Proceedings of the XXth International Congress on Ancient Bronzes

Resource, reconstruction, representation, role

EDITED BY
PHILIPP BAAS

BAR INTERNATIONAL SERIES 2958 | 2019

Published in 2019 by
BAR Publishing, Oxford

BAR International Series 2958

Proceedings of the XXth International Congress on Ancient Bronzes

ISBN 978 1 4073 5589 4 paperback
ISBN 978 1 4073 5592 4 e-format

DOI https://doi.org/10.30861/9781407355894

© the editor and contributors severally 2019

COVER IMAGE *Detail of the "Tübinger Waffenläufer" (Photo: Thomas Zachmann, copyright: Institute of Classical Archaeology, Eberhard Karls University Tübingen)*

The Authors' moral rights under the 1988 UK Copyright,
Designs and Patents Act are hereby expressly asserted.

All rights reserved. No part of this work may be copied, reproduced, stored, sold, distributed, scanned, saved in any form of digital format or transmitted in any form digitally, without the written permission of the Publisher.

Links to third party websites are provided by BAR Publishing in good faith and for information only. BAR Publishing disclaims any responsibility for the materials contained in any third party website referenced in this work.

BAR titles are available from:

BAR Publishing
122 Banbury Rd, Oxford, OX2 7BP, UK
EMAIL info@barpublishing.com
PHONE +44 (0)1865 310431
FAX   +44 (0)1865 316916
www.barpublishing.com

Of Related Interest

Archaeology, Art and Ethnography of Bronzes of Nepal
Mala Malla
Sub-series: South Asian Archaeological Series, 13

Oxford, BAR Publishing, 2011   BAR International Series **2208**

The Relief Plaques of Eastern Eurasia and China
The Ordos Bronzes, Peter the Great's Treasure, and their kin
John Boardman

Oxford, BAR Publishing, 2010   BAR International Series **2146**

Statues et statuettes en bronze de Cilicie avec deux annexes sur la main de Comana et les figurines en bronze du Musée de Hatay
Ergün Laflı and Michel Feugère

Oxford, BAR Publishing, 2006   BAR International Series **1584**

Casting Experiments and Microstructure of Archaeologically Relevant Bronzes
Quanyu Wang and Barbara S. Ottaway

Oxford, BAR Publishing, 2004   BAR International Series **1331**

Metalworking Technology and Deterioration of Jin Bronzes from the Tianma-Qucun Site, Shanxi, China
Quanyu Wang

Oxford, BAR Publishing, 2002   BAR International Series **1023**

For more information, or to purchase these titles, please visit **www.barpublishing.com**

Contents

Preface viii
Carol C. Mattusch

Vorwort ix
Philipp Baas

Part I. Reconstruction

1. Innovation and Tradition – Greek Bronzecasting Workshops 3
   Gerhard Zimmer

2. Casting large statuary in Classical Antiquity: Thoughts from India and Egypt 13
   Paul Craddock

3. Past and Recent Metal Analyses of the Germanicus Statue from Amelia 25
   Alessandra Giumlia-Mair, John Pollini

4. The Brescia Winged Victory: Ongoing Diagnostic Work, Conservation Treatment and Restoration 35
   Francesca Morandini, Stefania Agnoletti, Annalena Brini, Andrea Cagnini, Monica Galeotti, Anna Patera, Simone Porcinai

5. Projet d'une nouvelle étude technologique de l'Aurige de Delphes: les premiers résultats 45
   Sophie Descamps-Lequime, Benoît Mille, Nancy Psalti

6. The Bronze Antikythera Ephebe Revisited: Technical Features and Casting Technique 57
   Kosmas A. Dafas

7. Bronze Cast on Decorated Iron Sheets. An Unusual Manufacturing Technique in Iron Age Italy 67
   Joachim Weidig, Nicola Bruni, Fabio Fazzini

8. Artful illumination: Technical study of four Hellenistic bronze lamps from the eastern Black Sea site of Vani 75
   Jeffrey Maish, David Saunders, Nino Kalandadze, Marc Walton

9. Corinthian Helmets in the Hermitage Museum 87
   Nadezda Gulyaeva

10. A New Look at an Old Technology: Insights into the Metallurgy of Tin Bronze during the Iron Age of Luristan 91
    Omid Oudbashi

11. Drahtziehen in der Bronzezeit? Zu den drei Ziehbronzen aus dem Hort von Isleham, Cambridgeshire 101
    Ilyas Özşen

12. Bronze Circulation in the Aegean in the 2nd millennium BC: Technological Investigations of Bronze Finds from the Minoan Peak Sanctuary at Ayios Yeoryios sto Vouno, Kythera 107
    Emilia Banou, Aikaterini Panagopoulou

13. La Tomba Principesca di Roscigno: Greci e indigeni nelle élites dell'Italia Meridionale 117
    Silvia Pacifico, Rossella Luciano

14. Authepsa: A Singular Brass Container from Augusta Emerita (Mérida, Spain). History and Interpretation of the Object 125
    Rafael Sabio González, Cristina Isabel Mena Méndez

15. Technology Matters: The Kal-e Chendar Bronze Statuary from the Seleucid to the Parthian Periods 131
    Gunvor Lindström

Part II. Resource

16. How the Greeks manipulated the composition of their bronze coins. Case studies.................145
Maryse Blet-Lemarquand

17. Corinthian bronze: was it just wrought high-tin bronze?.................155
Jean-Marie Welter

18. Fragments of large-scale bronze statues in context of so-called scrap metal deposits in Dacia and Moesia Inferior.................165
Cristina-Georgeta Alexandrescu

19. Roman bronze vessels with signs of repair from Sarmatia.................177
Mikhail Treister

20. Recycling Economy in the Production of Roman Bronze Statues from the Limes Region. Results of the Research Project „Roman Bronze Statues from the UNESCO World Heritage Limes".................189
Frank Willer, Roland Schwab, Manuela Mirschenz

Part III. Representation

21. Tre bronzi greci da Porticello (Reggio Calabria).................201
Fabiano Fiorello Di Bella

22. Roman Bronzes of Augusta Emerita (Hispania). Representation: Iconography and Models.................211
Trinidad Nogales Basarrate, José María Murciano Calles

23. Who was in Charge of Fastening Bronze Statues on their Bases? A Case Study of Two Classical-Group Bases from Delphi.................223
Rachel Nouet

24. Scharnier, Tülle oder Zapfen. Beobachtungen an hellenistischen Bronzelampen mit Statuettendekor.................237
Norbert Franken

25. Iconografie "funerarie" nella piccola plastica bronzea romana.................247
Margherita Bolla

26. Small Objects, Multiple Perspectives: The Case of the Genius of Grumentum.................257
Giulia Bison

27. From the Roman noblemen to the European connoisseurs: the "Paramythia bronzes" and the allure of the Antique.................265
Antonia Tzortzatou

28. Collecting Bronzes in an Early Twentieth-century American Museum of Natural Science and Anthropology.................275
Philip Kiernan

Part IV. Role

29. Geometric Bronze Animal Figurines at Olympia – Who Dedicated What and Why?.................287
András Patay-Horváth

30. Bronzegefäße von Olympia: Ritual und Repräsentation, Statusänderung und Deponierung.................299
Beat Schweizer

31. Pinakes, Waffen und Statuen – Zur öffentlichen Präsentation von Bronzen am Außenbau griechischer Peripteraltempel.................307
Daphni Doepner

32. A bronze foundry of Classical times in the sanctuary at Kalapodi (Central Greece).................319
Johanna Fuchs

33. Copper-based offerings from the sanctuaries of Poseidon and Athena at Sounion, Attica: typological and analytical investigation.................331
Zetta Theodoropoulou Polychroniadis, Vana Orfanou

34. Bronzes of Arcadian Orchomenos: A Review of Old and New Finds.................345
Stamatis A. Fritzilas

35. **Paphian obstacles to powerful Death. A set of surgical tools found in the Agora of Paphos** 359
    Maciej Wacławik

36. **About Löwenkannen: La Löwenkanne del Museo Archeologico di Verona** 367
    Marina Castoldi

37. **Bronze Vessels from the Etruscan Necropolises of Bologna (540 – 350 BC): Preliminary Notes** 373
    Giulia Morpurgo

38. **The Kegs from the "Celtic" Graves of Santa Paolina di Filottrano. Misadventures and misunderstandings** 381
    Nicoletta Frapiccini

39. **Bronzeobjekte aus der römischen Garküche auf dem Monte Iato (PA)** 389
    Eva Riediker-Liechti

40. **Roman bronzes of *Augusta Emerita* (Spain). A functional approach** 397
    Nova Barrero Martín, Rafael Sabio González

Previous International Bronze Congresses and Publications 405

Preface

Since 1970, the International Bronze Congress has been the major forum for scholars whose research enhances our knowledge of the art, culture, and technology of bronzes in the Classical world. The twentieth International Congress on Ancient Bronzes was held from April 17 to 21, 2018, at the Institute for Classical Archaeology of Eberhard Karls Universität in Tübingen, at the generous invitation of the Institutsdirektor Professor Dr. Thomas Schäfer.

The topics under consideration, consisting of Resource, Reconstruction, Representation, and Role of ancient bronzes, drew 78 papers and 120 participants from more than twenty countries. The Congress was beautifully organized and skillfully orchestrated by Dr. Philipp Baas and Dr. Dieta Svoboda-Baas. Nearly forty papers were submitted for publication, and they have been ably and quickly edited by Philipp Baas, with the assistance of the members of the Advisory Board for the Bronze Congresses, Sophie Descamps-Lequime, Eckhard Deschler-Erb, Norbert Franken, Alessandra Giumlia-Mair, Nadezda Gulyaeva, Despina Ignatiadou, Annemarie Kaufmann-Heinimann, Susan Stock, and myself. We are grateful to Director Thomas Schäfer and to Philipp Baas and Dieta Svoboda-Baas for having made the Twentieth International Bronze Congress a great success and a memorable occasion.

Carol C. Mattusch
Chair, Advisory Board

Vorwort

Philipp Baas

Vom 17.–21.04.2018 fand am Institut für Klassische Archäologie der Eberhard Karls Universität Tübingen der „XXth Congress on Ancient Bronzes" statt. Diese Veranstaltung blickt auf eine lange Tradition zurück, die 1970 mit dem ersten „Congress on Ancient Bronzes" in Nijmegen begann. Die breit aufgestellten Konferenzen bringen und brachten seitdem nicht nur Forschende verschiedener Disziplinen, sondern auch Expertinnen und Experten aus ganz Europa, und im Falle Tübingens, Georgien, Großbritannien, dem Iran, Israel, Russland, der Schweiz und den USA zusammen.

Unter den Oberthemen „Resource, Reconstruction, Representation, Role" trafen sich 120 Wissenschaftler und Wissenschaftlerinnen sowie Interessierte, die den 78 Vorträgen lauschten. Der Band ist nach diesen Oberthemen gegliedert. Dazu seien zwei Anmerkungen erlaubt. Da die Themen so offen formuliert waren und sind, war es eine Herausforderung die eingegangen Beiträge einem bestimmten Themenkreis zuzuweisen. So kann man beispielsweise die Beiträge von Gunnvor Lindström, Rachel Nouet und Jean-Marie Welter ohne weiteres jeder der Kategorien zuordnen. Damit erklärt sich jedoch auch der Überhang bei den Themenkomplexen *Reconstruction* (15) und *Role* (12), wohingegen *Resource* (5) und *Representation* (8) gewissermaßen Juniorpartner zu sein scheinen.

Anders als die bisherigen Kongresse war es die Intention in Tübingen, das Material der Bronze an sich in den Fokus zu stellen, um einen weiteren Blick, auch abseits des Figürlich-ornamentalen, zu ermöglichen. Da gerade in der deutschsprachigen Forschung im Bereich der Klassischen Archäologie in den letzten Jahrzehnten ein Trend zurück zur reinen Kunstgeschichte zu beobachten ist, wollten wir auch modernen, technologischen Ansätzen eine Plattform anbieten. Ziel war ein Nebeneinander traditioneller und innovativer Ansätze, die so auch in dem vorliegenden Band vertreten sind. So geht es nicht nur um das Endprodukt aus Bronze, sondern ebenso um materialwissenschaftliche und metallurgische Aspekte sowie die Produktion von Bronzeobjekten, seien es Werkzeuge, Münzen, Statuetten etc. Der klassischen Erschließung aus einem Materialcorpus heraus stehen technische Analysen zur Seite. Aus unserer Sicht erfüllte die Konferenz, und damit dieser Band, den stets formulierten, oftmals nicht umgesetzten Anspruch der Inter- und Multidisziplinarität. Expertinnen und Experten sowohl aus den Bereichen Restaurierung, Materialwissenschaft, Grabungsarchäologie sowie Numismatik als auch kunsthistorisch arbeitende Kolleginnen und Kollegen besprechen Objekte, Befunde, Werkprozesse, Analysewerkzeuge und Kontexte. Abgerundet wird diese Zusammenschau durch bspw. eine eher ethnologische Analyse (Craddock) und Beiträge, die vor allem auf antike Verwendungs-, aber auch Recyclingpraxis abzielen (Treister, Schweizer, Willer et al.) und so den Lebenszyklen und Verwendungsbiographien der Objekte nachspüren.

Bei einem solchen Band stellt sich häufig die Frage nach der inhaltlichen Klammer oder der übergeordneten Fragestellung: Dieser Band soll als Plattform fungieren, die neue Funde und Objekte zeigt, Bekanntes in ein neues Licht rückt und schließlich Altes wie Neues kontextualisiert. Doch vor allem soll er als Plädoyer für eine Pluralität der Methoden verstanden werden. Es gilt zu zeigen, was möglich ist, sowohl mit traditionellen als auch innovativen Ansätze, aber auch wo die jeweiligen Methoden an ihre Grenzen stoßen. Der Blick soll nicht eingeengt werden auf eine einzelne Region, Epoche, Gattung oder Methode, sondern geweitet für die Möglichkeiten und Diversität der Objekte in Raum und Zeit, vor allem aber für die sich aus der Kombination unterschiedlicher Analyseansätze ergebenden Mehr-Erkenntnis in unserer Deutung von bereits Vergangenem.

Ich bin einer Vielzahl von Menschen zu Dank verpflichtet, die einen wichtigen Anteil an dem Erfolg der Konferenz und der Genese des Bandes hatten. Zuvorderst dem „Standing Commitee" des „Congress on Ancient Bronzes", das mir in der Vorbereitung der Veranstaltung und besonders bei der Redaktion des Bandes mit Rat und Tat zur Seite stand: Sophie Descamps, Eckhard Deschler-Erb, Norbert Franken, Alessandra Giumlia-Mair, Nadezda Gulyaeva, Despina Ignatiadou, Anne-Marie Kaufmann Heinimann und Susan Stock.

Carol Mattusch hat als Chair einen unglaublichen Enthusiasmus bewiesen, als sie sich bereit erklärte, sämtliche Beiträge nach dem Review noch einmal Korrektur zu lesen und auch die Formalia zu überprüfen. Der Herausgeberin der „British Archaeological Reports" und „BAR Publishing", Birgit Thaller, danke ich für die Aufnahme in die Reihe „BAR International Series". Die Betreuung durch Lisa Eaton, Ruth Fisher und Jacqueline Senior von Seiten des Verlages war hervorragend und äußerst professionell.

Dann danke ich den Kolleginnen und Kollegen des Instituts für Klassische Archäologie der Eberhard Karls

Philipp Baas

Universität Tübingen. Johannes Lipps, Richard Posamentir und Thomas Schäfer haben die Konferenz wohlwollend begleitet. Manuel Flecker, Martin Dorka-Moreno und Stefan Krmnicek haben mich engagiert bei der Planung und Ausrichtung unterstützt. Hanni Töpfer hat wie immer durch ihre organisatorischen Fähigkeiten und ihren Überblick garantiert, dass Konferenz und Publikation überhaupt möglich waren.

Viele fleißige Hände haben mit angepackt, um diese Mammut-Konferenz zu bewältigen: Bea Böse, Anna Galeano, Matthias Kalisch, Larissa Lazar und Marco Werkmann haben als fleißige Helferlein eine reibungslosen Ablauf der Veranstaltung garantiert.

Zuletzt gilt mein Dank meiner Frau Dieta-Frauke Svoboda-Baas, die mich sowohl bei der Ausrichtung der Konferenz und der Entstehung des Bandes maßgeblich in allen Aspekten unterstützt hat.

Part I

Reconstruction

Innovation and Tradition – Greek Bronzecasting Workshops

Gerhard Zimmer

Katholische Universität Eichstätt

Gerhard.Zimmer@ku.de

Abstract: In den letzten Jahrzehnten wurden zahlreiche Werkstätten für den statuarischen Bronzeguss in den Ländern des östlichen Mittelmeeres freigelegt und untersucht. Neue Erkenntnisse zu der dort angewandten Technik wurden experimentell auf ihre Richtigkeit hin überprüft. Wir sind nun in der Lage, technische Innovationen chronologisch einzuordnen und andererseits werkstatteigene Kniffe zu unterscheiden. Ein wenig ist dabei in den Hintergrund getreten, dass es auch handwerkliche Traditionen gibt, welche vom 5. Jh. v. Chr. bis in die Moderne hin gleich geblieben sind. Auf dem jetzigen Stand der Forschung ist es möglich, mit Werkstattresten Namen bekannter Bronzegießer zu verbinden.

Keywords: Bronzecasting; Workshop; Tradition; Statuary, Mediterranean

In the year 1838 the future Prussian field marshal Helmuth von Moltke went on a journey to eastern Anatolia as part of his mission as an instructor for the Osmanian army. There he also visited the city of Tokat, where bronze products of high esteem were produced up to the early modern age. It is therefore no wonder that Moltke wanted to see "the famous copper smelteries of the Chalybes". His high expectations were deeply disappointed. In his journal "Under the crescent moon" he writes:

> "Two rows of small ovens, like baking ovens, below sordid wooden sheds, bellows, which are maintained by the breath of men, and a stock of charcoal, that is the whole apparatus of the famous copper smelteries of Tokat" (Moltke 1841).

The disappointment of the young military man is easy to understand when we consider the environment of 19th century Prussia. There, for example, decorative iron-casting had achieved huge improvements at the turn of the century. Industrial plants like the smeltery of Sayn from the year 1830 had a high aesthetic standard which could compare to the architecture of contemporary buildings of the Glyptothek in Munich and the Old Museum in Berlin.

The boom of the iron industry was based upon a technical innovation, the invention of the so-called Kupol-oven. That was a shaft-oven, with which raw iron could be smelted with an unheard-of acuteness. So it was possible to produce even delicate jewellery. No wonder that the travellers from Central Europe expected appropriate workshop-constructions in the Osmanian Empire as well.

Archaeological research behaved quite similarly in the 20th century, when it came to the discovery of workshops for statuary bronze casting. Long known works like the "Betender Knabe" (Praying Boy) in Berlin or the Charioteer of Delphi, as well as the many new finds from the sea, above all the Riace Warriors, were so perfect that one could only imagine their production in well-equipped workshops. That hindered our way to understanding the technique and above all the insight into innovative progress for a long time.

Moreover, since the beginning of the 20th century, the research in Greek bronzecasting technology was clouded by the statement of academic engineers, that the lost wax casting process had been used basically unchanged during the course of millennia. Kurt Kluge especially spread and consolidated that opinion in the time between the two world wars.

Now, after decades of intense research on workshops, we are able to ask about innovation. Before we apply our modern questions to antiquity, though, we have to check if that is legitimate. We have to ask if technical innovation was perceived as something positive back then as well.

Here the Greek historian Thucydides can help. The first book of his *Histories* covers the backstory of the Peloponnesian War. To warn the Lacedaemonians of the danger the Athenians pose, an envoy from Corinth holds a speech and mentions the following reasons:

> "They are natural innovators, quick to have ideas and then to put their plans to action" (1,70); "… your practices are antiquated compared to those of the Athenians. Inevitably, it is the new that prevails, in this as in other fields of expertise" (1,71).

"ἀνάγκη δὲ ὥσπερ τέχνης αἰεὶ τὰ ἐπιγιγνόμενα κρατεῖν" (1,71)

thus it seems completely legitimate to put the question of innovation as incitement for the development of bronze casting at the centre of our research, a question that plays an important role in the industrial age.

1. Experiments and the search for the big format

The use of cast bronze for statuary sculpture was preceded by a long period of technological development during a time we do not know very much about, due to lack of material evidence. This development took place from the 9th through the 6th century BC.

One testing field for experiments on bronze casting were the tripod votives (Kiderlen 2010, 108). Cauldrons with three supporting legs initially were household items for heating food. As early as the 9th century BC, due to their increasing size and ornamental moulding, they become prestigious objects, which are mentioned as prizes in the Homeric epics. The starting point for the increasing size and the canonisation of the form was the ability to smelt pure copper and use it for the casting of fine ornaments.

Different techniques were necessary for the production of a tripod. The cauldron itself was chased out of a cast copper blank. The lug handles that were attached to the rim of the cauldron were cast and supported by human figures, which were also cast out of solid copper or tin bronze with a high copper content. Not a single tripod votive is fully preserved, but the approximate proportions of the devices are known. It can be calculated from the diameter of the ring-formed handles that there must have been tripod votives of 4 metres in height on the Acropolis in Athens. Together with their pedestals those were widely visible monuments (Scholl 2006, 52).

From a metallurgical point of view, the tripod votives were highly sophisticated works of art. The chasing of the cauldron, the casting of the ring-formed handles and the figures as well as the connection of the separate constructive elements with rivets put high demands to the abilities of artisans and offered room for improvement. The increasing height was another incentive for innovations.

The evidence for workshops during the early age in Olympia, Akovitika and Eretria is scarce. The new insights result therefore from numeric calculations and experimental recasts at the Foundry Institute in Aachen.

During the scientific work on the Geometric tripod legs the high number of casting flaws had always been striking, more so since starting with the 6th century the bronzes astonish us in their perfection, and careful correction of most flaws. In Geometric times the pursuit of perfection obviously played a subordinate role to function.

The numeric calculation and experimental recasts of a small tripod showed clearly that the flaws happened mostly from low smelting temperatures, since the use of clay crucibles did not allow for the necessary overheating of the pure copper with a melting temperature of 1054 degree C° (Fig. 1.1). The areas in which the melt solidified early defined in the numeric calculations corresponded with the observations made on the originals from Olympia (Gußtechnik 2013).

The experiments also showed that the burnt form had to be fixed vertically in a pit with the mount of the cauldron pointing downwards. Only in this position were the casting flaws the same as in the originals.

According to the results of the calculations the artisans could only cast tripod legs up to a certain size, one metre probably being the upper limit. The legs of the huge votives could only be produced with the traditional technique of chasing, brought to a high form of perfection. We therefore see that there were some innovative approaches in casting that met their limits in the amount of smelt, the too low

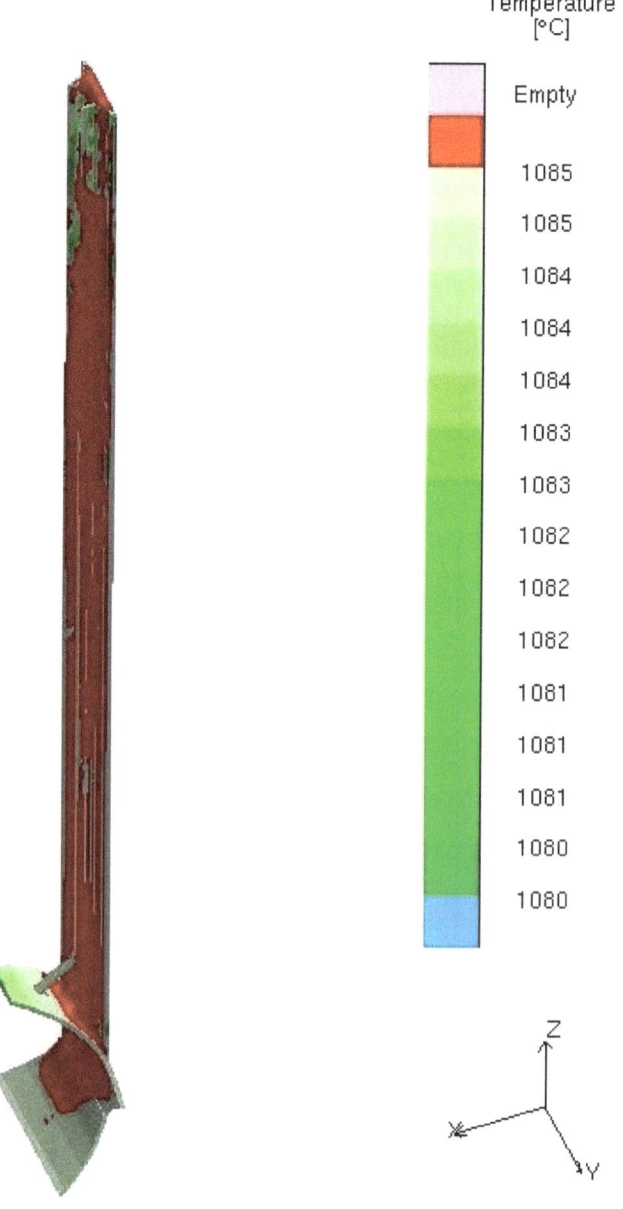

Figure 1.1: Filling temperature of a tripod-leg (Photo: Foundry-Institut, Aachen)

heat and probably other parameters as well. Here we have a situation in which innovation and tradition coexisted for a longer time, probably hinting at different workshops.

In Archaic times the casting technology had developed so far that it took the leading role in the production of large votives. Since such experimental phases of single workshops are usually marked by different trials, it was difficult to identify the most promising developments. The Samian griffin-cauldrons offered the best examples for our analysis, since all the alloys are known and Ulrich Gehrig published all griffin-protomes in an extensive volume (Gehrig 2004). The artefacts in question are big chased cauldrons, with griffin protomes, their beaks wide open. Here too the wish of increasing the size of the highly prestigious votives led to the artisans' search for new technical solutions. In the production of the griffins' heads, above all, we can observe attempts for innovation. Among the early examples are some that are chased. The toreutic work is so perfect that it was impossible to perceive a weld. All the rest of the griffin-protomes are cast. We witness a quick and thorough change of technology here. Formal quality therefore cannot have been the reason for that. The chased and the cast griffins are not different in iconography nor details, which is why the technical details of the casting are of special importance. As with the tripods' legs the size of the griffin protomes plays a decisive role. The big ones, over 20 centimetres in height, are hollow-casts done by the lost-wax-process.

Most of the findings are satisfactory from a metal-casting point of view, but there was a problem concerning the correct construction of the supply lines for the smelt. After the numeric calculations we may assume that some of the workshops experimented with this so-called gating until the cast was a success. Flaws in the breast and back areas point to falsely set gates which, together with too little overheating, resulted in less satisfactory results.

The uniformity of the griffins on one cauldron came about because a clay mould consisting of different parts was used to produce the wax form, as reconstructed by Ulrich Gehrig (Gehrig 2004, 124).

The biggest problems for the interpretation were posed by three spoiled castings of small griffins' heads. One that was particularly well preserved was used for reconstructing the casting process. Gehrig recently proposed the use of unit moulds with which the griffins of one series would have been cast (Gehrig 2004, 121–128). The spilt griffin's head would then have been a spoiled cast during a common process.

Since we don't have any workshop finds of stone or metal moulds, we can only imagine such a permanent mould consisting of clay- or silt-like material.

The experiments in Aachen therefore concentrated on the search for a mixture of clay that was stable enough to cast at least six griffins' heads (Fig. 1.2). In spite of the addition of different temper and a wide range of test runs it was not possible to produce a mould that would have met the requirements (Fig. 1.3) (Wirth et al. 2016). The spoiled griffins are probably the product of a workshop that experimented without success during the experimental phase in the Archaic period. The future lay in the further development of the lost wax process.

In the 6th century the workers of the leading workshops were familiar with hollow-casting. There were probably

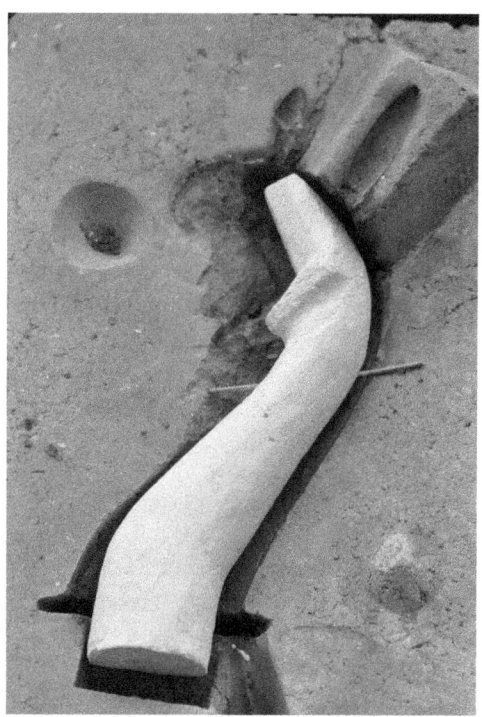

Figure 1.2. Clay mould for a griffin head (Photo: Author)

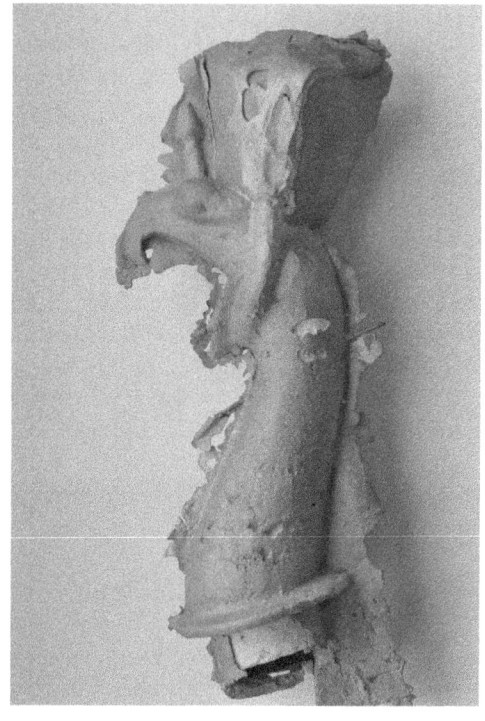

Figure 1.3. Cast of a griffin head (Photo: Author)

still some difficulties with heating the cast and handling the supply lines. Connecting the cast parts also still posed a problem, which is why connections with rivets remained important. That was the state of the art when the so-called "Archaic Foundry" created statues in the Agora of Athens in the years around 530 BC (Mattusch 1988, 54–59).

For a long time, it was believed that the cult statue for the older temple of Apollo Patroos was produced here. Recently it has become clear that the apsidal building next to the pit which lay underneath the later temple was a workshop only (Goette 2001, 79). Thus here we have the first stationary workshop with a casting pit outside a sheltered workspace.

Inside the pit there were various fragments of a mould that could be put together to form a kouros of half life-size. The mould was composed of several layers of clay which had taken different colours during the burning out. There were neither inlet pipes nor drains, nor a fixture on the bottom of the pit to divert or gather the discharged wax. It looks as though the method that had proved itself for statuettes was still in use: The form was heated somewhere else and carefully lowered into a pit for the cast (Zimmer 1990, 27–29).

According to Carol Mattusch's findings the pit contained fragments of moulds of two heads. Either a second head for the kouros was cast here because the first one was flawed, or the head belonged to a different kouros, a consideration we cannot exclude if we are looking at a stationary workshop here. The soldering and welding technology was so well developed that casting in different parts now offered the opportunity to increase the size of the statues.

Thus Greek founders had laid the foundation for producing life-sized statues and reaching the prime of bronze casting in the 5th century BC. The two Riace warriors may serve as an example here once more. The Berlin Foundry Cup from the time around 480 BC documents how naturally the casters mastered and used piece-casting.

For the further developments, Athens played an important role, not least because in recent decades extensive foundry-features have been unearthed there. In addition to a workshop at the Kerameikos there is a huge site on the southern slope of the Acropolis as well as a workshop in front of the House of Parliament that was in use during the second half of the 5th century BC. In the recent past another workshop of the 5th century was discovered in the Agora. This competitive situation was particularly favourable in the search for innovation.

2. The 5th century BC – new challenges

How can we imagine the working progress in such a pit? This is best shown by an experiment that was conducted in the year 1995 at the city of Murlo in Tuscany. It originated from a collaboration between the Foundry Institute at Aachen and the "Antikensammlung Berlin" as part of a course of the "Archaeologia sperimentale" led by Edilberto Formigli (Hackländer – Formigili 1997). The dimensions of the pit were laid out for the casting of a statue of about 1,28 metres high.

The centre of the pit was lined with clay bricks at the sides and isolated. On a pedestal in the middle the wax form was assembled and the inlet pipes and drains for the liquid bronze were attached.

Since it was a hollow casting, the wax form had to be filled with clay and tamped, which proved difficult, because the wax form was on the verge of caving in due to the weight.

When the works had advanced so far, the wax form was clad in several layers of clay having different consistencies. The inner layer was particularly fine and was applied with a brush, so as to reproduce all the details of the form.

In the end the wax form had disappeared within a cylindrical structure with a funnel and an air vent at the top. After the interior of the pit had been closed with two clay-brick walls towards the steps, it was heated for two nights and one day with wood that was stacked around the form inside the pit and permanently stoked.

After that, the wax flowed out and the form was burnt and dried, so that liquid bronze could be poured in. When the bronze had set and the whole pit cooled down a little bit, the casters smashed the form and pulled the raw cast out of the pit to work on it somewhere else. Up to that point all work took place in and around the pit, and it becomes clear why those installations formed the core of every workshop.

A parallel experiment at Aachen vividly shows how such a raw cast looked after the mould was broken (Zimmer 2012, 25, fig. 25).

This short overview shows us at how many points an innovation could set in and how many changes could result in an innovation.

The newest insights on the state of the art at the middle of the 5th century BC come from the newly found huge casting pit at the southern slope of the Acropolis in Athens (Zimmer 2009; Kasapoglou 2013; Zimmer 2016). It is carved into the soft bedrock oriented in a north south direction. Its length is 12 metres, its width 3,5 metres, its depth consistently 3,20 metres, measured from the top at the northern entrance. The walls of the interior run vertically and were roughly smoothed with a pick (Fig. 1.4).

Inside the pit the fixtures for burning out the moulds have been conserved in hitherto unknown detail. In the middle there is a big mould base on which remains of the mould are preserved in the form of a canal. Its course points to the cast of a female garment, a peplos of monumental size (Fig. 1.5).

Figure 1.4. Casting pit at the southern slope of the Acropolis (Photo: Author)

Figure 1.5. Detail of the casting pit (Photo: Author)

The verification of the casting of a female statue of colossal measurements is delivered by part of a mould assembled from seven fragments, used for the casting of a 1-metre-long fold. Since both ends are broken off, the fold may have been much longer still. The outside has been burnt at a very high temperature, for it is red and very hard. The clay was tempered with fine grit. On the inside we see the characteristic dark colour resulting from the contact with the hot melt. The composition of the mould of three layers of differently tempered clay is standard practice for the findings from this pit.

I shall not repeat all the arguments at this point: Carbon dating and ceramics point to the middle of the 5th century as the date of production. The cast monumental peplos-statue was the bronze statue of the Athena of Phidias, later called Promachos, that was standing on the Acropolis, widely visible at 9 metres in height. Concerning the appearance, for the present we can say that the arrangement of the fold bears a certain resemblance to the Angelitos-Athena (Borbein 1995, 262–263; Tölle-Kastenbein 1980, 56) and maybe we can discern the archetype in a copy from

Figure 1.6. Imprint of iron bands (Photo: Author)

Hadrianic times in Madrid (Schröder 2004; Zimmer 2016, 231–236).

Within the framework of our topic I want to try to show you what further course the innovations took by pointing out some technical details.

Among the mould fragments of the outer layer there is one group that shows brownish to intensely red traces on the inside, which according to our experience so far have to be interpreted as imprints of iron bands. What all fragments have in common is that they are usually not very thick-walled, that is the iron bands were located quite close to the outside of the mould. Almost all of the preserved surfaces with imprints of iron sheet plates were flat and rectangular. The clay layers that came in contact with the sheet metal are finer then the outer layer, but they do not reach the fineness of the inner facing. The red colour gives us further hints concerning the working procedure. When building the mould, the metal sheets made of iron were inserted into the moist clay. To avoid cracking, the mould could not be allowed to dry out too fast. The bigger the mould the longer the drying took. Probably the iron lay embedded in the moist clay for several weeks and thus had time to gather rust on the surface. A Fe-connection was formed. In the phase of heating the mould, temperatures over 400°C were reached. At such a heat the FeO turned into Fe_2O_3 with the conspicuous reddish-brown colour.

One adaptation that does not seem spectacular at first sight was achieved with two fragments (Fig. 1.6). Each shows the imprint of an iron band. Both together show, however, that the bands crossed approximately at a right angle. To us that means that at least one mould was built so as to be surrounded by a net of iron bands running vertically and horizontally, to absorb the enormous pressure that arose during the building of the mould out of moist clay as well as at the filling of the huge mould with molten bronze. At the same time it becomes clear what is the purpose of the thin outside layer on top of the iron bands, which gives the impression of being applied quite carelessly. That layer would prevent the iron bands from getting too much heat during the bake-out of the mould. Under unfavourable circumstances they could otherwise expand very much and

Figure 1.7. Mould-fragment with imprint of a nail-head (Photo: Author)

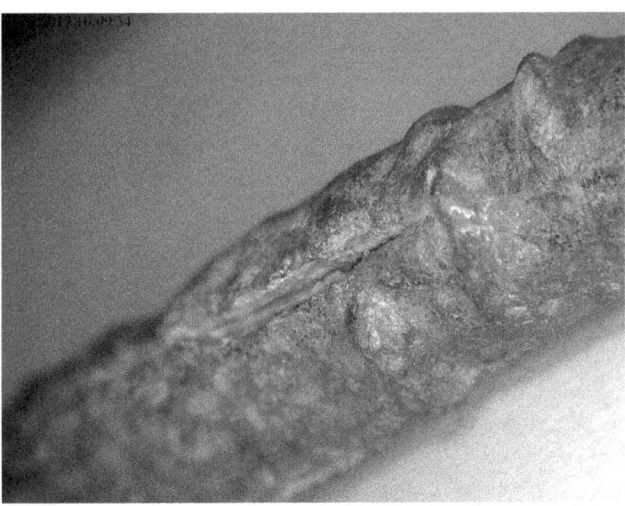

Figure 1.8. Nail with slanting grooves (Photo: Author)

thus themselves contribute to the instability of the mould. From these production-steps we can comprehend how many innovative thoughts in the details were necessary to create that monumental statue.

The use of chaplets is proven by mould-fragments with imprints of nail-heads. The nails had round heads, which were slightly convex and had a diameter of about 4 cm (Fig. 1.7). The heads are embedded in a flat clay surface and provide proof that the chaplets were level with the second layer.

On principle, such chaplets could be either bronze or iron. If they are bronze, they merge with the wall of the statue and only have to be cut away on the outside. After smoothing the surface they are no longer visible.

The other option for the founder was to use iron nails, which were pulled or pushed out of the wall after the cast. The remaining opening was closed by a small plate or patch and thus became virtually invisible, as we know from many examples.

The microscopic picture of red coloured fringes of such an imprint also hinted at the corrosive products of iron. Thus the record of the mould fragments proves the use of iron nails as chaplets.

In the meantime the restoration of the iron finds from the excavation actually produced nails that were used as chaplets.

One is a well preserved head with a diameter of 3,8 cm. The shaft of the nail has only been preserved to a length of 5 cm, the cross section measures 1,2 to 1,2 cm at most, with corrosion having roughened the surface.

The examination of the nail-head with a microscope brought another interesting observation: Within the corrosion-layer there was the imprint of a straw, which could only have gotten there if the head was in contact with the outer layer of the mantle, which was quite heavily grogged. The nail-fragment thus confirms that the chaplets were pushed through the second layer, with which they were level, as in this experimental set-up.

A second nail has been preserved to a length of 9 cm., with a bent tip. Such nails are common for house-building and are frequently found on excavations. The nail from our excavation shows a distinctive feature, which could be of importance for its use in a bronze-casting workshop. At a distance of 3–5 cm from the tip slanting grooves are visible on the preserved surface (Fig. 1.8). They are there to keep the nail from slipping out of the clay core of the mould and they are a sign of high strain. We may assume that the nails were specially produced for this workshop by a smith. Originally the nails seem to have been about 20 cm long. Considering the size of the cast parts and the force operating on the chaplets that surely is appropriate.

The number of fragments that survive from bellows nozzles is quite low. The nozzles were built from several layers of clay. Through intense contact with the fire they melted and vitrified at the opening.

According to the size of the cast parts the bellow nozzles were large-dimensioned. The air duct with a diameter of about 8 cm rivals the biggest we know up to now. The fragment of a bellow nozzle consists of highly grogged clay, built in layers and burnt hard. The outer layer is grogged with small stones and coloured grey. The air duct is burnt dark red on the inside. On the one long side we have, for a length of 11 cm, the imprint of an iron rod, whose side length was 10 mm. The dimension of the other ridge is unknown, though it was probably smaller. We have to see the rod as a stabilizing element that was used to fix the bellows above the crucible.

Up until now we only know such an attachment of the bellows with the help of rods from two right-angled bellows nozzles from Olympia which come from a workshop of around 440 BC (Heilmeyer – Zimmer 1987). The construction of such bellows shows that innovation must have taken place in the preparation of the melt as well.

Through the finds from Athens we get to know little that goes beyond what is already known about the melting of bronze and the preparation for casting. Finds from other workshop-contexts, especially from Olympia, have made clear that the bronze alloys were not melted in shaft furnaces, but in transportable crucibles and were poured into the mould through a funnel. In Olympia, remains of crucibles were found, which were mounted on a frame of iron and thus were so stable that they could be lifted with two rods.

So we see two lines of innovation: a greater amount of molten bronze had to be transported to the funnels and that metal had to be heated above the melting point of pure copper. The new form of the nozzles as well as the construction of movable crucibles with iron frames allowed for that demand.

The conclusions from the findings in Olympia were experimentally tried out. It turned out that the melting temperature was best reached by preheating the crucible from below, while achieving the main heat through the use of bellows nozzles from above (Zimmer 2016).

For the question of innovation, the complex excavations underneath the Leophoros Amalias south of the House of Parliament in Athens are of the utmost importance (Parlama – Stampolidis 2001, 149–161). They were undertaken in preparation for the building of the Metro in the early 1990s.

The workshop of the 5th century BC lay approximately 250 m east of the Themistoklean city-wall. That area was not included in the city before the extension of the wall under the reign of Hadrian.

Taking into account the traffic, the position of the workshop was exceptionally favourable, since the road that left the city through the so-called Diochares-gate and led eastwards into the urban hinterland was close by. The workshop was thus easily accessible from the city. We can imagine quite well that interested pedestrians or clients would visit the shop, as shown on the Berlin Foundry Cup. On the other hand, raw material like clay, wood, charcoal, sand or other materials needed could be delivered from the environs right to the doorstep.

For the work in a foundry, the access to a suitable amount of water was as important as the connection to the road network. Here the proximity of the Eridanos River and its spring are important. The river had its source at the slope of Mount Lykabettos, and crossed the whole city from east to west before leaving it at the Kerameikos next to the Holy Gate. Outside the Themistoklean wall in that region it also supplied water to craft producers such as potters and metal workers.

The Parliament site was a stationary workshop that produced bronzes for several decades until the early 4th century BC. Four casting pits were discovered in a

Figure 1.9. clay mould for casting a lifesized finger (Photo: Author)

peristyle courtyard. They were not all in use at the same time, but all are laid out in a space-saving manner, so as to allow circulation in the workshop. They are set up for casting Life-sized statues and partially constructed in a way that they could be used for more than one casting project. Smashed moulds were ground to dust and kept in one place in the courtyard to use as temper.

We have hints that point to the casting of female statues through many folds which suggest a peplos. In addition there is the fragment of a clay mould with which a lifesized finger was cast (Fig. 1.9) (Zimmer 2018, 128, fig. 17).

The burnt clay mould for the production of a mouth which is characteristic for the 5th century BC is especially interesting (Fig. 1.10) (Zimmer 2018, 128, fig. 18). It is not the casting mould itself, but some sort of mould to produce lips made of wax. Those wax lips were cut to fit, clad in clay, cast and added to the head, as we learned by studying the Warrior A from Riace (Formigili 1984, 130–132).

The existence of such a matrix speaks for the production of several statues of the same size and we may compare them to the forms that are hung up on the wall on the Foundry Cup (Zimmer 1982, 46, fig. 4). Together with the multiple uses of the casting pit, that procedure shows how in Classical times the setting of norms is also reflected in the technique.

The kind of perfection in handling the gating technique in our workshop is shown by the fragment of a big riser opening (Fig. 1.11). The riser or vent was attached to a funnel that was broken and is now lost. In it, three air vents were integrated. The fragment broke off so "conveniently" that one can envision the complex arrangement of the pouring channels in 3D (Zimmer 2018, 128, fig. 20).

As usual the venting pipe was built in three layers. First the channels formed from wax rods were clad in a 5 – 7 mm thick facing. The gaps were later filled with grogged clay and spread all around. In the end a 1-cm-thick layer allowed for a smooth surface. The two outer layers took on a red colour due to the burning process. It is clearly

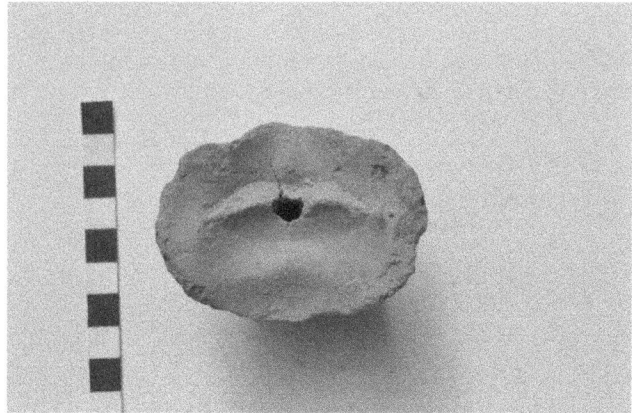

Figure 1.10. The burnt clay mould for the production of a mouth (Photo: Author)

Figure 1.11. Fragment of a big riser opening (Photo: Author)

visible how the workers did not succeed in pressing the easily kneadable clay into all of the cavities. That was not necessary, because at such a high point of the form or mould the pressure that was generated by the rising molten metal could not be very great and the air vent was already above the cast piece

It is astonishing in any case with what complexity the channels crossed each other in three dimensions. Before these finds it was never possible to study this feature in such detail. The feature shows that already in the 5th century BC there was a great deal of knowledge, gained by experience, concerning the elaborate gating technique. Up to now we thought that such elaborate pipes were an invention of the Hellenistic period. They were, in any case, an innovation that helped reduce the number of flawed castings.

An innovation whose date of invention we do not exactly know concerns the heating of the pits. In the workshops of the 5th century BC the casting mould stood on a base. The wax ran out through one or two openings and was removed from the heating area in vessels, before the mould was heated dry. In the early 3rd century BC we can see an elaborate new technique in Rhodes, where the wax was diverted out of the heating area through an underground channel. With some probability that technique was already in use during the 4th century BC. It rapidly replaced the old technique completely, since it was much safer.

So we see how the search for innovation in the workshops accompanies the development of bronze art at all periods. Innovations may take hold rapidly or be used alongside traditional methods for a while. There are those developments that allow for larger dimensions, those that save skilled labour, but also those that increase workplace safety. Nearly all of them are only possible if bronzeworkers, casters, ironsmiths and potters are working together in one workshop, or at least sharing their knowledge.

For the question of the wax form the new pit at the south slope of the Acropolis has brought new insights, which are the more important since in this area it is hard to make any secure statement owing to the scarcity of finds. Up to now it was only clear that pure beeswax was used for the production of wax models in antiquity. Beeswax has one drawback that is especially noticeable during the composition of a model: Its shiny and slightly transparent surface makes it problematic if not to say impossible to judge the plastic qualities and accuracy of detail. That is why the wax had to be mixed with a substance that improved the optical quality, more so when the last refinements were done to the wax image in the pit.

The problem for us lies only in the proof of those substances. The use of fine coal particles derived from ground charcoal, as documented in the Renaissance, suggests itself. The wax is coloured dark gray or black, depending on the amount of addition. Its look should be close to that of modern industrial wax. Such an addition cannot be proven, though, since the remains of the coal dust that were still in the pipes after burning the form were burnt at latest when the liquid bronze was filled in.

The finds from the Acropolis pit now, for the first time, give further hints as to the colouring of the wax. On a few mould fragments that got little heat, there was a clearly discernible layer of brown-red colour on the inside (Fig. 1.12). The analysis of the probe by the Democritos-Institute showed that it is an accumulation of ferrite (Fe_2O_3), a common feature of local Attic clay, which is not surprising, seeing that it certainly comes from the Attic clay pits. The amount of the accumulation supports the idea that the ferrite was mixed with the wax to improve the optical quality. That method is still used by artists today to achieve a uniformly reddish-brown colouring of the wax. If now, as shown in the analyses, the clay has hardly gotten any heat, the wax ran out slowly and the ferrite accumulated at the bend. Probably that mould part was damaged during the slow heating at the beginning and was not used afterwards. Thus we have the rare opportunity to prove the addition of ferrite to the wax. In this context the features of a workshop of Roman times in Petra (Jordan) are interesting as well (Grawehr 2010, 135). There plaster moulds of small bronze objects, such

Figure 1.12. Mould fragments with a layer of brown-red colour on the inside (Photo: Author)

as oil lamps or fulcra, were discovered, which were used to produce wax models. What was striking were the traces of red colour on the surface of the plaster, whose analysis identified them as haematite, that is Fe_2O_3. The workshop was active during the 1st century AC and shows that in connection with bronze work wax was often mixed with ferrite. We can therefore account for a crafting tradition here that endured for millennia.

3. Innovation and workshop tradition

Technical innovation is always connected to the owner or master craftsman of the workshop. Surely there were some very conservative masters and others that tried out new things. Up to now, due to the contingency of the findings we could not even think about naming famous masters, if we set aside the Phidias cup in Olympia. Now the evaluation of the finds from the southern slope of the Acropolis suggests that a similar technique was used there as in Olympia. Above all that concerns the innovative use of iron.

In bronze casters' workshops, vessels with names were found on different occasions. The best known is the so called Phidias cup from Olympia (Heilmeyer 1981, 447–448), but in the workshop of the Mylonas plot in Rhodes we also found a fragment inscribed with the name of Euboulos (Kantzia – Zimmer 1989, 520).

Among the sherds from the workshop of Phidias in Olympia Wolfgang Schiering found one engraved with the letters R A. Though they cannot be interpreted, there was a parallel among the ceramics of the Athenian workshop. With that we can certainly say that Phidias and his staff worked in both workshops.

Among the many fingerprints on the clay fragments surely there are his as well. The old saying of "discerning hands", that played in the German Archaeology an important role in the occupation with the works of Phidias, this gains a new meaning.

For the workshop underneath the Leophoros Amalias, I can only add a few thoughts: we may assume that, because of its preferential position, it belonged to a wealthy and well known master, who worked until the first years of the 4th century BC.

Among the mould fragments one group caught my eye that I did not understand at first. There were fragments of concave folds and especially tonguelike structures, that must belong to ending of concave folds. Such fold forms appear above all at the height of the belly, underneath the apoptygma. But as the depressions of the folds normally are quite small, the fragment with a width of 6,5 cm is too big. We also know similar folds at the height of the legs, where they can take on bigger dimensions, especially from the end of the 5th century BC. That design of folds is there to point out the particular materiality of the peplos and can take on a formulaic character. That form of fold design does not show actual buckle folds, it just hints at the consistency of the fabric.

Of course that form of characterizing folds exists frequently at the end of the 5th century BC, not least on the korai of the Erechtheion. On the other hand we find it especially striking on the group of Prokne and Ithys by Alkamenes and on copies of other works by Alkamenes (Schuchhardt 1977, 126). I end with the proposal that in the workshop underneath the Leophoros Amalias in front of the Parliament in Athens we can see the domain of that important master of the late Classical period.

Bibliography

Borbein, A.H., 1995. *Das alte Griechenland: Geschichte und Kultur der Hellenen*. München.

Formigli, E., 1984. La tecnica di costruzione delle statue di Riace. In: Due bronzi da Riace, *Bollettino d'arte*, Serie Special Vol. I, 107–143. Rom.

Gehrig, U., 2004. Die Greifenprotomen aus dem Heraion von Samos. In: *Samos IX*. Bonn.

Goette, H. R., 2001. *Athens, Attica and the Megarid: an archaeological guide*. London.

Grawehr, M., 2010. *Eine Bronzewerkstatt des 1.Jhs. n.Chr. von ez Zantur in Petra/Jordanien. Petra ez Zantur IV. Ergebnisse der Schweizerisch-Liechtensteinischen Ausgrabungen.* Mainz.

Gußtechnik geometrischer und früharchaischer Zeit: Zum Aufkommen monumentaler Weihegeschenke aus Bronze in der griechischen Frühzeit, 2013. Abschlußbericht des von der Fritz-Thyssen-Stiftung geförderten Projektes. Cologne.

Hackländer, N. – Formigli, E., 1997. Experimente zur Brenntechnik in einer Gußgrube. In: Zimmer, G. – Hackländer, N. (ed.), *Der Betende Knabe: Original und Experiment*, Frankfurt am Main, 93–98.

Heilmeyer, W. D., 1981. Antike Werkstättenfunde in Griechenland. In: *Archäologischer Anzeiger*, 440–453.

Heilmeyer, W. D. – Zimmer, G., 1987. Die Bronzegießerei unter der Werkstatt des Phidias in Olympia. In: *Archäologischer Anzeiger*, 239–299.

Kantzia, C. – Zimmer, G., 1989. Rhodische Kolosse. Eine hellenistische Bronzegußwerkstatt. In: *Archäologischer Anzeiger*, 497–523.

Kasapoglou, E., 2013. Neotera anaskafikadedomena apo dyo mnemeia tis notias klityos tis Akropolis: chalkourgeia kai chorigiko mnimeio tou Nikia. In: *Mousio Kykladikis technis, Archaiologikes Symboles*, Tomos B: Attiki, Athen. 45 – 50.

Kiderlen, M., 2010. Zur Chronologie griechischer Bronzedreifüße des geometrischen Typus und den Möglichkeiten einer politisch-historischen Interpretation der Fundverteilung. In: *Archäologischer Anzeiger*, 91–104.

Mattusch, C. C., 1988. *Greek Bronze Statuary. From the Beginnings through the Fifth Century B.C.* Ithaca and London.

Moltke, Helmuth von, 1841. *Unter dem Halbmond. Erlebnisse in der alten Türkei 1835–1839*. Berlin.

Parlama, L. – Stampolidis, N. Chr., 2001. *The City beneath the City. Finds from excavations for the Metropolitan Railway of Athens*. Athens.

Scholl, A., 2006. ΑΝΑΘΗΜΑΤΑ ΤΩΝ ΑΡΧΑΙΩΝ. Die Akropolisvotive aus dem 8. bis frühen 6. Jahrhundert v.Chr. und die Staatswerdung Athens. In: *Jahrbuch des Deutschen Archäologischen Instituts 121*.

Schröder, S.F., 2004. *Katalog der antiken Skulpturen des Museo del Prado. 2. Idealplastik*. Mainz.

Schuchhardt, W. H., 1977. *Alkamenes: mit einer Bibliographie der Schriften von W.-H. Schuchhardt*. Berlin.

Tölle-Kastenbein, R., 1980. *Frühklassische Peplosfiguren. Originale*. Mainz.

Wirth, M. – Ellerbrok, R. – Bührig-Polaczeck, A., 2016. Greifenprotomen: Gußtechnik früharchaischer Zeit. Rekonstruktion eines Fehlgusses. In: Zimmer, K. B. (ed.), *Von der Reproduktion zur Rekonstruktion – Umgang mit Antike(n) II*, Rahden, 223 – 228.

Zimmer, G., 1982. *Antike Werkstattbilder*. Berlin.

Zimmer, G., 1990. *Griechische Bronzegußwerkstätten: zur Technologieentwicklung eines antiken Kunsthandwerks*. Mainz.

Zimmer, G., 2009. Ergastiria Chalkoplastikis. In: *Egnatia 13*, 211–223.

Zimmer, G., 2012. Kupfer, Zinn und Silber. In: Cain, H.-U. (ed.), *Lust auf Farbe: die neue bunte Antike*, Leipzig 22–31.

Zimmer, G., 2016. Searching for the Goddess. In: Giumlia-Mair, A. – Carol C. Mattusch, C.C. (eds.), *Proceedings of the XVIIth International Congress on Ancient Bronzes*, Izmir, 231 – 236.

Zimmer, G., 2018. Werkstätten für Großbronzen im klassischen Griechenland. In: Martin Bentz, M. – Helms T. (eds.), *Craft production systems in a cross-cultural perspective*, Bonn, 119–132.

2

Casting large statuary in Classical Antiquity: Thoughts from India and Egypt

Paul Craddock

Dept. of Scientific Research, The British Museum, London, WC1B 3DG

pcraddock@britishmuseum.org

Abstract: Our understanding of the foundry practices of Classical antiquity is hampered by *lacunae* in the usual sources of evidence. In particular there are no surviving descriptions or workshop manuals so that the casting of large statuary had to be virtually reinvented in the Renaissance after a gap of almost 1000 years. By contrast in India the production of major castings has a continuous history of over 1000 years and, because the actual casting of the idols is part of the ritual, there are detailed technical instructions that must be adhered to by the founders who belong to an exclusive caste authorised to produce items for temple use. Studying the early and present practice from India and Nepal it is clear that they differ significantly from our interpretation of Classical practice.

The evidence of casting practice in Egypt in the late second and early 1st millennia BC, based on sites such as Qantir and Thebes, as well as on the surviving bronze figures, seems very different from that proposed for Greece. This is strange as Egypt is supposed to have inspired the rapid development of bronze statuary production in Greece from the 7th century BC.

Renaissance and later European casting technology differed significantly from Classical practice, including the introduction of true refractory crucibles that were capable of holding large volumes of liquid metal. The small quantities of metal in the much smaller crucibles of earlier periods would have been difficult to keep molten flowing through the large complex moulds with elaborate systems of feeding channels in use today and envisaged for the past.

Based on evidence from Egypt and India it is possible to reinterpret how the moulds may have been orientated in the Classical casting pits, significantly reducing the distance the metal had to flow.

Keywords: Casting; foundry; mould; bronze; statuary

Introduction

The study of classical bronze foundry technology can be approached through written records, archaeological evidence and the surviving bronzes themselves. The first suffers from several gaps in the potential sources of information that are available in other parts of the world, notably South Asia. In particular there are no surviving practical manuals. Instead, research has to fall back on inferences and analogies scattered through the classical literature to endeavour to gain some insight into contemporary practice. Such information as can be deduced from the Classical literature has been summarised by Zimmer (1985). The earliest "hands on" manual in western literature is that of Theophilus, compiled around 1100 AD (Smith – Gnudi 1942), followed centuries later by that of Biringuccio (Hawthorne and Smith 1963). By contrast, in India there are the detailed descriptions of the casting technology in texts such as the *Śilpaśātra*

and the *Mānāsāra* dating back at least a thousand years (Reeves 1962; Sarawasti 1936; Krishnan 1976). These texts describe every aspect of temple activity, including its construction and layout. This extends to the bronze idols, prescribing not only their dimensions and composition but also the methods by which they were to be made. It should be stressed that these were not just helpful tips, but strict ritual practices that must be adhered to, as they are to this day by the traditional metalsmiths, the *sthāpati*.

Also, the casting of large statuary ceased in the mid first millennium AD and there was a gap of almost a thousand years before it commenced again on a regular basis. It is often assumed that because the style and subject of the Renaissance bronzes were based on Classical antecedents that the technology must also be very similar. But this is not necessarily the case. Technology in Europe generally by the 1500s was very different from that of Classical antiquity, across a wide range of subjects. Renaissance smiths looking for existing contemporary casting practice for large bronzes would have turned to the foundries producing bells or cannon. Cannon were always cast set vertically in a pit and the molten metal run in directly from the melting (cupola) furnace in one operation as described by Biringuccio (Smith – Gnudi 1942, 249–255). This is probably the origin of the Post Medieval European tradition of casting statuary in a vertical position. By contrast the production of large copper alloy statuary in South Asia has a continuous history through many centuries and still flourishes (Reeves 1962; Krishnan 1976; Lo Boe 1981; Craddock – Hook 2007; Levey et al. 2008; Anfinset 2011; Craddock 2015; Shakya 2017).

The archaeological evidence that is available for the study of Classical casting technology are the foundry sites that have been excavated (Heilmeyer et al. 1987; Schneider 1989a and b), illustrations of foundries on some Greek ceramics, the so-called "foundry vases", and of course the surviving statuary. These should provide unambiguous physical evidence of the processes, but this is often not the case. The most prominent features at the Classical foundry sites are the pits in which it is believed the statuary was cast (Thompson 1948; Mattusch 1977a; Zimmer 1999), but how they actually functioned is largely a matter of conjecture (see below). To cast a statue weighing hundreds of kilograms a large installation for melting the metal must have existed within a very short distance of the moulds in the pits, yet apparently few have been identified. By contrast, in Egypt at the same period, hearths have been found for melting large quantities of metal, but with no real evidence for the actual casting arrangements, certainly no casting pits (Pusch 1990 and 1994; Scheel 1989, 25–27). The well-known Greek "foundry" vases should be of assistance (Mattusch 1980 and 2008; Schwandner et al. 1983; Zimmer 1982), but in fact only create more problems. It is certainly very difficult to relate the scenes depicted on the vessels with the excavated foundry sites. If the furnaces are associated with foundries then it is puzzling that no casting pits, moulds, pouring metal or even crucibles are shown. The functions of the furnaces depicted on the vases have been variously described as for melting the wax, melting the bronze in crucibles, melting the bronze directly, for annealing and softening the various components during the assembly of the statues and even as chimneys (Hoffman – Konstam 2002). Even the forms of the furnaces depicted create problems (Oddy – Swaddling 1985). Most of them clearly have a large hemispherical lidded vessel set on top. A shaft furnace operates by drawing air in at the base, then through the shaft where the reaction takes place, expelling air and waste gases from the top. The pot on the top prevents this happening, thereby negating the whole point of the shaft. The vessels are clearly depicted and such a vessel of the appropriate shape and size and with its base suitably encrusted with soot has been found in the foundry at the Heraion on Samos (Schmidt 1972, 77). Various explanations for the presence of the pots have been made, none of them satisfactory.

Finally, the examination of many of the surviving bronze statues often leaves some doubt over the methods by which they were cast. Reports on some famous and well-studied pieces such as the Riace figures and the Chatsworth Apollo for example are far from unanimous in the casting methods proposed. The Riace bronzes have been claimed as either direct (Lombardi – Vidale 1998) or indirect (Formigli 1984) castings. At least it was agreed that they were lost wax castings. The Chatsworth Apollo has been variously described as a sand casting (Wace 1938), a piece moulding (Maryon 1956, 476–477), an indirect lost wax casting (Haynes 1968 and 1970), a direct lost wax casting (Hemelrijk 1982) or a combination of direct and indirect (Mattusch 1988, 154–159) and more recently as an indirect casting again (Bouquillon et al. 2006). See Mattusch (1988 22–26), for a good discussion on the development of ideas on Classical casting methods. As she remarked when noting these changes in opinion (1988, 157), "it appears that scholars may have been more concerned with disputing previous scholarship than with examining the evidence provided by the bronze itself".

Difference between Ancient and Renaissance foundry techniques

As noted in the introduction, there are fundamental differences between ancient and Renaissance casting methods. Zimmer (1990, 4) remarked "dass die moderne Bronzegusstechnik zur Kenntnis der antiken Technologie wenig beitragen kann" that is, an awareness of modern bronze casting technology is hardly relevant to the study of bronze casting in antiquity. In the thousand years between Classical antiquity and the Renaissance there had been major advances in technology and this is reflected in the methods developed for the casting of large statuary. Having to virtually reinvent large statuary casting techniques from scratch, the founders would have based their methods on existing large casting techniques, notably for bells and ordnance.

Not least there had been major developments in ceramic technology. Studies of early crucibles and other metallurgical refractories show that in general their ceramic bodies were no different from the contemporary range of domestic pottery (Freestone – Tite 1986), although sometimes heavily tempered with vegetal matter, chopped straw and husks being especially favoured (Craddock 2014). These had poor refractory properties and could not withstand the high temperatures required to melt copper alloys for long without collapsing. However, as most melting operations were of fairly short duration this was of no great concern. The hearths upon which the crucibles would have been heated were quite simple affairs, so that a controlled heating raising the temperature uniformly would have been impossible and the crucibles would have been exposed to quite extreme temperature gradients, causing most ceramic bodies to split. Here the relatively open structure of most early ceramic coarse wares, especially if vegetal tempered, would have been an advantage, as incipient cracks due to unequal heating would have been stopped by the first void encountered. The big problem with early crucibles was their physical weakness, especially at high temperatures. This placed severe restrictions upon the weight of molten metal that could be safely carried in them, and thus their capacity was limited. Studies by Tylecote (1976, 16–19), Freestone and Tite (1986), Bayley and Rehren (2009) etc. concur that the maximum capacity of crucibles before the Post Medieval Period was of the order of a few kilograms of molten metal.

Crucibles from the Pheidias foundry at Olympia were apparently not even fired before use, which would have rendered them extremely weak (Heilmeyer 1969; Zimmer 1990; Schneider – Zimmer 1984; Schneider 1989a and b; Zwicker 1984). The Olympia crucibles were estimated to have been hemispherical with diameters of about 450 mm and depths of about 250 mm. This could give a theoretical capacity of about 12 litres if filled to the top, which equates to approximately 70–80 kilograms of metal, although it is very unlikely that they were so full. More realistically, experimental reconstructions successfully melted 11 kilograms of bronze (Zwicker 1984). This compares with crucible capacities of up to 100 kilograms regularly used in modern foundries for major statuary (Bruni 1994, 104–106). The apparently unfired Olympia crucibles would have been very weak, and it would have been impossible to lift them, so that it was suggested that they were merely tilted to pour the molten metal. To cast a major statue would have required many such loads of molten metal poured in quick succession; it is difficult to understand how this could be done from crucibles that could not be moved.

Volling and Zimmer (1995) suggested that the crucibles may have been reinforced with iron rods. This idea was based on the discovery at Olympia of a cross made up of two strips of iron of 8 x 7 mm and 12 x 12 mm cross section encased in clay. It was envisaged that these rods went all through the body of the crucible actually in the clay terminating as handles at each side thus effectively dividing it up into four segments. This would surely cause weakness along the contact zones of the iron and clay especially during heating; perhaps wisely, Zwicker did not include iron supports in his experimental crucibles. It seems more likely that these pieces of iron were part of an armature in the clay core of a major casting.

These large putative tilting crucibles are really more akin to a cupola furnace where the metal is melted and when a sufficient quantity has built up inside it is run out directly into the mould with no crucibles involved. The history of this process is very uncertain with no certain evidence of being used before the 16th century, in Europe in the *Pirotechnia of Vannoccio Biringuccio*, 1540 (Smith – Gnudi 1942, 258–260), and in South Asia in the *Bāburnāma*, 1520s (Beveridge 1922), both for casting cannon.

The well-known Bronze Age stone mould for casting oxhide ingots from Ras Ibn Hani, in Syria (Lagàrce et al. 1983) has a large deep channel cut in to it leading into one of the ears of the ingot. This looks very like a channel along which molten metal could have been run from a putative cupola furnace. The reconstruction drawing of the Agora foundry (Anon., 1982) in the popular booklet produced by the American School of Classical Studies at Athens, shows the shaft furnace operating as a cupola with the molten metal about to be run into the adjacent buried moulds. Subsequent interpretations of the foundry do not follow this interpretation, and, as stated above, no evidence of these furnaces have been found at a foundry site, and on the depiction of the vases themselves there is no real evidence that they were engaged in the melting of metal.

The first crucibles for holding molten metal to be made from truly refractory ceramics, capable of withstanding high temperature, thermal gradients and of sufficient strength to enable many kilograms of metal to be safely lifted and poured, were only developed towards the end of the Medieval period in Europe. They were produced in southern Germany/Austria using the special clays found in that region (Martinón-Torres et al. 2008; Martinón-Torres – Rehren 2009). These contained graphite, which formed a very refractory temper. The clays were also refractory, consisting mainly of alumina and silica and little else. The clays were heated to very high temperatures in excess of 1300°C causing the aluminium silicate mineral mullite to be formed and it was from this pre-heated clay that the crucibles were made. They have excellent thermal properties, and can withstand temperatures well in excess of 1500°C without deformation, are resistant to cracking and are strong. The excellence of the crucibles was widely appreciated and they were soon in use all over Europe and beyond and of ever increasing size.

The large quantities of molten metal in each pouring, now made possible in the new crucibles, had a much larger heat content, which in turn meant that they could be safely poured into longer and more complex feeder systems than hitherto without the danger of cooling and solidifying prematurely. Vasari (Bettarini – Barocchi 1987, 206) described how the sculptor della Porta had run the molten bronze down feeder channels in order to cast his bronzes from the bottom. From his comments this was a clearly a noteworthy and unusual innovation in early 16th century Italy, but what is the evidence from antiquity? Haynes (1992, 32) and Mattusch (1977a and b; 1988, 54–55, figs 4.4 and 4.10) discussed this problem and noted that the only more or less intact mould of a major casting to have been found, a two thirds life-size Apollo or *kouros*, of the 6th century BC, from the Archaic Foundry in Athens (Figure 2.1) (Mattusch 1977a and b; 1988, 54–59, fig. 4.4) had no evidence for vents or pouring channels, so it was believed the metal must have been poured directly into the mould from the top. However, the mould for a small Greek figure (Zimmer 1990, 114. 208, no. 8.3.82, fig. 69) was for a bottom pour, and Formigli (1984, 117, n. 49 and fig. 12) assumed a bottom pour for the Riace bronzes, but without giving any evidence.

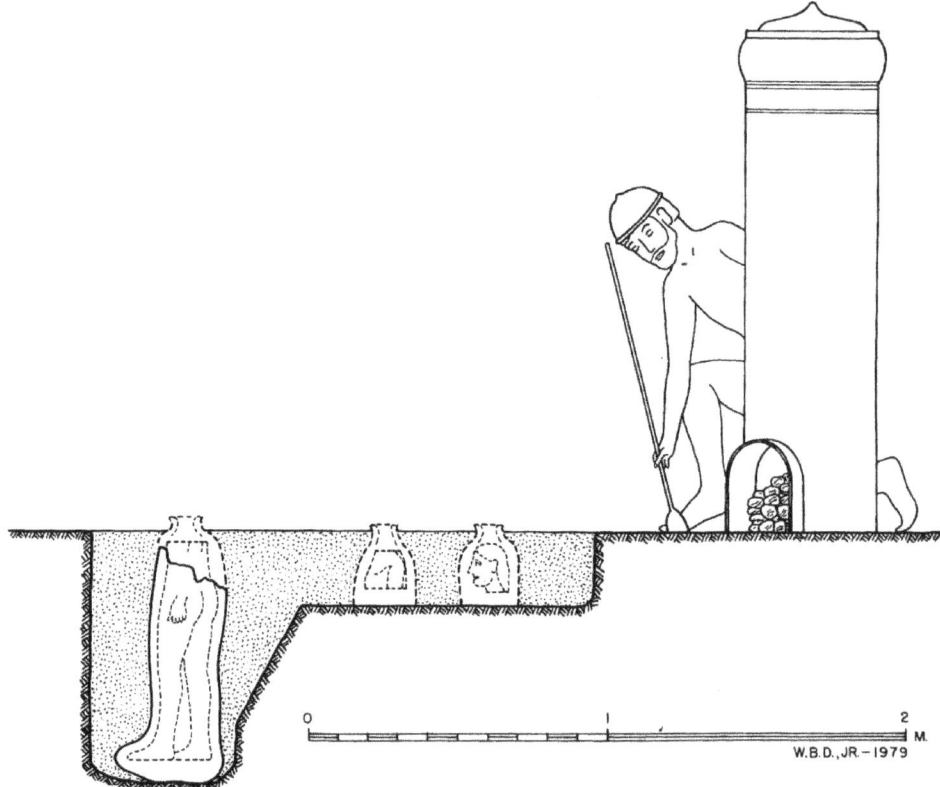

Figure 2.1. Reconstruction of the casting pit next to the Temple of Apollo Patroos, in the Athenian Agora. As clearly shown here, if complete, the torso mould would have stood well above the top of the trench, which seems very unlikely, whereas reclining along the trench would have enabled easy casting at locations along the back etc. (From Mattusch 1982, fig. 25)

Casting the bronze in antiquity

The limitations of the strength, and thus the size of the early crucibles raise two questions. How were sufficient quantities of metal, needed for major castings, melted simultaneously, and how were the moulds arranged so that the relatively small quantities of metal in each crucible pour got safely to its destination and joined the rest of the metal from previous pours before it had begun to solidify. If the metal had begun to set then the incoming molten bronze would not merge with it but instead would set against leaving a distinct, very visible and weakening boundary, known in English as a cold shut. There would also be the very real danger of small quantities of metal actually setting in the feeder channels before they even reached the main mould, thereby blocking them.

Melting the bronze

The Egyptian solution was to have long hearths that could accommodate many crucibles containing bronze that could be melted simultaneously and then presumably poured in quick succession. Major foundries with this arrangement have been excavated at Qantir (ancient Pi-Ramesse) in the Eastern Delta, dating to the 18th/19th Dynasty, in the second half of the second millennium BC (Pusch 1990; 1994 and 1998) (Figure 2.2) and at a foundry adjacent to the funerary temple of Seti I, dating from the Ptolemaic Period (Scheel 1989, 25–27). The long hearths at Qantir could have melted up to 100 crucibles simultaneously, and each crucible is likely to have contained between one and two kilograms of copper alloy. Multiple hearths have not been found in Greece but arrangements for heating large numbers of crucibles must surely have existed, unless some form of cupola furnace was used (see above). Hoffmann and Konstam (2002) recognised the problem posed by small crucibles for pouring large quantities of bronze into major castings and proposed a novel solution. They suggested that there must have been a huge fixed crucible set directly above the mould in the top of the casting pit with a fire surrounding it and with a "furnace vase" shaft furnace demoted to just acting as the chimney. When sufficient bronze had been melted it was released down into the mould, which was set at an angle in the pit (see below). The crucible was in fact acting as a cupola furnace and innovative though the suggestion is, there is no evidence at all that it was the solution adopted. The large crucible from Olympia (see above) might be construed as evidence for Hoffman and Konstam's giant crucible. However their crucible was envisaged as being heated from the outside around the sides and beneath, whereas the Olympia crucible had clearly been heated from above and within.

Arranging the moulds

The problem is that small individual quantities of metal would quickly dissipate their heat and begin to solidify prematurely, a disaster for any casting operation, as outlined above. Thus the mould had to be so constructed

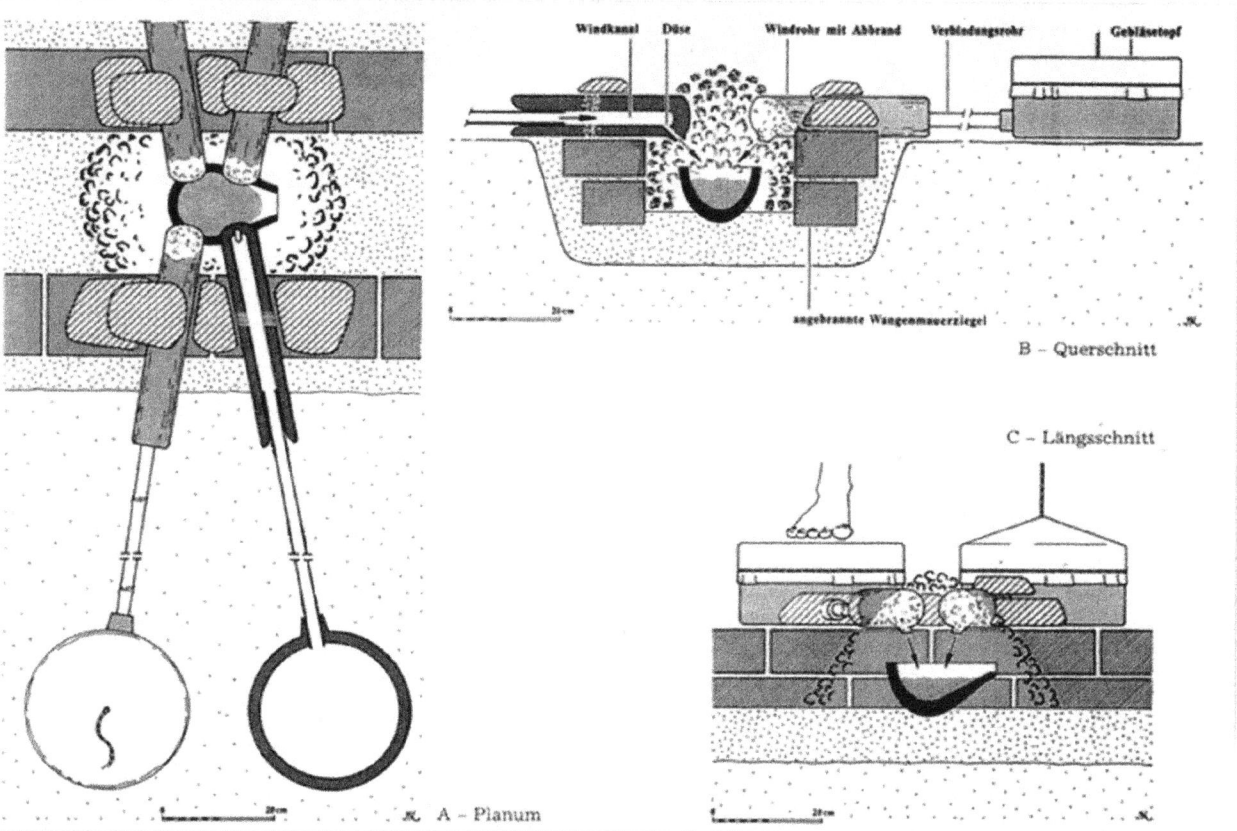

Figure 2.2. Reconstruction of sections across and along an individual hearth at Qantir, Egypt, fed with air from the foot bellows through the tuyeres. There were long lines of these hearths presumably operating together enabling large numbers of crucibles each containing relatively small amounts of bronze to be melted simultaneously. (from Pusch 1994)

that the metal had the least distance to flow. The solution in both Egypt and in South Asia for large castings was to lay the mould inclined at a slight angle to the horizontal with multiple pouring channels. The best evidence for this from Egypt is the scene depicting the casting of a temple door, painted on the walls of the tomb of Rekmire (TT100) of the 18th Dynasty at Karnac (Davies 1943; Wainwright 1944; Garenne-Marot 1985) (Figure 2.3). Judging by the size of the figures around the mould it would have been about 3 m long and had about 16 pouring cups arranged along the top. The mould is at a slight angle and presumably the pouring sequence would have started at the lowest cup and worked up, pouring each crucible in quick succession to ensure the previous pouring had not begun to solidify before the next had joined it. To facilitate this it is likely that the mould would have been heated. There is no such fire shown around the Rekmire mould, but at the Qantir foundry the foundations of a brick structure were found that had been strongly heated. This, the excavators believed, was where the moulds had been heated and the casting took place. Statuary moulds would have been laid on their fronts with the pouring channels in the back. The remains of these channels survive as stubs on the backs of some major statues of the Third Intermediate Period (Craddock 2017) including a figure of Osiris, EA 60717, in the British Museum, a figure of a female N 3390 (Delange et al. 1998, figs 15 and 16) and the famous figure of Karomama, N 500, in the Louvre (Aucouturier et al. 2004).

Casting major statuary bronze lying face down on the casting pit has always been the practice in South Asia (Craddock 2015), as well as in Nepal and Tibet (Hykin et al. 2007) and the evidence is rather more direct. In the instruction manual, the *Mānasāra*, which is believed to have been compiled in the Gupta period, in the early centuries AD it specifically states that pouring channels are to be fitted into the back, the shoulders and the neck of the figure to be cast (Sarawasti 1936). Several failed statuary castings that had been discarded have been found with the remains of their casting channels in the back and buttocks. The *Śilpaśātra* texts instruct that minor faults in a casting could be repaired but that castings with major faults must be abandoned. The castings include a 13th century Nataraja figure now in the Chennai Museum; it has the casting channels on the back of the figure complete with the impressions of the conical cups still filled with bronze attached. A figure of *Bālā-Krishna*, now in the Los Angeles County Museum of Art that had clearly failed during casting, has along the back and legs of the casting a series of protuberances. Johnson (1972) correctly interpreted these as the stubs of the original pouring channels, but then conjectured that they led to a common pouring cup. In fact it is more likely that each pouring channel had its own pouring cup directly above as surviving on the Nataraja figure (Figure 2.4). Finally, of course, there is the continuing practice of the *sthāpati* working in Tamil Nadu in southern India (Craddock – Hook 2007; Craddock

Paul Craddock

Figure 2.3. Wall painting in the tomb of Rekmire of the 18th Dynasty at Karnac, Egypt, showing the pouring of metal into numerous pouring cups set in the top of the slightly inclined mould for casting the frame of a bronze door. (S. La Niece)

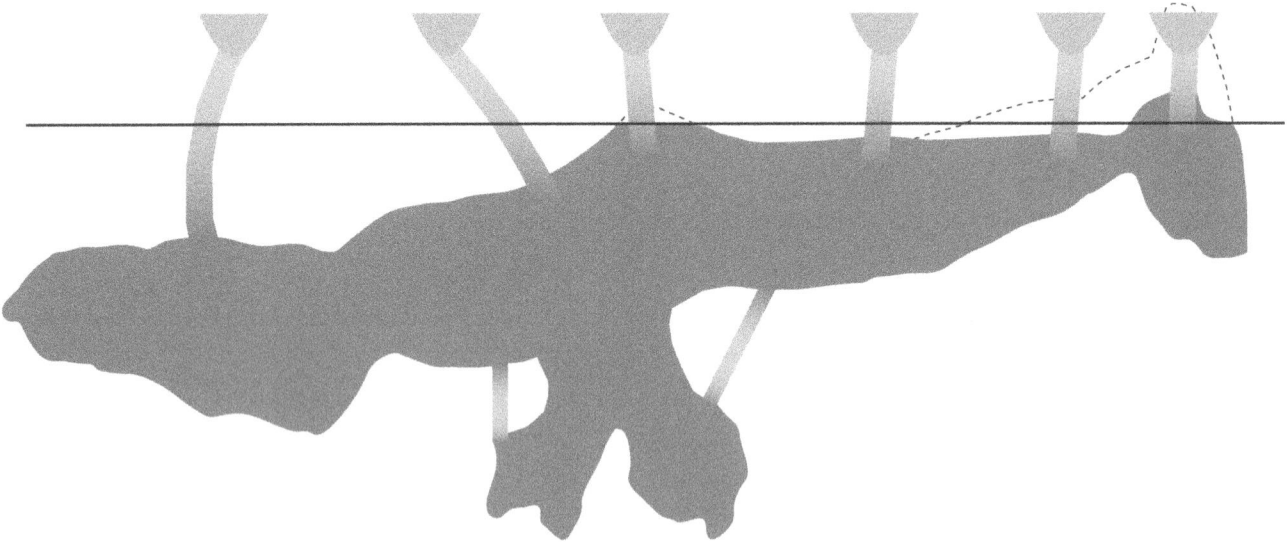

Figure 2.4. A figure of *Bālā-Krishna*, now in the Los Angeles County Museum of Art that had clearly failed during casting. It has along the back and legs a series of pouring channels surviving up to the horizontal line. Above that they have been drawn leading up to separate entry points, thus cutting the distance to be travelled by the molten bronze to a minimum. (redrawn from Johnson 1972)

2015). Major statuary is still cast with the moulds laid in shallow pits at slight angle, although, as a concession to progress, modern refractory crucibles with a capacity of 100 kilograms are used, pouring into a common cup feeding numerous channels into the back of the casting (Figures 2.5 and 2.6).

From Egypt to Greece

In the Third Intermediate Period (1070 BC to 664 BC) there were significant developments in bronze casting technology. Large numbers of bronze figures were produced in a number of regional centres (Hill 2007b). These were

Figure 2.5. Shallow casting pit in which the major statue of Shiva Nataraja (Figure 2.6) has just been cast, lying face down at a slight angle. Swamimalli, Tamil Nadu 1986. (P.T. Craddock)

often quite large and were the first sizeable hollow lost wax castings. Many were made by the traditional direct process, with the wax modelled around a clay core, with or without an armature (Taylor et al. 1998). Others were made by the indirect process as suggested by Roeder (1956, 522–523) and confirmed by more recent radiographic studies (Craddock 2017). In this process the wax models were made up of several separately formed wax impressions taken from plaster piece moulds. The various wax sections were then assembled and stuck together with more wax. This created a local thickening along the joins that was not removed from the inside surfaces of the wax. After this the core was added. On casting this was translated into the bronze and can be detected radiographically (Figure 2.7). In antiquity the cores were always solid, liquid plaster cores poured into the mould are another Post Medieval innovation. In contrast to the contemporary direct castings these indirect lost wax castings have thin walls (1 to 2 mm thickness) with no evidence of armatures in their cores, both characteristics of the indirect technique (Mattusch 1977a).

The Greeks themselves acknowledged the strong influence of Egypt on various aspects of their culture not least in technology, especially on sculpture and sculpting (Anthes 1963). In this assimilation of Egyptian culture and technology Samos was to play a significant role (Kyrieleis 1990; Bianchi 1990; Haynes 1992, 48–49; Jantzen 1972; Weitz 2005; Śliwa 1983; Mattusch 1988, 45–47).

From the end of the 8th century BC there were rapid developments in Greek bronze casting technology, especially in the production of figures (Mattusch 1988 and 2008). Quite suddenly large true hollow lost wax castings were being made locally, some almost certainly being moulded by the indirect process. There are several references in the Classical literature to the introduction of bronze casting to Greece and more specifically to Samos and the sculptors Rhoikos and Theodoros. The Classical literature include references to Rhoikos and Theodorus of Samos, in Pausanias (8,14,8; 9,41,1 and 10,38,6), as being the 'first to melt bronze and cast statues' (Jones 1933, 416–417; Jones 1935, 362–363. 600–601) and in Pliny (*Natural History* 35.152, Rackham 1952, 372–373), state that they introduced clay modelling. See also Diodorus (1.98.5–9; Oldfather 1933, 336–337) for a slightly different account; Telekles and Theodorus, sons of Rhoikos, used Egyptian schemes for planning their sculpture, and also commented upon the similarity between early Greek and Egyptian sculpture (Diodorus 1.97.6, Oldfather 1933, 332–333).

From the continuing excavations on Samos, especially those at the great temple to Hera (Jantzen 1972; Kyrieleis 1990), a number of major Egyptian bronze statues of the Third Intermediate Period have been found. These are most prolific from the 25th Dynasty (752–656 BC) and succeeding Saite Period (664–525 BC). Therefore, by the 7th century BC at the latest, the Samians would have been familiar with Egyptian bronze statuary that was technically superior to anything produced locally.

As well as several indirect lost wax castings, there are also the substantial remains, from the Heraion excavations, of the large figure of a man (Hill 2007b, 110–113, Cat 38, Archaeological Museum Samos, B 1312. 160. 126. 1525 and 1690); it is significantly larger and more advanced in technique than others from Samos. It was found in several pieces including the head, torso and arms, and is estimated to have originally stood between 660 and 680 mm tall. The torso is a direct hollow lost wax casting made around a core supported by an iron armature, and with separate hollow cast arms. These incorporate technical features, new to Greece, but which would soon begin to appear in indigenous castings, including true hollow castings made around a clay core supported by iron armatures (Schorsch 2007, 91). The arms could be cast separately, often attached mechanically to the torso by means of tangs or mortice and tenon joins, together with fusion welding, all in the Egyptian manner.

Thus it seems likely that the Greeks adopted many of the bronze casting techniques of the Egyptians. Could this also have extended to the position of the moulds?

Paul Craddock

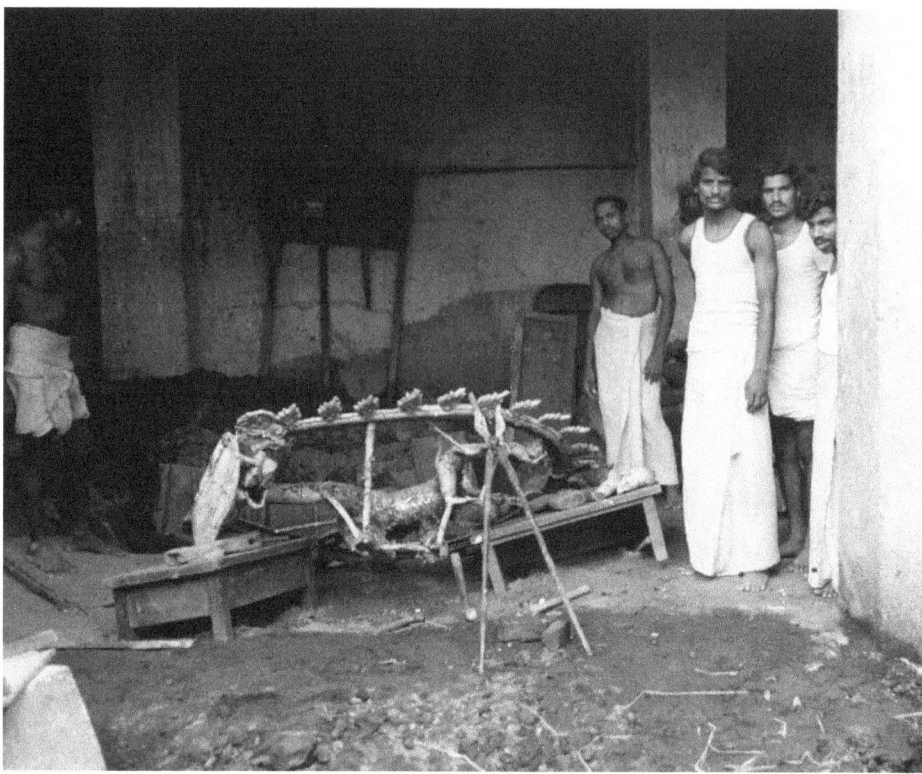

Figure 2.6. Large *Shiva Nataraja* casting just removed from the casting pit (Fig. 5). Note the whole assemblage has been cast in one, and the complex arrangement of feeders and risers now lying underneath as the casting has been turned over. Swamimalli, Tamil Nadu 1986. (P.T. Craddock)

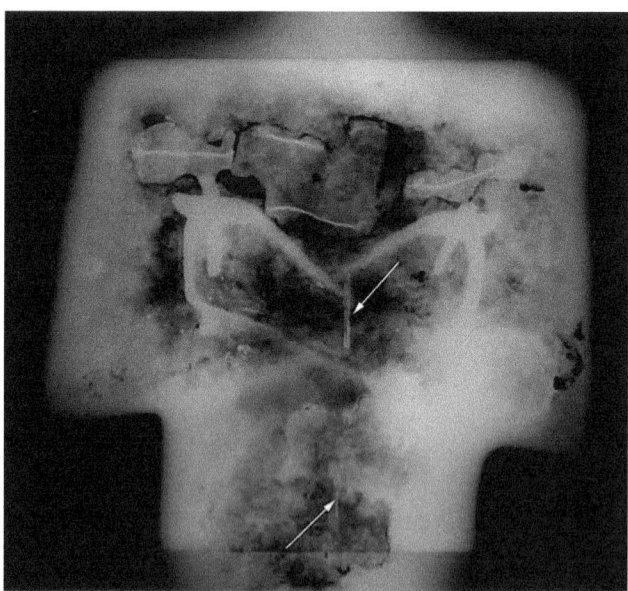

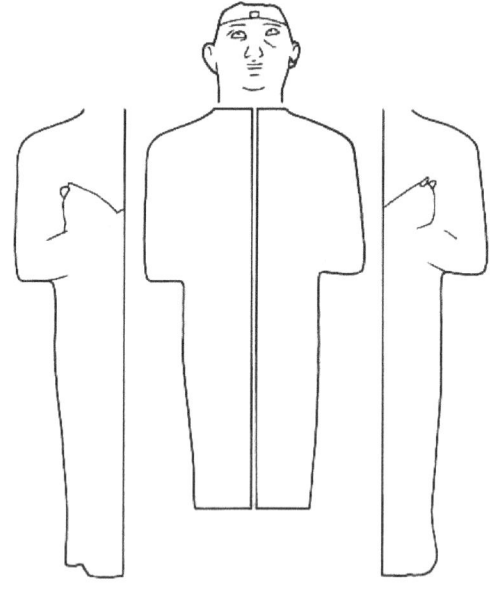

Figure 2.7A. Radiograph of the torso of a figure of Osiris, BM EA 60719, (Fig. 2.7B), showing 2 thin lines of vertical thickening running down centre, (arrowed) indicative of wax to wax joins. The upper line is on the chest the lower line is on the back.

2.7B. Simplified drawing of the four sections of the Osiris torso (Fig. 2.7A) showing the principal straight thickenings. Those on the front and back were revealed by radiography (Fig. 2.7A), those on the side by endoscopy. These are likely to be the remains of wax to wax joins. The head was likely to have been moulded separately. (B. R. Craddock)

The Greek casting pits are generally ovoid (Mattusch 1977a; Zimmer 1999) and seem unnecessarily long to accommodate a mould standing vertically. Also they are often rather shallow, if a substantial section of a life-size figure, typically the torso and lower limbs, was to be cast vertically. Two examples will illustrate the problem. The first was a small casting pit found at the Archaic Foundry in the Athenian Agora, which contained the substantial mould fragments of the major casting mentioned above (Figure 2.1). If, as seems likely, the statue had been cast in that pit then there are problems if is it assumed that the mould was cast upright. From the surviving mould fragments it is clear that the complete casting would have

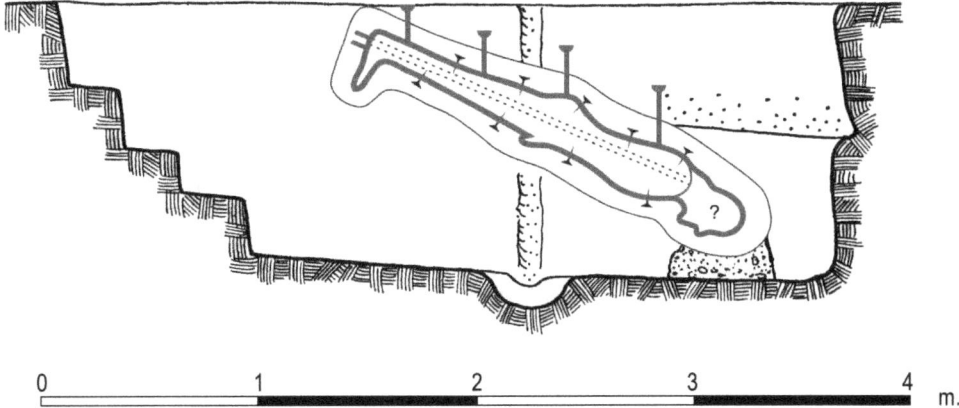

Figure 2.8. The casting pit from the Athenian Agora with the addition of a life size mould of human figure, which fits quite well when lay on its side in the pit, but would be impossible to cast vertically. The arrangement of the pouring channels is taken from the Indian and Egyptian evidence. (P. Craddock and A. Simpson, adapted from Thompson [1948, Fig. 7] and Hoffmann and Konstam [2002]).

been over a metre tall, but the pit is only 850 mm deep, and as Mattusch (1988, 56) states "the pit is not deep enough to have contained the mould for the entire statue and no bricks were found with which the pit walls might have been built up to an appropriate height.". Mattusch suggested that the statue was in fact cast in sections, and certainly the head is likely to have been cast separately, but the substantial surviving sections from head to chest show no signs of joins and suggest that the legs and torso were likely to be have been a single casting. The problem is immediately resolved if the mould was laid along the 1.7m length of the trench / pit, which is otherwise unused with perhaps the distal, foot end, in the deep section of the pit with the vessel for collecting the wax beneath.

The other is perhaps the most complete casting pit to have been found on the Agora (Thompson 1948, pl. 48.1 and Fig. 7; Mattusch 1977a) (Figure 2.8). Its dimensions were 3.78m by 1.7m and 1.4m deep for the main pit, 4.8 m long including the stairs. Thus, although large it is again quite shallow if it was to hold a major mould vertically. The small tile plinth at one end was interpreted as supporting the vessel that caught the molten wax escaping from the mould and is 300 mm thick leaving only 1.1m to the top of the mould. In addition there is the thickness of the mould itself at the base and the provision of a pouring cup and feeders at the top, leaving only about 900 mm for the length of the actual casting. Such a pit as this was surely dug to accommodate a major casting, such as a life-size figure although on the currently accepted vertical arrangement most of the space is redundant. A major mould could be easily accommodated and all the space used, if it was laid along the pit, inclined at a slight angle down to the plinth where the wax collected (Figure 2.8). A series of grooves were observed in the sides and across the centre of the pit. It was suggested that these held shuttering inserted to hold the sand or loam filling the pit during the casting operation. This explanation works for the central grooves, but why was shuttering necessary along the sides of the pit? A major mould would have been a heavy but fragile item and, if laid along the pit, would have needed support from beneath and from the sides, not least to ensure that the pouring cups remained in exactly the correct orientation throughout the pouring operation. A possible explanation for the grooves would be to hold a supporting framework.

Hoffmann and Konstam (2002) have already proposed that the moulds lay at an angle, but still include a complex series of feeder channels supplying metal to the mould from the bottom. However, there is no evidence for their proposed cupola / crucible set in the casting pit above the mould, necessary for melting the considerable quantities metal and, as already noted, pouring the metal in small quantities through such a complex arrangement would have been very hazardous. A much simpler arrangement would be to have a series of separate pouring channels feeding directly into the figure, ensuring the molten metal only had short distances to travel, such as was used in South Asia and in Egypt for major castings as depicted in Figure 2.8.

Conclusion

The production of large hollow bronzes developed significantly in Greece in the first part of the first millennium BC, especially during the Archaic period. During this period, particularly on Samos, there was significant contact with Egypt. There, during the Third Intermediate Period, the production of large hollow lost wax casting by the indirect method had developed through the first centuries of the first millennium BC. The Egyptian influence both in technology as well as design is clear from a comparison of the Egyptian bronze statuary found on Samos with the local productions.

Despite the similarities so obvious on the actual statuary, the arrangements for their production seem quite different. In particular the complex hearth arrangements for the simultaneous melting of many crucibles to ensure a steady supply of metal to the moulds, which have been found in Egypt, are apparently absent in Greece, yet installations serving a similar function must have existed. The Greek moulds were contained in large pits surrounded by soil for support and also for ease of pouring the metal. No such pits have been found in Egypt and it is suggested here that the statuary moulds were laid face down to pour the metal into a series of short pouring channels along the mould's length, as depicted on the Rekmire wall painting, and as was standard practice in other parts of the world, notably India. Given the Egyptian influence on Greek casting technology, it is probable that this influence extended to the arrangements of the mould in the pit, laid at an angle rather than vertically as currently reconstructed. This arrangement has the great merit that it reduces to a minimum the distance travelled by the molten metal between crucible and mould.

These are only suggestions based on observations made in other places and at other times. There still remain the problems of the evidence for the melting of large quantities of metal, the positions of the moulds and the arrangement and numbers of feeding channels.

Acknowledgements: The author acknowledges the great help of Alessandra Giumlia-Mair in the preparation of this paper.

Bibliography

Anfinset, N., 2011. *Social and Technological Aspects of Mining, Smelting and Casting Copper*. Bochum: Deutsches Bergbau Museum.

Anthes, R., 1963. Affinity and Difference between Egyptian and Greek Sculpture and Thought in the 7th and 6th Centuries BC, *Proceedings of the American Philosophical Society*, 107, 60–67.

Aucouturier, M. – Delange, E. – Meyoyas, M., 2004. Karomama, Divine Adoratrice, *Techne*, 19, 7–16.

Bayley, J. – Rehren, Th., 2009. Towards a functional and typological classification of crucibles. In: S. La Niece – D.R. Hook – P.T. Craddock, ed., *Metals and Mines*. London: Archetype Books. 46–55.

Bettarini, R. – Barocchi, P., ed., 1987. *Georgio Vasari: Le Vvite dè de' più excellent eccellenti pittoni pittori, scultori e architettori*. Testo VI, Firenze: Sansoni.

Beveridge, A.S., 1922. *The Bābur-nāma in English*. London: Luzac.

Bianchi, R, S., 1990. Egyptian metal statuary of the Third Intermediate Period, (circa 1070–656 B.C.), from its Egyptian antecedents to its Samian examples. In True and Podany, 1990. 61–84.

Bouquillon, A. – Deschamps, S – Hermary, A. – Mille, B., 2006/7. Une nouvelle etude de l'Apolion l'Apollon Chatsworth, *Revue Archéologique 2006/7*, 227–261.

Bruni, F., 1994. *La fusione artistica a cera persa*. Venezia-Marghera: Edizioni Arte in.

Craddock, P.T., 2014. Refractories with a purpose II: Ceramics for casting, *The Old Potter's Almanack*, 19 (1), 1–17.

Craddock, P.T., 2015. The metal casting industries of South Asia: Continuity and innovation, *Indian Journal of History of Science*, 50 (1), pp. 55–82.

Craddock, P.T., 2017. From Egypt to Greece via India. In: P. Eisenach – T. Stöllner – A. Windler, ed., *The RITak Conference 2013–14, Der Anschnitt Beiheft*, 34, Bochum: Bergbau Museum. 229–242.

Craddock, P.T. – Hook, D.R., 2007. The Bronze Industries of South India: A Continuing Tradition?. In: J.G. Douglas – P. Jett – J. Winter, ed., *Scientific Research on the Sculptural Arts of Asia*, Washington DC: Freer Gallery. 75–89.

Davies, N. de G., 1943. *The Tomb of Rekh-Mi-Re at Thebes*. New York: Arno.

Delange, E. – di Mantova, A. – Taylor, J., 1998. Un bronze Égyptien méconnu, *Revue du Louvre*, 5, 67–75.

Formigli, E., 1984. La technical di construzione delle statue di Riace. In: *Dua Due Bronzi da di Riace*, Bolletino d'Arte, serie speciale 3, Roma. 107–142.

Freestone, I.C. – Tite, M.S., 1986. Refractories in the Ancient and Preindustrial World. In: W.D. Kingery, ed., *High-Technology Ceramics Past, Present and Future. Ceramics and Civilisation III*, Westerville, Ohio, American Ceramic Society. 35–64.

Garenne-Marot, L., 1985. Le travail du cuivre dans l'Égypte Pharaonique d'après les peintures et les bas-reliefs, *Paleorient*, 11, 85–100.

Hawthorne, J.G. – Smith, C.S., trans. and ed., 1963. *On Divers Arts: The Treatise of Theophilus*. Chicago: University of Chicago Press.

Haynes, D., 1968. The technique of the Chatsworth Head, *Revue Archéologie*, 1, 101–112.

Haynes, D., 1970. Ancient Bronze-Casting Methods, *Archäologischer Anzeiger*, 4, 450–452.

Haynes, D., 1992. *The Technique of Greek Statuary Bronze*. Mainz: Philip von Zabern.

Heilmeyer, W. D., 1969. Gießereibetriebe in Olympia, *Jahrbuch des Deutschen Archäologischen Instituts*, 84, 1–28.

Heilmeyer, W-D. – Zimmer, G. – Schneider, G., 1987. Die Bronzegiesserei unter der Werkstatt des Phidas in Olympia, *Archäologischer Anzeiger 1987*, 239–299.

Hemelrijk, J., 1982. Piece casting in the direct process, *Bulletin Antike Beschaving* 57, 6–15.

Hill, M., 2007a. Heights of Artistry: The Third Intermediate Period (c.a. 1070–664 B.C.), in Hill 2007b. 51–63.

Hill, M., 2007b. (ed) *Gifts for the Gods: Images from Egyptian Temples*. New York: Metropolitan Museum of Art.

Hoffmann, H. – Konstam, N., 2002. Casting the Riace Bronzes: Modern Assumptions and Ancient Facts, *Oxford Journal of Archaeology*, 21 (2), 153–166.

Hykin, A. – Neweman, A. – Cummins, J., 2007. Casting compassion: the technical study of a large bronze from Tibet. In: J.G. Douglas – P. Jett – J. Winter, ed., *Scientific Research on the Sculptural Arts of Asia*. Washington DC: Freer Gallery. 90–100.

Jantzen, U., 1972. *Samos 8: Ägyptische und orientalische Bronzen aus dem Heraion von Samos*. Bonn: Deutsches Archäologisches Institut.

Johnson, B. B., 1972. Krishna Rājamannār bronzes: An examination and treatment report. In: P. Pal, ed., *Krishna: The Cowherd King*. Los Angeles: Los Angeles County Museum of Art Monograph Series 1.

Jones, W.H.S., trans., 1933 and 1935. *Pausanias: Description of Greece III and IV*. London: Heinemann.

Krishnan, M.V., 1976. *Cire Perdue Casting in India*. New Delhi: Kanak.

Kyrieleis, H., 1990. Samos and some aspects of ancient Greek bronze casting. In True and Podany, ed., 1990. 15–31.

Lagàrce, J. – Lagàrce, E. – Bounni, A. – Saliby, N., 1983(Nov.). Les Fouilles à Ras Ibn Hani (Syria), *Comptes Rendus, Academie des Inscriptiones et Belles Lettres*. 249–290.

Levy, T.E. – Levy, A.M. – Sthapathy, D. – Sthapathy, S., 2008. *Masters of Fire: Hereditary Bronze Casters of South India*. Bochum: Deutsches Bergbau Museum.

Lo Bue, E., 1981. Casting of devotional images in the Himalayas. In: W.A. Oddy – W. Zwalf, ed., *Aspects of Tibetan Metallurgy*. London: British Museum Occasional Paper 15. 69–80.

Lombardi, G. – Vidale, M., 1998. From the Shell to its Content: The Casting Cores of the two Bronze Statues from Riace (Calabria, Italy), *Journal of Archaeological Science*, 25, 1055–1066.

Martinón-Torres, M. – Freestone, I. – Hunt, A. – Rehren, Th., 2008. Mass-produced mullite crucibles in medieval Europe: manufacture and material properties, *Journal of the American Ceramic Society*, 91, 2071–2074.

Martinón-Torres, M. – Rehren, Th., 2009. Post-medieval crucible production and distribution: a study of materials and materialities, *Archaeometry*, 51(1), 49–74.

Maryon, H., 1956. Fine Metalwork. In: C. Singer – E.J. Holmyard – A.R. Hall – T.I. Williams, ed., *A History of Technology II*, Oxford: Oxford University Press. 449–492.

Mattusch, C.C., 1977a. Bronze and Iron-working in the Area of the Athenian Agora, *Hesperia*, 46 (4), 340–79.

Mattusch, C.C., 1977b. Molds for an Archaic Bronze Statue from the Athenian Agora, *Archaeology*, 30, 326–332.

Mattusch, C.C., 1980. The Berlin Foundry Cup, *American Journal of Archaeology*, 84, 435–44.

Mattusch, 1982. *Bronzeworkers in the Athenian Agora*. Princeton: American School of Classical Studies.

Mattusch, C.C., 1988. *Greek Bronze Statuary: From the Beginnings Through the Fifth Century B.C.* Ithaca: Cornell University Press.

Mattusch, C.C., 2008. Metalworking and tools. In: J.P. Oleson, ed., *The Oxford Handbook of Engineering and Technology in the Classical World*. New York: Oxford University Press. 418–438.

Oddy, W.A. – Swaddling, J., 1985. Illustrations of Metalworking Furnaces on Greek Vases. In: P.T. Craddock – M.J. Hughes, ed., *Furnaces and Smelting Technology in Antiquity*. London: British Museum Occasional Paper 48. 43–58.

Oldfather, trans., 1933. *Diodorus Siculus I*. London: Heinemann.

Pusch, E.B., 1990. Metallverarbeitende werkstätten der frühen Ramessidenzeit in Quantir-Piramese / Nord, *Ägypten und Levante*, 1, 75–113.

Pusch, E.B., 1994. Divergierende Verfahren der Metallverarbeitung in Thebes und Qantir? *Ägypten und Levante*, 4, 145–170.

Pusch, E.B., 1998. High temperature industries in the Late Bronze Age Capital Piramese (Qantir), A Quasi-Industrial Bronze Factory. In: F.A. Esmael, ed., *Proceedings of the 1st International Conference on Ancient Egyptian mining and metallurgy and conservation of metallic artifacts*. Cairo: Ministry of Culture, Supreme Council of Antiquities. 121–132.

Rackham, H., trans., 1952. *Pliny: The Natural History VIII*. London: Heinemann.

Reeves, R., 1962. *Cire perdu casting in India*. New Delhi: Crafts Museum.

Roeder, G., 1956. *Ägyptisches Bronzefiguren. Mitteilungen aus der Ägyptischen Sammlung 6*. Berlin: Staatliche Museen zu Berlin.

Sarawasti, S.K., 1936. An ancient text of casting metal images, *Journal of the Indian Society of Oriental Art*, 4 (2), 139–141.

Scheel, B., 1989. *Egyptian Metalworking and Tools*, London: Shire Books.

Schmidt, G., 1972. Heraion von Samos: Eine Brychon-Weihung und ihre Fundlaage. *Mitteilungen des Deutsches ArchäologischesArchaeologisches Institut, Athenische Abteilungen*, 87.

Schneider, G., 1989a. Investigation of crucibles and moulds from bronze founderies in Olympia and Athens and the determination of provenances of bronze statues. In: Y. Manniatis, ed., *Archaeometry: Proceedings of the 25th International Symposium*, Amsterdam: Elsevier. 305–310.

Schneider, G., 1989b. Bronze casting at Olympia in Classical times, *MASCA Research Paper in Archaeology*, 6, 17–24.

Schneider, G. – Zimmer, G., 1984. Technische Keramik aus antiken Bronzegußwerksttäten in Olympia und Athen, *Berliner Beiträge zur Archäometrie*, 9, 17–60.

Schwandner, E.-L. – Zimmer, G. – Zwicker, U., 1983. Zum problem der Öfen griechischer Bronzegiesser, *Archäologischer Anzeiger 1983*, 803–807.

Schorsch, D., 2007. The manufacture of metal statuary: "Seeing the workshops of the temple". in Hill 2007b. 189–199.

Shakya, R.J., 2017. *The Gilded Buddha: The Traditional Art of the Newar Metal Casters in Nepal*. Basel: Librum.

Śliwa, J., 1983. Egyptian bronzes from Samos in the Staatliche Museen (Antiken-Sammlung) in Berlin. *Etudes et Travaux*, 13, 380–392.

Smith, C.S. – Gnudi, M.T., trans. and ed., 1942. *The Pirotechnia of Vannoccio Biringuccio*. Chicago: Basic Books.

Taylor, J. – Craddock, P. – Shearman, F., 1998. Egyptian hollow-cast bronze statues of the early first millennium: The development of a new technology, *Apollo*, 148 (437), 9–14.

Thompson, H.A., 1948. Excavations at the Athenian Agora 1947, *Hesperia*, 17, 149–196.

True, M. – Podany, J., eds., 1990. *Small Bronze Sculpture from the Ancient World*. Malibu, California: The J. Paul Getty Museum.

Tylecote, R. F., 1976. *Metallurgy in Archaeology*. London: The Metals Society.

Volling, T. – Zimmer, G., 1995. Bewegliche Tiegel. – Ein Neufund in Olympia, *Archäologischer Anzeiger 1995*, 661–666.

Wace, A.J., 1938. The Chatsworth Head, *Journal of Hellenic Studies*, 58, 90–95.

Wainwright, G.A., 1944. Rekmirè's metal-workers, *Man*, 44, 94–98.

Weitz, K., 2005. Ägyptische Bronzevotive in grieschischen Heiligtümern. In: H. Beck – C. Bol – M. Bückling, ed., *Ägypten, Griechenland, Rom: Abwehr und Berührung*. Frankfurt: Städelsches Kunstinstitut und Städische Galerie / Liebighaus. 133–137.

Zimmer, G., 1982. *Antike Werkstattbilder*. Berlin: Staatlichen Museen.

Zimmer, G., 1985. Schriftquellen zum antiken Bronzeguss. In: H. Born, ed., *Archäologische Bronzen, Antike Kunst, Moderne Technik*. Berlin: Dietrich Reimer. 38–49.

Zimmer, G., 1990. *Griechische Bronzegusswerkstätten*. Mainz: Philip von Zabern.

Zimmer, G., 1999. Tecnologia delle fonderie del bronzo nel V secolo a.C. In: E. Formigli, ed., *I Grandi Bronzi Antichi*. Siena: Nnuova Iimmagine Eeditrice. 49–66.

Zwicker, U., 1984. Metallographische und analytische Untersuchungen an Proben aus den Grabhungen der Bronzegießerei in der Phidias-Werkstatt von Olympia und Versuche zum Schmelzen von Bronze in flachen Tiegeln, *Berliner Beiträge zur Archäometrie*, 9, 61–94.

3

Past and Recent Metal Analyses of the Germanicus Statue from Amelia

Alessandra Giumlia-Mair, John Pollini

AGM Archeoanalisi

University of Southern California

giumlia@yahoo.it

Abstract: The statue of Germanicus was discovered over 50 years ago outside the ancient town of Ameria (Amelia), Italy. There are several theories regarding the construction of this sculpture: A 2008 monograph suggested that it originally portrayed King Mithridates VI and that after his defeat by Sulla, the statue was brought to Rome, where the head was replaced first with that of Sulla and finally, around a century later, with one of Germanicus. An alternate theory posited that from the beginning this was a statue of Germanicus in all its parts and that there were no substitutions. In a paper published in 2017, John Pollini proposed that the original head represented Caligula and that it was replaced with a head of Germanicus after Caligula's assassination and damnation in 41 AD. For the present study, several XRF and ICP analyses, employing the most recent technology, were carried out on the various parts of the statue with the aim of finding an answer to a number of still open questions.

Keywords: Bronze Statue; Germanicus; XRF; SEM-EDX; ICP; Corinthium Aes

Introduction

A magnificent, slightly over life-size cuirassed bronze statue of Germanicus (Fig. 3.1), the adopted son of the emperor Tiberius and his designated successor, was discovered over 50 years ago (1963) outside of the city-walls of the ancient town of *Ameria* (Amelia, Italy), not far from the principal town gate. The conservation and restoration of this exceptional work of art in Perugia took many decades. The head of the statue was sent to Amelia in 1987 for a temporary exhibition, since the restoration of the body had not yet been completed. Only in the spring of 2001, when Amelia opened an Archaeological Museum, was the restored statue finally returned to the town.

In a monograph on the statue, Giulia Rocco suggested that it originally portrayed King Mithridates VI, an enemy of Rome in the 80s BC, and that after his defeat by Sulla, Mithridates' statue was brought to Rome, where its head was replaced first with that of Sulla and about 100 years later with that of Germanicus (Rocco 2008). In a recent article Andrea Salcuni posited that the statue always represented Germanicus and that the disproportionate parts are due to the Roman habit of taking casts from already existing statues and putting them together to produce a new image without worrying too much about the exact size and compatibility of scale of the reproduced parts (Salcuni 2014). This is certainly true in the case of many Roman statues. Their limbs are often in awkward positions and rather disproportionate; however, this theory does not explain why the rivets (Fig. 3.2) still visible on the separately worked "collar" of the cuirass were broken off (as already rightly pointed out by Rocco 2008, 538–531), and also why they are far too low to have been attached to the neck of the portrait head of Germanicus (Fig. 3.3). If all parts of the statue had been produced *ad hoc,* the rivets would have been positioned so as to fix the head to the body, but as it is, it seems clear that the neck attachment of the original head was completely different. In his recent article John Pollini (2017) proposed that the head of Germanicus was substituted not for that of Mithridates and then Sulla, but only once, for that of Germanicus' son Caligula, after the latter's assassination and damnation in 41 AD. To determine the nature of the statue's production, the authors of the present article, John Pollini and Alessandra Giumlia-Mair, received in 2017 a Loeb Classical Library Foundation grant and received permission from the Soprintendenza Archeologia, Belle Arti e Paesaggio dell'Umbria to carry out scientific bronze analyses of this statue.

Previous Analyses

Years ago, when the fragments of the Germanicus statue were still being restored, three different persons or groups of persons carried out some metal analyses on single samples taken from the statue. Clearly these were all "destructive" examinations, because pieces of metal were removed. The first examination was apparently an analysis carried out by optical emission spectrometry of a sample

Figure 3.1. Over life-size cuirassed bronze statue of Germanicus from the Roman town of *Ameria* (Amelia) Italy: Photo J. Pollini

Figure 3.2. Remains of three broken off rivets on the fragment of the inside of the collar of the cuirass, indicating that the head was replaced: Photo A. Giumlia-Mair

Figure 3.3. The gap between the neck of Germanicus and the collar of the cuirass, indicating that the head of Germanicus was not originally a part of the cuirass: Photo J. Pollini

taken from the back of the neck and presented by Ada Capasso Carola in a paper at a meeting in 1964 but never published. Although the data are supposedly available in the library of the Istituto Centrale di Restauro in Rome, we have not been able to find these documents. Instead, all the file cards on the Germanicus statue at the Istituto Centrale di Restauro expressly say that no analysis had been carried out on the statue. Nevertheless, the results of the 1964 analysis are reported in the 1987 catalogue of the exhibition in which the head of Germanicus was presented to the public with the following results: 86.76% Cu; 12.70% Sn and Pb 0.45%. This very high tin percentage and the low lead, however, suggest that the results in the catalogue are not reliable and that there must have been some problem with the analyses. If the alloy contained such a high amount of tin, the metal would be a very light golden color, but the parts of the statue that are exposed (where the patina is absent because it was damaged when the statue was excavated) look very reddish, as do copper alloys with lower tin contents.

Optical emission spectrometry involves heating the sample to thousands of degrees Celsius by using an electrical high voltage source. The material is vaporized at the surface, resulting in the atoms being excited and releasing element-characteristic emission lines that can be measured by an optical system. This method is a surface analysis that has to be carefully employed only on areas as free of corrosion as possible (see below). We have to keep in mind that over 50 years ago, the methods and procedure used when analyzing ancient bronzes were rather rudimentary.

The second analysis of some part of the statue, and certainly the most useful one among the earlier examinations, was that published in 1974 by Grazia Dassù and Giovanna Alessandrini in a rather obscure technical Italian journal called *La termotecnica* (Dassù – Alessandrini 1974). The authors were more interested in the superficial corrosion phenomena than in the composition of the bronze. The paper can almost be considered a "historical" document because its title was "New analytical methods in the study of bronzes and excavation patinas." The authors presented in Italy the use of a scanning electron microscope with energy dispersive X-ray spectrometer (henceforth SEM-EDS) as a new method for analyzing ancient bronzes. However, at that time SEM-EDS had already been employed in laboratories specializing in ancient materials, such as the British Museum Research Laboratory in London and the Rathgen Forschungslabor in Berlin. The values given for the Germanicus statue in the paper are 85.55% Cu; 10.21% Sn and 0.65% Pb. One destructive metal sample for metallography was taken, albeit from a corroded part (as becomes clear from the description in the paper). The metallic part of the large sample could have been used for a proper quantitative analysis with atomic absorption spectrometry (AAS), which in that period was a common and a very precise method, but that was not done. AAS is rather time-consuming because the sample has to be cleaned, dissolved in acids, and diluted to a measurable solution, and then the single elements have to be determined one by one. By contrast, SEM-EDS is very fast, and the sample can be examined and analyzed in a very short time.

Regrettably, Dassù and Alessandrini's 45-year-old paper does not say from where their sample was taken, so that analysis cannot help us further in the discussion of the reuse of the cuirass and the replacement of the head. In their work the authors commented on the "low significance of the values from the quantitative point of view", stating that the alloy ought to contain over 7% of tin (Dassù – Alessandrini 1974, 450) and underlining the fact that: 1) no noble patina was present on the fragment but only a rough, porous corrosion overburden; 2) what they call a tin layer was present under the corrosion overburden; and 3) chlorine was present under the tin layer. This is a clear statement that the authors knew that the results of the analysis were not reliable and that there were problems with the phenomenon of re-deposition of tin oxide on the surface that occurred before the formation of the patina. The details given in the discussion imply that on the surface of the fragment analyzed there were complex corrosion phenomena commonly found on ancient bronzes.

When a copper-based alloy containing tin and lead is subjected to oxidizing conditions, the first element attacked by corrosion is tin; the second is lead. This phenomenon is regulated by the order of reactivity of metals or Galvanic series. In this case the tin oxidized and leached out because of the action of chlorine and water in the soil. We must also note that lead that is not soluble in copper and its alloys builds globules in the metallographic structure that can be smaller or larger depending on the lead percentage. The globules consist of only lead and are more prone to corrosion than bronze, so the corrosion mechanisms going on in the metal are much more complex than just leaching out of the tin. In addition, the tin that had leached out re-deposited on the surface as tin oxide and was then covered by the patina and then by the growing corrosion overburden (Dassù – Alessandrini 1974, 450). This is important because the tin oxide also filled some of the cavities left by lead in the upper layers of the alloy. Even after the polishing and mounting of the samples in resin there must have been enough tin oxide in the crevices and interstitial cracks of the corroded metal to produce tin results that are too high. This was without doubt the reason for the very high tin and low lead results of the 1964 analysis as well. The 1974 description in the paper of Dassù and Alessandrini is still useful for our purposes, since it describes in detail the results of the very destructive metallography carried out on the bronze and clearly mentions the tin oxide layer under the corrosion overburden (Dassù – Alessandrini 1974, 443. 445).

Around the end of the 1970s or the beginning of the 1980s a further analysis was carried out on another metal sample from the statue (Leoni 1991). In this case, too, the method was optical emission spectrometry, a surface analysis, apparently followed by wet chemistry. However, in 1985 the analyst sent a letter to the Soprintendenza apologizing for the delay in sending the results and stating that he had lost the file in which he kept the data when he moved to a new house. He nevertheless had the following results collected on "a drapery" presumably a section of the *paludamentum* ("commander's cloak") "by spectrography" (a surface analysis): 85.99% Cu; 11.95 Sn and 0.82% Pb. The same results were published in two almost identical papers in 1991, in which the author indicates that the person represented is the "emperor [sic] Germanicus" (Leoni 1991; Leoni et al.1991). In one of the two publications the corrosion phenomena on the statue are compared with those taken from the Ephebe from Selinunte (dated to the 5th century BC), some sort of stud or ornament from a grave at Quinto Fiorentino (dated to the 7th century BC), a medieval bell and three statues cast by the Flemish artist Giambologna, who lived in Italy in the late Renaissance (1529–1608). The choice of individual pieces for comparison is definitely peculiar. The second 1991 paper only compares the patina from the statue of Germanicus with that of the Ephebe from Selinunte and the stud and medieval bell (but not the Renaissance statues). In both papers the same results mentioned above (85.99% Cu; 11.95 Sn; 0.82% Pb) are given. This means that six years later Leoni still had not found the missing file with his results.

Leoni took a very large bronze sample, apparently from the *paludamentum* (Fig. 3.4), and mounted it in resin for metallography (he mentions the large amount of material available for his study and presents a micrograph that even shows the folds of the "drapery"). However, even this large sample was not used for a proper quantitative analysis: the topic of both 1991 papers is the phenomenon of depletion of tin from bronze. The depletion of tin was described long ago by several scholars (cf., e.g., Cottrell 1967, 526–528) as a preferential attack on this particular component of the alloy in the presence of an electrolyte as a result of an electrochemical oxidation-reduction process (or redox). This is common knowledge among scientists and conservation experts working on ancient bronzes (cf., e.g., Cronyn 1990, 214–219). However, it was clearly new to Leoni, who apparently used to work on modern industrial materials. He must have been quite

Figure 3.4. Polished section of the metallographic sample taken by Leoni (2.5 cm; image enlarged 3x): After Leoni et al. 1991, fig. 1.

impressed by it, because he published two papers on this actually well-known phenomenon: one (together with other people) with the title "On the detinning phenomenon on archaeological bronzes"; the second (by himself) with the title "A particular corrosion phenomenon on the 'Fiorenza' of Giambologna". He described it as a "singular form of corrosion" and concluded his English abstract with "On the analogy with the terms 'dezincification' we propose 'detinning' as a new term to indicate the similar phenomenon found on bronze". The usual term employed for this common phenomenon is "destannification" (cf., e.g., Wang – Merkel 2001).

It must be underscored that both papers by Leoni (1991) and Leoni et al. (1991) completely miss the phenomenon of tin oxide deposition under the corrosion overburden, described by Dassù and Alessandrini in their 1974 article, although both 1991 papers mention Dassù and Alessandrini (1974). The point of explaining all this is that the high tin content found in the statue by Leoni was, again, due to tin oxide deposition.

In 1987, on the occasion of the exhibition of the head of the Germanicus statue in Amelia, a company called "AB2 Art" made radiographs, an ultrasonic examination of the head, and took a sample for metallography from the back of the neck. The analytical method employed is not mentioned, but the results seem to indicate that also in this case a surface method, most likely SEM-EDS, must have been used because among the listed elements detected by this analysis (beside 85.65% Cu; 12.20% Sn and 0.55% Pb, which again are far too high for tin and too low for lead) are sulfur, silicon and chlorine (elements from the soil). The destructive metallographic samples were again taken, rather surprisingly, from the same area at the back of the neck from which metallographic samples had been removed for the 1964 analysis.

It should be pointed out that ever since the invention of methods of analysis different from wet chemistry, it is common practice for any kind of report, paper, article on any kind of analysis to clearly state the method and the parameters employed for the measurements, so as to give the readers an idea of the precision and accuracy of the results.

To sum up briefly: Four different surface analyses produced tin results between 10 and almost 13% Sn and very low lead results under 1% for at least three different parts of the statue: the head, the *paludamentum,* and probably the cuirass. The high tin and low lead results are due to alteration phenomena, such as the re-deposition of tin oxide on the metal under the corrosion overburden layer, as described by Dassù and Alessandrini (1974). Very destructive samples for metallography (which needs a noticeable piece of non-corroded metal) had been taken at least three different times and probably four, with the aim of checking the degree of corrosion of the statue. There is no doubt that the statue was cast, so this was certainly not the reason for carrying out destructive metallography, which is normally done to determine the production technique of ancient bronzes. All those who had analyzed the Germanicus statue in past years had a large amount of material available to them for a proper quantitative analysis, but they only used it for metallography and surface analyses. As a result, the prior data are unreliable, which led Rocco to comment in her 2008 monograph:

"È provato come questi dati non risultino determinanti, rispetto a quelli ricavabili da altri elementi tecnici e stilistici…" ("It is proven that these data are not decisive, as compared to those deducible from other technical and stylistic factors") (Rocco 2008, 663–664, n. 457).

Further, a fragment of 2 square millimeters is sufficient to serve as a sample for metallography, but some of the samples that had been taken were unnecessarily large, like those taken from modern industrial alloys that have no quantity limitation. New analyses for solving the problems regarding the construction and the originality or replacement of the various parts of the statue were clearly needed.

Methods of Analysis

The new analyses carried out on the statue were first around 30 X-ray fluorescence spectrometry measurements. This method is well known in archaeology (cf. Lutz et al. 1996; Helmig et al. 1989; Longoni et al. 1998; Mendoza Cuevas – Perez Gravie 2011; Ferrence – Giumlia-Mair 2018) and has been used and improved upon for decades (Hahn-Weinheimer et al. 1995; Lutz et al. 1996). The main advantage is that XRF is a non-destructive method and that the elements can be determined all in one measurement. Although XRF is a surface analysis, various experiments carried out in the past by comparing the results of XRF and AAS analyses have demonstrated that over 90% of the XRF results were well within ± 20% of the corresponding AAS results (when carried out by experienced analysts). The calculated correlations for tin and lead, two of the most important alloying elements, range from 0.84 to 0.97. This demonstrates that the method is reliable and precise, if the parameters are respected and appropriate standards are employed. Different standards of known composition for all elements, produced by AGM Archeoanalisi for the analysis of ancient metal alloys, were employed during the measurements. These standards of known composition, as similar as possible to ancient alloys, represent an important tool, when the results are evaluated. Particular interference effects, for example, enhanced results for elements such as iron in a copper matrix or similar phenomena, could be exactly monitored and taken into account when calculating the results. Whenever possible the analyses were performed on bare metal, free of patina and corrosion. This was not too difficult because there are many spots on the statue that had been nicked by modern tools during excavation, resulting in exposure of the bare metal surface beneath the patina.

The equipment employed for this study was specially developed for the analysis of archaeological and Cultural Heritage artifacts that cannot be brought to a laboratory. This equipment includes an X-ray source, a transformer, a stabilizer and a tripod with several devices that control stability and position, as well as a computer with dedicated software. The spectrometer has a Si(Li) detector and operates at a maximum voltage of 50 kV and a maximum current of 0.35 mA. The XRF measurements are performed by illuminating with x-ray a small, flat, cleaned area on the object for a short time (typically 3–5 minutes). If necessary, however, the measurement time can be longer, as when the spot analyzed is very small. The x-rays are emitted by a miniaturized x-ray tube. The irradiated area has a diameter of around 1.5–2 mm, but by using the in-built collimator the analyzed spot can be reduced or enlarged, as required by the size of the object, the detail to be analyzed (for instance an inlay or a small area fee of corrosion) and the surface texture. The measurements of the sample are taken at a fixed angle and from a fixed distance. An audible signal rings when the position is correct, and a laser pointer indicates the exact spot of measurement. The quoted detection limits for some of the most significant elements are (given in ppm): Cu 0.1; Pb 200; Sn 200; Fe 250; Co 200; Ni 150; As 5; Sb 510; Ag 200.

Because of the size and manner of display of the statue of Germanicus, it could not be moved or touched in any way. Since the figure is over two meters in height and is set on a high base, an over three-meter-high scaffolding was needed to perform the analyses. The results of the XRF analyses are reported here in the table of results (table 3.1.). These XRF results were quite different from those in the analyses carried out in 1964, 1974, ca. 1980 (published in 1991) and 1987 (see above). Since then, additional fragments of the statue that had not been returned to Amelia were discovered in storage in the National Archaeological Museum in Perugia. With the permission of Soprintendente Dr. Mercalli (Soprintendenza Archeologia, Belle Arti e Paesaggio dell'Umbria) and the kind help of Dr. Elena Roscini, archaeologist at the same Soprintendenza, it was decided to carry out by means of Inductively Coupled Plasma Optical Emission Spectrometry (ICP-OES) a second, high-precision analysis of these and other fragments already in the Amelia Museum that could not be attached to the restored statue of Germanicus.

While XRF does not detect light elements, ICP-OES can detect all elements in very low concentrations. The ca. 10 mg drillings, taken with a jeweler's drill using thin bits with a diameter of 0,8mm (i.e. as thin as a needle) from the "re-discovered" fragments, were weighed as carefully as possible, put into pyrex flasks and dissolved in a fume-cupboard with *aqua regia* (i.e., 1 volume of concentrated nitric acid [HNO_3] to 3 volumes of concentrated hydrochloric acid [HCl]). The tiny holes left by the drill in the fragments were sealed with paraffin to avoid corrosion. The flasks were gently heated to ensure complete dissolution of the samples. After total dissolution at a controlled low temperature (60°C) 1 ml more of *aqua regia* and distilled water (up to 10 ml) were added to prepare the solution for analysis. Several standard solutions covering the concentration range were prepared as well. Specifically employed was a multichannel spectrometer system (polychromator) that can simultaneously detect all elements present in the solution, from trace levels to major elements. Because this procedure is very sensitive, only samples that are very small in size are needed for this analysis. The heart of the system is an ICP torch set in a water-cooled coil carrying high frequency current. The flame of the torch burns at temperatures of 6000°K up to 10,000°K, so that the injected sample solution is atomized and partly ionized. The radiation emitted is resolved into component radiations by means of a diffraction grating and converted to an electric signal that can be quantitatively measured by comparing the intensity of radiation with the specific wavelength for each element. The quoted standard deviation is ca. 1% (Thompson – Walsh 1983, 94). The results of the ICP analysis are given in the table of results (Tab. 3.1.).

Discussion of the Results

From the table of results (Tab. 3.1.) it becomes immediately evident that there are two groups of data that can be quantitatively distinguished because of their different tin and lead content. All higher tin and lead percentages (between 7.9% and 10.82% Sn and 5.6% and 8.64% Pb) have been determined in the pieces belonging to the cuirass (with the exception of the inlays). The 1–2% differences are due to corrosion and to minor instrumental variation, but the data are rather consistent and can be considered reliable. The ICP analyses carried out on the fragments confirm this trend as well. A further discriminant is represented by slightly enhanced (at trace level) cobalt, nickel and antimony percentages in several measurements carried out on the cuirass. All this seems to indicate that the cuirass is indeed a reused part of an older statue as hypothesized by all scholars (with the exception of Salcuni 2014) who have discussed the construction of this work of art (see especially Rocco 2008 and Pollini 2017).

The range of the tin and lead data of parts of the statue other than the cuirass is lower. Consequently, we have to differentiate between the various parts that were assembled in constructing the statue originally because,

Alessandra Giumlia-Mair, John Pollini

Table 3.1. Percentage of elements by weight in the bronze at 36 parts of the statue

no.	object	part	method	Cu	Sn	Pb	As	Sb	Fe	Ni	Ag	Zn	Co	Bi	Mn	Au
1	spear	point	XRF	93	6.3	0.3	tr	tr.	0.3							
2	spear	sauroter	XRF	93	6.2	0.2	tr	tr	0.2							
3	spear	shaft	XRF	91	6.9	1.3	0.2	tr	0.5		tr		tr		tr	
4	1st pteryx	base	XRF	84	8.2	7.3		0.2	0.2	tr					tr	
5	1st pteryx	black inlay	XRF	97	2.2	0.4	tr	tr	0.3		tr					tr
6	1st pteryx	satyr	XRF	83	8.7	7.9	tr	tr	tr						tr	tr
7	sword fitting	hook	XRF	95	4.1	tr		tr	0.2							
8	cuirass	front	XRF	85	7.9	6.1	tr	0.3	0.6		tr	tr	tr		tr	
9	cuirass	front	XRF	84	8.4	6.3		tr	0.8	tr	tr	tr	0.2			
10	Scilla	tail	XRF	81	9.8	7.8		0.3	0.8	tr	tr	0.3	tr	tr	tr	
11	cuirass	black inlay	XRF	96	1.9	0.9	tr		0.4		0.2					0.3
12	epomis	right	XRF	83	9.7	6.5	0.2	tr	0.2		tr		tr		tr	
13	cuirass	black inlay	XRF	96	1.9	0.9		0.2	0.4		0.2		tr		tr	0.2
14	sword	blade	XRF	95	3.8	0.7		tr	0.3	tr						
15	sword	taenia	XRF	95	4.1	0.7	tr	tr	0.2	tr						
16	cuirass	Scilla	XRF	87	6.3	5.6		tr	0.4		tr		tr		tr	
17	tunic frg.		XRF	93	4.6	0.9			0.7			0.3				
18	tunic frg.	repair	XRF	94	3.5	0.8	0.2		0.5		tr	0.4	tr			
19	r.Victoria	l.arm	XRF	93	3.1	1.7			0.2			1.3				
20	l.Victoria	body	XRF	95	2.9	tr			0.2			0.8				
21	head	top	XRF	93	5.2	1.4	tr	tr	0.4			tr				
22	cloak	frg.	XRF	89	6.7	2.3		0.2	1.3	tr						
23	r.sleeve		XRF	97	1.8	0.5			0.3		tr					
24	r.sleeve	repair	XRF	91	8.2	tr		tr	tr							
25	r.arm	forearm	XRF	90	6.4	3.1		tr	0.3	tr			tr		tr	
26	r.hand	forefinger	XRF	96	2.6	0.9			0.4	tr						
27	r.foot	top	XRF	93	4.7	1.8		tr	0.3							
28	l.foot	top	XRF	95	2.9	1.4			0.4							
29	l. tenon		XRF	3	18	64			12					3		
30	l.arm	forearm	XRF	94	4.3	1.2			0.4						tr	
31	l.hand	back	XRF	94	3.5	1.8			0.3							
32	solder	frg.	XRF	tr	36	62			1.9							
33	l.knee	frg.	ICP	91	5.22	1.48		0.03	0.62	0.023	0.03	0.005			0.02	
34	cloak	frg.	ICP	90	6.23	1.59		0.04	0.41	0.022	0.03	0.004			0.01	
35	spear	shaft	ICP	90	7.94	1.04			0.77	0.023	0.03	0.004			0.02	
36	pteryx frg.	base	ICP	80	9.36	8.64	0.02	0.32	0.53	0.096	0.08	0.004	0.04		0.05	
37	epomis	right	ICP	81	10.82	6.76	0.02	0.27	0.48	0.103	0.09	0.003	0.05		0.06	

quite often, different batches of metals were employed for the separate castings. Nevertheless, all the analyzed parts show tin results at the highest around 6.5% and lead at around 1%. It is important to underscore that the few slightly higher lead percentages (up to ca. 1.75% with a single outlier of 2.3% Pb in the cloak) are certainly only due to the non-homogeneous distribution of lead globules in the metallographic structure that are not relevant for this discussion. The very low lead content and the moderate tin content suggest that perhaps these parts of the statue were originally planned to be amalgam-gilded. The technique of amalgam-gilding (also called fire-gilding or mercury-gilding) has been known since Hellenistic times (Craddock 1995, 302; Giumlia-Mair 2001; 2002a and b). This gilding process involves the mixing of gold filings, gold leaf or pieces of gold wire with mercury to form an amalgam that could be spread on the surface to be gilded. Good quality copper-based objects to be amalgam-gilded usually contained very low amounts of tin and lead (and zinc as well) or at least as little as possible because these elements (lead in particular) tend to combine with the amalgam and produce spots on the gilding. In later Roman times the metalworkers did not work as carefully as they had earlier, and they employed alloys with very high lead content, sometimes covering the more visible spots with a piece of gold leaf. By contrast, in the first century AD, most probably and particularly in the case of statues of members of the imperial family, a high lead content was generally avoided. In the Middle Ages and Renaissance the deleterious effect of lead for gilding was certainly known (see, e.g., Theophilus Presbyter, *De diversis artibus*, LXVIII, *Qualiter deauretur auricalcum* [sic]), but only relatively small gilded objects for ritual use, such as chalices, were made of alloys without (or at least with very low) zinc-, tin- and lead-content.

In the case of the Amelia sculpture, it may have been one of a series of statues of Germanicus being produced in workshops in Rome to satisfy the need of cities and towns of Italy or other parts of the empire to honor this much-loved Roman military general and member of the Julio-Claudian family. Under Caligula's successor Claudius, a multiplicity of images of Germanicus would have served to confirm the dynastic legitimacy of Claudius, who greatly admired and promoted the memory of his brother Germanicus. Because of a high demand for commemorative or honorific statues of Germanicus, it may have been decided to reuse for the Amelia sculpture a pre-existing statue of Caligula. This sort of reuse may also have been the case with other bronze statues that originally represented Caligula, especially those that had been set up in Rome before his assassination and damnation.

Notably, the two appliqué figures of Victoria (Fig. 3.5), which had been attached to the cuirass, have a composition that is more similar to that of the head of Germanicus and the limbs than to the cuirass. This confirms Rocco's hypothesis that they had been applied when the breast- and back-plates were reused, as their style is very different from the rest of the skillfully decorated cuirass. Regrettably, the *Saltantes Lacenae* ("Spartan Dancers") and the palmettes appliqués could not be analyzed because they could not be reached by the XRF beam, but most probably they, like all the other separately cast appliqués on the cuirass, were added in a second phase, as indicated by their workmanship, which likewise looks much less skillful than that of the other decorations that were cast as part of the cuirass itself. The composition of the *paludamentum* on Germanicus' left shoulder is similar to that of the head and the other parts, with only ca. 6% of tin and 2% of lead. Therefore, this cloak also has to be considered an addition to the cuirass. The parts of the statue with the lowest lead content are the spear and sword with its accessories, but obviously these elements were separately cast; therefore, the fact that their alloy is slightly different from the rest of the statue is not surprising. The results of the analyses do not show much difference among the other separately cast parts of the statue, except for minimal discrepancies due to corrosion and small instrumental variations, so there is no reason to think that they are not also part of the second phase of the statue.

Black *Corinthium Aes* Inlays on the Cuirass and *Pteryges* of the Germanicus Statue

The black stylized sea-wave inlays (Fig. 3.6) under the figure of Skylla on the Amelia statue's cuirass and the palmette inlays on the skirt of the decorated leather straps (*pteryges*) attached to the lower edge of the cuirass are all examples of *Corinthium aes*, an artificially patinated alloy containing small amounts of precious metals that, after a treatment in an aqueous solution containing copper salts, turns a black, purple-black or blue-black color. The analysis of the inlays revealed that the alloy consists of copper with around 2% tin, less than 1% lead, 0.3% of gold, silver and iron, and traces of arsenic. The low percentages of gold and silver are too regular and too high to be considered an impurity because in Roman times copper was apparently always refined to recover precious metals and therefore contained only ca. 0.0002–0.001% Au and 0.02–0.1% Ag, amounts that would not be detectable with XRF. As several experiments (Giumlia-Mair and Lehr 2003) and the analyses of ancient pieces have shown (see for instance Giumlia-

Figure 3.5. Detail of Victoria applique on the right side of the cuirass (Note: The workmanship of this figure is much lower than that of the relief scenes which are part of the cast of the cuirass): Photo A. Giumlia-Mair

Figure 3.6. The black wave pattern under Skylla are inlaid in *Corinthium aes*: Photo A. Giumlia-Mair

Figure 3.7. Artificial black patina on the palmette inlays of *Corinthium aes* on the *pteryges* (presently regrown after having been removed during modern conservation): Photo J. Pollini

Mair – Craddock 1993a and b; Craddock – Giumlia-Mair 1993; Giumlia-Mair 1993; Giumlia-Mair 2015b), this small amount of precious metal is sufficient to produce the desired coloration on the alloy. With a variation in the amount of iron and arsenic, it is possible to change the color nuance and obtain instead of black, a purple-black or blue-black color. One of the characteristics of this alloy is the self-induced "re-growth" of its patina, after it has been damaged. This also happened with the palmette inlays on the *pteryges* (Fig. 3.7). The artificial black patina was probably removed when the statue was first cleaned, but over time it has been slowly reforming, becoming first reddish-brown and then black.

This kind of alloy is known from ancient times, with the earliest examples discovered thus far being Egyptian and dating to the mid-19th century BC: a statuette of the crocodile god Sobek and that of Pharaoh Amenemhat III, both from the Fayum (Giumlia-Mair 1997). Gold and silver inlaid daggers from the Shaft Graves at Mycenae, dated to the mid-16th century BC, are made of the same alloy (Giumlia-Mair – Craddock 1993a). In the Roman period, the black-patinated alloys appear in the 1st century BC – 1st century AD, when they become the "rage" (*furor*) in Rome, as Seneca the Younger notes (*Brev. Vit.* 12,2). Pliny the Elder describes *Corinthium aes* as "the most highly praised" copper alloy (*HN* 34,6), and "more precious than silver and almost as precious as gold" (*HN* 34,1). Objects made of this material were sought as collection pieces by wealthy Romans, including Augustus, who, according to Suetonius (*Aug.* 70,2), supposedly proscribed some men in order to confiscate their "Corinthian vases" (*vasa Corinthia*), most likely antique Corinthian vessels that were decorated with this costly black alloy. Tiberius seems to have nominated *Corinthiarii*, important civil servants, to look after his collection (cf. Murphy-O'Connor 1983, 80). Seneca (*Brev. Vit.* 12,2) also mocked the collectors who spent their days playing with their "rusty (i.e. patinated) metal inlays" (*aeruginosis lamellis*), while Pliny the Younger (*Epist.* 3,6,1) mentioned the beautiful patina of the Corinthian statuette he bought.

Figure 3.8. Small statue of emperor Nero in the British Museum, wearing a cuirass inlaid with *Corinthium aes* and silver: Photo J. Pollini

Among other examples of Roman cuirassed statues with inlays made of Corinthian alloy is a rather exceptional small statue of Nero in the British Museum, wearing an elaborately decorated cuirass with silver and black inlays (Fig. 3.8). The inlays were analyzed and are made of a Corinthian alloy (Stapleton et al. 1995). Another outstanding example is a large section of intricately inlaid drapery that probably belonged to a statue of Caracalla from the ancient city of Volubilis in Morocco (Giumlia-Mair – Craddock 1993a). Fragments of a cuirassed statue in the City Museum of Turin are less well known and have not been analyzed thus far; however, they also appear to be inlaid with silver and a black patinated alloy (Giumlia-Mair 1993; Mercando – Zanda 1998, 112–117).

Conclusions

The "destructive" analyses performed on samples taken from the statue of Germanicus in Amelia in 1964, 1974, ca. 1980 (published in 1991) and 1987 were all imprecise and – with the exception of those of Dassù and Alessandrini (1974) – did not take into account the phenomenon of tin oxide deposition under the corrosion overburden, described in the 1974 paper. As a result, all of the percentages obtained are too high in tin and too low in lead. Many analyses carried out in past years are just plain wrong because they were performed by people who were used to working with such modern materials as steel and aluminium and who had very little to no experience with ancient metals. Many examples of bad analyses of ancient materials can be found in the archaeological literature. For instance, in the otherwise excellent volume *Römische Bildnisse aus Bronze*, Götz Lahusen and Edilberto Formigli collected all analytical data available at that time (Lahusen – Formigli 2001) but did not critically evaluate these data. In short, a large number of such published analytical results are clearly incorrect. Regrettably, however, these types of analyses are used and cited in scientific publications by archaeologists. Such data only create confusion and are more problematic than useful. It is, therefore, very important that archaeologists become aware of the many difficulties with analytical data published in the past (see also Giumlia-Mair 2015a, 172).

Several conclusions have been reached in our study. To begin with, there is no doubt that the original head was pried off and replaced with that of Germanicus. The cuirass and *pteryges* are decorated with inlaid *Corinthium aes*. The composition of all other parts of the statue might have been planned for amalgam-gilding because of the rather low tin and the very low lead content. Perhaps it was decided not to gild the surfaces because of the presence of the black inlays on the cuirass and *pteryges*. The cuirass is slightly too large for the head and the rest of the body. The appliqués were added later in a second phase, most probably to adapt the motifs on the cuirass to highlight the military victories of Germanicus. The composition of the statue suggests that the head and the limbs were made by following one kind of metallurgical recipe, while the cuirass and the left *epomis* ("shoulder clasp") contain higher percentages of tin and lead, and some of the trace elements, such as cobalt, nickel and antimony, seem to be higher than in the other parts.

As demonstrated by Cadario, the "Butrint" type cuirass on the statue is known only after the battle of Actium won by Augustus in 31 BC (Cadario 2004; see further Pollini – Giumlia-Mair 2019). This and the fact that the patinated alloy *Corinthium aes* first comes into widespread use in the Roman world at the time of Augustus allow for a date for the cuirass in the 1st century AD. It is quite likely to have originally been part of a statue of Caligula that after his assassination and damnation was reused for the Amelia statue of his father, the beloved general Germanicus.

Bibliography

AB2 Art, 1987. Le indagini scientifiche. *Il volto di Germanico. A proposito del restauro del bronzo, catalogo della mostra, Amelia 1987*. Rome: Cedis Editrice, 42–48.

Cadario, M., 2004. *La corazza di Alessandro: Loricati di tipo ellenistico dal IV secolo a.C. al II d.C.* Milan: Edizioni Universitarie Lettere Economia Diritto.

Cottrell, A., 1967. *An introduction to metallurgy*. London: Edward Arnold Publ.

Craddock P.T., 1995. *Early metal mining and production*. Edinburgh: Edinburgh University Press.

Craddock, P.T. – Giumlia-Mair, A.R., 1993. Hsmn-Km, Corinthian bronze, shakudo: black patinated bronze in the ancient world. In: La Niece, S. – Craddock, P., eds., *Metal plating and patination. Cultural, technical, and historical developments*. Oxford: Butterworth-Heinemann, 101–127.

Cronyn, J.M., 1990. *The elements of archaeological conservation*. London: Routledge.

Dassù, G. – Alessandrini, G., 1974. Nuovi metodi d'indagine nello studio dei bronzi e delle patine da scavo. *La termotecnica*, 28(8), 441–452.

Ferrence, S.C. – Giumlia-Mair, A., 2018. Minoan status symbols: tweezers,"weaving hooks" and cosmetic scrapers. In: Lapatin, K. – Daehner, J., eds., *Artistry in bronze. The Greeks and their legacy*. Proceedings of the 19th Bronze Congress, October 13–17, 2015. Los Angeles: The Getty Museum.

Giumlia-Mair, A., 1993. Il caso di industria, la metallurgia del bronzo e Plinio. *Quaderni della Soprintendenza Archeologica del Piemonte*, 11, 76–97.

Giumlia-Mair, A., 1997. Early instances of *shakudo*-type alloys in the West. *Bulletin of the Metals Museum. Sendai, Japan*, 27, 3–15.

Giumlia-Mair, A., 2001. Colouring treatments on ancient copper alloys. *Revue de Métallurgie, Cahiers d'informations Techniques*, 98 (9), 767–776.

Giumlia-Mair, A. and Craddock, P.T., 1993a. *Das schwarze Gold der Alchimisten*. Mainz: Philipp von Zabern Verlag.

Giumlia-Mair, A. – Craddock, P.T., 1993b. Irogane alloys in classical antiquity. *Bulletin of the Metals Museum. Sendai, Japan*, 20, 3–18.

Giumlia-Mair, A. – Meriani, S. – Lucchini, E., 2002a. Indagini archeometallurgiche su dorature antiche: analisi tecniche e varianti. In: Giumlia-Mair, A., ed., *XV Congresso Internazionale sui Bronzi Antichi "Produzione e Tecnologia"*. Montagnac: Éditions Mergoil, 338–343.

Giumlia-Mair, A., 2002b. Technique and composition of equestrian statues in Raetia. In: Mattusch, C.C. – Brauer, A. – Knudsen, S.E., eds., Proceedings of the 13th Conference on Ancient Bronzes, Cambridge, Massachusetts, 1996, Portsmouth, Rhode Island, *Journal of Roman Archaeology, Supplementary, Series* 39, 92–97.

Giumlia-Mair. A., 2015a. Techno-Chronology? Alloy composition and the use of technical features for the dating of ancient bronzes. In: Daehner, J.M. – Lapatin, K., eds., *Power and Pathos. Bronze sculpture of the*

Hellenistic world, Los Angeles: Getty Publications and Florence: Giunti Editore, 167–181.

Giumlia-Mair, A., 2015b. Polychrome production of a Romano-Egyptian workshop. In: Deschler-Erb, E. – Della Casa, Ph., eds., *New research on ancient bronzes.* Acta of the XVIIIth International Congress on Ancient Bronzes. Zurich Studies in Archaeology, 10, 305–310.

Giumlia-Mair, A. – Lehr, M., 2003. Experimental reproduction of artificially patinated alloys identified in ancient Egyptian, Palestinian, Mycenaean and Roman objects. In: Bellintani, P. – Moser, L., eds., *Metodologie ed esperienze fra verifica, riproduzione, comunicazione e simulazione.* Atti del convegno, Comano Terme-Fiavè (Trento), Italy. Trento: Provincia autonoma, Ufficio beni archeologici, 291–310.

Hahn-Weinheimer, P. – Hirner, A. – Weber-Diefenbach, K., 1995. *Röntgenfluoreszenzanalytische Methoden – Grundlagen und praktische Anwendung in den Geo-, Material- und Umweltwissenschaften.* Braunschweig Wiesbaden: Vieweg Verl.

Lahusen, G. – Formigli, E., 2001. *Römische Bildnisse aus Bronze. Kunst und Technik.* Munich: Hirmer Verlag.

Leoni, M., 1991. Un particolare fenomeno corrosivo sulla "Fiorenza" del Giambologna. *Rivist OPD Restauro*, 3, 52–56.

Leoni, M. – Diana, M. – Guidi, G. – Perdominici, F., 1991. Sul fenomeno della destannazione nei manufatti bronzei di provenienza archeologica. *La Metallurgia Italiana*, 83(11), 1033–1037.

Longoni, A. – Fiorini, C. – Leutenegger, P. – Sciuti, S. – Fronterotta, G. – Strüder, L. – Lechner, P., 1998. A portable XRF spectrometer for non-destructive analyses in archaeometry. *Nuclear Instruments and Methods in Physics Research A 409*, 407–409.

Lutz, J. – Pernicka, E., 1996. EDXRF analysis of ancient copper alloys. *Archaeometry.* 38(2), 313–323.

Mendoza Cuevas, A. – Perez Gravie, H., 2011. Portable energy dispersive X-ray fluorescence and X-ray diffraction and radiography system for archaeometry. *Nuclear Instruments and Methods in Physics Research A 633*, 72–78.

Mercando, L. – Zanda, E., eds., 1998. *Bronzi da Industria.* Rome: Edizioni De Luca.

Murphy-O'Connor, J., 1983. Corinthian Bronze. *Revue Biblique* 1, 80–93.

Pollini, J., 2017. The Bronze Statue of Germanicus from Ameria (Amelia). *American Journal of Archaeology*, 121(3), 425–437.

Pollini, J. – Giumlia-Mair, A., 2019. The statue of Germanicus from Amelia: New Discoveries, *American Journal of Archaeology*, 123 (4), 675–686.

Rocco, G., 2008. *La statua bronzea con ritratto di Germanico da* Ameria *(Umbria)*, Atti della Accademia Nazionale dei Lincei, Anno CDV-2008, classe di scienze morali, storiche e filologiche, memorie, serie 9, volume 23, fascicolo 2. Rome: Bardi Editore.

Salcuni, A., 2014. Le incongruenze della statua loricata di Germanico da Amelia. Note sull'uso di modelli parziali nella produzione di grande plastica in bronzo in epoca romana. In: Kemmers, F. – Maurer, T. – Rabe, B. eds., *Legis Artis*, Bonn: Habelt, 129–144.

Stapleton, C. – Bowman, S.G.E. – Craddock, P.T. – La Niece, S. – Youngs, S., 1995. Corinthium aes and black bronzes in the early medieval period. *The Antiquaries Journal*, 75, 383–390.

Thompson, M. – Walsh, J.N., 1983. *A Handbook of inductively coupled plasma spectrometry.* Glasgow and London: Blackie Publ.

Wang, Q. – Merkel, J., 2001. Studies on the redeposition of copper in Jin bronzes from Tianma-Qucun, Shanxi, China. *Studies in Conservation*, 46(4), 242–250.

4

The Brescia Winged Victory: Ongoing Diagnostic Work, Conservation Treatment and Restoration

Francesca Morandini, Stefania Agnoletti, Annalena Brini, Andrea Cagnini,
Monica Galeotti, Anna Patera, Simone Porcinai

Brescia Museums Foundation (Morandini)

MiBAC, Opificio delle Pietre Dure di Firenze

morandini@bresciamusei.com

Abstract: The statue is one of the few Roman bronzes known from northern Italy. Since its discovery a number of hypotheses about its origin and date have been advanced, with reference to its iconography, resemblance to similar pieces and technique of manufacture. Collaboration between the Brescia Council, Brescia Museums Foundation and the Florence Opificio delle Pietre Dure has enabled the formulation of a project for studying, conserving and restoring the statue.

This paper presents the results of scientific investigation and preliminary tests regarding the treatment of surfaces to determine the most appropriate conservation operations.

Keywords: Roman Bronzes; Winged Victory; Conservation; Restoration Project; Scientific Investigation of Patina

The statue's history (by Morandini)

The bronze statue represents a winged female figure which would originally have displayed to viewers a shield on which she had just finished writing, using a stylus held in the fingers of her right hand. Her left foot was placed on some object, probably a helmet, and the shield would have been held between her left arm and bent left leg; neither shield, stylus nor helmet has survived (Fig. 4.1).

The statue, almost two metres high, was made by lost wax casting; some areas have been finished with a chisel and the band around the hair is damascened (most recently: Formigli – Salcuni 2011, 5–24).

It was discovered in July 1826 during archaeological excavations conducted by the Brescia Ateneo di Scienze, Lettere e Art at the *Capitolium* temple of Roman *Brixia*; the statue was found between two walls bordering the temple's western chamber, together with numerous other bronzes.

These important finds led to the establishment in 1830 – inside the temple unearthed during this most successful excavation campaign – of the *Museo Patrio* (Fig. 4.2), which was visited by the most illustrious scholars of the epoch (Panazza 2004).

The Winged Victory would have once been displayed in one of ancient *Brixia*'s principal public buildings, perhaps the *Capitolium* itself – and was then concealed, along with other works, in an inter-wall cavity in the late Imperial building, for reasons that are not entirely clear. Perhaps they were hidden to keep them safe, or maybe this was a hoard of metal items waiting to be melted down and given new forms and functions.

Hidden in the same place together with the Victory were found numerous other bronze sculptures and architectural temple furnishings, including six Imperial epoch portrait heads, a figured sword belt from an equestrian statue and another without relief decoration, a gilt *appliqué* showing a prisoner, a statue's arm, moulded and damascened frames, three bands with cylindrical ends, several smooth frames, and numerous smaller pieces of bronze (Formigli – Salcuni 2011, 35–52; for details about cult statue throne frames, see Franken 2002).

The exact year is unknown, but probably the first restoration of the Victory was attempted in about 1834: a metal frame was built inside the statue in order to connect the wings and arms, which were found detached and placed near the body. This ingenious structure consists of a rectangular-in-section iron bar that extends from the nape to the lower limit of the chiton, with some mechanically connected and interlocking side-pieces to which the arms and wings are joined. To attach the vertical bar to the bronze, the inside of the statue was filled with an admixture of various rather compact materials, some of organic origin (Miazzo 1994–1999).

Figure 4.1. Brescia, Museo di Santa Giulia. Bronze statue of Winged Victory (1st cent. AD) (Archivio Fotografico Musei Civici Brescia).

Figure 4.2. The Winged Victory in the Museo Patrio, Brescia: the missing shield and helmet have been reconstructed, probably using wood and plaster (photograph c. 1915, Archivio Fotografico Musei Civici Brescia).

Numerous studies have been made of the bronze, and interpretative hypotheses been proposed for the bronze, which came to be identified with the Roman goddess Victoria (summary in Morandini 2011).

News of Brescia's Winged Victory spread quickly throughout Europe, to the extent that days before the battle of Solferino in June 1859, Napoleon III came to visit the Museo Patrio – and (as recorded in contemporary chronicles) was so struck by the statue and its allegorical significance that following his triumph in the battle he asked for a copy of it. Brescia did its utmost to satisfy this request, making the first plaster cast by direct contact, from which a bronze copy was then produced – and which today is on display in the Louvre (Morandini 2009; Le Breton 2019; Panazza 2009 and 2011).

The first analyses of the bronze of which the Victory is made, conducted by Gian Giacomo Arnaudon, director of the Royal Arsenal of Turin chemical laboratories, also date to this period. The diagnostic operations carried out in 1861 were among the first archaeometric studies ever conducted on an archaeological bronze. These analyses revealed the composition of the alloy (Arnaudon 1861; Taddia 2010, 122. 124–125; Morandini 2011, 10–11; see below).

Gabriele D'Annunzio wanted a copy of the Victory – but without wings – for his residence, the Vittoriale degli Italiani, and Giosuè Carducci praised the statue in "Alla Vittoria" after seeing it in the *Museo Patrio*.

Diagnostic studies, partial maintenance operations and examinations of different types have been conducted over time to ensure the statue's good state of preservation and to better understand its history, in particular its origin, date, and physical and technical characteristics.

During World War II the Victory was removed from the *Capitolium* and hidden in the grounds of a villa south of Brescia; checks on its state of preservation at the end of the war involved thorough-going examinations and conservation treatment, conducted in 1948 in Rome at the Istituto Centrale del Restauro (now Istituto Superiore per la Conservazione ed il Restauro), with further analyses of the alloy composition (Borrelli 1950, 30; see below).

Research on the statue was taken up again 50 years later when in 1998 the new *Museo della Città* was opened in the monumental complex of Santa Giulia. The Winged Victory was dismantled and moved to a new display location (not far from the previous one).

The temporary removal of wings and arms, that were still attached to the 19th century frame, allowed partial checks on the sculpture's interior. These have resulted in interesting observations concerning its history, archaeology and technical features, together with antiquarian considerations, opening a fruitful new season of studies on the statue (Miazzo 1994–1999; Moreno

2002; Ferretti, Miazzo 2011; Morandini 2009; Morandini 2011; Panazza 2009; Panazza 2011; Salcuni 2011.

According to an earlier hypothesis the statue was made in Hellenistic times as Aphrodite (therefore without wings and with a partially different posture), brought to Rome as war booty, turned into a Victory by the addition of wings, and finally donated to Brescia as an imperial *ex voto* for the temple (Moreno 2002 with previous bibliography).

A subsequent study of Roman bronzes in north Italy dates the Winged Victory to the Roman era, specifically to Julio-Claudian times, and for the first time furnishes hard evidence that the statue's body was originally made together with the wings and arms (Formigli – Salcuni 2011, 5–24).

The diagnostic studies carried out in the same period involved the use of strain gauges and acoustic emission measurements, which highlighted the statue's generally poor condition, due to improper functioning of the internal support for wings and arms, and deterioration of the organic components present in the material that anchors this frame. The existence of these problems was reconfirmed in 2018, underlining the urgent need for taking corrective action with regard to the Winged Victory's mechanical state and the condition of its surfaces, accompanied by an overall study of its history and interpretation.

Conservation Project (by Patera, Brini, Agnoletti)

When found, the Winged Victory statue was in a good state of preservation, with the exception of some *lacunae* in the wing-tips and fingers. The eyes were also missing, as were the deity's specific attributes, which would certainly have been present originally. The detached arms had been positioned "at the sides of the statue" while the wings, also removed, were found "one above the other" at the head. These brief notes on the statue's condition at the time of discovery may be found in various accounts published in the Commentari dell'Ateneo di Brescia (extracts given in Nicodemi 1926 *passim* and Bonardi 1937 *passim*) and in the Museo di Brescia catalogue (Labus 1838, 136–141, figs. XXXVIII. XXXIX. XL), which also contains the first illustrations of it.

After the sensational discovery, the interest of scholars and the academic world focused mainly on the stylistic examination and identification of the subject sculpted in bronze; for this reason, the 19th century descriptions known to us mainly focus on formal aspects, without providing detailed information useful for studying its conservation history and technological characteristics.

The discoverers, and in particular Giovanni Labus who first studied the statue, were principally concerned with reassembling the figure's various parts (wings, arms and body) and identifying the missing attributes (helmet, shield and stylus) that are typical of a Winged Victory.

On that occasion, the eye sockets were filled with coloured sheet metal that is still present on the statue; it is likely that other operations were also carried out on the surfaces: some areas were abraded (damascening) and waxy substances were applied.

In the following decades, this restoration of the statue was questioned by some scholars, not only due to disagreement with the reconstruction proposed by Labus, but also because of reportedly incorrect positioning of the wings on the back and poor joining of the left arm to the shoulder, not properly fitting the edges of the fracture and thus lowering the position of the arm (Rizzini 1910, 275; Nicodemi 1926, 47–48).

Subsequent 19th-century interventions on the statue can be traced back to the above-mentioned plaster cast made for Napoleon III, other probable operations of the same type, left evident traces on the bronze surface which were still partly visible when the Victory was transported to Rome to repair the damage suffered during its transfer from the museum during World War II (also mentioned above). At the ICR the various types of deterioration were recorded (Fig. 4.3 and 4.4), and the results of the conservation treatment given were later published (Borrelli 1950).

The recently initiated programme of studies on the Winged Victory (see above) has provided the basis for the conservation project currently being drawn up, which is the result of collaboration between the Brescia Council, owner of the statue, the Brescia Museums Foundation, which manages the city museum heritage, and the Ministry for Cultural Heritage and Activities, represented by the Archaeology, Fine Art and Landscape Superintendency of the Provinces of Brescia and Bergamo, and the Florence Opificio delle Pietre Dure (a specialized cultural heritage conservation institute). The conservation work and other activities currently underway are funded by private firms, the Brescia Council, and the Brescia Museums Foundation.

The first conservation objective is the removal of the 19th century internal metal support that no longer seems sufficient to safely fulfil the function of attaching the wings and arms for which it was designed (Fig. 4.5).

Various inspections carried out recently through the gaps left by the removal of the arms indicate that at least in the upper part, the material that attached the frame seems to have lost the cohesion necessary to fix it solidly to the bronze statue.

Moreover, non-invasive investigations carried out through acoustic emission measurements have highlighted stresses within the statue, due to the weight of the wings on the back and the postural asymmetry this causes, also due to the no-longer-perfect functioning of the anchoring system. In 1950, during the conservation work conducted in Rome, plans were made to eliminate this weighty structure, but were abandoned because of the complexity of the problem (Borrelli 1950, 33). The controlled removal of the support

F. Morandini, S. Agnoletti, A. Brini, A. Cagnini, M. Galeotti, A. Patera, S. Porcinai

Figure 4.3 and 4.4. The statue without wings probably in about 1948, just before it was moved to Rome for conservation treatment in the Istituto Centrale per il Restauro (now ISCR) (Archivio Fotografico Musei Civici Brescia).

Figure 4.5. Detail of the statue's back showing the two holes for attachment of the wings (Archivio Fotografico Musei Civici Brescia).

(now possible due to technical improvements) will allow the design of a new structure for attaching the arms and wings that will permit the display of the sculpture in conformity with conservation requirements.

This occasion will give us the opportunity to examine the internal surfaces for the first time since its re-assembly and to obtain precious details about the technical bronze casting and processing processes.

The study of these data, combined with the results of the scientific investigations currently in progress, may eventually confirm, after almost two centuries of contrasting interpretations, that the bronze was made during the early Imperial era. The latest findings seem to point in this direction, and the idea that the sculpture began its existence as a Hellenistic original has now been abandoned. It seems likely to date to the second quarter of the 1st century AD on the basis of certain formal features (Salcuni 2011, 20ff.; Salcuni 2014, 130ff.), as well as the characteristics of the processing technique (Formigli 2011, 12ff). We are currently carrying out further analyses to better understand the history of this statue (see below).

The conservation project also involves cleaning the external surface, which is largely covered by earthy encrustations and deposits of various kinds, including waxy residues, colouring materials and resins left from previous interventions.

The scientific analyses discussed below were conducted in order to identify the origin of these materials, partly so as to select the most suitable products for their removal. Also in this case conservation work provides an opportunity to acquire new information about the statue, such as for example the possible presence of gilding on the surfaces, which at present may only be detected in small areas on the arms.

Scientific investigations (by Cagnini, Galeotti, Porcinai)

Before starting any conservation operations, an extensive investigation of the alloy and of the surface composition was conducted with the aim of making informed decisions regarding treatment and getting to know more about the statue's manufacturing technique and conservation history. Although priority was given to non-invasive analytical techniques (portable X-Ray Fluorescence – XRF-and Reflection Fourier Transform Infrared Spectroscopy – FTIR), it proved necessary to sample some fragments of the encrustation layer and of the patina. Very small flakes were investigated by transmission micro-FTIR, and in some cases, they were embedded in polyester resin and ground to prepare polished cross-sections. These were studied with optical microscope and Scanning Electron Microscope (SEM), equipped with energy dispersive X-ray analysis (EDX) probe.

XRF measurements were performed using an XGLab Elio portable spectrometer (incidence angle 90°; spot size 2.5 mm) equipped with a Si-Drift detector (active depth=500 μm, Take-off angle=63.5°, Sample-detector distance=14mm) and a Rh anode. For reflection FTIR, we used an ALPHA Bruker spectrometer. Spectra (200 scans) were collected with a spectral range of 400–7000 cm^{-1}, 4 cm^{-1} resolution, background on gold plate, collecting areas of 4 mm diameter and processed using OPUS software.

The analyses on samples were performed using a Continuum Infrared Microscope linked to a Nicolet Nexus FTIR spectrometer, with a spectral resolution of 4 cm^{-1} (128 scans) in transmittance mode.

An EVO® MA 25 Zeiss scanning electron microscope equipped with an Oxford EDS X-MAX 80 mm^2 microprobe and AZTEC® system with a 20 keV voltage was used for SEM-EDX. Samples were coated with a carbon film prior the analysis. Optical microscopic observations were performed with a Zeiss Axioplan microscope. Interestingly, the alloy of the Victory has been investigated many times: early analytical data by the Italian chemist Gian Giacomo Arnaudon date back to 1860 (Arnaudon 1861, 177–178). He reported a composition with 9.44% tin, 80.70% copper, 7.68% lead, 1.91 % zinc with traces of iron. Later analysis on two samples from the body of the Victory gives slightly different results, reported in Table 4.1 (Formigli 2011, 19; Ferro 2011, 19). More spots were tested with portable XRF in order to find out possible differences between the body and the wings (Ferretti 2011, 18). In the latter case, the thick layer of encrustation plays a significant role in the elements' ratio. Inconsistencies of results due to different analytical techniques, effect of encrustation thickness and of uneven lead distribution in the alloy, and poor quality of samples point to the need for reliable quantitative analyses: these are planned for when the surface will be cleaned up. In fact, removal of soil and thinning of the corrosion layer will make it possible to use non-invasive means (portable XRF) more confidently for a semi-quantitative survey. Further on, a few metal samples will be taken from selected areas.

While the analysis of the alloy will be presented in an upcoming publication, preliminary results on the surface composition and the patina layer are reported here. They indicate the widespread presence of lead in the outer part of the surface, confirming the outcomes of past XRF investigations (Ferretti 2011, 18). Lead was detected in quite thin layers on protruding areas and also in thicker deposits in flatter areas. FTIR spectra, obtained from both surface reflectance and μ-transmission on samples, show that lead is in the form of carbonate and hydroxycarbonate. Figure 4.6 shows a cross-section of a sample (images with optical and electron microscope). The dense greenish matrix has a complex composition that includes many carbonates (calcium, lead, copper), phosphates (lead, calcium, and mixed Ca-Pb phosphates), and silicates. In the SEM image elongated crystals of lead carbonates, formed by the recrystallization process, are clearly visible. (Fig 4.6).

In particular, SEM-EDX analysis of individual particles included in the green encrustation identifies phases containing either silicon and copper, or copper plus calcium and silicon (Fig. 4.7). These phases can be interpreted as copper silicates and calcium copper silicates, and are widespread in the light green matrix. Thick green encrustation also includes dihydrated calcium sulphate and quartz particles. Malachite is widespread on the surface, partly in the matrix containing copper silicates, and partly as a separate phase, as may be seen in Figure 4.8, where an agglomeration of malachite overlies a white layer of calcium carbonate. Calcium carbonate is also present as little 'stones', several millimetres across, spread all around the surface. Copper (and lead) chlorides and hydroxychlorides were also detected; for example,

Table 4.1. Quantitative composition of the alloy of the Winged Victory (ND, not detected), (after Formigli 2018, 18 and Ferro 2011, 19)

Method	Cu%	Fe%	Zn%	Pb%	Ag%	Sn%	Sb%	Au%
ICP-MS	88.38	0,38	0,02	8,41	0,28	ND	0,06	0,17
SEM-EDX	84	ND	ND	7	ND	9	ND	ND

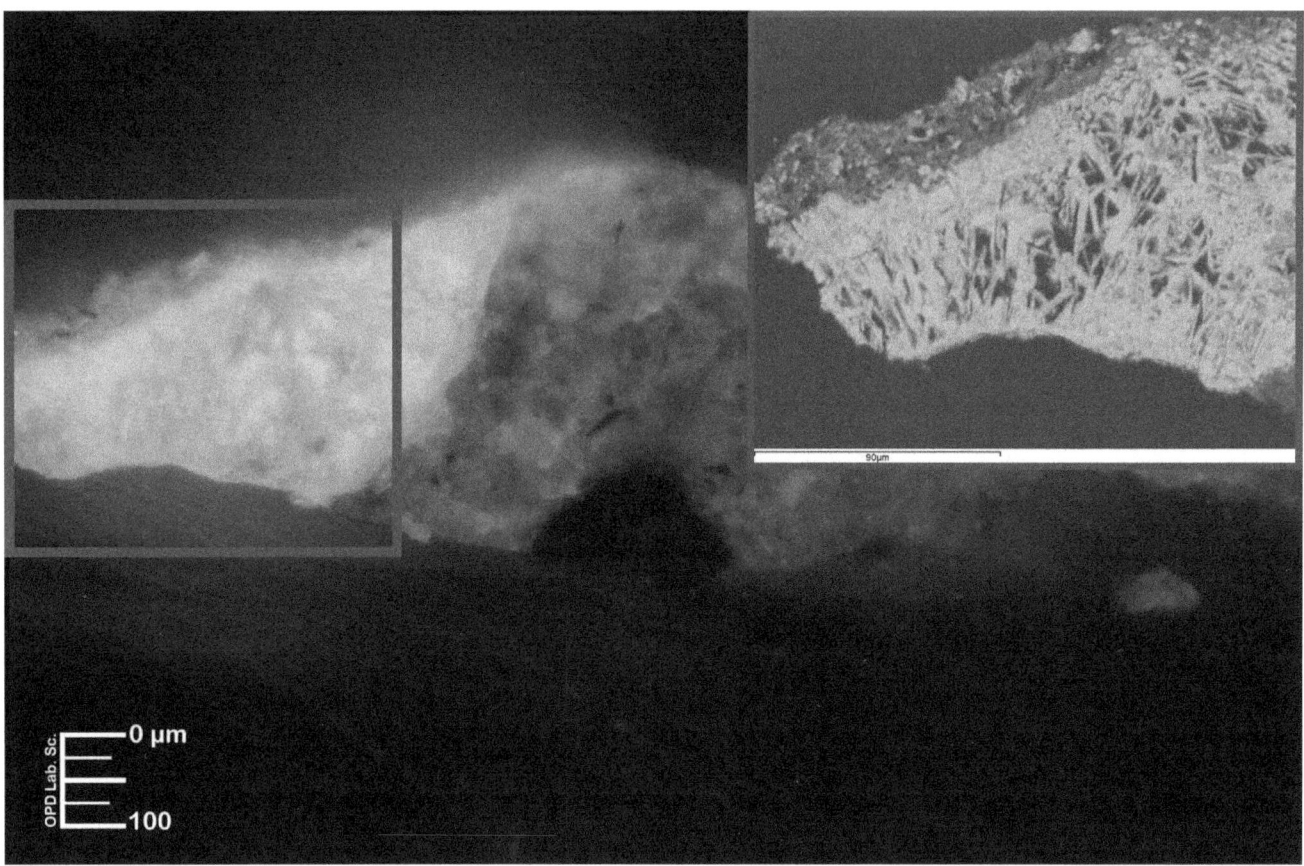

Figure 4.6. Optical microscope image of cross-section of the encrustation layer. The area in the red square is shown in the SEM-BSE image.

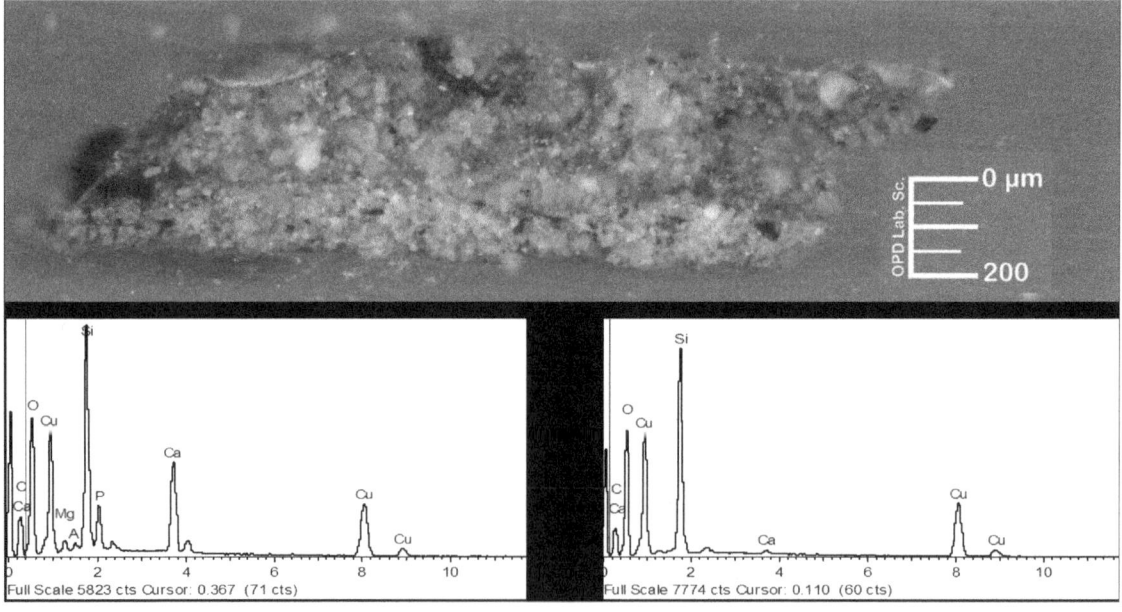

Figure 4.7. Optical microscope image of cross-section of the light green matrix of the encrustation with SEM-EDX spectra of individual green particles.

FTIR spectra identify the presence of atacamite (Fig. 4.7 and 4.8).

In spite of the presence of tin in the alloy (roughly around 9%), no tin was found in the superficial layer investigated so far. This might be due to the fact that the sampled volume does not include the complete characteristic stratigraphy of buried bronze, as described in the literature (Robbiola – Porter 2006). Indeed, in this preliminary phase of the work, only limited sampling was performed, and no samples including the entire thickness of the patina down to the alloy were taken. After this general survey, further investigations will be focused on particular areas and a few samples with complete stratigraphy down to

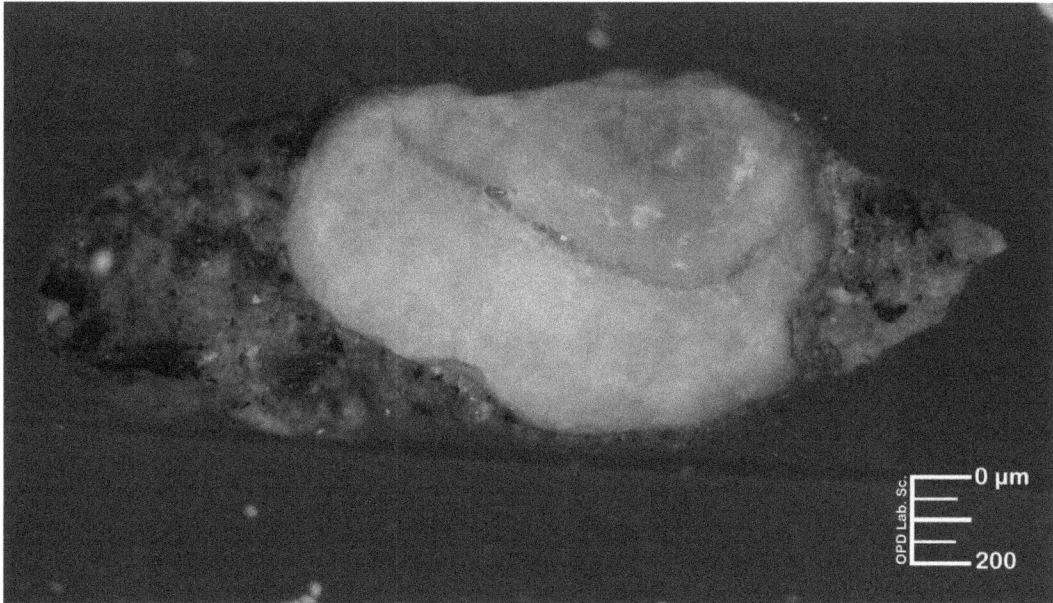

Figure 4.8. Optical microscope image of cross-section showing an agglomeration of malachite overlying a white layer of calcium carbonate.

the alloy will be taken from hidden parts of the statue. It is expected that these samples will enable us to acquire a deeper knowledge of the composition of the patina. Apart from the extensive presence of soil-derived elements, other compounds, coming from past conservation actions, indicate that our examination is limited to the outer layer of the patina/encrustation and that the layered system indicated by Robbiola is to be found underneath. In fact, FTIR spectra reveal the presence of protective and/or finishing compounds, such as animal wax and poly-methyl-methacrylate. Other compounds – copper carboxylates and oxalates – are related to the interaction of lipids with alloy corrosion compounds.

In some spots on the surface, featuring very dark colour and smooth appearance, SEM-EDX analysis shows the presence of copper and sulphur, with no oxygen. These data indicate that a sulphide-based artificial black patina is present.

In general, the interpretation of the analytical data is not straightforward, because the sculpture has undergone various conservation treatments since its discovery, and was reburied during World War II. No documentation exists on the sculpture's state of preservation after it was first unearthed, and there are no records concerning the 19th-century treatments. The existence of plaster replicas of the Victory provides a possible explanation for the remains of dihydrated calcium sulphate, a material used for casting. With regard to the high amount of lead and its needle-like crystal form, this element could come from the corrosion of the sculpture, with its high-lead alloy (roughly in the 7%–8% range, Ferro 2011, 19; Formigli 2011, 18), but it might also have come from the burial environment. In fact, no detailed information is recorded on the sculpture's discovery context and it is possible that the lead could have migrated either from nearby objects made of lead or high-lead bronze, or from building components such as piping. This hypothesis is also compatible with the results of previous XRF investigation, which revealed an uneven distribution of this element on both sides of the Victory, with higher content on the back. Calcium carbonate and/or lead carbonate could be responsible for the white efflorescence covering the surface of the Victory described by the conservators before the treatment carried out at the ICR in 1948 (Borrelli 1950, 32).

While the copper silicates and calcium copper silicates may be explained by reactions between copper corrosion compounds and soil, questions and doubts arise with regard to the origin of malachite. On one hand, malachite is one of the typical compounds found in buried bronzes (Robbiola – Hurtel 1997), yet we must consider the possibility of its artificial application to colour the sculpture (Risser – Saunders 2013, 41–55). In fact, the 1948 ICR report mentions an impressive list of treatments and compounds that might have considerably affected the surface composition and appearance. The authors of this report describe a first quick rinsing with distilled water to remove a whitish crystalline deposit, then they applied a very dilute solution of caustic soda. According to the ICR conservators, this treatment uncovered the old patina, with a dark green colour. Then a treatment aimed at stabilizing the patina ("fissazione della patina") was performed with sulphuric acid, while a subsequent patina consolidation ("consolidamento") was done with copper acetate and copper hydrogencarbonate. The use of these two compounds, in combination with acidic and basic solutions, may have left on the surface various forms of copper carbonates and acetates, not easy to differentiate from naturally formed ones, like, for example, malachite. The 1948 records refer to treatment with sodium sulphide to make particularly light-coloured areas less evident. The outcome of this patina treatment may be clearly seen in the dark areas featuring copper and sulphur alone.

Notwithstanding the invasiveness of the past operations described above and the doubts about the origin of some copper-containing compounds, analyses show evidence of materials applied in the plaster-casting process, and of compounds from the soil and from the interaction of soil and alloy corrosion products. The presence of these substances indicates that the cleaning of the Victory's surface was not as harsh as one might expect from the account of the 1948 conservation operations. Organic materials and their transformation products, on the other hand, have a clear origin in protection/finishing treatments. Besides the wax applied in 1948, Paraloid was used in subsequent surface treatment in 1998, after dusting the surface and removing old organic coatings. In the current project, preliminary cleaning trials were carried out on the surface of the statue with the aim of finding an effective way to remove natural and synthetic organic materials. The tests were monitored with portable digital microscope and reflectance FTIR, to check, respectively, the effects on the surface and the efficacy of the cleaning methods.

After this preliminary inquiry, many questions remain open about the surface characterization, in particular the investigation of inner alteration layers, next to the alloy, containing cuprite and other oxides. Comparison with fragments taken from inside the sculpture will help to differentiate between naturally formed compounds and those added artificially. The possible presence of pigments and binders used on discoloured areas will be explored carefully; this investigation will also be extended to the wings and arms.

Bibliography

Arnaudon, J., 1861. Analyse d'un bronze antique (époque romaine) statue de Brescia. *Le technologiste ou archives des progrès de l"industrie française et étrangère*, (22), 177–178.

Bonardi, F., 1937. Brescia archeologica. Ricerche sulla storia dell'archeologia e degli scavi romani di Brescia. La scoperta del tempio di Vespasiano e della statua della Vittoria (1825–1826) (da documenti inediti). *Aevum*, (XI, 3), 323–329.

Borrelli, L., 1950. Il restauro della Vittoria di Brescia. *Bollettino dell'Istituto Centrale del Restauro*, (1), 29–35.

Ferretti, M. – Miazzo, L., 2011. Analisi chimico-fisiche. In: Formigli – Salcuni 2011, 17–18.

Ferro D., 2011. Analisi chimico-fisiche. In: Formigli – Salcuni 2011, 19.

Formigli E., 2011. Analisi chimico-fisiche. In: Formigli – Salcuni 2011, 18–19.

Formigli, E. – Salcuni, A., eds., 2011. *Grandi bronzi romani dall'Italia settentrionale*, Frankfurter Archäologische Schriften, Bonn.

Franken N. 2002, Nuove osservazioni sui troni monumentali di divinità nel Capitolium di Brescia, In: F. Rossi, ed. 2002. *Nuove ricerche sul Capitolium di Brescia. Scavi, studi e restauri*. Milano, 191–195.

Labus, G., 1838. Osservazioni archeologiche intorno ai monumenti figurati esposti nel Museo. In: G. Nicolini – R. Vantini – G. Labus 1938. *Museo Bresciano Illustrato*, I. Brescia, 121– 219.

Le Breton, E., 2009. La Vittoria alata nelle raccolte del Louvre. In: Lucchesi Ragni – Mondini – Morandini 2009, 67–75.

Le Breton, E. 2019, La Victorie ailée de Brescia dans la gypsothèque du musée du Louvre: d'une statue en plâtre à une fonte en bronze, *Monuments et mémoires de la Fondation Eugène Piot*, (97), pp. 69-93.

Lucchesi Ragni, E. – Mondini, M. – Morandini, F. eds. 2009. *Napoleone III a Brescia e a Solferino. La Vittoria celebrata 1859–2009*. Milano.

Miazzo, L., 1994–1999. Considerazioni di restauro in occasione dello spostamento della Vittoria alata di Brescia, *Sibrium*, (23), 471–478.

Morandini, F., 2009. Dalla scoperta di una statua antica alla nascita di un simbolo. La Vittoria alata di Brescia. In: Lucchesi Ragni – Mondini – Morandini 2009, 53–57.

Morandini, F., 2011. Integrazioni e restauri sulla Vittoria alata di Brescia. In: Formigli – Salcuni 2011, 7–12.

Moreno, P., 2002. Iconografia e stile della Vittoria di Brescia, In: F. Rossi, ed. 2002. *Nuove ricerche sul Capitolium di Brescia. Scavi, studi e restauri*. Milano,119–157.

Nicodemi, G., 1926. Il deposito di bronzi romani rinvenuto a Brescia il 20 luglio del 1826. *Commentari dell'Ateneo di Brescia per l'anno 1926*, (1927), 27–55.

Panazza, P., 2004. Archeologia e coscienza storica. Il ruolo dell'Ateneo nella formazione dei musei cittadini. In: S. Onger, ed. *L'Ateneo di Brescia (1802–2002). Atti del convegno storico per il bicentenario di fondazione*. Brescia, 503–537.

Panazza, P., 2009. *Brescia per Napoleone III: la Vittoria alata e il palazzo della Loggia*, In: Lucchesi Ragni – Mondini – Morandini 2009, 59–65.

Panazza, P., 2011. La Vittoria alata di Brescia: repliche, calchi e fortuna iconografica nel XIX secolo. In: Formigli – Salcuni 2011, 25–34.

Risser, E. – Saunders, D., 2013. The restoration history of the bronze Apollo and Diana from Pompeii. In: E. Rissen – D. Saunders eds. *The restoration of ancient bronzes. Naples and beyond*. L. A.: The J. Paul Getty Museum, 41–55

Rizzini, P., 1910. Illustrazione dei Civici Musei di Brescia. Catalogo dei bronzi Etruschi, Greci e Romani che si conservano nel Museo dell'età romana. *Commentari dell'Ateneo di Brescia per l'anno 1910*, (1911), 273–357.

Robbiola, L. – Hurtel, L., 1997. Standard nature of the passive layers of buried archaeological bronze: The example of two Roman half-length portraits, in I. MacLeod – S. Pennec – L. Robbiola eds., *METAL 95, International Conference on Metals Conservation*, James and James Science Pub., London, 109–117.

Robbiola, L. – Portier, R., 2006. A global approach to the authentication of ancient bronzes based on the characterization of the alloy-Patina-Environment system, *Journal of Cultural Heritage* 7(1), 1–12.

Salcuni, A., 2011. Inquadramento archeologico/storico-artistico. In: Formigli – Salcuni 2011, 20–24.

Salcuni, A., 2014 Le incongruenze della statua loricata di Germanico di Amelia. Note sull'uso di modelli parziali nella produzione di grande plastica in bronzo di epoca romana. In F. Kemmers – Th. Maurer – B. Rabe (eds.), *Lege Artis. Festschrift für Hans-Markus von Kaenel*, Bonn 2014, 129–144.

Taddia, M., 2010. Il bronzo della Vittoria, *La chimica e l'industria*, 9, 122–125.

5

Projet d'une nouvelle étude technologique de l'Aurige de Delphes: les premiers résultats

Sophie Descamps-Lequime, Benoît Mille, Nancy Psalti

Musée du Louvre, département des Antiquités Grecques Etrusques et Romaines

Centre de Recherche et de Restauration des Musées de France (C2RMF)

Direction de l'Éphorie des Antiquités de Phocide, Musée archéologique de Delphes

sophie.descamps@louvre.fr

Abstract: Since its discovery in 1896, the Delphi Charioteer has been intensively studied. As a ca. 470's statue, it represents an exceptional evidence for the knowledge of bronzes' manufacturing techniques. Nevertheless, technological information has yet to be more specific. This is the reason why a complete re-examination of the statue and of the other preserved fragments of the chariot group has been decided by the Ephorate of Antiquities of Phokis which signed an agreement with the French School at Athens and the Louvre Museum to make further investigation. The fifteen years-collaboration between the Louvre and the Centre de Recherche et de Restauration des Musées de France on Ancient bronzes' techniques gives the scientific frame for such an investigation.

Keywords: Delphi Charioteer; Bronze; Technological Study; Metal Composition; Polychromy

Les grands bronzes, tant grecs que romains, sont extrêmement rares et leur contexte de découverte livre, le plus souvent, au mieux un *terminus ante quem* pour la date de leur création. Aussi l'Aurige de Delphes, identifié comme l'un des jalons majeurs de la sculpture antique, occupe-t-il une place privilégiée. Mais si le groupe auquel il appartenait a fait l'objet de nombreuses études stylistiques et épigraphiques depuis sa découverte en 1896 (Fig. 5.1), si l'on peut le dater à quelques années près – entre 470 et 466 d'après le raisonnement de Claude Rolley (1990) – et si l'on connaît l'emplacement de sa base dans le sanctuaire d'Apollon ainsi que l'identité de son commanditaire (Chamoux 1955; Jacquemin – Laroche, 2009), il n'a bénéficié depuis plus d'un siècle que d'examens technologiques superficiels (Homolle 1896; Hampe 1941; Chamoux 1955). C'est la raison pour laquelle l'Éphorie des Antiquités de Phocide a signé une convention avec l'École française d'Athènes et le musée du Louvre, pour reprendre et compléter, en collaboration avec le Centre de Recherche et de Restauration des musées de France, l'étude de cet ex-voto fameux, qui célébrait un Deinoménide vainqueur aux jeux pythiques. Les résultats d'une première mission effectuée en mai 2017 dans le cadre de la préparation du projet, ont été très prometteurs. Ils démontrent notamment déjà que l'Aurige a constitué un support privilégié pour les nombreuses innovations techniques qui se sont manifestées en Grèce à l'époque du style sévère. Ils ont permis aussi de définir les moyens analytiques qui devraient être déployés afin de préciser

les procédés de fabrication du groupe et de reconstituer sa polychromie originelle. Les méthodes d'analyse ont beaucoup évolué ces dernières années. Bon nombre des équipements concernés sont devenus portables, de sorte que l'étude pourra être réalisée sans déplacer la statue. De plus, la compréhension des techniques antiques a considérablement progressé et le projet pourra ainsi également s'appuyer sur une connaissance grandement actualisée des savoir-faire mis en œuvre par les sculpteurs antiques (Descamps-Lequime – Mille, 2017).

Comme en témoignent les archives de l'École française d'Athènes et celles de la Bibliothèque de l'Institut de France à Paris (fonds Homolle), les premières observations visuelles ont été très peu documentées à l'époque de la mise au jour du groupe mais elles fondent aujourd'hui encore la connaissance technologique de la statue. Très peu de photographies ont été prises directement pour illustrer les observations dont il est fait mention dans les diverses publications: aucun cliché n'est conservé de l'intérieur de la statue, pourtant accessible à plusieurs reprises alors que le torse était désolidarisé de la partie inférieure de la tunique; aucun relevé graphique n'a été établi.

Des réponses définitives doivent ainsi être apportées à des questions demeurées ouvertes depuis 1896, qu'il s'agisse de la nature des alliages des pièces principales et des incrustations (décor du bandeau, des sourcils, des lèvres et des dents), du procédé de fonte employé, de l'épaisseur

Figure 5.1. l'Aurige de Delphes en 1937, cliché n°22401, © photothèque de l'École française d'Athènes.

des parois de bronze, des techniques d'assemblage (mécaniques ou soudage par coulée secondaire), de l'emplacement des joints – existe-t-il vraiment un joint à hauteur de la calotte crânienne et un autre qui suivrait le tracé de l'encolure ? –, des caractéristiques des éléments rapportés (extrémités du bandeau, mèches sur les tempes, cordon, ceinture, yeux, rênes) ou encore des techniques de réparure.

La première mission "du projet Aurige" s'est déroulée du 22 au 24 mai 2017 à Delphes, alternant séances dans les salles d'exposition et dans la réserve des bronzes. Une évaluation de l'état de conservation des fragments préservés du groupe de l'Aurige a été effectuée et des capteurs climatiques ont été posés. Parallèlement à l'observation visuelle attentive de l'ensemble des éléments constitutifs de l'ex-voto ainsi que des autres fragments de grande statuaire de bronze retrouvés sur le site, la majorité des pièces a été soumise à une analyse de composition élémentaire par fluorescence X portable (pXRF). Deux des principaux objectifs de cette mission sont développés ci-après: confronter d'une part ce nouveau regard jeté sur l'Aurige aux descriptions des publications antérieures; déterminer précisément d'autre part les tâches à effectuer et les moyens à engager pour mener à bien une étude très approfondie du groupe statuaire.

Technique de fonte

Le montage actuel de l'Aurige ne permet pas d'observer facilement l'intérieur de la statue. Les renseignements recueillis sont donc pour l'instant de portée limitée et notre démarche a surtout consisté à confronter nos observations avec celles qui ont été publiées antérieurement. Soulignons tout d'abord la méthode, la précision analytique et la clairvoyance de Théophile Homolle décrivant dès 1896, alors qu'il y avait encore si peu d'éléments de comparaison, un bronze creux, fondu et non martelé, avec des parois épaisses de 8 à 13 mm, un noyau dans tous les éléments du groupe et la présence d'une tige de fer, "sorte d'armature", dans la partie inférieure de la statue (368–369). Ses observations ont cependant été négligées durant des décennies à la suite de la publication de Kurt Kluge (1929, 16–30), qui excluait l'emploi de la fonte à la cire perdue à cause du caractère lisse des parois internes de l'Aurige, de leur épaisseur et de leur irrégularité. L'originalité de cette hypothèse qui faisait de la statue une sorte d'*unicum* et l'autorité acquise par Kurt Kluge dans le domaine des grands bronzes antiques, donnèrent un grand retentissement à sa théorie. Il fallut attendre la publication de François Chamoux, en 1955, pour rétablir le fait que l'Aurige n'a pas été coulé au moyen d'un procédé spécial, et arriver à la notion de "fonte à la cire perdue". Cette hypothèse est aujourd'hui unanimement acceptée, la question étant toutefois de savoir s'il s'agit du procédé direct (fonte à la cire perdue sur positif), du procédé indirect (fonte à la cire perdue sur négatif) ou d'une association des deux procédés (Mattusch 1988, 27. 134–135). Claude Rolley optait encore en 1994 pour le procédé direct (67). Il conviendrait de vérifier les épaisseurs des parois, François Chamoux ajoutant aux dimensions données par Théophile Homolle que l'épaisseur du bronze dépassait "25 mm en certains points, comme par exemple dans les gros plis de la *xystis*" (1955, 61). Les mesures que nous avons pu effectuer directement sur la statue, en bas de la tunique et dans la cassure à hauteur de la ceinture, confirment globalement les données anciennes: une épaisseur toujours supérieure à 6 mm, en moyenne 7.5 mm, pouvant atteindre 11 mm dans les plis. Nous n'avons pas mis en évidence les très fortes surépaisseurs signalées par François Chamoux, mais seule une infime partie de la statue est actuellement accessible. Nos observations confortent en revanche l'hypothèse selon laquelle la statue est issue d'un procédé de fonte en creux à la cire perdue: l'Aurige s'inscrit sur ce point sans aucune difficulté dans le corpus des grands bronzes antiques. Il est cependant indéniable que la variabilité des parois métalliques est importante. Il conviendrait de cartographier et de mieux comprendre ces surépaisseurs avant d'apporter des conclusions sur le type de procédé à la cire perdue mis en œuvre, direct ou indirect. Par ailleurs, il serait indispensable de comparer les noyaux encore présents dans les différents fragments préservés du groupe (jambes des chevaux notamment). À l'époque où François Chamoux publiait sa monographie sur l'Aurige, le noyau de la statue "matière noirâtre et compacte" avait dû "être retiré à l'occasion de travaux de restauration et de nettoyage: il [s'était] alors résolu en poussière et c'est sous cette forme qu'il [était] encore conservé à Delphes." Quant à la "tige de fer" signalée par Homolle, il en subsistait "trois tronçons rouillés" (1955, 61).

Techniques d'assemblage

Dès 1896, Théophile Homolle précisait que l'Aurige avait été fondu en sept parties principales – la tête, le torse, les deux bras, la partie basse de la tunique depuis la ceinture et les deux pieds (369). François Chamoux ajoutait toutefois (1955, 60), à la suite de Kurt Kluge, la calotte crânienne comme huitième partie, une pièce coulée séparément pour des raisons techniques d'ajustage des yeux et des lèvres (Haynes 1957, 364; Mattusch 1988, 133–134). On qualifiera pour la suite ces parties principales comme étant des "coulées primaires". Les techniques d'assemblage qui les unissent n'ont pas été étudiées jusqu'à présent ou elles l'ont été très peu, et souvent les opinions divergent.

Théophile Homolle et François Chamoux s'accordaient sur le fait que les deux pieds étaient soudés sur un plateau qui ferme le bas de la tunique. Homolle précisait ainsi que les parois de la statue "sont reliées entre elles, à 0m15 environ au-dessus du bord inférieur de la jupe, par un disque de bronze, légèrement convexe et percé de deux trous où s'engagent les pieds" (Homolle 1896, 368) et Chamoux que

> "la suture entre les pieds et le reste du corps est très apparente [...] cachée par le bord de la *xystis* [elle est] exécutée d'une façon grossière mais très solide. La jambe, à l'endroit où elle s'arrête, s'élargit en un rebord, qui vient s'appliquer par une soudure contre la surface plane fermant la *xystis* vers le bas; en outre, des morceaux de bronze grossièrement traités sont soudés de place en place, à cheval sur le rebord des jambes et le fond de la *xystis* de façon à former des encoches où chaque pied se trouve fermement maintenu."

Notre examen confirme la présence d'un assemblage soudé, et révèle l'existence, à l'arrière de chaque cheville, de deux protubérances en forme de parallélépipède rectangle qui correspondent aux bassins d'alimentation par où ont été effectuées les coulées secondaires d'assemblage (Fig. 5.2). Il s'agit très vraisemblablement de soudures par fusion au bronze liquide, mais il reste néanmoins à comprendre le détail de ces soudures, et le mode de fabrication de la grande paroi transversale, possiblement coulée en même temps que le bas de la tunique à moins qu'elle n'ait été coulée à part puis soudée. François Chamoux avait noté le rôle purement utilitaire de cette paroi, dont l'aspect intérieur ne pouvait déjà plus être étudié à son époque car tout le bas de la statue était rempli de plâtre. Il signale que Pierre de La Coste-Messelière avait pu observer avant 1940 la présence

> "au fond de la jupe, [de] deux goujons carrés identiques à celui de la plante des pieds qui est antique" (Chamoux 1955, 59 n. 7).

Figure 5.2. vue de la paroi fermant le bas de la tunique et des deux protubérances métalliques à l'arrière de la cheville: elles correspondent aux bassins d'alimentation des coulées secondaires effectuées pour souder les pieds à cette paroi, © C2RMF, B. Mille.

Selon Théophile Homolle, l'assemblage à mi-corps avait été obtenu de façon mécanique: "Le torse semble avoir été posé sans scellement sur la jupe, la ceinture formant comme une espèce de douille" (1896, 369). Pour François Chamoux, il s'agissait d'une soudure (1955, 60). Sa description de la ceinture, "restée adhérente tantôt à la partie supérieure, tantôt à la partie inférieure du corps", est particulièrement précise. Les renforts de restauration moderne ajoutés sur la ceinture et la visibilité trop limitée de l'intérieur de la statue ne permettent pas, pour l'instant, de se forger une opinion définitive sur ce point.

Les bras s'engageaient "dans les emmanchures, profondes de 2 à 3 cm et fermées par une paroi transversale, ellemême percée d'un large orifice où venait s'encastrer le tenon du bras" (Chamoux 1955, 60). Cela n'indique toutefois pas comment ils étaient maintenus: assemblage mécanique ou soudure, combinaison des deux procédés. Une investigation plus approfondie du bras droit et de la cavité d'encastrement du bras gauche serait nécessaire pour répondre à cette question.

En ce qui concerne la tête, les propos de François Chamoux, sans photographies et sans relevés graphiques, n'ont pas été bien compris par certains auteurs lorsqu'il écrivait:

> "La tête avait été fondue à part, car on remarque un rebord saillant à la hauteur du cou: là se trouvait la soudure entre la tête et le torse. Mais la liaison est si parfaite qu'elle reste absolument invisible du dehors même à l'examen le plus attentif" (1955, 60).

Il était bien question du cou, comme répété plus loin dans le texte (1955, 63) et à aucun moment François Chamoux ne dit que la jonction était dissimulée par l'encolure en V de la tunique (Mattusch 1988, 133. 172). Il fallut attendre la découverte des guerriers de Riace en 1972 et l'étude

Figure 5.3. détail du cou sous l'oreille gauche. La trace ténue de deux auréoles elliptiques pourrait signaler la présence d'une soudure en cuvettes, © C2RMF, B. Mille.

de leur technique de fabrication par Edilberto Formigli (1984, 124–126, fig. 23–24) pour prendre connaissance de l'existence d'un procédé de soudage dit "en cuvettes", déjà remarquablement maîtrisé vers 460 av. J.-C. En variant les conditions d'éclairage dans la zone du cou à mi-hauteur, il a été possible de repérer les traces elliptiques qui, selon toute vraisemblance, signalent ce procédé (Fig. 5.3). Les propos de François Chamoux (1955, 64) étaient en fait prémonitoires:

> "Dans ces assemblages faits à chaud … on arrivait presque à une fusion locale du bronze, à laquelle la soudure ajoutait encore son effet. L'exemple de l'Aurige montre combien la liaison ainsi obtenue était solide."

La mise en évidence de la technique dite "en cuvettes" pour la fabrication de l'Aurige serait une importante nouveauté. Elle appuierait fortement une hypothèse récemment formulée selon laquelle ce procédé de soudage, très efficace et déjà parfaitement mis au point dans le deuxième quart du Ve siècle av. J.-C., aurait joué un rôle primordial dans le développement spectaculaire de la grande statuaire de bronze à l'époque du style sévère (Mille 2017, 302–311). Selon François Chamoux (1955, 60 et n. 3), qui s'appuyait sur une observation de Pierre de la Coste-Messelière, la ligne de suture, à la hauteur du bandeau, "parfaitement invisible du dehors, [est] sensible au doigt à l'intérieur." Cette suture correspond-elle vraiment à une soudure, qui indiquerait que la calotte, coulée séparément puis soudée, était rapportée? Ne pourrait-il s'agir plutôt d'un joint entre deux pièces de cire? Cela impliquerait alors de façon certaine l'usage d'un modèle intermédiaire en cire, et donc une fabrication de la tête au moyen du procédé indirect de fonte à la cire perdue. Il faudra mobiliser plusieurs techniques d'examen non destructif (radiographie gamma, endoscopie, ultrasons) pour espérer pouvoir répondre à ce type de questions.

Éléments rapportés par coulée secondaire

Quelques coulées secondaires, destinées à accentuer le caractère plastique de certains détails, complètent les sept ou huit coulées primaires. Mentionnons ainsi les zones de mèches en forme de triangle, situées à l'avant de l'oreille sur les tempes et que prolonge un favori qui existait dans le modèle en cire avant la coulée. Il faudrait vérifier si ces deux zones correspondent bien à des éléments fondus à part et rapportés, comme indiqué précédemment (Chamoux 1955, 61; Hampe 1960, 71). Il faudrait déterminer aussi si le nœud et les extrémités du bandeau à l'arrière de la tête ont été rapportés par soudage après coulée secondaire, ce que pensait, avec François Chamoux, Denys Haynes (1957, 364), ou s'ils ont été directement ajoutés à la tête par surcoulée. Il faudrait vérifier également si l'annulaire droit de l'Aurige était rapporté, comme l'avait observé Pierre de la Coste-Messelière (Chamoux 1955, 52, n. 1).

Incrustations polychromes

Les matériaux qui composent les incrustations du bandeau sont véritablement exceptionnels (Fig. 5.4). Il y a tout d'abord, dans les méandres et les croix, un fil plat d'un métal très altéré, dont les produits de corrosion remplissent les creux de l'incrustation et sont de couleur très blanche. Ce fil a jusqu'à présent été décrit comme de l'argent (Homolle 1897, 198–199; La Coste-Messelière 1943, 327; Chamoux 1955, 52) mais les analyses réalisées par pXRF révèlent qu'il est en étain. Ce métal, qui n'a

Figure 5.4. détail du bandeau incrusté, © EFA, Rachel Nouet.

pas l'éclat de l'argent, avait une couleur mate, grise à blanche, en fonction de l'épaisseur de la couche d'oxyde d'étain qui recouvrait l'incrustation. C'est la première fois que l'on observe l'utilisation de ce matériau pour le décor incrusté d'un grand bronze. Si l'on replace l'Aurige dans le contexte historique de l'époque, cela ne déprécie en rien la statue, bien au contraire. La présence discrète d'étain, assurément volontaire, n'était-elle que d'ordre esthétique? Sans développer davantage cette question ici, nous signalerons que les attestations d'étain comme métal de parure sont de plus en plus nombreuses en contexte méditerranéen des VIe et Ve siècles et que cette pratique était éminemment symbolique si on la relie à l'importance prise par le commerce de l'étain à cette période (Mille – Artioli 2017). On trouve ensuite deux autres fils droits, également plats, qui encadrent le motif de méandres et de croix. Ils sont constitués d'un métal qui apparaît très noir et se révèle être à l'analyse pXRF du cuivre non allié. Cette couleur sombre, très homogène d'aspect, pose question: est-ce la couleur rouge du cuivre qui était recherchée ou bien la couleur noire, résultat d'une patine intentionnelle? Et s'il s'agit en effet d'une patine volontaire, par quel moyen a-t-elle été obtenue? L'analyse en mode "mining" des deux fils ne détecte pas plus de soufre à ces endroits qu'ailleurs sur la statue. Cela signifie que la patine noire ne semble pas résulter d'un traitement chimique au soufre, un procédé attesté à partir de la seconde moitié du IIe siècle avant notre ère (Willer 1994). Peut-on envisager alors l'hypothèse d'un "cuivre noir", c'est-à-dire d'un cuivre susceptible de développer, parce qu'intentionnellement allié à une faible quantité d'or et/ou d'argent, une patine noire très résistante? Seule une analyse de composition élémentaire à l'aide d'un appareil pXRF plus sensible pointant précisément sur les deux fils permettrait de vérifier ce point, qui, s'il était avéré, ferait remonter la pratique grecque associée au "bronze de Corinthe" de plusieurs siècles (Descamps-Lequime 2015; Aucouturier – Mathis – Robcis 2017).

La zone des yeux est particulièrement complexe (Fig. 5.5). L'incrustation des sourcils n'a pas été remarquée tout de suite. Le premier auteur à la mentionner est Peter Bol (1978, 90). Ils sont pourtant bien visibles à cause de leur corrosion, qui est plus sombre que celle du bronze environnant. Les cils supérieurs et inférieurs sont a priori constitués de feuilles métalliques insérées de chant entre paupières et globes oculaires, à la manière de celle qui a été récemment rétablie dans l'œil droit du guerrier B de Riace (Donati 2013, 270–271, fig. 310). Ces feuilles devraient, en principe, être en cuivre, non en bronze. Les yeux, intacts, de l'Aurige sont composés de plusieurs matériaux, que l'examen visuel identifie mal. Théophile Homolle observait ainsi:

> "l'œil même est composé de matières colorées, au vrai le fond blanc (pâte), la prunelle brune et la pupille noire (pierres; onyx, sans doute)" (1896, 368).

Pierre de La Coste-Messelière parlait de "pâte d'émail blanc, et pierres sombres" (1943, 327). François Chamoux précisait que:

> "Le fond de l'œil est fait d'une pâte blanche; l'iris d'un marron très clair est entouré d'un cercle noir et enserre étroitement le rond noir de la pupille." et plus loin qu'il s'agissait de "[…] pâte de verre et pierres de couleur pour les globes oculaires" (Chamoux 1955, 53. 64).

Et Carol Mattusch (1988, 130):

> "The wide eyes […] are inlaid with white paste set with chestnut-colored irises and black onyx pupils."

À la décharge de ces différents auteurs, aucun des matériaux employés n'a pu être encore véritablement identifié et caractérisé. Rien n'est dit en outre de la matière du fin cercle clair à fort éclat métallique qui marque la séparation entre le blanc de l'œil et l'iris; rien non plus de la caroncule lacrymale, dont le logement est bien visible et que l'on pourrait supposer constituée d'une pierre rosâtre comparable à celle, maintenue par deux petits crochets, qui a été mise en évidence à l'angle interne de l'œil droit du guerrier A de Riace (Donati 2013, 269–270, fig. 305). L'analyse de cette grande diversité de matériaux imposera le recours à une combinaison de techniques analytiques sans contact: cartographie XRF, spectrométrie Raman et diffraction X.

Les lèvres sont également des éléments rapportés, qui se distinguent comme les sourcils par leur corrosion aujourd'hui plus sombre. Leur analyse pXRF a montré qu'elles ont été réalisées à partir de cuivre non allié, c'est-à-dire d'un métal de cuivre rouge. Mais doit-on les considérer comme des lèvres relativement épaisses (Bol 1978, 91–92, n°s 409–410), coulées à part et insérées dans le modèle intermédiaire en cire de la tête avant la fonte ou introduites après la coulée de la tête, ou bien encore comme de fines feuilles métalliques plaquées (La Coste-Messelière 1943, 327) ? François Chamoux, qui parle de lèvres "recouvertes d'une pellicule de cuivre" (1955, 52), rapporte une observation due à Georges Daux, selon laquelle (1955, 53 et n. 1)

Figure 5.5. détail de l'œil gauche et du sourcil incrusté, © **C2RMF, B. Mille.**

"Les lèvres sont bordées extérieurement d'une légère saillie. Une petite ouverture est visible à chaque commissure."

Haynes (1957, 364) associait ces ouvertures à la possibilité d'intervenir depuis l'intérieur de la tête à cause de la soudure différée, selon lui, de la calotte crânienne:

"The separation of the cranium was no doubt due, as C[hamoux] suggests, to the need to get inside the head after casting to [...] secure the (?) copper plating of the lips (for that, surely, must be the purpose of the holes at each end of the mouth and of the bar of lead found inside it)."

Lors de sa conférence, donnée à Tübingen dans le cadre de ce même colloque, Gerhard Zimmer a présenté un moule destiné à la confection de lèvres, moule mis au jour à Athènes, place Syntagma, à l'occasion de fouilles récentes de vestiges de grande fonderie datés des Ve et IVe siècles av. J.-C.

Le dispositif, à l'intérieur de la bouche, est particulièrement élaboré. Si Théophile Homolle avait émis très tôt l'hypothèse de la présence d'une "lame d'argent pour exprimer la blancheur des dents" (1897, 195 n. 4), cette hypothèse, reprise par Roland Hampe (1941, 16 n. 1 à gauche), avait été rejetée par François Chamoux, à la suite de l'examen effectué par Pierre de La Coste-Messelière assisté de Gilliéron, la lame d'argent étant alors interprétée comme de la soudure (1955, 52 n. 2). Dans le même temps, François Chamoux mentionnait la découverte par George Daux d'un morceau de plomb "grossièrement travaillé, courbé en arc-de-cercle", situé derrière les dents, puis son analyse par le laboratoire du Musée National d'Athènes (1955, 61, fig. 7 et n. 4). Ce morceau est sans doute aujourd'hui entièrement retiré. Il est indéniable que les dents – quatre incisives (Rolley 1994, 346) – sont mises en valeur par un placage (Fig. 5.6; sur la "redécouverte" du placage des dents, voir Mattusch 1988, 130; Rolley 1990, 287. 289, fig. 2; Pollini 2000, 52 et n. 74). La tentative de détermination par pXRF du placage qui recouvre les dents est restée infructueuse, la zone étant trop en retrait. Celui-ci reste donc à caractériser avec un appareil pXRF pouvant opérer à une plus grande distance de travail. La lamelle de plomb jouait sans doute un rôle de support pour le placage (Rolley 1990, 289, n. 7) et n'était pas liée à la fixation des lèvres.

D'autres éléments rapportés complètent la statue et lui conféraient vraisemblablement une polychromie métallique subtile en jouant sur la teneur en étain de l'alliage. Ces pièces venaient ajouter leurs couleurs à celles de la tête, en particulier un cordon croisé en huit, constitué d'un métal cuivreux et destiné à ajuster la tunique sur le corps de l'Aurige – il en reste un petit fragment dans le dos, à proximité de l'aisselle gauche – et la large ceinture, placée haut, qui permettait de masquer également l'assemblage entre les parties supérieure et inférieure du vêtement. Il convient aussi de mentionner les rênes: la main préservée de l'Aurige tenait encore trois des quatre rênes des chevaux de droite, au moment de la découverte de la statue. Quelques fragments n'ont pu être remontés et sont conservés en réserve. Soulignons que tous ne sont pas rigoureusement de la même largeur, ce qui pourrait révéler l'existence d'autres types de sangles.

La fixation de la statue

La photographie de la découverte, le 28 avril 1896, de la partie inférieure de l'Aurige est le seul témoignage de l'état originel des plantes des pieds, avec, en effet, sous le pied gauche de la statue, le remplissage du plomb qui maintenait un goujon quadrangulaire et creux. Ce goujon servait à la fixation mécanique de l'œuvre, non sur la base – il aurait été inutile et la disposition du plomb aurait été tout autre – mais sur la plateforme métallique du char. Homolle (1897, 188–189) avait décrit "un boulon carré, haut d'environ 1 centimètre, taillé à arêtes vives, complètement dégagé de toute soudure" et avait parfaitement conclu qu'un tel scellement ne convenait pas à la pierre: "le personnage était fixé, non sur la dalle de calcaire, mais sur le palier en bronze du char". Ses propos avaient été repris à juste titre par Chamoux (1955, 54): "Lors de la découverte, on pouvait voir sous le pied gauche de l'Aurige un des goujons carrés qui servaient à le maintenir sur le char. Les autres avaient été arrachés au moment de la catastrophe". Deux prises de vue effectuées par Jean Bousquet en 1939 (Chamoux 1955, pl. XX. 2 et 3) montrent que le goujon, associé aux tiges et au plomb du montage moderne, existait encore à cette date. La campagne photographique de 1948 (Chamoux 1955, pl. XIX.2–4 et XX.1) ne permet pas cependant de juger de son maintien dans le nouvel environnement moderne de soclage de la statue. Il serait important de pouvoir vérifier la présence de ce goujon et de le documenter, pour éviter que l'on continue à proposer de placer

Figure 5.6. détail des lèvres et des dents, © C2RMF, B. Mille.

l'Aurige directement sur l'un des blocs de calcaire de la base (Jacquemin – Laroche 2009, 12–13).

Les autres fragments du groupe de l'Aurige

Parmi les autres éléments associés au groupe, trois jambes fragmentaires (inv. 3485, 3538, 3597) et une queue (inv. 3541) des chevaux du quadrige ainsi que le bras d'enfant (inv. 3535) ont pu être examinés en mai 2017. Les zones de fractures ont montré que l'épaisseur des parois était du même ordre que celles qui avait pu être relevées sur l'Aurige (6 mm pour le bras, 7 à 10 mm pour les fragments de chevaux). Les trois jambes fragmentaires et le bras d'enfant conservent encore leur noyau de coulée, d'aspect compact, gris-sombre à noir; on note également l'existence d'armatures en fer de section quadrangulaire (env. 12 x 7 mm), au moins dans deux des jambes de cheval. Si François Chamoux avait bien noté que

"la cassure [des deux membres postérieurs, inv. 3485 et 3538] s'est produite à mi-jambe, aux environs immédiats de la suture avec le corps" (1955, 40),

il n'avait pu observer le fait que cette cassure, produite immédiatement sous une soudure, restitue par endroits très fidèlement la forme en demi-ellipse du procédé dit en "cuvettes" (Fig. 5.7). La queue s'est également brisée à hauteur d'une soudure, mais cependant au-dessus du joint: du métal de soudure est nettement visible et un petit morceau du corps du cheval est demeuré adhérent à la queue. Ce dernier détail avait déjà été mentionné par François Chamoux (1955, 40). On remarque sur les jambes des chevaux la présence de quelques grandes réparations (rondes ou rectangulaires), qui dissimulent des défauts de fonderie et améliorent l'état de surface du bronze. Il faudrait vérifier les observations de François Chamoux sur les fragments des deux jambes postérieures, qui seraient des fontes pleines jusqu'au genou inclus puis des fontes creuses dans la partie haute, et sur la face interne desquelles la "châtaigne" était rapportée:

"Cette pièce existe encore sur la jambe droite, mais elle a disparu sur la jambe gauche, où se distingue encore son logement" (1955, 40).

Par ailleurs, le sabot antérieur gauche (inv. 3597) "contient encore un peu de plomb antique" (Homolle 1897, 172, fig. 2; Chamoux 1955, 40; Haynes 1957, 364) qui pourrait être analysé en comparaison de celui qui se trouve sans doute encore sous le pied gauche de l'Aurige.

D'autres fragments, retrouvés dans la même zone que l'Aurige – la "maison Kounoupis" – selon le Journal de la Grande Fouille, tels un pied gauche d'homme de grandeur naturelle (inv. 3563, 455), et un fragment de jambe postérieure de cheval coupée un peu au-dessus et presque immédiatement au-dessous du genou (inv. 3675, 465; Rolley 1990, 289–290, fig. 5) seront à étudier attentivement. On signalera surtout le fragment de chevelure (inv. 3616) exhumé le 9 mai 1896 (459), le même jour que le coussinet de joug (inv. 3618). Inexplicablement, il a toujours été omis dans les publications sur l'Aurige – il est actuellement en réserve – et l'hypothèse selon laquelle il pourrait avoir appartenu au groupe semble n'avoir jamais été formulée. Par ses caractéristiques technologiques et les dimensions que l'on peut restituer de la calotte crânienne correspondante, il serait tout à fait compatible avec le bras d'enfant (inv. 3535). Seules des analyses très approfondies du métal de cette pièce, comparées à celles du bras, valideront ou infirmeront cette nouvelle hypothèse.

Résultats des analyses pXRF

Les analyses ont été effectuées de façon totalement non destructive en ayant recours à un équipement portable de fluorescence X (pXRF). Le spectromètre utilisé est un Niton XL3t, les rayons X sont produits par une anticathode d'argent, un détecteur refroidi par effet Peltier collecte les rayons X réémis par la cible. Les conditions opératoires ont le plus souvent été les suivantes: diamètre du faisceau 3 mm et utilisation en mode "metals electronics" (tension d'accélération 50 kV, durée d'une acquisition 30 s, collecte du spectre de haute énergie, Z > Ca). De plus, dans quelques cas nous avons cherché à détecter les éléments légers, l'appareil ayant alors été utilisé en mode "mining" (durée d'une acquisition 120 s, pendant laquelle quatre tensions différentes sont appliquées, permettant d'obtenir quatre spectres, deux consacrés aux hautes énergies, et deux aux basses énergies, c'est-à-dire Z compris entre Mg et Ca). Au total, cinquante-huit points d'analyse ont été effectués: quarante sur la statue de l'Aurige et dix-huit sur les autres éléments du groupe (chevaux, bras d'enfant ainsi que rênes conservées en réserve). Par ailleurs, trente-trois autres fragments ont également été analysés, avec pour objectif de confronter la composition de l'Aurige à celle des autres grands bronzes découverts à Delphes.

Figure 5.7. vue de la zone de fracture de la jambe postérieure de cheval inv. 3538, on perçoit distinctement le noyau de coulée (terre gris-noir au plus profond de l'ouverture), et la succession de demi-ellipses du bord de la paroi métallique, caractéristique d'une préparation pour un soudage en cuvettes, © C2RMF, B. Mille.

En ce qui concerne les analyses en mode "metals electronics", nous avons vérifié la qualité des mesures en analysant des matériaux de référence certifiés: justesse et précision sont globalement très bonnes. Il faut cependant considérer les résultats sur les métaux archéologiques comme semi-quantitatifs puisque les analyses ont été effectuées directement en surface (profondeur analysée inférieure à 0,5 mm). Les analyses intègrent à la fois les composés de corrosion nécessairement présents et le substrat métallique sous-jacent (si la profondeur altérée n'est pas trop importante). La quantification effectuée est donc surtout le reflet de la composition des couches de corrosion qui couvrent l'objet, et non la composition originelle de l'alliage. On sait de surcroît que la corrosion des alliages cuivreux, et tout particulièrement des bronzes, peut globalement être décrite comme le résultat d'une décuprification (Piccardo – Mille – Robbiola 2007). Lorsqu'une analyse de surface est effectuée, telle que par la méthode pXRF, il en résulte une surévaluation apparente de tous les éléments chimiques hormis le cuivre. Le phénomène se produit dans des proportions extrêmement variables et impossibles à prédire, mais on constate que les éléments d'alliage tels que l'étain et le plomb sont systématiquement surévalués (doublés voire triplés), et que la teneur en certaines impuretés telles que le fer, peut être multipliée par dix (Orfanou – Rehren, 2015).

Nous avons utilisé dans quelques cas le mode "mining" de l'appareil pour mettre en évidence la présence d'éléments plus légers que le manganèse. Pour ces analyses, la limitation précédente s'applique, mais s'y ajoute en outre le fait que l'algorithme de calcul utilisé pour la quantification est adapté aux matrices à base d'éléments légers tels que les silicates, et non aux matrices métalliques. Les résultats des analyses en mode "mining" sont donc à considérer uniquement de façon qualitative. Ils indiquent seulement la présence ou l'absence de tel ou tel élément. On comprendra donc que les résultats obtenus par pXRF sont à interpréter avec précaution. Ils se révèlent cependant essentiels car il est assuré que la composition de la corrosion est en relation directe avec celle du métal originel. En conséquence, de nombreuses informations peuvent être déduites de ces analyses comme l'identification des types d'alliage et la mise en évidence d'impuretés caractéristiques autorisant la confrontation entre les différentes pièces et zones du groupe statuaire.

Les compositions relevées par pXRF semblent indiquer l'emploi d'au moins deux variantes d'alliage cuivreux, qui sont fonction de la teneur en étain: l'une à plus de 10 % d'étain, et l'autre moins fortement alliée (Diagramme 5.1). Dans ces bronzes, il n'y a pas ou peu de plomb ajouté. Le maximum relevé est de 6,9 % et la plupart des teneurs oscillent entre 1 et 5 %. Rappelons que ces teneurs sont très vraisemblablement surévaluées. On remarque par ailleurs et surtout que les groupes de composition sont nettement corrélés avec la technique métallurgique et le type d'élément à fabriquer. Ainsi, le premier ensemble réunit les coulées primaires et les coulées secondaires: il concerne l'Aurige et tous les fragments qui lui sont associés. L'alliage serait un bronze à fort étain: pour ce groupe, la teneur minimum relevée par pXRF oscille entre

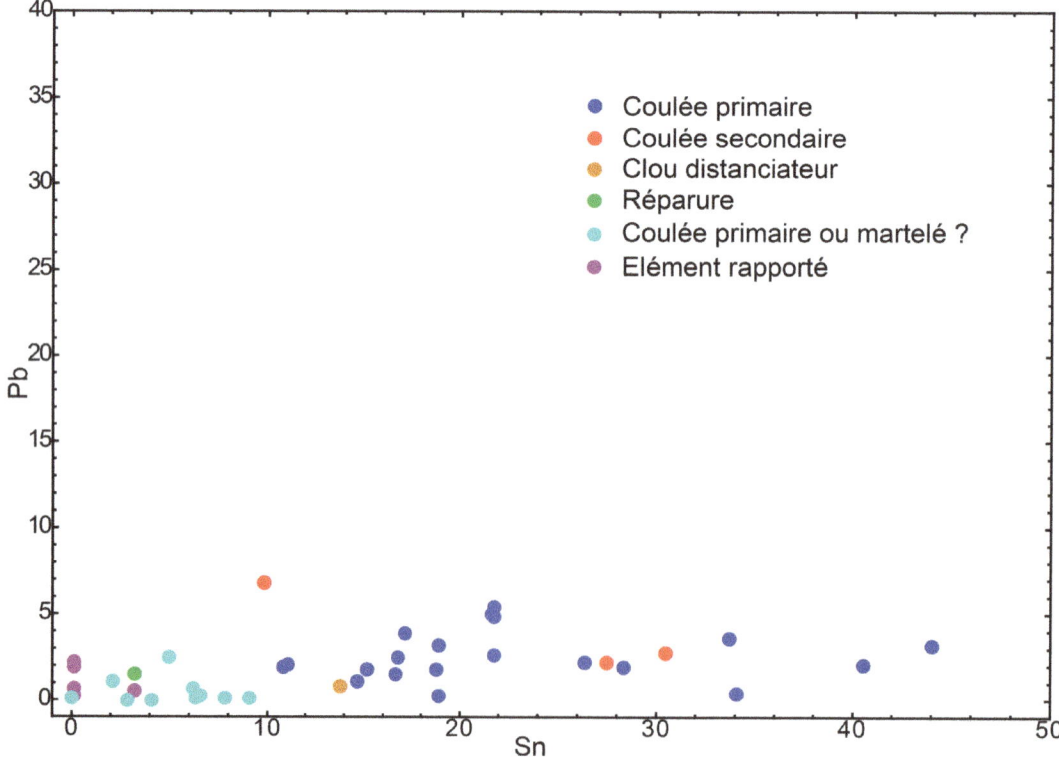

Diagramme 5.1. résultats pXRF en étain et plomb des alliages cuivreux du groupe de l'Aurige, analyses directement effectuées en surface. À noter que les teneurs sont fortement influencées par la composition des couches de corrosion, © C2RMF, B. Mille et D. Robcis.

10 et 11 %. Cette valeur est conforme à ce que l'on connaît pour les autres grands bronzes de la période (Mille 2017, 311–314). L'homogénéité de composition des différentes coulées primaires et secondaires du groupe de l'Aurige ne peut être cependant discutée: la majeure partie de nos analyses affichent des valeurs trop élevées pour l'étain, jusqu'à 44%! Ce résultat est la manifestation évidente du phénomène de corrosion par décuprification précédemment évoqué, qui conduit à un très important enrichissement en étain de la surface de ces bronzes. Seuls des micro-prélèvements de métal pourraient caractériser précisément l'alliage de ces coulées primaires et secondaires.

Le second groupe de composition est défini par un ensemble de pièces rapportées, qui pourraient avoir été fabriquées par martelage (rênes des chevaux). Les mesures pXRF indiquent que ces pièces ont été élaborées à partir d'alliages cuivreux à plus faible teneur en étain (dans tous les cas moins de 10 % d'étain, 4 mesures sur 10 autour de 6 %). La ceinture de l'Aurige pourrait se classer dans ce groupe, à moins qu'il ne s'agisse d'une troisième variante de bronze, à teneur encore plus faible en étain (2 à 3 % d'étain d'après les mesures pXRF). En tout état de cause, ces bronzes à faible étain, donc de couleur rosée, contrastaient incontestablement avec le ton jaune pâle du bronze à fort étain des grandes pièces coulées de l'Aurige. Comme pour les lèvres ou les sourcils, la cordelette qui enserrait le haut de la tunique est en cuivre rouge.

Les analyses pXRF donnent également une première image de la composition en impuretés des alliages cuivreux concernés même si le spectre obtenu est non seulement très partiel – la technique pXRF n'étant pas d'une très grande sensibilité – mais est lui aussi altéré par les surfaces corrodées, ce qui ne permet pas de mener l'exploitation quantitative des résultats. Toutefois, malgré le faible nombre d'éléments chimiques détectable par pXRF (au mieux six), un premier résultat déterminant a été obtenu (Diagramme 5.2). Il s'avère que les alliages utilisés pour réaliser les coulées primaires et secondaires du groupe de l'Aurige sont tous marqués par de fortes teneurs en bismuth, à l'exception du bras d'enfant. Indice de la présence d'un "jockey" pour évoquer une ou plusieurs victoires à la course au cheval monté (Jacquemin

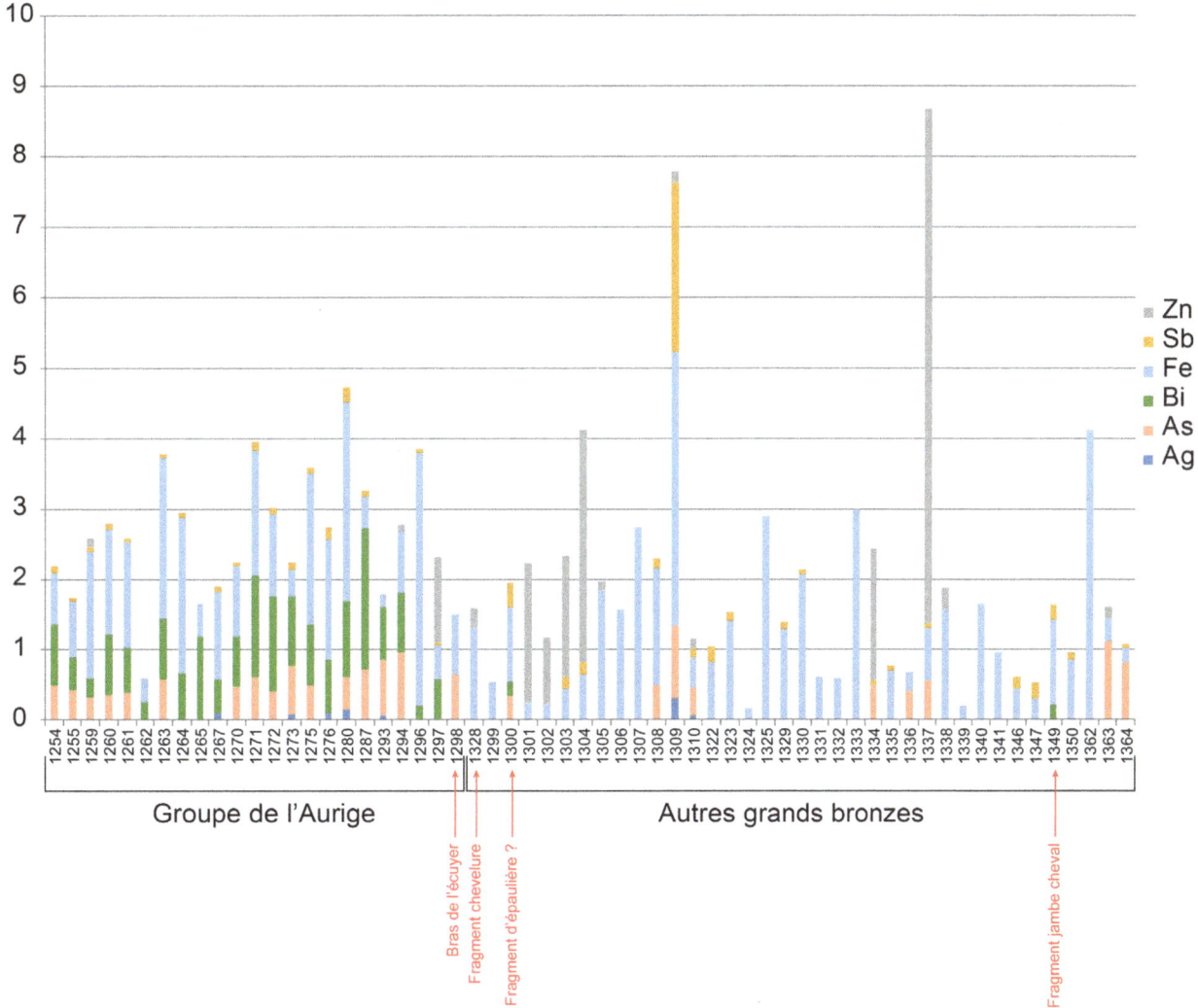

Diagramme 5.2. résultats des analyses pXRF. Spectre d'impuretés des alliages cuivreux du groupe de l'Aurige (à gauche) et des autres fragments de grands bronzes conservés au musée de Delphes. Seules les analyses de coulées primaires et secondaires sont représentées, © C2RMF, B. Mille et D. Robcis.

– Laroche 2009, 8–9) ou d'un palefrenier, ce bras a fait l'objet de nombreuses discussions (Hampe 1960, 70). Des analyses sur prélèvements seront requises pour faire le clair sur son appartenance au groupe de l'Aurige ou non, en particulier par la détermination comparée de la composition élémentaire des alliages cuivreux et de la composition minéralogique et chimique des noyaux. On notera que l'on ne détecte pas non plus de bismuth dans le fragment de chevelure: l'association des deux éléments reste donc possible dans l'état actuel de notre connaissance de leur composition. À deux exceptions près, sur lesquelles il conviendra de revenir, les autres fragments de grands bronzes conservés à Delphes ne sont pas composés de ce bronze fortement marqué par le bismuth.

Une conclusion provisoire

Des résultats nouveaux et importants ont ainsi été obtenus dès cette première mission d'étude technologique de l'Aurige, notamment sur les questions de polychromie métallique. Outre le ton jaune pâle de l'alliage de base de la statue et les couleurs diversement rosées des rênes comme de la ceinture, la palette de l'Aurige comportait trois ou quatre tons supplémentaires au moins, grâce aux éléments métalliques rapportés. Les analyses pXRF ont montré que les lèvres et les sourcils incrustés ont été réalisés à partir de cuivre non allié, c'est-à-dire à partir d'un métal de couleur rouge, ce qui est habituel pour la grande statuaire grecque de la fin du VIe siècle et de la première moitié du Ve siècle (Descamps-Lequime 2015). À ce titre, la technique d'élaboration de l'Aurige s'inscrit bien dans ce qui est connu des procédés de la période du style sévère. Comme on le sait pour la grande statuaire de bronze, l'essentiel de la polychromie était concentré sur la tête, ce que confirme la statue. Par son décor, le bandeau ajoutait un contraste supplémentaire, opposant au jaune de l'alliage cuivreux de base, le blanc gris mat de l'étain et le noir du cuivre vraisemblablement patiné.

La première mission effectuée à Delphes en mai 2017 avait pour but de confronter les connaissances déjà acquises à une observation directe du groupe et aux résultats d'une série exploratoire d'analyses par fluorescence X portable. Ce travail préliminaire était destiné à poser les bases d'un véritable projet de recherche sur l'Aurige en déterminant les actions prioritaires et les moyens scientifiques à engager pour les mener à bien. Il s'est avéré qu'il fallait utiliser des techniques avancées de contrôle non destructif pour étudier les procédés de fonte comme d'assemblage, et pour approfondir la caractérisation non destructive des éléments décoratifs contribuant à la polychromie de la statue. Il fallait nécessairement aussi documenter très précisément la composition chimique des matériaux constitutifs des différents éléments du groupe commémoratif par des analyses sur prélèvements (bronze et noyau). Une telle étude, s'il est possible de la conduire à son terme, serait le gage d'une réelle avancée sur la mise en œuvre technologique de la grande statuaire de bronze à l'époque du style sévère. Elle permettrait de mieux définir l'apparence originelle de l'Aurige, les modalités de sa création, sa provenance aussi et de confirmer l'appartenance enfin à l'ex-voto delphique de certains des bronzes qui lui sont traditionnellement associés.

Remerciements: cette mission n'aurait pu aboutir sans l'implication d'Alexandre Farnoux, Directeur de l'École française d'Athènes et de Jean-Luc Martinez, Président directeur du musée du Louvre. Qu'il nous soit permis de leur exprimer ici notre profonde gratitude.

Nous remercions également vivement l'équipe du musée de Delphes pour sa très grande disponibilité, et tout particulièrement Athanasia Regli, responsable du service de restauration et Christos Pantermakis, restaurateur, ainsi que Rachel Nouet, membre de l'EfA, et Dominique Robcis, du C2RMF, qui nous ont accompagnés et beaucoup aidés dans cette entreprise.

Références bibliographiques

Aucouturier, M. – Mathis, F. – Robcis, D., 2017. Les bronzes noirs antiques, nouvelles observations et mécanismes de création. In: S. Descamps-Lequime – B. Mille, eds. *Bronzes grecs et romains: études récentes sur la statuaire antique.* (Techné, 45), 114–123

Bol, P., 1978, *Grossplastik aus Bronze in Olympia (*Olympische Forschungen IX). Berlin: W. de Gruyter und Co.

Chamoux, F., 1955. *L'Aurige* (Fouilles de Delphes. Tome IV, Monuments figures: sculpture, fasc.5). Paris: De Boccard.

Descamps-Lequime, S., 2015. The Color of Bronze: Polychromy and the Aesthetics of Bronze Surfaces. In: J. Daehner – K. Lapatin, eds. *Power and Pathos. Bronze Sculpture of the Hellenistic World.* [exhibition: Florence, Palazzo Strozzi, 14 March–21 June 2015; Los Angeles, The J. Paul Getty Museum, 28 July–1 November 2015; Washington DC, National Gallery of Art, 13 December 2015–20 March 2016]. Los Angeles: Getty publications, 151–165.

Descamps-Lequime, S. – Mille, B., 2017. Progrès de la recherche sur la statuaire antique en bronze. In: S. Descamps-Lequime – B. Mille, eds. *Bronzes grecs et romains: études récentes sur la statuaire antique.* (Techné, 45), 4–13.

Donati, P., 2013. Die Gesichter der Bronzen von Riace. In: V. Brinkmann, ed. *Zurück zur Klassik. Ein neuer Blick auf das alte Griechenland.* [Exhibition: Frankfurt am Main, Liebieghaus Skulpturensammlung, 8. Februar bis 26. Mai 2013]. Munich: Hirmer Verlag. 269–273.

Formigli, E., 1984. La tecnica di costruzione delle statue di Riace. In: L. Vlad Borreli – P. Pelagatti, eds. *Due Bronzi da Riace. Rinvenimento, restauro, analisi ed ipotesi di interpretazione 1–2* (Bollettino d'arte 3, serie speciale). Rome, 107–142.

Hampe, R., 1941. Der Wagenlenker von Delphi. In: P. Arndt, ed. *Brunn-Bruckmann's Denkmäler griechischer und römischer Skulptur.* Munich: Brunn-Bruckmann. 786–790.

Hampe, R., 1960. Delphes 4,5: Chamoux, L'Aurige. *Gnomon*, 32, 60–73.

Haynes, D. E. L., 1957, Notices of Books: Chamoux (F.), Fouilles de Delphes. Tome IV, Monuments figures: sculpture. Fasc. 5. L'Aurige, Paris, De Boccard, 1955. *The Journal of Hellenic Studies*, 77 (2), 363–364.

Homolle, T., 1896. Statue de bronze découverte à Delphes, séance du 5 juin 1896, appendice. *Comptes rendus des séances de l'Académie des Inscriptions et Belles-Lettres,* 40 (4), 362–384.

Homolle, T., 1897. L'Aurige de Delphes. *Monuments et mémoires de la Fondation Eugène Piot, 4*(2), 169–208.

Jacquemin, A. – Laroche, D., 2009. Regards nouveaux sur deux quadriges delphiques. In: M. Denoyelle – S. Descamps-Lequime – B. Mille – S. Verger, eds. 2012. *"Bronzes grecs et romains, recherches récentes". Hommage à Claude Rolley, 16–17 juin 2009*, [e-book] Paris Collections électroniques de l'INHA. Available through INHA website https://journals.openedition.org/inha/3245 [Accessed July 2012], 8–13.

Kluge, K, 1929. Die Gestaltung des Erzes in der archaisch-griechischen Kunst. *Jahrbuch des Deutschen Archäologischen Instituts, 44*, 1–30.

La Coste-Messelière (de), P., 1943. *Delphes*, Paris: Du Chêne.

Mattusch, C. C., 1988. *Greek Bronze Statuary. From the Beginnings through the Fifth Century B.C.* Ithaca and London: Cornell University Press.

Mille, B. – Artioli, G., 2017. Les objets launaciens: composition élémentaire du métal, composition isotopique du plomb. In: J. Guilaine – L. Carozza – D. Garcia – J. Gasco – T. Janin – B. Mille, eds. *Launac et le launacien, Dépôts de bronzes protohistoriques du sud de la Gaule*, Montpellier: Presses universitaires de la Méditerranée, 130–177.

Mille, B., 2017. *D'une amulette en cuivre aux grandes statues de bronze, évolution des techniques de fonte à la cire perdue, de l'Indus à la Méditerranée, du 5e millénaire au 5e siècle av. J.-C.* Thèse de doctorat en cotutelle de l'ED 395 " Milieux, cultures et sociétés du passé et du présent " en préhistoire (Nanterre), et du département de géosciences en archéométrie (Fribourg), Université de Paris-Nanterre et Université de Fribourg, 2 volumes, 132. 484.

Orfanou, V. – Rehren, T., 2015. A (not so) dangerous method: pXRF vs. EPMA-WDS analyses of copper-based artefacts. *Archaeological and Anthropological Sciences*, 7(3), 387–397.

Piccardo, P. – Mille, B. – Robbiola, L., 2007. Tin and copper oxides in corroded archaeological bronzes. In: P. Dillmann – G. Béranger – P. Piccardo – H. Matthiesen, eds. *Corrosion of metallic heritage artefacts*, Cambridge, England: Woodhead Publishing Ltd, 239–262.

Pollini, J., 2000. The Riace Bronzes: some new observations. *Kölner Jahrbuch*, 33, 37–56.

Rolley, C., 1990. En regardant l'Aurige. *Bulletin de Correspondance Hellénique*, 114, 285–297.

Rolley, C., 1994, *La sculpture grecque, des origines au milieu du Ve siècle* (Vol. 1). Paris: Picard.

Willer, F., 1994. Fragen zur intentionellen Schwarzpatina an den Mahdiabronzen. In: G. Hellenkemper Salies, ed. *Das Wrack. Der antike Schiffsfund von Mahdia.* [Exhibition: Bonn, Rheinisches Landesmuseum Bonn, 8. September 1994–29 Januar 1995]. Köln: Rheinland Verlag. GmbH, 1023–1031.

6

The Bronze Antikythera Ephebe Revisited: Technical Features and Casting Technique

Kosmas A. Dafas

Ephorate of Antiquities of Lesvos

kosmas.dafas@gmail.com

Abstract: Found in the sea off Antikythera in the beginning of the twentieth century, the so-called *Antikythera ephebe* is a Greek large-scale Late Classical bronze preserved today in fairly good condition. Although issues concerning style, dating, artistic provenance, and interpretation have been discussed aplenty in scholarship, little attention has been given to exploring the technical aspect of the statue. This study focuses on its technical features and investigates the exact casting method used for its creation. Through scrutiny of the technical features and the interior of the statue this paper suggests that the Antikythera ephebe was cast with the use of moulds, by the indirect method, in at least sixteen large sections that were joined together after casting during cold working. The results of this study shed light on the technical aspect of the Antikythera ephebe and also contribute to our better understanding of contemporary large-scale bronze statuary and the casting techniques used during the Classical period.

Keywords: Antikythera Ephebe; Casting Techniques; Bronze Statues; Greek Bronzes; Large-Scale Bronze Statuary

The slightly over life-size bronze statue of the Antikythera ephebe (Fig. 6.1) (height 1.96 m, height of head 23.5 cm) is exhibited in the National Archaeological Museum of Athens (Inv. X13396).[1] The statue, part of the cargo of an ancient shipwreck, was found by chance in 1900 by Symian sponge divers in the sea off the north-east coast of the small island of Antikythera in Greece. Apart from the Antikythera ephebe, the cargo of the ship consisted mainly of marble and bronze statues, most of them fragmentary, as well as the so-called *Antikythera mechanism*, and clay, metal, and glass vessels. The ship, which most probably set sail from Asia Minor or the Aegean islands and was on its way to Italy, was wrecked off Antikythera between 80–50 BC (Stais – Tsountas – Kourouniotis 1902, 145–172; Svoronos 1911, 1–83; Bol 1972, 7. 43–120; Price 1974, 8–9. 21–62; Houser 1987, 183–185; Houser 1983, 91; Throckmorton 1970, 40–47. 113–168; Yalouris 1990, 135–136; Ridgway 1997, 341–342; Himmelmann 1994, 849–855; Morrow 1985, 115; Edwards 1965, 18–27; Grace 1965, 5–17; Robinson 1965, 28–29; Weinberg 1965b, 30–39; Kavvadias 1901a, 95–102; Kavvadias 1901b, 205–208; Frost 1903, 217–236; Ralph 1965, 48; Parker 1992, 55–56; Dafas 2008, 5–24, with bibliography, extensively consulted, but inadequately cited in: Kaltsas – Vlachogianni – Bouyia 2012, 17–292).

The ephebe, when extracted from the sea, was preserved in fragments that were later pieced together; some missing parts of the body were supplemented with modern material (Karouzos 1970, 59–79; Bol 1972, 19; Kaltsas 2002, 248–249). Its current condition is satisfactory, but the base of the statue, the items once held in the hands, the distal phalanx of the middle finger of the left hand, the lower right eyelash, and the pupils of the eyes are not preserved.

The statue depicts a nude, beardless ephebe, standing in a relaxed contrapposto pose, with his right arm bent at the elbow, raised upwards and extended forwards in an oblique direction to the right (Fig. 6.1) (for a detailed description, Dafas 2008, 28–33; Dafas 2013, 100–103; Dafas 2019, 70–71). The arrangement of the palms and fingers provides clear evidence that the figure once held in each of his hands an object that is now missing (Fig. 6.1 and 6.2).

Though refraining from going into detail here on issues that concern style, dating, artistic attribution, and

---

[1] This paper is based on the conclusions I drew on the casting technique of the bronze Antikythera ephebe in my MRes (Dafas 2008, 45–56) and my PhD theses (Dafas 2013, 103–109). These conclusions — first briefly presented in the form of an article (Dafas 2015, 137–146) — have been reviewed and enhanced with additional illustration for this publication. The photographs used in this paper were either taken by the author himself or originate from the archive of the National Archaeological Museum of Athens and were obtained during the study of the statue at the museum for the purposes of the author's PhD thesis. The drawing of the ancient seams/joins of the ephebe (Fig. 6.7) was also the work of the author. The conclusions and the majority of the photographic material presented in this paper were first published in a monograph (Dafas 2019) by the Institute of Classical Studies in London (BICS Supplement 138), under the title 'Greek Large-Scale Bronze Statuary: The Late Archaic and Classical Periods'.

Figure 6.1. The Antikythera ephebe: front view (from the photographic archive of the National Archaeological Museum, Athens, K. Xenikakis – © Hellenic Ministry of Culture and Sports, Archaeological Receipts Fund).

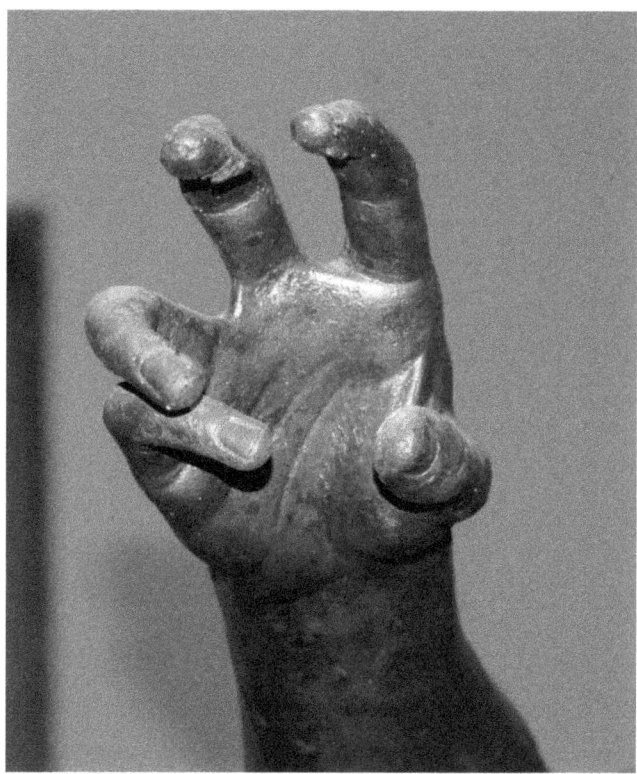

Figure 6.2. The Antikythera ephebe: detail of the right hand (photograph by the author) (National Archaeological Museum, Athens – © Hellenic Ministry of Culture and Sports, Archaeological Receipts Fund).

interpretation, it is essential to make a few remarks of crucial importance to set the scene: on stylistic grounds, the Antikythera ephebe should be dated to 340–330 BC (Dafas 2008, 57–66; Dafas 2013, 109–112; Dafas 2019, 76–77; Karouzou 1967, 157–158; Arnold 1969, 207–210; Bol 1972, 20–23; Houser 1987, 179–180. 190; Houser 1983, 92; Todisco 1993, 102; Yalouris 1994, 29–34. 262; Rolley 1999, 294; Maderna 2004, 320–321; Süsserott 1938, 171–172; Lullies – Hirmer 1957, 22. 69; Bieber 1961, 7–9. 12; Robertson 1975, 409. 470; Stewart 1990, 13–14. 175–176. 185; Ridgway 1997, 339–342. 365. 368–369; Kaltsas 2002, 248).

Despite the statue's frequent association with the Corinthian sculptor Euphranor (Karouzou 1967, 157–158; Bol 1972, 20–23; Houser 1987, 179–180. 190; Houser 1983, 92; Todisco 1993, 102; Yalouris 1994, 29–34. 262; Rolley 1999, 294), its attribution to an artist from the third generation of the school of Polykleitos' followers is more plausible (Arnold 1969, 207–210. For a critical review of the issue, Dafas 2008, 67–78; Dafas 2013, 112–115; Dafas 2019, 77–79).

The ephebe is most frequently interpreted as a depiction of Paris (Stais 1905, 51; Bieber 1910, 159–173; Karouzou 1967, 157; Bieber 1961, 12; Richter 1974, 164; Rolley 1999, 294; Kaltsas 2002, 248) or Perseus (Svoronos 1911, 20–28; Picard 1948, 267–277; Arnold 1969, 207; Lullies – Hirmer 1979, 112; Palagia 1980, 34; Stewart 1990, 185; Todisco 1993, 102–103; Roccos 1994, 345–348, no. 65), and reconstructed with either an apple or Medusa's head in his right hand, respectively. Although there is no general consensus on this issue, the second theory is more probable and has fewer weaknesses than the first (for a critical review on the issue, Dafas 2008, 79–88; Dafas 2013, 115–120; Dafas 2019, 79–83).

Let us now turn our attention to the technical aspect of the statue, beginning with its restoration and conservation. After its discovery in 1900, the ephebe was subjected to chemical cleaning, which was conducted by the chemist Othon Rousopoulos (1856–1922), and which lasted until June 1901. The negative consequences of this process were the corrosion of the bronze epidermis to a greater extent and the loss of the greenish patina, which had once been preserved on several areas of the bronze surface, and which was replaced by a darker greyish colour (Svoronos 1911, 15. 19; Stais – Tsountas – Kourouniotis 1902, 150; Karouzos 1970, 59).

The fragments of the ephebe were roughly pieced together by Panagiotis Kaloudis (1840–1917), the senior technician of the National Archaeological Museum of Athens at that time. In 1902, the statue was restored by the French artist Alfred André (1839–1919). Several missing parts of the shoulders, torso, abdomen, and buttocks were mended with modern material, and the epidermis of the statue was completely covered with a thick layer of colophony, a natural resin, which made it dull, adding further to the dark hue. Although André succeeded in constructing an effective armature, he failed to retrieve the original stance of the figure: the right leg was not attached to the lower torso in the correct position, and several other fragments of the chest were incorrectly joined (Svoronos 1911, 15. 19–20; Karouzos 1970, 59–60).

As the result of André's efforts was deemed unsatisfactory, it was decided that the bronze statue should undergo a second restoration, which took place much later, between 1948 and 1953. The project was carried out by sculptors and other staff-members of the National Archaeological Museum of Athens, under the supervision of the director of the museum at that time, Professor Christos Karouzos (1900–1967) (Fig. 6.3). André's metal armature was retained; the colophony was removed from the bronze surface, while the head, right arm and leg, and many fragments of the lower front trunk were set properly in their correct positions. The original height of the figure, stance and colour of the bronze were restored. The facial features, the details of the elaborate locks of hair, but most of all, the statue's plasticity and the rhythmic movement of its limbs into space were revealed, as the ephebe regained its proper three-dimensional character (Karouzos 1970, 59–79; Bol 1972, 19).

Moving on to the casting technique of the statue, so far in scholarship there have been only a few general references to the ephebe having been cast in pieces (Bol 1985, 19; Houser 1987, 186–187; Mattusch 1996, 88). However, there is no detailed discussion of the actual number of separately cast sections of the statue or of the exact casting method, direct or indirect, used for its manufacture. Caley, in 1970 (38–43), and Houser, in 1987 (187), referred to the results of chemical analyses conducted on the alloy of the statue, which showed that unleaded bronze, containing 84.74% copper and 14.79% tin, was used for its creation. Another technical detail was reported by Tzachou-Alexandri and Andreopoulou-Mangou in 2000 (89. 91), who described use of the common '*oval basins*' method for the joining of the separately made limbs of the Artemision god, the Riace statues, the Marathon boy and the Antikythera ephebe.

One cannot help but wonder why the archaeologists, conservators and technicians at the National Archaeological Museum of Athens made no attempt to systematically study the interior of the statue during its restoration, which is of crucial importance in understanding its casting technique. The fragmentary state of the ephebe (Fig. 6.3) would certainly have facilitated a thorough exploration of its interior. I was fortunate enough to have access to the photographic archive of the National Archaeological Museum of Athens for the purposes of my PhD thesis (Dafas 2013, 103–109, pls 66e. 67–70) and to examine the interior of the statue through the photographs taken when it was still in pieces (Figs 6.3–6.5. 6.8). Combining this evidence with the technical features of the statue still visible on its exterior, I have drawn my conclusions on the exact casting method used for its manufacture. First let us turn our attention to elucidating the separate sections in which the ephebe was cast.

During the second restoration of the ephebe, Karouzos (1970, 77) traced some — but not all — of the ancient seams of the statue: a horizontal seam at the front part of the upper torso at the level of the nipples; a horizontal seam at the level of the buttocks and the hips; two horizontal seams around the middle part of the thighs, one of which is also visible in an image from the museum's archive (Dafas 2013, pl. 69b; Dafas 2019, pl. 69b) (Fig. 6.4); another one along the middle part of the left instep; and traces of two smaller seams in the pubic area.

Karouzos does not mention if the seam between the buttocks and the hips extended to the front part of the lower torso as well (1970, 77), but, fortunately, an image

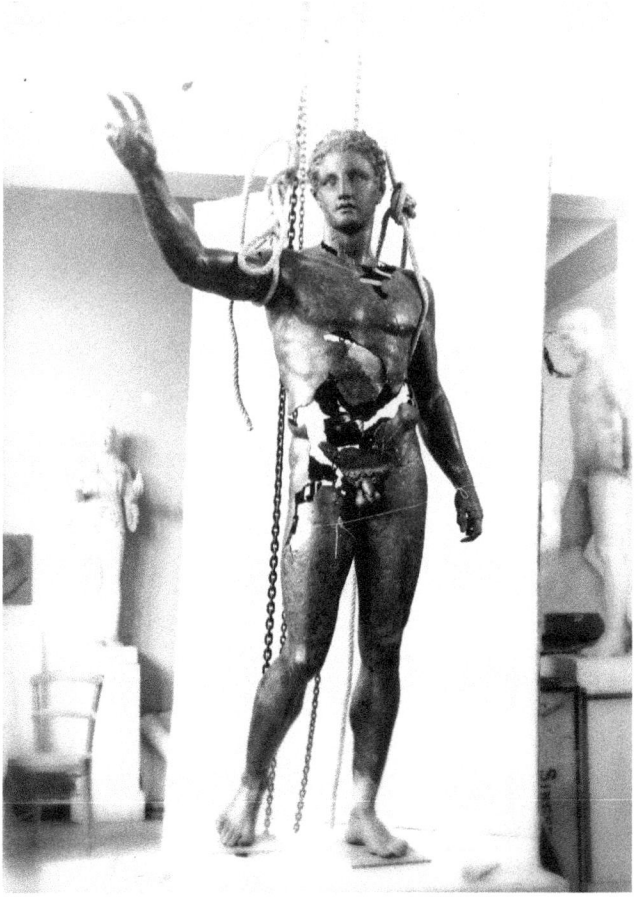

Figure 6.3. The Antikythera ephebe during its second restoration (from the photographic archive of the National Archaeological Museum, Athens – © Hellenic Ministry of Culture and Sports, Archaeological Receipts Fund).

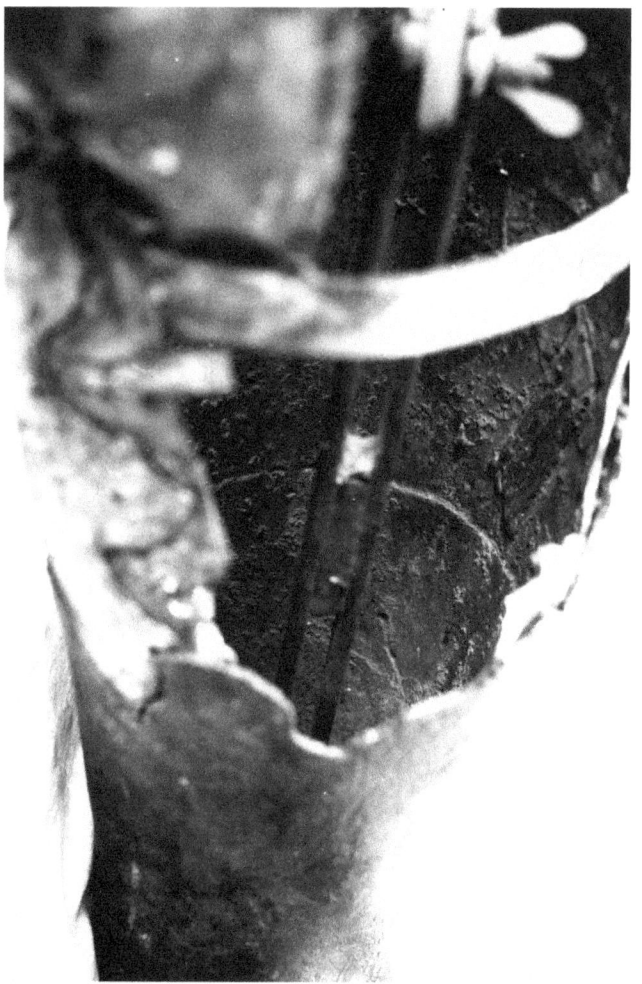

Figure 6.4. The Antikythera ephebe: detail of the interior of the right thigh (from the photographic archive of the National Archaeological Museum, Athens – © Hellenic Ministry of Culture and Sports, Archaeological Receipts Fund).

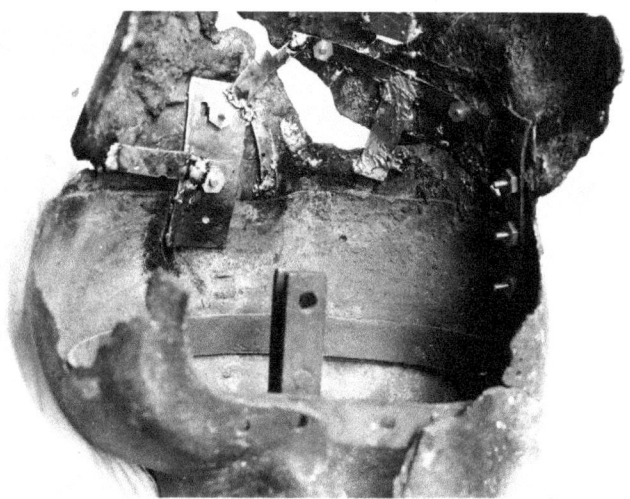

Figure 6.5. The Antikythera ephebe: details of the interior of the left part of the lower torso (from the photographic archive of the National Archaeological Museum, Athens – © Hellenic Ministry of Culture and Sports, Archaeological Receipts Fund).

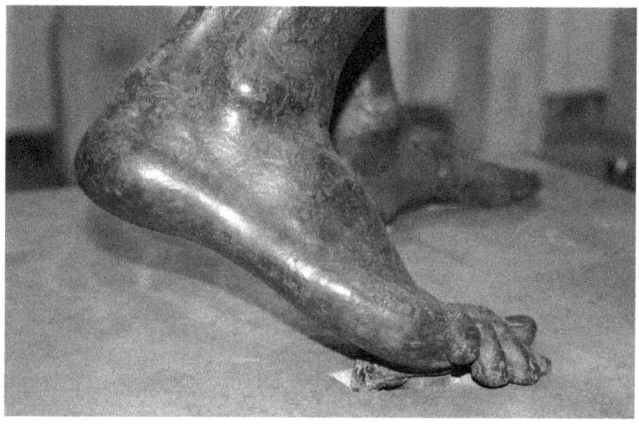

Figure 6.6. The Antikythera ephebe: detail of the right foot (photograph by the author) (National Archaeological Museum, Athens – © Hellenic Ministry of Culture and Sports, Archaeological Receipts Fund).

from the museum's archive (Dafas 2013, pl. 69a; Dafas 2019, pl. 69a) (Fig. 6.5) clearly shows that the seam also runs through the front part of the preserved lower torso, roughly following the shallow grooves of the groin and crossing the area between the abdomen and the pubic area. One might argue that this 'seam' should be interpreted as a trace left from the mould-lining process. However, the totally different appearance and overall shape of the technical marks left from the mould-lining process on the interior of a bronze leg in the Louvre (Inv. Br.69) (Bouquillon et al. 2006, 227–261, fig. 15) is a strong indication that the seam in the ephebe's lower torso should be interpreted as a joint seam between the separately made sections of the statue in this area. No seams were detected in the area of the head and the upper limbs. In all probability, this is due to the bad state of preservation of the base of the neck, since the original bronze surface in this area is not preserved (Dafas 2013, 105, pl. 68b; Dafas 2019, 73, pl. 68b; Bol 1985, 19; Mattusch 1996, 88). Yet, considering that the head and arms of *all* late Archaic and Classical large-scale bronzes preserved today have been cast separately, it is safe to conclude that the same applies to the ephebe (Dafas 2013, 104–109. 205–212. 226–233; Dafas 2019, 6–12. 74–75. 117–144; Bol 1985, 19; Mattusch 1996a, 88; Houser 1987a, 186–187). Evidence of this — at least in the case of the arms — consists in the faint traces of the seams still visible on the external surface of the statue at the base of the arms close to the shoulders (Dafas 2013, pls 58. 60–62; Dafas 2019, pls 58. 60–62) (Fig. 6.1). Finally, another faint trace of a seam is preserved along the middle part of the right instep (Dafas 2013, pl. 66; Dafas 2019, pl. 66) (Fig. 6.6), which is not reported/discussed by Karouzos.

Bearing in mind all the aforementioned observations, we can conclude that the head, together with the neck, was separately cast in one section and then attached to the torso at the base of the neck. The arms were also cast separately and attached to the torso at the base of the shoulders. The seams would in all probability roughly follow the shallow grooves that render the subdivisions of the muscles in this area, as in that way it would be easier for the bronze-worker to conceal the traces of the joining process during cold working. Both hands could also be separately cast, as in the case of the Artemision god (Athens, National Archaeological Museum, Inv. X15161) (Tzachou-Alexandri — Andreopoulou-Mangou 2000, 86–95) and the Riace statues (Reggio Calabria, National Archaeological Museum, Inv. 12801-2) (Formigli 1984, 107–142). The torso was cast in two large sections: the upper part, from the base of the neck to the level of the nipples, and the lower part, from the nipples to the pubic area, without the pubic hair and the genitals. The latter were made in two separate parts as well. Each of the legs was cast in two sections: from the groin to the middle of the thigh; and from the middle of the thigh to the middle of the feet. The front part of each foot, together with the toes, was also made separately. Last but not least, the objects the ephebe once held in his hands were cast separately and attached both mechanically and metallurgically to the palms and fingers (on the separately made objects in the hands, see also Bol 1985, 19; Houser 1987, 186–187; Mattusch 1996, 88). As already mentioned, the traces still visible on the surface of the palm and the fingers provide the evidence (Figs 6.1 and 6.2). In conclusion, the Antikythera ephebe was cast in at least sixteen separate sections (Fig. 6.7).

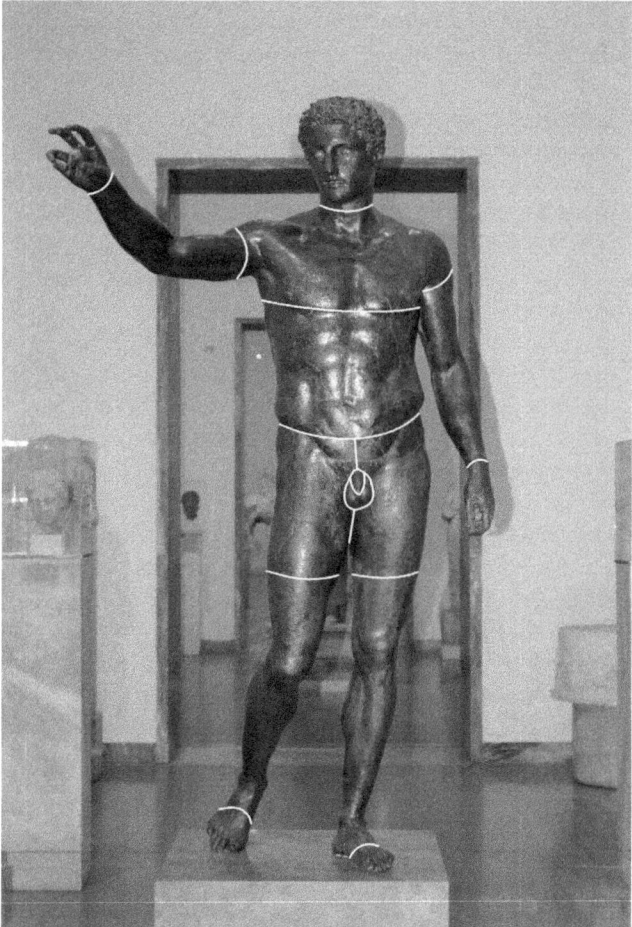

Figure 6.7. The Antikythera ephebe: front view with schematic drawing of the ancient seams/joins of the statue (photograph by the author / drawing of seams by the author) (National Archaeological Museum, Athens – © Hellenic Ministry of Culture and Sports, Archaeological Receipts Fund).

— including the missing items of the hands — that were joined together both mechanically and metallurgically during cold working (Dafas 2008, 45–56; revised in Dafas 2013, 103–109; Dafas 2015, 141 and Dafas 2019, 73).

Moving on to the exact casting method used for the manufacture of the ephebe, it is of crucial importance to bear in mind that the bronze walls are only 3–3.5 mm thick. This measurement was first reported by Houser in 1987 (314–315). In the direct method, the clay core bears no details except for the general anatomical features of the figure. All details are rendered in the wax which is applied on the dry surface of the core with special tools and by hand; hence, a considerable amount of wax is needed for this process. The greater the amount of wax applied on the core, the greater the thickness of the bronze walls of a statue becomes. The thickness of the bronze walls of a statue cast by the direct method cannot measure only a few millimetres, as is the case with the indirect method. In the indirect method, the initial model is a complete piece of work that bears all the details of the figure to be cast, and not only its general anatomical characteristics, as happens in the direct method. Thus, after mould-taking, all the details are impressed on the interior of the moulds in the negative. The wax applied on the interior of the moulds is but a very thin layer, as there is no need for the bronze-workers to further work the wax with their hands to render any details. As a result, the bronze walls of a statue cast by the indirect method are thinner than those of a statue cast by the direct method; it is in fact as thin as the wax layer applied on the interior of the moulds (Dafas 2008, 45–47; Dafas 2013, 231–233; Dafas 2019, 10–11; on direct and indirect casting techniques in general, Bol 1978, 71–78; Formigli 1984, 107–142; Bol 1985, 118–135; Rolley 1986, 33–40; Houser 1987, 313–326; Mattusch 1988, 15–22; Stewart 1990, 38–40; Zimmer 1990, 127–155; Haynes 1992, 24–33; Stewart 1997, 47–56; Hemingway 2000, 39–43; Hemingway 2004, 3–9). Considering that the bronze walls of the Antikythera ephebe measure only 3–3.5 mm in thickness, it is impossible that the direct method was used for its manufacture (Dafas 2008, 45–56; Dafas 2013, 103–109; Dafas 2015, 143; Dafas 2019, 74).

The second important factor is the interior of the statue, unfortunately inaccessible today due to its state of preservation. In Karouzos' study, only a small part of the interior of the statue is visible (1970, figs 4–7). Nevertheless, through the photographs in the archive of the National Archaeological Museum of Athens that were taken during the restoration of the statue, when it was still in pieces, one can discern with no difficulty that the bronze walls of the statue are indeed extremely thin (Dafas 2013, pls 66e. 67–70; Dafas 2019, pls 66e. 67–70) (Figs 6.3–6.5). The inner surface of the statue clearly reproduces its external contours in the negative in every detail. This key feature is extremely significant and can be technically explained only by the use of moulds. Consequently, it is safe to deduce that the bronze statue of the Antikythera ephebe was cast by the indirect method (Dafas 2008, 45–

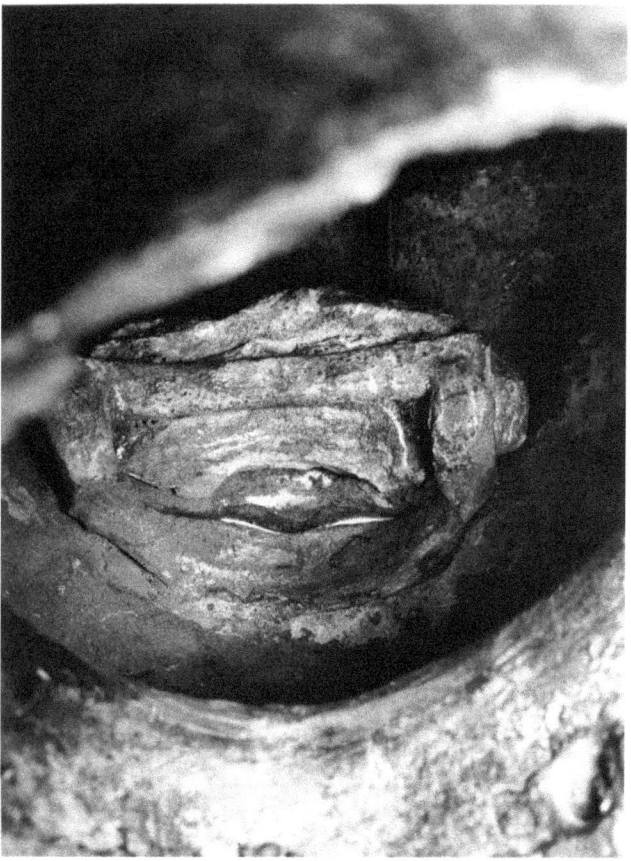

Figure 6.8. The Antikythera ephebe during its second restoration: detail of the interior of the head (from the photographic archive of the National Archaeological Museum, Athens – © Hellenic Ministry of Culture and Sports, Archaeological Receipts Fund).

56; Dafas 2013, 103–109; Dafas 2015, 143; Dafas 2019, 74).

Having said that, though, a combination of both methods, direct and indirect, was used for the casting of the ephebe's head. Part of the interior of the head is visible in an image from the archive of the National Archaeological Museum of Athens (Dafas 2013, pl. 70c; Dafas 2019, pl. 70c) (Fig. 6.8), also reproduced in Karouzos' article (1970, fig. 9). The contours are relatively rough in general, but the overall shape of the nose is reproduced in the negative to a certain degree. The inner surface of the head that corresponds to the hair is not visible, but it is safe to assume that it is rough and does not bear the impressions of the locks of hair in the negative (for a detailed discussion on the issue, Dafas 2008, 52–53; Dafas 2013, 107–108. 205–212; Dafas 2019, 74–75. 139–144). The locks of hair were fully rendered in solid wax after the removal of the moulds and before the placement of the clay investment (on the same issue, see also Haynes 1992, 59–60; Mattusch 1988, 19–21. 134). All the details of the locks, such as the fine incisions, were executed with special tools after casting, during the cold working phase (on this, see also Bol 1985, 20).

Numerous small round holes and larger rectangular depressions are visible all over the bronze surface of the statue. These technical imperfections, which were carefully concealed during the cold working phase, are visible today, due to the poor state of preservation of the bronze epidermis. Many of them were caused either by the iron pins, used to secure the position of the core within the outer clay investment during baking and casting, or the vents, used for the exit of the gases caused by the high temperatures during the baking and casting processes. Some of them were obviously caused by technical faults during casting, such as air bubbles and other casting slips. These imperfections were repaired during cold working: small square or rectangular metal patches were hammered into the imperfections in the bronze surface (Dafas 2008, 53–54; Dafas 2013, 108. 228–229; Dafas 2015, 143; Dafas 2019, 8. 75; on cold working in large-scale bronze statuary in general, Bol 1978, 78–81; Bol 1985, 138–156; Rolley 1986, 37–40; Houser 1987, 327–337; Mattusch 1988, 20–21; Haynes 1992, 92–120; Hemingway 2000, 44; Hemingway 2004, 9. 12–13).

The Antikythera ephebe bears inlaid eyes, eyelashes, lips, teeth, and nipples, which were separately made and placed in position during cold working, before the final joining process of the separately cast sections of the statue was undertaken. Three different materials were used for the eyes: white glass paste for the eyeballs; brownish stone for the irises; and a different material for the missing pupils. Fringed metal sheets were used to render the eyelashes of the figure. The eyes were attached to these sheets and inserted into the ocular cavities from the outside, probably before the fastening of the head to the torso. The aforementioned image from the interior of the ephebe's head (Dafas 2013, pl. 70c; Dafas 2019, pl. 70c) (Fig. 6.8) shows that the rear part of his eyes was held in position with the help of soldering material. As also seen in Karouzos' images (1970, figs 1–3. 9) – which are not discussed or explained in his text – the lips were separately cast in copper, fastened to a metal frame and inserted into the mouth cavity from the inside, before the attachment of the head to the torso. Behind the slightly open mouth, a separately made metal plate was fastened into place to render the teeth of the figure. The Cyrene Berber (London, British Museum, Inv. GR1861.11-27.13 – Bronze 268) is a close comparandum demonstrating the use of the same techniques for the production and insertion of the eyes, lips, and teeth. Finally, the nipples of the ephebe were separately cast in copper and inserted into the corresponding cavities of the torso (on the insets of the statue, Dafas 2008, 54–55; Dafas 2013, 108–109. 228–229; Dafas 2015, 144; Dafas 2019, 75; Stais – Tsountas – Kourouniotis 1902, 149; Svoronos 1911, 21; Karouzos 1970, 61, figs 1–3. 9; Bol 1978, 93–98; Houser 1983, 92–94; Formigli 1984, 136, fig. 35; Bol 1985, 19–20. 148–156, figs 104–108; Houser 1987, 180–181. 187. 328; Haynes 1992, 106–112, fig. 9, pl. 11–12; Mattusch 1996, 88; Ridgway 1997, 359, n. 35; Tzachou-Alexandri – Andreopoulou-Mangou 2000, 92).

The Antikythera ephebe was once mounted on a stone base which is not preserved today. Lead tenons, also now lost, anchored the statue to its base; this can also be inferred from the technical marks preserved on the undersides of its feet, also seen in Karouzos' images (1970, figs 10–11) (Fig. 6.6). The whole interior of the left foot was filled with molten lead reaching approximately to the level of the ankle. A different technique was used for the right foot: a metal projection, intentionally left protruding from the ball of the right foot (Fig. 6.6), was inserted into the cavity of the stone base of the statue (Houser 1987, 187. 293–294, fig. 11.8). Molten lead was then poured into the same cavity of the base and the interior of the foot, which on cooling would fasten the foot to the base, holding it firmly in position (Dafas 2008, 55–56; Dafas 2013, 109. 232–233; Dafas 2015, 144; Dafas 2019, 76; on mounting techniques in general, Bol 1978, 85–87; Formigli 1984, 137, fig. 36; Bol 1985, 160–163. 168, figs 117. 120–121; Mattusch 1988, 110–111; Haynes 1992, 102–103, fig. 8).

As this article has shown, the study of the technical features and the interior of the bronze Antikythera ephebe can help us determine the exact casting method used for its manufacture. It also significantly enhances our knowledge of contemporary casting techniques used in large-scale bronze statuary of the Classical period. Of course, the scrutiny of all surviving examples of the period (Dafas 2019) is of crucial importance in reaching further conclusions on these issues.

Acknowledgements

I would like to thank Dr Nikolaos Kaltsas, former director of the National Archaeological Museum of Athens, for granting me permission to study and photograph the Antikythera ephebe; Dr Maria Lagogianni-Georgakarakos, current director of the National Archaeological Museum of Athens, for granting me permission to use the images included in this article; Dr Georgios Kavvadias and Dr Maria Chidiroglou, senior curators at the National Archaeological Museum of Athens, for providing me with additional images from the photographic archive of the Museum and for helping me obtain the image rights permission for this publication. This article is dedicated with all my love to my wife Eleni.

Bibliography

Arnold, D., 1969. *Die Polykletnachfolge. Untersuchungen zur Kunst von Argos und Sikyon zwischen Polyklet und Lysipp* (*Jahrbuch des Deutschen Archäologischen Instituts: Ergänzungsheft* 25), Berlin.

Bieber, M., 1910. Der Paris des Euphranor und Jünglingsköpfe aus dem IV. Jahrhundert v. Chr., *Jahrbuch des Deutschen Archäologischen Instituts* 25, 159–173.

Bieber, M., 1961. *The Sculpture of the Hellenistic Age*, 2nd edition. New York.

Boardman, J., 1975. *Athenian Red-figure Vases: the Archaic Period. A Handbook*, London.

Bol, P.C., 1972. *Die Skulpturen des Schiffsfundes von Antikythera* (*Mitteilungen des Deutschen Archäologischen Instituts, Athenische Abteilung: Beiheft* 2), Berlin.

Bol, P.C., 1978. *Grossplastik aus Bronze in Olympia* (*Olympische Forschungen* 9), Berlin.

Bol, P.C., 1985. *Antike Bronzetechnik: Kunst und Handwerk antiker Erzbildner*, Munich.

Bouquillon, et al. 2006. Une nouvelle étude de l'Apollon Chatsworth, *RA*, 227–261.

Caley, E.R., 1970. Chemical Composition of Greek and Roman Statuary Bronzes. In: S. Döringer – D.G. Mitten – A.R. Steinberg, ed., *Art and Technology. A Symposium on Classical Bronzes*, Cambridge, 37–49.

Cavalier, K.R., 2000. An Old Saw. In: Mattusch – Brauer – Knudsen 2000, 81–85.

Dafas, K.A., 2008. *Ο χάλκινος έφηβος των Αντικυθήρων* (MRes thesis, Aristotle University of Thessaloniki, [pdf]. Available at: http://ikee.lib.auth.gr/record/103313/files/gri-2008-1406.pdf) [Accessed on 25 June 2019].

Dafas, K.A., 2013. *Greek Large-scale Bronze Statuary Revisited: The Late Archaic and Classical Periods* (PhD thesis, King's College London).

Dafas, K.A., 2015. The Casting Technique of the Bronze Antikythera Ephebe. In: Z. Theodoropoulou-Polychroniadis – D. Evely, ed., *Aegis: Essays in Mediterranean Archaeology presented to Matti Egon by the scholars of the Greek Archaeological Committee UK*, Oxford, 137–146.

Dafas, K.A., 2019. *Greek Large-scale Bronze Statuary: The Late Archaic and Classical Periods*, (monograph) *BICS Supplement 138*, the Institute of Classical Studies (*ICS*), London.

Edwards, G.R., 1965. The Hellenistic Pottery. In: Weinberg 1965a, 18–27.

Formigli, E., 1984. La tecnica di costruzione delle statue di Riace. In: L.V. Borrelli – P. Pelagatti, ed., *Due bronzi da Riace: rinvenimento, restauro, analisi ed ipotesi di interpretazione* (*Bollettino d'Arte Ser. spec.* 3), vol. 1, Rome, 107–142.

Frost, K.T., 1903. The Statues from Cerigotto, *Journal of Hellenic Studies* 23, 217–236.

Grace, V.R., 1965. The Commercial Amphoras. In: Weinberg 1965a, 5–17.

Haynes, D.E.L., 1992. *The Technique of Greek Bronze Statuary*, Mainz.

Hemingway, S.A., 2000. Bronze sculpture. In: R. Ling, ed., *Making Classical Art. Process and Practice*, Stroud, 37–46.

Hemingway, S.A., 2004. *The Horse and Jockey from Artemision. A Bronze Equestrian Monument of the Hellenistic Period*, Berkeley and London.

Himmelmann, N., 1994. Mahdia und Antikythera. In: G. Hellenkemper-Salies, ed., *Das Wrack. Der antike Schiffsfund von Mahdia*, 2, Cologne, 849–855.

Houser, C., 1983. *Greek Monumental Bronze Sculpture*, New York and Paris.

Houser, C., 1987. *Greek Monumental Bronze Sculpture of the Fifth and Fourth Centuries BC*, New York.

Kaltsas, N.E., 2002. *Sculpture in the National Archaeological Museum, Athens*, Los Angeles.

Kaltsas, N. – Vlachogianni, E. – Bouyia, P., ed., 2012. *The Antikythera Shipwreck. The Ship, the Treasures, the Mechanism*, Athens.

Karouzos, C.I., 1970. Χρονικὸν τῆς ἀνασυστάσεως τοῦ χαλκίνου Νέου τῶν Ἀντικυθήρων, *Ἀρχαιολογικὴ Ἐφημερίς*, 59–79.

Karouzou, S., 1967. *Ἐθνικόν Ἀρχαιολογικόν Μουσεῖον, Συλλογή γλυπτῶν: Περιγραφικός κατάλογος*, Athens.

Kavvadias, P., 1901a. Ἀνακοίνωσις περὶ τῶν ἐκ τῆς παρὰ τὰ Ἀντικύθηρα θαλάσσης ἀγαλμάτων, *Πρακτικά τῆς Ἀρχαιολογικῆς Ἐταιρείας Ἀθηνῶν*, 95–102.

Kavvadias, P., 1901b. The Recent Finds off Cythera, *Journal of Hellenic Studies* 21, 205–208.

Lechtman, H. – Steinberg, A., 1970. Bronze Joining. A Study in Ancient Technology. In: S. Döringer – D.G. Mitten – A.R. Steinberg, ed., *Art and Technology. A Symposium on Classical Bronzes*, Cambridge, 5–35.

Lullies, R. – Hirmer, M., 1957. *Greek Sculpture*, London.

Lullies, R. – Hirmer, M., 1979. *Griechische Plastik. Von den Anfangen bis zum Beginn der romischen Kaiserzeit*, 4th edition, Munich.

Maderna, C., 2004. Die letzten Jahrzehnte der spätklassischen Plastik. In: P.C. Bol, ed., *Die Geschichte der antiken Bildhauerkunst. II. Klassische Plastik*, Mainz, 303–382.

Mattusch, C.C., 1980. The Berlin Foundry Cup. The Casting of Greek Bronze Statuary in the Early Fifth Century BC, *American Journal of Archaeology* 84, 435–444.

Mattusch, C.C., 1988. *Greek Bronze Statuary. From the Beginnings through the Fifth Century BC*, Ithaca, NY.

Mattusch, C.C., 1996. *Classical Bronzes. The Art and Craft of Greek and Roman Statuary*, Ithaca, NY.

Mattusch, C.C. – Brauer, A. – Knudsen, S.E., ed., 2000. *From the Parts to the Whole. Acta of the 13th International Bronze Congress, Held at Cambridge, Massachusetts, May 28–June 1, 1996 (Journal of Roman Archaeology Suppl. 39)*, 1–2, Portsmouth, R.I.

Morrow, K.D., 1985. *Greek Footwear and the Dating of Sculpture*, Madison, Wis.

Neils, J., 2000. Who's who on the Berlin Foundry Cup. In: Mattusch – Brauer – Knudsen 2000, 75–80.

Palagia, O., 1980. *Euphranor (Monumenta Graeca et Romana* 3), Leiden.

Parker, A.J., 1992. *Ancient Shipwrecks of the Mediterranean and the Roman Provinces (British Archaeological Reports Int Ser.* 580), Oxford.

Picard, C., 1948. *Manuel d'archéologie grecque: La sculpture.* III. *Période classique–IVe siècle*, Paris.

Price, D.J. de S., 1974. *Gears from the Greeks. The Antikythera Mechanism – A Calendar Computer from ca. 80 BC (Transactions of the American Philosophical Society* 64.7), Philadelphia, 1–70.

Ralph, E.K., 1965. Carbon-14 Date for the Antikythera Shipwreck. In: Weinberg 1965a, 48.

Richter, G.M.A., 1974. *Ἀρχαία ελληνική τέχνη*, Athens.

Ridgway, B.S., 1997. *Fourth-Century Styles in Greek Sculpture*, Madison, Wis.

Robertson, M., 1975. *A History of Greek Art*, 1–2, London.

Robinson, H.S., 1965. The Early Roman Pottery. In: Weinberg 1965a, 28–29.

Roccos, L.J., 1994. LIMC VII, 345–348, no. 65, s.v. Perseus.

Rolley, C., 1986. *Greek Bronzes*, London.

Rolley, C., 1999. *La sculpture grecque: 2. La période classique*, Paris.

Stais, V., 1905. *Τὰ ἐξ' Ἀντικυθήρων Εὑρήματα: Χρονολογία, προέλευσις, χαλκοῦς ἔφηβος*, Athens.

Stais, V. – Tsountas, C. – Kourouniotis, K., 1902. 'Τὰ εὑρήματα τοῦ ναυαγίου τῶν Ἀντικυθήρων,' *Ἀρχαιολογικὴ Ἐφημερίς*, 145–148.

Steinberg, A., 1973. Joining Methods on Large Bronze Statues. Some Experiments in Ancient Technology. In: W.J. Young, ed., *Application of Science in Examination of Works of Art. Proceedings of the Seminar: June 15–19, 1970, Conducted by the Research Laboratory, Museum of Fine Arts, Boston, Massachusetts*, Boston, 103–138.

Stewart, A., 1990. *Greek Sculpture. An Exploration*, I-II, New Haven and London.

Stewart, A., 1997. *Art, Desire, and the Body in Ancient Greece*, Cambridge.

Svoronos, I.N., 1911. *Τὸ ἐν Ἀθήναις Ἐθνικὸν Μουσεῖον*, 1, Athens.

Süsserott, H.K., 1938. *Griechische Plastik des 4. Jahrhunderts vor Christus. Untersuchungen zur Zeitbestimmung*, Frankfurt.

Throckmorton, P., 1965. The Antikythera Ship. In: Weinberg 1965a, 40–47.

Throckmorton, P., 1970. *Shipwrecks and Archaeology. The Unharvested Sea*, London.

Todisco, L., 1993. *Scultura greca del IV secolo: Maestri e scuole di statuaria tra classicità ed ellenismo*, Milan.

Tzachou-Alexandri, O. – Andreopoulou-Mangou, H., 2000. Some Remarks on the Bronze God of Artemision. In: Mattusch – Brauer – Knudsen 2000, 86–95.

Weinberg, G.D., 1965a. *The Antikythera Shipwreck Reconsidered* (*Transactions of the American Philosophical Society* 55.3), Philadelphia.

Weinberg, G.D., 1965b. The Glass Vessels. In: Weinberg 1965a, 30–39.

Yalouris, N., 1990. The Shipwreck of Antikythera. New Evidence of Its Date after Supplementary Investigation. In: J.P. Descoeudres, ed., *Εὐμουσία. Ceramic and Iconographic Studies in Honour of Alexander Cambitoglou*, Sydney, 135–136.

Yalouris, N., 1994. *Ελληνική Τέχνη. Αρχαία Γλυπτά*, Athens.

Zimmer, G., 1990. *Griechische Bronzegusswerkstätten. Zur Technologieentwicklung eines antiken Kunsthandwerkes*, Mainz.

7

Bronze Cast on Decorated Iron Sheets. An Unusual Manufacturing Technique in Iron Age Italy

Joachim Weidig, Nicola Bruni, Fabio Fazzini

Albert-Ludwigs-Universität Freiburg

Soprintendenza Archeologia Belle Arti e Paesaggio dell'Umbria

Independent researcher

achim.weidig@gmx.de

Abstract: During the excavations of the Iron Age necropolis of Piazza d'Armi in Spoleto (Umbria, Italy), four mace-head-shaped sceptres were uncovered: they date to the mid-7th century BC. Two of them were cast in bronze and two were made of two light-weight metal halves, both fixed to a wooden shaft; of particular note is not only the unique figurative decoration with religious and mythological motifs but also the uncommon production technique in which the bronze was cast over the engraved iron sheet.

Keywords: Spoleto-Piazza d'Armi; Sceptre; 7th Century BC; Lost-wax Casting

Iron objects with inlaid decoration in copper, bronze or silver were already recognized in the funerary traditions of the great necropolises of central Italy (Abruzzo, Umbria, Marche) of 700–500 BC, but they have never been analysed in a systematic way. Of particular interest is the discovery of a new technique (= technique A) in which the bronze was cast over an engraved iron sheet. In the bi-metallic decoration three principal techniques were already known, subdivided into further varieties:

B) Inlaying
var. B1) Inlaying iron into bronze
var. B2) Inlaying bronze/copper into iron
C) Sandwich technique—two iron sheets with a sheet of bronze between them

Technique A – Bronze cast on decorated iron sheets

During the 2008 rescue excavations of the Iron Age necropolis of Piazza d'Armi in Spoleto (Umbria, Italy), four relatively inconspicuous objects were uncovered. Only the following investigations revealed them as mace-head-shaped sceptres.

Two of the heavy finials found in tomb 8 had been cast in bronze and were fixed to the wooden shaft with an iron nail (see technique B). They date to the mid-7th century BC. The other two mace-sceptres, however, had each been made of two light-weight metal halves, nailed to wooden shafts of about 55 cm in length. Of particular note is not only the unique figurative decoration with religious and mythological motifs but also the uncommon production technique (Fig. 7.1–7.2) (Weidig 2015; Weidig in press a; Weidig in press b; Weidig – Bruni 2017). The dome-shaped halves of the mace-sceptres had been forged from iron, the decoration was cut à jour. The bronze was cast on the iron sheets, thus closing the openwork. Radiological analyses clearly verified this technique. The liquid bronze created small air pockets and slightly encased the iron framework also on the front. Radiographs demonstrate that the actual motifs are significantly thicker and drawn in more detail than visible to the naked eye. Corrosion of the bi-metallic sceptres created a thick patina/corrosion layer, which completely hid the figurative decoration at the time of excavation.

Within the Italic territory, this exceptional technique is known from only one other context: the iron-bronze sheets from Pitino di San Severino Marche (Marche) (Fig. 7.3). Their function is until now unknown: they most likely served as coverings of an object in organic material, placed in the wealthy tomb of a woman (tomb 14) buried in the second half of the 7th century BC. Like the sceptres of Spoleto, the inside of the sheets is completely covered in bronze, while the exterior presents an anthropomorphic and zoologic decoration finished in engraved iron (cut "à jour") before the bronze was melted over it. Small air bubbles recognizable in the radiographs clearly demonstrate that the bronze was poured onto the iron and not hammered.

Technique B1 – Inlaying iron into bronze (Fig. 7.4)

A similarly chromatic effect may have also been created for the sheets for the Etruscan chariot from Populonia (Tuscany) (Emiliozzi et al. 1997, 155–177) (fig. 7.4A),

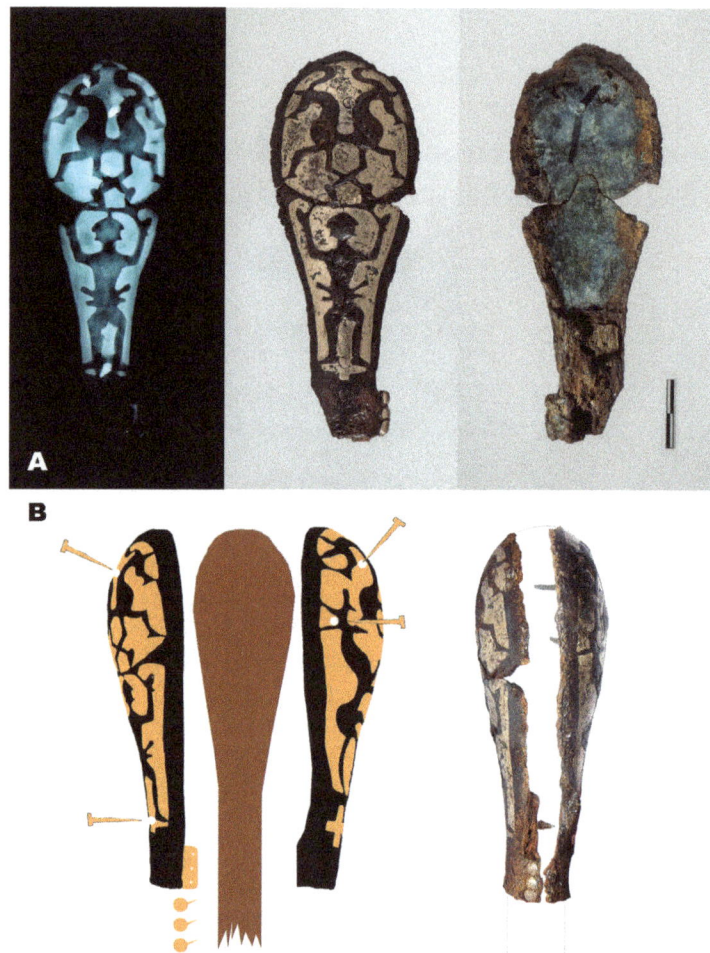

Figure 7.1. Technique A – Bronze cast on decorated iron sheets: A) Spoleto - Piazza d'Armi, tomb 8, a-side of the first mace-head-shaped sceptre made of two light-weight metal halves (radiography, front side and back side); B) Graphic reconstruction of the first mace-head sceptre nailed to a wooden shaft. Exhibited: Museo Archeologico Nazionale Spoleto, ItalyImage: © J. Weidig, Polo Museale dell'Umbria, S. Bonamore, N. Bruni.

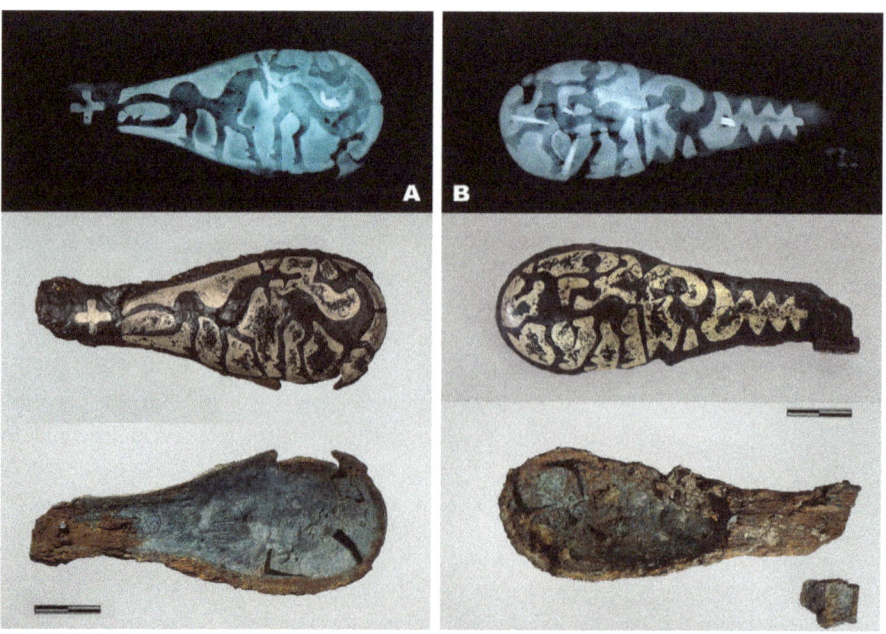

Figure 7.2. Technique A – Bronze cast on decorated iron sheets: A) Spoleto - Piazza d'Armi, tomb 8: b-side of the first mace-head-shaped sceptre made of two light-weight metal halves (radiography, front side and back side); B) and back side). a-side of the second mace-head-shaped sceptre made of two light-weight metal halves (radiography, front side). Exhibited: Museo Archeologico Nazionale Spoleto, ItalyImage: © J. Weidig, Polo Museale dell'Umbria

Bronze Cast on Decorated Iron Sheets. An Unusual Manufacturing Technique in Iron Age Italy

Figure 7.3. Technique A – Bronze cast on decorated iron sheets: Pitino di San Severino Marche, necropolis of Monte Penna, tomb 14: the central piece of the eight Iron-bronze sheets. Exhibited: Museo Archeologico Nazionale delle Marche, Ancona, Italy. Image: © J. Weidig, Museo Archeologico Nazionale delle Marche

Figure 7.4. Technique B1 – Inlaying iron into bronze: A) Bronze sheet from Populonia, "Tumulo dei carri"; B) Bronze belt buckles probably from Murlo, Poggio Civitate; C) Predator protome from Palestrina; D) Mace sceptre from Veio, Monte Michele, tomb 5. Exhibited/Kept: A) Museo Archeologico Nazionale Firenze, Italy; B) British Museum, London, GB, reg.no. 1977.2.-14.3-4; C) Archäologische Staatssammlung München, Germany; D) Museo Nazionale Etrusco di Villa Giulia, Roma, Italy. Image: A) Emiliozzi, 1997, 171, fig. 11; B) Haynes, 1985, 248, n. 11, fig. 11; C) Knauß – Gebauer 2015, 65, fig. 3.39, cat. 84; D) Boitani, 2001, fig. on page 116.

some Etruscan belt buckles from Murlo (Siena) (Fig. 7.4B), and a belt in the British Museum (Swaddling 1978; Haynes 1985, 248 n.11) . Those, however, were produced in bronze work with iron fillings – just like the well-known predator protome from Palestrina/Praeneste (Knauß – Gebauer 2015, 65–67, fig. 3.39a–c, Cat. Nr. 84 and fig. 3.40, Cat. Nr. 85.) (Fig. 7.4C), which has already been compared with similar Caucasian works by W.L. Brown (Brown 1960, 21–22, pl. Xa).

The mace-sceptre from the tomb of the princess n. 5 of the Monte Michele necropolises in Veio (670–650 BC) was also finished using this technique (Boitani 2001, 113–118. 115 n.I.G.8.15) (Fig. 7.4D). The 65 cm wooden shaft, decorated with silver nails, terminates in a cast bronze head with inlaid floral designs in iron. It was found in a war chariot, next to the weapons and casket-urn that contained the ashes of the man.

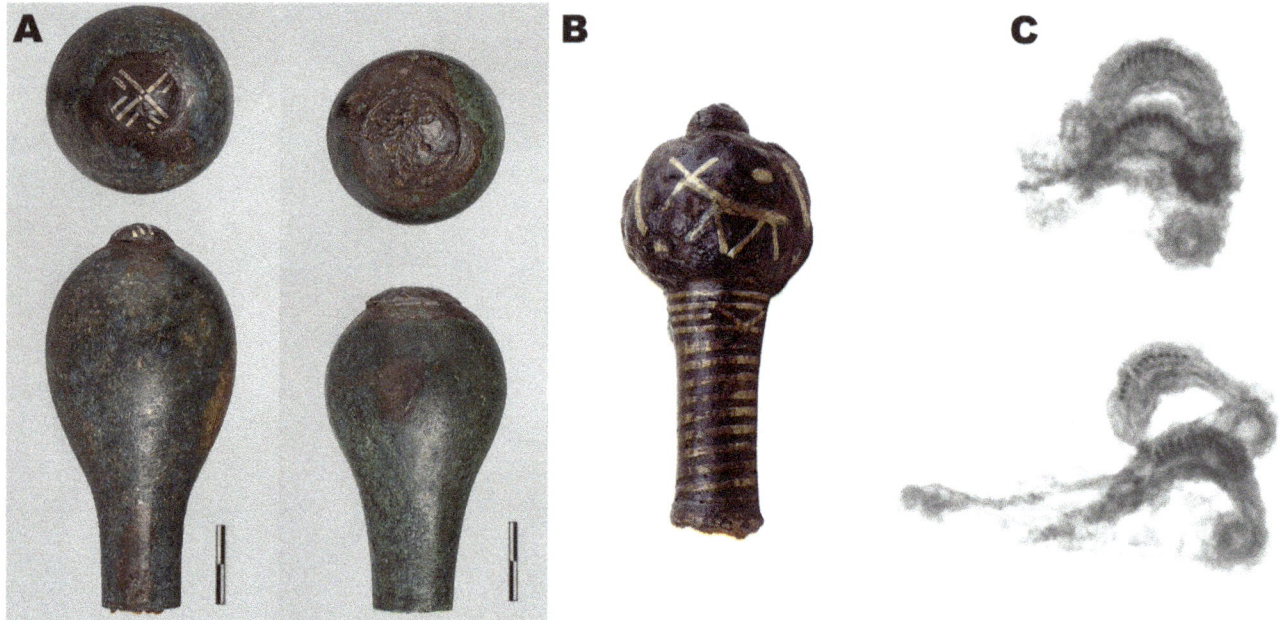

Figure 7.5. Technique B2 – Inlaying bronze/copper into iron: A) Spoleto - Piazza d'Armi, tomb 8: third and fourth mace-head-shaped sceptres cast in bronze with iron nails on the top; B) Iron mace sceptre from Pitino di San Severino, tomba 31; C) Radiography of iron fibulae from Spoleto - Piazza d'Armi, tomb 9. Exhibited: A, C) Museo Archeologico Nazionale Spoleto, Italy; B) Museo Archeologico Nazionale delle Marche, Ancona, Italy. Image: A) © J. Weidig, Polo Museale dell'Umbria; B) Colonna – Franchi Dell'Orto 1999, n. 453, fig. 53;) © J. Weidig.

Technique B2 – Inlaying bronze/copper into iron (Fig. 7.5)

Quite common in Apennine and Adriatic Central Italy is the inlaying of iron objects with wires of copper or bronze. It was used for the most part for decorations on iron brooches (Fig. 7.5C), scabbards for daggers or swords, belt buckles and bridles, but rarely on sceptres. In Spoleto, in the mace-sceptre cast in bronze the iron nail was inlaid with a copper cross (Fig. 7.5A), while the famous iron mace-sceptre from tomb 31 in Pitino di San Severino (Marche) was inlaid in copper with geometric and quadruped motifs (Colonna – Franchi Dell'Orto, 1999, n. 453, fig. 53) (Fig. 7.5B).

Technique C – Sandwich technique (Fig. 7.6)

However important the chromatic effect was, even if technique A could not be applied, certain mid-7th-century belt buckles from the necropolises of Fossa and Bazzano exhibit it. Two iron sheets decorated "à jour" with geometric motifs were completed; between these a thin sheet of bronze was placed, which was reminiscent of gold-plaiting; they were then closed with studs, which, in the case of Bazzano, Otefal 2002, t. sn. 2 were part of a variety of belt buckle of the so-called Capena type. (Fig. 7.6A) (Weidig 2014, 211, fig. 68A, 1235, n.1, pl. 375 T.S.n.2,1). In tomb 365 from Fossa a belt buckle was found together with a great

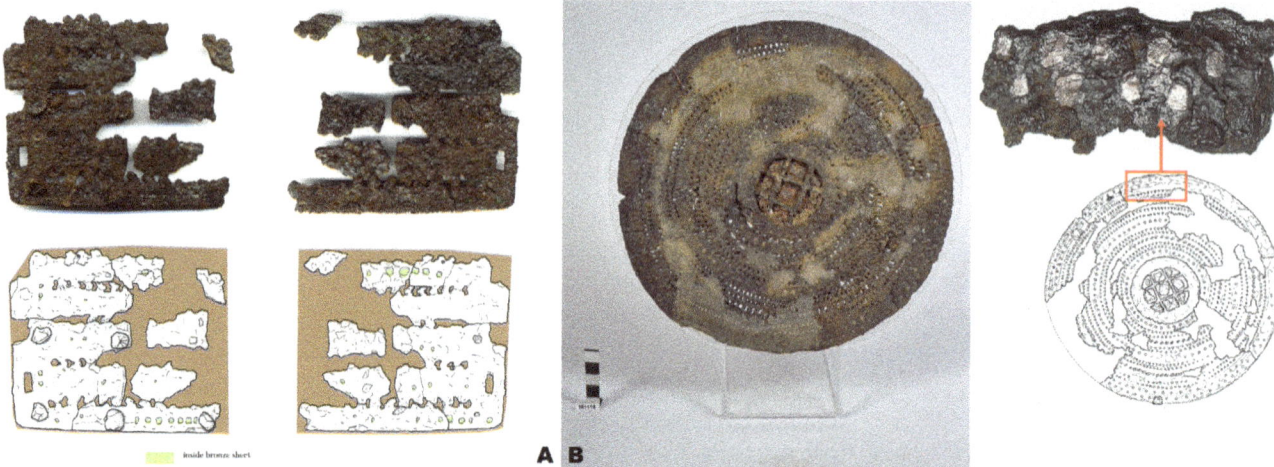

Figure 7.6. Technique C – Sandwich technique: A) Belt buckle from Bazzano, Otefal, tomb s.n. 2; B) Iron disc from Fossa, tomb 365. Exhibited/Kept: A) MUSE' Nuovo museo Paludi di Celano, Centro di restauro, Celano, Italy; B) Museo Archeologico Nazionale d'Abruzzo Villa Frigerj, Chieti, Italy. Image: A) © J. Weidig; B) photo: courtesy of Museo Archeologico di Chieti; draw: D'Ercole – Benelli 2014, 225 fig. 185.

iron disc, part of a female ornamental, cut "à jour" with central amber decoration and bronze insert along the border (Fig. 7.6B) (D'Ercole – Benelli 2004, 226, pl. 185): probably the bronze sheet was inserted using the sandwich technique.

The sceptres from Spoleto, nevertheless, are surely more sophisticated and labor-intensive, because the bronze casting was completed over the convex iron layers and already decorated "à jour."

The uniqueness of the sceptres from Spoleto complicates an identification of a workshop commissioned with their production. Although the figurative motifs follow Etruscan templates, they have been adapted to and refined for an Italic iconography.

The reproduction of the sceptres in iron and bronze (Fig. 7.7) by Fabio Fazzini

The study of the originals

The major indicators of the production methods of the originals are observable on the back side of the sceptre. In the half displaying the hunting scene, parallel grooves are noticeable, carried out probably with a file to level any irregularity in the bronze. In the exemplar decorated with the horse-master, one notices instead, in the center, what appears to be a crack, but is in reality an interruption of the casting caused by the cooling of the metal during melting. Still in the same half some missing bronze in the manes of the horses is noticeable. Such a shortage was probably caused by the iron at its coldest temperature, which caused the casting to be arrested.

It appears then quite probably to be a lost-wax casting with sprues placed in view of the face, which would have easily facilitated the removal of all canals and would have rendered the pouring of the bronze much easier, which would have easily flowed by means of gravity into all the parts of the object. The casting interruption visible only on the back side of the half with the horse-master is a clear indicator of the presence of two insertion canals, placed in the upper part of the object. The pouring was interrupted only in the lower part, due to the cooling of the alloy, while in the upper part, where the bronze was still fluid because of its proximity to the entrance funnel, no such interruption is visible. Other indicators include the voids created in correspondence to the equine manes, also on the same half. If the canals had been placed on the reverse side, it would have been impossible at that point to have a void in the material. At certain points, one may notice differences between the decorations visible on the originals and those that have become observable through the radiographs. It thus appears evident that some of the details of the ornaments in iron were encased in the pouring of the bronze. In light of this data acquired from the originals, the production of experimental copies proceeded.

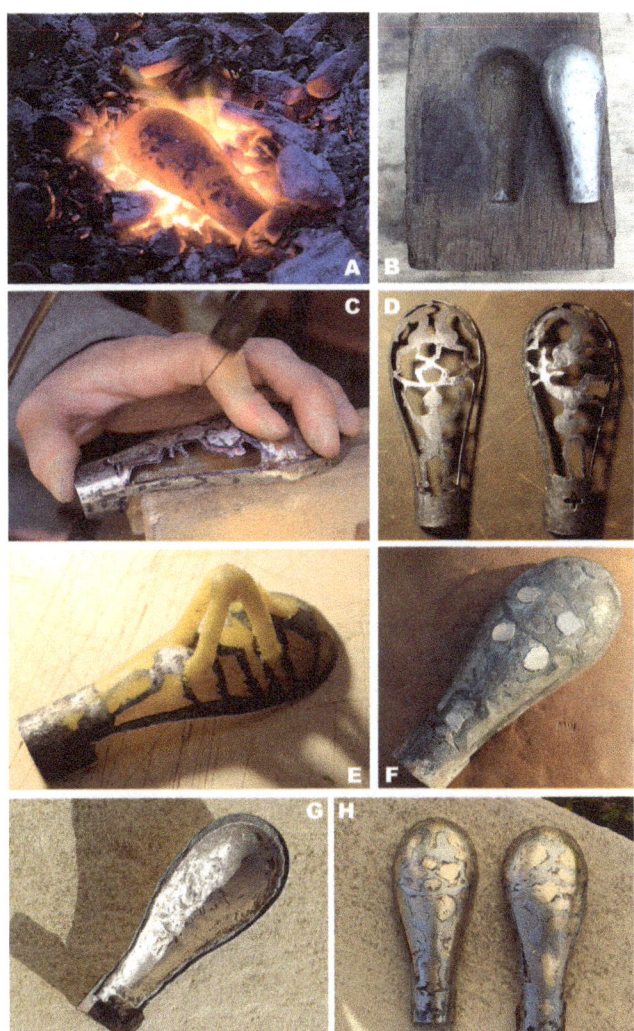

Figure 7.7. Reproduction of the first sceptre in iron and bronze: A) iron sheet heated in a forge; B) mould fashioned in negative on an oak log; C) decoration of the sheet by "openwork" method using a fretwork saw; D) sheets at the end of the decoration process; E) preparation for the lost-wax casting; F-G) one of the metal halves after the bronze melting, front and back side; H) metal halves after chasing and polishing process. Image: © Fabio Fazzini for Astra onlus.

The experimental copies

First it was necessary to produce two sheets in iron. Noting that the dimensions of the sceptres end up being almost identical, it is logical to suppose the use of a sort of mould to make both sides. In order to produce the sides in similar dimensions, a mould was fashioned in the negative, created out of an oak log. The sides were obtained from a sheet of soft iron .7 mm thick. The sheet was heated in a forge and was positioned on the wooden form already placed in a water bath to prohibit combustion on contact with the molten metal. With a ball peen hammer, the metal was pushed to the middle of the form. The process was repeated again and again, with various cycles of forging and hammering. Later, after the form of the sheets was well defined, excess material was cut off. After the removal of the excess, the round shape of the sides was corrected with light cold-hammering. At the end of this process, the pieces were refined and polished to create a surface as homogenous as possible.

After the forging phases came the preparatory designs for the decorative motifs. Decorations on the leaves were obtained by the "openwork" method, using a fretwork saw. At the conclusion of this long process, the pieces were prepared for the lost-wax casting.

Lost-wax casting

The voids of the openwork process were filled with a sheet of beeswax. The wax sheet was applied by pushing it in from the back side so that it partially came out of the voids, thus guaranteeing perfect adherence to the iron support. Once the excess wax was removed from the external part, the surface was then rendered homogenous paying attention not to leave any residual traces on the iron portions of the decoration. At the end of this phase, the vents and gates were positioned (spruing). In the central part of the sceptre's two halves, four sprues topped with cone-shaped funnels were positioned. Meanwhile two vents were positioned on the upper and the lower parts of the halves respectively. All of these elements were inserted directly into the filler wax of the voids. The halves being completed, they were then covered in a protective coat or investment. The molds, after having dried, were then baked allowing the wax to flow out of the internal portions. Once the baking of the molds was finished, the actual melting began (pouring). After that, the sprues were removed and finishing touches were applied (chasing). The surface was polished as much as possible to exhibit the metals as a cohesive whole without impurities or irregularities. After refining the pieces, the iron was hot-burnished in order to render its color darker and to throw into relief the lighter color of the bronze. The casting, as in the originals, still retains minute imperfections. In the part of the sceptre with the horse-master a slight shortage of bronze is noticeable in the background to the left, caused by the overly fast release of gas through the canals during the fusion process. In both parts, meanwhile, some iron elements of the decoration were completely encased by the bronze. This phenomenon was caused by the dip in some of the details of the iron layer, owing to the heat during the casting and baking, which rendered the metal too soft, causing it to fold toward the lower part. Finally, the sceptre's halves were mounted with bronze nails on a wooden support fashioned from a lathe-turned piece of hornbeam.

Conclusions

The results of the experiment positively confirm the hypotheses made from the observation of the workmanship visible on the originals. The final outcome was perfectly aligned with the originals, some defects notwithstanding, which we might say were amplified in the copies but still observable in the originals, too, for instance in the disappearance of certain parts of the fretwork decoration encased by the fusion.

Acknowledgements

Joachim Weidig is grateful to Dott. Mario Pagano and Dott. Tommaso Casci Ceccacci (Soprintendenza Archeologia delle Marche) for the permits to study the bronze discs from the Pitino necropolis at San Severino and for the analysis of the iron-bronze sheets from tomb 14 in the year 2015; Dott.ssa Silvia Bonamore and Fabio Milazzo for the Radiographs and Alessandra Sena for further information of the tomb 14.

Bibliography

Boitani, F., 2001. La tomba principesca n. 5 di Monte Michele. In: A. M. Moretti Sgubini, ed. 2001. *Veio, Cerveteri, Vulci. Città d'Etruria a confronto*. Rome, 2001, 113–118. 115 n.I.G.8.15. (for the sceptre of Veio)

Brown, W. L., 1960. *The Etruscan Lion*. Oxford, 21–22.

D'Ercole, V. – Benelli E., ed., 2004. *La necropoli di Fossa II. I corredi orientalizzanti e arcaici*. Pescara.

Emiliozzi, A. – Romualdi, A. – Cecchi, F. – Fiesoli, F. – Gennai, F. – Pecchioli, R., 1997. I veicoli dal tumulo dei Carri di Populonia. Necropoli di San Cerbone (Rep. 123-124.). In: A. Emiliozzi, ed., 1997, *Carri da guerra e principi etruschi*, Roma, 155–177.

Haynes, S., 1985. Etruscan Bronzes. London, 248 n.11.

Jucker, H., 1970. Etruscan Votive Bronzes of Populonia. In: S. Doeringer – D. G. Mitten – A. Steinberg, ed., 1970. *Art and technology. A symposium on classical bronzes*. Cambridge; London, 195–219.

Knauß, F. S. – Gebauer, J., ed., 2015. *Die Etrusker von Villanova bis Rom. Exhibition Staatliche Antikensammlung und Glyptothek München*. München, 65–67, fig.3.39a–c, Cat. Nr. 84 and fig. 3.40, Cat. Nr. 85..

Manca, M.L. – Weidig, J., ed., 2014. *Spoleto 2700 anni fa. Sepolture principesche dalla necropoli di Piazza d'Armi*. Spoleto: Soprintendenza ai Beni Archeologici dell'Umbria.

Swaddling, J., 1978. Etruscan bronze belt claps with iron inlay. In: *Studi Etruschi*, 46, 43–53.

Weidig, J., in press a. *Früheisenzeitliche etruskische und italische Zepter*. Jahrbuch RGZM.

Weidig, J., in press b. *Ikonographie und Deutung der figürlichen Szenen auf den Zeptern von Spoleto*. In: Festschrift für Markus Egg. RGZM.

Weidig, J., 2014. *Bazzano. Ein Gräberfeld bei L'Aquila (Abruzzen). Die Bestattungen des 8.–5. Jahrhunderts v. Chr. Untersuchungen zu Chronologie, Bestattungsbräuchen und Sozialstrukturen im apenninischen Mittelitalien*. Monographien des Römisch-Germanischen Zentralmuseums, Mainz, Nr. 112, 223–224. 1235 n. 1, tav. 375.

Weidig, J., 2014. Spoleto. Le tombe a circolo della necropoli orientalizzante di Spoleto, Piazza d'Armi. In: S. Rafanelli, ed., 2014. *Circoli di pietra in Etruria*. Catalogo della mostra, 192–197.

Weidig, J. – Bruni, N., 2015. Strutture tombali plurime a Spoleto. Elementi di differenze cronologiche, sociali e gruppi familiari nel VII sec. a.C. In: G. M. della Fina, ed., 2015. *La delimitazione dello spazio funerario in Italia dalla protostorica all'età arcaica. Recinti, circoli, tumuli*. Atti del XXII Convegno Internazionale di studi sulla storia e l'archeologia dell'Etruria, Orvieto. Annali Faina 22, 535–571.

Weidig, J., 2015. Studi sulla necropoli orientalizzante di Spoleto, Piazza d'Armi. Una visione preliminare. In: F. Gilotta – G. Tagliamonte, ed., 2015. *Sui due versanti dell'Appennino. Necropoli e distretti culturali tra VII e VI sec.a.C*. Atti del seminario Santa Maria Capua Vetere. Biblioteca di Studi Etruschi, 55, 47–77.

Weidig, J., 2015. I draghi appenninici. Appunti sulle raffigurazioni degli animali fantastici italici tra Abruzzo, Umbria e Marche. In: M.C. Biella – E. Giovanelli, ed., 2015. *Nuovi studi sul bestiario fantastico di età orientalizzante nella penisola italiana*. Quaderni di Aristonothos, 5, 247–272.

Weidig, J. – Bruni, N., 2017. The inheritance of power: King's sceptres and the infant princes of Spoleto Umbria. *Etruscan News,* 19(1), 6–7.

Weidig, J. 2017. Die Vererbung von Macht – Kleinkindergräber mit Waffen und Statussymbolen. In: J. Leskovar – R. Karl, ed., 2017. *Interpretierte Eisenzeiten. Fallstudien, Methoden, Theorie*. Tagungsbeiträge der 7. Linzer Gespräche zur interpretativen Eisenzeitarchäologie. Studien zur Kulturgeschichte von Oberösterreich, 47, 195–214.

Weidig, J. – Bruni, N. – Riva, A., 2017. Le sacerdotesse di Spoleto e il banchetto per l'aldilà – Nuovi studi sugli Umbri. *Spoletium*, 52–53, 161–167.

Weidig, J. – Bruni, N., 2018. Little heirs of an Umbrian royal family from the 7th century BC. In: J. Tabolli, ed., 2018. *From invisible to visible. New data a methods for the archaeology of infant and child burials in pre-Roman Italy*. Proceedings of the international conference Trinity College Dublin (24–25 April 2017). Studies in Mediterranean Archaeology (SIMA), CXLIX, 113–121.

8

Artful illumination: Technical study of four Hellenistic bronze lamps from the eastern Black Sea site of Vani

Jeffrey Maish, David Saunders, Nino Kalandadze, Marc Walton

J. Paul Getty Museum (Maish, Saunders)

Georgian National Museum Tiblisi

Northwestern University

jmaish@getty.edu

Abstract: The 2007 discovery of a large hoard at Vani, in the Republic of Georgia, yielded a rich trove of ancient bronzes and iron implements. Four large bronze lamps – two with elephant heads, one with performing Erotes, and another depicting Zeus in the form of an eagle carrying the youthful Ganymede – were a particular focus of conservation efforts and study. Cleaning revealed surfaces in an excellent state of preservation, while technical study and chemical analysis pointed to a variety of production techniques and sources for the materials, suggesting that the lamps and their materials were collected from a broad region of the eastern Mediterranean/northern Anatolia and/or were produced over an extended period of time around the late 2nd–early 1st century B.C.

Keywords: Vani; Bronze; Lamp; Hoard; Analysis

Introduction

Four large bronze lamps were recovered in 2007 as part of a hoard at the ancient Colchian settlement of Vani in the Republic of Georgia. The site is located in the Rioni River valley inland from the ancient Black Sea port of Phasis. Its earliest phases date to the 8th century B.C., with its final destruction around 50 B.C. perhaps by Pharnaces, king of the Bosphorus, and Mithridates VII, ruler of Pergamon. The sanctuary site has remnants of several temple structures and, following preliminary surveys in the 1930s and 40s, excavations by the Georgian Academy of Sciences began in 1947 (see Kacharava – Kvirkvelia 2008; Chichinadze – Kvavadze 2013). A selection of finds from the site formed the basis of the exhibition *Wine, Worship and Sacrifice: The Golden Graves of Ancient Vani*, organized in 2007–2009 by the Georgian National Museum, the Freer Gallery of Art and Arthur M. Sackler Gallery at the Smithsonian Institution and the Institute for the Study of the Ancient World (ISAW) in New York, with additional showings at the Fine Arts Museum in Houston, the Fitzwilliam Museum in Cambridge and the J. Paul Getty Museum in Los Angeles. Two lamps featuring elephant heads from the 2007 hoard were included in the exhibition at ISAW in 2008, and all four were exhibited at the J. Paul Getty Museum in 2009.

The hoard of metal artifacts was discovered by chance adjacent to a temple complex at the base of an ancient wall (Akhvlediani 2008; Akhvlediani – Kacharava – Matiashvili 2010; Akhvlediani et al. 2016). The source or purpose of the deposit is unknown but objects probably originated in a temple inventory (see Andrianou 2009 on furnishings in Greek houses and tombs). The objects may have been buried ritually at the bottom of the hill, hidden for protection prior to an invasion, or perhaps looted and deposited following a battle. The hoard is rich in bronze objects, including bowls, vessel-stands, couch (*kline*) leg parts and lamps, but also held two iron candelabra, a mass of iron projectile points and even a small deposit of beeswax. The authors reported previously on the bronze *kline* parts found in the pit (Maish et al. 2016) and continue here with an analysis of the four elaborately decorated three-arm bronze lamps, alongside a single-nozzle lamp from the same hoard. The lamps are remarkable for their subject matter, style and methods of manufacture, and their size alone suggests that they were used in a large architectural space such as a temple or sanctuary.

The lamp with Ganymede and Zeus and that with Erotes figurines were cleaned at the Getty as part of a collaborative project with the Georgian National Museum in preparation for their display (see Appendix below and http://www.getty.edu/art/exhibitions/vani/lamps.html). Conservation involved mechanical cleaning, with a scalpel and with some air abrasion using a soft grit abrasive. Some mild acid was also used in one area to break down a carbonate deposit. Cleaning under the microscope revealed a fine blue-green patina and well-preserved details, for example, of the eagle feathers on the Zeus and Ganymede lamp. The project provided the opportunity for a detailed study of the lamps, including radiography and inductively coupled plasma mass spectroscopy (ICP-MS) analysis of elemental and lead isotope compositions. The investigation revealed not only that the lamps were stylistically different, but also that they appear to have been manufactured by different methods.

The burial environment and preservation

The site of Vani in general, and the burial pit in particular, is characterized by a sandy soil (probably eroded from the parent rock), a lack of destructive soluble salts, and possible reduced water exchange with the surrounding environment. The pit itself was excavated in antiquity from soft sandstone (Georgian "tiri"), a material forming part of the present day geology of the site. This sandstone is fairly soft so may have been easily excavated with metal tools. In the millennia following deposition, the pit formed a fairly stable environment for the inorganic material, particularly the buried copper alloys. Burial environments with sandy soil generally allow for greater permeability of atmospheric gases. Elsewhere this soil type has been found to permit a greater dissolution of carbon dioxide, leading to the formation of carbonic acid and eventual formation of metal carbonates on bronzes. In tandem with the rapid carbonate formation and dissolution of copper is the rapid formation of protective tin oxide in the underlying tin-rich layer. These tin oxidation layers may in part account for the unusual blue-green patina evident on several Vani bronzes (compare, for example, a similar patina on an Etruscan mirror, Harvard Art Museum inv. 1977.216.2311). The presence of iron within the pit may also have conferred some initial anodic protection to the bronze. Iron is low on the chemical galvanic series and readily donates electrons, in effect "sacrificing" itself to protect metals higher in the series such as copper. Iron may have therefore conferred some initial protection to the bronzes in the pit and, in some instances, metallic cores remain in the iron objects.

The three-nozzle bronze lamp type

The three-nozzle lamp form is designed for suspension although, with a foot, it may also be used on a tabletop or stand (Franken 1996, 291–302, figs. 8–18 provides an overview of several examples). Suspension points coupled with three nozzles rendered these lamps more suitable for the illumination of larger spaces. Suspension is achieved either by the use of chains attached to perforated lugs or by integrating a locking lid that has a hanging point. In the latter case the lid is firmly locked to the lamp; it may slide through slots in the rim and lock with a twist. The relationship of lids to the overall lamp design is exemplified by a lid with griffin heads from the Mahdia wreck (Franken 1994, 294).

Large bronze lamps are uncommon, and the three-nozzle variety even more so. The form could be standardized but details modified or augmented to make unique creations (the basic form of the six-nozzle lamp discussed below has some similarities to three-nozzle examples from Mahdia and Pompeii discussed by Franken 1994, 291–302). Parallels are further limited by the unusual style and iconography of each Vani lamp, although we can compare Hellenistic single and double lamps with long narrow nozzles and flat tops, such as British Museum Q3544 and Q3561 (Bailey 1996, 8 and 10 respectively). Although of later 1st-century-A.D. dates, British Museum Q3650 (Bailey 1996, 34) includes depictions of elephant heads and the two-nozzle British Museum Q3649 (Bailey 1996, 33) includes lions protruding from unfurled leaves similar to the Vani six-nozzle lamp.

Three-nozzle elephant lamp or incense burner (Georgian National Museum N07:1-07/323, H: 11 cm. x L: 44 cm.)

The use of elephant models, particularly on lamps, is unusual, and the fairly accurate depictions of the heads on this example prompts a brief review of elephant characteristics and historic ranges. Elephant populations in the first centuries B.C. included two African varieties – the smaller (*loxodanta Africana pharaoensis*) used by the armies of Carthage, and the larger African bush elephant (*l. africana*) – and two Asian elephant types, the Indian *Elephas maximus* and Syrian subspecies *E.m. asurus* (extinct around 100 B.C.) The overall rendering in this bronze includes small ears and a head with two slightly protruding lobes, features characteristic of Asian varieties (Fig. 8.1). Such specific and accurate detail suggests the artist had some familiarity, perhaps even contact, with this elephant type. Asian elephants were first used for war in India and subsequently became a trade commodity as part of negotiated political alliances in Asia and Eastern Europe. They are depicted in various media, including contemporary bronze and lead weights from Syria (*e.g.*, J. Paul Getty Museum 96.AC.142 and 96.AI.146).

Wax modeling

Radiographic and visual examination reveals fine internal vertical and horizontal linear features. Based on the precision of the joins, as well as the absence of metal flow (characterized by join thickness and variation of material density), these features can be identified as wax-to-wax joins. Their presence suggests that the lamp was modeled

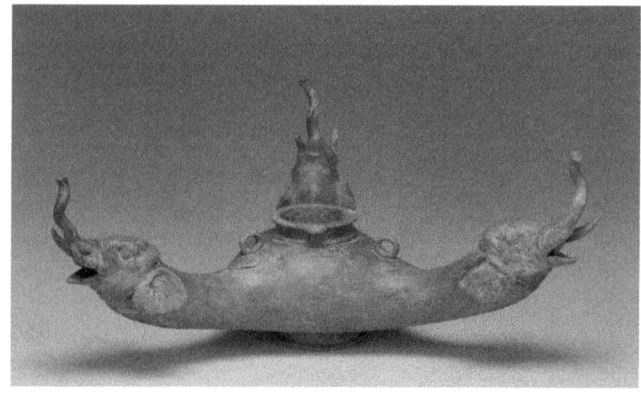

Figure 8.1. *Three-nozzle elephant lamp or incense burner*

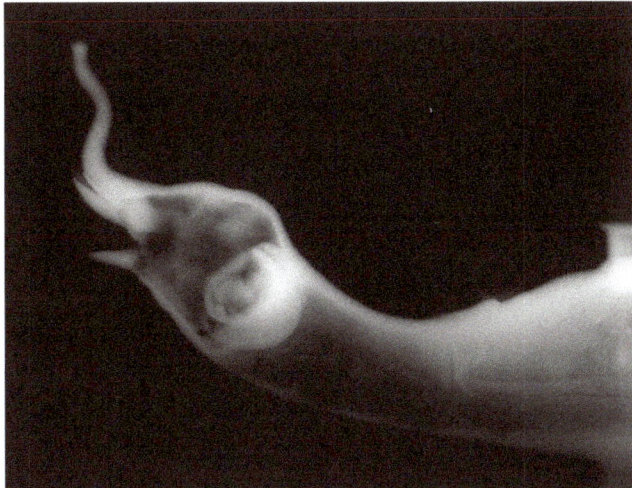

Figure. 8.2. Radiograph of *Three-nozzle elephant lamp*

and assembled from multiple wax components. The main body of the lamp was formed by shaping and joining upper and lower curved clam-shell shapes (perhaps created for a simpler unornamented type); wax sheets may have been pressed into molds to attain these upper and lower forms. The seam between the upper and lower section is visible in radiographs as wax thinning, where core material intruded internally into the wax-to-wax seam. Vertical seams indicate that the elephant heads were formed separately and joined to the central lamp body in the wax (Fig. 8.2). Radiographs also indicate variable wax thicknesses in the heads, suggesting some direct wax manipulation. Each separate elephant head could have been formed directly through external and internal shaping, with the trunks, tusks and ears attached later in the wax. Each trunk's extension over the mouth/nozzle openings suggests that this vessel might better be classified as an incense burner; used as a lamp, the trunks would have been immediately above the emerging flames.

The dimensions of each elephant's head are similar, albeit with some slight variations. The trunks are roughly the same lengths, with variations in curvature visible from the top. A comparison of left ears to right ears shows enough similarities to indicate that they were formed in left and right ear molds respectively (Fig. 8.3). The right ears are slightly flatter and squarer whereas the left ears have greater relief. The ring stand and neck collar were formed separately and attached to the lamp, and their dimensional regularity suggests that a turning method was used for both. The center of the lamp bottom was indented slightly. The swivel lid – detached from the neck/collar and missing on discovery – was probably a simple round disk. Such a lid could not have been used as a suspension point.

Casting

Radiographs do not show chaplets or repaired chaplet holes, suggesting possible core support through the elephants' mouths. Evidence of oval cast-in fills or repairs

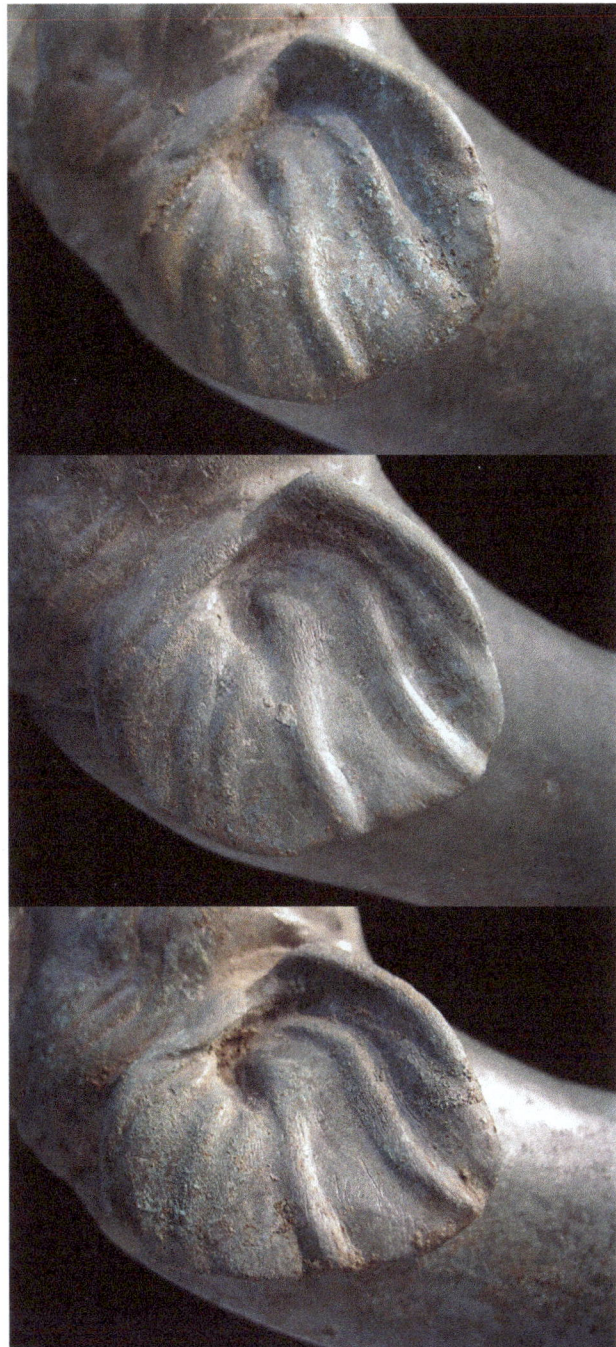

Figure 8.3. Detail of Elephant-ears

below one of the heads may indicate that the supports extended through the lower wax wall (below the heads). This would have allowed head details to be invested without the intrusion of a core support system and the lamp cast as a single piece.

Post-cast joining

The lamp body was finished smoothly, and visible surface striations may be remnants of polishing. There is an unusual repeating 'tire track' pattern under one nozzle. Since it was largely hidden, it may offer evidence of a rolling tool, possibly used in flattening and shaping a wax sheet. It could also be evidence of tool 'chatter' from post-cast finishing. The small hanging loops were probably added at this stage, although the underlying foliate design may have been part of the casting.

The six-nozzle elephant lamp

(Vani N07:1-07/324, H: 12 cm. x L: 41 cm.)

The six-nozzle lamp (Fig. 8.4) includes three elephant-heads (as with 07/323) and three torch bearers – Herakles, a satyr (or possibly Dionysos), and a Maenad (or possibly Ariadne). Compared to the other elephant lamp, the heads are depicted in a more schematic or generic manner. Besides casting, shaping of this lamp involved turning, soldering, incision, riveting and cold punch-work to create a series of draped necklace-like designs.

Examination reveals that the lamp was assembled from multiple components which were joined after casting. Three of the nozzles are formed in part by the torches each figure holds. These figures emerge from foliate designs on the central body between each elephant nozzle. A similar but smaller Hellenistic lamp with three flaring nozzles and masks of Medusa, Pan and Satyr between them can be found at the Istanbul Archaeological Museum (inv. no. 894 from Thessaloniki: see Atasoy 2005). The other three nozzles are formed by the elephant trunks. Comparison to the bronze lamp from the Mahdia shipwreck (Franken 1996, 296) suggests that these elephant trunks are modifications of a more standard lamp form with flared spouts. The lamp design also incorporates a turned foot.

The deep 'bayonet-style' neck has slots on either side of the neck interior (compare the grape-leaf lamp discussed below). Since the lamp itself has no loops, it is possible that the lid incorporated a means of suspension; when locked with a twist, a lid with loop could be used for hanging the lamp. A simpler three-nozzle lamp with a deeply slotted bayonet lid was found in the Mahdia shipwreck, which in turn parallels a lamp from Pompeii with a large finial-topped lid that provided the point of suspension (Tunis, Musée du Bardo F111; Museo Archeologico Nazionale di Napoli 72181; see Franken 1994, 291–302).

Wax modeling

The basic form of this lamp was initially modeled in the wax. The three protruding elephants' heads were modeled using a repousse-style technique by application of outward pressure to develop the heads. Three open cylinders were added in the wax over perforations between each elephant's head. Viewed from below, the walls of the lamp's body curve slightly outwards adjacent to each figure, indicating that the lamp was probably designed originally with six nozzles. The three figures holding torches have solid arms and heads but hollow torsos. The torches were also modeled separately and have small cast 'lips' pinned to the torch openings. The regularly shaped neck and foot were turned (turning marks are visible on the bottom of the foot).

Figure 8.4. The six-nozzle elephant lamp

Figure 8.5. Drawing of six-nozzle elephant-lamp

Casting and joining

The lamp was cast in multiple components: 1) the lamp body with elephant nozzles, 2) the three figures, 3) three torches and three torch lips. The figures were cast with stomach openings which matched openings in each torch (see Fig. 8.5). Once soldered together, the figure assemblages were slipped over the cylindrical openings in the lamp and soldered in place. Lamp oil could be wicked through the figures' abdomens to the torches.

Post-cast detailing

Sharply defined decorative details of the elephants' heads suggest repetitive use of post-cast incision and punch work. Individualized punched designs were added above each elephant's head. Round and horseshoe-shaped punching approximately 2.4 mm in diameter (the latter perhaps produced by an angled round punch) produced circular chain links, while a pointed graver was used to create the fine texture around the elephants' eyes. Broader chisel-type cuts were used to roughen the elephants' skin and to create a contrast with the smooth skin of the torch bearers.

Ganymede and Zeus lamp

(Vani N07:1-107/326 H.15 cm., W. 31 cm., L. 33 cm.)

The Ganymede lamp has the most sophisticated casting and joining of the four large lamps (Fig. 8.6). Zeus, in the form of a large eagle, carries Ganymede in his

Figure 8.6. Ganymed and Zeus Lamp

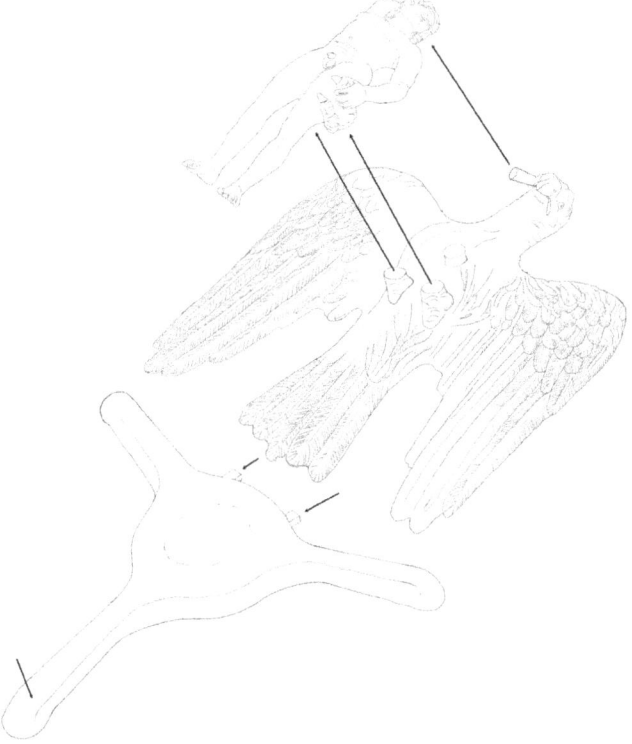

Figure 8.7. Drawing of Ganymed and Zeus

claws, and the youth in turn grasps the eagle's head. The composition is widespread in Hellenistic and Roman art, occurring in diverse media, and can be traced back to a lost bronze by the fourth-century BC sculptor Leochares (see Sichtermann 1988, 163–166, nos. 192–256.)

In contrast to the elephant lamps, the two figures are ornamental additions to a standard three-nozzle lamp form. Hanging loops are attached to the lamp part, which itself would be largely hidden when suspended. The eagle has large, intricately decorated wings folded at their leading edges to create volume. The bird was cast as an open shape with no back, evidently to be viewed from below. Ganymede's torso is hollow with a large casting porosity (visible in radiographs) in the lower solid leg, as well as a large solid central plug. The head and upper torso of the figure are likewise open, and radiographs of the legs show evidence in areas of an irregularly shaped core.

Wax models

The lamp includes sculpted detail in inaccessible locations, such as the eagle's stomach, which indicates that the figures were fashioned separately and joined in the wax. Irregular cavities within the legs suggest direct work over a support, possibly organic. By working in the wax, the sculptor was also able to contour and fit Ganymede's body more closely to the eagle, and develop Ganymede's grip on the bird (which as a consequence produced his slightly enlarged glove-like hands). To facilitate post-cast metallurgical joining, the wax assemblage was cut above the eagle's talons (which were cast with the human figure), while Ganymede's outstretched lower arm was cut and cast with the eagle. This left the eagle model without feet, and Ganymede's lower arm attached to the eagle's head. Similarly, for casting, the wax Ganymede would have had talons attached to his back and a truncated lower left arm. A considerable effort was made to render details of the eagle feathers, and these may have been enhanced further following casting.

Casting

Computed tomographs and visual observation support our interpretation of this lamp as being composed of three separate castings: a more standard three-nozzle lamp form; the eagle; and the Ganymede figure (Fig. 8.7). Radiographs show a large cylindrical plug at the center of the composition. This corresponds to the probable "sprue" for the eagle, which was simply cut off following casting and left unfinished, as it was hidden by the Ganymede figure. Gaps on the interior of the eagle's legs indicate joining and reworking of separately cast parts.

Post-cast joining

The components were metallurgically joined at three points between the Ganymede and eagle, and at three points between the lamp and eagle. The eagle's legs and Ganymede's left arm were soldered together. Evidence of the joins can be seen in the form of a discoloration of Ganymede's left wrist and file markings and gaps on the inside of each eagle leg. Two tabs connect the leading edges of the eagle's wings to the lamp body, and the eagle's tail is tacked to the bottom of one lamp nozzle.

Lamp with Erotes

(Vani N07:1-07/327, H: 26 cm. x L: 42 cm.)

The lamp form was shaped with three nozzles and a flat upper surface with a central, hinged lid (Fig. 8.8). It is notable for its comparative lack of detailing, and its simple contours and unusual flat-topped shape are similar to a single-nozzle Sarmatian lamp excavated at Klimenkovski Farm in the Ukraine (see Treister 2003, 299) Smaller examples with flat top profiles can also be found in the British Museum (Q3544; Q3561; Q3652; Bailey 1996, 8. 10 and 34) and the Istanbul Archaeological Museum (inv. no. 1132 from Homs, Syria in Atasoy 2005). During treatment we found a small fragment of charcoal, identified as hornbeam (Cartwright 2009), a local wood still encountered in Georgia. The fragment was radiocarbon dated to 2248 +- 35 BP, a date earlier than expected (Rafter AMS Report 2009).

The lamp has top and bottom loops for suspension, so clearly was meant for the interior illumination of a large space. The lower set of loops were presumably for suspending a secondary decorative element or lamp. The top loops are laid out in a roughly equilateral-triangle pattern and the circular opening of the lamp is precisely laid out within this pattern. Four small Eros figures were attached to the top of each nozzle and the lid – a lute player, a kithara player, a dancer and a torch-bearer.

Modeling and casting

The absence of wax-to-wax (or solder) join features in radiographs suggests that the entire lamp shape may have been modeled directly over a core. If the charcoal found inside the lamp is to be interpreted as manufacturing remains, this could suggest that wax was modeled over a wooden core support – although clay is more likely. The lamp has oval repairs on the curved lower surfaces beneath each nozzle, possibly where support pins, used to suspend the core, penetrated the upright wax model. If the lamp were cast inverted, the core would have been supported through the four lamp openings (three nozzles and central lid), obviating the need for additional supports. Inverted casting may have been problematic as the flat horizontal surface might not have filled evenly, causing air or gas bubbles to be trapped during casting.

Radiographs reveal that the four Eros figures are solid castings. Their weights following cleaning were: dancer – 513 gm., torch bearer – 521 gm., lute player – 524 gm. and kithara player – 579 gm. Similarities between all four suggest that the basic model was the figure alone (i.e., the dancer), with versions manipulated slightly and accessories added, increasing their weight to varying degrees. Metal porosities are visible in radiographs and one figure has an ancient post-cast repair.

The mounting location for each of the Eros figures was ascertained through study of their bases alongside raised

Figure. 8.8. Lamp with Erotes

rectangular deposits that were observed on the top of each spout. The latter were defined through cleaning, and following analysis, were found to be predominantly lead oxides. This confirmed our initial thoughts that the four figures had originally been attached with a leaded solder. Each figure's base has a slightly different profile – some have sharp corners while others were slightly rounded – and these corresponded closely to the solder remains, providing firm evidence for their placement. The Erotes were reattached during the recent conservation project by making separate epoxy interfaces and adhering them with a reversible acrylic adhesive.

Grape-leaf lamp

(Vani N07:1-07/325, H: 16.5 cm. x L:35 cm.)

The ornate single-spouted grape-leaf lamp (Akhvlediani et al 2016, fig. 11) was found with the other multiple-nozzle lamps in the hoard and was studied at the Georgian National Museum in Tbilisi in 2010. Although it has a carrying handle, the lamp is fairly large and differs from smaller more portable bronze and terracotta lamps. It could have been used as a table lamp, carrying lamp, hanging lamp, and possibly even as a post-mounted lamp. The upper portion is covered with detailed depictions of leaves and garlands, and the intricate detailing suggests lost wax casting.

Some leaves are perforated or indented with small 1-mm-diameter depressions, probably created in the wax. Their depth and regularity suggest that they may have been mounting locations for lost elements, perhaps glass or silver inlay (compare the silver additions on the bronze lebes, Getty 96.AC.51). These would mimic dewdrops, which could have been further highlighted by the nearby lamp flame. The size, shape and undercutting of the leaf covering the handle suggests that it was cast separately and metallurgically joined to the lamp. Four points of connection between leaf and lamp were identified – at the leaf base along a central rib to the main handle; to two vine projections; and at the leaf midpoint to an elongated curling tendril.

There are two aligned rectangular notches on the top of the nozzle with an associated small, oval surface loss between what was most probably an attachment point for a lost element. The attachment may have been a small figure, a protective shield/reflector or perhaps the location of a soldered hanging loop (compare the Roman lamp BM Q3779; Bailey 1996, 64). The lamp has several other possible points for chain attachment; there are two cylindrical posts on either side of the nozzle base, as well as two cast rings on either side of the handle. Although these may have been used, they appear well integrated into the overall relief design of the lamp and may not be entirely functional. The handle also has two aligned, rectangular perforations, possibly for insertion of a ground post in the absence of a table or ceiling suspension.

Slots in the lid's opening would have accommodated two vertical tabs or keys which, when rotated, would have locked the lid in place. This unusual 'bayonet' mechanism is shallower than that seen for the six-nozzle elephant lamp discussed above, and may be more typical for lids that are combined with figures (see, for example, Naples no inv. number (Mutz 1972, 141 fig. 399–402), where a small bronze figure locks to the heavy lid which in turn rests on the lamp; a two-nozzle lamp from Pompeii with a lid figure (Naples Inv. 72251; Pernice 1925, 58, fig. 78); and a double-nozzle lamp with a standing figure (Naples 72280; Pernice 1925, pl. XVI)). The deeper form seen on the six-nozzle lamp was perhaps intended to be load-bearing and designed for the suspension of the whole.

Elemental Analysis (Tab. 1)

Small drilled samples were analyzed by inductively coupled mass spectroscopy (ICP-MS; undertaken by Marc Walton) for major, minor and trace elements, as well as lead isotope compositions (see also Kuparadze et al. 2008; Khakhuatayshvili 1999; Treister 1996 and Tsetskhladze 1995). Results are presented in Table 1. Elemental compositions range from 2.4–20.5 % Pb and 5.1 – 9.8% Sn. Additional results for lead isotopes (^{206}Pb, ^{207}Pb and ^{208}Pb) are also presented below (for Hellenistic comparanda, see Hook – Craddock 1996, 155–162, specifically Q3554, Q3561, Q3649, Q3650, and Q3652).

Lead (Pb)

Lead levels in both the six-nozzle elephant lamp (14.42%) and three-nozzle elephant lamp (9.19%) are elevated compared to the other two lamps. Hook and Craddock 1996 (144) suggest lamps of lower lead content could be pre-Hellenistic, while alloys with slightly higher lead contents are of Hellenistic date. Higher lead content in the three-nozzle elephant lamp perhaps allowed for better flow of molten metal into a detailed mold at a lower melting point. Use of a highly leaded alloy may have facilitated later cold working, such as the surface punch-work.

Tin (Sn)

Tin content for all lamps is low, from 3.24 to 5.42%, consistent with Mediterranean bronze lamps produced from 300 to 1 B.C. Tin content in lamps increases significantly in the first century A.D. (see Sn Histogram in Hook – Craddock 1996, 147).

Zinc (Zn)

The alloy of the Ganymede lamp has slightly elevated levels of zinc compared to the other three large lamps. Elevated zinc levels could suggest re-use of metal. However, zinc levels are generally low (0.5% or lower), which is consistent with Hellenistic production. Zinc in significant levels does not appear in lamp alloys until the end of the 2nd century A.D. (see Hook – Craddock 1996, 148).

Iron (Fe)

The iron levels in the Ganymede and Eros lamps are slightly elevated, a possible indication of earlier production (Bailey 1996, 152). Iron can be used to change the alloy color, but more likely reflects reuse or poor smelting control.

Arsenic (As) and Cobalt (Co)

Trace elements are the most distinct with the Ganymede lamp. The arsenic levels are slightly elevated (0.06%) compared to the other lamps, and may be an additional

Table 8.1. Elemental Analysis

Lamp	Cu	Sn	Pb	Zn	Fe	Ni	Mn	P	As	Sb	S	Co	Ag	Bi
07/323	85.68	3.24	9.19	0.31	0.31	0.05	0.00	0.01	0.04	0.02	0.00	0.07	0.056	0.025
07/324_1	81.23	3.30	14.42	0.28	0.10	0.02	0.01	0.01	0.05	0.02	0.01	0.06	0.037	0.043
07/324_2	58.06	5.54	35.53	0.00	0.09	0.03	NR	NR	0.25	NR	NR	0.03	0.35	0.13
07/324_3	78.20	5.03	16.12	0.00	0.02	0.10	NR	NR	0.18	NR	NR	0.05	0.25	0.06
07/325_1	70.37	3.30	25.49	0.00	0.05	0.04	NR	NR	0.26	NR	NR	0.11	0.33	0.05
07/325_2	69.37	3.81	26.12	0.00	0.00	0.15	NR	NR	0.23	NR	NR	0.03	0.27	0.02
07/326	86.71	4.50	6.33	0.55	0.57	0.02	0.01	0.01	0.06	0.13	0.00	0.00	0.166	0.012
07/327	87.70	5.42	4.69	0.30	0.79	0.01	0.00	0.01	0.01	0.03	0.01	0.01	0.119	0.015

Key: 07/323 3-nozzle elephant burner, 07/324 6-nozzle elephant lamp (sample 1 body; sample 2 from weld area of satyr to torch; sample 3 from weld area bottom of calyx), 07/325 lamp with grape leaf, 07/326 Ganymede lamp, 07/327 lamp with Erotes

indicator of earlier production. Arsenic may be introduced from arsenical copper in the alloy. Cobalt levels (as in the three-spout elephant lamp and grape-leaf lamp) are slightly elevated, though not significantly.

Lead isotope analysis (Tab. 2 with Diagram 8.1)

Isotopic results clearly exclude Laurion as a source for lead, as well as Sardinia and Spain (on the use of lead isotope analysis for source identification, see Pollard 2009 and Gale 2009 and Kuleff 2006). Two lead isotope plots show the different potential associations of the lamps and, for additional reference, the Vani torso (Georgian National Museum 2/996-43; Kacharava – Kvirkvelia 2008, 45), to isotope fields in A) Bulgaria (Rhodope Mountains are ellipses 6 and 7) and B) the Turkish Black Sea coast (see Kuleff et al 2006 and Sayre 2001). A sample of Georgian galena (lead ore) was also analyzed and found to lie outside the isotopic fields associated with the lamps (below graphed in the upper right).

Table 8.2. Lead Isotype Analysis

Lamp	$^{208}Pb/^{206}Pb$	$^{207}Pb/^{206}Pb$	$^{206}Pb/^{204}/Pb$
3-nozzle elephant	2.0773	0.8382	18.67
Standard deviation	0.0011	0.0014	0.09
%RSD	0.05	0.17	0.50
6-nozzle elephant	2.0781	0.8384	18.53
Standard deviation	0.0029	0.0011	0.09
%RSD	0.14	0.13	0.46
Zeus and Ganymed	2.0862	0.8458	18.70
Standard deviation	0.0017	0.0008	0.13
%RSD	0.08	0.10	0.69
Erotes	2.0819	0.8407	18.53
Standard deviation	0.0016	0.0005	0.07
%RSD	0.08	0.06	0.38
Vani Torso	2.0795	0.8387	18.5962
Standard deviation	0.0016	0.0018	0.1636
%RSD	0.08	0.22	0.88
Georgian galena	2.0992	0.8499	18.79
Standard deviation	0.0003	0.00088	0.05
%RSD	0.01	0.10	0.27

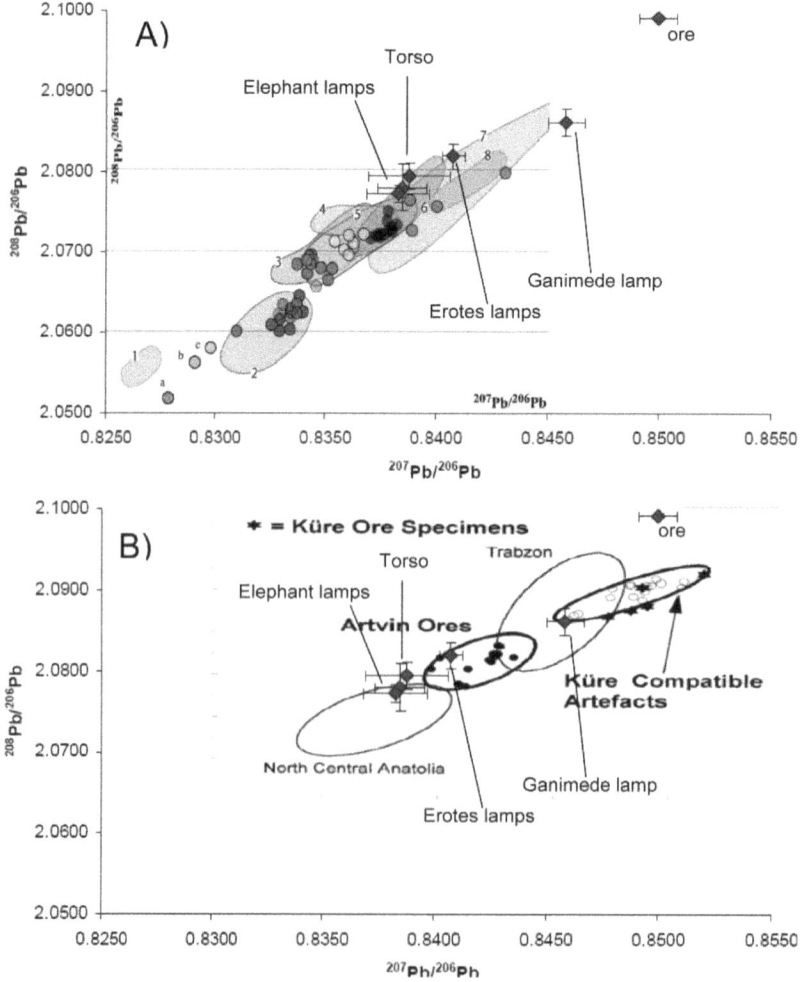

Diagram 8.1. Lead Isotope plots showing the different potential associations of the lamps to isotope fields in A) Bulgaria and B) the Turkish Black Sea coast. For further information see Kuleff et al. 2006.

Discussion and Conclusions

The lamps from the Vani Hoard are remarkable for both their variations in style and their production methods (see Barr-Sharrar 1994 for further lamp parallels). In addition to its characteristic punch-work surface designs (probably produced post-casting), the six-nozzle lamp is distinct for its complex multi-part assembly. Assembled figural parts were fitted over pre-formed lamp tubes through which oil flowed to the individual torches. This lamp is additionally distinguished by its high lead content and stylistically simpler modelling.

A streamlined wax modeling process is apparent in the three-nozzle elephant head lamp (or incense burner), where wax-to-wax joins are clearly visible in radiographs, and molds were probably used in the production of the wax models for the left and right ears. Wax was also modeled to vary the curvature of each elephant trunk. In contrast to the six-nozzle elephant lamp, the rendering of the elephants' heads is fairly naturalistic, with features identifiable as those of an Asian elephant.

The Ganymede lamp was carefully formed in three parts which were joined together in the wax. Conceptually different from the other examples, the figures attach below and hide a more standard lamp form. The figures were developed separately, as evidenced, for example, by the inaccessible detail of the lower eagle-body. Additional feather details of the eagle were probably incised in the wax. Particular care was taken to form the bonds between eagle and Ganymede in the hands and talons, and the wax was carefully divided for casting at locations which would simplify metallurgical joining. Metallurgical joins were effected at both the eagle's legs and Ganymede's lower arm at the eagle's head. The lamp itself was attached to the back of the eagle at three tabs. Analysis of the bronze alloy highlights higher levels of several trace elements than in the other lamps.

The lamp with Erotes pairs a simple lamp form with four small, more fully rendered figures. Similarities between these figures suggest that they may be based on a common model, although this would require further comparisons for confirmation. Whereas joins in the six-nozzle and Ganymede lamps were effected through fusion-type welding (using a bronze alloy), the Erotes were attached to the upper lamp surface using a lead-based solder. Perforated lugs above and below the lamp suggest that other elements, perhaps even a second lamp, were suspended below. Holes in the walls immediately below the lamp openings were filled following casting and may have been locations for a type of core support.

The six-nozzle elephant lamp is technologically distinct, while the other three large lamps share similarities. For example, the Erotes lamp and the three-nozzle elephant lamp both include post-cast fills in their spouts, possibly points of core support. The lamps' alloy compositions vary primarily in lead content, with additional variation noted in some minor and trace elements. Compositional dissimilarities suggest different ore sources or possible metal recycling. The two elephant lamps are distinct from one another as regards style and technology, but their isotopic ratios are closer to one another than to the other two lamps. Interestingly, the six-nozzle elephant lamp, presumably worked more extensively after casting, had the highest quantity of lead in its alloy (the addition of lead presumably making the surface softer for post-cast working). The Ganymede lamp by contrast had a lower lead content but was higher in some trace elements.

Isotopic plots of lead for these lamps indicate sources extending along the northern section of Anatolia to Bulgaria to the west and to the east towards the Rioni basin in Georgia, e.g., Artvin, Trabzon and Rhodope. Anatolian lead sources are within close proximity to Vani, but the Trabzon source for the Ganymede lamp could indicate production by a different workshop. This could also point to a variation in a workshop's lead sourcing. In addition to lead source locations, consideration should also be given to possible Asian elephant "models" to the south and east of Vani, and Sarmatian parallels to the north in the Ukraine for the profile of the Erotes lamp. These factors highlight Vani's position at a crossroads in the eastern Black Sea region. If workshops were close to the lead sources, this would place them in northern Anatolia or perhaps even in the vicinity of Vani itself, where bronze workshop remains (including slag, chaplets and a small pit) have been found (Kacharava – Kvirkvelia – Chi 2008, 75; Gigolashvili 2008). Variations in the lamps' styles and technologies suggest production by different workshops and/or in different time periods. Further research is needed to fix the dates of the lamps, but based on the stratigraphy of the excavation, analysis of organic materials found within one, as well as the lamps' styles, subject and iconography, the late Hellenistic period (late 2nd to early 1st B.C) is likely.

Appendix – Cleaning of the Ganymede and Erotes lamps

Removal of the dirt and iron compounds from the Ganymede lamp revealed a fine and richly detailed surface. The heavy sand encrustation was removed by application of distilled water and cleaning mechanically with metal and wooden tools. Soil was also removed from the interior. Exterior cleaning produced a slightly variegated surface as iron was deposited in areas buried in contact with projectile points. Some areas, notably Ganymede's torso, were stained orange-brown by the attached iron spear points. In general the lamp cleaning revealed a compact overall blue-green patina with fine surface detailing. One area of the figure also retained a purplish cuprite patina.

The thin carbonate crust on the Erotes lamp and figures was cleaned mechanically under a binocular microscope revealing a blue-green patina. The patina was thin, and the underlying metal was well preserved. A few areas preserved formations of fibrous malachite (resembling textile pseudomorph) and areas of the surface also preserved markings from wax or metal polishing. Adhered remnants of iron projectile points were removed, leaving reddish to black staining in areas. The interior of the lamp was filled with a sandy soil with a small clay component. The interior was carefully excavated and, as noted, several grams of charcoal were found in the main lamp chamber. Soil samples were bagged for future study.

The lid of the Erotes lamp was locked open by copper corrosion products which were determined to be slightly soluble in a weak acid. Cleaning elsewhere on the lamp showed a high-level metal preservation with little mineralization, so the hinge corrosion was removed with the dropwise application of dilute nitric acid (the concern being to avoid dissolution and weakening of a completely mineralized hinge). Gas evolution indicated carbonates were being reduced. This area was then rinsed with de-ionized water. The lid was closed after a week of gradual cleaning.

Bibliography

Andrianou, D. 2009. *The Furniture and Furnishings of Ancient Greek Houses and Tombs*. Cambridge: Cambridge University Press.

Akhvlediani, D. 2008. A Hoard from Vani. *Iberia-Colchis – Researches on the Archaeology and History of Georgia in the Classical and Early Medieval Period* 4: 129, 210 (English summary).

Akhvlediani, D. – Kacharava, D. – Matiashvili, N. 2010. Report on the work done in 2007 on the Former City Site of Vani. *Journal of Georgian Archaeology* 19: 33–45.

Akhvlediani, D. et al. 2016. The Hoard from the City-State of Vani, *Bulletin of the Georgian National Academy of Sciences* 10(2), 182–191.

Atasoy, S., 2005. *Bronze Lamps in the Istanbul Archaeological Museum – An illustrated catalogue*. BAR International Series 1436. Oxford: BAR Publishing.

Bailey, D.M. 1996. *A Catalogue of the Lamps in the British Museum IV, Lamps of Metal and Stone, and Lampstands*. London: British Museum Publications Ltd.

Barr-Sharrar, B. 1994. The Bronze Lamps. In: Hellenkemper-Salies, G. et al., ed., *Das Wrack. Der antike Schiffsfund von Mahdia*, Köln Rheinland-Verlag GmbH, 639–655.

Cartwright, C. 2009. *British Museum wood identification report*.

Chichinadze, M., – Kvavadze, E., 2013. Pollen and Non-pollen Palynomorphs in Organic Residue from the Hoard of Ancient Vani, (Western Georgia). *Journal of Archaeological Science* Vol. 40 no. 5 May 2013, 2237–2253.

Franken, N., 1996. Candelabrum Corinthium. In: *Neue Forschungen zum Schiffsfund von Mahdia*. Bonner Jahrbücher 196. 276–309.

Gale, N.H., 2009. A response to the paper of A.M. Pollard: What a long, strange trip it's been: lead isotopes and archaeology. In A. Shortland et al., ed., *From Mine to Microscope – Advances in the Study of Ancient Technology*. Oxford: Oxbow Books. 191–196.

Gigolashvili, E. 2008. Bronze Statuary and Bronze Production in the Ancient City Site of Vani. *Iberia-Colchis: Researches on the Archaeology and History of Georgia in the Classical and Early Medieval Period* 4: 14–18 (with English summary, 201–202).

Hook, D. – Craddock, P. 1996, Appendix. The Scientific Analysis of the Copper-alloy lamps: aspects of Classical alloying practices. In: Bailey, D.M., *A Catalogue of the Lamps in the British Museum IV, Lamps of Metal and Stone, and Lampstands*, London: British Museum Publications Ltd. 144–163

Kacharava, D. – Kvirkvelia, G. – Chi, J. Y. 2008. *Wine, Worship and Sacrifice: The Golden Graves of Ancient Vani*. Princeton: Institute for the Study of the Ancient World in association with Princeton University Press.

Khakhuatayshvili D.A. 1999. The Archaeometallurgy of the Asian Old World. *University Monograph 89, MASCA Research Papers in Science and Archaeology* 16, Vincent Pigott Ed., University Museum, University of Pennsylvania.

Kuleff, I. – Iliev, I. – Pernicka, E. – Gergova, D. 2006. Chemical and lead isotope compositions of lead artefacts from ancient Thracia (Bulgaria). *Journal of Cultural Heritage* Volume 7.4, 244–256.

Kuparadze, D. M. et al. 2008. Ancient Georgian Metallurgy and its Ore Base. In: Gurova, M. – Kostov, R. – Gaydarska, B., ed., *Geoarchaeology and Archaeomineralogy, Proceedings of the International Conference, 29–30 October 2008, Sofia*. Sofia: St. Ivan Rilski. 248–252.

Maish, J. – Walton, M – Saunders, D. – Kalandaze, N., 2016. Technical Study of the Bronze Kline Legs from Vani. In: A. Giumlia-Mair – C. Mattusch, eds. *Proceedings of the XVIIth International Congress on Ancient Bronzes, Izmir*, Monographies Instrumentum 52, Autun: Editions Mergoil. 103–109.

Mutz, A., 1972. *Die Kunst des Metalldrehens bei den Römern*. Basel and Stuttgart: Birkhäuser Verlag.

Pernice, E., 1925. *Gefässe und Geräte aus Bronze. Hellenistische Kunst in Pompeii*, Band IV, Berlin & Leipzig: Verlag von Walter de Gruyter & Co.

Pollard, N.H., 2009. What a long, strange trip it's been: lead isotopes and archaeology. In: A. Shortland et al., ed., *From Mine to Microscope – Advances in the Study of Ancient Technology*. Oxford: Oxbow Books. 181–189.

Rafter GNS Science, 2009. AMS Result, NZA 32939. September 29, 2009, Lower Hutt, NZ.

Sichtermann, H. 1988. "Ganymedes" *LIMC* IV. Zürich and Münich: Artemis Verlag. 154–169.

Treister, M. 1996. *The Role of Metals in the Hellenstic Era*. Leiden and New York: E.J. Brill.

Treister, M., 2003. Bronze Lamps of the Hellenistic period and the first centuries AD in the North Pontic Area. In: L. Chrzanovski, ed., *Lychnological Acts 1: actes du 1er Congrès international d'études sur le luminaire antique (Nyon-Genève, 29.9–4.10.2003)*. Montagnac: Editions Monique Mergoil. 293–299.

Tsetskhladze, G. R. 1995. Did the Greeks go to Colchis for Metals? *Oxford Journal of Archaeology* Volume 14(3), Blackwell Publishers, Oxford. 307–331.

9

Corinthian Helmets in the Hermitage Museum

Nadezda Gulyaeva

The State Hermitage Museum

npgulyaeva@mail.ru

Abstract: Five Corinthian helmets from the Ancient Department of the State Hermitage entered the museum in different years and from different collections. They could have been made by Greek craftsmen on the territory of Italy or brought from Greece. Four of them are made from one piece of metal, the last one, with movable cheek guards decorated with the figures of wild boars, represents a type of helmet transitional from Corinthian to Chalcidic. All of them are made from tin bronze, copper as basic element. Two-thirds of one helmet were completed, obviously, by restorers of the 19th century.

Keywords: Helmet; Cheek Guards; Corinthian; Greece; Hermitage

Five Corinthian helmets from the Hermitage represent a wide range of types of Corinthian helmet common in Greece and pre-Roman Italy in a certain period of time. All of them entered the museum in different years and from different collections. The Hermitage helmets provide an opportunity to follow the development and change of the Corinthian helmet throughout its existence.

The earliest of them, helmet No. B. 2355, entered the museum in 1935 from the Leningrad Institute of Linguistics and History (Gulyaeva 2008, 129). Its height is 22,3 cm (Fig. 9.1). It has almond-shaped eye holes and cheek guards that jut forward. This massive item, forged from a sheet of bronze, has a notch in the lower edge where the jaw ends and the neck begins. At the edges of the eye holes, the nose guard, the cheek guards and the lower edge, there are small holes intended for attaching an undercap that was wrapped from inside and fastened to the edge of the helmet. The inner cap was necessary for any metal casque since a helmet itself could protect from a cutting or chopping blow but not from a contusion.

An analogous helmet from Olympia dates to the second/third quarter of the 7th c. BC (Frielinghaus 2011, 268). Similar helmets, found in the Etruscan and Picenian necropolis, date to the 7th century BC (Stary 1981, 427–430). Most likely the helmet from the Hermitage was made in Greece in the middle of the 7 c. BC.

This casque is one of the earliest versions of the Corinthian helmet. Its nose guard is absent; maybe it was broken for a purpose, as that of the helmet from Olympia now in the Antikenmuseum, Berlin (Pflug 1989, 89, No.80). A hole, breaking and bending out of the back, the broken nose guard strongly suggest that the helmet came from a dedication of booty at a sanctuary. The motive for inflicting such damages might reflect the widespread custom, known also in Greece as "killing" swords and spear-heads that were being buried with the owner. Such "spoiled" helmets exist in some quantity in Olympia (Frielinghaus 2011) and in lesser numbers at Delphi and on the Athenian Acropolis.

The next two helmets entered the museum in 1862 with the collection of Marquis Campana (Guédéonow 1861, 40, 3–4). The first of them, No. B. 492, also made from one piece of metal, is intact (Fig. 9.2). Its height is 23 cm. It

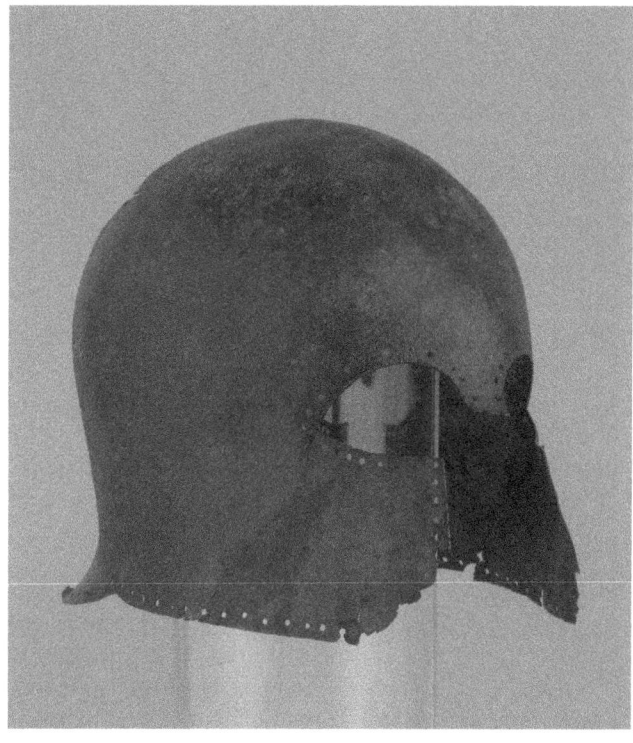

Figure 9.1. Helmet Inv. No. 2355 (Photos © The State Hermitage Museum)

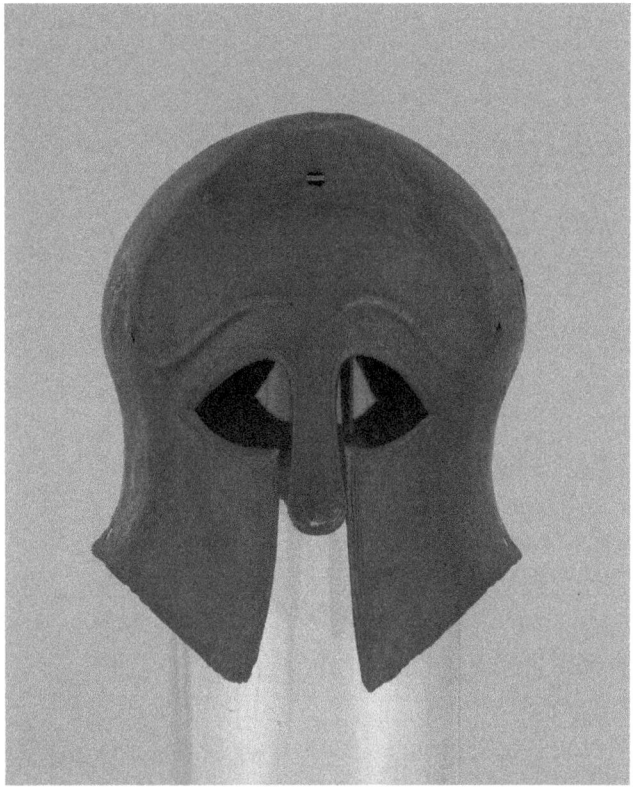

Figure 9.2. Helmet Inv. No. 492 (Photos © The State Hermitage Museum)

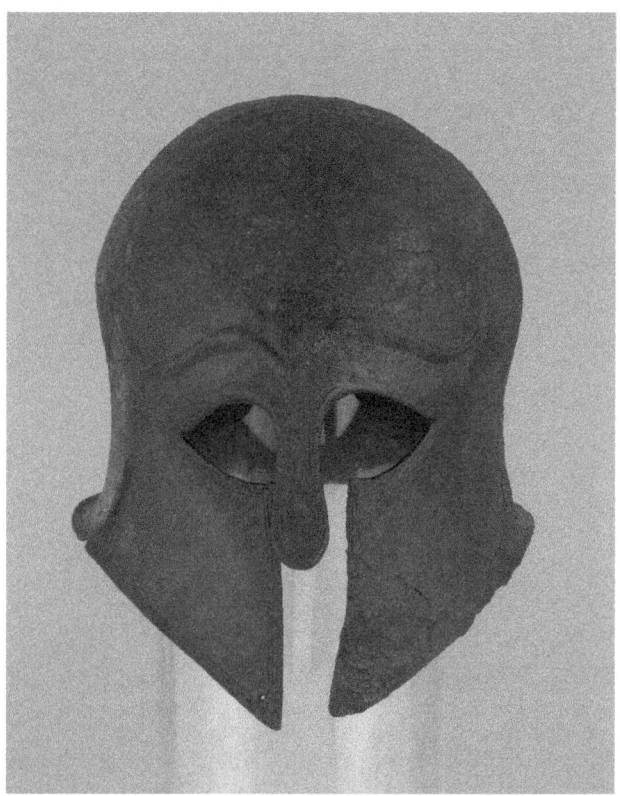

Figure 9.3. Helmet Inv. No. 578 (Photos © The State Hermitage Museum)

has almond-shaped eye holes, a tongue-shaped nose guard, and cheek guards that jut forward. Above the eye holes is a curved relief line, simulating eyebrows. The edge of the helmet is decorated with three parallel lines. On the lower edge under the ears on both sides there are small arrow-shaped incisions.

The helmet has no traces of crest fixtures. But earlier at the top of the helmet was a small figure of a swan, made of brass, with raised wings and an outstretched neck. The figure was attached to the helmet with a screw and a nut. Obviously it was made in the restoration workshops of its former owner Marquis Campana. The figure of the swan was removed as not belonging to the helmet and now the casque is shown in its original form.

An incised lotus-shaped ornament and lush leaves, which decorates the forehead of a helmet, are almost invisible. Such kind of decoration, not engraved but embossed, can be seen on two helmets; one from a private collection, found in Metapontum (Cahn 1989, 10–12), and another in the Antikenmuseum, Berlin (Pflug 1989, 56). They are dated to the second quarter/third of the 6th c. BC.

Helmet No. B. 578, similar to the previous one, is only partially intact (Fig. 9.3). Its height is 21 cm. The only surviving parts of the helmet are the front part with the nose guard, the right cheek guard and two thirds of the rim. The whole cranium was restored during the 19th century. Most likely the master restorers of the Marquis Campana "supplemented" this helmet in order to make it appear complete. Probably the helmet with the swan was taken as a model. It is possible that on the absent part of the helmet there was also a lotus flower above the bridge of the nose. The largest number of helmets of this type was found in Italy. We suggest that both of these helmets, which belong to the Myros group, were made in South Italy in the second quarter of the 6th century BC.

The fourth helmet No. B. 700, found near Catania (Sicily), came to the Hermitage in 1887 from the Tzarskosel'skij arsenal, Russian Count Saltykov being its previous owner (Gulyaeva 2008, 134). Its height is 19 cm (Fig. 9.4). The edge of the helmet is bent outward at almost a right angle for additional protection of nape and neck. It is a sleek helmet, very light and elegant, with a narrow pointed nose guard and fixed cheek guards. Although the left half of the helmet closer to the back of the head is badly preserved, large fragments were lost, and it lacks its left cheek guard, the helmet retains its original shape. A slender relief goes along the edges of the nose and cheek guards and the entire lower edge around the neck. In the places where the cheek guards pass into the nape part there are arrow-shaped incisions. Extremely close to this helmet is the one from Olympia dating to the middle/third quarter of the 6th c. BC (Frielinghaus 2011, 365–366). Possible dating of the helmet from the Hermitage is in the middle of the 6th c. BC.

Cheek pieces of the Corinthian helmet were pretty flexible. While a helmet was pulled down over the head cheek pieces fit tightly to a face. That is why once off the

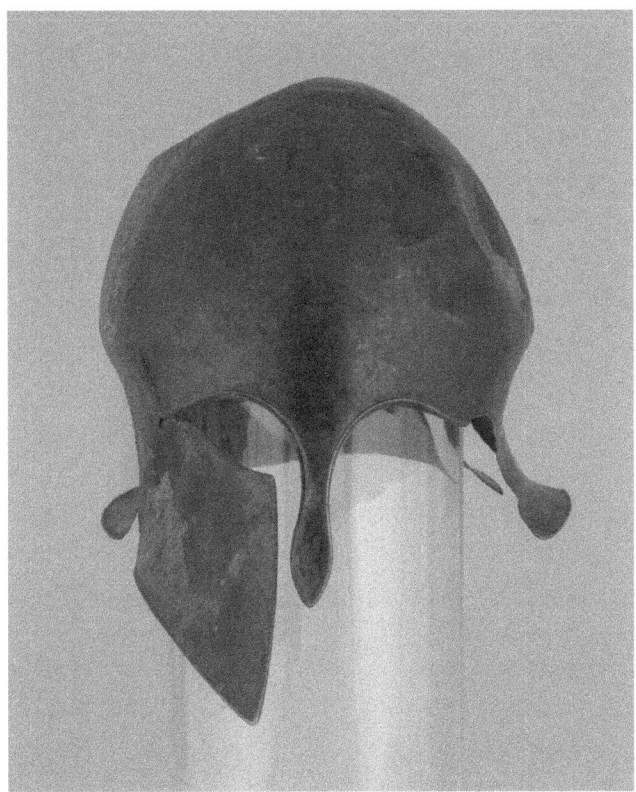

Figure 9.4. Helmet Inv. No. 700 (Photos © The State Hermitage Museum)

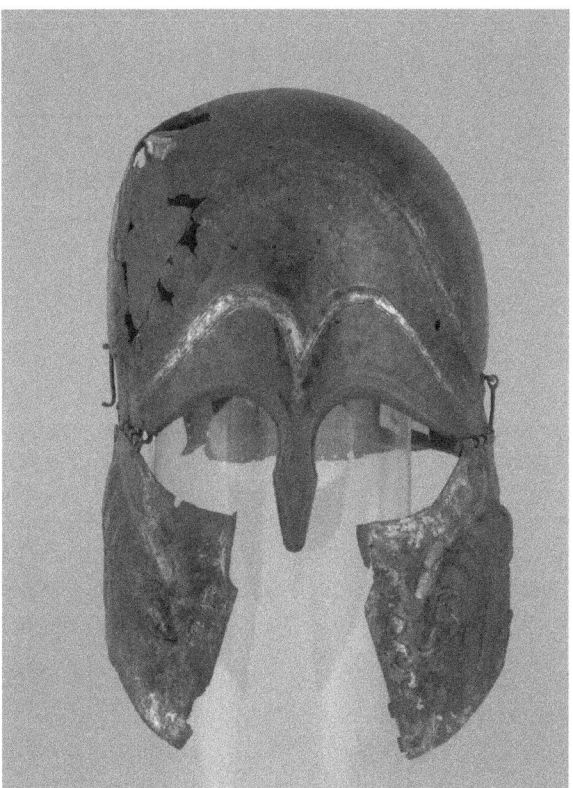

Figure 9.5. Helmet Inv. No. 536 (Photos © The State Hermitage Museum)

battlefield warriors could easily push it up to the top of the head and it continued to sit there tightly. However all these versions of the Corinthian helmet had one significant drawback – it was almost impossible to hear anything when it was on the head. Experiments in this area helped to develop a new version of the Corinthian helmet – the Chalcidian, which had a cutout around the ear area and cheek guards that were either rigidly fixed or hinged. An example of a transitional type from Corinthian to Chalcidian is the magnificent Etruscan-Corinthian helmet from the Hermitage No. B. 536 (Boriskovskaya 1990, 171–173). It is intact and in rather good condition; its height is 29 cm (Fig. 9.5). It has biconical nose guard and movable cheek-pieces on hinges riveted to the casque. A row of holes along the ear recess and bent neck guard was created for the attachment of padding to protect against heat and blows.

The thinness of the metal encouraged the master to make its decoration in hammered relief. The front side is visually separated from the cranium by the semicircular relief lug decorated with ovoids and locks of hair, like flames, under them. Above it comes a line with a wave ornament made of tin in a silver color. Below ovoids and locks goes a curved relief line simulating eyebrows painted in tin with a golden color. The movable cheek-pieces are decorated with relief figures of wild boars in such a way that the animals are facing each other. The boars were also covered with tin of a golden color, but this tinning only partially remains. A wave ornament made by tin of a silver color is also located at the edges of the cheek-pieces. The edge of the cheek guard, adjoining the nose guard, is bent outwards. Two hinges are riveted to the lower part of the left cheek guard in order to close the casque during a fight. The hinges of the right cheek guard are lost, along with an edge of the cheek piece itself. At the temporal part on both sides hooks are attached in order to fix raised cheek pieces.

This helmet, dating back to the beginning of the 5th c. BC, presumably was made in northern Italy by Greek or Etruscan masters. It entered the museum in 1862 with the collection of Marquis Campana. In the catalogue of the Campana collection it was reported that the helmet was found during archaeological excavations in a tomb at Vulci made by Principe di Canino Luciano Bonaparte (Cataloghi, Proemio al catalogo della classe II, p.VI). Evidently Marquis ordered its decoration, believing that thus the casque would look much more luxurious. So the helmet was crowned with three golden wreaths, which have now been removed. We can see how it look when it was in Campana's museum from the drawing in the archive of the German Archaeological Institute in Rome.

Corinthian helmets from the Hermitage were all made from sheet-bronze by Greek craftsmen, either in the territory of Italy or brought from Greece. All items were made from tin bronze, with copper as the basic element. The analyses were made in the Scientific and Technological Examination Department of the State Hermitage Museum by a roentgen-fluorescent method of the surface analysis (ArtTAX spectrometer) (Table 9.1)

Table 9.1. Surface analysis (ArtTAX spectrometer)

Helmet No.	Sn%	Pb%	Ag%	Zn%	As%	Co%	Sb%	Ni%	Fe%
B. 2355	14-16	<0,3	-	<0,8	-	-	<0,4	-	<0,3
B. 492 swan figure	5-8 2-4	<1 2-4	- -	- 13-15	<0,5 1-3	- -	- -	- -	- -
B. 578 (original part)	4-7	0,5	-	-	0,5-1	<0,2	-	<0,2	0,1-0,3
B. 700	14-17	traces	-	-	-	-	-	-	traces
B. 536	10-13	<0,4	traces	-	-	-	-	-	<0,3

Archaic Corinthian helmets appeared in Greece in the 8 century BC. Undoubtedly it was the most successful design for the Greek helmet, covering the whole head and having slits for the eyes, nose and mouth. In the 7th century BC, the Corinthian helmet acquired one characteristic feature – on the lower edge on both sides, in the place where the jaw ends, notches appear. This can be traced to helmets of the 7th and beginning of the 6 centuries BC. At the beginning of the 6th century BC, this recess deepens, becoming similar to the arrow-shaped incision. A Corinthian helmet with certain modifications existed in Greece until the beginning of the 5th century BC.

Bibliography

Boriskovskaya, S.P., 1990. Etruscan bronze helmets from the Campana collection in the Hermitage Museum. In: Die Welt der Etrusker, *Internationales Kolloquium.* Berlin, 24–26 Oktober 1988. Berlin: Akademie-Verlag.

Cahn, D., 1989. *Waffen und Zaumzeug. Antikenmuseum Basel und Sammlung Ludwig.* Basel: Gissler Druck Basel.

Cataloghi del Museo Campana, s. l., s. a.

Frielinghaus, H., 2011. Die Helme von Olympia. In: *Olympische Forschungen.* Bd. XXXIII, Berlin/New York: de Gruyter.

Guédéonow, E., 1861. *Notice sur les objets d'art de la Galerie Campana a Rome acquis pour le Musée Imperial de l'Ermitage.* Paris: Imprimerie Simon Baçon et compagnie.

Gulyaeva N., 2008. Sabello-Samnite Bronze Helmets of 8th–4th centuries B.C. In: *The World of Classical Antiquity. Art and archaeology. Transactions of the State Hermitage*, XLI. St. Petersburg: The State Hermitage Publishers, 124–145.

Pflug, H., 1989. *Scutz und Zier. Antikenmuseum Basel und Sammlung Ludwig.* Basel: Gissler Druck Basel.

Stary, P. F., 1971. Zur eisenzeitlichen Bewaffung und Kampfesweise in Mittelitalien (ca. 9. bis 6. Jh. v. Chr.). In: *Marburger Studien zur vor- und Frühgeschichte,* Bd. 3, Mainz am Rhein: Verlag Philipp von Zabern.

10

A New Look at an Old Technology: Insights into the Metallurgy of Tin Bronze during the Iron Age of Luristan

Omid Oudbashi

Art University of Isfahan

o.oudbashi@aui.ac.ir

Abstract: The development of metallurgy of tin bronze in Luristan has been a subject of interest for archaeologists. Tin bronze was first used during the Early Bronze Age in this region and was extended during the Iron Age of the Luristan region. There are few scientific works on this subject. In this paper, I shall describe and compare the results of chemical and microstructural analyses on some recently excavated bronze objects from Luristan and compare them with the previously studied Luristan objects. The results show that Luristan Bronzes are made of a variable tin-containing bronze alloy. The production of tin bronze may be by an uncontrolled alloying operation such as cementation or co-smelting. The copper ores used for bronze metallurgy in Luristan were sulphidic or a mixture of sulphidic/oxidic copper ores. Finally, the Luristan metalworkers used different manufacturing processes such as casting and thermo-mechanical operations.

Keywords: Luristan; Iron Age; Tin Bronze; Alloying; Microstructure

1. Introduction

The emergence of tin bronze metallurgy occurred during the late 4th and early 3rd millennia BC in the Near East (Nezafati 2006). It may have been started by accidental production of low-tin bronzes by the smelting of tin-bearing copper ores at the early stage; it developed as a deliberate copper-tin alloy in different ways (Pigott 2004; Coghlan 1975). Early evidence for tin bronze on the Iranian Plateau dates from the Late Chalcolithic/Early Bronze Age (about early 3rd millennium BC) (Oudbashi – Emami – Davami 2012). The use of tin bronze developed slowly during the third millennium BC alongside arsenical copper for the manufacture of different metallic objects. Cu-As was replaced with tin bronze on the Iranian Plateau during the second millennium BC (Late Bronze Age and Iron Age I), and tin bronze alloying was the main metallurgical activity during Iran's Iron Age (Overlaet 2004; Pigott 2004). Archaeological and scientific studies indicate that the tin bronze alloy was used to manufacture ritual and routine objects, as well as weaponry, with variable amounts of tin.

One of the outstanding metallurgical phenomena that occurred during the prehistoric period was the emergence of extensive tin bronze production in western Iran, in the region of Luristan. The ancient region of Luristan is located geographically in the western part of the Central Zagros orogeny in western Iran. Kabir Kuh (Kabir Mountain) divides it into two separate regions including Pish-i Kuh (eastern Luristan) and Pusht-i Kuh (western Luristan). The Luristan Bronzes are one of the best known categories of archaeological finds from the Near East (Fleming et al. 2005; Fleming et al. 2006; Muscarella 1988; Moorey 1969; Moorey 1982). They include a series of decorated bronze objects with a particular local style, dating to a large part of the Iron Age on the Iranian Plateau, ca. 1300–650 BC (Overlaet 2004, 330; Overlaet 2005, 11; Overlaet 2006).

Although Luristan Bronzes were produced in unusually large numbers, even for Iran, few have been found and recorded during formal archaeological excavations. Many were uncovered in illegal excavations carried out by local people during the late 1920s. (Overlaet 2006; Muscarella 1988, 112; Muscarella 1990, 478; Moorey 1964, 72). It has been determined that the majority of excavated bronzes came from graves, while many others served as votive offerings in sanctuaries (Oudbashi et al. 2013; Overlaet 2006).

A limited number of analytical studies have been performed on Luristan Bronzes, many of them on objects with unknown provenance, now in museums (Moorey, 1964), as well as some more recent studies of bronzes excavated at a few Iron Age sites in Luristan (cf. Oudbashi – Davami 2014; Oudbashi et al. 2013; Oudbashi – Hasanpour 2018; Fleming et al. 2006). I shall take a new look at the analytical studies of bronzes excavated at sites in Iron Age Luristan in an effort to understand tin bronze metallurgy of the first millennium BC in western Iran.

2. The Archaeological Context

Formal excavations of Iron Age sites in the Luristan region started when Luristan Bronzes began to appear in western museums. The early archaeological studies began with the excavations of the 1930s by Sir Aurel Stein and Eric F. Schmidt (the director of the Holmes expedition in Luristan) at some sites in Pish-i Kuh, such as the Surkh Dum sanctuary and the Khatunban graveyard (Stein 1940; Schmidt – van Loon – Curvers 1989). Excavations continued at such sites as Tepe Guran and Hamamlan by Belgian scholars (Thrane 1964), and in Pusht-i Kuh by the Belgian Archaeological Mission in Iran (BAMI) from 1965 to 1979 (Haerinck – Overlaet 1998; Haerinck – Overlaet 1999; Overlaet 2005; Overlaet 2006). These excavations and studies resulted in more accurate dating of the Luristan Bronzes culture and the Iron Age of the region (Haerinck – Jaffar-Mohammadi – Overlaet 2004). Excavations ceased after the 1979 Islamic Revolution in Iran, but, after more than 20 years, archaeological work began again with the excavation of Tappeh Nurabad (Tappeh Nourabad) during the last years of the 20th century (Sajjadi – Samani 1999).

The most important recent archaeological activity in the field is the discovery of the Iron Age sanctuary at the Sangtarashan site, which yielded a large collection of Luristan Bronzes. The Sangtarashan site is located in the Pish-i Kuh region in the southeast of the city of Khorramabad; it was excavated between 2006 and 2011 by M. Malekzadeh and A. Hasanpour (Oudbashi et al. 2013; Oudbashi – Hasanpour – Malekzadeh 2016). The bronzes from this site represent the largest collection of Luristan Bronzes discovered to date in an archaeological excavation. Other important excavations in the Pish-i Kuh region are the Iron Age graveyard of Baba Jilan and the Dia Ardizi settlement, both excavated by A. Hasanpour in recent years (Oudbashi – Hasanpour 2018; Palizvan 2017; Hasanpur – Hashemi – Overlaet 2015) (Fig. 10.1 and 10.2).

Although various archaeological sites from Iron Age Luristan have been excavated during the 20th and 21st centuries (Overlaet 2013; Overlaet 2004), the number of Luristan Bronzes discovered from those sites is insignificant in contrast to the many unprovenanced finds from illegal activities that are presently in museums worldwide.

3. Archaeometallurgical Studies on Luristan Bronzes

Relatively few technical and analytical studies have been performed on Luristan Bronzes. One of the earliest studies was undertaken on various bronzes in the Ashmolean Museum, and was published by P. R. S. Moorey (1964). All of the objects are unprovenanced; they have been dated to Iron Age Luristan. A smaller analytical project involved some Luristan Bronzes in the Nicholson Museum at the University of Sydney (Birmingham 1963). Some studies, however, have been directed towards single objects reported to be from Luristan, the goal being to characterize their production process (e.g. Birmingham – Kennon – Malin 1964; Scott 1991).

The study of the alloys of Iron Age bronzes that were excavated by the BAMI expedition in the 1960s and 1970s was undertaken during the 2000s. Analytical studies were performed on Iron Age tin bronzes from sites such as War Kabud, Kutal-i Gulgul and Bard-i Bal in Pusht-i Kuh (Fleming et al. 2005; Fleming et al. 2006). Metal finds from the Iron Age levels of Godin Tepe near Kangavar have also been analyzed (Frame 2010). This site has an archaeological sequence from the Neolithic to the Iron Age (6th to 1st millennium BC), but the importance of this site and its probable relation with Luristan Bronzes, make it well worth consideration for Luristan's bronze technology.

Recent excavations in the Luristan region have provided opportunities for analytical studies of the metallurgy of tin bronze during the Iron Age. There have been archaeometallurgical investigations of bronzes from Sangtarashan, Baba Jilan and Dia Ardizi (Oudbashi et al. 2013; Oudbashi – Davami 2014; Oudbashi – Hasanpour 2016; Oudbashi – Hasanpour 2018; Palizvan 2017). The archaeometallurgical study of tin bronze in Iron Age

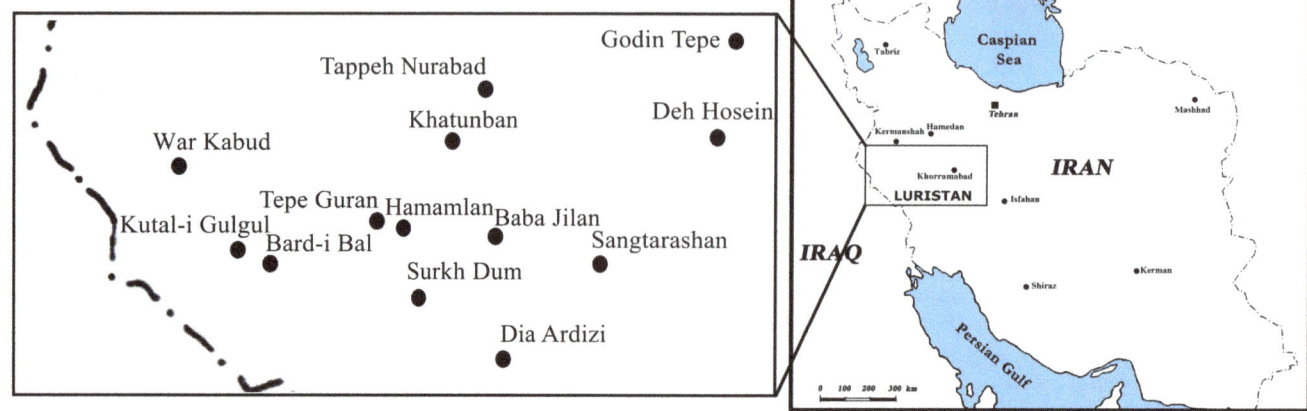

Figure 10.1. The map of Iran and the Luristan Region including the approximate location of archaeological sites mentioned in the text.

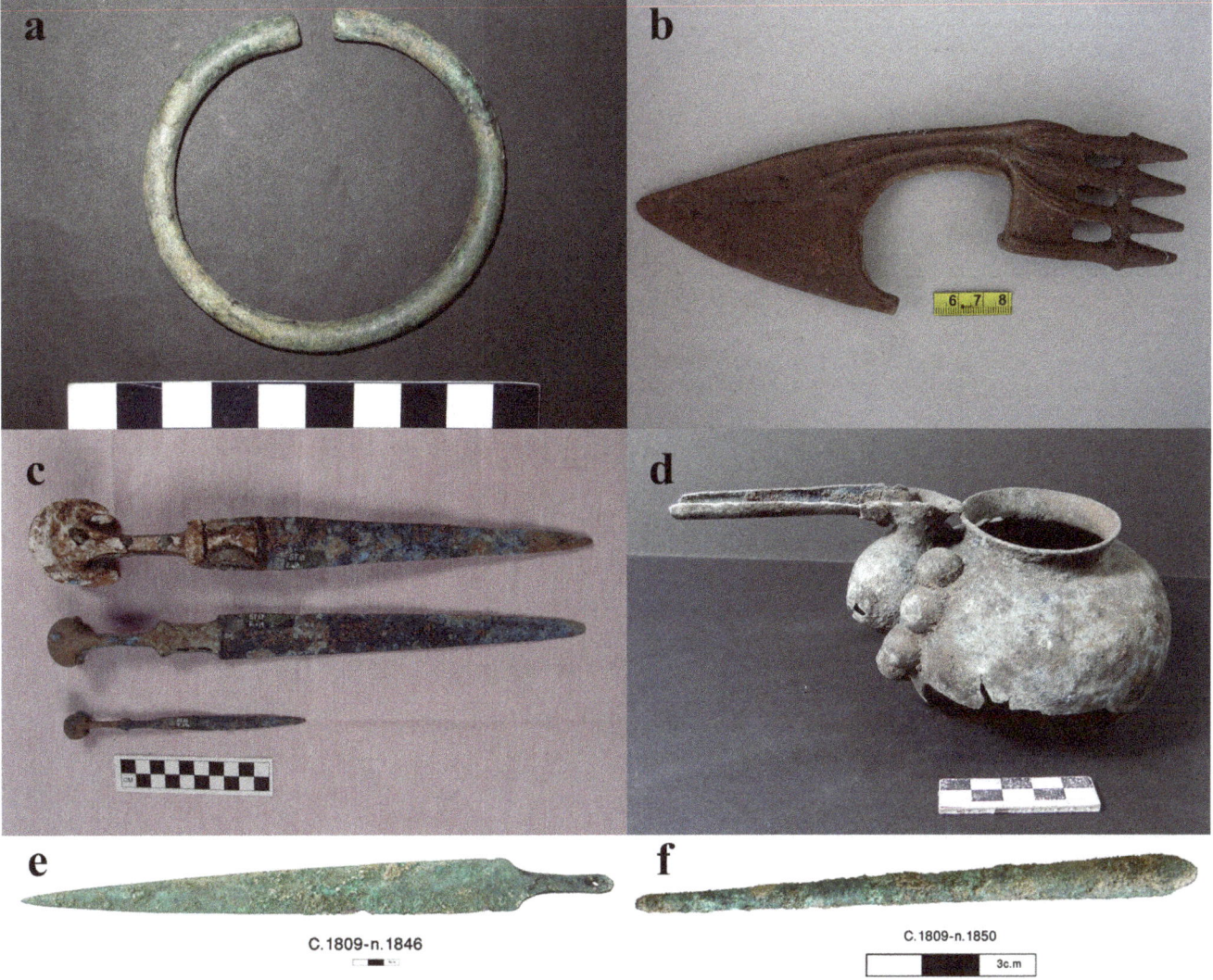

Figure 10.2. Some bronze objects discovered from the recent excavations in the Luristan region, a) a bronze bracelet from Baba Jilan, b) a decorated axe-head from Sangtarashan, c) three bronze daggers from Sangtarashan, d) a spouted bronze vessel from Sangtarashan, e) a dagger blade from Dia Ardizi, and f) a large pin from Dia Ardizi. It is worth noting that the Sangtarashan bronze collection is a variable collection including different types of objects. All photos are provided by the archaeological campaigns of the sites.

Luristan may also be expanded to include chemical and microstructural analyses of some unprovenanced objects, as well as of objects from the seven Iron Age sites at which Luristan Bronzes have been discovered.

A study of ancient sources for the copper and tin used during the Iron Age as raw materials for the production of Luristan Bronzes has been undertaken at the ancient mine of Deh Hosein in northeastern Luristan. Studies of the Deh Hosein mine have shown that this may well have been the resource that provided copper and tin for production of tin bronze during the Bronze Age and the Iron Age of western Iran, and thus probably for the Luristan Bronzes (Nezafati 2006; Nezafati – Pernicka – Momenzadeh 2006). The published works noted above, along with some short reports and case studies published in English or Persian, represent all the archaeometallurgical studies of Luristan Bronzes.

4. Analytical Studies

Apart from numerous bronzes said to be from Luristan and archaeometallurgical studies undertaken to identify the archaeometallurgy of tin bronze used on the western Iranian Plateau during the Iron Age, only metallic finds from seven excavated archaeological sites have been studied until now. They include metal objects from War Kabud, Kutal-i Gulgul and Bard-i Bal (Pusht-i Kuh), and Godin Tepe, Sangtarashan, Baba Jilan and Dia Ardizi (Pish-i Kuh). Table 10.1 presents the data about analytical studies performed on metallic finds from six sites. In total, 128 metallic objects attributed to the Iron Age of Luristan have been analyzed by various analytical methods, including ICP-OES, ICP-MS, PIXE, EPMA and SEM-EDS. Although some objects from Sangtarashan have been analyzed by both ICP-OES and SEM-EDS (Oudbashi et al. 2013; Oudbashi – Davami 2014; Oudbashi – Hasanpour – Malekzadeh 2016), only the

Table 10.1. The information about analysis of excavated bronze objects from the Iron Age of Luristan. Although, 128 objects are analyzed from these sites in total, results of analysis of 124 objects are considered in this paper.

Site	Analyzed Objects	Region	Analytical Method	Reference
Sangtarashan	38	Pish-i Kuh	ICP-OES; SEM-EDS	Oudbashi et al. 2013; Oudbashi – Davami 2014; Oudbashi – Hasanpour – Malekzadeh 2016
Baba Jilan	21	Pish-i Kuh	ICP-MS	Oudbashi – Hasanpour 2017
Bard-i Bal	6	Pusht-i Kuh	PIXE	Fleming et al. 2005
War Kabud	47	Pusht-i Kuh	PIXE	Fleming et al. 2006
Godin Tepe	9	Pish-i Kuh	EPMA	Frame 2010
Dia Ardizi	7	Pish-i Kuh	SEM-EDS	Palizvan 2017
Total	128			

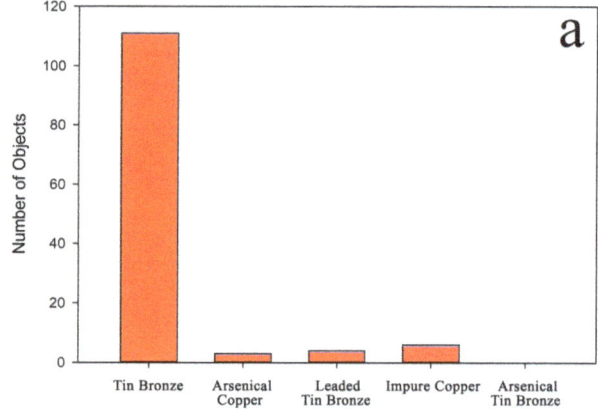

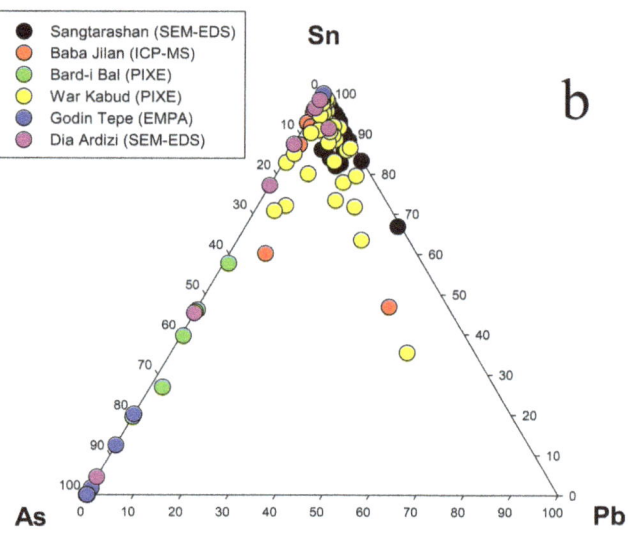

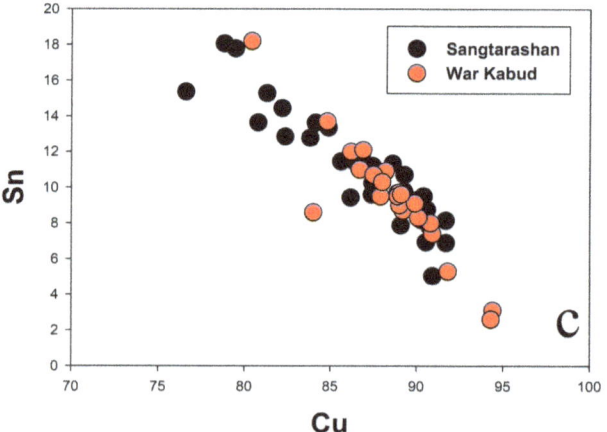

Figure 10.3. a) the columnar diagram showing the different types of copper alloys of the Luristan sites, b) ternary diagram of Sn-As-Pb based on the analysis of 124 analysed bronze objects from Luristan, c) scatter plot of Cu versus Sn in composition of bronze vessels from Sangtarashan and War Kabud showing no correlation between object's type and tin content in the Luristan Bronzes.

results of the SEM-EDS analysis (34 objects) are included in the following comparative studies. Of course, it is worth noting that some more objects from Bard-i Bal and Kutal-i Gulgul are analyzed too (in total 71 objects), but limited data from them has been published (Fleming et al. 2005). Thus, these brief data are not included here. In total, results of 124 analyzed objects from six sites of Luristan are considered here.

Results of analysis show that tin bronze (binary Cu-Sn alloy) was the main material used to produce metallic objects (Fig. 10.3a). Of course, arsenical copper (Cu-As alloy), leaded tin bronze (ternary Cu-Sn-Pb alloy), and impure copper have been detected as minor compositions applied in the copper alloys of that period. In many cases, tin alone was used as the main alloying element and arsenic and lead appear as impurities in the alloy from the use of metallic ores. Fig. 10.3b shows the ternary diagram of Sn-As-Pb in the composition of 124 objects analyzed. Clearly tin is the main constituent in many objects, while in some objects from Godin Tepe, War Kabud, Baba Jilan, and Dia Ardizi, arsenic and lead have been detected as major metallic constituents. On the other hand, the amount of Sn is variable, and arsenic has been measured in the few arsenical copper objects as varying from about 2 to 15 percent.

An important feature in the Luristan Bronzes is the variable tin content. Tin has been measured as ranging from about 2–3 wt% to about 20 wt% in different objects from different sites. It is especially visible in objects from War Kabud and Sangtarashan. For example, Fig. 10.3c presents the scatter plot of Cu versus Sn in the composition of the bodies of 54 bronze vessels, including 32 objects from Sangtarashan (EDS analysis) and 22 objects from War Kabud (PIXE analysis). In vessels from both sites, tin content varies from about 2.6 to 18.2 wt% in War Kabud (Fleming et al. 2006) and 5.05 to 18.06 in Sangtarashan

A New Look at an Old Technology: Insights into the Metallurgy of Tin Bronze during the Iron Age of Luristan

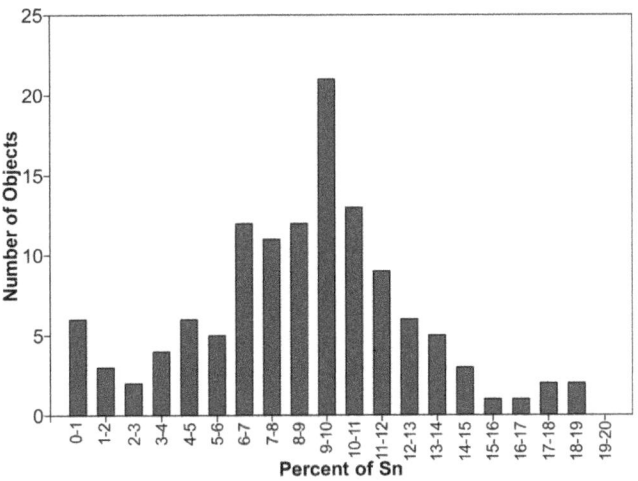

Figure 10.4. The columnar diagram of the distribution of tin content in different analysed bronze objects from Luristan.

(Oudbashi – Davami 2014; Oudbashi – Hasanpour – Malekzadeh 2016). Therefore, it is evident that there is no correlation between type of object and alloy composition (tin content) in the Luristan Bronzes. Also, the distribution of tin in different objects ranges between 6 and 11 wt%, most objects having tin content in this range (Fig. 10.4). On the other hand, the analytical studies show that there is no correlation between the tin content and the object's type of a Luristan Bronze.

Mesopotamian cuneiform texts note that a specific recipe based on proportion of copper and tin has been used for specific types of objects (Joannes 1997; Muhly 1973). Based on the Akkadian cuneiform texts, the known ancient Mesopotamian recipes often had a Cu/Sn proportion of 6:1, 8:1 as well as 9:1 (16.6, 12.5 and 11.11% of tin, respectively) for different types of bronze objects (Potts 1997; Joannes 1997; Helwing 2009, 210). It is evident that these recipes do not conform to the analytical results of the Luristan Bronzes. Yet it has been observed that the tin content of ancient bronzes could not have been easily controlled (Moorey 1994). Clearly the Luristan metalworkers did not use the Mesopotamian alloying traditions because that kind of control of tin content was difficult. This is evident from the composition of the bronze vessels from Sangtarashan and War Kabud. These vessels represent one of the most important types of bronzes in Luristan: in 54 objects, the tin content has been detected at levels ranging from about 2.5 to 18 per cent (please see Fig. 10.3c) (Fleming et al. 2006; Oudbashi – Davami 2014; Oudbashi – Hasanpour – Malekzadeh 2016).

Arsenic is an important element for the early metallurgy of copper in the prehistory of the Iranian Plateau. Analyses show that the Luristan Bronzes were not made of arsenical copper, and there is no evidence for a ternary Cu-Sn-As alloy (arsenical tin bronze) to make the bronze objects. Based on the literature, early copper objects have a significant amount of arsenic that may have been added to the copper accidentally owing to use of As-bearing copper ores during Neolithic and Chalcolithic periods (Pigott 2004; Thornton 2009; Oudbashi – Emami – Davami 2012; Thornton 2010). On the other hand, some evidence reveals that arsenical copper was produced deliberately at the end of the Late Chalcolithic period and in the Early Bronze Age on the central Iranian Plateau (Thronton – Rehren – Pigott 2009; Rehren – Boscher – Pernicka 2012; Thornton et al. 2002; Boscher 2016). Arsenical copper was replaced with tin bronze slowly during the Early and Middle Bronze Age (third millennium BC) and there is evidence of arsenical copper metallurgy during the third millennium BC in other regions of Iran (Meier 2011), earlier in western Iran (Luristan region) (Fleming et al. 2005; Begemann et al. 2008), though the process of replacing Cu-As with the Cu-Sn alloy occurred slowly throughout the Iranian Plateau during the Bronze Age (ca 3000–1500 BC). For this reason, it is clear that arsenical copper is a common alloy in the early metallurgy of the Iranian Plateau and was widely used even in the Bronze Age, though there is no evidence of extensive arsenical copper metallurgy during

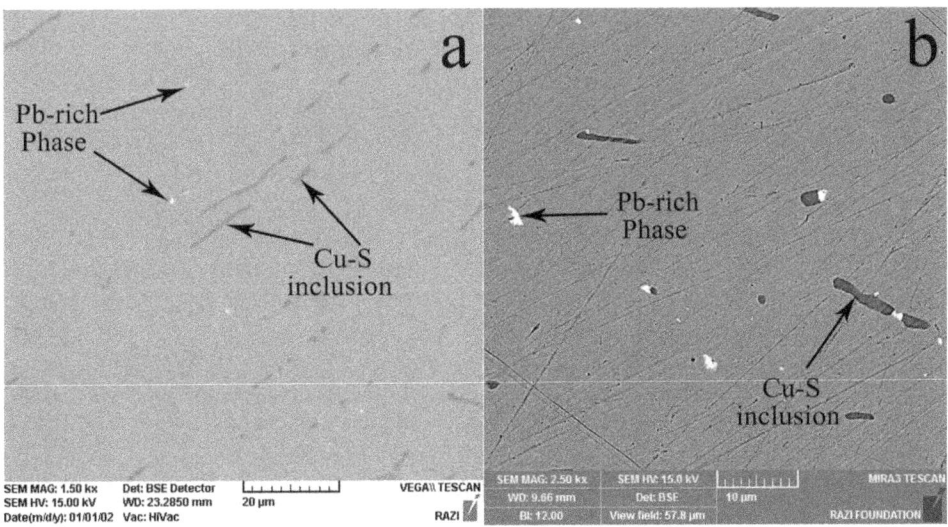

Figure 10.5. a) SEM-BSE micrograph of a bronze object from Sangtarashan, b) SEM-BSE micrograph of another object from Baba Jilan. Copper sulphide inclusions and lead globules are visible in the microstructure of the objects.

the Late Bronze Age and the Iron Age (Thornton 2009). This phenomenon is particularly noticeable in the Luristan Bronzes.

There is no evidence of the deliberate addition of lead to prehistoric bronzes in Luristan (Fleming et al. 2005; Fleming et al. 2006). In fact, lead has been considered as an impurity in the composition of prehistoric and Iron Age copper alloys in Iran. The few high-lead bronzes from Luristan may be the result of using lead-bearing copper ores, as observed earlier in other copper alloys from Iran (Oudbashi et al. 2019; Fleming et al. 2006; Coghlan 1975).

Microscopic studies revealed significant metallurgical features of tin bronze in Luristan. SEM-BSE micrographs from cross-sections show that the microstructure of many objects consists of the bronze solid solution matrix in which many dark and bright inclusions have been dispersed (Fig. 10.5). EDS analysis of these inclusions reveals that the dark inclusions are copper sulphide phases with low amounts of iron in some cases, while the very fine or large bright inclusions are the segregated lead globules (Oudbashi – Davami 2014; Oudbashi – Hasanpour – Malekzadeh 2016; Oudbashi – Hasanpour 2016; Oudbashi – Hasanpour 2018; Oudbashi et al. 2013; Palizvan 2017; Fleming et al. 2006). These microstructural features are very usual in almost all bronze objects from Luristan that were analyzed. On the other hand, the grain microstructure of the Luristan bronze under an optical microscope (metallography) shows that there are two different manufacturing and shaping procedures:

- Objects with microstructure including worked and annealed grains such as vessels, weapons (daggers, swords), decorative objects showing application of thermo-mechanical operations (cold working and annealed or hot-working) to shape the thin sheets, blades or rods.
- Objects with microstructure including cored dendritic structure, showing the use of casting. This microstructure can be seen in standards, axe-heads and some decorative objects.

The metallographic studies on a number of the Luristan Bronzes shows that these objects were shaped and manufactured by a range of metallurgical operations, from casting to hammering and heat treatment (for various examples of metallographic illustrations of the Luristan Bronzes see: Oudbashi – Davami 2014; Oudbashi – Hasanpour 2016; Oudbashi – Hasanpour 2018; Fleming et al. 2006; Palizvan 2017). In fact, the Luristan metalworkers used different metalworking techniques from those that were common elsewhere in the ancient world.

5. Bronze Metallurgy in the Luristan Iron Age

Despite the many bronzes that have been attributed to Luristan, the analytical studies of excavated bronzes is limited. Even this limited data, however, can help us to reconstruct the metallurgy of tin bronze during the Iron Age.

The first important feature of many Luristan Bronzes is the use of a binary copper-tin alloy to produce ritual and religious objects, although there is evidence of arsenic or lead as a major constituent in some objects that have been analyzed. The bronze objects have been made of variable-tin bronze alloy, and there is no correlation between the type of object and the composition, a common phenomenon in tin bronzes during the prehistoric period of the Iranian Plateau (Oudbashi – Naseri – Malekzadeh 2016; Oudbashi – Hasanpour – Malekzadeh 2016; Oudbashi et al. 2019). Based on the literature, there are five known procedures to produce tin bronze alloy that may have been used (Coghlan 1975; Pigott 2004; Oudbashi – Naseri – Malekzadeh 2016; Oudbashi – Hessari 2017):

- Addition of metallic tin to metallic copper and melting them together.
- Using a tin-bearing copper complex ore such as stannite (Cu_2FeSnS_4), a copper-tin ore commonly used in antiquity (Radivojević et al. 2013).
- Application of the method known as cementation in which tin ore (such as cassiterite) is added to metallic copper in the crucible.
- Co-smelting copper and tin ores in one crucible charge.
- And recycling and re-melting of broken or unusable bronze pieces to obtain small or large tin bronze ingots.

Considering the previously published reports about ancient tin bronze in Iran, it seems likely that metalworkers used co-smelting, cementation, or Cu-Sn complex ores to produce tin bronze. These are methods in which the composition and Cu/Sn proportion of the final product cannot be controlled, and the final product is a variable tin-copper alloy in each of the alloying processes. It should be noted that there is no evidence of tin smelting and metallic tin production in Iran itself, so that melting metallic tin and copper to produce tin bronze is not likely to have been used in the prehistoric period. On the other hand, re-melting or recycling broken bronze objects may produce bronze ingots/objects with a lower content of tin, as may be true of some low-tin bronzes in Luristan (Valério et al. 2010; Figueiredo et al. 2010). Thus the final method may have been used sometimes by the Luristan metalworkers. It appears that metalworkers in Luristan did not use any specific recipe – such as those that have been observed in Mesopotamia – to produce a tin bronze alloy with specific proportions of copper and tin. It may be due to three main reasons:

- A specific Cu/Sn proportion may not have been important to metalworkers in manufacturing the Luristan Bronzes because these bronzes were intended as ritual and religious objects: maybe no particular metallurgical characteristic was sought in the production of a tin bronze alloy. Thus, the metalworkers may have used any alloying method such as co-smelting, cementation, or simply using tin-bearing copper ores.

- Luristan metalworkers were not familiar with the Mesopotamian bronze technology noted in the ancient texts. Thus they used uncontrolled methods (one or more) to manufacture tin bronze objects.
- The third reason may be the difference between the explanations presented in the ancient texts and modern understanding of metallurgy. As noted above, one of the bronze production methods was cementation. If the metalworkers used cassiterite instead of metallic tin, the alloy would have been different each time. In other words, they may have used the ancient recipes, but the tin noted in the ancient texts means tin ore, cassiterite. Therefore, the bronze ingot or object would have been a different tin bronze alloy with each project.

The fact that Luristan metalworkers did not produce bronze objects with specific alloy composition shows that their alloying process was uncontrolled, and it could have been cementation or co-smelting. Of course, Cu-Sn complex ores may have been used in western Iran before the Iron Age (maybe during third millennium BC) (Nezafati 2006; Fleming et al. 2005; Begemann et al. 2008), but with respect to the composition and high quality of the Luristan Bronzes, it is more probable that they used the two alloying methods noted above. There is no evidence of the deliberate addition of other metallic elements, particularly arsenic or lead, as alloying/additive constituents in the metallurgy of the Luristan Bronzes. This feature is even visible in cast objects like maceheads from War Kabud (Fleming et al. 2006). In fact, there is no evidence of using Pb as an additive to improve the casting process, although it has been widely observed in later bronzes from Europe, India, and China, to obtain cast bronze with high quality and design (Mandal – Kumar Datta 2010; Chase 1994; Schiavon et al. 2013; Ingo et al. 2006; Quaranta et al. 2014). Clearly the metalworkers in Iron Age Luristan concentrated on the production of a copper-tin alloy, although there is some evidence that other elements entered into the composition of a limited number of objects as accidental impurities.

The main problem in the study of metallurgy in Luristan is that the sources of raw materials are unknown. Recent analytical studies on the ancient Deh Hosein mine located east of Luristan show that this mine was used during both the Bronze Age and the Iron Age to provide metallic raw materials. The main ore deposits are Cu-Sn complex ores that may have been used directly to produce a bronze alloy. Nevertheless, some evidence for high levels of arsenic is observed in the ore deposits of the Deh Hosein mine (Nezafati 2006). Furthermore, the presence of numerous copper sulphide inclusions in the microstructure of the Luristan Bronzes indicates that the sulphidic or a mixture of sulphidic and oxidic ores of copper were used as the sources for metallic copper (Rostoker – Pigott – Dvorak 1989). Apart from the smelting method used to produce metallic copper, these inclusions are the remains of ores that had not been transformed into metallic copper during the smelting process. However, the copper raw material used to produce Luristan Bronzes was obtained either from copper sulphide ores such as chalcocite-chalcopyrite or from sulphidic Cu-Sn complex ores such as stannite.

Based on the analytical and microscopic studies undertaken on some excavated bronzes from Iron Age Luristan, the following metallurgical and metalworking processes can be attributed to the bronze technology in this region:

- Extraction of raw materials (copper) from sulphidic or a mixture of sulphidic-oxidic copper ores; or direct use of copper and tin ores or Cu-Sn complex ores. It is likely that a crucible was used to smelt the copper ores or complex ores.
- Application of an uncontrolled alloying process such as co-smelting of copper and tin ores, cementation by using smelted metallic copper and cassiterite, or direct smelting of Cu-Sn complex ores. This crucible technology is likely to have been used for alloying processes.
- Production of large ingots by melting and casting small tin bronze ingots obtained from the direct or indirect processes explained above.
- Manufacture of different objects from the ingots, including the casting of sculptures or weapons such as axe-heads and mace-heads, and the application of thermo-mechanical operations to shape sheet-metal objects, blades and small decorative objects.

It is important to note that the first and second processes depend largely on the extractive metallurgical process used in Luristan, because if the metalworkers used co-smelting of copper and tin ores or direct smelting of the complex ores, then it is not necessary to consider the extraction of metallic copper. Otherwise, the extraction of metallic copper from the ores was necessary to obtain raw material for cementation with cassiterite. However, the quality, quantity, and variety of the Luristan Bronzes from both artistic and metallurgical points of view reveals a high level craftsmanship during the Iron Age in western Iran.

6. Conclusions

The Luristan Bronzes are one of the most interesting groups of objects in the archaeometallurgy of the ancient Near East. Many of them are scattered in museums around the world, with only a limited number having been discovered in formal excavations of Iron Age sites. Scientific studies that have been performed on bronzes excavated in Luristan in recent years include chemical and microstructural analyses. The results reveal an integrated metallurgical process for the production of the Luristan Bronzes, including the use sulphidic copper or complex copper and tin ores as metallic resources, and application of an uncontrolled alloying method. This might have been co-smelting of the copper and tin ores, cementation of the metallic copper with cassiterite, or direct smelting of Cu-Sn complex ores to produce a tin bronze alloy.

Luristan metalworkers were very familiar with common metalworking processes such as simple and complex casting methods, as well as with thermo-mechanical operations consisting of cold- and hot-working and annealing. Nevertheless, an understanding of Luristan Bronzes depends upon developing studies of different aspects, including archaeological and field investigations, mining and provenance studies, and analysis of significant numbers of excavated Luristan Bronzes. These will greatly enhance the available data about this important metallurgical resource from the ancient Near East.

Acknowledgements

The author is grateful from Dr. Ata Hasanpour, Dr. Mehrdad Malekzadeh and Samaneh Palizvan for their help and valuable information about the archaeological sites and their findings. The author also thanks the Deputy for Research of the Art University of Isfahan (AUI) and the Historical Metal Society (HMS) for financial support to participate in the 20th International Congress on Ancient Bronzes in Tübingen, 2018.

Bibliography

Begemann, F. – Haerinck, E. – Overlaet, B. – Schmitt-Strecker, S. – Tallon, F., 2008. An Archaeo-Metallurgical Study of the Early and Middle Bronze Age in Luristan, Iran. *Iranica Antiqua*, XLIII, 2–66.

Birmingham, J., 1963. Iranian Bronzes in the Nicholson Museum, University of Sydney. *Iran*, 1, 71–82.

Birmingham, J. – Kennon, N.F. – Malin, A.S., 1964. A "Luristan" Dagger: An Examination of Ancient Metallurgical Techniques. *Iraq*, 26, 44–49.

Boscher, L.C., 2016. *Reconstructing the Arsenical Copper Production Process in Early Bronze Age Southwest Asia*. PhD. University College London.

Chase, W. T., 1994. Chinese bronzes: casting, finishing, patination and corrosion, in *Ancient and Historic Metals: Conservation and Scientific Research*, In: D. A. Scott – J. Podany – B. B. Considine, ed., The Getty Conservation Institute, Los Angeles, 85–118.

Coghlan, H.H., 1975. Notes on the prehistoric metallurgy of copper and bronze in the Old World. In: T.K. Penniman – B.M. Blackwood, ed., *Occasional paper on technology 4*, 2nd ed. Oxford: Oxford University Press.

Figueiredo, E. – Silva, R.J.C. – Senna-Martinez – S.C., Araújo M.F. – Fernandes, F.M.B. – Inês Vaz, J.L., 2010. Smelting and recycling evidences from the late Bronze Age habitat site of Baiões (Viseu, Portugal). *Journal of Archaeological Science*, 37, 1623–1634.

Fleming, S.J. – Pigott, V.C. – Swann, C.P. – Nash, S.K. – Haerinck, E. – Overlaet, B., 2006. The Archaeometallurgy of War Kabud, Western Iran. *Iranica Antiqua*, XLI, 31–57.

Fleming, S.J. – Pigott, V.C. – Swann, C.P. – Nash, S.K., 2005. Bronze in Luristan: Preliminary Analytical Evidence from Copper/bronze Artifacts Excavated by the Belgian Mission in Iran. *Iranica Antiqua*, XL, 35–64.

Frame, L. D., 2010. Metallurgical investigations at Godin Tepe, Iran, Part I: The metal finds. *Journal of Archaeological Science*, 37, 1700–1715.

Haerinck, E. – Overlaet, B., 1998. *Chamahzi Mumah, An Iron Age III Graveyard*. Luristan Excavation Documents II. Acta Iranica 33, 3e série, Leuven: Peeters Publishers.

Haerinck, E. – Overlaet, B., 1999. *Djub-i Gauhar and Gul Khanan Murdah, Iron Age III sites in the Aivan plain*. Luristan Excavation Documents III. Acta Iranica 36, 3e série, Leuven: Peeters Publishers.

Haerinck, E. – Jaffar-Mohammadi, E. – Overlaet, B., 2004. Finds from Khatunban B-Badavar valley (Luristan) in the Iran National Museum, Teheran. *Iranica Antiqua*, 39, 105–168.

Hasanpur, A. – Hashemi, Z. – Overlaet, B., 2015. The Baba Jilan Graveyard near Nurabad, Pish-i Kuh, Luristan, *Iranica Antiqua*, 50, 171–212.

Helwing, B., 2009. Rethinking the tin mountains: patterns of usage and circulation of tin in greater Iran from the 4th to the 1st millennium BC. *TUBA-AR*, 12, 209–221.

Ingo, G. M. – De Caro, T. – Riccucci, C. – Angelini, E. – Grassini, S. – Balbi, S. – Bernardini, P. – Salvi, D. – Bousselmi, L. – Çilingiroğlu, A. – Gener, M. – Gouda, V. K. – Al Jarrah, O. – Khosroff, S. – Mahdjoub, Z. – Al Saad, Z. – El-Saddik, W. – Vassiliou, P., 2006. Large Scale Investigation of Chemical Composition, Structure and Corrosion Mechanism of Bronze Archaeological Artefacts from Mediterranean Basin. *Applied Physics A*, 83, 513–520.

Joannes, F., 1997, Metalle und Metallurgie, A. I. in Mesopotamien. *Reallexikon der Assyriologie und vorderasiatischen Archäologie*, 8, 96–112.

Mandal B. – Kumar Datta, P., 2010. Hot mold casting process of ancient East India and Bangladesh. *China Foundry*, 7(2), 171–177.

Meier, D.M.P., 2011. Preliminary Archaeometallurgical Investigations of Bronze Age Metal Finds from Shahdad and Tepe Yahya. *Iranian Journal of Archaeological Studies*, 1, 25–34.

Moorey, P.R.S., 1964. An Interim Report on some Analyses of "Luristan Bronzes". *Archaeometry*, 7, 72–79

Moorey, P.R.S., 1969. Prehistoric Copper and Bronze Metallurgy in Western Iran (With Special Reference to Lūristān). *Iran*, 7, 131–153.

Moorey, P.R.S., 1982. Archaeology and Pre-Achaemenid Metalworking in Iran: A Fifteen Year Retrospective. *Iran*, 2, 81–101.

Moorey, P.R.S., 1994. *Ancient Mesopotamian materials and industries, the archaeological evidence*. Oxford, Clarendon Press.

Muhly, J.D., 1973. *Copper and tin: the distribution of mineral resources and the nature of the metals trade in the Bronze Age*. New Haven, Connecticut Academy of Arts and Sciences.

Muscarella, O.W., 1990. Bronzes of Luristan, In: E. Yarshater, ed., *Encyclopedia Iranica*. Vol. IV, New York, Routledge & Kegan Publications, 478–483.

Muscarella, O.W., 1988. *Bronze and Iron: Ancient Near Eastern Artifacts in The Metropolitan Museum of Art*. New York: Metropolitan Museum of Art.

Nezafati, N., 2006. *Au-Sn-W-Cu-mineralization in the Astaneh-Sarband Area, West Central Iran, including a comparison of the ores with ancient bronze artifacts from western Asia*. PhD. Der Eberhard-Karls-Universität Tübingen.

Nezafati, N. – Pernicka, E. – Momenzadeh, M., 2006. Ancient Tin: Old Question and a New Answer. *Antiquity*, 80, 308.

Oudbashi, O. – Agha-Aligol, D. – Mishmastnehi, M. – Barnoos, V., 2019. The Elamite metalworkers: multianalytical study on copper objects and ingots from second millennium BC of southwestern Iran. *Archaeological and Anthropological Sciences*, 11, 2059-2072.

Oudbashi, O. – Hasanpour, A., 2018. Bronze alloy production during the Iron Age of Luristan: a multianalytical study on recently discovered bronze objects. *Archaeological and Anthropological Sciences*, 10, 1443–1458.

Oudbashi, O. – Hessari, M., 2017. Iron age tin bronze metallurgy at Marlik, northern Iran: an analytical investigation. *Archaeological and Anthropological Sciences*, 9, 233–249.

Oudbashi, O. – Hasanpour, A., 2016. Microscopic study on some Iron Age bronze objects from Western Iran. *Heritage Science*, 4 (8), 1–8.

Oudbashi, O. – Naseri, R. – Malekzadeh, M., 2016. Technical studies on the bronze age metal artefacts from the graveyard of Deh Dumen, southwestern Iran (third millennium BC). *Archaeometry*, 58, 947–965.

Oudbashi, O. – Hasanpour, A. – Malekzadeh, M., 2016. The Luristan Bronzes in Sangtarashan: Bronze Technology in Western Iran in the First Millennium BC. In: A. Giumlia-Mair – C. C. Mattusch, ed., *Proceedings of the XVIIth International Congress on Ancient Bronzes*, Izmir, Autun, Éditions Mergoil, 17–27.

Oudbashi, O. – Davami, P., 2014. Metallography and Microstructure Interpretation of some Archaeological Tin Bronze Vessels from Iran. *Material Characterization*, 97, 74–82.

Oudbashi, O. – Emami, S.M. – Davami, P., 2012. Bronze in archaeology: a review of the archaeometallurgy of bronze in ancient Iran. In: L. Collini, ed., *Copper alloys-early applications and current performance-enhancing processes*. Rijeka: InTech Open Access Publication, 153–178.

Overlaet, B., 2013. Luristan During the Iron Age, In: D. Potts, *Oxford Handbook of Iranian Archaeology*. Oxford: Oxford University Press, 377–391

Overlaet, B., 2006. Luristan Bronzes: I. The Field Research, In: E. Yarshater, ed. *Encyclopaedia Iranica Online*, Originally Published: November 15, 2006 Available at http://www.iranica.com/articles/luristan-bronzes-i-the-field-research.

Overlaet, B., 2005. The Chronology of the Iron Age in the Pusht-i Kuh, Luristan. *Iranica Antiqua*, XL, 1–33.

Overlaet, B., 2004. Luristan metalwork in the Iron Age. In: T. Stöllner – R. Slotta – A. Vatandoust, ed., *Persiens Antike Pracht. Bergbau Handwerk Archäologie, Exhibition Catalogue*. Bochum: Deutsches Bergbau-Museum, 328–338.

Palizvan, S., 2017. *Study of the manufacturing methods in some of the bronze objects of iron age in the Lorestan Dia Ardizi of Moorani, Luristan*. MSc. Art University of Isfahan (in Farsi).

Pigott, V.C., 2004. On the importance of Iran in the study of prehistoric Copper-Basemetallurgy. In: T. Stöllner – R. Slotta – A. Vatandoust, ed., *Persiens Antike Pracht. Bergbau Handwerk Archäologie, Exhibition Catalogue*. Bochum: Deutsches Bergbau-Museum, 24–43.

Potts, D.T., 1997. *Mesopotamian Civilization: The Material Foundations*. New York, Cornell University Press.

Quaranta, M. – Catelli, E. – Prati, S. – Sciutto, G. – Mazzeo, R., 2014. Chinese archaeological artefacts: Microstructure and corrosion behaviour of high-leaded bronzes. *Journal of Cultural Heritage*, 15, 283–291.

Radivojević, M. – Rehren, T. – Kuzmanović-Cvetković, J. – Jovanović, M. – Northover, J.P., 2013. Tainted ores and the rise of tin bronzes in Eurasia, c. 6500 years ago. *Antiquity*, 87, 1030–1045.

Rehren, Th. – Boscher, L. – Pernicka, E., 2012. Large scale smelting of Speiss and arsenical copper at Early Bronze Age Arisman, Iran. *Journal of Archaeological Science*, 39, 1717–1727.

Rostoker, W. – Pigott, V. – Dvorak, J., 1989. Direct reduction of copper metal by oxide-sulphide mineral interaction. *Archaeomaterials*, 3, 69–87.

Schmidt, E.F. – van Loon, M.N. – Curvers, H.H., 1989. *The Holmes expeditions to Luristan*. Chicago: The University of Chicago Oriental Institute Publications, 108, 2 Vols.

Sajjadi, M. – Samani, A., 1999. Excavations at Tappeh Nourabad, Luristan. In: A. Alizadeh – Y. Majidzadeh – S. Malek Shahmirzadi, ed., *The Iranian World, Essays on Iranian Art and Archaeology presented to Ezat O. Negahban*. Tehran, 85–130.

Schiavon, N. – Celauro, A. – Manso, M. – Brunetti, A. – Susanna, F., 2013. Iron-Age bronze statuettes in

Southern Portugal: combining archaeological data with EDXRF and BSEM + EDS to assess provenance and production technology. *Applied Physics A*, 113, 865–875.

Stein, A., 1940. *Old routes of Western Iran, narrative of an archaeological journey carried out and recorded by Sir Aurel Stein*. London.

Thornton, C.P., 2010. The rise of Arsenical Copper in Southeastern Iran. *Iranica Antiqua*, 45, 31–50.

Thornton, C.P. – Rehren, Th. – Pigott, V.C., 2009. The production of Speiss (iron arsenide) during the Early Bronze Age in Iran. *Journal of Archaeological Science*, 36, 308–316.

Thornton, C.P. – Lamberg-Karlovsky, C.C. – Liezers, M. – Young, S.M.M., 2002. On Pins and Needles: Tracing the Evolution of Copper-base Alloying at Tepe Yahya, Iran, via ICP-MS Analysis of Common-place Items. *Journal of Archaeological Science*, 29, 1451–1460.

Thrane, H., 1964. Archaeological Investigations in Western Luristan, preliminary report of the second Danish archaeological expedition to Iran. *Acta Archaeologica*, 35, 153–69.

Valério, P. – Silva, R.J.C. – Monge Soares, A.M. – Araújo, M.F. – Fernandes, F.M.B. – Silva, A.C. – Berrocal-Rangel, L., 2010. Technological continuity in early Iron Age bronze metallurgy at the south-western Iberian Peninsula-a sight from Castro dos Ratinhos. *Journal of Archaeological Science*, 37, 1811–1819.

11

Drahtziehen in der Bronzezeit? Zu den drei Ziehbronzen aus dem Hort von Isleham, Cambridgeshire

Ilyas Özşen

Humboldt-Universität zu Berlin

ilyas.oezsen@topoi.org

Abstract: The extent to which wire drawing was already used in antiquity is a much-discussed topic within archaeology. While the communis opinio assumes the 6th or 7th century A.D. for its beginnings, there are various indications that point to a much earlier occurrence of this production technique. A particularly early example are the three perforated bronze plates from the Isleham Hoard, which were already identified by Peter Northover as drawplates. However, his argumentation remains unconvincing. 3D-supported measurement methods and calculation formulas from material sciences were therefore used to re-examine these three plates in order to substantiate their suitability as drawplates.

Keywords: Wire Drawing; Isleham Hoard; Bronze Age; Wire; Tool

Im Jahre 1959 wurde bei Pflugarbeiten bei Isleham, Cambridgeshire der bis heute größte bronzezeitliche Hortfund Englands durch die beiden Brüder William und Arthur Houghton entdeckt (Britton 1960, 279). Die mehr als 6500 bronzenen Objekte wurden in einem keramischen Gefäß deponiert und waren größtenteils fragmentiert, weshalb Dennis Britton (1960, 280) bereits richtig erkannt hatte, dass es sich um ein Altmetalldepot handeln muss. Die Datierung des Depots erfolgt in die jüngste Phase der Spätbronzezeit, die in Südengland als Wilburton-Wallington-Phase bezeichnet wird (Northover 1995, 15–16), welche gleichzeitig mit Bronze Final II in Frankreich, Ha A2–B1 in Mitteleuropa und Montelius IV in Nordeuropa ist und absolutchronologisch eine Datierung in die zweite Hälfte des 11. Jh. v. Chr. bedeutet. Unter einer Vielzahl an Waffen, Werkzeugen und kleineren Gegenständen wurden auch drei teilweise fragmentierte bronzene Platten gefunden, die mit bis zu neun Lochungen versehen sind (Abb. 11.1). Bereits Britton (1960, 281) hatte die drei Platten unter Vorbehalt als Zieheisen, bzw. -bronzen, bezeichnet, was dann von Peter Northover (1995) in einem Artikel zu den drei Ziehbronzen aus dem Hort von Isleham aufgegriffen wurde.

Die Identifizierung der Objekte aus Isleham als Ziehwerkzeuge wurde vor allem durch Calista Fischer (1995, 10) in Zweifel gezogen, da die Lochungen, auch Hole genannt, insgesamt zu groß und zu wenig aufeinander abgestimmt seien. Diese Kritik an der vermeintlichen Eignung altertümlicher gelochter Metallplatten als Zieheisen wurde bereits von Ernst Foltz (1979, 217–218) formuliert und gibt die bis heute anhaltende Skepsis gegenüber dem Einsetzen des Drahtziehverfahrens vor dem Frühmittelalter wieder. Anstatt zum Ziehen von Draht sollen die Bronzeplatten aus Isleham als Nageleisen gedient haben (Fischer 1995, 10 Anm. 26), also einem Werkzeug, mit dem man einen Teil des Nagelschafts zu einem Nagelkopf umformt. Als Indiz hierfür betrachtet Fischer die von Northover beschriebenen konzentrischen Ringe, die sich bei einigen der Hole beobachten lassen und

Abb. 11.1. Drei teilweise fragmentierte Zieheisen aus dem Hort von Isleham, Cambridgeshire. Unten links: Isleham 1 (Inv. Nr. X.22.1), oben: Isleham 2 (Inv. Nr. X.22.2) und unten rechts: Isleham 3 (Inv. Nr. X.22.3).

die beim Umformen des Nagelschafts zu einem Nagelkopf entstanden sein sollen.

1. Herstellung

Die drei teilweise fragmentierten Ziehwerkzeuge aus Isleham wurden vor Ort im West Stow Anglo-Saxon Village untersucht, wofür ich mich bei Laura Parker vom Moyse's Hall Museum in Bury St Edmunds bedanken möchte. Die beiden vollständigen Ziehbronzen (Isleham 1 und 2) besitzen mindestens neun bzw. sieben Ziehhole, einige der Hole sind jedoch nicht intakt. Während ein Hol auf einer Seite des Ziehwerkzeugs vorhanden ist, sind auf der korrespondierenden anderen Seite kaum oder sogar keinerlei Spuren des Hols erkennbar. Solche Hole werden als „blind" bezeichnet. Die blinden Hole erlauben wichtige Rückschlüsse über die Anfertigung der bronzenen Ziehwerkzeuge, da es sich m.E. um Herstellungsfehler handelt.

Die drei Geräte aus Isleham wurden im Schalenguss aus einer stark bleihaltigen (>7–10 % Pb) Kupferlegierung gegossen (Northover 1995, 16). Bereits Pernicka und Eggert (1994, 1050–1051) hatten beschrieben, dass stark bleihaltige Bronzen bessere Reibungseigenschaften aufweisen; eine Eigenschaft, die gut für die Verwendung des Werkzeugs als Zieheisen passen würde. Die längs verlaufenden Gussnähte der Ziehbronzen liefern einen eindeutigen Hinweis auf das Herstellungsverfahren der Bronzeplatten, die im Zweischalenguss aus steinernen Formen gegossen wurden (Abb. 11.2). Weniger eindeutig ist jedoch das Verfahren, mit dem die Hole geformt wurden. Hierfür müssen beide Schalen mit konisch zulaufenden Stiften versehen gewesen sein. Die wiederverwendbare Gussform aus Stein bildet die Hole nicht selbst ab, da diese sehr dünnen Steinstege für die Hole nicht den Belastungen eines mehrfachen Gusses standgehalten hätten. Vielmehr dürften die Schalen Bohrungen für die Hole besessen haben, durch die man konisch zulaufende Stifte einführen konnte (Abb. 11.3). Denkbar wären dünne Stifte aus Ton, gehärtetem Holz oder Bronze, die bei einem Bruch einfach ersetzt werden konnten. Dass es zu einem teilweisen oder sogar vollständigen Bruch dieser Stifte während des Gießvorgangs kam, beweisen die blinden und fehlenden Hole der Ziehbronzen aus Isleham, weshalb die Ziehbronzen auch im Abfalldepot landeten und wieder eingeschmolzen werden sollten.

Es dürfte kein Zufall sein, dass meist die kleineren Hole der Ziehbronzen blind sind, da die teilweise unter 2 mm dicken Stege während des Gusses brachen. An dieser Stelle muss der Fundkontext betont werden, bei dem es sich um ein Altmetalldepot einer bronzezeitlichen Gießerei handelt (Britton 1960, 279 und Northover 1995, 15–16). Die drei bronzenen Ziehwerkzeuge aus Isleham sollten wieder eingeschmolzen werden, obwohl zwei der drei Objekte vollständig sind. In Verbindung mit den blinden Holen, die eindeutig Produktionsfehler darstellen, und den nicht abgearbeiteten Gussnähten und Gusskanälen, müssen die beiden vollständigen Ziehwerkzeuge als teilweise oder größtenteils dysfunktional betrachtet werden, während das kleinere Fragment (Isleham 3) Teil eines funktionalen, aber später gebrochenen Ziehwerkzeugs gewesen sein könnte. Kleinere Hohlräume an der Bruchstelle des Fragments weisen darauf hin, dass sich beim Guss entweder Luftbläschen gebildet haben, oder dass sich beim Erstarren der Bronze Innenlunker entstanden, die sich nachteilig auf die Stabilität der Bronzeplatte auswirkten (Abb. 11.4). Es ist anzunehmen, dass die Platte während eines Ziehvorgangs an dieser Stelle brach. Ein hierzu zusammengehöriges Fragment ist aus dem Hort von Isleham nicht bekannt.

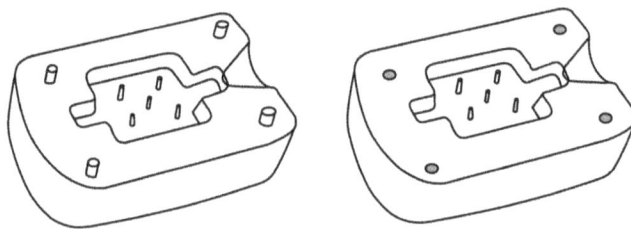

Abb. 11.3. Vorschlag für die beiden Schalen, die zum Guss von Isleham 2 genutzt wurden.

Abb. 11.4. Hohlraum innerhalb des Fragments Isleham 3. Vermutlich ist er auf eine Blasenbildung oder einen Lunker zurückführbar und somit auch verantwortlich für den Bruch der Bronzeplatte.

Abb. 11.2. Ziehbronze aus Isleham (Isleham 2) mit deutlich erkennbarer Gussnaht.

2. Vermessung und Berechnung der benötigten Ziehkraft

Die Hole der bronzenen Platten weisen vereinzelt einen Durchmesser von unter 2 mm auf, wodurch einer genauen Messung der Holdurchmesser mit konventionellen Mitteln wie einer Schieblehre Grenzen gesetzt sind. Northover (1995, 16) hatte bereits Werte für die Hole angegeben, doch eine genaue Differenzierung zwischen dem Anlauf bzw. Auslauf des Hols und dem tatsächlichen Durchmesser des Ein- bzw. Austritts war so nicht möglich. Mittels des Streifenlichtscanners ATOS 1 konnten 3D-Modelle erstellt werden, die für die genaue Bemaßung der Ziehhole genutzt wurden. Im fertigen Modell (Abb. 11.5) wurde der Umfang der Hole durch eine Auswahl der infrage kommenden Polygone bestimmt, wobei naturgemäß vorkommende Abweichungen zu idealisierten Kreisen durch eine Ausgleichungsrechnung optimiert wurden (*Gauß-Fitting*).

Die so gewonnenen Werte wurden in eine Formel eingefügt, die die Berechnung der benötigten Kraft für das Ziehen eines Drahtes ermöglicht (Tab. 11.2 und Tab. 11.3). Aus den Material- und Ingenieurswissenschaften (Rheologie) existieren eine Vielzahl an Arbeiten zum Drahtziehen (Kalpakjian – Schmid – Werner, 2011, 461–468), welche auch eine Formel zur Berechnung der benötigten Ziehkraft unter Berücksichtigung der Reibung angeben:

$$F = \bar{Y} A_f \left(1 + \frac{\tan \alpha}{\mu}\right)\left(1 - \left(\frac{A_f}{A_0}\right)^{\mu \cot \alpha}\right)$$

Die Fließspannung $\bar{Y}$ ergibt sich aus der Gleichung:

$$\bar{Y} = K \frac{\varepsilon^n}{1 + n}$$

Die Werte K (Formänderungsfestigkeit in *MPa*) und n (Verfestigungsexponent) stellen hierbei materialabhängige Konstanten dar, die man aus materialtechnischen Arbeiten entnehmen kann (Tab. 11.1). Geglühtes Kupfer besitzt beispielsweise eine Formänderungsfestigkeit (K) von 315 MPa und einen Verfestigungsexponenten (n) von 0,44.

Tab. 11.1: K- und n-Werte für verschiede Metalllegierungen (aus Kalpakjian, Schmid und Werner, 2011, S. 84 Taf. 2, 3).

Werkstoff	K (Formänderungsfestigkeit in *MPa*)	n (Verfestigungsexponent)
Kohlenstoffarmes Eisen (geglüht)	530	0,26
Kupfer (geglüht)	315	0,44
Messing CuZn15 (kaltgewalzt)	580	0,34

Tab. 11.2. Maße der Ziehole von Isleham 1 und die berechnete Ziehkraft.

Hol	Einlauf in *mm*	Auslauf in *mm*	Querschnittsminderung (von Auslauf zu Auslauf)	Ziehkraft für das Ziehen eines Kupferdrahtes in *N*
1	3,77 (Vs)	3,56 (Rs)	---	---
2	3,3 (Rs)	3,21 (Vs)	18,7 %	698
3	3,02 (Vs)	2,86 (Rs)	23,4 %	546,4
4	2,97 (Rs)	2,79 (Vs)	1,4 %	11,7
5	~2,8 (Vs)	2,14 (Rs)	41,2 %	483,8
6	2,52 (Rs)	1,95 (Vs)	17 %	115,8
7	2,18 (Vs)	--- (Rs)	---	---
8 (Rs blind)	--- (Rs)	1,93 (Vs)	---	---
9 (korrupt)	---	---	---	---

Tab. 11.3. Maße der Ziehole von Isleham 2 und die berechnete Ziehkraft.

Hol	Einlauf in *mm*	Auslauf in *mm*	Querschnittsminderung (von Auslauf zu Auslauf)	Ziehkraft für das Ziehen eines Kupferdrahtes in *N*
1	3,37 (Vs)	3,11 (Rs)	---	---
2	3,06 (Rs)	2,6 (Vs)	29,7 %	610,3
3	2,88 (Vs)	2,55 (Rs)	3,8 %	48,1
4 (kein Seitenwechsel)	3,03 (Vs)	2,33 (Rs)	16,5%	199,2
5	2,7 (Vs)	2,2 (Rs)	10,8 %	118,9
6 (Rs blind; kein Seitenwechsel)	2,52 (Vs)	---	---	---
7 (Rs blind)	---	~1,93 (Vs)	---	---

Abb. 11.5. 3D-Modell eines der bronzenen Ziehwerkzeuge aus Isleham, das mit einem Streiflichtscanner aufgenommen wurde (Isleham 1). Die grün hinterlegten Kreise wurden mittels einer Ausgleichsrechnung in die Hole eingebettet, wodurch die Maße mit einer hohen Präzision bestimmt werden konnten.

Die Reibung zwischen dem Draht und dem Ziehhol erhöht die Ziehkraft, da Arbeit zu verrichten ist, um die Reibung zu überwinden. Bei guter Schmierung mittels Wachs oder Fett liegt der Reibungskoeffizient μ üblicherweise bei 0,1. Neben diesem wird auch der Öffnungswinkel des Ziehhols relevant, was sich über den Tangens und Kotangens des Öffnungswinkels α ausdrückt. Diese Gleichung enthält nicht die in diesem Prozess ebenfalls auftretende redundante Arbeit, welche aber bei kleineren Öffnungswinkeln vernachlässigt werden kann (Kalpkjian Schmid und Werner, 2011, S. 462). Unter Berücksichtigung dieser Parameter ergeben sich bei Anwendung der Formel zur Berechnung der benötigten Ziehkraft für die beiden intakten Ziehbronzen Isleham 1 und Isleham 2 die Werte in Tab. 11.2 und 11.3.

Es wird deutlich, dass beim Ziehen eines geglühten Kupferdrahtes durch die Ziehbronzen aus Isleham Ziehkräfte von bis zu 700 Newton notwendig sind. David Sim und Jaime Kaminski (2012, 121) hatten für das manuelle Ziehen eines kohlenstoffarmen Eisendrahtes mittels einer Nachahmung des Zieheisens aus Vindolanda Werte von bis zu 2200 Newton als realistisch erachtet, wobei nicht bekannt ist, ob Winden oder andere Hilfsmittel im Altertum genutzt wurden. Die hier ermittelten Werte für die beiden intakten Zieheisen aus Isleham (Tab. 11.2 und Tab. 11.3) beweisen, dass das Ziehen eines Kupfer- oder Buntmetalldrahts mithilfe der Ziehbronzen möglich war.

3. Handhabung

Die Form von Isleham 1 erinnert an bronzezeitliche Ochsenhautbarren, während Isleham 2 eine rechteckige Form aufweist, die an den beiden Schmalseiten rechteckige „Ohren" besitzt. Die spitz zulaufenden Ecken von Isleham 1 und die „Ohren" von Isleham 2 könnten für die Arretierung der Ziehbronze gedient haben. Vorstellbar

Abb. 11.6. Vorschlag für die Arretierung von Isleham 2 in einem Baumstumpf.

Abb. 11.7. Reihenfolge der Ziehhole der Ziehbronze Isleham 1. Vorder- (X.1) und Rückseite (X.2) sind in der Klappansicht dargestellt. Farblich markiert wurden Ein- (grün) und Auslauf (rot). Weiß belassen sind die unsicheren oder unvollständigen Ziehhole.

wäre ein Baumstumpf, in dem man die Ziehbronzen vertikal eingelassen hat (Abb. 11.6).

Im Unterschied zu den eisenzeitlichen und römischen Zieheisen weisen die Ziehbronzen aus Isleham neben ihrer ungewöhnlichen Formgebung auch eine abweichende Handhabung auf. Während die Hole der späteren Zieheisen auf stets derselben Seite ihren Ein- bzw. Auslauf besitzen, alterniert die Seite des Ein- bzw. Auslaufs bei den Ziehbronzen aus Isleham (Abb. 11.7). Nach dem Ziehvorgang wurde der Draht also nicht auf derselben Seite wieder eingefädelt, sondern auf der gegenüberliegenden Rückseite.

Für eine gute Erreichbarkeit beider Seiten müssen die Ziehbronzen vertikal in einem Holzblock oder Stumpf eingesetzt worden sein. Die genaue Abfolge der Ziehhole ist nicht eindeutig, da die Hole auf der Fläche der Platten verteilt sind und nicht einem geraden Linienverlauf folgen. Erschwerend kommt hinzu, dass mehrere der Hole nicht mehr intakt („blind") sind oder teilweise ganz fehlen. Fehlende Hole können manchmal noch auf der Oberfläche erahnt werden, wobei nicht ausgeschlossen ist, dass strukturell notwendige Hole entweder vergessen oder während des Produktionsprozesses ohne sichtbare Spuren verlorengegangen sind. Die Fehlerhaftigkeit der Ziehbronzen wurde an anderer Stelle bereits erwähnt. Während Isleham 3 fragmentiert ist, sind Isleham 1 und 2 intakt; die Absicht des Einschmelzens kann nur über die mangelnde Funktionalität erklärt werden.

4. Resümee

Wie bereits eingangs erwähnt, wurde die Identifizierung der Objekte aus Isleham als Ziehwerkzeuge vor allem durch Calista Fischer (1995, 10) in Zweifel gezogen. Trotz dieser Kritik werden die Ziehbronzen aus Isleham in dem vorliegenden Text eindeutig als Drahtziehwerkzeuge interpretiert. Am Beispiel von Isleham 1 (Tab. 11.1) wird ein >3,56 mm starker Draht auf unter 2 mm Durchmesser reduziert. Es ist anzunehmen, dass der Draht mithilfe weiterer Ziehbronzen noch dünner gezogen werden konnte. Die berechnete Ziehkraft für das Ziehen eines Kupferdrahtes überschreitet nicht die 700 Newton, was weit unter den von Sim und Kaminski (2012, 121) angegebenen 2200 Newton liegt. Rein rechnerisch sind die Ziehbronzen aus Isleham geeignet für das manuelle Ziehen von weichgeglühtem Kupfer zu einem Draht. Drähte aus weitaus duktileren Metallen wie Gold und Silber, wären mit den Werkzeugen aus Isleham sogar noch einfacher zu realisieren.

Das Argument, dass die Dimensionierung und Abfolge der Hole nicht zum Drahtziehen geeignet seien, konnte durch materialtechnische Berechnungen nicht bestätigt werden, obwohl die Ziehbronzen aus Isleham teilweise produktionsbedingte Defekte aufweisen, weshalb sie auch wieder eingeschmolzen werden sollten. Des Weiteren ist die alternative Identifizierung als Nageleisen kritisch zu betrachten, da Nägel bis in die Neuzeit hin nur in verschwindend geringer Zahl rund gefertigt wurden und die Lochungen der Ziehbronzen aus Isleham entweder rund oder vereinzelt oval geformt sind. Dieses Identifikationskriterium zur Unterscheidung von Zieh- und Nageleisen wurde bereits von Bärbel Hanemann (2014, 332–334) erkannt. Nageleisen besitzen im Gegensatz zu Zieheisen und -bronzen vierkantig geformte Lochungen, um die vierkantigen Nagelschäfte aufzunehmen. Runde Lochungen würden zum Verkanten des Nagels führen und die Funktionalität als Nageleisen stark beeinträchtigen.

Gegen eine Identifizierung der Ziehbronzen aus Isleham als Nageleisen gibt es noch weitere Argumente: Die von Fischer als Hinweis für einen Nietvorgang angeführten konzentrischen Ringe um einzelne Hole treten sowohl am Ein- als auch Auslauf eines Hols auf, was für ein Nageleisen untypisch wäre, da die Nagelstifte auf der Seite des breiteren Einlaufs zu einem Nagelkopf umgeformt werden. Viel eher sind die Ringe Abdrücke der Stifte, die bei der Produktion übriggeblieben sind. Bei einem Nagel- oder Nieteisen wäre zu erwarten, dass sich Ein- und Auslauf auf der stets selben Seite der Platte befinden. Die Ziehbronzen aus Isleham hingegen wechseln die Seiten des Ein- bzw. Auslaufs nach jedem Hol. Der Draht wurde somit hin und her gefädelt.

Nicht geklärt werden kann, ob mittels der Ziehbronzen aus Isleham massive Drähte oder Blechdrähte gezogen wurden. Das Ziehen eines Drahts aus einem Metallblech konnte an den Kettenpanzergliedern des kaiserzeitlichen Kettenpanzers aus Zemplín nachgewiesen werden und wurde vom Autor in Zusammenarbeit mit Frank Willer vom LVR-LandesMuseum Bonn untersucht (Özşen – Willer 2016). Die errechneten Werte für die benötigte Ziehkraft (Tab. 11.2 und Tab. 11.3) lassen jedoch vermuten, dass auch massive Drähte aus Edelmetallen oder Kupferlegierungen mit den Ziehbronzen aus Isleham realisierbar waren. Somit stellen die Ziehbronzen aus Isleham mit ihrer Datierung in das 11. Jh. v. Chr. den frühesten Nachweis für die Verwendung des Drahtziehverfahrens dar. Die noch jüngeren Goldspiralen aus dem mittelbronzezeitlichen Hortfund von Gessel (Bz C2 ≈ 14 Jh. v. Chr.) weisen auf ihrer Oberfläche lediglich Riefen auf, die von den Bearbeitern als Ziehriefen bezeichnet werden (Lehmann – Vogt 2012, 30–31). Riefen auf der Drahtoberfläche eignen sich jedoch nur bedingt als Nachweis für ein Drahtziehverfahren, da die Drahtoberfläche Manipulationen unterliegen kann, wie beispielsweise einem Glättungsprozess. Hoffmann (1969, 449) ging sogar so weit, Riefen auf vermeintlich altertümlichen Drähten als Indikator für rezente Fälschungen zu betrachten, weshalb nur metallographische Analysen des Drahtinneren belastbare Beweise für die Drahtherstellung liefern können.

Das Drahtziehverfahren lässt sich zwar schon am Ende der Bronzezeit nachweisen, doch eine großflächige Diffusion dieser Innovation erfolgt erst ab der fortgeschrittenen Eisenzeit in Europa. Erklärbar wird dieser Prozess m. E. mit einer gestiegenen Nachfrage an großen Mengen von Eisen- und Buntmetalldrähten, die für Goldschmiedehandwerker so bisher nicht bestanden haben. Eine eingehende Untersuchung des technischen Innovationsprozesses des Drahtziehens im Altertum stellte das Dissertationsprojekt des Autors dar.

Bibliographie

Britton, D., 1960. The Isleham Hoard, Cambridgeshire, *Antiquity*, 34 (136), 279–282.

Fischer, C., 1995. Klein, aber fein: Beobachtungen zu einem Goldverbindungs- und Drahtherstellungsverfahren an einem spätbronzezeitlichen Fund aus Neftenbach (ZH). In: Primas, M. – Schmid-Sikimić, B., Hrsg., *Trans Europam: Beiträge zur Bronze- und Eisenzeit zwischen Atlantik und Altai. Festschrift für Margarita Primas.* (Antiquitas, 34). Bonn: R Habelt, 7–14.

Foltz, E., 1979. Einige Beobachtungen zu antiken Gold- und Silberschmiedetechniken, *Archäologisches Korrespondenzblatt*, 9, 213–222.

Hanemann, B., 2014. *Die Eisenhortfunde der Pfalz aus dem 4. Jahrhundert nach Christus.* (Forschungen zur pfälzischen Archäologie, 5). Speyer: Generaldirektion Kulturelles Erbe, Direktion Landesarchäologie, Außenstelle Speyer.

Hoffmann, H., 1969. 'Greek Gold' Reconsidered, *American Journal of Archaeology*, 73, 447–451.

Kalpakjian, S. – Schmid, S. R. – Werner, E., 2011. *Werkstofftechnik: Herstellung, Verarbeitung, Fertigung.* 5. Aufl. München: Pearson Studium.

Lehmann, R. – Vogt, C., 2012. Naturwissenschaftliche Analysen am Goldschatz von Gessel, *Berichte zur Denkmalpflege in Niedersachsen* (1), 28–33.

Northover, P., 1995. Late Bronze Age Drawplates in the Isleham Hoard. In: Primas, M. – Schmid-Sikimić, B., Hrsg., *Trans Europam: Beiträge zur Bronze- und Eisenzeit zwischen Atlantik und Altai. Festschrift für Margarita Primas.* (Antiquitas, 34). Bonn: R Habelt, 15–22.

Özşen, I. – Willer, F., 2016. Gezogener antiker Draht? Zur Drahtproduktion des Kettenpanzers aus Zemplín, *Restaurierung und Archäologie*, 9, 85–102.

Pernicka, E. – Eggert, G., 1994. Die Zusammensetzung der Bronzeobjekte von Mahdia. In: Hellenkemper Salies, G., Hrsg., *Das Wrack: Der antike Schiffsfund von Mahdia.* (Kataloge des Rheinischen Landesmuseums Bonn, 1). Köln: Rheinland-Verl., 1041–1061.

Sim, D. – Kaminski, J., 2012. *Roman Imperial Armour: The Production of Early Imperial Military Armour.* Oxford – Oakville, Conn.: Oxbow Books; David Brown Book Co.

12

Bronze Circulation in the Aegean in the 2nd millennium BC: Technological Investigations of Bronze Finds from the Minoan Peak Sanctuary at Ayios Yeoryios sto Vouno, Kythera

Emilia Banou, Aikaterini Panagopoulou

University of the Peloponnese

Ephorate of West Attica, Piraeus and the Islands

eban@otenet.gr

Abstract: The Minoan peak sanctuary at Ayios Yeoryios sto Vouno, Kythera, the only one identified with certainty outside Crete thus far, was excavated by Y. Sakellarakis (1992–1994) and E. Banou (2011–2015). Among other finds, many bronze artefacts were unearthed, including human figurines and figurine bases, votive limbs, cut-outs, and waste, implying that visitors were involved in trading metal in the southern Aegean and beyond during the Palatial period.

This paper presents the preliminary results of the investigation using XRF and SEM-EDS analysis of 13 objects from this site. These indicate the exploitation of different metal sources but also bronze recycling and special manufacturing techniques regarding copper alloying with lead or tin. Moreover, objects with a high copper content, probable ingot fragments and prills, denote *in situ* manufacturing.

Keywords: Kythera; Minoan sanctuary; Bronze votives; Bronze waste; Metal trade

In 1992–1994, on a prominent hill lying midway between the modern harbour of Diakofti and the village of Avlemonas, in the south-eastern part of the island of Kythera, the late professor Yiannis Sakellarakis brought to light a Minoan peak sanctuary, the only one identified with certainty outside Crete (Sakellarakis 2011) (Fig. 12.1). The 356-m.-high hill, named after one of the two Byzantine churches still standing on its top, rises on the western edge of a ridge, the highest peak of which is called Vigla, after the ruins of a probable Venetian tower still visible at its eastern end. Although not the highest point, the peak of Ayios Yeoryios sto Vouno, like Vigla, offers an uninterrupted view of the Aegean Sea towards the Laconian Gulf and Cape Maleas to the NE, as well as towards Crete to the SE. Indeed, under favourable weather conditions, such as the limpid days of late summer and early autumn, the peaks of Crete's White Mountains and Mount Ida are visible from the ridge, as is the island of Melos to the E. In other words, Ayios Yeoryios sto Vouno occupies a commanding position over the Aegean sea routes that criss-cross the strategically located island of Kythera, a fact also reflected in its probable later use as a garrison station, as well as in the name 'Vigla', meaning 'lookout point'.

Moreover, Ayios Yeoryios sto Vouno offers a direct view towards the promontory of Kastri, 3 km in a straight line to the W, where Coldstream and Huxley (1972) excavated a Minoan colony in the mid-1960s. The settlement at Kastri appears to have been the only substantial Minoan settlement in the area and probably on the whole island, situated at the edge of the island's widest and most fertile valley, according to the preliminary results of the Kythera Island Project directed by Broodbank (1999), which covered about one quarter of the island's surface.

The results of the 1990s excavations were published recently in five volumes (Sakellarakis 2011; 2012; 2013a; 2013b; Tournavitou 2014). The Minoan sanctuary at Ayios Yeoryios sto Vouno was established in MMIB but reached

Figure 12.1. Ayios Yeoryios sto Vouno, Kythera, from the E.

its acme in the MMIIIB-LMIA periods. Due to later occupation on the site, from late Roman times onwards, no secure architectural remains from the Minoan period were identified. It should be noted, however, that such remains also occur only rarely at Minoan peak sanctuaries in Crete. Movable finds included all three main categories of votives known from Minoan peak sanctuaries, namely terracotta human and animal figurines and votive limbs, but also less common ones, such as clay building models of profane or sacred character and landscape representations, stone offering tables, stone vessels and jewellery, stone tools and weights, and a potter's wheel-disc (Banou 2012). Without parallel, however, was the great number of bronze votives, mostly figurines of male and female adorants (84), but also some unique figurines, like those of a scorpion (Sakellarakis 1997; 2012a, 218–229; Banou – Davis 2016) and of a human tooth (Banou 2018, 4, fig. 4).

The importance of the finds led to the resumption of research at the sanctuary by the University of the Peloponnese in 2011–2015, under the direction of E. Banou (2017; 2018). Ten trenches were excavated, two on the northern and eight on the southern slope of the hill. Although no architectural remains associated with the sanctuary were discovered, among the movable finds are bronze human figurines of male and female adorants and votive limbs, bronze and lead votive blades and miniature swords, bronze sheets, bronze and lead waste, parts of terracotta human and animal figurines and votive limbs, and fragments of clay building models and stone vessels. The new investigations increased the number of bronze figurines to 110, which represents more than 40% of the Minoan bronze figurines known worldwide, and includes a unique find, namely a fragment of a bronze human foot from a 0.70–0.80 m tall figure (Banou 2016). One small fragment of a bronze bovine figurine or a limb is also unique, since bronze animal figurines have been reported so far only from caves.

Undoubtedly, the sanctuary served the needs of Kastri's inhabitants and the islanders in general, as modest everyday offerings in the form of stone tools and loom weights show. The great number and variety of bronze finds, however, some of which, like waste, indicate manufacturing *in situ*, could only be interpreted, we believe, as dedications from people involved with metals trade and manufacture outside Kythera, which has no metal ores. In other words, these people had easy access to the raw materials needed for their manufacture, which permitted them to offer bronze votives, even for a toothache, as the discovery of the bronze human tooth shows. These visitors could hardly be associated with the inhabitants of the nearby settlement, where, apart from a scraper and three tiny fragments of ingots, no metal finds were made (Broodbank et al. 2007). Rather, they would have been overseas visitors passing by the strategically located island in search of metals.

The search for metals, especially copper, tin, and lead, but also gold and silver, was of primary concern and the principal motive for the intensification of Minoan contacts with the southern Aegean and beyond during the Palatial Period, the Cyclades being a major copper source in the Protopalatial period, superseded by Lavrion and Cyprus in Neopalatial times (Banou 2018, with further bibliography). Kythera was ideally situated on the sea route from Crete to Lavrion but also to the Cyclades, which continued to provide copper in the 2nd millennium BC. Seafarers involved in metal circulation would have stopped at Kythera for provisions, or even to wait for suitable weather conditions before or after rounding Cape Maleas to the NE, a real maritime venture, as echoed in Strabo's well-known admonition: "Μαλέαν κάμψας επιλάθου των οίκαδε" ("If you are to go around Maleas, you would better forget your family"). Visiting the sanctuary and offering votives for the journey's success would have been a pious act accompanied by invocations for divine protection during the journey across the open sea and the safe return home, the latter probably symbolized by the building models of likely secular character dedicated at the sanctuary.

With this in mind, a doctoral study recently began by Aikaterini Panagopoulou at the University of the Peloponnese aims to clarify different aspects of copper exploitation, circulation, and manufacture in the Aegean in the middle of the 2nd millennium BC. The study is based on the sampling of 191 bronze and lead objects dated to the 2nd millennium BC, from the sanctuary, so that statistically valid conclusions can be drawn. Since the samples include bronze figurines and figurine bases, bronze and lead votive blades, bronze sheets and bronze wastes, observations regarding metal technology and circulation can also be made.

So far, a preliminary investigation of 13 objects found in 2011 and 2012 and dated to the Neopalatial period has been undertaken using X-ray Fluorescence and Scanning Electron Microscopy coupled with Energy Dispersive X-ray Spectroscopy in the Archaeometry Laboratory of the University of the Peloponnese. They were divided into three categories according to type: a) six cut-outs belonging to miniature blades and shapeless copper-based sheets, b) six copper-based metal lumps, most probably representing metal spills, as their small size and lack of defined shape indicate – they have an almost flat surface, and small holes visible on it may be due to steam escaping during melting – (Fig. 12.2), and c) one fragment from an originally circular figurine base (Fig. 12.3). The selection was based on the hypothesis that different alloys and techniques might have been used for different categories of objects, according to their function and value. All objects were conserved before examination by A. Panagopoulou in the Conservation Laboratory of the Archaeological Museum of Piraeus.

First, a portable X-ray fluorescence device (pXRF) was used to determine the chemical composition of the selected finds. This technique allows for the detection of trace amounts of heavy elements, such as antimony (Sb) and lead (Pb). The settings used were: yellow filter Al-Ti, accelerating voltage 40kV and current 12μA. The diameter of the X-ray beam was 3X3mm, and the measurement time for each spot analysis was 60 seconds.

Figure 12.2. Bronze BW_16 (right), BW_17 (left) and BW_18 (above).

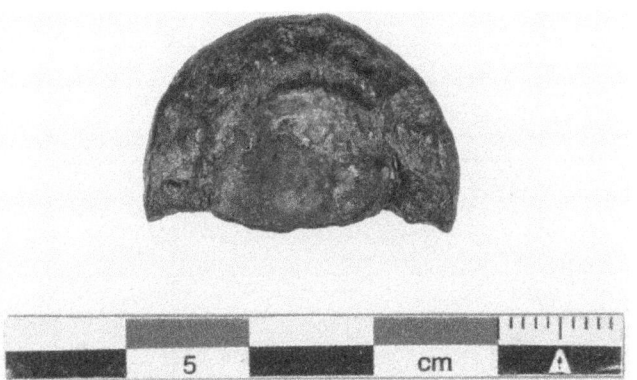

Figure 12.3. Figurine base (FB_03).

Second, bulk compositional analysis was carried out using a SEM-EDS system, in high vacuum, with secondary electrons, in a small spot size (40). The settings used were: accelerating voltage 20kV, working distance 15mm and collection time 90sec., and in 200X and 1400X magnifications. Elements like Sulphur (S) and Phosphorus (P) can only be detected with SEM-EDS analysis.

Tables 1 and 2 present the chemical composition of the objects analysed with pXRF. Tables 3 and 4 present the chemical composition of the same objects using SEM-EDS. The percentage of each element is recorded as the mean value (average) of all measurements taken.

The data are influenced by several factors, including the homogeneity of the metal and the presence of corrosion layers. Moreover, variations in measurements between the two methods are expected, due to the inhomogeneity of the particle distribution within the objects and measurements taken from different parts of them. During analysis with XRF especially, errors due to the geometry of objects may occur (Georgakopoulou – Bassiakos 2015, 348). Besides, the use of filter Al–Ti excluded the lighter elements from the measurements. Thus, elements such as Aluminium, Silicon, Sulphur, Chlorine and Calcium which may be present in the objects either naturally or as a result of corrosion – corrosion products and solid residues – could not be detected; on the other hand, elements present in very low concentrations, such as Nickel and Antimony were detected. Furthermore, the quantification of Lead and Arsenic, important elements for making copper alloys in the Aegean in the 3rd and the 2nd millennium BC respectively, is problematic in both methods because of the difficulty in distinguishing their peaks (Georgakopoulou – Bassiakos 2015, 349). Finally, the penetration depth of the two techniques differs, inasmuch as X-rays penetrate to a greater depth than the electron beam. Since the aforementioned factors can affect the normalization of

Table 12.1. Bronze Sheets. Concentration of elements (mean values) detected with XRF method expressed in % wt. (n.d.: non detected).

KYT_AYV	BS_01	BS_02	BS_06	BS_08	BS_10	BS_19
CuO	86.10	93.35	79.04	98.83	82.84	31.33
As$_2$O$_3$	0.63	0.32	0.05	0.13	0.01	1.14
SnO$_x$	1.38	1.93	0.27	0.24	0.21	9.35
PbO	2.81	1.72	0.26	n.d.	0.21	0.13
Fe$_2$O$_3$	0.82	0.74	1.16	0.18	1.21	0.33
ZnO	7.74	1.31	15.88	0.48	12.72	4.49
Ni	0.03	0.20	0.55	0.05	0.64	1.79
Sb$_2$O$_5$	0.11	0.11	0.26	0.04	0.18	0.17
Ag	0.10	0.06	0.31	0.04	0.25	50.47
MnO	0.06	0.05	0.20	n.d.	0.17	0.04
Co$_3$O$_4$	0.04	0.04	0.27	n.d.	0.22	n.d.
ZrO$_2$	0.09	0.12	0.87	n.d.	0.69	0.20
Nb$_x$O$_x$	0.07	0.07	0.72	n.d.	0.52	n.d.
Bi$_2$O$_3$	n.d.	0.02	0.16	0.02	0.12	0.56

Table 12.2. Figurine Base and Bronze Wastes. Concentration of elements (mean values) detected with XRF method expressed in % wt. (n.d.: non detected).

KYT_AYV	FB_03	BW_04	BW_05	BW_15	BW_16	BW_17	BW_18
CuO	76.05	77.88	72.25	73.35	85.94	83.82	87.57
As_2O_3	1.20	0.01	0.20	1.15	0.33	0.17	0.08
SnO_x	0.62	0.30	0.73	0.54	0.12	0.16	0.16
PbO	6.33	0.28	0.09	5.85	3.68	n.d.	0.10
Fe_2O_3	3.47	0.80	5.04	2.44	0.39	3.68	0.10
ZnO	8.91	17.05	17.87	13.50	6.92	9.89	10.88
Ni	0.45	0.68	0.24	0.35	0.27	0.73	0.63
Sb_2O_5	0.29	0.29	0.55	0.48	0.31	0.14	0.11
Ag	0.56	0.34	0.64	0.54	0.17	0.06	0.06
MnO	0.28	0.22	0.32	0.25	0.10	0.18	0.12
Co_3O_4	0.38	0.28	0.62	0.35	0.12	0.08	n.d.
ZrO_2	0.65	0.93	0.75	0.61	0.46	n.d.	0.06
Nb_xO_x	0.30	0.76	0.39	0.37	0.40	n.d.	n.d.
Bi_2O_3	0.12	0.17	0.32	0.21	0.79	0.23	0.13

Table 12.3. Bronze Sheets. Concentration of elements (mean values) detected with SEM-EDS method expressed in % wt. (n.d.: non detected).

KYT_AYV_	BS_01	BS_02	BS_06	BS_08	BS_10	BS_19
CuO	81.00	96.21	87.68	89.42	58.70	8.64
As_2O_3	0.60	0.40	0.76	0.42	1.50	0.51
SnO_x	2.92	0.64	0.67	0.55	0.30	0.83
PbO	2.49	0.31	0.90	0.62	0.79	0.84
FeO	0.79	0.48	0.43	0.59	1.49	0.66
ZnO	6.41	0.39	0.80	0.44	1.10	1.42
Ni	0.44	0.55	n.d.	n.d.	n.d.	1.43
Sb_2O_5	n.d.	n.d.	n.d.	n.d.	n.d.	n.d.
Ag	0.24	0.17	0.86	0.29	1.77	78.80
S	n.d.	n.d.	1.75	n.d.	n.d.	0.69
MgO	n.d.	n.d.	n.d.	n.d.	n.d.	1.02
Al_2O_3	2.14	1.31	n.d.	2.13	12.00	2.95
SiO_2	5.32	1.73	n.d.	5.72	33.46	3.24
P_2O_5	2.14	1.70	n.d.	1.03	n.d.	n.d.
Cl	2.00	n.d.	8.70	2.85	4.11	n.d.
K_2O	n.d.	n.d.	n.d.	n.d.	n.d.	n.d.
CaO	3.81	n.d.	n.d.	2.27	7.36	3.33

the measurements to 100% by raising the concentration of some elements against that of others, the element ratios and not the absolute values are taken into account to suggest the following preliminary results.

1. All objects analyzed are made of copper-based alloys containing both arsenic and tin, apart from BS_19 (Fig. 12.5)[1], which is made of a silver-copper alloy, also containing a small amount of tin (0.83 wt%) (Diagram 12.1).

The silver-copper alloy of BS_19 is unique. Silver-copper alloys have been detected in two EMII-III daggers from Mochlos and Pyrgos in Crete, in a much lower silver ratio though, and on three fragments of Neopalatial silver cups from the settlement at Kastri in Kythera. They are more common in Anatolia and Jordan in the 3rd millennium BC

---

[1] Weight: 2.1gr; Dimensions (max.): Length: 5.3cm; Width: 3.2cm; Thickness: 0.1cm; Excavation data: From rubble of retaining wall; Macroscopic description: Rectangular copper-based sheet with incised leg at the centre; on the perimeter repoussé dot decoration; suspension hole in the middle of the upper edge; yellowish colour on the front, silver appearance on the back; greenish and grey-black corrosion products appear locally in very thin layers; black spots unevenly distributed, mainly on the back.

Table 12.4. Figurine Base and Bronze Wastes. Concentration of elements (mean values) detected with SEM-EDS method expressed in % wt. (n.d.: non detected).

KYT_AYV	FB_03	BW_04	BW_05	BW_14	BW_15	BW_16	BW_17	BW_18
CuO	64.13	84.75	64.03	47.12	73.49	88.98	83.74	93.57
As_2O_3	2.43	0.50	0.61	1.60	0.36	0.94	0.84	0.57
SnO_x	0.58	0.29	5.70	0.81	1.53	0.25	0.78	0.60
PbO	14.18	0.23	n.d.	0.35	5.40	0.37	0.96	1.08
FeO	n.d.	0.50	3.89	28.82	1.59	0.34	6.61	0.40
ZnO	0.22	0.17	1.29	0.53	1.19	2.45	0.38	0.46
Ni	n.d.	0.46	n.d.	0.97	n.d.	n.d.	n.d.	n.d.
Sb_2O5	0.75	n.d.	n.d.	1.86	n.d.	0.53	n.d.	n.d.
Ag	n.d.	0.22	n.d.	n.d.	n.d.	0.14	0.30	0.59
S	n.d.	n.d.	0.85	n.d.	n.d.	n.d.	n.d.	n.d.
MgO	n.d.	n.d.	2.45	n.d.	n.d.	n.d.	n.d.	n.d.
Al_2O_3	1.37	3.57	8.04	4.99	4.90	1.79	n.d.	n.d.
SiO_2	16.53	10.80	18.33	11.32	14.92	9.63	2.80	n.d.
P_2O_5	1.91	n.d.	n.d.	n.d.	2.59	n.d.	n.d.	n.d.
Cl	4.81	2.14	4.12	n.d.	0.65	1,04	6.07	3.80

Figure 12.4. BW_05 under microscope.

(Broodbank – Rehren – Zianni 2007), with silver ratios ranging from 16% to 70% (Banou 2018, 8, with further bibliography). Apart from the deliberate addition of copper to silver in order to deceive, silver-copper alloys might have been used because of the different appearance they give to the items, since an alloy of even 50% copper and 50% silver may give an object a colour and a shine very similar to that of silver. Whatever the case, this votive shows that the metalworker of BS_19 possessed a good knowledge of this rare technique and its possibilities.

2. Other elements detected in almost all of the objects are Lead, Iron, Zinc, and Silver. Elements detected in trace amounts are Nickel, Antimony, Calcium, Aluminium, Silicon, Magnesium, and Chlorine.
  a. Generally speaking, iron and lead may be due to deliberate or accidental addition. Iron minerals may be used as a fluxing agent during smelting but they can also be present in the copper ore (Mangou – Ioannou 2000, 215). Iron concentration may also rise due to corrosion.

Figure 12.5. KYT_AYV_BS_19

The presence of lead in hammered objects is generally considered an impurity. In the case of moulded objects, however, it is considered a deliberate addition, because it lowers the alloy's melting point and improves the flow of the metal (Papadimitriou 2008, 282, 286). On the other hand, lead concentrations up to 4% wt are thought to be due to the presence of lead in the ore, and low levels of lead occur also commonly in copper smelting slags (Mangou – Ioannou 1997, 68–69; Georgakopoulou 2004, 9). Moreover, lead creates areas of heterogeneity in the alloy, resulting in a higher lead to copper ratio in the measurements, according to the examined area of the object (Georgakopoulou – Bassiakos 2015, 349; Papadimitriou 2008, 286). Thus, from the objects analyzed so far, only

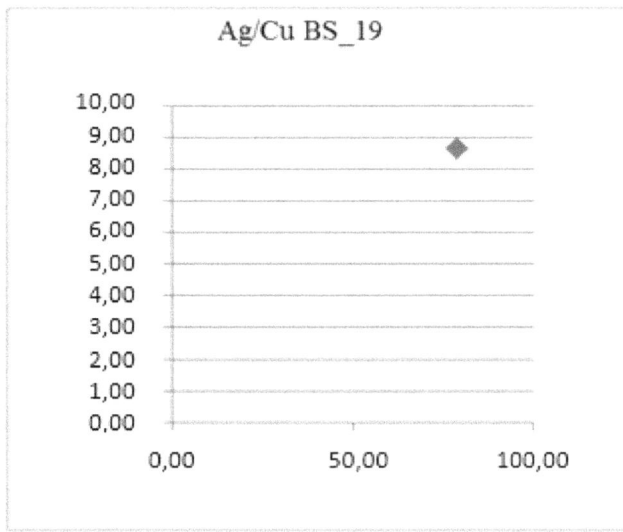

Diagram 12.1. SEM-EDS analysis: Distribution of copper and silver in BS_19.

FB_03 and BW_05 indicate the deliberate addition of lead, to improve castability.

  b. Lead, Zinc, Iron, Silver, and Antimony occur in multi-metallic ore deposits like that of Lavrion in Attica (Gale et al. 2009, 161–163). Antimony in trace concentrations is generally regarded as coming from the ore (Mangou – Ioannou 1997, 64) and is widely considered a common impurity of copper alloys (Papadimitriou 2008, 272).

The occurrence of zinc in prehistoric alloys is similarly thought to be accidental, since it is generally believed that it was not introduced to copper alloys in the Aegean until Hellenistic or Roman times (Papadimitriou 2008, 271; Welter 2003). It should be mentioned, however, that zinc occurs in copper alloys from Thermi in Lesbos, dated to the beginning of the 3rd millennium BC, in concentrations comparable to that observed in the objects from Kythera (Thornton 2007, 126, with further references). Therefore, we should not exclude the possibility that the makers (and most probably the dedicators) of some of the examined objects from the sanctuary were aware of the properties of copper-zinc alloys, which with an addition greater than 8 wt% zinc result in objects with a golden appearance (Thornton 2007, 124).

  c. Iron, Calcium, Aluminium, Silicon and Magnesium may be related to the smelting procedure, or to corrosion and soil remains. Calcium in particular may represent fuel residue during smelting. Moreover, the encrustations observed on all objects before conservation might have led to a higher calcium content.
3. Arsenic and Tin co-exist in the alloys, and arsenic occurs in low concentrations in all objects. Arsenical copper was used in the southern Aegean from the Early Bronze Age (Catapotis et al. 2011, 74) and remained popular until the beginning of the Protopalatial period, as studies of the smelting process at Chrysokamino have shown (Catapotis – Bassiakos 2006, 346; 351; Catapotis – Bassiakos 2007, 72–74), with the Cyclades considered the main copper source (Gale – Stos-Gale 2007, 106–107; Gale – Kayafa – Stos-Gale 2007, 14–15. 172; Sherratt 2007). In the Neopalatial period, Lavrion emerges as a principal copper source, followed by Anatolia and Cyprus, while exploitation in the Cyclades reaches its minimum (Gale – Stos-Gale 2007, 108; Gale – Kayafa – Stos-Gale 2007, 15).

The minimum presence of arsenic indicating deliberate addition is generally set at 1–1.2% wt. However, some push this limit to 2–2.5% wt, with arsenic acting as a de-oxidant preventing brittleness (Papadimitriou 2008, 277). Whatever the case, the only object that may show the deliberate addition of arsenic is the figurine base (FB_03) (Diagram 12.2). Another significant aspect of the addition of arsenic in this case is that it would have given the figurine a silvery appearance.

4. Tin is generally very low in the alloys from the sanctuary, with the exception of BS_01 and BW_05, which indicate deliberate addition. The co-existence of arsenic and tin in the others may be attributed to recycling (Diagram 12.3).
5. Regarding the bronze sheet group, a relatively low impurity level is evident, which would have improved the metal's ability to be hammered without cracking (Papadimitriou 2008, 279). Moreover, this group

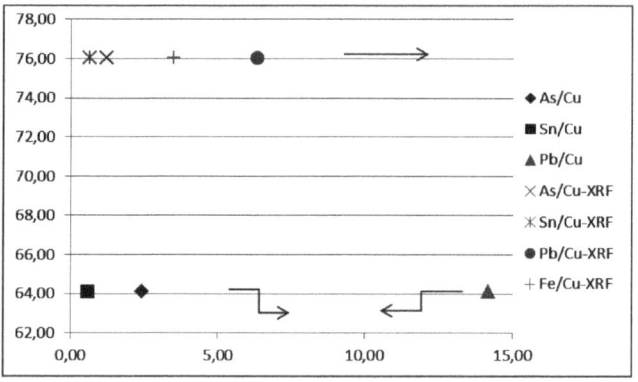

Diagram 12.2. Distribution of elements As, Sn, Pb, and Fe versus Cu in the figurine base (FB_03) in both techniques.

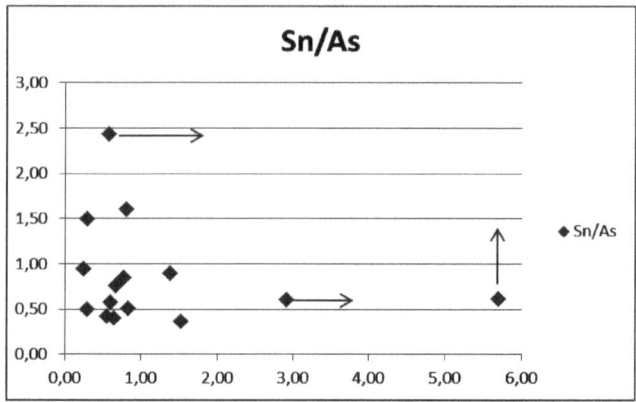

Diagram 12.3. Distribution of Sn and As using the SEM-EDS technique.

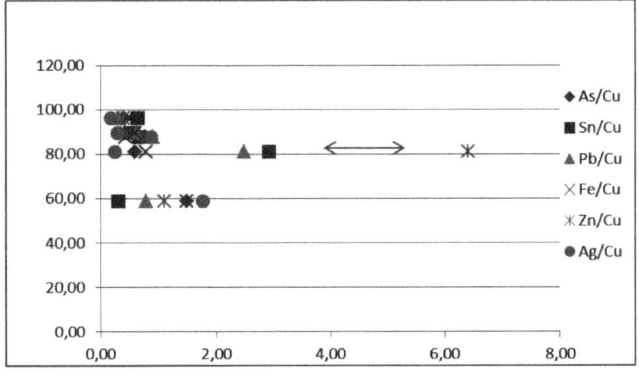

Diagram 12.4. Distribution of Arsenic, Tin, Lead, Iron, Zinc and Silver versus Copper using the SEM-EDS technique.

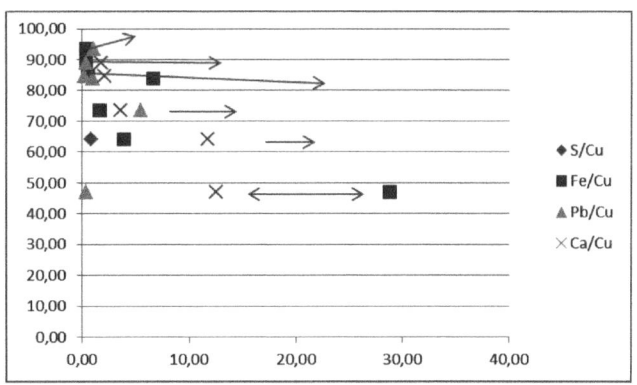

Diagram 12.6. Distribution of Sulfur, Lead, Iron and Calcium versus Copper in the waste assemblage measured by SEM-EDS.

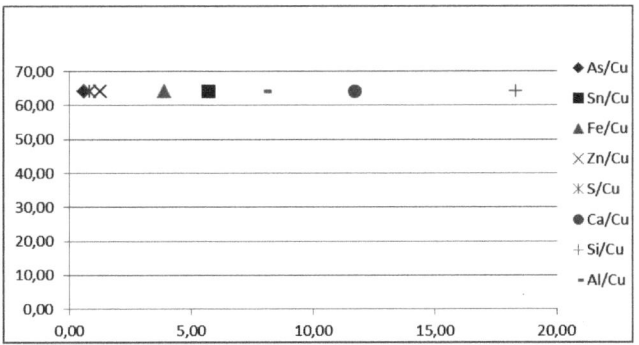

Figure 12.5. Element ratios versus Copper in KYT_AYV_BW_05, measured by SEM-EDS (mean values of measurements).

also shows a low iron concentration, which may also prevent damage during hammering. On the other hand, as far as BS_01 is especially concerned, the addition of tin would make the alloy harder. At the same time, the high lead concentration would improve fluidity. Such a combination of element concentrations may suggest controlling the alloy's melting point (Diagram 12.4).

6. As far as wastes are concerned, BW_05 (Fig. 12.4) also contains sulphur, as well as a significant amount of iron, but no lead. Sulphide minerals on Cyprus contain sulphur and iron but are usually lead-free (Bassiakos – Tselios 2012, 159; Charalambous et al. 2015, 96). But sulphur also occurs in the sulphide copper ores at Lavrion. Thus, different sources beyond the Cyclades, which the visitors to the peak sanctuary at the beginning of the Neopalatial period were aware of, might have been used for making the votives (Diagram 12.5).

7. BW_05 as well as BW_14 and BW_15 may be bronze spill residues indicating manufacture in situ. Moreover, BW_04, BW_16 and BW_18 show a low iron concentration, which, combined with their high copper ratio, may indicate that they originally belonged to ingots, and so could have been votives *per se*, or the results of manufacturing *in situ* (Diagram 12.6).

This brief presentation of certain aspects of the study of metal finds from the peak sanctuary at Ayios Yeoryios sto Vouno suggests that the sanctuary's visitors were well aware of the metal sources of their time, even distant ones. They were also well aware of the properties of the metals and used different manufacturing techniques related to the type and value of the dedicated objects. They might also have been involved in manufacturing *in situ*, a possibility further indicated by the rough manufacture of several bronze figurines, visible in the irregularities of their surface and caused by incomplete smelting or/and casting or by mould overuse. The study of a larger sample of bronze artefacts is expected to shed much more light on bronze circulation, technology, and manufacture in the Aegean in the middle of the 2nd millennium BC, during the apogee of Minoan colonisation and trade.

Acknowledgements

Our thanks are due to Dr. Jean-Marie Welter for bringing the paper of Thornton (2007) to our attention and for fruitful discussions regarding the presence of zinc in copper alloys.

Bibliography

Banou, E., 2012. Μικροαντικείμενα μινωικών χρόνων από πηλό, λίθο και πολύτιμες ύλες. In: Sakellarakis, Y. 2012a, 249–501.

Banou, E., 2016. Foot of a bronze figure from the Minoan peak sanctuary at Ayios Yeoryios sto Vouno on Kythera. In: E. Papadopoulou-Chrysikopoulou – V. Chrysikopoulos – G. Christakopoulou, ed., *ACHAIOS. Studies Presented to Professor Thanassis Papadopoulos*, Oxford: Archaeopress, 19–22.

Banou, E., 2017. Το μινωικό ιερό κορυφής στον Άγιο Γεώργιο στο Βουνό Κυθήρων: Τα νεότερα αποτελέσματα της αρχαιολογικής έρευνας (2013). In: D. Konidaris, ed., *Ι΄ Διεθνές Πανιόνιο Συνέδριο. Κέρκυρα, 30 Απριλίου – 4 Μαΐου 2014. Τα Πρακτικά. IV*, Corfu, 231–243.

Banou, E., 2018a. Επανέναρξη αρχαιολογικής έρευνας στο μινωικό ιερό κορυφής στον Άγιο Γεώργιο στο Βουνό Κυθήρων: 2011–2012. In: E. Zimi – A.V. Karapanayiotou – M. Xanthopoulou (eds), *Το Αρχαιολογικό Έργο στην Πελοπόννησο. Πρακτικά του Διεθνούς Συνεδρίου, Τρίπολη, 7–11 Νοεμβρίου 2012*,

45–57 [pdf]. Available at: http://ham.uop.gr/images/aepel1_all_final.pdf [accessed 16 January 2019].

Banou, E., 2018b. Minoans Overseas: The Peak Sanctuary at Ayios Yeoryios sto Vouno, *Procceedings of the 12*th *Interantional Congress of Cretan Studies, 21–25.9.2016* [pdf]. Available at: http://12iccs.proceedings.gr/el/proceedings/category38/32/343 [accessed 16 January 2019].

Banou, E. – Davis, B., 2016. The Symbolism of the Scorpion in Minoan Religion: A Cosmological Approach on the Basis of Votive Offerings from the Peak Sanctuary at Ayios Yeoryios sto Vouno, Kythera. In: E. Alram-Stern, F. Blakolme – S. Deger-Jalotzy – J. Weilhartner, ed., *METAPHYSIS, Ritual, Myth and Symbolism in the Aegean Bronze Age, Proceedings of the 15*th *International Aegean Conference, Vienna 22–25 April 2014* [Aegaeum 39], Leuven-Liege: Peeters,123–129.

Bassiakos, Y. and Catapotis, M., 2006. Reconstruction of the Copper Smelting Process, Based on the Analysis of Ore and Slag Samples. In: Philip P. Betancourt (ed.), *The Chrysokamino Metallurgy Workshop and its Territory* (Hesperia Supplement 36), 329–353.

Bassiakos, Y. – Tselios, Th., 2012. On the Cessation of Local Copper Production in the Aegean in the 2nd Millennium BC. In: V. Kassianidou – G. Papasavvas, *Eastern Mediterranean Metallurgy and Metalwork in the Second Millennium BC. A Conference in Honour of James D. Muhly, Nicosia Cyprous 2009,* Oxford and Oakville: Oxbow Books, 151–161.

Broodbank, C., 1999. Kythera Survey: Preliminary Report of the 1998 Season, *The Annual of the British School at Athens* 94: 191–214.

Broodbank, C. – Rehren, Th. – Zianni A. M., 2007. Scientific Analysis of Metal Objects and Metallurgical Remains from Kastri, Kythera, *The Annual of the British School at Athens* 102, 219–238.

Catapotis, M. – Bassiakos, Y. – Papadatos, Y., 2011. Reconstructing Early Cretan Metallurgy: Analytical Evidence from Kephala Petras, Siteia. In: Philip P. Betancourt – Susan C. Ferrence, ed., *Metallurgy: Understanding How, Learning Why. Studies in Honor of James D.Muhly*, Philadelphia, INSTAP Academic Press, 69–78.

Catapotis, M. – Bassiakos, Y., 2007. Copper Smelting at the Early Minoan Site of Chrysokamino on Crete. In: Peter M. Day – Roger C.P. Doonan (2007), *Metallurgy in the Early Bronze Age Aegean*, Oxford, Oxbow 68–79.

Charalambous, A. – Kassianidou, V. – Papasavvas, G, 2015. A comparative Study of Cypriot Bronzes Dated to the Late Bronze and the Early Iron Age. In: E. Photos-Jones, ed., *Proceedings of the 6*th *Symposium of the Hellenic Society for Archaeometry,* United Kingdom, Oxford: British Archaeological Reports Ltd 95–100.

Coldstream, J. N. – Huxley, G. L., 1972. *Kythera. Excavations and Studies Conducted by the University of Pennsylvania and the British School of Athens*, London: Faber and Faber Limited.

Gale, N.H. – Stos-Gale, A. Z., 2007. Cross-cultural Minoan Networks and the Development of Metallurgy in Bronze Age Crete. In: S. La Niece – D. Hook – P. Chaddock, ed., *Metals and Mines: Studies in Archaeometallurgy*, London, Archetype Publications in Association with the British Museum, 101–111.

Gale, H.N. – Papastamataki, A – Stos-Gale, Z.A. – Leonis, K. 1985. Copper Sources and Copper Metallurgy in the Bronze Age. In: T.P. Craddock – M. Hughes, ed., *Furnaces and Smelting Technology in Antiquity*, London: British Museum Occasional paper No 48, 81–102.

Gale, H.N. – Kayafa, M. – Stos-Gale, A.Z., 2007. Further Evidence for Bronze Age Production of Copper from Ores in the Lavrion Ore District. In: A. Giumlia-Mair – P. Craddock – A. Hauptmann – J. Bayley – M. Cavallini – G. Garagnani – B. Gimour – S. La Niece – W. Nicodemi – Th. Rehren, ed., *Proceedings of the 2nd International Conference: Archaeometallurgy in Europe*, Milan: Associazione Italiana di Metallurgia, 158–176.

Gale, H. N. – Kayafa M. – Stos-Gale, Z. A., 2008. Early Helladic Metallurgy at Raphina, Attica, and the Role of Lavrion. In: I. Tzachili, ed., *Aegean Metallurgy in the Bronze Age, Proceedings of an International Symposium Held at the University of Crete, Rethymnon, Greece, 2004,* I. Athens: Ta Pragmata, 87–104.

Georgakopoulou, M., 2004. Examination of Copper Slags from the Early Bronze Age Site of Daskaleio-Kavos on the Island of Keros (Cyclades,Greece), *Institute of Archaeo-Metallurgical Studies 24,* 3–12.

Georgakopoulou, M. – Bassiakos, Y., 2015. "Μεταλλουργικές δραστηριότητες και χρήση των μετάλλων στο Παλαμάρι". In: Λ. Παρλαμά – Μ. Θεοχάρη – Χ. Ρωμανού – Στ. Μπονάτσος, ed., *Ο Οχυρωμένος Προϊστορικός Οικισμός στο Παλαμάρι της Σκύρου, Διεπιστημονική Συνάντηση για το Έργο Έρευνας και Ανάδειξης,* 23–24 Οκτωβρίου 2012,. Athens: Ministry of Culture, Education and Religious Affairs, 347–366.

Mangou, E. – Ioannou, P., 1997. On the Chemical Composition of Prehistoric Greek Copper-based Artefacts from the Aegean Region, *The Annual of the British School at Athens*, Vol. 92, 59–72.

Mangou, E. – Ioannou P., 2000. Studies of the Late Bronze Age Copper-based Ingots found in Greece, *The Annual of the British School at Athens*, 95, 207–217.

Papadimitriou, G., 2008. The Technological Evolution of Copper Alloys in the Aegean During the Prehistoric Period. In: I. Tzachili, ed., *Aegean Metallurgy in the Bronze Age, Proceedings of an International*

Symposium Held at the University of Crete, Rethymnon, Greece, 2004, Athens: Ta Pragmata, 271–287.

Sakellarakis, Y. 1997. A Minoan Bronze Scorpion Figurine from Kythera. In: *Έπαινος Ιωάννου Παπαδημητρίου*. Athens, 423–472.

Sakellarakis, Y., 2011. *Κύθηρα. Το μινωικό ιερό κορυφής στον Άγιο Γεώργιο στο Βουνό. 1. Τα προανασκαφικά και η ανασκαφή*. Athens: Archaeological Society of Athens.

Sakellarakis, Y., 2012a. *Κύθηρα. Το μινωικό ιερό κορυφής στον Άγιο Γεώργιο στο Βουνό. 2. Τα ευρήματα*. Athens: Archaeological Society of Athens.

Sakellarakis, Y., 2012b. *Κύθηρα. Το μινωικό ιερό κορυφής στον Άγιο Γεώργιο στο Βουνό. 3. Τα ευρήματα*. Athens: Archaeological Society of Athens.

Sakellarakis, Y., 2013. *Κύθηρα. Το μινωικό ιερό κορυφής στον Άγιο Γεώργιο στο Βουνό. Μινωική λατρεία. Νεότεροι χρόνοι*. Athens: Archaeological Society of Athens.

Sherratt, S., 2007. The Archaeology of Metal Use in the Early Bronze Age Aegean – A Review. In: P. M. Day – R. C.P. Doonan, ed., *Metallurgy in the Early Bronze Age*, (Sheffield Studies in Aegean Archaeology 7), Oxford: Oxbow Books, 245–263.

Thornton, Ch. P. 2007., Of Brass and Bronze in Prehistoric Southwest Asia. In: S. La Niese – D. Hook – P. Craddock, ed., *Metals and Mining: Studies in* Archaeometallurgy, London: Archetype, 123–135.

Tournavitou, I. 2014. *Κύθηρα. Το μινωικό ιερό κορυφής στον Άγιο Γεώργιο στο Βουνό. 4. Κεραμεική της Εποχής του Χαλκού*. Athens: Archaeological Society of Athens.

Welter, J.M. 2003. The Zinc Content of Brass: A Chronological Indicator?, *Techne* 18, 27–36.

13

La Tomba Principesca di Roscigno:
Greci e indigeni nelle élites dell'Italia Meridionale

Silvia Pacifico, Rossella Luciano

Ministero dei beni e delle attività culturali

Museo Archeologico Provinciale di Salerno

silvia.pacifico@beniculturali.it

Abstract: The princely tomb of Roscigno, in the province of Salerno, presents an extraordinary collection of finds which are perfectly suited in order to analyze and rebuild a context symbolizing interlacing cultures. The particular nature of the grave is clearly evident from its structural features, displayed in such a isolated fashion, thus presenting an entryway with long dromos. The corpse was ushered by an iron carriage together with roughly 50 finds, mainly in bronze. Such wealth impels us to investigate the manner in which culture moves and manifests itself through the creation and the manufacturing of precious materials like bronze, silver and gold.

Keywords: Greeks; Royal Tomb; Bronze; Silver; Gold

1. Quadro storico geografico

Il massiccio degli Alburni domina un vasto territorio e separa le valli del Sele e del Calore che definiscono l'entroterra di Paestum, da quella del Tanagro che attraversa il Vallo di Diano. In questo contesto si colloca il paese di Roscigno crocevia di itinerari che attraversando tali vallate fluviali ha da sempre favorito i traffici dalle coste tirreniche e ioniche verso l'interno.

Il Monte Pruno di Roscigno costituisce lo sperone meridionale della catena degli Alburni. Sono già dal VI secolo segni di una comunità stabile sul tale Monte che "presenta un abitato piuttosto esteso, vicinissimo al Vallo di Diano, ma già in vista della costa e dominante la strada che dal colle scende verso Paestum" (de La Genière 1961, 75–88). Si tratta di un insediamento incentrato sul controllo delle principali vie di comunicazione che coinvolgono Etruschi e Greci della fascia tirrenica, ionica, Indigeni del Vallo di Diano e della Basilicata.

L'insediamento, strategico nella organizzazione territoriale dell'entroterra, occupa in forma sparsa, le alture e le pendici del Monte Pruno che ha ai suoi piedi i comuni di Roscigno, Corleto Monforte e Bellosguardo.

Tali valli almeno dalla fine del V sec. a.C. e durante tutto il periodo ellenistico furono vie di transito tra Poseidonia e le colonie greche dello Ionio. Le più recenti campagne di scavo condotte a partire dalla fine degli anni Ottanta del Novecento hanno consentito la definizione del tracciato della imponente fortificazione di età lucana e hanno restituito dati innovativi che offrono una diversa prospettiva per la ricostruzione delle dinamiche insediative e della organizzazione socio-politica ed economica dell'antico abitato, in relazione alla configurazione del paesaggio. Le indagini realizzate hanno apportato significativi elementi di novità, all'interno del quadro delle conoscenze finora noto dell'antico insediamento indigeno, la cui esplorazione è, tuttavia, da considerarsi ancora agli albori (Ferrara 2014, 183–233). In particolare, le maggiori novità si sono riscontrate nella individuazione, sui versanti sud-orientale, sud-occidentale e settentrionale, del circuito fortificato con la scoperta di due porte, una torre, un passaggio secondario e una postierla che meglio definiscono la fisionomia dell'impianto fortificato di Monte Pruno tra la metà del IV e la seconda metà del III sec. a.C. Le ricerche sul pianoro hanno, invece, chiarito le modalità insediative dell'antico abitato che si presenta in forme differenziate e disperse su un'ampia superficie, organizzato per nuclei sparsi, probabilmente pertinenti a diversi gruppi familiari, e con una articolazione funzionale degli spazi, abitativi, necropolici e produttivi.

I primi segni di una radicale trasformazione delle forme e dei modi d'insediamento e della cultura materiale si registrano sul Monte Pruno di Roscigno sul finire del V sec a.C. riflesso e conseguenza dell'arrivo di nuove genti, i Lucani che si insediano a Poseidonia e che determinano nel territorio profondi cambiamenti. A Roscigno il loro arrivo, la loro presenza, segna un momento significativo di passaggio, di trasformazione e organizzazione politica e territoriale. L'area di circolazione dei prodotti di matrice pestana è molto ampia ed estesa, tale prevalente componente nella cultura materiale del nostro insediamento indigeno, come evidenziato dalle recenti indagini al circuito murario, inserisce Roscigno nel circuito regionale da Fratte a Pontecagnano da un lato, da Roccagloriosa e Velia dall'altro.

Quel che accade nel V secolo e soprattutto tra la fine di questo secolo e l'inizio del IV non si può configurare come un "semplice" scontro etnico tra Greci e "Barbari" ma come l'incontro attraverso il confronto tra aristocrazie dominanti delle città che si trovano a doversi affrontare con blocchi emergenti indigeni fortemente strutturati attorno a cui iniziano a consolidarsi interessi delle plebi cittadine e rurali. Il mondo indigeno inizia ad apparirci configurato, in via di strutturazione e spesso in antagonismo con le città greche di cui comunque assimila i valori, e come protagonista dei processi che portano alla piena definizione dell'*ethnos* lucano. Tale determinazione non può configurarsi come la semplice discesa di gruppi provenienti dal Sannio, ma come esito del dinamico rapporto che vede le differenziate comunità intrecciarsi in un lungo periodo di contatti con l'ambiente greco coloniale campano e apulo.

Come in molti siti indigeni, la documentazione proviene prevalentemente dalle necropoli che restituiscono tracce sia dal punto di vista topografico, sia per quanto attiene le dinamiche sociali. I corredi della seconda metà del V secolo accanto alla manifestazione di oggetti che tradizionalmente esprimono il prestigio, ne presentano altri che indicano una più accentuata comprensione e adesione all'ideologia del banchetto e della caccia propria delle comunità greche in questo periodo. L'assenza delle armi e la presenza di simboli e rituali non più unicamente afferenti alle rappresentazioni arcaiche, pongono l'accetto su altri aspetti che configurano e caratterizzano le *élites* emergenti. Proprio le testimonianze che emergono dai centri indigeni compresi tra le valle del Sele e il Vallo di Diano esemplificano le complesse trasformazioni che avvengono durante il V secolo.

In particolare il nostro corredo di Roscigno può essere posto a confronto, come vedremo, con variegati contesti circostanti, come ad esempio quelli dei *basileis* dei centri apuli, modulati come la Campania, dalla influenza greca. Tale influenza deve dunque aver portato sino a quel salto strutturale e culturale che caratterizza l'affermazione di una nuova identità consapevolmente legata da comuni interessi politici ed economici, miranti al dominio dei territori e delle risorse fin ora prerogativa dei Greci.

Prima evidente testimonianza di tale processo è la tomba qui illustrata, che per l'associazione dei reperti può essere datata tra la fine del V e gli inizi del IV secolo a.C. ed evidenzia materialmente il cambiamento, l'evoluzione di una complessità di situazioni che caratterizzano la molteplicità delle componenti sociali nel loro incontrarsi e integrarsi.

2. Storia degli studi

Il Museo Archeologico Provinciale di Salerno possiede un ricchissimo archivio, all'interno del quale è possibile rintracciare le vicissitudini dei reperti archeologici che ne costituiscono la collezione: cartigli, documentazione di scavo e fotografie delle campagne intraprese nel salernitano a partire dalla fine dell'Ottocento. Il fascicolo n. 107 dell'Archivio Storico dei Musei Provinciali del Salernitano è dedicato ai rinvenimenti nell'area di Roscigno nel periodo compreso tra il 1928 e il 1938. Di particolare importanza per la ricostruzione del corredo della tomba principesca hanno avuto proprio le prime lettere e il primo inventario, redatto immediatamente dopo lo scavo, grazie ai quali è stato possibile ricostruire la natura della struttura sepolcrale.

La tomba principesca reca una straordinaria associazione di reperti, emblematica per analizzare e ricostruire un contesto simbolo di intrecci di culture. La natura peculiare della sepoltura appare fin dalle sue caratteristiche strutturali, presentandosi elitariamente isolata, con accesso attraverso un lungo *dromos*. L'inumato era accompagnato da un carro in ferro e da circa 50 reperti principalmente in bronzo.

La ricchezza e la particolarità di tale corredo spingono a indagare i meccanismi tramite i quali la cultura si muove e si manifesta nella creazione e lavorazione di materiali preziosi quali bronzo, argento, oro.

La rete straordinaria dei contesti si legge attraverso la materialità, gli oggetti pregni di biografie che ci parlano di chi li ha prodotti, usati e caricati di simboli e significati.

La sepoltura venne individuata nell'ottobre del 1938. Mentre si procedeva alla semina, sul pianoro alla sommità del Monte Pruno, nella proprietà Stio, affiorò prima

> "un tubo metallico, poi la base a tre gambe e ancora una lucerna a tre becchi e due vasi in bronzo",

così il dottor Resciniti, che era stato protagonista di diversi rinvenimenti archeologici nella zona, descrive in una lettera ad Antonio Marzullo, l'allora direttore del Museo Provinciale Vittorio Emanuele II, la scoperta. I lavori di scavo della tomba ebbero luogo dal 4 all'8 novembre dello stesso anno sotto la supervisione del prof. Marzullo che, il 9 novembre del 1938, comunica in una lettera (AMPS, 107-98) al Soprintendente Amedeo Maiuri le operazioni archeologiche, descrivendo così la struttura della tomba e le operazioni di recupero dei reperti:

> "Definita l'area sepolcrale, si è potuto accertare come questa si fosse ottenuta mediante taglio di un crepaccio nel banco naturale lapideo che si estende sul pianoro di m. Pruno, seguendo la pendenza del versante meridionale del monte: il taglio era stato favorito dalla formazione scistosa del banco lapideo, di cui infatti si sono definiti i filoni ai margini del recinto funerario. Il piano della tomba, alla profondità di un metro da quello superficiale al banco lapideo, è risultato ben definito dal taglio eseguito nel crepaccio in modo da ottenere un recinto rettangolare con le seguenti dimensioni: lungh. m. 5; largh. m. 3.30. Tale recinto aveva, sul lato orientale, un invito (alt. 0,15; prof. m. 1,15; largh. m. 2,85), su cui immetteva un "dromos" (largh. m. 1,70), aprentesi obliquamente verso SE

del lato stesso del recinto, fino a raggiungere dopo 2 metri, in leggero pendio, il piano superficiale del banco lapideo. Il recinto sepolcrale aveva, solo sul lato meridionale, una risega (alt. 0,15; largh. 0,45) per l'imposta del tumulo di pietre che copriva la tomba. Il tumulo (alt. 0,80) era, purtroppo, franato; sicchè la suppellettile si è spesso ritrovata in un ammasso di frammenti, talora anche non definibili, poichè le pietre del tumulo abbattutosi sulla deposizione avevano formato compatta lega coi sedimenti della maceria, a causa della permeabilità degli scisti calcarei. L'ardua investigazione è valsa, però, non solo a recuperare tutti gli oggetti e i frammenti della suppellettile sconvolta, ma anche ad accertare la disposizione del corredo funerario attorno alla deposizione, ch'era avvenuta in cassa di legno, com'è conferma nei chiodi rinvenuti accanto allo scheletro. Quest'ultimo, supinamente disteso, era lungo m. 1,80. Orientazione: EO. (…) Comunque è opportuno rilevare quanto segue, circa il carattere particolare della associazione di materiale nella suppellettile funeraria. La deposizione aveva sul fianco destro un prezioso insieme di materiale bronzeo; un candelabro, vasellame vario tra cui un'anfora del tipo c.d. "trozzella", oggetti pertinenti al "mundus muliebris", un gruppetto scultoreo raffig. un guerriero del tipo greco-italico nell'atto di incedere avendo il braccio sinistro. girato sulla spalla di una figura femminile panneggiata (alt. delle figg. 0,12), nonché un kantharos su piede in argento, già da Voi esaminato. Sullo stesso lato, verso i piedi della deposizione, erano gli avanzi di un carro in ferro. (…) La relazione completa sulla scoperta sarà inviata appena ultimata la ricostruzione della suppellettile."

Immediatamente successiva la risposta del Soprintendente in attesa di ulteriori indicazioni e del primo elenco completo.

Esposta presso il Museo Archeologico Provinciale di Salerno è stata oggetto di una prima pubblicazione da parte di Ross Holloway (Holloway 1982, 97–163) e di numerosi studi specifici fino alla fine degli anni '90, ma mai pienamente studiata nel suo complesso. Una importante stagione di restauri, eseguiti in seguito a continui spostamenti nel periodo bellico, interessò i materiali dopo la Seconda Guerra Mondiale, dando origine all'attuale stato del corredo. Purtroppo di questi interventi non si hanno notizie nell'Archivio.

3. Analisi dei reperti

Il vasellame in bronzo è quasi interamente di produzione etrusca e trova ampia diffusione in Campania.

Il candelabro (Fig. 13.1 e 13.2) rappresenta uno dei reperti di maggior interesse della sepoltura di Monte

Fig. 13.1. Il candelabro (Photo: Gaetano Guida – Direzione Musei e Biblioteche della Provincia di Salerno)

Fig. 13.2. Il candelabro (Photo: Gaetano Guida – Direzione Musei e Biblioteche della Provincia di Salerno)

Pruno, ha un'altezza complessiva di cm 148, 3 mentre la cimasa misura cm 14,2. Il fusto, con undici scanalature avente ciascuna alla sua estremità inferiore una linguetta rivolta verso l'alto, poggia su una base circolare decorata ad ovuli, con superiormente, un giro di gocce, da cui si dipartono tre piedi desinenti in zampe ferine, su dischetti staccati, alternate a palmette pendenti perforate al centro. Lo stelo termina superiormente nel piattello con funzione di raccogli gocce. La raggiera, infine, è composta da quattro bracci, delimitati ciascuno da volute, e su di essa un altro disco funge da base per la cimasa, costituita da un gruppo raffigurante un guerriero che cinge con il braccio le spalle della donna accanto a lui. L'uomo ha in mano una corta spada a costolatura mediana, porta un elmo dotato di un grande *lophos* con paragnatidi sollevate e indossa sul chitone una corazza in due pezzi; calza gli schinieri. La donna ha tra i capelli, con scriminatura centrale raccolti in due crocchie laterali, una corona, con la mano destra tiene il mantello sulla spalla e con la sinistra raccoglie le pieghe del chitone all'altezza della coscia. Le decorazioni ed i particolari dell'armatura dell'uomo e le vesti della donna sono stati ottenuti con il punzone circolare. Il candelabro è stato inserito nel gruppo C1 Dohrn (Dohrn 1959, 45–64) e trova confronti con esemplari da Spina (Hostetter 1986), Melfi-Chiuchiari, Locri e Carife- Piano la Sala (Bonifacio 2004, 237). Si tratta di un oggetto di lusso, collegato alla sfera del simposio che – secondo il modo greco di bere vino viene adottato anche dagli etruschi – doveva essere celebrato solo dopo il calare del sole. Poteva essere utilizzato nel gioco del *Kottabos*, con il quale i convitati si dilettavano a far cadere un piattello sovra impostato allo stelo con gocce di vino versate dalle proprie coppe.

La lucerna trilicne (alt. totale cm 12,5; diam. cm 8,5) in bronzo presenta uno dei tre becchi completamente integrato durante il restauro. È a base concava, cavità centrale con tre becchi disposti in senso radiale, equidistanti; asta verticale di sospensione, tubulare e desinente ad anello, fissata con quattro chiodi ribattuti sul fondo del serbatoio.

La *Schnabelkanne* (Fig. 13.3 e 13.4) ottenuta tramite un getto in bronzo e lamina ribattuta (h. cm 24,9; diam. cm 14, 8) è stata oggetto di un restauro invasivo negli anni '50 che ha prodotto integrazioni sia nel collo che nella spalla. Imboccatura obliqua, labbro a disco, collo distinto dalla spalla fortemente arrotondata, corpo ovoide che va rastremandosi verso la base piatta; l'ansa verticale, con scanalatura centrale delimitata da costolature e decorata lungo i margini, ribattuta sull'orlo e sul corpo, si sdoppia alla sommità in due bastoncelli desinenti in teste di serpente, che coprono la metà posteriore del labbro, mentre sul corpo termina in una palmetta dalle foglie aguzze e fortemente plastiche, delimitata su entrambi i lati da elementi serpentiformi fuoriuscenti dalle volute della palmetta stessa. La Schnabelkanne di Monte Pruno, importata dall'Etruria (si veda sulla categoria Bouloumè 1973), trova confronto con quella della tomba n. 89 della necropoli di Carife-Piano la Sala (Bonifacio 2004, 242–243, figg. 4–5), datata ugualmente alla fine del V secolo a.C.

L'*olpe* in bronzo (alt. totale cm 22,2, diam. orlo cm 8) ha subito anch'essa un restauro molto invasivo con forti integrazioni nella parte bassa del corpo e della base. Labbro estroflesso con orlo arrotondato e dentellato, breve collo concavo, corpo globulare, ansa verticale sopraelevata, con insellatura centrale, fissata con chiodini ribattuti sotto il labbro e desinente nell'attacco sul corpo in una *gorgoneion*. Base ad anello. Questo tipo è ampiamente attestato nei contesti etrusco-campani di Fratte (Greco – Pontrandolfo 1990), Nocera (D'Henry 1981) e Padula (Romito 2011, 188–200).

La brocca in bronzo (alt. totale cm 18,8; diam. orlo cm 6,5) è stata oggetto di integrazioni moderne sul corpo sopra l'attacco dell'ansa. Labbro estroflesso a disco

Fig. 13.3. La Schnabelkanne (Photo: Gaetano Guida – Direzione Musei e Biblioteche della Provincia di Salerno)

Fig. 13.4. La Schnabelkanne (Photo: Gaetano Guida – Direzione Musei e Biblioteche della Provincia di Salerno)

obliquo verso l'interno, corpo biconico, fondo piatto, ansa verticale sopraelevata con scanalatura centrale delimitata da costolature, fissata con chiodi ribattuti sotto il labbro e saldata sul corpo con una zampa ferina su fiore di loto fuoriuscente a volute. Il corpo, nella parte di maggior espansione, è decorato con una fascia orizzontale caratterizzata da foglioline d'edera legate da semicerchi, mentre motivi a fiori di loto sono incisi sotto il collo e sul piede. Le due zone delimitate da queste partizioni sottolineano la biconicità del corpo del vaso con sbaccellature terminanti a semicerchi, intermezzate da triangoli. Il labbro è ornato da un motivo ad ovuli.

Il boccaletto in bronzo (alt. cm 8; diam. orlo cm 7) è stato restaurato con integrazioni nel corpo e nel collo. Corpo ovoide, breve collo concavo con labbro fortemente svasato, fondo piano. Il corpo baccellato presenta 43 costolature, desinenti in piccoli semicerchi presso la base, ornata anch'essa con cerchi concentrici.

Il colino in bronzo (lungh. cm 27,8; diam. orlo cm 13,5) è mancante di quasi tutto il passatoio che è del tipo a profilo curvilineo carenato, con parete superiore inflessa, orlo piatto ispessito, ansa a nastro assottigliata verso l'anello di sospensione, desinente in due piccole volute. La decorazione incisa si sviluppa sulla superficie anteriore dell'ansa, e presenta, a partire dal recipiente, una testa femminile di profilo a destra, motivo a foglia dal contorno tratteggiato e, presso l'anello una foglia d'edera con terminazioni punteggiate. Al pari della brocca e della grattugia, il colino trova confronti nelle tombe delle necropoli etrusco-campane di Fratte (Donnarumma – Tomay 1990, 244 e 252), Nocera (Romito 2011) e Vico Equense (Bonghi Jovino 1982, t. 39/3, tav. 5, 2, 6).

La grattugia (lungh. cm 8; largh. cm 6), costituita da tre frammenti assemblati; consiste in una lamina rettangolare con bordo esterno liscio; i lati brevi sono stati ripiegati e ribattuti all'interno, i lati lunghi sono accompagnati da un incavo per la raccolta del cibo grattugiato. I fori sono stati eseguiti con uno strumento a sezione quadrata.

La *nestoris* in bronzo (Fig. 13.5) (alt. cm 57,8; diam. orlo cm 21,8) presenta integrazioni moderne all'orlo, al collo e sul corpo, di un'ansa e di sei rotelle. Breve collo a profilo fortemente concavo con labbro svasato, fissato con chiodi ribattuti sull'orlo superiore del corpo ovoide con spalla a parete tesa; piede cilindrico cavo, a terminazione ricurva con un piccolo cordone attorno all'orlo superiore; anse orizzontali a bastoncello fissate sul corpo con perni, anse verticali costituite da due parti saldate con chiodi ribattuti alla sommità dell'arco dell'ansa, ornate da otto rotelle sistemate a coppie mediante sbarrette alla sommità delle anse e presso l'attacco sul corpo. La decorazione a punzone, punteggiata, consiste in un ramo d'edera sul collo, palmette e fiori di loto alternati sulla spalla e capovolti sopra un motivo d'edera; all'altezza delle anse la decorazione con fiori di loto e palmette eretti, passando sotto le stesse anse, dimostra che queste sono un'aggiunta posteriore. Le anse verticali sono anch'esse ornate con palmette, doppia spirale e motivi a foglia su entrambe le facce esterne e dunque il decoro fu realizzato prima che fossero fissate al corpo e sull'orlo con chiodi ribattuti. La *nestoris* con decorazione floreale incisa rappresenta un unicum, nata come trozzella, successivamente adibita a *nestoris* con l'aggiunta delle anse orizzontali.

Il bacile in bronzo (alt. cm 12,8; diam. orlo cm 7) è stato restaurato nella parte della vasca, i chiodi per il fissaggio delle anse sono moderni. Ampio bacino apodo a vasca emisferica con pareti arcuate, largo orlo piano decorato con cerchietti punzonati, grosse anse fuse, a maniglia, desinenti in borchie sulla vasca dove erano fissate con chiodi ribattuti. Questo tipo di bacile è attestato in Apulia centro-meridionale, a Paestum (Pontrandolfo 1981, 104–107), a Duvanlij in Bulgaria (cit. in Holloway – Nabers 1982).

Le quattro *patere* in bronzo (alt. cm 3,7–4, 7; diam. orlo cm 26–26,7) hanno subito pesanti integrazioni durante i restauri degli anni '50, che purtroppo non permettono di stabilire con certezza la presenza di un'eventuale ansa mobile. Vasca profonda, parete tesa quasi verticale convessa in basso, breve orlo appiattito appena sporgente verso l'intero, base piatta indistinta.

I tre strigili in bronzo rinvenuti nella tomba principesca di Roscigno, oggetto di uno studio specifico da parte di Elena Carando (Carando 1998, 3–10), sono oggetti di fine fattura ed ottima lavorazione, con particolari caratteristiche morfologiche, confrontabili in ambito messapico e a Laterza, tutti prodotti in un'unica officina, individuabile probabilmente a Taranto. Il primo strigile (lungh. cm

Fig. 13.5. La nestoris (Photo: Gaetano Guida – Direzione Musei e Biblioteche della Provincia di Salerno)

21,8; largh. cm 3,5) con larga ligula molto arcuata, punta arrotondata, sezione aperta, passaggio al capulus con gradino e alette; *capulus* nastriforme sagomato, a profilo concavo, curvo; lungo attacco posteriore alla ligula a foglia lanceolata. Sulla faccia anteriore del *capulus* due incisioni: un uccello di profilo, immediatamente sotto un caduceo (attributo di Hermes) e successivamente una impressione a sigillo, raffigurante un attore comico in costume con *kalathiskos* (potrebbe essere una rappresentazione del dio), da leggersi ruotando l'oggetto di 180°. Il secondo strigile (lungh. cm 15,5; larg. cm 3,4) presenta una larga ligula molto arcuata, sezione aperta, passaggio al capulus con gradino e alette, *capulus* nastriforme sagomato a profilo concavo, curvo. Sulla faccia anteriore del *capulus* c'è una decorazione consistente in una impressione a sigillo, con l'immagine di una figura maschile nuda, stante, rivolta a destra (Apollo?). Il terzo strigile (lungh. cm 14; largh. cm 3) è molto lacunoso, si hanno due frammenti assemblati: parte del *capulus* e della ligula, sul retro della quale appare l'impronta dell'appendice foliata del *capulus*. I tre strigili sono realizzati in lamina di bronzo lavorata a sbalzo, molto sottile nella ligula e più spessa nel *capulus*. In ambiente greco lo strigile era utilizzato soprattutto da coloro che potevano dedicare molto tempo all'atletica – quindi fondamentalmente dalle élites cittadine – presso le classi dominanti non greche tale strumento assurge a simbolo dell'appartenenza del defunto ad un ceto sociale molto elevato, prescindendo totalmente da un suo reale uso in relazione ad attività sportive.

Il *kantharos* d'argento (Fig. 13.6 e 13.7) (alt. 18,4; diam. orlo cm 11,6); è mancante di una delle due teste sileniche più piccole e uno dei rinforzi interni dell'ansa. Alto labbro svasato a profilo leggermente concavo con orlo espanso, vasca a profilo convesso, stelo cilindrico centralmente ingrossato da una modanatura accompagnato sopra e sotto da scanalature, piede a calice esternamente scanalato, anse sormontanti a nastro con costolature centrali e laterali, con attacco sull'orlo e sul punto di giunzione tra il labbro e la vasca. Due coppie di teste sileniche in argento dorato, eseguite a sbalzo, erano applicate rispettivamente nel punto di attacco delle anse all'orlo e sull'esterno delle anse stesse nel punto dove queste presentano la costolatura centrale appiattita per uno spazio esattamente corrispondente ad ospitare dette testine, come ha sottolineato lo studio della Scheich (Scheich 1995, 12–28). Purtroppo durante i restauri degli anni '50 le teste sileniche più piccole furono collocate alle terminazioni degli elementi di rinforzo delle anse, sulla parte interna delle anse stesse, dove tutt'ora si trovano. Nel fondo interno un medaglione a sbalzo, sempre in argento dorato, con contorno perlinato a mò di moneta, rappresenta un'amazzone dal chitone e mantello svolazzante, il cui nome è riportato in dialetto dorico: *ANDPOMAXA*.

L'ornamento personale del defunto è costituito dalla sola corona d'argento con al centro la rosetta in lamina d'oro (Fig. 13.8), come a Taranto, Metaponto ed Eboli (Guzzo 1993), restando comunque un *unicum* per l'abbinamento dei due metalli preziosi. La rosetta (diam. totale cm 4,6) è costituita da una foglia d'oro ritagliata in modo da formare

Fig. 13.6. Il *kantharos* d'argento (Photo: Gaetano Guida – Direzione Musei e Biblioteche della Provincia di Salerno)

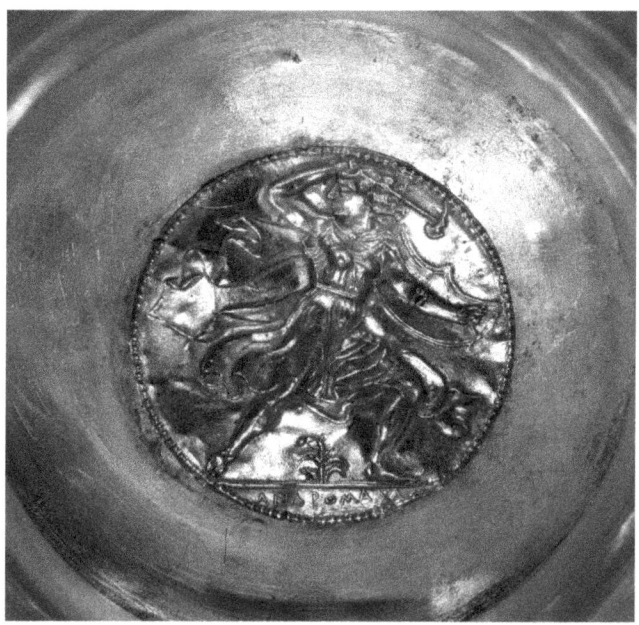

Fig. 13.7. Il *kantharos* d'argento (Photo: Gaetano Guida – Direzione Musei e Biblioteche della Provincia di Salerno)

una rosetta a sei petali di misura variabile, leggermente curvati verso l'alto, con striature molto fini; al centro, dove la rosetta presenta una perforazione dentellata, si trova una semisfera riempita di gesso, su cui la lamina è modellata assumendo forma leggermente conica. Le analisi (Paternoster – Rinzivillo 1995) condotte dimostrano che i due elementi di cui è composta la rosetta (petali e cuore) sono stati realizzati dalla stessa foglia d'oro. La corona d'argento (largh. max delle foglie da cm 1,7 a cm 3,1) è molto frammentaria e lacunosa, conserva solo sette foglie, mentre solo due gambi sono originali, gli altri sono integrazioni dovute al restauro degli anni '50. Allo stesso

Fig. 13.8. La rosetta in lamina d'oro (Photo: Gaetano Guida – Direzione Musei e Biblioteche della Provincia di Salerno)

restauro si deve il montaggio delle foglie sul plexiglass su cui oggi lo troviamo. È composta da un tubo, ottenuto curvando una lamina d'argento molto spessa, che funge da branca principale del ramo, dal quale partono, da entrambi i lati e senza simmetria, piccoli steli di foglie cuoriformi, di grandezza decrescente verso una estremità. Le analisi chimiche (Paternoster – Rinzivillo 1995) hanno confermato che la corona è stata realizzata con elementi ricavati da una foglia d'argento ritagliata e sagomata e hanno permesso di identificare gli elementi in ferro aggiunti a completamento dell'oggetto come il gambo di alcune foglie.

Accompagnano gli oggetti in metallo un ricco corredo in ceramica (si elencano qui per completezza gli elementi che lo compongono): un cratere a colonnette a vernice nera, che rientra in una produzione che dalla metà del V secolo a.C. accomuna Oliveto Citra, i centri del Vallo di Diano come Buccino, Satriano e Atena Lucana alle produzioni di area Peuceta e Messapica (Romito 2011); due *oinochoai* a figure rosse, con i nomi dei personaggi incisi in alfabeto dorico, sono ricondotte all'ambito della ceramica protolucana e attribuite al Gruppo di Schwerin (Holloway – Nabers 1982, 97–163) per la caratteristica dei motivi decorativi che riquadrano i pannelli figurati; al mondo greco appartiene il *rython* a testa d'ariete, la cui matrice, secondo Herbert Hoffmann (Hoffmann 1962, nn. 101–103. 105), ha prodotto altri quattro esemplari, in stile sub-mediaco, è inserito nella "Persian Class"; la *kylix* a figure rosse, in argilla rosata, vernice nera compatta e lucente che Holloway e Nabers (Holloway – Nabers 1980), seguendo Beazley (Beazley 1963, vol.2, 1297, n.4), attribuiscono al Pittore di Londra E 122.

Le due ruote del carro in ferro erano costituite da un telaio in legno rivestito da una struttura in ferro composta da due parti non collegate. Un battistrada con perni radiali equidistanti cm 15 inchiodati nel cerchione in legno, a sua volta sostenuto e rafforzato da due fasce laterali, collegate fra loro con chiodi ribattuti ogni 3 cm. Dal nucleo ligneo si dipartivano evidentemente gli elementi radiali destinati ad essere alloggiati negli spazi creati ogni 3 cm dai chiodi colleganti le due fasce laterali. Il raggio originario della ruota doveva aggirarsi intorno ai 40 cm. La presenza del carro, attestato a Ruvo del Monte (Bottini 1990) e Melfi-Chiuchiari (Cerchiai – Colucci Pescatori – D'Henry 1999), è indice della funzione militare del defunto unitamente ad una situazione economica molto prestigiosa.

4. Conclusioni

La posizione supina dell'inumato costituisce una netta differenziazione, sottolineata dalla composizione del corredo e dalla presenza del carro e una punta di lancia indicanti insieme ad altri elementi, il carattere maschile della sepoltura. La deposizione, probabilmente in cassa lignea come testimoniano i chiodi rinvenuti, differenzia il principe, probabilmente lucano o comunque legato a tale matrice, dai precedenti abitanti del territorio che seppellivano i propri defunti rannicchiati o incinerati, secondo un più antico costume riservato ai membri dell'aristocrazia, come testimonia la sepoltura 1100 a fossa ricoperta con tumulo di terra, con un corredo di 25 oggetti, rinvenuta nel 1993, posta nella stessa area e pertinente a un membro di spicco di almeno due generazioni precedenti (Ferrara 2014). Da ciò potremmo sostenere che tra i primi decenni del V sec. a.C., a cui appartiene la tomba 1100 e l'ultimo venticinquennio dello stesso secolo probabile riferimento temporale della tomba in oggetto, nella comunità che occupa il vasto territorio di Roscigno si assiste a una trasformazione dei rituali funerari propri delle genti lucane che si espandono sia sulla costa tirrenica che nelle aree interne.

Al di là delle articolazioni etniche, la tomba di Monte Pruno presenta numerose e già sottolineate analogie con la tomba 43 di Melfi. Al tempo stesso la nostra tomba sembra distinguersi dalla coppia di sepolture principesche di Melfi per una più coerente adesione ai modelli di tradizione greca, la cui portata è evidenziata dalla presenza di tre strigili in bronzo legati alla tradizione dell'*ephebia*, ma anche dalla presenza nel servizio da simposio di forme potorie come il *kantharos* e il *rython* che proiettano la pratica del consumo del vino verso una dimensione dionisiaca (Cerchiai – Colucci Pescatori – D'Henry 1999). Alcuni elementi in bronzo, come l'*oinochoe*, l'*olpe* e il colino sono riconducibili a officine etrusco-italiche. Si tratta di elementi diffusi nelle tombe di Bologna, Spina, e soprattutto nei corredi rinvenuti nella Campania meridionale sottoposta alla influenza etrusca come Nocera, Vico Equense, Fratte, nelle tombe di Melfi, e in alcuni centri apuli dell'entroterra. Il candelabro trova riscontri, fuori dalla Campania, con quelli di Marzabotto, Civita Castellana, Locri e in particolare l'iconografia del guerriero presente sulla cimasa, richiama l'oplita etrusco esemplificato dal Marte di Todi come da numerosi bronzetti votivi umbro-sabellici (Romito 2011). Nulla però ci dà la certezza di escludere che si trattasse di produzioni campane o lucane che abbiano molto risentito degli influssi etruschi quanto di quelli greci. Il *kantharos* e il boccaletto sono di provenienza greca, mentre le *oinochoai* sono fabbricate a Taranto e il bacile è proprio dei centri indigeni della Puglia.

La deposizione supina in cassa lignea e la composizione del corredo riflettono il sistema ideologico ben noto dalle necropoli pestane. La forma di *lekythos* attestata nella tomba principesca, come la presenza del *guttus* baccellato, testimoniano produzioni locali di larga diffusione e circolazione a partire poi marcatamente dalla metà del IV sec. a.C., proiettando l'insediamento di Monte Pruno verso la costa tirrenica

Il nostro defunto si presenta, come un capo dell'aristocrazia locale che sceglie forme di auto rappresentazione non più esclusivamente guerriere, aspetto privilegiato dagli antenati, ma accentuando altri valori simbolici inerenti alla pratica atletica e al rituale dionisiaco-simposiaco (corona di vite poggiante sul capo come simbolo del culto dionisiaco attraverso il tramite locale del rituale orfico, rappresentazione dionisiaca in una delle *oinochoai* trilobate a figure rosse, oltre che ceramica da banchetto, candelabro etc.).

Si tratta di uno dei primi rappresentanti di una élite dominante lucana che ha già preso possesso della Poseidonia greca e inizia a diffondersi, a integrarsi, a imporsi nel tessuto indigeno locale dell'entroterra.

Bibliografia

Beazley, J., D., 1963. *Attic red-figure vase painters.* Oxford. Vol.2, 1550–1551, n. 22, Group of Class W.

Bonghi Jovino M., 1982. *La necropoli preromana di Vico Equense.* Napoli.

Bonifacio R., 2004. Le tombe 89–90 della necropoli di Carife. In: La Regina A. – Caiazzo D., a cura di, *Safinim: studi in onore di Adriano La Regina per il premio I Sanniti.* Piedimonte Matese. Arti Grafiche Grillo, 237–259.

Bottini A., 1990. Il candelabro etrusco di Ruvo del Monte. In: *Bollettino d'Arte 59,* 1–14.

Bottini A e Guzzo P.G., 1986. Greci e indigeni nel sud della Penisola dall VIII secolo a.C. alla conquista romana. In: *Popoli e civiltà dell'Italia antica, VIII.* Roma, 11–390.

Bouloumiè B, 1973. *Les oinochoès en bronze du type "Schnabelkanne".* Roma.

Carando, E., 1998. Gli strigili della tomba "principesca" di Roscigno. In: *Apollo. Bollettino dei Musei Provinciali del Salernitano*.XIV. Electa Napoli, 3–10.

Cerchiai L. – Colucci Pescatori G. – D'Henry G., 1999. L'Italia antica: Italia meridionale. In: Emiliozzi E., a cura di, *Carri da guerra e principe etruschi: catalogo della mostra.* Viterbo, palazzo dei Papi 24 maggio 1997-31 gennaio 1998. 25–32.

De La Genière, J. *Ambre intagliate del Museo di Salerno,* in Apollo, 1, 1961, 75–88.

D'Henry G., 1981. Una tomba a Nocera della seconda metà del V secolo a.C.. problemi di inquadramento. In: *AION III,* 159.

Dohrn, T., 1959. Zwei Etruskische Kandelaber. In: *Römische Mitteilungen,* 66, 45–64.

Donnarumma R. – Tomay L., 1990. I corredidel VI–V secolo. In: Greco C. – Pontrandolfo A., a cura di, *Fratte. Un insediamento etrusco-campano.* Modena, 207–275.

Ferrara, B., 2014. Roscigno, Monte Pruno. Segni di trasformazione nell'insediamento tra la fine del V e il IV sec. a.C. In: Greco G., – Ferrara B., a cura di, *Segni di appartenenza e identità di comunità nel mondo indigeno.* Atti del Seminario di Studi. Napoli. Naus Editoria, 183–233

Guzzo, P. G., 1993. *Oreficerie dalla Magna Grecia. Ornamenti in Oro e argento dall'Italia Meridionale tra l'VIII ed il I secolo.* Taranto, 112. 114. 279. 318.

Greco C. – Pontrandolfo A., a cura di, *Fratte. Un insediamento etrusco-campano.* Modena

Hoffmann, H., 1962. *Attic Red-Figured rhyta.* Mainz. Nn. 101–103. 105.

Holloway, R. R. – Nabers, N., 1980. Le canthare d'argent de Roscigno (Monte Pruno, Salerne). In: *Aurifex 1, Etudes sur l'orfèvrerie antique. Studies in Ancient Jewelry.* Louvain-la-Neuve, 64–79

Holloway, R., – Nabers, N., 1982. The princely burial of Roscigno (Monte Pruno). In: *Revue des Archéologues et Historiens d'Art de Louvain.* XV, 97–163

Hostetter E. 1986. *Bronzes from Spina I.* Mainz am Rhein.

Nista L. – Capini S., a cura di, 2000. *Italia dei Sanniti. Guida alla mostra.* Milano. Mondadori Electa.

Paternoster, G., – Rinzivillo, R., 1995. La tomba principesca di Roscigno (Monte Pruno, Salerno): analisi mediante XRF degli oggetti ornamentali. In: *Apollo. Bollettino dei Musei Provinciali del Salernitano*.XI. Electa Napoli, 29–30

Pontrandolfo, A., 1982. *I Lucani. Etnografia e archeologia di una regione antica.* Milano, 104–107

Romito, M., 1996. La tomba principesca di Roscigno. In: *Posidonia e i Lucani. Catalogo della Mostra al Museo di Paestum per I Greci d'Occidente.* Napoli. Electa, 45. 94–100

Romito, M., 2011. *Salerno, "Provincia Archeologica". La politica culturale dell'Amministrazione Provinciale dal decennio prebellico al dopoguerra. Apollo XXIV–XXVI (2008–2010 Volume monografico).* Paestum. Pandemos, 188–200

Scheich, C., 1995. Nouvelles considerérations sur la tombe princiére de Roscigno (Monte Pruno, Salerne): étude tecnique des ornaments personnels en métal. In: *Apollo. Bollettino dei Musei Provinciali del Salernitano*.XI. Electa Napoli, 12–28

Trendall, A. D., 1967. *The Red-Figured Vases of Lucania, Campania and Sicily.* Oxford, 67–70

14

Authepsa: A Singular Brass Container from Augusta Emerita (Mérida, Spain). History and Interpretation of the Object

Rafael Sabio González, Cristina Isabel Mena Méndez

National Museum of Roman Art, Mérida

Independent researcher

rafael.sabio@cultura.gob.es

Abstract: This paper presents a hitherto unknown and never exhibited bronze receptacle from the collection of the National Museum of Roman Art in Mérida (Badajoz, Spain). The object belongs to the museum's historical collection and was located by the authors of this paper in the reserve collections. This oval receptacle has a hole in its upper section into which a tubular element is inserted. The object is thought to be a kitchen, or medical utensil for heating or cooling liquids held inside the receptacle by means of hot coals or ice placed in the tubular element. By inserting one part into the other, the temperature of the first is transferred to the content of the second without the heating or cooling material coming into contact with the foodstuff.

Keywords: Authepsa; Augusta Emerita; Roman bronze vessel

1. Introduction

The permanent collection of the National Museum of Roman Art in Mérida (Badajoz, Spain) houses an important collection of bronze finds, most of which date to the Early Imperial period and were found at the Mérida site. Among the finds is an interesting receptacle (inv. no 13591) which has never been exhibited. The shape of the object suggests an as-yet undocumented kitchen utensil from the *colony,* , of which there is only one recorded from across the entire Iberian Peninsula (Tomasevic Buck 2002). It has been difficult to properly identify the object, not only because of its unusual typology but because of the complex story behind its entry into the collection. We address both aspects in detail in this paper[1].

2. Description

The object in question consists of two separate elements which we will call A and B. The second (B) can be inserted in the hole in the first (A) (Fig. 14.1).

Element A is a receptacle 21 cm high with a maximum diameter of 20.5 cm. It has a flat bottom with a 11.5 cm diameter, an ovoid body and an opening with a flat rim around the tightly fitting insert B (it is currently separate but would originally have been joined to the rim). The body has various holes, particularly on the lower third of its surface, and is crossed by various precisely incised horizontal lines, some of which run in pairs. Halfway up

Figure 14.1. General view of the *authepsa* inv. no. 13591 (MNAR Photographic Archive/Lorenzo Plana).

---

[1] This work is part of the project titled InterArq- Arqueología e interdisciplinariedad: una investigación arqueológico-histórica sobre las relaciones interdisciplinares en la historia de la arqueología española (siglos XIX y XX) (InterArq Archaeology and Interdisciplinary Working: An Archaeological and Historical Investigation into Interdisciplinary Relationships in the History of Spanish Archaeology (19th and 20th Centuries), HAR2016-334033/Hist, funded by the State Research Agency (Spanish acronym AEI) and the European Regional Development Fund (ERDF, EU).

is a small circular hole with a diameter of 0.5 cm, framed by a circular corrosion mark with a diameter of 4 cm (Fig. 14.2). On the opposite side, near the mouth of the receptacle, is another round hole with a diameter of 1.5 cm (Fig. 14.3). It appears also to have been framed by a circular mark with a diameter of 4 cm. Slightly below this height are three equidistant hexagonal marks on the body of the object. They are around 3 cm wide and much fainter than the other marks already described. In fact, they are barely perceptible. Those correspond to hexagonal elements which were originally attached there. The part which is separated from the mouth comprises a ring with an inverted L cross-section. Its vertical section is 1 cm wide and is decorated externally with a series of relief ovals, below a 1-cm-wide everted rim.

Element B is a hollow tube 20 cm tall, which is slightly tapered and wider towards its base. This last part was possibly straight with a 9.3 cm diameter but does not survive. Its upper extreme has an internal diameter of 7 cm and continues as a horizontal rim 2.5 cm wide, with an off-center perforation of 1.2 cm in diameter, fitting perfectly over the separate everted rim of element A. This area demonstrates how the two parts were connected to make a single vessel.

3. History of the object

The find entered the collection on March 7th 1972, according to Volume III of the museum's records. The entry contains a short description of the object: "Pot with an internal cylindrical vessel. Bronze. Would have had a handle." The record states the following origin: "Casa Herrera". The field for method of acquisition is blank. In the 'remarks' field the find was given an identification number prior to becoming part of the museum collection: "No. 69" (Fig. 14.4).

All these data present a fundamental problem in that they are relatively imprecise and likely inaccurate in terms of the acquisition and the location of the finding, a site around seven kilometres north of Mérida's town centre. A late-antiquity basilica with opposing apses was found there in the 1940s. The basilica was first excavated in 1943 by José de Calasanz Serra Rafols, who handed over some of the finds to the museum in that same year (Serra Rafols 1943). His work was continued between 1968 and 1972 by the archaeologists Luis Caballero Zoreda and Thilo Ulbert (Ulbert – Caballero 1976) and by Ulbert in 1987 (Ulbert – Cruz Villalón 1990).

All of the materials found at the site have been dated to between the 4th and 8th centuries AD. Neither the shape nor the chronology of the object which we are interested in fit with the characteristics of any of the objects found in that context. Analysing the museum records reveals that the vessel marks the end of a series which started with various objects originating from the excavations at Casa Herrera. These include a piece of marble cymatium moulding (inv. no. 13586), a clay lamp (inv. no. 13587), and three ceramic jugs (inv. no. 13588–13590), all found during the excavation by Serra Rafols at Casa Herrera in 1943. However, unlike other finds handed over to the museum that same year, these did not become part of the collection until 1972. Their shape and the detailed information on these finds provided by Ulbert and Caballero in their work

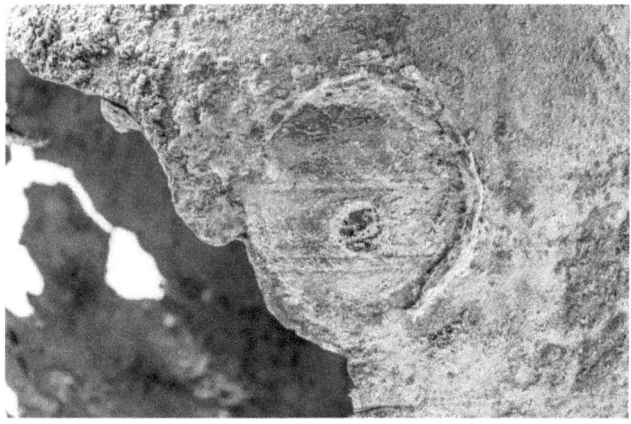

Figure 14.2. Detail of the middle hole and the mark of the application around it (MNAR Photographic Archive/ Lorenzo Plana).

Figure 14.3. Detail of the upper hole and the mark of the application around it (MNAR Photographic Archive/ Lorenzo Plana).

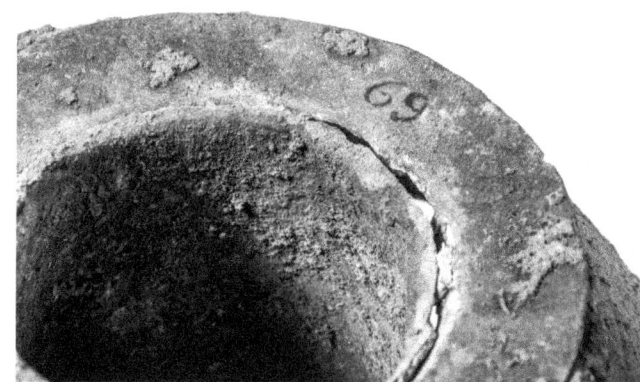

Figure 14.4. Detail of the own numbering inscribed on the authepsa (MNAR Photographic Archive/Lorenzo Plana)

on the basilica leave no doubt that they must have come from Casa Herrera. The ceramic items have their own numbers in the museum records (30. 35. 37 and 31) which relate to other finds also found in the 1943 excavation, but which were handed over to the museum during the 1968 campaign. This collection of objects remained in the possession of the archaeologist Serra Rafols until it was given to the museum in Mérida by the new custodians, following subsequent excavations.

It is possible that the physical similarities between our object and those just mentioned led to its being associated with these when it was handed over to the museum, along with the number 69 written on the base in identical lettering to that found on the finds from Casa Herrera (Figs. 14.4 and 14.5). However, aside from the problem arising from the shape of our vessel, that number does not appear to be connected to the list of other finds originating from Casa Herrera. The number on our find is 26 numbers apart from the last number corresponding to the finds which are linked to that site with certainty. Given all of the above, we can deduce that our vessel was found by Serra Rafols in 1943 along with the others and, like those, remained in his possession for research purposes, unlike the vast collection of finds which were in fact handed over to the museum in Mérida that year. From what we have been able to confirm regarding the 1943 accession, the number on this object may refer to a general record of materials from various interventions carried out in the city by that archaeologist. Only a very specific range in this document (nos 174–192) would correspond to Casa Herrera. Given what we know about the list of materials admitted in March 16th 1943, Serra Rafols handed over items originating not only from the aforementioned basilica but which were exhumed from other locations in the urban area surrounding the Mérida site, such as los Columbarios (nos 1–165), San Lázaro (nos 166–173), Miralrío (nos 193–194), Pancaliente (nos 195–221) and El Berrocal (no. 222). According to the list, the last two were excavated prior to the Civil War and not by Serra Rafols, and the finds were incorporated into the list before being handed over to the museum.

Given this information, it would be no surprise if there existed a second document (the whereabouts of which are unknown) containing a parallel list to the one dated March 16th 1943. The objects on this list would have been intended for future accession by the museum, so long as they remained in the possession of the archaeologist (perhaps for research purposes). However, Serra Rafols never published anything on the subject. The objects in this second hypothetical group must have been handed over by the archaeologist to Ulbert and Caballero, who deposited them in the Mérida museum between 1968 and 1972. This may have been where the confusion arose – perhaps a vessel of different origin slipped in among those found in Casa Herrera. What is certain from examination of the objects handed over to the museum by Serra Rafols in 1943 is that among those from *los Columbarios* is a small bronze object identified as number 130 in the list. It is described as a "Small polygonal bronze cup" and was more generically identified by the museum as a "finial". It is currently identified as inv. no. 4333 (Fig. 14.6). The cup is a perfect fit with one of the hexagonal marks near the mouth of our object, thus confirming the discovery of our vessel in the *Los Columbarios* area in 1943 (Fig. 14.7).

4. Functional interpretation

The object in question is identified as a mere "pot" in the records of the National Museum of Roman Art. This assertion is based largely on its shape and includes the extraordinary addition of an "internal cylindrical vessel". The inventory record does little to argue with this information. A small correction substitutes the Spanish word "puchero" (pot) for "olla" (pan), and provides summary information on its dimensions and its "beaded edging". Given its shape, however, it is not difficult to imagine a more unusual and specific purpose. Beyond simply containing a particular substance, the double cavity of the object must have been used to separate one substance from another with which it could have a beneficial interaction.

After analysing the existing literature on Roman bronze vessels, we have identified a singular receptacle designed

Figure 14.5. Detail of the own numbering inscribed on the jug inv. no. 13588 (MNAR Photographic Archive/Lorenzo Plana).

Figure 14.6. Handle inv. no. 4333 (MNAR Photographic Archive/Lorenzo Plana).

Figure 14.7. Location of the handle inv. no. 4333 on the authepsa (MNAR Photographic Archive/Lorenzo Plana)

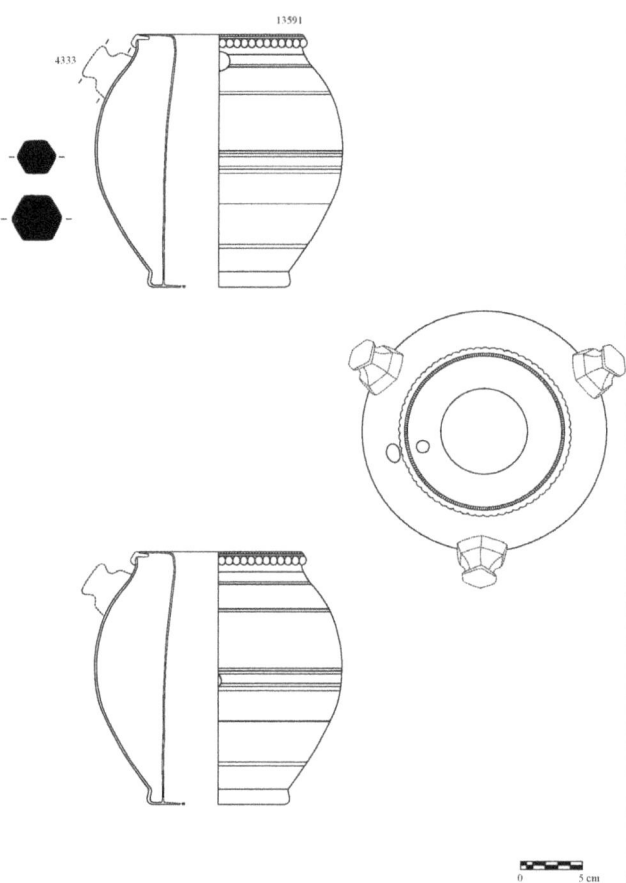

Figure 14.8. Profile, section and zenithal view of the authepsa with restitution of the handles (drawing by Cristina Mena).

specifically for heating a given substance and keeping it warm. Named *authepsa* in Greek, the body of the object contained two cavities: one for liquid, and the other for the coals which would provide the required heat. The main body of the object would not come into contact either with the fire or with the hot substance. Of the variety and diversity of *authepsae* catalogued by Tomasevic Buck in 2002, ours corresponds specifically to category A1, which contains 16 examples to date. The distinguishing features of this type are their ovoid shape and the presence of a tube for holding hot coals and which opens at its upper end.

The information provided by Tomasevic Buck enables us to interpret the two openings in the body of our object and the circles around them as the remains of a detached element which would have been used (at least the one in the centre of the body) for pouring the liquid contained in element A, with some form of valve to regulate the flow. Similarly, the three equidistant marks near the mouth would have been for inserting other elements to facilitate hanging the object on chains. As already seen, inv. no. 4333 is one of these additional elements. It has a simple hexagonal shape with an indentation near its finial, perhaps for attaching the chain used to support the object. We know nothing of the additional elements which would have been attached to the two existing holes in element A, except that they must have had a circular component. The precise decoration on the body and the beading around the mouth can also be found in other vessels from Tomasevic Buck's A1 category. The hole on the rim of element B would align with the upper hole on element A, and it displays signs of another element having been attached. However, we do not know if it would have been used for attaching a lid, for facilitating the flow of liquid in element A, or for both purposes (Fig. 14.8).

The various vessels analysed by Tomasevic Buck have been dated between the 1st and 3rd centuries AD. However, in the absence of more specific information, and with caution, we date our vessel to the Early Imperial period.

Bibliography

AA.VV., 1986. *Le collezioni del Museo Nazionale di Napoli*. Roma: De Luca.

Biroli Stefanelli, L. P., 1990. *Il bronzo dei romani. Arredo e suppellettile*. Roma, 1990.

Carandini, A., 1977. Alcune forme bronzee conservate a Pompei e nel Museo Nazionale di Napoli. *L'instrumentum domesticum di Ercolano e Pompei nella prima età imperiale*. Roma: L'Erma de Bretschneider, 163168.

Mutz, A., 1959. Bau und Betrieb einer römischen Authepsa (Samowar). *Ur-Schweiz*, 23.3, 37–48.

Serra Rafols, J. C., 1943. *Ingresos campaña excavaciones 1943* (unpublished report kept in the MNAR document archive).

Tomasevic Buck, T., 2002. Römische Authepsa, auch ein Instrument der ärztlichen Versorgung? *13. Bronze Congress: from the parts to the whole*, vol. II. Portsmouth: Journal of Roman Archaeology, 213–232.

Ulbert, T. – Caballero Zoreda, L., 1976. *La basílica paleocristiana de Casa Herrera en las cercanías de Mérida (Badajoz)*. Madrid: CSIC.

Ulbert, T. – Cruz Villalón, M., 1991. Nachuntersuchungen im Bereich der Frühchristlichen Basilika von Casa Herrera bei Mérida. *Madrider Mitteilungen*, 32, 185–207.

15

Technology Matters: The Kal-e Chendar Bronze Statuary from the Seleucid to the Parthian Periods

Gunvor Lindström

Deutsches Archäologisches Institut

gunvor.lindstroem@dainst.de

Abstract: After the conquest of Alexander the Great, Iran became part of the Seleucid Empire, a realm with strong ties to the West, until ca. 140/30 BC when Iran was incorporated into the Parthian Empire, centred in the East. This paper looks on mostly life-size Seleucid and Parthian period bronze statues discovered in the 1930s at Kal-e Chendar/Shami in Southwest Iran and since rarely studied. It argues that the statues constitute two groups in terms of style and iconography and technologically. This was the result of object studies at the National Museum of Iran that included art historical classification, 3D modelling and reconstruction, visual investigation focusing on casting technique, and pXRF.

Keywords: Hellenistic Art; Parthian Art; Iran; Casting Technique; Bronze Alloy

Introduction

In 1936, *The Times* of London ran a story by legendary archaeologist-explorer Sir Aurel Stein titled "Traces of Alexander the Great", detailing a cache of bronze sculptures accidentally discovered by newly-settled villagers at Kal-e Chendar near a ravine called Shami, high in the Zagros Mountains of southwest Iran (Stein 1936). The Shami bronzes, as they have come to be called – referred to here as Kal-e Chendar bronzes – are a group of mostly life-size sculptures, two nearly complete, and at least 9 others represented by one or more fragments. Although the sculptures certainly have no direct relation to Alexander himself, they date to the time after the Macedonian conquests of Persia, that is, the Hellenistic and Parthian period (3rd century BCE to 3rd century CE).

Because ancient bronze sculptures were usually melted down for their material, which was recycled into coins and other objects, only 100 to 200 bronze sculptures survive from the two centuries that comprise the Hellenistic period (323–23 BCE). The number of sculptures preserved in Kal-e Chendar is thus unusual. Had such an extraordinary number of bronzes been unearthed at a single site in the Mediterranean, this would certainly have caused a great stir among archaeologists. However, Iran was – and still is – outside the focus of classical archaeology. In addition, most of the sculptures belong to the art of the Parthian period that lasted in Southwest Iran from around 139 BCE to AD 224. Hence, they belong to "Parthian Art" which is often judged from a "classical" point of view to be stiff and rigid and therefore somehow inferior, a general sentiment that is rarely articulated but widely shared among historians of ancient Greek art. That is probably why the Kal-e Chendar sculptures have not received the attention they deserve until very recently.

This paper presents the first comprehensive, albeit preliminary, study of the Kal-e-Chendar bronze sculptures, which are of great importance because they represent the bulk of preserved bronze statues from the Hellenistic East. It introduces the sculptures from Iran to the debate on Ancient Bronzes that so far almost exclusively focused on bronze sculptures from the Mediterranean (for a rare exception cf. Meyers 2002). The study combines art-historical and technological perspectives and thus uses a research approach that plays an increasingly important role in research on ancient Mediterranean bronzes since the 1970s. In doing so, it goes back to the actual meaning of the word techné, which the Greeks used to describe the entire process – the art, the skill, and the craft of production (Mattusch 1996, 218).

Art-historical classification of the bronze statues

Only two bronze sculptures from Kal-e Chendar have been mentioned in scholarly literature with any frequency. The "Hellenistic Ruler" is a slightly larger than life head of a clean-shaven ruler portrait in Greek style (Lindström 2017, fig 22.1). Although the head is one of the very few Hellenistic ruler portraits preserved in the original, it is relatively rarely depicted in overviews and synopses of ancient Greek art. This is certainly due to the deformation of the bronze head that makes it impossible to identify the ruler. In contrast, the so called "Parthian Nobleman", a nearly two meter high and almost complete statue of a frontally standing man dressed in wide robes and trousers (Fig. 15.1 right), is considered a prime example of Parthian

Gunvor Lindström

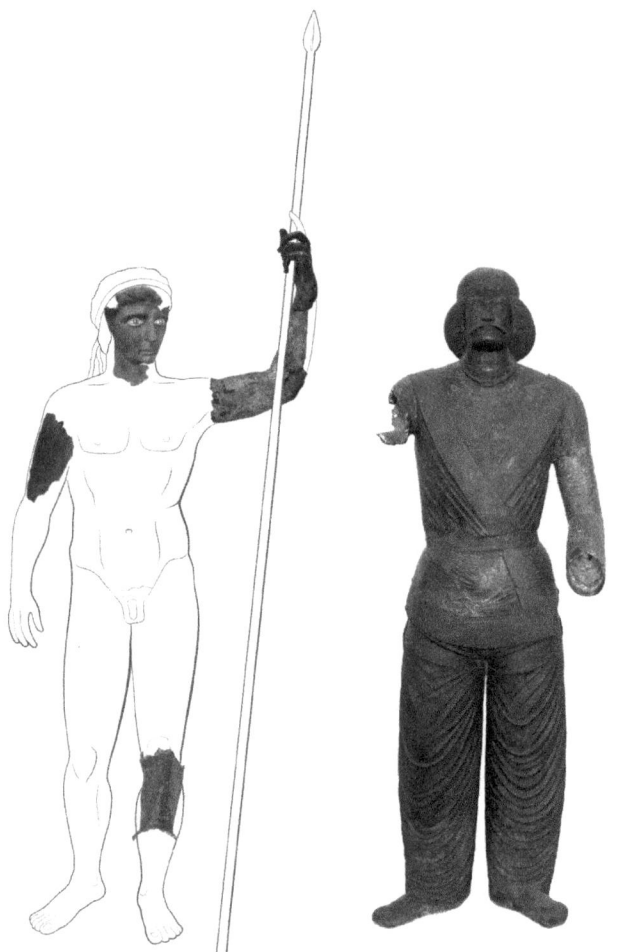

Figure 15.1 'Hellenistic Ruler' (National Museum of Iran, several fragments) and 'Parthian Nobleman' (National Museum of Iran Inv. 2401) from Kal-e Chendar/Shami.

art and illustrates almost every publication on the history of the Near East or on the Parthian period.

The most comprehensive survey of the number of Kal-e Chendar bronze statues is by Aurel Stein (1940) and André Godard (1937), although these initial publications do not illustrate all sculptures and fragments. Later publications deal with individual pieces, but they never include all finds (e.g. Kawami 1987; Mathiesen 1992; Fleischer 2016). A reasonably complete overview of the Kal-e Chendar bronzes was obtained only in 2015 with the author's own research that included object studies in the National Museum of Iran (Lindström 2017). These studies "rediscovered" several bronze fragments in the storage rooms of the museum. Moreover, previously unpublished bronzes were identified and, thus, added to the corpus that results in the current count of at least 11 bronze sculptures from Kal-e Chendar.

Despite the limited research on the Kal-e Chendar bronzes, several scholars suggested that they form two groups in terms of style and iconography (e.g. Mathiesen 1992, 165; Fleischer 2016, 270–271): On the one hand are "Greek" sculptures in heroic nudity and/or with attributes of Greek deities, the representative of which is the "Hellenistic Ruler". On the other hand are 'un-Greek' – respectively Iranian – sculptures in tunic and pants, of which the 'Parthian Nobleman' is the most complete statue. The classification resulted in an approximate dating of the "Greek" group to the 3rd or 2nd century BCE, that is the period after the Macedonian conquest of Persia, when the influx of elements of Greek art into the East was strong, presumably a response to the demands of Greek and other Western settlers in Persia and the more or less Hellenized local elites. In contrast, the "un-Greek" group of sculptures was generally dated to the Parthian period, which lasted in Southwest Iran from 139 BCE to roughly the early 3rd century CE. This dating is based on the observation that the Arsacid kings who ruled the Parthian empire turned away from the Hellenistic portrait conventions, at least as far as their representations on coins are concerned, by presenting themselves in long, loose robes, bearded and with longer hair. There were attempts to date the "Parthian Nobleman" more precisely, with a tendency to the 1st centuries BCE and CE (Kawami 1987, 66). However, dating of the Parthian Kal-e Chendar sculptures faces two problems. First, they lack comparative framework because they are the only large bronzes preserved from the Parthian empire. Secondly, even Parthian stone sculptures are known only from a few art centres quite distant from one other, namely Hatra, Palmyra, Dura Europos, and Nisa; and research on this art revealed that there was no uniform style of "Parthian Art" or "Art in the Arsacid Empire" (Invernizzi 2011; Jacobs 2014; Hauser 2014). In any case, the dating of the Kal-e Chendar bronzes, both the "Greek" and the "un-Greek" group is based on general assumptions about the historical conditions that favoured the transmission of Greek style and iconography, or that promoted a non-Greek visual culture, may it be called "Parthian", "Iranian" or simply "Oriental".

Current approach to a classification of the of the bronze statues

Although the Kal-e Chendar bronzes, namely the ruler portraits, were occasionally mentioned in the literature, they have never been investigated thoroughly, either individually or as a group. However, the 11 sculptures form a unique and promising subject for investigation, especially for a study that combines research on art and on technology. The Kal-e Chendar bronzes come from a single site but represent two successive periods, during which Southwest Iran was first part of the Seleucid Empire, a realm with strong ties to the West, and later part of the Parthian Empire, centred in the East. The sculptures thus have the potential to give valuable insights into transfer, adoption, and transformation of Hellenistic art in the East, not only in terms of style and iconography, but also in terms of technology.

As noted above, some scholars already assumed that the different style-groups of Kal-e Chendar sculptures were produced at different times and, hence, by different workshops. But this has been inferred rather than investigated and proven. However, the author's current research on the Kal-e Chendar bronzes revealed that the stylistic division of the Kal-e Chendar bronzes into two groups is carried through to technical differences, indicating a significant change in the production of bronze sculptures.

The paper first gives some background information on the discovery of the Kal-e Chendar statues in the 1930s, on the location and interpretation of the site itself, including the results of the recent Iranian-Italian fieldwork, and todays location of the bronzes. It will then present the results of the author's current research in three analytical steps: First, the research on the head of the "Hellenistic Ruler", whose facial features were reconstructed using photogrammetry and 3D technology. Based on the head's reconstruction it is here proposed to date this prime example of the "Greek" Kal-e Chendar bronzes in the years around 140 BCE. The second analysis is devoted to the reconstruction of the entire figure of the "Hellenistic Ruler", which was one of the spectacular results of the current project (Lindström 2017, 187 fig. 22.8, cf. here Fig. 15.1 left). Although the pieces of the figure do not directly join, the results of visual examination with a focus on casting technique and pXRF analysis proofed their belonging to the same statue. The same analytical methods are applied in a third step to additional bronze statuary from Kal-e Chendar, both from the "Greek" and the "un-Greek" group of sculptures, which indicates that the groups differ not only in terms of art, but also in terms of technology.

Discovery and Ancient Context

The sculptures, some almost complete but most as fragments, were discovered accidentally in 1935, during construction work. A few months later, in early 1936, the famous explorer Sir Aurel Stein visited Kal-e Chendar while on his "Fourth Expedition to Southwest Iran". During a rescue excavation over a few days he uncovered a small shrine enclosed by a wall of 23 by 12 meter, with an altar in the centre (Stein 1940, 130–134 and 141–146). The architecture of the sanctuary was largely destroyed, first by a fire, later by rebuilding and quarrying activity and finally by the foundation for the modern buildings. Nevertheless, Stein noted the find spots of the sculptures discovered a few months earlier by the local population and he unearthed additional, but smaller fragments of bronze statuary. According to the "local heads and others", nearly all the bronze pieces were found in a heap outside the enclosure, while the most intact statue of the find complex, the 'Parthian Nobleman' was from the central part of the shrine. Of the seven image bases preserved on site, Stein discovered only three bases *in situ*: two bases for larger statues were found on both sides of the central altar and another one with dowel holes for smaller statues stood close to the enclosure's wall. Even if Stein's own findings were not very significant in view of the high-quality statuary it was concluded that the site was once one of the most important religious places of ancient Elymais, at least during the Hellenistic an Parthian period.

After the discovery of the bronze statuary in 1935 and 1936, an agreement with the Iranian authorities allowed Sir Aurel Stein to temporarily send all objects to the British Museum for examination and study, subject to the subsequent division into half shares. But since most of the bronzes had been found before Stein's excavations by the locals, almost all the bronzes were sent back to Iran in 1937 or 1938. Only 20 smaller fragments accredited as British share remained in the British Museum and are now in the storage of the Department of the Middle East (The British Museum Collection Online).

Despite the importance of the site as one of the few sanctuaries in the Hellenistic East, there was no further archaeological research at Kal-e Chendar until very recently. The reasons for this include the isolated location of the site in the Zagros Mountains on an altitude of ca. 1000 m. However, from 2012 to 2016, the Iranian-Italian Joint Expedition in Khuzestan re-examined the site and discovered that the ancient ruins cover a much larger area than Stein had assumed (Messina – Mehr Kian 2014; Baqherian et al. 2016; Bucci et al. 2017; Bucci et al. 2018). In addition to the terrace partly excavated by Stein the walls of at least two other monumental terraces were identified, similar to those of Masjid-e Suleyman and Bard-e Nechandeh, sanctuaries that are also located in the mountainous Elymais (Ghirshman 1976). What is special about the sanctuary in Kal-e Chendar is that a large necropolis is built in the immediate vicinity. The Iranian-Italian team excavated only four of the 32 tombs identified, but they expect that hundreds will be discovered at the site in the future. The monumental impression of some tombs seems to relate to an aristocratic milieu that is also suggested by what remains of the funerary goods. For these reasons, the excavators assume Kal-e Chendar to be a dynastic sanctuary (already assumed by Sherwin-White 1984; Canepa 2015, 81). If so, some of the statues would relate to this function, namely the "Hellenistic Ruler" and the "Parthian Nobleman".

The "Hellenistic Ruler" portrait head

This author's investigations initially focused on the head of the "Hellenistic Ruler", which was cut in two pieces (NM 2475+2477) and heavily damaged in antiquity (Lindström 2017). Because of the damage and deformation this important piece of Hellenistic art in the East was often perceived as unattractive and was hardly noticed by the visitors of the National Museum of Iran. In addition, it was not possible to identify the depicted ruler. Therefore, one research objective was to reconstruct the original facial features and to use this reconstruction to identify the ruler and date the bronze portrait.

Based on a series of digital images and by means of photogrammetry, a three-dimensional model was created (Lindström 2017, fig 22.5). This, in turn, was modified by means of computer animation. There were a few areas of the face that remained relatively undamaged, such as the right side of the forehead to just below the eye; this area

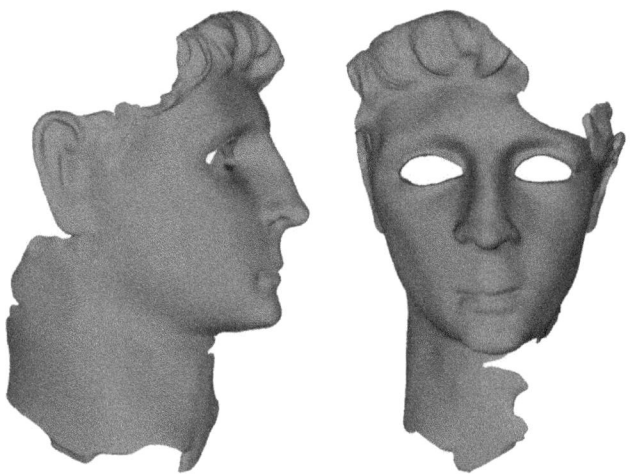

Figure 15.2 Digital 3D-reconstruction of the 'Hellenistic Ruler's' head.

was digitally copied, then mirrored to serve as a template on which the surface data of the left side of the face were applied. In addition, the dents created by hammering were compensated for, and parts with folding or bending, like the hair above the right ear, were put in place. The result of the reconstruction is a surprisingly youthful face of triangular shape with a broad forehead and a narrow chin; the jawline is not particular strong (Fig. 15.2). Short, curved strands of hair cover the forehead and form a tong slightly offset from the central axis. The nose is straight and not very prominent; it has a somewhat large distance to the upper lip. The mouth is narrow with small and tight lips. As one of the objectives was to make the original quality of this demolished head clear to a wider audience, the digital data of the 3D reconstruction were printed on the original scale and the print-out handed over to the National Museum of Iran, where it is now on display, right next to the original.

The second objective of the reconstruction was to come closer to an identification and thus to a dating of the bronze portrait. For this purpose the method of choice is to compare the bronze portrait to coin portraits of kings. For historical reasons alone, the search for the sitter can be limited to those rulers who were portrayed beardless and with short hair, and thus, the Parthian kings, always characterized by a beard or by long hair, are to be excluded. Because a portrait statue would be erected only for a ruler who actually controlled the region the search can also be limited to kings who, at least at some time, were in power in southwestern Iran. Therefore, the Kal-e Chendar portrait can either be a king of the Seleucid dynasty, who ruled in Iran and the neighbouring lands from 301 BCE on (for the portraits see Fleischer 1991; Houghton – Lorber – Kitt 2002; Houghton – Lorber – Hoover 2008), or of the local Elymaean kings, who took power in Elymais around 147 BCE and ruled intermittently until the Parthians captured Elymais around 139 BCE. The Elymaean kings of this short interphase, Kamnaskires and others, appear on their coins in fully Hellenistic style, with short hair and clean-shaven (for the coin portraits see Van't Haaff 2007). The bronze head can therefore be compared to coin portraits of almost all of the twelve Seleucid kings, who ruled the Hellenistic east, including southwestern Iran, and to the Elymaean kings of the interphase. As a basis for this comparison we can use the coins minted in Susa, the ancient capital of Susiana and Elymais (see also Le Rider 1965).

Although the facial features of the bronze portrait described above are not enough to identify the ruler, they may well lead to exclude certain identifications. For it is very unlikely that our bronze head represents Seleukos I, as he is never as youthful on the coins, or Antiochos I, who, like his father, is always characterized by a strong jawline that our portrait lacks. Antiochos II, Seleukos II, and Antiochos III are also unlikely because they are always characterized by a long, pointed nose – and our portrait doesn't have a prominent nose. In addition, Antiochos III is characterized by receding hairlines, a feature that is also typical for the portraits of his successors Seleukos IV and Antiochos IV – but our portrait has full hair. Antiochos V is to be excluded because he ruled only two years and was not important in the East. Demetrius I is also unlikely, because his coin portraits have a characteristic anastolé and a short nose-to-mouth distance, unlike our bronze portrait. It is certainly not Alexander Balas, because in contrast to the bronze head his coin portraits are characterized by a prominent jawline. And that brings us to Demetrios II, who, in his first reign (145–139 BCE), is depicted like the bronze head from Kal-e Chendar youthful and with a remarkably small, narrow mouth. However, during and after the succession conflict between Demetrios and Alexander Balas, the Seleucids had already lost control over Elymais. Thus, it is unlikely that an honorary statue of Demetrios II would have been erected in a sanctuary high up in the Zagros mountains. However, the Elymaean kings took over the mint of Susa, and the coins minted by Kamnaskires I and Okkonapses represent the local kings in a similar way as Demetrios II, with a small mouth and beardless. Hence, the sitter of our portrait could well be one of these Elymaean kings of the interphase, as already suggested by Robert Fleischer (2016, 280) and Matthew Canepa (2015, 85).

To summarize, although we cannot definitely identify the sitter of the Kal-e Chendar bronze portrait, a dating around 140 BCE is most likely. So the prime example of the 'Greek-style' group of bronze statues actually dates back to the time when Southwest Iran was still under strong Greek influence.

The "Hellenistic Ruler" statue reconstructed

A spectacular and unexpected outcome of the research on the head of the "Hellenistic Ruler" was the identification of previously unidentified remains of the same statue in the museum storage rooms, which allowed the reconstruction of the whole figure (Fig. 15.1 left). Leaning naked on a spear held with the raised arm, the statue followed the most popular format of Hellenistic royal figures. Although ruler representations of this type are supposed to be represented throughout the Hellenistic world, the Hellenistic king from Kal-e Chendar is now the first known for the regions of Iran and further east.

The bronze castings of the figure show similar proportions, which are in turn in accordance with the scale of the head. However, they represent the extremities: a fragment of the right arm (NM 2470), two joining fragments of the left arm (NM 2874 and 2473) that directly fit to the left hand (NM 2471), and a piece of the left leg from below the knee (NM 2478). Since the torso is missing not all fragments directly join. Hence, investigations moved to identifying other possible consistent features. In fact, a visual examination revealed long relief bands at the interior of all pieces of the extremities attributed to the "Hellenistic Ruler" (Lindström 2017, fig. 22.7). These indicate the use of a specific technique of lost-wax-casting, the indirect process that was commonly applied by Greek bronze sculptors from the early 5th century BCE on. The indirect method to model and cast a bronze statue has two main advantages over the simpler direct method: First, the indirect modelling allows any number of attempts to cast the figure. For example, if the casting of an arm failed, it was possible to repeat it, receiving in the result an exactly fitting piece. For this reason, the indirect method was of specific importance for casting large scale sculptures which were always cast in pieces. The second advantage of this method was the lining of the master moulds with wax, which results in thin and even metal walls (often only 0.3–0.5 cm). It also meant that less material had to be spent, so the casting was more economical.

All fragments of the arms and legs attributed to the "Hellenistic Ruler" show the long relief band at their interior surface: the piece of a leg from below the knee, the fragment of the right arm and both fragments of the left arm, the line observable at the larger of these fragments running into the interior of the left hand. These bands result from the lining of the master moulds with oblong, thin slabs of beeswax that were stuck together at their overlaps. Because during casting the wax was replaced by bronze, these "seams" are visible on the interior of the castings. However, lining with oblong wax slabs was suitable for tubular castings, like arms and legs, but it was not for spherical castings, like the head. And indeed, on the interior of the head no seams are observable. Apparently, in this case the hot wax was poured into the mould, the mould slued and swivelled around so that the wax was distributed evenly on the inner walls. However, at one spot at the interior of the right cheek it seems that the result of the application was not satisfying. Here, three parallel traces of a spatula can be observed that was obviously used to press the wax firmly to the mould (Fig. 15.3). These features are also evidence of the application of the indirect casting process. In addition to the visual examination of the castings, elemental analysis by portable XRF (pXRF) was performed by Daniel Steiniger from the DAI's Eurasia Department. Because pXRF provides results only at the surface where

Figure 15.3 Interior view of the 'Hellenistic Ruler's' head (National Museum of Iran Inv. 2075 and 2077), impressions of a spatula as evidence for indirect moulding and casting.

the metal composition is potentially altered by corrosion the measurements were taken at relatively "corrosion-free" areas, multiple spots on each of the bronzes were analysed, obvious outliers were excluded and the measured values were averaged. The results of the pXRF analysis show that the individual castings consist of a very similar alloy, a bronze with a tin (Sn) content of 5.5% to 8.8% and a considerable lower lead (Pb) content of around 1.8% to 5.4% (Diagram 15.1). To prove the validity of the pXRF surface analysis, additional measurements were performed on fresh cut sections, taken by the museum's conservator at the breaks of the head, the right and left arm, and the left leg. The results show a basic consistency with the values obtained at the bronze surface (cf. Diagram 15.1). The only outlier is the piece of the right arm, with a considerable higher amount of lead (16.5%). However, it is still highly probable that this fragment belongs to the same statue for it has a straight raised line at its interior surface that runs parallel to the length of the arm, thus indicating the use of a oblong wax plate to line the mould. As will be elaborated below, this feature is specific for the "Hellenistic Ruler" statue and cannot be observed at the pieces belonging to other sculptures from Kal-e Chendar.

As a result, the consistent technological features of the bronze pieces assigned to the "Hellenistic Ruler" indicate that they are produced as parts of one and the same statue. Its princely pose confirms that it represents a ruler. That the sculptor or workshop who made the statue in around 140 BCE not only applied Greek style and iconography, but also the indirect casting method demonstrates that he was also technically in a Greek workshop tradition.

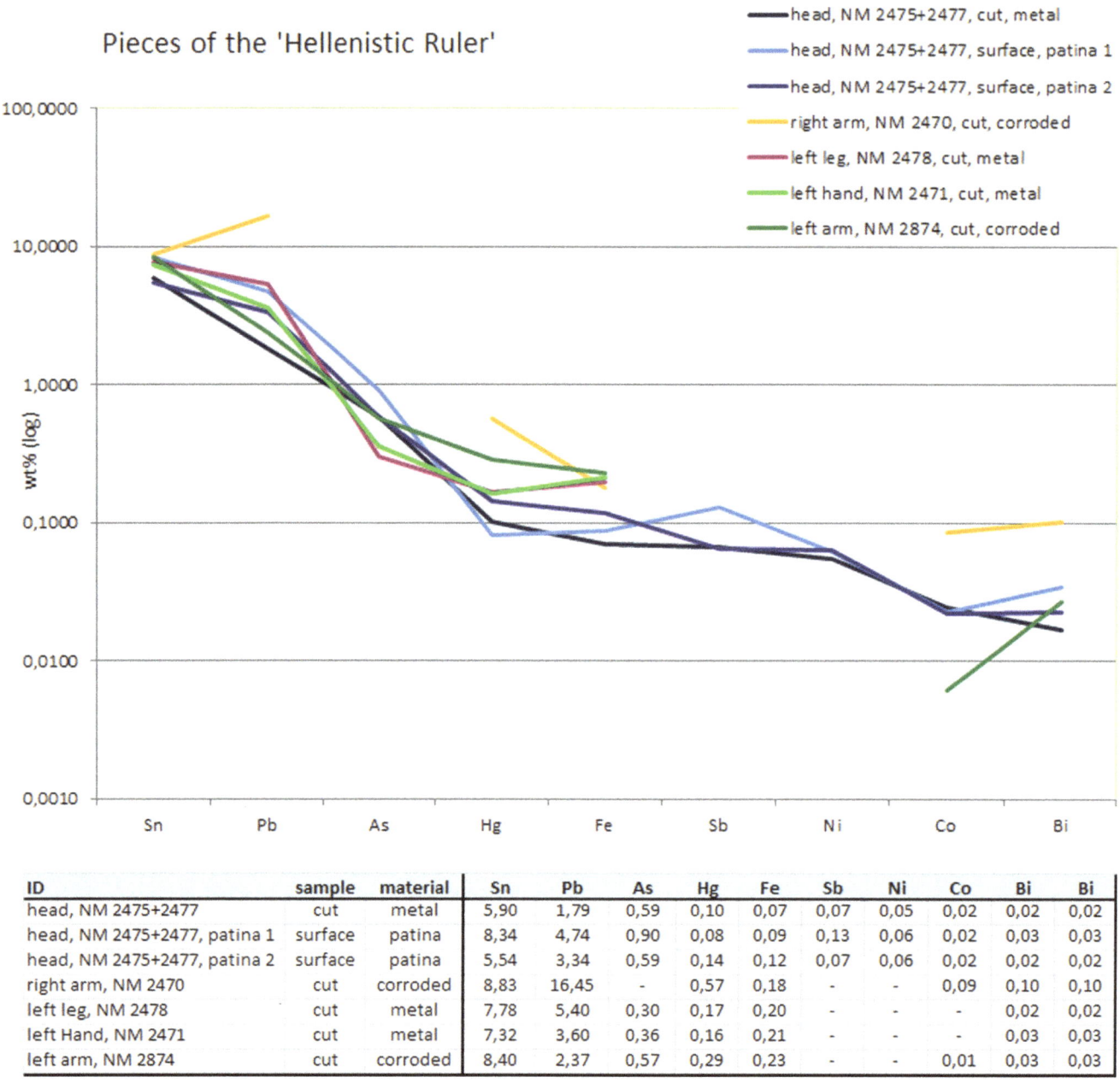

Diagram 15.1. Results of the pXRF analysis.

ID	sample	material	Sn	Pb	As	Hg	Fe	Sb	Ni	Co	Bi	Bi
head, NM 2475+2477	cut	metal	5,90	1,79	0,59	0,10	0,07	0,07	0,05	0,02	0,02	0,02
head, NM 2475+2477, patina 1	surface	patina	8,34	4,74	0,90	0,08	0,09	0,13	0,06	0,02	0,03	0,03
head, NM 2475+2477, patina 2	surface	patina	5,54	3,34	0,59	0,14	0,12	0,07	0,06	0,02	0,02	0,02
right arm, NM 2470	cut	corroded	8,83	16,45	-	0,57	0,18	-	-	0,09	0,10	0,10
left leg, NM 2478	cut	metal	7,78	5,40	0,30	0,17	0,20	-	-	-	0,02	0,02
left Hand, NM 2471	cut	metal	7,32	3,60	0,36	0,16	0,21	-	-	-	0,03	0,03
left arm, NM 2874	cut	corroded	8,40	2,37	0,57	0,29	0,23	-	-	0,01	0,03	0,03

Comparing the "Greek" and "un-Greek" bronzes from Kal-e Chendar

The above described technological features of the "Hellenistic Ruler" statue can only be considered unifying criteria if the other pieces from the same locality can be demonstrated to be different. Therefore, the other bronze castings from Kal-e Chendar were preliminary examined. As outlined above, they form two groups by motif and style: on the one hand 'Greek' figures and on the other hand 'un-Greek' representations in tunic and pants. To the "Greek-style" group of the "Hellenistic Ruler" belong three additional figures: a nude male statue, represented by a piece of the left lower leg (NM 2092; Stein 1940, pl. V.6), a statue with a club, apparently a Heracles (NM 2093; identified in the museum storage and here published for the first time, Fig. 15.4); and a small statuette represented by a panther skin, so presumably a figure of Dionysus (NM 2479; Stein 1940, pl. VI.14). The "un-Greek" group consists of the "Parthian Nobleman" (NM 2401), the back head of a life-size figure (NM 2476, now lost), and pieces of six additional figures, mostly presented by their extremities: a larger than-life right arm covered with a wide sleeve (NM 2474; Stein 1940, fig. 48); a life-size right hand which was obviously intended for insertion into an arm of a clothed statue, the sleeve of which would have covered the seam (NM 2472; Stein 1940, pl. V.5); a right arm with hand, sleeve and bracelet of two-thirds life size (NM 2091, Fig. 15.5); a statuette of a man in loose, long-sleeved robe, long trousers and boots of a supple material (NM 2090; Stein 1940, fig. 48); and left foot and ankle covered with a similar loose-fitting moccasin-like shoe (NM 2468; Stein 1940, pl. VI.16).

The question was if and how these castings differed from the fragments attributed to the "Hellenistic Ruler", in terms of casting technology and alloy composition. In addition, the comparative study of the entire group of bronze statuary from Kal-e Chendar was expected to show whether the grouping based on art historical criteria could be confirmed by technological criteria. This part of the study consisted of the same investigations as carried out on the fragments of the "Hellenistic Ruler", hence, visual examinations with a focus on casting technique and pXRF measurements to determine the alloys used to cast the figures.

With regard to the alloys, pXRF clearly confirmed the division of the bronzes into two groups. From the "Greek" group of bronzes, despite the pieces of the "Hellenistic Ruler" statue the panther skin NM 2479 and the Herakles" club NM 2093 were analysed, from the "un-Greek" group of sculptures the "Parthian Nobleman" NM 2401, the right hand NM 2472, the right foot NM 2468 and the right arm NM 2091. The method of measurement was as described above, measuring multiple spots on each casting, at the "Parthian Nobleman" even 16 spots. The results show that the "Greek" castings are bronzes – copper with a significant addition of tin – whereas the "un-Greek" castings are high leaded bronzes – copper with more lead than tin (Diagram 15.2). A striking difference is also evident in the trace elements: while the "Greek" bronzes contain no silver at all, the "un-Greek" bronzes have a relatively high content of silver (0.22 to 0.34 ppm). As it is unlikely that the silver was added to the alloy it can be regarded as a trace element and, therefore, is related to the ore source of the main metal components. In summary, this part of the investigation has found that the bronze sculptors and the workshops of the "Greek" and ""un-Greek" bronzes used different recipes and relied on different sources of metal ores.

With regard to the casting technology, relief bands at the inner bronze surface as at the "Hellenistic Ruler" resulting from indirect casting were only observed at the piece of a left leg (NM 2092) – nude and thus belonging to the "Greek" group of sculptures. But in contrast to the "Hellenistic Ruler" pieces, the relief band here runs horizontally, that is transverse to the direction of the

Figure 15.4. Fragment of a statue with a club, apparently a Heracles, from Kal-e Chendar (National Museum of Iran Inv. 2093).

Figure 15.5. Right arm of a statue with sleeve and bracelet from Kal-e Chendar (National Museum of Iran Inv. 2091).

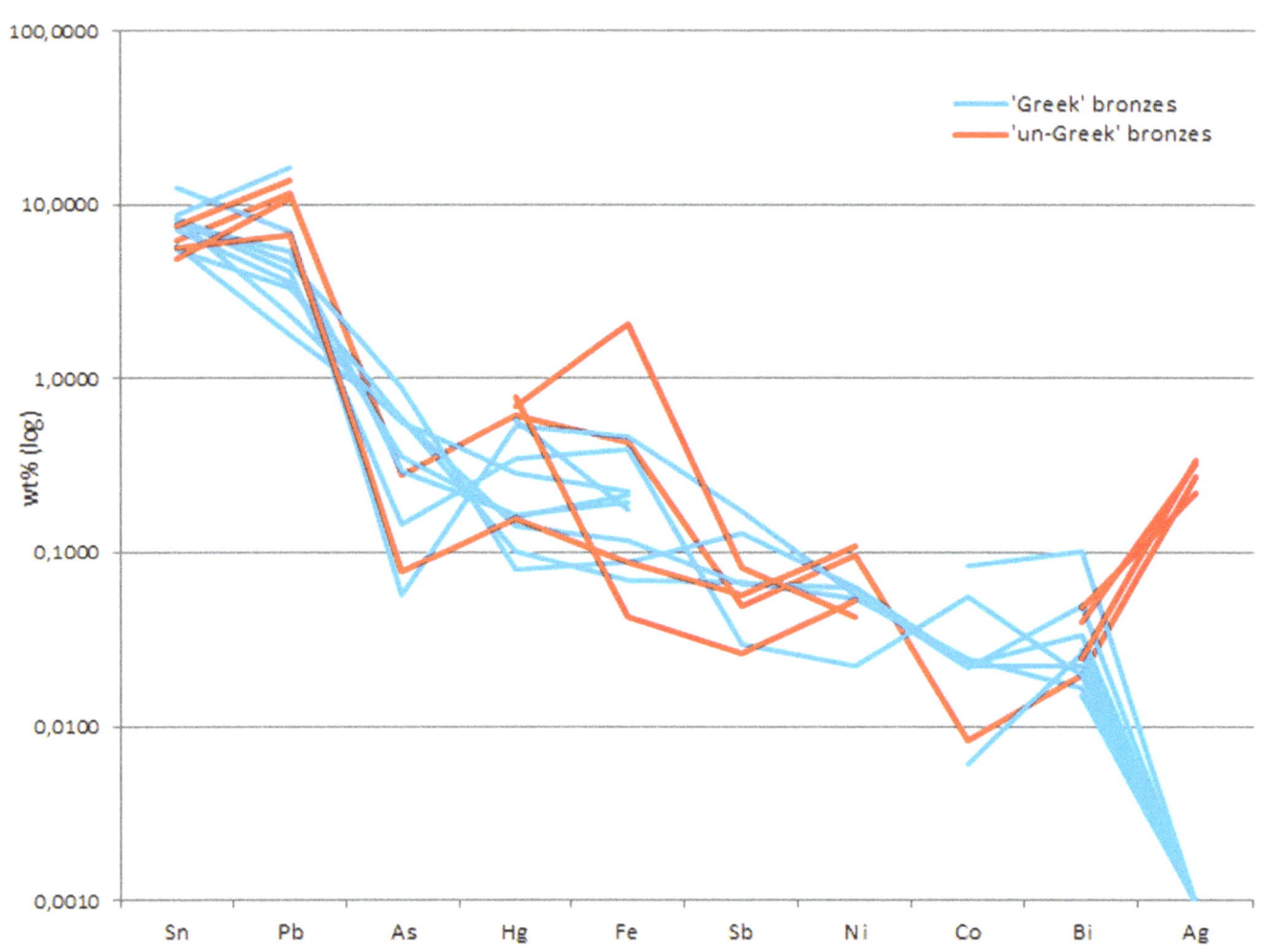

ID	sample	material	Sn	Pb	As	Hg	Fe	Sb	Ni	Co	Bi	Ag
head, NM 2475+2477	cut	metal	5,90	1,79	0,59	0,10	0,07	0,07	0,05	0,02	0,02	-
head, NM 2475+2477, patina 1	surface	patina	8,34	4,74	0,90	0,08	0,09	0,13	0,06	0,02	0,03	-
head, NM 2475+2477, patina 2	surface	patina	5,54	3,34	0,59	0,14	0,12	0,07	0,06	0,02	0,02	-
right arm, NM 2470	cut	corroded	8,83	16,45	-	0,57	0,18	-	-	0,09	0,10	-
left leg, NM 2478	cut	metal	7,78	5,40	0,30	0,17	0,20	-	-	-	0,02	-
left Hand, NM 2471	cut	metal	7,32	3,60	0,36	0,16	0,21	-	-	-	0,03	-
left arm, NM 2874	cut	corroded	8,40	2,37	0,57	0,29	0,23	-	-	0,01	0,03	-
panther skin, NM 2479	surface	patina	8,15	4,18	0,15	0,35	0,39	0,03	0,02	0,06	0,02	-
Heracles' club, NM 2093	surface	patina	12,55	7,13	0,06	0,54	0,46	0,17	0,06	0,02	0,05	-
'Parthian Nobleman', NM 2401	surface	patina	6,33	11,75	0,28	0,63	0,43	0,05	0,10	0,01	0,02	0,28
right hand, NM 2472	surface	patina	5,67	6,79	0,08	0,16	0,09	0,06	0,11	-	0,02	0,34
right foot, NM 2468	surface	patina	4,99	10,90	-	0,79	0,04	0,03	0,05	-	0,04	0,33
right arm, NM 2091	surface	patina	7,65	14,00	-	0,70	2,07	0,08	0,04	-	0,05	0,22

Diagram 15.2. Results of the pXRF analysis.

leg. Since the inner surfaces of the other castings could not be adequately examined without an endoscope or lighting device, it is not possible for the time being to make definitive statements about the particular casting technique used. One thing, however, is obvious at first sight: the metal walls of the "Greek" group of sculptures are relatively thin (0.3 to 0.5 cm), whereas the metal walls of the "un-Greek" group are considerably thicker (0.8 to 1.4 cm). This can be seen very well at the break of the right arm of the "Parthian Nobleman" (Fig. 15.6).

To summarize the comparative investigations on technology, the differences in alloy composition and thickness of the Kal-e Chendar bronze statuary confirms

Figure 15.6. View on the break of the right arm of the 'Parthian Nobleman' from Kal-e Chendar/Shami (National Museum of Iran Inv. 2401).

the stylistic classification into a "Greek" and "un-Greek" group. The sculptors and workshops involved in casting these bronzes obviously drew on different recipes and raw material sources for the bronze. While the workshops of the "Greek" statues obviously used indirect casting, the workshops of the "un-Greek" statues either did not apply this method or varied the method at a crucial point.

Discussion and future research

The thick metal walls of the "un-Greek" bronzes would actually speak in favour of direct casting process, in which the wax is modelled over a clay core, resulting in relatively thick and uneven wax layers and, hence, thick metal walls. However, since the development of the innovative, indirect casting process at the end of the 6th century BCE, the direct casting process was no longer used to produce large-scale sculptures, at least not in the geographical regions whose bronze castings are well-researched. This has to do with the two great advantages of indirect casting, namely lower material expenditure and reproducibility of the casting process. The latter was extremely important for casting large, complex forms, like life-size bronze figures.

Here it is assumed that the "un-Greek" Kal-e Chendar bronzes also were cast by the indirect process, at least the large statues. Logistical restrictions make the direct casting of life-size figures difficult, if not impossible. Because casting only succeeds if sufficient bronze can be kept at high temperature ready for pouring into the mould. Hence, the size of the castings is limited by the size of smelting furnaces and crucibles. Therefore, the life-size statues likely were cast in pieces. And in this case, the bronze sculptor had to make sure that the individual pieces actually fit together, which was most easily ensured by using the indirect modelling and casting process.

However, at this preliminary stage of investigation, piece casting can be proved only for one example of the "un-Greek" group of Kal-e Chendar bronzes, the 'Parthian Nobleman'. It was noted by Stein that the legs, the upper body and the head were found as separate pieces (Stein 1940, 131), most likely broken along the welding seams. As can still be observed at the exhibit, the head was definitely cast as a separate piece (cf. also Godard 1937, fig. 119) which, however, fitted that close to the body that it was not even necessary to weld it. Nevertheless, a close examination of the "un-Greek" group of Kal-e Chendar bronzes remains an important issue. An endoscope inserted for example into the 'Parthian Nobleman' may reveal precise traces of the applied casting method.

For the time being, it can only be stated that the workshops that produced the 'Greek' sculptures used all the advantages of the indirect process, the workshops of the "un-Greek" sculptures have foregone a significant advantage of this process, namely the saving of material. In addition, the alloys of the "Greek" and "Parthian" group of sculptures differ significantly in terms of trace elements, suggesting that the workshops used raw materials from different regions and that they were thus integrated into different trade-networks in raw materials. All in all, the differences indicate that the statues were made by different workshops that used different techniques and raw materials and certainly did not work side by side at the same period.

The reasons why the sculptors of the 'un-Greek' Kal-e Chendar bronzes accepted thick walls and an enormous material investment remain puzzling. Although the style of the "un-Greek" bronzes may not correspond to "classical" tastes, the executed cold work is certainly very high quality and shows a great craftsmanship of the bronze sculptors. Also lack of technological knowledge is unlikely to be the reason. Because, as stated above, for the casting of bronzes with thick walls a high amount of bronze needed to be heated at the right time and that was a challenge in terms of furnaces and crucibles.

A key to understanding the thick walls and high material investments of the "un-Greek bronzes" may be a finding from a region even further away from the Greek heartland than Kal-e Chendar. In 2004 and 2007, a foundry pit was uncovered in the temenos of the Oxus Temple, located in the South of Tajikistan (Boroffka – Mei 2013). From the filling of the pit, dating to the second half of the 2nd century BCE, come several moulds that were intended to cast large cauldrons with about 1 m in diameter. One of the moulds preserves the Greek dedicatory inscription expressly informing that seven talents of bronze were intended to cast the cauldron (Ivantchik 2013). As the weight of a talent varies between 25 and 39 kilos, depending on the weight system used, seven talents correspond to 175–275 kilos of bronze. The inscription thus not only proves a high material investment, but also that the amount of bronze was considered so prestigious that the dedicator wanted it to be visible on the edge of the cauldron. This inscription from the edge of the Hellenistic world is therefore an indication that a large material investment to cast an offering was considered as very prestigious. And hence, the prestige gained through an expensive dedication may have been a reason for commissioning and casting the thick-walled "un-Greek" Kal-e Chendar bronze statues.

Acknowledgements

I am grateful to Jebrael Nokandeh, the director of the National Museum of Iran for allowing me to work on the material from Kal-e Chendar, and I am especially appreciative to the museum's staff for their kind assistance (in particular Masoumeh Ahmadi and Firouzeh Sepidnameh). My sincere thanks go as well to Thomas Kersten, Maren Lindstaedt and Simon Deggim from the Photogrammetry and Laserscanning Lab of the HafenCity University Hamburg, to Daniel Steiniger from the Eurasia Department of the DAI for his pXRF analyses, to Vito Messina and Jafar Mehr Kian from the Iranian-Italian Mission to Khuzestan for providing valuable insights into their current work in Kal-e Chendar, to Helga Kosak from the Orient Department of the DAI for the reconstruction drawing, to Wolf-Dieter Heilmeyer for discussion of the project's results. Special thanks go to the CAWG and Wendy Laura Belcher, the author of *Writing Your Journal Article in 12 Weeks*. I also wish to convey my sincere gratitude to the Fritz Thyssen Foundation for funding this research project.

Bibliography

Baqherian, A. – Bucci, I. – Cellerino, A. – Foietta, E. – Mehr Kian, J. – Messina, V. – Rouhani Rankhoui, M., 2016. Preliminary report on the second season of excavation of the Iranian-Italian Joint Expedition in Khuzestan at Kal-e Chendar, Shami (6th campaign, 2013). *Parthica 18*, 31–52.

Boroffka, N. – Mei, J., 2013. Technologietransfer in Mittelasien – chinesische, griechische und skytho-sakische Interaktion in der Gusstechnik. In: G. Lindström – S. Hansen – A. Wieczorek – M. Tellenbach, ed., *Zwischen Ost und West. Neue Forschungen zum antiken Zentralasien. Wissenschaftliches Kolloquium 30.9.–2.10.2009 in Mannheim*. Archäologie in Iran und Turan 14. Darmstadt: Philipp von Zabern, 143–169.

Bucci, I. – Cellerino, A. – Faraji, M. – Foietta, E. – Mehr Kian, J. – Messina, V. – Rouhani Rankhoui, M., 2017. Preliminary report on the second season of excavation of the Iranian-Italian Joint Expedition in Khuzestan at Kal-e Chendar, Shami (7th campaign, 2014). *Parthica 19*, 9–26.

Bucci, I. – Cellerino, A. – Faraji, M. – Foietta, E. – Giusto, F. – Mehr Kian, J. – Messina, V. – Rouhani Rankhoui, M., 2018. Preliminary report on the third season of excavation of the Iranian-Italian Joint Expedition in Khuzestan at Kal-e Chendar, Shami (8th campaign, 2015). *Parthica 20*, 2018, 31–50.

British Museum Collection Online, 2018. Available at <http://www.britishmuseum.org/research/collection_online/search.aspx?searchText=Shami+Stein> [Accessed 8 October 2018].

Canepa, M., 2015. Bronze Sculpture in the Hellenistic East. In: J. M. Daehner – K. Lapatin, ed., *Power and Pathos. Bronze Sculpture of the Hellenistic World*. Los Angeles: Getty Publications, 83–93.

Colledge, M.A.R., 1977. *Parthian Art*. London: Paul Elek.

Colledge, M. A. R., 1987. Greek and non-Greek Interaction in the Art and Architecture of the Hellenistic East. In: A. Kuhrt – S. Sherwin-White, ed., *Hellenism in the East: the Interaction of Greek and non-Greek Civilizations from Syria to Central Asia after Alexander*. Berkeley/Los Angeles: University of California Press, 134–162.

Fleischer, R., 1991. *Studien zur Seleukidischen Kunst. Band 1*. Mainz am Rhein: Philipp von Zabern.

Fleischer, R., 2001. Portraitkopf eines Königs. In: *7000 Jahre persische Kunst. Meisterwerke aus dem Iranischen Nationalmuseum in Teheran: eine Ausstellung des Kunsthistorischen Museums Wien und des Iranischen Nationalmuseums in Teheran. Kunsthistorisches Museum, 22. November 2000 bis 25. März 2001, Kunst- und Ausstellungshalle der Bundesrepublik Deutschland, 10. August 2001 bis 6. Januar 2002*. Bonn: Kunst- und Ausstellungshalle der Bundesrepublik Deutschland, 227.

Fleischer, R., 2016. Der hellenistische "Königskopf" aus Šamī, Iran. In. H.-H. Nieswandt – H. Schwarzer, ed., *Man kann es sich nicht prächtig genug vorstellen! Festschrift für Dieter Salzmann zum 65. Geburtstag*. Münster: Scriptorium, 269–286.

Ghirshman, R., 1976. *Les terrasses sacrées de Bard-è Néchandeh et Masjid-i Sulaiman. L'Iran du sud-ouest du VIIIe s. av. n. ère au Ve s. de n. ère*. Mémoires de la Delegation Archéologique en Iran 45. Leiden and Paris: E. J. Brill.

Godard, A., 1937. Les statues parthes de Shami. *Athar-é Iran*, 2, 285–305.

Godard, A., 1962. *L'art de l'Iran*. Paris: Arthaud.

Hauser, St., 2014. "Parthian Art" or "Arts in the Arsacid Empire": Hatra and Palmyra as nodal points for cultural interaction. In: B. Jacobs, ed., ,Parthische Kunst"– Kunst im Partherreich: Akten des Internationalen Kolloquiums in Basel, 9. Oktober 2010. Duisburg: Wellem, 127–178.

Houghton, A. – Lorber, C. – Kitt, B., 2002. *Seleucid coins: A comprehensive catalogue. Part 1. Seleucus I through Antiochus III*. New York: Lancaster; London: The

American Numismatic Society; Classical Numismatic Group.

Houghton, A. – Lorber, C. – Hoover, O. D. 2008. *Seleucid coins: A comprehensive catalogue. Part 2. Seleucus IV through Antiochus XIII*. New York, N.Y.: Lancaster, London: The American Numismatic Society; Classical Numismatic Group.

Invernizzi, A., 2011. Parthian Art – Arsacid Art, Topoi. Orient-Occident 17, 189–207.

Ivantchik, A., 2013. Neue griechische Inschriften aus Tacht-i Sangin und das Problem der Entstehung der baktrischen Schriftlichkeit. In: G. Lindström – S. Hansen – A. Wieczorek – M. Tellenbach, ed., *Zwischen Ost und West. Neue Forschungen zum antiken Zentralasien. Wissenschaftliches Kolloquium 30.9.–2.10.2009 in Mannheim*. Archäologie in Iran und Turan 14. Darmstadt: Philipp von Zabern, 125–142.

Jacobs, B., 2014. Repräsentative Bildkunst im Partherreich. In: B. Jacobs, ed., „Parthische Kunst"– Kunst im Partherreich: Akten des Internationalen Kolloquiums in Basel, 9. Oktober 2010. Duisburg: Wellem, 77–126.

Kawami, T.S., 1987. *Monumental Art of the Parthian Period in Iran*. Acta Iranica. Textes et Mémoirs 13. Leiden: E. J. Brill.

Le Rider, G., 1965. *Suse sous les Séleucides et les Parthes: Les trouvailles monétaires et l'histoire de la ville*. Paris: Librairie Orientaliste P. Geuthner.

Lindström, G., 2017. The Portrait of a Hellenistic Ruler in the National Museum of Iran. In: J. M. Daehner – K. Lapatin – A. Spinelli, ed., *Artistry in Bronze: the Greeks and their Legacy: XIXth International Congress on Ancient Bronzes*. Los Angeles: J. Paul Getty Trust, 183–189.

Mathiesen, H.E., 1992. *Sculpture in the Parthian Empire: a Study in Chronology*. Aarhus: Aarhus University Press.

Mattusch, C.C., 1996. *Classical Bronzes. The Art and Craft of Greek and Roman Statuary*. Ithaca and London: Cornell University Press.

Messina, V. – Mehr Kian, J., 2014. Return to Shami. Preliminary Survey of the Iranian-Italian Joint Expedition in Khuzestan at Kal-e Chendar. *Iran* 52, 65–77.

Meyers, P., 2002. The casting process of the statue of Queen Napir-Asu in the Louvre. In: C.C. Mattusch – A. Brauer – S.E. Knudsen, ed., *From the parts to the whole. Acta of the 13th International Bronze Congress*. Journal of Roman Archaeology Supplementary Series 39. Portsmouth, R.I.: Journal of Roman Archaeology, 2000, 11–18.

Sherwin-White, S.M., 1984. Shami, the Seleucids and Dynastic Cult: a Note. *Iran* 22, 160–161.

Stein, A., 1936. Ancient Ways in Iran. A Fourth Journey I. Traces of Alexander the Great. *The Times*, 6 July 1936, 15–16.

Stein, A., 1938. An Archaeological Journey in Western Iran. *The Geographical Journal* 42, 313–342.

Stein, A., 1940. *Old Routes of Western Īrān: Narrative of an Archaeological Journey Carried Out and Recorded by Sir Aurel Stein*. London: MacMillan and Co.

Van't Haaff, P.A., 2007. *Catalogue of Elymaean coinage: CA. 147 B.C.–A.D. 228*. Lancaster, PA: Classical Numismatic Group.

Part II

Resource

16

How the Greeks manipulated the composition of their bronze coins. Case studies

Maryse Blet-Lemarquand

IRAMAT-CEB, CNRS/Université d'Orléans

lemarquand@cnrs-orleans.fr

Abstract: It is well known since the monograph published by Caley in 1939 that the quality of bronze coins minted by the Greeks was degraded, especially in the Hellenistic period. This question is reassessed, comparing different numismatic studies published during the past 30 years that provided metallurgical analyses of Greek bronze coins carried out by Fast Neutron Activation using a cyclotron.

Keywords: Greece; Bronze; Coins; Activation Analysis

Introduction

The first bronze coins were minted in the Greek world at the middle of the Vth c. BC, around a century and half after the first coins made of precious metals were struck (Grandjean 2013). The inception of bronze coinage is thought to be a decisive innovation because it marks the beginning of a fiduciary currency in which the metallic value of the bronze coin was much lower than its nominal value. According to Marcellesi (2010, 262), the nominal value of the Greek minted bronze was 4 to 10 times more than the commercial value of the raw alloy. The striking of bronze coins was a source of income for the Greek states besides the many other technical advantages of bronze coins mentioned by Marcellesi (2010, 261).

Metallurgical analyses show that the Greek minting authorities carefully checked the composition of their bronze coins, at least when they first adopted bronze for coinage. However, it has been known since Caley's monograph (Caley 1939) that the quality of the minted alloys generally appears to have been degraded over time.

We propose to examine case studies in order to answer these questions: What is the composition of early Greek bronze coins? What is the evolution of the composition over time? What about changes in the coins' metrology? What role does lead play in the bronze alloy? Could this evolution of composition always be interpreted as deliberate manipulation? What could result from a lesser control of the alloy to be minted?

Most of the analytical data considered here to tackle these questions was obtained since the late 80's at the IRAMAT – Centre Ernest-Babelon with a single method, FNAA or Fast Neutron Activation Analysis using a cyclotron, ensuring the full comparability of the contents. This method gives an average bulk composition of the whole coin for the 10 most important elements entering in the composition of copper and silver-copper alloys, and it is non-destructive (Beauchesne et al. 1988; Guerra – Barrandon 1998). Table 1 presents the different publications from which this analytical data comes. The general trends in the evolution of the alloys minted by each authority have already been summarized in an article

Table 16.1. Presentation of the main studies with compositional data obtained at the IRAMAT – Centre Ernest-Babelon for Greek bronze coins. All the dates are before our era.*coins and blanks.

Cities/ kingdoms	Date	Number of coins analysed by FNAA	Bibliographical references
Marseilles	from the end of the IVth c. (or 2nd half of the IIIrd c.) to the Imperial period	500*	Brenot and Barrandon, 1988; Barrandon and Picard, 2007; Pellé, 2011
Amphipolis	before 359 BC to the IInd c.	60	Beauchesne, 1986; Guerra and Picard, 1999
Thasos	from 390 to the beginning of the IInd c.	150	
Elis	from 350 to the Ist c.	42	Wojan, 2011; Wojan 2016
Miletus	from the IVth c. to the Ist c.	53	Barrandon and Marcellesi, 2005
Ptolemaic kingdom	From the end of the IVth c. to the Ist c.	128	Faucher and Lorber, 2010; Faucher, 2013

Table 16.2. Composition of early Greek bronze coins (for references see Table 16.1).

Cities/ kingdoms	Early series (denomination; typology)	Date	Number of analysed coins	Sn (%)	Pb (%)
Marseilles	Large bronzes; Apollo/ bull with symbol on the obverse	Last quarter of the IVth c. or (or 2nd half of the IIIrd c.)	13	2–6%	0.1–0.3%
Amphipolis	Chalkous; Apollo type	before 359	7 (?)	8–18%	< 2%
Thasos	Chalkous; Herakles weapons in an incuse square on the reverse	390–375	14	12–15% (11 coins) or 5–9% (4 coins)	< 1% (11 coins) or 3–7% (4 coins)
Miletus	Chalkous; lion/sun	380–370	5	8–12%	< 0.1%
Ptolemaic kingdom	Hemiobol	315/312–301	1	14%	< 0.1%

previously published (Blet-Lemarquand 2013, 42–49). The present paper focuses on coins made of bronzes or lead-bronzes, although recent publications have pointed out that other copper-based alloys or pure copper were also occasionally used to manufacture Hellenistic coins. The uses of pure copper and brass before the turn of the second and the Ist c. BC or in the Ist c. BC, particularly for Hellenistic coinages from Asia Minor and Northern Black Sea Coast, are reported in Smekalova, 2009 and Chameroy, 2012. Wojan proved a special series of "bronze" coins minted in Elis were actually made of pure copper (2016).

About the making of bronze coins

'Manipulation' in the context of the making of bronze

In the context of the making of bronze coins the expression 'manipulation of the composition' would suggest that the concentrations were strictly controlled and could be modified for different reasons. We wish to assess to what extent metallurgists could control the composition of bronze coins, examining what is known about the available raw materials. Manipulating the composition implies ways to reduce the constraints on the making of bronze; these constraints could affect cost on the one hand, or time on the other hand. How could both be reduced in the making of copper alloys?

Raw material for the making of blanks: ingots and bronze scraps

To make bronze, the metallurgist had at his disposal ingots of purified metals – copper, tin and lead – (fresh metals from mines) with very different cost. At the time of Pliny the Elder, one pound of tin cost 80 denarii against 7 for the same weight of lead (Pliny 34.161) meaning that tin was more than 11 times more expensive than lead. A Greek classical written source reports that tin was at least 6 times more costly than copper.

It is well known that recycled metals were a source for making coins as well. Pliny the Elder stated that the manufacture of bronze for statues required recycled metal besides metal in ingots – probably copper – and tin (Pliny 34.97). An advantage of using bronze scraps to prepare bronze is that it makes the melting easier (El Morr 2011). These scraps could be bronze waste from the coin workshop obtained from previous casts, old coins withdrawn from circulation because they were too worn or because the weight standard had changed, foreign coins that were not allowed to circulate, and also broken bronze artefacts. We have no idea of the cost of these different bronze scraps for recycling but they were very likely less expensive than freshly purified metals in ingots. This leads us to wonder how recycling could involuntarily affect the composition of the final bronze alloy. Ancient metallurgists were able to identify to a great extent the alloys of which scraps were made, using criteria such as colour, smell, taste, and behaviour while hammering and heating. However they very likely could not distinguish between closely similar grades of bronzes. Therefore, when ingots of purified metals were available, the bronzesmith was of course able to prepare an alloy of the quality specified by the authority. On the contrary, the melting of bronze scraps would necessarily have limited the strict control of the composition of coins. And, besides the metals, another valuable and essential material for the making of the alloy was charcoal.

The role of lead in bronze manufacture

The addition of lead to bronze had many advantages, both technical and economical. Lead was much more widespread and less expensive than tin. It was actually a by-product of the silver production obtained from lead ores and it is thought that it became more available in Greece in the course of the Vth c., when the issue of silver coins increased. Moreover, lead likely improved the castability of the alloy (Piccardo – Vernet – Ghiara 2017, 56, and see recent tests carried out in Mille 2017). Lead decreases the melting point of the alloy and thus helps to reduce the consumption of charcoal. If its addition remains at a reduced level (less than 10%), the colour is not modified, (Picon – Boucher – Condamin 1966), and the adulteration could probably not be detected by the users. On the contrary, the addition of higher proportions of lead makes the alloy's colour lighter and greyish. Nodules of lead can even be seen with the naked eyes on the surface of certain Greek coins (Griesser et al. 2012). Moreover, lead-rich bronze that contains 10% or more tin might jeopardise the casting because of segregation phenomena.

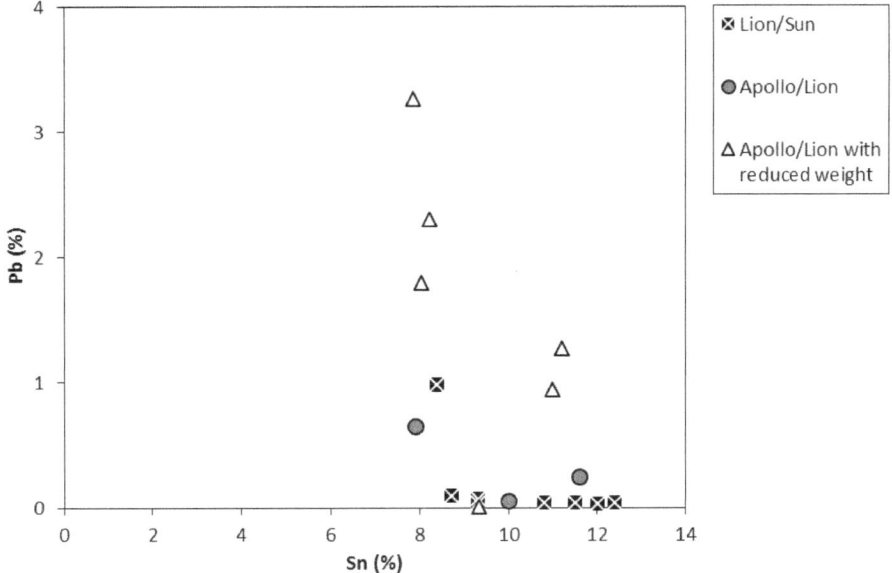

Diagram 16.1. Pb versus Sn for Miletus bronze coins dated c.380–370. Data from Barrandon – Marcellesi 2005.

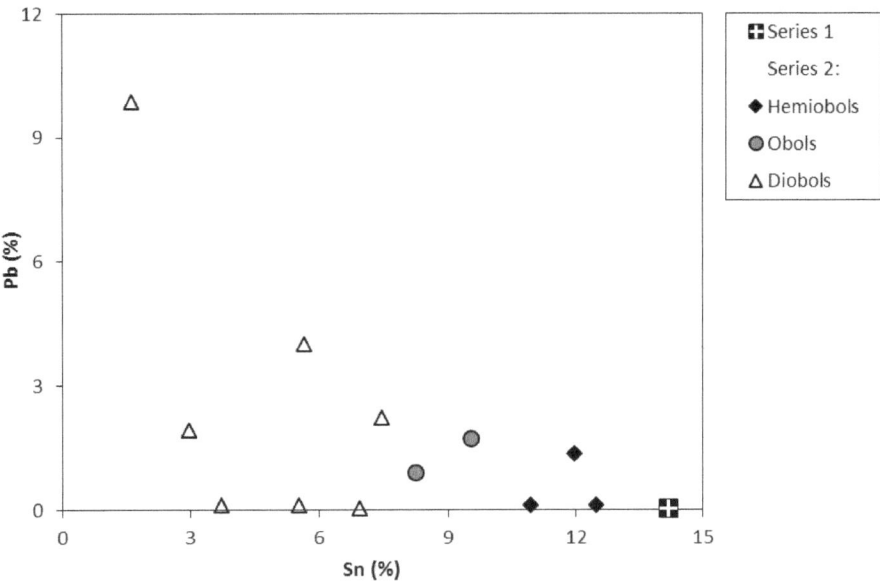

Diagram 16.2. Pb versus Sn for Ptolemaic bronze coins from Series 1 and 2. Data from Faucher 2013.

Under these circumstances, the bronzesmith would be well advised to lower the tin concentration. This view was supported by Picon, Boucher and Condamin (1966). As a consequence, the typical colour of bronze could not be retained when high proportions of lead were added. Thus massive additions of lead to the bronze to be minted could not remain hidden to the users of coins.

The composition of Greek bronze coins

Early Greek bronze coins

The low lead content found in early Greek bronze coins suggests that these alloys were produced by melting fresh metals, ingots of copper and tin, without recycling, which would have introduced lead coming from lead-bronze scraps. Special attention was paid to the manufacture of this new coinage. The 8–12% range for tin gave the liquid alloy a good fluidity and gave the coin a "golden" colour. We have hypothesized that this colour was thought to be attractive in order this new coin that didn't contain any precious metal and which value was largely fiduciary to be accepted by the people (Blet-Lemarquand 2013, 55). Bronze was expected to look golden in the ancient Greek world: Descamps-Lesquime (2013, 31) explained that bronze statues used to be regularly oiled to prevent the corrosion from growing and to keep the "golden" colour of the alloy.

Chronological evolution of Greek bronze coins' composition

For most of the Greek bronze coinages, the highest tin contents were found in coins belonging to the early series (see for instance the Ptolemaic bronzes, Diagram 16.2). As a general rule, high tin and a lead-free binary bronze

Table 16.3. Typology, date, weight standard and composition of the first bronzes struck in Miletus. Data from Barrandon – Marcellesi 2005. Average content ± 1 standard deviation.

Type	Date	Mean weight standard (g)	Sn (%)	Pb (%)
Lion/Sun	c. 380–370	2.1	10.3 ± 1.6	0.2 ± 0.3
Apollo/Lion	IVth c.	1.8	9.8 ± 1.9	0.3 ± 0.3
Apollo/Lion with reduced weight	IVth c.	1.0	9.3 ± 1.5	1.6 ± 1.1

alloy was no longer used for coins struck after the first series that inaugurated bronze coinage. The alloy of the following coins either contains lead as a minor element, or the tin concentration is reduced. Moreover, a concomitant reduction of the weight standard can often be seen.

The coinage from Miletus illustrates these general tendencies (Table 16.3 and Diagram 16.1). The earliest bronze coins show a lion on the obverse and a sun on the reverse; they are small denominations (chalkous) weighing about 2 g and made of 10% tin-bronze. The next type, with an Apollo's head on the obverse and a lion on the reverse, was minted in different denominations. This group of coins has exactly the same composition as the previous type. Then a reduction of the weight standard by 50% was carried out, and it appears that this is concomitant with a slight but significant increase in the lead content. This modification is not important enough to characterize the addition of lead, but could rather be interpreted as lesser control over the metals that were melted down. Bronze was spared with the weight reduction, and the quality of the alloy was slightly reduced, maybe from the use of bronze scraps.

The alloy of Ptolemaic bronze coins shows a degradation of quality that was carried out from the second series of coins. It is then characterised by a decline in the tin content and a small rise in the proportion of lead. The composition of the earliest series of the Ptolemaic bronzes is known from the analysis of one unique coin that contains 14% tin, and lead at the trace level, which is why we have to be cautious and this composition cannot be generalized (Diagram 16.2).

However, it is certain that the tin concentrations were reduced and the lead concentrations increased during the next series of coins. Most of the Series 2 specimens are made of binary bronzes with tin contents ranging from 13% to 2%, while lead concentrations tend to increase, although remaining less than 3%. It seems also that this variety of compositions for Series 2 is consistent with the denominations, the smallest coins containing more tin and rather less lead than the biggest ones (Blet-Lemarquand – Olivier, in press).

The next step in the evolution of Greek bronze coinage is the increase of lead content and the use of lead-bronzes. Caley (1939, 186) concluded that the proportions of lead had increased over the course of time and that at the latest period the lead content usually far exceeds that of tin. His conclusion is confirmed for all the Greek coinages considered here, especially at the end of the Hellenistic period. In Amphipolis and in Miletus, the lead content of coins rose to 15–20%. The concentration of lead increased to 20–35% in second-century Alexandrian bronzes (Faucher – Lorber 2010, 69), or 40% in the Marseilles bronzes (Barrandon – Picard 2007, 34; see the case of the large bronzes Table 16.4 and Diagram 16.3). However this general trend is different from what was observed in Thasian coins, where high proportions of lead (10–15%) were sometimes added in the fourth century to issue coins with the iconography and the weight of silver coins (Guerra – Picard 1999, 201–202).

Caley went further in the interpretation of his analysis of 70 Greek bronze coins and proposed a two-step process (1939, 188). 1. The copper content remained steady while lead increased and tin decreased; 2. The lead proportions increased to the detriment of both tin and copper. The first trend would come from the replacement of tin by a tin-lead alloy and the second one would be explained by "the addition of lead to bronze having the composition of that used in earlier coins" (Caley 1939, 189). The re-melting of the earliest coins is apparently not considered by Caley.

These trends were sought in the available analytical data, comparing the concentrations in copper, tin and lead with the chronology, and with the weight standard, if possible. The simplified evolution expressed by Caley could be sufficient to describe the alloy minted in Miletus. Most of

Table 16.4. Typology and composition of the large bronzes (Apollo/bull) struck in Marseilles. Data from Barrandon and Picard, 2007, especially 34.

Type	Mean weight (g)	Issue No.	Alloy composition	Date
Group 1 (symbol on the obverse)	15.6	1–9	Bronzes (Sn 2–6% ; traces of Pb)	Beginning of the last quarter of the IVth c. (or IIIrd c.)
Group 2 (symbol on the reverse)	10.4	10–17	Bronzes (Sn 3–8% ; traces of Pb)	Group 2 (symbol on the reverse)
Group 3 (symbol on the obverse or on the reverse)	10.3	18–24	3a: bronzes (Sn 3–8%; traces of Pb; sometimes Fe)	Third quarter of the IIIrd c. for 3c
	10.3	25–29	3b: bronzes (Pb < 3%)	
	7.5	30–39	3c: lead bronzes (Pb 10–30%)	

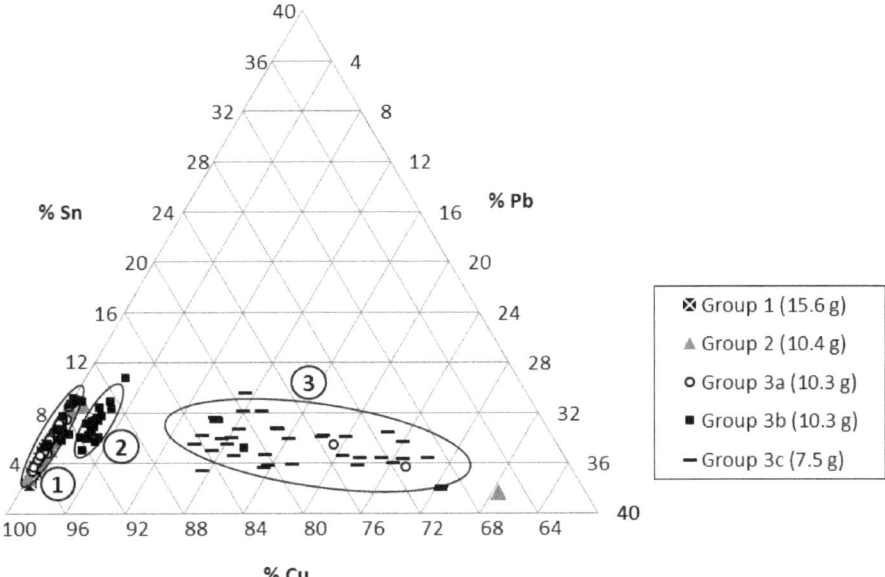

Diagram 16.3. Ternary diagram showing the Cu, Sn and Pb contents of the different groups of the large bronze coinage struck in Marseilles. Average weights between parentheses. See text for the comments on ellipses 1, 2 and 3. Data from Barrandon – Picard 2007.

the IIIrd c. bronze coins show a composition with tin being partially replaced by lead (Barrandon – Marcellesi 2005, 233), while lead often appears to be more important than tin in the second-century bronze coins. The substitution of a part of the tin by lead could be hypothesised for certain coins minted in Alexandria in the third c. (see Series 2, Diagram 16.2), but in the same series binary bronze coins were also struck. Therefore step 1 cannot have been a general rule for Greek bronze coinage; the recycling of bronze scraps that may have contained lead to manufacture new alloys appears to be more probable. For instance, the partial substitution of tin by a tin-lead alloy does not seem to exist in the Marseilles large coins, and the addition of lead in various amounts is more likely to have prevailed.

This first series of coins shows Apollo on the obverse and a bull on the reverse, and it is classified in three groups according to typology and weight (Table 16.4). Coins in groups 1 and 2 have more or less a similar composition (Table 16.4, Diagram 16.3), and are made of binary bronzes with 2–6% tin. A reduction of weight was carried out for group 2, suggesting that group 1 coins could have been re-melted to strike coins with a new weight standard (Barrandon – Picard 2007, 69). The next group split into three different subgroups – 3a, 3b and 3c – that are consistent with the typological classification, the weight standard and the alloy composition (Table 16.4, Diagram 16.3). Group 3a has a composition that is close to that of groups 1 and 2 (ellipse 1): all these coins are made of binary bronzes with 3–8% tin, with lead at trace levels. Some group 3b coins can be distinguished because they contain about 2.5% lead (ellipse 2). This noticeable and steady lead proportion in some group 3b coins could come from the intentional addition of a fixed proportion of lead to the binary bronze. Then there is a clear gap between groups 3b and 3c because all the group 3c coins contain between 10% and 30% lead while their tin contents range from 6% to 2% (ellipse 3). Moreover the mean weight of the group 3c coins was lowered if compared to 3b ones (7.5g against 10.3g). Thus, the reduced weight of the group 3c coins and the linear relationship between their copper, tin and lead concentrations could suggest that the previous coins from groups 2, 3a and 3b were massively re-melted and mixed with more and more lead.

In order to assess this hypothesis, a numerical mixing simulation for the major elements is shown in table 16.5. It reveals that the compositions of the group 3c coins could be explained by the dilution with varied proportions of lead of an alloy obtained from the melting-down of groups 2, 3a and 3b coins. The contents in minor and trace elements do not contradict this hypothesis of mixing (see for instance Blet-Lemarquand 2013, fig. 4 for Sb and Ag concentrations). A close examination of the available hoards would however be useful to help determine which coins circulated together, and then to support this hypothesis. The Olbia hoard was reassessed by Barrandon and Picard (2007, 53–62). It is composed of groups 2, 3a and 3b coins and doesn't contain any 3c coins. This composition would give weight to our hypothesis.

Distinction between bronze and lead-bronze from the data

It is generally accepted that 3% lead content is a threshold to characterize the deliberate adulteration of bronze with lead metal (see the definition of lead bronze in Piccardo et al. 2017 for instance). Caley (1939, 188) studied the distributions of lead content in Greek coins of the early series analysed by chemical methods: he concluded that lead concentrations of less than 2% could not be explained by intentional additions, while contents exceeding this value are usually the result of deliberate additions.

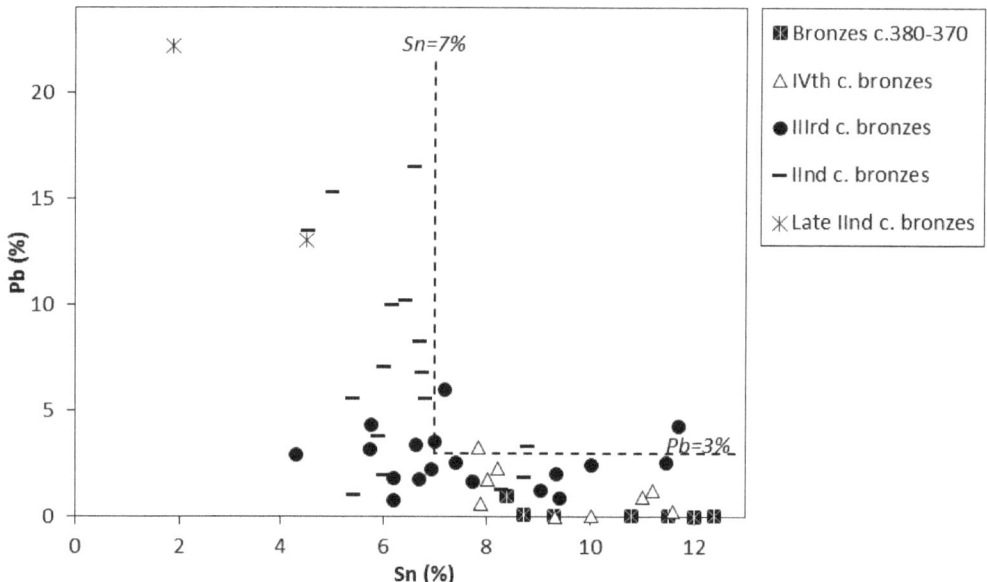

Diagram 16.4. Pb versus Sn for all the Miletus bronze coins analysed in Barrandon – Marcellesi 2005.

The value of 3% appears in fact to have a particular meaning in the composition of various Greek bronze coinages. For instance, the Marseilles large bronzes from groups 1 to 3b never contain more than 3% lead, while coins of the next subgroup are 10–30% lead-bronzes (Table 16.4 and Diagram 16.3). A simplified overview of the data available for the Miletus coins makes it clear that the 3% lead content plays a special role characteristic of deliberate adulteration (Diagram 16.4). Therefore, contents above this 2–3% threshold would adduce the proof of voluntary additions of lead in Greek bronze coins, whereas proportions below this range could rather generally result from uncontrolled additions of lead (impurities from the copper, recycling of bronze scraps). However this threshold probably depends on the type of objects, on the manufacture processes (casting, hammering, etc.) and on cultural practices. Picon, Condamin and Boucher (1968, 250) suggested a threshold of 6% lead for the statuettes and other cast bronzes from the Mediterranean Basin dated before our era, whereas Bourgarit and Mille (2003, 1551) came to the conclusion that the 1% lead concentration found in all the cast parts of the Vix crater was a voluntary addition.

Relation between the lead contents and the monetary manufacture techniques

It is well known that lead nodules in bronzes are detrimental to their deformability. For that reason, hammered antique bronzes, for which analysis was published by Craddock (1977), never contain more than 0.3% lead. Faucher (2017, 80; Blet-Lemarquand 2013, 53, fn. 52) reported archaeometallurgical experiments that he carried out with a 4% tin and 20% lead bronze alloy. Blanks were first cast in moulds and then struck between dies to receive images on both sides: most of the coins broke during the process of striking. This characteristic explains why some highly leaded bronze coins were only cast, pouring the hot and liquid bronze in a mould already incised with the monetary images and inscriptions. This is the case for the series of

Table 16.5. Mixing simulation. Data from Barrandon and Picard 2007, 126–132. Number of analysed coins between parentheses.* It is assumed that iron can be easily removed from bronze as dross because it is easily oxidised, as reported by Pernicka (1999, 165).

	Cu (%)	Sn (%)	Pb (%)	Fe (%)
Average composition of gr. 2 (55 ex.) + gr. 3a (86 ex.) + gr 3b (35 ex.) = alloy No. 1	90.6	5.7	0.9	2.4
Melting of 1 part of alloy No. 1 + 0.1 part of pure lead	84.5	5.3	10.1	*
Melting of 1 part of alloy No. 1 + 0.3 part of pure lead	71.2	4.5	24.3	*
Average composition of gr. 3c (36 ex.)	77.3	5.5	16.7	0.1

Ptolemaic coins that are indeed counterfeits produced by moulding official coins, especially in the 1st century BC (Faucher 2017, 76. 79). These latter coins are of poor quality and the facts that they were moulded using a highly leaded alloy cannot be debated. Is this example sufficient, however, to ensure that high contents of lead indicate that the coin was manufactured only by casting without any striking? The question is controversial. Faucher and Lorber (2010, 70) stated that "when the moulded coin is of good manufacture, it is very difficult to distinguish it from a struck one". Moreover, the microstructural and especially the texture-studies of coins are not very widespread for different reasons (preservation of the coins; cost and access to non-destructive approaches such as neutron or X-Ray diffraction). A close examination of the coins can give hints about the monetary manufacture techniques as evidenced by Faucher (2017, 73f.). Archaeological remains are another way to tackle the problem. Coin blanks were found in the excavations of the ancient mint of Marseilles. Some of them are rich in lead (25–35%) and could likely be attributed to the group 3c already presented with the weight, diameter and elemental composition criteria (Barrandon – Picard 2007, 64). These blanks were produced by casting and there is no reason to doubt that they were designed for striking.

Microstructural investigations carried out on lead-rich bronze coins and blanks have made it clear that the lead inclusions are of varying sizes and are inhomogeneously distributed over the width and depth of these objects (Barrandon – Picard 2007; Griesser et al. 2012; Griesser et al. 2016, Faucher 2017). Griesser and co-workers (2012; 2016) were able to pinpoint different spatial distributions that they have related to the casting technique chosen in antiquity, "vertical" or "horizontal". Furthermore, lead can be inhomogeneously distributed at all the scales of the cast alloy. Deraisme and Barrandon (2005) performed casting experiments of a 2% tin and 35% lead bronze in a connected-flan mould and determined the mean composition by FNAA of the blanks previously cut into two pieces. Discrepancies in the lead contents were observed between the blanks (Table 16.6), probably depending on how the liquid alloy had been mixed in the crucible before casting, according to the authors (2005, 9). They mentioned that the range of compositions noted for the blanks produced during a single casting is of the same order of magnitude as what is noted for bronze coins belonging to the same issue. The elemental data obtained for the group 3c coins from Marseilles is considered for comparative purposes (Table 16.7). The coins are classified into different issues on the criteria of the symbols put on their obverse and reverse (Barrandon – Picard 2007, 80f.). The variability expressed with the relative standard deviation is in fact generally much higher for real bronze coins from a particular issue than for the experimental blanks obtained from a single casting (Tables 16.6 and 16.7). This comparison suggests that the range of lead contents measured for coins belonging to a same issue can not only be explained by segregation phenomena but also chiefly results from the metals and alloys put in the crucible.

Conclusions

The comparison between different studies carried out on Greek bronze coins leads to various general conclusions. The elemental composition of bronze coins proves, if necessary, the skill of the ancient metallurgists and moreover reveals monetary-policy choices. As a matter of fact, the major elements of the bronze alloys are often relevant criteria, along with others, for building a relative chronology of the bronze issues. The investigations conducted on the Marseilles bronze coins by Barrandon and Picard (2007) give weight to this statement.

At this step of the researches we are able to give a general outline of the evolution of Greek bronze coins. The early coins are usually made of a real binary bronze having about 10% tin, that was certainly made from ingots of fresh metals without recycling. These coins must have had a "golden" colour that was very likely intentional – to make this new coinage without precious metal accepted by the users. Then, the partial substitution of tin by lead was sometimes used, or bronze scraps were mixed with copper and tin or with copper only to manufacture the alloy. These practices led to a slight rise in the lead concentrations to the detriment of the tin ones in the resulting alloy. The 3% lead content can actually be considered a threshold to prove the intentional addition of lead. Finally, the

Table 16.6. Average (AV), standard deviation (SD) and relative standard deviation (RSD) calculated for the Cu, Sn and Pb contents for blanks obtained with two different castings. Data from Deraisme – Barrandon – Pilon 2005.

	Cu (%)			Sn (%)			Pb (%)		
	AV	SD	RSD	AV	SD	RSD	AV	SD	RSD
1st casting (26 half blanks analysed)	64.7	2.1	3%	2.1	0.1	5%	32.7	2.0	6%
2nd casting (28 half blanks analysed)	62.4	3.5	6%	2.9	0.8	28%	34.5	3.5	10%

Table 16.7. Average (AV), standard deviation (SD) and relative standard deviation (RSD) calculated for the Cu, Sn and Pb contents for the group 3c bronze struck in Marseilles. "Nb" is the number of analysed coins. The different issues are distinguished. Data from Barrandon – Picard 2007.

Issue No.	Nb of coins	Cu (%)			Sn (%)			Pb (%)		
		AV	SD	RSD	AV	SD	RSD	AV	SD	RSD
30	4	80.8	2.2	3%	7.1	2.2	30%	11.6	1.2	10%
31	3	77.6	2.7	3%	5.2	1.4	27%	16.6	1.4	9%
32	8	80.1	4.8	6%	5.2	1.6	31%	14.2	5.8	41%
33	2	74.1	8.1	11%	3.3	2.0	62%	21.5	9.1	43%
34	4	82.2	1.2	1%	7.0	1.0	14%	10.2	0.2	2%
35	2	78.4	0.02	0.02%	6.0	2.9	49%	15.2	2.9	19%
36	1	73.3			4.4			21.5		
37	6	72.9	1.8	2%	4.8	1.0	21%	21.9	2.5	11%
38	6	73.7	4.6	6%	5.3	1.2	22%	20.6	4.6	22%

deliberate additions of lead to probably recycled bronze became widespread in Greek bronze coins in the second c., when lead contents reached 15–20%, or even more than 30%. This adulteration compelled the bronzesmith to manufacture coin blanks by casting and had of course many advantages for the minting authority. However, it could not remained hidden to the users. It did not seem to pose a major problem, meaning that bronze coins were widely accepted in Greek society.

A first comparison between the elemental composition of the coinage and the statuary was attempted by Blet-Lemarquand (2013, 53) for the Greek Classical and Hellenistic periods, and it highlighted some similarities. It would be interesting to go further with the comparison in order to determine relationships between both bronze productions and then place bronze coin manufacture within a general framework. The data gathered by Descamps-Lesquime and Mille for the antique statuary in the *Héphaïstos* database (2017, 6–11) could be a useful tool for initiating this comparison.

Acknowledgements

Most of the analysed coins were lent by the Département des Monnaies, médailles et antiques from the Bibliothèque nationale de France and the irradiations were carried out at the CEMHTI cyclotron (CNRS, Orléans). The author is indebted to the anonymous reviewer for incisive remarks and to critics who have improved this text. However, all conclusions are her sole responsibility.

Bibliography

Barrandon, J.-N. – Marcellesi, M.-C., 2005. Le monnayage de bronze aux types de Milet du IVe au IIe siècle avant J.-C.: l'apport des analyses métalliques. *Archäologischer Anzeiger*, 1, 227–242.

Barrandon, J.-N. – Picard, O., 2007. *Monnaies de bronze de Marseille. Analyse, classement, politique monétaire.* Cahiers Ernest-Babelon 10. Paris: Éditions du CNRS.

Beauchesne, F., 1986. *Analyse non destructive du cuivre et de ses alliages par activation à l'aide de neutrons rapides de cyclotron. Application à la numismatique.* Unpublished PhD Thesis. Université d'Orléans.

Beauchesne, F. – Barrandon, J.-N. – Alves, L. – Gil, F.B. – Guerra, M.F., 1988. Ion beam analysis of copper and copper alloy coins. *Archaeometry*, 30(2), 187–197.

Blet-Lemarquand, M. – Olivier, J., (in press) From one coinage to another: Pinpointing the melting down of coins in the Hellenistic world using archaeometric data. In: A. Bresson – D. Schloen – W. Shandruk, ed., *Proceedings of the conference 'Coin Circulation in the Ancient Greek World. Mapping and Networks', The University of Chicago Center in Paris, 17–18 May 2018'.*

Blet-Lemarquand, M., 2013. Les analyses élémentaires de monnaies de bronze grecques réalisées au Centre Ernest-Babelon de l'IRAMAT : méthode, résultats, synthèse. In: C. Grandjean – A. Moustaka, ed., *Aux origines de la monnaie fiduciaire. Traditions métallurgiques et innovations numismatiques. Actes de l'atelier international des 16 et 17 novembre 2012 à Tours.* Bordeaux: Ausonius Éditions, 39–56.

Bourgarit, D. – Mille, B., 2003. The elemental analysis of ancient copper-based artefacts by inductively-coupled-plasma atomic-emission spectrometry: an optimized methodology reveals some secrets of the Vix crater. *Measurement Science and Technology*, 14(9), 1538–1555.

Brenot, C. – Barrandon, J.-N., 1988. Les émissions de bronze à Marseille : apport des analyses. I. Les bronzes lourds. *Revue numismatique*, 6(30), 91–113.

Caley, E.R., 1939. *The composition of ancient Greek bronze coins.* American Philosophical Society Memoirs Vol. II. Philadelphie.

Chameroy, J., 2012. Chronologie und Verbreitung der hellenistischen Bronzeprägungen von Pergamon: der Beitrag der Fundmünzen. *Chiron*, 42, 131–181.

Craddock, P.T., 1977. The composition of the copper alloys used by the Greek, Etruscan and Roman civilisations: 2. The Archaic, Classical and Hellenistic Greeks. *Journal of Archaeological science*, 4(2), 103–123.

Deraisme, A. – Barrandon, J.-N., 2005. L'hétérogénéité des teneurs en plomb dans les monnaies de bronze antiques. *Revue numismatique*, 161, 5–15.

Deraisme, A. – Barrandon, J.-N. – Pilon, F., 2005. L'hétérogénéité des teneurs en plomb dans les monnaies de bronze antiques. In: C. Alfaro – C. Marcos – P. Otero, ed., *Actas del XIII Congreso Internacional de Numismática*, Madrid 2003. Madrid. 219–226.

Descamps-Lequime, S. – Mille, B., 2017. Progrès de la recherche sur la statuaire antique en bronze. *Technè: la science au service de l'histoire de l'art et des civilisations*, (45), 5–13.

Descamps-Lequime, S., 2013. De la cire à l'alliage cuivreux : techniques des bronzes grecs. In: C. Grandjean – A. Moustaka, ed., *Aux origines de la monnaie fiduciaire. Traditions métallurgiques et innovations numismatiques. Actes de l'atelier international des 16 et 17 novembre 2012 à Tours.* Bordeaux: Ausonius Éditions, 19–33.

El Morr, Z., 2011. *La métallurgie du levant au bronze moyen à travers les armes.* Unpublished PhD Thesis. Université Michel de Montaigne Bordeaux 3.

Faucher, T. – Lorber, C., 2010. Bronze coinage of Ptolemaic Egypt in the second century BC. *American Journal of Numismatics Second Series*, 22, 35–80.

Faucher, T., 2013. *Frapper monnaie : La fabrication des monnaies de bronze à Alexandrie sous les Ptolémées.* Alexandrie.

Faucher, T., 2017. Coin Minting Techniques in Ptolemaic Egypt: Observe, Analyze, Recreate. *NOTAE NUMISMATICAE – ZAPISKI NUMIZMATYCZNE*, XII, 71–90.

Grandjean, C., 2013. Une monnaie fiduciaire issue du monde colonial. In: C. Grandjean – A. Moustaka, ed., *Aux origines de la monnaie fiduciaire. Traditions métallurgiques et innovations numismatiques. Actes de l'atelier international des 16 et 17 novembre 2012 à Tours*. Bordeaux: Ausonius Éditions, 97–107.

Griesser, M. – Kockelmann, W. – Hradil, K. – Traum, R., 2016. New insights into the manufacturing technique and corrosion of high leaded antique bronze coins. *Microchemical Journal*, 126, 181–193.

Griesser, M. – Traum, R. – Vondrovec, K. – Vontobel, P. – Lehmann, E.H., 2012. Application of X-Ray and Neutron Tomography to Study Antique Greek Bronze Coins with a High Lead Content. *IOP Conference Series: Materials Science and Engineering*, 37.

Guerra, M.F. – Barrandon, J.-N., 1998. Ion Beam Activation Analysis with a cyclotron. In: W.A. Oddy – M.R. Cowell, ed., *Metallurgy in Numismatics Volume 4*, Royal Numismatic Society Special Publication No. 30. London: Royal Numismatic Society, 15–34.

Guerra, M.F. – Picard, O., 1999. L'alliage des monnaies de bronze (Amphipolis, Thasos, Maronée). In: C. Koukouli – A. Muller – S. Papadopoulos, ed., *Thasos. Matières premières et technologies de la Préhistoire à nos jours. Actes du Colloque International 26 – 29/9/1995 Thasos, Liménaria*. Paris, 195–206.

Marcellesi, M.-C., 2010. Adoption et diffusion de la monnaie de bronze dans le monde égéen : une évolution économique et institutionnelle. *Studi ellenistici*, XXIV, 255–270.

Mille, B., 2017. *D'une amulette en cuivre aux grandes statues de bronze : évolution des techniques de fonte à la cire perdue, de l'Indus à la Méditerranée, du 5e millénaire au 5e siècle av. J.-C.* Unpublished PhD Thesis. Paris 10.

Pellé, R., 2011. Un lot monétaire remarquable de petits bronzes massaliètes. *Revue numismatique*, 291–320.

Pernicka, E., 1999. Trace element fingerprinting of ancient copper: a guide to technology or provenance? In: S.M.M. Young – A.M. Pollard – P. Budd – R.A. Ixer, ed., *Metals in Antiquity*, BAR International Series 792. Oxford: BAR Publishing, 163–171.

Piccardo, P. – Vernet, J. – Ghiara, G., 2017. Mise en œuvre des alliages cuivreux : faire parler le métal grâce à la science des matériaux. In: M. Pernot, ed., *Quatre mille ans d'histoire du cuivre*. Ausonius Editions-Presses Universitaires de Bordeaux, 41–60.

Picon, M. – Boucher, S. – Condamin, J., 1966. Recherches techniques sur des bronzes de Gaule romaine. *Gallia*, 24(1), 189–215.

Picon, M. – Condamin, J. – Boucher, S., 1968. Recherches techniques sur des bronzes de Gaule romaine, III. *Gallia*, 26(2), 245–278.

Smekalova, T., 2009. The Earliest Application of Brass and "Pure" Copper in the Hellenistic Coinages of Asia Minor and the Northern Black Sea Coast. In: J.M. Højte, ed., *Mithridates VI and the Pontic Kingdom*, Black Sea studies, Volume 9. Aarhus University Press, 233–248.

Wojan, F., 2011. *Les Eléens (IVe siècle a.C.–IIIe siècle p.C.). Recherche de numismatique et d'histoire*. Unpublished PhD Thesis. Université de Tours.

Wojan, F., 2016. Un curieux monnayage de cuivre en Élide (Péloponnèse) à l'époque hellénistique. *Bulletin de la Société Française de Numismatique*, 71(4), 114–119.

17

Corinthian bronze: was it just wrought high-tin bronze?

Jean-Marie Welter

Independent Researcher

jean-marie.welter@pt.lu

Abstract: *Aes Corinthium* (Corinthian bronze) is one of the enigmatic metallurgical items mentioned by Pliny the Elder in his *Naturalis Historia*. It refers to a very highly praised material used to make tableware shaped by hammering. For Pliny, genuine Corinthian bronze had a silvery colour. Strangely enough, scholars have ignored this during the last centuries. The aim of the present work is to propose that the silvery, shining, wrought high-tin bronze with 20 to 25% of tin is a possible candidate for Corinthian bronze. Although no plate or bowl made with this alloy had apparently been identified in the Greco-Roman world, one cannot exclude imports from Asia, where the alloy (and its specific processing technology) was developed in the Indian sub-continent as early as the Iron Age.

Keywords: Corinthian Bronze; Wrought High-tin Bronze; Silvery Colour

Introduction

Corinthian bronze (*aes corinthium*) is the most mysterious copper alloy reported by ancient authors living between Rome and Alexandria. To quote Mattusch: it is *"famous, but elusive"* (Mattusch 2003). The epithet *elusive* is well merited, because until now, no archaeological object has been found which can be linked unambiguously to Corinthian bronze. Of course, such a link was hypothesized for various objects, often depending on the prevailing interpretation of the mysterious alloy. There are reasons why a clear-cut identification is almost impossible. According to the ancient authors, Corinthian bronze was used to fabricate luxury goods – mainly tableware shaped by hammering – and they were more highly rated than those made of silver and almost as high as those made of gold. The value of Corinthian bronze derived not so much from the cost of the metal, but rather from its processing. Consequently the quantity produced was limited. When falling into the hands of an ignorant individual, the artefact might be easily misused and eventually scrapped – contrary to silver and gold.

A difficulty results from the absence of consensus among scholars about the nature of the copper alloy and fabrication process which are covered by the term Corinthian bronze. For some scholars, Corinthian bronze was a kind of tin bronze with characteristic bulk properties. For others, the originality of Corinthian bronze resulted from the surface treatment of a purposely chosen alloy. Because of the absence of archaeological findings in the Greco-Roman zone, a recent trend followed by scholars is to check whether materials and techniques were developed in other civilisations which could support their interpretation of Corinthian bronze.

While studying the history of wrought bronze, I was puzzled by the fact that a large number of hammered bronze artefacts with tin contents up to 15% were excavated in the Greek-Roman-Celtic world, but none with tin contents in the range 20 to 25%. This is rather amazing, because the technique to fabricate wrought high-tin objects was developed millennia ago in India. It spread later over a large part of the Asian continent. Did it also diffuse to Europe? The question is justified in view of the commercial and cultural exchanges which existed already in ancient times between the two continents (see below). Possibly, the mysterious Corinthian bronze could relate in some way to wrought high-tin bronze. A first step would be to compare its properties with the ones mentioned sparely for Corinthian bronze in the ancient written records. In the following, this argument will be developed in more detail. The starting point is a discussion of the lengthy entry on Corinthian bronze given by Pliny the Elder in Book 34.6–8 of his *Naturalis Historia* (Plinius Secundus 1989). Most scholars agree that the paragraph is fundamental for understanding what Corinthian bronze could have been. For Pliny, an important characteristic of Corinthian bronze was the colour. The corresponding phrase in chapter 8 reads:

"Aeris tria genera: candidum argento nitore quam proxime accedens, in quo illa mixtura praevaluit; alterum, in quo auri fulva natura; tertium, in quo aequalis omnium temperies fuit."

"There are three kinds of bronze: a white one, the shine of which resembles the one of silver as much as possible, in which that mixture predominates; another one has a tawny golden colour; the third one is an equal combination of both."

There is no ambiguity in the statement: genuine Corinthian bronze has a colour close to that of silver. But Corinthian bronze could also be processed to produce derivate alloys with other colours, for instance one with tawny golden hue. Pliny gives no colour indication for the third bronze obtained by mixing the two other ones.

The question may be raised how knowledgeable Pliny was when he wrote his statement? When writing about any material, Pliny always emphasised the importance of colour as a key feature of its nature. Furthermore, he knew very well how the appearance of metals could be modified by surface treatments. He reports various techniques to tin objects to give them the lustre of silver, to plate artefacts with gold using mercury as a binder and even to blacken silver and copper by forming surface sulphides. He also indicates that copper turns black when melted and solidified under special conditions. Therefore we can assume that when Pliny writes that genuine Corinthian bronze has a silvery colour, he meant it. Furthermore, in case the colour of an object had resulted from a surface treatment, he would have mentioned it. As a *résumé*, in Pliny's view, the cited colours were characteristic for the various brands of Corinthian bronze he listed – and hence for the artefacts made with them.

Of course, there are other ancient texts written by authors living around the (eastern) Mediterranean to be considered. They cover a period extending roughly from the 5th century BC to the 10th century AC and can be linked to the Greek, the Roman and the Near Eastern/Egyptian traditions. A common feature of these texts is that, as a rule, the authors made affirmations about Corinthian bronze which give the impression that they knew perfectly the alloy about which they wrote. An exception was Pliny the Younger, who questions himself whether a statuette he bought because he liked the colour was made of genuine Corinthian bronze. The difficulty in interpreting the texts is that the authors mixed technical information about the material, its uses, and anecdotes concerning its history as well as moral considerations about its social impact. As we will see, one aspect leading to dissent in the scholarly world are explicit and implicit indications found in some ancient texts, that Corinthian bronze contained gold and silver. What seems clear is that objects made from Corinthian bronze were mainly tableware like plates, cups, basins.

Thus, they had to be produced by working a cast blank and by polishing the object in a finishing step. A final colouring surface treatment is highly improbable, considering the nature and use of these artefacts. The reason is that a thin surface film could have been easily abraded by wear (coloured inlays are another issue). Objects made from Corinthian bronze were already in use in ancient Greece, but became very popular in Rome at the end of the Republic period and during the first centuries of the Empire. Their high value led to forgery and in later periods even to the production of cast objects like statuettes. This could have been the reason for the concern that Pliny the Younger expressed in his letter to his friend Annius Severus (Plinius Caecilius Secundus 2014). The use of Corinthian bronze as a statuary alloy was first of all reported by authors writing at the end of the 1rst century AC and later on.

The reception of Corinthian bronze in modern times

Most relevant excerpts about Corinthian bronze have been quoted in various publications, so there is no need to report them exhaustively (Emanuele 1989; Giumlia-Mair and Craddock 1993; Murphy-O'Connor 1983). On the other hand, little attention has been given to the opinions expressed by scholars during modern times. Those scholars tried to interpret the ancient texts with the aim of proposing a material, its processing and its surface finish. Their focus lay on the appearance of the objects made from Corinthian bronze, in other words on their colour. As already mentioned, the chapter of the *Naturalis Historia* about Corinthian bronze was the starting point of the discussion. More recently, increased consideration was given to further texts and – as mentioned above –, scholars also enlarged the field of investigation. They investigated whether specific highly valued materials produced by other civilisations could match the description given in the Greco-Roman-Hellenistic tradition.

Already during the Italian Renaissance Corinthian bronze was discussed (Collareta 2008), but the first writer who considered Pliny's text in detail and expressed a personal view about the alloy was probably Louis Savot (Savot 1627). He started by putting Corinthian bronze on the same level as *electrum* (an alloy of gold and silver) and *aurichalcum* (for him an alloy of gold and copper [sic!]) (Darab 2012). He continued by correlating the colours of Pliny's three kinds of Corinthian bronze with their composition. For him, gold and silver were the main constituents in the golden (which he placed ahead) and silvery shining alloys, respectively. In the third alloy, the three metals, copper, gold and silver, were present in equal parts. He insists upon saying that the use of these alloys was given up long before Pliny's time. Indeed, many antique medals which were reported to consist of Corinthian bronze turned out to be just made of gilded copper alloys. Thereafter he discussed which alloy – pure copper, brass or bronze – could be best gilded. In any case, lead-containing metals like pot metal (*potin*) are unqualified for gilding. This restriction means that Savot had in mind fire gilding with a gold-mercury amalgam. He concluded by stating that Corinthian bronze had designated since antiquity any copper alloy – but first of all statuary bronze – which can be gilded. One difficulty with Savot's interpretation is that the copper content had to be very low in his ancient Corinthian bronze, in order not to shift the colours of gold and silver into the reddish corner (Manas 2018). Furthermore, supposing that Savot had been right, Pliny would have discussed Corinthian bronze in Book 33, which covers noble metals, and not in Book 34, which describes the other metals like copper, tin and bronze.

Two centuries later, Martin Heinrich Klaproth denied the presence of any gold and silver in Corinthian bronze

(Klaproth 1815). Although he admits that copper, gold and silver may have been melted together by chance during the sack of Corinth in the year 146 BC, as reported by various ancient writers, he says that no artefact with such a composition had been found. Klaproth considered that Corinthian bronze belonged to the same class of alloys as *aurichalcum* (or *orichalcum*), which for him was brass. The differences between "standard" brass and Corinthian bronze are for the latter a much narrower zinc concentration range, the absence of lead and tin and a very high surface polish. The weak point of equating Corinthian bronze and brass is that brass keeps its yellow colour up to a zinc content of 60%. Klaproth's interpretation of Pliny's text may have been based on the high reflectivity of polished brass, especially when the zinc content is in the range of 10 to 15%. The surface looks bright golden, with pink or even silver tinges, depending on the exact composition. A further argument he may have considered derives from Pliny' remark that both *aurichalcum* and *aes corinthium* were materials of the past. Klaproth also claimed that brass allows embossing coins, whereas bronze is too brittle and permits only the casting of coins. To support his interpretation of Pliny's text, Klaproth refers to a section of Aristotle's work known as *De mirabilibus auscultationibus* (On marvellous things heard) (Aristoteles 1981). Nowadays a large part of the content – especially the one dealing with metallurgy – is considered as having been excerpts from the lost book on metals by Theophrastus of Eresos (ca. 371–ca. 287 BC) (Halleux 1974). Section 62 (which will be again discussed below) reads:

> "They say that the copper of the Mossynoiki is extremely resplendent and white, not because it is alloyed with tin, but because it merges with an earth excavated in their territory."

For Klaproth the earth was calamine, which allows producing brass by cementation. He based his understanding of that earth on the origin of the German term for brass, *Messing* (in an older spelling *Mössing*). The term was considered to derive from the name of the tribe by the name of the Mossynoiki, who lived in western Pontus. Nevertheless, there is no way of accounting for a white metal with brass: as said, the alloy keeps its yellow colour with up to 60% of zinc.

Also at the very beginning of the 19th century, Johann Dominik Fiorillo, while reporting Bossi's investigations on natural patina (according to Fiorillo, the first ones based on scientific considerations) (Anonymus 1832), used the opportunity to discuss Corinthian bronze. Like Klaproth, Fiorillo did not share the view that Corinthian bronze contained gold and silver. For him, Corinthian bronze was nothing else than high purity copper. To support the view, Fiorillo refered to the section of Pausanias' description of Corinth where is mentioned that in this city the red-hot bronze was dipped into the water of the Peirene fountain (Pausanias 1918). Fiorillo implicitly assumed that the action of the water was to colour the metal light green. It is well known that some waters corrode copper and form a layer of greenish corrosion products, the so-called natural patina. In comparison to pure copper, its alloys, like bronze, need much more time to get patinated. As a further argument, Fiorillo quotes Pliny's description of *balantia*, a precious stone having the shape of an acorn (Plinius Secundus 2007). He says that there are two kinds of stones, one has a greenish colour and the other one is similar to Corinthian bronze. So Fiorillo completely misread Pliny's sentence and thought that it was Corinthian bronze which takes on a light greenish colour.

Even if Fiorillo's opinion of the colouring action of the water relied on wrong assumptions, it was shared by various scholars during the following decades. But more recently, Earle R. Caley reconsidered Pausanias' remark on the Corinthian practice to treat the red-hot bronze with water (Caley 1941). The problems with Pausanias' remark are that the surviving sentence is incomplete and that the Greek verb used by Pausanias to describe the action of the coppersmith is homonymous: it means as well *dip* (into water) as *dye* (with water). Caley was mostly interested in verifying the latter meaning. He analysed the ground water of the Corinthian area and found a rather high concentration of chloride ions. He linked the light green cupric chlorides found in the corrosion products of the bronze artefacts excavated at ancient Corinth to the specific soil and water environment in which the artefacts were buried for centuries. He continued by checking whether waters rich in chloride ions could corrode bronze within a few days. It turned out, that for getting any effect, the chloride concentration had to be almost on an order of magnitude larger than the one of the Corinthian underground water and that only the reddish cupric oxide was formed. Thus Caley rejected the use of the water of the Peirene fountain to dye bronze. He also refuted another interpretation of why Corinthian bronze was dipped into the Peirene water. Various scholars believed that the water rapidly cooled the bronze leading to a hardening of the metal. For Caley, rapid cooling simply allowed saving time after an annealing treatment of the bronze. Such softening thermal treatments were necessary to avoid crack formation during cold-working. Concerning the nature of Corinthian bronze, Caley apparently considered that the material could have been a high purity bronze with a tin concentration at the high end of the solid solution, i.e. with 10 to 15% (middle-tin bronze). He suggested that Corinthian coppersmiths discovered that some heat treatment allowed them to cold-work such alloys. As we will see below, cold-working can be performed once the dendritic microstructure of the cast blank has been homogenised. Caley's hypothesis suffers from two weak points. Firstly the colour of such bronze is golden – the best known object being the beautiful Derveni krater made of $CuSn15Fe0.1$ bronze. Secondly, objects made by hammering middle-tin bronze were not uncommon in the Greco-Celtic world.

Nevertheless, it was a very appealing suggestion. Having reviewed the ancient Greco-Roman texts mentioning Corinthian bronze as well as archaeological findings in the Corinthian area, Daniel Emanuele arrived at a similar conclusion (Emanuele 1989). Genuine Corinthian bronzes were (preferably) decorated vessels fabricated with middle-tin bronze – the reference being again the Derveni krater. He extended the designation of Corinthian bronze to any bronze object, vessel or even statuette, original or faked, related to the city of Corinth. Donald Engels also supported this point of view while discussing thoroughly the metal-working crafts at the time of the Roman Empire in the redeveloped and flourishing city of Corinth (Engels 1990).

At the end of the last century, suggestions again arose that the specificity of Corinthian bronze resulted from a surface treatment. The basic idea relied on the preferential thermal oxidation of copper in the Cu-Au-Ag system. One proposal suggested that the treatment consisted in gilding the surface by depletion – which is a different technique as the one proposed by Savot (Jacobson 2000; Jacobson – Weitzman 1992). The starting metal used for the fabrication of an object is an alloy in which gold is the main constituent. The copper oxide formed during the heating of the alloy was dissolved with an acid, leaving a thin porous layer of pure gold on the surface. The layer was compacted by polishing. Although the colour of the base alloy tends more towards a reddish shine, gilding by copper depletion gives the impression that the whole body consists of pure gold. This technique was extensively used in pre-Columbian South America (today's Colombia), by using a gold-silver-copper alloy called tumbaga (Lechtman 1979; Sparavigna 2016). Another proposal starts with copper alloyed with a few percent of gold and possibly silver (Aucouturier et al. 2017; Craddock 1982; Giumlia-Mair 2015; Giumlia-Mair – Mrav 2014; Giumlia-Mair – Craddock 1993). As gold atoms are insoluble in copper oxides, they precipitate as nanoparticles in the cuprite film formed during the high temperature oxidation of the alloy. The array of gold particles enhances the absorption of light and gives a black appearance to the surface. This technique was widely used in pharaonic Egypt to blacken inlays of luxury goods. Some artefacts were also found in the provinces of the Roman Empire, but the technique was superseded during the first century AC by the niello technique.

A problem with such thin films is their low resistance to wear. Thus their suitability for utilitarian ware is very limited. A visit to the Gold Museum in Bogotá shows that even in ornamental plaques, which were not subjected to intensive handling, large areas appear where the gold film had been abraded. Some goldsmiths today use the Egyptian technique to blacken jewellery, e.g. rings and artefacts like cups. But they have to protect the parts of the jewels which are in contact with human skin. Gentle handling of black cups does not deteriorate the surface film, but it is rather rapidly worn off by rubbing. Furthermore, as has already been said, models centred on surface treatments are not consistent with Pliny's writings on Corinthian bronze. Also, if Corinthian bronze had been an alloy based in essence on noble metals, Pliny should have discussed it in book 33. Concerning the black surface, one can at best hypothesize that it was the colour of the third type of Corinthian bronze, because Pliny did not disclose its colour. This would be a highly questionable assumption, because there are no arguments whatever supporting such an interpretation of Pliny's text. Furthermore, if the mixing of the silvery and golden Corinthian bronze types had resulted in a black one, Pliny would certainly have mentioned it.

As a conclusion, the most popular colour of Corinthian bronze accepted by scholars is the golden one: this colour appears only in second position in Pliny's text. Further colours brought forward are green and black ones, even if there is no reference in the *Naturalis Historia*. This leads to the question, why, apparently, did no scholar consider the silver-like colour ranked by Pliny as the true colour of Corinthian bronze? Were white copper alloys unknown in ancient times? Surely not, as archaeological findings reveal and as we learn from ancient writings, such as the already mentioned excerpt from Theophrastus' treaty on metals.

White copper alloys

"White" will be used here as a general term and covers nuances like very light yellow, silver-greyish and silver-white tints. The first of the two alloying techniques described in Theophrastus' treatise for whitening copper is clear. The colours of the copper-tin system will be discussed below in detail. The second technique is more mysterious. As already mentioned, Klaproth's assumption that the earth was calamine cannot be retained. It is much more probable that the earth is an arsenic-oxide-rich ore. It allows producing arsenic bronze in a similar way as brass by heating it with copper and charcoal in a crucible. The formed carbon monoxide reduces the arsenic oxide and the volatile arsenic vapours react with copper. Arsenic bronze becomes white for arsenic concentrations higher than 15% (Mödlinger et al. 2017; Radivojević et al. 2018). Therefore arsenic bronze has occasionally been used from antiquity until modern times. The drawbacks are the brittleness of the material and its toxicity.

The better technique to obtain a white alloy in ancient times was to alloy copper with tin. Unfortunately, Theophrastus gives no quantitative information about how much tin had to be added for obtaining a white colour. A hint can be found in the alchemist's treatise of Pseudo-Democritos written before the first century AC. The recipe describes a two step-process (Pseudo-Democritos 2011). Firstly, a special refining flux based on white magnesia is prepared. The second step reads:

> "Take four ounces of whitish copper, I speak of orichalcum; melt them with and add one ounce of tin which had been purified before and agitate manually the crucible, so to insure a good mixing of the substances. Pour half of the white flux. It will be the first operation,

because white magnesia does not embrittle metallic bodies and does not tarnish the brilliance of copper."

Thus tin was known to improve the whitening of copper, but also to make the alloy brittle. This could be avoided by fluxing the melt. Whether tin or the flux reduces tarnishing is not clear. As was already mentioned in discussing Klaproth's views on Corinthian bronze, the *orichalcum* may refer to brass with some 10 to 15% of zinc – an element which enhances the action of tin. Having in mind that the addition tin modifies the colour of copper, on can interpret Pliny's text as a description of how the change of colour proceeds. A description of the changes and a short explanation of the physical reason behind them will be given below (Diagram 17.1). To understand Pliny's text it is sufficient to know that already at a tin concentration of 4 to 6% (low-tin bronze), the reddish colour of copper turns into a brown-red one. At around 9% the colour is the one of tawny gold which gets lighter in the range of 12% (middle-tin bronze). By further increasing the tin content, the yellow colour of bronze vanishes and turns to white at concentrations above 20% (high-tin bronze). Bells metal with some 23% of tin is a good illustration for white bronze. When the bell is taken out of the mould, it has a greyish appearance. By mechanical polishing the colour becomes closer and closer to the one of silver. At even higher tin content, around 30%, bronze looks like silver. Such cast and highly polished bronze has been used for fabricating mirrors. Nowadays other alloying elements like aluminium, nickel, zinc or antimony allow to obtaining similar colours. The appearance of bronze can also be modified by surface treatments. For bells, a gold-like and brownish surface film is obtained by proprietary chemical and thermal surface treatments (or just by a careless, long-time exposure to the atmosphere). The formed tin and mixed tin/copper oxides have yellow and orange colours, respectively (Piccardo et al. 2007).

Having seen how tin modifies the colour of copper, two questions arise. The first one relates to Pliny's colour scheme, the second one to another consequence of alloying copper with tin, i.e. the impact on malleability. When Pliny writes that the bronze, in which the mixture (*illa mixtura*) predominates, has a colour close to the one of silver, we can only infer that the mixture is high-tin bronze. Although the Latin adjective *ill-e, -a, -ud* has many meanings (it can relate to what precedes or to what will follow, but it may also express pompousness), it refers here to the sentence in which Pliny tells us that the mixture emerged by chance during the conquest of Corinth, a highly questionable story (Darab 2015). How could one explain the formation of the second type of (Corinthian) bronze – the one which looks like tawny gold? As was mentioned, such a colour can be obtained by strongly reducing the tin content in the high-tin alloy or by applying a surface treatment. The characterisation of the third type of bronze obtained by mixing equal amounts of the two other ones suggests that the first possibility is the most obvious one. To conclude, the original silvery Corinthian bronze is high-tin bronze with some 22 to 25% of tin. Diluting it with roughly two parts of copper brings up a low- to middle-tin bronze with a brown-golden appearance and, eventually, mixing the two alloys gives a middle- to high-tin bronze in the range of 15% of tin with a brighter golden colour.

High-tin bronze

Having put forward the hypothesis that high-tin bronze is a possible candidate for Corinthian bronze, it necessary to review some of its properties and history and check how they fit into the descriptions given by ancient authors. The malleability of bronze is a critical aspect, as it controls mechanical shaping. Furthermore, increasing the tin content reduces the propensity for tarnishing and corrosion, because of the formation of a protective tin-oxide-rich surface layer. To start with, one should consider how the copper and tin atoms arrange themselves to form what is called a phase. A diagram showing which phases (usually identified with Greek letters) are stable at a given compositions and temperatures was already sketched by Heycock and Neville in 1901. In the following years the phase diagram was rather fully investigated by thermal analysis and metallographic studies and in 1905 Guillet could give an extensive overview of the Cu-Sn system (Guillet 1906). It suffices to consider the α-, β-, γ- and δ-phases for understanding the production of high-tin bronze objects. The solid solution (i.e. the α-phase having a face-centred cubic B2-structure) extends from 0 to 15 % of tin and is stable at all temperatures. It can be cold-worked once the dendritic casting structure has been dissolved with an adapted heat treatment (Welter 1996). The occurring work hardening makes intermediate annealing treatments necessary – the more impure the metal, the more frequent. A critical element to be avoided is lead. Rapidly cooling the metal, e.g. with water, reduces mainly the waiting time for the following cold-working step, but has only a minor metallurgical effect (see Caley's comment). It is almost impossible to hot-work the α-phase because of its grain boundary structure (Ozgowicz – Biscondi 1995). The three inter-metallic phases β, γ and δ are only stable at higher temperatures and have a much narrower range of

Table 17.1. Properties of cast, hot hammered and quenched CuSn25 samples. Both Brinell and Vickers hardness have been measured. The electrical conductivity values are indicated within the International Annealed Copper Standard and the International System of Units.

sample	thickness [mm]	tin content [XRF - %]	tin content [OES - %]
as-cast	4.0	26.9	25.1
hammered/ quenched	0.4	26.9	25.0

sample	hardness [HB 2.5]	hardness [HV 30]	electrical conductivity [%IACS/MSm^{-1}]
as-cast	354	388	~ 5.3 / 3.1
hammered/ quenched	259	284	~ 3.0 / 1.7

concentration. During recent years the prevailing view about the relationship between the β and γ phases has changed. It was accepted since the beginning of the 20th century that the two phases β and γ were separated by a narrow two-phase gap. Recent investigations revealed that the crystalline structure evolves continuously when the tin concentration is increased from the β- to the γ-phase – as was already hypothesised by the very earliest investigators (Fürtauer et al. 2013; Liu et al. 2004).

As the tin content of wrought high-tin bronze rarely exceeds 25%, it is sufficient to consider the β-phase. It is stable between 586 and 798 °C. The narrow tin concentration range between 22 and 26% reveals a highly stoichiometric phase. In terms of atoms, the composition reads Cu_5Sn, i.e. one tin atom for five copper atoms. On the lower concentration side, the phase is separated from the α-phase by a large two-phase region. On the higher side, we have (besides the γ-phase) the δ-phase. When the β-phase is slowly cooled, like in bell casting, it decomposes into the α- and δ-phases. Although the very brittle δ-phase is only stable above 350°C, a further decomposition will not occur for kinetics reasons. On the other hand, kinetic reasons allow freezing in the β-phase with a rapid cooling and thus preventing its decomposition on its way down to room temperature. The earliest metallographers already identified this possibility and could thus reveal the acicular (needle-like) microstructure of the β-phase (Behrens 1894; Guillet 1906).

The β-phase is not a specificity of the Cu-Sn system. It belongs to a series of inter-metallic phases identified in the 1920s by Hume-Rothery and named after him (Hume-Rothery 1926; Mizutani 2010). Their composition correlates with the valence electron per atom ratio of 3/2. Besides Cu_5Sn, this ratio also controls the existence of two further Cu_3Al and $CuZn$ phases ($CuZn$ forms with the high copper α-phase nowadays the most widely used brass alloy). Characteristics of these Hume-Rothery electron phases are their body-centred cubic A2-structure, their stability and their very low yield strength at high temperatures. Therefore they can easily be hot-worked. When the phases are quenched to room temperature, they loose most of their ductility and cold-working is impossible in complete contrast to the corresponding solid solutions.

Some experimental results

To learn more about the β-phase of bronze and to what extent its properties differ from the mixture of α- and δ-phases resulting from its decomposition, some preliminary tests were made. Three parts of copper and one part of tin were melted together and cast as a 4 mm thick plate. The brittle plate was easily broken into pieces. Some pieces were hot-worked down to 0.4 mm and water quenched. A first determination of the compositions of an as-cast and of a wrought piece were performed with a hand-hold XRF-analyser (Niton XL3T Goldd – Thermo Scientific) using the internal calibration curve of the instrument. A refined spark-emission OS-analysis (Spectrolab M11 – Spectro Analytical Instruments) of the pieces was made using a calibration curve covering the range from copper to high-tin bronze. This analysis may be considered as the more reliable one. It gave a tin content of 25%, a value slightly lower than the XRF-analysis. The hardness and the electrical conductivity (measured with eddy currents) of as-cast and wrought samples were also determined. Results are shown in table 1. In comparison to the as-cast blank, the wrought, i.e. hammered/quenched sample has lost almost one third of its hardness. In return, this means that the sample has gained in ductility. The high hardness provides good polishing properties and limits damaging the surface e.g. by wear. The electrical conductivities are extremely low, especially for the wrought sample: its electrical conductivity is some 35 times lower than the one of silver. According to the Wiedemann-Franz and Dulong-Petit laws, the ratio of the thermal diffusivity should be of the same order (Ziman 1964). Thus, when thin-walled cups of silver and high-tin bronze are held in the hand, the extraction of heat from the fingers is much smaller for the latter resulting into a warmer touch.

In the present context it appeared necessary to check to what extent the colours of as-cast and wrought high-tin bronze differ. Colorimetric measurements including specular light reflection were realized with a portable spectrophotometer (CM60D – Konica Minolta) within the range 400–700 nm. The reflection curves of polished samples are reported in figure 17.1, together with the reflection curve of pure silver. The figure shows also the reflection curves of wrought B20 bronze with some 20.4% of tin (XRF measurement). The sample is an industrially produced disk aimed for making cymbals. The 1.2 mm thick disk was cut out of a hot-rolled and water quenched coil. The slightly oxidised surface has a brown beige appearance coupled with an enhanced absorption of light. For comparison, the reflection curves of gold, copper and low- to middle-tin bronze are shown in figure 17.2 (Welter 2009) .

With the exception of silver, the curves exhibit an absorption edge for the visible light in the range 500 to 580 nm, an interval covering essentially the green colour. At higher wave-lengths, corresponding to yellow and red colours, the reflection is controlled by the rather free moving conduction electrons of the metal. These so-called s-electrons get excited by the incoming light rays, but rapidly relax and reemit part of the absorbed rays. The more time the electrons have to relax, the higher will be the rate of reemission and hence the reflectivity. As the electrical conductivity depends likewise on such a relaxation time, reflectivity and electrical conductivity are correlated to some extent. At lower wave-length, in the cyan and blue colour range, the light rays are sufficiently energetic to excite also electrons (named d-electrons) which are tighter bound to the atom's nuclei. Relaxation proceeds according to another mechanism involving predominantly no reemission of light. The absorption edge of copper starts around 600 nm. It explains the colour of the red metal. The edge of gold is lowered by some 50 nm

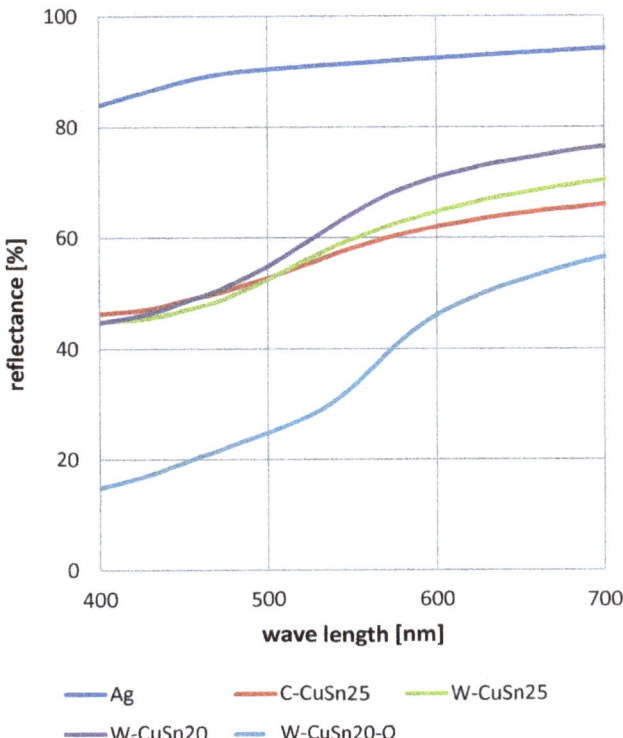

Figure 17.1. Reflectivity curves for silver and high-tin bronzes. Cast: C-, wrought: W-, oxidized: -O.

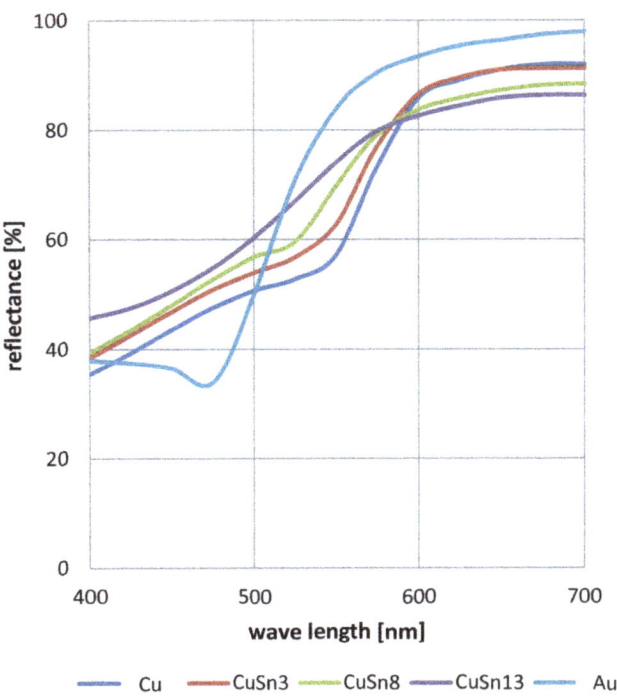

Figure 17.2. Reflectivity curves for gold, copper and low- and middle-tin bronzes.

toward shorter wave-lengths into the green colour range. Silver has its absorption edge in the invisible ultra-violet range. As silver is the metal with the highest electrical conductivity, it reemits light rays at all wave-lengths with the highest efficiency.

Alloying copper with tin leads to a modification of the electronic band-structure. The consequence is a shift of the absorption edge toward shorter wave-lengths and a weaker absorption in the blue colour range. On the red side of the light spectrum, the decrease of the electrical conductivity of the alloy reduces the reemission of light. Thus the colour of medium-tin bronze resembles more and more the one of gold – the best match being achieved for some 12% of tin. Increasing the tin content continues to slightly shift the absorption edge and to flatten the absorption curve. Thus the absorption-reemission behaviour of high-tin bronze is more equilibrated over the whole visible light spectrum. The low electrical conductivity makes that the bronze has not the bright colour of silver, but a more greyish shine.

The influence of the microstructure of high-tin bronze can apparently be neglected. For CuSn25 only a minimal difference occurs in the red colour range between the as-cast and wrought samples. The difference may be due to a slightly different polished surface finish. As the human eye has its highest sensitivity in the range of green colours, wrought Corinthian bronze cups and plates cannot be distinguished visually from statuettes cast with similar high-tin bronze. Thus forgers could very well sell such statuettes as being made of Corinthian bronze. As expected from the visual appearance of the oxidized CuSn20 sample, the absorption curve reveals a shift of the absorption edge toward higher wave-lengths and an increased emission of the light in the red colour range – of course at an overall lower level in comparison to the cleaned surface.

A brief history of wrought high-tin bronze

High-tin bronze was used as in Europe as a casting alloy for highly valued objects from the middle of the second millennium BC. One can mention wheel-shaped pendants (Heath et al. 1998), finger rings (Bottaini et al. 2017), coins (Sarthe et al. 2001) and mirrors (although the majority was made with middle-tin bronze). A polishing final treatment gave them a highly reflective silvery appearance, and one may venture the guess that this was one reason using high-tin bronze. On the other hand, apparently no wrought high-tin artefact has been unearthed until now in Europe, although they were produced in Asia. The history of wrought and cast high-tin bronze in Asiatic countries was recently reviewed by Shimizu (Shimizu 2010). It is sufficient here to mention some key points. The technique of processing high-tin bronze by the hot-working/quenching route was developed in the northwest part of the Indian subcontinent during the first millennium BC. It was rapidly adopted by the coppersmiths working in the south (Kerala) and east (Bengal) of India (Datta et al. 2008; Srinivasan 1994). From India the technology diffused to the eastern part of Asia along two routes. In the south, it spread to southeast Asia and first of all to Thailand (Glover – Bennett 2012; Rajpitak – Seeley 1979). In the north, it followed a route through China and Korea to Japan. On the western side of India, one has to wait for the early and middle Islamic period to see wrought high-tin bronze in the Middle East, and more specifically in what is now Iran (Melikian-Chirvani 1974; Mortazavi – Oudbashi

2010; Oudbashi et al. 2017). It was a popular substitute for silver and was known as white copper (Allan, n.d.). At the time of Corinthian bronze, the earliest western find is a hammered high-tin vessel excavated in a tomb located south of the Caspian Sea and dated to the 1st century BC (Shimizu 2010).

The fact that no wrought high-tin bronze artefact was found until now in Europe does not necessarily mean that the technology was unknown – e.g. in the eastern Mediterranean world. Nevertheless, it would seem more likely that such objects were imported in small quantities by land and sea from western Asia. The existence of east-west commercial routes has been identified for other achievements of Indian metallurgy, like crucible steel and brass (Srinivasan 2016). Within such a commercial network, Corinth would have been a trading post rather than a production centre. An argument for the knowledge of high-tin bronze, at least in the Hellenistic world, is a remark found in Strabo's *Geographia*. He reports that Alexander's general Nearchus mentioned a peculiar feature of Indian vessels: when they fall and hit the ground, they fracture like pottery. The statement could refer to high-tin bronze wares (Rajpitak – Seeley 1979). Although they gain some ductility through a final quench, they remain much more brittle than the low- to middle-tin vessels used in Europe: the latter just deform when mechanically impacted, whereas the former ones break and disaggregate into many pieces.

Conclusion

Wrought high-tin bronze is a material which should be considered when discussing what ancient writers had in mind when writing about Corinthian bronze. The alloy, both cast and wrought, has a silvery appearance. It acquires a golden shine by diluting it with copper. Although the intrinsic metal value is much lower than gold and silver, the demanding high-temperature forming process performed by highly skilled craftsmen strongly increases its value. Hot forging allows the manufacture of thin-walled table ware, and quenching the artefact restores some ductility, in contrast to the as-cast state. Furthermore, the high tin content insures excellent wear and tarnish/corrosion resistance. All these properties are in agreement with the information found in ancient texts about Corinthian bronze.

Acknowledgements

The experimental part could only be realised with the help of Jean Dubos (sample preparation), Wolfgang Schillinger (cymbal disc), Joachim Kreutner (XRF analysis), Tanja Hubrath (OES analysis & mechanical/physical measurements) and Chiara Petiti (colorimetry). Their contribution is gratefully acknowledged.

Bibliography

The translations from Latin, German, French and Italian are by the author.

Allan, J.W., n.d. Bronze ii. In Islamic Iran, in: *Encyclopaedia Iranica*. Encyclopaedia Iranica Foundation, New York, 471–472.

Anonymus, 1832. Versuch ueber die Patina oder ueber den natuerlichen und kuenstlichen Ueberzug der Bronzen, geschnittenen Steinen, Glaspasten, Statuen und Malereien (Aus Fiorillo's Nachlass). *Morgenblatt fuer gebildete Staende – Kunst-Blatt 97*, 385–388.

Aristoteles, 1981. Mirabilia, 2nd ed, *Aristoteles Werke* in deutscher Übersetzung. Akademie-Verlag, Berllin.

Aucouturier, M. – Mathis, F. – Robcis, D., 2017. Les bronzes noirs antiques – nouvelles observations et mécanismes de création. *Technè 45*, 115–123.

Behrens, H., 1894. *Das mikroskopische Gefüge der Metalle und Legierungen*. Leopold Voss, Hamburg und Leipzig.

Bottaini, C. – Vilaça, R. – Montero-Ruiz, I. – Mirão, J. – Cabdeias, A., 2017. Archaeometric contribution to the interpretation of the late bronze age "hoard" from Porto do Concelho (Mação, central Portugal). *Mediterrananean Archaeology and Archaeometry 17*, 217–231.

Caley, E.R., 1941. The corroded bronze of Corinth. *Proceedings of the American Philosophical Society 84*, 689–761.

Collareta, M., 2008. Aes corinthium: fortuna letteraria di un materiale antico, in: *L'industria Artistica Del Bronzo Del Rinascimento a Venezia e Nell'Italia Settentrionale*, Verona, 297–301.

Craddock, P.T., 1982. Gold in antique copper alloys. *Gold Bulletin 15*, 69–70.

Darab, A., 2015. Corinthium aes : die Entstehung und Metamorphose einer Anekdote, in: *Wiener Studien, Wiener Studien, Zeitschrift für klassische Philologie und Patristik*. Österreichische Akademie der Wissenschaften, Wien, 69–82.

Darab, A., 2012. Corinthium aes versus electrum. *Hermes: Zeitschrift für klassische Philologie 140*, 149–159.

Datta, P.K. – Chattopadhyay, P.K. – Mandal, B., 2008. Investigations on ancient high-tin bronze excavated from lower Bengal region of Tilpi. *Indian Journal of History of Science 43*, 381–410.

Emanuele, D., 1989. "Aes corinthium": fact, fiction, and fake. *Phoenix 43*, 347–358.

Engels, D.W., 1990. *Roman Corinth*. University of Chicago Press, Chicago and London.

Fürtauer, S. – Li, D. – Cupid, D. – Flandorfer, H., 2013. The Cu-Sn phase diagram, part I: new experimental results. *Intermetallics 34*, 142–147.

Giumlia-Mair, A., 2015. Polychrome production of a Romano-Egyptian workshop, in: Deschler-Erb, E. – Della Casa, P., ed., Zurich Studies in Archaeology, vol.

10 – *New Research on Ancient Bronzes*. Presented at the XVIIIth International Congress on Ancient Bronzes, Zurich, 305–310.

Giumlia-Mair, A. – Mrav, Z., 2014. The aes corinthium vessels from Egyed, Hungary. *Folia Archaeologica LVI*, 73–102.

Giumlia-Mair, A.R. – Craddock, P.T., 1993. *Das schwarze Gold der Alchimisten – corinthium aes*, Zabern Bildbände zur Archäologie. Philipp von Zabern, Mainz am Rhein.

Glover, I. – Bennett, A., 2012. The high-tin bronzes of Thailand, in: *Scientific Research on Ancient Asian Metallurgy*. Presented at the 5th Forbes Symposium, Archetype Publications, Washington, 101–114.

Guillet, L., 1906. *Etude industrielle des alliages métalliques*. H. Dunod et E. Pinat, Paris.

Halleux, R., 1974. Le problème des métaux dans la science antique, *Bibliothèque de la Faculté de Philosophie et Lettres de l'Université de Liège*. Société d'Edition "Les Belles Lettres," Paris.

Heath, D.J. – Trampuz-Orel, N. – Milic, Z., 1998. Wheel-shaped pendants: evidence of a late bronze age metal workshop in the Caput Adriae, in: *Ancient Metallurgy between Oriental Alps and Pannonian Plain*. Associazione Nazionale per Aquileia, Trieste, 53–70.

Hume-Rothery, W., 1926. Research on the nature, properties and conditions of formation of intermetallic compounds, with special reference to certain compounds of tin. *Journal of the Institute of Metals 35*, 295–299.

Jacobson, D.M., 2000. Corinthian bronze and the gold of the alchemists. *Gold Bulletin 33*, 60–66.

Jacobson, D.M. – Weitzman, M.P., 1992. What was Corinthian bronze. *American Journal of Archaeology 96*, 237–247.

Klaproth, M.H., 1815. *Chemische Abhandlungen gemischten Inhalts*. Nicolaische Buchhandlung, Berlin und Stettin.

Lechtman, H., 1979. A Pre-Columbian Technique for Electrochemical Replacement Plating of Gold and Silver on Copper Objects. *Journal of Metals 31*, 154–160.

Liu, X.J. – Wang, C.P. – Ohnuma, I. – Kainuma, R. – Ishida, K., 2004. Experimental investigation and thermodynamic calculation of the phase equilibria in the Cu-Sn and Cu-Sn-Mn systems. *Metallurgical and Materials Transactions A 35A*, 1641–1654.

Manas, A., 2018. Fifty shades of yellow. *Gold Bulletin 51*, 205–212.

Mattusch, C.C., 2003. Corinthian bronze: famous but elusive, in: Williams, C.K. – Bookidis, N., ed., *Corinth, the Centenary: 1896–1996, Corinth*. The American School of Classical Studies at Athens, Princeton, 219–232.

Melikian-Chirvani, A.S., 1974. The white bronzes of early Islamic Iran. *Metropolotan Museum Journal 9*, 123–151.

Mizutani, U., 2010. *Hume-Rothery rules for structurally complex alloy phases*. CRC Press, Boca Raton.

Mödlinger, M. – Kuijpers, M.H.G. – Braekmans, D. – Berger, D., 2017. Quantitative comparisons of the color of CuAs, CuSn, CuNi, and CuSb alloys. *Journal of Archaeological Science 88*, 14–23.

Mortazavi, M. – Oudbashi, O., 2010. *Influence of heat treatment in formation of martensitic structure in historical bronzes*. Presented at the International conference on materials heat treatment (ICMH 2010), Isfahan, 1–4.

Murphy-O'Connor, J., 1983. Corinthian bronze. *Revue Biblique 90*, 80–93.

Oudbashi, O. – Hasanpour, A. – Jahanpoor, A. – Rahjoo, Z. – 2017. Microscopic and microanalytical study on Sasanian metalobjects from western Iran: a case study. *STAR 3*, 194–205.

Ozgowicz, W. – Biscondi, M., 1995. High-temperature brittleness and interfacial segregation in tin bronzes. *Journal de Physique 5*, 315–320.

Pausanias, 1918. *Description of Greece – Books 1–2*, Loeb Classical Library. Harvard University Press, Cambridge.

Piccardo, P. – Robbiola, L. – Mille, B., 2007. Tin and copper oxides in corroded archaeological bronzes, in: Dillman, P. – Béranger, G. – Piccardo, P. – Matthiessen, H., ed., *Corrosion of Metallic Artefacts*, EFC Seies. Woodhead Publishing, 239–262.

Plinius Secundus, G., 2007. *Naturalis historiae, 2nd ed.*, König, R. and Hoppe, J. (eds.). Patmos Verlag, Düsseldorf.

Plinius Secundus, G., 1989. *Naturalis Historiae*, König, R. and Bayer, K. (eds.). Artemis Verlag, München.

Plinius Caecilius Secundus, G, 2014. *The complete work of Pliny the Younger, book III, letter VI*, Delphi Classics.

Pseudo-Democritos, 2011. *Scritti alchemici – con il commentario di Siesio, Textes et Travaux de Chrysopoeia*. S.E.H.A.-ARCHE, Paris-Milano.

Radivojević, M. – Pendić, J. – Srejić, A. – Korać, M. – Davey, C. – Benzonelli, A. – Martinón-Torres, M. – Jovanović, N. – Kamberović, Z., 2018. Experimental design of the Cu-As-Sn ternary colour diagram. *Journal of Archaeological Science 90*, 106–119.

Rajpitak, W. – Seeley, N.J., 1979. The bronze bowls from Dan Ta Phet, Thailand: an enigma of prehistoric metallurgy. *World Archaeology 11*, 26–31.

Sarthe, C. – Guerra, M.F. – Griffiths, D.R. – Lacey, A. – Nortover, P.J., 2001. Composition, simulation and manufacture of the Celts cast tin bronze, in: Bautista, P. – Barba, L., ed., *Presented at the 32nd International Symposium on Archaeometry*, UNAM, Mexico City, 1–10.

Savot, L., 1627. *Discours sur les médailles antiques.* Sébastien Cramoisy, Paris.

Shimizu, Y., 2010. Origin and diffusion of binary high-tin bronze wares: introduction of sahari into Japan, in: *Asian High-Tin Bronzes – Production Technology and Regional Characteristics.* University of Toyama, Tokyo, 137–144; annex: 22 pages.

Sparavigna, A.C., 2016. Depletion gilding: an ancient method for surface enrichment of gold alloys. *Mechanics, Materials Science & Engineering 2*, 96–106.

Srinivasan, S., 2016. Indian high-tin bronzes ad the Grecian and Persian world. *Indian Journal of History of Science 51*, 601–612.

Srinivasan, S., 1994. High-tin bronze bowl making in Kerala, South India, and its archaeological implications, in: *South Asia Archaeology 1993. Presented at the 12th international conference of the European association of South Asian archaeologists*, Suomalainen Tiedeakatemia, Helsinki, 695–706.

Welter, J.-M., 1996. Production of bronze strips by continuous casting and rolling at the end of the XXth century AC, in: Mordan, C. – Pernt, M. – Rychner, V., ed., *L'atelier Du Bronzier En Europedu XXè Au VIIIè Siècle Avant Notre Ère. Presented at the Bronze'96*, CTHS, Paris, 287–294.

Ziman, J.M., 1964. *Principles of the theory of solids.* Cambridge University Press, Cambridge.

18

Fragments of large-scale bronze statues in context of so-called scrap metal deposits in Dacia and Moesia Inferior

Cristina-Georgeta Alexandrescu

Institutul de Arheologie "Vasile Pârvan", Bucharest

cgetalexandrescu@gmail.com

Abstract: The finds of large bronze statues from Dacia and Moesia Inferior have been the object of dedicated studies in the past decades, lacking however analysis of their find-context. The present contribution presents several examples from military camps and civil settlements for which information on the findspot and/or archaeological context together with data on associated finds make it possible to bring into discussion the phenomenon of reusing bronze statues as a resource. Furthermore, it is possible – despite the high degree of fragmentation – to gain observations on technological details of the original statue.

Keywords: Large-scale Bronze Statues; Scrap Metal; Dacia; Moesia Inferior

Introduction

Bronze statues were the most expensive version of honorary monument known to the Romans. In his Oration to the Rhodians, Dio Chrysostom pointed out: "Apart from the beautiful sight which the entire world may enjoy, the great number of your statues brings you renown of another sort! For these things are manifestly a proof of your friendship for your rulers and of their respect for you" (*Or.* 31.149). In Diaconescu's (2005) opinion, since the habit of erecting statues became so typical for Roman mentality, one of the easiest ways of estimating the success of Romanisation in the first centuries of the Principate is to study the local attitude towards honorary statues (see also Pliny, *NH* 34.17 and Witschel 2016).

In everyday archaeological practice, fragments of bronze statues, especially unspecific and lacking decoration, are often listed among scrap finds; sometimes they are not even subject to further research. This tendency began to change in recent decades and, in some fortunate cases, it was even possible to re-evaluate older finds, as exemplarily proven in the project on finds from Germaniae (Gebrochener Glanz 2014). Bronze attracted both Romans and their enemies in order to reuse the material for different purposes. Therefore the collection of old metal was a common practice. This scrap metal was melted down and recast, often as weapons for the Roman troops, or even as new statues. Recycling metal was considered a more or less common practice, since the ancient texts like Pliny the Elder mentioned the scrap metal as being part of the usual recipes for copper alloys (*NH* 34.20.97).

In the provinces of Dacia and Moesia Inferior, the areas of interest for the present contribution (Fig. 18.1), the richness of finds of fragments of large bronzes is spectacular. Dedicated publications are however still missing. Selected fragments came into the scientific discussion through the catalogue entries by Gamer (1969), Pop (1978), Petculescu (1998) and Diaconescu (2005). The influence of the state of research and especially of the research strategy in analyses is complex, due to some characteristics: focus on military sites, irrespective of their surroundings, or of civil/rural settlements; a certain degree of disinterest in stratigraphic excavation, especially at military sites; publication of spectacular finds without specifying their context and the associated finds, causing loss of information on the initial correlation between the statue base and the fragments of statues, or fragments of metal finds and the context of a (possible) bronze workshop.

Methodologically, the study of large-scale bronze statues should be coordinated with the investigation of their bases (Kemkes 2017a). Most of them are identifiable only through the inscription and, if available, their shape, remains of socketing, and dimensions (Kemkes 2014a; Willer et al. 2017). It is common knowledge (also accepted by scholars) that even the smallest Roman fortlet might have had an impressive bronze statue (e.g. the 160 cm high base of a statue of Iulia Mamaea found in the *numerus*-camp Kleiner Feldberg in Taunus, next to small body and hair fragments of the bronze over-lifesize statue: Kemkes 2014a, 114–115).

In antiquity and post-Roman times, the attitude towards bronze/metal and stone was very different. Metal recycling was quite intense, while the reuse of stone depended on the shape and quality of the blocks and eventually proved to be more selective (Alexandrescu 2016a and 2016b). A final reuse of lithic materials was also the complete destruction

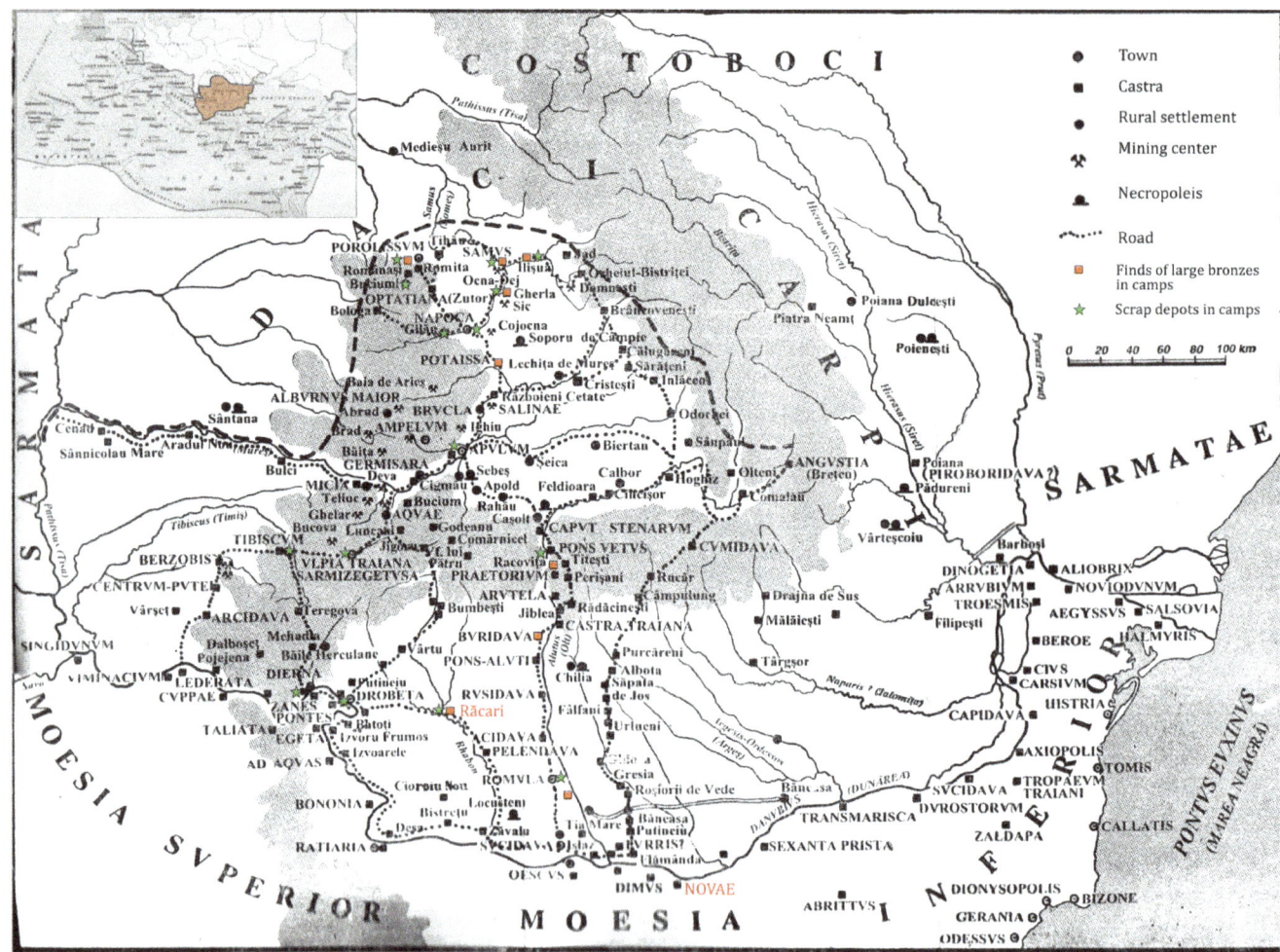

Figure 18.1. Map of Dacia and northern Moesia inferior (2nd–3rd centuries A.D.), with the marked finding places for metal workshop situations and finds of large bronzes in castra (the author, under use of Petolescu, 1995, Map 3).

in lime kilns, as in Novae (Sarnowski 2018). It has been observed – in the case of Rome and its provinces – that the Romans, without showing any religious or iconoclastic bias, reused the stone from funerary or official monuments, sometimes only decades after their initial dedication, depending on the circumstances and available materials (Alexandrescu 2016a and 2016b). For the area of interest here, it was a rather neglected aspect, considered usually at the provincial level or in comparative studies. Still, when registered, the information offers arguments for a closer look at this practice (Sarnowski 2018).

Regarding the finds of large bronzes, the usual analysis is aimed at differentiating the main categories: portraits, parts of human representations (with the male/female distinction), parts of animal representations, cuirassed statues, statues wearing drapery, representations of divinities etc. For a methodological overview, there are useful introductions by Sarge (2017) and in the exhibition catalogue Gebrochener Glanz (2014). The primary goal when dealing with fragments is to find hints at the complete statue and its identification, a fascinating and challenging task. For us, one further aspect is of interest: observations on the destruction of the statues – as can be most often observed on imperial portraits –, the degree of fragmentation and the number of pieces found in one context/spot, as well as the associated finds, when available. In addition, it is of great value if this context is documented and can be dated. Fragments of large-scale bronze statues are a more or less common feature in scrap metal deposits, even if an overview is not available, neither for military nor for non-military contexts (Stoll 1992, 86–88). The process of *damnatio memoriae* was one of the usual causes for systematic and official dismantling of statues or at least of portraits, with the direct consequence of collecting/ reusing the metal within the *aeraria* and workshops of the camp or its surroundings. It should now be accepted (as opposed to the traditional or widely accepted theses) that fragments of large bronze statues are not to be interpreted simply as the result of destruction by the enemies of the Romans. This is also the case for reused inscriptions, with or without images, that were reused as building material by the Romans themselves, without any relation to Christian communities. This aspect was considered, especially for the region under consideration, by Alexandrescu (2016a).

Statue bases are important indicators for the existence of statues at sites where perhaps no traces of statues were found. Examples found *in situ* are rare, as bases or fragments of slabs with inscriptions have usually been reused within the camp or nearby civil settlements. For the region of interest, again, Novae provides the most information (Sarnowski 1989 and 2018). In some cases, the reuse was established for the late 3rd century or a later context, after the end of the Roman province. 46 inscriptions from 17 military sites date from the reign of Hadrian to that of Gordian III. Due to the unknown archaeological contexts, the military/civil character of the finds cannot be evaluated. An overview, mainly descriptive, without systematic documentation of the characteristic details for bases of bronze statues, is possible thanks to Diaconescu (2005). The logistic requirements for this undertaking within collections in Romania remain an impediment. A preliminary map of the locations of finds is given by Alexandrescu (2017, fig. 2).

The newly published analysis by T. Sarnowski (2018) of the situation in Novae highlights the importance of observations on finds of inscribed stone monuments. He concludes that the statue bases from the *principia* of the fortress were used as building material in the episcopal complex only after a certain period had elapsed following the removal of the statues. This took place in quite a long process involving "the reuse of statues, statue bases and altars, and in other various dramatic moments and circumstances starting already from the first half of the 3rd century. In the meantime, the visitors of the *principia* probably could see some pedestals deprived of their statues" (Sarnowski 2018, 79–80).

One further interesting example is provided by a find in the 4th-century necropolis at Intercisa, where elements of two statue bases dated to the early 3nd century A.D. were reused (Visy 1983). The fact that several slabs from the two bases were used in the same area revealed that, at the time of material collection, the two bases were still in place, several decades after their dedication. In the *principia* of the auxiliary camp, in the basilica, archaeologists have observed traces of three statue bases, in their initial location.

Returning to the statue bases from Dacia, it is known that this kind of monument was also reused, especially in the 3rd century, during repairs in military camps. Details on the statues are not available. Often the description of the upper part of the base, possibly indicating the kind of statue it was bearing, was neglected by the publisher or that part might simply not be available any longer, especially if the stone was cut into shape suitable for its reuse. From the auxiliary fort in Micia and its surroundings, no less than ten statue bases have been recorded (Diaconescu 2005). Fragments of bronze statues came to light during the excavations in Micia, but no publication has yet been made, of the fragments, of their context, or of their possible relation to the bases (kind information from dr. L. Petculescu 2018). One of the rare cases of a statue base with documented upper surface is the base for a bronze statue of Herennia Etruscilla from Porolissum (AE 1944, 56). In the context of the present discussion, this site is best known for the statue of Caracalla that was reconstructed from fragments found over quite a large area (Gudea, et al. 1986; Lahusen – Formigli 2001, cat. no. 159). The latest analysis, though not a systematic or final investigation, shows that the portrait and some of the fragments of horses belong to a representation of Caracalla in a quadriga (Diaconescu 2005).

Moesia Inferior

The number of finds of large-scale bronzes from this province mentioned in publications is astonishingly low, being limited to the well-known head of Gordian III from the territory of Nicopolis at Istrum (Lahusen – Formigli 2001, cat. no. 189; Milceva 2005, cat. no. 30), to fragments of a cuirassed statue from the area of the auxiliary fort in Nigrinianis (Ivanov 1996), to random finds from equestrian statue(s) (Fig. 18.4) outside the main site in Troesmis (Barbu 1965, 399–400, cat. no. 17; Alexandrescu et al. 2016, 243, Kat. Nr. BZ 1, p. 346, plate 57), and to a bronze foot from Callatis (Barbu 1965, 399, cat. no. 16). Furthermore, there are the spectacular finds from Novae.

However small our corpus from Moesia Inferior, Novae (Fig. 18.2 and 18.3) is of high importance across the Roman Empire. In this case, there are also older finds dating back to the 70s and 80s of the last century (Sarnowski 1985 and 1989), some of them being published together with a larger amount of information on the archaeological context in 2016 (Čičikova 1992 and 2016).

First of all, there is the scrap metal deposit in the *aeraria* of the legionary camp, within the *principia* destroyed in approximately 316/317 AD (Sarnowski 1985, tab. 1), consisting of about 30 fragments of large bronzes (identified as fragments of depictions of emperors, of an equestrian statue, possibly of deities as well, judging by the attributes), fragments of weapons, coins, furniture, and lead, as well as tools for working metal (chisels, pincers, crucibles). Fragments were stored by size, in preparation for melting and recycling. T. Sarnowski considered the find as the usual deposit of scrap metal expected in a legionary camp and in a military centre as Novae, supplying material for repairs and small works within the army (Sarnowski 1985, 536–537).

Outside the camp in Novae was the so-called *villa extra muros* (Čičikova 1992 and 2016; Tomas 2017, 54–57), interpreted as a *praetorium*, the official residence of a legate, destroyed during one of the invasions in the middle of the 3rd century, which did not, however, affect the interior of the camp. Fragments of at least two bronze statues were found in the villa (at 1 and 2 on Fig. 18.2b). Fragments of two bases have also been preserved. One of the inscriptions is readable and was published soon after its discovery (AE 1990, 863; date: 238–244). The further use of the area and the new building works closed the level of the destroyed villa, covering the fragments of inscribed blocks as well as the remains of the bronze statues, the metal not being collected for reuse.

It was possible to reconstruct two portraits (Fig. 18.3), presumably of military officials, resembling the portraits

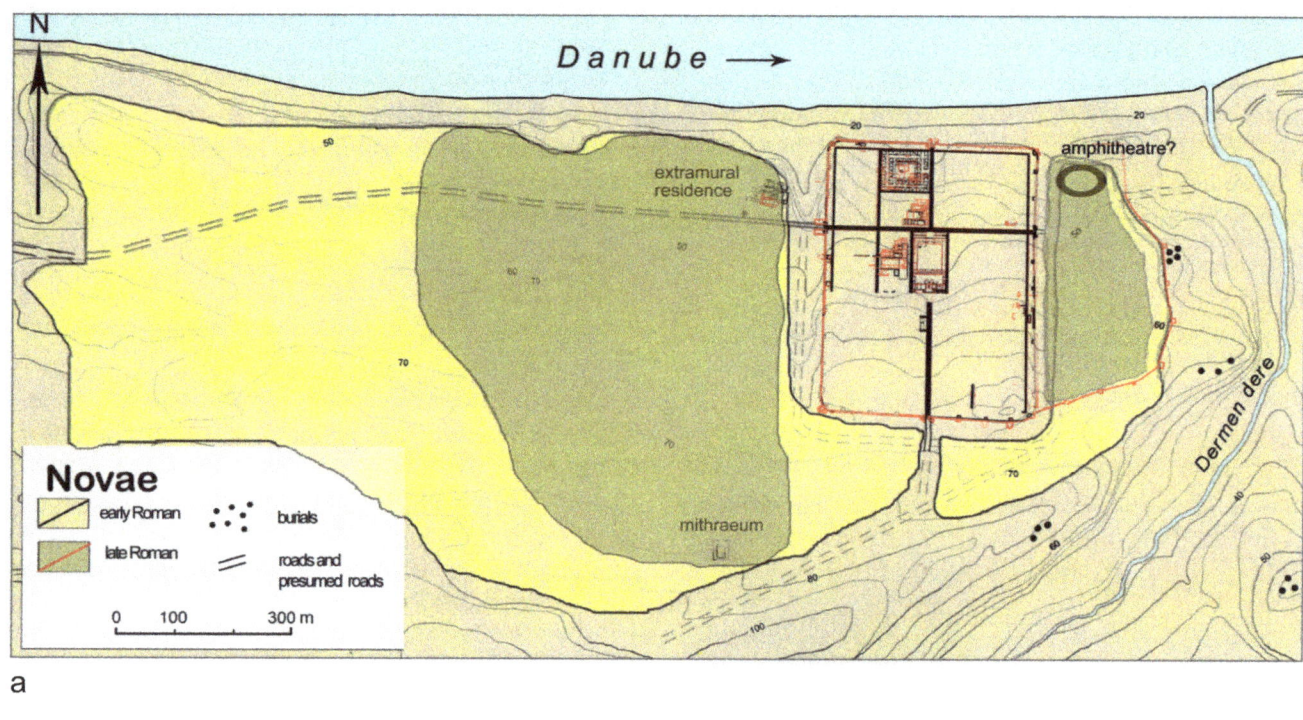

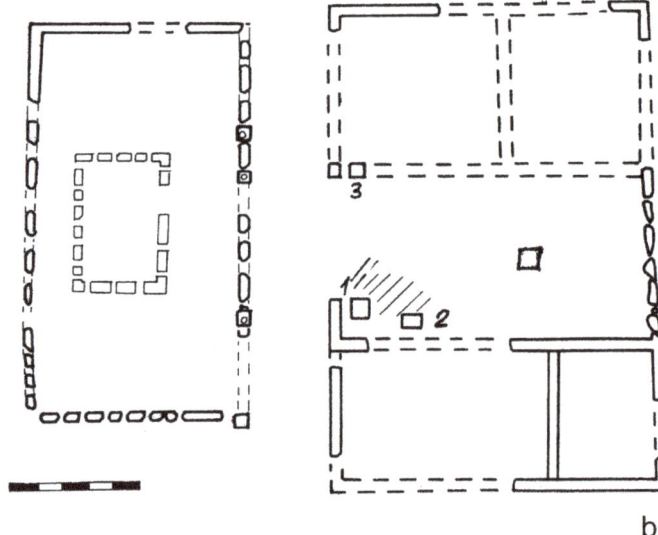

Figure 18.2. Novae general plan (a) and detail of the villa (b) (a: after Tomas, 2017, fig. 13; b: after Čičikova, 2016, fig. 1).

of the emperors Pupienus (238) and Gordian III (242), one of them wearing armour decorated with Medusa on the chest and Victory with *tropaion* on the *epomides* (Čičikova 2016). The statue of the young man is considered to have stood on the recovered base.

Dacia

The orange squares on the map (Fig. 18.1) show the recorded finds of large bronzes at nine camps in Dacia. More finds came from urban settlements near the military centre, without its being possible to identify the findspots of the bronze fragments (e.g Drobeta, Romula, Sucidava) or the archaeological context. As observed in Novae (Sarnowski 1989, 2018), the dismantling/destruction of a statue and its base occurred at different points in time, in some cases each step being far apart within a large time frame. At Drobeta, there is evidence for the reuse of a base for a statue of Antoninus Pius from the city in the Late Roman fort, the record of different phases of use being possible from mention of the *municipium* in the inscription (IDR II,1; CIL III 8017).

In Dacia, most bronze statues have been recovered in Apulum, Porolissum, Sucidava, Răcari and Slăveni (Gamer 1969; Pop 1978; Diaconescu 2005). None of the finds has been properly published, meaning that they lack the complete record, including findspot, context, measurements, complete description, and so on. It goes without saying that the most archaeological information is provided for the particularly spectacular fragments (for an overview see Alexandrescu 2017), while data are scarce for the bulk of the finds, and even the dates of contexts for the finds are unknown. It can be assumed that there are

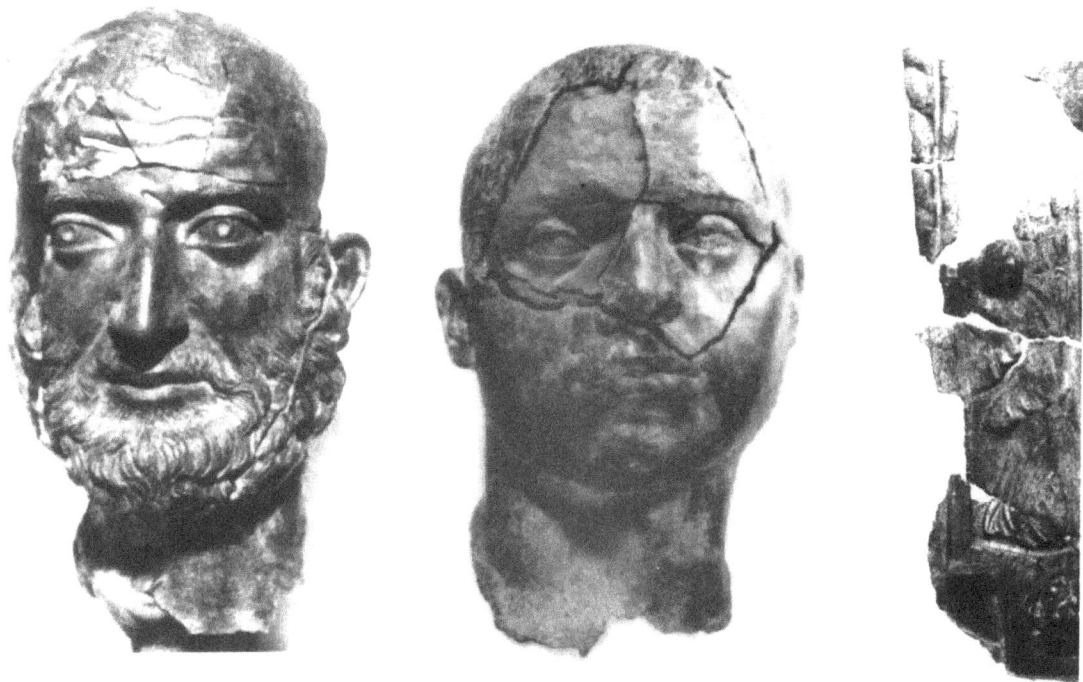

Figure 18.3. Novae – the heads and fragments of large bronze statues from the villa extra muros. (after Čičikova, 2016, fig. 3.5.12).

different contexts (in analogy to other Roman provinces) – lost collections of fragments, remains of deliberately destroyed statues, scrap metal deposits, workshop context. The differentiation of those contexts can be only hypothetical.

Bronze workshops (marked on Fig. 18.1 with green stars) in relation to so-called scrap metal deposits are also rare (Cociş 1995; Benea 2008). Only for Buciumi and Căşei is their military character probable. This means that the major finds in order to identify a workshop (specific tools, crucibles, dies, refuse, melted metal, slag, furnaces and/or ovens for bronze melting etc.) are not directly related to the deposits containing fragments of large bronzes (like Ilişua and Răcari). It is also important to establish if scrap metal deposits contained more or less fragmentary metal items, what were those items and what was their degree of fragmentation. The bronze workshops in Dacia seem to have been dealing with small pieces of civil and military use, of different technological complexity, but mainly confined to repairs (Cociş 1995; Benea 2008). The problem of bronze workshops within a military context, as analysed by M. Gschwind (1997) and Stoll (1995), is in Dacia lacking in sufficient data to allow for detailed discussion.

In the case of Ilişua, a clandestine mint is attested (Gaiu 2011; Găzdac et al. 2011, 119, cat. no. 233, pl. VII.3). In this auxiliary camp, the statue base of Iulia Mamaea, found in 1830, was perhaps reused in the civil settlement near the camp, (Alexandrescu 2015, 97) and may be related to some fragments of dress and of a female statue found 1983 in what was identified as a scrap metal deposit in the camp, but no direct link has been established (Alexandrescu 2015). It is, however, obvious that the statue was the subject of *damnatio memo*riae of the empress and her son. The dating of the scrap metal deposit is not given in the archaeological report.

Individual finds of fragments of bronze statues in rural areas must be assumed to have been brought there for recycling during Roman or post-Roman times, as was the case in Troesmis (Fig. 18.4), in Moesia Inferior. For example, gilded fragments of an equestrian statue were found in Arcalia (Domaszewski 1888; see also Petculescu 2003, cat. no. 7.8), in the surroundings of the northern Dacian limes, which are also of great interest as they attest to the application of ornaments to large bronzes in Dacia. Another example is a fragment of a saddle blanket (*tapetum*) from a gilded statue, found in a building east of the precincts of Ulpia Traiana Sarmizegetusa, and dating to the 4th–5th century A.D. (Alicu – Diaconescu 2008, 200. 202. 206).

The most famous examples – imperial portraits – are incidental finds, mainly found near or in rivers, like 'Traianus Decius' from Ulpia Traiana Sarmizegetusa, in Dacia (Lahusen – Formigli 2001, cat. no. 179), or Gordian III near Nicopolis ad Istrum in Moesia Inferior. One theory about these portraits is that they might have been lost in the crossing of the river.

The stockpiling of metals (Popović's "hoard horizon", 2008–2009) during the 2nd and 3rd centuries in the area of Dacia provides little information about large-scale bronzes, that is, whether the metal was collected and stored or buried as deposit. It is notable that the so-called treasures are not found on the left side of the river Jiu. Finds similar to the newly published illicit mint from a villa in the Hambacher Forst from Germania (Klages 2014), with

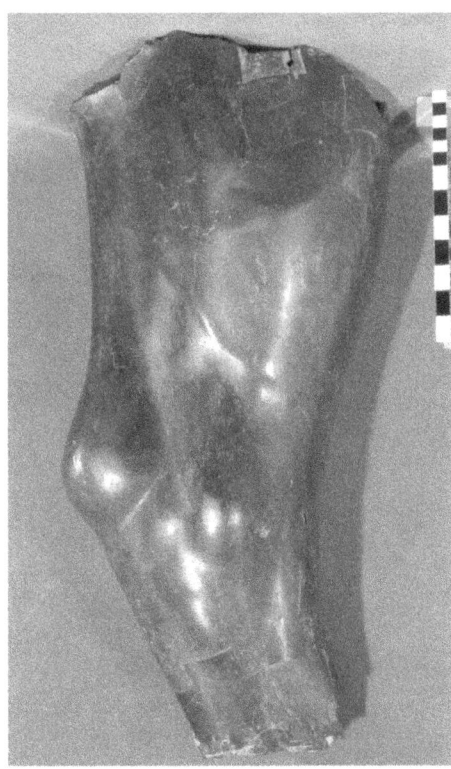
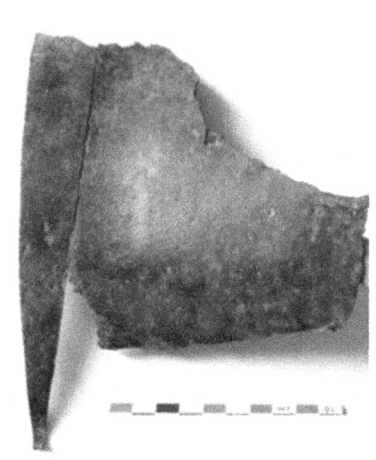

Figure 18.4. Troesmis – stray finds of equestrian statue(s) from the surroundings of the main site. (photos by the author).

coins and fragments of large bronzes are not yet available for study. A similar find in Dacia is the above-mentioned one made in the southern tower of the *porta praetoria* of the auxiliary camp at Ilişua, which lacks a proper record of the archaeological context (Protase – Gaiu – Marinescu 1996–1997, 41–42. 69–70). This find consisted of 20 fragments from several large bronzes with different degrees of fragmentation (Alexandrescu 2015), and also a rejected cast sestertius (Antoninus Pius), depicting on the reverse a design which does not match inscriptions in the RIC, whose publishers identified it as a provincial forgery (Găzdac et al. 2011).

The fragments of large-scale bronzes from Răcarii de Jos

In the area of the auxiliary fort in Răcarii de Jos in southern Dacia, excavations in the late 19th and first half of the 20th century found many fragments of large-scale bronzes (Tocilescu 1900; Florescu 1931; Bondoc – Gudea 2009 and 2017). The site is strategically located on one of the secondary roads connecting Drobeta and Romula, on the left side of the Jiu River; in the same area there are several sites with recorded finds of Roman materials over an area of more than 30 ha, though no systematic research has been possible up to now (Bondoc – Gudea 2009, 54).

Within the camp, additional small fragments of large-scale bronzes have been excavated as random finds since 2003. Information on the '3,000 fragments' mentioned in the first short report of Gr. Tocilescu (1900) is very limited. It was possible to pinpoint findspots of very few fragments (Fig. 18.5). A concentration or deposit is said to have been dug up in a fountain (probably in the *principia*) and in another place about 100 m to the West of the camp, this being also the largest deposit.

Nevertheless, the references in the archival material allow for some differentiation.

A diagnosis is possible for about 350 fragments of larger dimensions (Petculescu 2003, cat. no. 10. 11a–k. 12; Alexandrescu 2017; Bondoc – Gudea 2017). Most fragments are rather unspecific and very small (under 10 cm). Along with the fragments of statues, some of them bearing traces of fire, there have been found untypical bronze sheets and fragments of bronze items – vessels, statuettes, mirrors, a votive plate for Iupiter Optimus Maximus Dolichenus (Bondoc – Gudea 2009, 207, cat. no. 495, pl. XCII). In a recent publication on the bronze finds, Bondoc and Gudea consider the last mentioned fragment that may belong to the cuirass decoration of a statue (2017, 294–299).

It is difficult to draw conclusions on the provenance of several fragments from one statue, as with those from Răcarii de Jos, to date the largest concentration of fragments of large-scale bronzes from the region. They are preserved in three different collections, two of them in Bucharest and the third in Craiova, and have been cleaned and/or restored and published differently (Tocilescu 1900; Petculescu 2003; Alexandrescu 2017; Bondoc – Gudea 2017 – with results of some analyses by XRF-spectrometry). The same holds true for the finds of large bronzes from Romula, in two collections in Bucharest and

Fragments of large-scale bronze statues in context of so-called scrap metal deposits in Dacia and Moesia Inferior

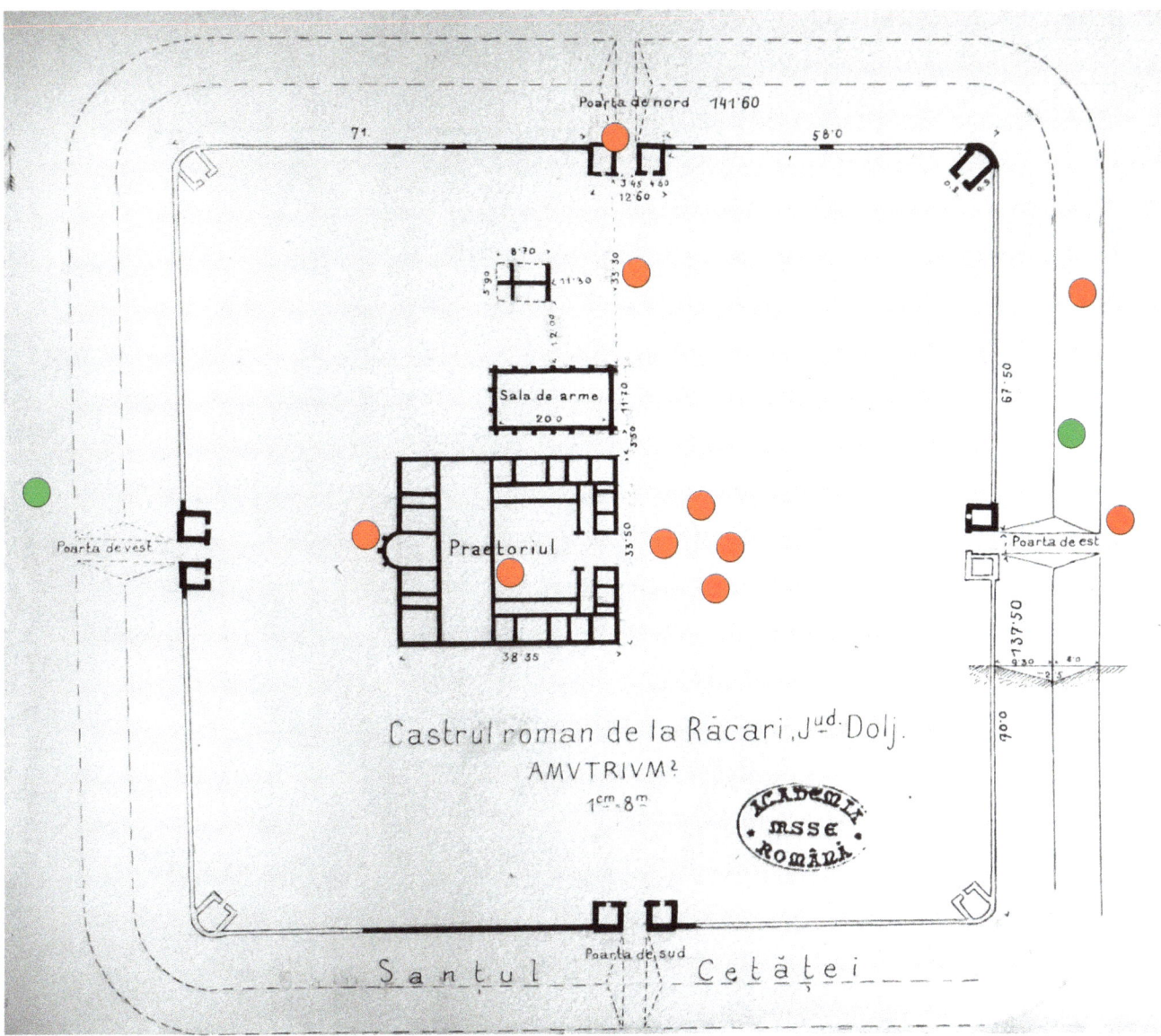

Figure 18.5. Răcarii de Jos – plan of the 19th century excavations with the marked finding spots, according to archival record. With green are marked the big scrap metal deposit (outside the camp, to the West), and the gilded horse leg (near the East gate), (the author, under use of the plan by P. Polonic).

one in Craiova, and from Porolissum, in Bucharest, Cluj-Napoca and Zalău. Proper and suitable material analyses, due to the technological characteristics of this category, would be very expensive and not necessarily definitive. Those, as well as basic documentation, would need a systematic datasheet in order to enable a comprehensive analysis of the excavated deposits. Good examples for this purpose appear in Gebrochener Glanz (2014) and Willer et al. (2017).

It is no longer possible to establish if the gilded fragments have been found only within the *principia* or in other spots as well. The degree of fragmentation is very different (Fig. 18.6). The initial statues identified were at least one equestrian and one depiction of a cuirassed deity. The gilded horse's leg (Fig. 18.7), bearing visible traces of gold leaf-gilding, came to light in the ditch at the Eastern gate (Information from the manuscripts of Gr.G. Tocilescu, mss. 5133, 214, preserved in the Library of the Romanian Academy, Bucharest).

The bronze fragments allowing diagnosis seem to belong to more than ten statues, which is quite a large number. There are fragments of two equestrian statues, one of which is gilded. Fragments of at least six imperial portraits (Bondoc – Gudea, 2017) and elements of about seven cuirassed statues can be identified. The possible combinations among those identified parts are numerous and cannot be solved definitively, as it was at least theoretically possible to reuse a statue, especially a cuirassed one, by changing its head.

From Răcari and nearby surroundings, no statue bases have been found up to now. In the *principia*, the 1897 reports mention the remains of a footing for a statue base (Tocilescu 1900), without a proper description.

The probability is high that scrap metal was collected from other sites and brought to Răcari for a workshop or just for storage in a strategically suitable location. Traces of fire may have been caused by the destruction of the initial

Figure 18.6. Răcarii de Jos – fragments of gilded bronze statues (photos by the author).

statue, by the deliberate use of fire for breaking up the statue, or by fire having been set to the area of the scrap metal deposit. A similar situation seems to have existed in Ilișua (Alexandrescu 2015). Due to the large quantity of fragments (in terms of both number and weight), the find in Răcari is quite different from the deposits in Novae and in other military centres.

The fort in Răcarii seems to have been abandoned by the Roman army in the middle of the third century (during the invasions of the Goths and the Carpi); there are no hints at violent events as at other sites in the province (e.g. Romula or Slăveni). In Slăveni, in the *principia* (IDR II, 500), a dedication to Phillipus Arabs made by the Ala I Hispanorum was found. The name of the emperor had not been erased. It is said that many fragments of large bronzes have also been found (Gamer 1968, 58; Tudor 1978, 307), although they have been not yet published, just mentioned by D. Tudor (author of the excavation) and scholars such as G. Gamer (1969) who worked on large bronzes during the 1960s. It is therefore not clear if the invasion caused the destruction of the fort, the *principia* and the statues.

For comparative purposes, the early Roman settlement of Lanau-Waldgirmes, with findspots of fragments from large bronze statues, provides an extreme example of violent destruction (Rasbach 2017, fig. 3). In this case, both the date of the forum and the date of the destructive invasion of the Germanic tribes are known.

The Roman sites near Răcarii are little investigated. It is not clear if the civil settlement near the camp was limited to a military *vicus* or if there was also an urban settlement from which the fragments of large-scale bronze statues could have been collected. The military *vicus* is less probable to have had bronze statues, due to the legal character of the settlement (Meyr – Flügel 2016, 162). The locations of larger ancient sites inside the province, such as Admutrium, Pelendava, Malva, which are known from ancient sources, are still subject to debate. As regards the likely distances travelled to collection sites, there is not sufficient information. It is also important to know the moment in time when the collecting was undertaken, during the lifetime of the Roman provinces or after 271–275 A.D. Theoretically, Drobeta or Romula could be possible collection sites, even though they are located at a

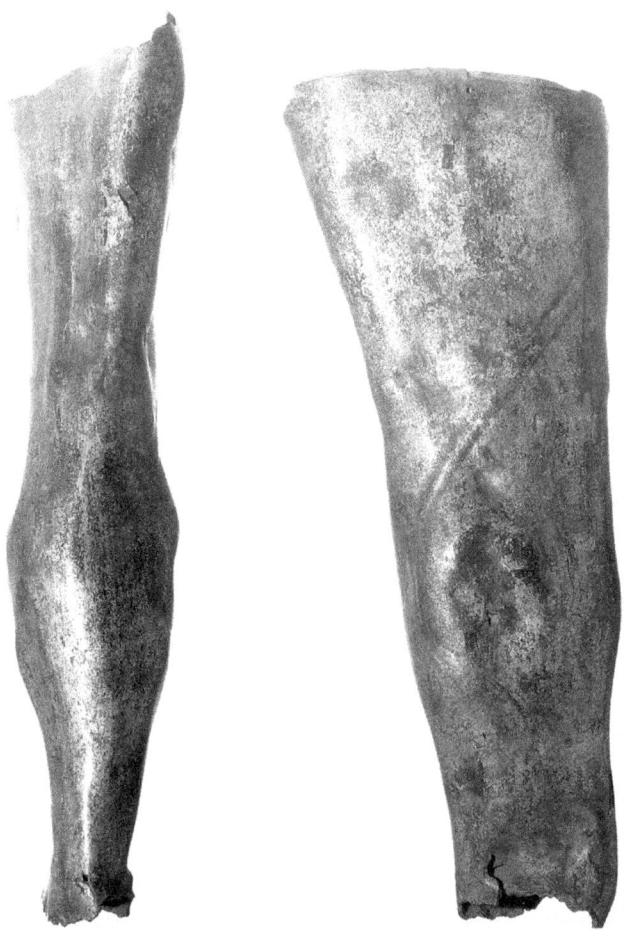

Figure 18.7. Răcarii de Jos – the gilded horse leg (photo by G. Chelmec, IAB).

distance of 3–4 days' travel (81–89 km). The large number of fragments of cuirassed statues brings into discussion also the forts on the *limes Alutanus* as places for metal collecting.

During the Roman use of the camp, reusing the stone material was common practice, and the same is assumed to be valid for the large bronzes depicting imperial persons that suffered *damnatio memoriae*. Remains from this process are considered to have been collected and reused by the army, such as is attested, for instance, in the camps of Aalen (Kemkes 2014b) and Novae. The post-Roman use of the camp of Răcarii de Jos, or to be more precise its post-military use, is the most probable explanation, at least for one of the scrap metal deposits outside the camp and the reuse of the large bronzes.

Conclusion and perspectives

In conclusion, large cuirassed and equestrian statues are well represented in Dacia and Moesia, and the quality of the statues is quite good. The gilded examples represented emperors. In only one case, at Răcarii de Jos, can it be assumed, owing to the smaller dimensions of a gilded shoulder *pteryges* fragment (Fig. 18.6), that it belonged to a statue of Mars.

The reason that the number of large bronzes and inscribed bases is large for Dacia and much smaller for Moesia Inferior is probably only a reflection of the state of research. It is obvious that, when dealing with this kind of finds, it is or at least should be necessary to approach both the finds themselves, their initial role and function, their original context, and their eventual reuse and recycling processes. The ancient behaviour towards metal-collecting is well illustrated by the situation in Augusta Raurica, where several 3rd-century workshops with their scrap-metal deposits containing fragments of large-scale bronzes and plates from their bases from the forum, dated to the first century, have been archaeologically investigated, (Witschel 2016, 131–134). This example, through its methodological approach, illustrates perfectly the potential information that can be provided by such scrap metal deposits as well as the need and importance of proper documentation and scientific approach.

The special interest shown towards this category of archaeological material in the last years will most certainly raise awareness among colleagues working at excavations and in museums, to re-evaluate and suitably record and publish both old and new finds. Areas of study can include: systematic record of statue bases and their findspots, though not all are easily accessible or known; stylistic analysis of recognizable fragments in order to get a closer time-frame on the 'fashion of one period'/*Zeitgeschmack*, corresponding to the observations made in Germania for cuirassed statues (Stoll 1992, 80–82); reconsideration of workshop finds and deposits of scrap metal in the area of interest; detailed documentation of the available fragments in order to build a record of technological details useful for comparison with already intensively studied finds from other provinces, as was the case in the *Grossbronzen am Limes* project (Gebrochener Glanz 2014; Willer et al. 2017).

The analysis of the Roman metals industry in Dacia and Moesia Inferior, including recycling processes, repairs, sources of materials such as tin and lead, the trade of materials, crafts and/or finished items, is far from advanced. These areas offer a wide range of possibilities for research in the years to come.

Abbreviations

AE = *L'Année épigraphique*.

CIL = *Corpus Inscriptionum Latinarum*.

IAB = Institutul de Arheologie "Vasile Pârvan", Bucharest.

IDR II = Florescu, G. – Petolescu, C.C., 1977, *Inscriptiones Daciae Romanae. Pars meridionalis, inter Danuvium et Carpatos montes*, București: Editura Academiei Republicii Socialiste România.

RIC = *Roman Imperial Coinage* (since 1923), London.

Bibliography

Alexandrescu, C.-G., 2015. Fragmente de statui din bronz descoperite în castrul roman de la Ilișua (jud. Bistrița Năsăud), *Revista Bistriței* 29, 93–112.

Alexandrescu, C.-G., 2016a. On the fate of sculpture in late Antiquity at the Lower Danube, in: Stirling, L. – Myrup Kristensen T., ed., *Afterlife of Roman Sculpture: Late Antique Reception and Response*, Ann Arbor: University of Michigan Press, 243–262.

Alexandrescu, C.-G., 2016b. Not just stone: lithic material from Troesmis – local resources and imports, in: Alexandrescu, C.-G., ed., *Troesmis – A Changing Landscape. Romans and the Others in the Lower Danube Region in the first century BC – third century AD. International Colloquium in Tulcea (7th–10th of October 2015)*, Cluj-Napoca: Editura Mega, 47–62.

Alexandrescu, C.-G., 2017. Römische Großbronzen aus den Provinzen Dacia und Moesia inferior: Funde aus den militärischen Anlagen, in: Kemkes 2017b, 150–157.

Alexandrescu, C.-G. – Gugl, C. – Kainrath, B., ed., 2016. *Troesmis I. Die Forschungen von 2010–2014*, Cluj-Napoca: Editura Mega.

Alicu, D. – Diaconescu, A., 2008. Recently Found Fragments of Bronze Statues from Colonia Dacica Sarmizegetusa, *Ephemeris Napocensis* 18, 197–206.

Barbu, V., 1965. Bronzes romains du Musée Archéologique de Constantza, *Dacia N.S.* 9, 387–402.

Benea, D., 2008. Ateliere de prelucrarea a bronzului, argintului și aurului în Dacia Romană, in: *Bibliotheca Historica et Archaeologica Universitatis Timisiensis (BHAUT) 9: Dacia în sistemul socio-economic roman: Cu privire la atelierele meșteșugărești locale*, Timișoara: Editura Universității de Vest, 107–179.

Bondoc, D. – Gudea, N., 2009. *Castrul roman de la Răcari: încercare de monografie. Interferențe etnice și culturale în mileniile I a. Chr.–I p. Chr.* 14, Cluj-Napoca: Editura Mega.

Bondoc, D. – Gudea, N., 2017. *Castrul roman de la Răcari II: clădirea comandamentului (principia): statuile de bronz și bronz aurit*, Craiova: Editura Antheo.

Čičikova, M., 1992. L'édifice à peristyle extra muros à Novae (Moesia Inferior), in: Niezgoda, A. – Niezgoda, E. – Zabecka, M., ed., *Studia Aegaea et Balcanica: In Honorem Lodovicae Press*, Warszawa: Wydawn. Uniwersytetu Warszawskiego, 235–243.

Čičikova, M., 2016. Deux statues-portraits en bronze de Novae (Mésie inférieure), *Studia Classica Serdicensia* 5: Monuments and Text in Antiquity and Beyond. Essays for the Centenary of Georgi Mihailov (1915–1991), 71–84.

Cociș, S., 1995. Ateliere de bronzieri în Dacia Romană, *Acta Musei Napocensis* 32/1, 383–391.

Diaconescu, A., 2005. *Statuaria majoră în Dacia romană*, Cluj-Napoca: Nereamia Napocae.

Domaszewski, A. von, 1888. Römischer Pferdeschmuck aus Siebenbürgen, *Archäologisch-epigraphische Mitteilungen aus Österreich-Ungarn* 12, 138–145, with pl. IV.

Gaiu, C., 2011. Vestigii ale metalurgiei bronzului în castrul roman de la Ilișua, *Revista Bistriței* 25, 169–178.

Gamer, G., 1968. Fragmente von Bronzestatuen aus den römischen Militäranlagen an der Rhein- und Donaugrenze, *Germania*, 46/1, 53–66.

Gamer, G., 1969. *Kaiserliche Bronzestatuen aus den Kastellen und Legionslagern an Rhein- und Donaugrenze des Römischen Imperiums. Inaugural Dissertation München*, Gießen: Gahmig-Druck.

Găzdac, C. – Gaiu, C. – Marchiș, E., 2011. *Arcobadara (Ilișua)*, Coins from Roman sites and collections of Roman coins from Romania 6, Cluj-Napoca: Editura Mega.

Gebrochener Glanz 2014. LVR-LandesMuseum Bonn, Archäologisches Landesmuseum Baden-Württemberg und Museum Het Valkhof Nijmegen, ed., *Gebrochener Glanz: Römische Großbronzen am UNESCO-Welterbe Limes. Begleitbuch zur Ausstellung "Gebrochener Glanz. Römische Großbronzen am UNESCO-Welterbe Limes" LVR-LandesMuseum Bonn vom 20. März bis 20. Juli 2014, Limesmuseum Aalen vom 16. August 2014 bis 22. Februar 2015, Museum Het Valkhof Nijmegen vom 21. März bis 21. Juni 2015*, Mainz: Nünnerich-Asmus Verlag.

Gudea, N. – Salanțiu, V. – Matei, A., 1986. Statuia ecvestră a împăratului Marcus Aurelius Antoninus (Caracalla) de la Porolissum. Propuneri pentru o reconstituire grafică, *Acta Musei Porolissensis* 10, 157–181.

Ivanov, R., 1996. s.v. Nigrinianis, *Enciclopedia dell'Arte Antica Classica e Orientale*, 2nd supplement, volume IV, 17–18.

Kemkes, M. 2014a. Zu Ehren des Kaiserhauses. Bronzebildnisse in militärischen Kontexten, in: Gebrochener Glanz 2014, 108–119.

Kemkes, M. 2014b. Kaiserstatuen als Metallschrott im Kastell Aalen, in: Gebrochener Glanz 2014, 131–134.

Kemkes, M. 2017a. Kaiserstatuen im militärischen Kontext – Das Zeugniss der Sockelinschriften und Postamente, in: Kemkes 2017b, 54–77.

Kemkes, M. 2017b. *Römische Großbronzen am UNESCO-Welterbe Limes*. Beiträge zum Welterbe Limes 9, Darmstadt: Konrad Theiss Verlag.

Kemkes, M. – Sarge, C. – 2009. Gesichter der Macht. Kaiserbilder in Rom und am Limes. Schriften des Limesmuseums Aalen 60, Stuttgart: Konrad Theiss Verlag.

Klages, C. 2014. Aus einer Statue wird Falschgeld, in: Gebrochener Glanz 2014, 158–159.

Lahusen, G. – Formigli, E. 2001. *Römische Bildnisse aus Bronze. Kunst und Technik*, München: Hirmer Verlag.

Meyr, M. – Flügel, C. 2016. Rom auch am Limes? Aspekte von urbanitas in römischen Militärsiedlungen, *Saalburg Jahrbuch* 59, 149–189.

Milceva, R., 2005. *Römische Skulptur im Archäologischen National Museum Sofia. Schriften des Zentrums für Archäologie und Kulturgeschichte des Schwarzmeerraumes*. Antike Skulptur in Bulgarien 1, Langenweißbach: Beier & Beran.

Petolescu, C. C. 1995. *Scurtă istorie a Daciei romane*, București: Editura Didactică și Pedagogică.

Petculescu, L., ed., 2003. *Antique Bronzes in Romania. Exhibition Catalogue*, Bucharest: Daim.

Pop, C., 1978. Statui imperiale din bronz în Dacia romană, *Acta Musei Napocensis* 15, 135–165.

Popović, I., 2008–2009. Characteristics of Balkan-Danubian treasures from the end of the 1st to the middle of the 3rd century, *Studii și Cercetări de Istorie Veche și Arheologie* 59–60, 33–51.

Protase, D. – Gaiu, C. – Marinescu, G., 1996–1997. Le camp romain et l'établissement civil d'Ilișua (département de Bistrița Năsăud), Rapports préliminaires et conclusions concernant les fouilles archéologiques effectuées dans le courant des années 1978–1995, *Revista Bistriței* 10–11, 27–110.

Rasbach, G., 2017. Waldgirmes – ein Bildersturm und seine Belege im Boden, in: Kemkes 2017b, 106–113.

Sarge, C., 2017. Geschaffen, verehrt, zerstört, verwertet... Überreste von Bronzestatuen aus der Germania inferior, dem Osten der Gallia Belgica und dem Norden von Germania superior, in: Kemkes 2017b, 26–39.

Sarnowski, T., 1985. Bronzefunde aus dem Stabsgebäude in Novae und Altmetalldepots in den römischen Kastellen und Legionslagern, *Germania*, 63/2, 521–540.

Sarnowski, T., 1989. Zur Statuenaustattung römischer Stabsgebäude, *Bonner Jahrbücher*, 189, 97–120.

Sarnowski, T., 2018. Novae in Lower Moesia. Building the Early Christian Episcopal Complex with Inscribed Pagan Stones from the Roman Legionary Headquarters, in: Klenina, E.J., ed., *Sacrum et profanum. Haec studia amici et collegae A.B. Biernacki septuagennio dicant*. Novae. Studies and Materials 6, Poznań: Instytut Historii UAM, 77–86.

Stoll, O., 1992. *Die Skulpturenausstattung römischer Militäranlagen an Rhein und Donau. Der Obergermanisch-Rätische Limes*. Pharos. Studien zur griechisch-römischen Antike 1, St. Katharinen: Scripta Mercaturae.

Stoll, O, 1995. Zu einigen Fragmenten von Bronzestatuen vom Kästrich in Mainz, *Mainzer Archäologische Zeitschrift* 2, 167–196.

Tocilescu, Gr. G., 1900. *Fouilles et recherches archéologiques* en Roumanie, București: Imprimerie du "Corps didactique" C. Ispasesco & G. Bratanesco.

Tomas, A., 2017. *Living with the Army I, Civil Settlements near Roman Legionary Fortresses in Lower Moesia*, Warsaw: Institute of Archaeology, University of Warsaw.

Tudor, D. 1978. *Oltenia romană*, 4th edition, București: Editura Academiei Republicii Socialiste România.

Visy, Z., 1983. Basen und Fragmente von Kaiserstatuen aus Intercisa, *Acta Archaeologica Academiae Scientiarum Hungaricae* 35, 73–85.

Willer, F. – Schwab, R. – Mirschenz, M. – Schneider, G., 2017. *Römische Bronzestatuen am Limes: archäometrische Untersuchungen zur Herstellungstechnik: Archäometrische Untersuchungen zur Herstellungstechnik*, Darmstadt: Verlag Philipp von Zabern.

Witschel, C., 2016. Die epigraphische und statuarische Ausstattung von Platzanlagen (fora) im römischen Germanien, in: Hensen, A., ed., *Das große Forum von Lopodunum*. LARES 1, Edingen-Neckarhausen: Edition Ralf Fetzer, 91–152.

19

Roman bronze vessels with signs of repair from Sarmatia

Mikhail Treister

Deutsches Archäologisches Institut, Zentrale Berlin

mikhail.treister@dainst.de

Abstract: The paper deals with Roman bronze vessels with signs of repair found in the nomadic burials of the 1st century BC – 3rd century AD in Asian Sarmatia. A considerable part of imported but already damaged vessels found their way into the burials. Depending on vessel type, from ca. 10% to more than 20% of all the imported vessels have been repaired, primarily with patches of various shapes, riveted from inside or outside. The question is where these repairs were executed: either the vessels were acquired by the nomads already repaired ("second-hand"), or this happened afterwards, examples of both cases are discussed in detail.

Keywords: Roman bronze vessels; repairs; nomadic burials; Sarmatia

The paper deals with Roman bronze vessels with signs of repair found in the nomadic burials of Asian Sarmatia, i.e. in the territory from the estuary of the Don River to the Urals and the steppes of West Kazakhstan, dated from the 1st century BC to the 3rd century AD (Fig. 19.1,1).

Vessels with losses

Many of the Roman vessels were damaged when they found their way into burials. The basins, found primarily in the Lower Don area, have lost stand-rings, as was the case with:

1) Eggers 96 / Tassinari S2121 basins from Kudinov Burial-mound no. 13/1961 (Fig. 19.2, 2) (Raev 1986, 18–21, pls. 13–14; Gossel-Raeck – Stutzinger 2003, 107, no. 70; Treister 2019, fig.4, 3) and
2) Sokolovskii Burial-mound no. 3/1970 (Raev 1974, 181–189, fig. 1–2; 1977, 139–42, figs.1–3; 1986, 18–21, pl.12),

or handles, which was typical for the later basins of Eggers 99–100 types:

1) basin from Kobyakovo Burial-mound no. 3/1983 with both handles missing (Fig. 19.2,3) (Guguev 1986, 72, no.1, pl. 48, 1; 2018, 64–65, no.1; figs.7.4. 8. 3; Treister 2019, fig. 4.6), or
2) the basin from Burial-mound no. 3/1991 near the station of Berdiya, with one of two handles lost (Fig. 19.2,1) (Mordvintseva – Sergatskov, 1995, 118, fig. 6.1; Sergatskov 2000, 70. 124, fig. 86.2; Skripkin 2013, 113 (ill. below), no. 230; Treister 2019, fig.4.1),

as well as jugs, oinochoes, amphoras and pateras:

1) The oinochoe (Fig. 19.2, 5) (Bespalyi – Bespalaya – Raev 2007, 33, no. 46, pl. 34.2; Bezuglov – Glebov – Parusimov 2009, 30. 45. 83, fig.13.3; Treister 2019, fig. 4.2) from Burial-mound no. 9/1987 of the Valovyi-I necropolis
2) The amphora (Fig. 19.2, 4) (Bespalyi – Bespalaya – Raev 2007, 33, no. 45. 126, pl. 37.1; Bezuglov – Glebov – Parusimov 2009, 31, fig. 14; 45. 82–83; Treister 2019, fig. 4.4) from the same burial.
3) The jug (Fig. 19.2, 6) from Burial-mound no. 3/1991 (Mordvintseva – Sergatskov 1995, 118, fig. 6.2; Sergatskov 2000, 70. 124, fig. 87.2; Skripkin 2013, 112 (ill. below left), no. 231; Treister 2019, 317, fig. 4.5) near the station of Berdiya.
4) The patera of the type Millingen found in the burial no. 2 of the Burial-mound no. 23/1978 in Lebedevka, Western Kazakhstan, lacks a handle (Moshkova 1982, 82.85, fig. 2.1–2; Treister, 2013c, 743, note 84).

It is worth noting that in each of these two burials named above were found two vessels with losses: one in the Lower Don area: Burial-mound no. 9/1987 of the Valovyi-I necropolis, another – in the Lower Volga area: Burial-mound no. 3/1991 near the station of Berdiya.

Vessels repaired with patches

Other vessels demonstrate ancient repairs or modification. The most widespread type of repair is closing the holes with patches of various shapes, usually rectangular, sometimes with rounded edges, which were riveted to the body of the vessels either from inside or outside.

The patches riveted outside are especially common. They were used to repair various categories of vessels, including pateras, as the piece from Burial-mound no. 9/1983 of Vysočino-V necropolis, where a rectangular patch covered

Mikhail Treister

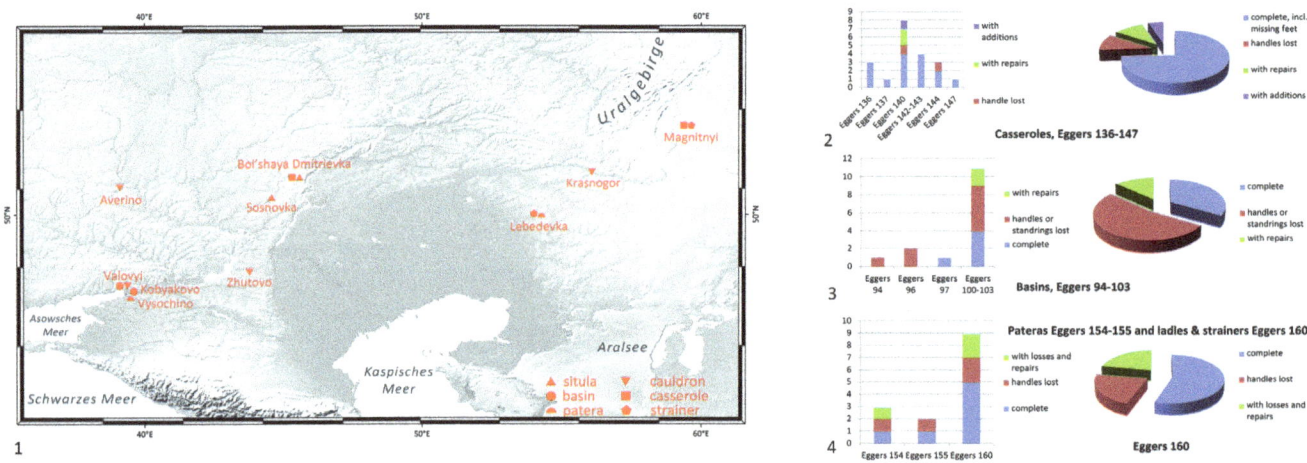

Figure 19.1. Map. Distribution of Roman bronze vessels with repairs in Asian Sarmatia. Map; 2 – chart and diagram, distribution of casseroles types Eggers 136–147 with repairs and losses; 3 – chart and diagram, distribution of basins types Eggers 94–103 with repairs and losses; 4 – chart and diagram, distribution of pateras types Eggers 154–155 and ladles/strainers type Eggers 160 with repairs and losses.

Figure 19.2. Roman bronze vessels with losses from Sarmatia. 1, 6 – Berdiya. Burial-mound no. 3/1991. Burial no. 1. Volgograd, Regional Local Lore Museum, inv.-no. 28007/22 (basin), 20 (jug); 2 – Kudinov. Burial-mound no. 13/1961. Burial no. 1. Rostov-on-Don, Regional Local Lore Museum, inv.-no. 2170/3; 3 – Kobyakovo. Burial-mound no. 3/1983. Burial no. 1. Tanais, Archaeological Museum-reserve, inv.-no. 394. AO 25/8; 4–5 – Valovyi-I. Burial-mound no. 9/1987. Burial no. 1. Azov, Historical-archaeological and paleontological museum-reserve, inv.-no. 25309/239 (amphora), 240 (oinochoe); Photographs, M. Treister, 2015.

the crack at the transition from the wall to the bottom (Fig. 19.3, 1–4) (Bespaly 1986, 76, pl. 60.3; Bespalyi – Luk'yashko 2008, 68, pl. LV.8; Treister 2019, 317, fig. 5.1–4), casseroles such as the find from Burial-mound no. 21/2010 near Magnitnyi in Trans-Urals, with a patch with rounded edges, which covered a hole in the wall (Fig. 19.3, 5–8) (Botalov – Ivanov 2012, 272. 276, fig. 4.1; 278, fig. 5.4; Treister 2016, 280. 282, fig. 2.4; Treister 2019, 317, fig. 5.5–8); basins, such as the piece with handle attachments of the rare type from the Burial-mound no. 25/1987 of the Valovyi-I necropolis. Also the crack on the rim of the basin was repaired with a brace (Bespalyi – Bespalaya – Raev 2007, 62, no. 29, pl. 76.2; Bezuglov – Glebov – Parusimov 2009, 53, fig. 29.2, 56. 58. 82).

The cauldron from Valovyj-I Burial-mound no. 6/1987 (Fig. 19.4, 5) has a big round external patch on the bottom (Fig. 19.4, 4–5), a somewhat smaller round patch on the bottom inside (Fig. 19.4, 3 and 6), and numerous rectangular patches (fig. 19.4, 1–2). Also two handles have lower attachments of different shapes – most likely during one of the repairs one of the attachments was also replaced (Abbaye de Daoulas 1995, 104, no. 130; Bespalyi – Bespalaya – Raev 2007, 22–23, no.5, pl. 22.4; Simonenko 2015, 37.38, fig.7.2–3). In general we meet numerous signs of repairs on the cauldrons. Other examples of cauldrons of different types and sizes with patches were found both in the Lower Volga basin (Demidenko 2016, 202, fig. 5.6. 205, no. 1. 211), South Urals (Shilov 1975, 161. 162, fig. 60.1; Demidenko 2008, 119, no. 32; fig. 120), and in a barrow in the Upper Don basin: the huge cauldrons from Averino show numerous patches, especially in the bottom (Medvedev 1996, 23–25; 1999, 112, fig. 56.6–7. 67.3–4; Simonenko 2015, 38. 39, fig. 6.6–7; Berezutskii 2017, 21–22).

Sometimes the patch was riveted inside the vessel – as on the wall of the basin Eggers 99–100 with missing

Roman bronze vessels with signs of repair from Sarmatia

Figure 19.3. Roman bronze vessels with patches. 1–4 – Vysočino-V. Burial-mound no. 9/1983. Ritual ground. Azov, Historical-archaeological and paleontological museum-reserve, inv.-no. 20200/136; 5–8 – Magnitnyi. Burial-mound no. 21/2010. Burial no. 1. Chelyabinsk, South-Urals State University, inv.-no. НТУ-ГИК 93. Photographs, M. Treister, 2015.

Figure 19.4. Bronze cauldron. Valovyj-I. Burial-mound no. 6/1987. Burial no. 3. Azov, Historical-archaeological and paleontological museum-reserve, inv.-no. 25309/176. Photographs, M. Treister, 2015.

Figure 19.5. Roman bronze vessels with patches. 1–4 – Kobyakovo. Burial-mound no. 3/1983. Burial no. 1. Tanais, Archaeological Museum-reserve, inv.-no. 394. AO 25/8; 5–7 – Sosnovka. Chance find, 1972. Volgograd, Regional Local Lore Museum, inv.-no. 8081/4. 1–5, 7 – photographs, M. Treister, 2015; 6 – drawing, N. Bespalaya, 2015.

handles found in Kobyakovo Burial-mound no 3/1983 (Fig. 19.5, 1–4) (Guguev 1986, 72, no. 1, pl. 48.1; 2018, 64–65, no. 1; figs.7.4. 8.3), and on a big bronze situla (Fig. 19.5.5–6), a chance find near Sosnovka in the Lower Volga area (Tsutskin 1974, 138–142; Skripkin 2013, 131 (ill. below left), no. 346; Treister 2019, 317, fig.7.4–7), bearing an inscription of the 2nd–3rd centuries AD to the effect that a certain Apollinarius Priscus took care that the money kept in the sanctuary of Ares Blekouros was used for manufacture and dedication to the sanctuary of the given vessel. Both the name of the dedicant and the epiklesis of the deity suggest strongly that this could refer to Thrace (Vinogradov 1997, 644–647; Saprykin 2003, 225–232).

Both external and internal patching are known on Roman bronze vessels found in the western and Danubian provinces of the Roman Empire. In some cases, as on casseroles from Noricum (Magdalensberg: Sedlmayer 1999, 84, pl. 33.4) and Dacia (Orheiu Bistriţei: Mustaţă 2017, 91–92, pl. LIX), the patches themselves are missing and only the holes along the break lines show that the repair was made in antiquity. In other cases, as in the vicus in Wederath, separate patches were found, without the vessels to which they should have been riveted (Bienert 2007, 157, no. 174). Infrequently the patches were not riveted but soldered, as on the outside of the casserole below the handle of the piece in the Rheinisches Landesmuseum Trier (Bienert 2007, 87, no. 75).

Patches riveted from outside occur on Roman bronze vessels of various categories and of various dates, including the casserole of the Augustan time manufactured by a metalsmith in Mainz (Petrovszky 2003, 117–118, fig. 75–76), on the vessels from Pompei (e.g., patera: Allison 2006, 56–57, no. 128, pl. 7.2–3), on the vessels of the late 1st–2nd century AD jug from Windischgarsten (Ruprechtsgerben 1985, 61–62, fig. 3), as well on the vessels which were still in use in late antiquity – a basin from Zwentendorf (Sedlmayer 1999, 55, pl. 21.3) and a bottle from the late 3rd-century-AD hoard from Navis-Mühlen (Tirol) (Kellner – Zemmer-Plank – Kellner, 1984, 60, fig. 5).

The patches riveted from inside occur on the 2nd century AD strainer of Eggers 160 type from Aventicum (Kapeller 2003, 108, no. 7) and on the jug Tassinari C1220 from Pompeii (Tassinari 1993, 52, type C1210), on the situla found in Paris: Bonnet 1989, 242–243, no. 234) and on the bronze plates from the 3rd century AD burial in Zomba, Pannonia (Bónis 1983, 115–18, fig. 14–16).

Among the Iron Age cauldrons in Europe it is rare to find a vessel without at least one repair and many have very extensive, overlapping repairs (Radnóti 1938, pl. XXVI.1; Roymans 2004, 156, nos. 111–113; Guštin – Kuzman – Preložnik 2014, 92, fig. 10; Joy 2014, 341–342). Although some of these could have been made at the time of manufacture, most were added throughout the life of the object. The fact that so much time was invested in their repair indicates that they were valued artefacts and also suggests they led long social lives (Joy 2014, 341–342). This was surely the case with the 3rd century AD bronze hammered cauldron from Waldürn, which demonstrates numerous patches riveted from inside (Weinrich-Kemkes 1993, 284, fig. 22). The materials published by Hans Drescher (Drescher 1963b, 46–47, fig. 3) show that riveted patches were a standard method of repair for Roman bronze vessels, particularly for cauldrons and situlae. The fragments of the cauldron from burial no. 16 in Harsefeld, Lower Saxony, show signs of numerous such repairs. A patch was positioned on the outside of the vessel so as to cover the area of the crack completely. On the interior, six small rectangular plates, which were fixed together with rivets through the holes in the patch and in the wall of the vessel (Wegewitz 1986, 81, fig. 15).

Vessels from the Burial-mound near Bol'shaya Dmitrievka in the Volga basin are rarely patched. The patch on the base of the casserole Eggers 140 from this burial is unusual: the added lamellar ring on the underside is attached with seven rivets (Fig. 19.6, 4–6) (Maksimov 1957, 157–159, no. 1, fig. 1; Shelov 1965, 266. 270, fig. 9.2; Schelow 1968, 243; Kropotkin 1970, 25, no. 58; 93, no. 802; Shilov 1973, 252, no. 1, fig. 1; 1975, 154, no. 1).

A situla of Bargfeld type from the same burial has an extremely rare type of repair: the bottom was completely renewed with a circular plate with rectangular projections along the edge, alternately wound from the outer and inner sides of the vessel's body (Fig. 19.6, 1–3) (Maksimov 1957, 158, fig. 2.1–2. 159, no. 2; Shelov 1965, 267. 270, fig. 9.3; Kropotkin 1970, 93, no. 802; Shilov 1973, 253, no. 2, fig. 2; 1975, 154, no. 1; Treister 2019, 317, fig. 7.1–3). This is the so called "jagged joint" ("zinnenartige

Figure 19.6. Roman bronze vessels with patches from Bol'shaya Dmitrievka. Burial-mound 96/1887. Saratov, Regional Local Lore Museum. 1–3 – inv.-no. 47796; 4–6 – inv.-no. 47795. 1–2 – drawings, N. Bespalaya, 2015; 3–6 – photographs, M. Treister, 2015.

Naht") of S. Bender (1992, 119). As has been shown, this technique, earlier considered to be first used from the 6th century AD, was already known to metalsmiths in the 3rd century AD, as proven by the finds from Moigrad in Dacia Porolisensis and Alba Iulia (Mustață 2017, 174–176, no. 100a–b, fig. 24; 365, pl. XCVII). This technique was also used to repair a cauldron found in the hoard from Mauer an der Url, dated towards the middle of the 3rd century AD, whose body was executed using such a joint (Noll 1980, 86–88, nos. 41. 43; pls. 32.41. 33.43; Bender 1992, 122). A similar piece was discovered at Nagyberki-Szalacska (Somogy, Hungary) (Radnóti 1938 123; Bender 1992, 122).

The correlation of repairs with vessel-types according to the finds in Sarmatia and from the western provinces of the Roman Empire and Germania Magna

To evaluate what percentage of the imported Roman bronzeware was found with losses and (or) repairs it is necessary to prepare e separate statistics. I took into account the more or less complete specimens with intact bodies (not the separate finds of handles or feet in robbed burials). The number of various categories of objects allows clear conclusions for only several categories of vessels.

Of 19 casseroles of various types according to Eggers' classification, most were found intact, although small feet which could have been originally soldered to the bottom were present in 4 cases. Also among the finds from the Roman provinces such vessels with feet are extremely rare: their absence did not prevent use of these vessels for their original function. In two cases a handle was completely missing; in two cases there were evident signs of repairs in the form of patches; and in one case the vessel was later decorated with a lower attachment of the handle of the jug riveted to its body. That means that in general only ca. 10% of them bear signs of repair. At the same time, if one discusses the types of casseroles separately, then those of Eggers type 140 / Petrovszky V.1, dated ca. 5–35 AD (Eggers 1951, 172, App. 60, pl. XII.140; Petrovszky 1993, 52–54; Karasová 1998, 34–35, map XIII, pl. IV.140; Erdrich 2001, 43; Bienert 2007, 78–79; Lund Hansen 2016, 230–231; Mustață 2017, 92–93), were repaired and modified much more often than those of the other types – the number of such vessels being exactly half of all of them (Fig. 19.1, 2).

The percentage of basins of the most common types with losses is much higher than is true of the casseroles. Seven or eight of 15 pieces were found without one or both handles or the stands; and two pieces (ca. 13.3%) had patches (Fig. 19.1, 3).

The percentage of basins is comparable to the percentage of strainers with losses Eggers 160/Petrovszky X.6, dated to 35/40–140/160 AD (Eggers 1951, 48. 85. 174, Taf. 13. 160, map 45; Kunow 1983, 27. 64. 75–76; Petrovszky 1993, 98–102; Sedlmayer 1999, 93; Erdrich 2001, 43–44; Kapeller 2003, 88. 135, no. 46, pl. 7; Bienert 2007, 93–94. 103–104, nos. 93–94; Luik 2016, 217, fig. 1.12; 218; Lund Hansen 2016, 231. 235; Mustață 2017, 98–101) – four of nine pieces have broken handles and in two cases the handles show signs of repair (ca. 22,2% of all vessels of this type) (Fig. 19.1.4).

In general, depending on the category of vessels, from ca. 10% to more than 20% of them were found with signs of repair. That the quantity of vessels being repaired in antiquity depended not on the duration of usage but rather on the weight of load of various types during daily use is known from publications by H. Drescher (1963a, 217–218; 1963b, 41–53), who studied repairs of Celtic and Roman bronze vessels; and confirmed by finds from Neupotz, which were often found without their handles which were soldered to the bodies (Künzl 2000, 607–614). Therefore it is clear why the Eggers basins (Eggers 99–100 / Petrovszky XV, 1–2; Eggers 1951, 169, pl. 10; Petrovszky 1993, 114–118; Tassinari 1993, type S4000, 221–238, pls. LVII–LXIX; Karasová 1998, 26–27, map X; pl. III. 100; Erdrich 2001, 44; Hrnčiarik 2013, 54, pl. XXXVIII. 389; Luik 2016, 216–218, fig. 1.9–10) By the considerable weight of the basins with water inside, attachment of handles by soldering was a weak point. The same is true with the long handles of strainers and dippers of Eggers 160–161 types which were broken and after that sometimes riveted, such as the finds from Bol'shaya Dmitrievka (Maksimov 1957, 157–159, nos. 1. 3, figs. 1. 3.1; Shelov 1965, 266. 270, fig. 9.1–2; Kropotkin 1970, 93, no. 802; Shilov 1973, 254–255, fig. 3.3; 1975, 154–155, nos. 1.3), Lebedevka, Burial-mounds no. 1/1966 (Bagrikov – Senigova 1968, 81, fig. 10. 21; 83) and no. 2/1966 (Bagrikov – Senigova 1968, 75–76. 81, fig. 10. 21), and Magnitnyi, Burial-mound no. 21/2010 (Botalov – Ivanov 2012, 272–273. 276, fig. 4.2; 278, fig. 5.2; Treister 2016, 282, fig. 2.5, 283). As for the hammered vessels (Blechkanne) with cast bronze handles, used for heating water, S. Künzl pointed out that the thin body of the jug was damaged more quickly than the handle, and that an old handle might be attached to a new body (Künzl 2000, 607). In practice however, we find more often in Sarmatia such vessels of Bolla type 1e (1979, 37–38; 1989, 104–105) without any handle (Treister 2018, 220–223, fig. 2–5) or with a new iron handle, which was further secured to the neck of the vessel with an iron loop (Treister 2018, 226, fig. 8.1. 8.3–4; 231–232), the same way in which vessels were repaired in the western provinces of the Roman empire (Radnóti 1938, 152, pl. LII.3; Bónis 1983, 108–111, no. 5, fig. 11; Miglbauer 2012, 72.75, figs. 2–3). In the spread of the Blechkanne type in the North Pontic area, the distribution of these vessels suggests not their import from the workshops of Thrace, but rather their manufacture in the workshops of the Kingdom of Bosporus (Treister 2018, 219, fig. 1; 232–233).

The only statistical data which I was able to find concerning the signs of repairs on Roman bronze vessels, comes from the vessels of Neupotz, and was published by S. Künzl (2000, 608, figs. 1–3). In her statistics the scholar differentiated vessels which have signs of 1–2 or 3 and more repairs. The vessels I am presenting, perhaps excluding some cauldrons, had usually only one repair, and to make the comparison clear, I neglected in these diagrams the number of repairs. It is absolutely clear that the vessels found in the Rhine near Neupotz were repaired much often than those from Sarmatia. At the same time, the vessels from Sarmatia frequently show much more considerable losses, such as the absence of handles, ring-stands, or feet.

Therefore it is of crucial importance to ask where these repairs were executed, whether the vessels were already repaired when acquired by the nomads ("second-hand"), whether this happened afterwards, or whether we have examples of both cases. I have already shown that all the types of repairs which we were able to study on the imported bronze vessels from Sarmatia, also the very rare types, find parallels on Roman bronze vessels from the western provinces of the Roman empire and Germania Magna. Some of the Roman vessels found in Germania Magna are thought to have been repaired by local German craftsmen (Stupperich 1995a, 148, note 22; 1995b, 75, fig. 15; Ekengren 2009, 149–152). Now we have to ask how the vessels were repaired by the nomads.

How the nomads repaired imported and locally produced vessels

An absolutely different technique was used for repair of a 4th-century-BC silver Achaemenid phiale, bearing an Aramaic weight inscription, from Sarmatian Barrow No. 1 near the village of Prokhorovka in the South Urals, secondarily used as phalera of a horse's harness, as well as large shoulder silver-gilt phalerae decorated in the centre with rosettes framed with garland belts, in the sloppy middle part – with curly rosettes, and with a guilloche pattern along the edge –, probably of Asia Minor manufacture in the last 3rd–early 2nd century BC found near Uspenskaya in the North Caucasus. The parts of these objects which were torn off in antiquity were accurately joined with the main parts by means of narrow silver strips, sewn crosswise in the holes, pierced especially along the torn-off edges. The mode of "sewing" together the edges with a narrow silver strip suggests the restoration not in a highly specialized toreutic workshop, but rather by a handicraftsman. This simple mode of repair is characteristic, for instance, of the wooden vessels with gold overlays from 4th-century-BC Scythian and Sarmatian burials (Treister 2006, 441–442; 2009, 119–120; 2013a, 98). A large copper cauldron from the 2nd–1st-century-BC Burial no. 4 in Burial-mound no. 27/1965 in Zhutovo between the Don and the Volga Rivers was repaired in the same way. The lower part of the cauldron was repaired from inside and outside with felt patches stitched to the edges of the holes with leather straps (Shilov 1975, 138, fig. 52.2; Mordvintseva – Shinkar' 1999, 139, fig. 6. 11; Demidenko 2008, 116, no. 2, fig. 124; Skripkin – Shinkar', 2010, 130, fig. 4A. 9; Brosseder 2011, 363, fig. 12. 19; Skripkin 2013, 93 (ill.

middle right), no. 159). The cracks in the bronze vessels were also repaired by pouring melted bronze ("Nachguß"; cast-on) from outside and inside, which was the case with the ancient repair of a Near Eastern bronze basin found in the vicinities of the 4th-century-BC princely barrow no. 1 in Filippovka in the South Urals (Treister 2013b, 117–118, no. A13.3.1.2; pls. I.53. II.19.3–4; figs. I.19.2. II.93.2), although this way of repair is attested also in case of a late 4th-century-BC Etruscan bronze mirror (Lie – Bewer 2014, 51–52, fig. 2.8).

For the sake of clarity in discussing the techniques of repair used by the nomads in the first centuries AD, I have chosen cauldrons of the local type, originating from the area farthest from the ancient centers of the North Black Sea area – from the burial-mounds of the Trans-Urals area. These are massive cast egg-shaped cauldrons dating to the late 2nd – mid 3rd centuries AD (Demidenko 2008, 20–21, type VIII; see, e.g. from Magnitnyi Burial-mound no. 21/2010: Botalov – Ivanov 2012, 271, fig. 1.8; 273). Many production defects, such as cracks and holes, were repaired by pouring melted metal into them, or by specially cast patches, which were inserted in the holes (Minasyan 1986, 75–77, fig.7), Although rare, some rectangular patches were riveted through the holes along the edge, as on the cauldron from Burial-mound no. 3/1997 of the Magnitnyi cemetery (Fig. 19.7) (Botalov – Gutsalov 2000, 51, fig. 14.7, 53; Treister 2019, fig. 6).

Conclusions

This survey proves that at least in the late 2nd and 3rd centuries AD the nomads were able to repair vessels with riveted patches. Not all such repairs were made by the nomadic smiths, to judge from the rare example of repair using jagged joints on the situla from Bol'shaya Dmitrievka (Fig. 19.6, 1–3) which suggests strongly that the nomads acquired the vessel already repaired. However, the majority of the vessels were acquired intact, and sometimes repaired during the course of use.

Moreover one should not exclude the vessels found in the burial-mounds of the Lower Don area (Fig. 19.1, 1) which could be repaired in the workshops of the neighboring Bosporan town of Tanais, though the distribution of the repaired vessels is more or less even and does not give any hints that this could really be the case.

One should also take into account that the nomads appreciated imported vessels, most probably considering them to be prestigious objects. Fragments of these vessels were often used as amulets, as in different intact burials both in the Lower Don area (Valovyi-I, Burial Mound no. 9/1987: ring-shaped handle: Bespalyi – Bespalaya – Raev 2007, 27, no. 4, pl. 30.3; Bezuglov – Glebov – Parusimov 2009, 28, no. 9; 30, fig. 13.1), and in West Kazakhstan (jug handle with the lower attachment in the form of a Silenus mask from Lebedevka (Bagrikov – Senigova 1968, 75. 76, fig. 5.1; Moshkova 2009, 105, fig. 4, 110; Treister 2015, 242–243, fig. 3.3–4) (Fig. 19.8, 1). In some

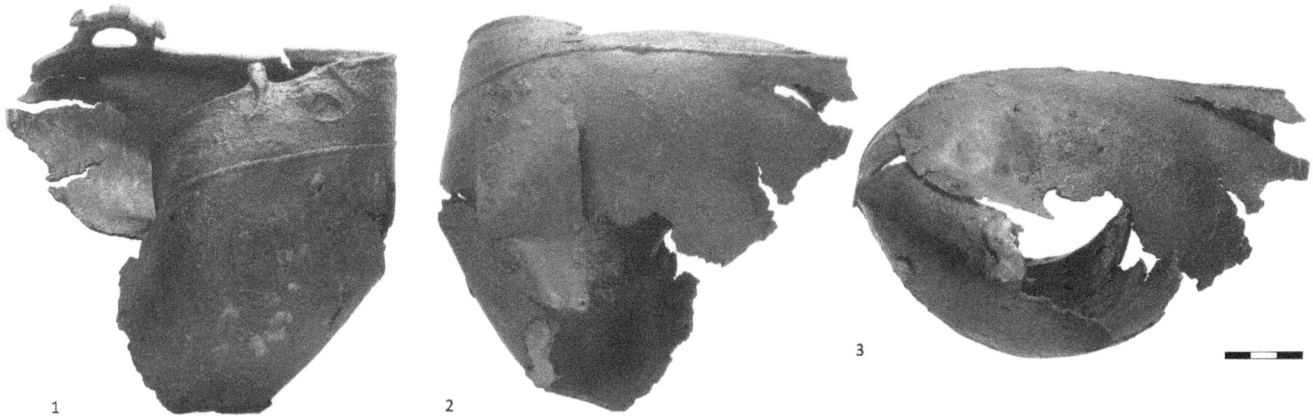

Figure 19.7. Bronze cauldron. Magnitnyi. Burial-mound 3/1997. Burial no. 1. Chelyabinsk, State Historical Museum of South Urals, inv.-no. Оф 6371/35. Photographs, M. Treister, 2015.

Figure 19.8. Secondary-used fragments of bronze vessels. 1 – Lebedevka. Burial-mound no. 2/1966. Astana, National Museum of the Republic Kazakhstan; 2, 3 – Valovyi-I. Burial-mound no. 9/1987. Burial no. 1. Azov, Historical-archaeological and paleontological museum-reserve, inv.-no. 25309/275 (2), 278 (4); 4 – Okhlebinino. Burial no. 230/1981. Ufa, Institute of Archaeology & Ethnology, Museum, inv.-no. 738/262. Photographs, M. Schicht (1), V. Terebenin (2, 3), S. Vorob'eva (4).

cases, they were secondarily used. That is testified by the additional holes, changing the function of the objects over time. Thus, the handle of the casserole found in the local burial in the Burial-ground Oklebinino in Bashkortostan (Ural area) was used as a detail of a belt (Fig. 19.8, 4) (unpublished), whereas the medallion of a patera with the image of Eros standing near the altar (Fig. 19.8, 3) (Bezuglov – Glebov – Parusimov 2009, 32–33, fig. 15.4; 83–84; Bespalyi – Bespalaya – Raev 2007, 28–29, no. 15, pl. 32.1) and the lower part of the strainer (Fig. 19.8, 2) (Bespalyi – Bespalaya – Raev 2007, 27, no. 5, pl. 30.4; Bezuglov– Glebov – Parusimov 2009, 28, no. 9; 41, fig. 21.6), both from BurialMound no. 9/1987 of Valovyi-I necropolis, as phalerae (?) or appliqués.

Thus imported bronze vessels were often used over a considerable period of time, which gives some reason to suggest that the repairs were made during that time. As an example of the durable usage of bronze vessels I refer to the intact burial of Magnitnyi Burial Mound no. 21/2010 in the Trans-Ural area, in which the bronze vessels dating to the 1st century and the first half of the 2nd century AD were found together with a 2nd-century glass beaker and a late 2nd-century enamelled brooch in the burial dated to first half of the 3rd century AD. All three imported bronze vessels had losses and two of them show signs of repair (Treister 2016, 279–286).

Abbreviations

KraSoob = Kratkie soobshcheniya Instituta arkheologii

RossArch = Rossiiskaya arkheologiya

SovArch = Sovetskaya arkheologiya

E. Deschler-Erb – P. Della Casa, ed., 2015. = *New Research on Ancient Bronzes. Acta of the XVIIIth International Congress on Ancient Bronzes* (Zurich Studies in Archaeology 10). Zurich: Chronos.

H.-U. Voß – N. Müller-Schneeßel, ed., 2016. = *Archäologie zwischen Römern und Barbaren. Zur Datierung und Verbreitung römischer Metallarbeiten des 2. und 3. Jahrhunderts n. Chr. im Reich und im Barbaricum – ausgewählte Beispiele (Gefäße, Fibeln, Bestandteile militärischer Ausrüstung, Kleingerät, Münzen).* Internationales Kolloquium. Frankfurt am Main, 19.– 22. März 2009. Bd. 1. Bonn: Habelt.

M. Treister – L. Yablonsky, ed., 2013.= *Einflüsse der achämenidischen Kultur im südlichen Uralvorland (5.–3. Jh. v. Chr.)*. Bd. 1. Vienna: Phoibos.

Bibliography

Abbaye de Daoulas, ed., 1995. *Entre Asie et Europe. L'or des Sarmates. Nomades des steppes dans l'antiquité. 17 juin – 29 octobre 1995*. Daoulas: Abbaye de Daoulas.

Allison, P.M., 2006. *The Insula of Menander at Pompeii. III. The Finds*. Oxford: Oxford University Press.

Bagrikov, G.I. – Senigova, T.N., 1968. Otkrytie grobnits v Zapadnom Kazakhstane (II–IV i XIV vv.). *Izvestiya Akademii Nauk Kazakhskoi SSR. Seriya obshchestvennye nauki*, 2, 71–89.

Bender, S., 1992. Zum Buntmetallkessel des sogenannten Seuso-Schatzes. *Archäologisches Korrespondenzblatt*, 22(1), 119–124.

Berezutskii, V.D., 2017. Bronzovye kotly iz sarmatskogo pogrebeinya Novochigol'skogo kurgannogo mogil'nika. *Vestnik VGU. Seriya: Istoriya. Politologiya. Sotsiologiya*, 2, 21–25.

Bespaly, E.I., 1986. Barrows with Roman Imports excavated by the Expedition of the Azov Regional Museum in 1979–84. In: B.A. Raev 1986, 75–78.

Bespalyi, E.I. – Bespalaya, N.E. – Raev, B.A., 2007. *Drevnee naselenie Nizhnego Dona. Kurgannyi mogil'nik «Valovyi 1»* (Materialy i issledovaniya po arkheologii Yuga Rossii. 2). Rostov-on-Don: Southern Scientific Centre, Russian Academy of Sciences.

Bespalyi, E.I. – Luk'yasho, S.I. 2008. *Drevnee naselenie mezhdurech'ya Dona I Kagal'nika. Kurgannyi mogil'nik us s. Vysochino* (Materialy i issledovaniya po arkheologii Yuga Rossii. I). Rostov-on-Don: Southern Scientific Centre, Russian Academy of Sciences.

Bezuglov, S.I. – Glebov, V.P. – Parusimov, I.N. 2009. *Pozdnesarmatskie pogrebeniya v ust'e Dona (kurgannyi mogil'nik Valovyi I)*. Rostov-on-Don: Media-Polis.

Bienert, B., 2007. *Die römischen Bronzegefässe im Rheinischen Landesmuseum Trier. Trier:* Rheinisches Landesmuseum.

Bolla, M., 1979. Recipienti in bronzo d'età romana in Lombardia. *Brocca rinvenuta* a Carobbio degli Angeli. *Rivista Archeologica dell'Antica Provincia e Diocesi di Como*, 161, 23–50.

Bolla, M., 1989. "Blechkannen": aggiornamenti. *Rassegna di Studi del Civico Museo Archeologico e del Civico Gabinetto Numismatico*, XLIII–XLIV, 95–118.

Bónis, É., 1983. Das kaiserzeitliche Bronzefund von Zomba. *Folia archaeologica*, XXXIV, 93–121.

Bonnet, J., ed., 1989. *Les bronzes antiques de Paris. Musée Carnavalet*. Paris: Paris-Musées.

Botalov, S.G. – Gutsalov, S.Yu., 2000. *Гунно-сарматы Урало-Казахстанских степей*. Chelyabinsk: Rifei.

Botalov, S.G. – Ivanov, A.A., 2012. Novyi kompleks kochevoi aristokratii gunno-sarmatskogo Vremeni v Yuzhnom Zaural'e. *Problemy istorii, filologii, kul'tury*, 4, 269–287.

Brosseder, U., 2011. Belt Plaques as an Indicator of East-West Relations in the Eurasian Steppe at the Turn of the Millennia. In: U. Brosseder – B.K. Miller, ed., *Xiongnu Archaeology. Multidisciplinary Perspectives of the First Steppe Empire in Inner Asia* (Bonn Contributions to Asian Archaeology, 5). Bonn: Rheinische Friedrich-Wilhelms-Universität, 349–424.

Demidenko, S.V., 2008. *Bronzovye kotly drevnikh plemen Nizhnego Povolzh'ya i Yuzhnogo Priural'ya (V v. do n.e. – III v. n.e.)*. Moscow: LKI Publ. House.

Demidenko, S.V., 2016. Vopinskoe pogrebenie s paradnoi konskoi upryazh'yu pozdnesarmatskogo vremeni v basseine reki Kurmoyarskii Aksai. *KSIAraSoob*, 244, 195–221.

Drescher, H. 1963a: Flickstellen und Reparaturen am keltischen und römischen Metallgeschirr. *Prähistorische Zeitschrift*, 61, 217–218.

Drescher, H. 1963b: Nachbesserungen und Reparaturen an keltischem und römischem Metallgeschirr. *Nachrichten aus Niedersachsens Urgeschichte*, 32, 41–53.

Eggers, H.J., 1951. *Der römische Import im freien Germanien* (Atlas der Urgeschichte, 1). Hamburg: Museum für Volkerkunde und Vorgeschichte.

Erdrich, M., 2001. *Rom und die Barbaren* (Römisch-Germanische Forschungen 58). Mainz: von Zabern.

Ekengren, F., 2009. *Ritualization – Hybridization – Fragmentation. The Mutability of Roman Vessels in Germania Magna AD 1–400* (Acta archaeologica Lundensia, Series prima in 4o, 28). Lund: Department of Archaeology and Ancient History, Lund University.

Gossel-Raeck, B. – Stutzinger, D., ed., 2003. *Steppengold. Grabschätze der Skythen und Sarmaten am unteren Don*. Frankfurt: Archäologisches Museum.

Guguev, V.K., 1986. The Burials in the Kobyakovo Barrow-Cemetery. In: B.A. Raev 1986, 71–72.

Guguev, V.K., 2018. Dva pogrebeniya s zapadnymi i vostochnymi importami s territorii Kobyakovskogo kurgannogo mogil'nika. In: I.N. Khrapunov, ed. *Krym v sarmatskuyu epoku* III. Simferopol: Nasledie tysyacheletii, 58–84.

Guštin, M. – Kuzman, P. – Preložnik, A., 2014. Celtic helmets from Hellenistic necropolises at Ohrid. In: M. Guštin and W. David, eds. *The Clash of Cultures? The Celts and the Macedonien World* (Schriften des Kelten Römer Museums manching 9). Manching: *Kelten Römer Museum*, 85–106.

Hrnčiarik, E. 2013. *Römisches Kulturgut in der Slowakei. Herstellung, Funktion, und Export römischer Manufakturerzeugnisse aus den Provinzen in der Slowakei* (Universitätsforschungen zur Prähistorischen Archäologie 222). Bonn: Habelt.

Joy, J., 2014. 'Fire Burn and Cauldron Bubble': Iron Age and Early Roman Cauldrons of Britain and Ireland. *Proceedings of the Prehistoric Society*, 80, 327–362.

Kapeller, A., 2003. La vaisselle en bronze d'Avenches / Aventicum. *ProAventico*, 45, 83–147.

Karasová, Z., 1998. *Die römischen Bronzegefässe in Böhmen* (Fontes Archaeologici Pragenses 22). Pragae: Museum nationale Pragae.

Kellner, H.-J. – Zemmer-Plank, L. – Kellner, E., 1984. Ein römischer Münzschatz von Navis-Mühlen im Wipptal. *Veröffentlichungen des Tiroler Landesmuseums Ferdinandeum*, 64, 57–236.

Kropotkin, V.V. 1970. *Rimskie importnye izdeliya v Vostochnoi Evrope (II v. do n.e. – V v. n.e.)* (Svod arkheologicheskikh istochnikov D1-27). Moscow: Nauka.

Künzl, S., 2000. Der zerbrochene Krug: Reparaturen an römischen Metallgefäßen. *Kölner Jahrbuch*, 33, 607–614.

Kunow, J., 1983. *Der römische Import in der Germania libera bis zu den Markomannenkriegen. Studien zu Bronze- und Glasgefäßen* (Göttinger Schriften zur Vor- und Frühgeschichte, Band 21). Neumünster: Karl Wachholtz Verlag.

Lie, H. – Bewer, F., 2014. Ex Aere Factum: Technical Notes on Ancient Bronzes. In: S. Ebbinghaus, ed., *Ancient Bronzes through a Modern Lens: Introductory Essays on the Study of Ancient Mediterranean and Near Eastern Bronzes*. Cambridge, MA: Harvard Art Museums, 38–63.

Luik, M., 2016. Buntmetallgefäße der mittleren Kaiserzeit zwischen Rhein und Pyrenäen. Ein Forschungsüberblick. In: *H.-U. Voß – N. Müller-Schneeßel 2016*, 215–228.

Lund Hansen, U. 2016: Kasserollen und Kelle- / Sieb-Garnituren als Indikatoren für Einsicht in den Übergang von der Älteren zur Jüngeren Römischen Kaiserzeit im Barbaricum. In: *H.-U. Voß – N. Müller-Schneeßel 2016*, 229–244.

Maksimov, E.K., 1957. Sarmatskoe pogrebenie iz kurgana u s. Bol'shaya Dmitrievka Saratovskoi oblasti. *SovArch*, 4, 157–161.

Medvedev, A.P., 1996. Mednye kovanye kotly iz Averinskogo kurgana na Srednem Donu. In: B.A. Raev, ed., *Antichnaya tsivilizatsiya i varvarskii mir (tezisy dokladov V arkheologicheskogo seminara)*. Novocherkassk: Museum of History of Don Cossacks, 23–25.

Medvedev, A.P., 1999. *Rannii zheleznyi vek lesostepnogo Podon'ya. Arkheologiya i etnokul'turnaya istoriya I tysyacheletiya do n.e.* Moscow: Nauka.

Miglbauer, R.M., 2012. Römische Tischsitten am Beispiel von Bronzegefäßen aus Ovilava/Wels. *Jahrbuch des Oberösterreichischen Musealvereines*, 157, 71–81.

Minasyan, R.S., 1986. Lit'e bronzovykh kotlov u narodov stepei Evrazii (VII v. do n.e. – V v. n.e.). *Arkheologicheskii sbornik Gosudarstvennogo Ermitazha*, 27, 61–78.

Mordvintseva, V.I. – Sergatskov, I.V., 1995: Bogatoe sarmatskoe pogrebenie u stantsii Berdiya. *RossArch*, 4, 114–124.

Mordvintseva, V.I. – Shinkar', O.A., 1999: Sarmatskie paradnye mechi iz fondov Volgogradskogo oblastnogo kraevedcheskogo muzeya. *Nizhnevolzhskii arkheologicheskii vestnik*, 2, 138–149.

Moshkova, M.G., 1982. Pozdnesarmatskie pogrebeniya Lebedevskogo mogil'nika v Zapadnom Kazakhstane. *KraSoob*, 170, 80–87.

Moshkova, M.G., 2009. Zhenskoe pogrebenie v kurgane2 iz Lebedevskogo mogil'nogo kompleksa (raskopki G.I. Bagrikova). In: A.G. Furas'ev, ed., *Gunny, goty i sarmaty mezhdu Volgoi i Dunaem*. St. Petersburg: Faculty of Philology and Arts, St. Petersburg State University, 99–113.

Mustață, S., 2017. *The Roman Metal Vessels from Dacia Porolissensis* (Patrimonium Archaeologicum Transylvanicum, 12). Cluj-Napoca: Mega Publ. House.

Noll, R., 1980. *Das Inventar des Dolichenusheiligtums von Mauer an der Url (Noricum)* (Der römische Limes in Österreich 30). Vienna: Österreichischen Akademie der Wissenschaften.

Otto, K.-H., 1948. Ein provinzialrömisches Bronzegeschirrdepot aus dem Elbtal bei Grieben, Kr. Stendal. In: K. Schwarz (Hrsg.), *Strena praehistorica. Festgabe 60. Geburtstag M. Jahn*. Halle: Niemeyer, 217–238.

Petrovszky, R., 1993. *Studien zu römischen Bronzegefäßen mit Meisterstempeln* (Kölner Studien zur Archäologie der Römischen Provinzen, 1). Buch am Erlbach: Verlag Marie Leidorf.

Petrsovszky, R., 2003. Die augusteische Kasserolle eines Mainzer Toreuten. Ein aktueller Fund aus Neuhofen, Kreis Ludwigshafen. *Archäologie in der Pfalz. Jahresbericht 2001*. Rahden: Verlag Marie Leidorf, 116–120.

Petrovszky, R., 2015. Der römische Hortfund von Lingenfeld (Lkr. Germersheim, Rheinland-Pfalz). In: *E. Deschler-Erb – P. Della Casa 2015*, 227–234.

Radnóti, A., 1938. *Die römischen Bronzegefässe von Pannonien* (Dissertationes Pannonicae, II/6).

Budapest: Institut für Münzkunde und Archäologie der P. Pázmány-Universität.

Raev, B.A., 1974. Bronzovyi taz iz 3-go Sokolovskogo kurgana. *SovArch*, 3, 181–189.

Raev, B.A., 1977. Vaisselle de bronze italique dans les tombes de la noblesse sarmate sur le Bas-Don. In: J.Ch. Balty – G. Faider-Feytmans – M.-E.Mariën, ed., *Actes des IIIes journées internationales consacrées à l'étude des bronzes romains* (Bulletin des Musées Royaux d'Art et d'Histoire 46). Bruxelles: Musées Royaux d'Art et d'Histoire, 139–149.

Raev, B.A., 1986. *Roman Imports in the Lower Don Basin* (BAR Intern. ser. 278). Oxford: British Archaeological Reports.

Roymans, N., 2004. *Ethnic Identity and Imperial Power. The Batavians in the Early Roman Empire*. Amsterdam: Amsterdam University Press.

Ruprechtsberger, E.M., 1985. Eine Bronzekanne aus Windischgarsten. *Jahrbuch des Oberösterreichischen Musealvereins Gesellschaft für Landeskunde*, 130, 61–70.

Saprykin, S.Yu., 2003. Greek Inscription on Bronze Cauldron from Sosnovka, Volgograd Region, Russia. In *Thracia XV. In honorem annorum LXX Alexandri Fol.* Sofia: In aedibus Academiae Litterarum Bulgaricae, 225–232.

Schelow, D.B., 1968: Der römische Import im Unterdon und Wolgagebiet in den ersten Jahrhunderten u. Z. In: J. Harmatta, ed., *Studien zur Geschichte und Philosophie des Altertums* (Kongress für klassische Philologie der Ungarischen Akademie der Wissenschaften, Budapest 1.–6. November 1965). Amsterdam: A.M. Hakkert, 238–246.

Sedlmayer, H. 1999: *Die römischen Bronzegefässe in Noricum* (Monographies Instrumentum, 10). Montagnac: Éditions Monique Mergoil.

Sergatskov, I.V. 2000. *Sarmatskie kurgany na Ilovle*. Volgograd: Volgograd State University Publ. House.

Shelov, D.B., 1965: Iltaliiskie i zapadnorimskie izdeliya v torgovle Tanaisa pervykh vekov n.e.. *Acta archaeologica Academiae scientiarum hungaricae*, XXV, 251–274.

Shilov, V.P., 1973. Metallicheskie sosudy iz kurgana u s. Bol'shaya Dmitrievka. *SovArch*, 4, 252–255.

Shilov, V.P., 1975. *Ocherki po istorii drevnikh plemen Nizhnego Povolzh'ya*. Leningrad: Nauka.

Simonenko, A.V., 2015. *Sarmatskie vsadniki Sedvernogo Prichernomor'ya*. 2nd ed. Kiev: Oleg Filyuk Publ.

Skripkin, A.S. – Shinkar', O.A., 2010: Zhutovskii kurgan no. 27 sarmatskogo vremeni v Volgo-Donskom mezhdurech'e. *RossArch*, 1, 125–138.

Skripkin, A.S., ed., 2013. *Arkheologicheskoe nasledie Volgogradskoi oblasti. K 100-letiyu Volgogradskogo oblastnogo kraevedcheskogo muzeya*. Volgograd: Izdatel'.

Stupperich, R., 1995a. Die Göldenitz-Gruppe. Figürlich verzierte Metallarbeiten des 3. Jhs. n. Chr. mit Weißmetallauflage. In: D. Rößler – V. Stürmer, ed., *Modus in rebus. Gedenkschrift für Wolfgang Schindler*. Berlin: Gebr. Mann, 144–152.

Stupperich, R. 1995b. Bemerkungen zum römischen Import im sogenannten Freien Germanien. In: G. Franzius, ed., *Aspekte römisch-germanischer Beziehungen in der Frühen Kaiserzeit* (Quellen und Schrifttum zur Kulturgeschichte des Wiehengebirgsraumes, B/1). Espelkamp: Verlag Marie Leidorf, 45–98.

Tassinari, S., 1993. *Il vasellame bronzeo di Pompei*. Rome: „L'Erma" di Bretschneider.

Treister, M.Yu., 2006. Falary iz stanitsy Uspenskoi (k voprosu o vremeni poyavleniya bol'shikh naplechnykh falarov ellenisticheskogo vremeni). *Drevnosti Bospora*, 10, 429–462.

Treister, M.Yu., 2009. Silver phialai from the Prokhorovka Burial-Mound No. 1. *Ancient Civilizations from Scythia to Siberia*, 15, 95–135.

Treister, M.Yu., 2013a. Edelmetallgefäße des achämenidischen Kreises aus dem südlichen Uralvorland. In: *M. Treister – L. Yablonsky 2013*, 69–108.

Treister, M.Yu., 2013b. Vorderasiatische Bronzegefäße aus dem südlichen Uralvorland. In: *M. Treister – L. Yablonsky 2013*, 111–118.

Treister, M.Yu., 2013c. Nomaden an der Schnittstelle von transeurasischen Karawanenrouten (Importobjekte aus den spätsarmatischen Gräbern von Lebedevka). In: T. Stöllner – Z. Samašev, eds. *Unbekanntes Kasachstan: Archäologie im Herzen Asiens*. Bochum: Deutsches Bergbau-Museum, 733–748.

Treister, M.Yu., 2015. Römische Bronzegefässe aus einem spätsarmatischen Grab (3. Jh. n. Chr.) der Kurgan-Nekropole Lebedevka in Westkasachstan. In: *E. Deschler-Erb – P. Della Casa 2015*, 241–246.

Treister, M.Yu., 2016. Kochevniki na perekrestke trans-evraziiskikh karavannykh putei (zapadnye importy v sarmatskom pogrebenii kurgana № 21 mogil'nika Magnitnyi). In: L.T. Yablonsky – L.A. Kraeva, ed., *Konstantin Fedorovich Smirnov i sovremennye problemy sarmatskoi arkheologii. Materialy IX mezhdunarodnoi nauchnoi konferentsii „Problemy sarmatskoi arkheologii i istorii", posvyashchennoi 100-letiyu so dnya rozhdeniya Konstantina Fedorovicha Smirnova*. Orenburg: OGPU Publ. House, 279–286.

Treister, M.Yu., 2018. Blechkanne. Mednye kovanye kuvshiny pervykh vekov n.e. v Severnom

Priechernomor'e i Sarmatii. *Drevnosti Bospora*, 22, 216–238.

Treister, M.Yu. 2019. Second-Hand for the Barbarians? Greek and Roman Metalware with Signs of Repair from the Nomadic burials of Scythia and Sarmatia. In: V. Cojocaru – L. Ruscu – T. Castelli – A.-I. Pázsint, ed., *Advances in Ancient Black Sea Studies: Historiography, Archaeology and Religion* (Pontica et Mediterranea VIII). Cluj-Napoca: Mega Publ. House, 313–345.

Tsutskin, E.V. 1974. Bronzovyi kotel s drevnegrecheskoi nadpis'yu. *Istoriko-kraevedcheskie zapiski*, 2. Volgograd, 138–142.

Vinogradov, Ju.G., 1997. *Pontische Studien*. Mainz: von Zabern.

Wegewitz, W., 1986. Bestattungen in importiertem Bronzegeschirr in den Urnenfriedhöfen der jüngeren vorrömischen Eisen- und der älteren römischen Kaiserzeit im Gebiet beiderseits der Niederelbe. *Hammaburg* N. F., 7 (1984–1985), 69–132.

Weinrich-Kemkes, S., 1993. Zwei Metalldepots aus dem römischen Vicus von Walldürn, Neckar-Odenwald-Kreis. *Fundberichte aus Baden-Württemberg*, 18, 253–323.

Recycling Economy in the Production of Roman Bronze Statues from the Limes Region. Results of the Research Project „Roman Bronze Statues from the UNESCO World Heritage Limes"

Frank Willer, Roland Schwab, Manuela Mirschenz

LVR-LandesMuseum Bonn

Curt-Engelhorn-Zentrum Archäometrie Mannheim

University of Bonn

frank.willer@lvr.de

Abstract: The question of recycled material in Roman bronze statues north of the Alps can be documented on the basis of production and material analyses. According to the zinc content, about a quarter of all analyzed fragments contained additions of brass scrap. One fifth of the samples from non-gilded statues contained significant traces of gold resulting from melted gilded statues. Identical alloys of statue-bronze and repair pieces and plates on the same fragment indicate the use of materials belonging to the same workshop, in which even old statue parts or faulty castings were recycled. The economic handling of metals is evident in many ways. Reversible assembly devices on imperial portraits where, if required, only the head had to be replaced, suggest the reuse of the statues.

Keywords: Recycling; Statue; Roman; X-ray Fluorescence Analysis

Project overview

The four-year research project "Roman Bronze Statues from the UNESCO World Heritage Limes" started in summer 2010 in order to record fragments of bronze statues from the northern Roman provinces *Germania Inferior*, *Gallia Belgica*, *Germania Superior* and *Raetia*. The main objective was to investigate the statues in an interdisciplinary way. Due to the ever-expanding number of statue fragments, our team of experts was not able to complete the last research work on production and archaeometric evaluation until 2017. The project was based on the cooperation between the Archäologisches Landesmuseum Baden-Württemberg, the Institute for Archaeological Sciences (Department II) at the Goethe University Frankfurt am Main and the LVR-LandesMuseum Bonn (LVR-LMB) and was financed by the Volkswagen Foundation, Germany, within the initiative "Research in museums" (Wessler 2011). Two dissertation projects at the Goethe University Frankfurt/Main focused on the archaeological analysis of installation sites and destruction contexts. A term paper in the field of conservation on a deposition of statue fragments in Groß-Gerau improved the understanding of repair techniques, gilding and the reuse of statue parts in Roman antiquity. Subsequently, a diploma thesis at the Academy of Fine Arts in Stuttgart in the field of conservation provided new insights into the gilding techniques observed on the statues (Bott 2011).

Since 2010, a parallel branch of research has also been devoted to Roman statue casting and the specific working methods in the Limes area. It is based on a combination of science, restoration and numerous experimental-archaeological tests. All investigations were carried out at the LVR-LandesMuseum Bonn in cooperation with the Curt-Engelhorn-Zentrum Archäometrie gGmbH in Mannheim and many other research institutions.[1] During the project, internal workshops took place in Bonn, Rastatt and Aalen, as well as a public symposium in Nijmegen. In addition, numerous research results were introduced at several meetings and conferences (Willer 2012, 10–17; Willer – Mirschenz 2015, 267–273; Willer et al. 2015, 239–245). In 2014, the team of archaeological and archaeometrical scientists presented characteristic bronze fragments and intermediate results of the project as part of the special exhibition "Gebrochener Glanz – Römische Großbronzen am UNESCO-Weltkulturerbe Limes" and in a catalogue of the same name to the public (Gebrochener Glanz 2014). The exhibition took place at

---

[1] The following institutions were involved: Bundesanstalt für Materialforschung und -prüfung (BAM), Gießerei-Institut der RWTH Aachen, Deutsches Bergbau Museum Bochum (DBM), Bronzegießerei Friedemann Sander in Bonn, Wieland-Werke AG in Ulm, Römisch-Germanishe Kommission Frankfurt am Main (RGK), Archäologosche Staatssammlung München, Landesmuseum Baden-Württemberg, Staatliche Akademie der Künste in Stuttgart, the Museum Het Valkhof in Nijmegen (NL), the Instituut Collectie Nederland in Amsterdam (NL) and the Universities of Berlin (FU), Bonn, Cologne, Freiburg, Eichstätt, Leiden and Nijmegen.

the LVR-LandesMuseum Bonn, the Limesmuseum Aalen and the Museum Het Valkhof in Nijmegen. Above all, it focused upon showing the results of the investigations of Roman production techniques, which were proven by experimental test series, analytical methods and reconstructions for the first time. Summaries of the results were published in several collected editions and journals (Kemkes 2015; Willer et al. 2016; Dövener et al. 2018).

Destroyed statues, their contexts and literature

In military camps and civil settlements of the Limes region, the Romans erected portraits and statues of the emperors and their families in large numbers. Moreover, in ritual contexts there must have been a great number of images of gods in the form of bronze statues. Many of these statues were likely destroyed during the crisis in the middle of the 3rd century AD or by *Damnatio memoriae* when an emperor had fallen out of favor. Most of the precious bronze was recycled afterwards (Mirschenz 2014; Willer 2014). Owing to fortunate circumstances, some of these statue fragments have been spared from remelting. Many of the larger parts of the statues, e.g. from the Limes fortress in Aalen, the legion camp in Bonn, Kalkar or Neuenstadt am Kocher, had already been smashed to crucible size (Fig. 20.1). Today, they allow an insight into the production technique and appearance of such life-size and larger-than-life bronze sculptures, even though the majority of smashed statues is often difficult to determine and to classify in detail. Nevertheless, fragments from bronze statues are important archaeological sources for the reconstruction of the imperial representation in the Limes fortresses and thus for the importance of the emperor's portrait within the Roman army. The same importance applies to bronze images of gods found in civilian contexts. It is remarkable that these findings were never systematically compiled in more than 150 years of intensive research on the Limes. Before this project was undertaken, most of them were stored as "forgotten old stock" in the depots of museums and other collections. Only a few fragments had been published since the end of the 19th century (Sarwey et al. 1892). They were briefly reviewed in the works of Gustav Gamer (1969) and Oliver Stoll (1992). Before the start of this research project, only a few well-preserved items like a horse head from Augsburg (Bakker 1985, 104–105; Bergemann 1990, 24. 29. 57 ff), the portrait of Gordian III from Niederbieber (Lahusen – Formigli 2001), and the so called "Traianus" from the Rhine near Xanten (Schalles 2010, 663–673) had been discussed in print. Comprehensive publications dealt with scrap fragments from *Colonia Augusta Raurica* in Switzerland (Janietz Schwarz et al.1996; Janietz 2000) and with the well-preserved statue of a young servant found near of Xanten (Schalles – Peltz 2012, 37–62).

Analytic methods, goals and results

In order to learn more about the production of the numerous statue fragments examined here for the first time, as well as about their appearance and history, all original findings were inspected and selected in an initial pre-evaluation, which was followed by non-destructive material testing procedures and archaeometric analysis. More than 1,000 fragments have been examined by radiography, which allows viewing through the material. Thus, it was possible to identify fragments that were obtained from one coherent context, but had originated from several statues broken into small pieces for further processing. In addition, they showed different types of casting defects, repairs, and soldering or welding seams that are not always macroscopically visible. To identify such working traces, measurements by means of the "Eddy-Current"-method" were carried out on more than 400 statue fragments to examine the conductivity of the metal alloy. Casting defects, welding seams, soldering or repairs have a considerable influence on the conductivity and thus make it measurable. In addition, the measurements provided initial indications of the qualitative composition of the metal alloy.

In order to determine the chemical composition of a bronze alloy by energy dispersive X-ray fluorescence analysis (see ED-XRF analyses below), small samples

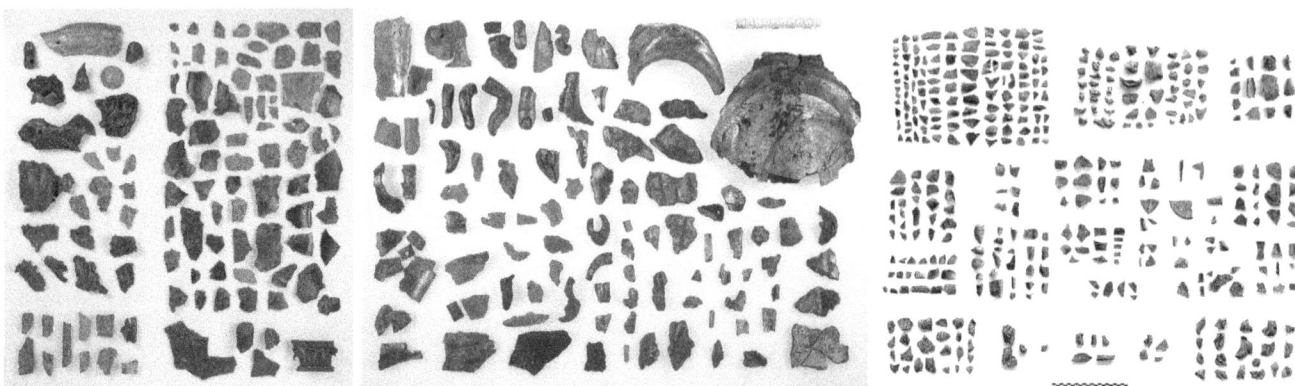

Figure 20.1. Statues smashed into small pieces. Left: Fragments from the legionary camp in Bonn come from partly larger-than-life sculptures. Middle: Mostly gilded parts of a female statue of gods originate from Kalkar, Alt Kalkar. Right: Fragments from Neuenstadt at the Kocher with hints to an armoured statue. Photo: Jürgen Vogel, LVR-LandesMuseum Bonn.

were taken from 554 selected statue fragments, using a very fine drill-bit. In addition, 120 of the 554 samples were examined by lead isotope analysis after successful X-ray fluorescence analysis. We used that method in order to identify the provenance of intentionally added lead. To study the microstructure and to determine surface finishing techniques such as gold plating or tin enrichment, we extracted small sections from a few selected fragments. These sections were examined by means of light microscope (LM) and scanning electron microscope (SEM) with attached energy dispersive X-ray spectrometer (EDX). Measurements of microhardness were carried out by the "Vickers test" method with a test force of 100 p (HV 0.1). In addition, we performed non-destructive X-ray fluorescence analyses on fragments from which samples could not be taken.

Computed tomography provided a three-dimensional view of the interior of the statues. Thus we were able to determine that the horses' heads from Augsburg (Fig. 20.3) and Waldgirmes were produced in the same way, despite the differences in chronological and geographical context. Technical similarity was indicated by identical assembly seams of the wax models' construction. Casting defects which are not visible from the outside, as well as repairs, soldering, welding and hidden traces of disassembly or recycling can be determined by this reliable method of analysis. Examinations by CT were applied to the bronze head of the emperor Gordian III found in Niederbieber (Fig. 20.2), the bronze head of the goddess Rosmerta of Mainz and the monumental bronze hand from Bregenz, for example. Three-dimensional documentation of surfaces by digital microscopy allowed us to determine tool traces, surface refinements, repairs or traces of destruction.

We found remains of the clay core on 15 statue fragments. The composition of the core material of 15 samples was determined by thin-section analysis. No standardized recipes were recognizable in the composition of core material, and thus it appears that the production of the statues was decentralized, with use of clay and tempering material available from the surrounding areas.

Ancient manufacturing processes were reconstructed in numerous experimental test series. For example, the portrait head of Gordian III from Niederbieber was examined by virtual casting simulation. During the entire research project, more than 5500 statue fragments from 134 locations were identified and scientifically recorded in an online database (www.grossbronzenamlimes.de).

About metal analyses and material properties

As mentioned above, the archaeometric investigations are based on different methods. Samples (50–100 mg) were usually taken with 0.8–1.0 mm fine drill-bits from the

Figure 20.2. Middle: Original portrait head of the Roman emperor Gordian III from Niederbieber. Left: X-ray with visible defects. Right: Computer tomography with insight into the interior without modern fillings. Photo: Christoph Duntze LVR-LandesMuseum Bonn.

fractured edges of the fragments which had previously been selectively freed from corrosion. Stationary X-ray fluorescence analysis (ED-RFA), was one of the essential methods of the research project. About ten percent of all recorded fragments were examined using this method, by which the element-composition of the alloys could be determined with high accuracy (Willer et al. 2016, see analysis table page 180–207). Besides the main elements of the alloys, minor elements could also be detected by this method, evidence that is of special interest in determining whether the statues contained recycled metal. The results of the analysis showed that more than the half of all samples contained relatively high lead (Pb) concentrations of 15–25%. About 67% of all samples had a tin content (Sn) of 6–9% (Diagram 20.1). Comparing the alloys from civil and military contexts, we observed no significant differences in the proportions of the main alloy constituents of copper, tin and lead. In civil contexts, the average copper content was 79.3%, tin 6.1% and lead 13.2%. In military contexts, the average copper content was 76%, tin 6.4% and lead 16.7%. Despite these high lead contents, which suggested savings in expensive tin, the tin contents are comparatively high in contrast to Roman statues from Italy. Therefore, we can see that not only scrap metal was recycled for statue casting, but also fresh tin must have been added. This observation coincides with the results previously obtained on the fragments with respect to their casting technique. Even from today's perspective, some statues, such as the horse head from Augsburg, were quite thin-walled castings (2–4 mm), and thus they were manufactured very economically (Fig. 20.3). If the bronze casters had used less suitable scrap, the risk of casting error would have increased. In order to decode the properties and qualities of the alloy types, modern material testing procedures were performed on re-cast bronzes under laboratory conditions. In addition, essential findings were obtained by means of experimental reproductions carried out under almost real conditions. These included observations concerning the casting conductibility of the liquid bronze, the solidification of the melt as well as workability in the cold state. It is important to note that the casting properties of modern bronze differ significantly from those of ancient

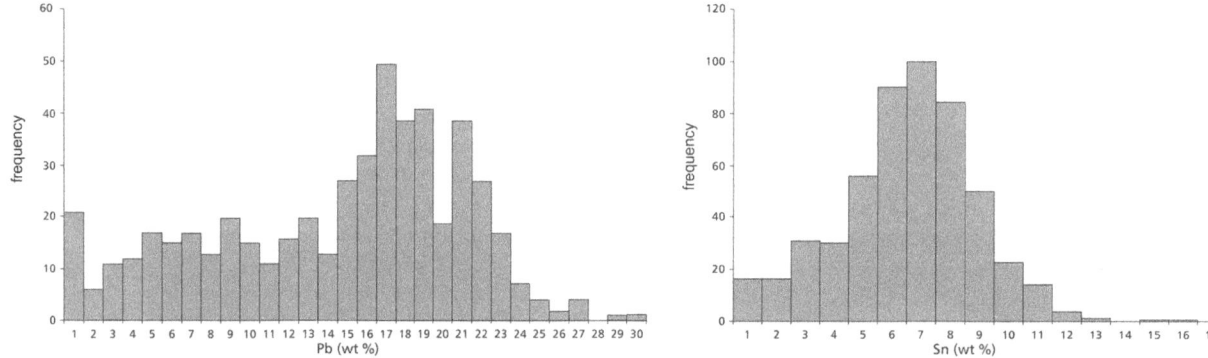

Diagram 20.1. Lead and tin contents of the analyzed samples. Credit: Roland Schwab CEZA Mannheim.

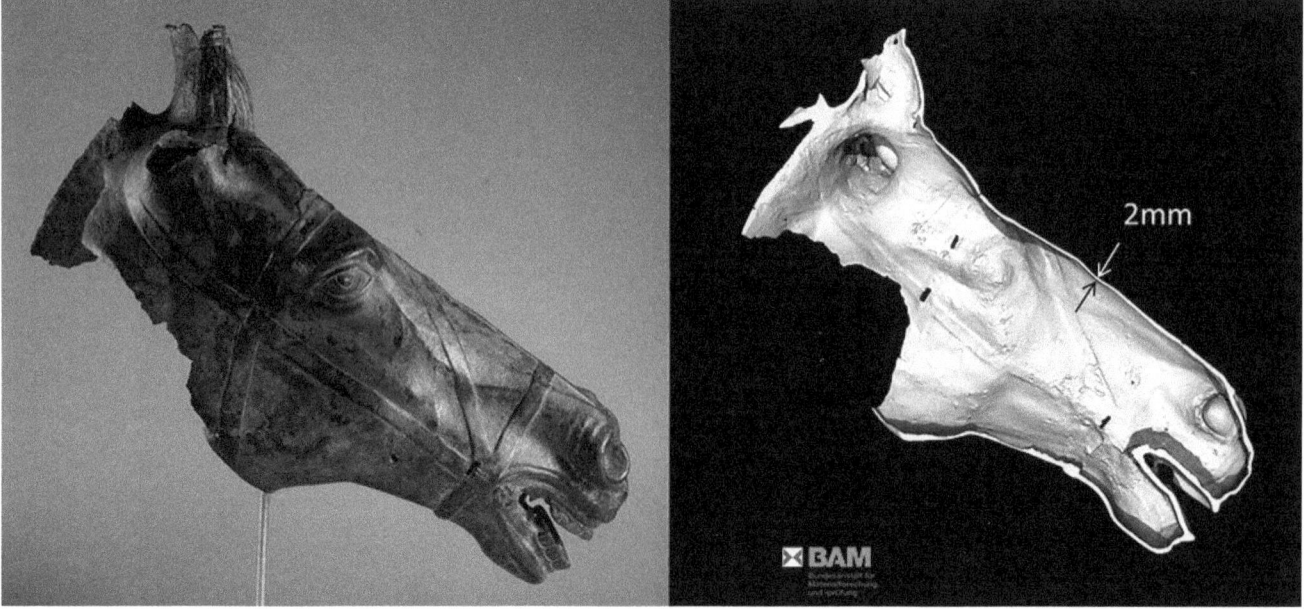

Figure 20.3. The horse's head from Augsburg is cast rather thin-walled. Measurements in the Ct profile show the sometimes very small material thicknesses in some areas. Photo: Fig. 20.3: Theo Gerhards und Frank Willer, LVR-LandesMuseum Bonn.

bronze. This can be traced back to modern ingredients such as phosphorus copper which was not available in ancient times (Ellerbrok 2014, 199). Despite the clear difference of casting conductibility compared to modern bronzes, the bronze of the Limes statues had quite good casting properties. It was also suitable for use under adverse conditions and enabled very thin-walled castings. Lead additives improve the casting properties of bronze, as the lead noticeably reduces the viscosity of the melt and increases the molds' filling capacity. In addition, the high lead content facilitates mechanical post-treatment, e.g. when casting channels (gate-systems) have to be removed or casting defects have to be repaired. However, the lead content affects the finishing techniques such as gilding. Fire- or diffusion-gilding of leaded bronze would form low melting surface (gold-lead), an unattractive gray layer (Anheuser 1999, 40–43; Willer et al. 2017, 88–89). Only a few statue fragments have been found to be fire- or diffusion-gilded. In contrast to fire-gilding or diffusion-gilding, where the bronze has to be heated for chemical bonding with the bronze, leaf-gilding is carried out in a cold state. For leaf-gilding, high lead contents do not play a role – as observed in many statues, to improve casting and processing properties. Consequently, the well-known leaf-gilding is the predominately observed gilding technology of the statues (Oddy et al. 1990, 103–124; Oddy 2000, 3–4). We have also found fire-gilded and additional leaf-gilded fragments of the Limes statues, unusually made of almost unalloyed copper with very low tin and lead contents. This high cupreous and reddish alloy is castable but presents a number of difficulties. It has a higher melting point than bronze alloys and tends to form shrinkage cavities, rough surfaces and even cracks due to the absorption of oxygen and hydrogen. Beyond that, it has a lower fluidity and thus less imaging accuracy than the standard Limes bronze alloys.

Minor elements in the alloy and their reference to recycling

Some minor elements like zinc or gold can be used as indicators for recycling, since these metals are not normal components of ancient bronze alloys and therefore they reveal the addition of scrap metal. Zinc came from brass objects, the gold probably from recycled gilded statue parts that were added to the crucible. About a quarter of all examined statue fragments show traces of zinc (Diagram 20.2). Gold can be found in nearly 20 percent of all samples. According to chronological criteria, brass objects (copper-zinc) seem to have been increasingly used as a supplement to statue-casting in the 2nd century AD. The dating results from an evaluation of the find contexts. This is not surprising, since brass alloys were the most commonly used copper alloy in the Roman Empire (Brüggler et al. 2012, 140). Presumably, at this time of greatest prosperity numerous statues of the first generation ended up in the crucible along with scrap metal. With regard to the use of zinc-containing material, there is no difference between military and civilian contexts. The recycling of brass objects was then equally pronounced – a fact that ultimately coincides with the results from northern England where the use of brass quantitatively does not differ significantly between civilian and military contexts (Dungworth 1997, 908). Pliny tells us about the use of recycled scrap to cast bronze statues:

"The metal is first fused and one third as much scrap bronze from old vessels that have been bought, is added... twelve and a half pounds of tin-lead alloy are added to every hundred pounds of molten metal" (Pliny NH 34.97, translation Caley 1970, 47).

However, the question is whether this recipe was also generally used for the technically difficult statuary casting. Counter-examples for the general application of this formula are gilded and ungilded statue parts from Bonn, Hambach, Kalkar, Trier and St. Mard, which were cast with very low tin and lead contents (1–2%) from almost unalloyed copper. This alloy is similar to that of the many rivet pins used to attach repair plates to the statues. Further examples of statues with a slightly higher lead content (2–6%) can be found in a group of mostly gilded statues from Bregenz, Groß-Gerau, Mainz, Mittelstrimmig, Nijmegen-Hessenberg, Trier as well as a fire-gilded fragment in Bonn from an unknown location. The small amount of tin and lead in the gilded statues may have technical reasons related to the gilding. The composition of these mostly gold-leaf-gilded statues with low tin and low lead content shows that Pliny's recipe specifications were not necessarily applied everywhere. If larger amounts of scrap are added when casting statues, this can have a very strong influence on the casting properties leading to casting defects. It is remarkable that Pliny mentions in his recipe that metal vessels (*ollaria*) are particularly suitable as a supplement to the casting:

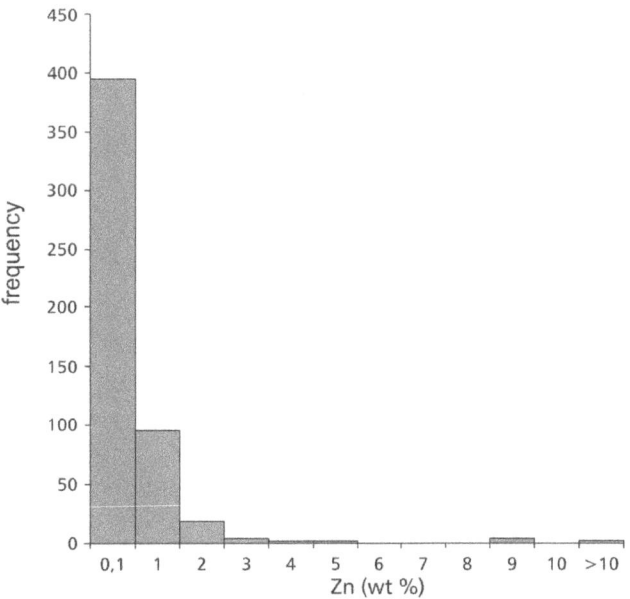

Diagram 20.2 The zinc diagram shows the frequency of the measured zinc content (Zn) in the Limes statues, which results from the additions of brass scrap. Credit: Roland Schwab CEZA Mannheim.

From the second half of the 2nd century onwards, metal containers often consisted of quite noble brass alloys (copper-zinc or copper-zinc-tin alloys). In contrast, additions of scrap metal, where the composition of the metal was unclear, were not useful for the manufacture of metal containers: by forging or pressing, the metal was subjected to enormous mechanical stress. Impurities or ungraded metal components which would have been added by the scrap would have worsened these required properties. In this respect, additions in the form of scrap from old metal containers are also suitable for the casting of statues, since the quality of the alloy of these objects was already recognizable by the production technique alone. Today we know that the zinc content of this scrap material has a positive influence on the casting of statues. It has to be considered that no modern smelter-reducing additives were available in antiquity. Similar to modern additives, brass can improve the melting and casting properties of bronze alloys. This is caused in particular by the zinc content. The copper content has no effect; it only becomes part of the new alloy. Measurements revealed that the bronze of the Limes statues is liquid at about 1100°C. Due to the relatively low boiling point of the zinc content (907°C), the zinc begins to evaporate and oxidize gradually in the melt. The zinc vapour and zinc oxide have a deoxidizing effect on the melt, which in turn reduces the negative loss of tin and copper. In addition, the zinc decreases the hydrogen solubility of the liquid copper content, minimizing the formation of gas bubbles and thus reducing casting defects (Ellerbrok 2014, 199). If the founders make the best use of this positive effect of burning off the zinc during melting and casting, only small amounts of the zinc will remain in the melt.

With the exception of the Raetian site of Künzing, brass was found as an aggregate for statuary casting mainly in the northern area of investigation (Willer et al. 2016, 83). Many of the fragments examined were gold-plated. This raises the question of their reuse. As we could see from a number of fragments from Groß-Gerau, an attempt had been made to scrape off the precious gilding, but without success (Fig. 20.4). This attempt would have been profitable, as calculations showed that about 90–120 g of gold were needed to gild a life-size statue, as Roman gold leaf is about four times as thick as modern gold leaf. In the 2nd century, this quantity corresponded to 12–17 Roman aurei (gold coins). Like zinc, gold is not an alloying additive that is deliberately added to the molten metal and no accompanying element of copper. Therefore, the analyzed gold contents in the Limes bronzes result from the addition of reused gilded bronzes. Based on reference measurements, we were able to prove that about every fifth bronze contained recycled, formerly gilded statues. The majority of gilded fragments comes from civilian contexts. Here, 45% of the statue parts were gilded, as opposed to only 5% in the military sector. In contrast, the analyses of the samples clearly show that more than fifty percent of the fragments from civilian contexts contain gold, whereas in the military context this is the case for one third of the statues. Therefore we can assume that scrap from destroyed gilded statues, probably from civilian contexts, was traded and recycled for casting new statues in military contexts. Gold in the alloy was found in both gilded and non-gilded statues.

Another indicator of recycled material in statuary bronze may be traces of antimony (Sb) and arsenic (As). If the contents of these elements are increased, this may indicate the usage of complex sulphide minerals, like fahlores. Fahlores were available north of the Alps as one main source of raw materials for copper during prehistory. High antimony contents in bronzes are quite typical for

Figure 20.4. The back fragment of a diffusion-gilded male statue, where an attempt was made to scrape off the valuable gold after destruction. Photo: Frank Willer, LVR-LandesMuseum Bonn.

the late Iron Age objects from southern Germany, but also in France (Schwab 2014). Some samples, such as the horse's head from Waldgirmes, show remarkably high percentages (2%) of antimony. Their silver (Ag) content is also increased, while the measurements of arsenic were affected by the high lead contents. High antimony-bearing copper had usually not been used for Roman objects and the few known Roman copper mines in the investigated area were not used for metal mining, but for pigment extraction. Other presumed Roman mining activities have remained without evidence so far. In the Limes region, fahlore copper has only appeared in early datable finds such as Waldgirmes, Tawern-Metzenberg and a fragment in Aalen. We can assume that in the early phase of occupation around the turn of the century up to the 1st century A.D. either locally existing old material such as the "Potin coins", which had become invalid at this time, was used as an additive for the production of statues. Some younger fragments, such as parts of an equestrian statue from Isny, still show slightly elevated concentrations of minor elements, which might have different reasons.

Recycling traces on the statues themselves

Numerous statue fragments showed macroscopically visible signs of recycling. In addition to traces of reused metals in the alloys, there were also indications on the statues themselves. Some statues had to be repaired immediately after casting owing to casting defects. The stability of these areas was so endangered that the craftsmen had to reinforce these areas on the back with repair plates and copper rivets. Apparently, old broken statue parts were used as well. Repairs like a gilded garment fragment from Groß-Gerau and a gilded fragment of a relief from Mittelstrimmig, for example, consist of almost the same alloy as the rest of bronze statue (Fig. 20.5). Since the recipe is almost identical, it could be parts of destroyed or disused statues, which were also cast in this workshop. A second explanation would be that they were faulty castings kept in stock for the repair of statues. Another example of this technique is a gilded garment fragment from Kalkar. A relief fragment from Maastricht shows quite unusual traces of recycling. Here, the leg of a large statuette was attached to the assembly on the back-bronze plate with a rectangular metal dowel. At

Figure 20.5. Gilded statue parts from Mittelstrimmig (above) and from Groß-Gerau (below) also show repairs with fragments of old statues at the backs (right). These were fixed with rivet pins made of copper (usual technique). The alloys of the repair plates correspond to those of the cast statue. Photo: Frank Willer, LVR-LandesMuseum Bonn.

Figure 20.6. Recycling of statues in a Roman counterfeit workshop in Hambach-Niederzier. Parts of statues melt remains as well as counterfeit coins and their blanks consist of the same alloy. They prove the production of counterfeit money from bronze statues. Photo: Jürgen Vogel, LVR-LandesMuseum Bonn.

the foot of the figure it had been fixed with lead-tin solder. On the one side, the dowel showed elaborate floral inlays of silver and copper, as known from Roman furniture fittings such as clines.

Investigations of an illegal Roman workshop in Hambach revealed that parts of statues were used in order to produce counterfeit money (Fig. 20.6). In addition to statue parts, numerous coins and blanks were recovered which were used for coin production. It seems that for the sake of simplicity the fingers of a statue were cut into slices, from which coins were subsequently minted. Other parts of the statues first had to be melted down and poured into bars from which the coins were then minted. At some sites, such as Groß-Gerau, Kempten, Hambach-Niederzier or Bonn, we can even prove a further development of recycling: Here, owing to lack of materials, Roman statues were melted down. The remnants of melting and the sizes of the crucibles indicate the casting of smaller objects for daily use. Since bronze has been recycled over the centuries, it can be assumed that modern copper alloys still contain parts of Roman statues. The portrait head of Gordian III (Fig. 20.2) found in Niederbieber and the portrait of Severus Alexander found in Carnuntum both show hints for the reuse of statue parts. Both heads were not welded or annually soldered to the statue as usual. Rather, both bronzes feature an installation technique using rivet pins or lead soldering. This allowed an easy exchange of the portraits, while preserving the body of the statue.

Summary

An essential aspect of the research project was to prove recycling of Roman bronze statues as well as the use of scrap metal for the production of new statues. Parts of old statues were melted down to cast or to repair newly cast statues or, as the Hambach find shows, broken into pieces to convert them into counterfeit coins. Minor elements like zinc or gold in the alloys indicate the remelting of brass objects (Zn) or once-gold-plated statues (Au). Both recycling processes can be observed in civilian and military contexts. An increased antimony (Sb) content may indicate the recycling of pre-Roman artefacts made of copper from fahlore sources north of the Alps.

Bibliography

Anheuser, K., 1999. Im Feuer vergoldet, Geschichte und Technik der Feuervergoldung und der Amalgamversilberung, *AdR-Schriftenreihe zur Restaurierung und Grabungstechnik 4* (Stuttgart 1999).

Bakker, L., 1985. Reste monumentaler Kaiserstatuen und der Pferdekopf aus der Wertach. In: *Die Römer in Schwaben. Arbeitshefte des Bayerischen Landesamtes für Denkmalpflege 27* (München 1985) 104–105.

Bergemann, J., 1990. Römische Reiterstatuen. Ehrendenkmäler im öffentlichen Bereich. *Beiträge zur Erschließung hellenistischer und kaiserzeitlicher Skulptur und Architektur 11* (Mainz 1990).

Bott, K., 2011. *Vergoldungstechniken an römischen Großbronzen des UNESCO-Welterbe Limes. Untersuchungen zur Diffusionsvergoldung an Bronzestatuen.* Diplomarbeit. Staatliche Akademie der Bildenden Künste Stuttgart, Konservierung und Restaurierung von archäologischen, ethnologischen und kunsthandwerklichen Objekten (Stuttgart 2011).

Brüggler, M. – Dirsch, Ch. – Drechsler, M. – Schwab, R. – Willer, F., 2012. Ein römischer Schienenarmschutz aus dem Auxiliarlager Till-Steincheshof. *Bonner Jahrb. 212*, 2012, 121–152.

Caley, E.R., 1970. Chemical composition of Greek and Roman statuary bronzes. In: S. Doeringer, D.G. Mitten – A. Steinberg (eds.), *Art and technology. A symposium on classical bronze* (Cambridge 1970) 37–49.

Dungworth, D., 1997. Roman copper alloys. Analysis of artefacts from Northern Britain. *Journal Arch. Science. 24*, 1997, 901–910.

Dövener, F. – Schwab R. – Willer, F., 2018. Kleine Zeugnisse einstiger Größe. Vier Bronzestatuen-Fragmente aus Luxemburg. In: *Archaeologica Luxemburgensis 4. Bulletin du Centre National de Recherche Archéologique 2017/18*, 2018, 141–161.

Ellerbrok 2014: R. Ellerbrok, Experimenteller Nachguss des Gordiankopfes in Blei-Zinn-Bronze. In: *Gebrochener Glanz*, 199–200.

Gamer, R. 1969. *Kaiserliche Bronzestatuen aus den Kastellen und Legionslagern an Rhein- und Donaugrenze des römischen Imperiums* (Gießen 1969).

Gazda, E.K. – Hanfmann, G.M.A. 1970. Ancient bronzes: decline, survival, revival. In: S. Doeringer – D.G. Mitten – A. Steinberg, ed., *Art and technology. A symposium on classical bronze* (Cambridge 1970), 245–270.

Gebrochener Glanz, 2014. S. Willer, ed., *Gebrochener Glanz. Römische Großbronzen am UNESCO-Welterbe Limes.* Exhib. Cat. (Mainz 2014).

Janietz Schwarz B. – Roullier D., 1996. Ein Depot zerschlagener Grossbronzen aus Augusta Raurica. Die Rekonstruktion der beiden Pferdestatuen und Untersuchungen zur Herstellungstechnik. *Forschungen in Augst 20* (Augst 1996).

Janietz, B., 2000. Ein Depot zerschlagener Grossbronzen aus Augusta Raurica. Die Rekonstruktion der Gewandfiguren. *Forschungen in Augst 30* (Augst 2000).

Kemkes, M., ed., 2015. Römische Großbronzen am UNESCO-Welterbe Limes, Abschlusskolloquium des Forschungsprojektes, Beiträge zum Welterbe Limes 9 (Darmstadt 2015).

Lahusen G. – Formigli E., 2001. *Römische Bildnisse aus Bronze. Kunst und Technik* (München 2001).

Mirschenz, M. 2014. Zwischen Ruhm und Recycling. In: *Gebrochener Glanz* 143–151.

Oddy, W.A. – Cowell, M.R. – Craddock, P.T. – Hook, D.R., 1990. The gilding of bronze. Sculpture in the classical world. In: M. True – J. Podany (eds.), *Small Bronze Sculpture from the Ancient World* (Malibu 1990) 103–124.

Oddy, W.A., 2000. A history of gilding with particular reference to statuary. In: T. Drayman-Weisser, ed., *Gilded metals: history, technology and conservation* (London 2000), 1–19.

Pliny NH: Pliny, Naturalis Historia.

Sarwey, O. – Hettner, F. – Fabricius, E., 1892. *Der Obergermanisch-Rätische Limes des Römerreiches 1*. Im Auftrage der Reichslimeskommission (Heidelberg 1892).

Schalles, H.J., 2010. Kaiserbild oder Privatporträt? Das römische Bronzebildnis in Nijmegen. *Kölner Jahrb. 43*, 2010, 663–673.

Schalles, H.J. – Pelz, U., 2011. Der Xantener Knabe. Technologie, Ikonographie, Funktion und Datierung. *Xantener Ber. 22* (Darmstadt/ Mainz 2011) 37–62.

Schwab, R., 2014. Eisenzeitliche Kupferlegierungen und Kupferverarbeitung zwischen Alpen und Eifel, in S. Hornung, ed., *Produktion – Distribution – Ökonomie. Siedlungs- und Wirtschaftsmuster der Latènezeit, Universitätsforschungen zur prähistorischen Archäologie 248* (Bonn 2014) 149–162.

Scott, D.A. – Podany, J. 1990. Ancient Copper Alloys: Some Metallurgical and Technological Studies of Greek and Roman Bronzes. In: M. True – J. Podany, ed., *Small Bronze Sculpture from the Ancient World* (Malibu 1990) 31–60.

Stoll, O., 1992. Die Skulpturenausstattung römischer Militäranlagen an Rhein und Donau. Der obergermanisch-rätische Limes. *Pharos 1* (St. Katharinen 1992).

Wessler, A., 2011. Interdisziplinäre Forschung an Museen. Wissenschaftsförderung der VolkswagenStiftung. *Museumskunde 76*, 1/2011, 32–37.

Willer, F., 2012. Small Fragments of Large Statues: The Limes Project. In: G. Eggert – B. Schmutzler, ed., *Bronze Conservation*, June 22th – 23rd 2012, [Stuttgart 2012] 15–17.

Willer, F., 2014. Recycling – ein alter Hut. In: *Gebrochener Glanz*, 210–211.

Willer, F. – Mirschenz, M., 2015. Archäometrische und herstellungstechnische Forschungen an „Limesbronzen". In: E. Deschler-Erb – Ph. Della Casa, ed., *New Research on Ancient Bronzes. Acta of the XVIIIth International Congress on Ancient Bronzes*. Zürich Studies in Archaeology Vol. 10 (Zürich 2015) 267–273.

Willer, F. – Schwab, R. – Bott, K., 2015. Large Roman Bronze statues from the UNESCO World Heritage Limes. In: A. Hauptmann – D. Modarressi-Tehrani, ed., *Archaeometallurgy in Europe III, Der Anschnitt Beih. 26* (Bochum 2015) 239–245.

Willer, F. – Schwab, R. – Mirschenz, M., 2016. Römische Bronzestatuen am Limes. Archäometrische Untersuchungen zur Herstellungstechnik. *Bonner Jahrb. 216*, 2016, 57–207.

Willer, F. – Schwab, R. – Mirschenz, M., 2017. *Ergebnisse der archäometrischen und herstellungstechnischen Forschungen an den „Limesbronzen" .Römische Großbronzen am UNESCO-Welterbe Limes. Beiträge zum Welterbe Limes 9.* (Darmstadt 2017) 79—105.

Part III

Representation

21

Tre bronzi greci da Porticello (Reggio Calabria)

Fabiano Fiorello Di Bella

University of Messina

fdibella@unime.it

Abstract: The Porticello wreck (Reggio Calabria – Italy), found in 1969, is an extraordinary source of knowledge of Classical Greek bronze sculpture. The junction operations and compositional analysis of the fragments lead to at least two statues: an elderly male with *himation* and a young naked man. No fragment of the wreckage belongs to the third sculpture, namely the head from Basel. This paper provides a study of the Porticello bronzes as a whole through iconography and style. Such sculptures raise questions about Greek Classical art: how it develops and communicates with the viewer.

Keywords: Greek Bronze Sculpture; Porticello Bronzes; Porticello Shipwreck; Classical Greece

Premessa

Il contributo propone l'aggiornamento stilistico-iconografico dei problemi relativi ai frammenti bronzei dal relitto di Porticello (Reggio Calabria). Le vicende del relitto sono ben note alla letteratura archeologica (bibliografia in Paoletti 1991–92, 136–138): esso è stato rinvenuto nel 1969, all'entrata settentrionale dello Stretto di Messina, in corrispondenza della località calabra da cui prende il nome. Le operazioni di scavo iniziarono l'anno successivo (Owen 1970; 1971) e sono raccolte, per quanto concerne gli aspetti scientifici e tecnici, nella monografia ufficiale della nave (Eiseman – Ridgway 1987, 3–9). Lo studio dell'intero carico, notevolmente composito e comprendente anche materiale ceramico, così come il tentativo di tratteggiare la rotta dell'imbarcazione, è già stato affrontato dallo scrivente in un'altra sede (Di Bella 2016).

La *ratio* che anima il presente lavoro è, piuttosto, quella di sottolineare l'autosufficienza dei bronzi nel formulare considerazioni di natura archeologica e storico-artistica, secondo lo spirito del Convegno Internazionale sui Bronzi Antichi, giunto alla XX edizione. Per tenere fede al proposito, gli sforzi interpretativi esuleranno dalle questioni trasversali e rimarranno fermamente ancorati ai bronzi. In questo principio, seppur radicale, sta la volontà di dare voce ai materiali senza mediazioni, in quanto testimonianza privilegiata dello *Zeitgeist*. È altresì corretto mantenere la cronologia tradizionale del naufragio, ossia il 415–385 a.C., sicuro *terminus ante quem* anche per le sculture.

In questo modo, acquista valore il riferimento alla bronzistica classica come l'unico contesto possibile, non soltanto cronologico ma storico generale. Non sono ammissibili dunque i tentativi di postdatare i frammenti in virtù di presunte incongruenze tra questi ultimi e l'arte del V secolo a.C., favoriti dal presunto realismo della testa barbata inv. n. 17096 (Paribeni 1984, 12–14; Giuliano 1998).

In secondo luogo, è cura di chi scrive trattare i frammenti alla stregua di un nucleo organico e unitario. A tal proposito, la scelta di riunire tutti i bronzi di Porticello non intende fornire soltanto una panoramica aggiornata dello *status quaestionis*, ma promette di aggiungere nuovi elementi al dibattito. In conclusione, le soluzioni formali adoperate nell'anziano barbato richiamano l'arte delle grandi commesse classiche che, pur nella diversità dei materiali (marmo vs bronzo) e nella differente funzione (scultura architettonica-ideale vs *Rollenporträt*), restituiscono uno spaccato sociale fortemente coerente.

Il catalogo dei frammenti: alcune considerazioni

I frammenti bronzei di Porticello sono in tutto ventisei, conservati al Museo Nazionale di Reggio Calabria. Il loro numero si è ridotto a ventuno, a causa delle giunzioni operate durante i restauri (Di Bella 2016, 70). La maggioranza non proviene dallo scavo, ma è stata tratta in salvo dal saccheggio dei tombaroli. Fa eccezione la piccola partizione panneggiata inv. n. 19149 (17149 in Paribeni 1984, 6, n. 9) rinvenuta nella prima sezione del campo, nonché quella più a Nord, a ben m 37 di profondità (Eiseman – Ridgway 1987, 7). Questo tratto di panneggio, secondo B. S. Ridgway (1987, 89–90, n. S16), attacca con il frammento inv. n. 17079, contrariamente a quanto emerge dalle analisi scientifiche e dal catalogo di E. Paribeni (1984, 5–6, nn. 6. 9).

Le discrepanze nelle due edizioni – italiana e americana – dei frammenti del relitto, che hanno visto la luce quasi in contemporanea, sono ancora più marcate in relazione agli elementi più cospicui della lista: basti pensare al frammento inv. n. 17089, descritto da Paribeni (1984, 4, n. 3) come

> *"parte di torso virile* [...] La modellazione si limita a un largo affossamento in alto a sinistra che intenderei come un tratto dell'arcata epigastrica. I piccoli attacchi sporgenti in basso potrebbero indicare l'attacco dell'*himation*".

All'opposto, Ridgway (1987, 86, nn. S11–S12) pensa a un frammento "*probably from the outer side of a buttock*", erroneamente indicato come la controparte del frammento inv. n. 17087.

Conseguentemente, le conclusioni a cui giungono gli autori americani non potrebbero essere più lontane dall'articolo di Paribeni. Una presa di coscienza resa esplicita dai primi in fase di discussione (Eiseman – Ridgway 1987, 63).

Per fronteggiare le evidenti lacune nell'assegnare univocamente le partizioni anatomiche nude e panneggiate, un importante aiuto giunge dall'archeometria. Un vantaggio dell'edizione italiana è la presenza, in coda al catalogo, dei primi esami strumentali (Fiorentino – Marabelli – Micheli 1984). Le ultime analisi (Valtieri et al. 2007) hanno sostanzialmente confermato l'appartenenza dei frammenti a due gruppi, secondo una discriminante che fa capo ad alcuni elementi in traccia (bismuto, piombo e argento), la cui maggiore o minore presenza distingue due sculture (Ferretti et. al. 2007, 1516):

Il primo gruppo (*I*) è caratterizzato da valori relativamente alti degli elementi chimici in questione. A questo gruppo appartengono i pezzi riferibili alla statua di un anziano panneggiato;

Il secondo gruppo (*II*) presenta bismuto sotto il limite di rilevazione e segnali bassi degli altri componenti chimici. In questo gruppo confluiscono i pezzi di una figura giovanile nuda.

Al fine di raggiungere un punto di sutura convincente, in cui la classificazione composizionale confermi l'indagine stilistica, il presente lavoro terrà conto solo di quei frammenti la cui appartenenza a due statue è verificata dalle analisi 1984 e 2007. Espungendo i pezzi dubbi, il totale delle attribuzioni si conta nell'ordine delle nove unità: inv. nn. 17096, 17077/17078/17095, 17082, 17087–17088, 17090–17091, 17094, 19149.

La scelta di non prendere in considerazione dodici frammenti la cui appartenenza all'uno o l'altro dei gruppi succitati è incerta porta a escludere, purtroppo, i piedi inv. nn. 17092–17093/17083. Gli esami chimici non combaciano e neppure l'analisi stilistica pare univoca. Se nel catalogo di Paribeni (1984, 10) entrambi i piedi sono attribuiti alla statua di anziano, le indagini archeometriche assegnano il sinistro piuttosto al giovane nudo (Valtieri et. al. 2007, 178. 182). Queste ultime divergono invece per quanto riguarda il piede destro (Ferretti et. al. 2007, 1516–1517). Paribeni è stato probabilmente indotto in errore dalle deformazioni causate dai traumi subiti in antico dalle statue per staccarle dalle proprie basi, interpretate come segni realistici dell'età avanzata. Pertanto, allo stato attuale, i piedi non verranno tenuti in considerazione per la restituzione iconografica delle figure. È interessante notare comunque che essi conservano i resti del fissaggio a una base (Fiorentino – Marabelli – Micheli 1984, 21), elemento sufficiente per considerare le statue già esposte in antico e non di nuova fattura (Eiseman – Ridgway 1987, 78–80, n. S7/8).

L'esempio è paradigmatico per ritenere i bronzi *disiecta membra*: poiché frammentati e con i segni di antiche manomissioni, la loro origine violenta è certa (Di Bella 2016, 66 e nota 5). I bronzi fatti a pezzi svolgevano una funzione commerciale a causa del valore intrinseco del metallo. L'associazione con i lingotti e il metallo sfuso rinvenuto sul fondale (Eiseman – Ridgway 1987, 33–36) lascia pensare, ancora una volta, che le sculture erano destinate alla rifusione.

Il giovane nudo inv. nn. 17087–17088, 17090

Il *gruppo II* è molto esiguo, potendo contare unicamente su tre frammenti. Il pezzo maggiormente diagnostico è un tratto dell'anca con la cresta iliaca disegnata in alto e l'inizio della coscia destra (inv. n. 17087). La parte in corrispondenza del gluteo è ripiegata sul retro a causa delle compressioni, mentre la modellazione del lembo anteriore è notevolmente deformata, complicando la lettura del pezzo. Paribeni coglie probabilmente nel segno quando deduce, in base al contorno rilassato del gluteo e all'andamento dell'inizio della coscia, che la gamba destra è libera. Di conseguenza, il senso degli arti inferiori non corrisponde a quello canonico del Doriforo policleteo. È verosimile che "la gamba destra era scaricata e forse notevolmente spostata in avanti, per esempio con il piede appoggiato a un piccolo rialzo" (Paribeni 1984, 9, n. 12). Anche l'edizione americana è concorde nel ritenere il frammento generato dall'unione del muscolo dell'anca e buona parte del corpo esterno della natica fino all'inizio della coscia (Eiseman – Ridgway 1987, 85–86, n. S11).

Il colore, la tecnica di esecuzione e lo spessore contribuiscono a rilanciare l'ipotesi che il pezzo possa essere la controparte del gluteo inv. n. 17088. Che quest'ultimo partecipi alla costruzione sinistra della scultura, con la metà destra inv. n. 17087 svincolata dai compiti di sostegno, si evince ancora dal tratto fermo e deciso del bronzo. La gamba sinistra dunque è la gamba portante. D'accordo Ridgway (1987, 83, n. S10), che confronta la tecnica di realizzazione con quella dell'efebo di Anticitera. La struttura generale e il modellato, a differenza del corrispettivo destro, risultano qui ben decifrabili. I contorni morbidi del gluteo, insieme alla nudità, depongono a favore di una figura giovanile, che si distingue così dai frammenti panneggiati del *gruppo I* (inv. nn. 17077/17078/17095 + 17082, 19149).

L'ultimo frammento del *gruppo II* sono i genitali, cavati in due parti, entrambe vuote: lo scroto con una porzione di peli pubici e il pene (inv. n. 17090). L'irregolarità nella resa dei testicoli – il destro, maggiormente sviluppato e più in basso del sinistro – testimonia un cedimento della gamba destra e conferma la posa della statua con la sinistra a sorreggere il peso del corpo (Eiseman – Ridgway 1987, 81, n. S9). Il realismo dei genitali è ottenuto tramite la resa della pelle flaccida tra i due testicoli, allungata seguendo la postura della statua, secondo un modello comune anche ai bronzi di Riace. Le copie romane del Doriforo, dallo schema inverso, presentano infatti una resa identica e opposta, con il testicolo sinistro maggiormente dimensionato e rivolto verso il basso.

L'atleta (ca. 470 a.C.)

La scultura riconducibile al *gruppo II* risulta decisamente evanescente. L'assenza di frammenti attribuibili alla parte superiore della figura, quale il torso o le braccia, non consente di giungere alla comprensione dell'atteggiamento complessivo. Tuttavia, è altresì ragionevole fare affidamento su alcuni punti fermi non di poco conto:

1. La nudità
2. La giovane età
3. La ponderazione, con la sinistra portante e la destra flessa.

Quest'ultimo luogo è di notevole interesse per l'inquadramento cronologico dell'opera e che apre a due possibilità, entrambe legate alla presenza o meno del "passo", il motivo canonico di Policleto:

1. Presenza del contrapposto policleteo e del "passo", ma con il primo invertito negli arti inferiori rispetto al Doriforo
2. Assenza del contrapposto policleteo e del "passo".

Seguendo la prima ipotesi, il giovane di Porticello proseguirebbe la tradizione di personaggi dai lineamenti efebici tentativamente identificati come atleti, ma dalla natura ambivalente: si tratta dei marmi del tipo Westmacott, pure attribuito a Policleto (cfr. da ultimo Hallof – Lehmann – Kansteiner 2007, 62–64, n. 9.1 con bibliografia precedente), ma anche di bronzi tardoclassici quali gli efebi di Maratona e Anticitera (un confronto tra i due in Childs 2018, 112–114 con bibliografia precedente alle note 85–86). Se la paternità delle opere è decisamente incerta, sembra possibile individuare due distinti filoni, facenti capo a scuole separate (cfr. Todisco 1993, 102. 133, nn. 202. 298 con bibliografia precedente). L'efebo di Maratona sarebbe di derivazione attica, prassitelica in particolare, mentre il bronzo di Anticitera conserverebbe il ricordo dei nudi policletei e peloponnesiaci. La critica li colloca entrambi alla metà del IV secolo a.C. o poco dopo (fa eccezione Himmelmann 2009, 186).

Sussistono, ad ogni modo, delle caratteristiche comuni: le sculture, frontali, insistono sulla gamba sinistra portante, indietreggiando la destra flessa al ginocchio. Il piede così puntato al suolo realizza pienamente il "passo". Il fanciullo di Anticitera riprende il ritmo, la ponderazione e le proporzioni della maturità di Policleto. La corporatura è robusta e la muscolatura sviluppata, giacché la sensazione del movimento risulta temprata dalla possanza del torso, pur spostando il piede destro più indietro e più di lato rispetto a quello del bronzo di Maratona. Proprio l'esigenza di esprimere il moto precario emerge maggiormente in quest'ultimo, dalle proporzioni più snelle, esili e slanciate. In base alle precedenti osservazioni, la distanza tra le due scuole – o meglio tra gli stili – è legata alla tendenza di presentare figure maschili ora solide e bilanciate (Anticitera), ora adolescenziali e instabili (Maratona).

Rincresce che sul piede destro inv. n. 17093/17083, sicuramente piantato al suolo, divergano persino le analisi archeometriche: se fosse certificata la sua appartenenza al giovane, sarebbe la prova inoppugnabile della sua estraneità al modulo policleteo. Ciononostante, la transizione graduale dalla natica alla gamba nel frammento inv. n. 17087 indica che la coscia deve essere rivolta in avanti, piegata al ginocchio, con la parte inferiore in posizione di traino o leggermente avanzata (Eiseman – Ridgway 1987, 86, n. S11). In effetti, l'impressione complessiva dei frammenti del *gruppo II* sembra avere poco a che fare con la meticolosa costruzione della figura umana e con le ricerche sull'equilibrio dei corpi tipiche della seconda metà del V secolo a.C.

I migliori paragoni per la posa del giovane di Porticello sono due statuette di atleti dal Metropolitan, inv. nn. 08.258.10 e 07.286.87 rispettivamente, l'una in atteggiamento di orante (Fig. 21.1), l'altra come lanciatore del disco (cfr. Richter 1915, 48–53, nn. 78–79; 1917, 89–92; 1929, 55; Thomas 1981, 40–41. 97; Fuchs 1982, 48. 51–52, nn. 42. 48; Himmelmann 2001, 60; Smith 2007, 116. 120). Datate intorno al 470 a.C., il secondo è forse il prodotto di un'officina peloponnesiaca; l'orante, invece, è di provenienza ignota. Prima del passaggio a New York nel 1908, la statuetta faceva parte di una collezione privata inglese e, ancora prima, è attestata in Turchia. Dal punto di vista formale, dipende da stilemi magnogreci e sicelioti, ponendosi circa un decennio prima dell'atleta di Adrano. Il peso del corpo è tutto sulla gamba sinistra, mentre la destra è avanzata e reclinata al ginocchio. Il piede aderisce al suolo con la pianta piena. L'interpretazione complessiva, se il paragone coglie nel segno, acquista risalto maggiore alla luce dell'ipotesi di provenienza della nave sulla quale i bronzi erano trasportati, vale a dire la Sicilia (Paoletti 1991–92; Di Bella 2016, 66–69).

In definitiva, l'iconografia del giovane del *gruppo II* sarebbe molto vicina a quella dell'atleta su di un *alabastron* a fondo bianco da Tanagra e conservato a Berlino, Antikensammlung, inv. n. F 2258 (Fig. 21.2. Cfr. Beazley 1963, 405; 1971, 371; Carpenter 1989, 231; Kefalidou 1996, 65 y nota 68, 92–93. 205, n. Γ80 con

Figura 21.1. Atleta orante. Ca. 470 a.C. New York, Metropolitan Museum of Art, inv. n. 08.258.10: Public Domain.

Figura 21.2. Atleta vittorioso. Pittore della Fonderia, *alabastron* a fondo bianco da Tanagra, 480-470 a.C. Berlino, Staatliche Museen, Antikensammlung, inv. F 2258: da Kefalidou 1996, tav. 42, n. Γ80.

ulteriore bibliografia). Il modello di questa scena potrebbe essere una vera e propria scultura, vista la plasticità delle figure dipinte. Il ragazzo sta fissando con la mano destra una benda sulla sua testa, mentre con la sinistra regge un bastone. Un attributo possibilmente non del tutto estraneo al bronzo di Porticello: "Oltre a numerosi tasselli un piccolo foro quadrangolare sull'anca si trova in corrispondenza di una zona più spessa di rinforzi all'interno, come a indicare un contatto con la mano o con un'asta" (Paribeni 1984, 9, n. 12).

Intermezzo: la testa inv. n. 145848

La testa di anziano inv. n. 17096 non è l'unico volto restituito dal relitto calabro: fin dalla scoperta, è stata segnalata alle autorità la testa di un uomo maturo, barbato, con una benda sottile che gira intorno al capo (*tainia*). Dell'eccezionale rinvenimento si persero però le tracce con altrettanta rapidità, fin quando – l'8 febbraio del 1993 – l'Antikenmuseum di Basilea lo riconsegnò ufficialmente allo stato italiano (la vicenda è ripercorsa con dovizia di particolari da Paoletti 1993 e, in occasione dell'ultimo restauro, da Malacrino – Di Cesare – Mantella 2018, 63). Da qui, all'inizio dell'anno molti quotidiani regionali e nazionali dedicarono alcune pagine alla cerimonia di consegna (Paoletti 1993, 5). La chiara rispondenza del pezzo ai motivi della Grecia classica e l'espressione austera

"frutto dello stile del tempo e dell'esecutore, piuttosto che indicazione di carattere o di *pathos*" (Malacrino – Di Cesare – Mantella 2018, 64)

hanno subito fatto pensare a una statua di Zeus, come si evince dai titoli di alcune importanti testate giornalistiche del tempo.

Quasi fosse una moderna spy story, la prova tangibile dell'appartenenza della testa al relitto calabro fu una sorta di identikit fornito alla Soprintendenza da chi per primo aveva dato notizia del furto. Il disegno, invero più vicino a un ritratto individuale, presenta però la profonda frattura alla radice del naso che si riscontra sul bronzo (Fig. 21.3). Un colpo subito già in antico a causa della necessità di staccare la testa dal corpo. Violenze come questa hanno provocato diverse crepe che si sono fatte strada in corrispondenza delle zone più difettose, dal momento che la testa è frutto di un getto imperfetto (Prisco 1996, 638, n. 10; Malacrino – Di Cesare – Mantella 2018, 67–68).

Il bronzo, stando all'analisi delle patine, è di sicura provenienza da ambiente marino. Tuttavia, manca un attacco tra i pezzi che certifichi a scanso di equivoci la presenza della testa di Basilea sulla nave di Porticello. In realtà, la composizione della lega è sostanzialmente identica a quella del giovane nudo, con l'assoluta mancanza di piombo aggiunto (Prisco 1996, 638). Dal momento che questo elemento è ampiamente presente nei frammenti del *gruppo I*, è possibile che la discrepanza sia da attribuire alle officine coinvolte e all'uso di leghe di bronzo differenti già in origine (cfr. Ferretti et. al. 2007, 1516), piuttosto che agli effetti della corrosione marina. I fenomeni causati da quest'ultima, come la costituzione di patine, sono invece simili in tutti i frammenti di Porticello.

Figura 21.3. Testa di Basilea. Relitto di Porticello, ca. 440 a.C. Reggio Calabria, Museo Archeologico Nazionale, inv. n. 145848: © MArRC, foto F. F. Di Bella.

Le diversità con la testa di Basilea riguardano più propriamente il piano tecnico: la qualità del getto, il modo di operare le saldature e i chiodi distanziatori (Prisco 1996, 638, n. 10; Prisco – Fiorentino 2003, 53–54). Queste dissonanze possono essere facilmente spiegate: la natura commerciale di un'imbarcazione che conserva in stiva prodotti alimentari (anfore a maggioranza greco-occidentale e punica) e i bronzi frammentari destinati alla rifusione, non esclude più luoghi di approvvigionamento dei prodotti. La destinazione ultima dei bronzi di Porticello, giunti ai nostri giorni privi dello status di statue votive e/o onorarie, è prosaicamente il riciclo. Pertanto, è perfettamente possibile che gli elementi scultorei dei *gruppi I-II* siano stati tratti dallo stesso contesto, mentre la testa inv. n. 145848 provenga da un'altra razzia o da un diverso emporio. Ciò spiegherebbe le anomalie nella realizzazione di questa terza scultura dal relitto. L'analisi isotopica, infine, rivela che il rame adoperato per la produzione della testa proviene da miniere cipriote (Malacrino – Di Cesare – Mantella 2018, 69).

L'analisi stilistica della testa va dal 460 al 430 a.C. La breve storia degli studi sul bronzo suddivide tale lasso di tempo in tre caselle cronologiche da un decennio l'una. Le ultime ricerche lo collocano entro l'orizzonte severo (Malacrino – Di Cesare – Mantella 2018, 65), più precisamente la fase tarda (460–450 a.C.: Paoletti 2005, 518). Sono stati avanzati confronti con notissime opere di scultura dalla Grecia e dalle colonie, quali il dio di Capo Artemision e lo Zeus sulla metopa con scena di *hieros gamos* dell'Heraion di Selinunte. Il decennio seguente (450–440 a.C.) è stato chiamato in causa da M. C. Parra (2008, 88), a causa della vicinanza con la testina bronzea dal santuario di Apollo a Cirene, forse Arcesilao IV (cfr. Richter 1965, 105 con bibliografia precedente). E. Lattanzi (1996, 638, n. 10) ha piuttosto ricavato un preciso confronto con alcune copie di originali greci degli anni 440–430 a.C., quali il "Münchner König", l'Anacreonte Borghese e il cosiddetto Capaneo di Villa Albani, derivato da una figura incidentata sullo scudo dell'Atena Parthenos fidiaca, dedicata nel 438/7 a.C. secondo lo scolio 605α alla *Pace* di Aristofane. La proposta conclusiva sul pezzo è di "una sua collocazione intorno alla metà del V secolo a.C., probabilmente in ambito non attico, non privo di influenze dello stile tardo-severo". Posizione minoritaria è quella di Ridgway (2010), che abbassa la datazione della testa di Basilea fino al 420 a.C., in pieno stile ricco.

Il già citato riferimento al nudo dalla Gliptoteca di Monaco, inv. n. 295 (cfr. Vierneisel-Schlörb 1979, 117–135, n. 11 con bibliografia precedente), è calzante (Fig. 21.4). Si tratta di una figura maschile matura con un torso muscoloso e superiore al vero. Il peso del corpo ricade sulla gamba sinistra, ferma, mentre la destra in riposo realizza il "passo". Il braccio destro si distende lungo il fianco e l'avambraccio sinistro è sollevato. Il marmo gira la testa di tre quarti a sinistra, ruotandola leggermente verso il basso. Il capo è cinto dalla *tainia* che tiene saldi i riccioli dei capelli.

In mancanza di qualsivoglia partizione anatomica appartenente alla testa di Basilea, il paragone può aiutare a visualizzare anche qui una scultura completa di poco superiore al vero (testa del "Münchner König" h m 0,39; testa di Basilea h m 0,343). L'andamento della barba è lo stesso del tipo di Monaco, con ciocche che si addensano cospicue sulla sommità del mento, a flussi lenti ma copiosi. Nell'esemplare marmoreo c'è però una diffusa plasticità, dovuta forse più all'autore dell'archetipo che al copista, laddove il secondo fa un uso della materia denso e pastoso per richiamare la sensibilità del primo. In alcuni punti del bronzo il tratto diventa invece calligrafico, come per i baffi, in ogni caso ben distinti dal resto della peluria in entrambe le opere. È nella capigliatura che la somiglianza raggiunge il picco più alto: la *tainia*, da cui sporgono alcune ciocche in alto, è posta alla stessa altezza, non coprendo del tutto la fronte e lasciando ricadere su di essa i capelli a lumachella. La lunghezza dei capelli è analoga: libera la nuca e non copre a sufficienza le orecchie. Nondimeno, il labbro inferiore è ugualmente marcato e carnoso.

Se l'alveo stilistico corrisponde, anche se non a tal punto da poter parlare di "archetipo comune" (Lattanzi 1996, 638, n. 10), il "Münchner König" possiede una certa inclinazione del volto che dona alla figura un'aria pensosa, certamente intenta in un atteggiamento specifico o colta durante l'esecuzione di un'azione concreta. È stato giustamente notato, infatti, che la statua non sostava isolata nello spazio, ma volgeva lo sguardo a una dirimpettaia posta alla sua sinistra (Vierneisel-Schlörb 1979, 118, n. 11). Al contrario, la frontalità della testa di Porticello conferisce una sensazione di maggiore ieraticità, a cui partecipano le labbra serrate, lasciando immaginare un contesto meno dinamico. La statua è di certo di un tipo ideale, non necessariamente legata a una narrazione di gruppo. La lettura iconografica dell'opera, a questo punto, è frenata dall'assenza degli attributi, limitati alla benda che evidenzia il lignaggio regale della personalità rappresentata.

Il "dio" di Basilea (ca. 440 a.C.)

Il contesto cronologico della testa di Basilea, a cui rimedia parzialmente il "Münchner König", anch'esso variamente inquadrato, trova un terreno più sicuro nelle opere ceramografiche. Si tratta dell'officina del Pittore di Kodros, "*old-fashioned*" (Boardman 1989, 98), che nelle sue fasi iniziali (ca. 440 a.C.) preferisce soggetti del mito, spesso uomini maturi, barbati e dalla corporatura possente (lo studio di riferimento è Avramidou 2011, 71–82 per le molte relazioni tra i suoi vasi e la scultura contemporanea). Il Pittore di Kodros dipinge figure dal profilo solenne, dagli occhi abitualmente larghi e ben spalancati. Il suo classicismo è rivolto a un'introspezione che non è quella, psicologica, dell'età dello stile severo, ma è già ricca di morale. Ad esempio, i personaggi maschili della cosiddetta Erichthonios Cup, una *kylix* attica a f.r. da Berlino, Antikensammlung, inv. n. F 2537, sono un buon paragone per il "dio" di Basilea (Fig. 21.5. Cfr. Beazley 1963, 1268.2, 1689; Carpenter 1989, 356; ora Avramidou 2011, 23. 33–36. 87, n. 2 con ulteriore bibliografia; Walter-Karydi 2015, 174). Il secondo re da sinistra verso destra del lato B della coppa, [ΑΙ]ΓΕΥΣ, indossa una benda sottile ornata da foglie dalla disposizione geometrica; il volto non accompagna il movimento del corpo, ma è totalmente eretto; i baffi affusolati che incorniciano le labbra sono ben distaccati dalla barba, mentre i capelli corti lasciano scoperto l'orecchio come nella testa di Basilea.

Palese è la differenza con il volto, ugualmente orientato verso sinistra, dell'Eracle dipinto sul lato A del celebre cratere dei Niobidi (cfr. Beazley 1963, 601.22. 1661; 1971, 395; Carpenter 1989, 266; ora Giuliani 2015 con bibliografia precedente). Datato al 460–450 a.C., mostra l'eroe visibilmente provato dalla stanchezza, solcato dalle rughe e corrucciato nell'espressione, acuita dal labbro inferiore piegato alle estremità. La clava puntata verso il basso materializza l'attesa, affinché il *ponos* – simboleggiato dalla leonté – appaia insieme premio e fardello. La testa di Basilea si pone dunque nel decennio seguente, laddove gli stilemi severi cedono a un tipo di rappresentazione che procede per sottrazione. Come nel bronzetto cirenaico, somigliante nel *ductus* di capelli e

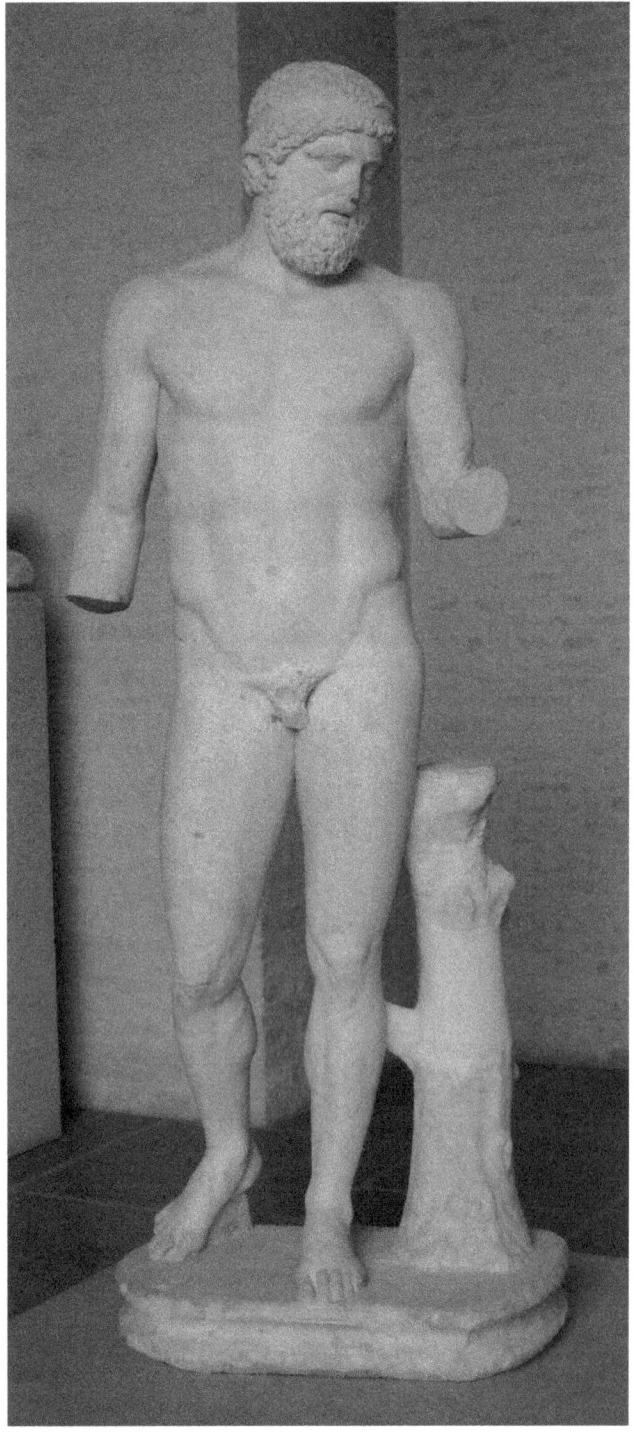

Figura 21.4. "Münchner König". Ca. 440 a.C. Monaco, Gliptoteca, inv. n. 295: Public Domain.

Figura 21.5. Pittore di Kodros, lato B di *kylix* attica a f.r. da Tarquinia, 440-430 a.C. Berlino, Staatliche Museen, Antikensammlung, inv. n. F 2537: da Walter-Karydi 2015, 175, fig. 95b.

barba, vanno scemando quei moderati elementi realistici che, in età protoclassica, compaiono accanto ai tratti idealizzati.

Conclusioni: l'anziano panneggiato inv. nn. 17096, 17077/17078/17095 + 17082, 17091, 17094, 19149 e la Kentaurenmaske

Venendo al *gruppo I*, ovvero all'anziano panneggiato, le riflessioni si fanno più complesse, giacché le possibilità analitiche offerte dal materiale disponibile si ampliano enormemente rispetto alle precedenti sculture esaminate. La figura, stante, è dotata di una veste che si interrompe al di sopra del ginocchio scoprendo l'anca, mentre l'andamento elastico delle pieghe richiama un pesante *himation*. La mano sinistra inv. n. 17094 stringe un oggetto cilindrico (*skeptron*). L'avambraccio sinistro e il tratto di gomito inv. n. 17091 formano insieme un angolo retto ad accompagnare proprio il gesto della mano. La testa inv. n. 17096, fortemente segnata dai *topoi* dell'età avanzata (fronte pronunciata, sopracciglia inarcate, guance emaciate, zigomi marcati, naso adunco), è incorniciata dai baffi imponenti e da una barba lunghissima (Fig. 21.6). Ciocche dell'acconciatura ricadono fino alle spalle. Un incavo preposto per l'inserzione di un attributo circondava il capo, girando anche sulla fronte, senza che spuntino i capelli a causa della stempiatura progressiva: dovette trattarsi di una benda, oggi perduta, più sottile rispetto alla *tainia* della testa di Basilea.

Figura 21.6. Anziano barbato. Relitto di Porticello, 445-440 a.C. Reggio Calabria, Museo Archeologico Nazionale, inv. n. 17096: © MArRC, foto F. F. Di Bella.

Non molto è possibile aggiungere all'analisi stilistico-iconografica già condotta da chi scrive (Di Bella 2016, 69–83), ma vale la pena richiamare alcune importanti acquisizioni:

1. La cronologia del 445–440 a.C., dal confronto stilistico tra il panneggio inv. nn. 17077/17078/17095 e quello delle lapitesse delle metope partenoniche 10 e 12 Sud
2. Il volto, leggermente piegato verso il basso, di un venerabile anziano assorto in un dialogo interiore. Non è un filosofo, ma un poeta-vate iconograficamente affine ai grandi Omero ed Esiodo, tutti caratterizzati dalla lunga barba, dalla fronte segnata da rughe leggere e dalla stempiatura
3. La benda sottile, segno dell'autorità
4. Il bastone, attributo normativo dell'età avanzata, con la stessa valenza della benda (cfr. AP II, 311–349; Hes. Th. 30–32; Paus. 9.30.2)
5. Il particolare della veste sollevata per mostrare l'arto scoperto (inv. nn. 17077/17078/17095 + 17082) riafferma ancora una volta la progressione età, saggezza, autorità. L'invalidità non è sgradevole ma, al contrario, richiama un particolare importante nella definizione del ruolo del personaggio.

Le rughe e soprattutto la barba lunghissima hanno favorito i molti collegamenti con i centauri delle metope del Partenone. È stata più volte ribadita l'associazione con Chirone, protagonista di un non altrimenti noto gruppo scultoreo composto dal giovane Achille e da un terzo personaggio (Ridgway 1986, 68; 1993; 2004, 350–364. 572–581. 759–760. 767–768; dubitativamente 2010, 338 con nota 34; Eiseman – Ridgway 1987, 99. 106). Spendere qualche parola in merito a questa teoria è di nuovo necessario, vieppiù che recentissimamente H. A. Shapiro (2018, 292–293) rinforza il parallelismo menzionando il "ritratto" di un centauro (Chirone?) su un cratere a campana attico a f.r. degli anni del Partenone, attribuito al Pittore di Eupolis e proveniente da una collezione privata.

L'interpretazione di tratti distintivi, fisionomici secondo la terminologia moderna, risponde a un modello che cambia di volta in volta a seconda del contesto. Gli antichi, in età classica, nell'osservare le immagini di intellettuali come il vate di Porticello, non dovettero avere in mente mostri quali i centauri. I ritratti traggono spunto dalle fattezze dei centauri per ragioni pratiche e non spirituali, non simboleggiano lo status protestatario della dedica. B. Schweitzer (1963, 170), in un famoso passaggio, considera i centauri, i sileni e le maschere teatrali i prototipi del ritratto: la vecchiaia, l'origine barbarica, la natura silenica e la *Kentaurenmaske* appartengono al regno dell'abnorme e del brutto, separati dall'espressione individuale soltanto da un semplice passo.

Qual è lo *Schritt* di cui parla il grande studioso tedesco? È chiaro che manca un tassello. Il comune habitat tra i primi ritratti – spesso uomini in là con gli anni – e i centauri è innegabile. Se non è la vicinanza caratteriale, poiché

Fabiano Fiorello Di Bella

Figura 21.7. Busto di Pindaro. Archetipo 460-450 a.C. Musei Capitolini, Sala dei Filosofi, inv. 60 (calco in gesso):
© Institut für Klassische Archäologie Tübingen, Gipsabguss-Sammlung, inv. G 1074, foto F. F. Di Bella.

gli intellettuali non sono outsider sociali, cosa spinge gli artisti a mutuare le iconografie dai centauri?

L'omogeneità dei lineamenti somatici tra intellettuali ed esseri mostruosi è un fattore prettamente stilistico, certamente arduo da contestare: il centauro della metopa partenonica 26 Sud, ad esempio, ha la barba nello stesso schema del bronzo di Porticello, appena sotto il labbro e ai lati del volto (Di Bella 2016, 79). Una metopa in cui coesistono componenti aggiornate e persistenze severe, in linea con la disomogeneità che caratterizza gli indirizzi figurativi del cantiere del Partenone. Altri esempi:

1. Ancora nell'età dello stile severo, il ritratto di Pindaro (Fig. 21.7) è comparabile con il centauro D del frontone Ovest del tempio di Zeus a Olimpia. In questo caso la somiglianza diventa perfetta sovrapponibilità specie per la parte superiore della testa (cfr. Bergemann 1991, 175–176. 186)
2. L'Anacreonte Borghese è molto vicino al centauro 2 Sud del Partenone, forse addirittura a esso ispirato (cfr. Voutiras 1980, 77–91; *contra* Giuliani 1982, 54)
3. L'anonimo ritratto da Firenze, inv. n. 13768, datato al terzo venticinquennio del V secolo a.C., presenta una struttura della testa compatta e massiccia, paragonabile al centauro della metopa partenonica 29 Sud (cfr. De Tommaso 2013 con bibliografia precedente).

La metà superiore dei volti di queste immagini-ritratto è identica ai centauri; differisce, invece, quella inferiore che, impassibile nei primi, diventa movimentata nei mostri tramite la tensione dello zigomatico. Il fatto non è casuale: in questo modo le rughe da espressione di violenza (*pathos*) si tramutano in un rimando all'attività mentale (*ethos*). Il cambiamento di significato del medesimo tratto esteriore, dovuto al contesto e arricchito di segni realistici (nodo della barba, orecchie dalla cartilagine dilatata), esclude ogni analogia di senso tra i personaggi della storia e le creature ostili alla norma (satiri, sileni, centauri). I centauri, quindi, non costituiscono dei confronti pertinenti per l'identità dell'effigiato, ma sono indizi dell'uso di medesimi schemi classici per figure mitologiche indifferenziate e per i ritratti degli uomini di pensiero (cfr. Bergemann 2007, 37 e critica in Ridgway 2010, 338). Accanto a esseri semiferini, quali centauri e sileni, compaiono venerabili anziani solcati da identiche grinze, accomunati dalla matrice su cui ricavare l'immagine personalizzata.

Fino al tardoarcaismo, l'uomo è *kalos kai agathos*: una figura ideale che non può e non vuole mostrare tratti personali. Così, si può separare il divino e il mortale solo per mezzo degli attributi, come nel caso dei *kouroi*. Gli artisti, in seguito, per raffigurare una tipologia umana nuova, l'intellettuale, dovranno trovare nuovi stimoli. Non potendo attingere al passato prepersiano, caveranno i riferimenti dai volti dei centauri, slegati da canoni estetici e da significati sopraindividuali. I centauri entrano nella formularità delle officine classiche per tramandare alcune personalità specifiche. Tra queste, un ruolo di primo piano spetta al coltissimo vate di Porticello.

Bibliografia

Avramidou, A., 2011. *The Codrus Painter: Iconography and Reception of Athenian Vases in the Age of Pericles*. Madison: The University of Wisconsin Press.

Beazley, J. D., 1963. *Attic Red-Figure Vase-Painters*. Seconda edizione. Oxford: Clarendon Press.

Beazley, J. D., 1971. *Paralipomena: Additions to* Attic Black-Figure Vase-Painters *and to* Attic Red-Figure Vase-Painters *(Second Edition)*. Oxford: Oxford University Press.

Bergemann, J., 1991. Pindar. Das Bildnis eines konservativen Dichters. *Mitteilungen des Deutschen archäologischen Instituts. Athenische Abteilung*, 106, 157–189.

Bergemann, J., 2007. Attic Grave Reliefs and Portrait Sculpture in Fourth-Century Athens. In: P. Schultz – R. von den Hoff, a cura di, *Early Hellenistic Portraiture: Image, Style, Context*. Cambridge: Cambridge University Press. 34–46.

Boardman, J., 1989. *Athenian Red Figure Vases. The Classical Period: A Handbook*. London: Thames & Hudson.

Carpenter, T. H., 1989. *Beazley Addenda: Additional References to* ABV, ARV2 *and* Paralipomena. Seconda edizione. Oxford: Oxford University Press.

Childs, W. A. P., 2018. *Greek Art and Aesthetics in the Fourth Century B.C.* Princeton-Oxford: Princeton University Press.

De Tommaso, G., 2013. Ritratto di filosofo (?). In: M. G. Bernardini – M. Lolli Ghetti, a cura di, *Capolavori dell'archeologia. Recuperi, Ritrovamenti, Confronti.* Roma: Gangemi Editore. 214, n. 44.

Di Bella, F. F., 2016. Il relitto di Porticello e l'iconografia del vate. Ritratto di ruolo e contesto in età classica. *Quaderni di Archeologia. A cura dell'Università degli Studi di Messina*, 6, 61–88.

Eiseman, C. J. – Ridgway, B. S., 1987. *The Porticello Shipwreck. A Mediterranean Merchant Vessel of 415–385 B.C.* College Station: Texas A&M University Press.

Ferretti, M., et. al., 2007. In Situ Study of the Porticello Bronzes by Portable X-Ray Fluorescence and Laser-Induced Breakdown Spectroscopy. *Spectrochimica Acta*, B(62), 1512–1518.

Fiorentino, P. – Marabelli, M. – Micheli, M., 1984. Indagini e intervento di conservazione sui reperti bronzei di Porticello. *Bollettino d'Arte*, 69(24), 15–24.

Fuchs, W., 1982. *Scultura greca*. Traduzione P. Orlandini. Milano: Rusconi immagini.

Giuliani, L., 1982. Rezension zu E. *Voutiras, Studien zu Interpretation und Stil griechischer Porträts des 5. und frühen 4. Jahrhunderts* (1980). *Gnomon*, 54(1), 51–56.

Giuliani, L., 2015. *Das Wunder vor der Schlacht: ein griechisches Historienbild der frühen Klassik*. Basel: Schwabe Verlag.

Giuliano, A., 1998. Porticello, In: G. Capecchi, et. al., a cura di, *In memoria di Enrico Paribeni*, vol. I. Roma: Giorgio Bretschneider Editore, 207–210.

Hallof, K. – Lehmann, L. – Kansteiner, S., 2007. Polyklet. In: S. Kansteiner et. al., a cura di, *Text und Skulptur. Berühmte Bildhauer und Bronzegiesser der Antike in Wort und Bild*. Berlin-New York: Walter de Gruyter. 62–74, n. 9.

Himmelmann, N., 2001. *Die private Bildnisweihung bei den Griechen. Zu den Ursprüngen des abendländischen Porträts*. Wiesbaden: Westdeutscher Verlag.

Himmelmann, N., 2009. *Der ausruhende Herakles*. Paderborn: Verlag Ferdinand Schöningh.

Kefalidou, E., 1996. *ΝΙΚΗΤΗΣ. Εικονογραφική μελέτη του αρχαίου ελληνικού αθλητισμού*. Thessaloniki: Aristoteleio Panepistimio Thessalonike.

Lattanzi, E., 1996. Testa maschile barbata. In: G. Pugliese Carratelli, a cura di, *I Greci in Occidente*, Catalogo della mostra (Venezia, Palazzo Grassi, aprile-dicembre 1996). Milano: Bompiani, 637–638, n. 10.

Malacrino, C. G. – Di Cesare, R. – Mantella, G., 2018. Testa maschile barbata, detta "Testa di Basilea". In: C. Bertelli – G. Bonsanti, a cura di, *Restituzioni 2018. Tesori d'arte restaurati*. Venezia: Marsilio Editori. 60–69.

Owen, D. I., 1970. Picking Up the Pieces. The Salvage Excavation of a Looted Fifth Century B.C. Shipwreck in the Straits of Messina. *Expedition*, 13(1), 24–29.

Owen, D. I., 1971. Excavating a Classical Shipwreck. *Archaeology*, 24, 118–129.

Paoletti, M., 1991–92. La nave di Porticello. Una rotta siciliana. *Klearchos*, 33–34(129–136), 119–148.

Paoletti, M., 1993. La "testa di Basilea" e il saccheggio di Porticello. *Magna Graecia*, 28(1–3), 5–7.

Paoletti, M., 2005. La scultura greca. I bronzi del relitto di Porticello. In: E. F. Ghedini, a cura di, *Lo stretto di Messina nell'antichità*. Roma: Edizioni Quasar, 515–523.

Paribeni, E., 1984. Le statue bronzee di Porticello. *Bollettino d'Arte*, 69(24), 1–14.

Parra, M. C., 2008. L'arte greca in Italia meridionale, tra scoperte, riscoperte, ricezione. In: M. L. Catoni, a cura di, *La Forza del Bello. L'arte greca conquista l'Italia*, Catalogo della mostra (Mantova, 29 marzo-6 luglio 2008). Milano: Skira, 78–91.

Prisco, G. – Fiorentino, P., 2003. Prime considerazioni sulla testa di Basilea alla luce dell'intervento di restauro. In: A. Meluccio Vaccaro – G. De Palma, a cura di, *I Bronzi di Riace. Restauro come conoscenza*, vol. I. Roma: Artemide Edizioni, 85–96.

Prisco, G., 1996. Appendice. Osservazioni tecniche. In: G. Pugliese Carratelli, a cura di. *I Greci in Occidente*, Catalogo della mostra (Venezia, Palazzo Grassi, aprile-dicembre 1996). Milano: Bompiani, 638–639, n. 10.

Richter, G. M. A., 1915. *The Metropolitan Museum of Art. Greek, Etruscan and Roman Bronzes*. New York: Gilliss Press.

Richter, G. M. A., 1917. *The Metropolitan Museum of Art. Handbook of the Classical Collection*. New York: Metropolitan Museum of Art.

Richter, G. M. A., 1929. *The Sculpture and Sculptors of the Greeks*. New Haven: Yale University Press.

Richter, G. M. A., 1965. *The Portraits of the Greeks*. London: The Phaidon Press.

Ridgway, B. S., 1986. The Bronzes from the Porticello Wreck. In: H. Kyrieleis, a cura di, *Archaische und klassische griechische Plastik: Akten des Internationalen Kolloquiums vom 22.-25. April 1985 in Athen*, vol. II. Mainz: Verlag Philipp von Zabern, 59–69.

Ridgway, B. S., 1993. Nuove considerazioni sui bronzi di Porticello. *Magna Graecia*, 28(1-3), 1–4.

Ridgway, B. S., 1995. Lo stile severo. Lo stato della questione. In: N. Bonacasa, a cura di, *Lo stile severo in Occidente: aspetti e problemi*. Roma: L'Erma di Bretschneider, 35–42.

Ridgway, B. S., 2004. *Second Chance: Greek Sculptural Studies Revisited*. London: The Pindar Press.

Ridgway, B. S., 2010. The Porticello Bronzes Once Again. *American Journal of Archaeology*, 114(2), 331–342.

Schweitzer, B., 1963. *Zur Kunst der Antike. Ausgewählte Schriften*, vol. II. Tübingen: Ernst Wasmuth Verlag.

Shapiro, H. A., 2018. Portrait of a Centaur. In: T. Greub – M. Roussel, a cura di, *Figurationen des Porträts*. Paderborn: Wilhelm Fink Verlag. 279–294.

Smith, R. R. R., 2007. Pindar, Athletes, and the Statue Habit. In: S. Hornblower – C. A. Morgan, a cura di, *Pindar's Poetry, Patrons, and Festivals From Archaic Greece to the Roman Empire*. Oxford: Oxford University Press, 83–139.

Thomas, R., 1981. *Athletenstatuetten der Spätarchaik und des Strengen Stils*. Roma: Giorgio Bretschneider Editore.

Todisco, L., 1993. *Scultura greca del IV secolo. Maestri e scuole di statuaria tra classicità ed ellenismo*. Milano: Longanesi.

Valtieri, et al. 2007. Il "filosofo" restituito. Indagini sui frammenti bronzei del "Relitto di Porticello" conservati nel Museo Archeologico Nazionale di Reggio Calabria. *Quaderni PAU. Rivista semestrale del Dipartimento Patrimonio Architettonico e Urbanistico dell'Università di Reggio Calabria*, 17(33–34), 177–184.

Vierneisel-Schlörb, B., 1979. *Glyptothek München. Katalog der Skulpturen. Band II. Klassische Skulpturen des 5. und 4. Jahrhunderts v. Chr.* München: C. H. Beck.

Voutiras, E., 1980. *Studien zu Interpretation und Stil griechischer Porträts des 5. und frühen 4. Jahrhunderts*. Bonn: Thesis Rheinische Friedrich-Wilhelms-Universität.

Walter-Karydi, E., 2015. *Die Athener und ihre Gräber (1000–300 v. Chr.)*. Berlin: Walter De Gruyter.

22

Roman Bronzes of Augusta Emerita (Hispania). Representation: Iconography and Models

Trinidad Nogales Basarrate, José María Murciano Calles

Museo Nacional de Arte Romano. Mérida (Spain)

trinidad.nogales@cultura.gob.es

Abstract: A study of the bronze figures from public and private spaces found at Augusta Emerita, in the capital of Lusitania, which are preserved at the Museo Nacional de Arte Romano (National Museum of Roman Art) in Mérida. The pieces are mostly sculpture and public in nature, reflecting the importance and early presence of bronze in official spaces, where they were combined with marble elements as ornamental public material. The iconographic evolution and diversity of bronzes from the private sphere, which are essentially aspects of domestic furnishings, give us an idea of the importance of provincial workshops in western Hispania.

Keywords: Hispania; Province of Lusitania; Colony of Augusta Emerita; Iconography; Bronze Workshops

State of the question[1]

Augusta Emerita, capital of the province of Lusitania in Western Hispania, is a World Heritage archaeological site that we understand better each day (Nogales 2004; Dupré 2004; Álvarez – Mateos 2011). Pieces from large public and private spaces – performance spaces, fora, necropoleis, and houses – are preserved at the Museo Nacional de Arte Romano (MNAR) in Mérida. The collection of bronzes from Augusta Emerita is currently one of the most important in Hispania, for both number and quality of pieces, many of which are quite exceptional.

Given the importance of MNAR's collection of bronzes, as the museum's research team that studies them, we have deemed it essential to complete two complementary bodies of work: first, a functional and typological approach to bronzes in general, and, secondly, an analysis of the iconography, meanings, and models of the bronzes presented here.

The first approach to the study of bronzes in Mérida was published by one of our team members in the catalogue of the exhibition "Los Bronces Romanos en España" (Nogales 1990), which was held in conjunction with the "11th International Congress on Ancient Bronzes" in Madrid in 1990. In the nearly three decades since, knowledge about these pieces from Mérida has improved considerably given that the findings occurred in recent decades, with the most significant ones being made known to the scholarly community in a series of exhibition catalogues (Lozano 1998; Alba – Álvarez 2012; Barrero 2014).

Decorative bronze was present in the colony since its foundation in the age of Augustus around the year 25 BC. It became particularly abundant, along with the emerging presence of marble, which was scarce at first, transforming bronze into a noble material of choice accompanied by local stones such as granite and limestone (Nogales 2003). It maintained its constant presence throughout the early Roman empire (Nogales 2011). Production would continue on until late antiquity, the Visigothic period, and, later, the Islamic world.

One of the greatest problems when attempting to study the bronzes from Emerita is a frequent lack of context. Few have an exact origin, and many of those with an origin came from excavations of smelting workshops, where they were about to be melted down for reuse, which was the leading cause of their disappearance. Therefore, the archaeological context of their discovery is not always valid when trying to determine their original point of origin. We will return to the question of their contexts below, when we fit them into the city's historical evolution.

In order to facilitate their analysis, we have classified the bronze figures from Mérida in two large groups.

1. Bronzes from public spaces
2. Bronzes from private areas

---

[1] This research falls within the scope of the Ministry of Science, Innovation, and University's national R&D project titled "Augusta Emerita and the Early Years of the Roman Province of Lusitania in the Augustan Age" ("Augusta Emerita y los Inicios de la Provincia Romana de Lusitania en Época de Augusto", 2015–2017, HAR2014-52958-P).

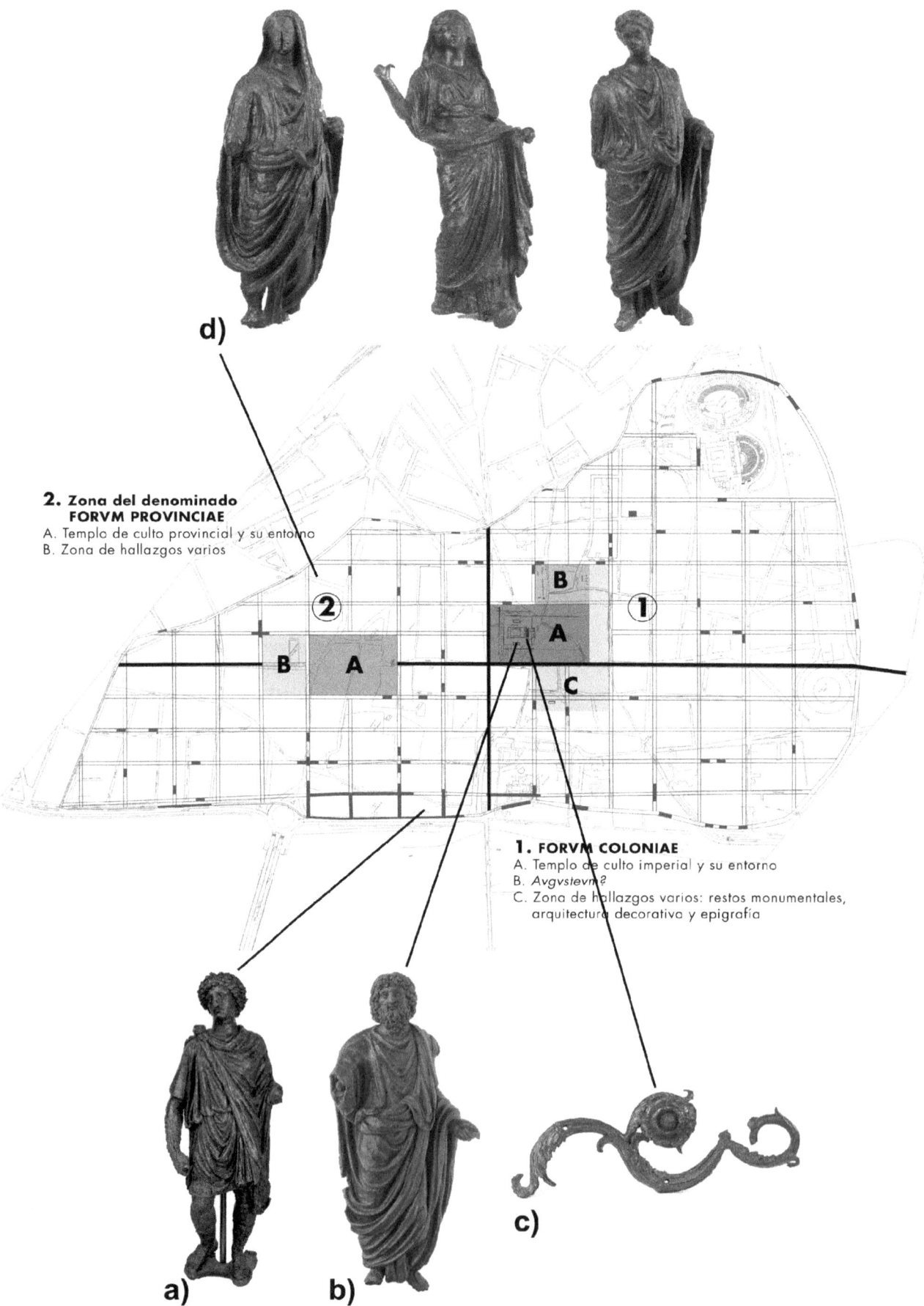

Figure 22.1. Plan of *Augusta Emerita* fora with location of pieces with archaeological context. 1.- Colonial *forum*: a and b) Figurative statuary group: *genius* and *prouincia*, s. II d.C.; c) Augustan decorative architectural scroll. 2.- Provincial *Forum*: d) *Simulacra* of imperial cult of the Tiberian era. (Elaborated by the authors according to Álvarez and Nogales 2003 plan and photographs of the Photo Archive MNAR).

Bronzes from public spaces (Fig. 22.1)

Bronze came to dominate the decoration of public spaces (Fig. 22.1) in the first years of the colony during the Augustan period, essentially in the forum of the colony and in the theatre (Nogales – Gonçalves – Lapuente 2008, 415–422). In both of these areas, bronze was used as the main form of decoration before the emergence of marble during the first phase of urban expansion. From its extensive use in the period from Tiberius to Claudius, marble joined bronze as the decorative material for monuments throughout the imperial period until late antiquity (Nogales 2011). We have good examples of marble sculptures, but the same is not true of bronze elements, which have disappeared owing to problems regarding their preservation and also because they could easily be melted down and reused.

Bronzes in the colonial forum temple: Augustan architectural decoration and statuary groups from the 2nd century AD.

The colonial forum in Mérida is comprised of several successive areas. In its initial Augustan phase is the so-called Temple of Diana, which was dedicated to the imperial cult (Álvarez – Nogales 2003). The building was constructed of local granite, which had all of its components and orders plastered and painted in various colours, including its columns, capitals, plinths, and friezes.

Decorative scroll in bronze (Fig. 22.1c)

A singular example of this official Augustan architecture in bronze before the mass introduction of marble into monumental decoration is a foliage scroll (inv. 18524) from the temple (Álvarez – Nogales 2003, 418–419, fig. 3).

Traces of gilding can be seen, and the object was possibly placed on a red stucco architectural base, of which hardly any remains are observed. The bronze would complement vibrant granite decorations covered with multi-coloured plaster similar to what has been preserved in both the theatre at Metellinum (modern Medellin), as well as in Emerita (Nogales – Merchán 2018, 530–532; Fernandes – Nogales 2018, 432–434).

The use of local stone with bronze appliqués in numerous public spaces was common in decorative architecture of the Republican and Augustan periods, for instance, in northern Italy (Rossignani 1969). The piece from Mérida recalls bronze elements from the altar of the forum of Asisium (Gros – Theodorescu 1987). Therefore, as pre-marble architectural decoration, figured bronze is an important remnant of this early phase of urban development.

The bronze architectural decorations in Augusta Emerita cannot have been an isolated case and, as can be deduced from this single surviving piece, they must have been removed for reuse. Many works in granite from this first phase of the colony's history show signs of perforations and holes, such as the podium of the so-called Temple of Diana (Álvarez – Nogales 2003, 149–150, plates 23–24) or the bronze letters preserved from the monumental inscriptions found in the theatre (Nogales, 1990, 104–105). These remains attest to the presence of both an epigraphical and ornamental use of bronze that has since been lost.

Statuary group from the 2nd century AD (Fig. 22.1a and b)

During the temple's excavations, other important sculptures attributed to a monument with applied bronze pieces were found in one of the pools that lay alongside the temple (Álvarez – Nogales 2003, 278–279, fig. 60; Nogales 2007, 484–490). The most important of them was a bronze sculpture designed to be attached that has been identified as a *Genius Senatus* (inv. 18438, Fig. 22.1b), a fully-formed, life-sized bare male leg (inv. 18439) and various perforated plates (inv. 18440 and 18441), presumably for affixing images. Due to its iconographic parallels, the *Genius* can be dated to the middle of the 2nd century AD (Álvarez – Nogales 2003, 254–257, fig. 50, plate 81).

Another appliqué figure was found together with marble not far from a burial area of the colony in a possible smelting workshop dating to the 5th century AD (inv. DO2012/5/1, Fig. 22.1a). It has been identified as a figure of Diana the Huntress from the domestic sphere (Ayerbe 1999). However, after an exhaustive analysis of the piece, we prefer to identify it as a personification of a Roman province, perhaps Mauretania because of iconographic parallels (Nogales 2007, 484–490). Both the *Genius Senatus* and this figure of a province date to the 2nd century AD and come from the same workshop. With their similar crafting technique and scale, they must form part of an allegorical group from the official sphere. Integrated into a representation of the provinces, which was typical of that time, they are full of symbolism representing the annexation of new provinces within the *oikumene* of the Roman Empire.

A close study of the details of both pieces, together with their morphology, iconography, style, and technique, allows us to attribute them to the same workshop. An *officina* at Mérida must have carried out this important allegorical study of the provinces, perhaps under the supervision of Roman authorities. The cycle of Rome and the provinces proliferated throughout the Empire in the most diverse media: reliefs, mosaics, paintings, and applied arts. This monument was later added to the repertoires of marble statuary of Augustan and Julio-Claudian dynastic cycles in the colony's oldest temple of the imperial cult to demonstrate the *koine* of the *imperium*, a theme that became well developed especially from Hadrian's time onwards (Nogales 2007, 489–490).

Bronzes in the provincial forum: Imperial cult statue *simulacra* (Fig. 22.1d)

The provincial forum complex, which was decorated completely in marble, also had an ambitious iconographic programme, which we have analysed extensively (Nogales 2007, 497–513). Although the large statues were of marble, several of the most important sculptural works in the monumental complex were made of metal, both gold and bronze. In terms of precious metal, well-known is an inscription from a small pedestal mentioning a gold image of the emperor Titus, which must have had an important place in this forum (Nogales 2007, 505–506).

Near the provincial forum, three small votive statuettes were found that were earmarked for smelting. The objects in this complex were from the period from Tiberius to Claudius, which we have identified as a dynastic period dedicated to the imperial cult (Nogales 2007, 510–512, fig. 14).

The statues' poor state of preservation, particularly of their faces, complicates their precise definition. However, we believe that they represent an individual *capite velato*, perhaps a *Genius* or Augustus, a veiled Livia and Tiberius with a crown.

A robed individual (inv. 37399), with his head covered (*capite velato*), is dressed in an expansive toga and appears rather aloof. We believe that this object should be related to the imperial cult, representing the *genius Augusti* or the deified emperor himself, as its iconography resembles that of the first *princeps* (Nogales 2007, 510, fig. 14a).

The female figure (inv. 37397), which could be a representation of Livia, wears a tunic and cloak, a *túnica* and *a palla*, covering her head and recalling the Livia from the basilica at Ocriculum, now in the Vatican (Alexandridis 2004, 129, fig. 4.2), since both open their arms in a similar gesture of prayer. There is a square perforation on the back of this statue, above which the inscription PRO can be seen. This may indicate that the object had a votive function, since it perhaps alludes to a vow for Livia's *salus* (*pro salute*) after she had initially overcome the illness that was eventually to cause her death in AD 29 (Nogales 2007, 510–511, fig. 14b).

The third image is that of a slender male figure in a toga (inv. 37398). This image is unparalleled in that the individual is wearing a civic crown (*corona civica*), for which reason we think that it is the representation of an emperor. Its face is so badly damaged that it is difficult to be certain about its iconography, but it could represent Tiberius or Claudius (Nogales 2007, 510–511, fig. 14c).

The three figures could presumably be interrelated, as their equivalent large-scale marble statues that stood in the temple of the provincial cult built during the Tiberian period could not have done without statues of Tiberius' mother Livia, Divus Augustus, or the emperor's *Genius*. It is quite a full repertoire of images where bronze was used as part of the site's religious iconography.

What use could these pieces have had? We have associated them with the *simulacra* of the imperial family that could have been used for dynastic cult processions that would have started from this provincial forum, as Duncan Fishwick has argued in his studies of this phenomenon (Fishwick 2007). The *Vicomagistri* relief in the Vatican shows this type of procession, where the officiants carry small *simulacra*, each representing a protective Lar. The three bronzes from Mérida could have been part of a processional dynastic group, which would explain their detail and high symbolic value (Nogales 2007, 512–513).

Public statues of illustrious citizens: a *togatus* and an equestrian statue

A statue of a toga-wearing individual from the colony's early years (Fig. 22.2)

The MNAR's collection includes the right foot of a semi-colossal bronze statue wearing a shoe, without clear origins (inv. 7483). It must have been part of a large, fully-formed male statue.

It is preserved up to the base of the leg near the shin, which is slightly inclined. This helps to reconstruct the statue's position, with the body inclined slightly forward. At its base there is a large iron spike, which could have served to attach it to the pedestal. The interior is filled with lead

Figure 22.2. Foot with *calceus equester* of a semi-colossal statue (MNAR Photo Archive / Lorenzo Plana Photo Archive).

to give the image stability, given its large size and weight (Nogales 1990, 106).

The type of shoe worn, a *calceus*, may categorise it in the group associated with the *ordo equester*, which is characterised by its simplicity when compared to the *calceus patricius* or *calceus senatorius*. This type of shoe, a *calceus equester*, appears on numerous togate statues from the Roman provinces, generally individuals from different social backgrounds that were illustrious in their community. We also know of at least one representation of an emperor where it is used as footwear for travelling that is comfortable and simple: on the Arch of Trajan at Benevento (for these parallels, see Goette 1988, 459–464).

Given that the edge of the cloth would not have covered the ankle, the figure seems to have been dressed in a short toga, a *toga exigua*, the use of which was restricted to the Republican and early Augustan period (Goette 1990, 20–29). We would, therefore, seem to be dealing with one of the first public statues in bronze from the colony of Augusta Emerita, at a moment when homage was paid to an important individual from the first years of the colony's history.

These bronze statues must have been typical in the first years of the Romanisation process as honours to local heroes, statues of whom adorned public spaces and fora. The equestrian statue in gilded bronze found in the forum of the colony of Norba Caesarina (Cáceres) is from a similar period, and could represent that colony's patron, L. Cornelius Balbus (Cerrillo – Nogales 2014, 72–75, fig. 8 and 10), associated with a granite pedestal.

These public bronze statues of local personalities must surely have come from the same workshop where craftsmen were familiar with Roman models. Later, the arrival of extensive marble statuary would lead to the gradual and proportional decline in bronze work.

Equestrian statue in a public space (Fig. 22.3)

An interesting figurative group found in a smelting workshop from the Morerías area of Mérida includes an individual in a horse-drawn chariot, galloping and accompanied by a possible barbarian with a trophy who guards this military figure (inv. DO2012/1/5).

A priori, the piece could be interpreted as a figurative bronze appliqué for a larger work. Analysing the iconography, the best parallels lead us to think that these two figures were part of a *balteus*, a decoration displaying symbolic elements that was placed on a horse's neck (Braemer 1994).

The best parallels are the two *baltei* from Brescia and Aosta, which are magnificent examples of these special decorative elements from bronze equestrian statues studied by François Braemer (1994, 75–79). An analysis of the Cartoceto bronze statue group helps us evaluate the overall format of this statue from Mérida (Pollini 1993).

Figure 22.3. Appliqué of equestrian group *balteus* (MNAR Photo Archive / José Luis Rodríguez).

Without a doubt, a public context would justify work of this quality and size, perhaps placing it in the forum of Augusta Emerita. Sadly, the lack of a fixed origin impedes any further advance regarding its public use and location.

Bronzes from private areas

The scarcity of bronze pieces that can clearly be attributed to the public sphere makes it possible to present a rather systematic examination of what remains, as we have seen up to this point. This is not the case with private bronzes, which are more abundant and heterogeneous. A typological analysis of them can be found in the article by Barrero and Sabio in this same volume. However, here we shall focus on the iconographic panorama of these few pieces in order to illustrate their heterogeneity, and to show the semantic richness that is also found in these private contexts.

In short, the collection of private bronzes can be divided into two groups based on their functions: on one hand, we have ornamental statues with no use other than the strictly decorative and, on the other hand, we have functional objects for daily use that are decorated with motifs expressing their owner's tastes and mentality.

Before explaining these examples, we would like to list briefly the possible contexts of discovery within the city because, again, there is a wide range of examples.

Context of appearance

In the public sphere, the use of bronze is attested thanks to a series of pieces, whose state of preservation is poor in many cases, owing to the fact that they have all been reused. This is particularly the case with those that originated in public spaces, as periods of renovation occurred there based on changed political, social, and even aesthetic assumptions of those in power. This led to large-scale sculptures and architectural decoration, which is the commonest use given to noble and semi-noble materials in these complexes. They were recycled over and over again, meaning that what we have in archaeological finds is only a small fraction of what was originally displayed there.

This situation contrasts with the private sphere, where similar processes of reuse were not usually the norm, at least not as extensively or as well organised by central authorities. Of course, reuse and recasting to create new materials occurred extensively for reasons of economic viability, and to take advantage of resources. However, a strictly political cause, requiring a change in mentalities, did not occur to the same degree as it did in the public sphere. In addition, the archaeological processes that have tended to seal off these private spaces favour the conservation of finds and need to be taken into account. This is not often the case with the processes that took place in the public sphere.

The two most frequent private spheres in which bronze objects with strong iconographic content have appeared are private houses and burial areas. In both cases, situations exist that encapsulate, as we have argued, the objects in a closed archaeological context. In the domestic sphere, it is typical for rooms to collapse and be renovated later, with objects of great archaeological relevance being lost inside. As an example, one may cite the appearance of a beautiful, banquet-themed fretted plate. It was found among the calcined remains of a door in some private baths that has been interpreted as a possible peephole (Ayerbe – Alba 1998), which was deposited in the MNAR for preservation by the CCMM (inv. DO2012/1/7).

In the funerary sphere, there is obvious interest in preserving the objects found in a burial deposit, regardless of their nature. There are abundant examples of such collections of materials. Just to cite some well-known cases, highlights of the MNAR's collection are the grave goods with medical instruments that have recently been studied by Bejarano (2015, with literature). A third private space in which bronze pieces survive are the many dumping sites that are found at the periphery of the city outside the walls. Here, relevant objects were again preserved and sealed off thanks to the constant discarding of waste (Acero 2018). In this same vein, the MNAR has recently carried out archaeological interventions in a plot adjacent to the museum where an extension will be added to the current building. During this work, an important dumping site was discovered, which is currently in the process of being studied and has already provided interesting discoveries of all types of materials.

Lastly, a fourth possible type of survival space may be termed industrial, as objects that were forgotten when they were being prepared for recasting have frequently been found in metal workshops. An example from Mérida is the collection of pieces found in a Visigothic smelting workshop (Ayerbe 1999; Nogales 2007, 484–490) that include two objects that have already been discussed in the section above on bronze figures found in the public sphere: the personification of Mauretania (inv. DO2012/5/1) and the appliqué with an emperor mounted on a horse (inv. DO2012/2/5).

Small statuary: a galloping horse figure (Fig. 22.4)

A piece that could possibly be attributed to a context similar to the one just described is the figure of a galloping horse (inv. 30215; Mélida 1925, 319–320, no. 1145; García 1949, 450, no. 480; Nogales 1990, 263, no. 187; Nogales 2000, 77–78). It was found in 1924 together with other interesting bronze pieces while a hole was being dug on the grounds of a house in the calle Calvario (Mélida 1925, 319). Due to the date of its discovery, we do not know the piece's exact archaeological context. However, in view of the heterogeneity of the group of objects, and the house's location in an area outside the city walls, it is highly likely that it was one of these recasting workshops. Today, the materials found there form part of the MNAR's collection, including a figure of a wrestler (inv. 30332), an architectural palmette (inv. 30118), a possibly piece from furniture (inv. 32531), and the three imperial figurines (inv. 37397–37399) discussed above.

Nevertheless, they are materials that could also fit with Mélida's suggestion that they should be interpreted as a group of ornamental furnishings and votive offerings associated with a cult building located nearby. However, in our view, this hypothesis must be rejected because, as previously mentioned, the objects' diverse character, with some being eminently public and associated with official worship of the emperor (in the case of the three imperial figures analysed in the previous section), while others, such

Figure 22.4. Galloping horse figure (MNAR Photo Archive / Lorenzo Plana).

as the one in question here, appear more easily associated with the decoration of domestic spaces.

The small, 45 cm long figure of a horse must have had a now-lost rider whose only remains are a hollow on the horse's back. What is preserved is partially fragmented, yet its high technical quality is undeniable, so much so that Mélida (1925, 320) evoked the Parthenon reliefs when discussing the figure's head, stating that it was "very fine art". However, the most immediate and closely related iconography, both in terms of its mood as well as its execution, is the statuette of Alexander the Great on horseback found near the Theatre of Herculaneum (Calcani 1997; Moreno 2002; Cadario 2010, the latter with an extensive updated bibliography), which is surely a reminder of the statue that Lysippos created for the Granicus monument. We only have this reproduction of the work from Herculaneum. However, as is widely documented for these famous Greek works, an able artisan from Mérida could have inspected models of these small statuettes that circulated throughout the Empire. The lack of rider impedes our ability to be sure that it is another copy, or simply another representation that uses Lysippos' statue as a model. Another horse that is also from Herculaneum and shares a similar format (Moreno 2002, fig. 243), has been associated with the one Alexander is riding. They must, therefore, be a pair, shown together on a piece of furniture, probably a table, as part of the ornamentation of an important household.

Functional objects

Lamp component (Fig. 22.5)

Other pieces connected to private contexts are purely functional, but their important symbolic and iconographic content merits their inclusion here (see, in this volume, the chapter by Barrero and Sabio, who provide an in-depth discussion of the typology of these objects). Among them, the most notable is a circular object in the form of a plate (diam. 49 cm) that must have been part of a lamp, candelabra, *thymiaterion*, or similar instrument (for different models, see Testa 1989), either as a support or as another decorative element around the shaft of such a support (inv. 24240).

As already mentioned, its circular form, with a hole in the middle, would have allowed it to fit onto the shaft that supported it. Its profile is not flat, but slightly curved at the centre, which means that the object cannot have served as a base. The decoration is comprised of four circular registers, one figurative and the others with stylised foliage motifs. The largest of these has several foliage friezes, which comprise hollow scrolls placed in a regular, alternating manner with vine leaves and bunches of grapes. It combines silver niello decoration for the leaves and scroll branches with gilding for the grapes. In terms of the friezes, they comprise fourteen representations of wreaths and festoons, which are also decorated with niello (in this case, applied to the *taenia* that wraps around them).

Figure 22.5. Component of possible *lampadarius* with vegetal decoration and figurative appliques of muses and Apollo (MNAR Photo Archive / Lorenzo Plana).

What most interests us about the piece is the iconographic identification of the small appliqué figures. As we have already mentioned, there are fourteen of them, of which nine have been lost. Only the mark of their attachment remains, accompanied by the outline of a support, which allows some of their silhouettes to be identified. Only six figures have been lost almost entirely, which makes their identification impossible. It is clear that these are the nine Muses, accompanied by five other figures, one of which could be Apollo (Aznar – Gaztelu – Yllán 1990, 23. 282; Nogales 1997). All of the preserved Muses appear to be dressed in a *stola*, represented by the V-shaped folds that are formed around the neck, and the folds that fall straight from the shoulders down the sides. Their *stolae* are gathered up under the chest with a wide belt, and each of the figures is adorned with a crown. The piece's iconography continues to be studied and merits a full discussion elsewhere.

Pieces of a chariot (Fig. 22.6)

In terms of functional objects, Mérida has several pieces from a chariot, which are traditionally considered to be rein-holders, and are currently the source of much debate (for their use and function, and the current controversy, see Barrero and Sabio). Two, and possibly a third – this one, inv. 30140, in a form different from the other two, with a tendency towards verticality and with an added handle –, form part of the collection of the MNAR, and all are characterised by having a central axis with rings or spaces presumably to pass reins through. The decoration of two of them (inv. 26438 and 30140) is comprised of zoomorphic motifs: the first with a panther or lion (Molina – Mora 1982; Nogales 1990) and swan protomes, the second with pairs of animals hunting each other (García 1949, 446, no. 474; Molina – Mora 1982; Nogales 1990).

Figure 22.6. Pieces of a cart with figurative and hunting decoration (MNAR Photo Archive / Lorenzo Plana and José Luis Rodríguez).

A high degree of naturalism is presented in the hunting scene, with animals in the most noteworthy and representative poses for their species: one pair is comprised of a lion with its front claws on the hindquarters of a ram that is turning its head back in terror; the other pair is composed of a hunting dog, perhaps a greyhound, that is biting the leg of a hare. Both scenes are exemplary displays of different hunting methods: the goal of the lion is to mount its prey in order to reach its jugular or another main artery, while the dog's goal is to firmly bite any part of the animal and drag it off.

The artisan shows a great ability to observe details like the dog's collar, the tensed muscles of all the animals and their respectively ferocious and terrified expressions. Even if all of these details make the piece outstanding, there are others that place it more in the category of what has been termed "provincial art", particularly noticeable in the face and proportions of the hare, which are rather unrealistic. With regard to the hare's size, which is too large, this could be due to the need to balance the piece in terms of composition, as the four figures are all of a similar size.

The third piece, traditionally called a rein-holder, was submitted to the MNAR by the CCMM, with inv. DO2012/1/8 (Barrero 2013, with reference to the previous bibliography). Combined with panther and lion protomes, the main motifs are two figures with iconography that is typical of scholars and is common from the Hellenistic age onwards: nude torsos covered only by a cloak, with a *volumen* and diptych respectively. At first interpreted as philosophers, a new theory (Sastre 2010, 79) associates them with the Christian sphere, given that the piece appears to date from the 4th century, thanks to the context of its discovery (for all the details, see Barrero 2013). Therefore, these could be figures of Peter and Paul, who were assimilated to the Hellenistic representation of philosophers at a time when Christian iconography was being configured on the basis of Greco-Roman artistic traditions (Zanker 2000).

Despite having diverse themes, the three "rein-holders" both share a feeling of refined and ornate luxury. The panther has a multi-faceted meaning, which could be related to the Bacchic cycle that was widely used in the private sphere to convey festive connotations or events that were held in the amphitheatre. On the other hand, however, like the animal hunting motif, they could be associated with the use of hunting activities as a sign of the power and high purchasing power of the local elite (Trinquier – Vendries 2009). A similar argument could be made for the pair of philosophers or saints. Activities connected to erudition were also associated with the leisured class, given that only individuals in such a position could afford to dedicate themselves to this kind of work, a concept that continued also as a literary theme (Dosi 2006, 95–102).

Possible peephole (Fig. 22.7)

Lastly, we shall include another functional piece with strong iconographic content, which is also presented in the article dedicated to the MNAR's collection regarding its functionality and typology (Barrero and Sabio, in this volume). We recommend reading this article for related details concerning the location of their discovery. (We will see shortly how the context is also important when trying to understand the piece's iconography.) The relevant artefact is a 19-cm-wide fretwork plate that is part of the CCMM's collection currently held at the MNAR (inv. DO2012/1/7, Ayerbe – Alba 1998; Ayerbe 1998; Ayerbe 2012). Represented on it is a banquet or symposium scene

Figure 22.7. Possible peephole with mythological banquet scene (MNAR Photo Archive / José Luis Rodríguez).

(and not a *thiasos*, as was described by Ayerbe 1998), laid out as a frieze and framed by a band of foliage scrollwork with fruit. In the Roman period, they took advantage of the said frame to perforate the plate for attachment.

The full-length figures maintain a rich variety of poses and moods, celebrating a banquet at which wine and grapes are being served. That, together with the presence of maenads and satyrs with their characteristic attributes, makes us think of a Bacchic symposium, although this one is presided over by Mercury at the centre of the scene, with his *caduceus* and emblematic ram below him.

The scene's subject and the exquisite manner of its composition recall sarcophagi with Bacchic themes. The figures are crowded together in a jumbled manner, each in contact with another, with no background. The composition favours the piece's manufacture, but this is also observed in the aforementioned sarcophagi. Although there is no absolutely identical pattern shared between them, all of the postures and mood visible in the piece from Mérida, even the least obvious ones, are also represented quite frequently on sarcophagi: for example, the satyr stepping on the krater (Matz 1968–1975, vol. 2, 121, in this case a basket) or the basket with its lid that has fallen under the cupbearer (Matz 1968–1975, vol. 2, taf. 105), which is a reference to the basket from which a snake emerges, a symbol of the god Bacchus (for example, Matz 1968–1975, vol. 2, taf. 138).

The only unusual element in the group is the figure of Mercury, placed in the centre and providing the scene's axis. He takes the place of Bacchus, who would normally have been presiding over the symposium, as all of the elements described are characteristic of a bacchanalian celebration. Ayerbe related these circumstances to the imperial cult, given that Mercury is the tutelary god of Augustus, with the bronze plaque symbolising the peace and prosperity experienced throughout the Empire (Ayerbe – Alba 1998 and Ayerbe 1998). However, these political references seem strange to us in a private leisured context such as in the baths where they were found.

We think that the piece should be interpreted as a type of syncretism, which is often observed in Roman households. This is manifested in all types of art, although it is particularly relevant in mosaics where dissimilar scenes are often combined. Well-known examples from Augusta Emerita include the mosaics from the calle Sagasta (inv. 14151, Blanco 1978, 30–32, no. 9), in which Muses, Horae, Victories, poets and philosophers appear together with Egyptian scenes, or from the travesía de Pedro María Plano (inv. 36192, Álvarez 1990, 37–49, no. 3), where Orpheus, Erotes, scenes of professions – harvesting, hunting –, fighting, and Nilotic scenes are combined. There is an iconographic motif of Mercury transporting an infant Bacchus to the island of Nisia, but this does not correspond to our scene. According to the *Lexicon Iconographicum Mythologiae Classicae* (III.1, *s.v.* Bacchus, 561, Carlo Gasparri) the only association between Mercury and Bacchus as adults is found in a *lararium*, again in a private sphere, in a scene in which Bacchus is associated with other family or domestic divinities (see no. 98, 99 and 121). We also know of a sarcophagus with the Bacchus-Mercury pair (Zimmer 1982, 218, no. 177), which is once again a scene from the private sphere that wishes to bear witness to tutelary gods, this time in a funeral context.

As for the decorative piece under discussion, we believe that it is meant to represent the tutelary divinities of the family within a relaxed leisured context. The presence of Mercury, possibly the tutelary god, in a festive environment is a sort of game that makes sense in the context of baths, while ownership could also be explained by observing the location of the house itself. This house is located next to the wall, on a street that ends at a small entrance gate to the city, in the so-called Area (Manzana) II of the Morerías site (for its place in the urban plan, see Alba 1997, which has also been confirmed orally by the excavator, in this case Alba himself). It is quite easy to imagine how important commerce and transport may have been to the economic life of the family, which would explain why Mercury, the god of merchants and travellers, was represented in this home. Furthermore, the baths were previously *tabernae* integrated into the home (Alba 1997, 290–291), and so we find activities associated with the business of the *domus* once again. In fact, Ayerbe mentioned the possibility that the piece could have been extensively reused due to the number of holes it has of varying sizes and locations, leading us to imagine that it was originally set up in another location.

This summary presentation of some of the bronzes from private contexts that are preserved at the MNAR has helped, we hope, to reconstruct something of the cultural milieu of the city of Mérida during the Roman period. In sum, the horse statuette, the support with the Muses, the various "rein-holders", and the supposed peephole all belonged, at different stages, to a sphere of refinement and worship, with diverse references ranging between cult art and more popular art, as was common for Roman *domus* ornamentation.

Acknowledgements

We thank Prof. Jonathan Edmondson for the corrections and comments provided. We are also grateful for the conversations with our colleague Rafael Sabio, who was the first to comment on the meaning of the interpretation of the peephole.

Bibliography

Alba Calzado, M., 1997. Ocupación diacrónica del área arqueológica de Morería (Mérida). *Mérida. Memoria de Excavaciones Arqueológicas*, 1 (1994–1995), 223–244.

Alba Calzado, M. – Álvarez Martínez, J.M., ed., 2012. *El Consorcio y la arqueología emeritense. De la excavación al Museo*. Mérida: Consorcio de la Ciudad Monumental Histórico-Artística y Arqueológica de Mérida y Ministerio de Educación, Cultura y Deporte.

Alexandridis, A., 2004. *Die Frauen des Römischen Kaiserhauses*. Mainz am Rhein: Philipp von Zabern.

Álvarez Martínez, J.M., 1990. *Mosaicos romanos de Mérida. Nuevos hallazgos*. Mérida: Ministerio de Cultura.

Álvarez Martínez, J.M. – Mateos Cruz, P., ed., 2011. *Actas del Congreso Internacional 1910 – 2010: El Yacimiento Emeritense*, Mérida.

Álvarez Martínez, J. M. – Nogales Basarrate, T., 2003. *Forum Coloniae Augustae Emeritae. Templo de Diana*. Mérida: Asamblea de Extremadura.

Acero Pérez, J., 2018: *La gestión de los residuos en Augusta Emerita. Siglos I a.C.–VII d.C.* Madrid: Consejo Superior de Investigaciones Científicas.

Ayerbe Vélez, R., 1998. Mirilla. In: M. Almagro-Gorbea – J.M. Álvarez Martínez, ed., *Hispania. El legado de Roma*, Madrid: Dirección General de Bellas Artes y Bienes Culturales, 605, no. 268.

Ayerbe Vélez, R., 1999. Escultura romana en bronce hallada en Morería. *Mérida. Memoria de Excavaciones Arqueológicas*, 3(1999), 339–346.

Ayerbe Vélez, R. 2012. Mirilla. In: M. Alba Calzado – J.M. Álvarez Martínez. ed., *El Consorcio y la arqueología emeritense. De la excavación al Museo*. Mérida: Consorcio de la Ciudad Monumental Histórico-Artística y Arqueológica de Mérida, 128.

Ayerbe Vélez, R. – Alba Calzado, M., 1998. Mirilla. In: M. del Lozano Barolozzi, ed., *Ana-Barraeca. Confluencia de culturas*. Mérida: Consorcio de la Ciudad Monumental Histórico-Artística y Arqueológica de Mérida, 89–90.

Barrero Martín, N., 2013. *Catálogo de toréutica de la Antigüedad Tardía (siglos IV–VIII d.C.) del Museo Nacional de Arte Romano. Bronces y orfebrería*. Mérida: Museo Nacional de Arte Romano de Mérida.

Bejarano Osorio, A., 2015. *La medicina en la Colonia Augusta Emerita*, Badajoz: Instituto de Arqueología de Mérida.

Braemer, F., 1994. Le balteus et ses problems. In: Ronke, J., ed., *Akten der 10. Internationalen Tagung über antike Bronzen*, Freiburg, 18–22 July 1988. Stuttgart: Kommissionsverlag, 75–95.

Cadario, M., 2010. Bronzetto equestre di Alessandro Magni da Ercolano. In: E. La Rocca, ed., 2010. *I giorni di Roma*. Milan: Skira, 290–291.

Calcani, G., 1997. L'immagine di Alessandro Magno nel gruppo equestre del Granico. In: J. Carlsen – B. Due – O.D. Due – B. Poulsen, ed., *Alexander the great. Reality and myth*. Rome: L'Erma di Bretschneider, 29–39.

Cerrillo de Cáceres, E. – Nogales Basarrate, T. 2014. Colonia *Norbensis Caesarina* (Cáceres). In: T. Nogales – M.J. Pérez del Castillo, de., *Ciudades Romanas de Extremadura*. Mérida: Museo Nacional de Arte Romano, 57–83.

Dosi, A., 2006. *Otium. Il tempo libero dei Romani*. Rome: Quasar.

Dupré, X. ed., 2004. *Mérida. Colonia Augusta Emerita. Las capitales provinciales de Hispania 2*. Rome: L'Erma di Bretschneider.

Fernandes, L. – Nogales Basarrate, T., 2018. Teatro romano de Olisipo: programas decorativos teatrales de Lusitania. In: C. Márquez – D. Ojeda, ed., *Actas de la VIII Reunión de escultura romana en Hispania*. Córdoba, 431–455.

Fernández de Avilés, A., 1958. Pasarriendas y otros bronces de carro romanos hallados en España. *Archivo Español de Arqueología*, 31 (1958), 3–63.

Fishwick, D. 2007. Imperial processions at Augusta Emerita. In: T. Nogales – J. González, de., *Culto Imperial: política y poder*. Mérida, 18–20 May 2006. Rome: L'Erma di Bretschneider, 29–47.

García and Bellido, A., 1949. *Esculturas romanas de España y Portugal*. Madrid: Consejo Superior de Investigaciones Científicas.

Goette, H. R., 1988. *Mulleus – embas – calceus*. Ikonografische Studien zu Römischen Schuhwerk. *Jahrbuch des Deutschen Archäologischen Institut*, 103 (1988). 401–464.

Goette, H.R., 1990. *Studien zu römischen Togadarstellungen*. Mainz am Rhein: Philipp von Zabern.

Gros, P. – Theodorescu, D., 1987. L´autel du Forum d´Assise. *Mélanges de l'École française de Rome*, 99 (2, 1987), 693–710.

Lozano Barolozzi, M. del M., ed., 1998. *Ana-Barraeca. Confluencia de culturas*. Mérida: Consorcio de la Ciudad Monumental Histórico-Artística y Arqueológica de Mérida.

Molina, M. – Mora, G., 1982. Una nueva teorías sobre los llamados pasarriendas: en torno a una pieza de carro del Museo de Mérida. *Archivo Español de Arqueología,* 55 (1982), 205–212.

Moreno, P., 2002. *Alessandro Magno. Imagini come storia*. Rome: Libreria dello Stato.

Nogales Basarrate, T., 1990. Bronces romanos en Augusta Emérita. In: M. Aznar – L. Gaztelu – C. Yllán, ed., *Bronces romanos en España*. Madrid: Centro Nacional de Exposiciones. 103–115.

Nogales Basarrate, T., 1997. Lampadario con figuras alegóricas. In: J., Arce – S. Ensoli – E. La Rocca, ed., *Hispania Romana. Desde tierra de conquista a provincia del Imperio*. Madrid: Electa, 363, no. 109.

Nogales Basarrate, T., 2000. *Espectáculos en Augusta Emerita: Espacios, imágenes y protagonistas del ocio y espectáculo en la sociedad romana emeritense*. Badajoz: Ministerio de Educación, Cultura y Deporte.

Nogales Basarrate, T., 2003. Colonia Augusta Emerita (Mérida): Von der Granitstadt zur Marmorstadt. *Actas del Congreso Die Stadt als Grossbaustelle. Von der Antike bis zur Neuzeit*. Berlin, 7–11 November 2001. Berlin: Deutsches Archäologisches Institut, 82–87.

Nogales Basarrate, T., ed., 2004. *Augusta Emerita. Territorios, Espacios, Imágenes y Gentes en Lusitania Romana*. Mérida: Ministerio de Cultura.

Nogales Basarrate, T., 2007. Culto Imperial en *Augusta Emerita*: imágenes y programas urbanos. In: T. Nogales – J. González, ed., *Culto Imperial: política y poder.* Mérida, 18–20 May 2006. Rome: L'Erma di Bretschneider, 449–541.

Nogales Basarrate, T., 2011. Escultura romana en Augusta Emerita. In: J.M. Álvarez Martínez – P. Mateos Cruz, ed., 2011. *Actas del Congreso Internacional 1910–2010: El Yacimiento Emeritense*, Mérida, 411–462.

Nogales Basarrate, T. – Gonçalves, L.G. – Lapuente, M.P., 2008. Materiales lapídeos, mármoles y talleres en Lusitania. In: T. Nogales – J. Beltrán, ed., *Marmora Hispana: Explotación y uso de los materiales pétreos en la Hispania Romana*. Rome: L'Erma di Bretchsneider, 408–466.

Nogales Basarrate, T. – Merchán, M.J., 2018. Teatro romano de Metellinum. Programa escultórico-decorativo. In: C. Márquez – D. Ojeda, ed., *Actas de la VIII Reunión de escultura romana en Hispania*. Córdoba, 527–551.

Pollini, J., 1993. The Cartoceto Bronzes: Portraits of a Roman Aristocratic Family of the Late First Century B.C. *American Journal of Archaeology*, 97, 423–446.

Rossignani, M.P., 1969. *La decorazione architettonica in bronzo del mondo romano*. Contributi dell'Istituto di archeologia, 2, 44–98.

Sastre de Diego, I., 2010. *Los primeros edificios cristianos de Extremadura. Sus espacios y elementos litúrgicos. Caelum in terra*. Mérida: Asamblea de Extremadura.

Testa, A., 1989. *Candelabri e thimiateria*. Rome: L'Erma di Bretschneider.

Trinquier, J. and Vendries, C., eds. 2009. *Actes du colloque international Chasses antiques. Pratiques et représentations dans le monde grécp-romain (III s. av.–IV s. apr. J.-C.)*. Université Rennes II, 20-21 September 2007. Rennes: Presses Universitaires de Rennes.

Zanker, P. 2000. Dal culto della "paideia" alla visione di Dio. In: S. Ensoli – E. La Rocca, de., *Aurea Roma. Dalla città pagana alla città cristiana*, Rome: L'Erma di Bretchneider, 295–300.

Zimmer, G., 1982. *Römische Berufsdarstellungen*. Berlin: Gebr. Mann Verlag.

Who was in Charge of Fastening Bronze Statues on their Bases? A Case Study of Two Classical-Group Bases from Delphi

Rachel Nouet

French School at Athens

rachelnouet@gmail.com

Abstract: The examination of signed bases with traces of attachment provides some valuable information on the process of creating a bronze sculpture. This paper will focus on two well-known group bases from the Classical period in Delphi: the Navarchs' and the Arcadians' monuments. Both presented several bronze statues made by different famous sculptors, as shown by the associated signatures and Pausanias' testimony, as well as by the numerous preserved footprints and inscriptions identifying the characters. We will consider how the cross-examination of literary, epigraphical, and technical evidence demonstrates that the installation on these bases was not the responsibility of the sculptor or his workshop, but was assigned to one or several other dedicated teams.

Keywords: Statue Bases; Fastening Techniques; Delphi; Craftsmanship; Labour Division

While fastening a figure on its base constitutes one of the last stages in the manufacturing process of a sculptural monument, the ancient techniques have not so far drawn much attention from scholars, with the noteworthy exceptions of Raubitschek (1938; 1943) on Attic bronze and marble statue bases from the Archaic to the end of the 5th century BCE, and a study by Willer (1996), focusing on the fastening techniques for bronze statues based on preserved statues, followed by a second article (Willer 2000), centered on Roman bronzes. Other scholars provided some paragraphs on the question in more general works on the manufacturing process of Greek bronzes, as for example Bol (1978, 84–85; 1985, 160–162); but no comprehensive study has yet been dedicated to the subject. It is probably due to the very few preserved original bronze statues which present a clearly identified and properly registered and studied mounting system – the best known case being that of the Riace warriors studied by Formigli (1984, 135–136, and figs. 17. 19. 20. 36, 120. 122. 123. 137). However, the excavations of ancient sites provided a large number of empty bases whose top face has often preserved holes and mortises. These traces help us not only to understand the different methods used to fasten a statue on its base throughout antiquity, but also to approach, in some ways, statues that have disappeared. Through these traces, information can be obtained on their material and scale, but also often on their number and position on group bases and, in some instances, their posture.

These bases are also very useful because they often present dedicatory or honorific inscriptions, which allow us to date them. Moreover, some of them even bear the sculptor's signature. Since original bronze statues whose authors are known are so rare, the combination of signatures and technical features, such as our mounting traces, provides valuable information about the role and involvement of the sculptor or his workshop at this final stage of the manufacturing process. Some questions might then arise: would it be possible to define some technical features specific to a sculptor or a workshop, through the examination of the mounting traces on signed bases? Can we apprehend to what extent the sculptor was responsible for the mounting of the statue? Is it even possible to identify some teams dedicated to this operation?

In order to answer these questions, the first step is to compare similar traces (i.e., traces left by the same fastening system) on bases signed by the same sculptor. Subsequently, these traces should be compared to similar ones on contemporaneous bases signed by other sculptors. This will allow the identification of specific features, if they exist. However, not so many bases signed by the same sculptor are preserved which present intelligible traces left by the same technique. Moreover, since they were not meant to be visible, these traces were often carved quite roughly, with simple tools. Thus, one could argue that, over time, even a single craftsman might have left very different traces.

That is why I will focus in this paper on two well-known group bases from the Classical period, the original exposition context of which is located in the lower part of the so-called "Sacred Way" in the Apollo sanctuary at Delphi: the bases of the Navarchs and of the Arcadians. Both held several bronze statues, made by different famous sculptors, each of whom produced several different figures. This is evidenced both by the identified signatures and by Pausanias' testimony. They also preserve numerous footprints, all belonging to the same technique, and inscriptions identifying the characters. Thus, they each offer what could be defined as a "closed-context" for comparing traces of statues: the mounting of the statues on each monument was made at the same time and of course in the same place and, on each base, each sculptor made several figures. While the exact reconstitution of the monuments remains difficult (especially for the Navarchs group), I will try to show how the cross-examination of literary, epigraphical, and technical evidence presented by such large groups helps us to better understand this stage of the manufacturing process – the installation. However, before beginning the study of these two bases, I would like to make some remarks on the technique employed here and how it allows us to compare traces left on bases.

The "sole technique"

Without going into too much detail, I will focus in this paper on the technique used in both our case-studies, usually called the "sole technique". It was first described by Bol (1978, 85, figs. a–e) as the "Sohlentechnik", which he thought belonged to the Hellenistic Period. In both the direct and indirect lost wax casting processes, the surface of the bronze statue supposed to touch the ground was usually left open already on the wax prototype, either entirely or in parts. Contrary to the idea expressed by Bol (1978, 84–87; 1985, 160–162), there was no real chronological evolution concerning these openings: the Riace statues show entirely open bronze soles (Triches 1984, 78–79, figs. 11–14.a–d, pl.XI, and figs. 46–47); examples of partly open bronze feet are given by the Poseidon from Cape Artemision (ca. 460 BCE), according to Bol (1978, 84–85) – for which I could not find a full picture of the soles, only of the toes of the statue (Arch. Delt. 13, 1930/1933, fig. 41) – the standing foot of the Antikythera Youth, usually dated to the third quarter of the 4th c. BCE (Willer 1996, 361, fig. 24), but also both feet of the 2nd quarter of the 5th c. Delphi Charioteer (Chamoux 1955, fig. 1, pl. II). They surely had a technical purpose during the casting, since openings in the bronze walls prevented the accumulation of gas (Willer 1996, 568). According to Formigli (1984, 112–114), they may also have provided the opportunity to maintain the inner core by the use of metal rods crossing through the legs and feet. But these openings also served later for the mounting of the statue on the base, as attested by the preserved bronze statues and the traces on bases.

On bases, the "sole technique" can easily be identified by the cuttings corresponding to the feet of the statue. The one under the standing foot, which was set flat on the ground, has an extended oval shape, sometimes very similar to footprints or soles. When the statue is in a so-called "Polykleitan" stance with the other foot on the toes, the mortise under the latter is a simple round or oval hole. These mortises are usually 6 to 8 cm deep, and larger at the bottom (Fig. 23.1). The sole under the standing foot is always smaller than the actual bronze foot – approximately one third. These proportions were first suggested by Arnold (1969, 24–25), from the observation of traces left on Classical bases from Olympia, preserving the outline of the feet around the mortises (the Kyniskos (*IvO* 148) and the Aristion (*IvO* 165) bases). Another later example that I examined supports the same conclusion, the 2nd-century base erected in honour of the epimelet Apel[…] on Delos (*ID* 1666): the left foot of the bronze statue, preserved on its top surface, is about 30 cm long, that is one third longer than the empty 23,5-cm-long "sole" of the second foot.

Once the cuttings had been carved, the bronze statue was placed on the base, with each opened foot upon the dedicated "sole". Some lead was poured inside the feet, in order to fill them and the mortises, and thus form lead tenons to anchor the statue to the base. This lead tenon can be seen on several bronze statues and feet discovered in ancient shipwrecks, as for example on the Antikythera statue feet wearing sandals (Bol 1972, 32–34; von den Hoff 1994, 151; Kaltsas et al. 2012, 62–101, especially cat. 31–34, 90–91). Indeed, Willer (1996) demonstrated that these types of tenons (only made of lead) could not have been made in the workshop. Given the dimensions of their bases, large-scale statues could only be mounted in the field; the presence of such tenons on statues from shipwrecks shows that they were not produced for export, but had been removed from their original context and shipped away. Moreover, examination of lead tenons and mortises show that their shapes overlap and that they bear the same irregular surface.

On bases, this kind of cutting in the shape of the foot appeared for the first time during the second quarter of the 5th c. BCE, in order to mount medium to large-scale bronze statues. The first well-attested bases with the "sole" technique are dated around 460–450 BCE. The Mikythos base in Olympia is surely dated between 467 and around 455 BCE; even if some statues were taken by Nero, and some blocks show clear evidence of reuse, the block B bears the original fixation traces, which are a "sole" for the left foot, and a round hole for the right foot set on the toes (Eckstein 1969, 33–42, figs. 4,6 [top], 7 [bottom]). In Delphi, two bases with "soles" are usually dated around 450: the Gortynian base, inv. 1657 (Pomtow 1918, 62, n° 88; Pouilloux 1976, n° 456), and the base offered by Phayllos' children, inv. 1618 (Pomtow 1909, 35; Pouilloux 1976, n° 453). Until the end of the century, it was used among other techniques, such as the "dowel" and the "lead tenon" techniques. These are characterised on bases by circular or oval single holes (one under each heel, or two by foot), but differ in the use of a metal dowel, which is present in the "dowel technique" but absent in the "lead tenon" one. These two systems were first both described as the one and only "tenon technique" ("Zapfentechnik") by Raubitschek (1938) because they left the same kind of traces on bases. However, remains of metal dowels are to be seen on several bases dating from the Archaic period to the mid-5th-c. BCE, for example in Athens on the Heortios and Ophsiades base (EM 6318) from the Acropolis (Raubitschek 1949,

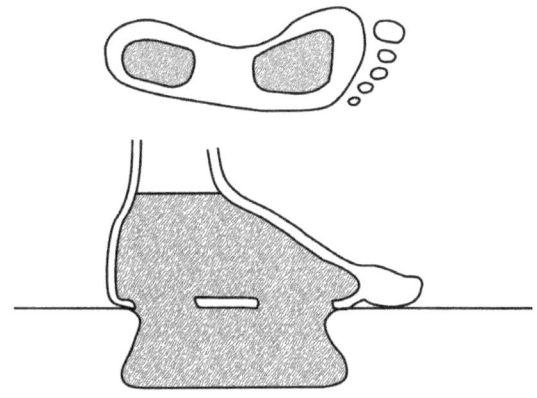
Two small openings
(Cape Artemision God; type A according to P. C. Bol)

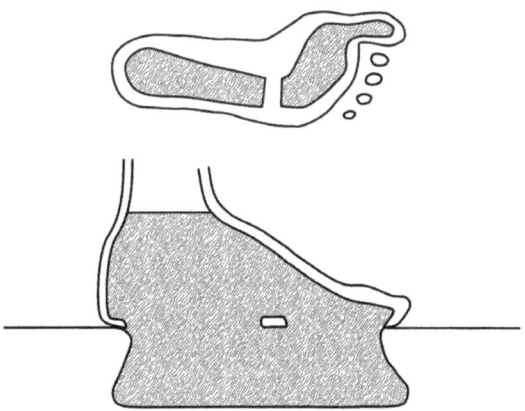
Two large openings
(Antikythera Youth; type B according to P. C. Bol)

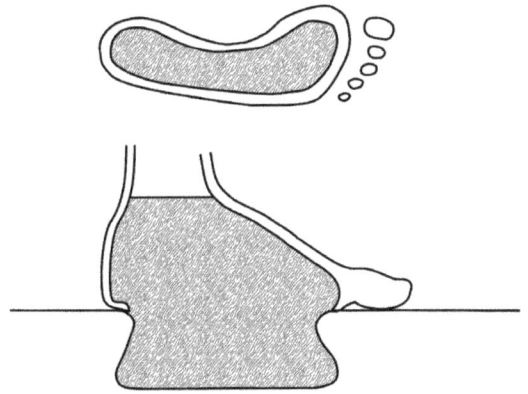
One big opening under the whole sole except the toes
(the Berlin "Praying Boy")

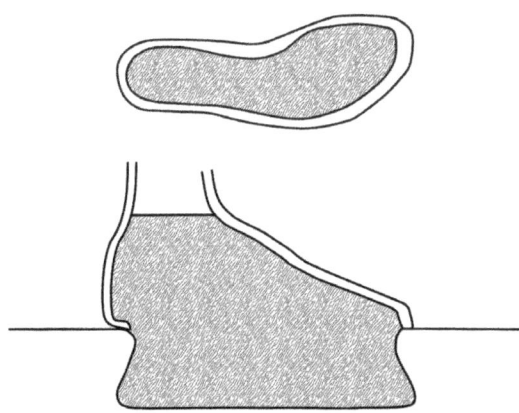
One big opening under the whole sole except the toes
(the Antikythera "Philosopher", with shoe)

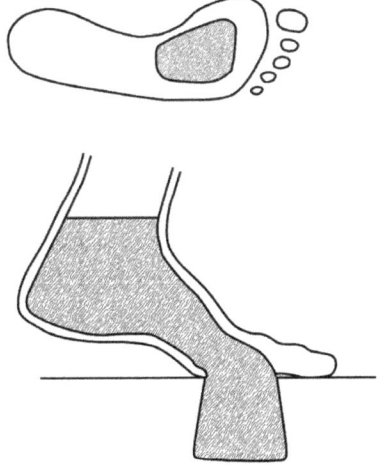
Free foot fixation

Sketch of the mortises on the base («Polycletean stance»)

Figure 23.1. The "sole" technique (R. Nouet).

n° 40; Kissas 2000, 231–232, B183). But there is no dowel preserved in the lead tenon under both feet of the Riace warriors (Triches 1984, 78–79, pl. XI, and figs. 46–47; Formigli 1984, 135–137, fig. 36). The hypothesis suggested by Formigli (1984) that, initially, the rods that formed the inner armature of the statue extended out of the feet and served for the mounting of the statue cannot be proven; either way, in their preserved state, they were both only mounted by lead tenons. As has been shown in my PhD thesis (Nouet, to be published in the BEFAR collection), other techniques were used at different times to fasten bronze statues: during the Archaic period, the so-called "Samian technique", first identified and named "Samische Technik" by Raubitschek (1938), and, from the beginning of the 4th c. onwards, the "tenon under the dress" technique for bronze figures dressed in a long *chitōn* touching the ground, whose bottom surface was left entirely open; animal statues were fixed under their paws or hooves, either with metal dowels or with a lead tenon. But from the end of the 5th c. BCE onwards, the "sole" technique prevailed for human standing statues whose garment did not touch the ground.

In techniques where only lead was used to fasten the statue on the base, such as in the "sole" technique, various hypotheses have been suggested to explain how the lead could have been poured to fill the foot and the mortise, and various solutions were surely used throughout antiquity. Some rare bases show horizontal pouring channels on the side of the "soles", indicating that lead was poured from the outside. For example, little horizontal pouring channels have also been noted on the side of some cuttings on the Marathon base in front of the Athenian Treasury (Amandry 1998, 84–85, figs. 4 a–b) and on the Epigons monument (Bommelaer 1992, 290–291, figs. 32–34, pl. 45) in Delphi. However, the vast majority presents only the soles, which were, as we have seen, smaller than the actual bronze feet, and made it impossible for the lead to be poured from the outside. It means that, in these cases, lead had to be poured through an opening in the foot or leg, which was closed afterwards on the spot. Since the middle toe, or even the whole front part of the foot, were often made separately, especially on Classical bronzes, it has been thought that these openings might have been used, and the rest of the foot then welded on the spot (Formigli 1984, 120–123, figs. 17–20). But the study and restoration of some ancient bronze statues also showed square openings, already mentioned by Bol (1985, 162–163), at the back of the feet and legs that could have been used. Indeed, X-ray images from the Mahdia Agon showed a small square plate (about 3 cm wide) located on the legs right above the lead level; instead of being inserted into a chisel-made square socket, as is the case when repairing minor cast defaults, the plate had been inserted and welded into a straight-edged square opening through the bronze wall. This shape indicates that the opening was not a cast default, but was already made on the wax model, and therefore had some technical purpose. It would indeed have been useful to create an additional connection between the inner core and the mould during the casting, but also, more interestingly for us, to pour the lead inside the leg in order to fasten the statue to the base (Willer 1996, 158, n. 293).The plate is preserved on the free leg, but not on the standing one. I think that the large rectangular plates that can be seen on X-ray images of the Riace warriors' legs, which were also already made on the wax prototypes, could have played the same role, a possibility not mentioned by the authors (Micheli – Vidale 2003, 125–126, fig. 235 (statue B), 176–177 and figs. 366–367 (statue A)).

In either hypothesis, when no traces of a horizontal pouring channel is preserved on the base, the statue had to have openings in the feet or the legs to pour the lead, which had to be closed once the statue had been fastened on the base. That means that the sculptor, or someone from his workshop, had to be there, not only to arrange separate fragile elements or to oversee the general setting, but also to actually finish the statue on the spot. However, one can wonder whether the mounting itself (carving the mortises, setting up the statue, and pouring the lead inside the foot) was done by the sculptor or his workshop, or by an independent team. Is it possible to find some specific features in the traces left on the bases that could be linked to a sculptor or his workshop?

In order to answer this question, I tried to compare traces on bases signed by the same sculptor, but also contemporary traces on bases signed by different artists. "Soles" on bases are difficult to compare because they often bear traces of later removal: these traces sometimes strongly alter their shape, making it difficult to observe the original tool marks. But, even in the case of well-preserved "soles", some bases that supported one statue show cuttings which are quite different in shape and length from one foot to the other. Therefore, the shape is not a criterion per se. Given these difficulties, the only solution is to combine criteria: shape and size are to be considered, as well as the regularity and precision of the tool marks, and the layout of the footprints. Following this method, it becomes possible to distinguish footprints, to identify the various monuments' modifications, and, occasionally, different "hands" for the mounting.

Case-studies

As mentioned earlier, the monuments of the Navarchs and the Arcadians in Delphi offer the rare opportunity to compare mounting traces in association with sculptors. First, they supported bronze groups fixed by the same technique: they each offer a strictly contemporary context for multiple traces. Second, they each supported several statues signed by different sculptors: one can compare traces from the same sculptor as well as those from different sculptors on the same base. Finally, thanks to their inscriptions as well as to Pausanias' descriptions, they are both well dated: they can testify for a practice existing between the end of the 5th and the first half of the 4th c. BCE.

The Navarchs' base (Atlas 109) (Fig. 23.2, reproduced from Bommelaer 2015, pl. II)

The monument, mentioned by Pausanias (10.9.7–11) in the lower part of the so-called "Sacred Way" in Delphi, was erected by the Lacedemonians to celebrate their victory at Aigos Potamos in 404 BCE. The problems of the exact location of the monument, its plan, or the exact sequence of the preserved inscribed blocks remain largely unresolved. G. Roux provided evidence that the monument did not stand in the niche located to the north of the "Sacred Way"

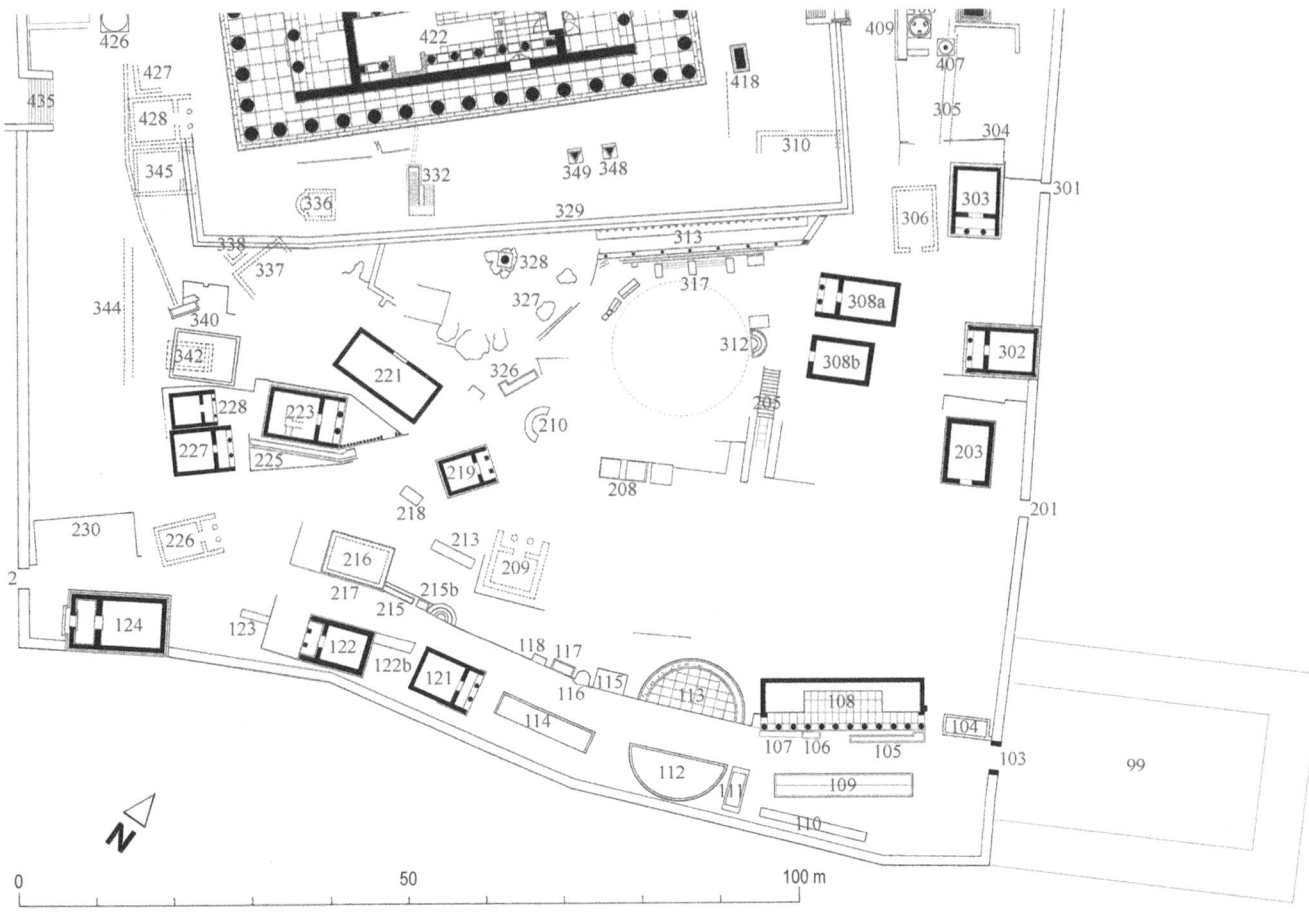

Figure 23.2. Reconstructed map of the monuments along the "Sacred Way" at the end of the 2d c. CE (Bommelaer 2015, pl. V, EFA).

above the Arcadians monument (*Atlas* 108), which is, in fact, Hellenistic, but was surely placed where Pausanias described it, on the southern side of the Sacred Way. However, the exact foundations are missing, and the order in which Pausanias describes the statues is problematic, as was again recently stated by Bommelaer (2011, 104, esp. fig. 2; 2015, 132–134), reflecting on the block sequence. Nevertheless, according to Pausanias, it supported at least thirty-seven bronze figures made by nine different artists. In his description, the author indeed mentions two series of statues displayed in two rows, one behind the other. In the first one he names nine figures: six gods (the Dioscuri, Zeus, Apollo, Artemis and Poseidon), a statue of Lysander crowned by Poseidon, and two crew members of the admiral vessel (the seer Agias and the pilot Hermon). A mounting inscription (κάρυξ) located between the feet of a statue on block X (inv. 30957) indicates the presence of a herald not mentioned by Pausanias. According to most scholars, he was probably placed in the front row, with Hermon and Agias. In the "back" row (ὄπισθεν), Pausanias mentions twenty-eight Lacedemonian generals. In addition to the characters, he also indicates the sculptors' names; five artists designed the nine characters of the first row: Antiphanes of Argos realized the Dioscuri, Athenodoros of Arkadia Zeus and Apollo, Dameas of Arkadia Artemis, Poseidon and Lysander, Pison of Kalaureia the seer Agias, and Theokosmos of Megara the pilot Hermon; and four sculptors, Tisandros, Alypos of Sikyon, and Patrokles

and Kanachos worked together to create the twenty-eight statues of the second row.

A total of twelve inscribed blocks from the top course of the base have been discovered and identified by their inscriptions. Numbers used below are taken from Bourguet (1929, n° 50–53. 55–58. 61–67), except for the block inv. 2598, which he tentatively attributed to this monument, but which more likely belonged to the monument of the Kings of Argos (*Atlas* 113) (Pouilloux – Roux 1963, 46–51). They do not follow the original sequence of the blocks in the monument, which remains doubtful. The actual block XII was not at first attributed to the base: it was published by Bourguet (1929, n° 562) with the inventory number 2610, and completed and attributed to the base by Bousquet (1961, 71–74). These numbers are used by most scholars (de la Coste-Messelière 1953, 182–189; Bousquet 1961, 71–74; Pouilloux – Roux 1963, 16–19. 30–36. 55–60; Bommelaer 1971, 43–64; 2011; 2015, 132–134). On these blocks, we can count the footprints of at least fifteen bronze statues, from both the first and the second row, but they are not all well preserved. Some of them attest to modifications of the original display, which prevent us from using them as evidence here (Bommelaer 1971, 45–46 and fig. 3). I will focus on a few blocks from the back row where footprints are clearly readable and might correspond to original statues, and where characters and sculptors can be identified.

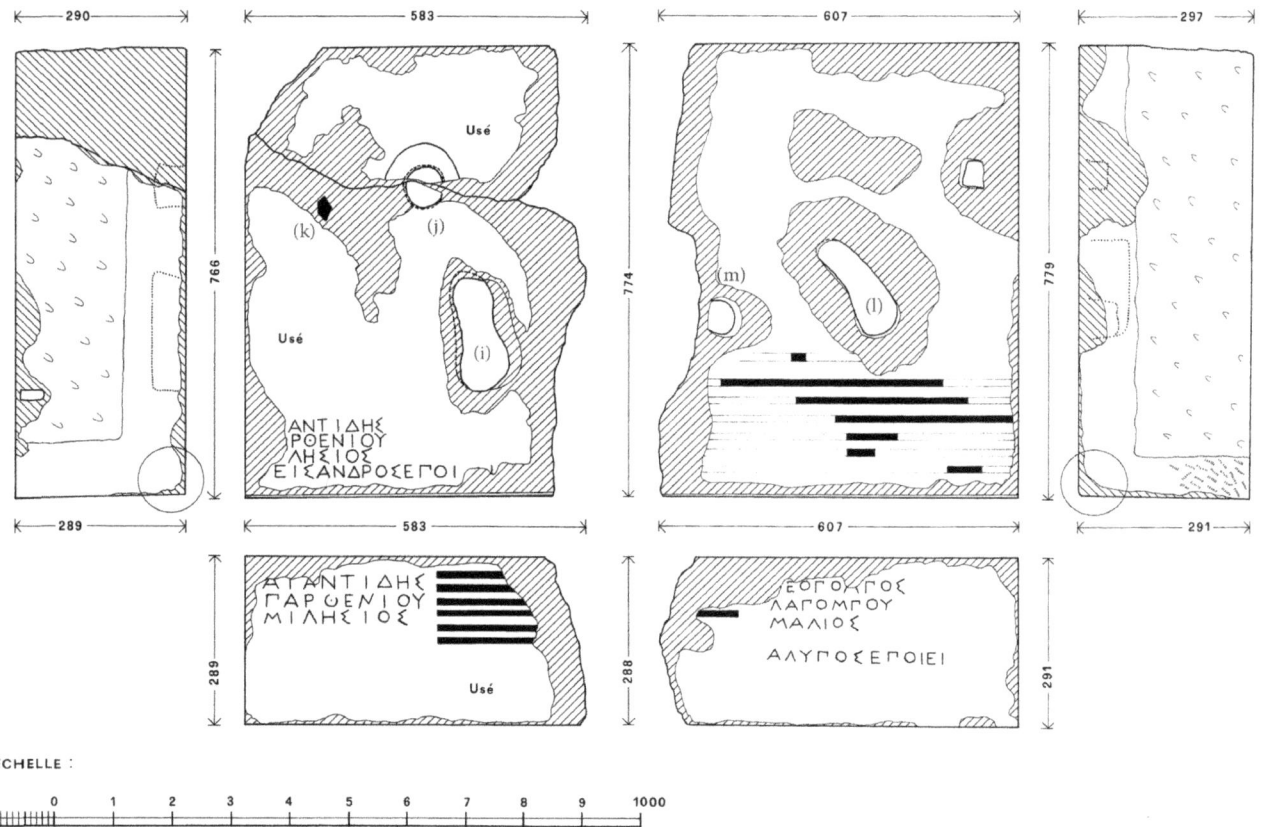

Fig. 23.3. Block V, inv. 2722 (left) and 2799 (right), with the new fragment at the back of inv. 2722: Aiantides and Theopompos (P. Ognolec, EFA).

The block V consists of three fragments: the connection between inv. 2722 (left) and inv. 2799 (right) was known from the first publications (Bourguet 1929, 33, fig. 12); a new fragment was added later by Bommelaer (1971, 46, fig. 5) at the back of inv. 2722. On it, we can see the footprints of two different statues (Fig. 23.3). To the left, the character's name, Aiantides of Miletos, is inscribed on the front face, and repeated on the top face along with the sculptor's name, Teisandros (Bourguet 1929, n° 55. 57). To the right, the character's name, Theopompos of Melos, and the sculptor's name, Alypos, are both inscribed on the front face (Bourguet 1929, n° 56). Pausanias, in his enumeration of the statues from the back row, mentions Aiantides of Miletos at the end of the series of statues attributed to Tisandros, right before he begins the series of statues made by Alypos of Sikyon, which starts with a certain Theopompos of Myndos, more probably to be identified with our Theopompos of Melos (Pausanias 10.9.9–10). The problem of the succession of these statues has been examined by Bommelaer (1971, 45–47).

Both statues were attached by a "sole" under the standing left foot, and a simple round hole under the right foot, set on the toes; these are (i) and (j) for Aiantides and (l) and (m) for Theopompos, according to the numbering of the mortises here added on the figures and used in Nouet (to be published in the BEFAR collection). They stood on the same leg, but their stances are actually quite different, as the footprints indicate: Aiantides stood with the right foot set far away in the back and nearly aligned with the left one, in an unbalanced stance which implies the presence of a support, surely fixed into the little hole (k) that remains left to (j). By contrast, Theopompos stood with the right foot on the side at the left heel's level, in a quite opened and balanced stance. Nonetheless, the "soles" carved on the base to fasten the standing left foot of both statues are very similar: they have the exact same shape (their internal side is curved, they present straight edges, large heels, and a neat flat bottom) and size (0,20 m long and 0,06 to 0,08 m wide), except for their depth (Aiantides' sole is 0,065 m deep and Theopompos' 0,085 m) (Fig. 23.4). Therefore, these two statues, which were set side by side

Figure 23.4. Block V, Aiantides and Theopompos (R. Nouet).

on the same block, were made by two different artists who represented them in two different postures – if not different styles – while their footprints are nearly identical.

Other statues made by the same artist Alypos on the same base, but on different and maybe distant blocks (Bommelaer 2011, 104, fig. 2), left very different traces. On block VI (inv. 2716), Autonomos of Eretria is named in the inscription on the front face (Bourguet 1929, n° 61), and on block VIII (inv. 2632), Apollodoros of Troezen (Bourguet 1929, n° 64). There is no signature for either one of them, but both characters were attributed to Alypos of Sikyon by Pausanias (10.9.10). Autonomos was represented with the right standing foot advanced (o), and the left foot on the toes (p), distant in the rear from the standing foot (Fig. 23.5). Apollodoros was represented standing quietly on his two feet, the standing left foot (y) slightly turned outwards, the right foot advanced and more strongly turned outwards (x) (Fig. 23.6). Whereas both statues were made by the same sculptor, their footprints do not share the same size and shape. Autonomos' footprint has roughly the same size as Theopompos' footprint on block V (0,215 m long, 0,045/0,08 m wide and 0,07 m deep), but it has a very different shape, which appears to be more rectangular, with an irregular bottom. As for Apollodoros' footprints on block VIII, even if their shape is similar to the ones on block V, they are much smaller (0,04 m wide, 0,05–0,06 deep, and 0,135 m (right)/0,165 m (left) long), but also distinct from the sole of Autonomos on block VI.

As regards the size of the footprints, we could argue that it reflected the size of the statue: this is true for other bases (such as the Arcadians, as we shall see), and is especially verified in the Hellenistic period. But in this particular instance, it does not seem to be the case. The footprint of Autonomos, a simple general who, according to Pausanias, stood in the second row, measures 0,215 long, whereas Pollux, a divine figure standing in the front row, left a footprint which is only 0,18 m long; and Apollodoros, a general from the same rank as Autonomos, left a much smaller footprint (0,165 m long). Since it would be difficult to assume that gods in the front row were smaller than generals in the second row, one can assume that, on this base, the size of the footprints was not linked to the actual size of the bronze statues, and may be due to the teams of craftsmen operating the mounting.

On this monument, the traces of two statues made by different sculptors on the same block V share the exact same shape and size for their standing foot, whereas the traces of two statues made by the same artist, but on different and maybe distant blocks (VI and VIII), are very different. There is no match between footprints and signatures here: it seems clear that the sculptors or their workshops were not responsible for the mounting of their own statues, but that different teams (at least two) of specialised craftsmen worked independently, following a different, but maybe also spatial logic (as suggested by the block V). This division of work may be more relevant for the many "back row" statues, where each sculptor's workshop mentioned by Pausanias (10.9.7–11) was in charge of more than seven statues: Teisandros made twelve statues, Alypos seven, and Patrokles and Kanachos ten.

The Arcadians' base (Atlas 105)

The monument was erected right in front of the Navarchs, across the Sacred Way (Fig. 23.2). Mentioned by Pausanias as the "monument of the Tegeans" (10.9.5), it was in fact dedicated by the Arcadian *koinon*, in order to celebrate their common victory with the Thebans in Laconia in 370/369 BCE (Bourguet 1929, n° 3). As the preserved inscriptions and Pausanias' description testify, the statues represented the heroic genealogy of the Arcadians, led by Apollo. The base is made up of two long courses of limestone, the lower one in grey limestone from the Profitis Ilias quarry, the upper one in black limestone. The nine blocks from the lower course were found *in situ*, except for a few fragments from block I, in the numbering of the first publication (Pomtow – Bulle 1906, 461–492, pl. XXIV; reused in Bourguet 1929, n° 3–46). The black limestone top course (0,321 m high) was also made up of nine blocks, five of which are fully preserved (blocks I, II, IV, V and VII). All nine were found nearby: block I was found on the stairs at the *temenos* entrance, the others were discovered to the South of the Sacred Way, under the Convert house 503. The base was meant to be read and seen from the East (the right) to the West (the left); Apollo, Kallisto and Nike began the row, followed by Arkas, son of Zeus and Kallisto, his four sons Apheidas, Elatos, Azan and Triphylos, and his grandson Erasos, son of Triphylos. The top course supported the dedicatory inscription, the characters' names and the signatures; the lower courses supported later decrees in honor of Arcadians.

These nine blocks show multiple cuttings to fasten the statues. We know from Pausanias as well as from the preserved inscriptions on the front of the base that four different sculptors made the nine statues: Pausanias of Apollonia, whose signature is preserved on the second block, made Apollo (block I) and Kallisto (block II) (Bourguet 1929, n° 3–4); Daidalos of Sikyon's signature is not preserved, but Pausanias mentions that he made the Nike on block III and Arkas on block IV (Bourguet 1929, n° 5–6); Antiphanes of Argos's signature appears on blocks V and IX, in relation with Apheidas (block V), Elatos (block VI) and Erasos (block IX) (Bourguet 1929, n° 7–8. 11); finally, Samolas of Arkadia, whose name appears on block VII, made Azan on this block and Triphylos on block VIII (Bourguet 1929, n° 9–10).

All those statues seem to have been fixed using the "sole" technique, at least those whose traces are well-preserved. Traces on blocks II, III, and VI are difficult to read, because the blocks are damaged, but also because they show signs of rearrangements of the statues, which is attested by the first block. Block II consists of three fragments; it supported the statue of Kallisto, but the exact display of the cuttings is hard to understand, maybe due to the later rearrangement of the monument; it seems

Rachel Nouet

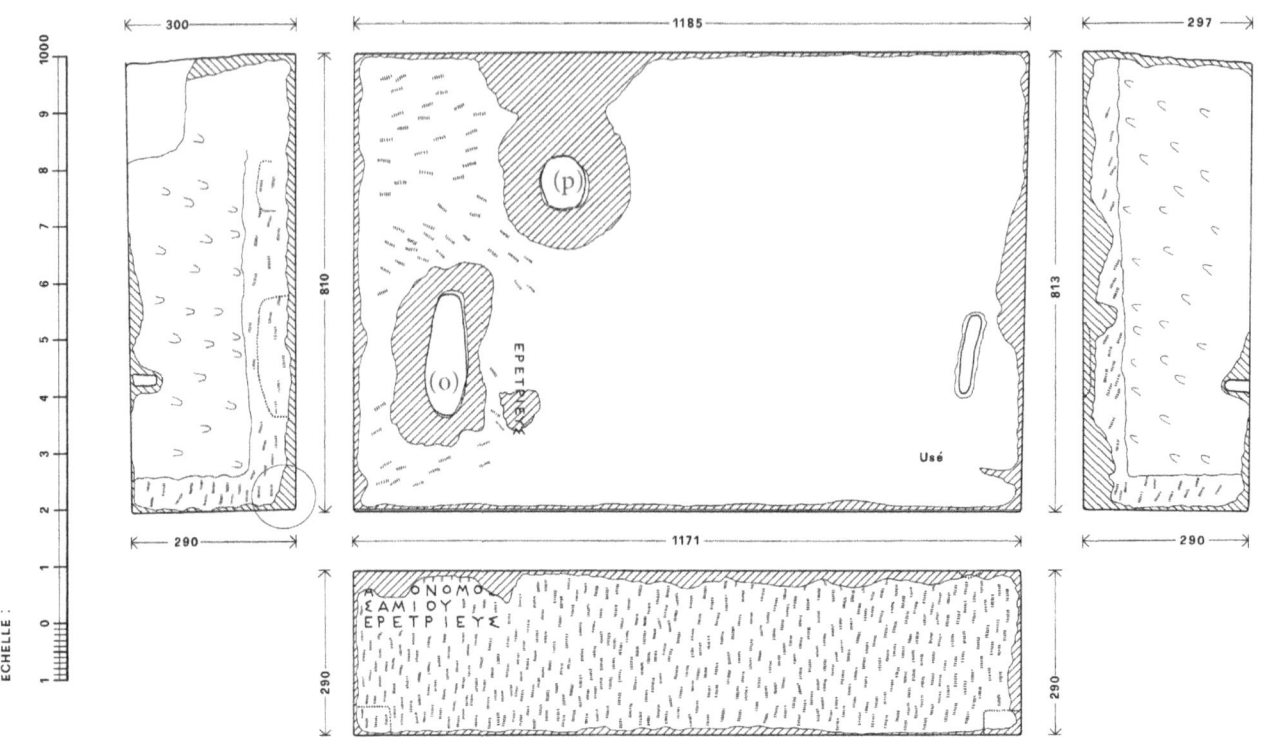

Figure 23.5. Block VI, inv. 2715. Drawing (P. Ognolec, EFA) and photography (R. Nouet).

that at one point the statue was turned toward Apollo, with the left foot advanced and set flat on the ground, but the general pose remains unclear. Only the right part of block III, which supported Nike's statue, is preserved, with the traces of what seems to be half a "sole", which remains unclear in the absence of the rest of the block. The preserved part of block VI, which supported Elatos' statue, shows multiple cuttings and holes that either point to a modification of the statue, or to the fixation of a complex attribute or a decoration set, but no well-preserved "sole". Some cuttings on other blocks were clearly meant to fasten attributes or other objects: for example, on block IV, we

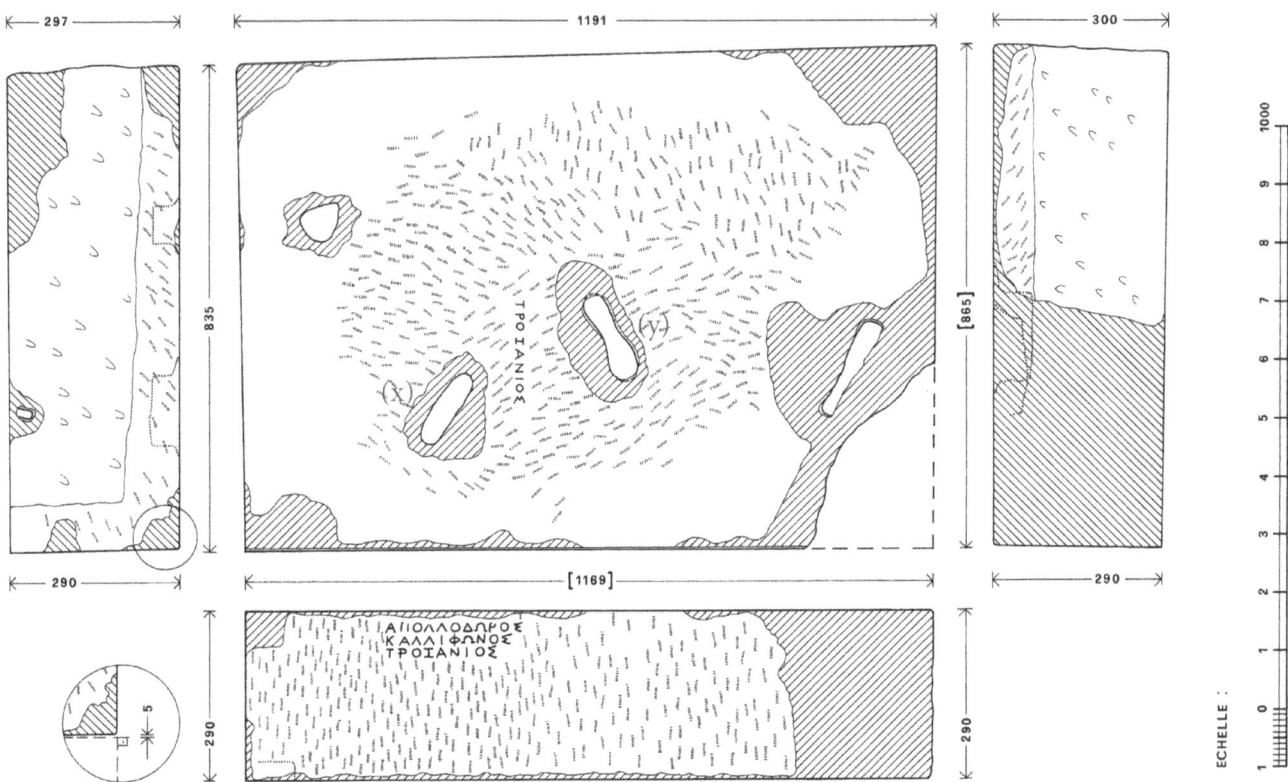

Figure 23.6. Block VIII, inv. 2632. Drawing (P. Ognolec, EFA) and photography (R. Nouet).

can see that Arkas' statue was standing with his right foot placed flat forward, fastened by a "sole", while his left was on the toes, fastened by a single round hole. He was probably leaning with his left arm on a shield, fastened on the three cuttings located to the right of the block. Other attributes or decoration elements are more doubtful, for example the traces on block VII. But let us focus on the preserved "soles" (Fig. 23.7).

The statue on block I (inv. 1813–1815), as we have seen, represented Apollo. On the top surface, there are two sets of footprints, which cannot possibly belong

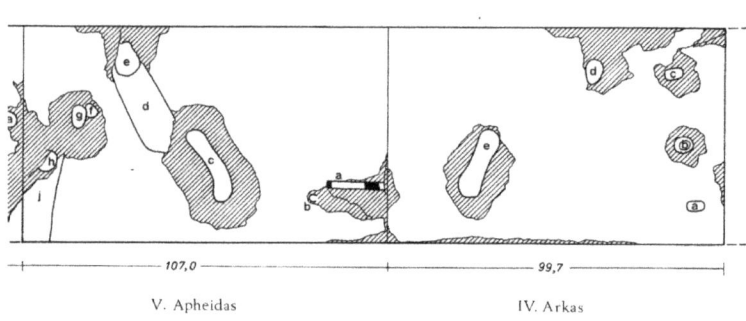
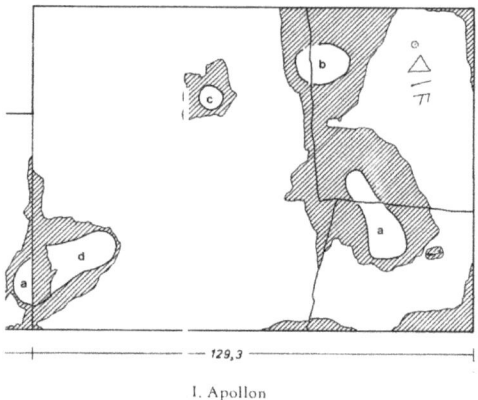
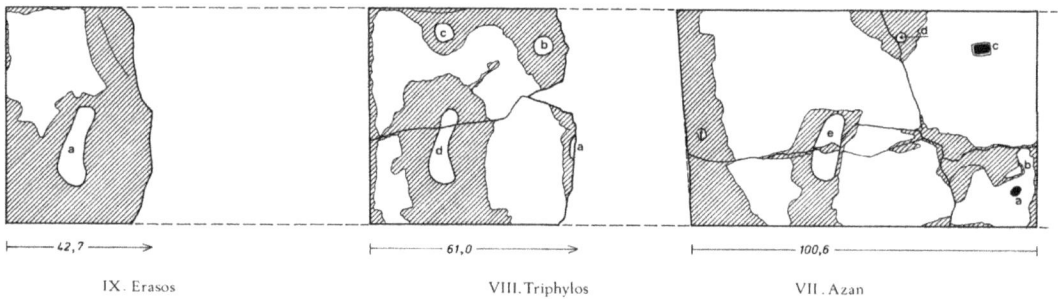

Figure 23.7. Drawings of the blocks I, IV, V, VII, VIII and IX of the Arcadians' base (D. Laroche, EFA).

to contemporary statues, as was shown by Bommelaer (2011, 129). Statue (1) had the left foot advanced in "sole" (a), and the right was on the toes in hole (c), in a well-balanced "polykleitan" stance, while the other (2) had the right foot far advanced and turned towards the left of the viewer in "sole" (d), and the left foot on the toes in hole (b), in a much more dynamic posture (Fig. 23.7). "Soles" do not have the same shape – the heel is narrow on the first statue's sole, whereas the whole mortise has an oval shape on statue (2) –, and they are not worked in the same way: we can observe regular tool marks and a flat bottom on statue (1)'s footprints, as opposed to the rougher work and the more irregular bottom of statue (2)'s cuttings (Fig. 23.8, above). As we shall see, statue (2) was most certainly erected later than the other, and replaced it.

Indeed, statue (1)'s footprints are very similar to, if not bigger than, the other well-preserved footprints on the base: those of Arkas, Apheidas, Triphylos and Erasos, respectively, on blocks IV, V, VIII and IX. Their outline is clear-cut, the bottom is flat and meticulously worked, and the shape is identical, with a narrow heel, a straight or outwardly curved external side, and a curved inner side (Fig. 23.8). For Apheidas on block V, we can see one complete "sole" (c) for the left foot, set forward approximately at the center of the block, but two single holes (e) and (g) to the left side of it, that could correspond to the right foot of the statue. It has been thought that the right foot was flat on the ground, fastened by these two holes (Pomtow – Bulle 1908; Arnold 1969, 23–24); but in that case this foot would be much bigger than the left one (0,28 m long compared to 0,225 m for the left one), and this kind of technique (one "sole" and two single holes for feet set flat on the ground) has no parallel. I believe that the right foot was in fact set on the toes, fastened only by one of the two single holes; other traces actually point to some attribute or decoration, or to a later remodeling of the group.

Thus, the examination of footprints allows us to interpret the mortises for statue (1) on block I as the original ones, while the mortises for statue (2) should be seen as traces of a later substitute. But it also shows that all well-preserved footprints from the original state of the monument share the same shape, and also the same size (between 0,20 m and 0,23 m long, except for Apollo (0,30 m long) presumably represented bigger), even if several different sculptors made the statues. Here it seems that the same team was in charge of mounting all the statues.

Conclusion

The examination of the footprints left on these bases is indeed very interesting regarding the actual process of mounting a statue on its base, in spite of the difficulties arising from the state of preservation. Differences in

Who was in Charge of Fastening Bronze Statues on their Bases?

Block 1 - Apollo (Pausanias), sole a

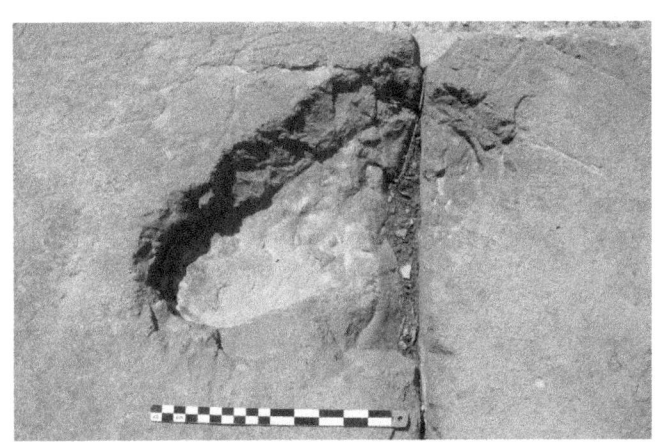

Block I/II - Apollo, sole d

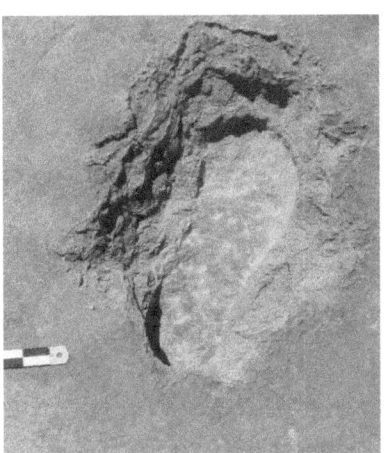

Block IV - Arkas (Daidalos)

Block V - Apheidas (Antiphanes)

Block VIII - Triphylos (Samolas)

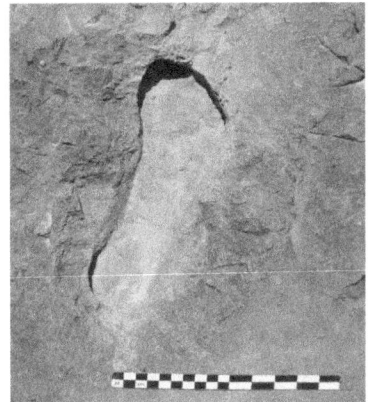

Block IX - Erasos (Antiphanes)

Figure 23.8. Comparisons of "soles" from the Arcadian base (R. Nouet).

shape and aspect among the cuttings do matter, but their close similarities are also significant. On the Navarchs' monument, which had numerous figures, the great variety of the preserved "soles" could stem from the different positions of the statues, and, above all, from the modifications that seem to have altered the figures and the whole group throughout time. Even the differences between "soles" used to fasten statues from the same sculptor could be explained by the size of the monument: it surely took some weeks to mount all the statues on the base, and the same artist (or workshop) could have varied in his way of carving the mortises. However, what is informative is the very close similarities between two "soles" carved to fasten two statues made by different sculptors on the same block: as we have seen, they were worked in the same way and surely by the same "hand". The Navarchs' monument is the only one I examined for which the presence of several mounting teams, independently from the sculptors' signatures, is attested; the multiplicity of "hands" here is probably owed to the exceptional size of the monument, since it seems that the mounting work was distributed to different teams, probably according to a spatial logic, which did not match the sculptural one.

It is also the close similarities among the "soles" carved on the Arcadians' base that lead us to identify only one single "hand" for the mounting of the statues, as opposed to the numerous sculptors who worked on the monument. Although these two examples are different, they both lead to the same conclusion: for these monuments made by several different sculptors, the division of work – as shown by the mounting traces – does not match the signatures. Admittedly, it is possible that the multiple teams mounting the statues on the Navarchs' base, or the team that worked on the Arcadians' base, belonged to the sculptors' workshops. However, what is certain is that each sculptor did not take care solely of his own statues. As we have seen, that does not mean that sculptors were absent during the mounting phase: they surely were there to supervise the general layout, but also to finish up details, and the statues themselves after the lead had been poured to anchor them on the base. However, there were other teams dedicated to at least carving the "soles" on the base, the identity of which still remains unknown.

One can wonder if the division of labour can be extrapolated as a general rule, from the end of the 5th c. onwards, for big monuments, or even for smaller ones. In lack of further evidence, this remains a tentative hypothesis. As we have seen, the big bases studied above are exceptionally informative: they form a closed context and present statues made and signed by different sculptors, as well as mounting marks that are readable and that belong to the same general technique. Such bases are, however, rare. A thorough study of signed bases with mounting traces from other sites and contexts could well shed additional light on this question in the future.

Acknowledgements

The author thanks Prof. J.-Fr. Bommelaer, who gave her access and granted the use of unpublished drawings made in a project of his.

Abbreviations

Atlas = Hansen, E. – Algreen-Ussing G. eds., 1975. *Fouilles de Delphes. II, Topographie et architecture. Sanctuaire d'Apollon. Atlas, relevés exécutés par un groupe d'architectes danois*. Paris: de Boccard.

ID = *Inscriptions de Délos*.

IvO = Dittenberger, W. – Purgold, K., 1896. *Olympia: die Ergebnisse der von dem deutschen Reich veranstalteten Ausgrabung. 5: Die Inschriften von Olympia*. Berlin.

SD = Bommelaer 2015.

Bibliography

Amandry, P., 1998. Le socle marathonien et le trésor des Athéniens. *Bulletin de Correspondance Hellénique*, 122, 84–85.

Arnold, D., 1969. *Die Polykletnachfolge, Untersuchungen zur Kunst von Argos und Sikyon zwischen Polyklet und Lysipp. JDAI* suppl. 25. Berlin: De Gruyter.

Bol, P. C., 1978. *Grossplastik aus Bronze in Olympia. Olympische Forschungen*, 9. Berlin: de Gruyter.

Bol, P. C., 1985. *Antike Bronzetechnik*. Munich: Beck.

Bommelaer, J.-Fr., 1971. Note sur les Navarques et les successeurs de Polyclète à Delphes. *Bulletin de Correspondance Hellénique*, 95, 43–64.

Bommelaer, J.-Fr., 1992. Monuments argiens de Delphes et d'Argos. In: M. Piérart, ed., 1992, *Polydipsion Argos. Argos de la fin des palais mycéniens à la constitution de l'État classique. Actes du colloque de Fribourg (7–9 mai 1987). Bulletin de Correspondance Hellénique*, suppl. 22. Paris: de Boccard, 265–303.

Bommelaer, J.-Fr., 2011. Delphica 3. Le monument des Navarques. *Bulletin de Correspondance Hellénique*, 135, 199–235.

Bommelaer, J.-Fr., 2015. *Guide de Delphes: le Site*. 2^d ed. Paris: de Boccard.

Bourguet, É., 1929. *Fouilles de Delphes. III, Épigraphie. 1, Inscriptions de l'entrée du sanctuaire au trésor des Athéniens*. Paris: de Boccard.

Bousquet, J., 1961. Inscriptions de Delphes. *Bulletin de Correspondance Hellénique*, 85, 69–97.

Chamoux, Fr., (1955). *Fouilles de Delphes. IV, Monuments figurés: Sculpture. 5, L'Aurige*. Paris: de Boccard.

de la Coste-Messelière, P., 1953. Trois notules delphiques. *Bulletin de Correspondance Hellénique*, 77, 177–189.

Eckstein, F., 1969. *ANATHEMATA, Studien zu den Weihgeschenken strengen Stils im Heiligtum von Olympia*. Berlin: Gebrüder Mann Verlag.

Formigli, E., 1984. La tecnica di costruzione delle statue di Riace. In: G. B. Triches, ed., 1984. *Due bronzi da Riace: rinvenimento, restauro, analisi ed ipotesi di interpretazione. Bollettino d'arte*, serie spe. 3. Rome: Istituto poligrafico e zecca dello Stato. 107–142.

von den Hoff, R., 1994. *Philosophenporträts des Früh- und Hochhellenismus*. Munich: Biering und Brinkman.

Kaltsas, N. – Vlachogianni, E. – Bouyia, P. ed., 2012. *The Antikythera Shipwreck. The ship, the treasures, the mechanism. Exhibition. National Archaeological Museum, April 2012–April 2013*. Athens: Kapon Editions.

Kissas, K., 2000. *Die attischen Statuen- und Stelenbasen archaischer Zeit*. Bonn: Dr. Rudolf Habelt.

Micheli, M. – Vidale, M., 2003. *I bronzi di Riace: restauro come conoscenza. Volume secondo, Scavo dell'interno delle due statue*. Rome: Artimide.

Palagia, O., 2017. Euphranor. In: Seaman, K. – Schultz, P. ed., *Artists and Artistic Production in Ancient Greece*, Cambridge: Cambridge University Press, 124–140.

Pomtow, H., 1909. *Delphica II. Vorläufiger Bericht über die Ergebnisse einer neuen Reise nach Delphi*. Berlin.

Pomtow, H., 1918. Neue delphische Inschriften. *Klio*, 15, 1–77.

Pomtow, H. – Bulle, H., 1906. Studien zu den Weihgeschenken und der Topographie von Delphi. *MDAI (A)*, 31, 437–563.

Pouilloux, J., 1976. *Fouilles de Delphes. III, Épigraphie. 4, Inscriptions de la terrasse du temple et de la région Nord du sanctuaire*. Paris: de Boccard.

Pouilloux, J. – Roux, G., 1963. *Énigmes à Delphes*. Paris: de Boccard.

Raubitschek, A., 1938. Zur Technik und Form des altattischen Statuenbasen. *Bulletin de l'Institut Archéologique Bulgare*, 12, 132–179.

Raubitschek, A., 1949. *Dedications from the Athenian Akropolis. A Catalogue of the Inscriptions of the Sixth and Fifth Centuries B.C.* Cambridge Mass.: Archeological Institute of America, Supplementum Inscriptionum Atticarum, vol. VII.

Triches, G. B., ed., 1984. *Due bronzi da Riace: rinvenimento, restauro, analisi ed ipotesi di interpretazione. Bollettino d'arte*, serie spe. 3. Rome: Istituto poligrafico e zecca dello Stato.

Willer, F., 1996. Beobachtungen zur Sockelung von bronzenen Statuen und Statuetten. *Bonner Jahrbücher*, 196, 337–370.

Willer, F., 2000. Neue Beobachtungen zur Herstellungs- und Versockelungstechnik antiker Bronzestatuen. *Kölner Jahrbuch*, 33, 565–573.

Scharnier, Tülle oder Zapfen. Beobachtungen an hellenistischen Bronzelampen mit Statuettendekor

Norbert Franken

Johannes Gutenberg-Universität, Mainz

norbert.franken@gmx.de

Abstract: From the Archaic period right down to Late Antiquity, particularly elaborate bronze lamps used to be decorated with free-standing figural representations. In Hellenistic times, mainly the fill holes for oil and, more rarely, the wick holes were covered with a lid crowned by statuettes. Unfortunately, not all lamps of this kind have survived in their entirety. To identify isolated bronze statuettes, for instance, as former lamp decoration elements, it takes both a sound knowledge of material and a thorough analysis of the technical features. Depending on the type of lamp, a distinction has to be made between figures fastened by soldering, lids fixed by means of a hinge, and covers with a socket or a tenon on the bottom. It is the lids of the latter category – with statuettes depicting Erotes, dancers, actors or other members of Dionysus' entourage, usually attached to the center of a lamp with two or three nozzles (bilychnis / trilychnis) in the way of a bayonet closure – that will constitute the subject-matter of my paper.

Keywords: Hellenistic Bronze Lamps; Figural Decoration; Egypt; Near East

Einleitung

Von archaischer Zeit bis in die Spätantike war es üblich, besonders große und prachtvolle Bronzelampen, insbesondere mehrschnauzige Lampen, wie Bilychnes, Trilychnes etc. oder allgemein Polylychnes, mit freiplastischem Figurenschmuck zu versehen. Wohl vor allem zu etruskischen Lampen gehörten Statuetten, die sich an einem schwanenkopfförmigen Haken aufhängen ließen und so auch heute noch – als isolierte Einzelfiguren – leicht als Teile von Lampen zu erkennen sind (Franken 2015 mit zahlreichen Nachweisen). Auch an griechischen Bronzelampen hellenistischer Zeit wurden vor allem die Öllöcher, seltener die Dochtlöcher, gelegentlich mit statuettenbekrönten Deckeln verschlossen. An spätantiken Bronzelampen (vor allem an Bilychnes), wie vereinzelt bereits in der frühen Kaiserzeit (Franken 2010, 246–247, Abb. 1–2), findet sich freiplastischer Dekor schließlich nur noch auf den Handhaben (Franken 2007). Doch soll der mythologische, heidnische, christliche oder jüdische Schmuck dieser späten Lampen nicht Thema unserer Untersuchung sein.

Wir wollen uns stattdessen ausschließlich mit den hellenistischen Bronzelampen beschäftigen, obwohl von ihnen nur sehr wenige im Original erhalten sind. Zudem sind auch diese oft nur in einem leidlich vollständigen Zustand überliefert oder sie befinden sich im Kunsthandel bzw. an Orten, wo sie für eine gründliche Untersuchung nicht zur Verfügung stehen. Der häufig unvollständige Erhaltungszustand erklärt sich aus der üblichen Fertigung dieser Lampen in mehreren separat gegossenen und danach zusammengesteckten und zusammengelöteten Einzelteilen. So besteht etwa die große Trilychnis aus Mahdia nach der Rekonstruktion des Verfassers (Franken 1996; zustimmend: Rolley 1998, 309) aus nicht weniger als zwölf Einzelteilen. Durch die Ungunst der Überlieferung kommt es allerdings dazu, dass vielen dieser Lampen im heutigen Zustand Füße, Deckel oder Teile des Bildschmucks fehlen, ohne dass dies heutigen Bearbeitern auffällt bzw. einer Erwähnung wert wäre. Doch ist gerade in diesen Fällen eine gründliche Autopsie und Beschreibung des Erhaltungszustandes wichtig, um nicht die Zufälligkeiten der Erhaltung zum Kriterium einer typologischen Einordnung zu machen.

Aufgrund der ungünstigen Ausgangssituation soll es hier weniger um die Lampen selbst als um den mutmaßlich zugehörigen Figurenschmuck gehen. Es lässt sich nämlich feststellen, dass offenbar schon im Altertum viele Figuren mutwillig von den Lampen abgebrochen bzw. entfernt worden waren. Andere könnten – entweder mit Absicht oder aus Unkenntnis – durch die Hand neuzeitlicher Sammler oder Kunsthändler von ihren Lampen abgenommen worden sein, um sie auf einem separaten Sockel neu aufzustellen. Möglicherweise schätzte man eine qualitätvolle Statuette als kostbares Einzelstück höher als eine Lampe mit Figurenschmuck. Ähnlich wie bei römischen Büstengewichten, bei denen frühe Sammler und Kunsthändler die ästhetisch störende und zudem an die Unvollständigkeit des Erhaltenen erinnernde Öse auf dem Oberkopf nicht selten abgearbeitet haben (Franken

1994, 24), dürften Zapfen und Tüllen an der Unterseite der Lampeneinsätze manchmal als störend empfunden worden sein. Wie sich zeigt, hat man diese aber nicht immer abgeschnitten, sondern mitunter auch nur in einen modernen Sockel eingelassen und auf diese Weise versteckt. Um aber auch die isolierten und manipulierten Statuetten als ehemaligen Lampenschmuck bestimmen zu können, bedarf es sowohl solider Materialkenntnis als auch gründlicher Beachtung und Analyse der technischen Indizien, worüber noch zu sprechen sein wird.

Grundsätzlich sind drei verschiedene Arten figürlichen Lampenschmucks zu unterscheiden. Dazu gehören erstens mittels einer kleinen Standplatte aufgelötete Figuren, wie sie bislang nur eine prächtige, 26 cm hohe Trilychnis mit vier Statuetten musizierender Eroten aus Vani (Georgien) zeigt (Vani, Georgisches Nationalmuseum Inv. 07:1-07/327: Akhvlediani et al. 2016, 184–185, Nr. 9, Abb. 10; Kat. Rom 2011, Abb. S. 133 unten), zweitens Figuren an mittels Scharnier befestigten Klappdeckeln und schließlich drittens Figuren, die mit einer an der Unterseite befindlichen Tülle bzw. einem Zapfen in die Lampe eingelassen sind. Es ergibt sich somit folgende Ordnung:
- aufgelötete Figuren mit Standplatte,
- in einem Stück mit dem Klappdeckel gegossene Figuren,
- zum Einsetzen bestimmte Figuren mit Zapfen oder Tülle an der Unterseite.

Die zuletzt genannten, in das zentrale Ölloch einer zwei- oder dreischnauzigen Bronzelampe eingesetzten Figuren von Eroten, Tänzern, Schauspielern und anderen dionysischen Gestalten sollen den Schwerpunkt meiner Betrachtung bilden.

Klappdeckel mit figürlichem Schmuck

Der Vollständigkeit halber seien zuerst einige Beispiele hellenistischer oder in hellenistischer Tradition stehender Bronzelampen mit figürlich geschmückten Klappdeckeln erwähnt.

Verhältnismäßig häufig begegnen Tierfiguren (z. B. Mäusen) auf den Klappdeckeln. Vollständige Beispiele dieser Art haben sich nur selten erhalten:
- New York, MMA Inv. 64.195. Aus Ägypten. L 14 cm. Fischer 1965, 2–3.
- London, BM. Aus Ägypten? L 15,9 cm bzw. 18,3 cm. Bailey 1996, 8–9, Nr. Q 3548. Q 3549, Taf. 4)

Gelegentlich finden sich Lampen, auf deren Klappdeckeln noch die Füße und andere Reste abgebrochener menschlicher Figuren zu erkennen sind:
- Berlin, ANT – SMB Inv. 10050. Aus Priene. L 25 cm. Raeder 1983, 57, Nr. 279, Abb. 8 b;
- Chicago, Art Institute. Gift of M. Phillips & J. Phillips, 2000.511. Angeblich aus Sri Lanka. L 24,9 cm. Unveröffentlicht).

Aufgrund der Spurenlage dürfte es sich bei den verlorenen Figuren meist um tanzende Eroten oder verwandte Figuren des dionysischen Umkreises gehandelt haben. Daneben beleuchten aber auch isoliert erhaltene Figuren, die durch eine runde Standplatte mit seitlicher Öse als Lampendeckel zu erkennen sind, das über Darstellungen von Tieren, wie Vögeln, Mäusen und Hunden (Bailey 1996, Taf. 63), hinausgehende thematische Spektrum, zu dem zum Beispiel Schauspieler der Neuen Komödie gehören:
- Berlin, ANT – SMB Inv. 32573: schreitender Mime; Dem Berliner Altbestand nicht zuzuordnen, darum vielleicht identisch mit verschollenem „Schauspieler" Dresden, Skulpturenslg. Inv. ZV 852. Von Antonio Sciarrino, Palermo 1890 erworben. Maße unbekannt. Unveröffentlicht.
- AO unbekannt, ehem. Slg. Fouquet. Aus Ägypten. H 6,1 cm. Perdrizet 1911, 73–74, Nr. 109, Taf. 27 unten: auf Altar sitzender Schauspieler;
- Tel Aviv, Kunsthandel. Unveröffentlicht: vollständige Lampe mit stehendem Schauspieler auf dem Deckel),

Weiter gibt es tanzende und sitzende Eroten:
- Ein tanzender Amor in orientalischem Gewand (Klagenfurt, LM Inv. 1722. Von der Gurinaalpe. H 6,8 cm. Fleischer 1966, 85–86, Nr. 101, Taf. 57),
- Amsterdam, APM Inv. 8035. Aus Ägypten. H 4,4 cm. van Gulik 1940, 55, Nr. 78, Taf. 18;
- Kopenhagen, Thorvaldsen-Mus. Inv. H2053. FO unbekannt. H 4,3 cm. Melander 2009, 169–170, Abb. 129; Melander 2014, 18, Abb. 9)

Ebenso treten Kinderdarstellungen auf:
- Leiden, RMO Inv. B 1952/1.2. Aus dem Libanon. H 3,5 cm. Unveröffentlicht;
- London, BM. Aus Lykien. H 3,3 cm. Bailey 1996, 52, Nr. Q 3731, Taf. 63)

Diesen drei Kategorien ähnliche Gestalten gehören ebenfalls zum Repertoire der Figuren.

Für Heiterkeit beim antiken Betrachter sorgte wohl auch eine 1952 in der ‚Ville Royale' von Susa (Iran) gefundene hellenistische Lampe, auf deren Deckel die Figur eines lesenden Affen sitzt (Paris, Louvre. DAO Inv. Sb 3866; Aus den Grabungen von R. Ghirshman in Susa). Wie eine jüngere Studie (Ilgner 2004) zeigen konnte, eröffnet das auch an figürlichen Tonlampen begegnende Thema jedoch noch eine Vielzahl weiterer möglicher Erklärungen.

Bei den Lampendeckeln mit figürlichem Schmuck fällt auf, dass die Tierfiguren in aller Regel mit ihrem Schnabel bzw. ihrer spitzen Schnauze nach vorne weisen, was ergonomisch die Handhabung des Deckels mit nur einem Finger erleichtert. Die Figur eines aggressiven Schwans (Rom, MNR Inv. 256288. FO unbekannt. L 16 cm. de'Spagnolis – De Carolis 1983, 52, Nr. VII.1, Abb. S. 53 oben) steht offenbar in der Tradition der von Alain Pasquier behandelten Gruppe (Pasquier 2008; vgl. dazu jetzt Franken 2019 im Druck, mit weiteren Erklärungen und Literatur). Nur an der oben genannten Lampe aus Susa befindet sich hinter dem Affen ein senkrechter Stift, der es ermöglichte, den Deckel mit dem Daumen zu öffnen und zu schließen. Ähnlich leicht zu handhaben waren die Deckel mit menschlichen Figuren. Zugleich setzte aber die gewünschte Handhabbarkeit der Größe der Figuren gewisse Grenzen. Da höhere Figuren beim Öffnen bzw. Umlegen des Deckels mit dem Lampengriff kollidieren bzw. das Gleichgewicht der Lampe gefährden würden, erreichte der Statuettenschmuck der aufklappbaren Lampendeckel kaum einmal eine Höhe von mehr als 8 cm. Überhaupt sind die meist nur einschnauzigen, seltener zweischnauzigen Lampen mit Klappdeckelchen insgesamt deutlich bescheidener in ihren Dimensionen und ihrer künstlerischen Qualität als die Lampen mit eingesetzten Figuren.

Schon dieser zwangsläufig unvollständige Überblick über die hellenistischen Bronzelampen mit figürlich gestaltetem Klappdeckel lässt erkennen, dass die Deckel zu den verschiedensten Typen gehören, was sich zum Beispiel daran zeigt, dass bei manchen Klappdeckeln die Ösen direkt an der Deckelplatte ansetzen und bei anderen ein längerer ‚Arm' vom Scharnier zur Deckelplatte führt. Ein ähnliches Ergebnis würde wohl auch die Betrachtung aller Lampen mit Scharnierösen (für verloren gegangene Deckel) erbringen. Doch kann eine vollständige Zusammenstellung aller Beispiele hier nicht geleistet werden und muss einer noch zukünftig zu schreibenden, sicher ertragreichen Arbeit zur Typologie vorrömischer Bronzelampen des 7.–1. Jahrhunderts v. Chr. vorbehalten bleiben. Eine bereits früher vom Verfasser angeregte Dissertation zu diesem Thema konnte leider nicht abgeschlossen werden.

Einsatzfiguren

Im zweiten Kapitel meines Beitrags möchte ich mit der hellenistischen Bronzestatuette eines tanzenden Satyrs der Berliner Antikensammlung (Kat. 1; Abb. 24.1) beginnen, die den Anlass darstellte, sich mit dem figürlichen Schmuck hellenistischer Bronzelampen und hier vor allem mit den in das zentrale Ölloch eingesetzten Figuren zu beschäftigen. Der 16,3 cm hohe Satyr erschien dem Verfasser hinsichtlich seines antiken Ursprungs zunächst mehr als verdächtig. Dies lag hauptsächlich an der für antike Bronzen ähnlicher Größe sehr ungewöhnlichen Form einer runden und verhältnismäßig dicken Standplatte und ebenso an seiner Herkunft aus dem Nachlass des berüchtigten Münzfälschers und Kunsthändlers Carl Wilhelm Becker (1772–1830), aus dessen Besitz die Statuette unbekannten Fundorts bereits 1837 für das nur wenig früher im Museum am Lustgarten eröffnete Königliche Antiquarium erworben worden war.

Bei näherer Betrachtung zeigt die Berliner Satyrstatuette aber eine Oberfläche, wie sie für Bronzen aus alten Sammlungen nicht ungewöhnlich ist. Man meint zwar an einigen Stellen unter einem dünnen (wohl modernen) Farbüberzug das blanke Metall zu ahnen. Doch gibt es auch

Abb. 24.1. Satyrstatuette Berlin, Antikensammlung – SMB Inv. Fr. 1835 (Kat. 1) (Foto: Staatliche Museen zu Berlin, Antikensammlung, Johannes Kramer).

stellenweise dickere Verkrustungen, die für eine zumindest teilweise original erhaltene Patina sprechen. Auffällig ist in diesem Zusammenhang der Zustand der Unterseite der in einem Stück mitgegossenen und darum ebenso zweifellos antiken runden Standplatte. Es zeigen sich dort deutlich rezente Schnitt- bzw. Feilspuren, die dafür sprechen, dass hier in nachantiker Zeit eine Tülle bzw. ein Zapfen entfernt wurde, mit der bzw. dem die Statuette einst auf dem Ölloch einer Bronzelampe befestigt gewesen sein dürfte. Genaueres ist nicht mehr erkennbar. Auch bleiben Sinn und Zweck eines unregelmäßig trapezförmigen Lochs in der Standplatte unklar.

In jedem Fall aber könnte man sich den im Aposkopein-Gestus heran tänzelnden Satyr, der sein Spiel auf der Panflöte (Syrinx) wohl nur für einen kurzen Augenblick unterbrochen hat, auch aus motivischen Gründen sehr gut als Bestandteil einer hellenistischen Bronzelampe vorstellen.

Als Lampeneinsatz diente vielleicht auch die nur wenig größere Statuette eines in gedrehter Haltung schreitenden und dabei die Doppelflöte spielenden Satyrs in Florenz (Kat. 2). Doch mahnt die Beobachtung, dass zumindest bei einigen Statuetten der Florentiner Sammlung solche runden Standplatten zweifellos das

Ergebnis einer modernen Restaurierung sind, hier zu besonderer Vorsicht. Zudem sind die verfügbaren technischen Beschreibungen (Arbeid – Iozzo, 2015) leider überwiegend unzureichend. Da es kaum jemals möglich sein wird, den Satyr in Florenz und alle anderen als Lampenschmuck in Frage kommenden Figuren eingehend im Original zu betrachten und es darüber hinaus wenig Sinn macht, auch alle unsicheren Stücke mit der gleichen Gründlichkeit zu diskutieren, sei er hier nur unter Vorbehalt aufgenommen. Überhaupt ist die unten stehende Zusammenstellung lediglich als ein vorläufiger und nach Belieben zu erweiternder Auswahlkatalog zu verstehen. Nicht in ihr enthalten sind auch die fünf oder sechs in den Vesuvstädten gefundenen Bronzelampen mit Statuettenschmuck, die sich heute im Neapler Museum befinden (Valenza Mele 1981, 37–39. 71–72, Nr. 58. 59. 61. 167. 168, Abb.; Nr. 167 nicht abgebildet?), da ihre Bearbeitung einem anderen Forschungsprojekt vorbehalten bleibt. In dem ansonsten sehr gründlichen Katalog von Valenza Mele vermisst man Detailfotos oder Zeichnungen, die die Verbindungen zwischen Lampen und Figuren besser nachvollziehbar machen würden. Stattdessen scheinen auf einigen Fotos (Valenza Mele 1981, Abb. zu Nr. 59) die Zapfen sogar einer Retusche zum Opfer gefallen sein.

Interessanterweise lassen sich trotz der geringen Zahl von Beispielen mehrere Stücke nennen, die sich so sehr ähneln, dass sie zweifellos zu Lampen desselben Typs gehörten oder sogar in derselben Werkstatt entstanden sein dürften. Dazu gehört eine angeblich aus Oberägypten stammende Bronzefigur aus der bedeutenden Sammlung des ehemals in Kairo wohnhaften, französischen Arztes Dr. David Marie Fouquet (1850–1914) (Kat. 3; Abb. 24.2–5). Nachdem der Verfasser die verschollene Bronze mit Hilfe der Museumsdatenbank im Rijksmuseum van Oudheden in Leiden wieder finden konnte, lässt sie sich genauer beschreiben. Der linke Arm ist knapp unterhalb der Schulter abgebrochen und mitsamt einem möglichen Attribut verloren. Bei dem in der rechten Hand gehaltenen Objekt könnte es sich aber um ein Plektrum handeln, weshalb Amor hier wahrscheinlich als Kitharaspieler dargestellt war.

Motivisch und stilistisch auf das Engste verwandt ist eine gleichfalls 17,8 cm hohe, also exakt maßgleiche Kleinbronze, die sich vor mehr als zwanzig Jahren im New Yorker Kunsthandel befand (Kat. 4; Abb. 24.6). Hier zeigt Amor eine charakteristische Armhaltung, die vermuten lässt, dass er einst die Doppelflöte (griech.: *auloi*; lat.: *tibiae*) spielte.

Die mir dank der kollegialen Hilfsbereitschaft des verantwortlichen Kurators, Ruurd B. Halbertsma, vorliegenden Fotos der Leidener Statuette zeigen deutlich, dass sich unterhalb der runden Standplatte eine nach unten offene Tülle befindet. Es zeigt sich also, dass die Figur nur lose, d. h. ohne jede Art von Befestigung durch einen Bajonettverschluss oder einen zusätzlichen Sicherungsstift, in die jetzt fehlende Lampe eingesteckt war. Doch lassen sich unter hellenistischen Bronzelampen, wie sich zeigen wird, auch andere Arten von Befestigung bzw. Sicherung nachweisen.

Stilistisch den beiden Amorfiguren nicht unähnlich, doch mit nur 11,8 cm Höhe wesentlich kleiner ist eine angeblich aus Syrien stammende Schauspielerstatuette, die sich zuerst in der Sammlung des bekannten französischen Archäologen Henry Seyrig (1895–1973) in Beirut befand. Wie vorliegende Fotos zeigen, war die unter der Standfläche erhalten gebliebene (aus ästhetischen Gründen lediglich zeitweilig in einem modernen Sockel versteckte) Tülle quer gelocht, wodurch sie mit Hilfe eines dünnen Stiftes auf der heute fehlenden Lampe befestigt werden konnte. Dies ist eine relativ einfache Art der Befestigung, wie sie sich auch an etruskischen Bronzelampen findet, die der Verfasser erstmals zusammengestellt hat (Franken 2003: Die dort 355–356 Abb. 4 behandelte Lampe der einstigen Sammlung Cook befindet sich jetzt in Atlanta, Michael C. Carlos Museum Inv. 1998.13.4). Auf der Oberseite dieser Lampen befindet sich als Einfassung des Öllochs ein kurzes, ebenfalls quer durchbohrtes Rohr, sodass man sich unschwer vorstellen kann, nach welchem Prinzip Lampen und Figuren zusammengesteckt waren. Obwohl an einer etruskischen Trilychnis in Agde (Franken 2003, 361, Abb. 9) durchaus auch Masken der Neuen Komödie vorkommen, erscheint es wegen der signifikant verschiedenen Verbreitung der Lampen und der angeblich syrischen Herkunft der Schauspielerstatuette wenig glaubhaft, dass die ganz und gar hellenistisch wirkende Figur zu einem etruskischen Leuchter gehört haben könnte. Ähnlich wie im Fall der Amorstatuetten (Kat. 3– 4), die einer ägyptischen Werkstatt entstammen dürften, bleibt hier nur zu hoffen, dass in Zukunft weitere Lampen und zugehörige Statuetten aus gut beobachteten Kontexten oder mit glaubwürdigen Fundortangaben auftauchen mögen, die dabei helfen können, unsere Fragen nach den zugehörigen Lampentypen und ihrer Verbreitung zu beantworten.

Am Ende dieser notgedrungen unvollständigen Liste figürlicher Bekrönungen hellenistischer Bronzelampen gilt es noch auf ein wahrlich ‚herausragendes' Stück einzugehen, für das die tatsächliche Funktion als Lampenschmuck bislang nicht erkannt wurde, obwohl es schon seit langem zu den Glanzlichtern der Ägyptischen Abteilung des Athener Nationalmuseums zählt. Es handelt sich um die 45 cm hohe Statuette eines wohl Marsyas darstellenden, einstmals die Doppelflöte spielenden und dazu ekstatisch tanzenden Satyrs, die aus Tanais im Nildelta (ET) stammen soll und 1885 mit der Sammlung des damals in Alexandria ansässigen, griechischen Baumwollfabrikanten Ioannis Dimitriou (1826–ca. 1900/1910) erworben wurde.

Trotz ihrer ungewöhnlichen Größe lässt die Zurichtung der Unterseite keinen anderen Schluss zu, als dass auch der ‚Marsyas Dimitriou' Teil eines großen Leuchters war. Deutlich erkennt man auf den zuletzt veröffentlichten Fotos eine senkrechte Tülle mit einem kleinen seitlichen Vorsprung am unteren Ende, wie man ihn für eine

Abb. 24.2–5. Amorstatuette Leiden, Rijksmuseum van Oudheden Inv. 1954/10.1 (Kat. 3) (Foto: Rijksmuseum van Oudheden).

Norbert Franken

Abb. 24.6. Amorstatuette Ehemals Kunsthandel New York (Kat. 4) (Photograph Courtesy of Sotheby's, Inc. © 2019)

Befestigung nach dem Prinzip des Bajonettverschlusses braucht. Aus ästhetischen Gründen wird man eine Lampe rekonstruieren müssen, die einschließlich der Statuette ebenso hoch wie breit gewesen sein dürfte, wodurch man auf eine Breite bzw. einen Durchmesser von rund 55–60 cm kommt. Mehrschnauzige Lampen dieses Formats sind zwar ungewöhnlich, aber im erhaltenen Bestand durchaus belegt. Hierzu zählen neben dem bekannten subarchaisch-etruskischen Leuchter in Cortona mit 60 cm (Krauskopf 1988, 332, Nr. 24 Abb.; van der Meer 2014, 289–302) auch eine Lampe der frühen Kaiserzeit in St-Germain-en-Laye mit 54 cm Durchmesser (Reinach 1913, 77–79, Taf. 1–2). Eine Höhe von beachtlichen 43,3 cm erreicht auch die einst zu einem gewaltigen etruskischen Leuchter gehörende Gruppe von Jason mit Flügeldämon in Florenz (Arbeid – Iozzo 2015, 126–127, Nr. 93, Farbtaf. S. 120). Auch die drei hellenistischen Trilychnes aus dem spektakulären Hortfund von Vani (Georgien) sind nur wenig kleiner (Akhvlediani et al. 2016). Ob der so nur in groben Zügen rekonstruierbare Marsyasleuchter aber einst in einem Palast, einem Tempel oder einem öffentlichen Gebäude hing, wird man wohl nie mit Gewissheit entscheiden können. Doch erscheint er einer Residenz der Ptolemäer gewiss nicht unangemessen.

Will man an dieser Stelle ein vorläufiges Fazit ziehen und dabei auch alle anderen bekannten Stücke berücksichtigen, so ist festzuhalten, dass sich die figürlichen Einsätze hellenistischer Bronzelampen nach technischen Kriterien stark unterscheiden. Abgesehen von massiven zylindrischen Zapfen (Valenza Mele 1981, 39, Nr. 61) gibt es längere (Franken 1996, 308–311, Abb. 21) oder kürzere Tüllen, wobei letztere sowohl gelocht (Kat. 5) als auch ungelocht (Kat. 3–4) sein können. Sowohl die voll gegossenen Zapfen als auch die hohl gegossenen Tüllen (Kat. 6) können zudem mit einem kleinen Vorsprung für einen Bajonettverschluss versehen sein, wobei es aus den Vesuvstädten auch Beispiele für Stifte und Zapfen gibt, die augenscheinlich erst sekundär zum selben Zweck hinzugefügt wurden (Valenza Mele 1981, 38. 72, Nr. 59. 168).

Alles das spricht dafür, dass wir von einer großen typologischen Vielfalt solcher Lampen ausgehen müssen. Selbst wenn man auch diejenigen Lampenkörper mit in die Betrachtung einbezieht, bei denen sich die ehemalige Existenz eines figürlichen oder gefäßförmigen Aufsatzes noch aufgrund der für Bajonettverschlüsse notwendigen Schlitze am Rand des Öllochs und somit nur indirekt nachweisen lässt, bleibt die Gesamtzahl der Beispiele für eine differenziertere Typologie vorläufig zu schmal.

Neben den schon früher behandelten Bronzelampen des Typus Mahdia, die von einem kleinen Greifenkessel oder der Statuette eines auf einem Altar sitzenden Schauspielers bekrönt waren und einer wohl in Delos oder Athen zu lokalisierenden griechischen Werkstatt zuzuschreiben sind (Franken 1996), konnte hier mit zwei Amorstatuetten (Kat. 3–4) auch eine ägyptische Produktion wahrscheinlich gemacht werden. Ob es daneben, etwa in Italien (Kat. 1–2) oder im Orient (Kat. 5), weitere Herstellungszentren für Bronzelampen mit Statuettenschmuck gab, müssen zukünftige Untersuchungen klären.

Auswahlkatalog

Kat. 1 Tänzelnder Satyr mit Panflöte (Abb. 24.1)

Berlin, Antikensammlung – SMB Inv. Fr. 1835. Fundort unbekannt, 1837 aus Nachlass C. W. Becker erworben. H 16,3 cm. – Lit.: Toelken 1850, 17, Nr. 59; Friederichs 1871, 391, Nr. 1835; Furtwängler 1880, 19 mit Anm. 2; Kat. Berlin 1924, 64, Taf. 58; Neugebauer 1951, 27. 68; Jucker 1956, 72; Kat. Berlin 1988, 250 f. Vitr. 19,1, Nr. 19; Klages 1997, 136 f. 156, Nr. N 10; Franken 2011 unter Fr. 1835 (mit weiterer Lit.).

Kat. 2 Tänzelnder Satyr mit (ergänzter) Doppelflöte

Florenz, Museo Archeologico Inv. 2343. Fundort unbekannt. H 17 cm. – Lit.: Milani 1912, 169, Taf. 137. 2; Loewy 1914, 118, Nr. 241, Taf. 140; Möbius 1970, 53; Wrede 1986, 189 ff., Taf. 69,3–4; Klages 1997, 141, Nr. 7, Abb. 7; Arbeid – Iozzo 2015, 102 f., Nr. 56 mit Abb.

Kat. 3 Amor (ehemals) mit Kithara ? (Abb. 24.2–5)

Leiden, Rijksmuseum van Oudheden Inv. 1954/10.1. Angeblich aus Unterägypten, zuerst in Sammlung Fouquet, 1954 von einem Kunsthändler in Nimwegen (Nijmegen) erworben. H 17,8 cm. (Die Angabe von 15 cm in der Museumsdatenbank bezieht sich wohl nur auf die Höhe der Statuette ohne die Tülle.). – Lit.: Perdrizet 1911, 10, Nr. 4, Taf. 5 unten rechts; Reinach 1924, 178, 7.

Kat. 4 Amor (ehemals) mit Doppelflöte (Abb. 24.6)

AO unbekannt. Zuerst im Besitz von K. J. Gladman Esq., dann im Kunsthandel New York. Fundort unbekannt. H 17,8 cm. – Lit.: Kat. New York 1997, o. Pag. Nr. 374 Abb.

Kat. 5 Schauspieler der Neuen Komödie (Abb. 24.7)

AO unbekannt. Aus Syrien. Erst Sammlung Seyrig in Beirut, später im Kunsthandel Basel, in Sammlung Dr. Louk van Roozendaal (Oss) und zuletzt im Kunsthandel London. H (gesamt) 11,8 cm. – Lit.: Bieber 1961, 104,

Abb. 24.7. Schauspielerstatuette Ehemals Kunsthandel London (Kat. 5) (Repro nach: Mitten – Doeringer, 1967, 121 Nr. 120).

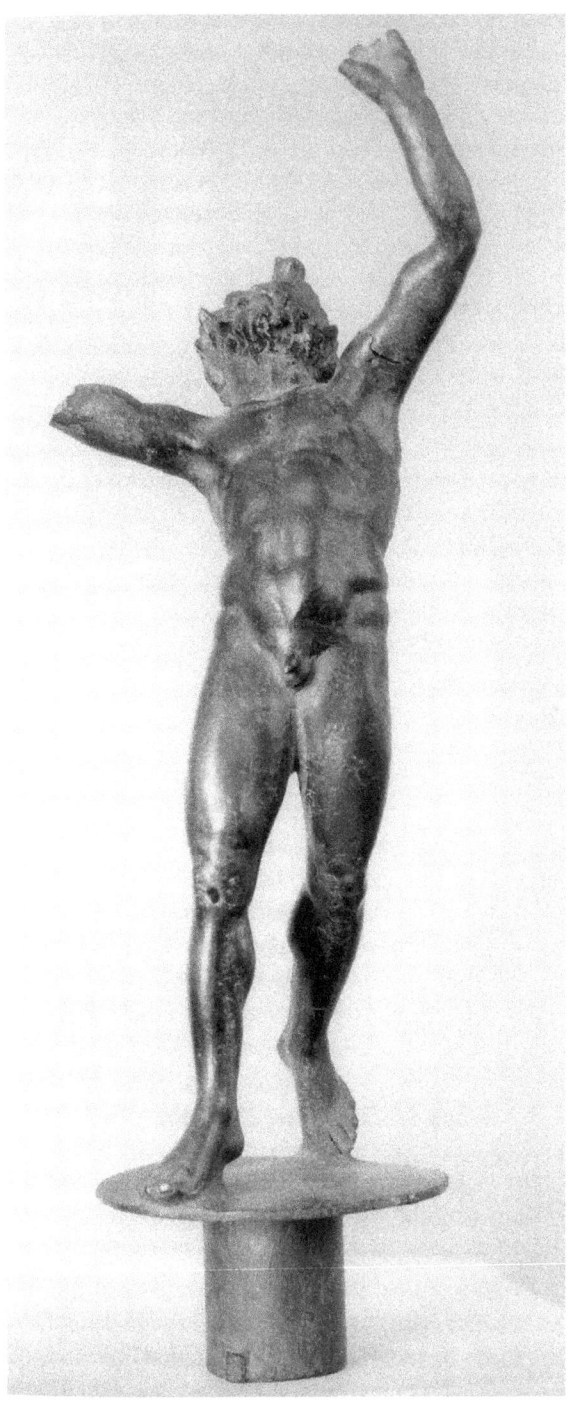

Abb. 24.8. Marsyasstatuette Athen, Nationalmuseum Inv. AEG 7531 (Kat. 6) (Repro nach: Bergmann 2008, 121–124, Abb. 17–18.

Abb. 404 a–c (Tülle weitgehend unsichtbar); Mitten und Doeringer 1967, 121, Nr. 120 Abb.; Kat. Basel 1982, 61, Nr. 123, Taf. 40 (Tülle in modernem Sockel verborgen); Seeberg 1988, 272 f., Abb. 5; Forge – Lynch 2018, o. Pag. Nr. 17 mit Farbtaf.

Kat. 6 Tänzelnder Satyr (ehemals) mit Doppelflöte. Marsyas (Abb. 24.8)

Athen, Archäologisches Nationalmuseum (Ägyptische Abteilung) Inv. AIG 7531. H 45 cm. Aus Tanais (Nildelta, Ägypten). 1885 aus Sammlung Dimitriou erworben. – Lit.: Mylonas 1885, Sp. 227–232, Taf. 6; Cavvadias 1894, 98, Nr. 7531; Stais 1907, 298; Reinach 1908, 51, 3 („suspect"); Bulle 1912, Sp. 194–196, Abb. 44 („einem modernen Fälscher mag man so viel Schönheit nicht zutrauen, ... eher ... der Nachguss eines antiken Werks"); J. Sieveking im Text zu Brunn-Bruckmann, Taf. 760, Abb. 1; Segall 1966, 34–36, Abb. 14; Klages 1997, 155f., Nr. N6 ohne Abb. („neuzeitlich"); Bergmann 2008, 121–124, Abb. 17–18.

Danksagung

Bei der Vorbereitung des Beitrags wurde mir vielfältige Hilfe zuteil, für die ich Thomas M. Weber-Karyotakis (Amman), Annika Backe, Marianne Bergmann, Martin Maischberger, Uwe Peltz (alle Berlin), Claudia Klages (Bonn), Philip Kiernan (Kennesaw, GA), Valeria Sampaolo (Neapel) und Nele Schröder-Griebel (München) sehr herzlich danken möchte. Ebenso danke ich Ruurd Halbertsma (Leiden) für freundliche Überlassung zahlreicher Fotos. Diese Untersuchung ist Teil eines seit Juli 2017 unter der Leitung von Detlev Kreikenbom an der Johannes-Gutenberg-Universität Mainz laufenden DFG-Projekts zu figürlichen Bronzen im Nahen Osten und auf der Arabischen Halbinsel. Tieferen Einblick in die Materialgruppe verdankt der Verfasser ferner dem von Ruth Bielfeldt (München) geleiteten Projekt „Neues Licht aus Pompeji" und mehreren mit freundlicher Genehmigung des Direktors Paolo Giulierini (Neapel) ermöglichten Forschungsaufenthalten im Archäologischen Nationalmuseum Neapel, worüber an anderer Stelle zu berichten sein wird.

Bibliographie

Akhvlediani, D. – Amaghlobeli, B. – Chi, J. – Chichinadze, M. – Kalandadze, N. – Kacharava, D. – Maish, J. – Kvirkvelia, G. – Lordkipanidze, N. – Saunders, D. – Tsereteli, M. – Walton, M., 2016. The Hoard from the City-Site of Vani, *Bulletin of the Georgian National Academy of Science 10(2)*, 182–191. Online: http://science.org.ge/bnas/t10-n2/28_Akhvledi.pdf (zuletzt aufgerufen am 19. 5. 2019)

Arbeid – Iozzo, Hrsg., 2015. *Piccoli Grandi Bronzi. Capolavori greci, etruschi e romani delle collezioni medicco-lorense nel Museo Archeologico Nazionale di Firenze*, Ausst. Florenz. Florenz.

Bailey, D. M., 1996. *A Catalogue of the Lamps in the British Museum IV. Lamps of Metal and Stone, and Lampstands*. London.

Bergmann, M. 2008, *Zu den Tempelfassaden im Eingang der Casa del Fauno*, in: Pirson – Wulf-Rheidt, 2008, 121–124

Bieber, M., 1961. *The History of the Greek and Roman Theater*. Oxford.

Bulle, H., 1912. *Der schöne Mensch*. München – Leipzig.

Cavvadias, P., 1894. *Les musées d'Athènes. Musée National, Antiquités mycéniennes et égyptiennes*. Athen.

de'Spagnolis, M. – De Carolis, E. 1983. *Museo Nazionale Romano I. Bronzi IV,1 Le lucerne*. Rom.

Fischer, H. G. 1965. Reports of the Departments: Egyptian, in: *The Metropolitan Museum of Art Bulletin 24, 2 (October) 54*; 2.–3.

Fleischer, R., 1966. *Die römischen Bronzen aus Österreich*. Mainz.

Forge, O. – Lynch, B., 2018. *Ancient Art from the Van Roozendaal Collection*. Oliver Forge – Brendan Lynch, London 2018.

Franken, N., 1994. *Aequipondia. Figürliche Laufgewichte römischer und frühbyzantinischer Schnellwaagen*. Diss. Bonn. Alfter.

Franken, N., 1996. Candelabrum Corinthium. Zu sakralidyllischen Bildelementen im späthellenistischen Wohnluxus am Beispiel eines Bronzekandelabers und einer Bronzelampe aus Mahdia, in: Neue Forschungen zum Schiffsfund von Mahdia, *Bonner Jahrbücher 196*, 276–311.

Franken, N., 2003. Etruskische Bronzelampen, *Römische Mitteilungen 110*, 353–363.

Franken, N., 2007. Leda und der Schwan. Beobachtungen zu Bildtradierung und Werkstattorganisation an spätantiken Bronzelampen mit figürlichem Schmuck, *Mitteilungen zur Spätantiken Archäologie und Byzantinischen Kunstgeschichte 5*, 9–19.

Franken, N., 2010. PARS PRO TOTO. Beobachtungen zur Funktionsbestimmung figürlicher Bronzen am Beispiel römischer Lampen, Leuchter und Laternen, in: Zwischen Orient und Okzident. Festschrift für H. Hellenkemper, *Kölner Jahrbuch 43*, 245–256.

Franken, N., 2011. *Bilddatenbank ›Antike Bronzen in Berlin‹* <http://ww2.smb.museum/antikebronzenberlin/>

Franken, N., 2015. *Der Leipziger Perseus. Ein wiederentdecktes Meisterwerk etruskischer Bronzekunst*, Festgabe des Archäologischen Instituts der Universität Leipzig zur Erinnerung an Johann Joachim Winckelmann. Leipzig.

Franken, N., 2019, im Druck. *Sklavenschicksale. Drei ikonographische Kapitel über hellenistische und römische Kleinbronzen*.

Friederichs, C., 1871. *Antike Geräthe und Broncen im Alten Museum*. Düsseldorf.

Furtwängler, A., 1880. Der Satyr aus Pergamon. *40. Berliner Winckelmannsprogramm*. Berlin.

Gschwantler, K. – Bernhard-Walcher, A., Hrsg., 1988. *Griechische und römische Statuetten und Großbronzen*. Akten der 9. Internationalen Tagung über antike Bronzen. Wien, 21.–25.4.1986. Wien.

Ilgner, C., 2004. Lesen im Lichte des Phallus – „vergnügliche Zügellosigkeiten der Töpferkunst in Knidos", *Boreas 27*, 255–263.

Jucker, I., 1956. *Der Gestus des Aposkopein*. Zürich.

Kat. Basel 1982. *Kunstwerke der Antike. Auktion 60*. Münzen und Medaillen AG Basel. 21.9.1982.

Kat. Berlin 1924. *Führer durch das Antiquarium I. Bronzen*. Berlin 1924.

Kat. Berlin 1988. *Antikenmuseum Berlin – Die ausgestellten Werke*. Berlin 1988.

Kat. New York 1997. Antiquities and Islamic Art, *Sotheby's New York 17.12.1997*.

Kat. Rom 2011. *Il vello d'oro. Antichi tesori della Georgia*, Ausst. Rom 2011. Rom.

Klages, C., 1997. *Tanzende Satyrn. Untersuchungen zur Typologie und Ikonographie hellenistischer Kleinkunst*, Diss. Bonn. Bonn.

Krauskopf, 1988. *LIMC IV, 1 (1988)* 330–345 s. v. Gorgones in Etruria (I. Krauskopf).

Loewy, E., 1924. *Griechische Plastik*. Leipzig.

Melander, T., 2009. *Thorvaldsens antikke bronzer*. Kopenhagen.

Melander, T., 2014. *Thorvaldsen's Roman Lamps*. Kopenhagen.

Milani, L. A., 1912. *Il R. Museo Archeologico*. Florenz.

Mitten, D. G. – Doeringer, S., Hrsg., 1967. *Master bronzes of the Classical World*, Ausst. Cambridge/Mass. Cambridge/Mass.

Möbius, H., 1970. Vier hellenistische Skulpturen. *Antike Plastik X*. Berlin.

Mylonas, K. D., 1885. Ο εν τη συλλογή Ιωάννου Δημητρίου χάλκους Σάτυρος, *AEphem* Sp. 227–232.

Neugebauer, K. A., 1951. *Die griechischen Bronzen der klassischen Zeit und des Hellenismus*. Berlin.

Pasquier, A., 2008. À propos du goût alexandrin: la lampe au Pygmée du musée du Louvre, *Monuments Piot 87*, 5–30.

Perdrizet, P., 1911. *Bronzes grecs d'Egypte de la collection Fouquet*. Paris.

Pirson, F. – Wulf-Rheidt, U., Hrsg., 2008. Austausch und Inspiration. *Kulturkontakt als Impuls architektonischer Innovation*. Kolloquium 28.–30.4.2006 Berlin anlässlich des 65. Geburtstages von A. Hoffmann. Mainz.

Raeder, J., 1983. *Priene. Funde aus einer griechischen Stadt*. Berlin.

Reinach, S., 1908. *Répertoire de la statuaire grecque et romaine II*. Paris

Reinach, S., 1913. Le lampadaire de Saint-Paul-Trois-Châteaux, *Revue Archéologique 21*, 77–79

Reinach, S., 1924. *Répertoire de la statuaire grecque et romaine V*. Paris

Rolley, C., 1988. Les bronzes grecs et romains: recherches récentes, *Revue Archéologique (2)*, 291–310.

Seeberg, A., *Bronzes Referring to New Comedy*, in: Gschwantler – Bernhard-Walcher 1988

Segall, B., 1966. Tradition und Neuschöpfung in der frühalexandrinischen Kunst. *119./120. Berliner Winckelmannsprogramm*. Berlin.

Stais, V., 1907. *Marbres et bronzes du Musée National*. Athen.

Toelken, E. H., 1850. *Leitfaden für die Sammlung antiker Metall-Arbeiten*. Königliche Museen Berlin. Berlin.

Valenza Mele, N., 1981. *Catalogo delle lucerne in bronzo*. Museo Nazionale di Napoli. Rom.

van der Meer, L. B., 2014. The Etruscan Bronze Lamp of Cortona, its Cosmic Program and its Attached Inscription, *Latomus 73*, 289–302.

van Gulik, H.C., 1940. *Catalogue of the Bronzes in the Allard Pierson Museum*. Amsterdam.

Wrede, H., 1986. Pan und das Lederhalfter, *Römische Mitteilungen 93*, 190–203.

25

Iconografie "funerarie" nella piccola plastica bronzea romana

Margherita Bolla

Musei Civici di Verona

margherita.bolla@comune.verona.it

Abstract: In the search about the role of figural bronzes in the Roman funerary sphere, the finds have been investigated as far as possible and the information for the chronology of the figurines has been examined on the basis of dated tombs. Some "funerary" iconographies are now being considered to understand their meaning and use, despite the difficulties arising from the widespread lack of reliable information on the contexts of discovery. Claude Rolley had noted the rarity of these subjects, mentioning the iconographies of the "sad" Attis and of the Cupid with inverted torch; to these, bronzes representing the dead can be added, that is the less rare and well-studied *larvae*, but, in relation to their meaning, it seems that there are no really funerary iconographies among the Roman small-scale bronze statuettes.

Keywords: Roman Bronzes; "sad" Attis; "funerary" Cupid; Somnus; Larvae

Nella ricerca sui bronzetti figurati in ambito sepolcrale in età romana, sono stati finora indagati i ritrovamenti nell'Impero e oltre i suoi confini e sono state esaminate le informazioni utili per la cronologia delle figurine derivanti dalla datazione delle tombe (v. *Appendice*).

Si considerano ora alcune iconografie correntemente definite come "funerarie", per comprenderne il significato e l'uso, nonostante le difficoltà generate dalla diffusa mancanza di informazioni attendibili sui contesti di ritrovamento. Claude Rolley (1998, 293) aveva rilevato la rarità dei soggetti funerari nella piccola plastica bronzea, citando in particolare l'Erote con torcia rovesciata e l'Attis "triste"; si esaminano quindi dapprima queste raffigurazioni e a seguire le cosiddette *larvae convivales*.

"Eroti funerari"

Nella piccola bronzistica, il termine "funerario" è spesso attribuito genericamente agli Eroti con fiaccola quando questa è rivolta verso il basso, ma si deve innanzitutto espungere una serie di Eroti incedenti con corpo talvolta in torsione, che reggono nella mano destra la fiaccola inclinata verso il basso ma sollevata rispetto al terreno e discosta dal corpo o addirittura orizzontale come a Bavay (Kaufmann-Heinimann c.s.), mentre nella sinistra possono avere un attributo perlopiù perduto, talvolta una conchiglia (Petit 1980, 49 n. 8) o una sfera (Kent Hill 1949, 31, n. 55, tav. 15). La torsione del corpo e la posizione delle gambe indicano una danza, in cui la fiaccola – usata nel mondo greco nella lampadedromia (Pellegrini 2009, 211-212) – viene inclinata verso il basso nel turbinio del movimento.

Diverso il caso delle raffigurazioni di "Erote" alato con fiaccola rovesciata che giunge fino a terra, collegato dagli studiosi alla Morte (Dunbabin 1986, 187), per il gesto di estinzione della luce e per la notevole frequenza dell'immagine su monumenti sepolcrali, ben diffusi ad esempio in Italia settentrionale (Marchini 1973). Però, come già avvenuto per gli "Eroti funerari" lapidei (Hermary – Cassimatis – Vollkommer 1986, 938-939; Poli 2015), che non rappresentano la Morte ma il Sonno (definito nelle iscrizioni *aeternus*, *aeternalis*, *perpetuus*), anche per le raffigurazioni in bronzo con torcia rovesciata bisogna domandarsi se non fossero raffigurazioni di questa divinità minore compagna di *Asklepios/Aesculapius*.

Hypnos/Somnus è raffigurato in età romana in due versioni, per le quali Gil Renberg (2016, 678. 683) accoglie le definizioni di "attiva" e "passiva", proposte nel *LIMC*: la prima è un adolescente in corsa, con ali nei capelli, talvolta con corolle di papaveri come attributo (Becatti 2018, 59-80); la seconda è appunto un "erote" addormentato o quasi, che – se stante - si sostiene a una fiaccola rovesciata reclinando il capo (per *Somnus* come fanciullo disteso, Becatti 2018, 81-92). L'iconografia stante è presente ad esempio in un rilievo in marmo rinvenuto nell'Asklepieion di Ulpia Traiana Sarmizegetusa, accanto alle divinità principali Esculapio e Igea (Varga 2015).

Nella bronzistica compaiono entrambe le versioni, quella di *Somnus* in corsa, abbastanza diffusa, con presenze anche in larari domestici (Lochin 1990, 597-598; Becatti 2018, 77-80), e quella "passiva" stante, attestata invece da un *corpus* esiguo: un bronzetto rinvenuto a *Lutetia* nel 1907, con fiaccola rovesciata posta sotto l'ascella e clamide pendente dalla spalla (Fig. 25.1; Bronzes Paris

Figura 25.1. Bronzetto da Lutetia (da *Bronzes Paris*, 1989).

1989, 58-59, n. 11); una figura di decorazione di carro da Codogno (provincia di Lodi), acefala, con corona nella mano sinistra e fiaccola rovesciata tenuta con la destra, senza gambe incrociate e presumibilmente senza testa reclinata (Bolla 2010, 128, fig. 9), il cui significato poteva essere illuminato dagli altri ornamenti del veicolo, non pervenuti; infine un bronzetto, attualmente disperso, dal Piemonte, con testa reclinata, che si appoggiava presumibilmente sulla fiaccola rovesciata, perduta (l'arco nella vecchia fotografia, Fig. 25.2, è un'aggiunta moderna; Assandria – Vacchetta 1897, 41-42, tav. II; Bolla 2002, 122, n. 1). Quest'ultima statuetta è stata ritrovata nel XVII secolo nella zona della Roncaglia a Bene Vagienna, in probabile associazione con altre: un famoso Esculapio, oggi al Cincinnati Art Museum, e due busti-*appliques* di Vittoria e di Satiro, dispersi; l'accostamento a Esculapio assume qui un particolare rilievo, poiché contribuisce all'identificazione di questo bronzetto (e di quelli analoghi) con *Somnus*. Un'iconografia parallela è la raffigurazione di *Somnus* come uomo maturo, appoggiato a un bastone (Lochin 1990, 606-607, con esclusione del bronzetto da *Timna*, Segall 1955, 212-214, fig. 8), diffusa su sarcofagi nel II-III secolo (Becatti 2018, 96-97) e attestata nella piccola bronzistica in due elementi da Ercolano, di cui uno riprodotto graficamente nel Settecento, ritenuti all'epoca una coppia di ornamenti di recipiente, ma forse parte di altro arredo (Fig. 25.3; Bronzi Ercolano 1771, 30. 418).

Le statuette bronzee citate non paiono dunque di per sé pertinenti all'ambito funerario, poiché non rappresenterebbero la Morte ma il dio minore *Hypnos/Somnus*, eventualmente collegato alla sfera curativa delle divinità salutari Esculapio e Igea (Stafford 2003, 97; Renberg 2016, 682 nota 14; Becatti 2018, 42-45).

"Attis triste"

Altra iconografia da esaminare è quella dell'"Attis triste", con il mento appoggiato alla mano, che compare nella piccola plastica bronzea in figure intere e busti, entrambi per applicazione (che non sembrano interpretabili come Cautes o Cautopates, poco attestati nella bronzistica e caratterizzati dalla presenza della torcia, ad es. Menzel 1986, 33, n. 73, tav. 38). Come noto, le raffigurazioni di "Attidi" sono molto diffuse su monumenti sepolcrali e sono state oggetto in tempi recenti di indagini volte a comprendere se si tratti proprio di Attis compagno di Cibele oppure di una generica figura di orientale rinviante a popoli con i quali i Romani si scontrarono, quali i Parti e altri (Landskron 2003).

Dai bronzetti da considerare vanno esclusi a priori quelli in atteggiamento non "triste" oppure con caratteristiche sicuramente riconducibili ad Attis, come la presenza di attributi specifici (ramo di pino, *pedum*) o il ventre scoperto. Gli altri, che qui interessano, sembrano poco diffusi; si ricordano ad esempio quelli da Bourges (Reinach, II.1, 1908, 479.7), Samboseto nel Parmense (Fig. 25.4; Bolla 2016, 189, ancora come Attis) e Tanneto (in provincia di Reggio Emilia; Bolla 2015-2018, 2), che potrebbero essere barbari orientali in atteggiamento "sottomesso", e, in quanto *appliques*, potrebbero aver fatto parte di "historische Reliefs im Kleinformat" (Kreilinger 1996).

Larvae

Le raffigurazioni in bronzo di scheletri o *larvae* (sul termine Guzmán Almagro 2013), sono state indagate in modo esauriente da Katherine Dunbabin (1986). Secondo l'interpretazione della studiosa, ampiamente condivisa, esse rappresentano il morto ma non una personificazione della Morte; ricordando l'immanenza di questo evento ineluttabile, esortavano a gioire pienamente della vita, in particolare nell'ambito del banchetto, importante momento sociale nel mondo antico. Non sono quindi ritenute realizzate a scopo "funerario", pur rappresentando il corpo umano dopo la decomposizione della carne. Agli esemplari citati da K. Dunbabin si possono aggiungere alcune testimonianze, in parte già menzionate da Mario Iozzo (2015).

Gli scheletri in bronzo sono noti in due tipi principali: colati in un sol pezzo (quindi rigidi) oppure snodabili. Il tipo rigido è rappresentato finora da cinque esemplari:

- dall'Etruria; agli inizi del Novecento conservato a Parigi nella collezione Courtot; Reinach 1913, IV, 440, n. 1; Causey Frel 1980, 171 nota 2; Dunbabin 1986, 196;

Figura 25.2. Bronzetti da Bene Vagienna, in parte dispersi (da Assandria, Vacchetta, 1927).

- probabilmente rinvenuto a Mesnil-Esnard (Seine-Maritime) nel 1823 o 1828, agli inizi del Novecento conservato a Rouen, attualmente disperso (Fig. 25.5); alt. cons. cm 7; Reinach 1904, III, 205, n. 4; Espérandieu – Rolland 1959, 56, n. 105, tav. XXXV (ivi è indicata la corrispondenza con l'esemplare già a Rouen); Causey Frel 1980, 171 nota 2; Dunbabin 1986, 196; Iozzo 2015, 112 (lo considera dubbio);

- conservato a Paris, Musée du Louvre, dalla collezione Campana (formatasi in Italia); alt. cons. cm 9,5; de Ridder 1913, 98, n. 710, tav. 49; Causey Frel 1980, 171 nota 2; Dunbabin 1986, 196 nota 52, fig. 6;
- da Elche, Ibarra y Manzoni 1879, 164, tav. X; Reinach 1924, V.2, 400, n. 3;
- conservato a Stockholm, Medelhavsmuseet (n. inv. MM 18583); alt. cons. cm 6,5; *non vidi*, con un anello

Figura 25.3. Bronzetto di *Somnus* maturo (da *Bronzi Ercolano*, 1771).

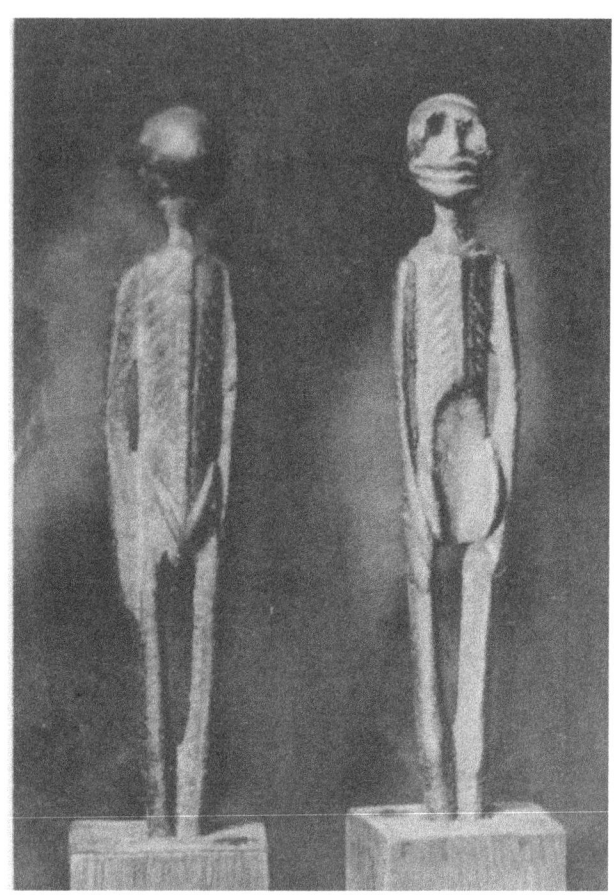

Figura 25.5. Scheletro probabilmente da Mesnil-Esnard, disperso (da Espérandieu, Rolland, 1959).

Figura 25.4. Figura di orientale da Samboseto (Milano, Civiche Raccolte Archeologiche).

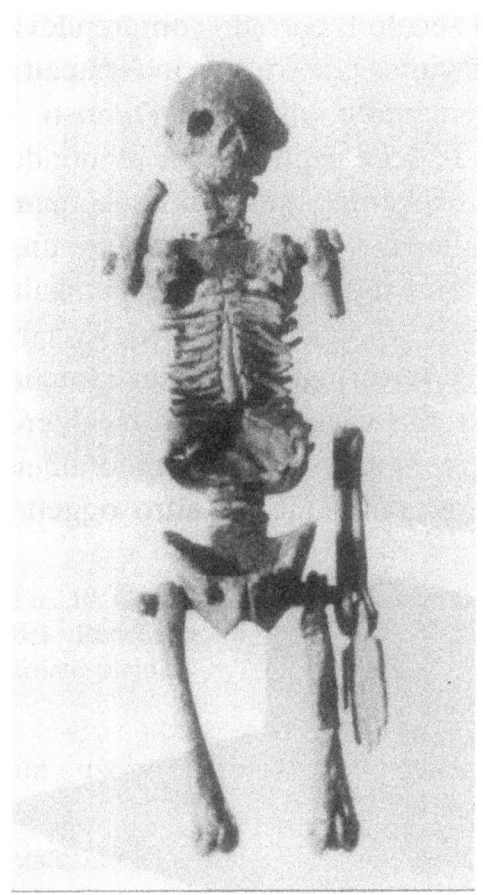

Figura 25.6. Scheletro da Patù (da Small, 2011).

di sospensione sul cranio, riferito a questa categoria da Dunbabin 1986, 196-197 nota 55

Gli scheletri rigidi sono accomunati dalla compattezza della struttura (braccia aderenti al corpo, gambe unite) e dallo scarso spessore, caratteristiche funzionali a una presa agevole, così che de Ridder propose un loro utilizzo come manici, ritenuto possibile da Dunbabin. Poiché tutti sono mancanti della parte inferiore delle gambe e dei piedi (l'altezza totale si aggirava attorno agli 11 cm), non è possibile ipotizzare di quale strumento o recipiente facessero parte. Non sono identici nei dettagli: ad esempio quello conservato al Louvre sembra presentare un resto di capigliatura. I luoghi di rinvenimento sono la penisola italica, la Gallia e la penisola ispanica. La mancanza di qualsiasi dato di contesto suscita dubbi sull'appartenenza di questi scheletri "rigidi" all'epoca antica, alla quale sono però concordemente attribuiti da tempo, forse per le scarse conoscenze anatomiche in essi espresse. In generale, riguardo all'antichità degli scheletrini, va tenuta presente la considerevole diffusione delle cosiddette "morticine" in metallo e in altri materiali, almeno dalla fine del Quattrocento, come *memento mori* con significato tendenzialmente opposto a quello delle *larvae* antiche (Caetani Lovatelli 1895, 10-13, fig. 2-3; Vertova 1992; Di Nola 2001, 85-86).

A parte va considerato un bronzetto del British Museum, con corpo non del tutto scheletrito e braccio destro piegato verso il ventre (il sinistro è mancante, come i piedi), definito da K. Dunbabin (1986, 196 nota 51) come *Hautskelett*, che potrebbe aver avuto funzione diversa da quella delle *larvae* e forse significato analogo a quello di una statuetta di uomo emaciato e con un piede deforme, proveniente dai dintorni di Soissons, fornita di iscrizione in greco e ritenuta votiva (Waser 2010, 93. 149, n. C1.1, fig. 256-257).

Gli scheletrini snodabili, più diffusi, sono stati divisi in due sottotipi – stanti e semisdraiati (in atteggiamento di banchettanti) – da K. Dunbabin.

Fra gli scheletrini snodabili stanti, alcuni presentano la gabbia toracica quasi chiusa:

- conservato a Roma, Museo Nazionale Romano, già nel Museo Kircheriano (da prima del 1757); privo della parte inferiore; Dunbabin 1986, 196
- da Perugia, rinvenuto nel 1875 sul lato nord della piazza Vittorio Emanuele; già collezione Giuseppe Bellucci, confluita nel Museo archeologico di Perugia; Causey Frel 1980, 171 nota 2; Dunbabin 1986, 196 (immagine in Caetani Lovatelli 1895, 5)
- da Patù (Veretum) – loc. Mariane, tomba (inumazione di adulto, probabilmente maschio), datata al pieno II sec. a.C., scheletrino privo della parte inferiore delle gambe, alt. cons. cm 10,7 (Fig. 25.6); Delli Ponti 1994; Auriemma 1998, 131 nota 30; Small 2011, 535-536, fig. 12; Iozzo 2015, 112;

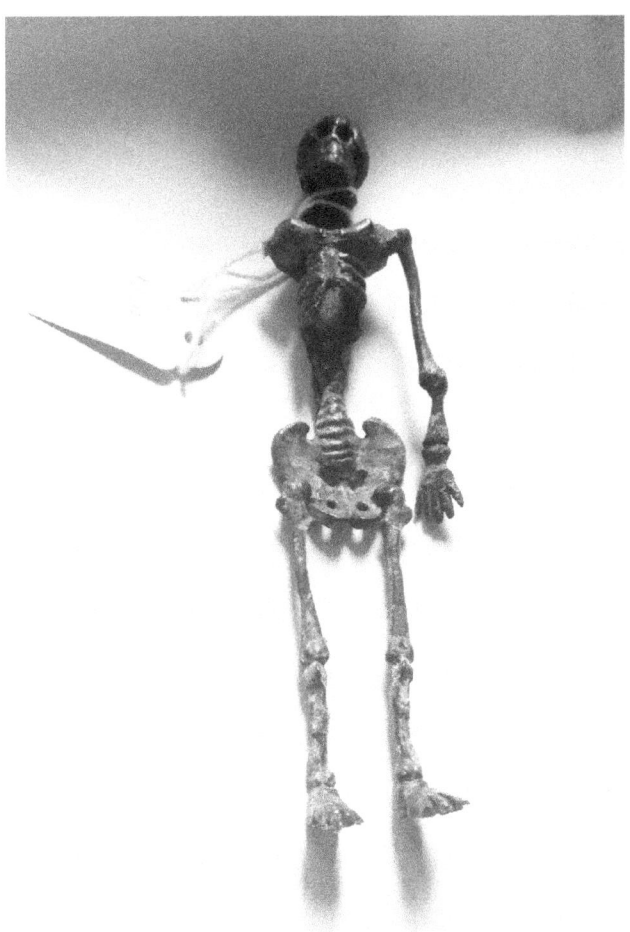

Figura 25.7. Scheletro conservato a Catania (© Comune di Catania – Museo Civico Castello Ursino).

- vendita Helbing, 28 ottobre 1913, n. 538; Reinach 1924, V.2, 400, n. 2;

Altri presentano nella gabbia toracica una più lunga apertura frontale triangolare:

- già nel museo dei Benedettini di Catania, confluito nel Museo Civico di Castello Ursino, n. inv. 1797 (Fig. 25.7, cortesia Valentina Noto e Floriana Cappadonna); alt. cm 10,7; mancante del braccio destro e forse di parte delle costole (quindi di non sicura collocazione tipologica); Dunbabin 1986, nota 56;
- conservato a London, British Museum, collezione Pourtalès, n. inv. 1865,0103.41; solo parte superiore, alt. cons. cm 4,2; Walters 1899, 270, n. 1682; Causey Frel 1980, 171 nota 2; Dunbabin 1986, 196, fig. 2;
- conservato a London, Science Museum, (https://collection.sciencemuseum.org.uk/objects/co90020/memento-mori-roman-199-bce-500-ce-memento-mori, consultato 6 gennaio 2019), n. inv. A629420 (Fig. 25.8); privo di parte della gamba destra, cui è stato sostituito il braccio sinistro, alt. cm 11; Iozzo 2015, 112;
- conservato a Dresden; privo della parte inferiore delle gambe, alt. cons. cm 6,8; Causey Frel 1980, 171 nota 2; Dunbabin 1986, 196, fig. 3;

Figura 25.8. Scheletro (London, Science Museum).

- conservato a München, Antikensammlungen; privo della parte inferiore, alt. cons. cm 5; Causey Frel 1980, 171 nota 2, fig. 3; Dunbabin 1986, 196;
- conservato a Malibu, J. Paul Getty Museum; privo della parte inferiore, alt. cons. cm 6,6; Causey Frel 1980; Dunbabin 1986, 196, fig. 4;

Scheletrini snodabili banchettanti:

- inviato nel 1671 da Roma da parte di Ottavio Falconieri a Leopoldo de' Medici; conservato a Firenze, Museo Archeologico Nazionale, lungh. cm 8,8; Dunbabin 1986, 185-186, fig. 1; Iozzo 2015, 211-212 (l'anfora da vino tenuta dallo scheletro viene datata in base alla tipologia dal tardo I sec. a.C. al tardo II sec. d.C.); Iozzo 2017, n. 20 (con datazione al tardo I sec. d.C.);
- conservato nel XIX secolo a Arolsen, nella collezione del principe di Waldeck; alt. cons. cm 9,5; Dunbabin 1986, 198 nota 58.

Frammenti:

- conservato nella collezione Gorga (Museo Nazionale Romano, Roma), un braccio (in tre elementi movibili, lungh. cm 7,4), Ligabue 2012;
- parte di femore in bronzo (alt. cons. cm 4,8), nel mercato antiquario, https://auctions.bertolamifinearts.com/de/lot/5590/roman-bronze-fragmentary-femur-of-a-larva-/ (consultato 24.06.2016).

È stato ritenuto parte di una *larva* anche un piede trovato ad Albano prima del 1898, conservato al Museo Gregoriano Etrusco (Caliò 2000, 182, n. 338, 738-739; Iozzo 2015, 112), ma dalla sua lunghezza (cm 7) deriverebbe un'altezza della figura intera di circa 40 cm, decisamente anomala rispetto alle *larvae* note; inoltre la sua fattura è molto più naturalistica e complessa rispetto ai piedi di scheletrini conservati (negli esemplari conservati allo Science Museum of London, a Firenze e a Catania).

Sono attestate in totale una quindicina di *larvae*; si tratta quindi di un'iconografia non rara.

Sono anche testimoniati scheletrini in materie diverse dal bronzo:
- in argento, snodabile, rinvenuto nel 1873 a Pompei, nell'atrio della casa di *L. Volusius Faustus* (Sarnataro 2002, 404, insieme con oggetti preziosi, vasellame da banchetto, strumenti), lacunoso, alt. cm 8,6; con gabbia toracica chiusa; conservato a Napoli, Museo Archeologico Nazionale, n. inv. 109688; Dunbabin 1986, 196; Pappalardo 1986, 212 n. 47: "pare di bronzo, anche se custodito tra gli argenti"; Cassetta 2006 (argento); Castiglione 2006, 50;
- in argento, frammento di cranio, Napoli, Museo Archeologico Nazionale, Medagliere, n. inv. 78288, dalle città vesuviane; Cassetta 2006; in bronzo, secondo Sarnataro 2010-2011, 202;
- in avorio, da Perugia, rinvenuto nel 1770 in "un'olla cineraria rotta", alla Pila, a sud della città, in un podere dei Padri Serviti; secondo Dunbabin 1986, 197, nota 56, potrebbe trattarsi di una bambola stilizzata, ma nella *Lettera del Professor Luigi Canali a Gio. Battista Vermiglioli* (Vermiglioli 1813, 109-118) è citato come "bello scheletro" e messo in relazione alle fonti antiche sulle *larvae*;

Da fonti letterarie romane sono menzionati scheletrini:
- in argento, *larva* citata da Petronio nel *Satyricon* (Dunbabin 1986, 188, 195-196);
- in legno, poiché nel *De Magia* (o *Apologia*), Apuleio viene accusato di aver fatto realizzare uno scheletrino in legno per pratiche magiche (evidentemente diffuse) e si difende affermando che si trattava di un piccolo Mercurio (Dunbabin 1986, 248-250).

Le *larvae* rimaste sono dunque perlopiù in bronzo, di altezza massima attorno ai 15 centimetri circa; solo per due di esse è sufficientemente noto il contesto della scoperta (Patù; Pompei, in una casa dal "tenore di vita medio", Sarnataro 2002, 405). Di particolare importanza lo scheletro trovato a Patù (l'antica *Veretum*), poiché proviene da una tomba, pur mantenendo probabilmente il medesimo significato delle *larvae* usate nei banchetti (cfr. Dunbabin 1986, 237-247). La datazione del contesto al pieno II sec. a.C. (parecchio dopo la conquista romana della Messapia) amplia all'indietro il *range* cronologico di diffusione degli scheletrini in ambito romano, collocato da Dunbabin (1986, 231-233) soprattutto fra l'avanzato I sec. a.C. e il I sec. d.C. Il ritrovamento è inoltre interessante per la collocazione all'estremo limite meridionale della penisola italica e in collegamento con il vicino scalo marittimo commerciale di Torre San Gregorio, in cui sono attestati rapporti con Grecia, Epiro, Africa e Oriente in genere (per rapporti fra Apulia ed Egitto in età ellenistica, Ghisellini 1993, 54-64). Ciò induce a chiedersi se lo scheletro di Patù non sia l'"anello mancante" per la dimostrazione dell'ipotesi di K. Dunbabin (1986, 210-212) di una elaborazione dell'iconografia degli scheletrini in ambito egizio ellenistico (alessandrino) e di un loro successivo trasferimento al mondo romano; resterebbe da chiarire come siano avvenuti il passaggio dall'uso di materiali organici a quello del bronzo e la trasformazione delle raffigurazioni da rigide a snodabili. Il fatto che in Egitto provengano, probalmente da sepolture, diverse raffigurazioni del "defunto scheletrico" potrebbe spiegare il contesto di Patù, al di fuori dell'ambito domestico. Altra ipotesi (Small 2011) è che lo scheletrino trovato in Puglia documenti, con il resto del corredo (privo di elementi di tipo indigeno), l'assimilazione alla cultura romana, perlomeno riguardo agli usi del banchetto; in tal caso la *larva* potrebbe esser giunta a Patù dall'Urbe.

Oltre a Patù, altri luoghi di rinvenimento degli scheletri snodabili sono Perugia (in bronzo e in avorio, il secondo forse da tomba), le città vesuviane (argento) e forse l'Asia Minore (bronzo). I luoghi di ritrovamento sicuri si situano quindi per ora prevalentemente nella penisola italica centrale e meridionale; all'Italia in genere vanno anche presumibilmente riferite (per vicende collezionistiche) altre quattro testimonianze in bronzo.

Da ricordare infine nell'ambito della piccola bronzistica un apparentemente unico esemplare di teschio (Paris, già collezione Dutuit), sormontato da una farfalla, considerato un *aequipondium* per il caratteristico riempimento in piombo (fornito di anello di sospensione; alt. cm 4,5; peso 455 g; Petit 1980, 177 n. 95), funzione messa in dubbio per la mancanza di confronti da N. Franken (1994, 76, 82 (nota 139), 170 n. B62*). Anche alle raffigurazioni di crani, con o senza la farfalla (simbolo dell'anima), è stata attribuita la stessa valenza delle *larvae*, con possibilità di uso nei banchetti per ricordare la fragilità della vita (Dunbabin 1986, 212-215); tuttavia, se il cranio conservato a Parigi fosse un *aequipondium*, un suo uso nell'ambito del simposio sarebbe poco probabile.

In conclusione, accettando l'interpretazione fornita da molti studiosi per le *larvae* e le identificazioni sopra proposte per gli "eroti" con torcia rovesciata e le figure in abito orientale, si arriverebbe a dire che non sono per ora attestate iconografie realmente funerarie nella piccola plastica romana in bronzo.

Appendice. Bronzetti in contesti sepolcrali: aggiornamento

Si segnalano, senza pretese di esaustività, alcune aggiunte agli elenchi sinora editi di rinvenimenti di bronzetti figurati (non decorativi) in ambito funerario (Bolla 2013; Bolla 2015). Alla bibliografia del bronzetto di pigmeo combattente dalla via Collatina a Roma, sono da aggiungere Chew 1995, 135 n 6, 140-141; Waser 2010, n. A2a12, fig. 78 (con ulteriori riferimenti). Il nano da una tomba di Tongeren (Waser 2010, 44, 130 n. A3a9, fig. 126) esula dal tema dei bronzetti a tutto tondo in contesti funerari, in quanto balsamario.

Italia
- Patù/*Veretum* (provincia di Lecce), scheletrino, v. sopra
- "presso Negarine presso Corrubbio di Valpolicella" (provincia di Verona), entro un "sarcofago", (contesto probabilmente medioimperiale o tardoantico), rinvenuto *ante* agosto 1886, Mercurio, identificato di recente nel Museo Archeologico al Teatro romano di Verona, Bolla 2013, 21; Bolla 2017, 16, fig. 6; Arzone 2018, 6

Crimea sudoccidentale (al di fuori dell'Impero romano)
- necropoli Belbek IV: tomba 3, 50-75 d.C., piccola erma; tomba 223, 125-150 d.C., Erote; tomba 233, fine II-inizi III sec. d.C., Erote; sono parti di vaso o arredo, trasformate in amuleti, secondo Zhuralev (2015)

Queste acquisizioni non modificano il panorama finora delineato, relativo a meno di una novantina di bronzetti, pochissimi in rapporto alle migliaia di sepolture di età romana finora scoperte. Si segnala qualche aggiunta anche per le divinità in piombo da tombe (Bolla 2013, 13-14): in Italia, a *Abellinum*, in tomba di fanciulla datata alla seconda metà del II sec. d.C., una piccola edicola con Venere anadiomene e una figura più piccola variamente identificata come Eros o Priapo (Pescatori 2013, fig. 23); forse in una tomba di Cornus (Sardegna), edicoletta con Venere anadiomene e Eros (Baratta 2013); in Gallia, a Narbonne, prima del 1836, in tomba a inumazione di bambina o adolescente, statuina femminile nuda con anello da sospensione sul dorso, in piombo, alt. cm 3 circa, amuleto (Pech 1847, 230-231, ill., e Galliou 1979, 527-528, con proposta di datazione della tomba alla media età imperiale, solo sulla base del rito seguito). Baratta (2013, 500-501, fig. 6) ritiene di provenienza funeraria anche l'edicola con Venere di Louvignies-Bavay (v. Bolla 2013, nota 62). Riguardo alle presenze in contesti funerari di raffigurazioni di divinità in piombo, sembra ora prevalere, rispetto a Mercurio, la figura di Venere.

Bibliografia

Arzone, A., 2018. Le monete d'oro rinvenute nella tomba romana di Corrubbio (Verona). *Verona illustrata*, 31, 5-23.

Assandria, G. and Vacchetta G., 1897. Augusta Bagiennorum (Scavi, Museo, antichità romane trovate nel suo territorio). *Atti della Società di Archeologia e Belle Arti per la provincia di Torino*, VII, 1, 29-43.

Auriemma, R., 1998. Archeologia della costa salentina: l'approdo di Torre San Gregorio. *Studi di Antichità*, 11, 127-148.

Baratta, G. 2013. Sulle edicole plumbee con raffigurazione di Venere Anadiomene della Sardegna. *Tharros Felix*,

5, a cura di A. Mastino, P.G. Spanu, R. Zucca. Roma: Carocci, 493-512.

Becatti, G., 2018. *Hypnos - Somnus: il demone custode e l'erote dormiente. Studio iconologico del dio del sonno dall'antichità all'epoca moderna*, (Artes, IX). Bruxelles-Roma: Istituto Storico Belga di Roma.

Bolla, M., 2002. Bronzetti romani di divinità in Italia settentrionale: alcune osservazioni. *Bronzi di età romana in Cisalpina. Novità e riletture (Antichità Altoadriatiche*, LI), a cura di G. Cuscito e M. Verzár-Bass. Trieste: Editreg, 73-159.

Bolla, M., 2010. La decorazione bronzea per carri in Italia settentrionale. *Lanx* [e-journal], 5, 107-167. https://doi.org/10.13130/2035-4797/613.

Bolla, M., 2013. Bronzetti in contesti funerari di età romana. *Lanx* [e-journal], 15, 1-50. https://doi.org/10.13130/2035-4797/3734.

Bolla, M., 2015. Datazione di bronzetti da contesti funerari romani. *New Research on Ancient Bronzes*, Acta of the XVIIIth International Congress on Ancient Bronzes (*Zürich Studies in Archaeology*, 10), a cura di E. Deschler-Erb, Ph. Della Casa. Zürich: Chronos Verlag, 137–146.

Bolla, M., 2015-2018. Statuette in bronzo da Taneto. *Pagine di Archeologia. Studi e materiali*, 2015-2018 (edito 2017), 1, 1-8.

Bolla, M., 2016. Eastern Bronzes in Northern Italy. *Proceedings of the XVIIth International Congress on Ancient Bronzes* (Izmir, 2011), Monographie-Instrumentum 52, a cura di A. Giumlia-Mair, C. Mattusch. Autun: Éditions Mergoil, 183-196.

Bolla, M., 2017. Novità sui bronzetti romani dal territorio veronese. *Studi Veronesi. Miscellanea di studi sul territorio veronese* [e-journal], II, 9-35. http://www.veronastoria.it/ojs /index.php/StVer/article/view/73.

Bronzes Paris 1989. *Les bronzes antiques de Paris (Collections du Musée Carnavalet)*. Paris: Musée Carnavalet: Paris-Musées.

Bronzi Ercolano 1771. *De' bronzi di Ercolano e contorni incisi, II. Statue* (*Delle antichità di Ercolano*, VI). Napoli: Regia Stamperia.

Caetani Lovatelli, E., 1895, Di una piccola larva convivale in bronzo. *Monumenti Antichi*, 5, cc. 5-16.

Caliò, L.M., 2000. *La collezione Bonifacio Falcioni* (*Museo Gregoriano Etrusco. Cataloghi*, 6), I. Città del Vaticano: Direzione generale dei monumenti, musei e gallerie pontificie.

Cassetta, R., 2006. Larva. *Argenti. Pompei, Napoli, Torino*, catalogo mostra (Torino, 2006-2007), a cura di P.G. Guzzo, Milano, 89 n. 41.

Castiglione, M., 2006. In argento plane studiosus sum: un'esibizione di privata luxuria. *Argenti. Pompei, Napoli, Torino*, catalogo mostra (Torino, 2006-2007), a cura di P.G. Guzzo. Milano: Electa, 45-59.

Causey Frel, F., 1980, A Larva Convivalis in the Getty Museum. *The J. Paul Getty Museum Journal*, 8, 171-172.

Chew, H., 1995, Une statuette de Pygmée en bronze d'époque romaine à Davron (Yvelines). *Antiquités Nationales* 27, 1995, 133-144.

Delli Ponti, G., 1994. Un singolare ritrovamento tombale a Patù. *Scritti di antichità in memoria di Benita Sciarra Bardaro*, a cura di C. Marangio e A. Nitti. Fasano: Schena, 47-52.

Di Nola, A.M., 2001, *La nera signora. Antropologia della morte e del lutto*, Roma (I ed. 1995): Newton Compton.

Dunbabin, K., 1986. Sic erimus cuncti... The Skeleton in Graeco-Roman Art. *Jahrbuch des Deutschen Archäologischen Instituts*, 101, 185-255.

Espérandieu, E. and Rolland, H., 1959. *Bronzes antiques de la Seine Maritime* (*Gallia*, Suppl. XIII). Paris: Centre national de la recherche scientifique.

Franken, N., 1994. *Aequipondia. Figürliche Laufgewichte römischer und frühbyzantinischer Schnellwaagen*. Alfter: Verlag und Datenbank für Geisteswissenschaften.

Galliou, P., 1979. La pseudo-Angerona du Musée de Morlaix (Finistère). *Latomus*, 38, 2, 1979, 525-529.

Ghisellini, E., 1993. Una testa femminile alessandrina da Egnazia: considerazioni sui rapporti tra l'Apulia e l'Egitto tolemaico. *Xenia Antiqua*, II, 45-70.

Guzmán Almagro, A., 2013. Demonios, fantasmas y máscaras en la Antigüedad: consideraciones sobre el término larua y sus significados. *Emerita, Revista de Lingüística y Filología Clásica*, LXXXI, 1, 183-202.

Hermary, A., Cassimatis, H. and Vollkommer R. 1986. Eros. *LIMC*, III. Zürich; München: Artemis, 850-942.

Ibarra y Manzoni, A., 1879. *Illici, su situation y antigüedades*. Alicante: Publicaciones del Instituto de Estudios Alicantinos.

Iozzo, M., 2015. Scheletrino da tavola. *Piccoli Grandi Bronzi. Capolavori greci, etruschi e romani delle collezioni mediceo-lorenesi*, catalogo della mostra (Firenze, 2015), a cura di B. Arbeid, M. Iozzo. Firenze: Polistampa, 111-112 n. 74.

Iozzo, M., 2017. Bronzi. *Leopoldo de' Medici. Principe dei collezionisti*, catalogo della mostra (Firenze, 2017), a cura di V. Conticelli, R. Gennaioli, M. Sframeli. Livorno: Sillabe, 260-263, 266-267, 280-281, nn. 17-18, 20, 27.

Kaufmann-Heinimann A., c.s. Le trésor de Bavay - un ensemble de statuettes hors norme. In corso di stampa nel catalogo della mostra *Nouveaux regards sur le trésor de Bavay* (Bavay, Forum antique, 2018-2019), https://nordoc.hypotheses.org/3372.

Kent Hill, D., 1949. *Catalogue of Classical Bronze Sculpture in the Walters Art Gallery*. Baltimore: Trustees of the Walters Art Gallery.

Kreilinger, U., 1996. *Römische Bronzeappliquen. Historische Reliefs im Kleinformat (Archäologie und Geschichte, 6)*. Heidelberg: Verlag Archäologie und Geschichte.

Landskron, A., 2003. Ein tanzender Orientale in Tarragona. *Jahreshefte des Österreichischen Archäologischen Instituts in Wien*, 72, 141-148.

Ligabue, G., 2012. Bambole. *Il Museo delle Antichità Etrusche e Italiche. III. I bronzi della collezione Gorga*, a cura di M.G. Benedettini. Roma: Casa Editrice Università La Sapienza, 520-521 n. 1609.

Lochin, C., 1990. Somnus. *LIMC*, V. Zürich; München: Artemis, 591-609.

Marchini, G.P., 1973. Rilievi con geni funebri di età romana nel territorio veronese. *Il territorio veronese in età romana*, Atti del convegno (Verona, 1971). Verona: Accademia di agricoltura, scienze e lettere, 357-438.

Menzel, H., 1986. *Die römischen Bronzen aus Deutschland. III. Bonn*. Mainz am Rhein: Philipp von Zabern.

Pappalardo, U., 1986. Gli argenti. *Le collezioni del Museo Nazionale di Napoli. I mosaici, le pitture, gli oggetti di uso quotidiano, gli argenti, le terrecotte invetriate, i vetri, i cristalli, gli avori*. Roma: De Luca, 90-101, 206-216.

Pech, L., 1847. Lettre a M. Ad. De Longpérier sur quelques monuments antiques inédits. *Revue Archéologique*, IV, 228-234.

Pellegrini, E., 2009. *Eros nella Grecia arcaica e classica. Iconografia e iconologia*. Roma: Giorgio Bretschneider.

Pescatori, G., 2013. Abellinum (Atripalda). Introduzione. *Fana, templa, delubra. Corpus dei luoghi di culto dell'Italia antica (FTD) - 2: Regio I: Avella, Atripalda, Salerno*. Paris: Collège de France; disponibile a: http://books.openedition.org/cdf/3909.

Petit, J., 1980. *Bronzes antiques de la Collection Dutuit. Grecs, hellénistiques, romains et de l'Antiquité tardive*. Paris: Musée du Petit Palais.

Poli, N., 2015. A proposito del papaver somniferum raffigurato su due monumenti funerari da Aquileia. *Studia archaeologica Monika Verzar-Bass dicata (West and East, Monografie, 1)*, a cura di B. Callegher. Trieste: EUT Edizioni Università di Trieste, 147-153.

Reinach S. I-VI, *Répertoire de la statuaire grecque et romaine*: I, 1920 (nuova ed.); II, 1, 1908 (2 ed.); II,2, 1909 (2 ed.); III, 1904; IV, 1913; V, 1-2, 1924; VI, 1930; Paris: Editions Ernest Leroux.

Renberg, G.H., 2016. *Where Dreams May Come. Incubation Sanctuaries in the Greco-Roman World (Religions in the Graeco-Roman World, 184)*. Leiden-Boston: Brill.

de Ridder, A., 1913. *Les bronzes antiques du Louvre. I. Les figurines*. Paris, Editeur Ernest Leroux.

Rolley, Cl., 1998. Les bronzes grecs et romains: recherches récentes. *Revue Archéologique*, 1998-2, 291-310.

Sarnataro, T., 2002. Le patere con manico dall'area vesuviana e la loro funzione domestica. Case-study; la Casa di L. Volusius Faustus (I 2, 10). *I Bronzi Antichi: Produzione e tecnologia*, Atti del XV Congresso Internazionale sui Bronzi Antichi (Grado-Aquileia, 2001) (Monographies Instruumentum, 21), a cura di A. Giumlia-Mair. Montagnac: Éditions Mergoil, 393-406.

Sarnataro, T., 2010-2011. *Privata luxuria all'ombra del Vesuvio. Le argenterie vesuviane: problemi di iconografia, cronologia, botteghe*. Tesi di dottorato (Università degli studi di Napoli Federico II).

Segall, B., 1955. Sculpture from Arabia Felix. The Hellenistic Period. *American Journal of Archaeology*, 59, 3, 207-214.

Small, A. M., 2011.Vino e acculturazione in Apulia nell' orizzonte ellenistico-romano. *La vigna di Dioniso. Vite, vino e culti in Magna Grecia*, Atti del 49° Convegno di Studi sulla Magna Grecia (Taranto, 2009). Taranto: Scorpione, 517-541.

Stafford, E.J., 2003. Brother, Son, Friend and Healer: Sleep the God. *Sleep*, a cura di T. Wiedemann e K. Dowden. Bari: Levante, 71-106.

Varga, T., 2015. Hypnos and the incubatio ritual at Ulpia Traiana Sarmizegetusa. *Acta Musei Porolissensis*, XXXVII, 241-251.

Vermiglioli, G.B., 1813. *Saggio di bronzi etruschi trovati nell'agro perugino*. Perugia: F. Baduel.

Vertova, L., 1992. La Morte secca. *Mitteilungen des Kunsthistorischen Institutes in Florenz*, 36, 103-128.

Walters, H.B., 1899. *Catalogue of the Bronzes, Greek, Roman and Etruscan, in the Department of Greek and Roman Antiquities, British Museum*. London: Longmans and Co.

Waser, M., 2010, *Behinderte in der hellenistisch-römischen Kleinplastik. Bronzefiguren*, Diplomarbeit (Klassische Archäologie). Wien (http://othes.univie.ac.at/12794/).

Zhuralev, D., 2015. Bronze Statuettes from the Necropolis Belbek IV in the southwestern Crimea. *Bosporos Studies*, XXXI, 276-286 (riassunto in inglese).

26

Small Objects, Multiple Perspectives: The Case of the Genius of Grumentum

Giulia Bison

National Etruscan Museum of Villa Giulia

giulia.bison@beniculturali.it

Abstract: This paper deals with the bronze statuette of a Genius discovered near a temple in the Forum of the Roman city of Grumentum. Bronze statuettes in context are quite rare: therefore, issues concerning its inclusion in the archaeological record, its relationship with the nearby sacred building and its dating are analyzed, as well as its economic, personal and symbolic value. In so doing, I raise several methodological questions and reflect on how these objects have been studied so far and how their informative potential could better be exploited by considering them from different points of view.

Keywords: Bronze Statuettes; Context; Residuality; Biography of Objects; Methodology

Introduction

This paper will deal with a bronze statuette discovered near one of the most important temples in the Forum of the Roman city of Grumentum and how it provides a useful case study for reflecting on the different perspectives from which it is possible to look at these objects.

In ancient times, *Grumentum* (modern Grumento Nova, Italy) was an important settlement of the upper Agri Valley at the crossroad between commercial routes connecting the Tyrrhenian and the Ionian Sea (Giardino 1992).

Founded in the first decades of the 3rd century BC, the city became a Roman colony in 59 BC. As a direct consequence of this change in its status, it was equipped with new walls, roads, an aqueduct and a Forum. The latter formed the core of its political and commercial life, and it featured a Basilica and three temples: the so-called Temple C (probably devoted to the imperial cult), the Capitolium and the Round Temple (Mastrocinque 2016) (Fig. 26.1).

This sacred building was constructed during the first half of the 1st century AD at the southeastern corner of the Forum on a circular podium with no *cella* and a single row of 18 columns. The space around it was delimited by a colonnaded porch on three sides; so far, no useful elements have emerged to identify the cult to which it was devoted (Soriano 2016; Soriano – Saracino 2016) (Fig. 26.2).

Figure 26.1. Map of Southern Italy showing the geographical collocation of Grumentum

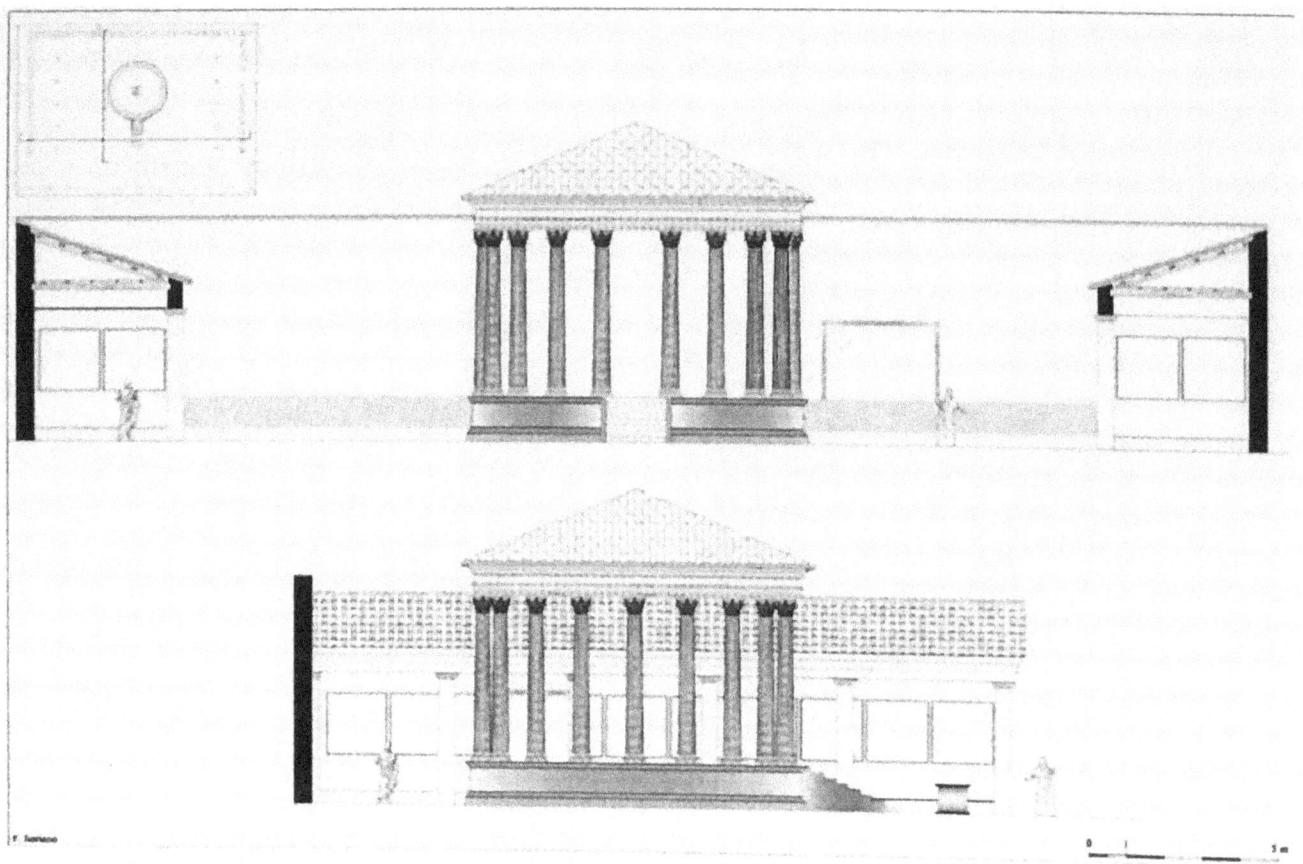

Figure 26.2. Reconstruction of the Round Temple (from Soriano – Sarracino 2016)

The bronze figurine in question was found northeast of the temple, in the space between the temple and the porch, in a layer whose characteristics will be more fully described below.

Description

The bronze statuette (6,2 cm height; 2,6 cm width; weight 50 grams) depicts a standing male figure wearing a toga, a fold of which covers the head (*velato capite*), and a sleeved tunic which forms a series of V-shaped folds on the chest. The toga is richly draped over the figure, which bears the weight on the right leg, while the left is slightly bent forward; the right foot is almost completely worn away, while the left does not show traces of means for attachment. The right arm is slightly flexed and bent forward, and the corresponding hand is holding a *patera umbilicata*; the left arm is bent and held close to the body, and in the hand is a *volumen* (Fig. 26.3).

The head is turned to the right, and the face has clearly discernible features, with big, round eyes, straight nose and a well-defined jawline. Some locks of hair are visible on the forehead, and in the space between these and the veil, other elements can be interpreted as the vines and leaves of a vegetal crown (Fig. 26.4).

The formal characteristics and attributes suggest an identification of the figure as a Genius, a divine entity protecting individuals and, by extension, everything that has a vital evolution, such as places, buildings, cities or associations (Daremberg – Saglio 1969, 1488–1494); iconographic attestations of *Genii togati* are rather numerous throughout the Empire, both as statuettes and in the form of *appliqués*, in a chronological period ranging from the 1st to the 3rd centuries A.D.

The range of functions assigned to this divinity is very wide, and these can change significantly according to the variation in attributes exhibited by the individual *Genii* (Kunckel 1974): while the presence of the sacrificial *patera* in the right hand is a constant feature, the left hand shows a series of variations in ritual objects (such as the *acerra*, or the *Cornucopia*), which serve to shift the identity of the subject, or at least to make it more easily identifiable.

As for the Genius of Grumentum, the presence of the *volumen* in the left hand would suggest its identification with a votive offeror, although other bronzes with similar attributes are often classified as *Genius patrisfamilias* (the protector of the head of the family) (Izquierdo Peraile – Moreno Conde 2000), or alternatively, even as simple representations of *Pontifices*, as shown in other items from France (Rolland 1965) and Italy (Mansuelli – Vergnani 1964, n. 171. 294) (Fig. 26.5).

The devotion to the Genii was revived by the institution of the cult of the *Genius Augusti*, following the religious reform of the *Vici* and the *Compita* accomplished between 12 and 7 BC (Alföldi 1973). Therefore, Genius statuettes

Figure 26.3. Bronze statuette of a Genius from Grumentum (Author)

Figure 26.4. Detail of the facial features (Author)

became widespread as a particular kind of quality production, no doubt reserved for the middle and upper classes as an expression of their support for the themes and schemes of the official public religion through the choice of a specific iconography (Adamo Muscettola 1980). In this respect, it is not unlikely that the "Julio-Claudian" resemblance of the Genius (to which I will return shortly) could have represented a sign of this acceptance.

The greatest stylistic and compositional similarities with our figurine can be found, in particular, in two statuettes from Austria (Fig. 26.6): the first comes from Kugelstein, and is dated to the Julio-Claudian age; even more interesting is the other one, found in Carnuntum, as it is the only published specimen with the attribute of the crown even if, in this case, the wreath of leaves is placed on the head above the toga, and not covered as in our specimen (Fleischer 1967).

The archaeological data: provenience

Considering this statuette and its findspot, the very first thought would be that of a direct connection between the statuette and the temple: the figurine could have been a votive gift to the deity worshipped in the Round Temple, as was customary in the Graeco-Roman world (Thomas 1992; Cadario 2015).

The dedication of statuettes in sanctuaries is a religious practice typical of both ancient and contemporary devotion; nonetheless, the discovery of bronze figurines in the excavation of sacred places is quite rare. The majority of the statuettes found "in context" come from Late Antique deposits, especially in the western provinces of the Empire, when the insecurity caused by continuous invasions led many to hide these objects, to avoid their being pillaged or destroyed: therefore, only a very careful examination of the context can provide help in clarifying the circumstances in which they were discovered (Kaufmann-Heinimann 1998). Furthermore, very often the real evidence of a small bronze's votive function is provided by an engraved inscription mentioning the name of the divinity to which it was devoted, rather than by its findspot.

Figure 26.5. From left to right: Genius patrisfamilias (from Izquierdo Peraile – Moreno Conde 2000), Pontifices (from Rolland 1965; Mansuelli – Vergnani 1964)

Figure 26.6. Geniuses from Kugelstein (left) and Carnutum (right) (from Fleischer 1967, 140, nn. 186–187, tav. 99)

Anyway – quite surprisingly – a relationship between the statuette and the temple does not seem highly probable, because the data pertaining to its findspot do not allow us to make that hypothesis.

As a matter of fact, in this specific case the context is not particularly helpful in providing information on the use and function of the statuette, because the Genius was found amid a thick layer of debris adjacent to the temple, placed between the latter and the surrounding colonnaded porch, which has been interpreted as an elevation of the flooring to create new paving for the whole area of the temple. Analysis of coins and pottery sherds points to the second half of the 2nd century AD as the most probable dating.

In the case of the Genius, therefore, the nature of the context makes it quite unlikely that it was a votive gift dedicated to the temple, first because it is difficult to imagine votive objects discarded in such a disrespectful way, and second because no other cult-related finds have been found in the same layer, nor in the whole area.

Moreover, if the main question that arises is *how* this statuette ended up in that context, its formal characteristics also lead us to question its chronological relationship with the layer to which it belongs.

Dating issues: a residual object?

The very nature of bronze statuettes, and their close stylistic links with large statuary, has led to the development of a tradition of studies based on iconographic and stylistic observations, which proved a reliable tool for the general classification of these pieces: in this case, for instance, some specific characteristics, such as the richness in the folds of the toga, the general look of the facial features and hairstyle show that the small Genius dates to the Julio-Claudian period, considerably earlier than its archaeological context.

If we look at the statuette from the standpoint of the archaeological laws of stratigraphy and dating, we should simply consider it a residual object (upon the topic: Carver 1983; Guidi 1994; Giannichedda 2008); but the concept itself of residuality, when applied to particular items such as bronze statuettes, can open up multiple meanings, because the chrono-typological incongruence of some finds with their stratigraphic context can have more than one explanation, especially when we take into consideration the duration of the life of this kind of item.

As objects having multiple functions and meanings, bronze statuettes were often considered treasured family possessions and could therefore be passed from generation to generation: this has been well proven by numerous finds from household shrines, where bronzes from different periods were assembled together, sometimes forming proper collections, a use which has presented a major obstacle to the creation of a reliable paradigm for the dating of these finds. Therefore, this bronze statuette could have been an heirloom, representing a family heritage and, at the beginning of its story, its particular resemblance to the portraits of Emperor Augustus could also have represented a sign of adherence to a specific political ideology.

But first and foremost, the Genius statuette must have been a symbol of devotion and religious faith: the search for divine protection over oneself and one's whole family. As a matter of fact, bronze figurines were not only dedicated in temples and worshipped in domestic shrines: they were usually carried around by their owners, in portable altars while travelling, or even as amulets (Cadario 2015, 57): in the end, this may be the most probable reason for discarding the small Genius, which could, for instance, have slipped out of a bag or a pocket and been lost.

In this sense, it is possible to further interpret its residuality and consider it a "dispersed object", that is, in the definition given by Maria Bonghi (2006, 721) as "an object inserted in layers that do not allow an adequate formulation, such as surface layers and fillings".

Obviously, this can only be a suggestion, as some questions are destined to remain unanswered: it serves as another demonstration, if there were any need, that when attempting to reconstruct the life of an artifact, archaeologists are forced to confront what is only its final stage, which is not always clearly reconstructible in its entirety.

Methodological aspects in the study of bronze figurines

Leaving aside the possible interpretation proposed, it seems appropriate to dwell on some methodological aspects concerning the study of bronze statuettes. When trying to reconstruct how the figurine came to be included in the archeological record, the only thing that can be excluded with certainty is its intentional discard: as already pointed out, in fact, such objects had for their owners not only a considerable economic value, but also a significant symbolic meaning.

The first aspect leads us to reflect upon the fact that to date small-scale bronzes have been studied primarily from a stylistic point of view, not as a manifestation of material culture. The main reason for this is that in the past most of these objects were not recovered in proper stratigraphic excavations, and therefore lacked contextual data; also, their intrinsic characteristics made them more similar to artwork than, say, humble pottery, and were thus considered in a completely different way.

Consequently, the issues related to the economic aspects concerning the production-consumption and production-exchange relationships were neglected or considered of minor importance: past studies seem to show an almost complete lack of interest in how these objects were manufactured and traded, thus making their stories incomplete (Giannichedda 2015, 493).

It is true that the data concerning the manufacture of a bronze object can best be provided by the recovery of related production structures, moulds and/or unfinished items; but the lack of evidence from the field could partly be balanced by focusing on an in-depth analysis of technological aspects, such as the reconstruction of manufacturing processes, characterization of raw materials through non-invasive methods and careful observation of construction, decoration and finishing techniques, on both historical collections and recently excavated objects.

On the other hand, focusing on some as-yet-overlooked phenomena might bring in some fresh information: for example, we know that sanctuaries played an important economic role in managing, directly or indirectly, workshops dedicated to the production of objects which the devotees could buy and then offer to the divinity

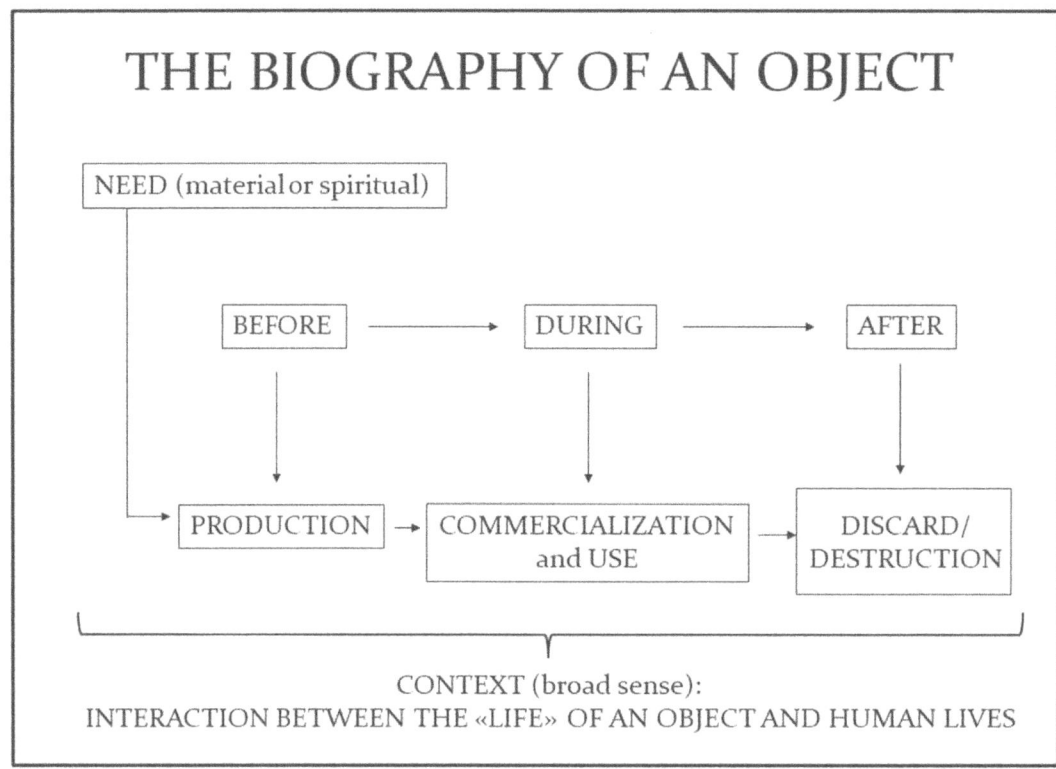

Figure 26.7. The biography of an object (Author)

(Malrieu 2005), while another branch of production of bronze figurines was dedicated to the market for souvenirs (Kunzl – Koeppel 2002); this is something that should be taken into consideration, by paying attention to the possible traces on-site, and during the subsequent phase of research.

This kind of combined methodology could provide information on the basic facts of production, on economic processes, exchange dynamics and social phenomena, helping us to get a clearer view of everything concerning (before, during and after) bronze figurines, shedding new light also on the diverse meanings attached to them, thus allowing us to reconstruct their stories from technological, economic and social perspectives (Kopytoff 1986, 66–68).

Moreover, the study and understanding of bronze statuettes from contexts could benefit significantly from considering their associations with other archaeological materials, rather than simply studying them as isolated "precious" objects. Inserting figurines into this general framework, though, does not mean they have to be acritically assimilated to every other find in a given context: recognizing the diversity of approaches such material deserves remains of paramount importance, while considering the mutual relationships between different items of material culture that can be key in the reconstruction of their biographies.

On the other hand, while taking into consideration the aspects related to material culture, we should not forget the equally important symbolic aspects which are very often behind certain kinds of objects and nonetheless are closely interconnected with their material characteristics (Hurcombe 2007, 211).

Concluding remarks

To conclude, it is important to stress that the aim of this article is not to answer questions concerning the identification of this statuette, or to give a conclusive explanation for its presence in the vicinity of a temple, but rather to offer a reflection on the multiple perspectives which can be considered when approaching bronze figurines from excavations, starting from some key points which can help us in reconstructing their biographies (Fig. 26.7).

The starting point for any interpretation must always be the context, as the ultimate reliable source of information on the sequence of events the objects went through during the different stages of their life: every possible hypothesis regarding a given find must always be considered in light of the data provided by the excavation.

From here, it is possible to start analyzing objects inside a general framework which must consider the possible relationships between different finds, recognizing that all are the expression of human actions and thoughts, to different degrees and in different ways. Looking at them from a single point of view can restrict the scope of interpretation and prevent us from grasping their informative potential in full.

A balanced methodology, combining the analysis of data from excavation with the contribution of research on aspects relating to production, as well as symbolic aspects, is the best way to reconstruct the biography of an object, and to shed light on how the lives of artifacts intersected with those of the human actors with which they interacted (Appadurai 1996).

As a closing remark, these words by Linda Hurcombe (2007, 196) seem to be particularly relevant to this case study:

"Metallurgy...has a significant division between those who study the objects produced and those who study the technologies and the archaeological remnants of metallurgical processes"

It is highly desirable that such a division will become progressively smaller in the future.

Bibliography

Adamo Muscettola, S., 1984. Osservazioni sulla composizione di larari con statuette in bronzo di Pompei ed Ercolano. In: Gehrig, U. – Faider-Feytmans, G.M., ed., *Toreutik und figürliche Bronzen römischer Zeit: Akten der 6. Tagung über antike Bronzen*. Berlin, Germany, 13–17 May 1980. Berlin: Staatliche Museen Preussischer Kulturbesitz, Antikenmuseum, 9–32.

Alföldi, A., 1973. Die zwei Lorbeerbäume des Augustus, Antiquitas, 3, 14. 18 ss.

Appadurai, A. ed., 1986. *The Social Life of Things: Commodities in Cultural Perspective*, Cambridge: Cambridge University Press

Bonghi, M., 2006. *Prospettive di pensiero e di prassi archeologica. Appunti in margine alla classificazione e all'interpretazione dei materiali archeologici di Tarquinia*. In: Studi di protostoria in onore di Renato Peroni. Florence: All'Insegna del Giglio, 718–722

Cadario, M., 2015. Le statuette in bronzo in contesto tra culti, ornamenta e pezzi da collezione. In: Arbeid, B. – Iozzo, M., ed., *Piccoli grandi bronzi. Capolavori greci, etruschi e romani dalle collezioni mediceo-lorenesi nel Museo Archeologico Nazionale di Firenze*. Catalogue of the exhibition (Florence, National Archaeological Museum, March 20th – June 21, 2015). Florence: Polistampa, 53–58

Caver, M.O.H., 1983. Valutazione, strategia e analisi nei siti pluristratificati. *Archeologia Medievale*, 10, 49–71

Daremberg, C. – Saglio, E., 1969. *Dictionnaire des antiquités grecques et romaines*. Graz: Akademische Druck

Fleischer, R., 1967. *Bronzen aus Österreich*. Mainz am Rhein: Verlag P. von Zabern, 140, nn. 186–187, tav. 99

Giannichedda, E., 2008. Lo scavo, i residui, l'affidabilità stratigrafica. *Facta. A journal of Roman material culture studies*, 1, 51–64

Giannichedda, E., 2015. Casi specifici e considerazioni generali sui tecnocomplessi dell'Italia settentrionale. In: Santangeli Valenzani, R. – Molinari, A. – Spera, L., ed., *L'archeologia della produzione a Roma (secoli V–XV)*. Proceedings of the international Conference, Rome, Italy, 27–29 March 2014. Bari: Edipuglia, 493–502

Giardino, L., 1992. *La città di Grumentum. Da Leukanie a Lucania. La Lucania centro orientale fra Pirro e i Giulio- Claudii*. Exhibition catalogue, Venosa, Italy, November 8 1992 – 31 March 1993. Roma: Istituto Poligrafico dello Stato, 91–93

Guidi, A., 1994. *I metodi della ricerca archeologica*. Roma-Bari: Laterza, 58

Hurcombe, L., 2007. *Archaeological Artefacts as Material Culture*. London; New York: Routledge

Izquierdo Peraile, I. – Moreno Conde, M., 2000. *Creencias, simbolos y ritos religiosos. Los Dioses Lares*. Madrid: Museo Arqueologico Nacional de Madrid

Kaufmann-Heinimann, A., 1998. *Götter und Lararien aus Augusta Raurica. Herstellung, Fundzusammenhänge und sakrale Funktion figürlicher Bronzen in einer römischen Stadt*. Augst: Römermuseum

Kopytoff, I., 1986. The Cultural Biography of Things: Commoditization as Process. In: Appadurai, A., ed. *The Social Life of Things: Commodities in Cultural Perspective*. Cambridge: Cambridge University Press, 64–91

Kunckel, H., 1974. Der römische Genius. *Mitteilungen des Deutschen Archäologischen Instituts. Römische Abteilung*, Ergänzungsheft 20

Kunzl, E. – Koeppel, G., 2002. *Souvenirs und Devotionalien. Zeugnisse des geschäftlichen, religiösen und kulturellen Tourismus im antiken Römerreich*. Mainz am Rhein: P. von Zabern

Malrieu, A., 2005. Le rôle économique des sanctuaires romains: thésaurisation et investissement des fonds sacrés. *Topoi. Orient – Occident,* 12/13, 95–116

Mansuelli, G. A. – Vergnani, M., eds., 1964. *Arte e civiltà romana nell'Italia settentrionale dalla repubblica alla tetrarchia*. Bologna, Palazzo dell'Archiginnasio, 20 settembre–22 novembre 1964. Bologna: Edizioni Alfa

Mastrocinque, A., ed. 2016. *Grumentum and Roman Cities in Southern Italy*. Oxford: BAR Publishing International Series 2830

Rolland, H., 1965. *Bronzes Antiques de Haute Provence*. Paris: Editions du Centre national de la recherche scientifique

Soriano, F., 2016. Il complesso del tempio rotondo: lettura stratigrafica e architettonica. Nuovi dati dalle campagne di scavo 2012–2014. In: Mastrocinque, A., ed., *Grumentum and Roman Cities in Southern Italy*. Oxford: BAR Publishing International Series 2830, 99–110

Soriano, F. – Saracino, M., 2016. Lettura crono-stratigrafica e proposta interpretativa delle prime fasi di occupazione del Settore M dell'area forense di Grumentum. In: Mastrocinque, A., ed. *Grumentum and Roman Cities in Southern Italy*. Oxford: BAR Publishing International Series 2830, 87–98

Thomas, R., 1992. *Griechische Bronze-Statuetten*. Darmstadt: Wbg Academic

From the Roman noblemen to the European connoisseurs: the "Paramythia bronzes" and the allure of the Antique

Antonia Tzortzatou

Ephorate of Antiquities of Thesprotia

atzortzatou@culture.gr

Abstract: The papers aims at unraveling the intriguing story of the so called "Paramythia hoard", one of the most controversial assemblages of ancient bronzes, unearthed at the end of the 18th century in the area of Paramythia (Thesprotia, Epirus). From the Ottoman-held Epirus and after a long and adventurous journey to European capitals, the Paramythia bronzes became precious acquisitions of the most eminent connoisseurs of the era and the greater part of them ended up in the collection of the British Museum.

Keywords: Paramythia Bronzes; Epirus; Society of Dilettanti; Antiquarianism

In 1792, in the area of Paramythia (today a municipal unit of Thesprotia, Epirus), local peasants accidentally unearthed an impressive group of bronze statuettes and reliefs depicting deities and mythological figures, which became widely known as the "Paramythia bronzes" or the "Paramythia hoard". It still remains one of the most controversial assemblages of ancient bronzes, frequently cited in the international literature with regard to the dating of the objects, their findspot and the context in which they were used in antiquity. Even more intriguing, though, is the chronicle of the hoard's dispersion and the changes of hands since its initial discovery. Through the history of the hoard and its long and adventure-filled journey to European capitals, the historical and social circumstances prevailing in Ottoman-held Epirus emerge, as do the idiosyncrasies of European collectors in the late eighteenth and the early nineteenth century (Tzortzatou – Lazou 2019). This was a period during which the classical ideal was sought through the monuments of antiquity and the first national museums were set up in Europe, deriving from private and royal collections (Chatzidimitriou 2012; Tolias 2012, 80–86).

From 1732, London was home to the Society of Dilettanti (Cust – Colvin 1914; Redford 2008), members of which were the most renowned collectors of the day, among them some of the persons who played a central role in the story related here. The Society's nature and aims are eloquently captured in the celebrated oil-paintings and caricatures of the period (Redford 2008, 20–21. 98–101. 103. 129–142). The members were an exclusive club of aristocratic intellectuals and artists who combined indulgence in amusement, copious drinking and witty importunity with the study of classical antiquity and the systematic collection of works of art.

In Epirus, during the same period, Ali Pasha's star was at its zenith. Having succeeded in putting the pashalik of Ioannina under his control and by exploiting the weakness of the central power and the diplomatic relations of the period, he quickly became the almighty ruler of an extensive territory (Arsh 1963, 144 ff.; Panagiotopoulos 2009, 15–126). European powers which had consulates in his capital of Ioannina endeavoured, through official agencies and clandestine agents, to infiltrate his court in order to win his favour and to turn the political situations to their advantage, as well as to secure, in some cases, the permit to transport antiquities and to conduct excavations. Indicative, among other things, is the letter of 23 May 1806 from François Pouqueville, consul of France in Ioannina, in which he informs the French Minister of Foreign Affairs of the existence of important antiquities in Corinth and Athens, and requests permission to use his influence on Ali Pasha, so as to acquire these antiquities for the museums of Paris (Siorokas 1985, 45–46).

This feverish hunt for antiquities, within the general frame of political involvements, caught the antiquarian interests of Ali Pasha, which began from archaeological curiosity and extended to 'excavations' in search of coin hoards and ancient sculptures (Panagiotopoulos 2009, 88–89). Characteristic of Ali's investigations at Nicopolis in 1812–1813 are the reports written by the Danish philologist and antiquarian Peter Oluf Brønsted (Karabelas 2001, 23–24. 29–33) and the British physician Henry Holland (Holland 1815, 74. 441–442; Karabelas 2009, 193–194. 204–206), who visited the area at that time.

Ali Pasha may well have appreciated the aesthetic value of his acquisitions, but he primarily collected antiquities as part of his well-known mania for amassing and hoarding

(Panagiotopoulos 2009, 23–24. 91–97; Koupari 2010, 425), or in order to offer them as gifts to his choice guests and to European leaders to whom he was amicably disposed. Among these were the British traveller, military envoy and later British consul in Epirus, William Martin Leake, to whom Ali Pasha gave a marble bust of the orator Aeschines from Bitolia (Bitola or Monastir), a city today in North Macedonia, which Leake later donated to the British Museum (Karabelas 2008, 47–48, note 9, fig. 2). In April 1807, 120 vases that had been confiscated from the residence of the Italian painter Giovanni Battista Lusieri, official representative of Lord Elgin in Athens, were sent by Ali Pasha to France as a gift to Napoleon Bonaparte (Gennadios 1930, 33–37; Σιορόκας 1985, 49–54).

At that period, chance finds of ancient objects were, of course, common. They were dug up by peasants in the fields and were displayed or sold to foreign travellers eager to acquire antiquities. In the case of the Paramythia bronzes, the man who found them was almost certainly ignorant of their true value, but he found a way of profiting from them by selling them as metal to a coppersmith in Ioannina. We have no idea how many pieces were melted down in his furnace before they came to the attention of a Greek merchant from Ioannina, who had seen similar sculptures in the collection of a Russian nobleman. Confident that he would make a great profit, he purchased the objects and sent a specimen to his contact in Russia (Walpole 1820, 481; Edwards 1870, 407), where at that time, in circles close to the imperial family, the first collections of artworks and antiquities were being assembled, which subsequently formed the core of the Hermitage Museum collection (Chatzidimitriou 2012, 67–69). Purchase of the Paramythia bronzes was about to be finalized by Empress Catherine II herself, but she died suddenly in November 1796, before the transaction was completed (Society of Dilettanti 1835, lxv, para. 80; Edwards 1870, 407; Penny 1982, 71). After her death, another adventure began for those objects that had reached Russia.

Most of them are said to have been bought by a Polish connoisseur, Christopher von Wierislowsky (or Wiessiolowski): statuettes of Apollo (Fig. 27.1.i), Zeus or Poseidon (Fig. 27.1.ii), Ganymede or a Lar (Fig. 27.2.v), Castor (Fig. 27.2.iii), Dione or Aphrodite (Fig. 27.2.iv), Aphrodite adjusting her sandal (Fig. 27.4.i), seated Zeus Serapis (Fig. 27.1.iv), figurine of a ram with Odysseus, in relief (Sharpe 2017, fig. 16.7), clinging to its belly, and a disc with the head of Apollo in relief (Fig. 27.3). This assemblage of nine pieces then passed into the collection of the British aristocrat and one of the most eccentric and controversial members of the Society of Dilettanti, Richard Payne Knight (1751–1824), to whose personality and actions there are abundant references (Edwards 1870, 401–412; Michaelis 1882, 119 ff.; Clarke – Penny 1982; Redford 2008). Knight had already bought a bronze statuette of Zeus from the same hoard (Fig. 27.1.iii), which was initially in the possession of a Greek merchant in Smyrna and reached Britain via a Greek dragoman in the Turkish Embassy in London, Thomas Amaxari (Society of Dilettanti 1835, lxv, para. 80; Clarke – Penny 1982, 133, cat. no. 34; Penny 1982, 71; Sharpe 2017, 141, note 46).

In Knight's opinion *"magnitude and beauty cannot be united"*, which is why he liked to acquire small antique artworks, while he was particularly proud of his collection of bronzes – *"his jewels in bronze"* as he characteristically called them – which no other collector of the day dared to rival (Michaelis 1882, 119–120; Walters 1899, xiv; Walters 1915, 3). Impressed by the figure of Zeus, which aroused great expectations in him, Knight sent an agent who located and purchased the aforesaid objects from Wierislowsky. It is not clear whether the deal was clinched in Russia (Edwards 1870, 408) or whether the pieces had already left for Warsaw (Swaddling 1979, 103; Penny 1982, 71). Whatever the case, as soon as they reached London, Knight lost no time in showing off his new acquisitions to the eminent collector Charles Townley, who estimated their value as £585 (Penny 1982, 71). Little is known about the fortunes of a further six statuettes that had ended up in Russia. These sculptures are reported as representing a Zeus similar to the one in Knight's collection, a naked bearded Satyr, an Eros, a triple Hecate, a draped female figure, probably Hera, and a Hercules. The first five pieces are said to have been bought by the Russian Czernicheff family or by Count Golovkin (M. de Golovkin), while it is not clear who purchased the statuette of Hercules (Society of Dilettanti 1835, lxv–lxv, para. 80; Walters 1899, xiv; Walters 1915, 2; Swaddling 1979, 104; Penny 1982, 71; Sharpe 2017, 140).

A few years later, the Earl of Aberdeen (George Hamilton Gordon, fourth Earl of Aberdeen, 1784–1860) entered the circle of the Society of Dilettanti. Cousin of Lord Byron, this intellectual antiquarian and later Prime Minister of Great Britain (1852–1855) had recently returned from his grand tour to Greece, where he had not neglected to obtain antiquities, either from the excavations he zealously carried out on the Pnyx in Athens in 1804, or from various purchases (Michaelis 1882, 118. 147–148. 249; Cust – Colvin 1914, 136. 147. 283; Gennadios 1930, 31–32. 38. 51–56. 101; Redford 2008, 17). Aberdeen showed Knight two bronzes from the Paramythia hoard –the right arm of a statuette and a bull's hoof (Sharpe 2017, fig. 16.10–11) –, which the latter purchased, thus having in his collection twelve objects from the same group (Society of Dilettanti 1835, lxv, para. 80; Edwards 1870, 408; Michaelis 1882, 118. 120; Walters 1899, iv, 38, nos 280.1–2; Walters 1915, 2; Swaddling 1979, 104; Penny 1982, 71).

Meanwhile, back in Epirus, the first British traveller to visit Ali Pasha's capital, in 1795 and later in 1798, was the distinguished naturalist and collector of paintings John Hawkins (ca. 1758–1841), who became a member of the Society of Dilettanti in 1799 (Michaelis 1882, 118–119. 212–213; Cust – Colvin 1914, 145. 281). His combined botanical and antiquarian interests must have brought him to the area towards the end of his travels with Professor John Sibthorp's team engaged in compiling *Flora Graeca* –one of the rarest and most precious illustrated botanical

Figure 27.1. Drawings of the statuettes of Apollo, Zeus or Poseidon, Zeus and seated Zeus Serapis in the publication of the Society of Dilettanti *Specimens of Antient Sculpture* (after Society of Dilettanti 1809, pl. XLIII. XXXII. LIII. LXIII).

publications (Krimbas 2004; Rizopoulou 2007)– while he was preparing his essay on Dodona (Walpole 1820, 473–488). Hawkins relates how he acquired his own share of the Paramythia hoard (Walpole 1820, 481–483; Smith 1904b, 219), namely the bronze statuette of seated Hermes (Fig. 27.2.ii) and the relief depicting the visit of Aphrodite to Anchises on Mount Ida or Aphrodite and Paris from the Judgement of Paris (Fig. 27.2.i):

"Shortly after my arrival at Yanina, in the month of June, 1795, I received a present from a merchant of that city, Demetrio Vassíli, a bronze figure of a Mercury, in the most finished stile of Greek workmanship. I learnt, upon enquiry, that it had been brought thither about two years before, together with many other bronze figures of equal beauty, from Paramythia" (Walpole 1820, 481; Smith 1904b, 219).

Hawkins also speaks about the Greek merchant who managed to rescue most of the bronzes from the melting furnace, purchasing them at a very low price and then making a handsome profit by sending them to Moscow

Figure 27.2. Drawings of the relief with the mythological scene and the statuettes of Hermes, Castor, Dione or Aphrodite and Ganymede or a Lar in the publication of the Society of Dilettanti *Specimens of Antient Sculpture* (after Society of Dilettanti 1835, pl. XX–XIV).

(Walpole 1820, 481; Smith 1904b, 219). On hearing his friends in Ioannina extolling the beauty and the excellent condition of the remaining objects of the Paramythia group, which were equal in every way to the statuette of Hermes, Hawkins expresses his disappointment that he had not been in the area a couple of years earlier. Keen to learn more about the finds, he asked Ali Pasha to provide him with an escort to visit Paramythia. Ali, even though a particularly solicitous host to his British guest, refused his request because he was on hostile terms with the inhabitants of Paramythia and thus could not guarantee Hawkins's safety (Walpole 1820, 481–482). The dangers faced by foreign travellers at that time in the area of Paramythia are described vividly by the British consul William Eton, who then serving as a translator in France, visited Ali Pasha in Ioannina in 1792 – that is, the year in which the hoard was found:

"All strangers, Turks, Europeans, Greeks, or others, who happen to pass on their territory, or are caught by them, are carried to their public market, and there sold…A stranger might travel into these mountains, and would be treated hospitably by the inhabitants, if while he was in a neighbouring country, he put himself under the protection of a Paramathian, who would give security for his being brought back safe" (Eton 1809, 369–370).

On his second journey, in May 1798 (Walpole 1820, 482), Hawkins purchased the bronze relief with the mythological scene. He mentions that it had been found one or two years earlier, which confirms that after the find was made in 1792, and with now the obvious motive of profiteering, unscrupulous operators returned to the region. Hawkins tried once again to visit Paramythia, securing the promise of hospitality from prominent Muslim families who were just then ratifying the peace with Ali Pasha. However, he did not succeed on this occasion either, as he had no leeway to deviate from the programme of his trip.

The question reasonably arises as to why during all these years, from 1792 to 1798, nothing about the discovery and the fortunes of the precious bronzes from Paramythia became known to the vigilant and intelligent vizier, who learnt immediately about whatever was happening in his territory. It seems that he had not yet discovered the magical and profitable world of antiquity, which was opened up for him by the stream of foreign travellers to Ottoman-held Greece in the early nineteenth century and mainly through the competitive antiquarian inquiries of the two consular officials serving in his seat, Pouqueville and Leake (Panagiotopoulos 2009, 88). Moreover, Ali must have been kept particularly busy in that period by machinations and planning operations against rival pashas of southern Albania and the Souliots, in combination with his efforts to extricate himself from sultanic authority, and after that the overtly expansionist policy he followed between 1796 and 1798 (Arsh 1963, 203–209). To the above should be added the hostile relations with the Muslim agas of Paramythia, while we can be certain that in the chronicle of the discovery and dispersal of the hoard all moves would have been made in the utmost secrecy, in the framework of an informal agreement of confidentiality between the transacting parties, for fear of Ali Pasha.

Just as much interest in the Paramythia bronzes, the exact identification of the site and the circumstances of their finding was shown by other official envoys and travellers who were in the region during the first decades of the nineteenth century, such as William Martin Leake (Leake 1835, 62), Henry Holland (Holland 1815, 458–459), Thomas Smart Hughes (Hughes 1820, 304–305), François Pouqueville (Pouqueville 1826, 136–137) and later Robert Curzon (Curzon 1849, 239). The important find had become particularly celebrated among aristocratic and artistic circles in Britain, through the publishing activity of the Society of Dilettanti, thus rekindling interest in the antiquities and historical topography of Epirus.

Figure 27.3. Drawing of the head of Apollo in the publication of the Society of Dilettanti *Antiquities of Ionia* **(after Society of Dilettanti 1797, ix).**

Published in *Antiquities of Ionia* (Society of Dilettanti 1797, ix) is an inaccurate drawing of the relief head of Apollo (Fig. 27.3). The two volumes of *Specimens of Antient Sculpture* followed, in 1809 and 1835, in which are gathered together the choicest sculptures and small-scale artworks from private collections of members of the Society of Dilettanti. Included there is the presentation of the greater part of the Paramythia bronzes (Figs. 27.1–2): Zeus or Poseidon, Apollo, Zeus and seated Zeus Serapis in the first volume (Society of Dilettanti 1809, xliii, para. 78, xlvi, para. 83, xlviii, para 86, liii, para. 93 with pl. XXXII. XLIII–XLIV. LII–LIII. LXIII), the relief with the mythological scene and the statuettes of Hermes, Castor, Dione or Aphrodite and Ganymede or a Lar in the second volume (Society of Dilettanti 1835, pl. XX–XXIV).

These two publications are imbued with the spirit imposed by Richard Payne Knight for presenting sculptures in a manner that does not mislead the reader, giving particular importance to the provenance as well as the detailed description of their state of preservation (Redford 2008, 146–150). Following the same logic, the drawings of the sculptures by the gifted draughtsman and engraver John Samuel Agar (ca. 1770–1835), whose work Knight held in high esteem (Redford 2008, 150–158. 168–171), aim at enhancing the details of the figures, but noting as clearly as possible the actual or hypothetical restorations: as in a variation of the figure of Zeus from Paramythia, in Knight's collection, on which are rendered in bold lines – as hypothetical graphic restorations – the sceptre, the thunderbolt and the *himation* (Society of Dilettanti 1809, pl. LII; Redford 2008, 148, fig. 7.5).

Knight may have been opposed to any kind of interventions in the sculptures in his collection and was vociferous in his polemic against the logic of restorations (Redford 2008, 144–147), but this was not the case with the overwhelming majority of collectors, who often resorted to arbitrary restorations in order to give to the

Figure 27.4. The statuette of Aphrodite adjusting her sandal, before and after restoration (after Walters 1899, pl. VII; Walters 1915, pl. XXV).

sculptures the beauty and value of completeness and to make them more spectacular, closer to the archetypes from which they were considered to derive, or to import the static balance necessary for displaying them. The Hermes in John Hawkins's possession had been restored from the outset, not only with the rock on which the figure would have sat but also with two further attributes of the god: a cockerel that stands next to him and a tortoise upon which he rests his right leg (Fig. 27.2.ii). These restorations are owed exclusively to the imagination of John Flaxman (1755–1826), one of the most important sculptors of his generation (Redford 2008, 196). Flaxman's inspiration for them was a statuette of Roman times in the Knight Collection, which represents Hermes sitting on a rock and holding a purse (*ballantion*), flanked by a goat, a cockerel and a tortoise at his feet (Society of Dilettanti 1835, pl. XXI; Walters 1915, pl. XXVI). It is also very likely that he was aware of the famous bronze statue of a seated Hermes from the 1758 excavations in the Villa of the Papyri in Herculaneum. However, no one yet knew that this work had undergone many restorations, among them the addition of the rock, thus giving the public the impression of an intact and perfectly preserved sculpture with Lysippian influences (Mattusch 2013, 34–36). Flaxman also made minor completions at damaged points on the relief with the mythological scene in Hawkins's collection, which have today been removed (Society of Dilettanti 1835, pl. XX; Smith 1904a, 100).

Presumably after Knight's death, restorations were made to the statuette considered to depict Dione. Initially the right hand and the spear-sceptre was restored, as well as a gold shield in the left hand, while added later was part of a draped himation below the figure's waist (Fig. 27.2.iv); all these restorations were removed in the following years (Walters 1899, 37, no. 279, pl. VI). Smaller interventions were made to the figure of Aphrodite (Fig. 27.4.i–ii), who acquired calves – possibly for reasons of stability– years after it entered the British Museum (Walters 1899, pl. VII; Walters 1915, pl. XXV).

After Knight's death in 1824, his entire collection came into the possession of the British Museum, the twelve bronzes from Paramythia included (British Museum inv. nos 1824,0428.1, 1824,0490.4, 1824,0405.2, 1824,0453.4, 1824,0453.5, 1824,0453.6, 1824,0429.1, 1824,0437.2, 1824,0478.1, 1824,0405.3, 1824,0415.11, 1824,0473.1. See Sharpe 2017, 610–611, fig. 16.1–16.12). As is recorded characteristically:

"The addition of Mr. Knight's Greek coins made the British Museum superior, in that department, to the Royal Museum of Paris; the addition of his bronzes raised it above the famous Museum of Naples" (Edwards 1870, 412).

In 1904, John Hawkins's widow gifted the bronze Hermes statuette (Fig. 27.2.ii) to the British Museum (British

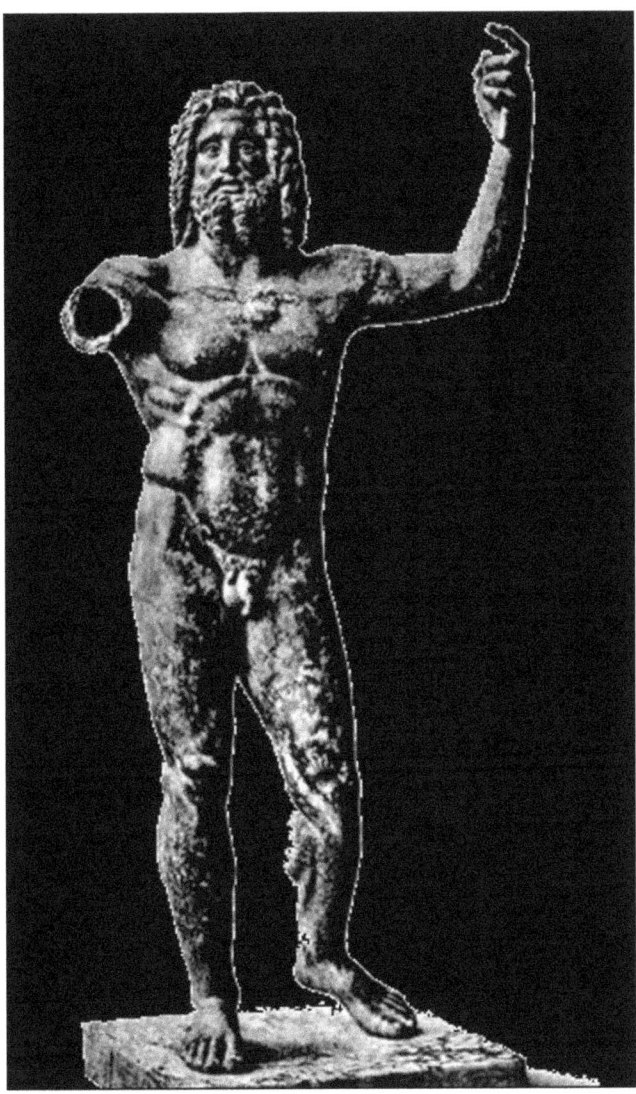

Figure 27.5. The statuette of Zeus Soter at the Museum of Constantinople (after Collignon 1885, pl. XIV).

Museum inv. no. 1904,1010.1. See Smith 1904b, 219; Walters 1915, 2; Sharpe 2017, 611, fig. 16.14) That same year, the relief with the mythological representation of Aphrodite – Anchises or Aphrodite – Paris (Fig. 27.2.i) was sold in the famous Hawkins Auction by Christie's for almost £2,250. The British Museum, although not financially in a position to do so, could not let the opportunity pass and eventually succeeded in making the purchase, with the contribution of the National Art Collections Fund and the Friends of the Museum (British Museum inv. no. 1904,0702.1. See Smith 1904a, 9; Walters 1915, 2; Sharpe 2017, 611, fig. 16.13).

Various other bronze objects in the British Museum collection from the Knight bequest have been linked with the Paramythia hoard, but their identification is not clear or sufficiently documented. Among them are a small silver statuette of Zeus Serapis, a terminal figure of Hermes, a statuette of Apollo and a female bust, probably Aphrodite (British Museum inv. nos 1824,0478.2, 1824,0460.10, 1824,0405.5 and 1824,0490.5. See Walters 1899, 180, 211, 272, nos 992, 1232, 1703; Walters 1915, pl. XXI; Walters 1921, 3, fig. 3, no. 6; Swaddling 1979, 104, pl. 56, fig. 15–16).

In 1885, almost a century after the finding of the Paramythia hoard, two bronze objects were added to the collection of the Museum of Antiquities in Constantinople (inv. nos 749–750). These are a figurine of an ox and a statuette of Zeus Soter (Fig. 27.5), which were said to have been found in the vicinity of Ioannina in March of the previous year (Collignon 1885). If these too belonged to the same assemblage (Walters 1899, 36; Krapsitis 1960, 322. 335, no. 21, fig. XII; Krapsitis 1972, 293. 295. 300, no. 21, fig. XII), they would have been discovered by chance or in organized clandestine excavations that are recorded during that period in the wider area of Photike in Paramythia (Krapsitis 1972, 306; Mouselimis 1994, 25). Moreover, as we shall see below, the Roman colony of Photike, which was founded in the first century BC and flourished in the first centuries of the Christian era (Dakaris 1972, 201–202; Hatzopoulos 1980; Samsaris 1994), seems to have been the findspot of the Paramythia bronzes. The most characteristic known find from illicit digging in Photike at that time, which somehow escaped the fortunes of the two bronze objects in the Constantinople Museum, was a marble sarcophagus with relief scenes from the Dionysian cycle, an excellent example of Attic art of the second century AD, which was brought to light in 1871 (Krapsitis 1972, 301–307; Mouselimis 1994, 18–24). The Ottoman authorities had approved the dispatch of the sarcophagus to Constantinople (Mouselimis 1994, 23), usual practice at that time for finds from excavations conducted by foreign missions in lands of the Ottoman Empire and which remained, after the official share out, in government hands (Chatzidimitriou 2012, 58–59; Manopoulos 2015, 609–610), as well as for stray finds brought to light by peasants, which were confiscated by or handed over to the local authorities (Chatzidimitriou 2012, 43–44). However, it seems that the high cost of the undertaking led to the cancellation of its journey.

The lack of any measures to protect antiquities in lands of the Ottoman Empire, as well as the competitive policy of acquiring archaeological treasures pursued by European governments as a means of boosting their national prestige, brought to the collections of the major European museums a significant portion of the antiquities purloined from Epirus in the eighteenth and nineteenth centuries. The Paramythia hoard is an explicit example of this activity in which avaricious peasants, discreet antiquarian travellers, crafty foreign officials, as well as the local authorities themselves were usually involved. It remains a precious yet enigmatic assemblage of bronzes that to this day, more than two hundred years after the first publication, continues to be debated in the international bibliography (Sharpe 2017), and which still leaves the field open for research, diverse approaches and new deliberations. And the truth is that we can actually know little more than what the objects themselves tell us and the frequently vague and contradictory references of texts of the period and from the archives of their owners.

Despite the views that have been expressed concerning the findspot or the original provenance of the bronzes (Paramythia or Dodona), it is now commonly accepted that they come from modern Liboni, near Paramythia, the area that has been identified as the territory of the Roman colonia of Photike (Hammond 1967, 580–582; Dakaris 1972, 173–174; Swaddling 1979, 103; Tzouvara-Souli 1979, 53–54; Samsaris 1994, 69–70; Sharpe 2017, 134–138). Or at least some of them did, since we cannot rule out the possibility of intentional hoodwinking of potential purchasers by cunning middlemen. Owing to the growing interest in the Paramythia bronzes, it is very likely that antiquities from elsewhere appeared on the market, purported to come from the Paramythia hoard, a phenomenon familiar also for finds from excavations at Dodona (Manopoulos 2015, 607–608, note 68).

One further issue that has preoccupied research is the dating: objects that stylistically and iconographically seem to date to Hellenistic times, such as the relief with the mythological scene (Aphrodite – Anchises or Aphrodite – Paris), coexist with others that are clearly Roman, such as the male household deity (Lar). The most recent studies of the hoard (Swaddling 1979; Sharpe 2017) propose the dating of the objects to the early second century AD, which view is corroborated by the results of earlier chemical analyses of twelve of the bronzes in the British Museum. These analyses point to a similar elemental composition, a common workshop and possibly a common source of ore for the majority of the objects. Nevertheless, the relief with the mythological scene, which most probably dates from the fourth century BC, remains problematic. No analysis of this piece has been made and it has been argued that perhaps it did not belong to the same assemblage (Swaddling 1979, 104; Sharpe 2017, 141, note 47).

It is not known from which region and under what circumstances the bronzes came into the home of a Roman nobleman in Photike, some as decorative items, others within the context of a domestic shrine (Dakaris 1972, 173–174; Sharpe 2006, 96–102. 198–201; Sharpe 2017). Neither is it known whether they were in fact hidden deliberately by their owner, for security reasons in a moment of danger, such as the Herulian invasion in AD 267 (Sharpe 2017, 138–139), or if the Roman who hid them left with the hope of finding them again but never returned. Fate, however, led them from the hands of the prosperous Roman "collector" of the period of the revival of classical antiquity in the second century AD into the collections of British connoisseurs of the eighteenth century, a period of reverence for the ancient world. Throughout this course, they remained desirable acquisitions for those seeking to be linked with the elegance, the good taste and the moral values of ancient Greek art, prestigious objects and, later, admirable artistic treasures in the collection of one of Europe's greatest museums.

Bibliography

Arsh, G.L., 1963. *Η Αλβανία και η Ήπειρος στα τέλη του ΙΗ΄ και στις αρχές του ΙΘ΄ αιώνα. Τα δυτικοαλβανικά πασαλίκια της Οθωμανικής Αυτοκρατορίας* [*Albania and Epirus in the late 18th and early 19th century. The western Albanian pashaliks of the Ottoman Empire*]. Translated from German by A. Dalla, 1994. Athens: Gutenberg. [in Greek]

Chatzidimitriou, A., 2012. Ο εκπατρισμός των ελληνικών αρχαιοτήτων και η συμβολή τους στη συγκρότηση των πρώτων αρχαιολογικών συλλογών και μουσείων [Expatriation of Greek antiquities and their contribution to the establishment of the first archaeological collections and museums]. In: S. Matthaiou – A. Chatzidimitriou, ed., *«Ξενιτεμένες» ελληνικές αρχαιότητες. Αφετηρίες και διαδρομές* [*"Expatriated" Greek antiquities: Departures and trajectories*]. Athens: National Hellenic Research Foundation / Institute for Neohellenic Research. 33–78. [in Greek]

Clarke, M. – Penny, N., ed., 1982. *The arrogant connoisseur: Richard Payne Knight, 1751–1824*. Manchester: Manchester University Press.

Collignon, M., 1885. Bronze grec du musée de Tchinli-Kiosk à Constantinople. *BCH*, 9, 42–45.

Curzon, R., 1849. *Visits to monasteries in the Levant*. London: John Murray.

Cust, L. – Colvin, S., 1914. *History of the Society of Dilettanti*. London: Macmillan and Co., Printed for the Society.

Dakaris, S., 1972. *Θεσπρωτία. Αρχαίες Ελληνικές Πόλεις 15* [*Thesprotia. Ancient Greek Cities 15*]. Athens: Athens Centre of Ekistics. [in Greek]

Eton, W., 1809. *A survey of the Turkish empire, in which are considered I. Its government..., II. The state of the provinces..., III. The causes of the decline of Turkey..., IV. The British commerce with Turkey..., with many other important particulars*. London: Luke Haniard & Sons.

Edwards, E., 1870. *Lives of the founders of the British Museum with notices of its chiefs augmentors and other benefactors, 1570–1870*. London: Trübner and Co.

Gennadios, I., 1930. *Ο Λόρδος Έλγιν και οι προ αυτού ανά την Ελλάδα και τας Αθήνας ιδίως αρχαιολογήσαντες επιδρομείς, 1440–1837. Ιστορική και αρχαιολογική πραγματεία* [*Lord Elgin and the prior to him archaeological invaders in Greece and in Athens in particular, 1440–1837. A historical and archaeological treatise*]. Reprint 1997. Athens: The Archaeological Society at Athens. [in Greek]

Hammond, N.G.L., 1967. *Epirus. The geography, the ancient remains, the history and the topography of Epirus and adjacent areas*. Oxford: Clarendon Press.

Hatzopoulos, M., 1980. Photice. Colonie romaine en Thesprotie et les destinées de la latinité épirote. *BalkSt*, 21, 97–105.

Holland, H., 1815. *Travels in the Ionian Isles, Albania, Thessaly, Macedonia, &c. during the years 1812 and 1813*. London: Printed for Longman, Hurst, Rees, Orme, and Brown.

Hughes, Th.S., 1820. *Travels in Sicily, Greece and Albania, Vol. II*. London: Printed for J. Mauman.

Karabelas, N., 2001. Ο Δανός αρχαιολόγος Peter Oluf Brønsted στην Πρέβεζα [The Dane archaeologist Peter Oluf Brøndsted in Preveza]. *Πρεβεζάνικα Χρονικά [Prevezanika Chronika]*, 37–38, 5–38. [in Greek]

Karabelas, N., 2008. Ο Άγγλος λοχαγός William Leake στο νομό Πρέβεζας [The British captain William Leake in the region of Preveza]. *Ηπειρωτών Κοινόν [Epiroton Koinon]*, 2, 44–127. [in Greek]

Karabelas, N., 2009. Ο Άγγλος γιατρός Henry Holland στην περιοχή της Πρέβεζας [The British physician Henry Holland in the region of Preveza]. *Πρεβεζάνικα Χρονικά [Prevezanika Chronika]*, 45–46, 143–215. [in Greek]

Koupari, N. 2010. Η τέχνη στην αυλή του Αλή Πασά. Οι μαρτυρίες των περιηγητών [Art in the court of Ali Pasha. Travellers' testimonies]. *Ηπειρωτικά Χρονικά [Epirotika Chronika]*, 44, 413–441. [in Greek]

Krapsitis, V., 1960. *Ταξίδι στην Ήπειρο [Travel in Epirus]*. Reprint 1970. Athens. [in Greek]

Krapsitis, V., 1972. *Θεσπρωτικά [Thesprotian]*. Reprint 1973. Athens. [in Greek]

Krimbas, C., 2004. H.W. Lack with David J. Mabberley, The Flora Graeca Story, *The Historical Review/La Revue Historique*, I, 275–285.

Leake, W.M., 1835. *Travels in northern Greece, Vol. IV*. London: J. Rodwell.

Manopoulos, G., 2015. Η πρώτη συστηματική ανασκαφή της Δωδώνης (1875–1876) [The first systematic excavation of Dodona (1875–1876)]. In: G. Papageorgiou – K. Petsios, ed., *Ιστορία – Λογιοσύνη: Η Ήπειρος και τα Ιωάννινα από το 1430 έως το 1913. Πρακτικά Α´ Πανηπειρωτικού Συνεδρίου (28 Φεβρουαρίου – 3 Μαρτίου), Τόμος Β´ [History – Erudition: Epirus and Ioannina from 1430 to 1913. Proceedings of the 1st Epirote-wide Conference (28 February – 3 March 2013), Vol. II*. Ioannina: University of Ioannina – Society for Epirotic Studies – Foundation for the Studies of Ionian and Adriatic Space – Joseph & Esther Gani Foundation. 593–613. [in Greek]

Mattusch, C.C., 2013. Appearances can be deceiving. The presentation of bronzes from Herculaneum and Pompeii. In: E. Risser – D. Saunders, ed., *The Restoration of Ancient Bronzes: Naples and Beyond*. Los Angeles: The J. Paul Getty Museum. 30–40.

Michaelis, A., 1882. *Ancient marbles in Great Britain*. Translated from German by C.A.M. Fennel. Cambridge: Cambridge University Press.

Mouselimis, S., 1994. *Ιστορία της Φωτικής. Ιστορική και αρχαιολογική έρευνα Θεσπρωτία [History of Photike. Historical and archaeological research]*. Athens. [in Greek]

Panagiotopoulos, V., 2009. *Αρχείο Αλή Πασά Γενναδείου Βιβλιοθήκης της Αμερικανικής Σχολής Αθηνών, Τόμος Δ´, Εισαγωγή – Ευρετήρια – Γλωσσάρι [The Ali Pasha Archive at the Gennadius Library of the American School of Classical Studies at Athens, Vol. D, Introduction – Index – Glossary]*. Athens: National Hellenic Research Foundation / Institute of Historical Research.

Penny, N., 1982. Collecting, interpeting, and imitating ancient art. In: M. Clarke – N. Penny, ed., *The arrogant connoisseur: Richard Payne Knight, 1751–1824*. Manchester: Manchester University Press. 65–81.

Pouqueville, F.C.H.L., 1826. *Voyage de la Grèce, Tome Second*. Paris: Fermin Ditot, Père et Fils.

Redford, B., 2008. *Dilettanti. The antic and the antique in eighteenth-century England*. Los Angeles: The J. Paul Getty Museum and the Getty Research Institute.

Rizopoulou, S., 2007. Flora Graeca. *Νεύσις [Neusis]*, 16, 34–44. [in Greek]

Samsaris, D.K., 1994. *Η ρωμαϊκή αποικία της Φωτικής στη Θεσπρωτία της Ηπείρου. Ιστορικογεωγραφική και επιγραφική συμβολή [The roman colony of Photike in Thesprotia, Epirus. Historic-geographic and epigraphic contribution]*. Ioannina. [in Greek]

Sharpe, H.F., 2006. *From hieron and oikos: The religious and secular use of hellenistic and greek imperial bronze statuettes*. [pdf] PhD Thesis, Indiana University. Available at: https://www.academia.edu/4468030/From_Hieron_and_Oikos_A_Study_of_Bronze_Statuettes_from_Hellenistic_and_Imperial_Greece [Accessed 1 February 2019].

Sharpe, H., 2017. The Paramythia bronzes: expressions of cultural identity in Roman Epirus. In: J.M. Daehner – K. Lapatin – A. Spinelli, ed., *Artistry in bronze: the Greeks and their legacy. XIX International congress on ancient bronzes, The J. Paul Getty Museum, Los Angeles, October 13–17 2015*. Los Angeles: The J. Paul Getty Museum and the Getty Conservation Institute. 134–143.

Siorokas, G.A., 1994. Από τη δράση των Γάλλων στα Γιάννενα του Αλή Πασά. Το κυνήγι των αρχαιολογικών θησαυρών [On the activity of the French at Ioannina of Ali Pasha. The hunt of archaeological treasures], *Ηπειρωτικό Ημερολόγιο [Epirotiko Imerologio]*, 7, 43–56. [in Greek]

Smith, C., 1904a. The new bronze relief in the British Museum. *The Burlington Magazine for Connoisseurs*, 6 (20), 99–101.

Smith, C., 1904b. A bronze statuette from Paramythia. *The Burlington Magazine for Connoisseurs*, 6 (21), 219–221.

Society of Dilettanti, ed., 1797. *Antiquities of Ionia published by the Society of Dilettanti, Part the Second*. London: W. Bulmer and Co. for George Nicol.

Society of Dilettanti, ed., 1809. *Specimens of Antient Sculpture, Ægyptian, Etruscan, Greek, and Roman: Selected from Different Collections in Great Britain, by the Society of Dilettanti, Vol. I*. London: T. Bensley for T. Payne, and J. White and Co.

Society of Dilettanti ed., 1835. *Specimens of Antient Sculpture, Ægyptian, Etruscan, Greek, and Roman: Selected from Different Collections in Great Britain, by the Society of Dilettanti, Vol. II*. London: W. Nicol for Payne and Foss.

Swaddling, J., 1979. The British Museum hoard from Paramythia, north-western Greece: classical trends revived in the 2nd and 18th centuries AD. In S. Boucher, ed., *Bronzes hellenistiques et romains: Tradition et renouveau: Actes du Ve Colloque international sur les bronzes antiques, Lausanne, 8–13 mai 1978. Cahiers d'Archéologie romande 17*. Lausanne: Bibliothèque historique vaudoise. 103–105.

Tolias, G., 2012. Διασπορά, εντοπιότητα και εθνική κληρονομιά. Οι ελληνικές αρχαιότητες κατά τους τελευταίους προεπαναστατικούς χρόνους [Dispersion, nativeness and national heritage. Greek antiquities during the last pre-revolutionary years]. In S. Matthaiou – A. Chatzidimitriou, ed., *«Ξενιτεμένες» ελληνικές αρχαιότητες. Αφετηρίες και διαδρομές* [*"Expatriated" Greek Antiquities: Departures and trajectories*]. Athens: National Hellenic Research Foundation / Institute for Neohellenic Research. 79–104. [in Greek]

Tzortzatou, A. – Lazou, Th., 2019. Συλλεκτισμός και αρχαιότητες στην Οθωμανοκρατούμενη Ήπειρο. Η περίπτωση του «θησαυρού της Παραμυθιάς» [Antiquarianism and the antiquities in Epirus during the Ottoman rule. The case of the Paramythia "Hoard"] In: I.P. Chouliaras – G.Th. Pliakou, ed., *Thesprotia I. 1st International Conference on the Archaeology and History of Thesprotia, Igoumenitsa, 8–11 December 2016, Proceedings*. Ioannina: Ministry of Culture and Sports – Ephorate of Antiquities of Thesprotia. 631–644. [in Greek]

Tzouvara-Souli, X., 1979. *Η λατρεία των γυναικείων θεοτήτων εις την αρχαίαν Ήπειρον. Συμβολή εις την μελέτην της θρησκείας των αρχαίων Ηπειρωτών* [The cult of female deities in ancient Epirus. Contribution to the study of the religion of the ancient Epirotes]. Ioannina: University of Ioannina. [in Greek]

Walpole, R., ed., 1820. *Travels in various countries of the east; being a continuation of Memoirs relating to European and Asiatic Turkey*. London: Printed for Longman, Hurst, Rees, Orme, and Brown.

Walters, H.B., 1899. *Catalogue of the Bronzes, Greek, Roman, and Etruscan, in the Department of Greek and Roman Antiquities, British Museum*. London: Printed by order of the Trustees.

Walters, H.B., 1915. *British Museum. Select Bronzes, Greek, Roman, and Etruscan, in the Department of Greek and Roman Antiquities*. London: Printed by order of the Trustees.

Walters, H.B., 1921. *Catalogue of the silver plate (Greek, Etruscan and Roman) in the British Museum*, London: Printed by order of the Trustees.

Collecting Bronzes in an Early Twentieth-century American Museum of Natural Science and Anthropology: The Example of the Buffalo Museum of Science

Philip Kiernan

Kennesaw State University

pkierna1@kennesaw.edu

Abstract: This article presents an overview of a collection of ancient bronze artefacts owned by the Buffalo Museum of Science to provide a glimpse into the collecting philosophy of an early 20th-century American museum of natural history and anthropology. Single examples of non-Classical bronzes from the Levant, the Caucasian Steppes, and Luristan, as well as Cypriote, Greek, Etruscan, and Roman pieces are examined in detail, along with their origins and the probable motives behind their acquisition. The museum's preference for bronzes of particular periods and cultures suggests a desire to illustrate the universal characteristics of what were then considered to be primitive societies. These characteristics include a love of animal imagery, and a schematic rather than a naturalistic mode of representation.

Keywords: Bronzes; Buffalo Museum of Science; History of Collecting; Chauncey Hamlin

Introduction

Students and scholars of ancient bronze objects will be well aware that there are several important collections of Greek, Roman, and related material in North America. For the most part, however, these collections are in large museums and galleries dedicated to art and archaeology. It may come as a surprise that small collections of ancient bronze artefacts can also be found in some very different institutions, including museums dedicated to Natural History and the Sciences. The Buffalo Museum of Science is one such institution which owns a collection of ancient bronzes.

The author is currently directing a study of these bronzes together with students from Kennesaw State University, which is supported by a grant from the university's Center for Excellence in Teaching and Learning. A temporary exhibition of 39 of the bronzes from the Buffalo Museum of Science, entitled *Discovering Bronzes,* opened at Kennesaw State University's Bentley Rare Book Room in April 2019. I am most indebted to Kathy Leacock, head of collections at the Buffalo Museum of Science, for the opportunity to work with this material, and for the assistance of Rebecca Klie, Collections Assistant and Manager of the Education Collections.

The Buffalo Museum of Science's collection includes Greek, Roman Etruscan, Egyptian, Near Eastern, and Early medieval pieces, as well as objects from other cultures more distantly related to the Classical world. Mostly acquired in the first half of the 20th century, these bronzes are almost entirely unstudied. This article presents a small number of these pieces to give a sense of the collection and its qualities, but also to try and illustrate what the entire collection can tell us about the collecting policies and philosophy of those who assembled it.

At first glance, the collection gives that impression that these objects were acquired almost randomly as a result of the whims of patrons and chance opportunities. But this is not the case. Like the other objects acquired by the Buffalo Museum of Science, the bronzes were never meant to be great works of ancient art, but were rather specimens representative of what were then considered to be primitive cultures and developing civilizations. These objects were meant to illustrate characteristics and steps in a universal process of development believed to be common to all human societies.

Buffalo and Its Museums

As the nineteenth century turned into the twentieth, the city of Buffalo in the western corner of New York State had become one of the most important industrial cities in the United States. Located on the Niagara River, and at the mouth of the Erie Canal, Buffalo was an important transit point for goods, especially grain, moving from the Great Lakes to the east coast. Around 1900, Buffalo also became a major centre for the production of steel. By the late 1950s, however, the opening of the St. Lawrence Seaway made the Erie Canal redundant, and the city's fortunes went into sudden and rapid decline. At the height of Buffalo's prosperity, local industrialists, traders, socialites, and philanthropists ensured that their native city acquired all of the cultural trappings and institutions fitting to an early 20th-century metropolis, and this included museums.

In 1861, the Buffalo Society of Natural Sciences was formed with just over 100 members. In the following year, the city's Historical Society and Fine Arts Academy were also established. For the remainder of the 19th century these three institutions shared quarters, but saw their respective collections and membership bases grow enormously. In 1901, the Historical Society moved into a dedicated building that had originally been constructed as the pavilion for the State of New York in the Pan-American Exhibition, which was hosted by Buffalo that year. The two porches of the building, designed by George Cary, were inspired by the Parthenon, and contained pedimental sculptures depicting allegories of industry and trade. In 1905, the Fine Arts Academy was gifted a building by John J. Albright, which is today the Albright-Knox Art Gallery. Another neoclassical building, designed by E.B. Green, the gallery included a porch based on the Erectheion, with caryatids carved by the American sculptor Augustus Saint-Gaudens. In 1929, after a lengthy fundraising campaign, a dedicated building, known as the Buffalo Museum of Science, was constructed to house and display the collections of the Society of Natural Sciences. The museum remains in this location and is still in operation today (Goodyear 1994, 10–33; Leacock 2012).

As might be expected, the bulk of the Buffalo Museum of Science's collections belong to the domains of strict Natural History and the Sciences – botany, entomology, zoology, astronomy, geology, palaeontology, and so on. Since the 19th century, however, the museum had actively acquired objects pertaining to the archaeology of both the region and the New World in general. For example, at the close of the great Pan-American Exhibition, the museum acquired numerous objects from Africa and South America that had been used in the displays and presentations of foreign governments and companies during the exhibition. These acquisitions expanded to include numerous other world cultures, past and present, and were housed in the museum's Department of Anthropology and Ethnology. As of 1994, the collection of what is now known simply as the Anthropology Department contains approximately 300,000 objects.

The great driving force behind the expansion of the Buffalo Museum of Science, and its anthropology collection in particular, was Chauncey J. Hamlin (1881–1963), who presided over the Buffalo Society of Natural Sciences from 1920 to 1948. Hamlin is also a major figure in the history of both American and international museology. He was one of the founders of the International Council of Museums, and served as its first president from 1946 to 1953. He was also president of the American Association of Museums from 1923 to 1929. A very wealthy and influential man, Hamlin aggressively acquired artefacts from different world cultures, both through dealers and during his own very extensive world travels (Goodyear 1994, 51–56). One of his most significant acquisitions was a group of 300 Chinese jade objects ranging from the late Neolithic period to the Han Dynasty that Hamlin purchased during and shortly after a trip to China in the 1930s (Hartman 1975).

The collections of the Anthropology Department of the Buffalo Museum of Science consist of specimens from numerous cultures and periods, including the ancient European and Mediterranean worlds. The names of the museum's galleries as it was organized in 1929 give a sense of the anthropological school of thought in which it was grounded. They included a "Hall of Primitive Races" and a "Hall of Civilization" and, by 1932, a "Hall of Primitive Art" which would later be transformed into a "Hall of Early Technology." By 1941, many of the anthropological artefacts were displayed in a series of alcoves along the "Corridor of Time" the opening of which roughly corresponded with the publication of a new book by Phelps H. Clawson, then curator of anthropology (Goodyear 1994, 132–147).

Entitled "By their Works", Clawson's (1941) book presents a narrative of various primitive groups and developing civilizations across world history, and their key characteristics. The idea seems to be that certain characteristics, technologies, and artworks are common in a universal history of human development. The book is filled with photographs of the specimens of these cultures owned by the museum, as well as replicas (described in their captions as "casts") of famous objects, such as the Venus of Willendorf. The illustrations include several ancient bronze artefacts owned by the museum. At no point, however, does Clawson's narrative refer to any of the museum's pieces directly or explore them in any detail. Apart from occasional brief articles in the magazine *Hobbies*, which the museum published for its members, the collection of both bronzes and other types of artefact is largely unpublished.

The Bronzes

Among the 300,000 artefacts now housed in this department, the museum's records classify nearly 1,000 as bronzes. Of these artefacts, 399 may be said to pertain to the ancient cultures of Europe, including Mediterranean and Classical groups, as well as neighbouring and outlying cultures connected to them (Diagram 28.1). It is important to note that the classifications of the objects in the museum presented here are based on the museum's own records of the collection. Many of the attributions made in the early years of the museum, and also by those who donated and sold pieces to it, may well be incorrect. Nonetheless, the records do present a rough a picture of the collection.

The Non-Classical Bronzes

By far the largest group of bronzes in the collection were made by the nomadic tribes of the far eastern Steppes, most of which probably belong to the Ordos and Xiongnu

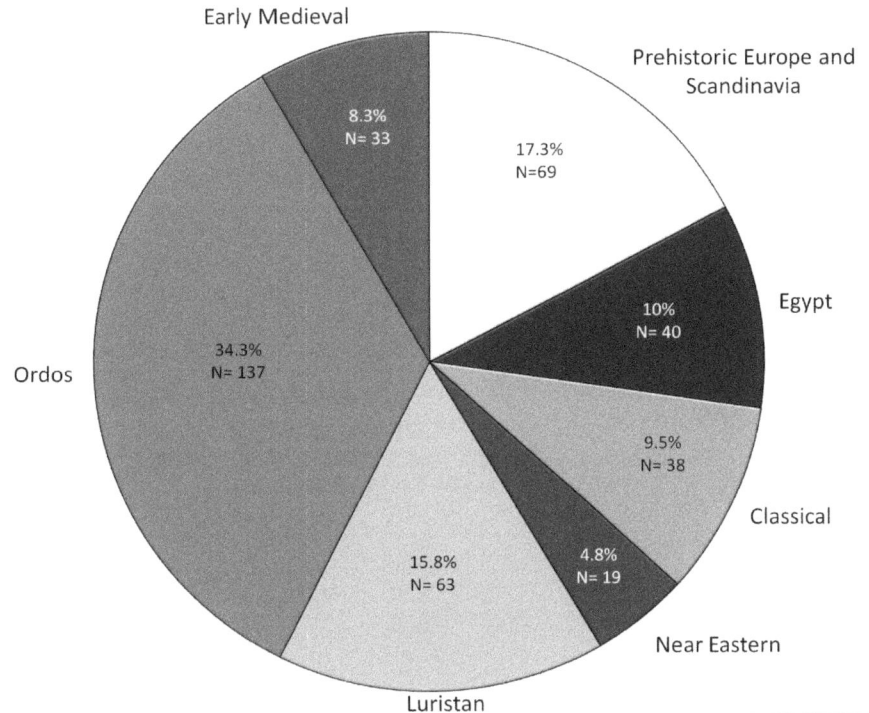

Diagram 28.1. Bronze Artefacts in the Buffalo Museum of Science from the Classical World and Related Cultures according to the Museum's Records

cultures of the sixth to second centuries B.C. These people may be broadly seen as the distant relatives of the Scythian tribes who were known to the inhabitants of the Greek world. Their graves were often filled with buckles and other adornments in which curvilinear depictions of animals were a common theme. The place of the so-called "animal style" in barbarian art and in the art of the prehistoric Steppes became a popular topic in the late 1920s, when it was the subject of a series of lectures and a book by the ancient historian Michael Rostovsteff (1929).

Though undoubtedly from the Caucasus, a large bronze buckle acquired some time before 1941 is also classified within this same group (Fig. 28.1). Though not accessioned until 1951, the piece appears as an illustration (without commentary) in Clawson's book (1941, 28). The centre of the open work bronze is dominated by a large stag, executed in a distinctive curvilinear style. A tongue and hook on the back side confirm the plaque functioned as a belt buckle. It was acquired prior to 1941, and, along with other buckles like it, was at the time considered to be a pre-Scythian artefact, dating between 1,000 and 800 B.C. More recent discoveries in the 1970s and 80s, however, have since placed these pieces at the very other end of the spectrum, between the first and second centuries A.D. (Bunker 1981, 182–184, cp. no. 942; Muscarella 1988, 439–441, cp. nos. 581–584, esp. 582–583.) The curvilinear open-work representation of a stag inside the rectangular buckle is at least similar to the more easterly Ordos bronzes in its subject matter (an animal) and its use of non-naturalistic style.

With 69 objects, the next largest group of bronzes consists of artefacts that belong to the Bronze Age and pre-Roman Iron Age of western Europe and Scandinavia. Most of the pieces in this group are examples of tools, weapons and dress accessories, such as fibulae and arm rings. These pieces illustrated not only developments in early technology, such as the shift from flanged to socketed axes, but could also demonstrate the fundamentals of prehistoric typology. The same is true of the early medieval pieces, which consist mostly of buckles, fibulae, and other adornments of the Franks and other "barbarian" groups. Several of the prehistoric pieces were obtained either in trade or by purchase from the National Museum of Archaeology in Copenhagen, and the National Historical Museum of Sweden in Stockholm.

A similar number of pieces in the collection belong to the so-called Luristan bronzes, which flooded western art markets in the 1920s and 1930s. Plundered from burials in the mountainous Luristan region of western Iran, most of these artefacts are thought to date between the late third millennium and the seventh century B.C. The study of these bronzes has been greatly frustrated by the absence of good archaeological excavations of the cemeteries in which they were found, and by the fact that forgeries of the pieces are very common. As with the Ordos bronzes, animals, both real and mythical, are a major theme of the Luristan bronzes, most of which were pieces of functional or ceremonial objects, such horse-trappings, pins, and pole-tips.

A few of the Luristan bronzes are hammered vessels, including a conical drinking cup decorated with a relief scene in the repoussé technique (Fig. 28.2) that was donated to the museum by Hamlin in 1951. This type of conical cup, sometimes erroneously described as a *situla*,

Philip Kiernan

Figure 28.1. Belt buckle with open-work representation of a stag. Caucasus. 1st–2nd century A.D. Acquired prior to 1941, accessioned 1951. 8.5 x 9.8 cm (Inv. No. BR153, Illustration by Emily Huffmann).

Figure 28.2. A conical bronze drinking cup from Luristan with ostrich-egg hunting scene. 1000–800 B.C. H. 16 cm, Dm. 7 cm. (Inv. No. C20027. Illustration by Chloe Redstone)

is a well-known form amongst the Luristan bronzes, and was probably produced between about 1000 and 800 B.C. (Moorey 1981, 82–89; Muscarella 1988, 244–248). Unlike other Luristan bronzes, the reliefs on the cups often share themes and motifs more in common with the art of other Near Eastern cultures. The cup in Buffalo depicts a male hunter armed with a bow holding the egg of an ostrich, facing the very bird from which he has presumably stolen it. Pointed shapes below the feet of the bird denote a hilly landscape. An almost identical cup has been published by Moorey (1981, no. 434), and the same scene appears on a cylinder seal found in Aleppo in 1922 and now in the British Museum (Fig. 28.3). Ostrich eggs were prized luxury commodities in the first millennium B.C., with carved and painted eggs traded widely across the ancient world (Falsone 1993).

When a short article (Ackerman 1946) appeared on the Luristan bronzes in a 1946 issue of the museum's magazine, *Hobbies*, it was prefaced by the following comments of an anonymous editor in the museum (quite possibly Hamlin himself):

"Wherever one turns to inquire into the subject of man's earliest aspirations towards artistic expression, one finds the universal impulse to picture, carve, or model the animals which conditioned the life about him... everywhere throughout the globe one finds evidence of this fact."

For the museum, the acquisition of the bronze collection were simply trying to illustrate that perceived universal impulse.

A very small number of bronzes in the Buffalo Museum of Science belong to other areas of the ancient Near East, of which some of most striking are a group of six figurines purchased by Hamlin from an aged Eustache de Lorey in 1950. De Lorey (c. 1865? – c. 1955?), was a mysterious adventurer, diplomat and archaeologist active in the Arab world in the late 19th and early 20th century. Between 1922 and 1930 he served as the founder and director of the *Institut Français d'archéologie et d'art musulmans* in Damascus, after which he returned to Paris, publishing and lecturing on the art and archaeology of the Near East and early Islamic world (Avez 1993, 135–155).

The figurines that Hamlin acquired from de Lorey are fine examples of a class of bronze figurines that is commonly found in the northern Levant and southern Turkey, and dates to the first half of the second millennium B.C. Probably functioning as votive offerings, the same forms, gestures, and designs are repeated in both clay and bronze statuettes. One common type (Fig. 28.4, left) represents a male figure with upraised right arms, which in some examples hold weapons, such that type is usually referred to as a smiting god (Negbi 1976, 8–9, figs. 7–8; Seeden 1980; Muscarella 1981, 360–262, nos. 486–487). Another common type depicts a woman with exaggerated genitalia clasping her breasts in both hands (Fig. 28.4, right). Not surprisingly, these figurines are routinely associated with a fertility goddess (Negbi 1976, 60–84, cp. no. 1550–1552).

Figure 28.3. Impression from a travertine cylinder seal from Aleppo, 12th century B.C. (British Museum, Inv. No. 1922,0511.280, Courtesy of the Trustees of the British Museum)

The facial features in all of these figurines from the Levant is remarkably schematic, and it is easy to see the link to the museum's ongoing theme of primitive art. In the overly simplistic comparative anthropology and museology of the early 20th century, the style of these figurines could easily be matched with objects in other media from Africa, South America, or Australia.

Figure 28.4. Two of the figurines acquired from Eustache de Lorey. Left: The smiting god, H. 12 cm; right: fertility goddess, H. 10 cm. Northern Levant area, 2000–1500 B.C. Buffalo Museum of Science, inv. nos. C16958 and C16953.

Philip Kiernan

Figure 28.5. Left: Geometric horse, supposedly from Olympia, L. 8 cm (Inv. No. C12846), Right: Supposedly Etruscan horse, actually from Cyprus, 1050–650 B.C., L. 7.3 cm. (Inv. No. C12889).

The Classical Bronzes

The bronzes from the world of classical antiquity are the second smallest group in the collection, but are nonetheless still revealing of the intentions that lay behind the museum's collecting, and are not without interest in their own right. Of the 38 bronzes that may be placed in this category, 23 were classified by the museum as Etruscan, 10 as Greek, and five as Roman. Of these pieces, very few belong to the Greek Classical and Hellenistic periods, or the Roman Imperial period. The reason for this, however, is fairly obvious.

If the museum aimed to acquire examples of primitive art, early civilization, and technological innovations, the Classical, Hellenistic, and Roman periods were simply deemed too advanced. The museum was not, one suspects, motivated to acquire great examples of naturalistic art, which was probably thought to be the prerogative of Buffalo's Albright Knox Art Gallery. Instead, these bronzes were meant as illustrations of stages of development of the Greek and Italic worlds before they reached their ultimate high points.

The museum's records describe only seven of these bronzes as figurines, with all the rest being weapons, tools, and items of adornment. The readily identifiable non-figural pieces include three strigils, several fibulae, including a large *navicella* fibula (inv. no. C15418, acquired from Count Walewski), and a smaller *sanguisuga* fibula (inv. no. BR 238, purchased from J. Khayat in 1944) that was supposedly found near Hama in northern Syria. Other functional pieces include a large but heavily restored late Archaic Greek mirror with siren grip (inv. no. BR 225), which was supposedly found near Athens, and a somewhat dubious Etruscan mirror (inv. no. C15924, acquired from J. Khayat in 1947) engraved with a scene of Athena and Perseus examining the head of Medusa in a pool.

Two of the bronzes that fall into the classical group are representations of horses; one is Greek, the other supposedly Etruscan (Fig. 28.5). Both were purchased from the Brummer Gallery in New York City, a major supplier of pieces to the museum, with branches in Paris and New York that operated from 1906 to 1949. The Brummer Gallery sold artworks and artefacts to America's larger museums, including the Metropolitan Museum of Art, the Walters Art Gallery, and Harvard's Fogg Museum of Art. It was also patronized by America's wealthiest collectors, including such prominent figures as Randolph J. Hearst and John D. Rockefeller (Carter 2018). While the Anthropology and Ethnography department of the Buffalo Museum of Science never aspired to be in the same league with the collections of these museums, Chauncey Hamlin and the Buffalonians behind the Museum of Science were very much moving within the same circles as these wealthy Americans. It is perhaps worth noting at this point that if Hamlin had wished to collect high-end Classical, Hellenistic, and Roman bronzes, he most certainly could have afforded to do so.

Fortunately, many of the inventory and sales records of the Brummer Gallery have been digitized by the Metropolitan Museum of Art, and can be accessed freely online. These records often allow the interesting pathways of objects purchased from the Brummers by the Buffalo Museum of Science to be traced. The first of the two bronze horses is one such piece. The Museum purchased the piece on Jan. 28th 1938, and it was accessioned in the museum's records the following month. The horse had supposedly been found at Olympia, which is a perfectly plausible findspot for this common form of a Geometric Greek votive offering.

The Buffalo horse statuette belongs to a group of statuettes identified by Heilmeyer as the products of a Lacedaemonian workshop at Olympia, and by Zimmermann as part of the so-called Giamalakis group. The latter group is named after a group of bronzes donated to the Heracleion Museum in 1962, which were supposedly found on the plain of Lassithi on Crete. Both authorities date horse figurines of this group to the 730s B.C. (Zimmermann 1989, 299–303, nos. GIA 1–82; Heilmeyer 1979, 130–134, nos. 539–607, esp. nos. 560–564).

The Brummer card for the horse (card X814) includes a black and white photo of the horse statuette without the wooden base on which it is mounted today, a base that also appears in a photograph of the piece in Clawson's book (1941, 74). More interestingly, the Brummer card records the piece as part of a consignment which the Greek dealer Zoumpoulakis had left with the Brummer gallery on Oct. 27th 1934. The same Brummer records (card X1122) also inform us that the Buffalo Museum of Science purchased the horse together with a large Geometric amphora, which features processions of warriors and chariots in two friezes. This amphora had been sent by Zoumpoulakis directly to the Metropolitan Museum of Art, who had declined it, and then sent it to the Brummers, who evidently acted on Zoumpoulakis' behalf. The Brummer card for the amphora describes and pictures the amphora in large fragments. But one again, this same vessel appears restored on the dustcover of Clawson's 1941 book.

Apart from this little glimpse into the intricacies of the trade and speedy restorations made in 1930s America, the purchases also suggest a degree of planning or strategy by the Buffalo Museum of Science. The geometric depiction of the horses on both the amphora and the bronze clearly complement one another. Moreover, they are a phase in the development of Greek art before naturalism became the norm, and long before the floruit of the Greek world. In a museum employing a comparative approach, the pieces could be related to other artefacts from primitive cultures of the world.

The second bronze horse (inv. no. C12889) was purchased from the Brummer gallery in March of 1938, and was thought to be Etruscan. Perhaps its rather triangular neck and straight legs were seen as a pendant to the recently acquired Olympian horse, but the object is very different from any Greek Geometric bronze. The underside is hollow and open, while the center of the body is pierced with a hole. The animal's giraffe-like neck terminates in a tiny head with round open sockets for eyes and an open mouth. While these abnormalities may have led the Brummers to make the Etruscan attribution, the piece is also quite unlike any Etruscan bronze.

In fact, an almost identical horse exists in Berlin (Antikensammlung, Inv. Nr. Misc. 8105, 10). In this case, the horse was found in the 19th-century excavations of ancient cemeteries Ayia Paraskevi at Nicosia on Cyprus (Hermary 2001, 157, no. 86; Ohnefalsch-Richter 1893, 180, no. 387,2 and pl. no. 2), and should be dated to that island's Royal period (1050–600 B.C). The hole in the back of both horses was perhaps used to suspend the piece, but could also have been intended to attach a mounted rider. The misattribution of this object is a good example of why the collection requires careful study, and may yield further surprises.

While the Cypriote bronze horse was quite incorrectly attributed to the Etruscan world, the attribution of a small statuette (Fig. 28.6) also purchased from the Brummer Gallery in 1938 to the same culture was quite correct (Clawson 1941, 78). The rather flat representation stands on pointed feet, from which an ancient peg extends into a modern base. The woman pulls at the clothing of her chiton with her left hand, while her right arm is broken at the elbow. One of the most striking aspects of this piece is the extent to which details were incised after casting. The folds in the chiton are indicated by curved lines, and the patterning of the cloth by a series of circles and crosses, while the hem is of the garment is denoted by a series of triangles in a border just below the neck.

The gesture of the left hand was taken directly from Greek marble korai, such as the Antenor kore, which began to be carved in the later sixth century B.C. (Fuchs 1969, 167–172). The attenuated style of this piece, however, is decidedly Etruscan, as is her conical hat, which can be found on numerous Etruscan bronze korai and in other depictions of Etruscan women (Richardson 1983, 243). The flat body and extensive cold work on the Buffalo kore allow it to be placed in a group of Etruscan bronze korai described by Colonna (1970, 88–90, nos. 212–223) as the "Gruppo Vöcklabruck", after an example found in the Austrian town of that name (Fleischer 1967, no. 227, pl. 95). Several examples have been found north of the Alps.

Colonna (1970, 88–90) suggested a production center in Umbria as a working hypothesis, and, in line with other authorities on Etruscan bronzes (e.g. Richardson 1983, 308–316, her Series C, Group 3A ("Perugia"), saw these pieces as late Archaic (520–450 B.C.). Miari (2000, 274–275) also described korai of this sort as "provincial," suggesting Umbria, the Po Valley and Northern Etruria as production centers. Haynes (1985, 62 and 214–215) saw extensive engraving and flat shape on Etruscan figurines as typical of Umbria and Northern Italy.

The elongated face of the Buffalo kore is decidedly daedalic, with large bulging eyes, a protruding chin, and a faintly smiling mouth. Along with the rather schematic nature of the piece, it is likely that this simplified and crude face was another attraction for the Buffalo Museum of Science. The piece seemed to fit into a category of primitive art, employing a degree of simplification could easily be compared to the primitive faces and schematized bodies of the Syro-Hittite statuettes of the Levant and some of the Luristan bronzes. By contrast, a more naturalistic kouros or kore would have not met the museum's needs at all. Such a work would have represented the achievements of an advanced culture, not its early development.

Perhaps only two of the Roman bronzes owned by the Buffalo Museum of Science can really be considered

Figure 28.6. Etruscan kore, Late Archaic, 520–450 B.C., H. 10.3 cm. (Inv. No. C12888)

figural pieces. One of them (inv. no. C24004) is a finial from a folding bronze tripod depicting a young Bacchus. These tripods and their finials have been studied extensively by Klatt (1995), and the Buffalo example has had the characteristic hook that extends from the back of these bronzes carefully removed and filed away. This piece was a chance donation made in 1981, which can hardly be connected to the collection development plans of the early museum. The second Roman piece is a statuette depicting Cerberus (inv. no. C15633), which was purchased by Hamlin in Paris from the antiquities dealer Le Veel in 1946 (Fig. 28.7). The Buffalo card index describes the piece as coming from Cappodocia, presumably a piece of information obtained from Le Veel.

At least at first glance, the Cerberus seems to be a rather surprising outsider in the usual scheme of the collection, for the mythical guardian of the entrance to the underworld is a remarkably attractive piece of naturalistic representation. The canine head on the right side of the creature's body licks its right forepaw, while the central and left heads are twisted backwards to look behind the animal. The tail is broken near the base, and the right hind paw is also lost.

An almost identical Cerberus was acquired by the British Museum (inv. 1772,0302.75) with the collection of Sir William Hamilton (1730–1803), the British Ambassador to the Kingdom of Naples, antiquities collector, and at one time owner of the Portland Vase. Another very similar piece is now in the cabinet of the Bibliothèque Nationale (Babelon – Blanchet 1895, 340–341, no. 793), and arrived there around 1874 with the collection of A. Oppermann (1808–1877). Described as a piece of mediocre quality by Babelon and Blanchet, this piece, as well as the Buffalo and British Museum pieces, probably date to the second or third centuries A.D. Bronze statuettes of Cerberus seated or standing with a snake wrapped around his body, are slightly more numerous, and are usually thought to be products of Hellenistic or Roman Egypt (Babelon – Blanchet 1895, nos. 790–792; and British Museum, inv. nos. 1866,1006.1 and 1919,0620.8).

Perhaps the Buffalo Cerberus would also have been seen as "mediocre" in quality by Babelon and Blanchet, and it must be admitted that the details of the three heads are decidedly rudimentary, nonetheless the posture and proportions are still far more naturalistic than most of the other figural bronzes in the Buffalo Museum of Science's collections. It may well be that Hamlin purchased this piece on a whim, having been charmed by its connection to a famous monster of Greek mythology, but it is just as likely that he felt the Cerberus was connected to the museum's mission. Like the fantasy animals of the Luristan and Ordos bronzes, the three-headed dog reflected a connection to the animal world which the museum perceived as an important aspect of early man and his art.

Figure 28.7. Cerberus statuette. Second or third century A.D. L. 4.9 cm, H. 5.9 cm (Inv. No. C15633)

Conclusion

The bronzes presented here give a taste of the nature of the Buffalo Museum of Science's collection. The periods and cultures emphasized by the collections were those that were largely neglected by the Fine Art galleries of the day. Though only a very small part of the enormous collection assembled by the Anthropology and Ethnography Department in Buffalo, the bronzes nonetheless provide a glimpse into the sorts of themes and philosophies that influenced the acquisitions policies of a Science and Natural History Museum in the first few decades of the 20th century.

By and large the pieces in the collection were chosen for their potential to illustrate a view of world history in which primitive man shared certain characteristics in virtually any time period or geographical setting. These characteristics included a lack of naturalistic representation in the figural arts, an interest in fertility, and a close connection with the animal kingdom. Just like the botanical and zoological collections, the bronzes were specimens of human society that existed as a natural phenomenon that could to be studied using the same guidelines across time and space. Needless to say, anthropologists and museums have long since abandoned this approach, but its legacy has nonetheless left an interesting collection of ancient bronzes in Buffalo.

Bibliography

Ackerman, P. 1946. The Luristan Bronzes. Their Source, Meaning and Relations. *Hobbies*, 26(3), 150–158.

Avez, R. 1993. *L'Institut français de Damas au Palais Azem (1922–1946) à travers les archives*. Damascus: Presses de l'Ifpo. [doi: 10.4000/books.ifpo.7405]

Babelon, E. – Blanchet, J.-A. 1895. *Catalogue des bronzes antiques de la Bibliothèque nationale*. Paris: Ernest LeRoux.

Carter, M. 2018. "The Brummer Gallery Records: A Fuller Picture" On *In Circulation* – blog Post of the Libraries of the Metropolitan Museum of Art. Oct. 31st 2018. [online] available at <https://www.metmuseum.org/blogs/in-circulation/2018/brummer-gallery-records> [accessed Jan. 25th 2019].

Colonna, G. 1970. *Bronzi votivi umbro-sabellici a figura umana. I. periodo 'arcaico.'* Florence: Sasoni.

Bunker, E. 1981. Ancient Art of Central Asia, Mongolia and Siberia. In: P.R.S. Moorey – E.C. Bunker – E. Porada – G. Markoe, ed., *Ancient Bronzes, Ceramics and Seals. The Nasil M. Heermaneck Collection of Ancient Near Eastern, Central Asiatic, and European Art*. Los Angeles: Los Angeles County Museum of Art, 13–138.

Falsone, G. 1992. Nuove coppe metalliche di fattura orientale. *Vicino Oriente* 8(2), 83–112.

Fuchs, W. 1969. *Die Skulptur der Griechen*. Munich: Hirmer Verlag.

Goodyear, G.F. 1994. Society and Museum – A History of the Buffalo Society of Natural Sciences 1861–1993 and the Buffalo Museum of Science 1928–1993. *Bulletin of the Buffalo Museum of Sciences 34*. Buffalo: Buffalo Society of Natural Sciences.

Haynes, S. 1985. *Etruscan Bronzes*. London: Sotheby's Publications.

Hermary, A. 2001. Les statuettes en bronze à Chypre à l'époque des Royaumes. *Archaeologia Cypria* 4, 145–164.

Leacock, K. 2012. Happy Anniversary! Celebrating 150 Years of Buffalo's Cultural Institutions. *Western New York Heritage*, 2012, Spring, 8–17.

Miari, M. 2000. *Stipi Votive dell'Etruria Padana*. Corpus delle stipe votive in Italia 11, Regio 3.3. Rome: Bretschneider.

Moorey, P.R.S. 1981. The Art of Ancient Iran. In P.R.S. Moorey – E.C. Bunker – E. Porada – G. Markoe, ed., *Ancient Bronzes, Ceramics and Seals. The Nasil M. Heermaneck Collection of Ancient Near Eastern, Central Asiatic, and European Art*. Los Angeles: Los Angeles County Museum of Art, 139–186.

Muscarella, O.W. 1988. *Bronze and Iron. Ancient Near Eastern Artifacts in the Metropolitan Museum of Art*. New York: The Metropolitan Museum of Art.

Ohnefalsch-Richter, M. 1893. *Kypros, die Bibel und Homer. Beiträge zur Cultur-, Kunst- und Religionsgeschichte des Orients im Alterthume. Mit besonderer Berücksichtigung eigener zwölfjähriger Forschungen und Ausgrabungen auf der Insel Cypren*. Berlin: Asher.

Richardson, E. 1983. *Etruscan Votive Bronzes, Geometric, Orientalizing, Archaic*. Mainz: von Zabern.

Rostovsteff, M. 1929. *The Animal Style in South Russia and China*. Princeton: Princeton University Press.

Seeden, H. 1980. *The Standing Armed Figurines in the Levant*. Prähistorische Bronzefunde 1.1. Munich: C.H. Beck.

Part IV

Role

29

Geometric Bronze Animal Figurines at Olympia – Who Dedicated What and Why?

András Patay-Horváth

Eötvös Loránd University

pathorv@gmail.com

Abstract: According to the prevailing *communis opinio*, Geometric bronze animal figurines found at Olympia represent domesticated cattle and horses, which were in this form put under the protection of the divinity. This view is challenged here for various reasons: I suggest that the bovids depicted were feral, and that the figurines were offered by foreign aristocrats visiting the sanctuary especially for the sake of hunting these animals. In a similar way, the horse figurines are interpreted as depicting feral horses, which were presumably captured and taken away by the visitors.

Keywords: Dedication Practices; Aristocrats; Animals; Hunting

At Olympia the earliest dedications were small votive figurines made of clay and bronze. Several thousands have been discovered in the so-called „Black stratum" (Furtwängler 1890, 2–6), and one can hardly guess how many were actually dedicated. On the basis of previous studies (e.g. Furtwängler 1890, Heilmeyer 1979, Herrmann 1964, Zimmermann 1989 summarized and thoroughly discussed by Andrews 1994, 34–150), it seems to be safe to conclude that the bronze figurines were produced during the 9–8th centuries either by distant workshops in Argos, Korinth and Lakonia or by itinerant bronzesmiths coming from these regions and working temporarily at Olympia. The reason(s) for their dedication have, however, been sought in vain and this paper addresses this problem, because it has received only cursory treatment so far (Heilmeyer 1979, 195–197; Pilali 1986, 160; Sinn 2010, 81; Bevan 1986, 89, 204–206).

Apart from some singular pieces and the human figures, the bronze figurines represent two kinds of animals: horses and cattle. Heilmeyer (1979, 196) gives the following statistics: „53,84% Rinder, 45,21% Pferde", in absolute numbers (Heilmeyer 1979, 275): 1885 cattle and 1583 horses out of a total of 4042. (Cattle figurines are often clearly meant to depict bulls, but the sex is not always indicated. Since there is not a single figurine showing a cow suckling a calf, the terms 'bovids' or 'bulls' are used here as the synonyms of 'cattle'.)

The horses have been studied more thoroughly and mainly from an art historical perspective (Herrmann 1964). According to the communis opinio (Heilmeyer 1979; Rolley 1994, 97–101; Coldstream 2003), their rendering is not uniform, but displays characteristic features attested in different regions of the Peloponnese, and can thus be used to identify the manufacturers' place of origin. The bulls or bovines are equally various, but have fewer parallels elsewhere. The largest group that is most similar to the material from Olympia both in general appearance and in terms of chronology, comes from Crete. Pilali (1985) enumerates 172 pieces, most of them from Hagia Triada, Phaistos and Psychro, Schürmann (1996) lists 325 geometric bull figurines from a single sanctuary, Syme Viannou or Kato Syme. In other sanctuaries and regions there are only occasional finds (Patay-Horváth 2015, 100–101) or, in the case of the Kabeirion, they are mainly later series (Schmaltz 1980; Langdon 1982, 596). In fact the Geometric bull figurines from Olympia account for ca. 75–80% of all the comparable contemporary material. (Diagram 29.1a) The percentage is similar in the case of horse figurines (Diagram 29.1b), the main difference being that the surviving material is not uniformly scattered but concentrated almost exclusively on Crete.

The assemblage of the material in Olympia, i.e. the relative percentages of the species depicted, require special attention. As already mentioned, at least 90% of the bronze material is made up of cattle and horses, which are represented continuously (i.e. without much fluctuation over the centuries under discussion) in more or less equal numbers (*pace* Snodgrass 1987, 206). This ratio is unparalleled elsewhere, as in most cases horses account for the majority of votive figurines, and when the cattle/bulls are more numerous, as in the case of Crete or the Theban Kabeirion, the horses are almost entirely missing. (According to Zimmermann 1989, 293, there are 7 bronze horse figurines known from Crete, four of them decorating vessels and coming from the Ideaen cave.) Moreover, if we look at the role played by the two animals in Greek cult, we see that while bulls were the most prestigious and

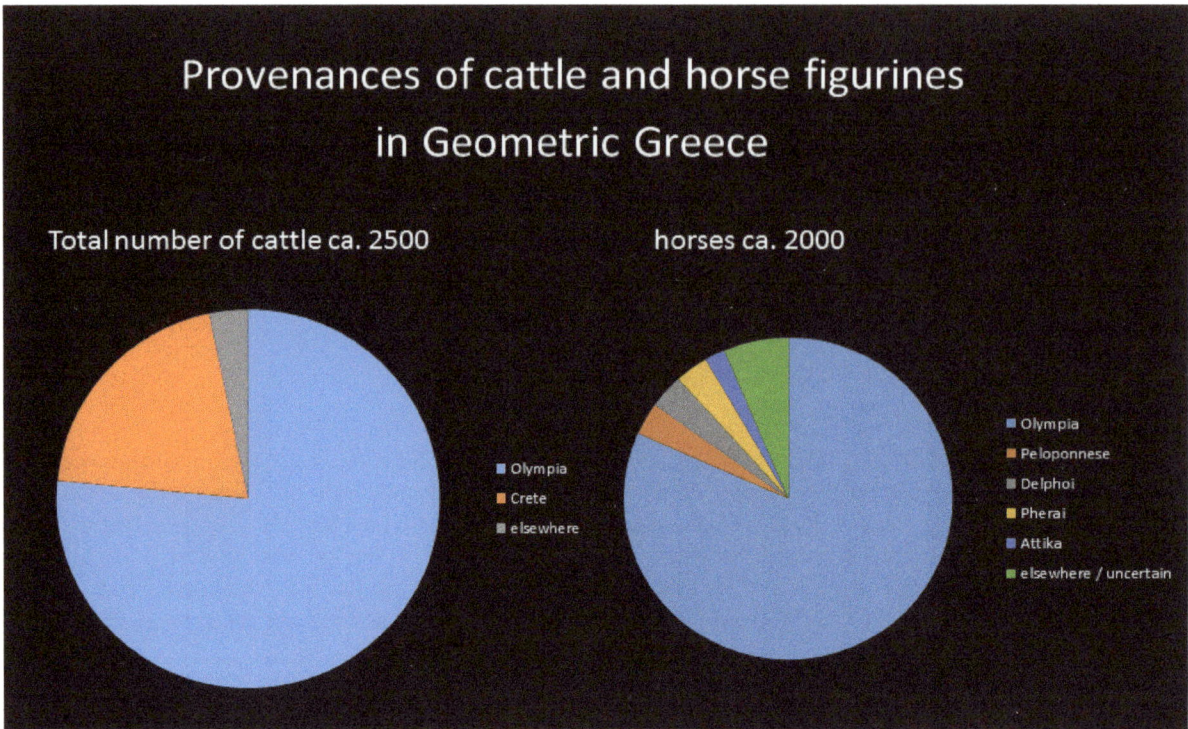

Diagram 29.1. Provenances of cattle (left) and horse figurines (right) in Geometric Greece.

ubiquitous animals sacrificed, horses were almost never used for this purpose. So what was the common factor in the equally remarkable numbers of horse and cattle figurines? Is there actually a common factor? Considering the large numbers involved, the approximately equal proportions are unlikely to be accidental, and because the two groups were produced by similar workshops it is possible that they were dedicated by the same group of people and at a similar frequency. So even if the reason for their dedication was not exactly the same, it can be safely assumed that it was comparable.

The large number of the figurines at Olympia cannot simply be explained by the ordinary sacrificial customs observed all over Greece, and except for Snodgrass (1989/1990, 292), apparently no one is inclined to assume a direct link with real animal sacrifices, even for the bovids. In such a case, one would certainly be surprised to find that in later centuries the dedication of bull figurines practically disappeared, while the sacrificial practices remained basically the same. Also in the Kabeirion in Boiotia, where bronze cattle figurines are similarly abundant and indeed almost the only species represented throughout several centuries, the analysis of the archaeozoological material has shown (Schmaltz 1980) that in reality these animals were sacrificed less fequently in comparison with ovicaprids, which are, however only sporadically represented among the votives. According to the available archaeozoological data (Hägg 1998; Forstenpointer 2003), this sacrificial pattern prevailed in most Greek sanctuaries. Assuming some kind of correlation with actual sacrifices performed in the sanctuaries, the generally low frequency of dedicating bull figurines or statues in Greek sanctuaries can be regarded as normal. This underlines the exceptional character of the cattle figurines at Olympia and suggests that another explanation is needed for their dedication, just as in the case of the Kabeirion.

At the sanctuary of Hermes and Aphrodite at Kato Syme on Crete and the Theban Kabeirion, the figurines could be dedicated to any divinity, just as the living bovids could be sacrificed for any god or goddess), and as most Geometric santuaries did not receive cattle figurines in similar numbers, it is equally clear that chronological factors were not responsible either. A common feature of the cults involved, such as fertility or initiation, can be perhaps supposed, but some more specific local factor seems more likely. One could imagine for examplethat after winning a great number of horses and cattle during a raid, as related by Nestor (Hom. Iliad 11.670–761), the victors would have dedicated some figurines representing the booty or the share of the gods. Such a practice is, however, not indicated by the epic: the gods were regularly honoured with animal sacrifices and not with figurines. The commemoration of animal sacrifices in the form of statuettes is not very likely either, since in later centuries, when similar sacrifices were regularly held, it was by no means usual to erect a monument depicting the sacrificial animal and horses were certainly not sacrificed at all.

Given the differences in the ritual role of horses and cattle, it was supposed that the dedication of these animal figurines was simply motivated by the everyday living conditions or personal emotions of the dedicators, who were supposed to be mainly ordinary local peasants. In this respect it is interesting to note that concerning cattle and horses were generally quite different and are therefore not likely to account for the roughly equal numbers of the figurines (Lorenz 2000, 324–325). If this were true, horse figurines should far outnumber cattle, as is the case in most other sanctuaries.

The prevailing opinion (Heilmeyer 1972, 87–88; Sinn 1981, 37–38; Morgan 1993, 22; Schürmann 1996, 219–220; Taita 2009, 378–379) thus takes the figurines as a reflection of the living conditions of the dedicators themselves, and suggests that the most valuable animals were in this form put under the protection of the divinity. (As far as I can see, it was only Herrmann 1980, 69, n. 67 who criticized this view, but he did not offer any alternative explanation and his short remark has largely gone unnoticed.) This hypothesis could perhaps explain the presence and the large number of animal figurines in Olympia, if the underlying notion of a large-scale pastoralism during the Geometric period in the surrounding region could be substantiated, but this is essentially quite an improbable assumption, as demonstrated e.g. by Cherry 1988, 27–29 (against Snodgrass 1987) and Howe 2008, 13–25. 34–38. At any rate, the traditional explanation certainly does not account for the conspicuous gaps in the distribution pattern. One wonders, for instance, why in Crete the method would have been applied only to cattle, rams, and goats, but not to horses, and why most well-to-do farmers/herders in ancient Greece applied this method practically exclusively to their horses and did not choose this simple option for their cattle even in those areas which show marked environmental similarities with Olympia, being well-suited or even renowned for cattle rearing and/or are clearly in close contact with this sanctuary. The most conspicuous instance belonging to both categories is in the case of the Argolid, where the Heraion attracted only horse dedications, whereas Thessaly is a prime example of the first and Lakonia of the second. So this should not be taken as the definitive explanation for the dedication of animal figurines.

First of all, the identity of the dedicators should be clarified. In general, they are supposed to be local ones, but the implications of such a hypothesis have not been recognized, so they deserve to be mentioned here.

Assuming local dedicators, it would be first unexplained, why local people around Olympia would and could have attracted bronzesmiths or their products from distant regions. In Crete, the sanctuary of Kato Syme was certainly unable to do so. It is obviously possible to assume that local people around Olympia were more prosperous than those on Crete and could afford elaborate and expensive dedications, in much greater quantities, since Elis was renowned for its agrarian wealth from the late Classical period (Xen. Hell. 3.2.26; Polyb. 4.73; Livy 27.32.9). Mythology also located large herds of cattle in this region (Hom. Il. 11.670ff; Paus. 5.1.9), but clearly identifiable dedications made by individuals from Elis (attested by dedicatory inscriptions) are practically unknown at Olympia at any time (most important in this context is certainly their absence during the Archaic period) and large numbers of dedications offered by individual inhabitants from the neighbourhood are therefore not very likely at such an early period either. The absence of individual votive inscriptions is of course an argumentum *e silentio*, but it is perhaps more relevant than other similar arguments, since there are some collective dedications made by the Eleans and other local peoples which are attested by inscriptions on a few metal vessels (Siewert 1991), so the absence of personal dedications can not be attributed to a general lack of interest in inscribing votives.

On the other hand, assuming local dedicators and considering the parallel case of the Kabeirion, it is not apparent why the dedications would have been made, both on Crete and in Olympia, only during the Geometric period, and why the supposed dedicators ceased to continue this practice in later centuries. General trends can be invoked for this change (Snodgrass 1989–1990), but as the large numbers seem to be a local speciality at both places, and since they seem to be unrelated, one would expect an equally local cause for the abandoning of the practice as well.

As the figurines were relatively easy to produce and therefore cheap, and because they are present in large numbers, one might suppose an equally large number of relatively poor dedicators and mainly local ones. But low costs imply poor dedicators only if we assume that each dedicator left just one figurine (or a few) and nothing else in the sanctuary, and this is by no means certain (all might have dedicated dozens or even hundreds of figurines at a single occasion and also other objects as well); the large numbers are likely to result from the large number of visitors, but may be also explained by recurring visits by the same, relatively small group of visitors, who may have come from any distance.

Supposing therefore external dedicators in Olympia is more likely, even if it is not immediately clear why all (or at least most of them) would have come from the Argolid, Korinth and Lakonia to Olympia, and why they offered such simple and inexpensive votive dedications and only during the Geometric period. At any rate, the producers of the figurines came mainly from the same areas as those of the large tripod cauldrons and it is therefore reasonable to suppose that the accumulation of small dedications in Olympia is equally due to the exceptionally strong attraction and supraregional importance of the sanctuary, and that it is not a purely local phenomenon. This consideration actually argues for the assumption that the dedicators of the figurines were of the same origins as their producers, that they were most probably external visitors of the sanctuary, coming mainly from the north-east and southern Peloponnese. And if they came from such distant areas, they are likely to have been wealthy enough to afford such a trip. I think it is reasonable to assume that they were identical with the dedicators of the tripod cauldrons, because otherwise (assuming that the number of figurines indicates roughly the number of dedicators or the number of their visits) the numerous figurines would require a high number of relatively wealthy dedicators in addition to those dedicating the tripods, all of them able to afford a visit to the distant sanctuary. Numerous well-to-do visitors are not very likely to be found anywhere during the Geometric period and are especially unlikely to be present at Olympia before ca. 700 B.C., when the first pits were dug to provide drinking water for a large number of people (Mallwitz 1988; 1999, 196–199). That, on the other hand, the two groups of dedications were intimately connected is clearly shown by the bulls' heads on the earliest cauldron handles (Maass 1978, 18, n. 26) and by the numerous horse figurines on the later ones. It would be therefore quite logical to search for a cult context, which could account for dedicating both types of object (i.e. tripod cauldrons and animal figurines) by the same group of dedicators.

The animal species represented also corroborate this view. The most important common feature of cattle and horses in ancient Greece was that they were valuable belongings (horses in particular can be termed „luxury items" or „prestige goods") and their relatively cheap representations could therefore be seen as expressing notions connected with wealth and status. If they were dedicated by people wealthy enough to own and to use these animals, they could express their success and pride but also their anxiety about them; if on the contrary they were dedicated by those who were simply eager to acquire them, the figurines could stand for their hopes. The material from the sanctuary at Kato Syme can help to decide this question. Here the bovine figurines disappeared, similarly to those at Olympia, and were replaced by representations of the dedicators themselves, who are characterized as aristocratic hunters (Langdon 2008, 89–94). The dedicators were thus not ordinary or poor local people, but the wealthiest of the surrounding region. The same is most probably true for Olympia as well. For the question of whether the well-to-do „aristocratic" visitors at Olympia were local or mainly external, we have a valuable source of information, namely the victors in the equestrian events. The available data (Moretti 1955) clearly show that these victors always came from outside the surrounding region, suggesting that the wealthy horse-owners, were descendants of the dedicators of the horse figurines, and were (like their manufacturers) also of foreign origin. Of course local aristocrats cannot be excluded altogether, but they are not likely to account for a large percentage of the dedications.

The sheer quantity of the horse figurines points in the same direction as well. From the nearly contemporary literary sources, i.e. Homer and Hesiod, it is evident that horses were used exclusively for pulling the chariots of the aristocratic warriors and played no role in agricultural activities on a subsistance level (Lorenz 2000, 103–105). Horses (whether few or many) in the possession of ordinary farmers or herdsmen can therefore be practically excluded, and it is appropriate to assume that horse figurines were connected with and dedicated by wealthy people, who can be termed as the elite (Morgan 1993, 23). The relatively even distribution and (in comparison with Olympia) low numbers of the horse figurines all over Greece, (Diagram 29.2) even in regions which were essentially well-suited for horsekeeping (e.g. Argolid, Thessaly), show that horsebreeding and the dedication of horse figurines were indeed restricted to the elite and there is nothing to suggest that it would have been otherwise in the case of Elis. In other words, the dedication of horse figurines does not reflect the large number of horses, but that of wealthy

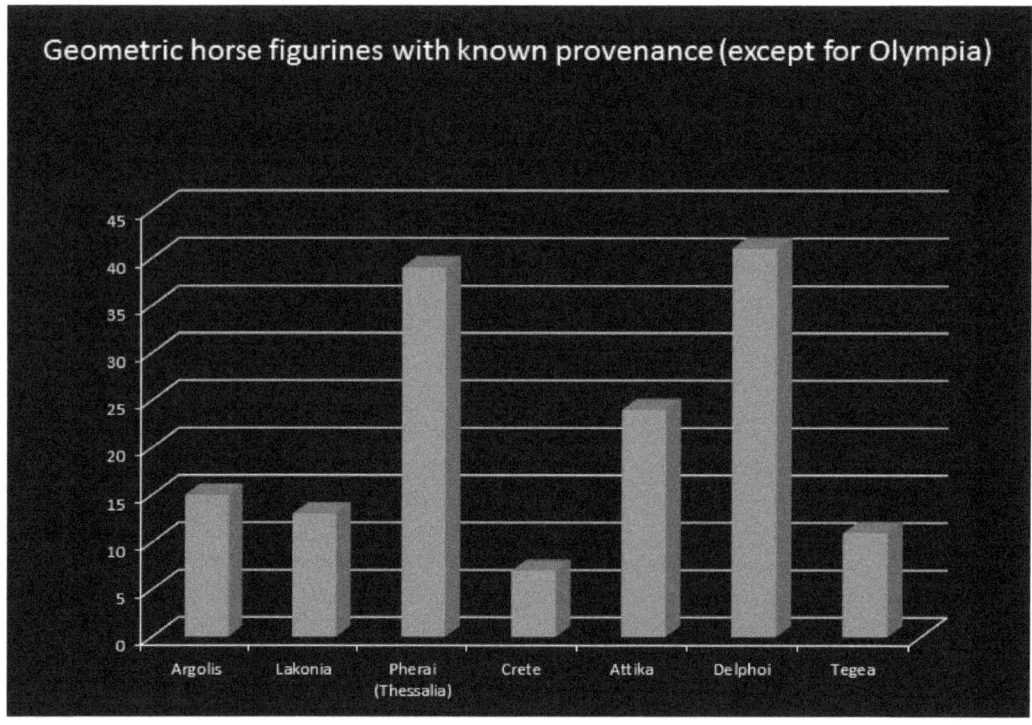

Diagram 29.2. Geometric horse figurines with known provenance (except for Olympia).

aristocrats. The large number of horse figurines cannot therefore result primarily from local dedicators, since it is quite unlikely for Elis to have developed horsebreeding aristocrats in such large numbers.

So, even if the exact reason for dedicating the animal figurines still remains mysterious, one might safely conclude with Herrmann (1972, 72) and Eder (2006, 554 n. 5) that most of the dedicators must have been foreign aristocrats visiting the sanctuary on a regular basis.

But why would well-to-do people have dedicated such simple figurines instead of objects which could readily reflect their wealth and status? The answer lies partly in the assumption, mentioned above, that these offerings were probably only part of their dedications, the most impressive ones being the tripods. It is even conceivable that the figurines were not only or not primarily dedicated for representing the wealth or status of the dedicators (the terracotta ones are especially ill-suited for such a purpose), but presumably to fulfil some kind of ritual obligation, like throwing a coin into the Fontana di Trevi nowadays. This would explain their large number as well as their relatively low costs, their often careless renderings and the use of bronze as well as clay.

It remains to be asked, what this ritual obligation could have been, or why „aristocrats" from a wide region visit Olympia regularly and why did they develop the strange habit of dedicating among other things small animal figurines at this particular sanctuary, so far away from their homes? At this point, it is time to return to the identification of the figurines in the hope of finding a conclusive answer to these problems.

The cattle are usually described and interpreted as domesticated bulls and cows, but the pose, along with the form and the size of their horns, are strongly reminiscent of those of aurochs (*Bos primigenius*, Bojanus 1827): they are often inward-curving and the angle formed by the skull's axis and the horns is less than 60 degrees (Fig. 29.1). These are the characteristic features enabling a distinction between the two species (van Vuure 2005, 120–135). In addition, the horns are much longer than those of domesticated cattle (*Bos taurus*). These features are not uniformly observable on all the figurines (Fig. 29.2), but they occur very frequently and in all periods and workshops identified among them (Heilmeyer 1979, Nr. 90–91. 230–236. 246–247. 383–386. 390. 391. 412–416. 511. 513. 583. 585. 763. 767. 774. 778. 781. 783. 826. 827. 856. 857. 881–889). They are not restricted to the bronze figurines, but are equally present in the clay figurines (Heilmeyer 1972, 124–125) and can be thus termed as constant features which are definitely not to be regarded as personal, regional or chronological idiosyncrasies. The resemblance to anatomical reality and the contrast with bovine figurines clearly depicting normal domesticated cattle in other Greek sanctuaries of the Geometric period (e.g. Delphi, Tegea, Lousoi and the Kabeirion) strongly suggest that the rendering of the horns at Olympia is not a general convention of Greek Geometric art, but a realistic element of the otherwise schematically-modelled animals. This is at least strongly suggested by the only pair of yoked oxen figurines found at Olympia, which obviously depict domesticates with large horns curving outwards. (Fig. 29.3)

Comparing the figurines from Olympia with depictions of ordinary domesticated cattle elsewhere in Greece, such as those found at the Theban Kabeirion, the formal differences are clearly recognisable and strongly suggest that they are not incidental. This has already been pointed out by Schmaltz (1980, 12) An interesting difference between the two groups is discernible in their chronology as well: the series of bulls disappears from Olympia after the Geometric period, whereas they continue for several centuries at the

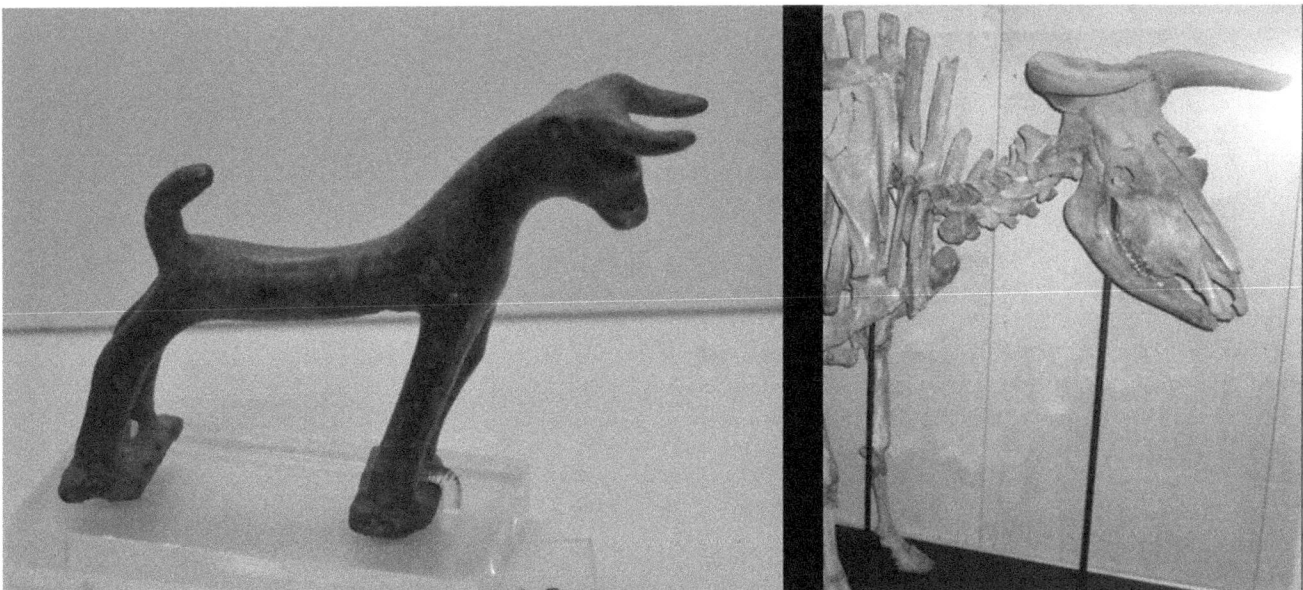

Figure 29.1. Bronze bovid figurine (Olympia B 5252) and the skeleton of an aurochs bull. (Photo: Author).

Figure 29.2. Random selection of animal figurines from Olympia. (Photo: Author).

Figure 29.3. Pair of yoked oxen (Olympia B 5618). (Photo: Author).

Kabeirion. This fact also supports the hypothesis that in Olympia the figurines represent not domesticated but wild animals and strongly suggests that their disappearance is not due to some change in the dedicatory practices, but can be explained by the extinction of the species resulting from excessive hunting and the spread of domesticated cattle in the region. It is after all these causes which led to the extinction of this animal in other periods and regions as well (van Vuure 2005, 72–78).

Moreover, even if there are no skeletal remains of aurochs in Olympia (Benecke 2006a; 2006b), there is some osteological evidence for their presence on Crete (Pilali 1985, 124; Persson 1993; Nobis 1996), the only place where similar representations are attested in considerable quantities. Admittedly, the archaeozoological material dates from the Bronze Age and most recently the identification of these remains has also been challenged (Vigne 1999, 300; Shapland 2010, 122). Yet, one of the famous cups from Vapheio clearly shows the capturing of a bull with a net and two passages in Homer (Il. 12.22–23; Od. 16.295–296) can be interpreted as evidence for the presence of wild cattle in Greece. Finally, a gloss in Hesychius (s.v. κατράγοντες) explaining a word as a special Laconian term for wild cattle shows that these animals were certainly present on the Peloponnese (Keller 1887, 53–60; 1909, 341–343). In addition, the species may have found ideal conditions in the vicinity of Olympia and was likely to have been extremely rare elsewhere in Greece (van Vuure 2005, 48–52. 245–258). By the time of Herodotus (7.126) it seems to have been extinct in all Greece, but was to be found in Macedonia and its horns were still imported to Hellas. The bulls were certainly impressive in size and were surely regarded as exclusive game animals in Geometric Greece as well, since as their numbers were decreasing, the hunting of aurochs generally became a privilege of the aristocracy (van Vuure 2005, 55–64).

One might object that besides the many figurines with typical aurochs-like horns, there are many others without this feature. But the overwhelming majority of them can be certainly compared to feral bovids, i.e. domesticated animals that escaped human control and lived as wild animals (Fig. 29.4). Such animals are genetically identical with the domesticated *Bos taurus*, but their appearance may come close to the aurochs. Their osteological remains cannot be distinguished from their domesticated counterparts and assuming therefore not wild but feral animals could perfectly account for the archaeozoological evidence both at Olympia and on Crete. It is therefore highly probable that after the collapse of the Bronze Age, many domesticated animals became feral, especially in those regions like Elis, where human populations decreased rapidly and the natural environment was favourable for large herbivores. Crossbreeds of wild/feral and domestic animals are also possible and supposing that the manufacturers carefully depicted at least the horns of the animals, this could explain the large variability among the figurines as well.

Ethnographic parallels can also help to explain the numerous representations of the animals and the dedication of the images in a sacred place: the miniature figurines are

Figure 29.4. Feral bovids (in the Camargue) compared to bronze figurines from Olympia. (Photo: Author).

used by hunters either to effect the successful catch or as thank offerings of the wild animals after the hunt for a god or goddess, to ensure the regeneration of animals for the following hunt (Karjalainen 1927, 5–6; Holmberg 1927, 83–99. 510–512; Ivanov 1958; Paulson 1961, 27–35).

So hunting or capturing wild/feral animals might have been the only legitimate occasion for dedicating animal statuettes and this practice could perfectly account for the mass dedication of bronze and terracotta bovine figurines at Olympia. The material from Crete, especially the largest group found at Kato Syme, can be adduced as a parallel and clearly corroborates the above hypothesis. Geometric animal figurines disappear at this site roughly at the same time as in Olympia and since the worshipped deities and the artistic environment of the two sanctuaries are clearly different, it is unlikely that similar art historical or religious phenomena could have provoked the change in both cases. Instead, the real reason might be sought in the hunt itself, which is clearly attested by the sheet bronzes as the central cult element in Syme during the later centuries (Lebessi 1985). This was probably also the case earlier, the only difference being that the wild/feral cattle became extinct and could not be hunted any more. Consequently the species was not depicted any more, and dedicatory habits changed as well. Later literary sources (Ephoros, FrGrHist 70 F 149 = Strabo 10.4.21) clearly report that hunting played a decisive role in male initiation on Crete and this practice can definitely explain the dedication of hammered bronzes at Syme. It is reasonable to assume that initiation by hunting or the hunting itself did not start exactly with the appearance of the hammered bronze sheets, but originated much earlier and can therefore be used to explain the presence of Geometric bronze figurines at the same site. Seen from this perspective, the remaining animal figurines at Syme appear to belong to the same context of hunting: wild goats were certainly game animals and the rams may also have belonged to this category.

Pursuing this line of reasoning, one can find an easy explanation for the different kinds of animal figurines accompanying the bovids at Syme and in Olympia. The Cretan sanctuary was situated in a high mountain landscape providing optimal habitat for wild goats and rams, whereas the well-watered gentle hills and swampy lowlands around Elis and Olympia were ideal for feral horses. This is clearly attested by the Homeric epithet of the region, *hippobotos* (Od. 21.347), and in the famous story (Hom. Il. 11.670–761) related by *hippota* Nestor. Horses were of course not hunted to be sacrificed and eaten, like wild bovines, goats and rams, but they were presumably captured to be tamed and used as valuable and prestigious domesticated animals. This practice may have contributed considerably to the attraction of the region and may also explain the dedication of large numbers of horse figurines as well as the name and the prominent role of Hippodameia at Olympia. As the horses were captured and removed from their original living environment, a ritual restitution was considered appropriate, similar to the dedication of figurines representing ordinary game animals. In both cases, it was essential for the hunters to secure the procreation of the hunted or captured animals by mitigating the wrath of their former owner, the Master or Mistress of the animals.

In this way the dedication of all Geometric animal figurines can be explained more satisfactorily than by supposing owners or would-be owners of ordinary domestic animals making bronze dedications, since it was already pointed out for another context that „although subsistence was based largely on agriculture and herding, these subjects are notably absent from the art" (Russell 2012, 19). This observation seems equally valid for ancient Greeks as well. Moreover, the differences clearly observed between Syme and Olympia do not seem in this way haphazard, but clearly reflect the different natural environments of the two sanctuaries. In this respect, a good parallel to the area surrounding Olympia is offered by the Rhône delta, where feral horses as well as feral cattle live together in the Camargue (van Vuure 2005; Duncan 1992).

Regarding the disappearance of the figurines, the hypothesis of the extinction of the animals appears as a logical explanation. As Hughes (2014, 102) already observed in general „Hunting reduced wild cattle, sheep and goats to remnant herds and eliminated them from some islands in Classical times. This was only one of a series of extinctions of island fauna." The possible causes of these extinctions are discussed in more detail by Russell (2012, 176–186). Wild cattle were most probably consumed on the spot during the feasts in the sanctuary, while the horses were transported home by the visitors as valuable goods. For the *panegyris* the wild cattle were eventually replaced by their domesticated counterparts, but horse-breeding was hardly practised for a considerable time on a large scale. In addition to the lack of winners in the equestrian events referred to above, our sources do not mention *hippeis* or cavalry in Elis before the 4th century (Spence 1993, 7–8). This fact may be regarded as not especially significant since cavalry forces are practically unattested in the whole Peloponnese during the 6th–5th centuries, but would be nonetheless quite hard to explain, if the numerous horse figurines had really resulted from horsebreeding practised on an unusually large scale here. The scarcity of horses might explain on the other hand the curious habit (Herodot 4.30; Paus. 5.5.2; Plut. Mor. 303b) of restrictions concerning mules in Elis. The few horses available had to be strictly protected and even though mules were needed (as they were much more usable for everyday purposes), they were bred only occasionally. At any rate, domestication made the ritual processes connected with the animals obsolete and the dedication of animal figurines was thus abandoned.

The general importance of hunting in Mycenaean Greece, during the Dark Ages and afterwards in the Archaic period was already pointed out by different scholars (Lane Fox 1996, Barringer 2001; Hamilakis 2003; Buchholz et al. 1973; Eder 2006, 553–554, Langdon 2008, 252–255) It was proposed by Guggisberg (2008) that hunting lost its paramount place during the Geometric period and regained it only afterwards, but such a hypothesis of extreme fluctuation is not likely, and considering the above interpretation of Geometric bronze figurines, was no longer necessary.

In general, animal figurines are not a dominant class of dedications in major Greek sanctuaries. Especially after the Geometric period, statuettes or statues of animals on their own are rare compared to human or divine figures. Horse figurines are by far the most common dedications representing animals, but horses were status symbols and this fact is most probably the reason for their relatively frequent depiction. The Kabeirion bulls or the terracotta ones near Chania (Niniou-Kindeli 2003) are clearly exceptional and most probably explained by cultic reasons. In contrast, animal figurines are often found in great numbers in shrines frequented by hunters and ethnographical observations made quite recently among Siberian peoples also furnish the underlying rationale: large numbers of wooden figures depicting fishes and animals were placed at sacred trees in order to effect the successful catch of the species (Karjalainen 1927, 5–6). A similar reason can most probably account for the appearance of numerous animal figurines at Kato Syme and there can be little doubt that the same applies to the stone reliefs depicting various kinds of animals at Göbekli Tepe. This site was recently discovered and identified as the very first temple complex and even if archaeology cannot provide conclusive proof concerning the dedicators and the occasion for the dedication, the connection with hunting can hardly be denied (Schmidt 2006; Russell 2012, 62). It is therefore quite reasonable to assume that hunters were generally inclined to depict their most important or prestigious game animals and that these animal images were often gathered at sacred places or sanctuaries from the earliest periods in human history until quite recently.

Here the general resemblance to Paleolithic cave art might be considered as well. Although the exact purpose and meaning of these well-known and magnificent paintings is far from clear, it is absolutely certain that those who produced them, were hunters and that the depicted animals were wild ones and were usually hunted. Nevertheless, and similarly to the animal figurines at Olympia, the actual hunt is never depicted and wounded animals are also represented only sporadically (Leroi-Gourhan 1992, 277–278). In general, the large number of animal depictions found at Olympia and Kato Syme may be compared to the large herds of animals covering the walls of Paleolithic caves. Local variations in the fauna represented, like those between Olympia and Kato Syme, were also observed, in some caves the horses being accompanied by aurochs, in others by bisons (Leroi-Gourhan 1992, 370–372).

It is remarkable, however, that "the species most abundant in the art are not those most abundant in contemporary faunal assemblages. This is true both at the global level – with reindeer and red deer dominating animal bone remains, whereas bison and horses appear most frequently in the art –and at the local level." (Russell 2012, 14.) The artistic representations are therefore not to be connected with the regular subsistence hunt, but with special occasions, which already come close to hunting for sport. It is therefore only natural that the aristocrats of early Greece who visited Olympia for the sake of hunting for sport were eager to depict the animals in the way, that their prehistoric predecessors had done.

Bibliography

Andrews, T. K. 1994. *Bronzecasting at Geometric period Olympia and Early Greek Metal Sources,* PhD Dissertation Brandeis University.

Barringer, J, 2001. *The Hunt in Ancient Greece*, Baltimore: Johns Hopkins.

Baumbach, J. D. 2004. *The significance of votive offerings in selected Hera sanctuaries in the Peloponnese, Ionia and Western Greece* (BAR 1249). Oxford: BAR Publishing.

Benecke, N. 2006a. Die Tierreste. In: H. Kyrieleis, ed., *Anfänge und Frühzeit des Heiligtums von Olympia* (OlForsch 31) Berlin: De Gruyter, 247–248.

Benecke, N. 2006b. Animal Sacrifice at Late Archaic Artemision of Olympia. The Archaeological evidence. In: U. Tecchiati – B. Sala, ed., *Archaeozoological Studies in Honour of Alfredo Riedel*, Bolzano: Beni Archeologici, 153–160.

Bevan, E. 1986. *Representations of Animals in Sanctuaries of Artemis and other Olympian Deities* (BAR Int. 315) Oxford.

Buchholz, H-G. et al. 1973. Jagd und Fischfang (Arch. Hom II J) Göttingen:Vandenhoeck & Ruprecht.

Cherry, J. F. 1988. Pastoralism and the Role of Animals in the Pre- and Protohistoric Economies of the Aegean. In: Whittaker 1988, 177–195.

Coldstream, N. 2003. *Geometric Greece 900–700 B.C.,* London– New York: Routledge.

Duncan, P. 1992. *Horses and grasses; the nutritional ecology of equids and their impact on the Camargue*, New York: Springer.

Eder, B. 2006. The World of Telemachus: Western Greece 1200–700 BC. In S. Deger-Jalkotzy – I. S. Lemos, ed., *Ancient Greece. From the Mycenean Palaces to the Age of Homer*, Edinburgh: Edinburgh University Press, 549–580.

Forstenpointer, G. 2003. Promethean legacy: investigations into the ritual procedure of 'Olympian' sacrifice, in: Kotjabopoulou 2003, 203–213.

Furtwängler, A. 1890. *Die Bronzen und die übrigen kleineren Funde von Olympia*, Berlin: Asher.

Guggisberg, M. A. 1996. *Frühgriechische Tierkeramik : zur Entwicklung und Bedeutung der Tiergefäße und der hohlen Tierfiguren in der späten Bronze- und frühen Eisenzeit (ca. 1600–700 v. Chr.)*, Mainz: Zabern.

Guggisberg, M. A. 2005. Der Krieger als Jäger: Zur Bedeutung der Jagd in den 'Dark Ages', in: A. Alexandridis et al., ed., *Mensch und Tier in der Antike*, Wiesbaden: Reichert, 2008, 329–352.

Hamilakis, Y. 2003. The sacred geography of hunting: wild animals, social power and gender in early farming societies, in: Kotjabopoulou 2003, 239–247.

Hodkinson, S. 1988. Animal husbandry in the Greek polis, in: Whittaker 1988, 35–74.

Hägg, R. 1998. Osteology and Greek sacrificial practice, in: R. Hägg, ed., *Ancient Greek cult practice from the Archaeological Evidence*, Stockholm: P. Aströms, 49–56.

Herrmann, H-V. 1962. Zur ältesten Geschichte Olympias, *Athenische Mitteilungen* 77, 3–34.

Herrmann, H-V. 1964. Werkstätten geometrischer Bronzeplastik, *Jahrbuch des Deutschen Archäologischen Instituts* 79, 17–71.

Herrmann, H-V. 1972. *Olympia. Heiligtum und Wettkampfstätte*, München: Hirmer.

Herrmann, H-V. 1980. Pelops in Olympia, in: *Stele. Tomos eis mnemen N. Kontoleontos*, Athens, 59–74.

Heilmeyer, W-D. 1972. *Frühe Olympische Tonfiguren* (OlForschVII) Berlin: De Gruyter.

Heilmeyer, W-D. 1979. *Frühe Olympische Bronzefiguren. Die Tiervotive* (Olympische Forschungen 12). Berlin: De Gruyter.

Holmberg, U. 1927. *Finno-Ugric, Siberian Mythology*, Boston: Jones.

Howe, T. 2008. *Pastoral politics. animals, agriculture and society in ancient Greece.* Claremont: Regina Books.

Hughes, Donald J. 2014. *Environmental Problems of the Greeks and Romans. Ecology in the Ancient Mediterranean*, Baltimore: John Hopkins

Ivanov, S. W. 1959. Religiöse Vorwürfe in der Kunst der Völker Nordasiens vor der Revolution. In: *Opuscula Ethnologica Memoriae Ludovici Biró Sacra*. Budapest: Akadémiai, 113–136.

Karjalainen, K. F. 1927. *Die Religion der Jugravölker III*, Helsinki: Suomalainen Tiedeakatemia.

Keller, O. 1887. *Tiere des klassischen Altertums*, Innsbruck: Wagner (Nachdruck: Hildesheim: Olms, 2001).

Keller, O. 1909. *Antike Tierwelt I–II*, Leipzig: Engelmann.

Kotjabopoulou, E. (ed.), 2003. *Zooarchaeology in Greece. Recent advances* (British School at Athens studies No. 9) London.

Lane Fox, R. 1996. Ancient hunting: from Homer to Polybios. In: G. Shipley – J. Salmon, ed., *Human*

Landgon, S. 1982. Rev. of Schmaltz 1980, *American Journal of Archaeology* 86, 596–597.

Langdon, S. 2008. *Art and identity in dark age Greece, 1100–700 B.C.E.*, Cambridge: UP.

Lebessi, A. 1985 Το ιερό του Ερμή και της Αφροδίτης στη Σύμη Βιάννου, 1, 1. Χάλκινα κρητικά τορεύματα. (Βιβλιοθήκη της εν Αθήναις Αρχαιολογικής Εταιρείας, 102) Athen.

Lengerken, H. von 1955. *Ur, Hausrind und Mensch*, Berlin: Deutscher Bauernverlag.

Leroi-Gourhan, A. 1992. *L'art pariétal. Language de la préhistoire*. Grenoble: J. Millon.

Lorenz, G. 2000. *Tiere im Leben der alten Kulturen*, Wien: Innsbruck Univ. Press.

Maass, M. 1978. *Die geometrischen Dreifüsse von Olympia (*OlForsch 10), Berlin: De Gruyter.

Mallwitz, A. 1988. Cult and Competition Locations at Olympia. In: W. J. Raschke, ed., *The Archaeology of the Olympics*, Madison: Univ. of Wisconsin Press, 79–109.

Mallwitz, A. 1999. (bearb. von K. Herrmann), Ergebnisse und Folgerungen, in: XI. Bericht über die Ausgrabungen in Olympia, Berlin: De Gruyter.

McInerney, J. 2010. *The Cattle of the Sun. Cows and Culture in the World of the Ancient Greeks,* Princeton: University Press.

Meuli, K. 1946. Griechische Opferbräuche, in: Phyllobolia für Peter von der Mühll, Basel: Schwabe, 211–283=Gesammelte Werke, Hrsg. von Th. Gelzer, Bd. II, Basel: Schwabe 1975.

Moretti, L. 1957. Olimpionikai. I vincitori negli antichi agoni olimpici, MemLinc Ser VIII, Vol. VIII Fasc. 2.

Morgan, C. 1990. *Athletes and Oracles*. Cambridge: UP.

Morgan, C. 1993. The origins of pan-Hellenism. In: N. Marinatos – R. Hägg, ed., *Greek sanctuaries. New approaches*, London: Routledge, 18–44.

Niniou-Kindeli V. 2003. The Bull and the Sanctuary of Poseidon at Chania, Crete, in: Athanassopoulou, S. et al., ed., *Bull in the Mediterranean World. Myths and Cults*, Exhibition Catalogue Athens – Barcelona, 132–137.

Nobis, G. 1996. Der Auerochse oder Ur (Bos primigenius) auf Kreta. In: D. S. Reese, ed., *Pleistocene and Holocene Fauna of Crete and its Forst Settlers* (Monographs in World Archaeology No. 28), 263–272.

Patay-Horváth, A. 2015. *The Origins of the Olympic Games*, Budapest: Archaeolingua.

Paulson, I. 1961. *Schutzgeister und Gottheiten des Wildes (der Jagdtiere und Fische) in Nordeurasien*. Stockholm: Almqvist & Wiksell.

Persson, P. O. 1993. Ure in Chania auf Kreta, Tier und Museum 3(4): 121–123. (non vidi)

Pilali-Papasteriou, A. 1985. *Die bronzenen Tierfiguren aus Kreta* (PBF I,3), München

Robertson, N. 2010, *Religion and Reconciliation in Greek Cities: The Sacred Laws of Selinus and Cyrene*. Oxford: UP.

Rolley, C. 1994. *La sculpture grecque I*, Paris: Picard.

Schmaltz, B. 1980. *Metallfiguren aus dem Kabirenheiligtum bei Theben, Die Statuetten aus Bronze und Blei*, Berlin: De Gruyter.

Russell, N. 2012. *Social Zooarchaeology. Humans and Animals in Prehistory*, Cambridge: UP.

Sallares, R. 1991. *The Ecology of the Ancient Greek World*. Ithaca: Cornell University Press

Schmaltz, B. 1983. Mensch und Tier in der griechischen Antike. In: H. Müller-Karpe, ed., *Zur frühen Mensch-Tier-Symbiose*, München: Beck, 99–114.

Schmidt, K. 2006. *Sie bauten die ersten Tempel. Das rätselhafte Heiligtum der Steinzeitjäger*, München: Beck.

Schürmann, W. 1996. *Das Heiligtum des Hermes und der Aphrodite in Syme Viannou. II. Die Tierstatuetten aus Metall*, Athen: Archaeological Society.

Shapland, A. 2010. Wild nature? Human-Animal Relations on Neopalatial Crete, *Cambridge Archaeological Journal* 20, 109–127.

Siewert, P. 1991. Staatliche Weihungen von Kesseln und anderen Bronzegeräten in Olympia, *Athenische Mitteilungen* 106, 81–84.

Sinn, U. 1981. Das Heiligtum der Artemis Limnatis bei Kombothekra, *Athenische Mitteilungen* 96, 25–71.

Snodgrass, A. M. 1987 *An archaeology of Greece. The present state and future scope of a discipline*. Berkeley: Univ. of California Press.

Spence, I. G. 1993. *The cavalry of classical Greece,* Oxford: UP.

Taita, J. 2009. Fattori geografici e sviluppi cultuali. Il caso di Olimpia. In: E. Olshausen – V. Sauer, ed., *Die Landschaft und die Religion*, Stuttgart: Steiner, 375–388.

Ulf, Chr. 1997. Überlegungen zur Funktion überregionaler Feste im archaischen Griechenland. In: W. Eder – K.-J. Hölkeskamp, ed., *Volk und Verfassung im vorhellenistischen Griechenland*, Stuttgart: Steiner, 37–61.

Van Vuure, C. 2005. *Retracing the aurochs: history, morphology and ecology of an extinct wild ox*, Sofia: Pensoft.

Vigne, J.D. 1999. The large 'true' Mediterranean islands as a model for the Holocene human impact on the

European vertebrate fauna? Recent data and new reflections, in: N. Benecke, ed., *The Holocene History of the European Vertebrate Faunas: Modern Aspects of Research*, Rahden: Leidorf, 295–322.

von Reden, S. 2010. *Money in Classical Antiquity*, Cambridge, UP.

Zimmermann, J-L. 1989. *Les chevaux de bronze dans l'art géometrique grec*, Mainz: Zabern.

Whittaker C. R., ed., 1988. *Pastoral Economies in Classical Antiquity*, Cambridge Philological Society, Suppl. Vol. No. 14.

30

Bronzegefäße von Olympia: Ritual und Repräsentation, Statusänderung und Deponierung

Beat Schweizer

SFB 1070 RessourcenKulturen/Institut für Klassische Archäologie

Eberhard Karls Universität Tübingen

b.schweizer@uni-tuebingen.de

Abstract: Sanctuaries of ancient times are both, places of cult and sacrifice as well as spaces of social processes, for example feasting, political negotiations or construction of collective identities. So one perspective of contextualizing bronze vessels is directed at ritual and representation.

What is documented through excavations in sanctuaries like Olympia, has a lot more to do with uses or deposition of things, after being regarded as more or less monumental offerings or dedications, after being part of ritual implements. It is tried to focus on bronze vessels from Olympia with regard to changes of status as sacred things.

Keywords: Bronze Vessels; Ritual; Representation; Deposition; Change of Status

Ernst Curtius, der die Konzeption und Durchführung der archäologischen Ausgrabungen in Olympia von 1875 bis 1881 entscheidend prägte (Schweizer 2011), hatte als Ziel dieser später als Alte Grabung benannten Untersuchungen herausgestellt, „daß hellenische Bauanlagen von hervorragender Bedeutung als ein Ganzes zur Anschauung kommen, weil dadurch auch einzelne Denkmäler erst zum vollen Verständnis gelangen können" (Curtius 1876, 9). In gewissem Sinn wurde dabei schon damals das moderne Verständnis von griechischen Heiligtümern voraus gesetzt, nachdem sich auch Olympia sowohl als Ort von Kulten und Opferhandlungen verstehen lässt, zugleich aber auch als sozialer Raum der Feste, der politischen Aushandlungen und Machtkämpfe sowie der Konstruktionen kollektiver Identitäten (vgl. Hölscher 2002; Kyrieleis 2016), also als Kontext von Ritualen und zugleich von sozialen Repräsentationen. Jedoch ist der seinerzeit, in der Zeit der großen Grabungen des 19. Jahrhunderts erhoffte und propagierte, aber auch heute noch implizit als Forschungsziel angesehene direkte Einblick in die Lebenswelt antiker Gesellschaften, in das Alltagsleben und die Festtage der Städte und Heiligtümer, im Idealfall im Sinne der „Pompeii premise" (vgl. Allison 1992), von der Archäologie gar nicht zu erfüllen (Schweizer 2014). Dies zeigt sich deutlich schon daran, dass das Bild Olympias heute einerseits durch architektonische Überreste vom 6. Jh. v. Chr. bis in die spätrömische Zeit bestimmt ist (dazu nach wie vor Mallwitz 1972; vgl. Herrmann 2002). Andererseits stammt die Masse etwa der Kleinfunde, bestehend vor allem aus Bronzefunden, aber aus dem Zeitraum des 10.–5. Jahrhunderts v. Chr. (allgemein in der Zusammenschau: Herrmann 1972; Kyrieleis 2011).

Die große Zahl der Bronzefunde schon der Alten Grabung hängt zum einen an der Lage des Heiligtums im Alpheiostal mit seinen sandigen Böden. Vor der Grabung waren lediglich einige in europäische Sammlungen gelangte Schutzwaffen bekannter geworden, vor allem der erste der drei Helme mit den auf Hieron verweisenden Inschriften (Frielinghaus 2011, 448, Nr. L 2 neben 402, Nr. D 529. 448, Nr. L 1; Graells i Fabregat 2018, 373–376, Abb. 2). Dagegen endet das Bronzeinventar der sechs Kampagnen der Alten Grabung mit der Nummer 14471, auch wenn darunter auch funktionale Elemente wie Nägel und auch kleinste Fragmente fallen. Die Rolle Adolf Furtwänglers bei der Erfassung und Ordnung des Fundstoffs kann kaum hoch genug eingeschätzt werden (Furtwängler 1880; 1890). Dies ist für die Forschung zu den Bronzewaffen nochmals deutlich heraus gestellt worden (Graells i Fabregat 2018, 382 f.), gilt aber für alle Arten von Bronzefunden, soweit sie in Olympia vertreten sind, auch für die Gefäße. Dies passt auch zu dem von Curtius formulierten Anspruch:

„Es muss die Alterthumswissenschaft aber, wenn sie lebendig fortschreiten soll, ebenso wie die experimentelle Naturforschung, im Stande sein, die Quellen der Erkenntnis selbstthätig zu vermehren; sie muss sich von zufälligen Entdeckungen, welche, so glücklich sie sein mögen, immer nur ungenügende Ausbeute gewähren, unabhängig zu machen versuchen" (Curtius 1876, 9).

Die ‚Ausbeute' der Grabungen, der Alten wie der Neuen im 20. Jahrhundert, basierte jedoch nicht nur auf den topographischen Bedingungen, sondern auch auf der besonderen Befundsituation Olympias (Kyrieleis 2011,

61 f.). So wurde das Gelände der Altis zwischen dem 7. und 5. Jahrhundert v. Chr. wiederholt aufgefüllt oder erhöht. Schon die Ausgräber der Alten Grabung sind unterhalb der Bauten auf zwei sogenannte schwarze Schichten (Herrmann 1972, 55 f.; Mallwitz 1972, 85–87 mit 82 f., Abb. 6.2) gestoßen, die aufgrund der darin gefundenen Knochen und Holzkohlereste als umgelagerte Überreste der Opferhandlungen anzusehen sind (Kyrieleis 2002, 216 f.; 2006, 35–47; Bocher 2013, 356, Abb. 1; 2015, 51, Abb. 4.1). Während der Grabungen des 20. Jahrhunderts wurde darüber hinaus zwischen Echohalle, Hestia-Heiligtum und Mosaiksaal eine offensichtlich im 7. Jh. v. Chr. aufgefüllte Senke untersucht (Schilbach 1999a, 33–42). Auch bei den seit dem 6. Jh. v. Chr. belegten Anschüttungen der Bauphasen des aus Erdwällen bestehenden Stadions (Schilbach 1992) sind immer wieder Bronzegegenstände unter die Erde gekommen, die teilweise, z. B. Schilde, auf den ehemaligen Walloberflächen gesichert werden konnten. Vor allem im Südostgebiet und im Bereich des nördlichen Stadionwalls ist zudem eine große Zahl (171 bzw. 47) unverschalter, daher kurzfristig genutzter Brunnenschächte aufgedeckt worden (Mallwitz und Herrmann 1999, 188; Gauer 2012). Die zahlreichen Bronzeobjekte, auch die Bronzegefäße aus den Verfüllungen dieser Brunnen sind zum Teil vollständig oder nahezu vollständig erhalten. Vor allem mit diesen Befunden weicht Olympia von dem Muster ab, das schon 1836 L. Ross (1855, 111) und später S. Karusu (1979, 77) für die Funde von der Akropolis von Athen hervorgehoben hatten. Demnach gilt für Bronzegefäße aus den Schichten der Kultorte, dass in der Regel nur die gegossenen Zierelemente, Füße oder Henkel erhalten oder geborgen worden sind (für Olympia: Gauer 1991, 2; Kyrieleis 2011, 67 f.). Gefäßkörper aus Bronzeblech sind meist bis zur Unkenntlichkeit zerdrückt oder korrodiert aufgefunden worden und können selbst mit modernen Restaurierungsmethoden nicht immer gesichert oder erhalten werden.

Vor allem in Bezug auf monumentale geometrische Dreifüße und Kessel orientalisierender Zeit ist für Olympia davon ausgegangen worden, dass die Gefäße vor der Niederlegung in Schichten des Heiligtums entweder beschädigt oder bewusst zerstört worden waren, da anpassende Teile derselben Objekte in teilweise weit entfernt liegenden Befunden des sakralen Raums wieder aufgefunden worden sind. In den 1970er Jahren wurde dazu einerseits geschrieben, dass so „für altmodisch oder auch nur unansehnlich gehaltene Gegenstände" „unabsichtlich bewahrt" worden seien (Mallwitz 1972, 12), oder andererseits, dass die Bautätigkeit der klassischen Zeit „erwünschte Gelegenheit" bot, im Sinne von „Entrümpelungsaktionen" „Überflüssiges und Beschädigtes massenweise loszuwerden" (Herrmann 1972, 107. 88). Helmut Kyrieleis hat später allerdings Gefäßteile der zerstückelten frühen großen Weihgeschenke als *pars pro toto* interpretiert, die die Weihungen repräsentieren und daher erhalten werden sollten (Kyrieleis 2006, 95–98; 2011, 62; Bocher 2013, 357 f.). Insgesamt sind jedoch in den ‚schwarzen Schichten', in den Geländeauffüllungen, in den Wallschüttungen des Stadions und in den Brunnen Bronzegegenstände entsorgt, vergraben, der Sichtbarkeit entzogen worden.

Der erste Versuch, die Bronzefunde gattungsweise zahlenmäßig zu erfassen und zu interpretieren, geht auf Thomas Völling (2002, 91–100; vgl. Schweizer 2005, 363) zurück und ist von Heide Frielinghaus (2013) vertieft und in Bezug auf Waffenfunde auch von Raimon Graells i Fabregat (2016, 149) weiterverfolgt worden. Demnach sind etwa aus geometrischer Zeit über 4000 Tierfiguren, rund 50 Menschenfiguren und 90 Wagenvotive überliefert, aus archaischer Zeit ca. 3000 Waffen – rund 300 Beinschienen, 200 Schilde, 850 Helme, 450 Pfeilspitzen, 900 Lanzenspitzen und 500 Lanzenschuhe. 1300 Schmuckgegenstände bilden die einzige Fundgruppe, von der ein größerer Bestand dann auch aus römischer Zeit überliefert ist. Frielinghaus stellt den 3000–4000 Waffenfunden vor allem archaischer Zeit lediglich 130 Objekte klassischer bis römischer Zeitstellung gegenüber, die mit athletischer Ausrüstung verbunden werden können (Frielinghaus 2013, 364, Abb. 1). Untersuchungen zu Votivspektren einzelner Heiligtümer wie Olympia zielen in der Regel auf je nach Gattung unterschiedliche lokale Weihepraktiken (Olympia: Bocher 2013; Frielinghaus 2013). Im Fokus stehen aber auch allgemeiner das Bewahren des Materials (für Edelmetalle Linders 1989–1990), bewusste Zerstörungen für das Recyceln (Lindenlauf 2006; Lindström – Pilz et al. 2013, 269) und im Sinne ritueller Verformungen, Durchlochungen oder Faltungen (Frielinghaus 2006; 2011, 185–205; Graells i Fabregat 2018; Bocher 2016, 274–276). Oft steht auch der Versuch im Vordergrund, ursprüngliche Aufstellungskontexte zu rekonstruieren. So wurde für Olympia ausgehend von der Fundlage und mit Bezug auf Pfostenlöcher auf eine Aufstellung von Tropaia auf den Wällen des Stadions geschlossen (Schilbach 1992, 33), während andererseits die Aufstellung zahlreicher Panhoplien skeptisch gesehen und Einzelweihungen bzw. gattungsweise Weihungen in den Vordergrund gestellt wurden (Frielinghaus 2011, 167–170). In ereignisgeschichtlicher Perspektive wurde die Verbreitung unterschiedlicher Pfeilspitzenvarianten mit dem Kampf zwischen Eleern und Arkadern im Heiligtum im Jahr 364 v. Chr. (Baitinger 2001, 19 f. zu 18, Abb. 1) oder aber mit einem Tropaion der Perserkriege (Baitinger 2001, 22 f. zu 24, Abb. 2) verknüpft.

Manchmal werden Votivspektren auch in Bezug auf generelle Rekonstruktionen ritueller Praktiken (Ephesos: Klebinder-Gauß 2015) oder sakraler Regeln der Auswahl, Aufstellung und Bewahrung und späterer menschlicher Eingriffe als Überlieferungsfilter (Philia: Kilian-Dirlmeier 2002, 192 f.) gedeutet. Funde werden dann auch in Hinblick auf soziale Kontexte der Repräsentation (Kyrieleis 2016), der Identität und Ethnizität der Weihenden (Lindström – Pilz et al. 2013, 271–273), eventuell auch der Identität der Kultempfänger ausgewertet. Wenn auch die Rekonstruktion ritueller Praktiken, sozialer Repräsentationen, eventuell sogar historischer Ereignisse ein wichtiges Ziel der archäologischen Untersuchungen ist und bleibt, so hat, was durch Grabungen zuallererst dokumentiert werden kann, oft mehr zu tun mit der Niederlegung und der Behandlung von Dingen, nachdem diese ihren Status als mehr oder weniger monumentale Weihegaben oder Bestandteil ritueller Gerätschaften verloren haben. Dies ist jedoch nicht weniger von Interesse, weil Dinge und Monumente aller Kategorien in Heiligtümern sakral sind, und zwar in dem Sinne, dass diese dem täglichen oder gewöhnlichen Leben entzogen sind.

Im Weiteren sollen diese Perspektiven exemplarisch anhand von wenigen Gefäßen oder Gefäßteilen Olympias behandelt werden, denn die Anzahl der gefundenen Objekte liegt in der Größenordnung von 3000 Objekten (vgl. Frielinghaus 2013, 364f.). Sicher anzusprechen sind etwa 200–300 geometrische Dreifüße, 250–300 Greifenkessel, 100 Stabdreifüße, 600 Dinoi, Kessel oder Kratere, 100 Becken und Ringdreifußständer, 80 Hydrien, 25 Teller, 200 Eimer, 500 Schalen, Schüsseln, Kylikes, 250 Kannen, Kannenhenkel, 130 Becher, Kantharoi, Skyphoi, 30 Siebe, 50 Kellen und Löffel, 30 Salbölgefäße und weitere vereinzelte Stücke (nach der Literatur bei Schweizer 2005, 363 Anm. 42; Schweizer in Druckvorbeitung).

In genereller Sicht sind diese Gefäße „in weitestem Sinn mit der Zubereitung von Speisen und bzw. oder dem Symposion" verbunden worden (Frielinghaus 2013, 364). Dies beruht auf der zuletzt für Funde der Heiligtümer zunehmend vertretenen Differenzierung zwischen Weihgeschenk im engeren Sinn, genutztem Kultgerät oder der Infrastruktur zuzurechnenden Gegenständen (etwa Frielinghaus 2013, 363; Klebinder-Gauß 2015, 109). Jedoch dürften Gefäßgattungen oder Gefäßtypen nicht nur dem Konsum von Nahrung und Wein zuzuordnen sein, sondern auch der Libation (Phialen) und Reinigungsriten (Becken und Kannen), der Athletik (Aryballoi, Alabastra) und nicht zuletzt der Repräsentation. Einige der Gefäße wie die Dreifußkessel und die Greifenkessel sind paradigmatische Zeugnisse der Repräsentation von sozialem Status Einzelner, wenn nicht der Repräsentation ganzer Gemeinschaften. In späterer Zeit sind Weihgeschenke vom Format der Greifenkessel Weihungen von Poleis (Mattusch 1990). Nach Helmut Kyrieleis hatte mit „den Prunkvotiven […] ein überzeitlicher, auf Nachahmung und individuellem Prestigestreben beruhender 'monumentaler Diskurs' in den Heiligtümern eingesetzt" (Kyrieleis 1996, 106). Eine Passage bei Herodot (4.152) über eine Weihung des Kolaios im Heraion von Samos zeigt, dass Gefäße wie diese zum Wertvollsten gehörte, was gestiftet werden konnte:

„als daher das Schiff wieder nach Samos heimkehrte, brachte es einen reichen Erlös seiner Waren mit nach Hause wie nie ein griechisches Schiff, von dem wir genaue Nachricht haben, ausgenommen allerdings Sostratos, der Sohn des Laodamas aus Aigina. Mit ihm kann kein anderer den Vergleich aufnehmen. Die Samier nahmen den Zehnten von ihrem Gewinn, sechs Talente, und schufen ein ehernes Gefäß nach der Art eines argolischen Mischkruges; ringsherum springen Greifenköpfe an ihm hervor. Sie weihten dieses Gefäß ins Heraion." (Übersetzung J. Feix).

Nach Robin Osborne waren Greifen "part of the grand tripod cauldrons that seem to have been a standard way of putting great wealth on display" (Osborne 1998, 45). Dies bezieht sich jedoch nur auf ökonomische Aspekte der Erzählung. Kolaios und seine Mannschaft weihten ein Bronzegefäß, an das sich seine Geschichte heftete (Osborne 1996, 12), und Kolaios wurde so Bestandteil des kollektiven Gedächtnisses von Samos und später – durch Herodot – Teil der griechischen Geschichte als einer der Seefahrer mit dem größten Profit und so auch zu einer Figur, die archaischen Handel repräsentieren kann.

Ein anderes oder zumindest vielfältigeres Bild ergibt sich demgegenüber aus der Befundlage vergleichbarer Gefäße oder ihrer Fragmente in den Brunnen im Osten der Altis von Olympia. Unter der Prämisse, dass die Datierung der aufgelassenen Brunnen nicht nur die Zeit der Deponierung, sondern auch der Fragmentierung der darin deponierten Gefäße bezeugen, ergibt sich, dass geometrische Dreifüße wie auch Greifenkessel der orientalisierenden Zeit – oder zumindest Teile derselben – teilweise erst sehr lange, auch nach hunderten von Jahren nach der Produktion letztendlich entsorgt wurden, teilweise aber auch schon nach kurzer Zeit nicht mehr sichtbar waren (Schweizer 2005, 367, Abb. 6). Ein ähnliches Bild der Zeitspannen zwischen Weihung oder Ausstellung und Niederlegung hat auch Frielinghaus anhand der Befundlage für Helme und Beinschienen rekonstruiert (2011, 170–184. 536–545, Tabelle 3).

Selbstverständlich ist nicht genau zu klären, was mit Weihegaben passiert ist, die oder deren Teile lang nach der Produktion und möglicherweise nach einer langen Zeit der Ausstellung in Auffüllungen oder Brunnen deponiert wurden. Gute Hinweise auf Arten der Behandlung sakraler Gegenstände im Heiligtum von Olympia geben jedoch einige große, zum Teil ursprünglich figürlich durch Greifen- und Löwenprotomen sowie Sirenenattaschen verzierte Kessel. Selbstverständlich waren diese im 7. Jh. v. Chr. Repräsentationsobjekte wie der Krater des Kolaios. Gefunden wurden sie jedoch in Kontexten des 5. Jhs. v. Chr., und zwar installiert in Werkstätten, wohl um Wasser bereit zu stellen. Von besonderem Interesse ist in diesem Zusammenhang ein Kessel, der westlich der Altis in einer Anschüttungsschicht (der sog. Formenschicht bzw. Schicht E) vom Ende des 5. oder Anfang des 4. Jhs. v. Chr. gefunden wurde, zusammen mit Werkstattabfällen, Werkzeugen und auch ausgeschnittenen Blechstücken weiterer Kessel. Denn von diesem Gefäß abgerissene Greifen- und Löwenprotomen konnten von Hans-Volkmar Herrmann im Fundmaterial identifiziert und zugewiesen werden (dazu zuerst Herrmann 1966, 11–17). Und eines der verlorenen Teile wurde in einem Kontext des 7. Jhs. v. Chr. gefunden (die Befundlage zusammenfassend: Schweizer 2005, 368). Dies bedeutet, dass ein am Ende des 8., Anfang des 7.Jhs. v. Chr. hergestellter Kessel kurz nach der Aufstellung im

7. Jh. v. Chr. abgeräumt wurde. Abgerissene Protomen kamen in dieser Zeit in Aufschüttungen der Altis. Der Kessel mit den Protomenansätzen und Sirenenattaschen muss aber auf irgendeine Art aufbewahrt worden sein, um im späten 5. Jh. v. Chr. noch in einer Werkstatt genutzt zu werden. Der importierte oder in Olympia von auswärtigen Handwerkern hergestellte monumentale Kessel hatte seine Bedeutung als Weihgeschenk also schon nach relativ kurzer Zeit verloren. Man hatte offenbar keine Scheu, die oft als apotropäisch bezeichneten Greifen- und Löwenbilder abzureißen und den noch intakten Kessel einer anderen Nutzung zuzuführen.

Ein weiteres Beispiel stellt ein eventuell kyprischer Kessel des 7. Jhs. v. Chr. dar (Mallwitz – Herrmann 1999, 231, Taf. 51), der wohl zur Wasserversorgung bei Bauarbeiten der Mitte des 5. Jhs. v. Chr. eingesetzt worden war (Schilbach 1999b, 151). Auch bei diesem war der figürliche Schmuck teils abgerissen worden. Und in der Bronzegießerei in der Phidiaswerkstatt wurde ein intakter, aber unverzierter früher Kessel (Mallwitz – Schiering 1964, 43 Abb. 19. 44, Abb. 20; Gauer 1991, 179, Nr. Le 11) im mittleren 5. Jh. v. Chr. in neuer Funktion verwendet:

„Die Nutzung eines ursprünglich wertvollen Weihegeschenkes als Arbeitsgerät bereitet unserem Verständnis keine Probleme und erklärt sich aus der Menge solcher Votive und ihrer leichten Verfügbarkeit in einem Heiligtum wie Olympia" (Zimmer 1990, 39.41).

Dasselbe könnte auch für den großen Kessel gelten, von dem E. Dodwell berichtet hatte:

„A short time before my arrival a bronze lebes of large dimensions was excavated near the ruins of the temple: it was quite entire, and I had an offer of it for a trifling sum; but, as it was perfectly plain and unornamented, though extremely thin and finely worked, I declined the purchase, on account of the inconvenience of its size and form, which was that of a large cauldron" (Dodwell 1819 II, 330).

Alle diese Beispiele stehen für eine Veränderung des Status des Objekts, vom repräsentativen Weihgeschenk zum Bestandteil der Infrastruktur. Es handelt sich dabei aber nur in gewissem Sinne um eine ‚Profanierung' sakraler Objekte, denn diese Objekte sind nicht aus dem sakralen Raum entfernt worden.

Eine andere Art der Repräsentation bezeugen Inschriften, mittels derer sich eine Gruppe von unterschiedlichen Gefäßen – drei Kessel, eine Oinochoe sowie ein Infundibulum etruskischer Produktion (zum Typ die Liste bei Naso 2016, 161–169, die Verbreitung 159, Abb. 13.7) – als ein gemeinsam geweihtes Set, als ‚Staatsweihung' der Eleer rekonstruieren lässt (Siewert 1991, 81–84; Siewert – Taeuber, 2013, 218–222, Nr. 202–206). Die Inschrift lautet: „Dem olympischen Zeus die Eleier": ΤΟΙ Ζ[Ι] ΟΛΥΝΠΙΟΙ ΤΟΙ ϜΑΛΕΙΟΙ. Einer der Kessel trägt jedoch eine weitere Inschrift: „Zeus geweiht". ΙΑΡΑ ΔΙΟΣ, im Sinne von ‚dem Zeus gehörend'. Diese später angebrachte Inschrift kennzeichnete diesen als sakralen Besitz, wodurch dessen Status als Objekt staatlicher Repräsentation aufgehoben wurde. Allein der Zustand dieser Gefäße – deren Form ist bewahrt bis auf das Infundibulum – bezeugt, dass diese weder ausgesondert noch entsorgt wurden. Auch diese müssen in einer uns unbekannten Form konserviert worden sein.

In Tabelle 30.1 sind unterschiedliche Handlungen mit Dingen zusammengefasst, die zu primären bzw. sekundären, wenn nicht tertiären archäologischen Kontexten der in Heiligtümer geweihten oder dort benutzten Dinge führten (frühere Fassung Schweizer 2005, 366, Abb. 5, eine andere Differenzierung zwischen

Tabelle 30.1. Dinge im Heiligtum: Dinge, Praktiken, archäologische Kontexte

Rituelle Praktiken		Primärer Kontext		Sekundärer / Tertiärer Kontext
Weihegaben	Konserviert	Monumente	-----	
	Liegen Gelassen	Altarkontexte	Umgelagert	„Schwarze Schichten"
Rituelle Gegenstände	Abgeräumt	-----	Recycled	Werkstätten
			Entsorgt	Brunnen, *Bothroi*, Auffüll-Schichten
Gegenstände des Heiligtumsbetriebs	Kontinuierlich benützt	-----	Aufbewahrt	*[Thesauroi]*
	Verloren	-----	Umgelagert	Schichten

primären und sekundären Kontexten bei Frielinghaus 2011, 138 f.). Geweihte Gefäße konnten konserviert werden, wenn diese wie der Krater des Kolaios als Monumente stehen blieben. Weihegaben konnten liegen gelassen werden, wie vereinzelte Altarkontexte, etwa der Artemis-Altar in Olympia (Bocher 2015, 56–58), mit den Hinterlassenschaften noch *in situ* bezeugen. Dies sind primäre Kontexte. Wurden Schichten aber bewegt, wurden Dinge nicht intentionell umgelagert. Dies führte zu den sogenannten Schwarzen Schichten Olympias, aber auch anderer Heiligtümer. Häufig wurden Bereiche abgeräumt, Weihungen konnten teils oder ganz bewahrt, in Werkstätten recycled oder wieder verwendet („reuse" nach Lindenlauf 2006, 30; für Waffen Frielinghaus 2011, 206–209) werden oder sie wurden intentionell entsorgt in den Brunnen, den *Bothroi*, den Auffüllschichten und Geländeerhöhungen. Gegenstände konnten auch einfach verloren gehen und so Bestandteil der Fundschichten werden. Archäologisch nicht sichtbar sind natürlich zum einen die Objekte, die eingeschmolzen wurden und deren Material für neue Weihegaben oder rituelle Gefäße (Linders 1989–1990) eingesetzt worden ist. Archäologisch nicht sichtbar sind aber auch jene ebenfalls nur aus Schriftquellen oder Inventaren der Heiligtümer bekannten Objekte, die kontinuierlich benützt oder thesauriert worden sind (Lindström – Pilz et al. 2013, 268) wie etwa der von Kroisos nach Delphi geweihte Silberkrater des Theodoros aus Samos, der – so Herodot (1.51) – nach dem Brand des Tempels neu platziert und rituell benutzt wurde. Bronzefunde und insbesondere Bronzegefäße stammen dagegen – bis auf seltene Ausnahmen – aus den sekundären und tertiären Fundkontexten. Das heißt, was auch immer deren Status ursprünglich war, am Ende wurden sie nicht bewahrt, um gesehen werden, auch nicht um recycled oder eingeschmolzen zu werden. Das Material wurde aus dem Nutzungskreislauf genommen. Da es aber nicht aus dem Heiligtum entfernt wurde, begründete es vielleicht Sakralität des Geländes.

Auf der Ebene der ursprünglich mit Gefäßen verbundenen rituellen Praktiken können unterschiedliche Kategorien wie Repräsentation des sozialen Status von Einzelnen oder Gemeinschaften, Konsum von Wein und Nahrung, mit dem Kult verbundene Riten wie Libation und Reinigung unterschieden werden. Die Salbölgefäße kommen unter den Gefäßen wahrscheinlich dem am nächsten, was üblicherweise als Gabe an die Götter im Sinne der Kommunikation und Interaktion zwischen einem Individuum und einem Gott gesehen wird. Für eine Phase nach der Weihung oder Nutzung im Heiligtum konnte jedoch an einigen Beispielen ein Statuswechsel der Dinge nachgewiesen werden. Einige der Kessel wechselten von der Kategorie der repräsentativen Weihegabe zur Kategorie ‚Infrastruktur', ein anderer in gewissem Sinne umgekehrt von der Staatsweihung der Eleer, von einem Set des Konsums von Wein und Nahrung zur Kategorie ‚Heiliger Besitz'. Dies hat Astrid Lindenlauf als „reutilisation" bezeichnet, seinerzeit jedoch als „translation of waste to a new social and cultural status" verstanden (Lindenlauf 2006, 30). Ihre Beispiele bezogen sich auf die Verwendung von Dreifußbeinen als Schriftträger, darunter auch ein gehämmertes Dreifußbein, aus dem nach einer ersten Umwidmung als Schreibmaterial in einer zweiten Phase des Recycling kleine Blechteile ausgeschnitten wurden (Lindenlauf 2006, 31). Lindenlaufs „material reprocessing" bezieht sich dagegen auf technische, auch Material verändernde Prozeduren, wie sie die Sphyreleta aus Olympia (Borell – Rittig 1998) bezeugen (vgl. Schweizer 2005, 369–372; Lindström – Pilz et al. 2013, 269). Stimmt die Hypothese Ursula Seidls (1999), dass das Ursprungsmaterial dieser Sphyreleta – auch – späthethitische Gefäße waren, handelt es sich um eine Statusänderung innerhalb des Heiligtums, die Objektbiographien wie die eines silbernen Kraters aus Sidon bei Homer (Ilias 23.740–49) grundlegend erweitert. Dieser war eine Gabe von Phoinikern an Thoas, wurde über Jason und Hypsipyle an Euneos vererbt, von diesem als Lösegeld an Patroklos gegeben und wurde von Achill als Preis im Wettlauf zum Ruhm des Patroklos ausgesetzt und von Odysseus gewonnen. Aber ab dem Moment der Weihung und der rituellen Nutzung in den Heiligtümern sind alle Gefäße in Kontexte neuer, auch wechselnder Bedeutungszuschreibungen eingebettet.

Danksagung

Der Beitrag entstand im Rahmen des von der DFG geförderten SFB 1070 RessourcenKulturen an der Eberhard Karls Universität Tübingen, geht jedoch zurück auf ein Forschungsstipendium des Deutschen Archäologischen Instituts. Diesem gilt so mein besonderer Dank genauso wie dem Archäologischen Nationalmuseum Athen, dem Archäologischen Museum Olympia und der Ephorie für Altertümer, Elis. Gerne bedanken möchte ich mich darüber hinaus bei der Organisatorin und den Teilnehmern der Session „Bronze objects in sacred contexts: their function and meaning in Archaic Greek culture" des Tübinger Kongresses: Chiara Tarditi, Giacomo Bardelli, Raimon Graells i Fabregat, Valeria Meirano und Azzurra Scarci.

Bibliographie

Allison, P., 1992. *Artefact Assemblages. Not 'the Pompeii Premise'*. In: E. Herring – R. Whitehouse – J. Wilkins, Hrsg., *Papers of the Fourth Conference of Italian Archaeology 3. New Developments in Italian Archaeology I*. London: Accordia Research Centre, 49–56.

Baitinger, H., 2001. *Die Angriffswaffen aus Olympia*. Olympische Forschungen 24. Berlin: de Gruyter.

Bocher, S., 2013. Aspekte früher Ritualpraxis anhand des geometrischen Votivspektrums im Heiligtum von Olympia. In: I. Gerlach – D. Raue, Hrsg., *Sanktuar und Ritual. Heilige Plätze im archäologischen Befund. Menschen – Kulturen – Traditionen 10*. ForschungsCluster 4, Heiligtümer: Gestalt und Ritual, Kontinuität und Veränderung. Rahden: VML Leidorf, 355–361.

Bocher, S., 2015. Ash, Cones, Votives. Analysing the Black Strata in Early Greek Sanctuaries: Two Examples from Olympia, the Schwarze Schicht and the Altar of Artemis. In: P. Pakkanen – S. Bocher,

Hrsg., *Cult Material. From Archaeological Deposits to Interpretation of Early Greek Religion*. Papers and Monographs of the Finnish Institute at Athens 21. Helsinki: Suomen Ateenan-Instituutin Säätiö, 49–64.

Bocher, S., 2016. Dinge zwischen Menschen und Göttern. Zu Deutungsansätzen für Dedikationspraktiken in frühen griechischen Heiligtümern. In: S. Hansen – D. Neumann – T. Vachta, Hrsg., *Raum, Gabe und Erinnerung. Weihgaben und Heiligtümer in prähistorischen und antiken Gesellschaften*. Berlin Studies of the Ancient World 38. Berlin: Edition Topoi, 265–279.

Borell, B. – Rittig, D., 1998. *Orientalische und griechische Bronzereliefs aus Olympia*. Der Fundkomplex aus Brunnen 17. Olympische Forschungen 26. Berlin: de Gruyter.

Curtius, E., 1876. I. [Einführung]. In: E. Curtius – F. Adler – G. Hirschfeld, Hrsg., *Die Ausgrabungen zu Olympia 1. Übersicht der Arbeiten und Funde vom Winter und Frühjahr 1875–1876*. Berlin: Wasmuth, 9–11.

Dodwell, E., 1819. *A Classical and Topographical Tour through Greece, During the Years 1801, 1805, and 1806: in Two Volumes*. London: Rodwell and Martin.

Frielinghaus, H., 2006. Deliberate Damage to Bronze Votives in Olympia during Archaic and Early Classical Times. In: C. C. Mattusch – A. A. Donohue – A. Brauer, Hrsg., *Common Ground: Archaeology, Art, Science and Humanities*. Proceedings of the 16th International Congress of Classical Archaeology, Boston, August 23–26, 2003. Oxford: Oxbow, 36–38.

Frielinghaus, H., 2011. *Die Helme von Olympia. Ein Beitrag zu Waffenweihungen in griechischen Heiligtümern*. Olympische Forschungen 22. Berlin und New York: de Gruyter.

Frielinghaus, H., 2013. Beobachtungen zum Votivspektrum Olympias in archaischer und nacharchaischer Zeit. In: I. Gerlach – D. Raue, Hrsg., *Sanktuar und Ritual. Heilige Plätze im archäologischen Befund. Menschen – Kulturen – Traditionen* 10. ForschungsCluster 4, Heiligtümer: Gestalt und Ritual, Kontinuität und Veränderung. Rahden: VML Leidorf, 363–368.

Furtwängler, A., 1880. *Die Bronzefunde aus Olympia und deren kunstgeschichtliche Bedeutung*. Abhandlungen der Königlich Preußischen Akademie der Wissenschaften, Philosophisch-historische Klasse 1879.4, 3–106.

Furtwängler, A., 1890. *Die Bronzen und die übrigen kleineren Funde von Olympia*. Olympia: Die Ergebnisse der von dem Deutschen Reich veranstalteten Ausgrabung 4. Berlin: Asher.

Gauer, W., 1991. *Die Bronzegefäße von Olympia I. Kessel und Becken mit Untersätzen, Teller, Kratere, Hydrien, Eimer, Situlen und Cisten, Schöpfhumpen und verschiedenes Gerät*. Olympische Forschungen 20. Berlin und New York: de Gruyter.

Gauer, W., 2012. Brunnenfunde, Festgesandtschaften und Festgesellschaften. In: W.D. Heilmeyer – N. Kaltsas – H. J. Gehrke – G. E. Hatzi – S. Bocher, Hrsg., *Mythos Olympia. Kult und Spiele*. 31. August 2012 bis 7. Januar 2013, Martin-Gropius-Bau München: Prestel, 99–103.

Graells i Fabregat, R., 2016. Destruction of Votive Offerings in Greek Sanctuaries – The Case of the Cuirasses of Olympia. In: H. Baitinger, Hrsg., *Materielle Kultur und Identität im Spannungsfeld zwischen mediterraner Welt und Mitteleuropa*. Akten der Internationalen Tagung am RGZM Mainz, 22.–24. Oktober 2014. RGZM-Tagungen 27. Mainz: RGZM, 149–160.

Graells i Fabregat, R., 2018. Sobre el nacimiento de los estudios de armas defensivas antiguas griegas como disciplina arqueológica. *Annuario della Scuola Archeologica Italiana di Atene* 96, 2018, 369–388.

Herrmann, H.-V., 1966. *Die Kessel der orientalisierenden Zeit I. Kesselattaschen und Reliefuntersätze*. Olympische Forschungen 6. Berlin: de Gruyter.

Herrmann, H.-V., 1972. *Olympia. Heiligtum und Wettkampfstätte*. München: Hirmer.

Herrmann, K., 2002. Bauforscher und Bauforschung in Olympia. In: H. Kyrieleis, Hrsg., *Olympia 1875–2000. 125 Jahre Deutsche Ausgrabungen*. Internationales Symposion, Berlin 9.–11. November 2000. Mainz: von Zabern, 109–130.

Hölscher, T., 2002. Rituelle Räume und politische Denkmäler im Heiligtum von Olympia. In: H. Kyrieleis, Hrsg., *Olympia 1875–2000. 125 Jahre Deutsche Ausgrabungen*. Internationales Symposion, Berlin 9.–11. November 2000. Mainz: von Zabern, 331–345.

Karusu, S., 1979. ΤΕΧΝΟΥΡΓΟΙ ΚΡΑΤΗΡΩΝ. Fragmente bronzener Volutenkratere. *Athenische Mitteilungen* 94, 77–91.

Kilian-Dirlmeier, I., 2002. *Kleinfunde aus dem Athena Itonia-Heiligtum bei Philia (Thessalien)*. Römisch-Germanisches Zentralmuseum, Monographien 48. Bonn: Habelt 2002.

Klebinder-Gauß, G., 2015. Interpreting Votive Offerings from Early Archaic Deposits at the Artemision of Ephesos. In: P. Pakkanen – S. Bocher, Hrsg., *Cult Material. From Archaeological Deposits to Interpretation of Early Greek Religion*. Papers and Monographs of the Finnish Institute at Athens 21. Helsinki: Suomen Ateenan-Instituutin Säätiö, 107–121.

Kyrieleis, H., 1996. *Der große Kuros von Samos. Samos X*. Bonn: Habelt 1996.

Kyrieleis, H., 2002. Zu den Anfängen des Heiligtums von Olympia. In: H. Kyrieleis, Hrsg., *Olympia 1875–2000. 125 Jahre Deutsche Ausgrabungen*. Internationales Symposion, Berlin 9.–11. November 2000. Mainz: von Zabern, 212–220.

Kyrieleis, H., 2006. *Anfänge und Frühzeit des Heiligtums von Olympia. Die Ausgrabungen am Pelopion, 1987–1996*. Olympische Forschungen 31. Berlin: de Gruyter.

Kyrieleis, H., 2011. *Olympia. Archäologie eines Heiligtums*. Mainz: von Zabern.

Kyrieleis, H., 2016. Anathem und Gesellschaft. In: S. Hansen – D. Neumann – T. Vachta, Hrsg., *Raum, Gabe und Erinnerung. Weihgaben und Heiligtümer in prähistorischen und antiken Gesellschaften*. Berlin Studies of the Ancient World 38. Berlin: Edition Topoi, 237–246.

Lindenlauf, A., 2006. Recycling of Votive Offerings in Greek Sanctuaries. Epigraphical and Archaeological Evidence. In: C. C. Mattusch – A. A. Donohue – A. Brauer, Hrsg., *Common Ground: Archaeology, Art, Science and Humanities*. Proceedings of the 16th International Congress of Classical Archaeology, Boston, August 23–26, 2003. Oxford: Oxbow, 30–32.

Linders, T., 1989–1990. The Melting Down of Discarded Metal. Offerings in Greek Sanctuaries. In: G. Bartoloni – G. Colonna – C. Grottanelli, Hrsg., *Anathema. Regime delle offerte e vita dei santuari nel Mediterraneo antico*. Atti del Convegno internazionale, Roma, 15–18 giugno 1989. Scienze di Antichità 3/4, 281–285.

Lindström, G. – O. Pilz et al., 2013. Votivspektren von Heiligtümern. In: I. Gerlach – D. Raue, Hrsg., *Sanktuar und Ritual. Heilige Plätze im archäologischen Befund*. Menschen – Kulturen – Traditionen 10. ForschungsCluster 4, Heiligtümer: Gestalt und Ritual, Kontinuität und Veränderung. Rahden: VML Leidorf, 267–274.

Mallwitz, A., 1972. *Olympia und seine Bauten*. München: Prestel.

Mallwitz, A. – K. Herrmann, 1999. Ergebnisse und Folgerungen. In: H. Kyrieleis, Hrsg., *XI. Bericht über die Ausgrabungen in Olympia. Frühjahr 1977–Herbst 1981*. Berlin: de Gruyter, 181–284.

Mallwitz, A. – W. Schiering, 1964. *Die Werkstatt des Pheidias in Olympia 1*. Olympische Forschungen 5. Berlin: de Gruyter.

Mattusch, C. C., 1990, A Trio of Griffins from Olympia. *Hesperia* 59, 1990, 549–560.

Naso, A., 2016. Brian Benjamin Shefton and the Etruscan Bronze Funnels. In: J. Boardman – A. Parkin – S. Waite, Hrsg., *On the Fascination of Objects. Greek and Etruscan Art in the Shefton Collection*. Oxford: Oxbow, 155–172.

Osborne, R. 1996. *Greece in the Making 1200–479 BC*. London und New York: Routledge.

Osborne, R., 1998. *Archaic and Classical Greek Art. Oxford History of Art*. Oxford: Oxford University Press.

Ross, L., 1855. *Archäologische Aufsätze I*. Leipzig: Teubner.

Schilbach, J., 1992. Olympia, die Entwicklungsphasen des Stadions. In: W. Coulson – H. Kyrieleis, Hrsg., *Proceedings of an International Symposion on the Olympic Games*. Athen: Lucy Braggiotti Publications, 33–37.

Schilbach, J., 1999a. Abfolge und Datierung der Schichten unter dem Südteil der Echohalle. In: H. Kyrieleis, Hrsg., *XI. Bericht über die Ausgrabungen in Olympia. Frühjahr 1977–Herbst 1981*. Berlin: de Gruyter 1999, 33–54.

Schilbach, J., 1999b. Die Datierung der Schichten im Südostgebiet. In: H. Kyrieleis, Hrsg., *XI. Bericht über die Ausgrabungen in Olympia. Frühjahr 1977–Herbst 1981*. Berlin: de Gruyter, 70–151.

Schweizer, B., 2005. Fremde Bilder – andere Inhalte und Formen des Wissens. Olympia in der ›orientalisierenden‹ Epoche des 8. und 7. Jhs. v. Chr. In: T. L. Kienlin, Hrsg., *Die Dinge als Zeichen. Kulturelles Wissen und materielle Kultur*. Internationale Fachtagung an der Johann Wolfgang Goethe-Universität, Frankfurt am Main 3.–5. April 2003. Universitätsforschungen zur prähistorischen Archäologie 127. Bonn: Habelt, 355–382.

Schweizer, B., 2011. Ernst Curtius (1814–1896): Berlin – Athen – Olympia. Archäologie und Öffentlichkeiten zwischen Vormärz und Kaiserreich. *Saeculum* 61.2, 305–336.

Schweizer, B., 2014. Zur Authentizität archäologischer Stätten. Vergangenheit als Ressource. In: M. Fitzenreiter, Hrsg., *Authentizität – Artefakt und Versprechen in der Archäologie*, Workshop vom 10. bis 12. Mai 2013, Ägyptisches Museum der Universität Bonn, Internet-Beiträge zur Ägyptologie und Sudanarchäologie [IBAES] 15. London: Golden House Publications, 123–137.

Schweizer, B., in Druckvorbereitung. Die Bronzegefäße aus Olympia II. Schalen, Henkel- und Griffschalen, Becher, Skyphoi und Kantharoi, Kannen, Siebe, Infundibula und Schöpfkellen, Salbgefäße und Räuchergefäße sowie Villanova-Amphoren. *Olympische Forschungen*.

Seidl, U., 1999. Orientalische Bleche in Olympia. *Zeitschrift für Assyriologie* 89, 269–282.

Siewert, P., 1991. Staatliche Weihungen von Kesseln und anderen Bronzegeräten in Olympia, *Athenische Mitteilungen* 106, 81–84.

Siewert, P. – Taeuber, H., Hrsg., 2013. *Neue Inschriften von Olympia. Die ab 1896 veröffentlichten Texte*. Tyche Supplement 7. Wien: Holzhausen.

Völling, T., 2002. Weihungen in griechischen Heiligtümern am Beispiel des Artemisheiligtums von Kombothekra und des Zeusheiligtums von Olympia. In: L. Zemmer-Plank, Hrsg., *Kulte der Vorzeit in den Alpen. Opfergaben – Opferplätze – Opferbrauchtum*. Bozen: Athesia, 83–111.

Zimmer, G., 1990. *Griechische Bronzegußwerkstätten. Zur Technologieentwicklung eines antiken Kunsthandwerks.* Mainz: von Zabern 1990.

Pinakes, Waffen und Statuen – Zur öffentlichen Präsentation von Bronzen am Außenbau griechischer Peripteraltempel

Daphni Doepner

Institut für Archäologie und Kulturanthropologie, Bonn

d.doepner@t-online.de

Abstract: Starting from the findings not yet published at the archaic temple of Apollo in Syracuse (Sicily) the contribution studies briefly the permanent attachment of objects made of bronze (plates, weapons and statues) fixed on the outer parts of Greek *peripteroi*. This enlarges the current knowledge concerning technics of fixation and provokes to discuss the role played by temples as sites of exhibition in antiquity. The needs especially bronzes fulfilled at these prominent places must be considered and so a less known aspect of their function in ancient sanctuaries.

Keywords: Temples; Votivs; Decrees; Weapons; Statues

Einleitung

Tempel sind die auffallendsten Bauten griechischer Heiligtümer. Sie überragten schon in der Antike eine Umgebung, in der vieles – darunter auch Bronzen – zur Schau gestellt wurde, etwa Statuen, Reliefbilder, Dreifußkessel, Waffen oder sogar anikonische Steine und Pfeiler. Modelle und Rekonstruktionszeichnungen vermitteln heute eine ungefähre Vorstellung (etwa von den Situationen vor dem Zeus-Tempel in Olympia (Ausschnitt des Modells von A. Mallwitz bei Moustaka 1992, Taf. 24, Abb. 5); westlich des Parthenon auf der Athener Akropolis (Stevens 1940, Frontispiz) und im Stadtheiligtum von Metapont (Doepner 2002, Abb. 172). Vor diesem Hintergrund erstaunt, dass in der Forschung bisher nicht eigens hinterfragt wurde, in welchem Ausmaß der Tempel selbst – seine zumeist erhöhten, gut sichtbaren und z. T. auch durch das Dach geschützten äußeren Bereiche – zur dauerhaften öffentlichen Präsentation von Statuen und anderem genutzt wurde. Sein Außenbau wurde nur nebenbei mit einer knappen Zusammenstellung von Zeugnissen als einer von vielen üblichen Orten in griechischen Heiligtümern gewürdigt, an denen Weihgeschenke verschiedener Art in Erscheinung traten (Brulotte 1994, 279–281). Anlass für eine intensive Auseinandersetzung mit der genannten Frage gibt der Befund am Apollon-Tempel in Syrakus, der als erster monumentaler Peripteros des griechischen Westens gegen 580/70 v. Chr. im damaligen Zentrum der Polis auf der Halbinsel Ortygia errichtet wurde (Mertens 2006, 104–110 mit Abb. 158–170). Denn noch heute finden sich an den Stufen seiner Ostfront und an seinen Pronaos-Säulen Spuren der Befestigung verlorener, auch bronzener Objekte, die in die Zeit des funktionierenden antiken Heiligtums gehörten. Diese Spuren erstmals eingehend zu untersuchen und auch den Stellenwert der am Apollon-Tempel zu beobachtenden Phänomene im Rahmen der antiken Welt insgesamt zu ermitteln, waren die Ziele eines mittlerweile abgeschlossenen Projektes, das unter der Leitung von Martin Bentz an der Universität Bonn durchgeführt wurde und auch unerwartete neue Erkenntnisse zu anderen, bereits bekannten Tempelbefunden erbrachte. Der vorliegende Beitrag nutzt die Ergebnisse dieser umfangreichen Untersuchung, um zu hinterfragen, welche Arten speziell an Bronzeobjekten dauerhaft am Außenbau griechischer Peripteroi ausgestellt wurden und warum. Dabei kann hier freilich nur ein grober Eindruck vermittelt werden – quasi als Ausblick auf die noch anstehende ausführliche Publikation der Untersuchung. Vorab sei erwähnt: Über das Projekt wurde bereits vorläufig berichtet (Doepner 2015), allerdings mit der ein oder anderen Einschätzung, die nach neuen Beobachtungen zu korrigieren ist.

Die verschiedenen Phänomene

Mit den Befestigungsspuren am Apollon-Tempel lassen sich – wie im Folgenden zu zeigen sein wird – mit Gewissheit drei Arten antiker Bronzen in Verbindung bringen: Pinakes, Waffen und Statuen. Eine Umschau offenbart Entsprechendes auch an anderen Peripteroi der antiken griechischen Welt, wobei in Olympia zusätzlich noch Stelen überliefert sind. Insgesamt zeigt sich aber, dass die genannten Objektarten, obwohl sie mitunter gemeinsam an einem Tempel in Erscheinung traten, nicht zu einer einzigen Votivkonvention gehörten, die verschiedene ‚Spielarten' hatte, sondern vielmehr von drei verschiedenen Phänomenen zeugen, die hinsichtlich ihrer Verbreitung und Funktion unterschiedlich zu bewerten sind. Diese drei Phänomene werden daher im Folgenden zunächst jeweils eigens vorgestellt, um abschließend anhand der Gemeinsamkeiten überlegen zu können, warum Bronzen am Tempel fixiert wurden. Der Vollständigkeit

Daphni Doepner

halber sei an dieser Stelle noch erwähnt: Dass auf Basen, die auf den Stufen auflagen, befestigt oder angebaut waren, auch andere Arten von Bronzen existierten, etwa Dreifußkessel, kann aktuell nicht ausgeschlossen werden, doch es fehlen dafür sichere Indizien. Pausanias (5.10.4) sah vergoldete Kessel an den Ecken des Daches des Zeus-Tempels.

Pinakes und Stelen

An den Außenseiten der beiden Pronaos-Säulen in Syrakus waren mindestens 15 Pinakes befestigt. Davon zeugen noch heute Leeren, also Fassungen, die zur vollständigen Einfügung der Täfelchen in die Kanneluren eingearbeitet wurden (Abb. 31.1). Alle Pinakes waren ähnlich groß – max. circa 30 cm breit und etwa 40 cm hoch – und besaßen – soweit es das Erhaltene erkennen lässt – die Form von Ädikulen, also einen Giebel, häufig auch eine Basisplatte und Akrotere. Sie wurden zusätzlich durch vier bis fünf relativ massive Nägel in der Kannelur fixiert, die bisweilen auch in rechteckige Holzdübel eingetrieben wurden. Diese intensive Befestigung, die für Täfelchen aus Holz oder Ton nicht nötig gewesen wäre, zeugt von einigem Gewicht. Die scharf konturierten, mitunter sehr kleinteiligen Ausschnitte sprechen gegen Marmor oder Stein als Material und machen bronzene Pinakes einer Dicke von mindestens 0,5–1 cm wahrscheinlich. An den Innenseiten derselben Säulen – also bereits im Pronaos – und an der Vorderseite einer Ante des stark beschädigten Tempels zeugen kleinere Nagellöcher ohne zugehörige Leeren von weiteren, aber leichteren Täfelchen ähnlicher Form und Größe.

Bleche und massivere Pinakes aus Bronze dieser Art sind aus verschiedenen Gegenden der antiken griechischen Welt überliefert und mit Proxenie-Dekreten hellenistischer Zeit beschrieben. Sie nennen also die Privilegien, die eine Polis dem Bürger einer anderen Stadt zu seinen Ehren verlieh, weil dieser dort ihre Interessen vertreten hat. Dabei wurden Stelen oder Bronzetäfelchen mit solchen Dekreten nicht selten doppelt angefertigt und ein Exemplar an gut sichtbarer Stelle öffentlich in der verleihenden Polis ausgestellt. Das zweite gelangte zumindest in der Regel in die Geburtsstadt des Proxenos, um ihn auch dort zu ehren (Guarducci 1969, 28–30. 36). Zwei bronzene Pinakes der beschriebenen Art, die aus mehreren separat gefertigten Partien bestanden, wurden spätestens in der 1. Hälfte des 1. Jahrhunderts v. Chr. auch für einen Demetrios aus Syrakus ausgestellt, und zwar etwa gleichzeitig von zwei verschiedenen Poleis – Melite (Malta) und Akragas (Agrigent). Sie fanden sich allerdings nicht in Syrakus, sondern in Rom, wo der Geehrte womöglich lebte (Manganaro 1963, bes. Taf. 63. 64). Im Artemis-Heiligtum von Lusoi kamen bei Ausgrabungen Bleche mit Dekreten noch gemeinsam mit vielen Nägeln in Sturzlage hervor: Sie waren an den hölzernen Türpfosten des Propylons aufgehängt gewesen, bevor diese durch einen Brand zerstört wurden (Reichel – Wilhelm 1901, 19f. 64–77, Abb. 144–152). Literarische Quellen und Inschriften bezeugen die Veröffentlichung von Proxenie-

Abb. 31.1. Apollon-Tempel, Syrakus: Spuren der Befestigung von Pinakes an der Außenseite der südlichen Pronaos-Säule (Foto: Autorin)

Dekreten sowie von Schuldner- und Priesterlisten vor allem auch an Tempeleingängen (Reichel – Wilhelm 1901, 85–87). So bemerkt der griechische Historiker Polybios (12.11.2–3) aus dem 2. Jahrhundert v. Chr. leicht ironisch: Sein älterer Berufskollege Timaios sei bei der Arbeit so gründlich gewesen, dass er selbst die Proxeniedekrete an den Türpfosten der Tempel entdeckt habe. Timaios lebte von ca. 345–250 v. Chr. unter anderem auch in Syrakus, wo er mit 96 Jahren verstarb. Dies alles lässt vermuten, dass der beschriebene Befund am Apollon-Tempel in Syrakus die in hellenistischer Zeit überregional bekannte Konvention der Dekret-Publikation anhand bronzener Pinakes in Ädikulaform an Tempel-Eingängen besonders eindrücklich überliefert.

Doch auch der Hera-Tempel in Olympia, der als einziger weiterer Peripteros ähnliche Befestigungsspuren an den Säulen und Anten aufweist, wird mit dieser Praxis zu verbinden sein, die hier aber vielleicht schon früher und auch noch in der römischen Kaiserzeit ausgeübt wurde: An der südlichen Ante des Tempeleingangs sind außen Nagellöcher und Vertiefungen erhalten, die Eckstein auf die Fixierung langer, schmaler archaischer Bronzebleche mit Urkunden zurückführte (1969, 88, Nr. 18, Textabb. 24, Abb. 21. 96), jenen ähnlich, die – mit Dekreten dieser frühen Zeit versehen – aus Olympia erhalten sind (Dittenberger –

Purgold 1896, 9–14, Nr. 4. 17–20, Nr. 7. 57–60, Nr. 23) und deren Anbringung in Türbereichen Reichel und Wilhelm bereits zuvor angesichts des erwähnten Lusoi-Befundes vermuteten (1901, 86 mit Anm. 61). Die Pronaos-Säulen fehlen am Hera-Tempel. Es ist also nicht auszuschließen, dass auch an ihnen Tafeln fixiert waren. Dies gilt umso mehr, da in den Säulen der Peristasis zahlreiche Leeren für Pinakes existieren – darunter auch ädikulaförmige (Abb. 31.2) –, die noch heute das Erscheinungsbild des Tempels prägen und in seinen Zugangsbereichen vermehrt auftreten (Dörpfeld 1935, 170f.; Eckstein 1969, 96). Sieverling hat diesen Befund an den Säulen in ihrer leider noch nicht publizierten Magister-Arbeit (2008) eingehend studiert und auch unter den Relikten in Olympia nach Material gesucht, das zumindest mit seinen Maßen zu den Leeren passen könnte. Ihr zufolge wurde eine Position der Tafeln „auf Augenhöhe" angestrebt, und wohl keine Nägel, sondern Klammern verstärkten die Befestigung mancher Exemplare. Sie konnte zwar keine einzige zugehörige Tafel identifizieren, weist aber darauf hin, dass in einigen Leeren wegen der passenden Maße Bleche aus Bronze mit Urkunden verschiedener Art fixiert gewesen sein könnten, wie sie relativ zahlreich aus Olympia überliefert sind. Diese Bronzen wären dann auf Holztafeln montiert oder auf Stuck in den Leeren verklebt gewesen. Auch steinerne Tafeln mit Inschriften könnten angesichts des Erhaltenen eingefügt worden sein. Die Anbringung wiederverwendeter marmorner Ziegel des Zeus-Tempels, die römische Priesterlisten trugen, hält Sieverling sogar für sehr wahrscheinlich, denn von ihnen wurden – anders als im Falle der Bronzen – auch viele Exemplare im Bereich des Hera-Tempels gefunden. Zwischen den Säulen mit den Pinakes und vor der Cella-Wand an der Süd- und Ostfront des Tempels existieren auf dem Stylobat noch Spuren von auffallend vielen Stelen, die dort vornehmlich und an der Südseite sogar ausschließlich aufgestellt waren, darunter auch Exemplare aus Bronze (Eckstein 1969, 87–89. 90–96, Taf. 4). Bei den bronzenen Stelen handelte es sich um Tafeln, die mit ihrer Unterseite entweder ganz in den Tempel eingelassen oder verzapft waren. Eine eindrucksvolle, circa 60 cm hohe einst verzapfte Bronzestele mit Giebel ist sogar noch aus dem olympischen Heiligtum erhalten: Sie trägt ein Dekret der Eleer zu Ehren des Demokrates aus Tenedos aus der 1. Hälfte des 3. Jahrhunderts v. Chr. (Heilmeyer et al. 2012, 549 Kat. 14, 36). Hohe, schmale Bronze-Tafeln wurden

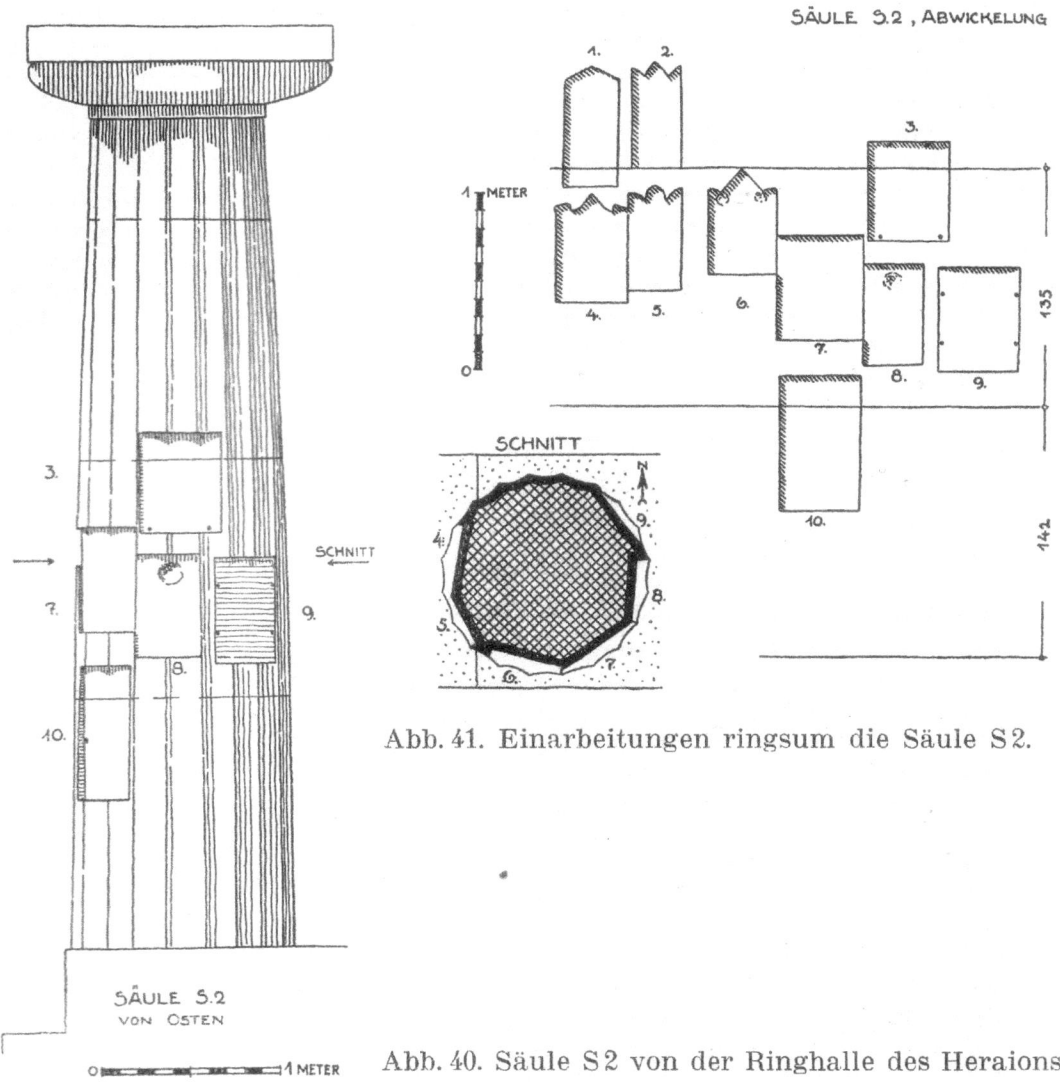

Abb. 41. Einarbeitungen ringsum die Säule S 2.

Abb. 40. Säule S 2 von der Ringhalle des Heraions.

Abb. 31.2. Hera-Tempel, Olympia: Spuren der Befestigung von Pinakes an einer Säule der Peristasis (aus Dörpfeld 1935)

am Hera-Tempel aber auch noch auf eine dritte Weise fixiert: anhand einer rechteckigen „Kanalbettung". Schon Eckstein verband die Spuren dieser Technik dort mit der Befestigung von Stelen (1969, etwa 94 [Joch 1 c)]). Eine Neuansicht des Befundes offenbarte, dass die Spuren jenen einer ‚samischen Einlassung' entsprechen, die bisher nur mit der Montierung von Bronzestatuen archaischer und frühklassischer Zeit in Verbindung gebracht wurde (etwa von Willer 1996, 347f., Abb. 7.8). Dabei wurde das Objekt auf einen Bronzekasten montiert, der dann in einen passend ausgehauenen Rahmen mit zentral leicht abgearbeiteter Innenfläche auf der Basis eingefügt wurde. Dafür, dass diese Technik am Hera-Tempel zur Befestigung von Bronzetafeln diente, sprechen die Maße und der Kontext der betreffenden Bettungen sowie Vorrichtungen, die in einigen Fällen die Stelen zusätzlich oben sicherten.

Vieles lässt annehmen, dass am olympischen Hera-Tempel nicht nur einige der erwähnten Bleche, Pinakes und Stelen, wie es bisher vermutet wurde (Eckstein 1969, 96; Sieverling 2008), der Publikation von Gesetzen, Ehrendekreten und ähnlichem gedient haben könnten, sondern alle: das exklusive Vorkommen von Dekreten am Propylon in Lousoi und an den literarisch und archäologisch bezeugten Tempeleingängen; die Uniformität der Täfelchen am Apollon-Tempel; das fast gänzliche Fehlen auch nur zum Teil erhaltener Votivtafeln mit figürlichen Darstellungen im Gegensatz zur erwähnten Menge an Resten von Blechen, Pinakes und Stelen aus Bronze oder Stein mit Dekreten, die in die beschriebenen Einlassungen hätten passen können; die nicht zufriedenstellenden anderen Erklärungsversuche der Pinakes am Hera-Tempel; und schließlich der Umstand, dass Befunde eine einst konzentrierte Aufstellung von Dekret-Stelen auch in anderen griechischen Heiligtümern wahrscheinlich machen. All dies kann aber freilich erst in der ausführlichen Publikation der Untersuchung dargelegt werden. Auf jeden Fall scheint bei der beschriebenen Praxis in Syrakus und Olympia Bronze gegenüber Stein oder Marmor als Material besonders geschätzt worden zu sein. Am Apollon-Tempel wird dies durch die einstige Existenz ausschließlich bronzener Pinakes an den Vorderseiten der Pronaos-Säulen deutlich. Und auch am Hera-Tempel waren Bleche und Stelen aus Bronze vor allem im Zugangsbereich anzutreffen.

Doch nicht alle Tempel in griechischen Heiligtümern dienten der Dekret-Publikation. Dies verdeutlichen die Seltenheit erhaltener Inschriften und das Fehlen von Fixierungsspuren an gut erhaltenen Stufen, Stylobaten, Säulen und Wänden, auch wenn freilich nicht ausgeschlossen werden kann, dass Texte einst in Farbe an Wänden und vielleicht auch in Kanneluren aufgetragen waren und heute verloren sind. Womöglich erfüllten in der Regel nicht die Tempel diesen Zweck, sondern andere Bauten – wie das erwähnte Propylon in Lousoi – und vor allem die Stelen in ihrer Umgebung und an den sakralen Wegen. Die Publikation von Dekreten erfolgte aber nicht nur in Heiligtümern, sondern auch auf der Agora. Dabei beschloss stets die Polis das Dekret und auch seine Gravur etwa auf einer Stele. Sie überließ aber mitunter wohl aus Kostengründen die Anfertigung dieser Stele dem Geehrten selbst und sogar die Wahl des öffentlichen Ausstellungsortes (Guarducci 1969, 35f.).

Waffen

Auf der Euthynterie der Front des Apollon-Tempels existieren zwei ähnliche runde, etwa 40 cm tiefe Löcher für den Einsatz von Pfosten, die einen Durchmesser von 15,5 und 17,5 cm besaßen. Sie liegen in einem Abstand von etwa zwei Metern zueinander (Abb. 31.3–4). Ein viereckiges Loch an prominenter Stelle neben der zentralen Zugangstreppe wird einen etwas schmächtigeren Balken gefasst haben, den die Stufe dahinter zusätzlich stützte.

Löcher, deren Form und Größe in etwa vergleichbar sind, fanden sich an verschiedenen Stellen in Olympia: Runde Exemplare sind in großer Zahl aus den Bereichen des Hera-Tempels aus der Zeit vor seiner Entstehung überliefert und vom Stadion-Südwall, wo sie in die 2. Hälfte des 6. Jahrhunderts datieren. Da sich in der Umgebung der letzteren viele bronzene Waffen und Rüstungsteile – auch mit Befestigungslöchern – fanden, wurde vermutet, dass die Pfosten hier und auch im Areal des Hera-Tempels zur Präsentation von Beutewaffen dienten (Frielinghaus in: Heilmeyer et al. 2012, 96f.; Baitinger 2011, 87, Abb. 57). Erhaltene Inschriften überliefern, dass es sich dabei nicht um private Votive, sondern um Weihungen von Poleis handelte (Philipp 2004, 145). Solche Male wurden – wie auch Siegesanatheme anderer Art im Heiligtum – von verschiedenen Städten Zeus wohl zum Dank geweiht, weil in Olympia ein bis ins 4. Jahrhundert v. Chr. überregional bedeutendes Kriegsorakel im Rahmen seines Kultes existierte. Es schickte seine Seher auch mit in den Kampf (Baitinger 2011, 77–80).

Viereckige Balkenlöcher sind in Olympia sogar mittig zwischen den Säulen der Peristasis des Zeus-Tempels erhalten. Sie wurden von Eckstein (1969, 70–83, Textabb. 17. 18. 22. 23, Abb. 20, Taf. 3) ebenfalls hölzernen Stützen von Waffenanathemen zugewiesen, jedoch in der Folgezeit in der Forschung nicht mehr beachtet. Wann die Löcher

Abb. 31.3. Apollon-Tempel, Syrakus: Pfostenlöcher in der Euthynterie der Ostfront (Foto: Autorin)

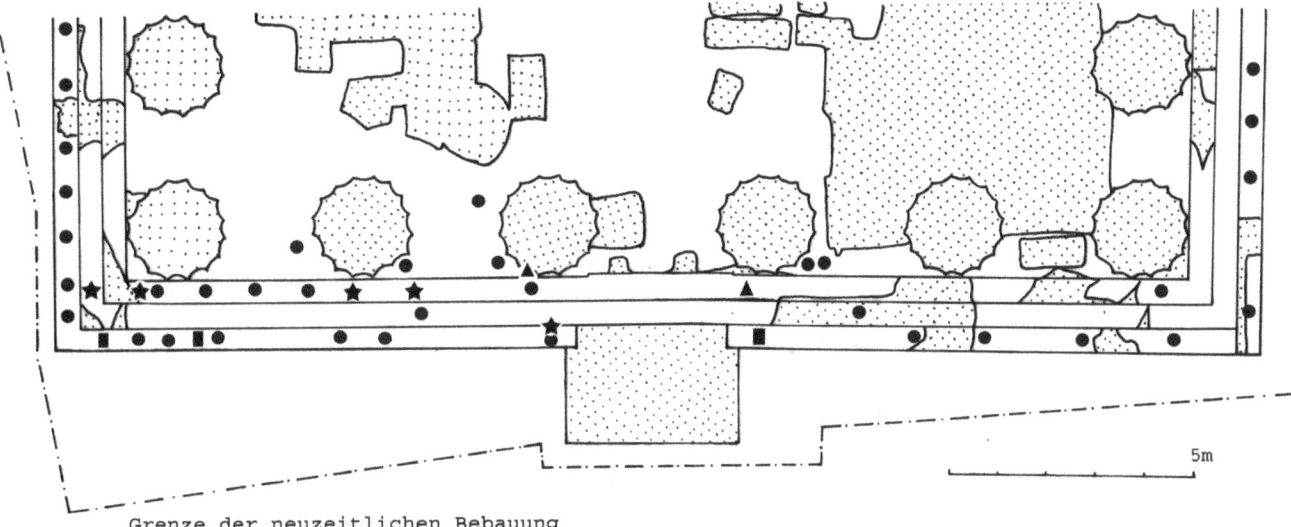

Abb. 31.4. Apollon-Tempel, Syrakus: Schematische Aufsicht der Ostfront mit Lage der Befestigungsspuren von Anathemen: Rechteck = für Pfosten/Balken mit bronzenen Beutewaffen; Stern = für Bronze-Statue; Dreieck = für Statue/Stele aus Stein oder Marmor; Kreis = für Objekt, dessen Art und Material unbekannt sind; gepunktet = zerstörter oder verdeckter Bereich (Zeichnung: Autorin unter Verwendung einer Bauaufnahme von Dieter Mertens)

innerhalb des langen Zeitraums ab der Fertigstellung des Baus im mittleren 5. Jh. v. Chr. bis zum Ende des kultischen Lebens im Heiligtum gegen 420 n. Chr. entstanden, ist letztlich unbekannt. Eine Zurschaustellung von Beutewaffen schon in klassischer Zeit, wie sie Eckstein vermutete, würde wegen des angesprochenen Kriegsorakels aber nicht verwundern.

Angesichts des Dargelegten ist zu vermuten, dass auch in den Pfostenlöchern auf der untersten Stufe des Apollon-Tempels in Syrakus Stützen zur Präsentation von Beutewaffen errichtet wurden. Ob die Beuteanatheme hier oder am Zeus-Tempel die Gestalt von Tropaia auf dem Schlachtfeld imitierten, ist allerdings genauso fraglich wie das einstige Aussehen der Waffenmale im offenen Areal von Olympia. Zumindest für einige der dortigen Fälle wurde wegen charakteristischer Löcher in Helmen eine Befestigung auf Pfahlspitzen und das Erscheinungsbild von Tropaia vermutet (Frielinghaus in: Heilmeyer et al. 2012, 96). Doch die gefundenen Rüstungsteile lassen sich (auch zahlenmäßig) nicht zu vollständigen Tropaia vereinen (Rabe 2008, 30–32). Auch sind Unterschiede im antiken Umgang mit einem tatsächlichen Tropaion auf dem Schlachtfeld und mit Spolienweihungen im Heiligtum zu bedenken (Graells i Fabregat 2017, 53–55).

Dass Beutewaffen das äußere Erscheinungsbild des Apollon-Tempels in Syrakus prägten, legt auch die schriftliche Überlieferung nahe: Laut Diodor (11.25.1) soll Gelon nach seinem Sieg über die Karthager bei Himera (480 v. Chr.) den besten Teil der Beute zur Seite gelegt haben, weil er die Tempel von Syrakus mit Beutewaffen ‚schmücken' wollte. Erst dann habe er von dem Rest vieles an die wichtigsten Tempel von Himera genagelt. Freilich konnten Beutewaffen auch ins Innere der Tempel gelangen (Rabe 2008, 29). Dennoch erweckt die Diodor-Stelle den Eindruck, dass gerade das gut sichtbare Äußere reich mit ihnen behangen worden sein

könnte. Vasenbilder und literarische Quellen überliefern tatsächlich eine Befestigung von Beutewaffen am Tempel-Außenbau, allerdings bisher nur „am Gesims, über der Tür oder an Türpfosten von Tempeln" (Rabe 2008, 28f. Anm. 191). Am Architrav könnten schon in archaischer Zeit die Helme und Räder von Streitwagen befestigt gewesen sein, deren Fragmente jüngst in Falllage am archaischen Südtempel im Apollon-Heiligtum von Kalapodi gefunden wurden (Niemeyer 2016, 21, Taf. 8,2). Zumeist wurden aber wohl im Bereich der Metopen ausgewählte Beuteschilde angebracht, die auch vergoldet sein konnten, wie jene am Apollon-Tempel in Delphi, von den Athenern nach der Schlacht bei Marathon geweiht und von den Aitolern nach dem Sieg über die Galater (Paus. 10.19.4). Es ist aber auch möglich, dass solche Schilde, eigens angefertigt wurden, also ohne den üblichen Holzkern und die Halterung auf der Innenseite, und ganz aus Bronze bestanden (Philipp 2004, 139 Anm. 864). Einzelne Schilde, die vielleicht sogar ganz aus Gold waren, das aus Beutegut finanziert wurde, erhielten eine besondere Positionen im Dachbereich. Die literarischen Quellen, die über alle diese Schilde berichten, vermitteln den Eindruck, dass sie von Poleis bzw. Feldherren voller Stolz nach besonders bedeutenden Siegen an die Tempel montiert wurden: Gelon wird aus der Beute seines Sieges über die Karthager um 480 bei Himera in Syrakus nicht nur den Athena-Tempel selbst finanziert haben, sondern auch den Schild an seinem Ostgiebel (Baitinger 2011, 112f.), der laut Athenaios (11,462 C) weithin sichtbar war. Pausanias sah im 2. Jahrhundert n. Chr. nicht nur die erwähnten Schilde in Delphi, sondern auch am Zeus-Tempel in Olympia am Giebel den goldenen Schild der Spartaner mit einer Inschrift darauf, die verkündete, dass er aus dem zehnten Teil der Beute des Sieges gegen die Argiver, Athener und Ionier bei Tanagra geweiht worden sei, sowie an den Metopen 21 vergoldete Schilde, welche der römische Feldherr Lucius Mummius 146 v. Chr. nach der Eroberung Korinths aus der Siegesbeute anbringen ließ (5.10.4–5). Alexander der Große brachte nach seinem Sieg am Granikos 334 v. Chr. Schilde am Gebälk des Parthenon an (Plutarch, Alexander 16.8) – von ihnen und von jenen des Mummius am Zeus-Tempel in Olympia zeugen sogar noch Befestigungsspuren (Stevens 1940, 64–66, Abb. 50. 51; Philipp 2004, 139 Anm. 863). Über die Motivation Timoleons, der von Korinth zur Unterstützung der Griechen in Sizilien gegen die Karthager ausgesandt worden war, ist von Plutarch (Timoleon 29.5–6) – und damit freilich erst aus der römischen Kaiserzeit – sogar Genaueres zu erfahren: Er soll nach seinem Sieg (341/340 v. Chr.) zusammen mit der Siegesbotschaft die schönsten erbeuteten Barbaren-Waffen zum Schmuck der auffälligsten Tempel nach Korinth geschickt haben, um so – Neid weckend – optisch seine Heimatstadt unter allen Griechenstädten auszuzeichnen und – unterstützt durch Inschriften – auf die große von den Korinthern und ihm erbrachte Leistung aufmerksam zu machen, dies alles den Göttern zum Dank.

Auch das Ausstellen bronzener Beutewaffen am Außenbau von Peripteroi war also eine überregional bekannte Praxis. Sie wurde aber nicht beliebig ausgeübt, sondern nur in Orakel- und – angesichts der Funde am archaischen Poseidon-Tempel in Isthmia (Jackson 1992, 142) – womöglich auch in Bundesheiligtümern, also in Heiligtümern, die von überregionaler Bedeutung und für das Miteinander verschiedener Poleis wichtig waren, sowie in repräsentativen Stadtheiligtümern. Dies gilt auch allgemein für Waffenweihungen (Baitinger 2011, 169), also ebenso für Beuteweihungen und Siegesmale, die im freien Areal und in kleineren Gebäuden der Tempelumgebung ausgestellt wurden. Da zudem in Olympia „die Sitte", Waffen zu weihen, angesichts des überlieferten Materials "ihren Höhepunkt ... in archaischer und frühklassischer Zeit" erreichte, „danach jedoch relativ rasch aufgegeben" wurde (Baitinger 2011, 87), erscheint es naheliegend zu vermuten, dass dort die Anatheme am Zeus-Tempel in der Tradition der älteren im Gelände standen und in griechischen Heiligtümern allgemein beide Ausprägungen letztlich zu einer Votivkonvention gehörten.

Statuen

Auf den Stufen des Apollon-Tempels in Syrakus können anhand der Befestigungsspuren insgesamt fünf Bronzestatuen identifiziert werden (Abb. 31.4). Sie stammten zumindest zum Teil, vielleicht aber auch alle aus archaischer bis hochklassischer Zeit. Zwei von ihnen standen in etwa einem Meter Abstand zueinander auf der Stufe unterhalb des Stylobats. Die Form ihrer auffallend großen Befestigungslöcher erinnert an archaische Figuren in aufrechter Haltung mit nur leicht versetzten Beinen. Vor allem der Vergleich mit den Montierungsspuren auf der Basis einer überlebensgroßen Bronzestatue des Apoll aus Delphi offenbart, dass hier zwei leicht überlebensgroße, hohl gegossene Statuen dieser frühen Zeit fixiert gewesen sein müssen (Doepner 2015, 85–87, Abb. 7–10). Zugleich wird deutlich, dass die Spuren die ältesten aktuell bekannten Zeugnisse zweier Fixierungstechniken sind, die ab dem 2. Viertel des 5. Jahrhunderts v. Chr. für Bronzestatuen üblich waren: der ‚Sohlenbettung' und der ‚peloponnesischen Technik'. Diese Techniken wurden von Willer anschaulich beschrieben (1996, 349–351. 353–356 bes. Abb. 9. 10). In beiden Fällen wurde die jeweilige Statue durch flüssiges Blei befestigt, das nach ihrer Aufstellung in dazu vorgesehene Öffnungen gegossen wurde, welche sich wohl in den Unterschenkeln der Figur befanden. Das Blei floss von dort in die Füße und durch deren offene Sohlen in Löcher, die zuvor extra dafür in die Basis eingearbeitet worden sind. Nach dem Erkalten des Bleis stand die Figur für den Betrachter dann wie von alleine fest auf ihrem Sockel, denn die Bleiverbindung unter den Statuen-Füßen war für ihn nicht sichtbar: Das Loch einer Sohlenbettung nahm mehr oder weniger den Raum unter der Fußsohle ein (die Zehen also ausgenommen); im Falle der Peloponnesischen Technik waren nur unter den aufliegenden Fersen und Ballen Löcher in die Basis eingebracht. Die Befestigungslöcher in Syrakus weisen allerdings statt der für beide Methoden später üblichen gerundeten Konturen viereckige auf. Dabei werden im Falle der einen Figur zwei Sohlenbettungen zu einer einzigen Einlassung für einen Bleizapfen vereint (Abb. 31.5). Im Falle der anderen Statue wurden zukunftweisend die Verankerungen beider Füße voneinander getrennt und unter dem linken Fuß zusätzlich zur Sohlenbettung die Löcher der Peloponnesischen Technik unter Ferse und Ballen eingebracht, also beide Befestigungsmethoden miteinander verbunden (Doepner 2015, 85f., Abb. 8. 9).

Am Apollon-Tempel sind noch zwei weitere Statuen durch Blei in Sohlenbettungen oder in Zapfenlöchern der Peloponnesischen Technik verankert worden, wobei

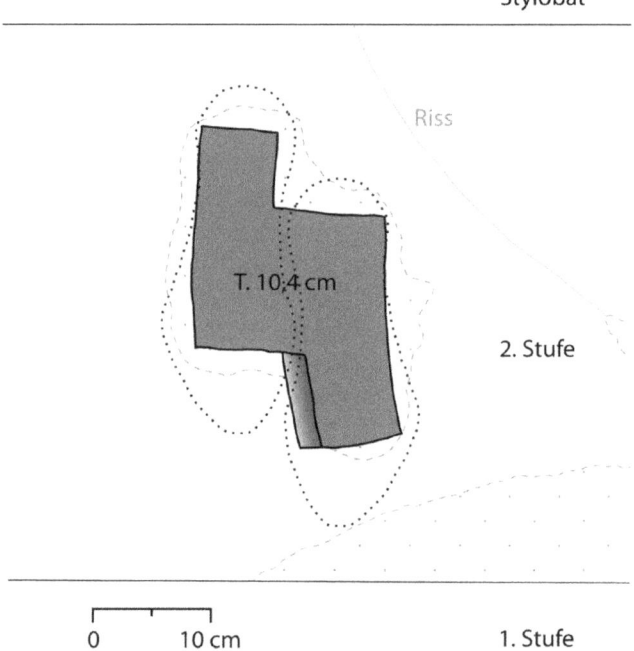

Abb. 31.5. Apollon-Tempel, Syrakus, Ostfront: Loch zur Befestigung einer Bronzestatue mit angedeutetem Umriss der einst aufliegenden Statuenfüße (Zeichnung: Autorin)

in einem Fall auch gesichert ist, dass Eisenstäbe mit vergossen waren, die aus dem Inneren der Figur unten herausragten und die Stabilität des Anathems zusätzlich sicherten. Diese beiden Statuen könnten wegen ihres Standmotivs in der klassischen Zeit des 5. Jahrhunderts v. Chr. errichtet worden sein. Allerdings blieben Standmotive, die damals entwickelt wurden, bis in römische Zeit hinein für neu geschaffene Statuen beliebt, so dass sie alleine nicht als Indiz für eine Datierung ausreichen. Nur eine Figur war am Apollon-Tempel in einer Samischen Einlassung befestigt – eine Technik, die vor allem zur Fixierung von Bronzestatuen und -statuetten archaischer und frühklassischen Zeit bekannt ist, am Hera-Tempel in Olympia aber auch bronzene Stelentafeln fixierte (s.o.). Am Apollon-Tempel sprechen die Größe des Einlassungsrahmens, seine Ausrichtung mit der Schmalseite nach vorn zum Betrachter und seine Lage im Vergleich zu den Befestigungsspuren gesicherter, direkt vergossener Bronzestatuen auch auf derselben Stufe aber tatsächlich für die Montage einer Bronzestatue. Zahlreiche Spuren stammen dort womöglich von weiteren Anathemen aus Bronze, die dann auch direkt in der Stufe vergossen worden wären oder auf eingelassenen, verzapften, verklammerten oder sogar nur aufliegenden Platten, Kästen oder höheren Basen aus Bronze bzw. Stein gestanden hätten. Womöglich wurden sogar Bronzen auf angebauten Steinbasen errichtet. In allen diesen Fällen sind die Spuren aber zu unspezifisch, um Marmorfiguren oder anderes ausschließen zu können. Dass hier nicht nur Bronzen aufgestellt wurden, legen Einlassungen nahe, die am ehesten mit einer kleineren Stele aus Stein und mit der Plinthe einer frühen Marmorstatue zu verbinden sind. Leeren für gerundete Plinthen, die von archaischer bis hellenistischer Zeit in Griechenland zur Fixierung von Marmorstatuen üblich waren, fehlen aber völlig. Vor diesem Hintergrund ist aktuell nicht zu ermessen, ob Bronzen auf den Stufen des Apollon-Tempels nur in geringer Zahl oder bevorzugt errichtet wurden (vgl. Abb. 31.4). Überdies kann nicht ausgeschlossen werden, dass Statuen aus diesem Material auch noch in nachklassischer Zeit auf die Tempelstufen gelangten.

Bei den fünf gesicherten Bronzen handelte es sich um aufrechte, relativ unbewegte Figuren, die Götter, Heroen oder Sterbliche, etwa Sieger in Wettkämpfen, wiedergegeben haben werden. Sie waren alle lebens- oder leicht überlebensgroß und wurden einzeln oder – im Falle der beiden eingangs erwähnten Statuen – vielleicht sogar als Paar geweiht. So werden sie sich optisch und funktional nicht von den Figuren aus Bronze oder anderem Material unterschieden haben, die in griechischen Heiligtümern normaler Weise in der Umgebung des Tempels und des zugehörigen Altars errichtet wurden oder entlang der ‚heiligen Straße', welche zu diesen Bauten führte. Die Funktion solcher Figuren hatte verschiedene Aspekte (Doepner 2002, 161 f. 171–173): Sie waren, wie wir durch erhaltene Votivinschriften wissen, Geschenke für die Gottheit, zumeist als Dank für eine erwiesene Wohltat, etwa für einen Sieg im Wettkampf oder in einer Schlacht. In Verbindung mit der Votivinschrift hielten sie den Stifter und den Anlass der Weihung dauerhaft in Erinnerung – der Gottheit und allen gegenwärtigen und zukünftigen Besuchern des Heiligtums gegenüber. (Solche Inschriften werden am Apollon-Tempel an den frühen, direkt in den Stufen vergossenen Bronzestatuen selbst existiert haben und auf den bronzenen Standflächen bzw. an den steinernen Basen der anderen Anatheme.) War ein sterblicher Mensch dargestellt, wurde er auf diese Weise zugleich geehrt. Dabei galten die Statuen – ähnlich den oben behandelten Waffen – auch als Schmuck (‚agalmata') des Heiligtums, der die Gottheit erfreuen sollte. Am Apollon-Tempel nahmen die Anatheme – an ausgesuchten Plätzen und auch unter gegenseitiger Berücksichtigung – die verschiedenen Stufen der Ostfront ein, wo sich der Zugang zum Tempelinneren befand. Dabei wurde nur selten ein Objekt durch ein anderes an Ort und Stelle ersetzt. So könnten hier Bronze-Statuen lange existiert haben, bis sie mit Sorgfalt – wie es der Befund zeigt – entfernt wurden.

Eine grobe Umschau unter den Befunden antiker Peripteroi offenbart mangels von Spuren, dass es in der antiken griechischen Welt wohl nicht üblich war, Bronze-Statuen wie in Syrakus dauerhaft zwischen den Säulen oder auf den Stufen des Außenbaus zur Schau zu stellen. Die wenigen bekannten, im Folgenden beschriebenen Ausnahmen in Athen und Olympia lassen aktuell sogar vermuten, dass dieses Phänomen nicht – wie die beiden anderen – mit einer vielleicht selten praktizierten, aber doch überregional bekannten Konvention zu verbinden ist, sondern nur in Sonderfällen auftrat, die jeweils eigens motiviert waren. Allerdings kann aktuell nur darüber spekuliert werden, ob eingeschränkte räumliche Möglichkeiten oder anderes den Sonderfall in Syrakus ausgelöst haben könnten.

Vom ‚Archaios-Naos' auf der Athener Akropolis sind wenige Teile des Stylobats und der stufenbreiten Euthynterie darunter mit Befestigungsspuren erhalten, die noch kaum bekannt sind. Die Spuren wurden Anathemen zugeschrieben, die dort errichtet wurden, als der archaische Tempel noch in Funktion war (Kissas 2000, 36 mit Anm. 204, Abb. 1. 2). Doch gibt es Hinweise darauf, dass zumindest drei der Objekte – darunter eine in einer Samischen Einlassung befestigte Bronze – erst nach der Zerstörung des Tempels durch die Perser um 480 v. Chr. aufgestellt worden sein könnten, als der Bau in großen Teilen nur noch als Ruine sichtbar war: Zwei Einlassungen (Kissas 2000, Abb. 1) befinden sich noch heute in situ dort, wo eine Säule der Peristasis und das Ende der Stylobat-Stufe des intakten Baus zu erwarten sind. Die Samische Einlassung (Kissas 2000, Abb. 2) könnte – falls sie nicht erst am Ort ihrer Wiederverwendung südwestlich des Parthenon entstand und auch keine Stele fixierte – wegen ihrer Ausrichtung auf der Stylobatplatte (mit ihrer Langseite zum antiken Betrachter) bereits eine klassische Figur befestigt haben. Erst die genaue Untersuchung der Tempelreste wird aber – wenn überhaupt – klären können, ob eine Fixierung von Anathemen am intakten Archaios Naos auszuschließen ist. Denn Bauteile mit

Montagespuren davon könnten ja auch zur Reparatur der Ruine wiederverwendet worden sein. Vor diesem Hintergrund sind Überlegungen über die Funktion des erwähnten Bronzeobjekts aktuell nicht ratsam.

Am Parthenon sind nur durch Verwitterungsspuren viereckige Standplatten oder Basen überliefert. Sie lagen ohne jede Befestigung jeweils vor einer Säule der Peristasis auf der Stufe darunter auf (Stevens 1940, 62f., Abb. 47. 48). Ob auf ihnen Bronzen errichtet waren ist aktuell genauso ungewiss wie die Datierung der Objekte. Der Befund veranschaulicht aber immerhin, dass einst mehr auf den Tempeln existiert haben könnte, als heute für uns fassbar ist.

In Olympia wurden an der Südseite des Zeustempels 27 und an der Ostfront des Hera-Tempels mindestens vier Bronzestatuen unmittelbar – also ohne Basis – in den Stylobat und in der Stufe darunter mit Blei vergossen. Eckstein, der auch diese Spuren publizierte, vermutete – Emil Kunze folgend – an beiden Tempeln eine Wiederaufstellung zumeist klassischer Originale zu ihrem Schutz vor dem Ansturm der Heruler im späten 3. Jh. n. Chr., und zwar innerhalb einer Umfassungsmauer, die damals angesichts der Bedrohung aus Spolien errichtet worden sei (1969, 70–84, Textabb. 19–23, Taf. 3 [Zeus-Tempel], 93–96, Taf. 4 [Hera-Tempel]). Diese These fand auch noch jüngst trotz der Kenntnis neuer archäologischer Untersuchungsergebnisse Zuspruch (Remijsen 2015, 38–42), die zu einem ganz anderen Verständnis der ‚Heruler-Mauer' veranlassen: Sie wird wegen der Konzentration der Splitter zerstörter Bronzestatuen hoch in der Stratigraphie des Heiligtums, der gleichartigen Verwendung von Spolien in der Mauer und in anderen Bauten sowie wegen schriftlicher Zeugnisse, die ein Ende der olympischen Feste erst gegen 420 n. Chr. belegen, erst im frühen 5. Jh. als Fluchtburg einer christlichen Domäne entstanden sein (Gutsfeld – Lehmann 2013, bes. 93–98, Abb. 11; Gutsfeld – Lehmann – Lehmann 2013). Dies führte auch zu einer Neuinterpretation der Spuren am Zeustempel: Während damals andere Bronzen „durch staatliche Behörden zerkleinert und abtransportiert" worden seien, habe der erste Pächter einige klassische Statuen auf der Südseite des Zeustempels zusammengestellt, weil er die Kunst dieser Zeit geschätzt habe und die Figuren dort – vom offenen Innenhof der Fluchtburg aus gut sichtbar – an die klassische Glanzzeit Olympias erinnern sollten (Gutsfeld – Lehmann 2013, 100f., Abb. 18).

Die erneute Untersuchung der Spuren auch vor Ort erbrachte detailliertere Informationen nicht nur über die verwendeten Befestigungstechniken, sondern auch über die einstige Größe und Haltung der Figuren sowie über die Verteilung von allem auf den Stufen. Sie erlauben es, die bisherigen Thesen zu überprüfen. Es bestätigt sich, dass hier Originale klassischer Zeit wieder aufgestellt worden sein werden, frühestens in der späten römischen Kaiserzeit – nach dem Besuch von Pausanias im 3. Viertel des 2. Jahrhunderts n. Chr., der sie sicher erwähnt hätte – und dass dies an beiden Tempeln im Rahmen einer Maßnahme erfolgte. Letzteres widerlegt allerdings die These, dass die Aufstellung zum Schutz der Figuren erfolgte. Der Hera-Tempel befindet sich nämlich außerhalb der Festungsmauer. Die Statuen wären dort also jedem Angriff ausgeliefert gewesen (Abb. 31.6). Zudem ist zu beobachten, dass die Figuren unter gegenseitiger Berücksichtigung erst nach und nach errichtet wurden und ihre Positionierung dabei ähnlichen Regeln folgte wie jene der Stelen auf dem Stylobat des Hera-Tempels. Daher wird das Aufstellen der Bronzen noch während des kultischen Lebens im Heiligtum erfolgt sein. Dies spricht gegen die angenommene Zurschaustellung durch den christlichen Domänenfürsten. Die Bronzen wurden vielmehr zuvor dort errichtet, wo sie für die Besucher gut sichtbar waren, die sich in wichtigen Arealen des funktionierenden Heiligtums aufhielten: auf der Feststraße südlich des Zeus-Tempels oder vor der Hauptfront des Hera-Tempels (vgl. Abb. 31.6).

Die Maßnahme der Aufstellung, die angesichts der Verteilung der unterschiedlichen Befestigungstechniken eine längere Zeit in Anspruch genommen haben könnte, kann nun auch genauer charakterisiert werden: Bei den Figuren wird es sich in der Regel, wenn nicht sogar ausschließlich um Siegerstatuen gehandelt haben. Sie waren fast alle etwas überlebensgroß – ein Maß, das übrigens zusammen mit dem Bronzematerial für Siegerstatuen in Olympia üblich war (Lehmann 2003, 31). Zumindest die Exemplare am Zeus-Tempel wurden nicht nur unter Beachtung der oben erwähnten Regeln errichtet, sondern auch nach heute unbekannten Kriterien sortiert: Gruppierungen, Paare und symmetrische Bezüge sind zu erkennen. Eine Sortierung nach Kunstlandschaften, der Herkunft der Sieger, ästhetischen Kriterien oder auch nach inhaltlichen Gemeinsamkeiten ist denkbar, vielleicht auch eine Mischung von allem, da bei einer sukzessiven Aufstellung mal das eine und mal das andere eine Rolle gespielt haben könnte. Allerdings wird man die Zusammenstellung der Figuren auf den Stufen nicht als museal bezeichnen dürfen, was auch bereits für Skulpturen festgestellt wurde, die im Inneren des Hera-Tempels aufbewahrt wurden (Krumeich 2008, 73–86): Erläuternde Inschriften fehlten, und manche Statuen standen äußerst dicht neben- und hintereinander, waren also nur auf Fernwirkung angelegt. Vielleicht wurde eine sukzessive Wiederaufstellung der Figuren nötig, weil die Bereiche des Heiligtums, aus denen sie stammten, nach und nach umgestaltet wurden. Jedenfalls werden klassische Siegerstatuen im 3. und 4. Jahrhundert n. Chr. auch noch in der Umgebung der Tempel zu sehen gewesen sein. Denn Pausanias erwähnt in seiner Beschreibung kurz zuvor „etwa 200 Siegerstatuen in der Altis des Zeusheiligtums" (Lehmann 2003, 26). Und angesichts der erwähnten Splitter hoch in der Stratigraphie ist damit zu rechnen, dass viele dieser Bronzestatuen erst in frühchristlicher Zeit zerstört wurden.

Vor weiteren Überlegungen zur Funktion der Figuren sei noch erwähnt, dass an verschiedenen Stellen auf den Stylobaten bzw. Stufen beider Tempel in Olympia

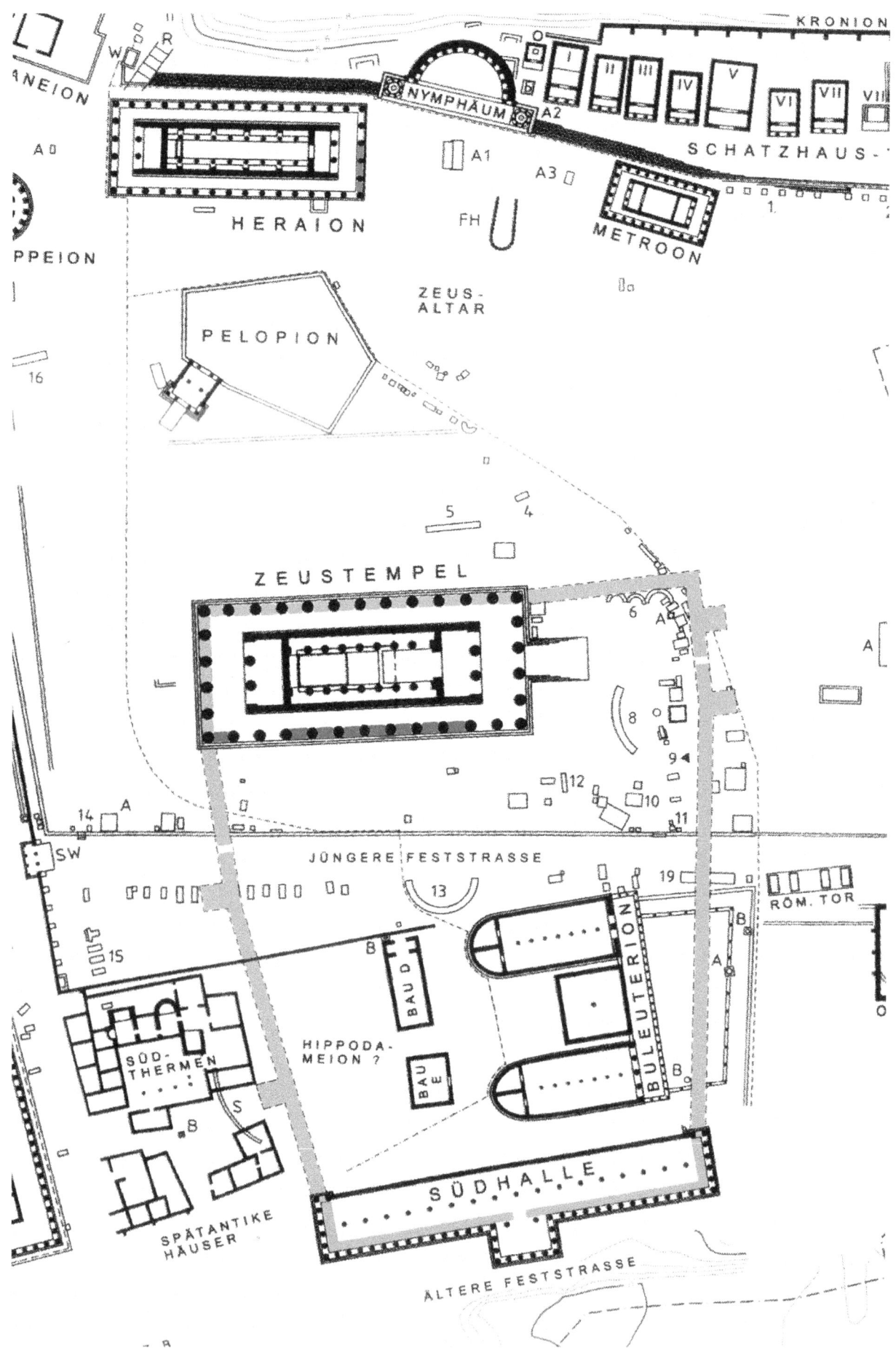

Abb. 31.6. Olympia: dunkelgrau = Bereiche der Peripteroi mit Bronzestatuen; hellgrau = Festungsmauer (durch D. Doepner eingefärbter Ausschnitt der Beilage von Kyrieleis, 2002, unter Berücksichtigung von Mallwitz, 1972, Abb. 87)

auf wenigen Basen Objekte standen, deren Aufstellung aufgrund anderer Eigenschaften nicht zu der beschriebenen Maßnahme gehörte. Da diese Objekte womöglich auch nicht aus Bronze bestanden, werden sie hier nicht mit berücksichtigt.

Überlegungen zur Funktion der am Tempel befestigten Bronzen

Folgende Beobachtungen lassen sich in Bezug auf alle Phänomene anstellen:

- Die Zahl der am Tempel montierten Bronzeobjekte war stets begrenzt.
- Ihre konkreten Anbringungsorte wurden immer bewusst gewählt.
- Die zumeist erhöhte Position auf den Stufen oder am Dach hob die Bronzen im wahrsten Sinne des Wortes räumlich und optisch aus der Umgebung hervor – eine Fernansicht wurde dabei oft regelrecht inszeniert.
- Die Montage am Tempel brachte die Objekte zugleich in eine größere Nähe zu den wertvollsten Utensilien des Kultes, darunter das Kultbild, die sich in der Cella befanden. Dies gilt besonders für bronzene Dekret-Tafeln, die den Zugang zum Tempel quasi säumten.

So verlieh der Tempel den an ihm fixierten Objekten Eigenschaften, durch die sie öffentlich als etwas Besonderes wahrgenommen werden mussten. Auf diese Weise publizierten sie mit Nachdruck die oben erwähnten Inhalte, die auch bei der Präsentation von Gleichartigem im offenen Areal des Heiligtums eine Rolle spielten – also etwa den Dank an die Gottheit, den Stolz auf einen errungenen Sieg, die Ehrung eines Genannten. Dies galt umso mehr, wenn Entsprechendes zu derselben Zeit in der Umgebung des betreffenden Tempels zu sehen war (also womöglich nur Ausgewähltes an ihm fixiert wurde), nur durch ältere Aufstellungen im Freien und in kleineren Bauten bekannt war oder zeitgleich in anderen Heiligtümern lediglich auf diese andere, weniger spektakuläre Weise präsentiert wurde. Das, was die Tafeln, Waffen und Statuen inhaltlich betonten, wird wiederum auch die Funktion des Tempels, an dem sie in Erscheinung traten, in der öffentlichen Wahrnehmung mit geprägt haben.

Doch die an den Peripteroi fixierten Objekte dienten nicht nur Stiftern und Rezipienten: Eine Ausstellung im Heiligtum und besonders eine exklusive am Tempel wird nicht ohne die Erlaubnis des Gremiums der Polis (oder der Amphiktyonie) erfolgt sein, das für die Organisation des Heiligtums zuständig war. Über das Wirken dieses Gremiums – wahrscheinlich das Kultkollegium –, das neben eigenen Interessen auch jene der Polis vertreten haben wird, ist nicht viel bekannt. Wenige erhaltene Dekrete überliefern immerhin, dass zumindest in einzelnen Heiligtümern hellenistischer Zeit das Anbringen von Weihgeschenken im Inneren von Gebäuden und im offenen Areal reguliert wurde, wenn ihre Menge drohte, Durchgänge oder die Sicht auf das Kultbild zu blockieren (Brulotte 1994, 259–261). Die aufgezeigten Phänomene boten gerade diesem Gremium vielfältige Möglichkeiten des finanziellen und anderen Zugewinns, der Selbstdarstellung, der ‚politischen' Einflussnahme und der Werbung, und es ist zu erwarten, dass diese Möglichkeiten genutzt wurden, auch wenn antike Quellen bisher darüber schweigen:

- Finanzielle Zuwendungen für die Anbringung am Tempel könnten dem Wohle des Heiligtums gedient haben.
- Eine Bronzetafel am Tempelzugang wird öffentlich die besonders große Bedeutung des auf ihr vermerkten Dekrets für die Polis zum Ausdruck gebracht haben bzw. – im Falle eines Ehren-Dekrets – die außergewöhnlich hohe Wertschätzung, die die Stadt der von ihr geehrten Person entgegenbrachte. Dies konnte auch politisch genutzt werden, um wichtige Verbindungen zu betonen und zu fördern. Priesterlisten, die die Namen der Amtsträger am Tempeleingang veröffentlichten und diese so zugleich besonders ehrten, werden der Selbstdarstellung des Kultkollegiums gedient haben.
- Durch ein weithin sichtbares eigenes Beuteanathem am Peripteros wird eine Polis nicht nur ihren eigenen militärischen Erfolg und damit sich selbst gefeiert haben, sondern auch die Wirksamkeit ihres Kultes und seines Personals. Umso wichtiger waren sicher fremde spektakuläre Beutemale am Tempel eines Orakelheiligtums, da sie optisch die Effizienz seiner Seher hervorhoben, zugleich die überregionale Bedeutung des Kultes demonstrierten und so für weitere Anfragen warben. Beutewaffen wie jene von Mummius in Olympia dürften aber auch politische Abhängigkeiten widergespiegelt haben.
- Eine frühe Bronzestatue am Apollon-Tempel in Syrakus wird die große Bedeutung des Votivanlasses und auch des Stifters für die Polis kundgetan haben. Zugleich bezeugte sie öffentlich die Effizienz des Kultes. Die klassischen Originalstatuen könnten jedoch in später römischer Zeit auf die Stufen der traditionell wichtigsten Tempel Olympias gelangt sein, um dort besonders augenfällig an die Kunstfertigkeit und die Agone der Zeit im elischen Heiligtum zu erinnern, die von seinen Betreibern als die glanzvollste empfunden wurde.

So dürfte die auf Dauer angelegte Präsentation am Außenbau der Peripteroi unsere Kenntnisse über die Funktion von Bronzen in griechischen Heiligtümern bereichern, indem sie die Organisatoren des Heiligtums in den Fokus der Aufmerksamkeit rückt.

Danksagung

Die Arbeit wurde von der Fritz-Thyssen-Stiftung finanziert und von der archäologischen Soprintendenz in Syrakus gefördert. Von den zahlreichen anderen internationalen Institutionen und Kollegen, die sie hilfreich unterstützten, seien hier nur jene genannt, die großzügig von ihnen angefertigte, aber noch nicht veröffentlichte Aufnahmen für das Projekt zur Verfügung stellten – besonders Dieter Mertens, der die Untersuchung auch anregte, und auch Arnd Hennemeyer und Anne Sieverling –, sowie Frank Willer vom LVR-Landesmuseum in Bonn, welcher mein

Verständnis der technischen Vorgänge in Bezug auf Bronzen erheblich förderte. Ich bin allen sehr dankbar.

Bibliographie

Baitinger, H., 2011. *Waffenweihungen in griechischen Heiligtümern.* Mainz: Verlag des Römisch-Germanischen Zentralmuseums.

Brulotte, E. L., 1994. *The placement of votive offerings and dedications in the Peloponnesian sanctuaries of Artemis*, 1-2. Thesis (Ph. D.) – University of Minnesota. Ann Arbor: University Microfilms International.

Dittenberger, W. – Purgold, K., 1896. *Die Inschriften von Olympia.* Olympia 5. Berlin: A. Asher & Co.

Doepner, D., 2015. Weihgeschenke am Apollon-Tempel in Syrakus: ein Vorbericht. *Kölner und Bonner Archaeologica*, 5, 79–89.

Doepner, D., 2002. *Steine und Pfeiler für die Götter. Weihgeschenkgattungen in westgriechischen Stadtheiligtümern.* Palilia 10. Wiesbaden: Reichert.

Dörpfeld, W., 1935. *Alt-Olympia: Untersuchungen und Ausgrabungen zur Geschichte des ältesten Heiligtums von Olympia und der älteren griechischen Kunst*, 1. Berlin: E. S. Mittler & Sohn.

Eckstein, F., 1969. *ΑΝΑΘΗΜΑΤΑ. Studien zu den Weihgeschenken strengen Stils im Heiligtum von Olympia.* Berlin: Gebr. Mann.

Graells i Fabregat, R., 2017. L'immagine muta del trionfo. Il *tropaion* sud-italico della Antikensammlung di München e il suo contesto. In: A. Pontrandolfo – M. Scafuro, Hrsg., *Dialoghi sull'archeologia della Magna Grecia e del Mediterraneo. Atti del 1. Convegno internazionale di studi, Paestum, 7–9 settembre 2016.* Paestum: Pandemos.

Guarducci, M., 1969. *Epigrafia greca, 2. Epigrafi di carattere pubblico.* Rom: Libreria dello Stato.

Gutsfeld, A. – Lehmann, S., 2013. Spolien und Spoliation im spätantiken Olympia, in I. Gerlach – D. Raue, Hrsg., 2013. *Sanktuar und Ritual. Heilige Plätze im archäologischen Befund.* Rahden/Westf: VML, Verlag Marie Leidorf, 91–104.

Gutsfeld, A. – Lehmann, N. – Lehmann, S., 2013. Olympia und seine zwei Leben in der Spätantike vom panhellenischen Heiligtum zur Domäne, *Gymnasium* 120, 2013, 1–18.

Jackson, A., 1992. Arms and Armour at the Panhellenic Sanctuary of Poseidon at Isthmia. In: W. Coulson – H. Kyrieleis, Hrsg., 1992. *Proceedings of an International Symposium on the Olympic Games, Athens 5–9 September 1988.* Athen: Deutsches Archäologisches Institut, 141–144 Taf. XXIII, 66–68.

Heilmeyer, W. D. – Kaltsas, N. – Gehrke, H.-J. – Hatzi, G. E. – Bocher, S., Hrgs., 2012. *Mythos Olympia. Kult und Spiele* (Katalog zur Ausstellung vom 31. 8. 2012 bis 7. 1. 2013 in Berlin, Martin-Gropius-Bau). München, London, New York: Prestel.

Kissas, K., 2000. *Die attischen Statuen- und Stelenbasen archaischer Zeit.* Bonn: In Kommission bei R. Habelt.

Krumeich, R., 2008. Vom Haus der Gottheit zum Museum? Zu Ausstattung und Funktion des Heraion von Olympia und des Athenatempels von Lindos, *Antike Kunst* 51, 2008, 73–95.

Kyrieleis, H., Hrsg., 2002. *Olympia 1875–2000. 125 Jahre deutsche Ausgrabungen. Internationales Symposion, Berlin 9.–11. November 2000.* Mainz: P. von Zabern.

Lehmann, S., 2003. „Der Mensch – Maß aller Dinge?" Zur Deutung griechischer Athletenstatuen. In: M. Lämmer – B. Ränsch-Trill, Hrsg., *Der „künstliche Mensch" – eine sportwissenschaftliche Perspektive?* Sankt Augustin: Academia, 17–39.

Mallwitz, A., 1972. *Olympia und seine Bauten.* München: Prestel-Verlag.

Manganaro, G., 1963. Tre tavole di bronzo con decreti di *proxenia* del Museo di Napoli e il problema dei proagori in Sicilia, *Kokalos* 9, 205–220, Taf. 63–67.

Mertens, D., 2006. *Städte und Bauten der Westgriechen. Von der Kolonisationszeit bis zur Krise um 400 vor Christus.* München: Hirmer.

Moustaka, A., 1992. Μορφή και συμβολισμός της Νίκης στην Αρχαία Ολυμπία, in W. Coulson – H. Kyrieleis, Hrsg., *Proceedings of an International Symposium on the Olympic Games, Athens 5–9 September 1988.* Athens: Deutsches Archäologisches Institut, 39–43, Taf. VIII. 22–26.

Niemeier, W.-D, 2016. *Das Orakelheiligtum des Apollon von Abai/Kalapodi: eines der bedeutendsten griechischen Heiligtümer nach den Ergebnissen der neuen Ausgrabungen.* Wiesbaden: Harrassowitz.

Philipp, H., 2004. *Archaische Silhouettenbleche und Schildzeichen in Olympia*, Olympische Forschungen 30. Berlin, New York: Walter de Gruyter.

Rabe, B., 2008. *Tropaia: τροπή und σκῦλα – Entstehung, Funktion und Bedeutung des griechischen Tropaions.* Rahden/Westf.: Leidorf.

Reichel, W. – Wilhelm, A., 1901. Das Heiligthum der Artemis zu Lusoi, *Jahreshefte des Österreichischen Archäologischen Institutes* 4, 1901, 1–89.

Remijsen, S. 2015. *The end of Greek athletics in late Antiquity. Greek culture in the Roman world.* Cambridge: University Press.

Sieverling, A., 2008. *Untersuchungen zu den Befestigungsspuren an den Säulen des Heratempels in Olympia* (unpublizierte Magisterarbeit an der Freien Universität Berlin)

Stevens, G. P., 1940. *The Setting of the Periclean Parthenon*, Hesperia Suppl. 3. Baltimore, Md.: American School of Classical Studies at Athens.

Willer, F., 1996. Beobachtungen zur Sockelung von bronzenen Statuen und Statuetten, *Bonner Jahrbücher* 196, 1996, 337–370.

32

A bronze foundry of Classical times in the sanctuary at Kalapodi (Central Greece)

Johanna Fuchs

German Archaeological Institute, Athens

JohannaFuchs@gmx.net

Abstract: Northeast of the modern village of Kalapodi in ancient Phokis (Central Greece) lies the archaeological site which can probably be identified with the oracular sanctuary of Apollo at Abai. Here, a number of (casting-)pits and other installations, as well as fragments of metallurgical ceramics like moulds and crucibles, bronze slag and vast numbers of bronze droplets, prove the former existence of a bronze foundry west of the Archaic South Temple. The workshop was engaged in the indirect lost-wax casting of large-scale bronze statuary. According to preliminary results, it was operating at the end of the 5th century BC.

Keywords: Bronze Foundry; Metallurgical Ceramics; Kalapodi; Greek Sanctuary; Workshop

Introduction

Since the 1970s, the German Archaeological Institute at Athens has been working close to the modern village of Kalapodi Phtiotidas in ancient Phokis (for an overview of the excavation history, see Niemeier 2013a; 2013b). Investigations at the site, which is probably identifiable with the oracular sanctuary of Apollo at Abai (Niemeier 2013b, 3–5; Prignitz 2014; Kopanias forthcoming), have revealed two neighbouring sequences of temple buildings. In recent years, excavations at the southern temple complex provided a number of successive cult buildings reaching from Mycenaean to Roman imperial times (for an overview, see Niemeier 2013a; 2013b). Excavations conducted from 2007 to 2012 under the supervision of Wolf-Dietrich Niemeier, and again in the years 2015, 2016, and 2018 with Katja Sporn as head of excavation, also revealed a number of (casting-) pits and other installations attributable to a bronze foundry (Niemeier 2010, 107f.; 2012, 96 with fig. 12; 2013b, 22; 2014, 30–31 with figs. 12. 13; Sporn 2016–2017, 197; Fuchs 2016–2017). Based on current work, this article presents an overview of the finds and findings from the workshop area and assigns them to a functional as well as chronological context.

Archaeological Record

The workshop remains are located within the centre of the sanctuary (for the latest results on the wider area now excavated, see Sporn 2016–2017; 2017). They are to be found immediately west of the so-called Archaic South Temple (Fig. 32.1). This late Archaic building was burned down during the destruction of the sanctuary by the Persians in 480 BC. After its demolition, this temple was left in ruins (Grigoropoulos 2015, esp. 80–81 with fig. 3). In place of the former Archaic North Temple, a new cult building, the first Classical North Temple, was erected (Felsch 2007, 17; Niemeier 2013b, 20–22). Therefore, when the craftspeople established their bronze workshop – presumably at the end of the 5th century BC, they set it up in a debris-strewn area. The establishment of bronze foundries in or close to abandoned or as yet unfinished buildings is a phenomenon that can be observed on a quite regular basis (Zimmer 1990, 157). Typically the artisans seem to have been looking for a degree of shelter that partly standing walls and/or roofs could provide. In Kalapodi, the damage to the Archaic South Temple was so severe that apparently not much was left upright. During excavation, not only fallen roof tiles but also burnt wooden beams and collapsed mudbricks were uncovered. Even large parts of the stone pediment of its western façade were found as they had fallen (Fig. 32.6) (Niemeier 2013b, 20–21; Hellner 2016–2017). However, the southern blocks had been removed in antiquity, apparently for the construction of the workshop. After the removal of some of the Persian rubble, the place in front of the former temple seems to have been reckoned by the bronze workers to fit their purpose. It was then wide enough, adequately flat and even, and the ground was appropriate for the creation of pits. However, since the dating and possible cultic function of the only known well in the area, situated in the southern *peridromos* of the first Classical North Temple (Felsch 2007, 18), remains still undecided, it is not yet clear where the water needed for the processing of the clay came from. With Zimmer (1990, 158), we have to assume that the sanctuary administration also had their say in the allocation of the workplace.

The remains of the bronze foundry cover an area of at least 75 m². Since the workshop has not been entirely

Johanna Fuchs

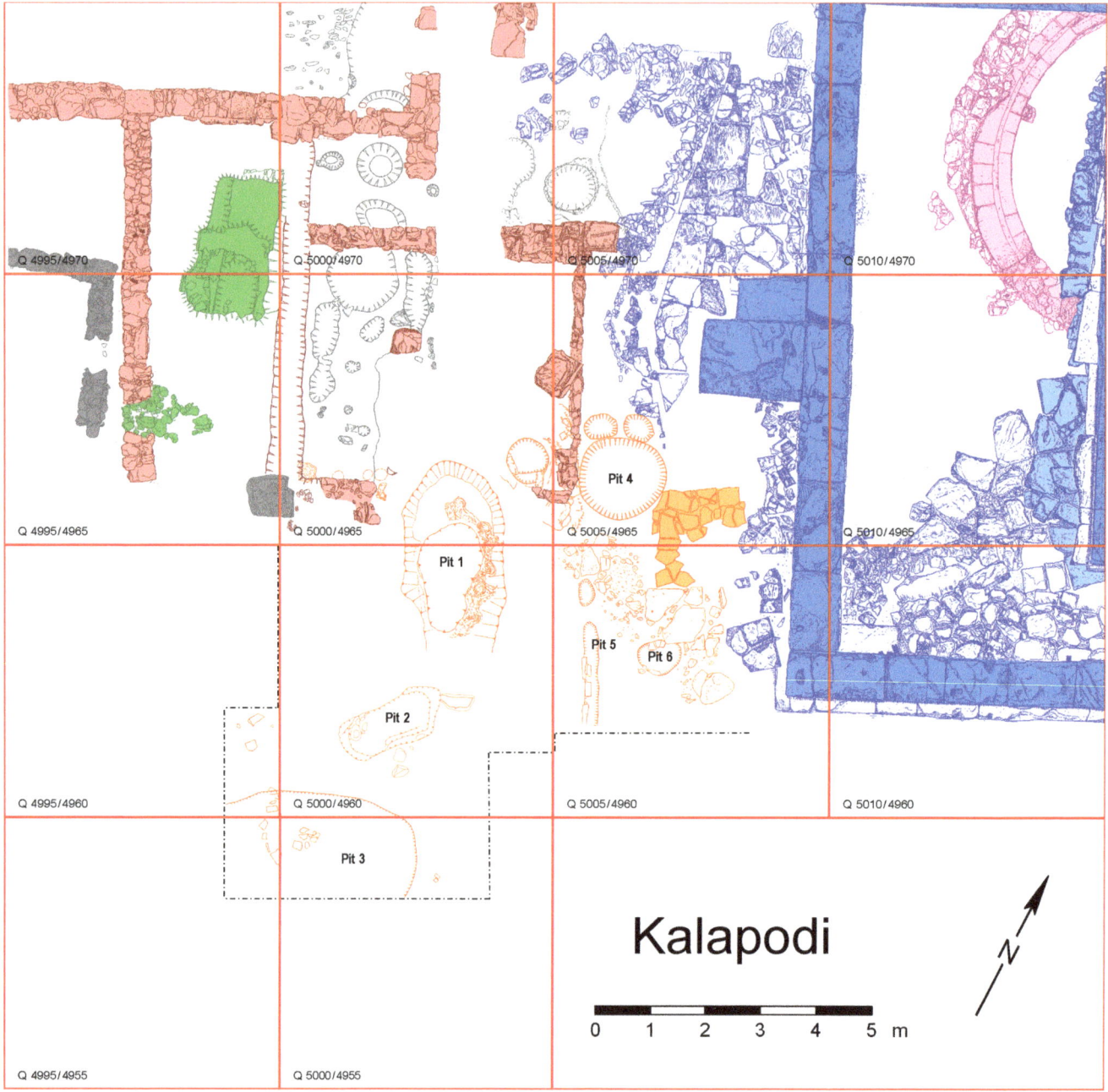

Fig. 32.1: Kalapodi, general plan of the bronze foundry (2018). Plan: German Archaeological Institute Athens (J. Fuchs, N. Hellner & H. Birk).

investigated and, according to the excavated results, would have extended further at least south and west of the investigated area, the size given has to be considered as a minimum.

In the centre of the excavated area lies a casting pit in the shape of a key-hole, that has been cut into the virgin soil (pit 1) (Fig. 32.1). Its maximum dimensions are 4.15 m from north to south and 1.75 m from west to east. The inner core of this pit, which is also formed like a key-hole, measures about 2.00 m x 1.20 m. Due to its exposure to fire it has taken on a red colour (Fig. 32.2). The eastern and northeastern sides of the pit´s core are coated with clay. To the north and northwest, sand was added to regulate the desired form.

Within said core, three clay pillars stood on a common clay base (Fig. 32.3). The middle pillar, with a diameter of 15–17 cm, is preserved to a height of about 20 cm. It is composed of a thick outer layer of coarse clay around a cylindrical core of finer clay, all enclosing a channel-like hole in the centre. The pillar is angled to the south, where it has a small ledge (cf. Fig. 32.2). When compared with other such finds, this installation can be interpreted as the base of a mould for casting. In its composition it shows similarities to a bigger and slightly earlier mould base erected in foundry pit 4, beneath the so-called Bau Z in the Kerameikos in Athens (Zimmer 1984, 64–76 with figs. 1–5; Zimmer 1990, 34–37 with figs. 4–6 and pl. 3d. e). Although they do not have the same layered composition as the one in the middle, it can be assumed that the two

A bronze foundry of Classical times in the sanctuary at Kalapodi (Central Greece)

Fig. 32.2: Kalapodi, bronze foundry, pit 1. General view from southeast. Photo: Neg. no. D-DAI-ATH-2017-32553 (W.-D. Niemeier).

clay pillars on either side of it (with a maximum diameter of 23 cm and 25 cm) also functioned as mould bases. To further ensure its stability, the eastern pillar is supported by an iron rod that has been jammed between the mould base and the wall of the pit (Fig. 32.3).

The three clay pillars interpreted as mould bases are erected on a common clay base, with a length of 45 cm and a width of 17 cm. While the middle and the western clay pillars are set directly on top of the base, the eastern pillar is partly built upon mould fragments. The clay base itself is heavily burned. Like the clay block situated behind the mould bases in foundry pit 4 beneath ›Bau Z‹ in the Kerameikos in Athens (Zimmer 1984, 65–66 with fig. 2), it might have primarily served to demarcate the positioning of the fire for melting the wax. The place in front of it shows intense scorch marks (Fig. 32.4). Attached to the base is a hand-crafted spout pointing south-southeast that was most likely used to divert the molten wax as it ran out of the middle mould base. A small pit lined with reused tile and mould fragments that lies south of the installation might have served to secure the position of a vessel for collecting the wax.

In the course of the excavation, it became obvious that the features as described above did not mark the full extent of pit 1. As was indicated by the presence of mould fragments in and beneath the fireplace, as well as its red outer rim of triangular shape – seemingly recoloured during a second heating, it became clear that the firing-place had been installed over an earlier mould base of greater dimensions, small traces of which were later

Fig. 32.3: Kalapodi, bronze foundry, pit 1. Detail of the three clay pillars interpreted as mould bases. View from northwest. Photo: Neg. no. D-DAI-ATH-2019-00333 (W.-D. Niemeier).

Fig. 32.4: Kalapodi, bronze foundry, pit 1. Detail of the clay board beneath the three clay pillars (cf. fig. 32.3). View from southeast. Photo: Neg. no. D-DAI-ATH-2019-00334 (W.-D. Niemeier).

found on a reddish-white clay area that was uncovered. Within the surface of that area, imprints of iron rods that might have served as reinforcements attest to a previous casting-event within pit 1. Therefore, we can assume at least two consecutive casting projects. During the first one, a mould with a base of about 0.85 m to 0.72 m was erected at the bottom of pit 1. After the casting, it was broken up and the pieces almost completely removed from the pit. A little later, a second base, intended for the casting of three smaller items (as indicated by the three ›pillar bases‹), was erected. The workers levelled the area formerly occupied by the first mould and then built the bases for the second casting on top of the same spot. They also lined the northern wall of the pit with clay and mould fragments from the first casting and further backfilled it with sand to better retain the heat. After the completion of the second casting, the pit was refilled with earth and waste material.

In the vicinity of the ›key-hole pit‹ (pit 1) several other pits of varying sizes and shapes have been uncovered (Fig. 32.1). To the south, there are two large pits that have a rather amorphous shape. Pit 2 is orientated in southwest-northeast direction. It has a maximum length of 2.50 m and a width of 1.25 m. Pit 3 measures at least 2.95 m from east to west and 2.00 m from north to south. It has not been entirely investigated and extends further west and south out of the excavated area. East of pit 1, we find a cluster of more or less circular pits with a maximum diameter of up to about 1.50 m (pit 4) and 0.80 m (pit 6), respectively. Although remains of a mould base have been preserved in pit 1 only, we can probably assume that at least some of the other pits, which were filled with fragments of metallurgical ceramics, bronze droplets and charcoal, also served as casting pits. Others may have been utilized to stand vessels in, as rubbish pits, etc.

Situated in the eastern part of the excavated area is the elongated pit 5, orientated in a north-south direction (Fig. 32.1). On its southwestern side is a lining of Corinthian roof-tile fragments. The dimensions of the pit, which has a width of about 40 cm, a depth of about 33 cm and a length of at least 2.00 m, in combination with the lining of tile fragments, recall Ptolemaic smelting installations discovered in Egypt. These structures, unearthed in the funerary temple of Sethos I in the Theban necropolis, consist of two parallel mud brick walls set 22 cm apart. Remains of metal and charcoal, fragments of crucibles, nozzles, and stone moulds found in between and immediately around them, as well as imprints of crucibles preserved by scorch marks within the walls, all attest to their function as crucible stands for the melting of metal (Scheel 1988a; 1988b). It might be that pit 5 in Kalapodi served as a similar kind of oven (for a discussion of various aspects of the smelting process in crucibles, see Zimmer 2006). Estimating the average crucible to have an upper diameter of about 40 cm (cf. examples from Olympia reconstructed by Völling – Zimmer 1995, 661–662 with figs. 1. 2; Zimmer 2006, 24–25 with fig. 1), the pit's dimensions would be enough to align and feed at least five crucibles. Additional support for this interpretation is the loose fill from pit 5 that contained many fragments of charcoal, as well as bronze droplets.

In the western part of the excavated workshop area in Kalapodi, there is a nearly rectangular area with a maximum length of about 1.20 m. It is characterised by a blackened surface and a concentration of heavily burnt

Fig. 32.5: Kalapodi, bronze foundry, fragments of metallurgical ceramics northwest of pit 4. View from southsoutheast. Photo: Neg. no. D-DAI-ATH-2019-00335 (W.-D. Niemeier).

olive pits in the middle. Together with finds of charcoal, bronze slag and bronze drops, it points to the positioning of another melting installation, whose appearance however remains unclear.

East of the pits was found a nearly rectangular platform of about 1.70 m to 1.80 m (Fig. 32.6). It is made of reused roof tiles from the first Classical North Temple. This platform most probably served as a base for the assembly and reworking of the cast during subsequent cold-working processes (for an overview of cold-working and montage in general, see e.g. Bol 1978, 78–87). A similar structure – though much bigger and made out of stone blocks – has been uncovered at the foundry site on the southern slope of the Acropolis in Athens (Zimmer 1990, 66–67; Zimmer 2002, 503; cf. also Zimmer 1990, 44–47 for a mudbrick installation in Phidias' workshop at Olympia).

A smaller installation at the northern edge of pit 3 most likely has also been used as a base for piecing together smaller parts of the cast. It is composed of a single layer of reused tiles, mud brick fragments, and stones with a maximum dimension of 0.50 m and is covered with ash, interspersed with bronze droplets and bronze slag.

Characteristic of the whole foundry area is the presence of charcoal and ash, as well as large quantities of small bronze drops, slag, accumulations of scrap, and also immense amounts of fragmentary metallurgical ceramics (Fig. 32.5). We find these both in the occupation layer and within the fill of the pits.

All the workshop structures seem to be rather ephemeral. Remains that would point to the existence of more permanent installations and proper buildings are missing in the excavated workshop areas in Kalapodi. Looking at other known foundry sites, this is a common finding (Zimmer 1990, 156). Although one would expect to find traces of roofs or hall-like structures that could protect the moulds, they are not often detectable (Zimmer 1990, 158). From personal experience during the experimental recasting of a bronze statue, Hackländer and Formigli (1997, 94) argue for the necessity of some kind of roof for the protection of the moulds from strong climatic influences. However, since these workshops were usually set up for a specific task only and abandoned after its completion (Zimmer 1990, 156), the artisans seem to have contented themselves with rather simple constructions (Hackländer – Formigli 1997, 94).

Movable Finds

After this short overview of the archaeological record, we now turn to the movable finds that were discovered within the workshop area. Among them are hundreds of fragments of metallurgical ceramics, filling almost one hundred boxes (Fig. 32.7). The most significant and characteristic of these – about 120 pieces – have been inventoried, catalogued, and photographed by the author.

The remains are heavily fragmented; generally they are less than the size of a fist. Their poor condition can be explained by the usual composition of metallurgical ceramics, their often low durability, and the casting process itself, which involved the breaking up of cores and moulds, as well as the reuse of raw material. Unfortunately, this makes it nearly impossible to find joins between individual fragments and complicates their identification (for the challenges in working with metallurgical ceramics, cf. e.g. Schneider – Zimmer 1984, 17). However, among the fragments, bellows nozzles, crucibles, remains of casting moulds, funnels and gates, vents, plugs, and point bars (mould supports or struts) could all be recognized. Thus, the whole range

Fig. 32.6: Kalapodi, Archaic South Temple. View from west. In the foreground the area of the bronze foundry with pit 4 and tile platform. Photo: Neg. no. D-DAI-ATH-2019-00336 (W.-D. Niemeier).

of ceramics required in casting is present: we can retrace the process from the building of the mould through the attachment of a funnel and gate system to the melting of the metal and the casting itself.

The metallurgical ceramics from Kalapodi consist of presumably local clay of a light brown to reddish-yellow colour (cf. Zimmer 1990, 159–160, with general thoughts on the use of local clay by bronze workers). It is mixed with gravel, lime, mica and organic materials in varying proportions. The examination of some of the fragments under the scanning electron microscope (SEM) by Anno Hein and Kyriaki Christodoulo revealed rather homogenous round and oblong pores with a diameter of around 100 μm within the microstructure of the fragments (Hein et al. 2017). They indicate the use of animal hair for tempering the clay. The adding of organic components and non-plastic inclusions is a well-known recipe for the construction of metallurgical ceramics (Zimmer 1990, 160). It is also attested in Olympia (Schneider – Zimmer 1984, 32. 34–45 with figs. 19–20) and Demetrias (Schneider 2003, 66 with pls. 14f. g. h). The mixture improved the refractoriness of the clay paste during firing operations, i.e. its resistance to the application of heat. The porosity generated by the voids made when the organic temper burned out during firing suppressed heat transference and loss and prevented the propagation of cracks (Hein – Kilikoglou 2011, 182).

Metallurgical ceramics were built up by hand. Therefore many fragments show finger marks. Usually the ceramics consist of more than one layer. Different layers can be distinguished by different tempering, but they do not necessarily have to have varied compositions. Between the layers sometimes there are regular gaps, where the connection between them has not been entirely achieved (Fig 32.7,1).

The biggest group among these fragments are those from the moulds (Fig. 32.7.1, 2, 3). They usually show a characteristic layer sequence, with increased coarse tempering as one moves out from the central and initial layer. The finest innermost layer has a greyish colour. Generally it is only a couple of millimetres thick and shows no tempering, apart from some small whitish inclusions and mica. Although an infrequent find, some mould fragments still preserve parts which may even show traces of the brush and tool marks that once were visible on the surface of the wax model. Being applied directly in a rather liquid form, this first and fine clay reproduces the surface subtleties of the wax model, in order to faithfully reproduce all the details of the figure. Once this first layer had dried, the next layer would have been applied. It is generally thicker and contains more temper. After this one had dried out, the next layer, even thicker, could be applied and so on. The outermost layers of the moulds all preserve finger marks. They also show an attempt to create

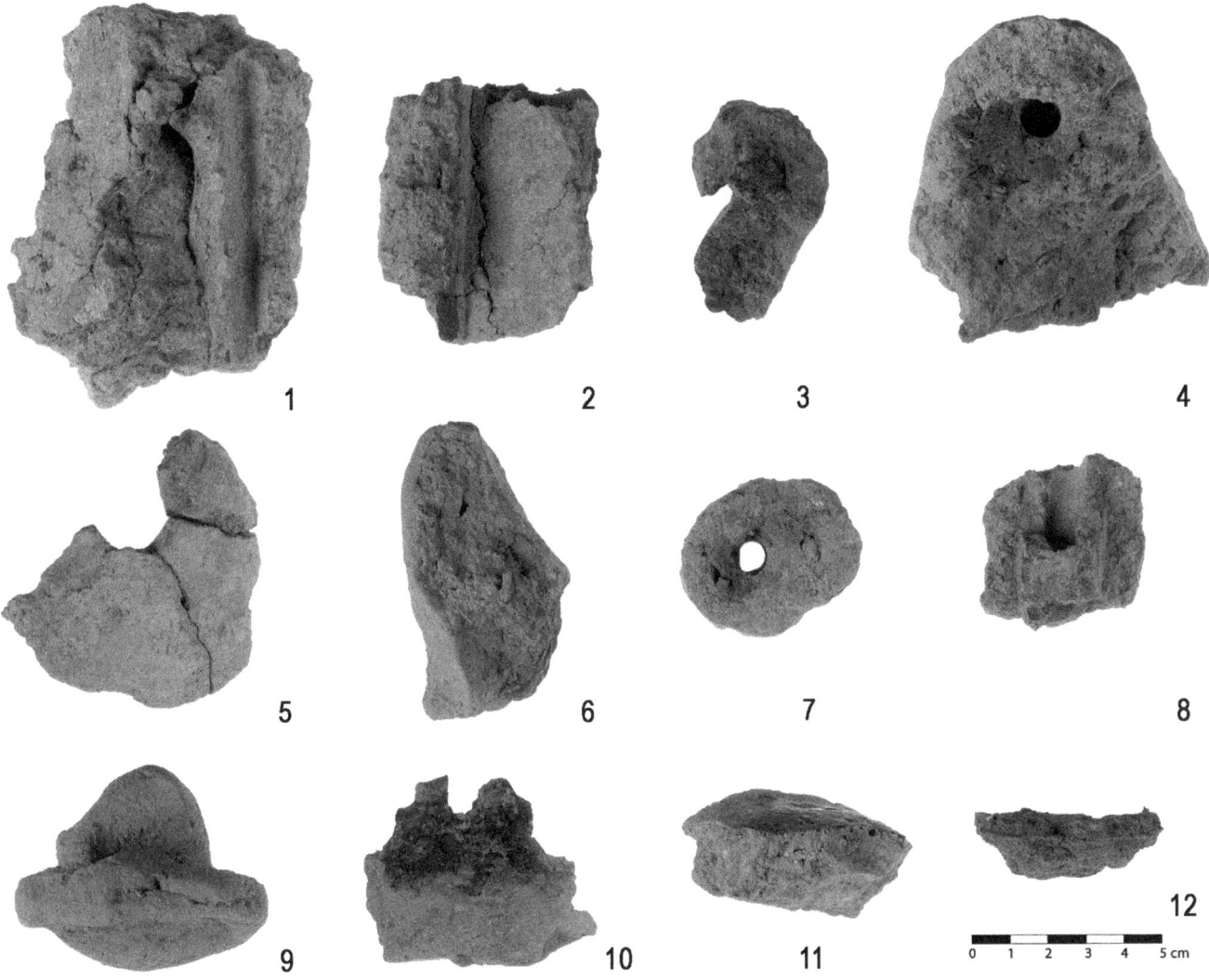

Fig. 32.7: Kalapodi, variety of metallurgical ceramics from the context of the bronze foundry. 1: mould fragment with attached vent (KAL11.193.022). 2: mould fragment (KAL11.193.041). 3: mould fragment (KAL11.193.040). 4: vent fragment (KAL11.193.021). 5: vent fragment (KAL08.303.003). 6: funnel fragment (KAL11.193.024). 7: vent fragment (KAL11.193.018). 8: vent fragment Inv. KAL11.218.015). 9: plug (KAL11.193.020). 10: fragment of a bellow nozzle (KAL15.099.016). 11: fragment of a bellow nozzle (KAL11.218.05). 12: crucible fragment (KAL11.218.004). Photo: Neg. nos. D-DAI-ATH-2016-05222, D-DAI-ATH-2016-05301, D-DAI-ATH-2016-05297, D-DAI-ATH-2016-05219, D-DAI-ATH-2016-05098, D-DAI-ATH-2016-05231, D-DAI-ATH-2016-05202, D-DAI-ATH-2016-05346, D-DAI-ATH-2016-05208, D-DAI-ATH-2016-05565, D-DAI-ATH-2016-05313, D-DAI-ATH-2016-05309 (J. Fuchs).

a smooth surface and avoid rough edges and angles (cf. Zimmer 2003, 32).

Unfortunately, even the closest examination of the mould fragments from Kalapodi did not reveal more detailed information about the cast object or objects. Enlightening fragments are missing, such as the face details from the so-called Archaic foundry in the Ancient Agora in Athens, where a one-half life-size figure of a *kouros* was cast (Mattusch 1975, 100–116 esp. 104 cat. 4 with pls. 14b. 15b; Mattusch 1977, 343–347 esp. 346–347 cat. nos. A 3. A 4 with pls. 80a. 81a. b). In Kalapodi, the only hints we have for the appearance of the cast item or items are mould fragments with corners and curved angles that could be read as representing drapery (Fig. 32.7.2, 3). Their sizes could be taken as hinting at a life-size figure;

an assumption that would be supported by the dimensions of the casting pit(s).

The biggest mould base we know of here is a triangular one of 0.85 m to 0.72 m that was erected at the bottom of pit 1. Assuming that the figure was cast in different pieces that were joined together later (for the separate casting of single pieces of large-scale bronze statues, see e.g. Dafas 2015, 141 with n. 25), the space would suffice for casting a large-size figure. The dimensions of the above mentioned platform, interpreted as a base for the assemblage of the sculpture during cold-working, would also support the assumption of a life-size figure. Measuring some 1.70 m by 1.80 m, the space is sufficient for a single statue. It would be large enough to handle, say, the over life-size bronze statue of Athena (height 2.35 m) now in the Piraeus

Archaeological Museum, that has a base area of under 1 m × 1 m¹. However, the space seems rather small for anything involving more than one figure.

Apart from the mould fragments, we also find traces of a gate and vent system. Gates channelled the molten bronze into the mould and vents allowed the escape of gases. The diameter of these pipes ranges from just under 1 cm to 3 cm. In addition to examples directly attached to the mould (Fig. 32.7.1, 4), there are also fragments of pipes that do not preserve any traces of how they were connected to the casting mould (Fig. 32.7.5, 7, 8).

To prevent dirt from entering the mould via the gates and vents, plugs were used to seal off the openings. Apart from a couple of fragments, two fully preserved examples have been found in the foundry context in Kalapodi. One of them (KAL11.193.020) has a roughly formed handle and convex bottom (Fig. 32.7.9). Baked into the surface of the plug are some bronze droplets. The clay, tempered with fine gravel, chalk, mica, and organic material, is well-fired. On the reverse of both examples there are traces of soot.

The metal for the casting was melted in crucibles. Low-fired on the outside, these vessels typically show a vitrified or even blistered inner surface (cf. Fig. 32.7.12). Bronze drops baked into the clay are also common. Since the crucible fragments are usually very small, they do not enable a further reconstruction of the vessels. One example preserves parts of a second layer of clay that was applied to an already vitrified surface, presumably to strengthen the vessel for a second use.

Close investigation of crucible fragments in Olympia enabled Völling and Zimmer (1995) to demonstrate that crucibles were also strengthened by metal reinforcements. In the same way, it can be argued that an iron ring (KAL11.193.004) found in the context of the bronze foundry might have been used to reinforce a crucible. The piece would point to a crucible diameter of about 25 cm.

To increase the heat of the flame and to reach the temperatures necessary to melt the metal, bellows were used. In Kalapodi only the ends of the nozzles nearest the heat have been preserved (Fig. 32.7.10, 12) (for better preserved examples from Olympia, see Schneider and Zimmer 1984, 25, fig. 9). They usually consist of more than one layer of clay. Marks within the pipes lead to the conclusion that they were built up around a rod that was removed by giving it a pull and a twist after the piece had dried out sufficiently. Vitrification and even slagging on the outside of the fragments are typical.

Pouring funnels were applied to guide the molten metal from the crucibles into the mould. At Kalapodi, about a dozen such fragments could be identified. Most significant are four matching rim fragments (KAL08.303.002, KAL08.305.001, KAL08.305.002, KAL08.305.003). Together they make up a funnel with rounded edge, a wall thickness of about 4.5 cm and an inner diameter of about 13 cm (Fig. 32.8). The piece is composed of two layers of clay, which, however, do not show any difference in their tempering. Other pieces have steep walls and round or tapered rims (Fig. 32.7.6). Because of their bad state of preservation, the diameter of these can be reconstructed only with difficulty. Usually it seems to be around 6 cm.

Point bars or struts, used to support the casting mould or parts of the funnel and gate system, could also be identified among the fragments of metallurgical ceramics. They are simple, hand-made clay rods with a diameter of about 4 cm to 5 cm. The tempering of the well-fired clay consists of fine gravel, chalk and organic material.

Within the workshop innumerable amounts of metal and slag fragments have been found. Typical of the whole area are numerous small bronze droplets. Most of these are residue from the melting and casting processes: they have a diameter of only half a centimetre. Apart from these small and amorphous fragments, there are also bigger pieces of iron, bronze and lead. Among them are parts of weaponry like the cheek pieces and nose protectors of bronze helmets of the Corinthian type, a bronze ferrule, and iron spearheads, as well as jewellery, like the heads of bronze needles and fibulae. All these would have been dedications originally, later collected by the bronze workers (for dedications of weaponry in Greek sanctuaries cf. Baitinger 2011; Frielinghaus 2011, 210–232; for the remelting of metal offerings in Greek sanctuaries, cf. Linders 1989–1990). We often find sets of two or more objects that seem to have been scheduled for reuse. Especially remarkable is an assembly of four fragments of large-scale bronze statues, and an amorphous bronze ingot with a total weight of about 20 kg. Tightly stacked, the objects were deposited immediately north of pit 5. Apart from such pieces that most probably were designated for remelting, there are others that have been (re-)used in a much more practical and immediate manner (for the reuse of scrap cf. e.g. Zimmer 1990, 160). Among them are an iron rod that has been jammed between the mould base within the ›key-hole pit‹ (pit 1), and the broken blade of a sword found nearby and most probably also used to support the mould (Fig. 32.3) (for mould supports made out of other materials, see Zimmer 1990, 135. 221–223). Other iron rods and an iron ring (all with rectangular sections) might have also served as reinforcements for the moulds and crucibles (for the reconstruction of a crucible with iron reinforcements, see Völling – Zimmer 1995; cf. Zimmer 2006). Some iron finds from the workshop area in Kalapodi are mentioned by Zipprich (2016–2017).

---

[1] cf. e.g. http://www.perseus.tufts.edu/hopper/artifactname=Piraeus+Athena&object=sculpture [accessed 15 January 2018]; http://www.latsis-foundation.org/eng/electronic-library/the-museum-cycle/the-archaeological-museum-of-piraeus [accessed 15 January 2018].

A bronze foundry of Classical times in the sanctuary at Kalapodi (Central Greece)

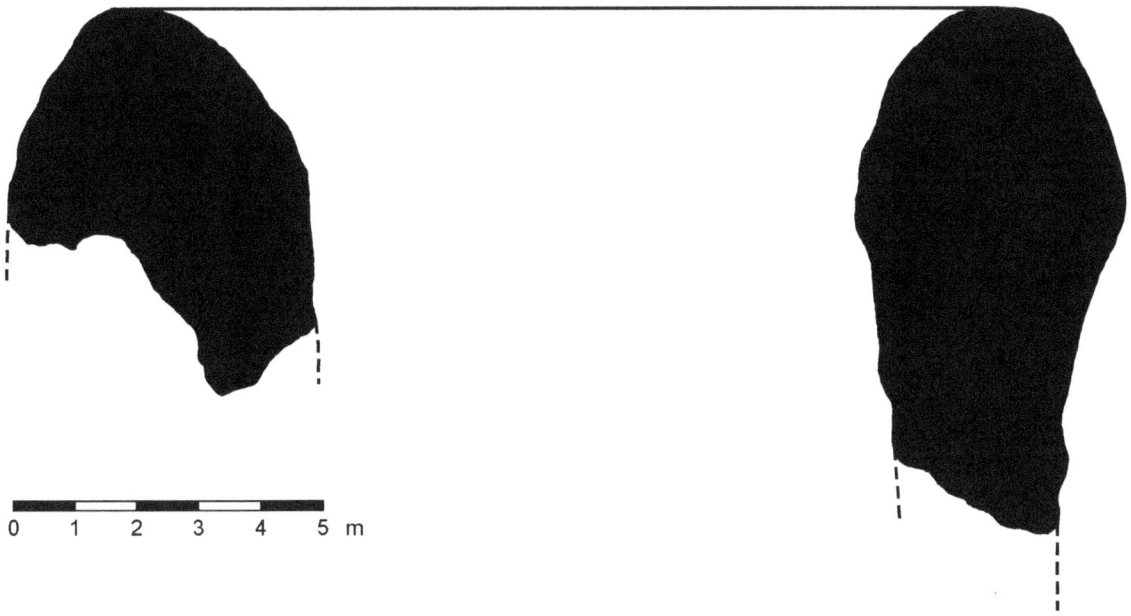

Fig. 32.8: Kalapodi, section of a funnel (KAL08.303.002, KAL08.305.001, KAL08.305.002, KAL08.305.003). Drawing: I. Vaporakis & J. Fuchs.

Casting Technique

From the archaeological record and the movable finds within the workshop area, we can draw the conclusion that the method applied in the bronze foundry in Kalapodi was the technique of indirect lost-wax casting. This rather intricate and lengthy procedure allows for more complex castings than the simpler technique of direct lost-wax casting. In the direct method, a wax model, formed over a clay core and covered by a mould, is burnt out. After baking, the hollow left by the burnt-out wax is filled up with molten metal. However, in the indirect method, moulds taken from a finished clay prototype are used to form wax impressions. Filled up with a core and surrounded with a clay mould, these are used to produce bronze copies of the original. This means that in contrast to the direct method, the model remains intact during the whole process, therefore providing the opportunity to repeat a casting in case something should have gone wrong during the operation (for the methods, see e.g. Mattusch 2002; Zimmer 2003, 38).

Chronological Context

As mentioned above, the bronze foundry was established within the debris of the Archaic South Temple destroyed by the Persians in 480 BC. Within the workshop area, we find numerous fragments of roof tiles from the first Classical North Temple reused in its installations (for the Classical roofs from Kalapodi, see Hübner 1994). Therefore the destruction of the Classical North Temple serves as a *terminus post quem* for the establishment of the foundry. Conventionally it is attributed to the earthquake of 426/425 BC (Felsch et al. 1980, 107; Niemeier 2013b, 22; for the earthquake, see also Rocchi 1998, 319 with n. 9). Since neither building material of the second Classical North Temple (cf. Felsch et al. 1980, 107), that replaced its predecessor, nor early Hellenistic pottery has been found within the context of the workshop, we have to assume that the workshop was active within the last quarter of the 5th century BC. This chronological bracketing is supported by the ground plan and the dimensions of the foundry pit that do have close parallels in e.g. the foundry pits near the Hephaisteion at the Athenian Agora (see Mattusch 1975, 116–124; Mattusch 1977, 348–356; Zimmer 1990, 60–62) or the western pit of the bronze workshop on the south slope of the Acropolis in Athens (see Zimmer 1990, 62–71). Both of them are dated to the 5th century BC.

Not only from the evidence of other foundry sites, but also in regard to the excavation results, which did not reveal stratigraphical evidence pointing to long-term operations, one has to assume that the workshop in Kalapodi was set up by craftsmen who were assigned to one specific task, i.e. the casting of one statue (see Zimmer 1990, 156 for the generally temporary lifespan of ancient Greek bronze foundries). This work most probably was intended to stand within the sanctuary. For though it is possible to move large-scale bronze statues, as exemplified by those that have been found among the cargo of sunken ships (like e.g. the so-called Antikythera ephebe; for the statue see Bol 1972, 18–24 pls. 6–9; Dafas 2015), it is much more convenient to manufacture them close to their intended location. In doing so, one could reduce the costs and dangers of transport and also enable the specialists to attend to the statue until it was finally erected in position (Zimmer 1990, 74. 157). Since (bronze) statuary often adorned sanctuaries, several bronze workshops within a *temenos* are frequently enough attested (Zimmer 1990, 157). Thus, they exist in the sanctuaries of Olympia (Zimmer 1990, 39–50; Heilmeyer – Zimmer 1987) and Nemea (Zimmer 1990, 50–57).

Due to the chronology applied to the findings in Kalapodi, a certain relationship between the casting and the second Classical North Temple can be assumed (for the temple, see Felsch 2007, 20–21; Niemeier 2013b, 22). Since the making of a large-scale bronze statue could easily have taken several years (Zimmer 1985, 45–47; Lazzarini 2003; Zimmer 2003, 40–41), even a contemporaneity between the construction work at the temple and the operation of the workshop seems possible. Niemeier (2013b, 22) suggested that the object cast within the bronze workshop might have been the cult image of the new temple. After the fulfilment of their order, the bronze artisans most likely left the sanctuary to take on other tasks elsewhere. The pits were refilled and the workshop area again abandoned until its reuse in Hellenistic and later times.

Acknowledgements

This paper is a slightly altered and extended version of an article that will be published in the proceedings of the international conference "Ancient Phokis. New approaches to its history, archaeology, and topography" at the German Archaeological Institute at Athens 30 March–01 April 2017. I would like to thank the heads of the Kalapodi excavation, Wolf-Dietrich Niemeier and Katja Sporn, for entrusting me with the publication of the bronze foundry at the site. I am especially grateful to Dimitris Grigoropoulos, who acted as trench director in the workshop area during the field seasons 2007–2012, and generously shared with me his documents, as well as to the local workmen Athanasios Mavroeidis and Ioannis Kasounis with whom I excavated in the area in 2015, 2016 and 2018.

Bibliography

Baitinger, H. 2011. *Waffenweihungen in griechischen Heiligtümern.* Monographien des Römisch-Germanischen Zentralmuseums 94. Mainz: Verlag des RGZM.

Bol, P. C. 1972. *Die Skulpturen des Schiffsfundes von Antikythera.* Berlin: Gebr. Mann.

Bol, P. C. 1978. *Grossplastik aus Bronze in Olympia.* Berlin: W. de Gruyter.

Dafas, K. 2015. The Casting Technique of the Bronze Antikythera Ephebe. In: Z. Theodoropoulou Polychroniadis – D. Evely, ed., *Aegis. Essays in Mediterranean Archaeology presented to Matti Egon by the Scholars of the Greek Archaeological Committee UK*. Oxford: Archaeopress, 137–146.

Felsch, R. C. S. – H. J. Kienast – Schuler, H. 1980. Apollon und Artemis oder Artemis und Apollon? Bericht von den Ausgrabungen im neu entdeckten Heiligtum bei Kalapodi 1973–1977. *Archäologischer Anzeiger* 1980, 38–118.

Felsch, R. C. S., ed., 2007. *Kalapodi II. Ergebnisse der Ausgrabungen im Heiligtum der Artemis und des Apollon von Hyampolis in der antiken Phokis.* Mainz am Rhein: Philipp von Zabern.

Frielinghaus, H. 2011. *Die Helme von Olympia. Ein Beitrag zu Waffenweihungen in griechischen Heiligtümern*, Olympische Forschungen 33. Berlin: De Gruyter.

Fuchs, J. 2016–2017. Untersuchungen in der Bronzewerkstatt (BW) und Ergebnisse zur technischen Keramik. In: K. Sporn, ed., Forschungen zur Anlage, Ausdehnung und Infrastruktur des Heiligtums in Kalapodi 2014–2016. *Athenische Mitteilungen* 131–132, 204–206.

Grigoropoulos, D. 2015. Hadrian, Abai and the Memory of the Persian Wars. In: D. Panagiotopoulos – I. Kaiser – O. Kouka, ed., *Ein Minoer im Exil. Festschrift für Wolf-Dietrich Niemeier.* Universitätsforschungen zur prähistorischen Archäologie 270, 75–98.

Hackländer, N. – E. Formigli 1997. Experimente zur Brenntechnik in einer Gußgrube. In: G. Zimmer – N. Hackländer, ed., *Der Betende Knabe. Original und Experiment,* 93–98.

Heilmeyer, W.-D. – G. Zimmer 1987. Die Bronzegießerei unter der Werkstatt des Phidias in Olympia. *Archäologischer Anzeiger* 1987, 239–289.

Hein, A. – V. Kilikoglou 2011. Technological Aspects of Bronze Age Metallurgical Ceramics in the Eastern Mediterranean. In: P. B. Betancourt – S. C. F. Ferrence, ed., *Metallurgy: Understanding How, Learning Why. Studies in Honor of James D. Muhly.* Prehistory Monographs 29, 181–187.

Hein, A. – K. Christodoulou – J. Fuchs 2017. A Classic Bronze Workshop at the Apollon Sanctuary of Kalapodi – Investigation of the Metallurgical Ceramics. Accessed via https://www.academia.edu/34507288/A_classic_bronze_workshop_at_the_Apollon_sanctuary_of_Kalapodi_-_Investigation_of_the_metallurgical_ceramics on 7 December 2017.

Hellner, N. 2016–2017. Sondage WG 2016 – Die Dachausbildung und der Westgiebel des Südtempels von Kalapodi. In: K. Sporn, ed., Forschungen zur Anlage, Ausdehnung und Infrastruktur des Heiligtums in Kalapodi 2014–2016. *Athenische Mitteilungen* 131–132, 206–211.

Hübner, G. 1994. Die klassischen Tempeldächer von Kalapodi (Phokis). In: N. A. Winter, ed., *Proceedings of the International Conference on Greek Architectural Terracottas of the Classical and Hellenistic Periods.* Athens. December 12–15, 1991, 171–180.

Kopanias, K. forthcoming. Das Straßennetz der Ostphokis und die Frage nach der Lokalisierung von Abai. Accessed via https://www.academia.edu/4580471/Das_Straßennetz_der_Ostphokis_und_die_Frage_nach_der_Lokalisierung_von_Abai on 8 January 2018.

Lazzarini, M. L. 2003. Rendiconti di spesa per l'esecuzione di statue di bronzo. In: A. Melucco Vaccaro – G. De Palma, ed., *I Bronzi di Riace. Restauro come conoscenza 1. Archeologia, restauro, conservazione,* 71–73.

Linders, T. 1989/1990. The melting down of discarded metal offerings in Greek sanctuaries. *Scienze dell'antichità. Storia. archeologia, antropologia* 3/4, 281–285.

Mattusch, C. C. 1975. *Casting techniques of Greek bronze sculpture. Foundries and foundry remains from the Athenian Agora with References to other Ancient Sources.* Ann Arbor: University of North Carolina.

Mattusch, C. C. 1977. Bronze- and Ironworking in the Area of the Athenian Agora. *Hesperia* 46/4, 340–379.

Mattusch, C. 2002. Statuaria in bronzo. Tecniche di produzione dal V al III secolo. In: A. R. Giumlia-Mair – M. Rubinich, ed., *Le arti di Efesto: capolavori in metallo dalla Magna Grecia,* 75–81.

Niemeier, W.-D. 2010. Deutsches Archäologisches Institut, Jahresbericht 2009. Abteilung Athen. Kalapodi (Abai). *Archäologischer Anzeiger* 2010/1 Beih., 106–108.

Niemeier, W.-D. 2012. Deutsches Archäologisches Institut, Jahresbericht 2011. Abteilung Athen. Kalapodi (Abai). *Archäologischer Anzeiger* 2012/1 Beih., 94–96.

Niemeier, W.-D. 2013a. Kultkontinuität von der Bronzezeit bis zur römischen Kaiserzeit im Orakel-Heiligtum des Apollon von Abai (Kalapodi). In: I. Gerlach – D. Raue, ed., *Sanktuar und Ritual. Heilige Plätze im archäologischen Befund.* Menschen, Kulturen, Traditionen 10, 33–42.

Niemeier, W.-D. 2013b. *Das Orakelheiligtum des Apollon von Abai/Kalapodi. Eines der bedeutendsten griechischen Heiligtümer nach den Ergebnissen der neuen Ausgrabungen.* Trierer Winckelmannsprogramme 25. Wiesbaden: Harrassowitz.

Niemeier, W.-D. 2014. Kalapodi, Griechenland. Die Arbeiten der Jahre 2012 und 2013. *Deutsches Archäologisches Institut. E-Forschungsberichte* 2014/3, 27–31. Accessed via https://www.dainst.org/documents/10180/367514/e-Forschungsberichte+2014-3+klein/d9a4c50e-3a37-4990-8596-dcf3d12d34dc on 12 January 2016.

Prignitz, S. 2014. Zur Identifizierung des Heiligtums von Kalapodi. *ZPE* 189, 133–146.

Rocchi, G. D. 1998. La sismicità della Focide orientale e della Locride. In: E. Olshausen – H. Sonnabend, ed., *Naturkatastrophen in der antiken Welt.* Stuttgarter Kolloquium zur historischen Geographie des Altertums 6. Geographica Historica 10, 316–328.

Scheel, B. 1988a. Metallverarbeitung in Theben. Der Fund einer Werkstätte aus der Ptolemäerzeit am Tempel Sethos' I. *Archäologie in Deutschland* 2, 18–23.

Scheel, B. 1988b. Fundobjekte einer ptolemäerzeitlichen Metallverarbeitungsstätte in Theben und Vergleichsfunde anderer vorderorientalischer Ausgrabungsplätze. *Studien zur Altägyptischen Kultur* 15, 243–254.

Schneider, G. – G. Zimmer 1984. Technische Keramik aus antiken Bronzegusswerkstätten in Olympia und Athen. *Berliner Beiträge zur Archäometrie* 9, 17–60.

Schneider, G. 2003. Untersuchungen von Proben technischer Keramik aus der hellenistischen Bronzegießerei in Demetrias. In: A. Furtwängler, ed., *Hellenistische Bronzegusswerkstätten. Lampenproduktion und -importe. Amphorenfunde.* Demetrias 6, 65–67.

Sporn, K. 2016/2017. Forschungen zur Anlage, Ausdehnung und Infrastruktur des Heiligtums in Kalapodi. Die Kampagnen 2014–2026. *Athenische Mitteilungen* 131–132, 204–206.

Sporn, K. 2017. Kalapodi, Griechenland. Neue Forschungen in der Umgebung der Tempelkomplexe. *Deutsches Archäologisches Institut. e-Forschungsberichte des Deutschen Archäologischen Instituts* 2017/1, 58–63. Accessed via https://www.dainst.org/documents/10180/321 5758/eDAI-F+2017-1/7be991fe-1f45-40ce-b678-a208e6476112 on 10 December 2017.

Völling, T. – Zimmer, G., 1995. Bewegliche Tiegel. Ein Neufund in Olympia. *Archäologischer Anzeiger* 1995, 661–666.

Zimmer G. 1984. Gießeinrichtungen im Kerameikos. *Archäologischer Anzeiger* 1984, 63–83.

Zimmer, G. 1985. Schriftquellen zum antiken Bronzeguss. In: H. Born, ed., *Archäologische Bronzen, antike Kunst, moderne Technik,* 38–49.

Zimmer, G. 1990. *Griechische Bronzegusswerkstätten. Zur Technologieentwicklung eines antiken Kunsthandwerks.* Mainz am Rhein: Philipp von Zabern.

Zimmer, G. 2002. Die Bronzegusswerkstatt des Pheidias am Südabhang der Akropolis. In: M. Maischberger – W.-D. Heilmeyer, ed., *Die griechische Klassik. Idee oder Wirklichkeit,* 501–506.

Zimmer, G. 2003. Hellenistische Bronzegusswerkstätten in Demetrias. In: A. Furtwängler, ed., *Hellenistische Bronzegusswerkstätten. Lampenproduktion und -importe, Amphorenfunde.* Demetrias 6, 9–68.

Zimmer, G. 2006. Die Suche nach dem Schmelztiegel. Ein deutsches Problem? In: A. Dostert – F. Lang, ed., *Mittel und Wege. Zur Bedeutung von Materialität und Technik in der Archäologie,* 23–36.

Zipprich, S. 2016–2017. Eisenfunde aus der Grabung 2016. In: K. Sporn, ed., Forschungen zur Anlage, Ausdehnung und Infrastruktur des Heiligtums in Kalapodi 2014–2016. *Athenische Mitteilungen* 131–132, 250–253.

Copper-based offerings from the sanctuaries of Poseidon and Athena at Sounion, Attica: typological and analytical investigation

Zetta Theodoropoulou Polychroniadis, Vana Orfanou

Greek Archaeological Committee UK

Aarhus University

zetta.theodoropoulou@gmail.com

Abstract: Copper-based artefacts of small size recovered by Valerios Stais (1897–1915) from the Poseidon and Athena sanctuaries at Sounion include weapons, miniature anthropomorphic and zoomorphic figurines and jewellery, all studied typologically and contextually by Theodoropoulou Polychroniadis (2015). The typological analysis is here complemented by the archaeometallurgical examination of a selection of copper-based objects. The combined results address their typology, technology and function, and make some initial observations on their provenance. This data set encourages further analytical exploration into the provenance and treatment of the metal alongside typological considerations in order to comprehend their pattern of original dedication and deposition around the time of the Persian Wars (480/479 BC).

Keywords: Archaic Period; Sounion; Votive Offerings; Copper-Based Alloys; XRF Analysis

Introduction

Sounion in context

'Holy' Sounion, (Odyssey 5.276–285), lies at the southeastern tip of Attica, in the Laureotike, continuously inhabited from the 6th millennium BC. One of the main centres of metallurgy in the Aegean, the region played a vital role in the growth and wealth of Athens. At its major settlement, Thorikos, there is evidence of mining, metallurgical activities and trade from the Neolithic to the Archaic period (Laffineur 2011, 26–27. 34–37). From the end of the 6th c. BC, under the Athenian state, the Laureotike developed as a flourishing industrial centre of mining and became an exporter of ores throughout the Eastern Mediterranean.

Cape Sounion with its two harbours rises 13 km south of Thorikos. By its strategic and geographical position, commanding sea routes between East and West, as well as its proximity to the mines of Laurion, it constituted a 'point of access to the outside world' (de Polignac 1995, 85). To the northeast of the promontory, at a distance of 500 m, rises a hill. This hill and the promontory were where early cult activity was based.

In the late 8th c. BC, the existing arrangement was transformed into the sanctuaries of Athena and Poseidon respectively. Both locales housed a hero cult, later transformed from sanctuaries funded by a local elite into major Attic religious centres. By the late 6th c. BC, Sounion was an integral part of Athenian territory. To consolidate its own territorial and political boundaries, the Athenian state invested in Sounion's defence and in the enhancement of the sanctuaries with monumental architecture. The erection of the Archaic temple of Poseidon started on the promontory around 490 BC; still incomplete, it was ravaged by the Persians in 480/479 BC. At the Athena sanctuary, a small temple in antis stood on the footprint of an earlier structure. The destruction of both temples resulted in large-scale removal of debris and site-levelling. Around 460 BC, the Classical temple of Athena was built southwest of the Archaic one, while that of Poseidon was erected by 440 BC on the stylobate of the Archaic one.

Excavations at Sounion

The only extensive archaeological project undertaken at Sounion to date is that conducted by Valerios Stais (1897–1915), funded by the Archaeological Society at Athens. Stais excavated the fortress and a sanctuary on the Cape, a *bothros*, a landfill and a triangular fissure, where *kouroi* were buried, believing that it was that of Athena. In 1900, his excavation revealed a major discovery: that of the Athena sanctuary, its *bothros* and landfill, northeast of the one he had initially dug, now identified as that of Poseidon. Concise reports were regularly forthcoming in the Archaeological Society's *PAE* and *AE* journals (Theodoropoulou Polychroniadis 2015) and comprise the only information on the Sounion excavations and finds. They lack important information on the find spots, mainly of the small-scale material, as well as on their stratigraphical contexts. Questions consequently arising about the sanctuaries' topography, their almost-untraceable structures, the patterns of their socio-economic growth and their early cults have been addressed by Theodoropoulou Polychroniadis (2015). On the Athena sanctuary and temples, a recent review has been made by Barletta (2017).

The finds

The assemblages of copper-based objects, despite their limited number, consist of a variety of items whose typology and provenance remain unclear. They are considered here typologically, with comparisons made, in an effort to suggest geographical connections. The finds derive from the Poseidon *bothros* and the Athena landfill. They are a mixture of functional and non-functional small-scale objects, all classified as votives.

Of 922 diverse small finds from both sanctuaries, 326 are of metal, but only 44 are copper-based (see Table 33.1). Of all the copper-based objects, the Poseidon *bothros* yielded the majority, while other metals were also recovered from the Athena landfill.

Aims and objectives

Given the limited documentation on vertical and horizontal distribution of the small finds, the need for more detailed examination became essential. A typological examination of the copper-based offerings from the Poseidon and Athena sanctuaries was aimed at clarifying their contextualisation, their role in the ritual process and, owing to Sounion's geographical location on trade routes, the impact of contacts from a wider Mediterranean perspective during the Archaic period. Comparative material has demonstrated the typological uniqueness of several Sounion finds, though their provenance remains problematic. Thus, an archaeometric examination of the objects was initiated, to address questions on their technology and how this related to their typology. The integration of the results from the typological/stylistic and analytical studies is intended to produce a more well-rounded interpretation of the votive assemblage at the sanctuaries.

Typological and stylistic examination

Poseidon sanctuary

The *bothros* is situated at the SE corner of the sanctuary. Its contents span the late 8th to the early 5th centuries. The assemblage comprises one anthropomorphic and one zoomorphic figurine, personal ornaments, weapons, a unique tool, and some oddments.

Anthropomorphic figurine

The dimensions of this standing figurine NM 14926.22 (NM and X[?] before figures in bold refer to numbering in the National Archaeological Museum, Athens), H. 6.5 cm, W. 3.7 cm, and the suspension-hole on its back suggest that it was either attached to a vessel or worn as an amulet (Stais 1917, 195, fig. 7; Hanfmann 1962; Seeden 1980, 128, pl. 114, no. 1819) (Fig. 33.1). Cast in the round, the figurine has a sturdy schematised body with disproportionally large ears, the right arm raised, both fists clenched, short legs

Table 33.1. Table showing findspot and numbers of copper-based votives at Sounion

Findspot	Both sanctuaries	Poseidon	Athena	Unclear findspot
Finds (no.)	44	24	13	7
Percent (%)	100	54	30	16

Fig. 33.1. Sanctuary of Poseidon: Reshef type figurine, National Archaeological Museum, Athens 14926.22 (Photo: Elias Eliades)

and small feet. It wears a plain conical helmet and a kilt. The composition and features, e.g. the kilt, are Levantine, resembling statuettes of the smiting warrior god, the so-called Reshef (cf. Seeden 1980, 151, group XI, pl. 107, no. 1756, Syria, pl. 109, no. 1774, N. Syria). The type, from Syria or Palestine, possibly imported via Cyprus, occurs in Greek sites from the LBA II–III until the Archaic period (Seeden 1980, 122–132, pl. 114; Gallet de Santerre 1987, 7–29; Sapouna-Sakellarakis 1995, pl. 44; Papapostolou 2010, 35–37, fig. 29). The proportions, rendering and the stance of the Sounion piece differ from examples from other Greek sites and the Levant. Despite the lack of exact parallels, the figurine alludes to an iconography common in the Levant and reinforces the belief that it is a Reshef-type effigy. According to the *bothros'* context, it is possibly dated to the late 8th c. BC (Theodoropoulou Polychroniadis 2015, 88–89. 122–123. 226).

It is unclear whether the figurine's deposition was connected to a cult centred on a male personality at the Cape, such as Poseidon or Heracles (Theodoropoulou Polychroniadis 2015, 120–122). If indeed dated to the late 8th c. BC, does it simply reflect the influence of Levantine figurines on local manufacture, or was it imported by a visitor to the Cape as an offering? The stylistic analysis of the figurine offers no clues as to its origin, manufacture and exact date. A comparable figurine from the sanctuary of Athena Itonia, dated to the end of the 8th c. BC, is a Levantine import (Kilian-Dirlmeier 2002, pl. 180, no. 1007).

Zoomorphic figurine

An animal figurine NM 14932.1, with a disc between its broken horns, is a bovine (Fig. 33.2). Its raised, punctured eyes, long trapezoidal muzzle, elongated cylindrical body, neck, legs and tail, all recall figurines of the late Geometric and mid-7th c. BC date from Olympia (Kyrieleis 2006, pl. 48, no. 119), Delphi (Perdrizet 1908, 53, fig. 167) and the Idaian Cave (Sakellarakis 2013, pl. 61γ), but without exact parallels.

Finger rings

The diameters of seven plain finger rings NM 14936.1, 14936.4, 14936.5, 14936.6, 14936.7, 14936.8, 14936.9

Fig. 33.2. Sanctuary of Poseidon: Figurine of a bovine, National Archaeological Museum, Athens 14932.1. Spiral finger rings, 14936.2, 14936.3. Arrowheads (from left to right) 14932.6, 14932.8, 14932.7, 14932.9, 14932.10, 14932.12, 14932.13. Ex-voto spearhead 14932.11 (Photo: Elias Eliades)

with an almost circular cross-section, vary between 1.7 cm and 2.2 cm (Fig. 33.2). They are classified as Type A at the Argive Heraion (Waldstein et al. 1905, 251–252, pls. 89–90 passim.) and group A1 at Kalapodi (Felsch 2007, 173–174, pls. 40–44), dated to the 6th or early 5th centuries BC. Their dimensions and weight suggest that these are finger rings and not decorative elements, as is the case with the intact and solid oval ring-handle X26862 of unknown find-spot made from a plain circular rod (cf. Tarditi 2016, 56, no. 21391/1).

Two rings NM 14936.2, 14936.3, made of a rod that is oval in section, with the ends coiled in small spirals, date to the late 8th c. BC. This spiral type, common in Mycenaean tombs, remained fashionable in the Peloponnese, Central Greece and Thessaly from the MG and LG periods onwards until the Early Archaic period (Kilian-Dirlmeier 1980, 250–251. 258, pls. 256–257). Comparanda are found in Lousoi (Mitsopoulos-Leon 2012, pl. 20, no. 176), Philia (Kilian-Dirlmeier 2002, pl. 10, no. 177), Kalapodi (Felsch 2007, pls. 37 and 39, nos. 645–647. 808), Kythnos (Touloumtzidou 2017, 212, no. 66), Ano Mazaraki (Petropoulos 2002, 91, fig. 14) and Olympia (Philipp 1981, 146–148, pl. 7, no. 42, pl. 16, nos. 538–541).

Weapons

The weapons deposited in the Poseidon sanctuary as items of importance and high value follow a practice seen widely in Greek sanctuaries (Fig. 33.2). They were also represented by purely symbolic miniature offerings, possibly related to a male rite of passage.

The Sounion arrowheads have no exact parallels. The question arises as to whether they were imported, or more likely were local products, intentionally manufactured as votives.

Arrowhead NM 14932.6, of Snodgrass's Type 2, spanning the Mycenaean period to the 7th c., has a wide and flat barbed blade and a long flat tang. It recalls arrowheads from Chios (Lamb 1935, pl. 32, nos. 15. 16), Olynthos (Robinson 1941, pl 120, no. 1911, Type C) and the sanctuary at Isthmus in Lemnos (Greco – Correale 2017, 32, fig. 6, Type 5), but has no exact parallels.

Two arrowheads NM 14932.8, 14932.7 with midrib and square tangs are of Snodgrass's Type 5a (1964, 154–155). Arrowheads from Chios (Lamb 1935, pl. 32, no. 10), Olynthos (Robinson 1941, pl. 121, no. 1924, Type D) and two from the Dictaean Cave (Boardman 1961, fig. 11, nos. 120. 126) of the Archaic period show broad similarities in shape with the Sounion one. Two further arrowheads with midrib NM 14932.9, 14932.10, also Snodgrass's Type 5a, have long, cylindrical tangs and are comparable to examples from Olynthos (Robinson 1941, pl. 120, no. 1895, Type A2).

A smaller, barbed arrowhead NM 14932.12 of Snodgrass's Type 2, is dated to the Archaic period. Its light weight (10 gr) and flat form imply that it was intended as a votive. Ex-voto arrowheads occur in Bassai (Kourouniotis 1910, 318, fig. 38) and Paestum (Giacco 2015, 33). A comparandum derives from the Dictaean Cave (Boardman 1961, fig. 11, no. 122).

A three-edged, leaf-shaped arrowhead NM 14932.13, with spur and a cylindrical socket, is classified as Snodgrass's Type 3B2 (1964, 151–152, fig. 10, no. 2) or Baitinger's type IIB2 (2001, 20–21). The type originates in the Near East in the 7th c. BC and was in use until after the Persian wars. Examples appear in Smyrna (Nicholls 1958–1959, 133, no. 138), Olynthos (Robinson 1941, pl. 125, nos. 2086. 2091, Type F), Athens (Broneer 1935, 114, fig. 4; Comstock – Vermeule 1971, 416, no. 595), Olympia (Baitinger 2001, pl. 8, nos. 227. 232. 233. 240. 241) and Nemea (Miller 1977, pl. 7a, BR 113; Miller 1984, pl. 42a, BR 1137).

Ex-voto spearhead NM 14932.11 has a leaf-shaped blade, sloping shoulders and a longish circular socket. It is classified as Snodgrass's Type Q1 (1964, 130, fig. 8f). Its shape is comparable to a full-size iron spearhead from Olynthos (Robinson 1941, pl. 127, no. 2149, Type A II). Similar miniature spearheads were found in Olympia (Baitinger 2001, pl. 67, no. 1347) and Philia (Kilian-Dirlmeier 2002, pl. 12, nos. 218–224).

Two holes on the blade of a miniature ex-voto double-axe NM 14926.3, an apotropaic and power symbol, suggest it was worn as an amulet. Comparanda are found in the sanctuaries of Artemis Orthia (Dawkins 1929, pl. 35), Lindos (Blinkenberg 1931, 391–392, nos. 1562. 1563), Emporio (Boardman 1967, 227, pl. 93, no. 407), Delphi (Perdrizet 1908, figs. 143. 144, nos. 650. 651), Olympia (Philipp 1981, pl 81, nos. 1335–1339. 1341), Lousoi (Mitsopoulos-Leon 2012, pl. 17, no. 137).

Tool

The only tool recorded by Stais, NM 14926.1 is an intact, cast, double-ended punch, with an X-like engraved pattern in an incuse square at both ends, possibly dated to the early 6th c. BC (Fig. 33.3). Several uses have been proposed by scholars (Calligas 1997, 143, pl. 18; Sheedy 2014, 26). At the 2015 International Conference on 'Mines, Metals and Money in Attica', Theodoropoulou Polychroniadis proposed its alternative use as a punch for stamping silver. The tool's dimensions, light weight and its design on both ends, being identical with that of a bronze truncated pyramid-shaped stamp from the Argive Heraion (NM 13987), imply that it too was used as a stamp. Stamps with an X imprint were also found in Tegea (Kilian-Dirlmeier 1979, pl. 14, nos. 214–216. 219. 223). Inscription IG I^3 8, (460–450 BC) discovered on the Cape, provides evidence on landing-taxes imposed on cargo ships anchoring at the harbours at Sounion. Local officials would weigh and confirm the fineness of silver before it was stored away in the Poseidon sanctuary. The tool therefore may have been deposited at the end of the 6th c. BC when local elite lost its authority after the Cleisthenic reforms.

Oddments

A pair of tweezers NM 14926.2, a bi-conical bead NM 14932.15 and a nail cap NM 14932.14 complete the assemblage from the Poseidon bothros. (For the sanctuary and temples of Athena, see Barletta 2017.)

The landfill inside the sanctuary is close to its eastern peribolos wall. Metalwork here is finer and more varied than that at the Poseidon sanctuary (Stais 1917, 201–202. 207–208, figs. 13. 17 and 18), dated from the late 8th to the early 5th c. BC. The copper-based objects consist of zoomorphic figurines, personal ornaments, ex-voto shields, tripods and oddments.

Zoomorphic figurines

A miniature hollow-cast recumbent bull NM 14932.22, bears a rectangular perforation below, indicating that it was attached to a vessel (Fig. 33.4). The bent and solid-cast left foreleg forms a space for a rivet. Its composition, size and rendering are closely paralleled by a fragmentary bull figurine from Isthmia, dated to the 5th c. BC (Raubitschek

Fig. 33.3. Sanctuary of Poseidon: Tool, National Archaeological Museum, Athens 14926.1 (Photo: Elias Eliades)

1998, pl. 12, no. 53). This close similarity implies that the Sounion bull is of a like date and possibly came from the same workshop.

A cast miniature stag NM 14932.23, has two affixed rings, one below the muzzle and one behind the front leg. It has a long, slender body and fleshed-out eyeballs, as well as an impressed cavity below its neck, suggesting that it was attached to a larger object as a decorative feature (Kilian-Dirlmeier 1979, 194, pl. 61, no. 1163; Perdrizet 1908, 48, fig. 151, no. 126). The stag's rendering, size and features resemble figurines decorating horse trappings from Luristan (Moorey 1974, pl. 14A; Waele 1982, 166, fig. 136, no. 250; Marangou 1996, 156, nos. 254. 255), implying that it was either imported or more likely imitates such figurines from the Near East, and providing evidence of trade networks and artistic influence in the 8th and 7th c. BC. (Cf. Jantzen 1972, 65, pl. 61, B895, BB756 and 74–80, pls. 74–79, from Luristan). Similar stag figurines in Greek sanctuaries of the late 8th and early 7th c. BC, e.g. the Samian Heraion (Jantzen 1972, 80–84, pl. 82, B154 from Caucasus), Camiros (Bernardini 2006, 43, pl. 22, no. 10), Olympia (Heilmeyer 1979, 148–151. 238. 252, pl. 68, nos. 507. 507a, pl. 85, no. 705) and Delphi (Kilian-Dirlmeier 1979, 149, pl. 60, no. 1141) were either imported or were imitations. The landfill context and the above comparanda suggest a date at the end of the 8th c. BC.

The bovine figurine NM 14926.5 with thick conical horns, a cylindrical body and short and sturdy legs was also likely applied to a large vessel. It parallels figurines from Olympia (Heilmeyer 1979, pl. 93, nos. 754. 757, pl. 110, no. 858; Kyrieleis 2006, 124, pl. 41, nos. 58. 59. 65) and from Asia Minor (Comstock – Vermeule 1971, 38, nos. 37. 38) dated to the LG–early Archaic periods.

The dimensions (4–5.4 cm) of the animal figurines from Sounion imply that they were decorative elements attached to vessels or pendants, from the late 8th to the early 5th centuries. The similarities in the rendering of the eyes of three animal figurines may argue they are from the

Fig. 33.4. Sanctuary of Athena: Miniature zoomorphic figurines, National Archaeological Museum, Athens, 14932.22, 14932.23, 14926.5 (Photo: Elias Eliades)

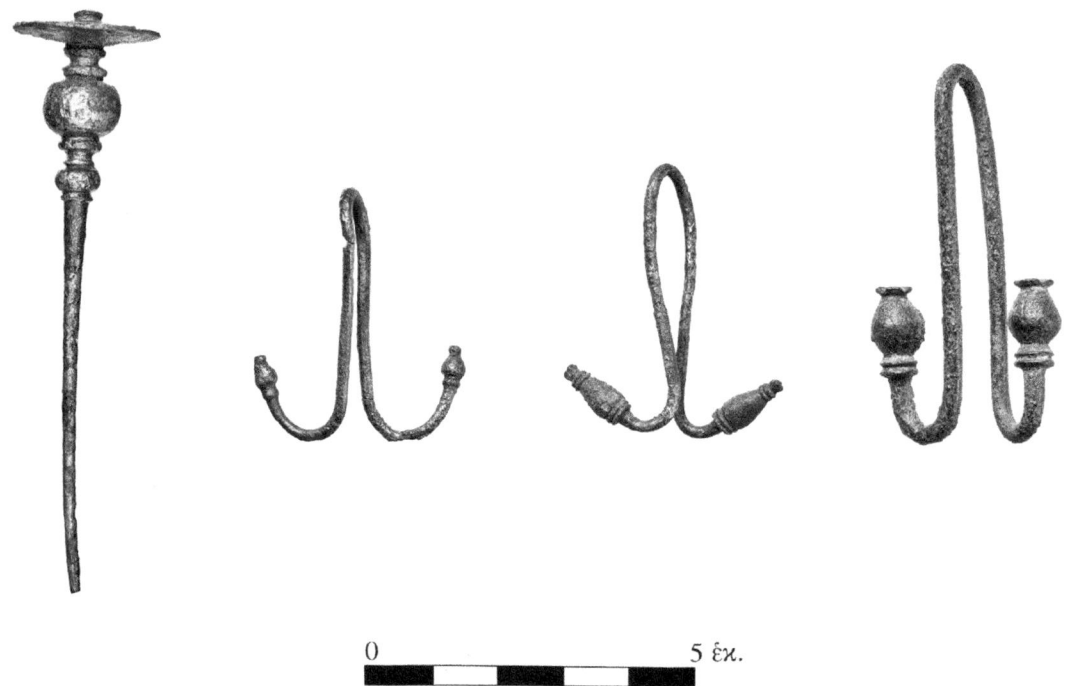

Fig. 33.5. Sanctuary of Athena: Pin, National Archaeological Museum, Athens 14932.18. Elongated spiral earrings (from left to right), with miniature pomegranates 14932.21, with elongated buds 14932.20, with large pomegranates 14932.19 (Photo: Elias Eliades)

same workshop. But with no exact parallels, it is unclear whether they were imported or local products.

Jewellery

In early Greek sanctuaries jewellery was a frequent dedication to female deities, favoured by women at times of transition in their lives (Fig. 33.5).

Only one pin, with two globules and a disc-shaped head, was found at Sounion, NM 14932.18. Typologically, it belongs to Dirlmeier's type BIVa (1984, 220. 226–229, pl. 89, nos. 3711. 3712. 3715) from the Archaic period and possibly from a Peloponnesian workshop. Its closest but not exact parallels are from Olympia (Philipp 1981, pl. 29, no. 94) and Akraiphia (Andreiomenou 2001, 505, fig. 54). Similar pins were found at Kythnos (Touloumtzidou 2017, 210, fig. 58), Kalapodi (Felsch 2007, pl. 28, no. 425, Type B IV), Philia (Kilian-Dirlmeier 2002, pl. 95, no. 1512), Argos (Waldstein 1905, pl. 80, nos. 417. 418), Perachora (Payne 1940, pl. 74, nos. 15. 17) and Lindos (Blinkenberg 1931, 126–127, pl. 12, no. 315).

Three 7th c. and intact elongated spiral earrings resemble examples from an Eastern Greek workshop (Laffineur 1978, 145. 152–154. 188–189). Their bodies (Castor 2008, 13–14) are made of a cast copper-based rod of circular cross section while their upturned ends are decorated, NM 14932.21 with miniature schematised pomegranates, NM 14932.20 with elongated buds, and NM 14932.19 with finials ending in well-shaped pomegranates. They are Laffineur's type C, fashionable in the 7th and early 6th c. BC, mainly in Asia Minor (Hogarth 1908, pl. 18, no. 41) and the eastern Aegean (Boardman 1967, fig. 144, nos. 351. 352; Lamb 1935, pl. 32, nos. 31–33; Blinkenberg 1931, pl. 12, no. 275). This type also occurs on the Greek mainland, at Argos (Waldstein 1905, pl. 92, no. 1554), Pherai (Kilian 1975, pl. 70, nos. 2–10) and Olympia (Philipp 1981, pl. 7, no. 398), but their finials, flat discs, beads or pyramidal tips, differ from the Sounion examples. From Kalapodi 2 earrings, however, (Felsch 2007, 194–195, pl. 47, no. 1889, Type A II and no. 1892, Type A III) have similar finials to NM 14932.20 and 14932.21, while an earring from the sanctuary at Kythnos has identical finials to NM 14932.19 (Touloumtzidou 2017, 210–211, fig. 62).

Ex-voto shields and tripods

Miniature shields NM 14932.5, 14932.4, plain, circular with a shallow convex profile and broad rims, are made of very fine copper-based sheet-metal (Snodgrass 1964, 33. 164–165) (Fig. 33.6). They are identical, bear no attachment holes, and date to the early Archaic period, as does a nearly identical parallel from Lindos (Blinkenberg 1931, pl. 63, no. 1566). Similar pieces come from Olympia (Furtwangler 1890, pl. 62, no. 1002; Maass 1978, 121, pl. 60), Philia (Kilian-Dirlmeier 2002, 17–18, no. 228), Bassai (Kourouniotis 1910, 315–316, fig. 36a, b), Akanthos (Kaltsas 1998, 65, pl. 72, no. 1124) and from the Kythnos sanctuary (Touloumtzidou 2017, 216, fig. 78). Such offerings were appropriate to an 'armed divinity' at Sounion, namely Athena.

Miniature tripods NM 14932.24, a, b, nearly identical, are made entirely of the same fine copper-based sheet. The legs are riveted to the plain and thin rim of the *lebes*, where a pair of loop-shaped handles are also fixed. These prestigious votive offerings at Archaic sanctuaries have many parallels,

Fig. 33.6. Sanctuary of Athena: (Top) Miniature shields, National Archaeological Museum, Athens 14932.5, 14932.4. (Bottom) Miniature tripods 14932.24a, 14932.24b (Photo: Elias Eliades)

e.g. from the deposit on the N. Slope of the Areopagos (Burr 1933, 621, fig. 87, no. 329), Eretria (Huber et al. 2003, pls. 42. 117, O25), Olympia (Maass 1978, pl. 60; Heilmeyer 1979, fig. 17, no. 143, fig. 18, no. 145), Ano Mazaraki in Achaia (Petropoulos 2002, table 3.3) and the Idaian Cave (Sakellarakis 2013, 83–85, pl. 58).

Two *lebetes*, NM 14932.3, 14932.17, belonging to miniature tripods in poor condition, retain the slots for the now-missing legs. They are made of thin sheet with rims turned inwards (cf. Heilmeyer 1979, 133, fig. 19, no. 146). Their modelling is identical with the *lebetes* of the tripods mentioned above, dated to the late 7th c. BC. Traces of soot on the handles and rim of one *lebes* suggest that it was burnt. If so, it and a few other items with signs of fire may be a *terminus ante quem* for the destruction of the sanctuaries by the Persians.

Oddments

An assortment of seven objects of unknown context completes the assemblage of bronzes, among which are one constructional element X26861 and two fragments of a copper-based hammered sheet X26858, X26859.

Analytical examination

Surface, non-invasive analyses (handheld XRF, LED microscope)

Method

Surface, non-invasive analysis was performed on 31 copper-based objects with a portable handheld X-ray Fluorescent (hhXRF) Spectrometer Bruker Tracer III

SD from the Laboratory of Archaeometry at the Dept. of History, Archaeology and Cultural Heritage Management at the University of the Peloponnese (Table 33.2). All analyses took place at the National Archaeological Museum in Athens with a collection time of 60 sec with a beam diameter of 3 mm, while the instrument operated at a voltage of 40kV and a current of 12 μA. During surface analysis, selected objects were examined with an LED handheld microscope in order to examine surface features. Results are presented in weight percent (wt%).

During the analysis, measurements of two certified reference materials (CDA510 and CDA360 from Metal Samples Co., Munford, Alabama, Demo Samples, Version L, provided by Bruker) were performed in order to monitor the instrument's accuracy, precision and detection limits (Table 33.3). Major elements came with a percentage deviation (δ relative) of <1%, which was higher for minor elements, as is expected for lower concentrations. For minor elements, a detection limit of 0.5 wt% was applied. Nevertheless, the surface hhXRF results were considered only as qualitative, as is customary for such non-invasive analyses of metallic surfaces of ancient objects, which most often show discrepancies when compared to the metal core (Orfanou – Rehren 2015). This qualitative approach of the surface analyses was performed as a first step in examining a larger sample with minimal invasion and to get an overview of the metals present in the objects, but not to discover the actual concentrations of each element.

Results (hhXRF)

Surface characterisation of the samples showed enrichment in zinc (see below). Zinc was detected in all 31 objects in variable amounts from <1 up to 33 wt% (10 wt% mean, 8

Table 33.2. Summary table of the objects analysed with hhXRF and µXRF

Find No.	Description	hhXRF	µXRF
X26858	thin sheet	x	x
X26859	thin sheet	x	x
X26860	nail cap	x	
X26861	pin	x	x
X26862	ring	x	
NM14926.1	tool	x	
NM14926.2a	tweezer	x	
NM14926.2b	tweezer	x	
NM14926.3	miniature double axe	x	
NM14926.5	animal figurine	x	
NM14926.22	warrior figurine (Reshef)	x	x
NM14932.1	animal figurine	x	
NM14932.10	arrowhead	x	
NM14932.2	earring	x	
NM14932.3	miniature tripod	x	
NM14932.4	miniature shield	x	
NM14932.5	miniature shield	x	
NM14932.6	arrowhead	x	
NM14932.7	arrowhead	x	
NM14932.8	arrowhead	x	
NM14932.9	arrowhead	x	
NM14932.10	arrowhead	x	x
NM14932.11	spearhead	x	
NM14932.12	arrowhead	x	
NM14932.14	nail cap	x	
NM14932.18	pin	x	
NM14932.19	earring	x	
NM14932.22	animal figurine	x	x
NM14932.23	animal figurine	x	x
NM14932.24a	miniature tripod	x	
NM14936.2	ring	x	
NM14936.7	ring	x	

Table 33.3. Analyses of certified reference material (CRM) provided by Bruker with the hhXRF; bd= below detection limit; δ rel.= percentage deviation

CRM	Values	Cu	Sn	Pb	Zn	Fe
CDA510	certified (wt%)	95.27	4.54	bd	0.03	bd
	analysed (wt%)	95.88	4.18	bd	0.1	bd
	δ rel. (%)	-0.6	9	-	-70	-
CDA360	certified (wt%)	60.99	bd	2.98	35.88	0.15
	analysed (wt%)	61.97	0.19	2.16	35.63	0.14
	δ rel. (%)	-1.6	nd	38	0.7	7

Table 33.4. Summary table of the hhXRF results showing mean, minimum and maximum values detected; bd= below detection limit

	Cu	Sn	Pb	Zn	As	Fe	Mn	Co	Ni	Ag	Sb
mean	85	1.1	1.2	11	0.6	0.5	0.1	0.1	0.2	0.2	0.2
max.	98	10	14	33	9	3.1	0.3	0.6	1.0	1.3	1.6
min.	56	0.1	bd	0.6	bd	bd	bd	bd	bd	bd	bd

Table 33.5. Detection limits of the µXRF in weight percent (wt%) used for the analysis of the sample as established with the analyses of certified reference materials (for more details see Orfanou et al., in prep)

µXRF	Sn	Pb	Zn	As	Fe	S
Detection limits	0.2	0.1	0.5	0.05	0.1	0.1

standard deviation). Tin and lead were detected in small amounts with means of 1 wt% for both elements and maximum values of 10 wt% tin and 14 wt% lead. Seven objects showed tin, six objects lead, and three objects both tin and lead >1%. Minor elements such as arsenic, iron, manganese, cobalt, nickel, antimony, silver and bismuth were also detected typically <1% (Table 33.4).

Invasive analyses (micro XRF)

Method

A selection of seven objects were additionally analysed invasively. The objects were sampled either by cutting a small piece from already fragmented artefacts (three objects) or by drilling (in the case of three complete objects) with drill bits of 0.5–1 mm in diameter (four objects). For each drilling a fresh bit was used in order to guard against any contamination. Samples were mounted in epoxy resin and polished following standard metallographic procedures. Bulk chemical compositions were obtained with a Bruker Tornado M4 benchtop micro X-ray Fluorescence (µXRF) at the Aarhus Geochemistry and Isotope Research (AGiR) Platform at the Dept. of Geoscience, Aarhus University. The µXRF's minimum detection limits, precision and accuracy for the different elements analysed were monitored with the routine analyses of certified reference materials (Table 33.5). For more details on the settings, see Orfanou et al. (in prep.). The µXRF results are considered representative of the objects' bulk chemical compositions away from any surface contamination.

Results (µXRF)

Analyses of the objects' metal cores showed no detectable zinc traces (Table 33.6). The objects consist mostly of copper between 89 and 99 wt%. Tin is present in low concentrations (mean <0.5 wt%, maximum of 1.5 wt%), as is lead (mean <1 wt%). Two objects showed lead contents between 3 and 6 wt% lead, i.e. animal figurine NM 14932.22 and warrior figurine 14926.22. Arsenic and iron were detected with means of <0.3 wt% and sulphur <0.1 wt%. Figurine NM 14932.22 was found to have a lead-tin filling (94 wt% lead, 4 wt% tin) and traces of arsenic (0.1 wt%), as further confirmed in a radiograph (Fig. 33.7).

Table 33.6. Compositional results of the invasive μXRF analyses; excluding the lead filling of a14932.22; all values in wt%; bd= below detection limit

Find no.	Cu	Sn	Pb	As	Fe	S
X26858	99	0.3	0.2	0.2	0.1	bd
X26859	98	bd	0.3	0.2	0.8	bd
X26861	99	bd	bd	0.2	0.2	bd
NM14926.22	94	0.2	2.9	0.8	0.7	0.1
NM14932.10	98	bd	0.7	0.4	0.1	0.2
NM14932.22	89	1.5	5.9	0.2	0.1	0.1
NM14932.23	97	0.4	0.3	0.3	bd	0.1
mean	96	0.4	0.8	0.3	0.3	0.1

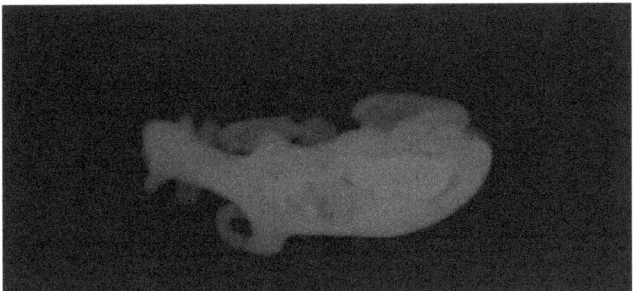

Fig. 33.7. Radiograph of animal figurine NM 14932.22 showing the two distinct metals, i.e. the copper-based metal for the figure and the lead for the filling (Radiograph: National Archaeological Museum, Athens; adapted by: Vana Orfanou)

Fig. 33.8. Photomicrograph of miniature shield NM 14932.4 with an LED handheld microscope, showing the characteristic orange lustre of the zinc-rich surface; magnification 10x, field of view 2.5 cm (Photomicrograph: Vana Orfanou)

Table 33.7. Compositional results of the surface hhXRF analyses of the group of objects analysed also invasively; note the high zinc contents; all values in wt%; bd = below detection limit

Find no.	Cu	Sn	Pb	Zn	As	Fe	Ni
X26858	98	bd	0.4	1.5	bd	bd	bd
X26859	89	bd	bd	8.3	bd	bd	0.5
X26861	86	bd	2.2	7.9	0.6	1.3	bd
NM14926.22	80	bd	1.4	16.0	bd	bd	bd
NM14932.10	94	0.9	bd	5.0	bd	bd	bd
NM14932.22	73	0.5	9.7	14	0.6	0.6	bd
NM14932.23	95	1.4	1.6	1.3	bd	bd	bd

Discussion of analytical results

Impact of conservation treatment

The surface zinc enrichment of objects noted during hhXRF analyses must be addressed before discussion of the analytical results. Copper-zinc alloys, i.e. brasses, were available from the Roman period when the necessary technology was introduced (Bayley 1998). Even though earlier brass objects are occasionally identified, these should be considered more as accidental occurrences, i.e. natural alloys as the result of smelting copper-zinc minerals, rather than as intentional production (Craddock 1978; Thornton – Ehlers 2003; Orfanou et al. 2014). Thus the Sounion assemblage with a *terminus ante quem* in the 8th c. BC is too early to have been made of brass.

Quickly it became apparent that the electrochemical cleaning of the objects in conservation treatment at the beginning of the 20th c. was responsible for the unlikely presence of zinc on their surface (pers. com. G. Moraitou). This method of cleaning ancient metals is still popular amongst conservators, and if conducted correctly, it should not have any impact on the objects' surfaces (Degrigny 2010). In the case of the Sounion assemblage, though, chipped zinc metal sheets were added in the electrolyte during cleaning along with the objects. This was possibly done to add the characteristic bright orange-ish lustre that a zinc-enriched surface would exhibit (Fig. 33.8). The process created a surface enrichment of the objects in zinc. Variation in the zinc content detected on the objects' surface could relate to the intensity and duration of the cleaning, from the nature of the corrosion products present in the first place or from post-cleaning treatment.

Thus, great caution is needed with the hhXRF results obtained from the sample which are not only semi-qualitative, but which can also be misleading on the alloys used. The effect on the objects' surface from the electrochemical cleaning extended beyond the surface enrichment in zinc. As seen in a comparison of Tables 33.6 and 33.7, the objects' surface was typically depleted in copper, whereas tin and lead behaved erratically – both their enrichment and depletion was observed, e.g. less tin was found on the surface of NM 14932.22, but more on 14932.23 (compared to the μXRF analyses). Even so, the discovery of the conservation treatment's impact adds an interesting detail to the objects' biographies.

Bulk compositions

The invasive μXRF analyses of the seven objects are considered as safely representative of the original bulk compositions. All samples contained <1.5 wt% tin. Tin amounts at these concentrations can occur from contacts between tin-rich copper ores, or equally from mixing scrap bronze. For lead, values up to 5 wt% can occur in ancient copper from naturally co-existing copper and lead minerals (Pernicka 1999). Five objects showed lead below <1 wt%, i.e. levels expected for natural impurities in copper. Figurines NM 14932.22 and 14926.22 with 6 wt% and with 3 wt% lead stand out. Whether their lead content came from smelting lead-rich copper ores, the mixing of leaded copper alloys or from intentionally adding small amounts of lead, they point towards a different technological practice when compared to the rest of the samples which bear only lead impurities. Figurine NM 14932.22 also contained the highest tin detected (1.5 wt%). This, with its higher lead content, distinguishes it even more. In the Archaic period, the prevalence of unalloyed copper noticed in the invasive analyses is surprising as most votive offerings comprise copper alloys, as analysed from elsewhere in Greece (e.g. Craddock 1977). Furthermore, the discovery of a lead-tin filling in the figurine's core further supports the hypothesis of it being originally an attachment on a large vessel, as mentioned above in the typological discussion. Lead-tin alloys were commonly used in antiquity for soldering purposes. All other minor elements, namely arsenic, iron and sulphur, were detected at impurity levels.

Oriental, orientalizing or local?

Bronze offerings appear in large quantities in Greek sanctuaries from the late 8th c. BC (de Polignac 1995, 14–15). Their limited number at Sounion implies that extensive recycling could have taken place, a norm often encountered in sanctuaries (Lebesi 2002, 189). Re-use is also observed in other spheres, e.g. Archaic column capitals from the ravaged Poseidon temple used at the Athena sanctuary as bases for awning posts (Dinsmoor 1974, 49) and columns re-used in the Classical long stoa of the Poseidon sanctuary (Stais 1920, 17). No such clear evidence for the copper-alloy votives can exist, since recycling of such items is hard to trace (Lindenlauf 2006, 31; Ponting – Levene 2015). In the Poseidon sanctuary's *bothros* one has a primary deposition, before 490 BC, while in the landfill of the Athena sanctuary finds are more likely discards after the Persian destruction (Theodoropoulou Polychroniadis 2015). The dedications discussed span the late 8th to the early 5th c. BC. Several finds, however, can be dated to the late 8th–7th c. BC, such as the Reshef figurine, the animal figurines, except for NM 14932.22, and the earrings, displaying influences of eastern prototypes. Thus, they are assigned to the period of transformation, innovation and change in Greek art and culture resulting from dissemination of ideas and techniques from the East (Burkert 1992). They are grouped with the large number of oriental/orientalising finds in Greek sanctuaries like Olympia, Samos and the Argive Heraion. Were these specially acquired items or purpose-made pieces ordered from a specific workshop for dedication? Were they brought by travellers as offerings or were they objects of everyday use that were 'converted' into dedications? It is unclear whether the Sounion finds were imports, the products of mobile craftsmen or possibly of locals versed in the techniques and styles of the East.

The abundance of metal in the Laureotike and the fact that we are dealing with offerings from significant sanctuaries where craftsmen tended 'to reinterpret rather than copy oriental models', as Aurigny notes (2017, 42), lead to the hypothesis that these objects were the product of local workshops (Voyatzis 1994, 162; Lebesi 2002, 185–192). This is further supported by their iconographic details, the absence of exact comparanda, and the results, so far, of the analytical examination.

Invasive analyses of five out of seven objects of various types X26858, X26859, X26861, NM 14932.10, 14932.23 showed uniformity in bulk composition, namely copper with only impurities of tin and lead, reflecting consistency in the technological choices during their manufacture. Given the limited size of the current sample analysed, the possibility that the objects were the output of several workshops cannot currently be excluded. Figurines NM 14926.22 with its elevated lead content and 14932.22 with additions of both lead and tin stand out compositionally, as they do typologically, raising further questions as to their geographical origin.

Conclusion

The assemblage discussed seems to follow the trend of the production and dedication pattern of votive offerings in contemporary sanctuaries, e.g. Lindos, Delphi, Olympia, Kalapodi. The quantity and type of metal offerings, as well as the statuary, being both prestigious and valuable, imply an elite of mine owners, traders and seafarers. This may establish the profile of visitors and dedicators at the Cape. The typological analysis of the objects advances research into the origin of the votives. It was coupled with metallurgical analyses to produce new evidence regarding their technology. Even though the bulk compositions were obtained from a limited sample (7 out of 44 objects), the archaeometric analysis provided new insights into the matter of distinct technological traditions. The results point to a local tradition of unalloyed copper production, while alloyed objects could be the products of different workshop(s), local or otherwise. Additional lead isotope analysis coupled with trace element analysis could prove useful in tracing the origin of the metal used for the Sounion votives, which could indeed be the Laurion mines.

Finally, scholars should be aware not only of the natural degradation that occurs during long-term burial of metals, but also of possible changes to the surface and substrate layers as a result of particular conservation treatments. Thus, as in the case of the Sounion assemblage, conservation treatment took place a century ago, but such assemblages long kept in museums are often the source for archaeometric analyses today.

Acknowledgements

The authors would like to thank the Director and staff at the National Archaeological Museum in Athens, who made this work possible and in particular: Dr George Kavvadias, Head of the Collection of Vases, Minor Arts and Metal Objects; archaeologists Alexandra Hatzipanagiotou and Nomiki Palaiokrassa, for their support on the project's aims; Dr Georgianna Moraitou, Head of the Department of Conservation, Scientific Research and Archaeometry for her input on the conservation treatment; conservators Sofia Spyridaki for her assistance during the hhXRF analyses, Makis Makris and Giorgos Kouros for their assistance with the sampling. We also thank Prof. Nikos Zacharias, Chair of the Dept. of History, Archaeology and Cultural Resources Management and Director of Laboratory of Archaeometry, University of the Peloponnese, for access to the hhXRF instrument; and Prof. Charles Lesher, Niels Bohr Professor, Department of Geoscience, Aarhus University for access to µXRF equipment at AGiR. VO would like to thank the Danish National Research Foundation for supporting her position during part of this work under the grant DNRF119 – Centre for Excellence for Urban Network Evolutions (UrbNet).

Authors' contributions: The overall project was designed by ZTP, who conducted the stylistic and typological examination. VO conducted the surface and invasive analyses. Both authors drafted the text and approved the final manuscript.

Bibliography

Andreiomenou, A., 2001. Το εργαστήριον χαλκοτεχνίας της Ακραιφίας (830–480 π.Χ.). Συμβολή εις την χρονολόγησιν ενίων τύπων κοσμημάτων. In: A. Alexandri – I. Leventi, ed., *Καλλίστευμα. Μελέτες προς τιμήν της Όλγας Τζάχου-Αλεξανδρή*. Athens, Ministry of Culture, 469–526.

Aurigny, H., 2017. Greek art in the seventh century BC: the example of bronzes from Delphi. In: X. Charalambidou – C. Morgan, ed., *Interpreting the seventh century BC. Tradition and innovation.* Oxford, Archaeopress, 38–46.

Baitinger, H., 2001. *Olympische Forschungen XXIX. Die Angriffswaffen aus Olympia.* Berlin and New York, De Gruyter.

Barletta, B.A., 2017. *The Sanctuary of Athena at Sounion.* Ancient Art and Architecture in Context 4. Princeton, ASCSA.

Bayley, J., 1998. The production of brass in antiquity with particular reference to Roman Britain. In: P.T. Craddock, ed., *2000 years of zinc and brass.* London, British Museum Press, 7–26.

Bernardini, Ch., 2006. *I bronzi della stipe di Kamiros.* Monografie della SAIA 18. Athens, SAIA.

Blinkenberg, C., 1931. *Lindos I. Les petits objets.* Berlin, De Gruyter and Cie.

Boardman, J., 1961. *The Cretan collection in Oxford: The Dictaean cave and Iron Age Crete*, Oxford, The Clarendon Press.

Boardman, J., 1967. *Excavations in Chios, 1952–1955: Greek Emporio.* BSA Supp. 6. London, Thames and Hudson.

Broneer, O., 1935. Excavations on the north slope of the Acropolis in Athens 1933–1934. *Hesperia*, 4(2), 109–188.

Burkert, W., 1992. *The orientalizing revolution: Near Eastern influence on Greek culture in the early archaic age.* Harvard University Press.

Burr, D., 1933. A Geometric house and a Proto-Attic votive deposit. *Hesperia*, 2, 542–640.

Calligas, P.G., 1997. A bronze die from Sounion. In: K.A. Sheedy – C. Papageorgiadou-Banis, ed., *Numismatic archaeology, archaeological numismatics. Proceedings of an international conference held to honour Dr Mando Oeconomides in Athens 1995.* Oxbow Monographs 75. Oxford, Oxbow, 141–147.

Castor, A., 2008. Archaic Greek earrings: an interim survey. *A. Anz.*, 1, 1–34.

Comstock, M. – Vermeule, C., 1971. *Greek, Etruscan and Roman bronzes in the Museum of Fine Arts, Boston.* Boston, Museum of Fine Arts.

Craddock, P.T., 1977. The Composition of the Copper Alloys used by the Greek, Etruscan and Roman Civilizations: 2. The Archaic, Classical and Hellenistic Greeks. *Journal of Archaeological Science*, 4, 103–23.

Craddock, P.T., 1978. The composition of the copper alloys used by the Greek, Etruscan and Roman civilizations: 3. The origins and early use of brass. *Journal of Archaeological Science*, 5, 1–16.

Dawkins, R.M., ed., 1929. *The sanctuary of Artemis Orthia at Sparta: excavated and described by members of the British School at Athens, 1906–1910.* JHS Supp. Paper 5. London, Macmillan.

Degrigny, C., 2010. Use of electrochemical techniques for the conservation of metal artefacts: a review. *Journal of Solid State Electrochemistry*, 14, 353–361.

Dinsmoor, W.B., Jr., 1974. *Sounion.* Athens, Lycabettus Press.

Felsch, R.C.S. ed., 2007. *Kalapodi II. Ergebnisse der Ausgrabungen im Heiligtum der Artemis und des Apollon von Hyampolis in der antiken Phokis.* Mainz, Philipp von Zabern.

Furtwängler, A., 1890. *Olympia. Die Ergebnisse der von Deutschen Reich veranstalteten Ausgrabung. IV. Die Bronzen und die übrigen kleineren Funde von Olympia.* Berlin, A. Asher and Co.

Gallet de Santerre, H., 1987. Les statuettes de bronze mycéniennes au type dit du "dieu Reshef" dans leur contexte égeen. *BCH*, 111, 7–29.

Giacco, M., 2015. Votive bronze objects from the sanctuary of Hera at the mouth of the Sele river (Paestum). In:

E. Deschler-Erb – P. Della Casa, ed., *New research on ancient bronzes. Acta of the XVIIIth international congress on ancient bronzes*. Zurich Studies in Archaeology 10. Zurich, Chronos Verlag, 29–38.

Greco, E. – Correale, A., 2017. L'edificio dell'istmo e le sue frecce rituali. In: A. Pontradolfo – M. Scafuro, ed., *Dialoghi sull'Archaeologia della Magna Grecia e del Mediterraneo*. I. *ATTI del I Convegno Internazionale di Studi, 7–9 Settembre 2016*. Paestum, Pandemos, 27–40.

Hanfmann, G.M.A., 1962. A Syrian from Sounion. *Hesperia*, 31, 236–237.

Heilmeyer, W.-D., 1972. *Olympische Forschungen VII. Frühe olympische Tonfiguren*. Berlin, De Gruyter.

Heilmeyer, W.-D., 1979. *Olympische Forschungen XII. Frühe olympische Bronzefiguren: Die Tiervotive*. Berlin, De Gruyter.

Hogarth, D.G. et al., 1908. *Excavations at Ephesus. The Archaic Artemisia*. London, British Museum Press.

Huber, S. et al., 2003. *Eretria XIV. Fouilles et recherches. L'aire sacrificielle au nord du sanctuaire d'Apollon Daphnephoros: un rituel des époques géométrique et archaïque*. Montreux, Gollion.

Jantzen, U., 1972. *Samos VIII. Ägyptische und orientalische Bronzen aus dem Heraion von Samos*. Bonn, DAI, in Kommission R. Habelt.

Kaltsas, N.E., 1998. *Άκανθος: η ανασκαφή στο νεκροταφείο κατά το 1979*. Athens, TAPA.

Kilian, K., 1975. *Fibeln in Thessalien von der mykenischen bis zur archaischen Zeit. PBF*, XIV, 2. Munich, Beck.

Kilian-Dirlmeier, I., 1979. *Anhänger in Griechenland von der mykenischen bis zur spätgeometrischen Zeit. PBF*, XI,2. Munich, Beck.

Kilian-Dirlmeier, I., 1980. Bemerkungen zu den Fingerringen mit spiralenden. *Jahrbuch des Römisch Germanischen Zentral Museums*, 27, 249–269.

Kilian-Dirlmeier, I., 1984. *Nadeln der fruhhelladischen bis archäischen Zeit von der Peloponnes. PBF*, XIII.8. Munich, Beck.

Kilian-Dirlmeier, I., 2002. *Kleinfunde aus dem Athena Itonia-Heiligtum bei Philia (Thessalien)*. Mainz, Verlag des Römisch-Germanischen Zentralmuseums.

Kourouniotis, K., 1910. Το εν Βάσσαις αρχαιότερον ιερόν του Απόλλωνος. *AE*, 271–331.

Kyrieleis, H., 2006. *Olympische Forschungen XXI. Anfänge und Frühzeit des Heiligtums von Olympia. Die Ausgrabungen am Pelopion 1987–1996*. Berlin, De Gruyter.

Laffineur, R., 1978. *L'orfèvrerie Rhodienne orientalisante*. École française d'Athènes, travaux et memoires 21. Paris, De Boccard.

Laffineur, R., 2011. 'Πολυάργυρος Θορικός. Thorikos rich in silver. The prehistoric periods. In: P.P. Iossif, ed., *'All that glitters...': the Belgian contribution to Greek numismatics, 29 September 2010–15 January 2011*. Athens, Belgian School at Athens, 26–40.

Lamb, W., 1935. Excavations at Kato Phana in Chios. *British Scholl at Athens*, 35, 138–164.

Lebesi, A., 2002. *Το ιερό του Ερμή και της Αφροδίτης στη Σύμη Βιάννου* III. *Χάλκινα ανθρωπόμορφα ειδώλια*. Βιβλιοθήκη της εν Αθήναις Αρχαιολογικής Εταιρείας 225 Athens, Η εν Αθήναις Αρχαιολογική Εταιρεία.

Lindenlauf, A., 2006. Recycling of votive offerings in Greek sanctuaries, epigraphical and archaeological evidence. In: C.C. Mattusch – A.A. Donohue – A. Brauer, ed., *Common ground: archaeology, art, science and humanities: proceedings of the XVIth international congress of classical archaeology, August 23–26, 2003, Boston*. Oxford, Oxbow, 30–32.

Marangou, L., 1996. *Ancient Greek art. The N.P. Goulandris collection*. Athens, N.P. Goulandris Foundation.

Maass, M., 1978. *Olympische Forschungen X. Die geometrischen Dreifüsse von Olympia*. Berlin, De Gruyter.

Miller, S.G., 1977. Excavations at Nemea, 1976. *Hesperia*, 46(1), 1–26.

Miller, S.G., 1984. Excavations at Nemea, 1983. *Hesperia*, 53(2), 171–192.

Mitsopoulos-Leon, V., 2012. *Das Heiligtum der Artemis Hemera in Lousoi. Kleinfunde aus den Grabungen 1986–2000*. Sonderschriften des Österreichischen Archäologischen Institutes 47. Vienna, Osterreichisches Archaologisches Institut.

Moorey, P.R.S., 1974. *Ancient bronzes from Luristan*. London, British Museum Press.

Nicholls, R.V., 1958–1959. Old Smyrna: the Iron Age fortifications and associated remains on the city perimeter. *British School at Athens*, 53–54, 35–137.

Orfanou, V. – Birch, T. – Lichtenberger, A. – Raja, R. – Barfod, G. – Lesher, C., in preparation. *Elemental and lead isotope analyses of Roman to early Islamic copper-based metalwork at Jerash*, Jordan.

Orfanou, V. – Doulgeri-Intzesiloglou, A. – Arachoviti, P., 2014. Archaeometric investigation of copper-based fibulae from the sanctuary of Thavlios Zeus at ancient Pherae: preliminary results [in Greek]. In: D. Karamberopoulos, ed. *Hypereia* 6. A. Volos: Epistimoniki Etaireia Meletis Feron-Velestinou-Riga, 213–222.

Orfanou, V. – Rehren, T., 2015. A (not so) dangerous method: pXRF vs. EPMA-WDS analyses of copper-based artefacts. *Archaeological and Anthropological Sciences*, 7(3), 387–397.

Papapostolou, I.A., 2010. Aspects of cult in early Thermos. *AE*, 149, 1–59.

Payne, H.G.C., 1940. *Perachora. The sanctuaries of Hera Akraia and Limenia*, I. Architecture, bronzes, terracottas, Oxford, The Clarendon Press.

Perdrizet, P., 1908. *Fouilles de Delphes* V. *Monuments figurés:petits bronzes, terres-cuites, antiquités diverses*. Paris, Albert Fontemoing.

Pernicka, E., 1999. Trace element fingerprinting of ancient copper: a guide to technology or provenance? In: S.M.M. Young – A.M. Pollard – P. Budd – R.A. Ixer, ed., *Metals in antiquity*. Oxford, BAR Publishing, 3–171.

Petropoulos, M., 2002. The Geometric temple at Ano Mazaraki (Rakita) in Achaia during the period of colonisation. In: E. Greco, ed., *Gli Achei e l'Identità Etnica degli Achei d'Occidente. Atti del Convegno Internazionale di Studi, Fondazione Paestum. Tekmeria* 3. Paestum and Athens, Pandemos, 143–164.

Philipp, H., 1981. *Olympische Forschungen* XIII. *Bronzeschmuck aus Olympia*. Berlin, de Gruyter.

Polignac, F. de, 1995. *Cults, territory, and the origins of the Greek city-state*, Chicago, University of Chicago Press.

Ponting, M. – Levene, D., 2015, Recycling economies, when efficient, are by their nature invisible: A first century Jewish recycling economy. In: Geller, M.J., ed., *The archaeology and material culture of the Babylonian Talmud*. London, Brill, 39–65.

Raubitschek, I.K., 1998. *Isthmia* VII. *The metal objects (1952–1989)*. Princeton, The American School of Classical Studies at Athens.

Robinson, D.M., 1941. *Excavations at Olynthos*. X. *Metal and miscellaneous finds: an original contribution to Greek life*. Baltimore, John Hopkins Press.

Sakellarakis, J.A. – Sapouna-Sakellaraki, E., 2013. *Το Ιδαίο Άντρο: ιερό και μαντείο*, III. Βιβλιοθήκη της εν Αθήναις Αρχαιολογικής Εταιρείας 281. Athens, Η εν Αθήναις Αρχαιολογική Εταιρεία.

Sapouna-Sakellaraki, E., 1995. *Die bronzenen Menschenfiguren auf Kreta und in der Ägäis*. PBF I.5. Stuttgart, F. Steiner.

Seeden, H., 1980. *The standing armed figurines in the Levant*. PBF I, 1. Munich, Beck

Sheedy, K.A., 2014. The Sounion 'Wappenmunzen die' revisited, *Νομισματικά Χρονικά* 32, 21–32.

Snodgrass, A.M., 1964. *Early Greek armour and weapons: from the end of the Bronze Age to 600 B.C.* Edinburgh, The University Press.

Stais, V., 1917. Σουνίου ανασκαφαί. *AE*, 168–213.

Stais, V., 1920. *Το Σούνιον και οι ναοί του Ποσειδώνος και Αθηνάς*. Athens, Η εν Αθήναις Αρχαιολογική Εταιρεία.

Tarditi, Ch., 2016. *Bronze vessels from the Acropolis: style and decoration in Athenian production between the sixth and fifth centuries BC*. Thiasos Monografie 7. Rome, Quasar.

Theodoropoulou Polychroniadis, Z., 2015. *Sounion revisited: The sanctuaries of Poseidon and Athena at Sounion in Attica*. Oxford, Archaeopress.

Thornton, C.P. – Ehlers, C.B., 2003. Early brass in the ancient Near East. *IAMS*, 23.3, 3–8.

Touloumtzidou, A., 2017. Small finds from the sanctuary of Kythnos. The bronze finds – Part 1. In: A. Mazarakis Ainian, ed., *Les Sanctuaires Archaiques des Cyclades*. Rennes, Presses Universitaires de Rennes, 200–231.

Voyatzis, M.E., 1994. An analysis of votive types recently found at Tegea. In: R. Hägg, ed., *Peloponnesian sanctuaries and cults. Proceedings of the ninth international symposium at the Swedish Institute at Athens, 11–13 June 1994*. SkrAth 4°, 48. Stockholm and Athens, P. Åströms förlag, 159–168.

Waele, E., de 1982. *Bronze du Luristan et d'Amlash: ancienne collection Godard*. Publication d'histoire de l'art et d'archéologie de l'Université catholique de Louvain 34. Louvain-La-Neuve, Institut supériore d'archéologie et d'histoire de l'art.

Waldstein, C., et al., 1905. *The Argive Heraeum* II. *Terra-cotta figurines, terra-cotta reliefs, vases and vase fragments, bronzes, engraved stones, gems, and ivories, coins, Egyptian, or Graeco-Egyptian objects*, Boston/New York, Houghton, Mifflin and Co.

34

Bronzes of Arcadian Orchomenos: A Review of Old and New Finds

Stamatis A. Fritzilas

Ephorate of Antiquities of Messenia

sfritzilas@culture.gr

Abstract: The aim of this paper is to examine the evidence of ancient bronzes found in the old (1913) and new excavations (2011–2014) of the Acropolis of Orchomenos in Arcadia, highlighting less-known or new material. Four groups of bronze objects are considered in connection with the monuments of the archaeological site. The first group consists of various votive offerings in the sanctuary of Artemis Mesopolitis. The second group consists of more than a dozen bronze plaques with decrees in a Doric dialect, which come from the destruction layer in the Eastern Stoa. The third group consists mainly of coins found in the first and recent excavations. The fourth group is also the various arrowheads from the period of the city's destruction. The reassessment of the old and new rare bronze objects in context provides a basic source of historical information that illuminates multiple aspects of human activity during the Classical and Hellenistic periods.

Keywords: Votive Offerings; Bronze Plaques; Coins; Arrowheads

History of research

During the 19th century, Orchomenos' rich historical past has lured a steady stream of travellers (Gell 1817, 144–145; Dodwell 1819, 425–428; Gell 1823, 368–371; Dodwell 1834, 30; Curtius 1851, 219–224; Bursian 1868, 203–206; Frazer 1898, 223–226). This was to be expected, because during the fourth and third centuries BC, the city of Arcadian Orchomenos, due to its significant military strength and key geographical position in the middle of the Peloponnesos, played an important role in the political and military conflicts of this turbulent era (Meyer 1939, 887–905; Nielsen 2004, 523–525). It was a long period marked by antagonism between the Achaean League, the Aetolian League, Sparta, and the kingdom of Macedonia (Petropoulos 2005, 9–22; Fritzilas 2014, 35–46; Maher 2017, 255–257). The ancient Agora of Orchomenos, being a public space that served both commercial, political and religious purposes, was situated in a plateau on the southern slope of the Acropolis. Earlier research found that the Agora plateau further developed on an entirely new monumental scale through the construction of retaining walls, large stoas, temples, and the theatre (Hiller von Gaertringen – Latterman 1911, 18–29) (Fig. 34.1). The Temple of Artemis Mesopolitis, the official sanctuary of the city of Orchomenos, was situated on the southernmost lower terrace of the Agora. The temple of Artemis with its altar was unearthed for the first time in 1913 during the excavations conducted by the French School at Athens (Ecole française d'Athènes) (Blum – Plassart 1914a, 71–88; 1914b, 447–478). Further research showed that during the second half of the fourth century and the early part of the third century BC, a large building program was implemented in the city (Winter 1987, 235–239; 1989, 189–200). It included the construction of new fortifications and the monuments of the Agora. Four groups of bronzes are studied in connection with the monuments of the archaeological site; they were found on the Acropolis of Orchomenos and came from the previous investigations of the French Archaeological School, as well as the new researches conducted by the Greek Archaeological Service during the period 2011–2014 (Fig. 34.2), as described in preliminary publications (Fritzilas 2011, 231–235; 2012a, 174–180; 2013, 198–199; 2014, 10–28; 2018, 183–190).

Votive bronze objects from the Sanctuary of Artemis Mesopolitis

The first group consists of various bronze objects, mainly votive offerings from the important sanctuary of Artemis Mesopolitis (Meyer 1939, 904; Jost 1985, 117–188), but also from other excavated monuments of the Agora. The group includes figurines, parts of vessels, pins, and other finds. A deposit in a *bothros* was discovered at a short distance from the sanctuary (Blum – Plassart 1914 a, 77–78). Many of the objects are fragmentary, and it is not always easy to identify their original discovery contexts. Excavations in the inner chamber (*sēkos*) of the temple also brought to light a late Archaic bronze mirror-handle shaped like a *korē* (NAM, inv.X 14618), as well as a bronze lion's head (NAM, inv. X 14617) (Fig. 34.3.1). Conspicuous among the finds now in the National Archaeological Museum in Athens is a female face mask made from a thin sheet of bronze (NAM, inv. X 14619) (Fig. 34.3.2). Other bronze miniature objects were included among the artifacts, such as bronze-discs (NAM, inv. X 14621/1–5), bronze kylix-

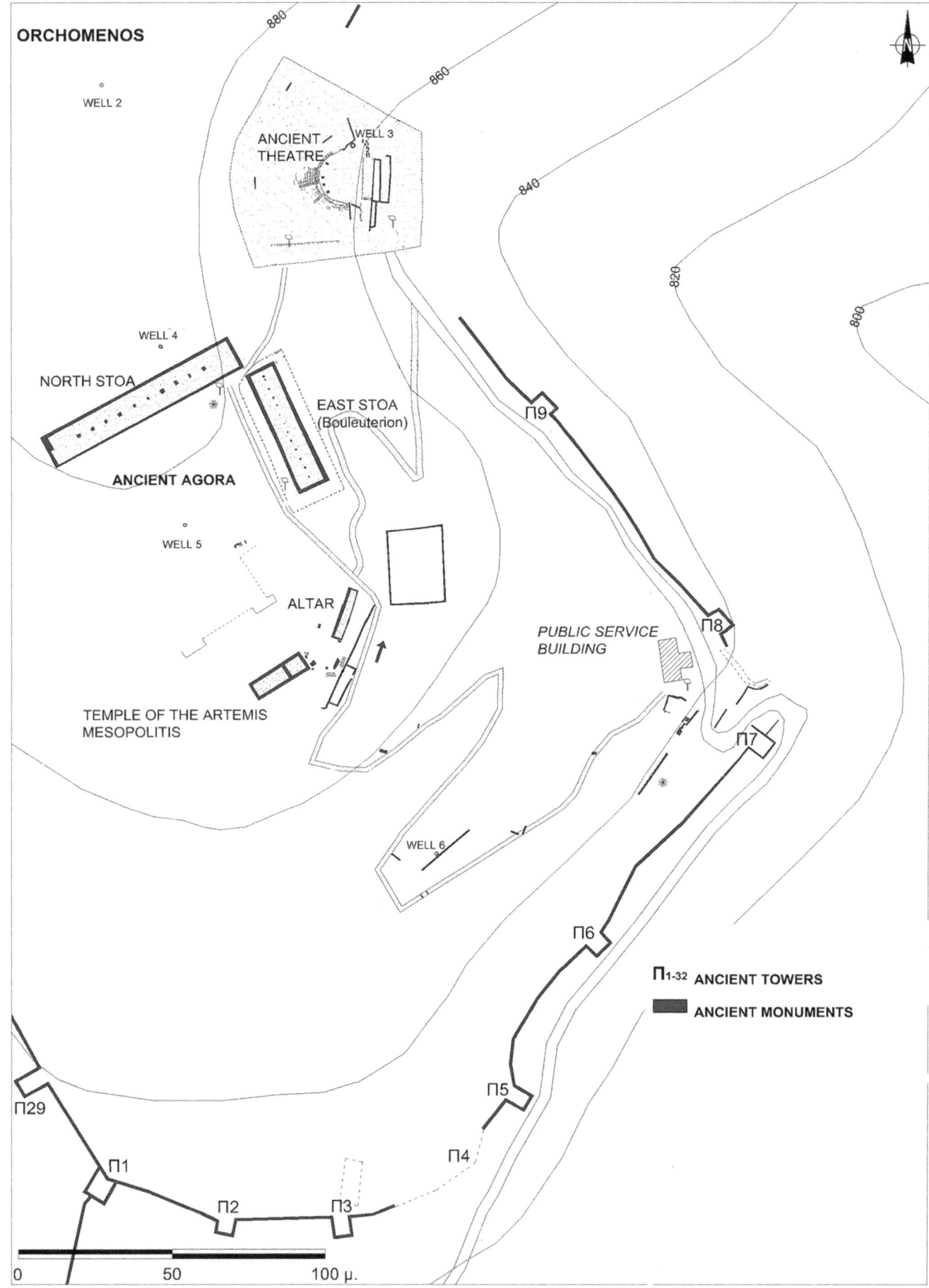

Figure 34.1. Ground plan. The monuments of the acropolis of Orchomenos (Drawing by S. Fritzilas and V. Zekios, 2014; courtesy Ephorate of Antiquities of Arcadia).

Figure 34.2. Aerial photo. The Agora of Orchomenos (Photo V. Fotinopoulos – Aerofilms, 2014; courtesy Ephorate of Antiquities of Arcadia)

handles (NAM, inv. X 19042 α–β) (Fig. 34.3.3), bronze vase-handles (NAM, inv. X 19043, X 19044, X 19046, X 19047 α–β) (Fig. 3.4), rims of bronze vessels (NAM, inv. X 19041), various parts of bronze vases (NAM, inv. X 19045), and parts of bronze fibulae (NAM, inv. X 19048, X 19049, X 19050, X19051 α–γ, X 19052 α–δ) (Fig. 34.3.5). Recently, another Archaic bronze pin was found while digging a trench for the utilities networks along the access road near the new public service building (AMT, inv. M 206, 15.7.2014).

Figure 34.3.1–5. Bronze votive offerings from the sanctuary of Artemis Mesopolitis. Photos and Compilation: S. A. Fritzilas. 34.3.1. NAM, inv. X 14618, 34.3.2. NAM, inv. X 14619, 34.3.3. NAM, inv. 19042A, 34.3.4. NAM, inv. X 19043, 34.3.5. NAM, inv. X 19049.

There are numerous parallels for such objects from other sanctuary sites. Bronze objects were extremely popular at Arcadian sites. Bronze votive offerings were also found at many other sanctuary sites in the Arcadian mountains. Their function was probably the same as the other items of jewelry and metal weapons dedicated in the Arcadian sanctuaries such as Asea, Tegea, Mantinea, Pallantion, Mt. Kotilion (Bassai), Mt. Aphrodision, Mt. Lykaion and Mt. Tetrazi (Ano Melpeia) (Kardara 1988, pl. 105–124; Tzortzi 2000, 36–41; Forsén 2003, 30–34; Baumer 2004, 31–41. 73–75. 138–141; Karagiorga-Stathakopoulou 2008, 128–139, Pl. 17–29; Baitinger 2011, 8. 56. 67. 88. 89. 90. 113; Romano – Voyatzis 2014, 618–622; Romano – Voyatzis 2015, 220. 242. 258; Karapanagiotou 2015, 106–107; Arapogianni 2017, 3–8).

Bronze plaques with proxeny decrees of the Orchomenians

The second group consists of more than a dozen bronze plaques with decrees written in a Doric dialect dating from the Hellenistic period, which were found in the destruction layer of the Eastern Stoa in the so-called *Bouleuterion* of the city (Blum – Plassart 1914a, 73; Douglas van Buren 1926, 56; McDonald 1943, 236–238; Martin 1944 112; Coulton 1976, 6, 269 fig. 97.2). The basis for this identification was the presence in the building of a series of bronze plaques inscribed with proxeny decrees issued by the city council (*Boulē*). It was through these decrees that the people of Orchomenos conferred the honorary title of *proxenos* to citizens of Peloponnesian and other cities. The bronze inscribed tablets were found some 10 cm. above the floor level. In all probability, they were kept on shelves, or were nailed on wood, or hung along the walls of the Stoa in order to be visible. Similar decrees and laws were often kept or displayed in such buildings, known from such well-preserved examples as that of Assos in the Troad (Arslan – Böhlendorf-Arslan 2014, 79–91) and the storage hall along the side of the Agora in Thasos (Grandjean – Salviat 2000, 62–72). Their discovery probably allows for the identification of the Stoa, or part of it, as the "Archives" (*Archeia*) of the polis, known from the well-preserved example at Megalopolis (Lauter-Bufe – Lauter 2011, 147–154). The precious bronze plaques carrying the proxeny decrees were transferred to the National Archaeological Museum of Athens where they are kept under the collective inv. no. 14613.

These small portable bronze tablets were used by the Orchomenians to record the decrees issuing the office of *proxenos* to citizens of Greek cities. The proxeny decrees of the third century BC. mention *proxenoi* from a total of seven Peloponnesian cities, five of which are Arcadian (Lousoi, Kaphyai, Megalopolis, Alea, and Tegea). There is also mention of *proxenoi* from Argos, Pellēne in Achaea, Athens, as well as the Aetolian League. These proxenoi would enjoy certain specific privileges during their stay in Orchomenos. The city often adds to the office the general honorific title of "benefactor" (*euergetēs*). The decree then goes on to list a number of privileges for each *proxenos*.

It was believed that the *proxenos* upon whom these privileges were bestowed would continue to be closely involved and show zeal in supporting the interests of the state that had deemed him trustworthy (Marek 1984, 1–4; Mack 2015, 4–12). The honours mentioned include *ateleia*, i.e. exemption from public burdens. There is also the privilege of *asylia*, which meant that the person of the *proxenos* was inviolable and his property on foreign soil could not be seized forcibly by the state. The decrees also record *epinomia*, in other words the right of pasture on communal grazing grounds. It was often the case that the privileges granted were hereditary, devolving upon the *proxenos*' offspring and their descendants, and applied in wartime as well as in peacetime.

Catalogue

1. NAM, inv. X. 14613/1. H 12 cm.
    The earliest bronze proxeny-decree recorded on a bronze plaque concerns three Athenians and dates from about 265 BC, during the early stages of the Chremonidean War (266–263 BC), when the people of Orchomenos originally allied themselves with the Athenians against Antigonus II Gonatas, king of Macedonia. Other allies of the Orchomenians at the time included Areus I of Sparta and Ptolemy II of Egypt. Nikasilaos is referred to as president of the council of the Orchomenians (προστάτης τῆς Ἁλιαίας), while Simmos is the eponymous magistrate of the year. The people of Orchomenos confer the office of proxenos upon three Athenian citizens, who are also granted epinomia, ateleia, and asylia, both in wartime and in peace. The three honorees are Kallippos, son of Moiroklēs, Aristeidēs, son of Mnēsithēs, and [Glauk]ōn, son of Eteoklēs.
    Bibliography: Blum – Plassart 1914b, 451–454, nr. 1; Fritzilas 2014, 99, nr. 12, fig. 118.

2. NAM, inv. X. 14613/2. H 10 cm.
    The second bronze plaque concerns proxenoi from the koinon of the Aetolians. The city-state of Orchomenos grants the honours of proxenia, euergesia, asylia to four Aetolians: Phillidas, Dorymenēs, Dorkinas, and Andro[la]os. The decree most probably dates from the period when Orchomenos was dominated by the Aetolian League, around 230–229 BC.
    Bibliography: Blum – Plassart 1914b, 454–457, nr. 2; Fritzilas 2014, 100, nr. 13, fig. 119.

3. NAM, inv. X. 14613/3. H 16 cm.
    The third proxeny decree set in bronze concerns Theoxis, son of Aleōs, from the city of Lousoi. The people of Orchomenos confer upon Theoxis of Lousoi the offices of proxenia and theorodokia. This is the only instance among the Orchomenian proxeny decrees in which the proxenos is simultaneously granted the privilege of theorodokia, an honour akin to the proxenia (Plassart 1921, 1–85; Perlman 2000, 13–17). As suggested, the duty of the theorodokos was to receive and offer hospitality to the theoroi, delegates from other states who were sent from place to place in order to announce their city's upcoming festivals.
    Bibliography: Blum – Plassart 1914b, 457–459, nr. 3; Fritzilas 2014, 101, nr. 14, fig. 120.

4. NAM, inv. X. 14613/4. H 14 cm.
    The fourth proxeny decree concerns Kleophaēs of Kaphyai. The city of Orchomenos awards the office of proxenos to Kleophaēs, son of Kleonikos from Kaphyai. The record of this act can be correlated with references to Orchomenian magistrates and priests. More specifically, Kalleidas was president of the council at the time, Daïthrasēs was the eponymous magistrate of the year, and Neodamos was counter of hands, that is, of votes. The name of this magistrate, rarely mentioned in ancient sources, clearly shows that the preferred method of voting in the council of the Orchomenians was by a show of hands, before the result was recorded by the secretary. The decree dates from the third century BC.
    Bibliography: Blum – Plassart 1914b, 459–461, nr. 15; Fritzilas 2014, 102, nr. 15, fig. 121.

5. NAM, inv. X. 14613/5. H 12 cm (Fig. 34.4)
    The fifth bronze proxeny decree concerns Lykiskos, the name of whose city of origin has not survived intact. The city of Orchomenos honours Lykiskos the proxenos with grants of ateleia and all other privileges usually awarded to benefactors. The record of this act may be correlated with the mention of Orchomenian magistrates and priests. More specifically, Thrasonidas was president of the council at the time, Minaichmos was counter of votes, and Sthenolaos was secretary. The plaque bears two holes on each corner. The decree dates from the third century BC.
    Bibliography: Blum – Plassart 1914b, 461, nr. 5; Fritzilas 2014, 103, nr. 16, fig. 122.

6. NAM, inv. X. 14613/6. H 15 cm
    The sixth proxeny decree recorded on a bronze plaque concerns Tyteas from the neighbouring city

Figure 34.4. Bronze plaque with proxeny-decree concerning Lykiskos. NAM, inv. X. 14613/5. Photo: S. A. Fritzilas

of Kaphyai. The city of Orchomenos once again awards Tyteas, son of Pantodamos, the titles of proxenos and euergetēs. The record of granting ateleia, enktesis (the right to acquire land property within the territory of Orchomenos), asylia, epinomia, and all other hereditary privileges given to proxenoi may be correlated with the mention of Orchomenian magistrates, more specifically Polykratēs, who was secretary (γραμματεὺς) at the time. The decree dates from the third century BC.
Bibliography: Blum – Plassart 1914b, 462–463, nr. 6; Fritzilas 2014, 104, nr. 17, fig. 123.

7. NAM, inv. X. 14613/7. H 9.5 cm
The seventh proxeny decree recorded on a bronze plaque was issued in favour of Ainēsandros of Megalopolis, and dates from the period around 235 BC. The council of Orchomenos confers upon Ainēsandros and his descendants the titles of proxenos and euergetēs. In addition to the usual privileges granted to all other proxenoi, he receives a grant of epixylia, i.e. the right to cut timber, which he then could transport to Megale Polis, the neighbouring Arcadian city from which the proxenos in question hailed.
Bibliography: Blum – Plassart 1914b, 463–464, nr. 7; Fritzilas 2014, 105, nr. 18, fig. 124.

8. NAM, inv. X. 14613/8. H 19 cm (Fig. 34.5.1).
The eighth bronze proxeny decree of the 3rd c. B.C. concerns Neoklēs, son of Thorsylochos, from Pellene (Achaia). The Orchomenians grant the office of proxenos and benefactor to Neoklēs, son of Thorsylochos and his descendants. More specifically, Kallippos was secretary of the theoroi (γραμματεὺς τῶν θεαρῶν), while Aigypios served as the priest of Artemis (ἱερεὺς τῆς Ἀρτέμιδος). The upper part of the tablet is decorated with a star. From this plaque we also gain the cult adjective of Artemis as Mesopolitis. The epithet of the goddess is given in the following manner: ΑΡΤΕΜΙΔΟΣ ΜΕΣΟΠΟΛΙΤΙΟΣ ΙΕΡΟΝ; the epithet "Mesopolitis", namely the goddess whose sanctuary was at the center of the polis, is mentioned only on this proxeny decree. This is clearly the same sanctuary of Artemis to which Diodorus Siculus (19.63.5) refers in describing the dramatic events of 315 BC in Orchomenos, when the supporters of Polyperchon who had taken refuge there were put to death.
Bibliography: Blum – Plassart 1914b, 464–465, nr. 8; Fritzilas 2014, 73, 106, nr. 19, fig. 125.

9. NAM, inv. X. 14613/9. H 24 cm
The next bronze proxeny decree of the 3rd c. B.C. refers to Hagēsimachos. The Orchomenian council confers on Hagēsima[chos] from the neighbouring city of Alea the title of proxenos. He is granted the privileges of ateleia, asylia, and epinomia, in war as well as in peacetime.
Bibliography: Blum – Plassart 1914b, 466–467, nr. 9; Fritzilas 2014, 107, nr. 20, fig. 126.

10. NAM, inv. X. 14613/10. H 13,5 cm
The tenth proxeny decree of the 3rd c. B.C refers to Pannis, son of Aigypios, from Argos. The city-state of Orchomenos grants him the post of proxenos and benefactor.
Bibliography: Blum – Plassart 1914b, 467–468, nr. 10; Fritzilas 2014, 108, nr. 21, fig. 127

11. NAM, inv. X. 14613/11. H 27 cm (Fig. 34.5.2)
The eleventh bronze proxeny decree refers to Larchippos, son of Stipakos, from Tegea. The city grants him the post of proxenos. Other privileges are ateleia, enktesis, asylia.
Bibliography: Blum – Plassart 1914b, 468–471, nr. 11; Fritzilas 2014, 109, nr. 22, fig. 128.

The aforementioned Hellenistic proxeny decrees recorded on bronze plaques mention three magistrates of the Boulē, called Βουλά or Ἁλιαία in the Arcadian dialect. The decrees in question record two Orchomenians as holding

Figure 34.5.1–2. Bronze plaque inscribed with proxeny-decrees concerning Neoklēs from Pellene and Larchippos from Tegea. Photos and Compilation: S. A. Fritzilas. 34.5.1. NAM, inv. X. 14613/8, 34.5.2. NAM, inv. X. 14613/9.

the office of the president of the council, who must have been seated in the city's Boulē, i.e. the Haliaea. The names of the two Orchomenians who held the office in question were Nikasilaos and either Kalleidas or Thrasonidas. The president of the council was assisted in his duties by the *cheroskopos* of the council, who counted the hands of those who took part in the vote (Nielsen 2002, 581). Naturally the secretary of the council was responsible for recording the vote tally. It is recorded in the tablets that the office of the counter of hands, that is, of votes in the Boule was held by Minaichmos and Neodamos. Sthenolaos, Polykratēs, Kallippos, and Aristarchos are mentioned as secretaries of the council.

Recent research (Fritzilas 2014, 65–69) suggests that it is possible to speculate about the actual location of the building in which the council of Orchomenos held its meetings, and where proxeny and privileges were debated, because the Eastern Stoa was probably used for archival storage. Contemporary practice in other cities suggests that the *Bouleuterion* would have been close to the Agora. Our recent research shows that there are remains of another sizeable building in the vicinity that could be a possible candidate: the large rectangular building that was revealed during clearing work conducted in recent years on an artificial plateau southeast of the East Stoa and to the east of the sanctuary of Artemis Mesopolitis (Fritzilas 2013, 198–199 fig.17–18). Earlier research (Winter 1987, 239) suggested that the *Bouleuterion* of the Orchomenos of the fourth century would have been near but not actually facing the Agora. Recent research (Fritzilas, 2014, 67 fig. 78) shows that the large four-sided building is strictly oriented on a north-nouth axis. The western side is about 24 meters long, the east 25, the north and south sides 18 m. The plan of the proposed *Bouleuterion* may be seen in the cuttings for its foundation walls. It seems clear that the auditorium faced east. The spacious hall of the building, which lay along the east side of the Agora and was originally dated to the fourth century BC., could be restored with wooden seats, and it is large enough to have accommodated 500 citizens, members of the Council.

The coins

The third group of bronze finds consists mainly of coins, found in earlier research and more recently during the project "Enhancement of the Archaeological Site of Orchomenos" (NSFR 2007–2013). More than one hundred coins of the late Classical – Early Hellenistic period were found in excavations and surveys between 2011 and 2014 (Fritzilas 2014, 80–86). They include coins issued by the city of Orchomenos, the neighboring Arcadian cities, and other well-known Peloponnesian cities, such as Corinth, Sicyon, and Argos. These bronze coins attest to the volume of trade between the city and other Greek urban centers during the Late Classical and Hellenistic periods. They also provide interesting data on the period prior to the city's destruction. The new coins from Orchomenos were transported to the Archaeological Museum of Tripolis for safekeeping. Fieldwork conducted by the French Archaeological School at Orchomenos in 1913 recovered 95 coins, which were handed over to the Numismatic Museum of Athens (Plassart 1915, 117–122). The recent excavations have added to our knowledge regarding the autonomous issues of the Orchomenos, known locally as Erchomenos (Spyropoulos 2013, 268). It is known that the Orchomenians produced a bronze coinage beginning in the mid-fourth century BC, and continuing to the end of the fourth century BC (Ziesmann 2005, 193–202; BCD Peloponnesos, 374–377; Hoover 2011, 239–242). This involved two denominations, and motifs featuring Artemis paired with a depiction of the death of Kallisto or the head of a young hero. The civic bronze coins all carry abbreviated inscriptions naming "The Erchomenians" as the issuing authority. On the reverse we usually read the letters "E" and "P" (Fig. 34.6). Specimens from both groups of coins, belonging to the years between 350 and 300 BC, have recently been discovered in Orchomenos. The iconography of the first group is marked by a helmeted bearded male head facing right (usually identified with local hero Orchomenos or Arkas) on the obverse, and Artemis aiming her bow on the reverse (Fig. 34.6.1). Coins of the second group bear the image of Artemis with a bow on the reverse and the helmeted head of Athena on the obverse. The third group of Orchomenian coins dating from the same period bear the head of Kallisto on the obverse and the image of a standing beardless naked hero with a spear and a shield on the reverse (Fig. 34.6.2). The Orchomenian Kallisto type refers to the terrible punishment meted out to the nymph by Artemis when the former gave birth to a son by Zeus. Kallisto was killed by an arrow shortly after the birth of her son Arkas, who would grow up to become the eponymous ancestor of the Arcadian peoples (Tsagari 2017, 161–163). The same two letters (EP) may also be seen on coins with Kallisto or Artemis seated on a throne on the reverse, while the obverse bears the head of Athena or a beardless hero, such as on a new bronze coin of Orchomenos (Fig. 34.6.3). Smaller denominations of the same period (*chalkoi*) display the first two letters of the city's name EP(XOMENIΩN) in laurel-wreath on the reverse and the head of Athena or a beardless hero on the obverse (Fig. 34.6.4).

Apart from the autonomous issues of the city of Orchomenos, finds include coins from other neighbouring Arcadian cities, such as Tegea, Mantinea, Pheneos, Kaphyai, as well as other major Peloponnesian cities, including Phleious, Corinth, Sicyon, and Argos. Stray finds of coins attest to the volume of trade between the city and other urban centers in the Greek mainland during the Late Classical and Hellenistic periods, revealing interesting data on numismatic circulation in the Peloponnesos, as well as the commercial ties and alliances between Orchomenos and other cities (Fritzilas 2014, 80–83, fig. 95–101).

Recent excavations reached down to the foundations of the North Stoa, where new undisturbed strata have been uncovered, mainly on the west side of the building (Fritzilas 2011, 233–234; 2012, 176). The so-called North Stoa is the longest edifice on the archaeological site, facing southwards to the Agora plateau. It is dated to the fourth century BC and is assumed to have had a commercial use.

Figure 34.6.1–4. Bronze coins of Orchomenos, autonomous issues. Photos and Compilation: S. A. Fritzilas. 34.6.1. AMT, inv. N11, OM. 3, 13.10.11 (unpublished), 34.6.2. AMT, inv. 25.10.2013, 34.6.3. AMT, inv. N. 70, OM. 27,11.1.2014, 34.6.4. AMT, inv. N 29, OM. 30, 13.9.2012.

The destruction layer that has been brought to light also included roof tiles, amphora sherds, West Slope pottery and third-century-BC bronze issues of Peloponnesian cities such as Tegea, Mantinea, and Sicyon.

In the East Stoa, where the lowest drums or plinths of at least six columns have been preserved, part of an undisturbed destruction layer was uncovered in 2014, including roof-tiles, mainly in its northwestern corner (elevation 874.65m). The dimensions of the undisturbed layer of roof-tiles were 5.5m (north-south) X 3.7m (east-west), located at a depth of 30–40cm near the last base of the colonnade. Among the scanty finds were iron nails from the roof beams, some fragments of bronze plaques, as well as a number of bronze coins of the Hellenistic period, indicating that the destruction of the building must have taken place in the last quarter of the third century BC (Fritzilas 2014, 64–67).

Among the various coins found, mostly of Peloponnesian cities, it is interesting to note the impressive presence of numerous bronze coins of Sicyon in the destruction layers that we excavated in the North Stoa, the South Stoa, the theatre, and other parts of the archaeological site (Fig. 34.7.1–4). These coins coincide with the period when the Achaean League was led by Aratus the Sicyonian, during which time Orchomenos had joined the Achaean League around 234 BC, as is attested by a decree regulating the terms of the agreement (AMT 3300: IG V (2) 344; Plassart 1914b, 447–449, fig. 1; Fritzilas 2012b, 250, fig. 479; Fritzilas 2014, 92–93, nr. 3, fig. 40). Aratos was elected general (*stratēgos*) of the Achaean League on numerous occasions (17 times between 245/4 and 213 BC) and regularly led the League to its maximum extent in the face of Macedonian, Spartan, and Aetolian League opposition (Skalet 1975, 98–104; Lolos 2012, 112). Sicyon was glorified through the many successes of Aratus and became the preeminent city of the Achaean League during his lifetime. Its importance and strategic location made Sicyon and the allied city-states, including Orchomenos, subject to frequent attack during the 'Cleomenic War' of 229/8–222 BC (against Cleomenes III of Sparta), as well as during the Social War (220–217 BC) against the Aetolian League (Cartledge – Spawforth 2002, 49–57. 61–64). After the Spartans defeated and nearly destroyed the cities of the Achaean League, Aratos invited Antigonus III Doson of Macedonia to help in the fight against the Aetolians and Spartans. The expansion of the Achaean League in the third and early second centuries BC created an extensive and virtually homogeneous coinage throughout the Peloponnesos. It was necessary, due to the League's frequent conflicts with Sparta and the Aetolian League, to coerce unwilling members in the wars in Greece (Hoover 2011, 3. 52–54).

Arrowheads and destruction layers

It is in connection to the above-mentioned evidence that we must research a small group of bronze arrowheads deposited in destruction layers throughout the archaeological site (Fig. 34.8.2–3), since they constitute indisputable evidence of the dramatic sieges and the violence of war that washed over the city, as we are told by ancient sources. A number of bronze arrowheads have been found in the temple of Artemis Mesopolitis and its immediate vicinity. Spearheads or arrowheads were often offered in a sanctuary dedicated to a female goddess (Fig. 34.8.1): we have some interesting parallels in Greek sanctuaries (Tarditi 2015, 48). Arms and armor represent dedications of personal objects, and those are believed to have been dedicated by adult males. This category of votives seems to have been especially popular in Arcadian

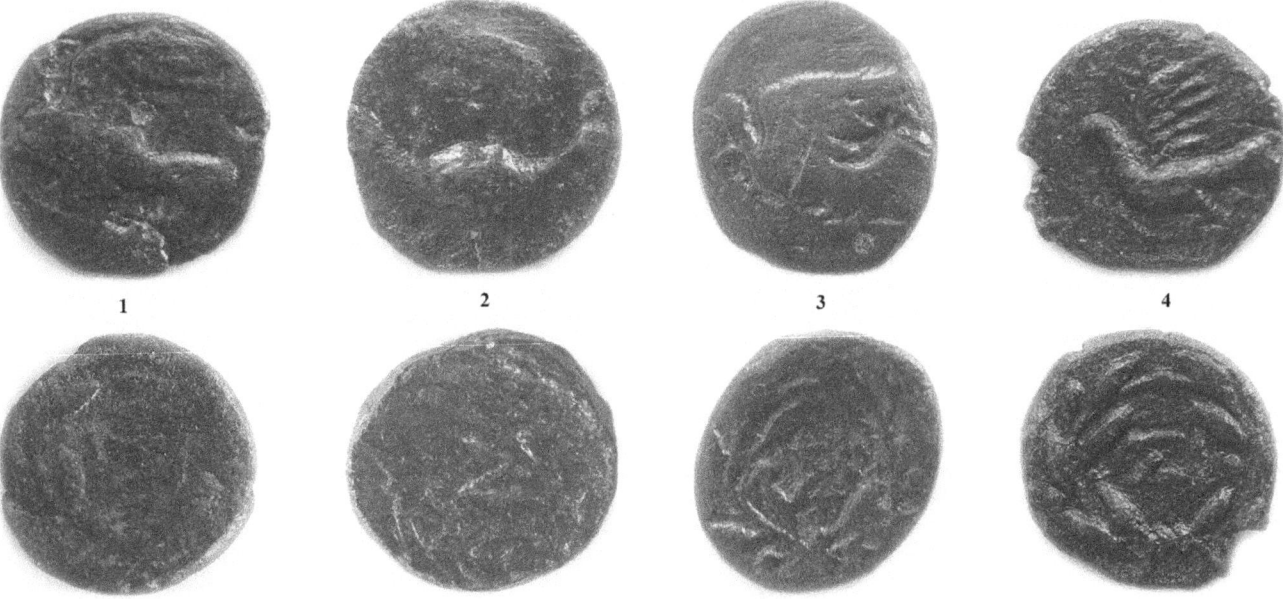

Figure 34.7.1–4. Bronze coins of Sicyon in the destruction layers of Orchomenos. Photos and Compilation: S.A. Fritzilas. **34.7.1. AMT, inv. N 9, OM 3, 30.9.2011, North Stoa (unpublished). 34.7.2. AMT, inv. N. 2, OM 2, 30.8.2011, East Stoa (unpublished). 34.7.3. AMT, inv. N 43, OM 3, 30.1.2013, North Stoa (unpublished). 34.7.4. AMT,inv. N 82, 06.03.2014, Theatre (unpublished).**

Figure 34.8.1–3. Bronze arrowheads from Orchomenos. Photos and Compilation: S. A. Fritzilas. 34.8.1. NAM, inv. X 14620.1-2, 34.8.2. AMT, inv. M 6, OM 7, 07.07.2011. Arrow-head in an excavation trench near Tower 7 (unpublished), 34.8.3a. AMT, inv. M 6, OM 7, 07.07.2011, 34.8.3b. AMT, inv. M 146, 28.3.2013, 34.8.3.c. AMT, inv. M 186, OM.28, 23.08.2013.

sanctuaries (Voyatzis 1990, 200–201; Voyatzis 1999, 131–140). Bronze arrowheads have been found in other parts of the Arcadian Orchomenos, deposited in destruction layers connected to the sieges of the Hellenistic period.

An arrowhead was found on a surface layer of the excavation trench near Tower 7, by the modern entrance to the archaeological site, during work aimed at widening and leveling the rising slope (Fig. 34.8.2–3a). The arrowhead was found in contact with the northern face of the fourth-century BC southeastern tower (Fritzilas 2011, 232, fig. 35–37). At a greater depth, approximately 65cm from the modern ground level, excavation unearthed a section of the earlier, fifth-century-BC enceinte mentioned by ancient authors such as Thucydides (5.61–62), Xenophon (Hell. 6.5.13), and Diodorus (12.79.2); the section of the walls in question was particularly weak. A second arrowhead was recovered near the public service building, on a terrace formed during Antiquity in order to facilitate the erection of buildings of the city of Orchomenos. The walls formed rectangular spaces belonging to some public building, probably a guard post of the ancient city, with an ancient well in the interior. A Hellenistic-era destruction layer was located, containing skyphoi decorated with Dionysian motifs and warriors. Other characteristic finds, apart from the arrowhead, included a silver Corinthian drachme, an iron spear-butt (sauroter), a snaffle bit (Giaccio 2015, 34, fig. 9), and the foot of a clay figurine depicting a warrior (Fritzilas 2018, 185).

Some bronze arrowheads (Fig. 34.8.2–3) must be related to the military operations that took place around Orchomenos during the Cleomenic War, when the city would play a pivotal dramatic role in military events. In 229 BC the city of Orchomenos was captured in a surprise attack by the Spartans under Cleomenes III (LGPN, III A 247, nr.11), who also annexed Tegea and Mantinea. Even though the Spartans managed to restore Orchomenos to their sphere of influence, the city harboured an anti-Spartan party, which had reached an agreement with Aratos (LGPN, III A 52, nr. 3), general of the Achaean League, to secretly hand the city over to him, although they proved unable to deliver. In 223 BC, however, Antigonus III Doson, king of Macedonia and guardian of his cousin's son, Philip V, stormed Spartan-held Orchomenos in the course of his Peloponnesian campaign. He then established a Macedonian garrison and an arsenal on the fortified acropolis of Orchomenos (Maher 2017, 257).

A similar arrowhead was found in 2007 in the destruction layer of Megale Polis, dating from 223/222 BC, when the Arcadian federal capital was destroyed in a surprise attack led by Cleomenes III (Fritzilas 2007, 335). The city's destruction layer, which was excavated during construction of the sewer system of modern Megalopolis, showed traces of fire and revealed parts of walls belonging to private residences of the Hellenistic city, as well as bronze coins of Sicyon displaying a dove on the obverse and the city's initial (Σ) within a wreath on the reverse;

both coins and pottery dated from the second half of the third century BC. We know it was at that time that the Arcadian city of Megale Polis, which had sided with the Achaean League and Macedonia, was razed to the ground after it was captured by treason, while its population fled to Messēne and the spoils, worth many talents, were transported to Sparta (Themelis 2015, 24). The systematic and multi-faceted study of the bronzes and the other groups of finds within their historical and cultural context is a fundamental source of historical data, shedding light on multiple aspects of human activity. The various objects found at Orchomenos indicate that this city-state played an important role in the production of bronze objects and bronze coinage during the fourth and third centuries B.C. Thus this research represents a reassessment of bronze objects within the excavation context and has led to insights regarding their use and date as part of human activities within the city of ancient Orchomenos.

Abbreviations

AMT = Archaeological Museum, Tripolis

BCD Peloponnesos = LHS Numismatics, Coins of Peloponnesos. The BCD Collection, Auction 96 (08-09/05/2006)

IG = Inscriptiones Graecae

NAM = National Archaeological Museum, Athens

LGPN = Lexicon of Greek Personal Names

RE = Pauly-Wissowa, Real-Encyclopädie der klassischen Altertumswissenschaft

Bibliography

Arapogianni, X., 2017. Unknown sanctuaries of Messenia before the foundation of ancient Messene. In: Themelis, P., Spathi, M. – Psaroudakis, K., ed., *Sanctuaries and Cults of Messene. From the pre-classical to the byzantine period. Proceedings of the International Archaeological Congress, Athens 25 October 2014*. Athens: Society of Messenian Archaeological Studies, 1–28.

Arslan, N. – Böhlendorf-Arslan, B., 2014. *Assos: Living in the Rocks. An archaeological guide*. 2nd ed. İnstanbul: Homerkitabevi ve Yayıncılık Ltd.Şti.

Baitinger, H., 2011. *Waffenweihungen in griechischen Heiligtümern. Monographien des Römisch-Germanischen Zentralmuseums 94*. Mainz: Römisch-Germanisches Zentralmuseum; Regensburg: Schnell & Steiner.

Baumer, L. E, 2004. *Kult im Kleinen: Ländliche Heiligtümer spätarchaischer Zeit; Attika – Arkadien – Argolis – Kynouria*. Internationale Archäologie, vol. 81. Rahden: Verlag Marie Leidorf GmbH.

Blum, G. – Plassart, A., 1914a. Orchomène d'Arcadie. Fouilles de 1913. Topographie, architecture, sculpture, menus objets, *Bulletin de Correspondance Hellénique (BCH)* 38, 71–88, pl. III. IV. V.

Blum, G. – Plassart, A., 1914b. Orchomène d'Arcadie. Fouilles de 1913. Inscriptions, *Bulletin de Correspondance Hellénique (BCH)* 38, 447–478.

Bursian, C., 1868. *Geographie von Griechenland. Peloponnesos und Inseln*. vol. 2. Leipzig: B. G. Teubner.

Cartledge, P. – Spawforth, A., 2002. *Hellenistic and Roman Sparta. A tale of two cities*. 2nd. ed. London and New York: Routledge.

Coulton, J.J., 1976. *The Architectural Development of the Greek Stoa*. Oxford: Clarendon Press.

Curtius, E., 1851. *Peloponnesos: eine historisch-geographische Beschreibung der Halbinsel*, vol. 1. Gotha: J. Perthes.

Dodwell, E., 1819. *A Classical and Topographical tour through Greece, during the years 1801, 1805, and 1806*, vol. 2. London: Rodwell and Martin.

Dodwell, E., 1834. *Views and descriptions of Cyclopian or, Pelasgic remains in Greece and Italy: with constructions of a later period*. London: A. Richter.

Douglas van Buren, E.,1926. *Greek Fictile Revetments in the Archaic Period*. London: John Murray.

Forsén, J., 2003. Previous Archaeological Research in the Asea Valley. In: J. Forsén – B. Forsén, ed., *The Asea valley survey: an Arcadian mountain valley from the palaeolithic period until modern times, Skrifter utgivna av Svenska Institutet i Athen, 4o = Acta Instituti Atheniensis Regni Sueciae*, 40 ; 51. Stockholm: Paul Åströms Förlag, 23–37.

Frazer, J. G., 1898. *Pausanias' Description of Greece*. vol. 4. London: Macmillan and Co., Ltd.; New York: The Macmillan Co.

Fritzilas, S., 2007. Μεγαλόπολη, (Νεκροταφείο, Οδός Σοφοκλέους, Οδός Αρχαίου Θεάτρου 71), *Archaiologikon Deltion (ArchDelt)* 66, Chron B΄1, 333–336.

Fritzilas, S., 2011. Ορχομενός, *Archaiologikon Deltion (ArchDelt)* 66, Chron B΄1, 231–235.

Fritzilas, S.,2012a. Ακρόπολη Ορχομενού, *Archaiologikon Deltion (ArchDelt)* 67, Chron B΄1, 174–180.

Fritzilas, S., 2012b, Ορχομενός. In: A. Vlachopoulos (ed.), *Αρχαιολογία – Πελοπόννησος*. Athens: Melissa Publishing House, 248–250. 574.

Fritzilas, S., 2013, Ακρόπολη Ορχομενού, *Archaiologikon Deltion (ArchDelt)* 68, Chron B΄1, 198–199.

Fritzilas, S., 2014. Ορχομενός Αρκαδίας. Οδηγός του Αρχαιολογικού χώρου. In: A. V., Karapanagiotou – S., Fritzilas, ed. & text, *Arcadian Orchomenos* . Tripolis: Ephorate of Antiquities of Arcadia.

Fritzilas, S., The Acropolis of Arcadian Orchomenos in 2012. In: E. Zymi – A.V. Karapanagiotou – M. Xanthopoulou, ed., *Το Αρχαιολογικό Έργο στην Πελοπόννησο (1ο ΑΕΠΕΛ). Πρακτικά του Διεθνούς Συνεδρίου*. Τρίπολη, 7–11 Νοεμβρίου 2012. Kalamata: University of Peloponnese, 183–190.

Giaccio, M.,2015. Votive Bronze Objects from the Sanctuary of Hera at the Mouth of the Sele River (Paestum). In: E. Deschler-Erb – P. Della Casa, ed., *New Research on Ancient Bronzes. Acta of the XVIIIth International Congress on Ancient Bronzes, Zurich 2013. Zurich Studies in Archaeology*, vol. 10. Zurich: Chronos Verlag, 29–38.

Gell, W., 1817. *Itinerary of the Morea: being a description of the routes of that peninsula.* London: Rodwell and Martin.

Gell, W., 1823. *Narrative of a journey in the Morea.* London: Longman, Hurst, Rees, Orme, and Brown.

Grandjean, Y. – Salviat, F., 2000. *Guide de Thasos. École Française d' Athènes, Sites et monuments 3*, 2nd ed. Paris: De Boccard Édition.

Hiller von Gaertringen, F. – Latterman, H. 1911. *Arkadische Forschungen*. Berlin: Konigl. Akademie der Wissenschaften.

Hoover, O. D., 2011. *Handbook of Coins of the Peloponnesos. Achaia, Phleiasia, Sikyonia, Elis, Triphylia, Messenia, Lakonia, Argolis, and Arkadia. Sixth to First Centuries BC*. Lancaster / London: Classical Numismatic Group, Inc.

Jost, M., 1985. *Sanctuaires et cultes d'Arcadie*, Etudes péloponnésiennes; 9. Paris: J. Vrin.

Karapanagiotou, A.V., 2015. *Μαντίνεια. Αρχαιολογικός Οδηγός*. In: Karapanagiotou, A. V., ed., *Mantineia. Archaeological Guide*. Tripolis: Ephorate of Antiquities of Arcadia.

Karagiorga-Stathakopoulou, Th., 2008. Investigating Archaic Mantineia, In: G. A., Pikoulas, ed., *Ιστορίες για την Αρχαία Αρκαδία : Proceedings of the International Symposium in honour of James Roy; 50 χρόνια Αρκάς (1958–2008), 9–10 May 2008*. Stemnitsa: Δήμος Τρικολώνων; Πανεπιστήμιο Θεσσαλίας, Τμήμα ΙΑΚΑ, 125–143.

Kardara, Ch., *Αφροδίτη Ερυκίνη: Ιερόν και μαντείον εις την Β.Δ. Αρκαδίαν*. Βιβλιοθήκη της εν Αθήναις Αρχαιολογικής Εταιρείας, vol. 106. Athens: The Archaeological Society at Athens.

Lauter-Bufe, H. – Lauter, H., 2011. *Die politischen Bauten von Megalopolis*. Darmstadt; Mainz: Philipp von Zabern.

Lolos, G. A. Σικυώνα. In: A., Vlachopoulos, ed., *Αρχαιολογία – Πελοπόννησος*. Athens: Melissa Publishing House, 112–116, 569.

Mack, W., 2015. *Proxeny and Polis. Institutional Networks in the Ancient Greek Word*. Oxford: Oxford University Press.

Maher, M.,2017. *The Fortifications of Arkadian City State in the Classical and Hellenistic Periods*. Oxford: Oxford University Press.

Marek, Ch., 1984. *Die Proxenie. Europäische Hochschulschriften: Reihe 3, Geschichte und ihre Hilfswissenschaften, vol. 123*. Frankfurt am Main; Bern; New York: Verlag Peter Lang GmbH.

Martin, R., 1944. Sur deux enceintes d'Arcadie, *Revue archéologique (RA)* 21, 97–114.

McDonald, W. A.,1943. *The Political Meeting Places of the Greeks* Baltimore: The Johns Hopkins Press.

Meyer, E., 1939, Orchomenos (4), *RE* 17, 887–905.

Nielsen, T. H., 2002. *Arkadia and its Poleis in the Archaic and Classical Periods*, Hypomnemata, vol. 140. Göttingen: Vandenhoeck & Ruprecht.

Nielsen, T.H., 2004, Arkadia. Orchomenos. In: M. H. Hansen, – T.H. Nielsen, ed., *An inventory of archaic and classical poleis*. Oxford: Oxford University Press, 523–525.

Perlman, P. J., 2000. *City and sanctuary in ancient Greece: the „theorodokia" in the Peloponnese*, Hypomnemata, vol. 121. Göttingen: Vandenhoeck und Ruprecht.

Petropoulos, M., 2005. Η Πελοπόννησος κατά την ελληνιστική εποχή. In L. Kypraiou, ed., *Ελληνιστική κεραμική από την Πελοπόννησο*. Athens: Hellenic Ministry of Culture, 6th Ephorate of Prehistoric and Classical Antiquities, 9–22.

Plassart, A., 1915. Orchomène d'Arcadie. Fouilles de 1913. Inscriptions, II (2e article), *Bulletin de correspondance hellénique (BCH)* 39, 53–127.

Plassart, A., 1921. Inscriptions de Delphes, la liste des Thèorodoques, *Bulletin de correspondance hellénique (BCH)* 45, 1–85.

Romano, D. G. – Voyatzis, M. E., 2014. Mt. Lykaion Excavation and Survey Project, Part 1: The Upper Sanctuary, *Hesperia* 83, 2014, 569–652.

Romano, D.G. – Voyatzis, M. E., 2015. Mt. Lykaion Excavation and Survey Project, Part 1: The Lower Sanctuary, *Hesperia* 84, 2015, 207–276.

Skalet, Ch. H., 1975. *Αρχαία Σικυών και Σικυώνια Προσωπογραφία*. Transl. N. Charlaugis. Αθήνα: Ιωλκός.

Spyropoulos, Th., 2013. *Λακεδαίμων*, vol. 2. Athens: Kardamitsa Publications.

Tarditi, C., 2015. Metal Finds from the Votive Deposits of the Archaic Sanctuary of Bitalemi, Sicily: Typological and Quantitative Remarks. In: E. Deschler-Erb – P. Della Casa, ed., *New Research on Ancient Bronzes. Acta of the XVIIIth International Congress on Ancient*

Bronzes, Zurich 2013. Zurich Studies in Archaeology, vol. 10. Zurich: Chronos Verlag, 43–50.

Themelis, P., 2015. *Ancient Messene*. Athens: Archaeological Receipts Fund.

Tsagari, D., Arcadian coins. Witnesses of the local mythology. In: E. Apostolou – Ch. Doyen, ed., *Coins in the Peloponnese. Proceedings of the sixth scientific meeting of the Friends of the Numismatic Museum. Argos, May 26–29, 2011*. Bulletin de Correspondance Hellénique Supplément 57 / Obolos 10. Athènes: École française d'Athènes, 2017, 159–166.

Tzortzi, K., 2000. *The Temple of Apollo Epikourios: a Journey Through Time and Space*. Athens: Committee for the Preservation of the Temple of Apollo Epikourios.

Voyatzis, M. E., 1990. *The early Sanctuary of Athena Alea at Tegea and Other Archaic Sanctuaries in Arcadia*. Götheborg: Paul Åströms Förlag.

Voyatzis, M.E., 1999. The Role of Temple Building in Consolidating Arkadian Communities. In: T. H. Nielsen – J. Roy, ed., *Defining Ancient Arkadia. Acts of the Copenhagen Polis Centre*, vol. 6. Copenhagen: The Royal Danish Academy of Sciences and Letters, 130–168.

Winter, F. E., 1987. Arkadian Notes I: Identification of the Agora Buildings at Orchomenos and Mantinea, *Echos du Monde Classique /Classical Views (EchCl)* 31, 235–246.

Winter, F. E., 1989. Arkadian Notes, II: The Walls of Mantinea, Orchomenos, and Kleitor, *Echos du Monde Classique /Classical Views (EchCl)* 33, 189–200.

Ziesmann, S., 2005. *Autonomie und Münzprägung in Griechenland und Kleinasien in der Zeit Philipps II. und Alexanders des Großen*. Bochumer altertumswissenschaftliches Colloquium, vol. 67. Trier: Wissenschaftlicher Verlag.

35

Paphian obstacles to powerful Death.
A set of surgical tools found in the Agora of Paphos

Maciej Wacławik

Jagiellonian University in Kraków

maciej.waclawik@gmail.com

Abstract: During the excavations carried out in 2016 under the Paphos Agora Project, a set of surgical tools was found in Trench II. It included a spatula, an ear probe, a hook and a pair of tweezers – all made of bronze – as well as two bone levers, one made of bronze and one of iron (unfortunately the iron lever was broken in half). The set was complemented by a small stone palette, which had been used both for preparing medicines and for sharpening blades. The palette had probably been installed as one of the walls of a wooden box decorated with bone ornaments, whose fragments were found together with a bronze lid and hinges. In the immediate vicinity of the set, glass vessels and a set of bronze coins were also unearthed. It seems that all these artefacts were part of the equipment of a surgery that functioned in the East Portico of the Agora in the first quarter of the second century AD.

Keywords: Surgical Tools; Ancient Roman Medicine; Agora of Nea Paphos

Introduction

In August 2016, during excavations carried out by the archaeological expedition from the Department of Classical Archaeology of the Institute of Archaeology, Jagiellonian University in Krakow, headed by Professor Ewdoksia Papuci-Władyka, a set of surgical tools and remains of a box were found. They were discovered within context 798 of Room (R.) 16 in Trench II in the East Portico of the Agora (Fig. 35.1). The ceramic material from context 798, as well as coins and other movable material, date to the Early Roman (ER) period, probably before 126 AD, when an earthquake destroyed the entire area (Miszk, forthcoming). After the excavations, the set was transferred to the Paphos District Museum (Inv. nos. PAP/FR 109/2016 – PAP/FR 117/2016). It has not yet been cleaned from the layers of corrosion and contamination, as there is a future possibility of conducting traceological tests and analyses of substances remaining on its surfaces.

The surgical set from the Agora in Paphos

The set consists of six tools and fragments of a box in which they were stored:

1. PAP/FR 109/2016 and PAP/FR 111/2016 – a bronze spoon (L: 154.02 mm; D: 2.5 mm) (Fig. 35.2).
   Below an oval bowl (max. W: 9 mm) a set of seven rings (D: 4.5 mm; W: 1.5 mm) grouped in three-one-three can be seen. An ovoid enlargement on the tip (L: 16.24 mm, max. W: 5.5 mm) of the spoon for crushing ingredients and mixing them had been broken off and was found separately, and because of that it received an individual inventory number.
   The tool was probably used for preparing medicines and applying them to wounds. It may also have served as a spatula for examining the upper respiratory tract – holding the tongue down and enabling a view of both pharynx and larynx.
   The tool should be classified as Variant D in the typology by E. Riha (1986, 69).

2. PAP/FR 110/2016 – a bronze ear probe or *ligula* (L: 146.35 mm; max. D: 3 mm) (Fig. 35.3).
   The circular head (D: 4.5 mm) is curved at an angle of 145° in relation to the arm. The tip is pointed and there are no rings on the arm. Therefore, there may have been some organic cladding on the handle of the ear probe that was not preserved.
   The tool was probably used to clean hard-to-reach spots, such as the inner part of an ear, and to apply medicine there. It may also have been helpful in removing stones from the urethra, as well as in obstructing the flow of blood during a phlebotomy. If the assumption regarding the organic handle is correct, the tool was probably also used as a cautery – the head could have been heated and veins or bleeding wounds could be closed with it.
   The tool should be classified as Variant E in the typology by E. Riha (1986, 60).

3. PAP/FR 112/2016 – Bronze tweezers/forceps (L: 115.08 mm) (Fig. 35.4).
   The drop-shaped head (L: 11 mm; max. W: 6.5 mm) of the tool, with a semi-globular appendix of three rings (respectively, D: 4.5 mm, W: 3 mm; D: 3 mm, W: 1

Figure 35.1. Map of fragment of Trench II (by W. Ostrowski and W. Winiarska, based on photos by A. Oleksiak).

Paphian obstacles to powerful Death. A set of surgical tools found in the Agora of Paphos

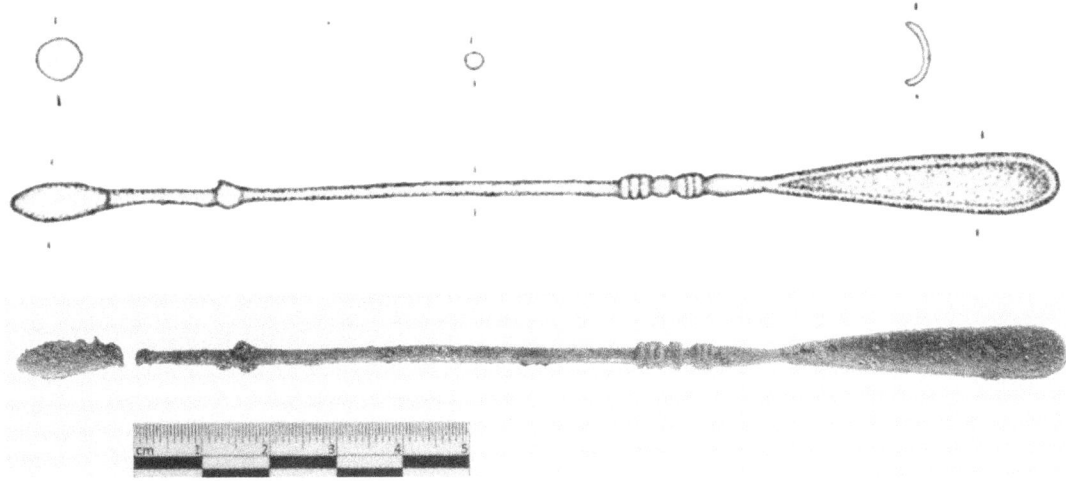

Figure 35.2. A bronze spoon PAP/FR 109/2016 + PAP/FR 111/2016 (photo by A. Oleksiak, drawing A. Jurkiewicz-Cora).

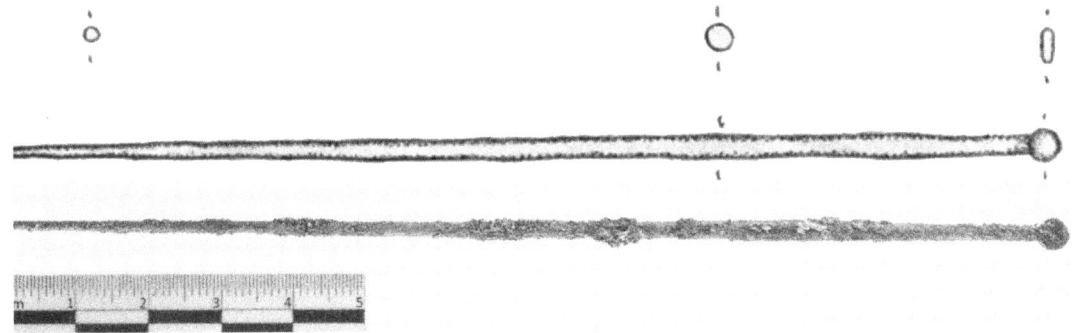

Figure 35.3. A bronze ear probe PAP/FR 110/2016 (photo by A. Oleksiak, drawing A. Jurkiewicz-Cora).

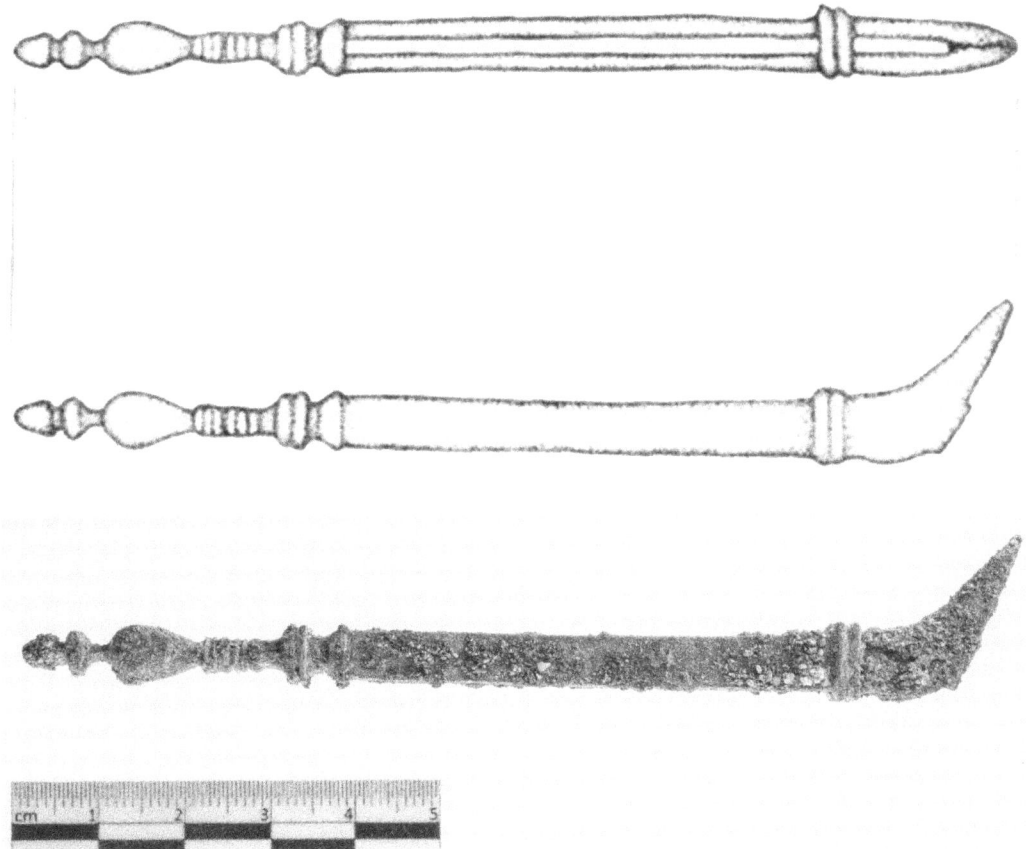

Figure 35.4. Bronze tweezers PAP/FR 112/2016 (photo by A. Oleksiak, drawing A. Jurkiewicz-Cora).

mm; D: 5.5 mm, W: 2.5 mm; L of appendix: 11 mm) on a circular foot (H: 3,5 mm; D: 2 mm) is connected by means of a circular foot (L: 14 mm; D: 3 mm) with six rings (D: 4 mm, W: 0.5 mm) on a double-circular base (D: 7 mm; W of the ring: 1.5 mm) with pointed arms, curved at an angle of 143° (L: 79.58mm; max. W: 10 mm) by a ring base (D: 7.5 mm; W: 1 mm), which is the *fulcrum* of the device. On the arms there is a two-ringed clamp (L: 9 mm; W: 2.5 mm; W of the ring: 1 mm) protecting the tool from deformation and blocking it during surgical interventions. It is smaller than the maximum width of the arms so as not to slide off them.

The tool should be classified as Variant E in the typology by E. Riha (1986, 37), as she dates it back to the third quarter of the first century AD based on the pottery sherds found nearby.

4. PAP/FR 113/2016 – An iron bone lever (L: 137.5 mm; D: 9 mm) (Fig. 35.5).

The tool was found broken into two matching pieces. Owing to the corrosion, it is very hard to say anything certain about it. One end seems to be curved, the other one forked.

5. PAP/FR 115/2016 – A bronze hook (L: 106.52 mm; D: 3.5 mm) (Fig. 35.6).

The head of the tool is of a semi-globular shape (D: 7 mm; H: 2 mm) and is based on a ring (D: 7 mm; W: 1 mm) with a semi-globular (D: 3.5 mm; H: 1 mm) appendix. The tip of the tool is curved at an angle of 124° in relation to the arm.

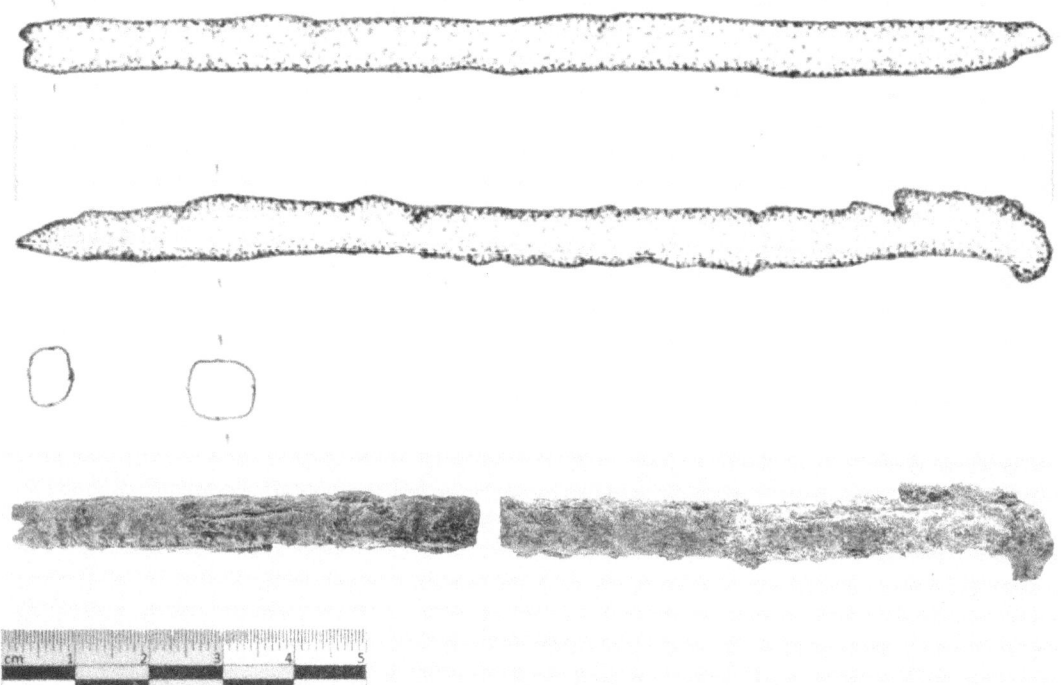

Figure 35.5. An iron bone lever PAP/FR 113/2016 (photo by A. Oleksiak, drawing A. Jurkiewicz-Cora).

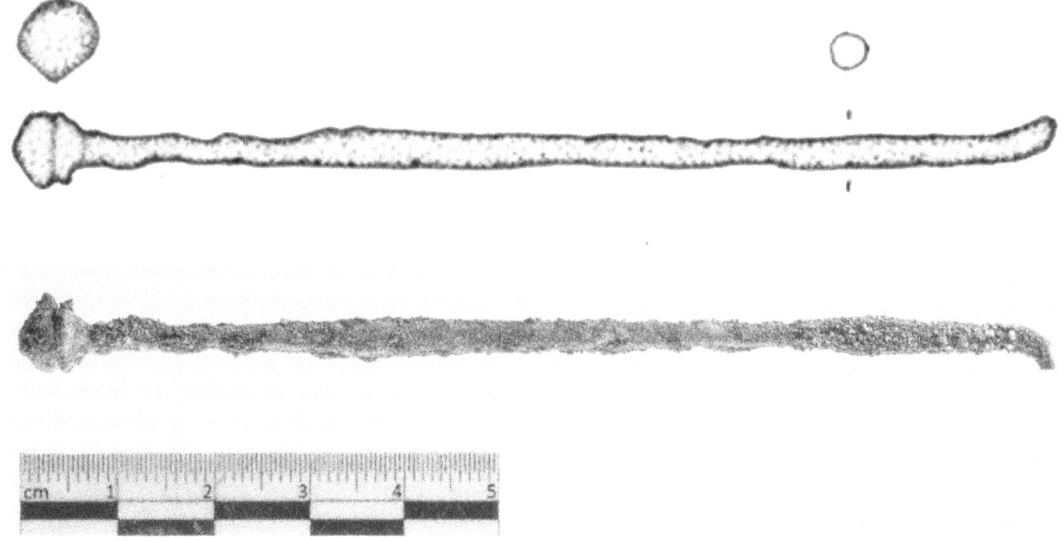

Figure 35.6. A bronze hook PAP/FR 115/2016 (photo by A. Oleksiak, drawing A. Jurkiewicz-Cora).

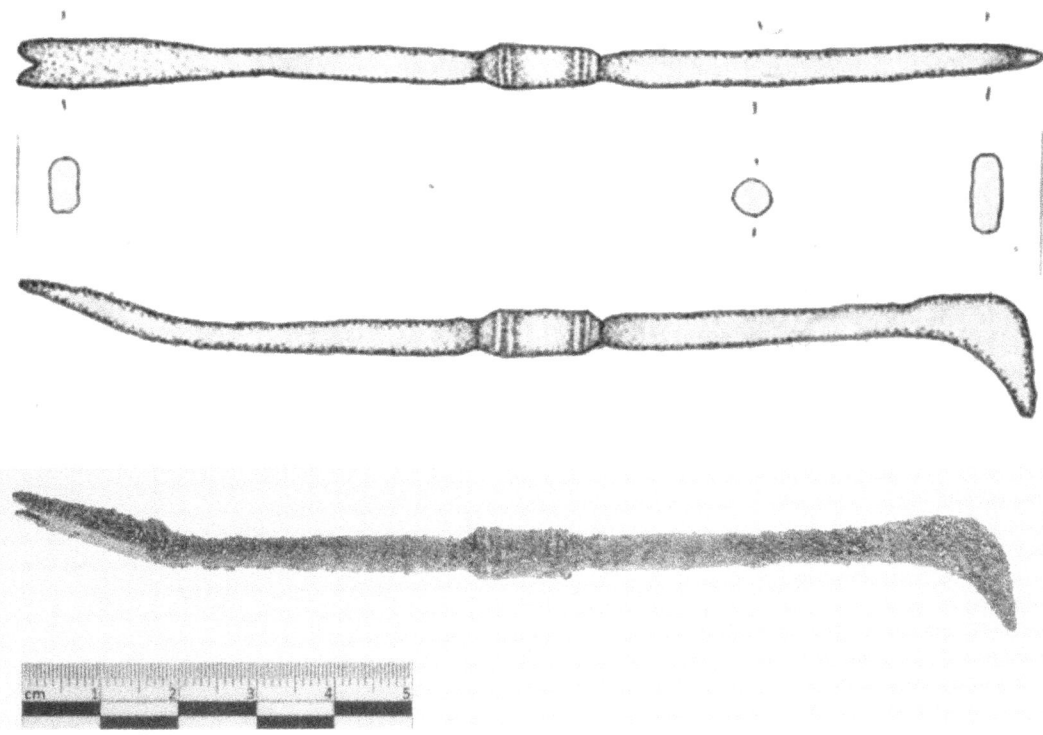

Figure 35.7. A bronze bone lever PAP/FR 116/2016 (photo by A. Oleksiak, drawing A. Jurkiewicz-Cora).

The tool was probably used to immobilize and separate the edges of wounds, sections of tissue and blood vessels during surgery, or to lift the latter. It may also have been used to locate foreign bodies in the wound, to hold fragments of flesh together, and to raise small pieces of tissue for excision (e.g. during tonsillectomy).

6. PAP/FR 116/2016 – A bronze bone lever (L: 127.88 mm; D: 5 mm) (Fig. 35.7).

   The object is similar to No. 4 above (PAP/FR 113/2016), but much better-preserved. The curved blade (max. W: 8 mm) is bent at an angle of 140° in relation to the arm (D: 4.5 mm) and is connected to a forked tip (W: 5.5 mm) by means of a finger handle (D: 6 mm) including two sets of two rings (W of each: 1 mm), which probably had a decorative function.

   Both tools No. 4 and No. 6 were used for levering fractured bones into a desired position and may also have been used for levering teeth – the curved blade to remove molars, the forked tip to remove incisors and canines. It was also possible to pull out a foreign body using the tool.

7. PAP/FR 114/2016 – A stone palette (L: 59.11 mm; W: 35.24 mm; Th: 7.9 mm) (Fig. 35.8).

   A rectangular palette, probably made of slate. Two edges are bevelled, the third one is profiled.

   The palette may have been used for crushing ingredients and mixing medicines, as well as for sharpening tools. It is also possible that the palette constituted one of the walls of the storage box, the fragments of which were found nearby.

8. PAP/FR 117/2016 – Fragments of a box

   The excavated material consists of a rectangular bronze lid (L: 150 mm; W: 36 mm; Th: 1 mm) with a handle, four bronze trapezoidal hinges (L: 19 mm; W: 14 mm; Th: 5.5 mm) and many fragments of bronze and iron fittings, as well as bone cladding. The marks imprinted on the iron corrosion allow one to assume that the box was made of wood. On two sides of the main axis of the lid, two fastening tabs are located. The handle is made of a single circular bronze wire (L: 22 mm; D: 0.5 mm), curved in four spots, attached to the

Figure 35.8. A stone palette PAP/FR 114/2016 (photo by A. Oleksiak).

lid by two other bent wires dragged through two holes located in it.

Discussion

All of the tools included in the set are made of metal – bronze or iron. These two materials were typically used for the production of surgical tools, mainly because of their lack of absorbency, which helped to maintain the hygiene of treatments (Michaelides 1984, 321; Bliquez 2014, 16–17). Similar objects were also made of wood or bones, but they served as cosmetic rather than medical tools, as these materials could absorb bodily fluids, such as blood or saliva. It is often hard to determine whether a tool was used for a medical or a cosmetic purpose, and only a larger context can help in making the final distinction (Künzl 1983, 5–6).

Related to the hygienic features of metals, particularly bronze, are also their antiseptic (bactericidal) properties. Copper and its alloys, as well as silver or gold, are natural antimicrobial materials whose properties had been exploited long before the concept of microbes became understood in the nineteenth century (Dollwet – Sorenson 1985). In this case, the lower price of copper and its alloys was an advantage over silver and gold. The hardness of metals, especially iron, was also an important factor in setting broken bones. The sharpness of metal surgical tools must be taken into consideration as well.

At the moment, it is hard to say anything certain about the possible decoration of the tools because they have not yet been cleaned. Only the profiling at the ends and at the grip-points is now visible. The goal was to increase friction and prevent the hand of a surgeon from slipping during an examination or a procedure performed on a patient. The analysis of analogies, with the hygienic aspects of the tools taken into consideration, leads to a conclusion that no additional decorations could probably be found on their surface (Michaelides 1984, 322). If any ornaments had been made, they probably would have been snakes or other symbols related to Asclepius, the divine physician. Similarities in the 'utility ornaments' found on the tools unearthed in the Agora of Paphos allow one to draw a conclusion that all the tools had been manufactured as a set and did not constitute individual elements.

Analogies

Similar tools were quite common and can be found in most museums around the world – e.g. in the National Archaeological Museum in Athens, Studium Biblicum Franciscanum in Jerusalem, the Vatican Museum, the British Museum, the University of Queensland Art Museum, etc. Their shape is defined by their purpose, hence the significant similarity between particular examples of items dating back to various centuries. Often the finds of tools are not published and information about their provenance is uncertain. The majority of other tools are often unearthed in burial sites, which makes the set from the Paphos Agora important in terms of the reconstruction of the daily practice of physicians in ancient times.

Very interesting from the Paphos perspective is also a Roman Surgeon's Tomb excavated in the Eastern Necropolis of ancient Paphos in 1983 (Michaelides 1984). The 64 surgical tools found in it include an ear probe (Cat. No. 7), spoons/probes (Cat. No. 8–9), bone levers – made both of bronze (Cat. No. 28. 29) and of iron (Cat. No. 16. 50. 53), as well as a stone palette (Cat. No. 19). The author dates the tomb to the mid-second/early third century AD, but he indicates that similar objects can be dated to the first century AD (Michaelides 1984, 331–332). Interesting is also an iron, key-like object (Cat. No. 62) of an uncertain purpose, because an almost identical item (PAP/FR 87/2014) – made of lead – was found during excavations in the Agora in the season of 2014 at the bottom of Well S.173, in a context dating to the Late Hellenistic period (Papuci-Władyka – Machowski – Miszk, 2018, 538).

The most recent publications are *The Tools of Asclepius* by L. J. Bliquez (2014), which discusses comprehensively all medical tools of both the Greek and the Roman worlds, and *Hygieia: Health, Illness and Treatment from Homer to Galen*, the catalogue of an exhibition organised in 2014 at the Museum of Cycladic Art in Athens with approximately 300 artefacts dating from the late 13th century BC to the 2nd/3rd century AD, including an inventory of the Paphos tomb (Stampolidis – Tassoulas 2014). Many items in that exhibition were published for the first time, including a Roman bronze hook (Cat. No. 175), similar to No. 6, Early Imperial tumour forceps (Cat. No. 178), not unlike tweezers No. 3. The artefacts also included three spoons, each with an olivary enlargement on the tip (Cat. No. 190) like No. 1, but with a different bowl, as well as four ear probes (Cat. No. 192), that look like No. 2.

The largest amount of information about discoveries of tombs containing medical tools can be found in *Medizinische Instrumente aus Sepulkralfunden der römischen Kaiserzeit* published by E. Künzl (1983). Künzl mentions a set of basic instruments similar to those found by our team, which was uncovered in the palaestra of Pompeii under a skeleton of a physician (Künzl 1983, 12). The set included, among other things, a spoon probe, two ear probes, two pairs of tweezers and two hooks. Tweezers and a hook were also found in tomb in Melosa dating to the early Imperial period (Künzl 1983, 40). Southwestern Asia Minor is the area from which came a hook, two spoons and five ear probes, similar to those found in the Agora of Paphos (Künzl 1983, 45). These objects date to the first half of the third century AD and are stored in the Römisch-Germanisches Zentralmuseum in Mainz. In a tomb in Vermand, which dates to a similar period, and in another one in Wancennes, dating to the imperial period, stone palettes were discovered (Künzl 1983, 68–70). The latter tomb also contained a spoon probe. Another spoon probe, very similar to No.1, but with a twisted bar, was found in a tomb dating to the second half of the first century AD and located in Roman Vicus Belginum in Wederath (Künzl

1983, 73). One more similar spoon probe, as well as an ear probe, were part of a set in a toolbox with one wall made of a stone palette found in the so-called Oculist Tomb in Lyon (Lasfargues 2012, 76). Tweezers very similar to No. 3 are part of a private collection in Paris – lost today – and were said to have been discovered in a grave located in the region of Paris (Künzl 1983, 74–78).

A grave from Rhemis, dating to the second half of the second century AD, contained, among other finds, seven pairs of tweezers and three hooks (Künzl 1983, 61–67). It is particularly interesting because of a small steelyard of a Pompeiian type (L: 125 mm) and fragments of a balance, which were also found there. A similar steelyard (L: 158 mm), dated to the first century AD, was found on the Agora in East Portico R.2, 10 metres north of the area where surgical tools were uncovered (Papuci-Władyka – Wacławik 2016; see also below). It may have been used for measuring the proper composition of medicines during their preparation (Bliquez 2014, 269). Other interesting tombs were discovered in Varna and in Noricum, and date to the second half of the second and third centuries AD, respectively (Künzl 1983, 112–116). In both of them, besides medical tools like spoons, complete glass vessels were excavated. They are of the same types as vessels found in R.16 and R.15 (PAP/FR 137–139/2016), directly to the north of R.16, where surgical tools were unearthed. They can also be regarded as part of a physician's equipment, and most likely contained base substances and solvents for medicines (Bliquez 2014, 278).

A possible "Office of a Paphos Surgeon" (or Physician) on the Agora?

The information presented above allows one to assume that a physician, presumably a surgeon, had his office on the Agora of Nea Paphos, which functioned most probably in the ER period and occupied the area of R. 15 and R. 16. The name "Office of a Paphos Surgeon" was used for the first time by E. Papuci-Władyka in "In the heart of the ancient city. Research of the Jagiellonian University in Krakow at the Agora and beyond in Paphos Archaeological Park, Cyprus. An exhibition of Photographs by Robert Słaboński", published in Kraków by Uniwersytet Jagielloński, on 28–30 and fig. on 45.[1]

It should be considered whether the office occupied a larger area and whether it had operated also in earlier periods, maybe even from the beginning of the functioning of the East Portico (For the development and functions of the rooms in Portico see Miszk, forthcoming). The evidence supporting this assumption can be the steelyard and the key-like object mentioned above. If they were also related to the surgeon's practice, as can be concluded from the analogies discussed above, probably also R. 2 and R. 13, where Well S.173 had been uncovered, could be considered as part of the office. This theory might also be confirmed by a stone mortar PAP16/II/1225/S1 found in R. 15 at a level approximately 60 cm below the surgical set. Similar mortars were used to grind substances in the preparation of medicines (Bliquez 2014, 263). If the office had operated here before, this mortar could have been part of its equipment.

This hypothesis is hard to confirm at present, however, mostly because the steelyard and the key-like object may have been used by merchants or officials working on the Agora. Also R. 2 seems to belong to an autonomous structure rather than the 'Office of a Paphos Surgeon', which is separated from it by a large channel. On the other hand, in the entire Trench II many basins and wells have been excavated and L. J. Bliquez (2014, 293) mentions that these structures were part of the equipment needed in a basic medical surgery. Maybe a closer analysis of the other artefacts will help to confirm or reject this hypothesis, because it is possible that more finds from the East Portico will be identified as related to a medical practice.

Acknowledgements

The title of this paper is inspired by a poem *On Death, without Exaggeration* by Polish Nobel Prize-winner W. Szymborska (available online http://www. visegradliterature.net/works/pl/ Szymborska%2C_Wisława-1923/O_śmierci_bez_przesady/ en/7552-On_Death%2C_ without_Exaggeration). The information about the set has been previously published by the author of a popular science text in *Antike Welt*, cf. Wacławik, 2018.

The author is deeply indebted to the Head of the expedition for sharing the materials, granting permission for publication, as well as for all other assistance. The Paphos Agora Project is financed by the Narodowe Centrum Nauki (NCN – National Science Centre, Poland) grant MAESTRO no. 2014/14/A/HS 3/00283.

The author is deeply indebted to Anna Sowul, MD and Aleksander Sowul, MD for substantive consultations in the field of surgery, as well as to Iwona Kasperczyk for enabling him to contact them.

Bibliography

Bliquez, L. J., 2014. *The tools of Asclepius*. Leiden – Boston: Brill.

Dollwet, H. H. – Sorenson, J. R., 1985. Historic uses of copper compounds in medicine. *Trace Elements in Medicine 2/2*, 80–87.

Künzl, E., 1983. *Medizinische Instrumente aus Sepulkralfunden der römischen Kaiserzeit*. Köln – Bonn: Rheinland Verlag.

Lasfargues, J., 2012. *Des objets qui racontent l'Histoire: Lugdunum*. Lyon: EMCC.

Michaelides, D., 1984. A Roman surgeon's tomb from Nea Paphos. *RDAC 1984*, 315–332.

Miszk, Ł., forthcoming. Stratigraphy and Architecture of the Agora. In: E. Papuci-Władyka, ed.,, *Paphos Agora Project (PAP) 1. Interdisciplinary Research of the Jagiellonian University in Nea Paphos (2011–2015): First Results*. Historia Iagellonica: Kraków .

---

[1] The booklet is available on-line: paphos-agora. archeo.uj.edu.pl/ documents/5871239/60438820/Papuci-Wladyka+2017+-+katalog. pdf/679b04e9-f0ce-4eb8-a1d4-80f942416c47.

Papuci-Władyka, E. – Wacławik, M. T., 2016. A bronze steelyard with an acorn-shaped counterweight from the Paphos Agora. *SAAC 20*, 137–147.

Papuci-Władyka, E. – Machowski, W. – Miszk, Ł., 2018. Paphos Agora Project (PAP) 2011–2014: First Preliminary Report on Excavation by the Jagiellonian Unversity in Krakow, Poland. *RDAC, New Series 1*, 533–569.

Riha, E., 1986. *Römisches Toilettgerät und medizinische Instrumente*. Augst: Römermuseum.

Stampolidis, N. C. – Tassoulas, Y., 2014. *Hygieia. Health, illness, treatment from Homer to Galen.* Athens: Museum of Cycladic Art & Hellenic Ministry of Culture and Sports.

Wacławik, M. T., 2018. Wie man sich in Paphos dem allmächtigen Tod widersetzte. Chirurgische Instrumente aus Nea Paphos auf Zypern. *Antike Welt 1/18*, 60–65.

36

About Löwenkannen:
La Löwenkanne del Museo Archeologico di Verona

Marina Castoldi

Università degli Studi di Milano

marina.castoldi@unimi.it

Abstract: A so-called Löwenkanne is kept among the bronze vessels in the Archaeological Museum at the Roman Theatre of Verona; the jug is part of a collection assembled in the nineteenth century by Carlo Alessandri. The provenance of the vessel is unknown, but part of the Collection was collected in Southern Italy and Sicily.

This type of decorative jug, whose handles are adorned with plastic lions, is produced during the 6th century BC by Greek and Etruscan workshops with wide distribution range. Numerous stylistic and decorative contacts between the various specimens led to the formulation of various typological groups, with chronology and distribution evidences that, however, were based on vessels coming mostly from Collections, in good conservation status, but without findplaces and contexts.

Starting from the analysis of the Löwenkanne of the Museum of Verona, this caratteristico type of jugs is take into account with particular reference to the types present in the contexts of the Italian peninsula, where Löwenkannen are attested in settlements and in cemeteries, and where they are included among the high quality artefacts.

The aim of the following paper consists in the archaeological evidence based on archaeological context data; I will try to highlight the role and function of these particular types of jugs, to be read in a circulation phenomenon of fine vessels characterizing the Archaic period.

Keywords: Löwenkannen; Archaic Bronze Vessels; Greek and Etruscan Bronze Workshops; Archaic Period

Il mio interesse nei confronti delle *Löwenkannen* nasce con una brocca del Museo Archeologico di Verona (Fig. 36.1–2) che, per la particolare conformazione dell'ansa, configurata plasticamente, all'attacco superiore, con una protome di leone aggettante sull'imboccatura e due corti bracci che, seguendo la curvatura del labbro, terminano con leoncini accovacciati fissati con un ribattino posto tra le zampe, rientra in questa particolare classe di recipienti.

Si tratta, come è noto, di brocche a collo distinto, labbro trilobato con lobo centrale più pronunciato e corpo ovoide su basso piede a tromba; l'ansa, che presenta sempre una protome di leone più o meno stilizzata aggettante sull'imboccatura, può avere bracci desinenti a leoncini, a teste di scimmia o a rotelle; l'attacco inferiore è invece sempre a forma di palmetta pendente, isolata o associata ad altri elementi plastici.

Questo tipo di brocca dall'ansa molto decorativa – con reminiscenze orientali ed esotiche nella scelta di protomi di leone (Tarditi 2014; Tarditi 2016, 310–313) e di scimmia (Stibbe 1999, 40), nonché nell'attacco a rotelle che caratterizza, come è noto, le cd. "oinochoai rodie" (Castoldi 1995, 35–36; Jurgeit 1999, 348–350) – è prodotta nel corso del VI secolo a.C. da fabbriche greche ed etrusche con ampio raggio di distribuzione.

Per l'inquadramento del tipo si può considerare ancora valido lo studio di Weber (1983), che rielabora e completa i contributi di Brown (1960), Kent Hill (1967) e Szilágyi (1968) e identifica tre tipi (A, B e C), a seconda della terminazione dei bracci dell'attacco superiore. La brocca di Verona, con terminazioni a leoncini, si inserirebbe in questo caso nel tipo B, datato dall'Autore a partire dalla prima metà del VI secolo (Weber 1983, 6–89) e attestato attraverso una serie greca, per la quale è stato riconosciuto l'epicentro nel Peloponneso, e una etrusca, che si connota per una resa meno plastica delle notazioni anatomiche e della criniera, in genere più stilizzata e con dettagli incisi (Kent Hill 1967, 43; Castoldi 1995, 39–44; Sannibale 2008, 69).

Marina Castoldi

Fig. 36.1. Brocca del Museo Archeologico di Verona (Foto: Gianluca Stradiotto)

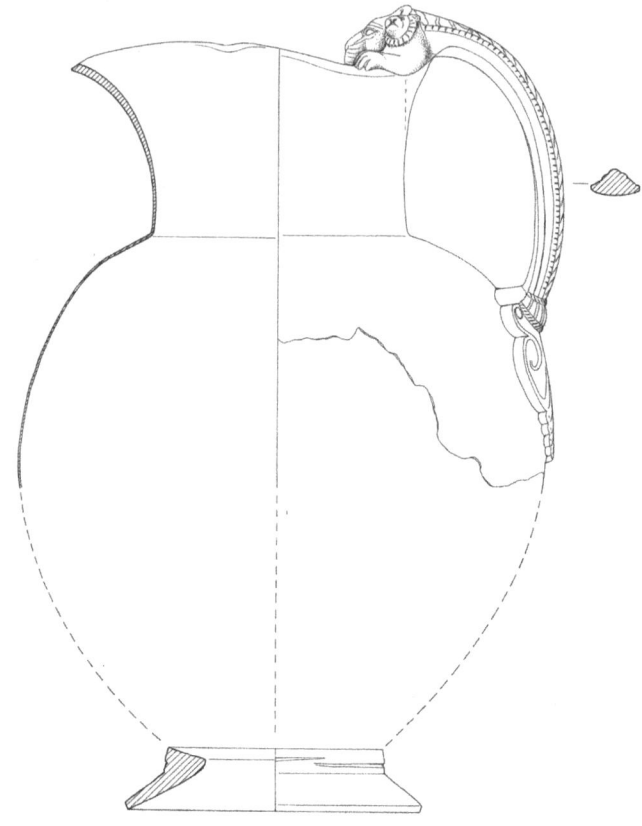

Fig. 36.2. Brocca del Museo Archeologico di Verona (Disegno: Raffaella Giacometti)

Più recente la proposta di Stibbe (1999) che, nell'ambito di un contributo sulle oinochoai in bronzo laconiche con decorazione plastica, istituisce per le *Löwenkannen* una tipologia più articolata, nella quale le oinochoai con protome leonina tra leoni recumbenti costituiscono il gruppo 4, suddiviso a sua volta in tre sottogruppi in base alla forma dell'attacco inferiore, che può essere variamente conformato (sottogruppo 4a), oppure a palmetta tra arieti (sottogruppo 4b), o ancora a palmetta con serpenti (sottogruppo 4c) (Stibbe 1999, 42–44). La brocca di Verona potrebbe inserirsi in questo caso solo nel gruppo 4a che tuttavia raccoglie soltanto tre *Löwenkannen* prive di contesto – una a Dresda, una a Oxford e una da Capua, ma attualmente dispersa – con caratteristiche, un po' anomale rispetto a quelle degli altri gruppi, che hanno indotto l'Autore ad attribuirle a una fase ancora sperimentale della produzione (Stibbe 1996, 362–363, tavv. 31. 32; Stibbe 1999, 42).

Il problema, come si deduce dagli elenchi forniti da Brown, Weber e Stibbe, è che le *Löwenkannen*, tra esemplari completi e anse, sono piuttosto numerose, ma quasi tutte provenienti da Collezioni o da vecchi scavi e quindi per la maggior parte prive di dati sia sulla provenienza, sia sul contesto d'origine. L'inquadramento è quindi quasi sempre affidato a criteri stilistici che prendono in considerazione soprattutto la resa degli animali, talora affiancati da protomi femminili, e degli elementi decorativi quale la palmetta dell'attacco inferiore.

Anche la *Löwenkanne* del Museo Archeologico di Verona è priva di dati di contesto; proviene infatti dalla collezione ottocentesca di Carlo Alessandri (1809–1894) (Civiche Raccolte Archeologiche di Verona, n. inv. 22139; Catalogo Alessandri n. 703. H cm 27,8; h con ansa cm 29,4; diam. mass. cm 19; diam. piede cm 10,5). La provenienza è ignota, sappiamo tuttavia che una parte della collezione, che annovera anche materiali di età romana, è stata raccolta in Italia meridionale e in Sicilia, dove lo stesso Alessandri si era più volte recato (Marchini 1972, 167–172).

La brocca è stata oggetto di un recente intervento di restauro che ha eliminato tutte le integrazioni ottocentesche: del corpo, in lamina, si conserva, benché molto lacunosa, solo la parte superiore, con l'ampio labbro trilobato, il largo collo distinto, cilindrico, la spalla convessa e l'inizio del ventre ovoide; sono invece meglio conservati, in quanto realizzati a getto, il piede e l'ansa, che, come si è detto, costituisce l'elemento caratterizzante del vaso in esame. Sulla base di un esame autoptico, il corpo è stato verosimilmente realizzato per battitura partendo da un abbozzo a getto (Pernot 2003, 266–267); il piede, a getto, è stato applicato con brasatura dolce; l'ansa con ribattini.

Se prendiamo in esame l'attacco superiore, notiamo che tutti e tre i leoni della brocca di Verona si caratterizzano per una testa tondeggiante con muso pronunciato, ben rifinito nei dettagli anatomici, particolarmente evidenti nella protome centrale: si distinguono gli occhi infossati, a mandorla e la fronte marcata da una ruga triangolare, il naso largo e tozzo, le fauci, sottolineate da un taglio a V, i baffi arricciati verso l'alto (Fig. 36.3). La criniera forma una sorta di cornice circolare intorno alla testa, il pelame è reso a tacchette radiali distanziate, chiaramente incise sul modello a cera; le orecchie del leone centrale sono massicce, con profilo superiore a semicerchio e sono collocate in primo piano ai lati della fronte; quelle dei leoncini sono invece più minute, sempre a semicerchio, ma poste dietro la criniera (Fig. 36.4).

Un confronto puntuale, per le grandi orecchie che interrompono, in modo insolito, lo svolgersi della criniera, è dato da un leone in osso del santuario di *Arthemis Orthia*, a Sparta, purtroppo rinvenuto in uno strato sconvolto, con materiali rimescolati (Dawkins 1929, 217, tav. CXIV.3); il leoncino, datato su basi stilistiche al VI secolo a.C., ha però il muso più squadrato, con naso molto allungato, anche se l'impostazione radiale della criniera, che qui ha però maggiore risalto plastico, richiama l'esemplare in esame. Si segnala anche un leoncino dall'Heraion di Samo, che reca un'iscrizione con la dedica da parte di uno Spartiate (Stibbe 1996, 369, n. 7, tav. 37.1–2; Rolley 2003, 140). Lo stesso particolare delle grandi orecchie frontali ritorna sulla *Löwenkanne* del Museo di Mainz, dove la protome di leone, definita da Stibbe *"ungewöhnliche"*, è fiancheggiata da musi di scimmie; è un pezzo, purtroppo privo di provenienza, che ha in comune con la brocca di Verona anche la forma del corpo, ovale e molto capiente, il disegno della criniera e l'attacco inferiore dell'ansa a palmetta incisa (Weber 1983, 210ss, I.A.1, tav. I; Stibbe 1996, 362, n. 28, tav. 30.2; Stibbe 1999, 39, 'gruppo 3B', fig. 11–12). Il disegno della criniera con ciocche a S più o meno ordinate ritorna però su brocche di produzione etrusca (Tombolani 1981, 36, n. 17; Sannibale 2008, 72, n. 37).

Secondo Stibbe, che inserisce la brocca di Mainz nella serie laconica, si tratterebbe di una fase ancora sperimentale della produzione, da collocare quindi all'inizio del VI secolo a.C., se non alla fine del secolo precedente (Stibbe 1996, 262 e nota 28). Il particolare delle orecchie poste in primo piano ritorna su un'ansa conservata a Berlino, proveniente dal santuario di Apollo Pizio di Melana, in Laconia, come rivela la dedica (Stibbe 1999, 41–42, fig. 18); il tipo di leone è tuttavia diverso, così come l'attacco inferiore, a palmetta plastica tra serpenti.

In linea di massima, pur non trovando, tra il materiale edito, un confronto puntuale, i leoni della brocca veronese sembrano allinearsi ai tipi considerati laconici (Rolley 2003, 140), che si caratterizzano per il muso largo e schiacciato, movimentato sulla fronte, tra gli occhi, da una ruga triangolare, e per la criniera circolare, a collare, resa a brevi tacche radiali, forse nel nostro caso più rade

Fig. 36.3. Brocca del Museo Archeologico di Verona (Foto: Gianluca Stradiotto)

Fig. 36.4. Brocca del Museo Archeologico di Verona (Disegno: Raffaella Giacometti)

e distanziate. Il particolare del triangolo con il vertice in alto è presente anche sulla protome centrale della brocca di Verona; si possono confrontare i leoni delle fibule laconiche (Stibbe 1996, 364–366, tav. 27.2–3, fig. 3) e il bel leone di Dodona, attribuito a officine laconiche (Bieg 2002, 107, fig. 128; Rolley 2003, fig. 98).

L'ansa ha fusto a nastro ingrossato, percorso sulla faccia a vista da costolature perlinate, e termina con un collarino decorato e con una piastra conformata a palmetta pendente da coppie di volute; i petali della palmetta e le volute sono incisi a cesello profilatore; nelle volute superiori sono i ribattini di fissaggio al ventre del vaso (Fig. 36.5). Sulla parte superiore dell'ansa, sul punto di appoggio del pollice, coppie irregolari di linee a S indicano la criniera, che continua sulla parte centrale del fusto con un motivo stilizzato a *chevrons*. Il piede è svasato, a tromba, e privo di elementi decorativi.

La palmetta dell'attacco inferiore ripropone a incisione il tipo, più diffuso per questa classe di brocche, della palmetta plastica (Fig. 36.6). Un buon modello, a rilievo, è offerto ancora una volta da un esemplare definito laconico, un attacco inferiore, forse di oinochoe, dal santuario di Apollo *Hyperteleatas* di Phoiniki, in Laconia, con palmetta pendente da due coppie di volute sovrapposte a rivoluzione interna; l'attacco è datato da Stibbe, su basi stilistiche, perché non ci sono dati di contesto, all'inizio del terzo quarto del VI secolo (Stibbe 1997, 45. 60, n. 90, fig. 19; Stibbe 2008, 20, n. 4, fig. 8). È un tipo di palmetta molto raffinata, a petali arrotondati, leggermente concavi, sormontata da grosse volute.

La palmetta della brocca di Verona, che ha una resa molto più corsiva, richiama quella di un'ansa di Mainz, con palmetta sormontata da una testa femminile con polos; è un pezzo abbastanza isolato, privo di contesto, per il quale è stata proposta, da Shefton, una produzione etrusca su

Fig. 36.5. Brocca del Museo Archeologico di Verona (Foto: Gianluca Stradiotto)

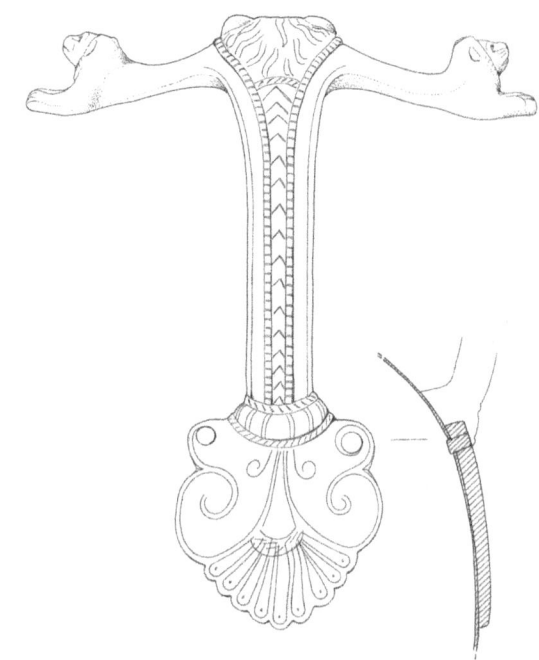

Fig. 36.6. Brocca del Museo Archeologico di Verona (Disegno: Raffaella Giacometti)

influsso dei prodotti laconici (Shefton 1992, 153 nota 31), ipotesi ripresa da Stibbe (Stibbe 1996, 361, nota 26. 373, tav. 29.1–2) e ancora da Naso, con proposta di datazione alla metà del VI secolo a.C., proprio a causa della palmetta graffita "che potrebbe costituire un'introduzione etrusca" (Naso 2003, 59, n. 92, tav. 33). In effetti, questo tipo di palmetta a piastra, con petali arrotondati di uguale lunghezza, riferita alla tradizione corinzia (Tarditi 2016, 268, fig. 51), è associata anche alle cd. "oinochoai rodie", che sembrerebbero precedere, nella produzione e nella diffusione in ambito italico, le brocche con protomi di leoni e sono ormai ben attribuite, con l'esclusione di pochi esemplari effettivamente rodioti, a fabbriche etrusche (Rolley 1987, 336–341; Castoldi 1995, 35–36; Jurgeit 1999, 348–350).

Un dato interessante, per una possibile anteriorità della palmetta incisa rispetto a quella a risalto plastico, è offerto anche dalla tomba 163 di Campovalano, datata alla prima metà del VI secolo (Chiaramonte Treré – d'Ercole 2003, 74–77, tav. 7 (D. Francone); 149 (C. Chiaramonte Treré), con una *Löwenkanne* con attacco inferiore a palmetta incisa fiancheggiata da due leoni (Zanco 1974, 38–39, n. 8, tav. 14–17; Weber 1983, 238).

Possiamo ricordare anche alcune *Löwenkannen* in bucchero rinvenute a Pontecagnano: mi riferisco a quattro oinochoai di grandi dimensioni e di alto livello qualitativo – provenienti le prime due dallo "scarico Granozio" di via Sicilia, la terza dalla tomba 4307 in località S. Antonio, la quarta dalla tomba 4306 della stessa necropoli – che riproducono fedelmente, soprattutto le prime due, più naturalistiche, le anse con protome di leone e leoncini accovacciati a tutto tondo, tanto da far pensare ad una diretta mutuazione dalla metallotecnica (Cuozzo 1993, 149, n.

1–4, fig. 1–10. 156–158). Gli attacchi inferiori delle anse ripropongono le palmette realizzate a incisione. I contesti, tutti collocabili nell'ambito del primo quarto del VI secolo a.C. (Cerchiai 1990, 4–9; Cuozzo 1993, 162–163), sottintendono che i modelli di bronzo, d'importazione o già di produzione locale, dovevano essere in circolazione anche in ambito italico all'inizio del VI secolo a.C.

Resta invece priva di contesto, ma forse di provenienza locale in senso lato, un'ansa del Museo di Lecce con protome di leone all'attacco superiore e bracci terminanti con protomi di scimmia e palmetta con volute incisa all'attacco inferiore (Delli Ponti 1973, 42, n. 64, tav. XLI). È un pezzo che Stibbe inserisce tra le palmette corinzie, ma attribuisce a fabbriche sud-italiche per la resa sommaria del motivo (Stibbe 1997, 48. 63 n. 103).

Se si prendono in considerazione i documenti provenienti dall'Italia, meglio contestualizzati, si può notare come il tipo della *Löwenkanne* sia diffuso abbastanza precocemente. Tra i pochi esemplari in contesto, le due oinochoai della tomba 1505 di Santa Maria Capua Vetere, località Fornaci (Johannowsky 1980, 447. 452. 460. 461; Benassai 1995, 185–186), attribuite da Stibbe a una produzione laconica ancora sperimentale (Stibbe 1999, 39, fig. 9–10, 43, fig. 20–21; Stibbe 2000, 11–14, n. 3. 4), forniscono un importante termine *ante quem* per l'associazione con un'hydria e un'oinochoe corinzie datate all'inizio del VI secolo a.C. (Stibbe 2000, 6 nota 11, tav. 4). Abbiamo visto come gli esemplari d'imitazione in bucchero da Pontecagnano confermino questa cronologia. Tra i recipienti di bronzo che facevano parte del corredo di questa ricca tomba, in parte andato disperso, figurano anche due hydriai laconiche e un'oinochoe di tipo 'rodio' (Stibbe 2000, 6, nota 11, n. 1. 2, tav. 3,6).

Si può notare anche che nelle *Löwenkannen* di Capua la palmetta è plastica, ma fiancheggiata da arieti o da leoni recumbenti, come nella brocca di Campovalano. Non abbiamo ancora il tipo più diffuso di *Löwenkannen* con attacco inferiore a palmetta plastica associata ad appendici 'ad ancora' o a serpenti (Tombolani 1981, 36, n. 17; Castoldi 1995, 39–40; Sannibale 2008, 69–84, n. 36–44), come nelle serie delle *plumpe Kannen*, datate dalla metà del VI all'inizio del V secolo e delle *Schnabelkannen*, datate dall'ultimo terzo del VI ai primi anni del V secolo (Adam 2003, 145). Sono analogie che evidenziano per le *Löwenkannen* etrusche un'area di fabbricazione analoga a quella delle ben note brocche a becco (Tombolani 1981, 36; Sannibale 2008, 69).

Riassumendo, accettando per le *Löwenkannen* una produzione laconica, mi sembra che si possa cogliere un arrivo precoce del tipo in territorio italico, già intorno all'inizio del VI secolo, con imitazioni in ceramica e, verosimilmente, in bronzo che evidenziano un interesse specifico per questa forma. Sulla base dei pochi elementi in contesto, è probabile che gli esemplari con attacco inferiore a palmetta incisa rappresentino effettivamente una fase 'sperimentale', da collocare nella prima metà del secolo. L'acme della produzione si avrebbe però nella seconda metà del secolo, in concomitanza con la produzione delle *Schnabelkannen*.

La brocca di Verona, dalla quale siamo partiti, potrebbe collocarsi verso la metà del secolo o poco dopo per la presenza dell'attacco a palmetta incisa, di tipo più antico, che però qui si associa a un attacco superiore meno plastico e naturalistico degli esemplari laconici d'importazione, come la brocca di Capua; dei leoncini, infatti, è ben riconoscibile solo la parte anteriore, il tronco e le zampe, mentre il resto del corpo è annullato e si fonde con i bracci di fissaggio al labbro del vaso. Sono notazioni che sono state considerate indicative di recenziorità rispetto agli esemplari con corpo più compatto, a forte risalto plastico, come quelli appena descritti (Stibbe 2006, 5–6).

Per quanto riguarda l'area di produzione non sarebbe da escludere, visti i numerosi riscontri per le protomi di leone, una produzione laconica, forse tarda e seriale; d'altro canto, il carattere un po' eclettico del pezzo potrebbe indirizzare anche verso una produzione magnogreca in senso lato, senza poter avanzare, in mancanza di dati di contesto, ulteriori considerazioni.

Il problema è che, come sempre, è difficile trovare vasellame di bronzo negli abitati ed è altrettanto problematico, in un panorama molto frammentato, proporre attribuzioni puntuali (su questi problemi cfr. Tarditi 1996, 201–205). In Italia meridionale, i recipienti di bronzo abbondano soprattutto nelle tombe del *milieu* indigeno; se togliamo alcuni casi un po' isolati e molto significativi, come il sacello ipogeico di Poseidonia, nelle *poleis* greche gli oggetti in bronzo in contesto sono molto pochi, soprattutto per l'epoca arcaica. E non è costume dei Greci farsi seppellire con vasi di bronzo. Sono le *elite* etrusche, picene, enotrie e japige che scelgono per l'Aldilà ricchi corredi, con arredi e vasellame di bronzo.

Queste *Löwenkannen* dovevano del resto essere considerate pezzi eccezionali, perché figurano nelle tombe più ricche, come la tomba 1505 di Capua, già ricordata, pertinente a un guerriero, membro di un clan gentilizio che si riserva uno spazio familiare all'interno della necropoli (Benassai 1995, 185–186). Del corredo facevano parte «cinque bacini ad orlo perlinato, otto piatti con orlo inciso a treccia, due oinochoai di tipo 'rodio', due olpette con ansa a palmetta tra serpenti, due oinochoai con anse a leoncini, una situla e due hydriai del gruppo *Telesstas*», oltre a due morsi di cavallo, diversi spiedi e ceramiche del corinzio antico finale (Gilotta 2009). Ma si può ricordare anche l'oinochoe della tomba 103 di Vaglio, in località Braida, con attacco superiore a leoni molto naturalistici e attacco inferiore a palmetta con serpenti. La brocca figura all'interno di un ricco corredo da banchetto e da simposio, in una tomba datata nella seconda metà del VI secolo (Bottini 2013, 141–142, fig. 3; Bottini, Setari 2013, 245–256).

Acknowledgement

Mi è gradito ringraziare Margherita Bolla, curatore dei Musei Maffeiano e Archeologico al Teatro romano di Verona, che ha gentilmente favorito la pubblicazione del pezzo e Chiara Tarditi, per i preziosi consigli.

Il restauro della *Löwenkanne* è stato eseguito dalla Ditta Ambra di Sant'Antonino Ticino (VA). Le fotografie sono di Gianluca Stradiotto (Verona); i disegni di Raffaella Giacometti (Verona).

Bibliografia

Adam, A.-M., 2003. Les vases de bronze étrusques. In: C. Rolley, ed., *La tombe princière de Vix*. Paris: Picard, 144–260.

Benassai, R., 1995. Sui deinoi bronzei campani. In: *Studi sulla Campania preromana*. Roma: G. Bretschneider, 157–205.

Bieg, G., 2002. *Der Bronzekessel aus dem späthallstattzeitlichen Fürstengrab von Eberdingen-Hochdorf (Kr. Ludwigsburg), Griechische Stabdreifüsse und Bronzekessel der archaischen Zeit mit figürlichem Schmuck*. Stuttgart: Theiss.

Bottini, A., 2013, Lusso e prestigio. Lo strumentario in bronzo a Torre di Satriano e nei centri "nord-lucani". In: M. Osanna – M. Vullo, ed., *Segni del potere. Oggetti di lusso dal Mediterraneo all'Appennino lucano di età arcaica*. Venosa: Osanna Edizioni, 137–143.

Bottini, A. – Setari, E., 2013, Braida di Vaglio. Le tombe 103 e 108. In: M. Osanna – M. Vullo, ed., *Segni del potere. Oggetti di lusso dal Mediterraneo all'Appennino lucano di età arcaica*. Venosa: Osanna Edizioni, 245–260.

Brown, W. L., 1960. *The Etruscan Lion*. Oxford: at The Clarendon Press.

Castoldi, M., 1995. *Recipienti in bronzo greci, magnogreci ed etrusco-italici delle Civiche Raccolte Archeologiche di Milano*. Milano: Comune di Milano.

Cerchiai, L.,1990. *Le officine etrusco-corinzie di Pontecagnano*. Napoli: Istituto Universitario Orientale.

Chiaramonte Treré C. – d'Ercole, V., 2003. *La Necropoli di Campovalano. Tombe orientalizzanti e arcaiche*, I. Oxford: BAR.

Cuozzo, M., 1993, Produzione di lusso, produzione corrente nel bucchero di Pontecagnano. Alcune considerazioni. In: M. Bonghi Jovino, ed., *Produzione artigianale ed esportazione nel mondo antico. Il bucchero etrusco*. Atti del Colloquio Internazionale (Milano 1990). Milano: Edizioni Et, 147–165.

Dawkins, R.M., 1929. *The Sanctuary of Arthemis Orthia at Sparta*. London: Mac Millian and Co.

Delli Ponti, G., 1973. *I bronzi del Museo Provinciale di Lecce*. Lecce: Amministrazione Provinciale.

Gilotta, F., 2009. Capua etrusca. In: M.L. Chirico, ed., *Lungo l'Appia: scritti su Capua antica e dintorni*. Napoli: Giannini, 19–28.

Kent Hill, D., 1967. Palmette with Snakes: a Handle Ornament on Early Metalware. *Antike Kunst*, 10, 39–47.

Johannowsky, W., 1980, Bronzi arcaici da Atena Lucana. *La Parola del Passato*, 35, 443–461.

Jurgeit, F., 1999. *Die etruskischen und italischen Bronzen sowie Gegenständen aus Eisen, Blei und Leder im Badischen Landesmuseum Karlsruhe*. Pisa-Roma: Istituti Editoriali e Poligrafici Internazionali.

Marchini, G., 1972. *Antiquari e collezioni archeologiche dell'Ottocento veronese*. Verona: Edizioni di Vita Veronese.

Naso, A., 2003. *I bronzi etruschi e italici del Römisch-germanisches Zentralmuseum*. Mainz: Verlag des Römisch-Germanischen Zentralmuseums, Bonn: In Kommission bei Habelt.

Pernot, M., 2003. Étude technique de quelques objets en bronze. In: C. Rolley, ed., *La tombe princière de Vix*. Paris: Picard, 265–277.

Rolley, C., 1987. Le bronzes grecs: recherches récentes. *Revue Archaelogique*, 2, 335–360.

Rolley, C., 2003, Le cratère. In: C. Rolley ed. *La tombe princière de Vix*. Paris: Picard. 77–143.

Sannibale, M., 2008. *La Raccolta Giacinto Guglielmi*. II. *Bronzi e materiali vari*. Roma: L'Erma di Bretschneider.

Shefton, B.B., 1992. The Recanati Group. A Study of some Archaich Vassels in Central Italy and their Geek Antecedents. *Mitteilungen des Deutschen Archäologischen Instituts – Römische Abteilung*, 99, 139–162.

Stibbe, C. M., 1996. Frauen und Löwen. Eine Untersuchung zu den Anfangen der lakonischen Bronzeindustrie. *Jahrbuch des Römisch-germanischen Zentralmuseums Mainz*, 43(1), 355–381.

Stibbe, C. M., 1997. Archaic Greek Bronze Palmettes. *Bulletin Antieke Beschaving*, 72, 37–64.

Stibbe, C. M., 1999. Laconian clay and bronze oinochoae with plastic decorations, Part II. *Bulletin Antieke Beschaving*, 74, 37–48.

Stibbe, C. M., 2000. Lakonische Bronzegefässe aus *Capua. Antike Kunst*, 43, 4–16.

Stibbe, C. M., 2006. Eine archaische Bronzekanne in Basel. In: C.M. Stibbe, ed., *Agalmata. Studien zur griechisch-archaischen Bronzekunst*. Leuven: Peeters, 1–15.

Stibbe, C. M., 2008. Laconian Bronzes from the Sanctuary of Apollo Hyperteleatas near Phoniki (Laconia) and from the Acropolis of Athene. *Bulletin Antieke Beschaving*, 83, 17–45.

Tarditi, C., 1996. *Vasi di Bronzo in area Apula. Produzioni greche ed italiche di età arcaica e classica*. Galatina: Congedo Editore.

Tarditi, C., 2014. Il motivo del leone nell'Atene arcaica: diffusione e stile nella produzione ateniese di vasellame in bronzo. *Erga-Logoi*, 31–63.

Tarditi, C., 2016. *Bronze vessels from the Acropolis. Style and decoration in the Athenian production between the sixth and fifth centuries BC*. Roma: Quasar.

Tombolani, M., 1981. *Bronzi figurati etruschi, italici, paleoveneti e romani del Museo Provinciale di Torcello*. Roma: L'Erma di Bretschneider.

Szilágyi, J. G., 1968. L'oenochoe de Mitrovica. *Acta Antiqua Academiae Scientiarum Hungaricae*, 16, 117–131.

Weber, T., 1983. *Bronzekannen. Studien zu ausgewählten archaischen und klassischen Oinochoenformen aus Metall in Griechenland und Etrurien*. Frankfurt am Main: P. Lang.

Zanco, O., 1974. *Bronzi arcaici da Campovalano*, Roma: Soprintendenza alle Antichità degli Abruzzi.

Bronze Vessels from the Etruscan Necropolises of Bologna (540 – 350 BC): Preliminary Notes

Giulia Morpurgo

University of Bologna

giulia.morpurgo2@unibo.it

Abstract: This paper presents the preliminary results of ongoing research dedicated to the systematic study of the bronze vessels and *instrumentum domesticum* recovered in the Etruscan necropolises of Bologna, which were dated between the middle of 6th and the middle of the 4th centuries BC. Within these contexts, bronze vases and tools represent a fundamental part of the grave goods, recalling not only the themes of banquet and wine consumption. Therefore, the research will analyse this particular category of objects, focusing on the major related aspects, such as the stylistic and chronological sequence, the role within the local funeral ritual and the identification of the production centres.

Keywords: Etruscan Bronze Vessels; Necropolises of Bologna; Trade; Workshop; Funerary Ritual

The necropolises of the main Etruscan sites of the Po Valley represent one of the main fields of study for the Chair of Etruscology at Bologna University. Specifically, the research is focused on the chronological and cultural phase called "Certosa", between the 6th century BC and the progressive Gallic occupation in the 4th century BC (Govi 2009; 2017; Gaucci et al. 2018).

Between the XIX and XX centuries, more than 5000 tombs of this phase have been brought to light: an extraordinary amount of data, which stands out for its significance to Etruscan funerary archaeology.

These necropolises are not only some of the richest and most extensive contexts in the whole of Etruria, especially for the period in question, but they are also a highly privileged survey sample, favoured in particular by a deposition system generally based on single burials. Accordingly, the problems related to the analysis of grave goods within multiple depositions can be excluded, which are very frequent in the chamber tombs of the Tyrrhenian area.

A systematic analysis of these finds, aimed at the complete publication of the contexts, has been accompanied over time by thematic studies dedicated, *inter alia*, to individual categories of material (Macellari 2002; Pizzirani 2009; Morpurgo 2018). In particular, the research aspires to outline commercial trends relative to this cultural area and local production characteristics (for example, on black-glazed ware, both Attic and Etruscan, see Govi 1999; Gaucci in press and Gaucci et al. 2017; on stone sculpture in Bologna, see Govi 2015, with earlier bibliography; on the ware from the Etruscan Po Valley see, Mattioli 2013 and in press).

The study recently undertaken, which focuses on bronze vessels from the tombs of Bologna dating from the period between the middle of the 6th and the middle of the 4th centuries BC, fits into this framework. As literary sources testify, in this period the city of *Felsina*/Bologna distinguished itself, earning the title of *princeps Etruriae*. Thus, it could be assumed that the city had a leading role in economic, political and territorial reorganization in the Po Valley (Sassatelli – Govi 2013; Sassatelli 2014). For the present, the study is limited to vessels and domestic instruments. However, it could be extended someday to other categories documented in these contexts, such as candelabras and other items of furniture.

Even if some of these items have been published in studies dedicated to specific vase shapes (e.g. Stjernquist 1967; Shefton 1988; Bouloumié 1973; Vorlauf 1997; Giuliani Pomes 1954; 1957) or frequently mentioned for comparative purposes in literature, the complete set of bronzes destined for burials has never been the subject of a specific study. Accordingly, a general overview of the phenomenon is lacking, which could be the only way to appreciate fully the various implications related to this key category of Etruscan handicrafts.

For these reasons, systematic research is needed in order to focus accurately on many closely related aspects such as, for example, the stylistic and chronological classification, their function within the local funeral ritual and the identification of local productions and imports.

Although the project has just begun, this conference has been an extremely valuable opportunity to present a preliminary evaluation of the results so far achieved, emerging problems and future prospects.

A little more than one thousand Etruscan tombs in Bologna can be dated from the middle of the 6th to the middle of the 4th centuries BC, mostly distributed along the ancient main roads that led to the city.

First, the research has focused on compiling as complete a catalogue as possible of the preserved bronze items, precisely documenting the variety and types. The systematic census collected more than 200 finds (Diagram 37.1), a significant number that, by itself, clearly illustrates their key role in funerary ritual, even more so if we are to consider the frequent pillaging carried out in the past within these necropolises.

Three main areas, albeit to differing extents, played central roles in the selection of grave goods from this period: the *symposium*, the female *charis* and the sacred sphere.

Because of their prevalence, bronze items referring to the preparation and consumption of wine should first be mentioned. This represents a major theme within the local funerary ideology and its importance could possibly be seen as the most obvious reflection of the process of Hellenization that involved the community of Bologna/ *Felsina* from the Late Archaic period onwards. Therefore, grave goods generally contained materials related to this theme, in particular, bronze objects and Attic pottery, expertly selected and included within more or less complex sets. In spite of the wide diffusion of the ideological model, it actually took shape through a broad selection of combinations. This variety could be interpreted as the reflection of the composite horizontal and vertical stratigraphy of society, even if we are not always able to grasp clearly, what was undoubtedly obvious for people living in those times.

According to the available data, there are no complete bronze symposium sets featuring all those elements that refer to specific acts performed during the symposium. The metal items were an alternative or, more often, an addition to pottery. For example, bronze mixing vessels are completely absent, only Attic ceramic versions being recorded. On the contrary, among large vases used to hold wine metal *situlae* and *stamnoi* are recorded. Bronze *oinochoai* used for pouring are rather rare, confirming the preference given, also in this case, to imported Attic pottery (Govi 1999, 161). Conversely, some specific uses seem to be fulfilled only by metal objects such as *simpula*, *olpai* or *kyathoi* for drawing and/or dosing, and *cola* for filtering mixed and spiced wine. Finally, two other items complete the range of bronze vessels used for the symposium that were recovered in these contexts: the so-called tray, a well-documented vessel used for several purposes (Caramella 1995, 163–164; Castoldi 1995, 10–14; Nati 2008, 46–47), and, albeit more rarely, graters. The latter were associated with the preparation of *kykeòn*, a wine-based beverage seasoned with cheese and mentioned in Homeric poems.

The available documentation seems to highlight how metal objects connected to the *graeco more* symposium first appeared among grave goods at the end of the 6th century, persisting at least until the end of the 5th century and the beginning of the 4th century BC. However, a more detailed study reveals a heterogeneous diachronic distribution of finds, which shows a significant incidence between the end of the 6th and the middle of the 5th centuries BC with an increase in the second quarter of the 5th century (Diagram 37.2). From this viewpoint, this period proved to be the golden age of Etruscan Bologna.

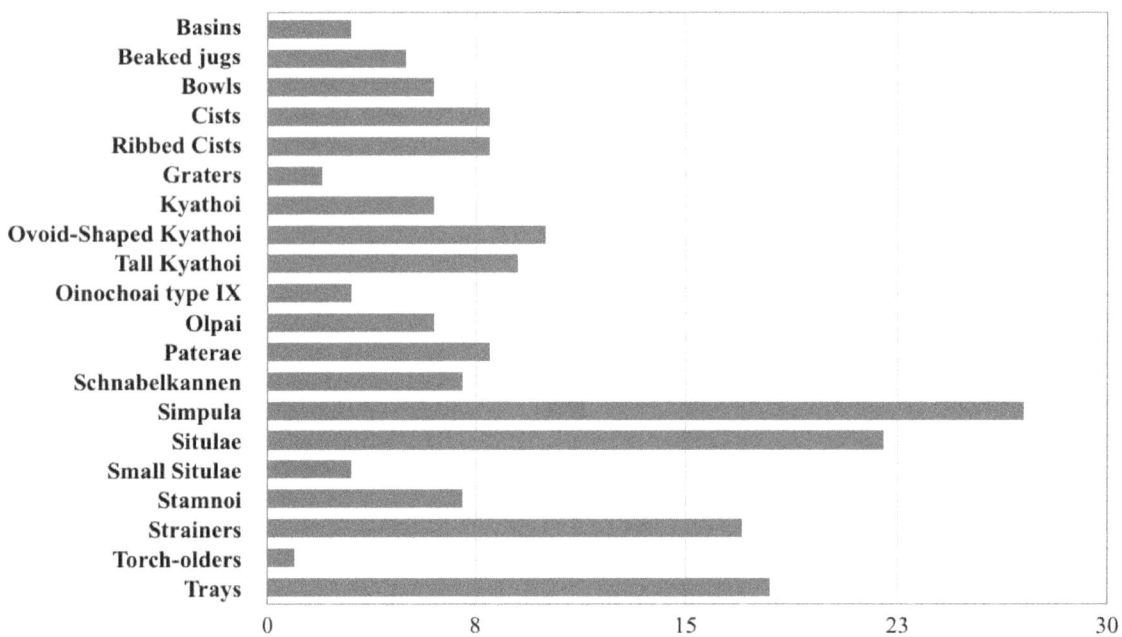

Diagram 37.1. Distribution of bronzes in the etruscan necropolises of Bologna by shape.

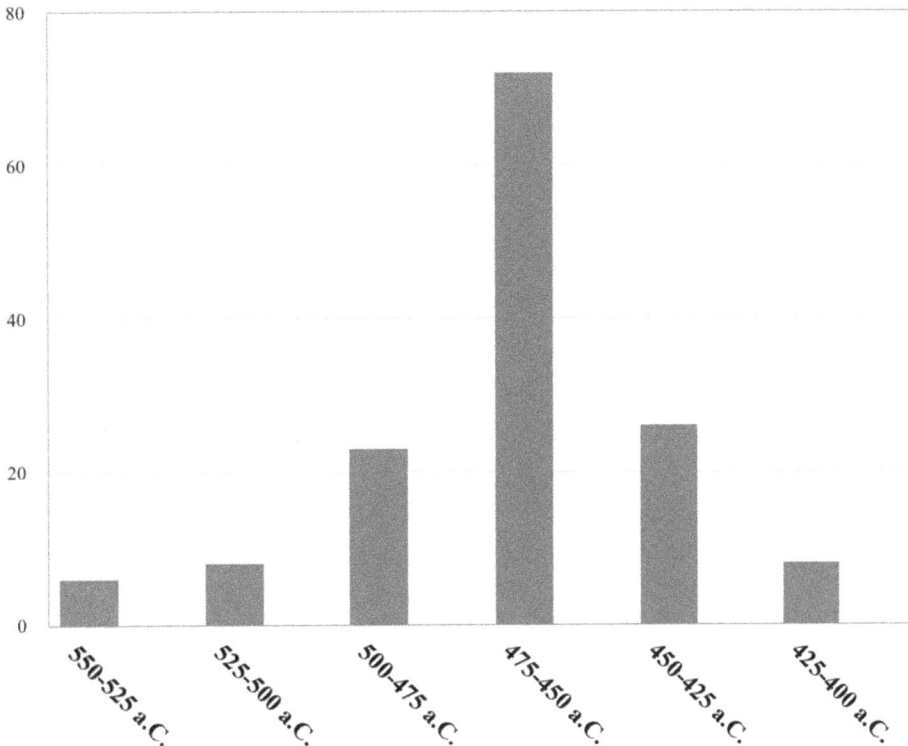

Diagram 37.2. Distribution of bronzes in the etruscan necropolises of Bologna by quarter century.

The spatial distribution is equally interesting: in spite of a considerable quantity of bronze vessels and utensils, their diffusion within the graves was much more limited. Frequently, various metal objects were assembled within a single funerary set with repeated combinations, hinting at specific logics.

Sets of grave goods combining all functions are rare and mainly dated from the second to the third quarter of the 5th century BC. As regards metal items, the selection of shapes shows considerable uniformity. According to documented cases, even the earliest, this fixed model consists of the stamnoid situla, ovoid *kyathos*, a pair of *simpula*, *colum* and tray, all of which were especially common shapes in the Etruscan Po Valley (Fig. 37.1). Clearly, these burials represent some of the most prestigious funerary contexts within the whole necropolis, where all the elements, even the monumental tomb-structure, seem to express the fact that they belonged to high-ranking individuals holding leading positions within the community.

A more concise reference to the consumption of wine is more frequent, a diffusion that reflects widespread wealth. In these cases, Attic pottery was found together with a single bronze vessel such as, for example, *simpula* and *colum*, or *simpula*, situlae, *kyathoi* and trays.

Thus, the documentation just reviewed, despite its diversity, proved the local community's total acceptance of a Greek-oriented model of wine consumption, with all its implications at a symbolic level. Other bronze vessels, always used to hold wine, seem to express a different place within the ritual, suggesting a possible reference to a local tradition.

In particular, this is the case with ribbed *cistae* with fixed handles (Fig. 37.2) forming part of the "Certosa Group" in the classification compiled by Berta Stjernquist (1967, 47–56). Thanks to the numerous finds, their production has been repeatedly attributed to a local workshop, operational between the end of the 6th and the beginning of the 4th centuries BC (Martelli 1982).

This shape, which claims a long, deep-rooted tradition in northern Italy and transalpine Europe, was found solely in cremations in Bologna, inside small pit-graves and large ditches. In both cases, the ribbed *cista* was always used as a cinerary urn and was never included with sets of bronze utensils and vessels used for the symposium.

As some recent studies suggest, the choice of this type of vessel might represent a sort of opposition to Attic kraters, which were used either to hold and prepare wine or to contain ashes. This choice possibly implies the deceased's desire to accentuate a tie with a genuine Etruscan tradition and with wine consumption customs differing from Greek ones (Sassatelli 2013). A clue to their strong social and ideological value is implied also by the spatial distribution of finds, usually recovered within coherent groups of graves that may indicate relationships among the deceased.

Although the symposium is definitely the dominant theme, the systematic study of necropolises dated to the "Certosa phase" is gradually bringing to light a much more complex and composite system of representation, which

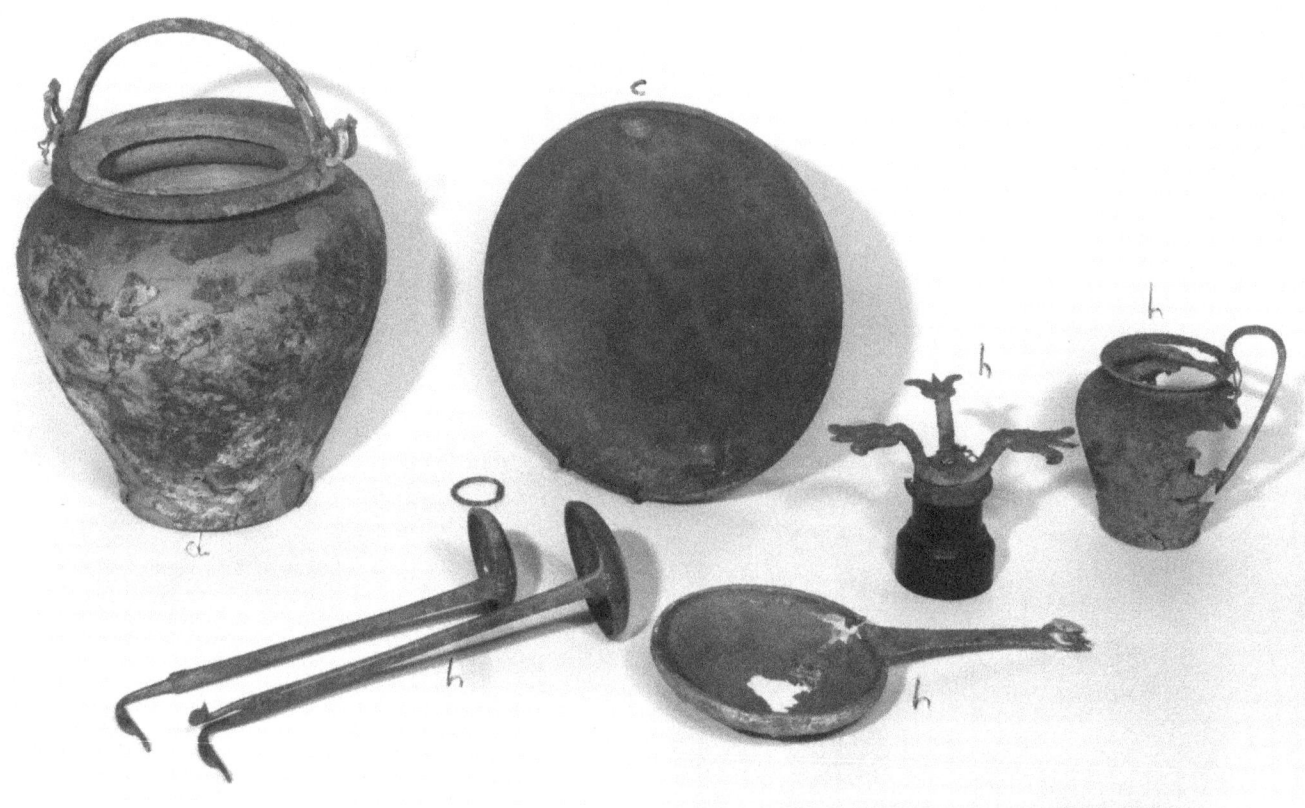

Fig. 37.1. Bologna, Certosa necropolis, tomb 117: bronze funerary equipment (from Govi 1999, 94, fig. 45; Archaeological Museum of Bologna).

Fig. 37.2. Bologna, Battistini necropolis, tomb 1: ribbed cist (from Morpurgo 2018, 779, pl. 172; ; Archaeological Museum of Bologna).

can no longer be related to this single model. Conversely, the plurality of social, political and religious reasons often firmly interwoven and displaying the local ideological heritage can be accurately analysed only as a complex funerary ritual system.

From this viewpoint, the study of bronze vessels and their mutual associations plays a prime role.

In particular, the self-representation of women and religion, often closely intertwined, seems to acquire a certain importance among the various semantic spheres.

The social value of marriage as a status symbol clearly comes to light in some tombs belonging to women of high social standing. Parts of the grave goods recall the theme through a recurring model, in which the bronze *cista* is usually combined with other elements, such as the *kibotion* and the mirror, which are closely linked to the *mundus muliebris* (Morpurgo 2017; in press).

In some of these tombs, the deposition of a tray and of a truncated cone-shaped *kyathos* also does not appear to be random. This combination could perhaps refer symbolically to pouring rites or even to the ritual washing of the bride, rather than to the symposium, hence creating a semantically coherent set with the aforementioned materials.

In Bologna, a similar combination consists of the bronze *oinochoe* and the bronze tray or *patera*. This pairing was endorsed on numerous occasions in previous studies and appears sometimes to form an independent unit referring to the ablutions that preceded the actual consumption of wine or, even in this case, to libation.

One of the most important finds in this sense is the Arnoaldi 133 tomb, a female burial dated to the middle of the 5th century BC (Macellari 2002, 320–323). Here, a coherent set, as outlined above, can be seen in the deposition of a bronze *phiale* and a bronze *Schnabelkanne* corresponding to Beazley Shape 6, of Etruscan origin albeit with northern Greek influences (Fig. 37.3). The latter vase has been the subject of in-depth studies over the years, which highlighted, *inter alia*, its close connection with the sacred sphere (Martelli 1976; Krauskopf 1980, 14, note 7; 1981; 2004; Colonna 1990).

The Certosa 86 tomb, also a female burial and dated to the second quarter of the 5th century BC, is another interesting complex from this point of view. The tomb contained a small tray and a Jacobsthal type *Schnabelkanne* (Bouloumié 1973, 12; Vorlauf 1997, 44, n. 60), perhaps not randomly included among grave goods that also featured an Attic bell-krater decorated with a libation scene (Govi 1999, 49–50, n. 20, fig. 19) (Fig. 37.4).

Besides the possibility to examine the presence and function of these elements within local rituals, which is not to be taken for granted as regards Etruria, places of production can be investigated, thanks to this extensive documentation. Indeed, the main obstacle to studying bronze vessels is the difficulty of attributing individual artefacts to specific artistic environments, including them within places of production that have already been identified or whose existence is testified by the artefacts themselves.

A preliminary and perhaps obvious observation is that there are no records of Greek bronze vessels in Bologna despite the large quantity of imported Greek pottery. The same statement can be extended to the whole of Etruscan Po Valley, suggesting that the demand was met entirely by Etruscan products.

Especially in the Late Archaic period, the area of Vulci distinguished itself among the cities that excelled in this production (Martelli 1983, 266; 1988; Riis 1998). However, the idea of various places of production is gradually taking hold, to such an extent that the whole of Etruria would seem to have been involved in this phenomenon (*Volsinii*, Chiusi, Populonia, Tarquinia and the Faliscan area). In general, the analysis of centres of production does not allow for a precise overview of the specific characteristics of each location, largely because of the mostly ordinary and standardised nature of the objects.

The theory that many bronze objects recovered in the Etruscan Po Valley may have been produced by local workshops has recently gained ground (e.g. Hostetter 1986, 201; Jurgeit 1986, 105–117; Sassatelli 1987, 79; Macellari 2002, 230, n. 10 and Pizzirani 2009, 73–74). Proof could lie in the vessels brought to light in this area, noteworthy for both quantity and chronology. Other important and relevant facts are the existence of a long and well-established tradition, especially in Bologna, and the identification of places of production, for example

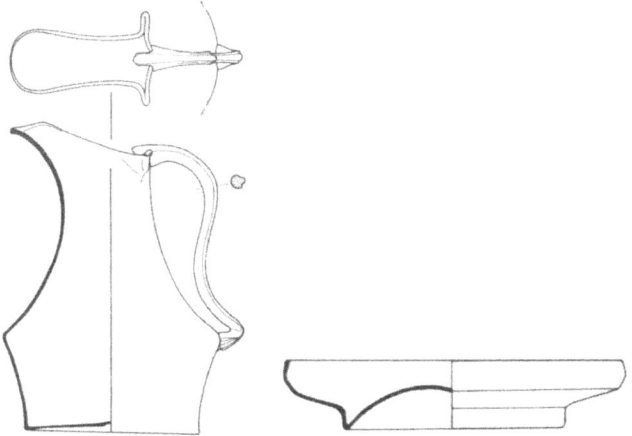

Fig. 37.3. Bologna, Arnoaldi necropolis, tomb 133: beaked jug and phiale (from Macellari 2002, pl. 37; Archaeological Museum of Bologna).

Fig. 37.4. Bologna, Certosa necropolis, tomb 86: funerary equipment (from Zannoni 1876–1884, pl. XXXXIII; Archaeological Museum of Bologna)

in Marzabotto, which are aligned on a technological and formal level with the Tyrrhenian area.

Therefore, a review of the issue seems to be necessary, starting with the objects and their characteristics. This is but a preliminary examination of an important and complex aspect of research, hindered by the fact that the types recorded herein belong to very common categories of bronze vessels, which rarely have plastic and decorative motifs that could serve as recognizable stylistic features. The brief observations that follow are to be taken as purely illustrative of possible approaches in a broad and systematic study, the only means by which to achieve the hoped-for results.

In this regard, an interesting case is represented by "ovoid-shaped *kyathoi*" corresponding to type C in the *kyathos* classifications compiled by Ludwig Husty (1990, 18–19).

This type, widespread in Etruria and beyond, is traditionally assigned to workshops of Orvieto and/or Vulci (Macellari 2002, 202, n. 2 and Sannibale 2008, 122–124, n. 69). It is no coincidence that the oldest example was found in Vulci's so-called "Tomb of the Warrior" in the Osteria necropolis, dated to 530–520 BC (Cristofani 1985, 300–303, n. 11.21.6). However, many scholars have previously stressed the significant concentration of this particular *kyathos* in the Etruscan Po Valley and especially in *Felsina*, where some of the earliest examples were recovered.

It is important to note that this type is recorded in Bologna and in the sites culturally linked to it and was included within symposium sets that, as already mentioned, are extremely uniform typologically (Fig. 37.1). In contrast, the shape is not recorded in Spina (Hostetter 2001). This difference can be attributed not only to the flow of trade, but also to specific ritual choices.

An examination of the available documentation makes it possible to single out two vessels with a handle ending in a feline paw on top of a leaf. The vases were both recovered in the Certosa 27 tomb, dated to the end of the 6th and the beginning of the 5th century BC, and in the Certosa 154 tomb, dated to 460–450 BC. The motif is frequently found on Etruscan *olpai* of the Weber III.BEtr.d type (1983, 399, pl. XV), but also occasionally recorded on ovoid *kyathoi* (Biella 2011, 191, II.b.1.6, pl. LXVI; Cianferoni 1992, 19, fig. 15; Gatti 1986, 54–55, fig. 213). Even if the earliest record refers once again to Vulci, an analysis of distribution seems to show a favoured presence of this category outside Tyrrhenian Etruria and especially in the Padania and Campania areas (Guzzo 1970; Baldelli 1977, 293, n. 12, fig. 4, tav. LXIII.1 und 3; Pontrandolfo – Rouveret 1992, 430–431).

The detail of the heart-shaped leaf, in one case additionally underlined inside with an engraved line (Fig. 37.5), prompts further observations. The motif is usually found on other categories of vessels, especially on the two-handled trays of A2 type of Gianluca Caramella's classification (Bini – Caramella – Buccioli 1995, 166), a production attributed to the Vulci area and especially popular in the Etruscan Po Valley (Fig. 37.6) and in transalpine Europe (Schaaf 1969; Naso 2003, 91, n. 139; Sannibale 2008, 58–59, n. 28–29). The presence of the same motif on a pair of Jacobsthal-type *oinochoai* is equally significant. These two, found in tombs of Bologna, were produced in Vulci and can be dated at the end of the 6th century BC (Bouloumié 1973, 14, pl. III, fig. 9–11; Vorlauf 1997, I, 166, type 2, II, 44–46, n. 61. 63, pl. 7.61 and 35.61).

In conclusion, even if a study of these ornamental details and of the vessels' morphological characteristics seems to refer to the Vulci area, their fortune in the Po Valley and especially in Bologna appears to be extremely significant, providing at least a clue to the existence of production

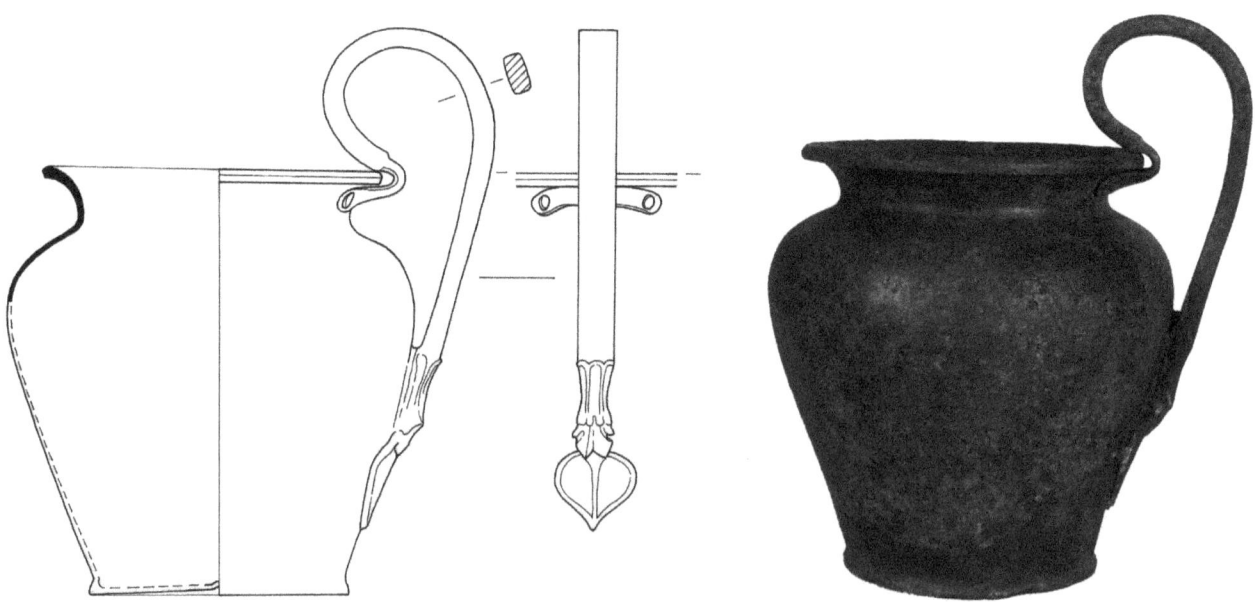

Fig. 37.5. Bologna, Certosa necropolis, tomb 154: ovoid-shaped kyathos (Archaeological Museum of Bologna).

Fig. 37.6. Bologna, Giardini Margherita necropolis, tomb 6: tray (from Govi 2005c, pl. 101; Archaeological Museum of Bologna).

intended for these markets. But the circulation of moulds and/or the transfer of skilled artisans, in relation to the undeniably Vulci-led tradition, cannot be discounted. As has already been proven for other categories of materials, it is very likely that, after importing bronze objects, the workshops of Bologna quickly equipped themselves to produce refined bronzes capable of satisfying the demands of customers with specific and high-level tastes.

Bibliography

Baldelli, G., 1977. Tomba con vasi attici da Monte Giove presso Fano. *Archeologia Classica*, 29, 277–309.

Biella, M.C., 2011. *La collezione Feroldi Antonisi de Rosa: tra indagini archeologiche e ricerca di un'identità culturale nella Civita Castellana postunitaria*. Pisa-Roma: F. Serra.

Bini, M.P. – Caramella, G. – Buccioli, S., 1995. *Materiali del Museo Archeologico Nazionale di tarquinia. I bronzi etruschi e romani, I–II*. Roma: G. Bretschneider.

Bouloumié, B., 1973. *Les oenochoes en bronze du type „Schnabelkanne" en Italie*. Rome: École Française de Rome.

Castoldi, M., 1995. Recipienti di bronzo greci, magnogreci ed etrusco-italici nelle civiche raccolte Archeologiche del Museo di Milano. In: *Rassegna di Studi del Civico Museo Archeologico e del Civico Gabinetto Numismatico di Milano: notizie dal chiostro del Monastero maggiore*, Supplementi, 15. Milano.

Cianferoni, C., 1992. I reperti metallici. In: A. Romualdi, ed., *Populonia in età ellenistica. I materiali delle necropoli*. Atti del seminario, Firenze 30 giugno 1986. Firenze: Il Torchio, 13–41.

Colonna, G., 1990. Vasi per bere e vasi per mangiare (a proposito di alcuni nomi etruschi di vasi). *Prospettiva*, 53–56/1, 30–32.

Cristofani, M., 1985. *Civiltà degli Etruschi*. Milano: Electa.

Gatti, E., 1986. Una tomba del Golasecca III A dal Sotto Ceneri. In: R. De Marinis, ed., *Gli Etruschi a Nord del Po*. Udine: Campanotto Editore, 54–55.

Gaucci, A., in press. A Challenging complexity. Black-Gloss Ware from the Hellenistica period in the Etruscan City of Spina. *BaBesch*, in press.

Gaucci, A. – Morpurgo, G. – Pizzirani, C., 2018. Ritualità funeraria in Etruria padana tra VI e III secolo a.C. Progetti di ricerca e questioni di metodo. In: G. Della Fina, ed., *Scavi d'Etruria*. Atti del XXV Convegno Internazionale di Studi sulla Storia e l'Archeologia dell'Etruria, Orvieto 15–17 dicembre 2017. Roma: Edizioni Quasar, 653–692.

Gaucci, A. – Minguzzi, V. – Gasparotto, G. – Zantedeschi, E., 2017. La ceramica etrusca a vernice nera di Valle Trebba: dati archeologici e archeometrici a confronto. In: Ch. Reusser, ed., *Spina. Neue Perspektiven der archaeologischen Erforschung*. Tagung an der Universität Zürich vom 4.–5. Mai 2012. Rahden/Westf., 127–138.

Giuliani Pomes, M.V., 1954. Cronologia delle situle rinvenute in Etruria. *Studi Etruschi*, 23, 149–194.

Giuliani Pomes, M.V., 1957. Cronologia delle situle rinvenute in Etruria. *Studi Etruschi*, 25, 39–84.

Govi, E., 1999. *Le ceramiche attiche a vernice nera di Bologna*. Imola: University Press Bologna.

Govi, E., 2009. L'archeologia della morte a Bologna: spunti di riflessione e prospettive di ricerca. In: R. Bonaudo – L. Cerchiai L. – C. Pellegrino, ed., *Tra Etruria, Lazio e Magna Grecia: indagini sulle necropoli*. Atti dell'Incontro di studio, Fisciano 5–6 marzo 2009. Paestum: Pandemos, 21–36.

Govi, E., ed., 2015. *Studi sulle stele etrusche di Bologna tra V e IV sec. a.C.* Roma: Edizioni Quasar.

Govi, E., 2017. Il progetto di ricerca sulla necropoli di Valle Trebba. Qualche spunto di riflessione. In: Ch. Reusser, ed., *Spina. Neue Perspektiven der archaeologischen Erforschung*. Tagung an der Universität Zürich vom 4.–5. Mai 2012. Rahden/Westf., 99–108.

Guzzo, P.G., 1970. Una classe di brocchette in bronzo. *Rendiconti Lincei*, Serie VIII, 87–110.

Hostetter, E., 1986. *Bronzes from Spina, 1. The figural classes. Tripod, kraters, basin, cista, protome, utensil stands, candelabra and votive statuettes*. Mainz am Rhein: Verlag Philip von Zabern.

Hostetter, E., 2001. *Bronzes from Spina, 2. Istrumentum domesticum*. Mainz am Rhein: Verlag Philip von Zabern.

Husty, L., 1990. Ein neuer etruskicher Gefässtyp ans der Frühlatènezeitlichen Adelsnekrpole Bescheid «Bei den Hübeln» Kreis Trier-Saarburg. *Trierer Zeitschrift*, 53, 7–54.

Krauskopf, I., 1980. La Schnabelkanne della collezione Watkins nel Fogg Art Museum e vasi affini. *Prospettiva*, 20, 7–16.

Krauskopf, I., 1981. Etruskische und griechische Kannen der Form VI im. 5. Jahrhundert. In: *Die Aufnahme fremder Kultureinflüsse und das Problem des Retardierens in der etruskischen Kunst*. Symposium des Deutschen Archäologenverbands, Mannheim 8.–10.1980. Mannheim: Vorstand des Deutschen Archaologen-Verbandes, 146–155.

Krauskopf, I., 2004. Wein-und Wasserkannen. Zur unterschiedlichen Exportsituation verschiedener etruskischer Schnabelkannen. In: M.A. Guggisberg, ed., *Die Hydria von Grächwil. Zur Funktion und Rezeption mediterraner Importe in Mitteleuropa im 6. und 5. Jahrhundert v. Chr*. Akten Internationales Kolloquium, Bern 12–13 Oktober 2001. Bern: Verlag Bernisches Historisches Museum, 127–135.

Jurgeit, F., 1986. *Cistenfüsse: etruskische und Praenestiner Bronzewerkstätten*. Roma: Consiglio Nazionale delle Ricerche.

Macellari, R., 2002. *Il sepolcreto etrusco nel terreno Arnoaldi di Bologna, 550 – 350 a.C.* Venezia: Marsilio editori.

Martelli, M., 1976. Recensione a A. Emiliozzi: "La Collezione Rossi Danielli nel Museo Civico di Viterbo". *Prospettiva*, 4, 42–46.

Martelli, M., 1982. Cista a cordoni di Cuma. In: Απαρχαι. *Nuove ricerche e studi sulla Magna Grecia e la Sicilia antica in onore di Paolo Enrico Arias*. Pisa: Giardini editori e stampatori, 185–190.

Martelli, M., 1983. Le manifestazioni artistiche. In: M. Cristofani, ed. *Gli Etruschi in Maremma. Popolamento e attività produttive*. Milano: Silvana, 223–284.

Martelli, M., 1988. La cultura artistica di Vulci arcaica. In: *Un artista etrusco e il suo mondo: il Pittore di Micali*. Roma: De Luca, 22–28.

Mattioli, C., 2013. *Atlante tipologico delle forme ceramiche di produzione locale in Etruria padana*. Bologna: Ante Quem.

Mattioli, C., in press. *Spina: abitato e necropoli di Valle Trebba. Aggiornamento all'Atlante tipologico delle forme ceramiche di produzione locale in Etruria padana*, in press.

Morpurgo, G., 2017. Sui kibotia tardo-arcaici dai sepolcreti etruschi di Bologna. *Studi Etruschi*, 79, 63–87.

Morpurgo, G., 2018. *I sepolcreti etruschi di Bologna nei terreni De Luca e Battistini (fine VI–inizi IV secolo a.C.)*. Bologna: Bononia University Press.

Morpurgo, G., in press. L'archeologia della salvezza a Bologna: una prospettiva di genere. In: *Iconografia e rituale funerario. I Seminari di Studi sul significato delle immagini nei contesti tombali*, Ravenna 10 dicembre 2018, in press.

Naso, A., 2003. *I bronzi etruschi e italici del Römisch-Germanisches Zentralmuseum*. Mainz: Römischgermanischen Zentralmuseum; Bonn: Habelt.

Nati, D., 2008. *Le necropoli di Perugia*. Città di Castello: Edimon.

Pontrandolfo, A. – Rouveret, A., 1992. *Le tombe dipinte di Paestum*. Modena: F. Cosimo Panini.

Pizzirani, C., 2009. *Il sepolcreto etrusco della Galassina di Castelvetro (Modena)*. Bologna: Ante Quem.

Riis, P.J., 1998. Vulcentia vetustiora. *A Study of Archaic Vulcian Bronzes*. Copenaghen: Munksgaard.

Sannibale, M., 2008. *La Raccolta Giacinto Guglielmi. Bronzi e materiali vari*. Città del Vaticano: L'Erma di Bretschneider.

Sassatelli, G., 1987. Un "nuovo" candelabro etrusco da Spina. Aspetti ellenizzanti nella cultura dell'Etruria Padana. In: *Celti ed Etruschi nell'Italia centro-settentrionale dal V secolo a.C. alla romanizzazione*. Atti del Colloquio Internazionale, Bologna 12–14 aprile 1985. Imola: University Press Bologna, 61–83.

Sassatelli, G., 2013. Etruschi, Veneti e Celti in area padana. Relazioni culturali e mobilità individuale. In: G. Della Fina, ed., *Mobilità geografica e mercenariato nell'Italia preromana*. Atti del XX Convegno Internazionale di Studi sulla Storia e l'archeologia dell'Etruria, Orvieto 14–16 dicembre 2012. Roma: Edizioni Quasar, 397–427.

Sassatelli, G., 2014. La Bologna etrusca tra Grecia ed Etruria. In: G. Sassatelli – A. Russo Tagliente, ed., *Il viaggio oltre la vita. Gli Etruschi e l'Aldilà tra capolavori e realtà virtuale*. Bologna: Bononia University Press, 99–109.

Sassatelli, G. – Govi, E., 2013. Etruria on the Po and the Adriatic Sea. In: J. MacIntosh Turfa, ed., *The etruscan world*. London and New York: Routledge, 281–300.

Schaaf, U., 1969. Versuch einer regionalen Gliederung frühlatènezeitlicher Fürstengräber. In: O.-H. Frey, ed., *Marburger Beiträge Zur Archäologie der Kelten. Festschrift für Wolfang Dehn zum 60*. Bonn: Taschenbuch, 187–202.

Shefton, B.B., 1988. Der Stamnos. In: W. Kimmig, hrsg. *Das Kleinaspergle. Studien zu einem Fürstengrabhügel der frühen Latènezeit bei Stuttgart*. Stuttgart: Kommissionsverlag, Konrad Theiss Verlag, 104–152.

Stjernquist, B., 1967. *Ciste a cordoni (Rippenzisten): produktion, funktion, diffusion*. Bonn: Habelt.

Vorlauf, D., 1997. *Die etruskischen Bronzeschnabelkannen. Eine Untersuchung anhand der technologisch-typologischen Methode, I–II*. Espelkamp: Marie Leidorf.

The Kegs from the "Celtic" Graves of Santa Paolina di Filottrano. Misadventures and misunderstandings

Nicoletta Frapiccini

National Archaeological Museum of the Marche

nicoletta.frapiccini@beniculturali.it

Abstract: The National Archaeological Museum of the Marche, in Ancona, exhibits the extraordinary funerary assemblage of the richest grave from the "Celtic" necropolis of Santa Paolina di Filottrano, which includes jewels, attic and bronze vessels and the reconstruction of a keg. This is not, however, the only specimen from the necropolis.

A second keg, very similar to the first one, was discovered in another tomb. Starting from the archival data, together with the comparison of the photographic documentation, this article identifies the original context of these kegs, one of which has recently undergone a new restoration and metallographic analysis.

Keywords: Keg; *cista;* Celtic Necropolis; Supplies; Ficoroni *cista*

The necropolis of Santa Paolina di Filottrano, not far from Ancona, was discovered in 1911, during agricultural work. The archaeological excavations continued until 1913, revealing twenty-eight graves, dating to around the mid of the 4th c. B.C. (Baumgärtel 1937; Landolfi 1987; Landolfi 1998a, Belfiore, in press). The rich funerary offerings in some of the graves, including gold jewelry, precious bronze vessels, and Celtic weapons (such as helmets and swords), very similar to the good graves of the nearby necropolises of Montefortino di Arcevia (Brizio 1901; Landolfi 1991a; Kruta 1992; Landolfi 1997) and San Filippo di Osimo (Dall'Osso 1915; Landolfi 1998b), led to the hypothesis that this too was a Celtic necropolis. Today, new and extensive research is in progress, starting with funerary offerings from the necropolis of Montefortino di Arcevia (Landolfi – Piana Agostinetti, in press), in an attempt to better define the contours of this distinct context. These studies help to clarify the real importance of the presence of the Senones to the north and especially to the south of the Esino River, where the literary sources placed the boundary of the Celtic territories (Landolfi 1987; Piana Agostinetti 1992; Kruta 1999). The necropolis of Santa Paolina di Filottrano, in particular, located south of the Esino River, attests to an encroachment of this border.

We know that two kegs come from the necropolis of Santa Paolina, and we can find their first descriptions in the excavation journal (Archive of Superintendence ABAP Marche, AV/4/3,5). The first was discovered in 1911, among the grave goods of the richest tomb (2), which yielded only a few bronze traces of a wooden keg. The second one was in tomb 20 (Fig. 38.1), a female burial discovered in 1913, which had rich funerary offerings, including bronze vessels, a mirror, gold and amber jewellery, recently studied by Valentina Belfiore (in press).

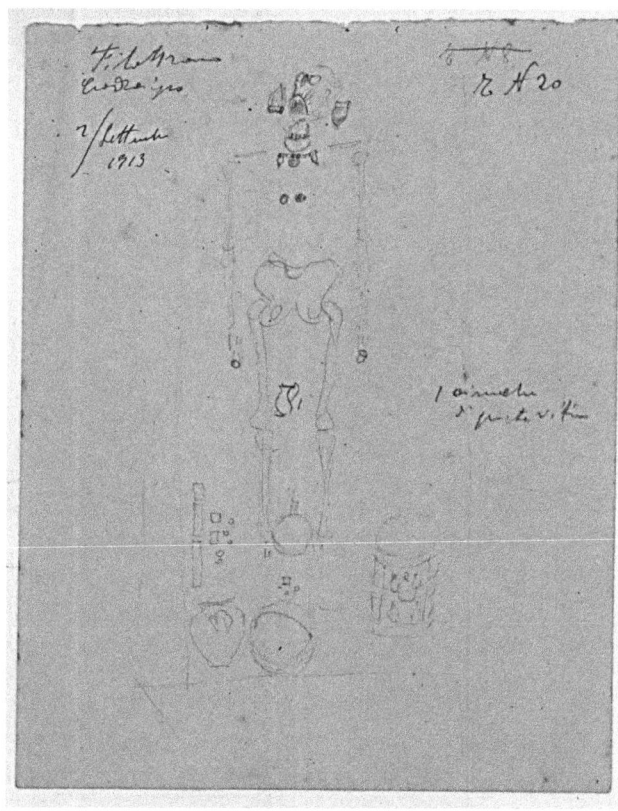

Figure 38.1. Santa Paolina di Filottrano, Tomb 20. Original drawings of the grave the and its supply (1913) (By Belfiore 2016).

Despite the description in the excavation journal, the two specimens are sometimes confused with each other. In that journal there is a description of the keg from grave 2 at the moment of the discovery, consisting of "bronze fragments with small impression bulbs and twisted nails, which were used to cover an unrecognizable object found near the foot (of the deceased)". The report also records the presence of fragments of a twisted bronze "double" handle, belonging to the same unrecognizable object. Four years later, in 1915, Innocenzo Dall'Osso described a cylindrical case among some funerary objects, without specifying the number of the tomb, which today we can recognize as grave 2. He also published a photo of this "wooden case" (Fig. 38.2), which shows two bronze bands at both ends that join the contiguous sides; a third bronze band is almost at the center, with rings hooked at a regular distance, one of which had the remains of a chain, very similar to those of the Praenestine *cistae*, and very similar to the wood, leather and bronze specimen in the National Museum of the Villa Giulia, in Rome (Bordenache Battaglia 1979, 18–21, n. VIII, Pl. XX). Four hemispherical bronze elements had been arranged in pairs between the bands, described as "big bolts". The two upper ones were hemispherical and smaller, while the lower ones were larger and almost conical in shape; probably four other elements were on the opposite site of the case. The opening of the case was at the top and a circular bronze lid with a handle closed it. Dall'Osso wrote of a "double handle" (1915, 250. 261), though in the photo it is clearly distinguishable as only one handle. All the bands had the same punched decoration, consisting of opposite pod-shaped elements along the edges, and a row of small circles in the middle.

In the following edition of the necropolis of Santa Paolina di Filottrano, in 1937, E. Baumgärtel for the first time attributed to the supplies of tomb 2 not a *cista*, but rather a keg (Fig. 38.3). We may suppose that in the meantime there was a revision of Dall'Osso's interpretation and a new re-assembly of the same bands. This hypothesis is perhaps supported by Baumgärtel, who wrote: "a considerable part of the bronze bands are restored" (1937, 242–243). The keg had "bronze hoops at both ends", which also covered the edges. Flat bronze plates bounded the keg above and below, joined along a side by a narrow band with rings, the only one preserved. The flat plates and the central band were very important, because they determined the length of the barrel, as Baumgärtel noted. However, the central band could be a fragment of the one on the case of Dall'Osso. In fact, the keg had only two rings, and there was not one on the opposite site, while the so-called *cista* showed a band that ran all around the case, with five rings in front and probably other rings on the opposite side. Nevertheless, the right ring still had the first link of a chain, exactly like one ring on the band of the so-called *cista*. The keg had a mouth with enlarged neck and horizontal rim, covered by a lid with a low, squarish arching handle passing through two rings with slender bud finials. The remains of a chain hung from the handle. The description of the ends reveals that there were bronze plates, which probably covered only a part of the surface. In the middle, a protruding element (described as a *tutulus*) had been fixed, and each side had a movable, twisted handle, as the excavation journal reported. Four hemispherical elements finish the top, while four conical feet supported the keg. All the bands were adorned with pod-shaped elements

Figure. 38.2. The keg from Santa Paolina di Filottrano, Tomb 2, reconstructed as a *cista* (by Innocenzo Dall'Osso, 1915 (by Innocenzo Dall'Osso, 1915).

Figure 38.3. The keg from Santa Paolina di Filottrano, Tomb 2, in a new reconstruction (by E. Baumgärtel 1937).

along the edges, among which ran a row of small circles. The side plate, on the other hand, is narrower, and presents only the opposing pod-shaped elements.

Today we have a new reconstruction of this keg (Fig. 38.4), which unfortunately has lost the spout, the original lid, the central band with rings, the flat plates, and the hemispherical elements. Nevertheless, we can recognize one of the two twisted handles on the top, the lid (but without the chain), the four conical feet, and the remains of the hoops, which cover only one edge and the adjoining side, where the central plate is located. Lacking the central band, the dimensions are only hypothetical, based upon those of the keg in tomb 20 from the same necropolis, which is much better preserved.

As for the lost central band, it looked like a foreign element of the keg, and such an element is not attested on any other similar specimen. It would seem to belong to a *cista* from which the other elements might have been lost. Dall'Osso probably integrated it with the remains of the keg, thereby creating a hybrid object, while on the specimen studied by Baumgärtel only a part of it was used as a keg band.

Dall'Osso also published a second keg, again as a *cista*, without the reference to the grave of origin (1915, 263. 265. 267–271). He specified that this fragile case had been dug up with the surrounding clod of earth and was subsequently restored in the laboratory. He published the figure of this keg before and after the restoration, and he describes it as a vertical case, pointing out the particular position of the opening in the middle of the body, rather than at the top. The excavation journal recorded the discovery of this second keg in tomb 20, and the drawings of the grave and its contents clearly show that it is surely the same object described and illustrated in the *Guide* by Dall'Osso. Nevertheless, some scholars attributed this precious keg to tomb 2, confusing this specimen with the previous one.

Later, in 1934, Pirro Marconi and Luigi Serra (1934, 21–22. 55) published the same object, once again as a *cista*, in their *Guide* to the new display in the Museum of Ancona, without reference to the grave from which it came. This new *Guide* described the case in the correct, horizontal position. Baumgärtel also recognized this specimen as a keg, doubtfully referring it to tomb 20 (1937, 243, Pl. XXV, fig. 2, Pl. XXVII, fig. 3 – this one erroneously attributed in the legend to grave II). Thanks to painstaking work in the laboratory, this keg still preserves all the bronze bands and the other elements in the correct position and, therefore, its dimensions are reliable (Fig. 38.5). This specimen still has the flat plate at the top, at whose center is the bronze spout, with short neck and flared rim, divided by a groove. A bronze lid, decorated with concentric and alternating rows of small circles and pod-shaped elements, closes the mouth. A bronze handle, with the remains of a chain, lifted the lid. The handle was secured to the lid by loops, through which the ends passed. At the bottom of the lid, the only loop preserved continues with a curved bar, perhaps useful to fix a plug, which perfectly matched the mouth. A refined cast decoration enriches the upper part of the keg, consisting of six swans in a resting position. Four of them are located at the four corners of the plate, facing outwards, while the other two are on both sides of the mouth of the keg, and bear two two-eyed attachments on their backs, through which the ends of the double handle are inserted. These two swans are so near to the lid that their beaks help to close it. Various hoops and bands cover the keg: two hoops are on each end, which fold over the edges, joining with the bands on the sides, in the centers of which is a round plate. Three bands on each side join the ends, while another one is placed vertically, in the center of the keg. It stands on four hemispherical feet attached to the lower bronze plate. The bands show the same decoration, only slightly different from the previous keg, consisting of pod-shaped elements alternating with circles along the edges, divided by a row of circles.

Figure 38.4. The current reconstruction of the keg from Santa Paolina di Filottrano, Tomb 2 (Photo by Nicoletta Frapiccini).

Figure 38.5. The keg from Santa Paolina di Filottrano, Tomb 20 (Photo by Nicoletta Frapiccini).

The ends, instead, show a circular band adorned by an external row of pod-shaped elements and an internal row of circles, which is reversed in the central plate.

This specimen from tomb 20 bears a close resemblance to a keg from Gualdo Tadino (Micozzi 2014), and also to another keg, until now unpublished, from tomb 9 of the "Gaulish" necropolis of San Filippo di Osimo (Fig. 38.6). This keg, mentioned by Marconi and Serra (1934) and by Baumgärtel (1937), has the same cast elements, consisting of six swans placed on the top plate, three of which have been reconstructed in modern times. The manufacture of these birds appears less refined than those of Santa Paolina, but they are of the same typology. Hoops, bands and plates have a slightly different adornment, consisting of more elongated pod-shaped elements, including a row of circles, while on the side the bronze plate covers the entire surface, as on the keg from Gualdo Tadino. At the center of this plate there is an isolated, circular element, surrounded by a smooth space and by three concentric series of circles and pod-shaped elements.

Figure. 38.6. The keg from San Filippo di Osimo, probably Tomb 9 (half of 4th c. B.C.) (Photo by Nicoletta Frapiccini).

A keg from Vallicelle di Camerino (Fig. 38.7) bears similar cast decoration (Landolfi 1999; Salvini 2003): there are four swans at the four corners and a couple of deer are placed at one of the attachments of the double handle, having been compared to similar wooden boxes in the form of animals (hind, dove, swan) from Praeneste, published by Bordenache Battaglia (1990, Pl. CCCXXXIX. CCCLXXXIV). This keg, furthermore, presents a new element in the punched decoration, which consists of a series of palmettes alternating with the usual pod-shaped motifs and circles. Also in this specimen, the circular plate at the end most probably covered the entire surface.

Finally, the analysis of the bronze plates generally assigned to a keg from Moscano di Fabriano (Fig. 38.8a) revealed that they could hardly fit this vessel, both for their shape and

Figure 38.7. Keg from Camerino, Vallicelle (MC) (by Landolfi 1999).

Figure 38.8a. Moscano di Fabriano (AN), isolated Tomb, bronze plates and a handle wrong attributed to a keg (Photo by Nicoletta Frapiccini).

their thickness. Instead, they would seem more suitable to covering other objects, perhaps a *cista*, or a box. However, the punched decoration is very interesting because it includes the same decoration of circles as the kegs, to which are added palmettes in the so-called Waldalgesheim style. In the same burial, moreover, a grater bears pod-shaped motifs identical to those on the kegs (Fig. 38.8b). This decorative repertoire is widespread not only on the plates of some helmets from Monte Bibele, published by Vitali (1988, 241–242, fig. 3, 280–281), but also on swords from Santa Paolina di Filottrano and Moscano di Fabriano, published by Landolfi (1998c, 159–162) and Rapin (2008, 243–246, fig. 3), and on the cheekguards of a helmet from San Filippo di Osimo (Fig. 38.8c).

These additional local comparisons widen the area of diffusion of such productions, and connect even more clearly the decoration of the kegs to the Celtic milieu. The decorative repertoire, like the punching technique, suggests that this production could perhaps be ascribed to local workshops, which would have given rise to a mixture of Praeneste's repertoire (handles and cast decoration) with some elements of Celtic taste. In this regard, see the interesting reflections of Marina Micozzi (2014, 341, with bibliography).

The use of these kegs is still in doubt. The hypothesis that they contained wine, to be extracted with a *kyathos* (as Jurgeit 2006, 594–595 and Micozzi 2014, 341–342), seems to be not entirely convincing, owing to the difficulties imposed by the narrow mouth and the shape.

The representation, on the Ficoroni *cista*, of a young man coming down from the Argo ship holding a keg in his right

Figure 38.8b. Moscano di Fabriano (AN) isolated Tomb, bronze grater with punched decoration of pod-shaped elements (Photo by Nicoletta Frapiccini).

Figure 38.8c. San Filippo di Osimo, Tomb 1, Cheekguards of helmet decorated with punched circles (Photo by Nicoletta Frapiccini).

hand and a *cista* in the left, and probably heading towards a source of water, led to the belief that the keg was used to draw water (Hill 1938, 276–277; Dohrn 1972; Bordenache Battaglia 1990, 211–226, n. 68 and Jurgeit 2006, 589–595). Nevertheless, in the same scene there appear many amphoras, one of which is located just below the fountain, clearly assigning this function to the amphora, not the keg. Furthermore, the young Argonaut with the keg and the *cista* turns his back to the fountain and seems instead to be heading towards the central group, where Pollux ties Amycus to a tree in the presence of Athena. Here is also represented a young man with a cage vase and a strigil, which strongly indicate care of the body after athletic competition. Perhaps the keg contained oil and was intended for this function which would have been well served by a narrow mouthpiece, its closure secured by a wooden or cork stopper. This connection with body-care, both male and female, could also be revealed by the presence of the cast zoomorphic decoration. Representations of birds and deer are often seen in relation to toiletry objects, such as wooden boxes containing make-up, and the mirror-handle from Praeneste, found within the same Ficoroni *cista* and other exemples. In particular, at Santa Paolina di Filottrano in the female tomb 2, the keg was found in association with a mirror, a cage vase and, perhaps, a *cista* (?), while in tomb 20 it was found in association with a mirror and a glass alabastron.

The valuable content, moreover, would be appropriate to such refined vessels, documented only by very few specimens. It cannot be excluded that they could have been more widespread, perhaps made only of wood and leather, without the precious bronze elements, which have been preserved until today in these rare examples.

Bibliography

Baumgärtel, E., 1937. The Gaulish Necropolis of Filottrano in the Ancona Museum. *The Journal of the Royal Anthropological Institute of Great Britain and Ireland*, LXVII, 231–286.

Belfiore, V., in press. The 'gaulish' necropolis of Santa Paolina di Filottrano (Ancona): the unpublished tomb 20. Some preliminary remarks. In: *L'età delle trasformazioni: l'Italia medio-adriatica tra il V e il IV sec. a.C. Nuovi modelli di autorappresentazione delle comunità a confronto e temi di cultura materiale. Atti del workshop internazionale*. Chieti 2016.

Bordenache Battaglia, G., 1979. *Le ciste prenestine. I.1 Corpus*. Roma: CNR

Bordenache Battaglia, G., 1990. *Le ciste prenestine. I.2 Corpus*. Roma: CNR

Brizio, E., 1901. Il sepolcreto gallico di Montefortino di Arcevia. *MAL*, IX, cc. 617–791.

Dall'Osso, I., 1915. *Guida illustrata del Museo Nazionale di Ancona*. Ancona: Stab. tip. cooperativo.

Dohrn, T., 1972. *Die Ficoronische Ciste in der Villa Giulia in Rom*. Berlin: Gebr. Mann Verlag

Hill, D. Kent, 1938. Notes of some bronzes made at Praeneste. *StEtr*, XII, 271–277.

Jurgeit, F., 2006. I recipienti a barilotto. *Scienze dell'Antichità. Storia Archeologia Antropologia*, 13, 589–595.

Kruta, V., 1992. Materiali senonici nel Piceno e arte celtica. In: *La civiltà Picena nelle Marche. Studi in* onore di Giovanni Annibaldi. Ancona, 10–13 luglio 1988. Ripatransone: Maroni, 388–401.

Landolfi, M., 1987. Presenze galliche nel Piceno a sud del fiume Esino. In: D. Vitali, ed., *Celti ed Etruschi nell'Italia centrosettentrionale dal V sec. a.C. alla romanizzazione. Atti del Colloquio Internazionale.* Bologna 12–14 aprile 1985. Imola: Santerno Edizioni. 443–468.

Landolfi, M., 1991a. Montefortino d'Arcevia. In: *I Celti.* Milano: Bompiani. 722–723.

Landolfi, M., 1991b. I Senoni dell'Adriatico dopo la battaglia di Sentinum. *Etudes Celtiques*, XXVIII, 219–234.

Landolfi, M., 1997. Montefortino di Arcevia. In: M. Pacciarelli, ed., *Acque, grotte e dei. 3000 anni di culti preromani in Romagna, Marche e Abruzzo.* Imola: Musei Civici. 172–179.

Landolfi, M., 1998a. Filottrano – Loc. Santa Paolina. In: E. Percossi Serenelli, ed., *Museo Archeologico Nazionale delle Marche. Sezione Protostorica. I Piceni.* Falconara: ERREBI, 166.

Landolfi, M., 1998b. Osimo – Loc. San Filippo – Necropoli. In: E. Percossi Serenelli, ed., *Museo Archeologico Nazionale delle Marche. Sezione Protostorica. I Piceni.* Falconara: ERREBI, 163–164.

Landolfi M. 1998c. Fabriano – Loc. Moscano. Contrada Serroni. In: E. Percossi Serenelli, ed., *Museo Archeologico Nazionale delle Marche. Sezione Protostorica. I Piceni.* Falconara: ERREBI, 159–162.

Landolfi, M., 1999. Decorazioni zoomorfe di bronzo. In: L. Franchi Dall'Orto, ed., *Piceni Popolo d'Europa.* Roma: De Luca, p. 279, n. 617.

Landolfi, M. – Piana Agostinetti, P., (in press). La necropoli celtica di Montefortino d'Arcevia: nuove ricerche. In: *Contacts et acculturation dans l'Etrurie classique: images, notions, artefacts. Colloque International.* Roma, 2–3 ottobre 2017.

Marconi, P., Serra, L., 1934. *Il Museo Nazionale delle Marche in Ancona.* Roma: La libreria dello Stato.

Piana Agostinetti, P., 1992. Sul territorio dei Senoni: un contributo toponomastico. In: *La civiltà Picena nelle Marche. Studi in onore di Giovanni Annibaldi.* Ancona, 10–13 luglio 1988. Ripatransone: Maroni, 402–431.

Rapin, A., 2008. Les Celtes et leurs voisins septentrionaux: nouveau outil d'analyses pour l'armament leténien du sud de l'Europe aux Ve et IVe s. av. J.-C. In: D. Vitali – S. Verger, ed., *Tra mondo celtico e mondo italico. La necropolis di Monte Bibele. Atti della Tavola Rotonda.* Roma, 3–4 ottobre 1997, 237–268.

Salvini, M., 2003. Il territorio camerte: un crocevia. In: *I Piceni e l'Italia medio-adriatica. Atti del XXII Convegno di Studi Etruschi ed Italici.* Ascoli Piceno – Teramo – Ancona, 9–13 aprile 2000. Roma: Istituti Editoriali e Poligrafici Internazionali, 171–180.

Vitali, D., 1988. Elmi di ferro e cinturoni a catena. Nuove proposte per l'archeologia del Celti in Italia. *Jahrb. Röm-Germ. Zentralmuseum Mainz*, 35, 239–284.

39

Bronzeobjekte aus der römischen Garküche auf dem Monte Iato (PA)

Eva Riediker-Liechti

Universität Zürich

eva.riediker-liechti@uzh.ch

Abstract: Between 1992 and 2007, the Institute of Archaeology of the University of Zurich excavated a Roman tavern on Monte Iato (Sicily). The numerous finds come from a massive destruction layer, which is possibly linked to an earthquake in the Early Imperial Period. This closed context allows the reconstruction of the inventory of the tavern. In addition to various pottery fragments some bronze objects were discovered. The detailed analysis of these items allows answering questions regarding the furnishings of the building, whereas the comparison with taverns at Pompeii and Herculaneum reveals possible peculiarities of the bar at Ietas. Moreover, through this study we may gain insight into the daily life of a Roman settlement in Sicily during the 1st century AD.

Keywords: Roman Sicily; Tavern; Ietas

Einleitung: Lage und Befund

Der Monte Iato, etwa 30 km südwestlich von Palermo gelegen, befindet sich im Hinterland Siziliens. Er erhebt sich hinter den heutigen Städten S. Cipirello und S. Giuseppe Iato. Auf dem Hügelplateau entstand im 8. Jh. v. Chr. eine Siedlung mit dem griechischen Namen *Iaitas* (später lat. *Ietas*), die bis ins Jahr 1246 bewohnt war, als Kaiser Friedrich II. die Stadt belagerte und zerstörte.

Die römische Phase begann laut Diodorus Siculus nach dem Ersten Punischen Krieg, als sich die Einwohner von Ietas den Römern ergaben. Zuvor war die Stadt Teil des punischen Herrschaftsgebietes (Diod. 23.18.5). Plinius der Ältere erwähnte, dass Ietas eine *civitas stipendiara* war (Plin. Nat. 3.91), also eine abgabepflichtige Siedlung.

Das Gebäude, welches im Folgenden Thema sein soll, liegt direkt südlich des Forums der römischen Stadt, mit einer eigens erbauten Verbindung zum Forum in Form einer Rampe (Mohr et al. 2018, 4–7). Es wurde zwischen 1992 und 2007 durch das Institut für Archäologie (Fachbereich Klassische Archäologie) der Universität Zürich freigelegt. Zum Vorschein kamen die Überreste eines Baus, der 4,10 x 21,00 m misst, einen rechteckigen Grundriss aufweist und aus zwei Räumen besteht, Raum A und Raum B (Fig. 39.1). Zahlreich aufgefundene Fragmente von Ess-, Trink- und Kochgefäßen, eine eingebaute, gemauerte Theke, diverse Tierknochenfunde sowie ein Backofen führten

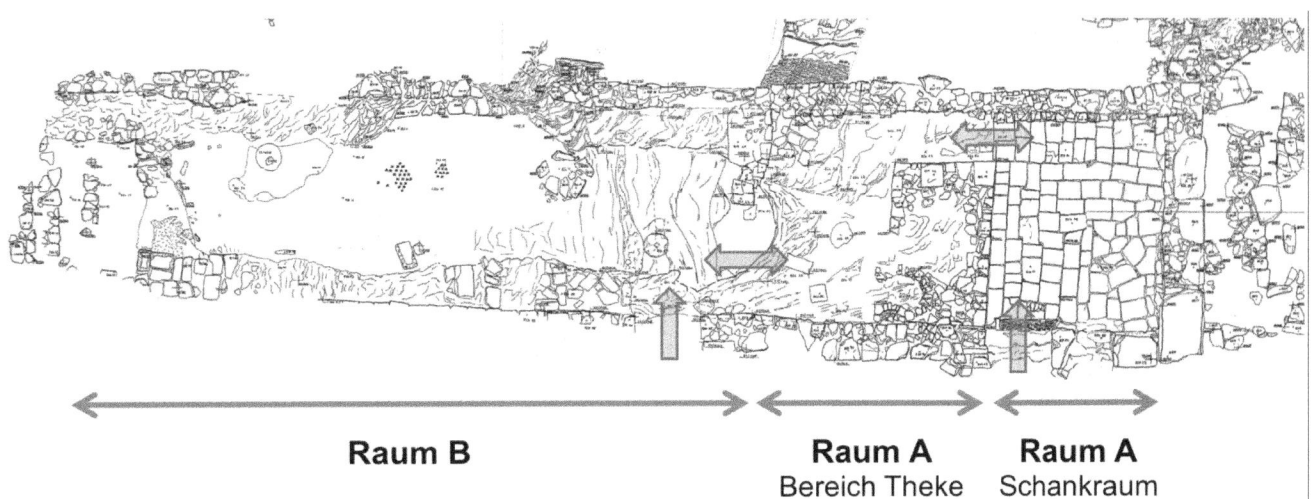

Fig. 39.1. Monte Iato, Grundriss der Garküche. Steinplan: Zürcher Ietas Grabung.

zur Deutung des Gebäudes als Garküche (lat. *popina*) (Isler 2001, 72). Die Funde stammen aus einer mächtigen Zerstörungsschicht, auf die man in beiden Räumen stieß. Die Zerstörung ist wohl auf ein Erdbeben zurückzuführen, das sich auch in anderen Bereichen der antiken Stadt nachweisen lässt, zum Beispiel im sog. Peristylhaus 1 (Hedinger 1999, 294–295). Aufgrund der Datierungen der Funde aus der Zerstörungsschicht muss dieses Ereignis in der frühen Kaiserzeit, um die Mitte des 1. Jh. n. Chr., stattgefunden haben.

Dieser geschlossene Befund erlaubte es, das gesamte Inventar der *popina* zu rekonstruieren. Damit ist es erstmals möglich, nicht nur die Einrichtung, sondern auch die Ausstattung einer kaiserzeitlichen Garküche umfassend vorzulegen und im Detail zu analysieren. Eine solche Analyse erfolgte im Rahmen einer Dissertation, die von der Autorin verfasst wurde und bereits vorliegt. Sie wird demnächst in Form einer Monographie in der Reihe „Zürcher Archäologische Forschungen" erscheinen. Die Katalognummern in diesem Artikel stammen aus der Dissertation.

Funde: Einleitung

Insgesamt wurden in der Zerstörungsschicht der *popina* 1623 Objekte entdeckt. Die Keramik macht die Hauptmenge der Funde aus und ist mit 72,6% vertreten (1178 Mindestindividuen). Sie lässt sich in Tafelgeschirr (20,9% der Funde) und Gebrauchskeramik (51,6%) unterteilen. Des Weiteren kamen in den beiden Räumen aber auch Objekte aus Eisen, Bronze und Glas sowie Öllampen und Münzen zum Vorschein.

Bronzeobjekte sind im Fundspektrum mit 3,5% vertreten. Es handelt sich um 57 Mindestindividuen, die nachfolgend im Detail besprochen werden.

Funde: Geräte aus Bronze

In diese Kategorie fallen 11 Bronzebleche, die als Beschläge von Truhen, Kästchen oder Möbeln aus Holz zu interpretieren sind. Dazu kommen drei Nägel, die jeweils noch in einem Plättchen aus Bronze stecken (z.B. Fig. 39.2). Diese drei Beispiele können ebenfalls als Beschläge gedeutet werden.

Toilettgeräte sind in der Garküche mit acht Objekten vertreten: Drei Spiegelscherben (für 1862 vgl. Deschler-Erb 1996, Nr. 193–199), zwei Ohrlöffel (vgl. Riha 1986, Nr. 264–401), zwei Strigiles (vgl. Riha 1986, Nr. 59–70) und eine Spatelsonde (Fig. 39.3) (vgl. Riha 1986, Nr. 587).

Bei einem weiteren Bronzeobjekt handelt es sich vermutlich um einen Schlossriegel (vgl. Hintermann 2000, Taf. 147, Nr. 35). Auch ein kleines Bronzemesser ist belegt. Hinzu kommen eine Nadel sowie drei Ringe, die wohl als Aufhängung gedient haben. Von einem Werkzeug oder Gerät aus Bronze hat sich nur das vierkantige

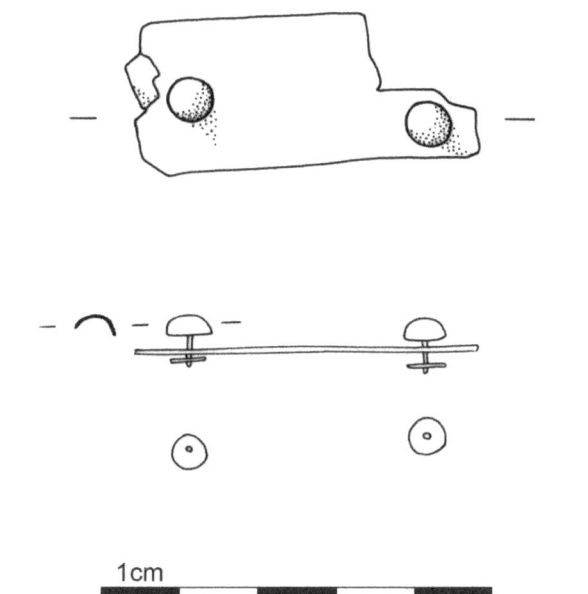

Fig. 39.2. Bronzebeschlag, Kat.nr. 1735. Zeichnung: Zürcher Ietas Grabung.

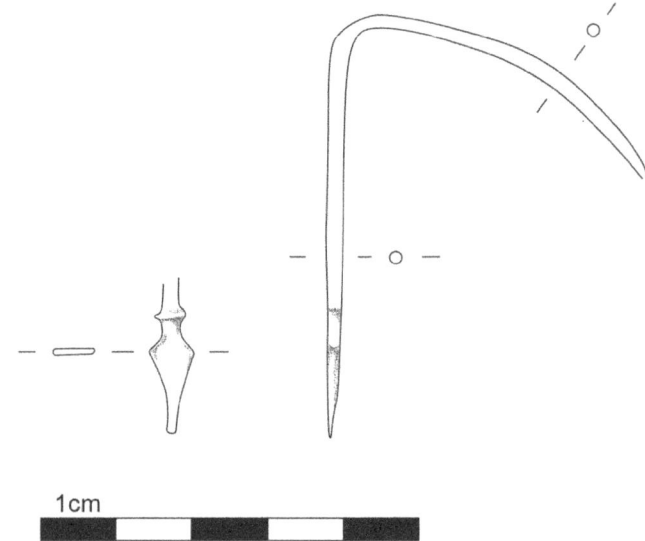

Fig. 39.3. Spatelsonde, Kat.nr. 1568. Zeichnung: Zürcher Ietas Grabung.

Verbindungsglied zum Griff mit ankorrodierten Eisenresten erhalten.

Funde: Bronzene Gefäße

Neun Fragmente können sicher als Elemente von Bronzegefäßen gedeutet werden.

Von zwei Weinsieben haben sich die Griffe erhalten. Der Griff 1652 (Fig. 39.4) weist eine annähernd quadratische Ansatzplatte auf, während Griff 1653 eine quadratische Ansatzplatte und zwei unterschiedlich hohe Arme zeigt. Weinsiebe dieser Form wurden vom Ende des 2. Jh. v. Chr. bis in tiberische Zeit hergestellt (vgl. Guillaumet 1991, 91, Fig. 3.3). Ein weiteres Grifffragment könnte von einem Becher oder einem Krug aus Bronze stammen (vgl. Tassinari 1993, 19), wobei die Masse des Fragments

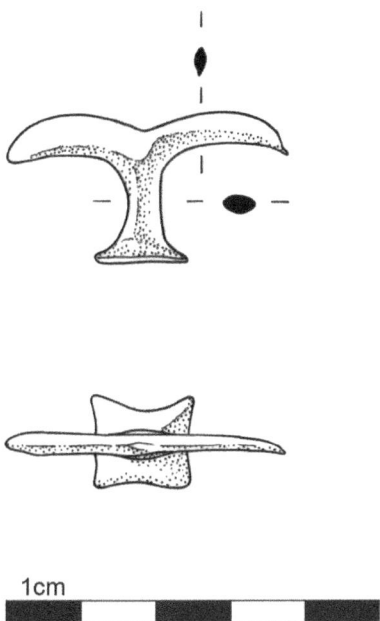

Fig. 39.4. Griff eines Weinsiebes, Kat.nr. 1652. Zeichnung: Zürcher Ietas Grabung.

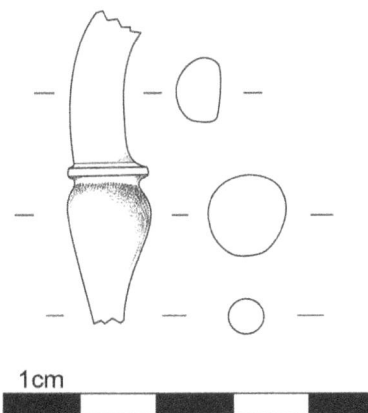

Fig. 39.5. Fragment eines Situlahenkels mit knospenförmigem Ende, Kat.nr. 1725. Zeichnung: Zürcher Ietas Grabung.

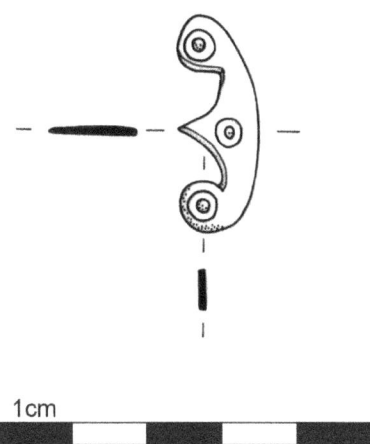

Fig. 39.6. Peltafüsschen einer Kasserolle, Kat.nr. 1731. Zeichnung: Zürcher Ietas Grabung.

Fig. 39.7. Widderkopf-Griff einer Griffschale, Kat.nr. 1819. Foto: Zürcher Ietas Grabung.

eher für einen Becher sprechen. Es weist eine dreieckige, spitz zulaufende Blattattasche auf. Der Henkel verfügt über einen dreieckigen Querschnitt. Ein Bruchstück eines ovalen Henkels mit knospenförmigem Ende gehörte wohl zu einem Eimer bzw. einer Situla der Form Eggers 18 (Fig. 39.5) (vgl. Bolla – Boube – Guillaumet 1991, 15, Fig. 8). Es sei anzumerken, dass Situlen der Form Eggers 18 ab der Phase LT D1 (ab Ende 2. Jh. v. Chr.) bis zur Mitte des 1. Jh. n. Chr. hergestellt wurden (Bolla – Boube – Guillaumet 1991, 14). Ebenfalls von zwei Eimern stammen die bogenförmigen Grifffragmente 1719 und 2026 (vgl. Tassinari 1993, 302–303).

Eine Kasserolle ist durch ein einzelnes peltaförmiges Füßchen bezeugt (Fig. 39.6). Jeweils drei solche Füßchen wurden, in einem regelmäßigen Abstand, am Boden von Kasserollen befestigt (Tassinari 1993, 128). Das peltaförmige Füßchen entspricht dem Tipo VII nach M.A. Hernandez Prieto, der im 1. Jh. n. Chr. und vielleicht noch zu Beginn des 2. Jh. n. Chr. produziert wurde (Hernandez Prieto 1985, 155. 160, Fig. 3). Ein weiteres Gefäßfüßchen mit konkaven Seiten gehörte zu einer Kasserolle, einer Schale oder einem Krug aus Bronze (vgl. Sedlmayer 1999, 113. 115, Taf. 51.6). Es lässt sich Hernandez Prietos Tipo II zuweisen, der in die 1. Hälfte des 1. Jh. n. Chr. datiert (Hernandez Prieto 1985, 154. 158, Fig. 1).

Von einer Griffschale stammt ein bronzener Widderkopf (Fig. 39.7). Für Widderkopf-Griffe existieren vielerorts Vergleiche. So sind beispielsweise in Pompeji mehr als 20 solche Stücke bekannt, von denen keine zwei Exemplare identisch sind (vgl. Tassinari 1993, 227, Fig. e). Solche Griffschalen wurden, zusammen mit einer Kanne, für die Waschung vor dem Bankett oder vor dem Opfer verwendet (Tassinari 1993, 232). Sie wurden erstmals in augusteischer Zeit produziert; einzelne Ausläufer lassen sich bis ins 6. Jh. n. Chr. verfolgen. Werkstätten existierten in den unterschiedlichsten Regionen des römischen Reiches (z.B. Italien, Gallien, Donauraum) (Nuber 1972, 38–73).

Ein D-förmiger Henkel sowie zwei omegaförmige Henkel (Fig. 39.8) könnten zu Gefäßen, aber auch zu Kästchen gehört haben.

Eva Riediker-Liechti

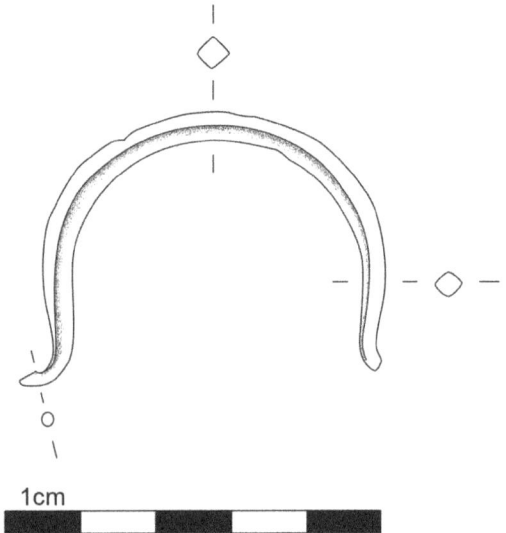

Fig. 39.8. Omegaförmiger Henkel, Kat.nr. 1816. Zeichnung: Zürcher Ietas Grabung.

Funde: Bronzeschmuck

Dieser Kategorie lassen sich fünf Gegenstände zuordnen. Ein Fragment stammt von einem herzförmigen Anhänger aus Bronzeblech, ein zweites von einem bronzenen Armreif. Bei den restlichen drei Objekten handelt es sich um D-förmige Gürtelschnallen aus Bronze (vgl. Deschler-Erb 1999, 180–183, Taf. 40).

Funde: Sonstige Objekte aus Bronze

Zu dieser Gruppe gehören sieben Nieten oder Nägel aus Bronze, welche in der *popina* entdeckt wurden.

Des Weiteren kam ein bronzenes Befestigungsblech einer Gladius-Scheide (Scheidenklammer) zum Vorschein (Unz – Deschler-Erb 1997, 15–16, Taf. 6–7). Dieser interessante Fund deutet auf die Anwesenheit eines Soldaten in der Garküche hin.

In der Zerstörungsschicht fand sich auch ein komplett erhaltener, vierkantiger Bronzehaken mit kegelförmigem Kopf (vgl. Friedrichs 1871, 322, Nr. 1533 hh)[1]. Dieser war vermutlich ursprünglich an der Wand befestigt.

Zwei massiv gegossene Bronzefragmente konnten nicht bestimmt werden.

Funde: Fundorte der Bronzeobjekte innerhalb der Garküche

Ein interessantes Bild bietet sich, wenn man bestimmt, in welchem Raum oder in welchem Bereich der Garküche die Gegenstände aus Bronze zum Vorschein kamen.

Im Schankraum, das heißt im östlichen Bereich von Raum A (zur Deutung dieses Bereichs als Schankraum: Riediker-Liechti 2015, 49; 2016, 6), fanden sich lediglich acht Bronzen. Hier wurden drei Toilettgeräte, ein Beschlag, ein Gefäßfragment (Siebgriff), ein Henkel, der herzförmige Anhänger und die Scheidenklammer eines Gladius entdeckt. Die geringe Menge der Bronzefunde, vor allem der Gefäße aus Bronze, zeigt, dass in dieser Zone wohl eher Keramikgefäße benützt wurde, die hier in großer Zahl (476 Mindestindividuen) freigelegt wurden.

Mehr als die Hälfte der bronzenen Objekte wurden im Bereich hinter der Theke entdeckt. Bei dieser Gruppe fallen einerseits die vielen Beschläge und Nägel ins Auge (insgesamt 15 Exemplare), die von hölzernen Kästchen oder dergleichen zeugen. Offenbar befanden sich solche Objekte bevorzugt im Thekenbereich. Vielleicht waren in diesen Behältern gewisse Gegenstände aufbewahrt, die das Personal der Garküche bei seiner Arbeit schnell benötigte. Andrerseits fallen die sieben Bronzegefäße ins Auge, die sich beim Einsturz des Baus in dieser Zone befanden. Besonders bei den drei Eimern und der Kasserolle macht es Sinn, dass sie hinter der Theke benützt wurden, da hier das Essen für die Gäste zubereitet wurde. Der bronzene Wandhaken war in diesem Bereich vermutlich an der Wand befestigt. Zusammen mit den drei Ringen, die in dieser Zone entdeckt wurden, diente er dazu, Gegenstände aufzuhängen. Es ist gut vorstellbar, dass gewisse Gefäße auf diese Weise verstaut wurden, damit sie weniger Platz einnahmen. Ein Beispiel für diese Praxis wären bronzene Bratpfannen aus Pompeji, an deren Griff ein beweglicher Ring angebracht war, an dem sie aufgehängt werden konnten (vgl. Tassinari 1993, 153, Nr. J2310. Nr. J2320).

In Raum B hingegen stieß man nur auf 14 bronzene Gegenstände. In dieser Zone des Baus wurde wohl geschlachtet oder große Fleischstücke zerkleinert, Mehl gemahlen und zum Teil Essen zubereitet. Eher überraschend ist dabei die Tatsache, dass auch der Widderkopf-Griff in Raum B zum Vorschein kam, würde man ihn aufgrund der Funktion der Griffschalen doch viel eher im Bereich für die Gäste erwarten, also im Schankraum. Möglicherweise wurde Raum B aber unterschiedlich genutzt und war zeitweise auch für die Gäste der Garküche zugänglich. Darauf deutet im Übrigen auch die Tatsache hin, dass die Wände dieses Raumes verputzt und bemalt waren. Auch das Bronzemesser lässt sich nicht gut mit der Deutung von Raum B vereinbaren, da es aufgrund seiner geringen Größe (L. 6,7 cm, B. Klinge 2,0 cm) nicht für grobe Arbeiten benutzt werden konnte, sondern vermutlich als Rasier- oder Federmesser Verwendung fand (Riha 1986, 28; Fünfschilling 2012, 182–184). Bei diesem Objekt handelt es sich wahrscheinlich um den persönlichen Besitz eines Gastes oder eines Mitarbeiters der Garküche.

Funde: Die Eisenobjekte

Im Zusammenhang mit der Untersuchung der Bronzeobjekte ist auch ein Blick auf die Funde aus Eisen interessant, die mit 156 Exemplaren vertreten

---

[1] Den Hinweis auf dieses Stück in der Antikensammlung Berlin verdanke ich Norbert Franken.

sind. Die häufigsten Eisenobjekte aus der *popina* sind lange Nägel mit großem, pilzförmigem oder flachem Kopf (Dm. meist zwischen 2,0 und 3,0 cm), von denen 93 Mindestindividuen entdeckt wurden. Diese Nägel besaßen eine dekorative oder konstruktive Funktion und können somit Hinweise auf Holztüren oder hölzerne Regale liefern, die sich nicht erhalten haben (Riediker-Liechti 2016, 7–8). Bei 14 Eisenobjekten handelt es sich um Fragmente von Scharnieren oder Verriegelungen. Diese waren ursprünglich an Türen, Truhen oder Kästchen befestigt. Auch acht Schlüssel verweisen auf Türen oder Schlösser. Des Weiteren fanden sich in der Garküche acht sichere und fünf unsichere Beispiele von Werkzeugen. Darunter sind zwei Sicheln, ein Sägeblatt, eine Hacke, ein Meißel und ein Stechbeitel. Außerdem wurden fünf Eisenmesser entdeckt. Ebenfalls aus Eisen bestehen sechs Schuhnägel (vgl. Schaltenbrand Obrecht 1996, Nr. 766–769), drei T-Nägel (vgl. Manning 1985, Pl. 62, R65–R69), die eine konstruktive Funktion besaßen, und sechs weitere Objekte.

Die Eisenfunde aus der Garküche umfassen also teilweise ähnliche Kategorien wie die Bronzefunde. Einerseits finden sich Hinweise auf hölzerne Elemente der Einrichtung in Form von Nägeln, Scharnierfragmenten oder Schlüsseln. Andrerseits wurden auch aus Eisen Objekte wie Werkzeuge entdeckt, die nicht direkt mit der Arbeit in einer Garküche in Zusammenhang stehen.

Vergleiche: Einleitung

In einem weiteren Schritt sollen nun die Bronzen aus der Ietiner *popina* anderen Inventaren von römischen Garküchen gegenübergestellt werden, um eine Antwort auf die Frage zu erhalten, ob es sich hier um eine typische Ausstattung eines solchen Lokals handelt, was die Bronzeobjekte anbelangt. Als Vergleiche bieten sich wegen der guten Erhaltung und der zahlreichen Beispiele an einem Fundort Schänken in Pompeji und Herculaneum an. Da es sich bei den untenstehenden Beispielen um Altgrabungen handelt, ist bei einer Analyse des Inventars natürlich Vorsicht geboten. Es wurden wohl kaum alle Funde verzeichnet und aufbewahrt. So entspricht das Verhältnis von Keramik zu Bronzegefäßen mit Sicherheit nicht der antiken Realität.

Vergleiche: Pompeji, Thermopolium der Fortunata (VI 3, 18–20) (Diagramm 39.1)

Dieses Lokal verfügt neben dem Schankraum über zwei weitere Räume, einen Speiseraum für die Gäste sowie eine Küche mit Herd und Latrine (Eschebach 1993, 165). Im Schankraum stieß man auf zahlreiche Gegenstände. Hier wurden 21 Keramikgefäße und vier tönerne Öllampen entdeckt, während sieben Münzen, ein Krater, eine Patera, eine Merkur-Statuette, zwei Tintenfässer, eine Lampe, drei Fragmente von Schlössern, zwei Ringe sowie ein kleiner Vogel aus Bronze bestehen. Des Weiteren kam hier ein Schlossfragment aus Eisen zum Vorschein. Die Gegenstände aus Glas umfassen fünf Gefäße, ein Kameo

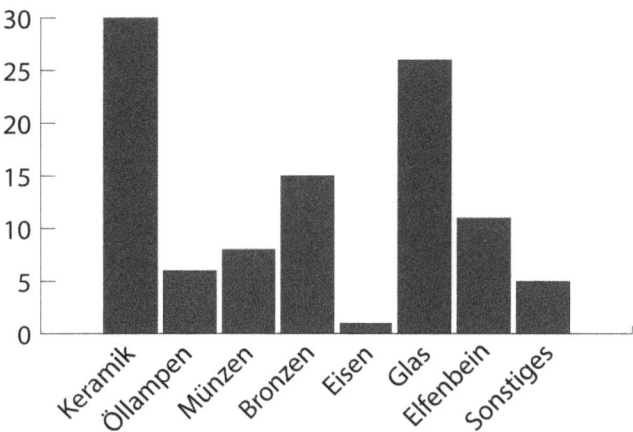

Diagramm 39.1. Funde aus dem sog. Thermopolium der Fortunata, Pompeji. Diagramm: E. Riediker-Liechti.

und 16 Spielsteine. Mehrere Objekte (ein Relieffragment, ein Phallus, vier kleine Löffel, eine Nadel, ein Würfel, ein Beschlag und zwei Stäbe) bestehen aus Elfenbein. Zudem wurden ein bearbeiteter Knochen mit zwei Löchern und drei runde Plinthen aus Marmor in diesem Bereich entdeckt (Fiorelli 1860, 80–82).

Für die rückwärtigen Räume wurden neun Keramikgefäße (u.a. zwei kleine Ölgefäße, ein Kochtopf, zwei Deckel, ein Mörser mit Tülle und zwei kleine Krüge), zwei Lampen aus Ton, ein Kochtopf, ein Becher und eine Patera aus Bronze, eine Bronzemünze, vier gläserne Gefäße sowie ein kleines Marmorkapitell als Funde verzeichnet (Pesando 1990, 114–115).

Vergleiche: Pompeji, Thermopolium des Suettius Certus (VII 13, 24) (Diagramm 39.2)

Bei diesem Bau handelt es sich um eine kleinere Garküche. Sie besteht aus einem Schankraum mit einer Treppe zum Halbgeschoss sowie einer Latrine und einem schmalen Gastzimmer (Eschebach 1993, 337). In diesen Räumen wurden vom Ausgräber drei Gefäße und drei Lampen aus Ton, sieben Bronzegefäße (darunter drei Kochtöpfe), eine bronzene Glocke, drei bronzene Tintenfässer,

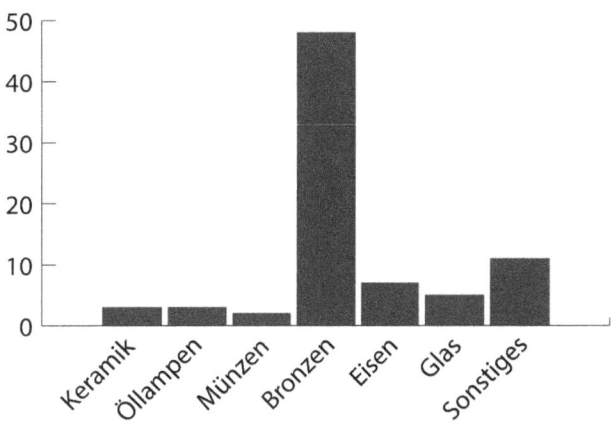

Diagramm 39.2. Funde aus dem sog. Thermopolium des Suettius Certus, Pompeji. Diagramm: E. Riediker-Liechti.

zwei Öllampen aus Bronze, eine bronzene Waagschale, eine Bronzefibel, eine Ahle, ein Vorhängeschloss, zwei medizinische Instrumente und eine Art Maß aus Bronze, eine Bronzenadel, fünf bronzene Möbelbeschläge und zwei Bronzemünzen als Funde verzeichnet. Außerdem kamen ein Eisenmesser, sechs Schlossfragmente aus Eisen, eine kleine Marmor-Herme, die vielleicht Bacchus wiedergibt, sowie ein marmorner Mörser mit Stößel zum Vorschein (Fiorelli 1862, 43–44).

H. Eschebach (1982, 252–253) erwähnt als Funde zudem ein Rohr, eine Feder, zwei Schmuckelemente, neun Haken, zwei Fassdauben, eine Schnalle, drei Ringe und drei aus Ringen gefertigte Ketten aus Bronze, zwei Karaffen und drei Perlen aus Glas, ein Gewicht sowie ein kleiner Bacchuskopf aus Marmor, vier Stücke einer Knochenflöte, zwei Garnspulen aus Knochen und karbonisierte Oliven.

Vergleiche: Herculaneum, Lokal IV 15–16 (Diagramm 39.3)

Diese Garküche verfügt hinter dem Schankraum über vier weitere Zimmer, die als Küche, Vorrats- und Speiseräume für die Gäste gedeutet werden. Im Schankraum fanden sich eine bronzene Pfanne, ein Bronzegefäß, ein Balsamarium aus Glas und vier bronzene Münzen, während im westlich anschließenden Raum acht Teller – bei sieben davon handelt es sich um Terra Sigillata-Gefäße –, zwei Krüge aus Ton sowie ein bronzener Krug entdeckt wurden. Im Zimmer dahinter kamen ein silberner Ring, eine Silbermünze, ein bronzener Kochtopf, ein Bronzekrug, drei Glöckchen aus Bronze, ein Keramikgefäß, zwei gläserne Balsamaria, Seile, Fragmente von mehreren Amphoren und ein Fragment eines Terra Sigillata-Gefäßes zum Vorschein (Monteix 2010, 384–385).

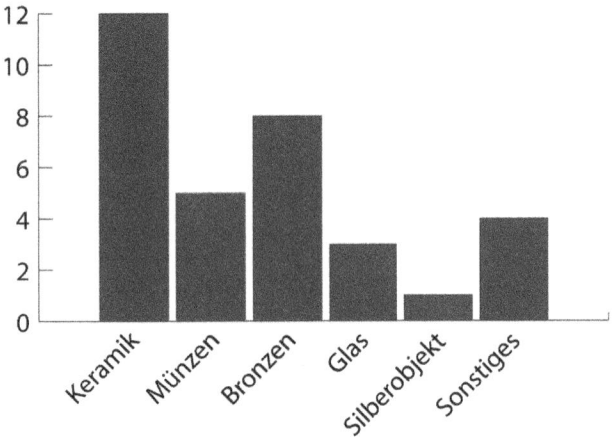

Diagramm 39.3. Funde aus dem Lokal IV 15-16, Herculaneum. Diagramm: E. Riediker-Liechti.

Vergleiche: Zusammenfassung

Was das Fundspektrum anbelangt, so lässt sich festhalten, dass neben Gegenständen aus Bronze, die man in einer Garküche erwarten würde – wie Geschirr, Beschläge, Griffe und Elemente von Aufhängevorrichtungen – sowohl in Pompeji als auch auf dem Monte Iato zudem Objekte wie Werkzeuge und Toilettgeräte zum Vorschein kamen. Wahrscheinlich handelt es sich hierbei um den persönlichen Besitz des Personals der Garküche, der im Schankraum selbst, hinter der Theke oder im Hinterzimmer (Ietiner *popina*: Raum B) aufbewahrt wurde. Die große Gesamtmenge der Funde, vor allem in Raum A, deutet darauf hin, dass in diesem Bereich ein Mezzanin (Zwischengeschoss) vorhanden war. Vielleicht haben wir es jedoch auch mit dem Eigentum der Gäste des Lokals zu tun, welche die Gegenstände in der *popina* verloren hatten.

In der beschriebenen Garküche in Herculaneum hingegen wurden, was die Objekte aus Bronze anbelangt, praktisch nur Gefäße entdeckt. Auffällig ist der hohe Anteil an Bronzegeschirr im Verhältnis zu den Gefäßen aus Ton. Vermutlich wurden bei der Ausgrabung nicht alle Funde verzeichnet und für die Aufbewahrung eher die vom Materialwert her wertvolleren Bronzeobjekte berücksichtigt.

Fazit

Ein beträchtlicher Teil der 57 Bronzeobjekte aus der Ietiner Garküche – Gefäße, Henkel, Beschläge und Ringe – stammen von der Einrichtung und der Ausstattung des Lokals. Es lassen sich folglich Möbel, Truhen oder Kästchen aus Holz rekonstruieren. Auch ergänzten einzelne Gefäße aus Bronze das umfangreiche Keramikinventar. Dabei sticht vor allem die bronzene Griffschale ins Auge, die man wohl eher im Kontext eines reichen Wohnhauses erwarten würde als in einer einfachen Garküche. Andere Bronzegegenstände wie Toilettgeräte, Schmuck oder Werkzeuge sind wohl als Eigentum des Personals oder der Gäste der *popina* zu verstehen.

Im Vergleich zur großen Zahl der Gefäße aus Ton sind die entdeckten Bronzegefäße äußerst spärlich. So stehen zum Beispiel eine oder zwei bronzene Kasserollen 202 Kochgefäßen aus Ton gegenüber. Es fragt sich, ob dieses Verhältnis mit dem Fundkontext zusammenhängt. Garküchen wurden den Schriftquellen zufolge hauptsächlich von der Unterschicht frequentiert (Riediker-Liechti 2016, 10) und boten eher einfache Gerichte an, sodass sich der Betreiber des Lokals wohl nur die günstigeren Tongefäße leisten konnte. Allerdings macht das teurere Tafelgeschirr (Terra Sigillata, römische Dünnwandkeramik, Schwarzfirnisgefäße) 28,9% der Keramik aus. Ein Blick auf die bronzenen Gefäße, die im Peristylhaus 1 auf dem Monte Iato, einem Wohnhaus der Elite, zum Vorschein kamen, zeigt jedoch, dass diese Erklärung zu kurz greift. In diesem Haus wurden nämlich nur zwei oder drei Bronzegefäße entdeckt (Hedinger 1999, 496. 536. 538). Vielleicht gelangten nur wenige solche Gegenstände als Importe nach Ietas. Möglicherweise war aber auch während des Erdbebens, das gewisse Teile der Stadt zerstörte, noch genügend Zeit, um wertvolle Objekte zu retten.

Bibliographie

Bolla, M., Boube, C. – Guillaumet, J.-P., 1991. Les situles. In: M. Feugère – C. Rolley, ed., *La vaisselle tardo-républicaine en bronze*. Lattes, 26 au 28 avril 1990. Dijon: C. R. T. G. R.

Deschler-Erb, E., 1999. *Ad arma! Römisches Militär des 1. Jahrhunderts n. Chr. in Augusta Raurica*. Augst: Römermuseum Augst.

Deschler-Erb, E., 1996. Die Kleinfunde aus Edelmetall, Bronze und Blei. In: Direktion der öffentlichen Bauten des Kantons Zürich, Hochbauamt, Abteilung Kantonsarchäologie, ed. *Ausgrabungen im Unteren Bühl*. Zürich: Fotorotar AG, 13–139.

Eschebach, L., ed., 1993. *Gebäudeverzeichnis und Stadtplan der antiken Stadt Pompeji*. Köln: Böhlau Verlag.

Eschebach, H., 1982. Die Casa di Ganimede in Pompeji VII 13,4. Ausgrabung und Baugeschichte. *Mitteilungen des Deutschen Archäologischen Instituts, Römische Abteilung*, 89, 229–314.

Fiorelli, G., 1862. *Pompeianarum antiquitatum historia II*. Neapel: s.n.

Fiorelli, G., 1860. *Pompeianarum antiquitatum historia I 2*. Neapel: s.n.

Friedrichs, C., 1871. *Berlins antike Bildwerke II. Geräthe und Broncen im Alten Museum*. Düsseldorf: Verlagshandlung Julius Buddeus.

Fünfschilling, S., 2012. Schreibgeräte und Schreibzubehör aus Augusta Raurica. *Jahresberichte aus Augst und Kaiseraugst*, 33, 163–236.

Guillaumet, J.-P., 1991. Les passoires. In: M. Feugère – C. Rolley, ed., *La vaisselle tardo-républicaine en bronze*. Lattes, 26 au 28 avril 1990. Dijon: C. R. T. G. R.

Hedinger, B., 1999. *Die frühe Terra sigillata vom Monte Iato, Sizilien (Ausgrabungen 1971–1988) und frühkaiserzeitliche Fundkomplexe aus dem Peristylhaus 1*. Lausanne: Édition Payot.

Hernandez Prieto, M. A., 1985. Propuesta de clasificación para los pies de recipiente de bronce romanos. *Museo de Zaragoza. Boletín*, 4, 151–161.

Hintermann, D., 2000. *Der Südfriedhof von Vindonissa. Archäologische und naturwissenschaftliche Untersuchungen im römerzeitlichen Gräberfeld Windisch-Dägerli*. Brugg: Aargauische Kantonsarchäologie.

Isler, H.P., 2001. Grabungen auf dem Monte Iato 2000. *Antike Kunst*, 44, 70–78.

Manning, W. H., 1985. *Catalogue of the Romano-British Iron Tools, Fittings and Weapons in the British Museum*. London: British Museum.

Mohr, M. – Reusser – C., Kolb, A. – Elsener, A., 2018. Forschungen auf dem Monte Iato 2017. *Antike Kunst*, 61, 88–107.

Monteix, N., 2010. *Les lieux de métier. Boutiques et ateliers d'Herculanum*. Rom: École française de Rome.

Nuber, H. U., 1972. Kanne und Griffschale. Ihr Gebrauch im täglichen Leben und die Beigabe in Gräbern der römischen Kaiserzeit. *Bericht der Römisch-Germanischen Kommission*, 53, 1–232.

Pesando, F., 1990. Le botteghe e le abitazioni dell'area meridionale dell'*insula* VI 3. In: Carocci, F. – de Albentiis – E. – Gargiulo, M. – Pesando, F., ed., *Le insulae 3 e 4 della regio VI di Pompei. Un'analisi storico – urbanistica*. Rom: Bretschneider. 111–148.

Riediker-Liechti, E., 2016. Takeaway in Antiquity – A Roman Tavern on Monte Iato (PA). *ATINER's Conference Paper Series*, [online] Available at: http://www.atiner.gr/papers/HIS2016-1968.pdf [Accessed 21 November 2018].

Riediker-Liechti, E., 2015. Eine *popina* auf dem Monte Iato. *Bulletin der Schweizer Arbeitsgemeinschaft für Klassische Archäologie*, 2015, 44–50.

Riha, E., 1986. *Römisches Toilettgerät und medizinische Instrumente aus Augst und Kaiseraugst*. Augst: Römermuseum Augst.

Schaltenbrand Obrecht, V., 1996. Die Eisenfunde. In: Direktion der öffentlichen Bauten des Kantons Zürich, Hochbauamt, Abteilung Kantonsarchäologie, ed., *Ausgrabungen im Unteren Bühl*. Zürich: Fotorotar AG. 141–228.

Sedlmayer, H., 1999. *Die römischen Bronzegefässe in Noricum*. Montagnac: Éditions Monique Mergoil.

Tassinari, S., 1993. *Il vasellame bronzeo di Pompei*. Rom: "L'Erma" di Bretschneider.

Unz, C. – Deschler-Erb, E., 1997. *Katalog der Militaria aus Vindonissa. Militärische Funde, Pferdegeschirr und Jochteile bis 1976*. Brugg: Gesellschaft Pro Vindonissa.

40

Roman bronzes of *Augusta Emerita* (Spain).
A functional approach

Nova Barrero Martín, Rafael Sabio Ganzález

National Museum of Roman Art – Mérida, Spain

nova.barrero@cultura.gob.es

Abstract: This article offers an approach to the study of the bronzes in the National Museum of Roman Art (hereinafter MNAR), grouped according to function. The collection of the MNAR is monographic about the colony *Augusta Emerita* (present-day Mérida, Spain), the capital of the Roman province of Lusitania, located at the western end of the Empire, in the southwest of the Iberian Peninsula.

Keywords: Hispania; Colony of *Augusta Emerita;* Province of Lusitania; National Museum of Roman Art, Roman Bronzes

Introduction[1]

The colony of *Augusta Emerita* was founded *ex novo* around 25 BC by discharged veterans from two of the legions that fought against the Cantabrians and Asturians in the northern Iberian Peninsula. A few years later, the *Pax Augusta* led to an administrative reorganisation of *Hispania*, creating a third province (Lusitania) with its capital at *Augusta Emerita*.

Today's city of Mérida is established upon the ancient colony's urban structure, with archaeological and architectural heritage that earned it the designation of UNESCO World Heritage Site in 1993. Mérida is the home of four aqueducts that supplied the city with water, the Iberian Peninsula's longest bridge, allowing communication across the Guadiana river, exceptional public spaces such as the so-called Temple of Diana and event locations (Roman theatre, amphitheatre, and circus), as well as public roads and certain burial and residential areas.

Founded in 1838, the National Museum of Roman Art is an institution with an extremely long history. Since the beginning of the 20th century, the Museum has been responsible for excavations carried out in the city, and has taken care of the archaeological finds. In 1986, the Museum embarked on a new phase with construction of the institution's new facilities designed by the architect Rafael Moneo, providing international visibility for the colony and province of Lusitania's heritage and the research done there.

This article aims to offer a glimpse at the current state of cataloguing with regard to the collection of bronzes, and the corresponding contextual difficulties. This work was completed with the contribution of the current volume of a specific study on models and iconographic aspects, which was completed by our colleagues Dr. Nogales and Dr. Murciano.

The study of the bronze collection of the MNAR differs from those found in an archaeological context and the materials whose only possibility of identification is a formal study, since there is no associated information. Beginning with the archaeological context, given the historical nature of the host institution and the different accession systems used, it should be explained that varying amounts of information on many objects have been lost. For this reason, we profit from recent accessions from newly discovered deposits in the city, this time excavated using modern methodology, which has allowed lost pieces of information to be rediscovered. These are primarily burial deposits, personal adornments, attire, or elements placed next to the body for a specific symbolic or emotional purpose.

Another important group of objects have been found in places outside their original context of use. For instance, casting pits have been found at the Morería archaeological site, where piles of objects of all kinds, related to both the public and private sphere, were gathered for remelting.

Typology

MNAR's current collection of bronzes includes more than 4,000 pieces. This project will provide a typology for the collection and will render it more widely known.

Given that some of the categories are possibly associated with both public and private uses, the precise reference

---

[1] This research falls within the scope of the Ministry of Science, Innovation, and University's national R&D project titled 'Augusta Emerita and the Early Years of the Roman Province of Lusitania in the Augustan Age' ('Augusta Emerita y los Inicios de la Provincia Romana de Lusitania en Época de Augusto', 2015–2017, HAR2014-52958-P).

for such criteria has been omitted from the classification. Nevertheless, this is tacitly established in the typology's general organisation: architectural elements (Group A) precede groups of objects more often associated with the public sphere (Groups B–C: epigraphy and sculpture); followed by those most often associated with the private sphere (Groups D–H: horse riding gear, professional tools, domestic furniture and tableware, and personal adornments). A final ninth group is collected in the section 'Various', which refers to multi-functional pieces or those not easily categorised.

Group A: Architectural elements

In this first group of objects, we will include all objects that imply an architectural function, regardless of whether they entail a certain ornamental character, while avoiding those that are intended purely for building ornamentation, which we will include in the sculpture group.

Among the purely architectural elements are those that fulfil a tectonic or a structural function associated with closures of doors and windows. Also among the bronzes associated with building structures are clamps (inv. Nos 2190–2193. 4847. 4849–4859. 4861–4863. 7392, and 7664) that were moved to the Museum from the Roman Theatre Warehouse, following the Spanish Civil War; known to have been found previously, they are linked to one of José Ramón Mélida's and Maximiliano Macías's excavations in the city between 1911 and 1936. It is very likely that they were found during the excavation of the Roman Theatre, where they would have been associated with iron building elements secured in place with lead (Sabio González 2012, type 60).

The Museum's collection includes two types of objects associated with jambs or hinges. The first group includes a pair of large jambs from excavations carried out at the Alcazaba site in 1971 (inv. no 12427), while the second group includes another large specimen linked to the same context (inv. no 12380), as well as smaller ones that were found in the Casa del Mitreo (inv. Nos 13390–13391. 13610 and 17174–17179). Finally, a thick bronze plate with equidistant orifices (inv. no 18441) was extracted from the Temple of Diana's western pool; the plate relates to a possible late use of the burial complex, perhaps associated with the monumental door's covering slats, although it has also been associated with an iconographic support of small figures (Álvarez Martínez – Nogales Basarrate 2003, 266–268).

Group B: Epigraphy

Two types of finds involve both bronzes and epigraphy. Bronze was used to make writing tablets used extensively by the Romans for the distribution of legal texts. Additionally, bronze letters were typically inlaid in stone. In the first category, Mérida has only the *tabula* of hospitality between the settlements of *Ugia* (Seville) and *Augusta Emerita* (inv. no 721) (Nogales Basarrate 1990, 105).

The bronze letters were pillaged owing to the value of their material and ease of removal; therefore only traces of their fixatives are left on their original support. There is a good example of this in Mérida on the *Aqua Augusta* aqueduct. An inscription on a marble support identifying the structure barely remains, with a puncture separating the two words of the short text (Stylow – Ventura Rodríguez 2013, cat. S-32). In contrast, other finds from Mérida include a small but valuable group of six letters (inv. Nos 29928–29930. 29935–29937) and four interpuncts (inv. nos 29931–29934) that appear to have been found in the Roman Theatre itself, where they must have been dropped during a hasty attempt at removal at the beginning of Late Antiquity (Nogales Basarrate 1990, 104–105; Stylow – Ventura Rodríguez 2013, cat. L-37). These elements are around 35 cm high on average, and are of a much larger size than those of the *Aqua Augusta* inscription, showing the appendage that moored it to the wall on one of their sides, as well as a gilded surface on the opposite side that would have shown a text, possibly alluding to the Theatre's inauguration by Agrippa in 16 BC.

Group C: Sculpture

As explained above, we include specimens associated with the public and private spheres in this group, as it may be difficult to tell the exact provenance of finds out of context. The iconography of Mérida's bronze collection is discussed in another paper in this volume.

From a typological perspective, architectural sculpture should be distinguished from sculpture in the round. The first group has formal and contextual characteristics quite similar to those of the inscriptions. Thus a prominent specimen would be a foliage rinceau in bronze (inv. no 18524), found during the 1973 excavations of the area surrounding the Temple of Diana site, which may be related to the appliqués that ornament the granite basement with stucco of that building (Álvarez Martínez – Nogales Basarrate 2003, 261–265). Similar to this specimen is fragment inv. no 29491, which lacks context, but which was discovered during excavations in the city between 1911 and 1936. Although having a different position, we also list the palmette (inv. no 30118) from Calle Calvario, along with sculptural appliqués.

With regard to sculpture in the round, we must distinguish pieces of large-scale statues from small-scale sculpture. In general, the former is associated with what we have already seen in the public sphere. Given the tendency to recycle, preservation in the city of Mérida tends to be quite limited, and there is only a vague association with a small group of limbs, which were sometimes discarded owing to the difficulty of reuse. Here we must include three life-sized statue legs: the first (inv. no 7483), from the Theatre Warehouse, may have been found during that site's excavation in the first third of the 20th century; the second (inv. no 9984) is from excavations on the site known as the Arch of Trajan in 1967; and the third (inv. no 18439) was discovered in the western pool of the

Temple of Diana site's square in 1972 (Álvarez Martínez – Nogales Basarrate 2003, 258–260). Of these pieces, two are associated with ancient burial sites, both colonial (inv. no 18439) and provincial (inv. no 9984), while the other two are connected to the city's event locations (Nogales Basarrate 1990, 106–107). A finger (inv. no 7790) may also be associated with the Theatre and Amphitheatre areas, along with two gilded garment fragments (inv. nos 6268 and 7782).

Medium-sized finds, also connected to the public sphere, include statuettes such as those identified with the Genius of the Senate (inv. no 18438) or the Province of Africa. Peculiarly, the first was found in the colonial forum's western pool in 1972 (Álvarez Martínez – Nogales Basarrate 2003, 254–257). Also of medium size is an enormous collection of specimens discovered in the Cerro del Calvario in 1924 (Nogales Basarrate 1990, 108–109). Of note here are the three small figures that were associated with emperor-worship (inv. nos 37397–37399). However, there are other statues of less certain context that, for their decorative character, could be more closely associated with the private sphere, such as a figurine of Hermaphroditus (inv. no 30331), a figure of a wrestler (inv. no 30332), and one of a horse (inv. no 30215). The shin-guard (inv. no 30211) is difficult to interpret, but may be of a votive nature (Nogales Basarrate 1990, 107). To the use of these last items, we might also mention a Venus statuette (inv. no 30142), which is perhaps connected to a lararium, and some small animal figures, which could be interpreted as toys, religious or votive objects (inv. no 37283).

Finally, we draw attention to a branched fragment in the Museum's collections, which should be interpreted as waste from the casting of sculpture, perhaps part of the gate system for a statue's hands or arms (inv. No 7784).

Group D: Harness and Military Equipment

The MNAR's collection of bronze horse harness has been studied recently, incorporating a series of important pieces that stand out owing to the quality of their craftsmanship and their typological individuality (Barrero Martín 2014). Nevertheless, it must also be noted that some of these objects raise doubts as to their correct interpretation.

Included among this functional group of pieces is the set of bit rings (inv. no 37084 and 37085), with a fretwork relief of Bellerophon riding Pegasus in his battle against the Chimera (Barrero Martín 2014, 43–47).

Likewise, two pieces of great interest have been interpreted as rein-holders, a panther (inv. no 26438) (Nogales Basarrate, 1990, pp. 115) and a philosopher (inv. no DO2012/1/8) (Alba – Ayerbe 1998, 99). In both cases, these are pieces with a hollow structure to loop through, with a fully-formed figure piece on the base and rings on each side, supposedly for the reins (Fernández Avilés 1958, 3–63). Another interpretation offered is their use as intermediate carriage pieces (Molina – Mora 1982, 205–210), as in the case of the feline appliqué (Rousséva-Slokoska 1994, 391–392, Fig. 8, with previous bibliography and other parallels), and with pieces of similar form and structure (see, for example, the carriage suspension harness from *Carnuntum* (Buora – Jobst 2002, 193, Fig. III.10 and III.11).

The case of the bronze identified as an insignia-holder is distinctive (inv. no 30140), and was found in the area surrounding the Theatre (Nogales Basarrate 1990, 199, Fig. 66). It is comprised of a hollow bronze tube flanked at the bottom by two appendages that double back to close in on themselves like a volute, finishing with two rosettes. A hunting scene is presented on both sides of the central shaft. On the right side is a clambering hare that is being chased by a collared dog that attacks the former's hind legs. On the left side, a mountain goat also attempts to scramble up the shaft pursued by a lion that, standing on its hind paws, digs its claws into the goat's haunch. Both scenes are placed next to the handle, which is decorated with stylised foliage volute.

Finally, the figure of a bound barbarian (inv. no 24429) (Fig. 40.1) is the decorative motif of an appliqué with a hollow shaft bent at a 90-degree angle, under which a zigzag fretwork structure appears. The base is preserved in two fragments that come together with two holes

Figure 40.1. Appliqué with a bound barbarian. Inv. no 24429. Height 17.4 cm Width 10 cm Photo. L. Plana. MNAR

to stud the shaft. Found in the peristyle of a *domus*, the context of its discovery leads one to think of its possible association as a furniture attachment, although it has also been interpreted as an insignia-holder. The figure of the barbarian is naked and bearded, his hands tied behind his back, following the theme's usual iconography.

Group E: Professional or personal tools

Ever since the forging of iron was introduced to human industry, bronze tended to be used only in certain professional spheres for more beautiful and ornate objects, where more subtle and visually appealing forms could be produced, owing to the material's greater adaptability.

Medicine and writing are two areas in which bronze objects from the Early Imperial Period have tended to concentrate, particularly at the Mérida site, where numerous medical tools have been found (Bejarano Osorio 2015). Ever since a *speculum magnum matricis* was found at the site (currently at the MAN in Madrid), scholarly attention has been drawn to the many and various medical instruments found at the ancient *Colony*. These are either for cutting or for inspection. Among the cutting instruments, there are lancets and certain types of special knives; the inspection instruments include a considerable series of probes linked to types that are well-identified by their Greek names. The cases containing these instruments will be added to the group, along with some important ancient boxes that were used to store pharmaceutical products.

The writing instruments are less widely known in Spanish bibliography than the medical instruments. For the systematic study of these instruments, the MNAR opened a line of research that was a pioneer on the peninsula (Alonso – Sabio González 2012; Sabio González – Alonso – Hidalgo Martín 2014; Sabio González – Alonso 2016). Even if the materials used in the *instrumenta scriptoria* were varied, bronze is used on those utensils to impart greater ornamental character, for which reason those were associated with individuals of a higher social status. There are four types of such objects : two for writing on wax; and two more for ink. The former include styli and spatulas, with four adorned specimens standing out for their geometric (inv. Nos 29216. 29267 and 30117) and, in one case, zoomorphic motifs (inv. no 7598). In the second group, a handle with a bust of Minerva (inv. no 13694) is of particular interest, as are a series of inkwells. Some of these inkwells are extensively decorated, from the base up, with three pieces showing a series of geometric motifs at their openings made from inlaid silver (inv. nos 15494 and DO2012/1/19), or even silver and gold (inv. no 23696). In contrast, the number of bronze reed-type pens is very small and uncertain, owing to the state of preservation of the finds (inv. No 36288).

Group F: Furniture and vessels

In a luxurious *domus*, the so-called "House of Marbles", an important series of tableware and furniture have been documented. Located next to the city's walls by the river, this house was renovated and extended during the 4th century AD, taking space away from the public road to reach 800 sq meters and provide greater luxury and comfort (Alba Calzado 1997, 285–315). A beautiful *oinochoe* found at the bottom of the well in the peristyle (inv. no DO2012/1/4) has a well-defined flaring shoulder, a wider cylindrical neck, crowned by an outward flaying mouth with a beak to facilitate pouring. The tapered body is balanced on a short foot with a hollow disk-shaped base. The handle was manufactured separately and is decorated with a winged griffin on the mouth of the jug, and a palmette or claw at the very bottom (Mosquera Müller – Alba Calzado 2012, 204, No. 66).

Two bronze appliqués were found on the calcined threshold of the house's private baths. The mythological-themed fretwork plaque with its central figure of Mercury (inv. no DO2012/1/7) would serve as a peephole or to facilitate steam ventilation on the door providing access to the baths (pers. communication with the excavator). This vent must have been for long-term use, as there are holes around the perimeter made at various later dates (Ayerbe Vélez – Alba Calzado 1998, 89–90). Besides this, the plaque of niello vegetal motifs reveals the versatility of such pieces, whose function would be difficult to determine if not for the contextualised discovery (inv. no DO2012/1/3) (Ayerbe Vélez 2012, 202, No. 65).

In relation to the furniture, a great number of bronzes of the collection are appliques that could have a very diverse function. This is the case for the appliqué in the form of a bust (inv. no 30141), which presents a hollow cast base. The naked bust maintains the blurred features of the face. The hair is centrally parted and gathered in a bun at the nape of the neck, with two strands of hair falling forward. Bulky curls surround the head. There is an upward hook at the back. Although this object was interpreted as an element of horse harness (Fernández de Avilés 1958, 57–59, Fig. 26 and 27), more direct parallels (Biroli Stefanelli 1990, 259–260, ilus. 98–100, cat. No. 17) appear to connect it to the top of a folding tripod. (Fig. 40.2).

A highlight of MNAR's collection is a piece that is interpreted as an enclosure's baluster (inv. no 6267). The piece consists of a large circular section of hollow trunk, adorned with protruding bent leaves, with a quadrangular base. Holes in the trunk indicate where other elements were inserted. The surviving five pomegranate-like objects (three of them attached, and two that have been separated) are filled with lead. (Fig. 40.3).

Vessels related to domestic equipment, but from unknown contexts, include the typical repertoire of patera handles with zoomorphic finials, and vessels such as the particularly interesting canteen (inv. no 6267) (Fig. 40.4) (Nogales Basarrate 1990, 293, No. 247).

The collection is very representative of vessels associated with hygiene and personal care. The more interesting of

Figure 40.2. Appliqué in the form of a bust. Inv. no 30141. Height 8 cm Width 4.7 cm Photo. L. Plana. MNAR

Figure 40.4. Canteen. Inv. no 29963. Height 13,5 cm. Photo. L. Plana. MNAR

cranium, and the sides of the head maintain traces of the handle's base. The right shoulder is bare, while the left shoulder is covered by a nebris or bacchic animal skin. The face is framed by thick wavy hair parted down the middle, with coarse curls marked with fine lines. The face is nicely cast, with well-defined pupils and irises. The piece appeared in a burial context as part of a ritual deposit, together with other glass and ceramic objects dating from the first half of the 2nd century AD. (Mélida Alinari 1929, 33, Lam. XX).

A highlight is the sculptural *oinochoe* in the shape of a woman's head (inv. no 209) (Fig. 40.5). The eye sockets are empty as they have lost the material that filled them, most likely glass. The woman wears a turban that is knotted at the forehead and is adorned with nielloed triangular geometric forms. There is a high-rise handle, a tri-lobed mouth and a circular base. There are Italian parallels from the 1st century BC and the beginning of the 1st century AD from Campania, which perpetuated a Hellenistic tradition. The feminine examples present this characteristic turban-like headdress with different variations, as well as the niello decoration (Biroli Stefanelli 1990, cat. n. 117–118, fig. 230–236).

Figure 40.3. Baluster with pomegranates. Inv. no 6267. Length 84.5 cm Photo. L. Plana. MNAR

the two anthropomorphic balsam flasks (inv. nos 8262, and 30139) represents a young male figure (Nogales Basarrate 1990, 301, No. 261) on a flared base with concentric mouldings. There is a lid on top of the

Greater problems were faced when attempting to interpret a container identified as a *balsamarium*, comprised of three independent parts: a situla, a plate, and a cover, that fit together to form a composite round container (inv. no

Figure 40.5. Figural *oinochoe*. Height 8.1. Width 3.8 cm Photo. L. Plana. MNAR

12152) (Nogales Basarrate 1990, 303, No. 266). Like the situla, the plate has an annular base, which has lost part of its edge. The cover is perforated at the top. All the objects have strigil-like decoration. The opening on the top, as well comparison with other parallels, has led to an interpretation of this object as an incense burner or cauldron. (Fig. 40.6)

A paper in this volume, by Rafael Sabio Gonzales, presents the city's first documented *Authepsa*, a singular type of container used to heat wine and keep it warm (Sabio González – Mena Méndez 2018).

The final group of objects is associated with the world of feminine care, including mirrors of various types, and items associated with cosmetics and the application of make-up and ointments, such as small spoons and tweezers.

Group H: Amulets and Personal adornments

The Museum's collection of phallic amulets (De la Barrera Antón – Velázquez Jiménez 1988, 211–214) is represented by a number of finds, and by variety of typology and quality (Fig. 40.7). Some of the larger ones may have had other uses, such as for horse gear, or they may be part of other multi-object items, such as lamps. They were symbols intended to bring good luck and ward off evil spirits.

The bronze objects of personal adornment of late antiquity were catalogued and studied by Barrero Martin (2014). Bracelets and rings have simple straps that are closed with slipknots, or overlapping ends that occasionally present punching decorations of repetitive geometric motifs. There is a significant increase in these materials during the late empire, while the use of more noble metals, such as gold or silver, is reduced. As for the earrings, open bronze rings predominate, with the head highlighted in the geometric button, which are common from the 4th century AD.

Figure 40.6. Composite container. Inv. no 12152. Height 14 cm Diameter 12 cm Photo. L. Plana. MNAR

Group I: Various

This last group includes pieces that cannot be placed in other groups by either function or form.

A highlight is the portable sundial, a *viatoria pensilia* (inv. no 37086), found by chance near Mérida (Arce 2002, 215–226). It takes the form of a slightly convex disk with an irregular opening at the centre and a small perforation to one side. Radially arranged inscriptions on part of the surface indicate the various Roman provinces. Two incomplete semicircles separate these names from a series of corresponding numbers. At a certain point, the list stops and six lines mark segments of parallel circles. The list itself or, more specifically, the mention of "Britannia Inferior", allows the dating of this object to between the time of the Severans and Diocletian's provincial reform. (Fig. 40.8)

A set of eight *crotalia* (inv. no Do2012/3/49) are part of a full set of female belongings dating between

Closing thoughts

Throughout this article, an attempt has been made to present the nature of MNAR's important collection of bronzes, and also some types and highlights. The purpose has been to spread information on the collection, to show new evidence, and to indicate cataloguing problems.

As a whole, we must underscore the lack of data to contextualise precisely many of the items in the Museum's collection, an aspect that is partially resolved with new finds from current excavations. The finds all come from burial sites or waste deposits, the latter intended for recycling activities.

The problem of dating the finds is made more difficult by the fact that, in the case of certain more recent excavations, the objects are found in silt and thus, in many cases, stylistic criteria constitute the only available ground on which to date them.

Bibliography

Alba Calzado, M., 1997. Ocupación diacrónica del área arqueológica de Morería (Mérida). *Mérida. Excavaciones Arqueológicas 1994–1995. Memoria 1.*, 285–315.

Alonso, J. – Sabio González, R., 2012. Instrumentos de escritura en Augusta Emerita. Los stili o estiletes. *Revista de Estudios Extremeños*, LXVIII.3, 1001–1024.

Álvarez Martínez, J. M. – Nogales Basarrate, T., 2003. *Forum Coloniae Augustae Emeritae. "Templo de Diana"*. Mérida: Asamblea de Extremadura.

Ayerbe Vélez, R. – Alba Calzado, M., 1998. Mirilla. *Ana –Barraeca. Confluencia de culturas.* Mérida, 89–90.

Ayerbe Vélez, R., 2012. Placa decorativa. In: J. M. Alvarez Martínez – M. Alba Caldazo, ed., *De la Excavación al Museo. El Consorcio y la Arqueología Emeritense.* Mérida. 202, nº 65.

Arce, J., 2002. Viatoria pensilia. Un nuevo reloj portátil del siglo III d.C. procedente de Augusta Emerita (Mérida). In *Mérida Tardorromana (300–580 d.C.)*, Colección Cuadernos Emeritenses 22. Mérida: Museo Nacional de Arte Romano, 215–226.

Barrero Martin, N., 2014. *Catálogo de Toréutica de la Antigüedad Tardía (siglos IV–VIII d.C.) del Museo Nacional de Arte Romano – Bronces y Orfebrería –*. Colección Cuadernos Emeritenses 38. Mérida: Museo Nacional de Arte Romano.

Bejarano Osorio, A., 2000. Intervención arqueológica en el antiguo solar de Campsa. *Mérida. Excavaciones Arqueológicas Memoria* 4. Mérida: Consorcio de la Ciudad Monumental, 315–331.

Bejarano Osorio, A., 2015. *La medicina en la Colonia Augusta Emerita.* Mérida: Instituto de Arqueología.

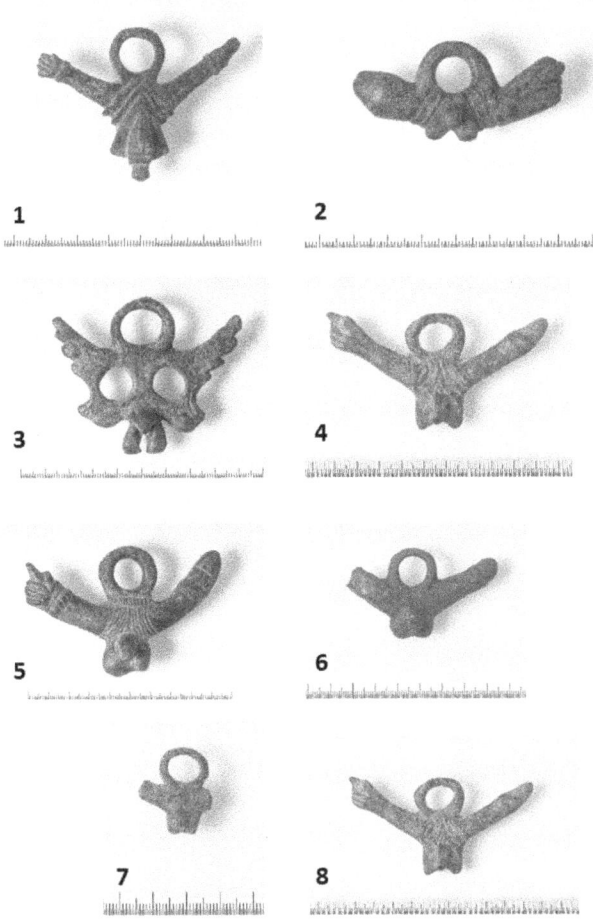

Figure 40.7. Phallic amulets (from left to right and from top to bottom). 1. Inv. no 205. Height 61 Width 96 mm. 2. Inv. no 206. Height 79 Width 63 mm. 3. Inv. no 6635. Height 64 Width 49 mm. 4. Inv. no 8229. Height 28 Width 60 mm. 5. Inv. no 24223. Height 26 Width 21 mm. 6. Inv. no 24319. Height 40 Width 68 mm. 5. Inv. no 30121. Height 42 Width 41 mm. 8. Inv. no 37282. Height 51 Width 96 mm.

Figure 40.8. *Viatoria pensilia*. Inv. no 37086. Diameter 13 Thickness 0.4 cm Photo. L. Plana. MNAR

the 1st century and the 2nd century AD. (Bejarano Osorio 2000, 315–331). These pieces are all the same and have lost only the element that would allow them to be affixed, and which would have been held in the central hole.

Biroli Stefanelli, L. P., 1990. *Il BRONZO dei romani: Arredo e suppellettile*. Roma: L'Erma" di Bretschneider.

Buora M. – Jobst, W., 2002. *Roma sul Danubio: da Aquileia a Carnuntum lungo la via dell'ambra*. Colección Cataloghi e monografie archeologiche dei Civici Musei di Udi-6. Roma: L'Erma di Bretschneider.

De La Barrera Antón, J. L. – Velázquez Jiménez, A., 1988. Amuletos romanos de Mérida. *Homenaje a Samuel de los Santos*. Mérida, 211–214.

Fernández de Avilés, A., 1958. Pasarriendas y otros bronces de carro romanos hallados en España. *Archivo Español de Arqueología 31 (*1958), 3–63.

Mélida Alinari, J. R., 1929. *Excavaciones de Mérida: el circo, los columbarios, las termas, esculturas, hallazgos diversos. Memoria de los trabajos practicados en 1926 y 1927*. Madrid: Junta Superior de Excavaciones y Antigüedades.

Méndez Grande, G., 2006. Desarrollo de un espacio agropecuario y funerario en la zona sur de la ciudad. *Mérida. Excavaciones Arqueológicas 2003* Memoria 9, 313–356.

Molina, M. – Mora, G., 1982. Una nueva teoría sobre los llamados pasarriendas: en torno a una pieza de carro del Museo de Mérida. *Archivo Español de Arqueología* 55 (1982), 205–210.

Mosquera Müller, J. L. – Alba Calzado, M., 2012. Oinochoe. In: J. M. Alvarez Martínez and M. Alba Caldazo eds., *De la Excavación al Museo. El Consorcio y la Arqueología Emeritense*. Mérida. 204, nº 66.

Nogales Basarrate, T., 1990. Bronces romanos en Augusta Emerita. In *Bronces romanos en España*, Palacio de Velázquez. Madrid, 103–115.

Rousséva-Slokoska, L., 1994. Appliques de Bronze Antiques de Chars Provenant de Pautalia/Sur le Problème de la Reconstitution. *Akten der 10 Internationalen Tagung über antike Bronzen*. Stuttgart: Kommissionsverlag – Konrad Theiss Verlag.

Sabio González, R., 2012. *Catálogo de la colección de hierros del Museo Nacional de Arte Romano*. Mérida: Museo Nacional de Arte Romano.

Sabio González, R. – Mena Méndez, C. I., 2018. Authepsa: un singular recipiente de bronce procedente de Augusta Emerita (Mérida, España). Historia e interpretación del objeto. Póster presentado en el XX Congress on Ancient Bronzes de Tübingen. (https://www.academia.edu/ 36534537/Authepsa_un_singular_recipiente_de_bronce_procedente_de_Augusta_Emerita_M%C3%A9rida_Espa%C3%B1a_._Historia_e_interpretaci%C3%B3n_del_objeto [19.09.2019])

Sabio González, R. – Alonso, J., 2016. Instrumentos de escritura en las colecciones del Museo Nacional de Arte Romano: estiletes y espátulas. *Mérida. Excavaciones Arqueológicas 2005. Memoria 11,* 481–506.

Sabio González, R. – Alonso, J. – Hidalgo Martín, L., 2014. Ars Scribendi. *La cultura escrita en la antigua Mérida*. Mérida: Ministerio de Educación, Cultura y Deporte.

Stylow, A. – Ventura Rodríguez, A., 2013. Las inscripciones con *litterae aureae* en la Hispania ulterior (*Baetica et Lusitania*): aspectos técnicos. *Actes I Congrés Internacional d'Arqueologia i Món Antic*. Tarragona: Fundació Privada Mútua Catalana. 301–339.

Previous International Bronze Congresses and Publications

1. Nijmegen, 1970.
"Tagung über römische Bronzegefäße im Rijksmuseum G. M. Kam in Nijmegen von 20. bis einschließlich 23. April 1970". Hektogr. Niederschrift 1970.

2. Mainz, 1972.
"Bericht über die Tagung 'Römische Toreutik,' vom 23. - 26. Mai 1972 in Mainz." Ed. Heinz Menzel, *Jb. RGZM 20* (1973), 258-282.

3. Brussels-Mariemont, 1974.
Actes des IIIes journées internationales consacrées à l'étude des bronzes romains Bruxelles-Mariemont 27. - 29. mai 1974. Bulletin des Musées Royaux d'Art et d'Histoire 46, 1974 (1977), 5-217.

4. Lyon, 1976.
Actes du IVe Colloque International sur les bronzes antiques (17. - 21. mai 1976). Annales de l'Université Jean Moulin, Lyon 1977, 5-236.

5. Lausanne, 1978.
Bronzes Hellénistiques et Romains. Tradition et Renouveau. Actes du Ve Colloque international sur les bronzes antiques Lausanne, 8. - 13. mai 1978. Cahiers d'Archéologie Romande 17 (1979).

6. Berlin, 1980.
Toreutik und figürliche Bronzen. Akten der 6. Tagung über Antike Bronzen 13. - 17. Mai 1980 in Berlin. Berlin, Antikenmuseum, 1984.

7. Székesfehérvár, 1982.
Bronzes Romains figurés et appliqués et leur problème techniques. Actes du VIIe Colloque international sur les Bronzes antiques, Székesfehérvár, 1982.
Alba Regia 21, 1984, 5-136.

8. Stara Zagora, 1984.
Unpublished.
Exhibition catalog: Ancient Bronzes, Stara Zagora: District Historical Museum, 1984.

9. Vienna, 1986.
Griechische und römische Statuetten und Großbronzen. Akten der 9. Tagung über antike Bronzen in Wien, 21. - 25. April 1986, ed. Kurt Gschwantler und Alfred Bernhard-Walcher. Vienna: Kunsthistorisches Museum, 1988.
Exhibition catalogue: *Guß + Form: Bronzen aus der Antikensammlung,* ed. Kurt Gschwantler et al., Vienna: Kunsthistorisches Museum, 1986.

10. Freiburg, 1988.
Akten der 10. Internationalen Tagung über antike Bronzen. Forschungen und Berichte zur Vor- und Frühgeschichte in Baden-Württemberg, 45 (1994)
Exhibition catalogue: Hans Ulrich Nuber, *Antike Bronzen aus Baden-Württemberg, Schriften des Limesmuseums Aalen 40,* 1988.

11. Madrid, 1990.
Bronces y Religion Romana. Actas del XI. Congreso Internacional de Bronces Antiquos, ed. J. Arce and F. Burkhalter. Madrid: Consejo Superior de Investigaciones Científicas, 1993.
Exhibition catalogue: *Los Bronces Romanos en España,* Madrid: Ministerio de Cultura 1990.

12. Nijmegen, 1992.
Acta of the 12th International Congress on Ancient Bronzes, Nijmegen, 1-4 June 1992, edd. S. T. A. M. Mols, A. M. Gerhartl-Witteveen, H. Kars, A. Koster, W. J. Th. Peters, and W. J. H. Willems, *Nederlandse Archeologische Rapporten 18* (Nijmegen 1995).

13. Cambridge Mass., 1996.
From the Parts to the Whole: Acta of the 13th International Congress on Ancient Bronzes, ed. C. Mattusch, A. Brauer, and S. Knudsen, *JRA supplement, 1999.*
Exhibition catalogue: *The Fire of Hephaistos: Large Classical Bronzes from North American Collections,* ed. C. Mattusch, Cambridge, Mass.: Harvard University Art Museums, 1996.

14. Cologne, 1999.
Antike Bronzen, Werkstattkreise:Figuren und Geräte, Cologne, 2000.

15. Udine, 2001.
I Bronzi Antichi: Produzione e tecnologia, Montagnac, ed. A. Giumlia-Mair, Montagnac 2002.

16. Bucharest, 2003.
The Antique Bronzes: Typology, Chronology, Authenticity, ed. C. Museteanu, Bucharest 2004.

17. Izmir, 2011.
Proceedings of the XVIIth International Congress on Ancient Bronzes, Izmir, eds. Alessandra Giumlia-Mair and Carol C. Mattusch, *Monographie Instrumentum 52,* Autun 2016.

18. Zurich, 2013.
New Research on Ancient Bronzes, ed. E. Deschler-Erb and P. Della Casa, *Zurich Studies in Archaeology* 10, 2015.

19. Los Angeles, 2015.
Exhibition catalogue: *Power and Pathos: Bronze Sculpture of the Hellenistic World*, ed. J. M. Daehner and K. Lapatin, Los Angeles: J. Paul Getty Museum, 2015.

Artistry in Bronze: The Greeks and Their Legacy: XIXth International Congress on Ancient Bronzes, eds. Jens M. Daehner, Kenneth Lapatin, and Ambra Spinelli, Los Angeles: J. Paul Getty Museum and Getty Conservation Institute, 2017.

20. Tübingen, 2018.
Bronzes: Resource, Reconstruction, Representation, Role.
Proceedings forthcoming 2019: Oxford: British Archaeological Reports.

Ingram Content Group UK Ltd.
Milton Keynes UK
UKHW051043190423
420352UK00007B/21